MW00789998

The New Roman Empire

The New Roman Empire

A History of Byzantium

ANTHONY KALDELLIS

Oxford University Press is a department of the University of Oxford. It furthers the University's objective of excellence in research, scholarship, and education by publishing worldwide. Oxford is a registered trade mark of Oxford University Press in the UK and certain other countries.

Published in the United States of America by Oxford University Press
198 Madison Avenue, New York, NY 10016, United States of America.

Library of Congress Cataloging-in-Publication Data
Names: Kaldellis, Anthony, author.
Title: The new Roman empire : a history of Byzantium / Anthony Kaldellis.
Description: New York : Oxford University Press, [2024] |
Includes bibliographical references and index.
Identifiers: LCCN 2023011420 (print) | LCCN 2023011421 (ebook) |
ISBN 9780197549322 (hardback) | ISBN 9780197549346 (epub) |
ISBN 9780197549339 | ISBN 9780197549353
Subjects: LCSH: Byzantine Empire—History. |
Byzantine Empire—Civilization.
Classification: LCC DF552 .K25 2024 (print) | LCC DF552 (ebook) |
DDC 949.5/02—dc23/eng/20230321
LC record available at https://lccn.loc.gov/2023011420
LC ebook record available at https://lccn.loc.gov/2023011421

DOI: 10.1093/oso/9780197549322.001.0001

Printed by Integrated Books International, United States of America

Contents

PART FIVE: TO THE BRINK OF DESPAIR

PART SIX: RESILIENCE AND RECOVERY

PART SEVEN: THE PATH TOWARD EMPIRE

PART EIGHT: A NEW PARADIGM

PART NINE: EXILE AND RETURN

PART TEN: DIGNITY IN DEFEAT

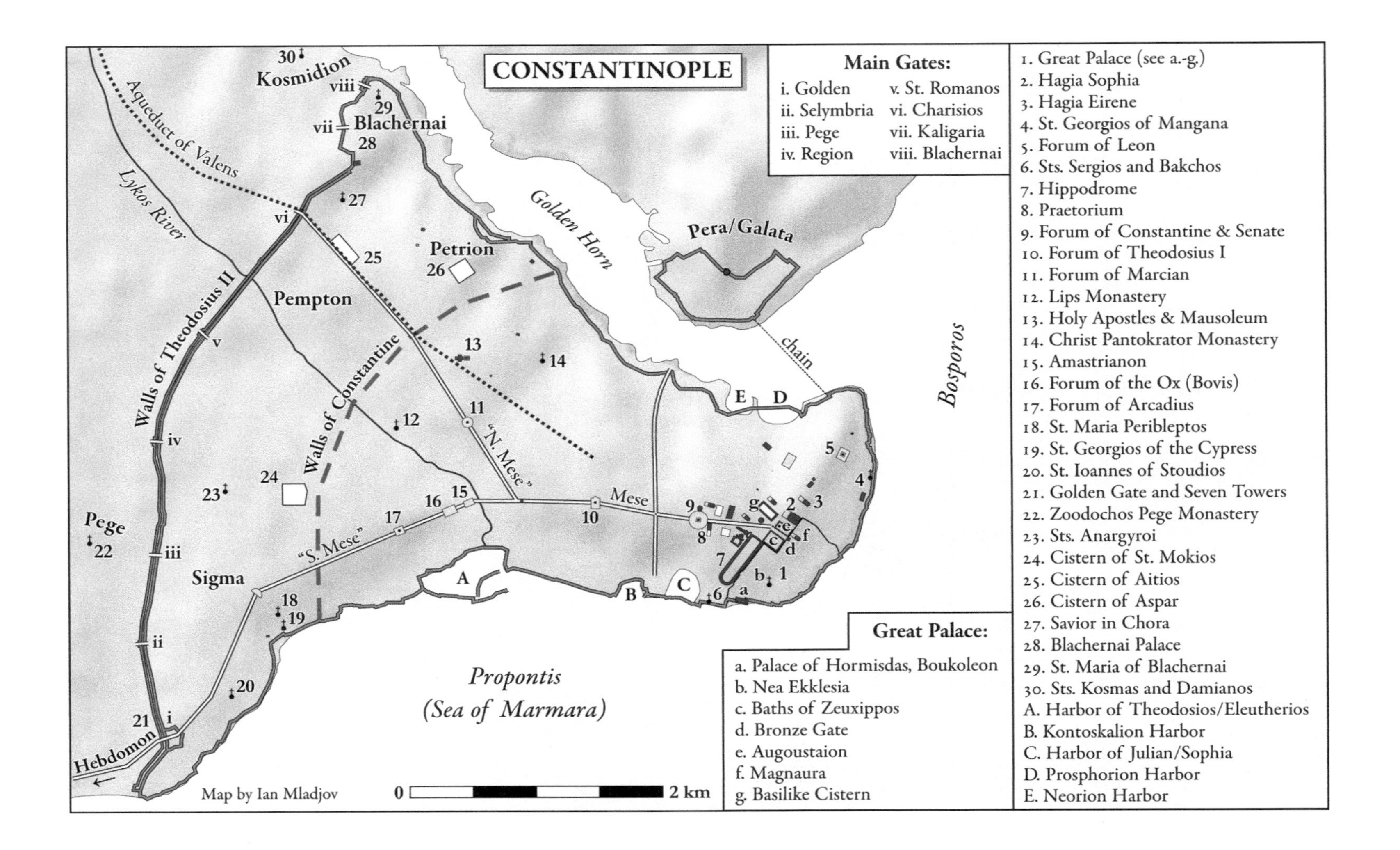

CONSTANTINOPLE
Main Gates:
i. Golden
ii. Selymbria
iii. Pege
iv. Region
v. St. Romanos
vi. Charisios
vii. Kaligaria
viii. Blachernai
1. Great Palace (see a.-g.)
2. Hagia Sophia
3. Hagia Eirene
4. St. Georgios of Mangana
5. Forum of Leon
6. Sts. Sergios and Bakchos
7. Hippodrome
8. Praetorium
9. Forum of Constantine & Senate
10. Forum of Theodosius I
11. Forum of Marcian
12. Lips Monastery
13. Holy Apostles & Mausoleum
14. Christ Pantokrator Monastery
15. Amastrianon
16. Forum of the Ox (Bovis)
17. Forum of Arcadius
18. St. Maria Peribleptos
19. St. Georgios of the Cypress
20. St. Ioannes of Stoudios
21. Golden Gate and Seven Towers
22. Zoodochos Pege Monastery
23. Sts. Anargyroi
24. Cistern of St. Mokios
25. Cistern of Aitios
26. Cistern of Aspar
27. Savior in Chora
28. Blachernai Palace
29. St. Maria of Blachernai
30. Sts. Kosmas and Damianos
A. Harbor of Theodosios/Eleutherios
B. Kontoskalion Harbor
C. Harbor of Julian/Sophia
D. Prosphorion Harbor
E. Neorion Harbor
Great Palace:
a. Palace of Hormisdas, Boukoleon
b. Nea Ekklesia
c. Baths of Zeuxippos
d. Bronze Gate
e. Augoustaion
f. Magnaura
g. Basilike Cistern
Kosmidion
Blachernai
Aqueduct of Valens
Lykos River
Golden Horn
Pera/Galata
chain
Bosporos
Petrion
Pempton
Walls of Theodosius II
Walls of Constantine
"N. Mese"
Mese
"S. Mese"
Pege
Sigma
Hebdomon
Propontis
(Sea of Marmara)
Map by Ian Mladjov
0
2 km

CONSTANTINOPLE & THE STRAITS

0 30 km
0 20 mi

Constantinople imperial capital
Nikomedeia provincial capital
approx. province borders
select Roman roads

Map by Ian Mladjov

Black Sea
Propontis
(Sea of Marmara)
Aegean Sea
Bosporos
Hellespont
THRAKE
HAIMIMONTOS
RHODOPE
EUROPE
HELLESPONTOS
ASIA
BITHYNIA
PHRYGIA SALUTARIS
Constantinople
Nikomedeia
Adrianople
Traianoupolis
Herakleia
Kyzikos
Nikaia
Long Walls of Anastasius
Walls
Makrolibada
Perperakion
Bourdepto
Ephraim
Boukelon
Hebros
Tonsos
Ardeskos
Probaton
Skopelos
Skopos
Brysis
Bizye
Karabizye
Thynias
Salmydessos
Sergentze
Ostodizon
Nike
Bourtoudizon
Boulgarophygon
Arkadioupolis
Mesene
Drouzipara
Plotinopolis
Didymoteichon
Pamphilon
Charioupolis
Regina
Zirinai
Gratianoupolis
Garella
Tzouroulon
Kalabria
Dymai
Bera
Maroneia
Kypsela
Kissios
Aproi
Raidestos
Heraion
Panion
Rousion
Ainos
Aphrodisias
Myriophyton
Ganos
Prokonnesos
Samothrake
Chersonesos
Tzympe
Kallipolis
Parion
Priapos
Halone
Artake
Imbros
Sestos
Koila
Madytos
Abydos
Lampsakos
Pegai
Zeleia
Elaious
Dardanos
Granikos
Poimanenon
Sigeion
Troy
Kenchreai
Tenedos
Skamandros
Skepsis
Alexandreia Troas
Antandros
Assos
Adramyttion
Hadrianoutherai
Palaiokastron
Attea
Philia
Delkos
Selymbria
Epibatai
Athyras
Region
Hebdomon
Neapolis
Hieria
Philokrene/Pelekanon
Rebas
Hieron
Chrysopolis
Chalkedon
Rouphinianai
Panteichion
Libyssa
Charax
Dakibyza
Helenopolis
Pylai
Kibotos
Prainetos
Artanes
Daphnousia
Kalpe
Sangarios
Maximianai
Tarsia
Kabia
Metabole
Trikokkia
Leukai
Tattaios
Kios
Kroulla
Daskyleion
Apameia
Platanea?
Lopadion
Kaisareia
Prousa
Apollonia
Bilecik
Hagios Nikolaos?
Söğüt
Miletoupolis
Mekestos
Tataula
Lamounia
Hadrianoi
Ryndakos
Dorylaion
Thymbrios
Hadrianeia
Tiberioupolis
Kotyaion
Nakoleia

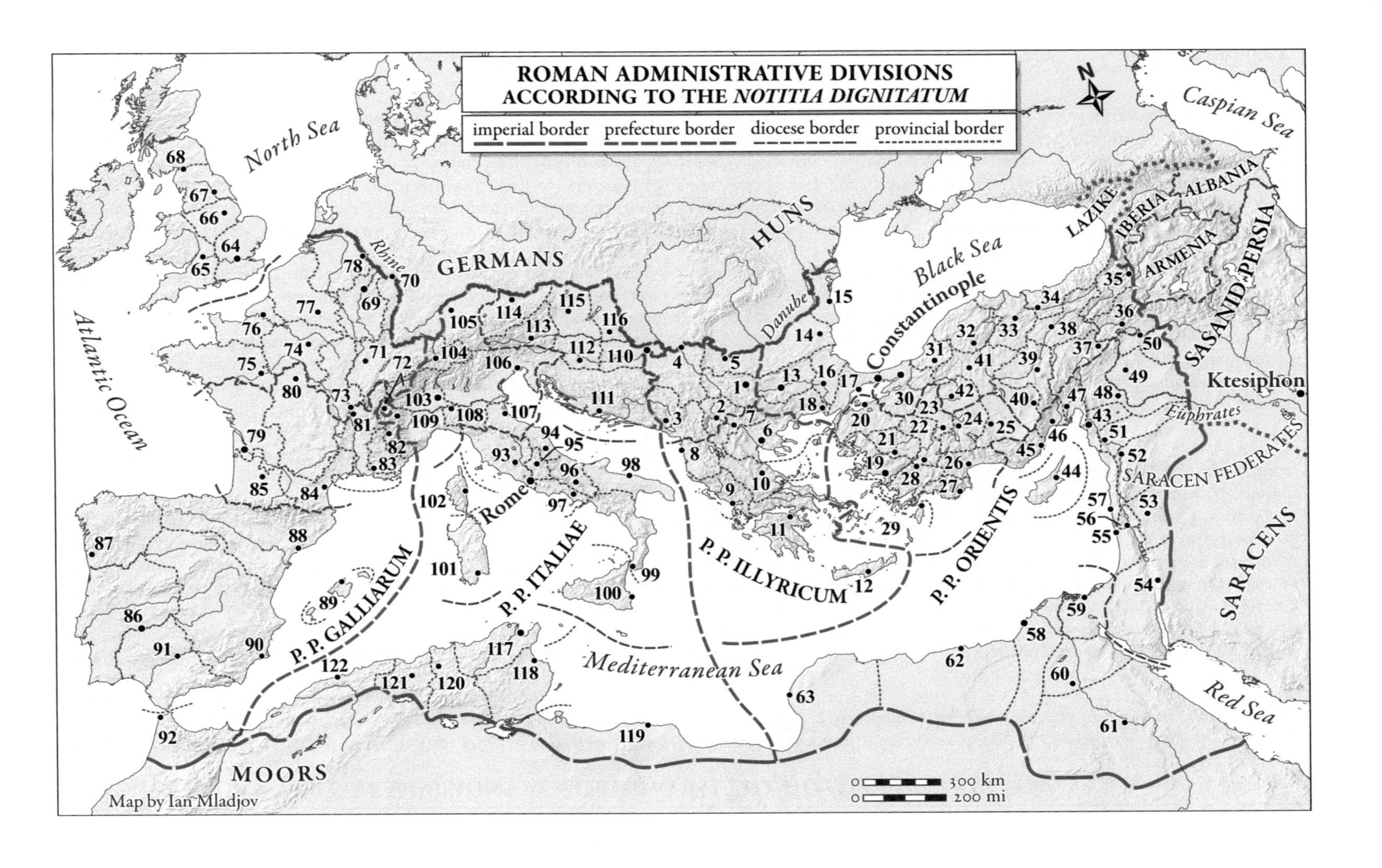

ROMAN ADMINISTRATIVE DIVISIONS
ACCORDING TO THE *NOTITIA DIGNITATUM*
imperial border
prefecture border
diocese border
provincial border
N
North Sea
Atlantic Ocean
Caspian Sea
Black Sea
Mediterranean Sea
Red Sea
Rhine
Danube
Euphrates
GERMANS
HUNS
LAZIKE
IBERIA
ALBANIA
ARMENIA
SASANID PERSIA
Ktesiphon
SARACEN FEDERATES
SARACENS
MOORS
Constantinople
Rome
P. P. GALLIARUM
P. P. ITALIAE
P. P. ILLYRICUM
P. P. ORIENTIS
300 km
200 mi
Map by Ian Mladjov

ROMAN ADMINISTRATIVE DIVISIONS ACCORDING TO THE *NOTITIA DIGNITATUM*

PRAETORIAN PREFECTURE OF ILLYRICUM: Diocese of Dacia: 1 Dacia Mediterranea (Serdica); 2 Dardania (Scupi); 3 Praevalitana (Doclea); 4 Moesia I (Viminacium); 5 Dacia Ripensis (Ratiaria); **Diocese of Macedonia:** 6 Macedonia I (Thessalonike); 7 Macedonia II Salutaris (Stobi); 8 Epirus Nova (Dyrrachion); 9 Epirus Vetus (Nikopolis); 10 Thessalia (Larissa); 11 Achaia (Corinth); 12 Creta (Gortyna).

PRAETORIAN PREFECTURE OF ORIENS: Diocese of Thraciae: 13 Thracia (Philippoupolis); 14 Moesia II (Markianoupolis); 15 Scythia (Tomis); 16 Haemimontus (Adrianople); 17 Europa (Herakleia); 18 Rhodope (Traianoupolis); **Diocese of Asiana:** 19 Asia (Ephesos); 20 Hellespontus (Kyzikos); 21 Lydia (Sardeis); 22 Phrygia Pacatiana (Laodikeia); 23 Phrygia Salutaris (Synnada); 24 Pisidia (Antiocheia); 25 Lycaonia (Ikonion); 26 Pamphylia (Perge); 27 Lycia (Myra); 28 Caria (Aphrodisias); 29 Insulae (Rhodes); **Diocese of Pontica:** 30 Bithynia (Nikomedeia); 31 Honorias (Klaudioupolis); 32 Paphlagonia (Gangra); 33 Helenopontus (Amaseia); 34 Pontus Polemoniacus (Neokaisareia); 35 Armenia Interior (Theodosioupolis); 36 Sophene et Gentes (Arsamosata); 37 Armenia II (Melitene); 38 Armenia I (Sebasteia); 39 Cappadocia I (Kaisareia); 40 Cappadocia II (Tyana); 41 Galatia I (Ankyra); 42 Galatia II Salutaris (Pessinous); **Diocese of Oriens:** 43 Syria I (Antioch); 44 Cyprus (Konstanteia); 45 Isauria (Seleukeia); 46 Cilicia I (Tarsos); 47 Cilicia II (Anazarbos); 48 Euphratensis (Hierapolis); 49 Osrhoene (Edessa); 50 Mesopotamia (Amida); 51 Syria II Salutaris (Apameia); 52 Phoenice Libanensis (Emesa); 53 Arabia (Bostra); 54 Palaestina III Salutaris (Petra); 55 Palaestina I (Kaisareia); 56 Palaestina II (Skythopolis); 57 Phoenice (Tyre); **Diocese of Aegyptus:** 58 Aegyptus (Alexandria); 59 Augustamnica (Pelousion); 60 Arcadia (Oxyrynchos); 61 Thebais (Ptolemais); 62 Libya Inferior (Paraitonion); 63 Libya Superior (Berenike).

PRAETORIAN PREFECTURE OF GALLIAE: Diocese of Britannia*: 64 Maxima Caesariensis (Londinium); 65 Britannia I (Corinium); 66 Flavia Caesariensis (Lindum); 67 Britannia II (Eboracum); 68 Valentia (Luguvalium?); **Diocese of Galliae**:** 69 Belgica I (Augusta Treverorum); 70 Germania I (Moguntiacum); 71 Maxima Sequanorum (Vesontio); 72 Alpes Graiae et Poeninae (Darantasia); 73 Lugdunensis I (Lugdnum); 74 Lugdunensis IV (Agedincum); 75 Lugdunensis III (Caesarodunum); 76 Lugdunensis II (Rotomagus); 77 Belgica II (Durocortorum); 78 Germania II (Colonia Agrippina); **Diocese of Septem Provinciae**:** 79 Aquitania II (Burdigala); 80 Aquitania I (Biturigum); 81 Viennensis (Vienna); 82 Alpes Maritimae (Ebrodunum); 83 Narbonensis II (Aquae Sextiae); 84 Narbonensis I (Narbo); 85 Novempopulana (Elusa); **Diocese of Hispaniae:** 86 Lusitania (Emerita Augusta); 87 Gallaecia (Bracara); 88 Tarraconensis (Tarraco); 89 Balearica (Pollentia); 90 Carthaginensis (Carthago Nova); 91 Baetica (Corduba); 92 Mauretania Tingitana (Tingis).

PRAETORIAN PREFECTURE OF ITALIA: Diocese of Italia: 93 Tuscia et Umbria (Volsinii); 94 Picenum Suburbicarium (Asculum); 95 Valeria (Reate); 96 Samnium (Beneventum); 97 Campania (Capua); 98 Apulia et Calabria (Barium); 99 Lucania et Brutii (Rhegium); 100 Sicilia (Syracuse); 101 Sardinia (Carales); 102 Corsica (Aleria); 103 Liguria (Milan); 104 Raetia I (Curia); 105 Raetia II (Augusta Vindelicum); 106 Venetia et Histria (Aquileia); 107 Flaminia et Picenum (Ravenna); 108 Aemilia (Placentia); 109 Alpes Cottiae (Segusio); **Diocese of Illyricum/Pannoniae:** 110 Pannonia II (Sirmium); 111 Dalmatia (Salonae); 112 Savia (Siscia); 113 Noricum Mediterraneum (Virunum); 114 Noricum Ripense (Ovilava); 115 Pannonia I (Savaria); 116 Valeria Ripensis (Sopianae); **Diocese of Africa:** 117 Africa Zeugitana (Carthage); 118 Byzacena (Hadrumetum); 119 Tripolitania (Leptis Magna); 120 Numidia (Constantina); 121 Mauretania Sitifensis (Sitifis); 122 Mauretania Caesariensis (Caesarea).

NOTE: borders are approximate; * arrangement hypothetical; ** Galliae and Septem Provinciae treated together in the *Notitia Dignitatum*. Compiled by Ian Mladjov

THE BALKANS IN LATE ANTIQUITY

imperial border
provincial border

1. Kula
2. Čomakovci
3. Sadovec
4. Taurision?
5. Bederiana?

0 50 km
0 30 mi

Map by Ian Mladjov

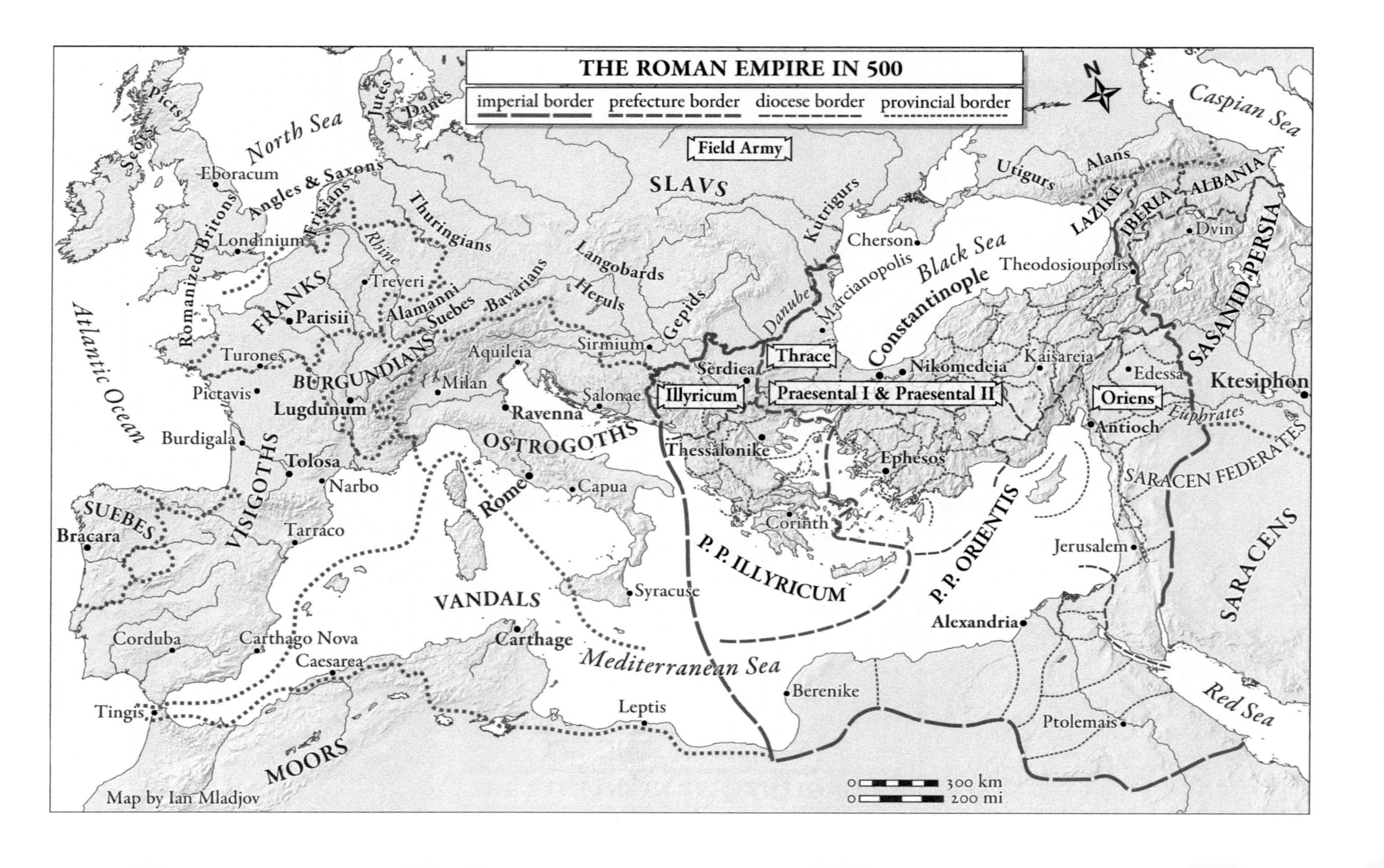
THE ROMAN EMPIRE IN 500
imperial border
prefecture border
diocese border
provincial border
Field Army
SLAVS
North Sea
Picts
Scots
Jutes
Danes
Eboracum
Angles & Saxons
Frisians
Thuringians
Romanized Britons
Londinium
Rhine
Treveri
FRANKS
Parisii
Alamanni
Suebes
Bavarians
Langobards
Heruls
Gepids
Danube
Kutrigurs
Utigurs
Alans
Caspian Sea
Cherson
Marcianopolis
Black Sea
Constantinople
Theodosioupolis
LAZIKE
IBERIA
ALBANIA
Dvin
SASANID PERSIA
Atlantic Ocean
Turones
Pictavis
BURGUNDIANS
Lugdunum
Aquileia
Milan
Sirmium
Serdica
Thrace
Nikomedeia
Kaisareia
Edessa
Ktesiphon
Salonae
Illyricum
Praesental I & Praesental II
Oriens
Euphrates
Ravenna
Antioch
Burdigala
VISIGOTHS
Tolosa
Narbo
OSTROGOTHS
Thessalonike
Ephesos
SARACEN FEDERATES
Rome
Capua
SUEBES
Bracara
Tarraco
Corinth
P. P. ILLYRICUM
P. P. ORIENTIS
Jerusalem
SARACENS
VANDALS
Syracuse
Alexandria
Corduba
Carthago Nova
Carthage
Caesarea
Mediterranean Sea
Berenike
Red Sea
Tingis
Leptis
Ptolemais
MOORS
0 300 km
0 200 mi
Map by Ian Mladjov

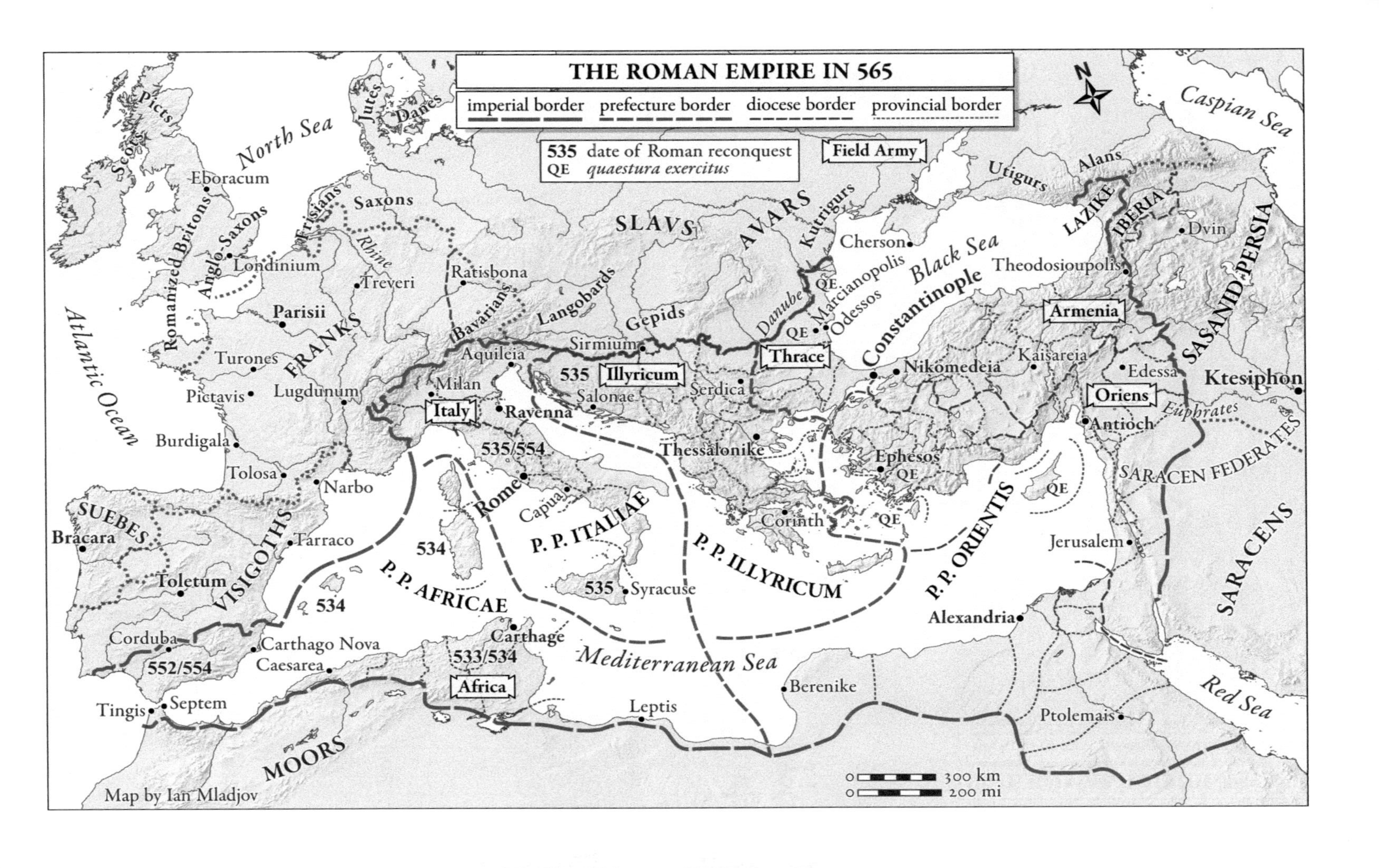
THE ROMAN EMPIRE IN 565
imperial border
prefecture border
diocese border
provincial border
535 date of Roman reconquest
QE quaestura exercitus
Field Army
N
Caspian Sea
North Sea
Atlantic Ocean
Black Sea
Mediterranean Sea
Red Sea
Picts
Scots
Eboracum
Romanized Britons
Anglo-Saxons
Londinium
Jutes
Danes
Frisians
Saxons
Rhine
Treveri
Parisii
FRANKS
Turones
Pictavis
Lugdunum
Burdigala
Tolosa
Narbo
SUEBES
Bracara
VISIGOTHS
Tarraco
Toletum
Corduba
552/554
Carthago Nova
Caesarea
Tingis
Septem
MOORS
Ratisbona
Bavarians
Langobards
SLAVS
Gepids
AVARS
Kutrigurs
Utigurs
Alans
Cherson
Danube
QE
Marcianopolis
Odessos
Constantinople
Theodosioupolis
LAZIKE
IBERIA
Dvin
SASANID PERSIA
Armenia
Sirmium
Aquileia
Milan
Italy
Ravenna
535
Illyricum
Salonae
Serdica
Thrace
Nikomedeia
Kaisareia
Edessa
Ktesiphon
Oriens
Euphrates
Antioch
535/554
Thessalonike
Ephesos
SARACEN FEDERATES
Rome
Capua
P. P. ITALIAE
Corinth
P. P. ILLYRICUM
P. P. ORIENTIS
Jerusalem
SARACENS
534
P. P. AFRICAE
Syracuse
Alexandria
Carthage
533/534
Africa
Berenike
Leptis
Ptolemais
0 300 km
0 200 mi
Map by Ian Mladjov

THE ROMAN EMPIRE IN 751
imperial border
strategides/other districts
Straßburg
Regensburg
SLAVS
SLAVS
FRANKS
Bavarians
Malamocco
Milan
Pavia
Aquileia
VENICE
AVARS
KHAZAR QAGHANATE
Dnieper
LOMBARDS
Luni
Ravenna
Sirmium
Alans
Corsica
Zadar
Split
BULGARS
Danube
Dorostolon
Cherson
Spoleto
SLAVS
Pliska
Varna
Black Sea
ABASGIA
K'ut'aisi
Rome
Ragusa
Serdica
Beroe
Mesembria
Constantinople
Trebizond
Theodosioupolis
Torres
Gaeta
Benevento
Dyrrachion
Philippoupolis
Adrianople
Nikomedeia
SARDINIA
Naples
Amalfi
THRACE
Euchaita
Amaseia
Cagliari
Thessalonike
Nikaia
ARMENIAKON
ARMENIA
Larissa
OPSIKION
Kamacha
Mantzikert
Palermo
SICILY
Amorion
Melitene
Tunis
Reggio
Thebes
THRAKESION
Kaisareia
Patrai
HELLAS
Ephesos
ANATOLIKON
Amid
Corinth
Athens
Chonai
ABBASID CALIPHATE
Syracuse
Edessa
Qayrawan
Methone
Attaleia
Tarsos
Harran
Malta
KIBYRRAIOTAI
Raqqa
Monembasia
Antioch
Aleppo
Rahba
Konstanteia
Euphrates
Gortyna
CRETE
Hims
Mediterranean Sea
Condominium with Caliphate
CYPRUS
0 200 km
0 100 mi
Damascus
Map by Ian Mladjov

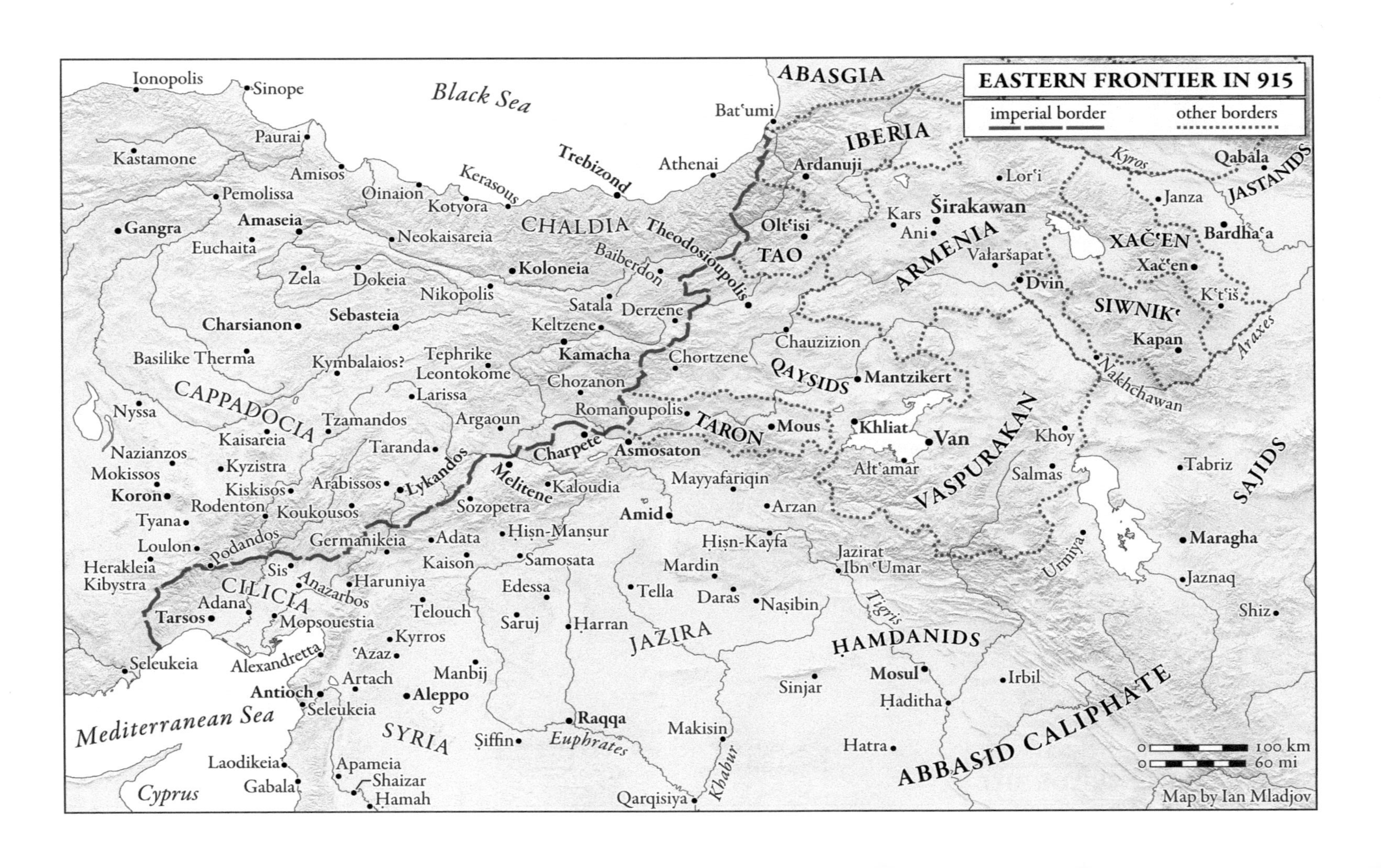
EASTERN FRONTIER IN 915
imperial border
other borders
Black Sea
Mediterranean Sea
Cyprus
ABASGIA
IBERIA
TAO
ARMENIA
XAČʿEN
SIWNIKʿ
JASTANIDS
SAJIDS
QAYSIDS
TARON
VASPURAKAN
CHALDIA
CAPPADOCIA
CILICIA
SYRIA
JAZIRA
ḤAMDANIDS
ABBASID CALIPHATE
Ionopolis
Sinope
Paurai
Kastamone
Amisos
Pemolissa
Gangra
Amaseia
Euchaita
Zela
Dokeia
Oinaion
Kotyora
Kerasous
Neokaisareia
Koloneia
Nikopolis
Trebizond
Athenai
Batʿumi
Ardanuji
Oltʿisi
Theodosioupolis
Baiberdon
Satala
Derzene
Keltzene
Kamacha
Chortzene
Chozanon
Romanoupolis
Charpete
Asmosaton
Charsianon
Sebasteia
Basilike Therma
Kymbalaios?
Tephrike
Leontokome
Larissa
Nyssa
Tzamandos
Argaoun
Kaisareia
Taranda
Nazianzos
Mokissos
Koron
Kyzistra
Kiskisos
Arabissos
Lykandos
Melitene
Kaloudia
Rodenton
Koukousos
Sozopetra
Tyana
Loulon
Podandos
Germanikeia
Adata
Ḥiṣn-Manṣur
Kaison
Samosata
Herakleia
Kibystra
Sis
Anazarbos
Haruniya
Adana
Tarsos
Mopsouestia
Telouch
Seleukeia
Alexandretta
Kyrros
ʿAzaz
Artach
Antioch
Seleukeia
Aleppo
Manbij
Edessa
Saruj
Ḥarran
Raqqa
Ṣiffin
Euphrates
Laodikeia
Gabala
Apameia
Shaizar
Ḥamah
Qarqisiya
Khabur
Makisin
Amid
Mayyafariqin
Arzan
Ḥiṣn-Kayfa
Mardin
Tella
Daras
Naṣibin
Jazirat Ibn ʿUmar
Tigris
Sinjar
Mosul
Ḥaditha
Hatra
Irbil
Chauzizion
Mantzikert
Mous
Khliat
Van
Alṭʿamar
Lorʿi
Kars
Ani
Širakawan
Valaršapat
Dvin
Khoy
Salmas
Urmiya
Nakhchawan
Kapan
Kʿtʿiš
Xačʿen
Bardhaʿa
Janza
Kyros
Qabala
Araxes
Tabriz
Maragha
Jaznaq
Shiz
0 100 km
0 60 mi
Map by Ian Mladjov

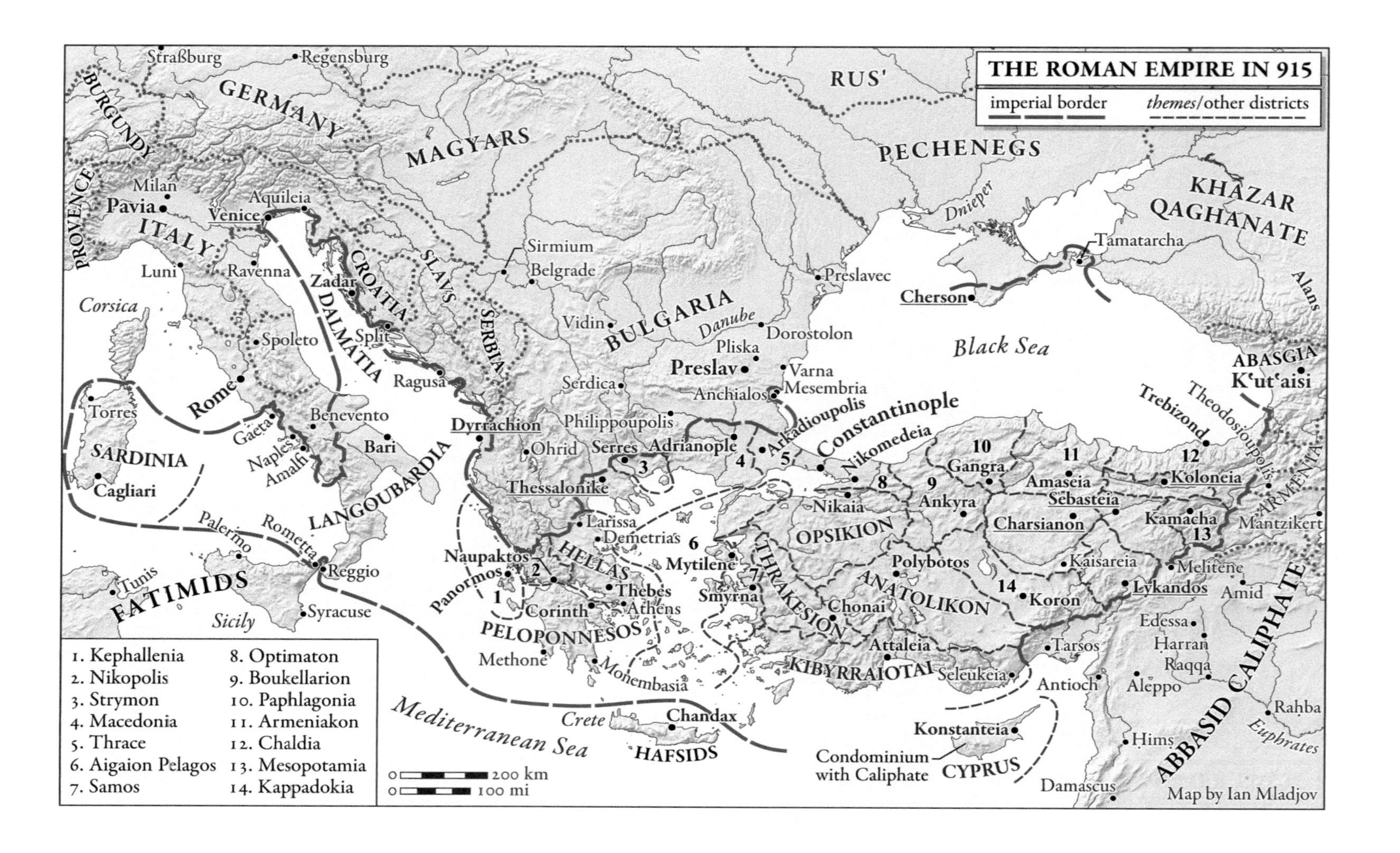
THE ROMAN EMPIRE IN 915
imperial border
themes/other districts
Straßburg
Regensburg
RUS'
GERMANY
BURGUNDY
MAGYARS
PECHENEGS
KHAZAR QAGHANATE
Dnieper
Tamatarcha
Alans
PROVENCE
Milan
Pavia
Aquileia
Venice
ITALY
Luni
Ravenna
Sirmium
Belgrade
Preslavec
Cherson
Corsica
Zadar
CROATIA
SLAVS
SERBIA
DALMATIA
Split
Spoleto
Vidin
BULGARIA
Danube
Dorostolon
Pliska
Black Sea
Preslav
Varna
Mesembria
Anchialos
ABASGIA
K'ut'aisi
Rome
Torres
Ragusa
Serdica
Philippoupolis
Adrianople
Arkadioupolis
Constantinople
Nikomedeia
Trebizond
Theodosioupolis
Benevento
Bari
Gaeta
Naples
Amalfi
SARDINIA
Cagliari
Dyrrachion
Ohrid
Serres
Thessalonike
LANGOUBARDIA
Nikaia
Gangra
Ankyra
Amaseia
Sebasteia
Koloneia
ARMENIA
Palermo
Rometta
Larissa
Demetrias
OPSIKION
Charsianon
Kamacha
Mantzikert
Naupaktos
HELLAS
Mytilene
Polybotos
Kaisareia
Melitene
Tunis
FATIMIDS
Reggio
Panormos
Thebes
Smyrna
THRAKESION
ANATOLIKON
Koron
Lykandos
Amid
Sicily
Syracuse
Corinth
Athens
Chonai
Edessa
Harran
Raqqa
PELOPONNESOS
Methone
Monembasia
KIBYRRAIOTAI
Attaleia
Seleukeia
Tarsos
Antioch
Aleppo
ABBASID CALIPHATE
Rahba
Euphrates
Mediterranean Sea
Crete
Chandax
HAFSIDS
Konstanteia
Condominium with Caliphate
CYPRUS
Hims
Damascus
0 200 km
0 100 mi
Map by Ian Mladjov
1. Kephallenia
2. Nikopolis
3. Strymon
4. Macedonia
5. Thrace
6. Aigaion Pelagos
7. Samos
8. Optimaton
9. Boukellarion
10. Paphlagonia
11. Armeniakon
12. Chaldia
13. Mesopotamia
14. Kappadokia

THE CAUCASUS IN 999

imperial border, 999 — expansion to 1045

969 date of Roman conquest

Temporary gains:
* Roman 949–979
** Roman by 971/5–979

0 100 km
0 60 mi

Map by Ian Mladjov

THE ROMAN EMPIRE IN 1054

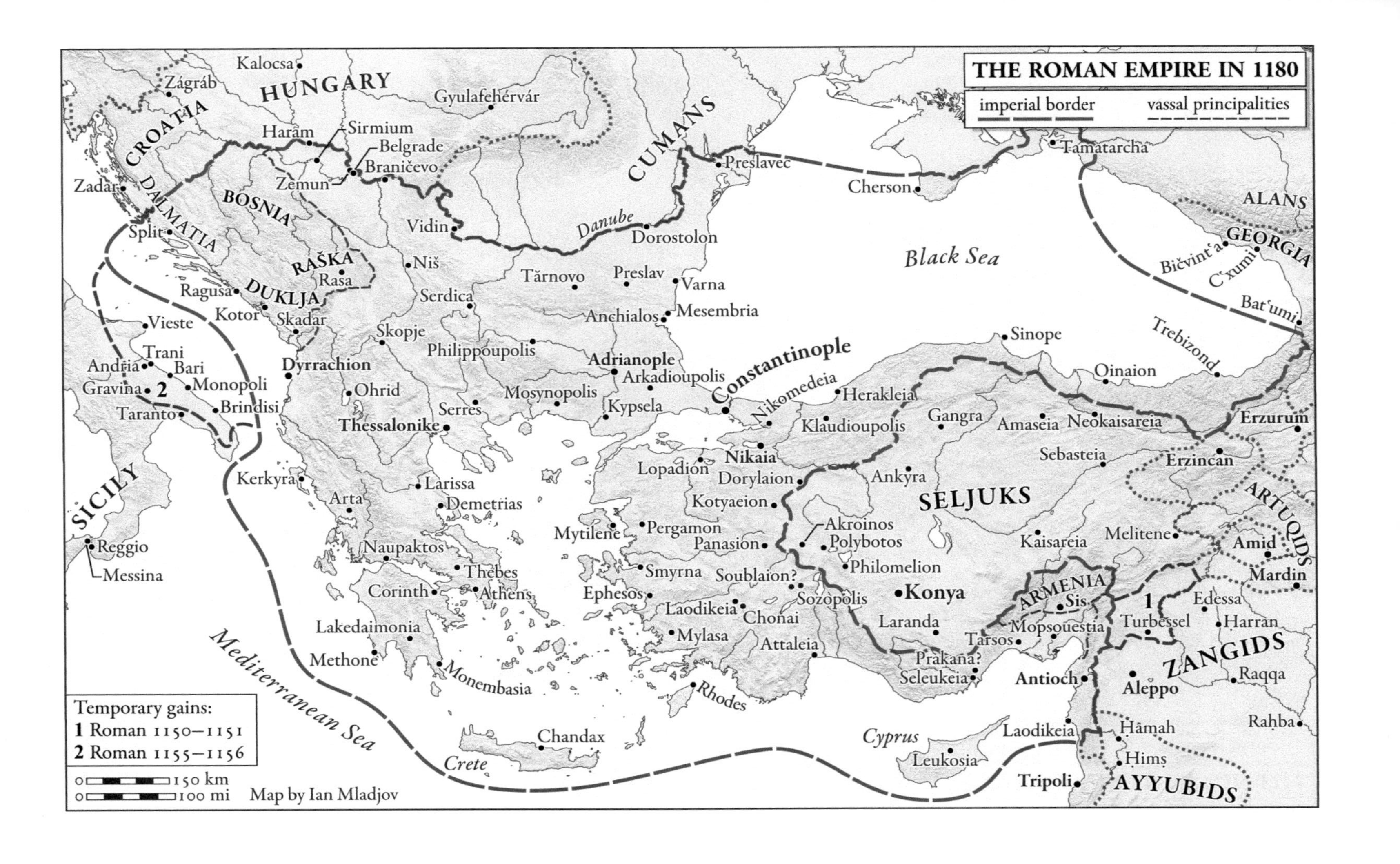
THE ROMAN EMPIRE IN 1180
imperial border
vassal principalities
HUNGARY
CROATIA
DALMATIA
BOSNIA
RAŠKA
DUKLJA
CUMANS
ALANS
GEORGIA
SELJUKS
ARMENIA
ARTUQIDS
ZANGIDS
AYYUBIDS
SICILY
Black Sea
Mediterranean Sea
Danube
Crete
Cyprus
Kalocsa
Zágráb
Zadar
Split
Ragusa
Kotor
Skadar
Rasa
Harām
Sirmium
Belgrade
Braničevo
Zemun
Gyulafehérvár
Vidin
Niš
Dorostolon
Preslavec
Cherson
Tamatarcha
Bičvint'a
C'xumi
Bat'umi
Trebizond
Oinaion
Sinope
Tărnovo
Preslav
Varna
Mesembria
Anchialos
Serdica
Skopje
Philippoupolis
Adrianople
Arkadioupolis
Constantinople
Nikomedeia
Herakleia
Klaudioupolis
Gangra
Amaseia
Neokaisareia
Erzurum
Erzincan
Sebasteia
Dyrrachion
Ohrid
Mosynopolis
Kypsela
Serres
Thessalonike
Nikaia
Lopadion
Dorylaion
Ankyra
Kotyaeion
Vieste
Trani
Andria
Bari
Monopoli
Gravina
Brindisi
Taranto
Kerkyra
Larissa
Arta
Demetrias
Mytilene
Pergamon
Panasion
Akroinos
Polybotos
Philomelion
Kaisareia
Melitene
Amid
Mardin
Reggio
Messina
Naupaktos
Thebes
Corinth
Athens
Smyrna
Soublaion?
Ephesos
Sozopolis
Konya
Laodikeia
Chonai
Laranda
Sis
Edessa
Turbessel
Harran
Lakedaimonia
Methone
Monembasia
Mylasa
Attaleia
Tarsos
Mopsouestia
Prakana?
Seleukeia
Antioch
Aleppo
Raqqa
Rhodes
Chandax
Leukosia
Laodikeia
Hāmah
Hims
Rahba
Tripoli
Temporary gains:
1 Roman 1150–1151
2 Roman 1155–1156
0 150 km
0 100 mi
Map by Ian Mladjov

THE ROMAN EMPIRE IN 1212

Roman states
other borders

HUNGARY
Sirmium
Belgrade
Braničevo
BOSNIA
CUMANS
Vicina
Hârşova
Danube
Dorostolon
BULGARIA
Vidin
SERBIA
Niš
Rasa
Ragusa
Kotor
Lipljan
Skadar
Serdica
Loveč
Tărnovo
Preslav
Karvuna
Varna
Mesembria
Anchialos
Skopje
Philippoupolis
Beroe
Adrianople
Arkadioupolis
Dyrrachion
Ohrid
Prosek
Melnik
Mosynopolis
Edessa
Serres
Rousion
Aulon
Thessalonike
EPEIROS
Kerkyra
Ioannina
Larissa
LATIN EMPIRE
Arta
Bodonitsa
Kephalonia
Naupaktos
Salona
Negroponte
Andrabida
Patras
Thebes
Zakynthos
Corinth
Athens
Akoba
ACHAEA
Argos
Aigina
Keos
Modon
Koron
Lakedaimonia
Naxos
Monembasia
VENICE
Candia
Crete
150 km
100 mi
Constantinople
Nikomedeia
Kyzikos
Poimanenon
Adramyttion
Mytilene
Pergamon
Magnesia
Smyrna
Nymphaion
Tralleis
Mylasa
Rhodes
GABALAS
Mediterranean Sea
Nikaia
Prousa
NIKAIA
Laodikeia
Chonai
Akroinos
Dorylaion
Kotyaeion
Polybotos
Philomelion
Attaleia
Kalonoros
Cherson
Black Sea
from Trebizond to Nikaia 1211/14
Amastris
Herakleia
Kastamone
Gangra
Ankyra
SELJUKS
Konya
Laranda
Seleukeia
Sinope
TREBIZOND
Trebizond
Amisos
Kerasous
Oinaion
Amaseia
Dokeia
Neokaisareia
Sebasteia
Kırşehir
Kaisareia
Erzincan
Erzurum
ARMENIA
Sis
Msis
Anazarbos
Tarsos
Ayas
Korykos
Antioch
Kantara
Nicosia
CYPRUS
Famagusta
Limassol
Laodikeia
Tortosa
Tripoli
Aleppo
AYYUBIDS
Hamah
Hims
Maraş
Melitene
Harput
Edessa
Harran
Raqqa
Euphrates
Rahba
ARTUQIDS
Mardin
Amid
Mayyafariqin
Mantzikert
AYYUBIDS
ZANGIDS
Kars
Ardanuji
GEORGIA
K'ut'aisi
Bat'umi
C'xumi
Bičvint'a
ALANS

Map by Ian Mladjov

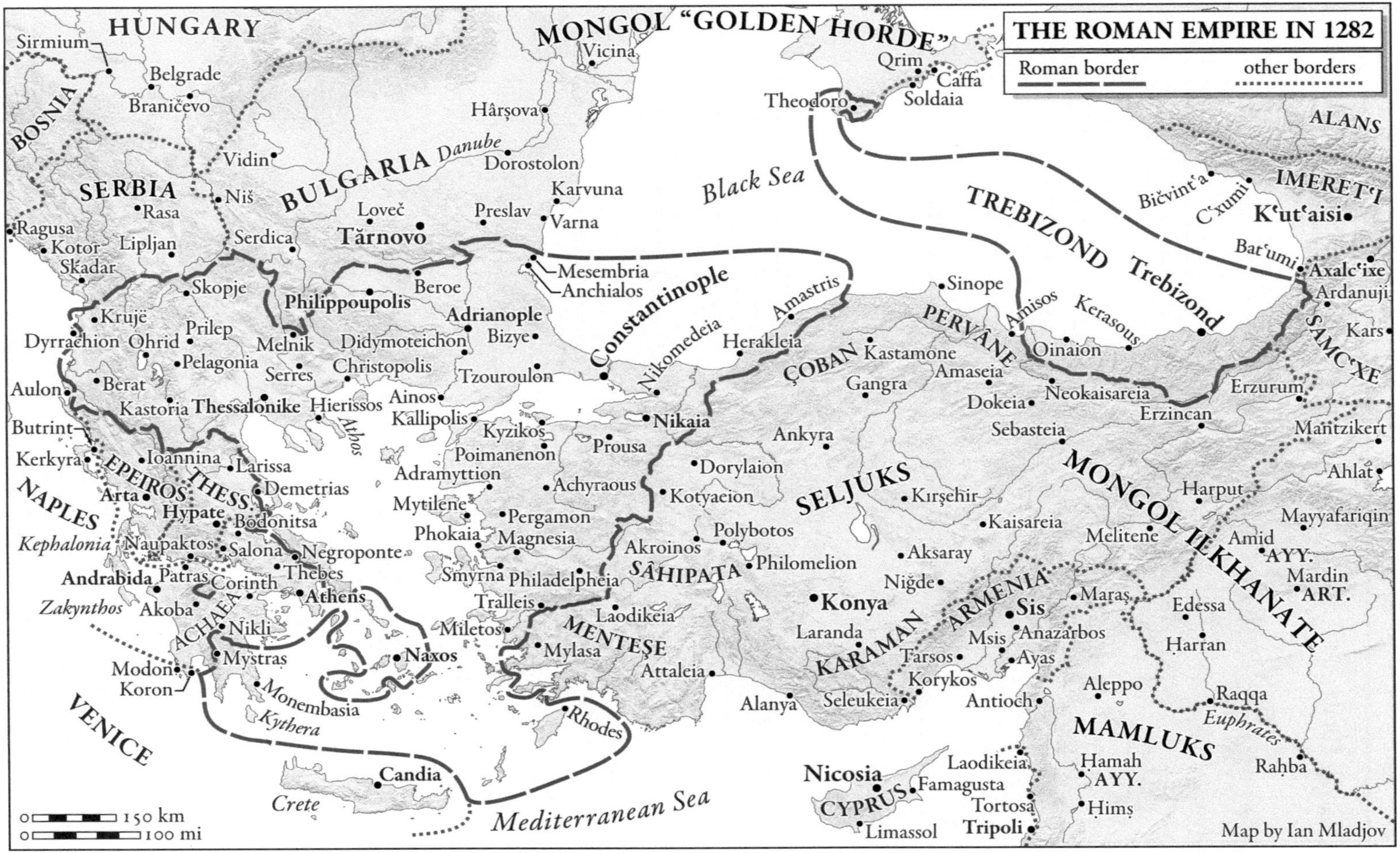
THE ROMAN EMPIRE IN 1282
Roman border
other borders
HUNGARY
MONGOL "GOLDEN HORDE"
Sirmium
Belgrade
Braničevo
BOSNIA
Vicina
Hârșova
Danube
Dorostolon
Vidin
SERBIA
BULGARIA
Niš
Rasa
Karvuna
Preslav
Varna
Loveč
Tărnovo
Ragusa
Kotor
Lipljan
Serdica
Skadar
Mesembria
Anchialos
Skopje
Beroe
Philippoupolis
Krujë
Prilep
Adrianople
Dyrrachion
Ohrid
Melnik
Didymoteichon
Bizye
Pelagonia
Serres
Christopolis
Tzouroulon
Berat
Aulon
Kastoria
Thessalonike
Hierissos
Ainos
Kallipolis
Athos
Butrint
Kerkyra
Ioannina
Larissa
EPEIROS
THESS.
Demetrias
Arta
NAPLES
Hypate
Bodonitsa
Kephalonia
Naupaktos
Salona
Negroponte
Andrabida
Patras
Corinth
Thebes
Athens
Zakynthos
Akoba
ACHAEA
Nikli
Mystras
Modon
Koron
Monembasia
Kythera
VENICE
Naxos
Candia
Crete
0 150 km
0 100 mi
Mediterranean Sea
Black Sea
Theodoro
Qrim
Caffa
Soldaia
Constantinople
Nikomedeia
Amastris
Herakleia
Kyzikos
Prousa
Nikaia
Poimanenon
Adramyttion
Mytilene
Phokaia
Pergamon
Magnesia
Smyrna
Philadelpheia
Tralleis
Miletos
Mylasa
MENTEŞE
Laodikeia
Attaleia
Rhodes
Achyraous
Kotyaeion
Dorylaion
Akroinos
Polybotos
Philomelion
SÂHIPATA
ÇOBAN
Kastamone
Gangra
Ankyra
SELJUKS
Kırşehir
Aksaray
Niğde
Konya
Laranda
KARAMAN
Alanya
Seleukeia
Korykos
Tarsos
Msis
Anazarbos
Ayas
Sis
ARMENIA
Maraş
Sinope
PERVÂNE
Amisos
Kerasous
Oinaion
Amaseia
Dokeia
Neokaisareia
Sebasteia
Kaisareia
Melitene
TREBIZOND
Trebizond
Erzincan
Erzurum
ALANS
IMERET'I
Bičvint'a
C'xumi
K'ut'aisi
Bat'umi
Axalc'ixe
Ardanuji
Kars
SAMC'XE
Mantzikert
Ahlat
Harput
MONGOL ILKHANATE
Mayyafariqin
Amid
AYY.
Mardin
ART.
Edessa
Harran
Aleppo
Antioch
Raqqa
Euphrates
MAMLUKS
Rahba
Hamah
AYY.
Hims
Laodikeia
Tortosa
Tripoli
Nicosia
Famagusta
CYPRUS
Limassol
Map by Ian Mladjov

THE ROMAN EMPIRE IN 1403
imperial border
other borders
HUNGARY
MOLDAVIA
WALLACHIA
BULGARIA
SERBIA
BOSNIA
OTTOMANS
SARUHAN
GERMIYAN
AYDIN
MENTEŞE
TEKE
HOSPITALLERS
VENICE
Fehérvár
Buda
Várad
Kalocsa
Kolozsvár
Szeged
Pécs
Temesvár
Szeben
Brassó
Bârlad
Monocastro
Chilia
Sirmium
Belgrade
Curtea de Argeş
Târgovişte
Golubac
Severin
Hârşova
Vidin
Danube
Dorostolon
Orjahovo
Ruse
Kruševac
Nikopolis
Niš
Vratica
Šumen
Karvuna
Varna
Kaliakra
Black Sea
Tărnovo
Loveč
Preslav
Peć
Priština
Serdica
Kotor
Prizren
Rosokastron
Mesembria
Anchialos
Sozopolis
Skadar
Stoponion
Velbužd
Beroe
Diampolis
Kruje
Stob
Skopje
Tzepaina
Philippoupolis
Constantinople
Edirne
Durazzo
Prilep
Strumica
Melnik
Bizye
Ohrid
Didymoteichon
Nikomedeia
Bitola
Serres
Peritheorion
Tzouroulon
Berat
Avlona
Edessa
Thessalonike
Raidestos
Kastoria
Ainos
Argyrokastron
Beroia
Hierissos
Kyzikos
Athos
Nikaia
Gallipoli
Butrint
Servia
Bursa
Ioannina
Kerkyra
Trikala
Larissa
Lemnos
Eskişehir
Parga
Arta
Pharsalos
Demetrias
Adramyttion
Balıkesir
Kütahya
Bonditza
Halmyros
Zetounion
Mytilene
Pergamon
Leukas
Hypate
Bodonitsa
Phokaia
Manisa
Angelokastron
Salona
Naupaktos
Negroponte
Karahisar
Kephalonia
Chios
Smyrna
Philadelpheia
Glarentza
Patras
Thebes
Ayasuluk
Zakynthos
Corinth
Athens
Andros
Aydın
Laodikeia
Akoba
Tenos
Argos
Miletos
Arkadia
Mylasa
Naxos
İstanoz
Mystras
Modon
Attaleia
Koron
Monembasia
Rhodes
Kythera
Candia
Crete
Mediterranean Sea
1 Roman Morea
2 Gattilusi
3 Tocchi
4 Bua Shpata
5 Buondelmonti
6 Zenebishi
7 Žarković
8 Muzaka
9 Thopia
10 Dukagjin
11 Balšići
12 Brankovići
13 Lazarevići
G Genoese possessions
H Hospitaller possessions
V Venetian possessions
0 100 km
0 60 mi
Map by Ian Mladjov

Introduction

The end was inevitable, though the Romans of the east held it at bay for over a thousand years. Their anxiety over it simmered during that millennium, finding expression in apocalyptic fiction. According to one scenario, which still resonates, the waters would rise and submerge the world, and the few survivors would tie their boats to the tip of the Column of Constantine and lament its passing.[1] Historical events also fueled the imagination. Raging infernos periodically tore through Constantinople, turning the porticos into rivers of fire and scorching that iconic Column. Urban insurrections led to armed clashes among the citizens in the forum around it and the surrounding streets. The Column was struck by lightning, which sheared off shards, and a mighty gale toppled the colossal nude statue of Constantine-as-Apollo that had stood at its top for almost eight centuries; the fallen statue was prudently replaced with a cross. History and apocalypse flirted around this monument in both pagan and Christian guises. It was said that Constantine had transferred the Palladium, a talisman of Athena that made cities impregnable, from Rome to Constantinople, burying it under the Column. When the Turks finally broke through in 1453, the rout was expected to reach only as far as the Column, whereupon an angel of God would appear and deliver a sword to a common man, who would drive the enemy to the borders of Persia.[2]

The Column of Constantine may be the worse for wear but it withstood the test of time: it still stands in modern Istanbul (see Figure 1 in chapter 1). It was built by Constantine the Great as a focal point for his new city and remains an iconic monument for a civilization that lasted over 1,100 years. Though other phases of Roman history are studied more, this was the longest one. The eastern Roman empire, known colloquially to its inhabitants as *Romanía*, was one of the most durable states the world has ever seen. Its existence spanned a fifth of recorded human history, hence the length of this book. At the start of our story, it encompassed about a fourth of a total global population of some 190 million; by the end, the Romans were but a tiny fraction of a global population that had nearly doubled. When we begin, most Romans worshipped the ancient gods of Olympos and knew a world of three continents, whereas the end of our story was witnessed by people who would, later in life, hear of the arrival of the Cross and Spanish empire to the New World. The Romans of the east did not survive for so long by praying or burying talismans to avert the apocalypse, though they did those things too. They survived by investing in institutions of resilience, pooling resources to promote common goals, and building consensus around shared values, especially regarding justice, social order, correct religion, and the common good. This book recounts their millennial tale, which was by turns exhilarating and agonizing but always fascinating. It is a story of resilience and adaptability framed against the backdrop of those institutions and shared values, as the east Romans struggled to survive and thrive during one of the most difficult and dangerous periods in history.

Like the ship of Theseus discussed by ancient philosophers, the Roman polity gradually changed its component elements over the centuries, but never lost its underlying identity. It built a new capital in the east, lost the old one in the west, converted to Christianity, absorbed new populations, forgot Latin to fully embrace Greek, and adapted its institutions to meet new challenges as they came. These changes took place gradually, over the course not only of generations but sometimes centuries, so they were not experienced as dramatic ruptures. Sudden ruptures generally came from the outside, from the exogenous shock of foreign invasion, such as the Arab conquests in the 630s, the Seljuk conquests of the 1070s, and the Fourth Crusade of 1203–1204. After each of these shocks, Romanía recovered and adjusted, until little by little it eventually succumbed. Through all this, it remained Roman and Orthodox, and these identities were the immovable foundations on which its institutions were built and rebuilt over the centuries.

Perceptions of this culture in the west have traditionally been quite different from what the reader will find in the following pages. Starting around 800 AD and continuing to our day, western scholars and institutions have invidiously denied that this polity and especially its people were Roman at all, concocting both sham pretexts and alternative names to justify this stance. Western ideologies—at first those of the papacy and the medieval German emperors, then the idea of "Europe" that emerged in early modernity—claimed the Roman tradition as their exclusive right. For a thousand years, they saw in the east a "Greek" society, attributing to that name a host of negative connotations derived from ancient Latin literature, such as perfidiousness and effeminacy. Later on, the thinkers of the Enlightenment cast the Greek empire as corrupt, theocratic, superstitious, and lacking a functional political culture. This model was more instrumental than historical, as its purpose was to discuss indirectly the flaws of Europe's own monarchies.

In the nineteenth century, a new Greek state appeared that aspired to reconstruct the eastern empire of Constantinople. This project was unwelcome to the western Great Powers, who saw it as an extension of Russian imperialism, and so western scholars dropped the term "empire of the Greeks," replacing it with the vacuous names "Byzantine" and "Byzantium," derived from the pre-Constantinian name of its capital. With its Romanness long placed out of bounds, they reimagined it now as a society organized primarily around Orthodoxy.[3] Its political thought was wrongly cast in purely theological terms, and exhibitions of its art projected a historically inaccurate image of exotic mysticism and "spirituality." Our modern scholarly traditions emerged from these medieval and early modern prejudices. In no other field of research is the identity of the people being studied denied so strenuously as in Byzantine Studies. The attested names of their state (*Romanía*, i.e., "Romanland") and vernacular speech (*Roméika*) do not even appear in standard reference works published in the twenty-first century.[4]

Yet now these obsolete ideologies and the cognitive dissonance required to maintain them are being swept away. What was formerly called "the empire of the Greeks" and more recently "the Byzantine empire" is quickly claiming its place as a direct continuation of the ancient Roman state and its culturally complex society. Better than calling it a "late" or "medieval" Roman empire, this book foregrounds an overlooked term used by the Enlightenment historian Edward Gibbon, who flagged it in two places as a "new" Roman empire.[5] Contrary to his narrative, however, its history was less a long decline and more an ongoing renewal of its basic modes. As late as the twelfth century, authors in Constantinople could still imagine it as "a new Rome, a wrinkleless Rome, a Rome forever young, forever renewed."[6] Yet paradoxically, it was also "born old."[7] It directly inherited Roman political traditions, Greek literature, and Biblical monotheism that were each about a thousand years old when New Rome was built. Its culture drew from a deep well fed by many streams. It was, in fact, the only civilization that combined these elements in their original Roman, Greek, and Christian forms, and it did so long before western theorists tried to define "Europe" in the same terms.[8] It was the new Roman empire, not the old, that gave these elements to the west, including curated versions of the corpus of Roman law, Greek literature and thought, and the Church Fathers and decisions of the Church Councils. Each of these traditions remained vital and active in New Rome, where their evolving interactions defined a fascinating culture.

The recovery of east Roman identity is not the only, or even the main, storyline of this book. Its primary goal is to explain, through a combination of narrative and analysis, the longevity of this polity and the renewable sources of its resilience. The argument rests primarily upon a reinterpretation of Roman governmentality that has been underway for some time. Specifically, the new Roman state successfully threaded the needle of (on the one hand) extracting enough resources to maintain, by premodern standards, an extraordinarily large military and administrative apparatus, while (on the other hand) not alienating its subjects and making them want to secede or topple the monarchy. At the same time, through a wide range of media it hammered home the message that taxes were used solely for the public good of the Roman people. The evidence suggests that this was no rhetorical ploy: it was an ideology that actually shaped the priorities and not just the persona of government. In this way, it achieved a considerable level of consensus and buy-in among all of its subjects, not just elites. As a result, during centuries that saw the domains of caliphs and Carolingians, Huns and Avars, and crusaders and Mongols come and go, as they succumbed to the centrifugal forces that pulled at all other premodern empires, New Rome endured.

This reading, therefore, directly refutes past views of the "late" empire as despotic, oppressive, totalitarian, and corrupt,[9] as well as cynical views, which are always fashionable, according to which it was run by distant elites in the capital for their own benefit without any commonality of interest between them and the provincial populations. It is easy to be cynical—and safer for scholars' reputations—but the evidence does not support this picture. By and large, it supports instead a different picture, which is currently gaining ground. According to this, the court recognized that it was both a practical and an ideological necessity to explain how its policies benefited the totality of its subjects. As it struggled to balance extraction with consensus, the monarchy projected responsiveness, accountability, and adherence to shared social norms, and its subjects duly held it to those standards. In New Rome, political legitimacy derived from the stewardship of the common good, as subjects were frequently keen to remind their emperors. It is not even clear that this was an "empire" in the conventional sense, a term with no clear equivalent in medieval Greek. It called itself—and was—the monarchy, or the polity, of the Romans.

This book presents a detailed narrative of New Rome's political, military, and Church history. Recent years have seen a proliferation of brief histories of "Byzantium" and concise introductions. While these serve a purpose, they tend to leap from one peak to the next to briskly cover a millennium in a couple hundred pages. A longer narrative, by contrast, can afford to explore the valleys and crags below, so that readers can appreciate the entire terrain and properly understand how it was all interconnected. A proper history must take the time to build a world, tell its story, and situate its protagonists. At the same time, following east Roman models of history it must also try to explain events.[10] Although we cannot (and therefore should not even attempt to) psychologize protagonists, we can instead situate their decisions and reactions within the range of possible options that their institutions, culture, and environment required, enabled, or impeded. It is sometimes enough to make sense of what happened, even if we cannot fully identify its causes.

This, in turn, calls for a rigorous analysis, parallel to the narrative and entwined with it, of the deeper structures of east Roman life, including economy (especially taxation), social stratification, ethnicity, demography, and the evolution of religious identity. A narrative that is not informed by such analysis is superficial. Conversely, theoretical models must work in practice too, and the testing ground for them is narrative. Deeper forces have, at some point, to appear on the surface, otherwise they are merely abstractions. Many of these abstractions have been put forward in the field of Byzantine Studies, promoting theological, national, or academic agendas but without robustly interfacing with events on the ground. Here these two entwined approaches, the narrative and the structural, are deployed dialectically.

Narrative does not mean that the book will focus on a few leadership cadres to the exclusion of the majority of the population. Quite the contrary, the purpose of this book is not merely to tell an exciting story—though it does that too—but to access the conditions and status of most people. This is done in various ways. First, large groups, especially provincials and the people of Constantinople, appear often in the sources, both acting and reacting, for they were regarded as legitimate stakeholders in the polity. Their consent, even if only tacit, was required for the legitimation of each new emperor and was deemed essential for the success of imperial policy. This was why emperors, bishops, and other elites sought to justify their actions in the eyes of public opinion, whether by posting notices in churches or assembling the people in the hippodrome, the forum of Constantine, or Hagia Sophia. The infrastructure of Constantinople was designed to facilitate large gatherings for precisely this reason. For their part, the people often intervened in elite political conflicts, in doctrinal controversies, and even in economic policy, usually decisively. These interventions are crucial for understanding the basic dynamics of society and the parameters of its political sphere.

Second, it is true that most large groups usually appear in the sources as aggregates that lack granular definition. Narrative sources mostly focus on a small cast of characters, including emperors, court and military officials, bishops, monks, and saints—most of them men. But they too are significant for the people's history, not only because they made impactful decisions but also because, as character-types that were expected to play familiar roles, they focalized the values, hopes, and frustrations of the majority.[11] Roman and Christian culture in all periods was a field of contestation and debate, and leadership figures became avatars of the issues of the day. They were watched closely. No one, not even the poorest farmer in the interior, was so isolated or indifferent as to long ignore what they were doing. Romanía was a highly interconnected society, buzzing with expectations, demands, reciprocity, suspicion, and anger.

Third, this book will push back against the idea that the Roman state, as a premodern state, was unable to significantly shape the lives of its subjects and could do little more than gather taxes or recruits from a distance and, therefore, that the study of the state is little more than the study of elites. The new Roman empire was, famously, an experiment in "big government," and its longevity is an indication of its success. Government reached all the way down to the local level and shaped the economic circumstances of most people, including what they could own, their property and inheritance rights, and how they calculated value in the first place; it defined their social status in relation to other groups; and, not least of all, it successfully established an official religion that defined not only what people believed but how they worshipped, married, were born, died, and were remembered. It also created a unified legal system and currency, an army that pooled resources from the entire territory for the purpose of common defense, and administrative hierarchies that reported to the capital. The horizons of time and space themselves were determined by the same institutions, for example the calendar, the schedule of tax payments, and the boundaries of villages, cities, and provinces. Not even the most hardened hermits could fully escape the grid of these institutions by fleeing to remote mountain tops or deserts. Understanding these institutions, therefore, significantly explains the parameters of daily life.

It was also through narrative that Christian Orthodox identity emerged. This book does not presuppose that there was always one ideal Orthodoxy waiting to be elaborated by successive generations. When Constantine gained control of the east in 324, no Christian could have imagined a version of the faith in which Jesus Christ was "consubstantial" with the God the Father but himself "in two Natures," with two "Wills" and "Operations"; or that icons, to which one prayed and bowed, would become central to worship; that the Greek and Latin Churches would split, among other reasons, over the "Procession of the Holy Spirit"; far less that monks, through a form of repetitive prayer, would be able to see the light of the operations of God. These beliefs accreted gradually through contingent controversies that could easily have yielded different outcomes. Therefore, the narrative parameters in which they unfolded essentially created Orthodoxy. After all, few people fully understood the theological issues, sometimes not even the leading theologians themselves. Instead, Christian identities formed around the narratives of persecution and righteousness, triumph and injustice, that evolved around the rival doctrines to the point where the latter became secondary. With a modicum of good will, theological compromises could usually be worked out, but neither side could forgive what it believed that it had suffered at the hands of its enemies. Through all this, most emperors tried to promote consensus and steer the ship of state safely to the other side. Orthodoxy was anything but static or settled.

Narrative is indispensable for research in Byzantine Studies, which more than many others is an intensely historicizing field. Byzantinists interpret every text, idea, figure, art, and material artifact against its immediate context, striving to pin it down it, if possible, to the year, month, or even day. Getting the narrative right has ramifications for research across the field, by opening new contexts of interpretation and closing others. While our understanding of some periods has long remained stable, others have been radically transformed by recent research. The present reconstruction will challenge and possibly surprise many experts by presenting both recent findings and original interpretations. It rests on the critical use of the sources, which are cited in the notes and synthesized with conclusions drawn from archaeology and scientific data, such as palynology. Another area of current scientific research—the study of fluctuations in historical climate—has received much attention recently but has not yet reached a point where its ambivalent claims can interface with the other material in this book. The work of integrating climate into this narrative is left to future historians, who will thereby be taking up, in their own distinctive way, a task that has been handed down by the ancients themselves.

The history of the New Roman Empire is one of the most fascinating tales in human history. It is at times Biblical, taking its cue from scriptural archetypes, and at times heroic, drawing on Homer and the classics. It is replete with saints and sinners. But behind the more colorful figures, there labored a host of bureaucrats, lawyers, military engineers, land surveyors, and tax collectors that kept the whole thing together. This is a story of a single society held together by a strong sense of its values and its identity, and by robust institutions that enabled it to survive the most dangerous millennium of human history. Germanic barbarians, Muslim conquerors, and Viking raiders all came and went, while Romanía endured to the very threshold of modernity, falling to the sound of cannonfire. How it did so will occupy our attention for the next thousand pages.

A Note on the Spelling of Names

The reader will find at the end of the book a glossary of important technical terms whose use could not be avoided; they are mostly offices, titles, and institutions of the east Roman state. "Byzantium" and "the Byzantines," which are misleading modern terms, are not used, except in the subtitle and a few rare references to modern perceptions.

The pre-Constantinian name of Constantinople is "Byzantion." It is also called the City, because that is what its residents frequently called it (ἡ Πόλις) in recognition of its size and importance. "The City" lies behind its modern Turkish name Istanbul, which derives from the Greek for "in the City" (*eis ten polin*); the expression had given rise to a name much like "Istanbul" even before the Turkish conquest. Other place-names are usually spelled according to their Greek form, unless they have overwhelmingly familiar English forms (e.g., Athens). Turkish forms are introduced only at the very end.

The names of individuals are spelled according to their most likely native language, or the language in which they wrote, which for most people in this book was Greek (e.g., Prokopios and Ioannes). The Latinization of Greek names ("Comnenus") and, worse, their Anglicization (e.g., "John") is an offensive form of cultural imposition. It is practiced for no other culture except "the Byzantines," whose very name as a people ("Romans") has likewise been deemed inadmissible in the west for centuries. It is time for this nonsense to end. An exception is made here for famous individuals who, by a subjective standard, are overwhelmingly well known by their English names, e.g., Julian, John Chrysostom, Justinian, and Basil II, as well as some western Europeans who came from multilingual backgrounds and whose names at the time were recoded in many variant forms. The same is true for the names of the important Church Councils, by which they are generally known, as opposed to the names of the cities in which they were held (e.g., Nicaea vs. Nikaia). Moreover, the names of emperors and high officials are Latinized down to ca. 520, because the highest echelons of government in Constantinople continued to operate in Latin until then, and these men appear here as its functionaries, regardless of their native language. Before the glossary, the reader will also find a list of state revenues and large payments, in gold solidi, by which other costs and values can be put into perspective.

Acknowledgments

This book would not be possible without all the excellent research of colleagues around the world, for which I am immensely grateful. If bibliographies did not eat up so much of the allotted word count, more of your publications could have been cited here. In the years that it has taken me to write this book, I have consulted with dozens of you on matters large and small, and I can discern now the influence of countless more conversations, debates, and lectures that took place years earlier. It is, unfortunately, impossible to thank everyone here individually, so a collective acknowledgement must suffice. For proof of my appreciation, I direct readers to the podcast "Byzantium & Friends" that I launched while writing this book. It remains to be seen whether that medium will have a longer shelf-life than this book you are reading.

The New Roman Empire exists only because Stefan Vranka, at OUP, asked me point-blank after dinner if I might be interested in writing it. Of course, I immediately said no. His support and frank advice helped immensely once I came around to it. Special thanks go out to others who also read long sections of this book and made valuable comments and corrections, especially Garth Fowden and my former students Scott Kennedy, Marion Kruse, and Brian Swain. Ian Mladjov also corrected many errors and provided the excellent maps for the books. The color plates and index were subvented by research funds that were provided by the Division of Humanities of the University of Chicago. Many of the images were generously made available by David Hendrix and Dumbarton Oaks. The medallion on the cover was judiciously recommended by Betsy Williams.

Finally, I am immensely grateful to young scholars around the world who are struggling—against the headwinds of neoliberal austerity, politicized hostility to the humanities, and the insecurities of adjunct employment and the project-grant system—to expand our knowledge of history and impart their love of it to the next generation of students.

PART ONE

A NEW EMPIRE

1

New Rome and the New Romans

New Rome

On 11 May, 330, the sun, rising behind the Asian hills across the Bosporos, shone for the last time on the ancient city of Byzantion. On that day, the emperor Constantine rededicated the city to himself and to the Fortune of Rome. Henceforth, Byzantion became Constantinople and, as New Rome, it would change the course of history. While the city below lay still in the predawn shadow, the sun reflected off its highest point, a colossal statue of Constantine himself. This was a gilded bronze nude with rays emerging from his head, a spear in his left hand, and a globe signifying universal dominion in his right. Standing atop a column of purple stone that was almost forty meters tall and banded with victory laurel wreaths, the colossus was a repurposed Apollo. It reinforced the emperor's long association with the Solar God and the first emperor of Rome. Over three centuries before, Augustus had chosen Apollo to project the serene power, eternal youth, and classical order of his new golden age. Constantine's statue alluded also to the colossus of Sol that stood beside the Coliseum in Rome and gave it its name, and it linked New Rome to nearby Troy, the ancient Roman homeland whose patron deity was Apollo. Constantine and his City thus picked up the thread of an old history: the Romans, children of Aeneas and heirs of Augustus, had returned home. Stories soon circulated that Constantine had brought his colossus from Troy and had intended to found his City there but was diverted by an apparition to the more advantageous location of Byzantion.[1]

Touched by the dawn, the gilded statue "blazed over the citizens like the sun."[2] It illuminated the forum of Constantine in whose center it stood, a circular paved plaza (see Figure 1). The forum was enclosed by a two-tiered colonnade of white marble and was bisected by the City's main boulevard, the Mese, which ran east-west, from the palace by the sea to the new land walls. As late as the tenth century, the marble columns were read cosmically, as gleaming stars attending upon the statue of Sun-Constantine.[3] At the northern arc of the forum stood a new Senate House flanked by a bronze colossus of Athena and statues that evoked Troy, such as the Judgment of Paris. The huge doors of the Senate came from the temple of Artemis at Ephesos and featured a bronze relief of the Gigantomachy, the battle of the gods against the serpent-legged Giants. It was precisely as a serpentine monster that Constantine had denigrated his rival emperor Licinius, whom he defeated in 324 in order to take over the eastern half of the empire. The victor founded his City in the aftermath of the war as a magnificent "monument to his triumph."[4] Augustus had likewise founded Nikopolis, his City of Victory, in Greece after the naval battle of Actium in 31 BC, when he defeated his rival Mark Antony. As Constantine also defeated his rival in a naval war, the southern arc of his forum was adorned with a fountain flanked by statues of twelve Sirens or Hippocamps on tall columns. The forum was thus a grand architectural image of the Constantinian cosmos, linking the City to Troy, Rome, victory, and the Apolline order of Augustus. It marked a glorious new beginning, fueled by civil war and built from its spoils.

Figure 1 Porphyry Column of Constantine, encased in an Ottoman base
Shutterstock/hdesislava

Constantinople was created between 324 and 330 through a series of arcane Roman rites. There was the *limitatio* in 324, when Constantine delineated the walls in the ground with a spear; the *inauguratio*, when omens were taken and a horoscope cast; and finally the *consecratio* and *dedicatio* of 11 May, 330, when the City was endowed with its new identity.[5] Experts in traditional cult ensured that the rites were performed properly and the emperor made a "bloodless sacrifice," one appropriate for a Christian, that bound the City to its new names. The focal point of its new destiny was the emperor's column and statue, but the City also featured traditional foci of Roman religion: a Capitolium and temples to Kybele and the Tyche (or Fortune) of New Rome. Christian thinkers struggled to discern the emperor's Christian beliefs in all this, or averted their gaze from the naked paganism on display. Ordinary Christians, by contrast, did what Romans had always done before imperial images: "they propitiated with sacrifices the image of Constantine standing on the porphyry column, honored it with lamps and incense, and prayed to it as a god."[6] Constantinople began as a Roman imperial foundation, not a Christian capital, a concept that did not yet exist.

After the forum rites of 11 May, the imperial procession moved along the Mese toward the Augoustaion, the open square before the palace named for the emperor's mother, the Augusta Helena, whose statue stood there. To the left was the Golden Milestone, or Milion, a massive tetrapylon (four piers joined by arches supporting a domed roof). Like its equivalent column in Rome, the Milion served as a symbolic zero point for measuring distances from Constantinople, the new center of the eastern empire. Behind it, to the north, was the Basilica ("Royal") Stoa, a colonnaded courtyard that hosted twin shrines for the goddess Roma and the Tyche of Constantinople, who was depicted on coins as an enthroned matron with a crown of walls. Panning clockwise around the square, the procession saw the foundations of the church of Hagia Sophia, whose construction had just begun; the entrance to the palace and a second Senate House; the Zeuxippos baths, a complex that would hold a collection of over eighty statues, many of heroes and scenes from the Trojan War; and finally, to their right, the hippodrome. This was the monumental core of New Rome, the nexus of imperial, spiritual, and popular power.

The day's events concluded with chariot races in the hippodrome, where the emperor appeared before the people wearing his new diadem set with precious stones. This was an innovation in imperial regalia, but otherwise the procession before the games, or *pompa circensis*, was a venerable part of Roman tradition. Chariot races featuring the Blue, Green, Red, and White teams were centuries-old at Rome and would continue for another nine hundred years at New Rome, until 1204, making them the longest-lived sporting events in world history. The proximity of the hippodrome to the Great Palace replicated that of the Circus Maximus and Palatine at Rome, as did the collection of artwork that was appropriated from other cities to adorn the central spine of the racetrack (see Figure 2). There was, for example, the Serpent Column from Delphi, which was dedicated by the Greeks who defeated the Persians at Plataea (479 BC); it now hinted at Constantine's planned campaign against the Sasanian Persian empire. There was a statue from Augustus' Nikopolis in Greece, reinforcing the link to Constantine's role model, and a statue of the she-wolf suckling Romulus and Remus. Plans were drawn up to bring an obelisk from Egypt—the Circus Maximus in Rome had one, after all—but that project stalled. The hippodrome was eventually endowed with the "built obelisk" that still stands toward the southern end of the spine. Originally, it was sheathed in bronze. The hippodrome was thus a museum of the empire's many histories and cultures. As one wit of that period put it, the new capital "was adorned with the nudity of all other cities,"[7] referring to the nudity of the statues themselves and the stripping bare of the provinces to adorn Constantinople. But many provincials also "took pleasure in seeing" their cultures represented in the new capital.[8]

The hippodrome was designed for the races, an avid passion of the people that, as many preachers complained, mired them in gambling, magic, anger, and factions. It was also a forum for the interaction of emperor and populace, where each gauged the other's mood. Estimates of its capacity range from 40,000

Figure 2 Obelisks on the axis of the hippodrome of Constantinople
Photo by Anthony Kaldellis

to 100,000. The people could gather there even when there were no races to protest an unpopular policy or emperor. The populace of the City, after all, was the *populus Romanus* and was recognized as such on Constantine's own coins; his successors called them *Romani cives*.[9] The point of interface between the palace and the people was the imperial box in the stands, the *kathisma*, which led to the palace through a spiral stairway. It was a multistoried building with artwork and a loggia of its own. Here emperors would be acclaimed, cheered, and exalted by tens of thousands of their loyal subjects—or booed, jeered, and deposed. The hippodrome was a stage on which regimes were made and unmade.

Constantine decreed an anniversary procession from the forum to the hippodrome to reenact the City's dedication. A wooden statue of himself, gilded in gold, holding a Tyche of the City, was placed in a chariot and accompanied by soldiers carrying candles. The procession would march around the turning post and stop before the imperial box, whereupon the emperor of the day, along with everyone else, would rise and kneel before the founder. This ceremony lasted until the reign of Theodosius I (379–395), or later. By the tenth century the City's birthday celebration was marked only by races and a liturgy in Hagia Sophia.[10]

Christian writers endowed Constantine with every virtue, an exaltation that continued after his death until he had become a paragon of imperial rule held up to future emperors. He was labeled "the Great" and, in recognition of his services to the Church, he was venerated, uniquely among emperors, as a saint "equal to the Apostles." Starting in the mid-fifth century, his successors would often be hailed as "new Constantines."[11] His conversion to Christianity and foundation of a New Rome were later seen as turning points, but they did not disrupt the continuity of Roman history. A tenth-century emperor understood the new empire as a phase in a larger story: it was "the Roman empire in Byzantion,"[12] less a new empire than a renewed one.

Laws, coins, poems, imagery, and monuments prove that Constantinople was intended from the beginning as a double of Rome in the east, as a "younger," "other," "second," or "new" version of it. It was endowed with many attributes for that role, such as a Capitolium (on the Mese, west of the forum), a bread dole for its people, and exemption from provincial administration: "it not only had the name," wrote a native in the early fifth century, "it had a corresponding Senate, popular organizations, and magistracies, and was subject to the modes and orders of the Romans in Italy."[13] Like Rome, it had fourteen administrative regions and was even imagined to have seven hills. More abstractly, Constantinople "partook in the Tyche and the name of Rome." That was how the Aristotelian philosopher and orator Themistios put it in a speech of 357. Themistios had been elevated to the eastern Senate by Constantine's son and heir, Constantius II (337–361), and charged with recruiting new men to that body. In 357, he led an embassy to Rome on behalf of the eastern Senate and tried to express the ineffable identity of the two cities. In his speeches, Themistios often called Rome the "metropolis" (i.e., mother city) of Constantinople and claimed the ancient Romans as its "ancestors." The one city had Romulus, the other Constantine.[14] Elder Rome retained a place of honor, at least for now, but eastern Romans would soon refer to their City simply as "Rome," without qualification, as if they were the same.[15]

How was it possible to imagine such a thing? No other state in history has copied-and-pasted its capital, the city from which it took its name, and bilocated it to a former frontier province. And why did Constantine do so?

Constantine's immediate concern after the civil war of 324 was to win over Licinius' former supporters and build up a body of loyalists in the east. He also wanted to showcase his victory and, like many past emperors, to exalt his name by refounding a city. Licinius had used Byzantion as a base and had likely embellished it as an imperial residence. Constantine had to erase the traces of his rival, just as he had done in Rome, where he had appropriated the buildings begun by his rival Maxentius, whom he defeated in 312. But one war cannot explain the grandeur in which Constantinople was conceived as a Second Rome, or the commitment to it by the subsequent emperors of the fourth century, few of whom spent much time there. For example, Valens (364–378) spent most of his reign on the move, fighting border wars along the Danube and in the east, but he too invested in the City, even though he did not belong to Constantine's dynasty; witness the impressive aqueduct named after him (see Figure 9). Early in his reign the City even supported a usurper, Procopius, giving Valens cause to abandon the project. Yet he did not. His successor Theodosius I also invested massively in building up the City and he spent most of his reign in it. Roman leadership was, therefore, committed to Constantine's plan for a New Rome in the east. Regardless of their dynastic and religious differences, all eastern emperors had sound strategic and political reasons to ensure Constantinople's success.

Strategic challenges

A capital in the east addressed two growing strategic challenges. The first was the empire's tendency to break into pieces, with the fault line running through Greece or Asia Minor, or directly along the Bosporos. The empire had fractured there between the rivals Octavian and Mark Antony, whose base was at Alexandria (43–31 BC); between Vitellius and Vespasian, also based at Alexandria (69); between Septimius Severus and Pescennius Niger, whose base was at Antioch, though much of the fighting took place around Byzantion (193–194); between Aurelian, who used Byzantion as his base in 271–272, and Zenobia of Palmyra, who seized a large part of Asia Minor; between Licinius and Maximinus Daia in 313, when Byzantion proved to be the pivot of the war; and between Constantine and Licinius in 324, when the fighting again took place on the Bosporos. Byzantion, the point of passage between two continents, Europe and Asia, and two seas, the Black Sea and the Mediterranean, had become the fulcrum of the eastern Roman world. Before the emperor Caracalla murdered his brother Geta in 211, the two had discussed partitioning the empire at the Bosporos, "a point provided by divine providence for dividing the continents." Caracalla would receive the west and place his armies at Byzantion, whereas Geta would take the east, with Antioch or Alexandria as his capital, and place his forces at Chalkedon, across the straits from his brother.[16] Byzantion had already become a watchword for imperial fracture.

The second challenge was the growth of foreign threats. Increasingly, these were more than a single emperor could handle. In the mid-third century, the empire was devastated by repeated barbarian invasions from across the Rhine and Danube, and from across the Euphrates by the militaristic Persian empire that had replaced the Parthians. More legions were transferred to the eastern provinces to meet this strategic development, putting more distance between Rome and the empire's concentrations of military power. Syria was too far to govern from Italy. Also, during that crisis, the frontier armies frequently took matters into their own hands, appointing their own emperors to defend the provinces provided they paid their soldiers generously. This had splintered the empire into a series of regional Roman states, which mimicked the original and replicated its institutions. During the third century, there were too many emperors at any time, popping up everywhere from Britain to Egypt.

This challenge was met by Constantine's predecessor, the reforming emperor Diocletian (284–305), who effectively turned the problem into its own solution by transforming hostile breakup into a system of power-sharing. Instead of having rival emperors who tore the empire apart, he took on colleagues to form an imperial college of two Augusti and two junior Caesars. Multiple emperors now operated quasi-autonomously in separate quadrants of the empire while still being coordinated through a single will, his own. They stayed with the armies, keeping them under control, and moved throughout the provinces to deal more effectively with barbarians and other rivals. Modern scholars call this regime the Tetrarchy, or Rule of Four (see Figure 3). Their regional headquarters included Trier and Milan in the west and Antioch, Nikomedeia, and Thessalonike in the east. From there, they could respond faster to trouble on the Danube and Euphrates than from Rome. The growing importance of the east in this system of collegiate emperorship is shown by the fact that between 284 and 395 the senior Augustus always chose the east as his own domain, save only Valentinian I (364–375).

Constantinople suited this new strategic pattern, being equidistant from the Euphrates and upper Danube. It could be supplied by sea from Egypt and the Black Sea. It controlled the Bosporos, the crucial bottleneck and sensitive breaking point of the empire. Yet after so many rounds of civil war, Constantine

Figure 3 Porphyry statue-group of the Tetrarchs in Venice, taken from Constantinople. It is just over 4 feet tall and embedded in the corner of the cathedral of San Marco.
Photo by David Hendrix

had realized that regional headquarters were not enough. His capital had to be more than a fortified advance base to use against rivals: it had to be a clamp that fastened the two halves of the empire together and made it harder for them to fracture. Constantinople was tasked with holding Europe and Asia together. More than just roaming emperors, the east needed a Rome of its own.

Constantine and his son Constantius achieved this by recruiting elites from the eastern provinces and focalizing their careers at New Rome. Thus, the east was socially and economically bound to the new capital, and the new capital was linked to the old through an open channel of senatorial transference. It was harder to break such a state: Constantinople succeeded. New Rome was henceforth the focal point of the Roman east, no longer a border between east and west. Thus, instead of emperors traveling around the provinces to secure their loyalty, they brought the cream of the eastern provinces to New Rome.[17]

The idea of Rome and Romanía

By this point in Roman history, "Rome" was less a physical city than an ideal of political community, and it had expanded to encompass the provinces. Mobility and inclusiveness were values embedded in the earliest layers of Rome's legend, as its national ancestors had moved from Troy to the banks of the Tiber. The *res publica* that emerged there was imagined less as a physical place than a community cemented by shared notions of justice and religion.[18] This idea was evoked vividly in times of civil war as each side claimed to represent the true *res publica*, even if it was not physically in Rome. In the war against Julius Caesar, Pompey and his followers reconstituted the fatherland in Thessaly. "Do not fear to abandon Italy and Rome," Pompey argued, "for our home is where our freedom is."[19] His faction acted as the true Rome in exile. Other Roman leaders did the same. In Alexandria, Mark Antony constituted a virtual Rome abroad with consuls, senators, law courts, and armies. Fears recurred under "bad emperors" that the government would be relocated to Alexandria.[20] The idea of a Roman move to the east was ancient.

As a community rather than a place, Rome expanded by absorbing its subjects through incremental grants of legal equality. Provincials joined the ranks of the Senate and the army in ever greater numbers, and eventually men of non-Italian origin reached the throne. Septimius Severus (193–211) was of Punic North African origin, his son Caracalla (211–217) was half-Syrian and half-Punic. Maximinus (235–238) was a Thracian. Non-Italian emperors were the rule after the mid-third century. Between 268 and 582, the vast majority of eastern emperors were of Illyrian (west Balkan) or Thracian origin and had a background in military service; the dynasty of Constantine (293–363) belonged to this group. During the third century, emperors not only came from the provinces, they spent most or all their reigns by the frontier. Maximinus was among the first to never visit Rome. The idea was even floated, by a Roman general from Antioch, that "Rome was wherever the emperor was."[21] After all, an emperor was accompanied by a large mobile court, including senators, jurists, a treasury, and soldiers, who were the Roman people under arms. After centuries of rule by senatorial emperors resident at Rome, the empire now began to be ruled by military emperors who patrolled its frontiers. After 268, emperors went to Rome only when they could not avoid it, and usually only to celebrate their reign. Rome was still unrivaled as a stage backdrop. Even so, a fourth-century senator noted that Rome's 1,100th anniversary—in 348—"was celebrated with none of the customary festivities, so drastically has the concern for the city diminished day by day."[22]

Not only were the new emperors provincials, the new Romans were too. In 212, Septimius Severus' son, Caracalla, bestowed Roman citizenship on all his free subjects, a boon that some called the "Divine Gift" (we call it the *Constitutio Antoniniana*, or Antonine Decree). Caracalla was paranoid and megalomaniacal, so a fit candidate for greatness. He desired the gods of Rome to receive prayers on his behalf from as many people as possible, so he made them all into Romans.[23] It was a giant leap, affecting possibly two-thirds of the empire's population or more, but in a direction in which Rome was already heading. The empire effectively now ceased to be a domination by Romans of everyone else; one might even say that it ceased to be an empire altogether. If Rome was wherever there were Romans, then the entire empire, from Britain to Egypt, became a Rome writ large. Formerly a city (*urbs*), Rome had become a world, the *orbis Romanus*. Now, all people in this world, except for its slaves and some barbarian newcomers, were Roman citizens, a principle enshrined in law, in both Latin and Greek.[24] This meant, as a jurist put it, that "Rome is our common fatherland."[25]

Rome could now be everywhere in the empire. Just as the imperial office could be duplicated so that two or four men could be animated by the same soul, the same could happen with Rome. Third-century emperors holding court in provincial cities took to calling them "Romes" and treating them as proxies for the old capital. Gordian III, who rebelled in North Africa, treated *Carthage* as a proxy Rome in 238, designating its civic institutions as surrogates for those of the capital. Once the great nemesis of Rome, Carthage had now become Rome. Diocletian treated his primary residence Nikomedeia as "the equal of the city of Rome," and his colleague Maximian did the same with Milan. Before 324, Constantine had claimed that "my Rome is Serdica" (modern Sofia).[26] Premonitions of a New Rome had thus been appearing throughout the provinces long before 324. Conversely, in this more equal Roman empire, there was no reason for Italy or even Rome itself to be treated as special. Diocletian had imposed taxes on Italy and subordinated it to regular provincial administration, and Constantine imposed taxes on all cities, including Rome, and on senators. Diocletian, who largely avoided Rome during his reign, ceased issuing coins that hailed *Eternal Rome* in the legend, issuing a coin throughout the empire that instead hailed the *Spirit of the Roman People*.[27] In 324 Constantine referred to his new eastern subjects as "the Roman people."[28]

Those millions of new Romans were not passive before this remarkable transformation, or indifferent to it. The idea of Rome as a "common fatherland" took hold among them. We know this because, out of these very developments, a name emerged that eastern Romans would give to their state and society for the next thousand years and more: *Romanía*, i.e., "Romanland." Already by the 350s provincial priests in southern Egypt understood, without requiring explanation, that "Rome was the metropolis of Romanía." The whole of the Roman world was being imagined as a vast city-state, a primary focus of political loyalty and identity. In the 360s, ordinary Christians in Cappadocia understood that Romanía was distinct from the *barbarikon*, the barbarian lands beyond the Danube.[29] The term *Romanía* does not appear in sources prior to the fourth century because it was a vernacular way of referring to the empire, not a term that a polished author would use.[30] It was also used in Latin in the west, but declined after the west fell in the fifth century. In the east, by contrast, it must have been ubiquitous. We hear it when the people of Constantinople are quoted directly, for example in making demands about who should be the "emperor for Romanía."[31] It became an official name of the state only in the eleventh century. Romanía reflected the idea that "the empire of the Romans should be imagined as a single, unified city," as the philosopher-senator Themistios put it in 366.[32]

Thus, the empire had "turned inside out."[33] As Elder Rome began to pay taxes and was ignored by emperors, a former frontier city was elevated to the status of imperial capital. But Constantinople was not an imperial imposition dropped into the midst of a Greek-Thracian world. It was created in a provincial world that had already become Roman and was experimenting with new forms of eastern Romanness. In a work dedicated to Valens, Constantinople was called the "second citadel of the Roman globe."[34] Constantinople was not the first but it was the greatest, most whole hearted and enduring attempt to create a second Rome. It grew by gathering up the resources, artwork, food, and loyalty of eastern Romans, who migrated to it by the thousands. Who were the first new Romans?

The new Romans

The old city of Byzantion had maybe 25,000 people. Before the outbreak of the plague in 542, so within two centuries, Constantinople had grown to about half a million residents. This implied an average annual increase of 2,200 people, though growth was not linear, at least not at first. But densely populated cities in premodern times were so unsanitary—what with the warm bacterial cultures that the Romans called baths and waste often tossed out from balconies onto the street below—that they were effectively death traps. People died of disease, fires, and violence at greater rates than they did in the countryside.[35] Constantinople may have *lost* 1% of its population each year, which means that it had to import that many merely to not shrink (and some estimates put the annual mortality higher, at 3%). By 540, then, it required between 5,000 and 6,000 people per year, in addition to those whom it needed in order to grow. In other words, Constantinople grew because of a vast and ongoing migration to it from the provinces.

What did half a million mean compared to the overall population of the eastern empire? Modern estimates for 164 (before the outbreak of the Antonine plague) put the total at about 25 million.[36] If we (arbitrarily) assume that the empire lost 10% of its population in the second-century plague and another 10% in the plague and wars of the third century, that leaves us with just over 20 million in the late third century, or possibly more, as ancient populations could grow by 0.1% a year in good times. By the early fourth century, 22 million would break down to roughly 4.5 million in Egypt, 4.5 in Syria-Palestine, 9 in Asia Minor, and 4 in the Balkans. On this estimate, the eastern empire had a smaller population than the greater Tokyo area today. But comparisons to modern countries reveal only that the latter have the technology to sustain huge urban populations. In premechanized societies, seven or eight people were required to work the land or with animals in order to feed one person who did not. Today one such person can feed two hundred or more.

With a ratio of 7/1 or 8/1 in favor of agricultural workers, the east could sustain at most 2–3 million people who did not work the land. These included the court, bureaucrats, soldiers, and urbanites such as lawyers, poets, beggars, sex workers, and craftsmen. The eastern empire had approximately 250,000 soldiers, though some did farm on the side.[37] Moreover, this 2–3 million (minus the soldiers) was not the maximum size of the entire urban population of the empire, as most cities were situated in the midst of an agricultural hinterland, making it possible for residents to commute to farms or stay overnight in a farmhouse during sowing and the harvest. Thus, agricultural and urban populations partially overlapped. Some cities, including Alexandria, Antioch, Carthage, Oxyrhynchos in Egypt, and possibly Sardeis had bread doles similar to that of the capital, financed through a combination of imperial and civic subventions. Emperors could control local politics by redirecting, withholding, or threatening to withhold this grain.[38]

Wealthy landowners mostly lived in cities and never touched a plow or a cow, while their farms were worked by slaves or tenants. The richest among these men made up the city councils. The eastern empire had about a thousand cities, which functioned as local units of governance. Council sizes varied, from fifty to several hundred men (called *decurions* in Latin, *bouleutai* in Greek). If we estimate an average of one hundred per council, we have a stratum of 100,000 wealthy men throughout the empire who controlled local politics. If we add their immediate families, we have half a million mostly urban people belonging to the councilor class. These were the people who wrote the vast majority of our sources.

By the time Constantinople reached the half-million mark, around 540, the population of the eastern empire had experienced two centuries of demographic growth.[39] It may have reached 27 million people, with a maximum nonagricultural potential of just over 3 million people. Constantinople would have claimed a large chunk of that potential for itself, absorbing population from the provinces. Around 470 some young Balkan peasants left their villages and hiked to Constantinople

> because at home they had to struggle constantly against poverty and all its attendant hardships, and they wanted to be rid of all that. They even walked on

> foot all the way to Byzantion carrying on their own shoulders sacks made of goat's hair that, by the time they arrived, contained only some baked bread.[40]

One of these men was the future emperor Justin I (518–527).

There are three indications that Constantine intended his City to grow on a massive scale. The first is its sheer dimensions. The territory enclosed by the Constantinian walls was roughly three times larger than that of ancient Byzantion, though at first it included mostly fields. Second, the hippodrome was expanded to accommodate more people than before, between 40,000 and 100,000 (estimates vary because only the outline of the racetrack survives, not the stands around it). And third, Constantine provided his new capital with a generous bread dole (the *annona*), which means that, in his projections, it would eventually be unable to feed itself from its own hinterland. Grain was traded on the open market, but Constantine also provided for the free daily distribution of 80,000 portions of bread, and oil was given to some as well.[41] Depending on their sizes, these portions could feed between 160,000 and 240,000 people. In the sixth century, one author on the dole was entitled to five loaves a day.[42]

The scale of the grain supply chain was immense: as the ships arrived from Egypt "they made the sea seem forested . . . a city upon the waves."[43] Their cargoes were unloaded into state granaries; state bakeries made the bread before dawn; and tens of thousands of "Roman citizens"—as they were called in the dole laws—lined up every morning at the distribution stations, placed atop a stepped platform. Each person held his bronze token, which recorded his name and the amount to which he was entitled. The senator Themistios, only one beneficiary among many, was joined by "cobblers, bath attendants, and leather-workers."[44] The military units stationed in the City received their rations separately. The people depended on this largesse and the efficient administration of its long supply line. Free or greatly discounted, bread became a right and emperors worked hard to ensure its delivery. Under Constantine adverse winds once held up the fleet and the people were discontented. The applause for the emperor in the hippodrome was tepid and Constantine fell into a foul mood. He reacted with deadly alacrity, executing a pagan philosopher on the charge of binding the winds with magic. The emperors deemed it more important to inspect the granaries than the treasury.[45]

Grain was imported from Thrace, the Crimea, Asia Minor, and Syria, but the greatest volume came from Egypt, credited against that province's tax liability. In the past, Egypt had sent much of its surplus to feed Rome. Hundreds of grain ships had been shuttling for centuries between Egypt and Italy on a nearly year-round basis. They were now diverted to the Bosporos. This meant that Constantine intended that Rome would shrink so that Constantinople could grow. Baby Rome literally snatched food from her mother's mouth.

The market supplied the City with vegetables and animal products from farms operating within the walls and in the hinterland.[46] Constantinople also had an abundant supply of fish. The confined channel and inlets of the Bosporos were ideal for industrial fishing. Byzantion had once exported fish around the Aegean, but now it was importing the people who ate the local fish. The latter were more sanitary than those of the Tiber river, which was an extension of Rome's sewer.[47] Even so, Constantine instituted funeral assistance for citizens of Constantinople: city life had many risks.[48]

In order to receive a bread token, it was at first expected and later required to build or own a house in Constantinople.[49] We glimpse the inducements used by Constantine to populate his City: build a house, that is, invest in New Rome, and receive free bread for life. Constantine offered even greater incentives to one group of desirable immigrants: senators from Rome. He built manors to lure them to his City; thus, there were walls and houses in Constantinople before its populace even arrived.[50] To those who followed him from Rome were soon added senatorial recruits from the eastern provinces. The first known are from Crete, Paphlagonia, Phrygia, and possibly Egypt.[51] It is unclear exactly when the Senate of New Rome was formally established as an institution separate from that of Rome, but senators had been attending upon emperors in the east since the third century, and they came to Constantinople when it was founded. Constantius bolstered the status of the eastern Senate in the 350s, when the western usurper Magnentius cut off his ability to recruit men from Rome. He established a commission, headed by Themistios, to recruit eastern notables into the new Senate, preferably men of wealth and culture. In elevating Themistios himself to the Senate, Constantius had seen it as a fair exchange in which one side bestowed "Roman dignity" while the other brought "Hellenic wisdom" —a fitting definition of the civilization to come.[52]

Themistios later boasted that he had increased the senators from 300 to 2,000. By 400, there were hundreds of positions in the imperial administration that conferred senatorial status, if not a few thousand, and some of them had a high turnover, which meant they produced senators faster.[53] Emperors could also elevate someone to senatorial rank independently of holding office. Well, the household of a senator was a small community in itself. It included extended family, slaves, and a host of dependents and attendants. Describing the aristocracy of Cappadocia, a bishop in the 370s listed their "stewards, accountants, farmers, craftsmen, cooks, bakers, wine-pourers, hunters, painters, and procurers of every type of pleasure." Another bishop listed jesters, mimes, musicians, dancing girls, boys with the hair style of girls, and shameless girls.[54] Dependents also included renters and hangers-on, who pursued their own livelihoods but acted as clients and henchmen of the grand lords. These passages exaggerate the extravagance of this class but reveal the secular and worldly tastes of an emerging Christian elite.

Some senatorial households in Old Rome included hundreds of people, but the wealth of the western senators outstripped that of their eastern counterparts—for now.[55] If we conservatively assign 30 people to the household of the average eastern senator, and assume that 2,500 senators lived in the capital by ca. 400, we arrive at 75,000 people in the City who were dependent on or connected to its leading men. They formed the core of the populace. Residency requirements were relaxed during the fourth century, so not all senators maintained a full household in the City.[56] But many who remained grew even wealthier and so had more servants. To them we must add thousands more who depended for their livelihood on the Great Palace and the palaces of lateral members of the imperial family, which began to proliferate toward the end of the fourth century. These urban estates hosted retail and merchant business.[57] Around 390, the pious noblewoman Olympias was giving away as charity her lands in Thrace, Cappadocia, and other provinces, along with her many manors in the City, including workshops and dwellings attached to them.[58] Constantinople was also a vast construction site, keeping thousands of craftsmen and artisans busy. Finally, there were military units stationed in the City, though these were relatively small. All these people, then, formed the core of the Constantinopolitan *populus Romanus* in its first burst of expansion. A significant fraction of the population was an extension of the court system, or at least the aristocracy.

Not everyone was happy with this massive investment in Constantinople. The City sucked up artwork from the provinces, from as far as Egypt and Antioch, along with thousands of the best people. The assets of the wealthiest councilors who moved to Constantinople could now no longer be taxed locally, shifting the burden onto those who stayed behind. One of the latter, Libanios of Antioch, spiced up his speeches with snide comments against this City that "lived in luxury off the sweat of others."[59] Still, he helped many acquaintances make the move. In a letter to Themistios, he playfully wrote that senatorial fish leaped out of the water and landed next to Themistios even while he slept.[60]

Constantinople's cost was prodigious. How did Constantine pay for it, right after a major war? He had Licinius' treasury to spend, but some discerned a link between this ambitious project and the new taxes that Constantine levied on senators, urban craftsmen, and merchants. These taxes, however, would not have produced enough revenue. Another handsome resource were the treasures of the ancient temples, which Constantine, a Christian, forced open and melted down to mint coins in huge quantities. This perk is rarely noted in modern discussions of Constantine's Christianity. Yet the link was noted by contemporaries, especially pagans, who were resentful and grew even more bitter as Constantinople became more Christian.[61] The gods, whose statues overlooked the bustle of the City, had subsidized its construction.

The crowds in the City's streets were of mixed origin, "from every part of the empire."[62] But in general they reflected the backgrounds of the new senators, who came from Hellenic regions and cities. The overwhelming majority of epitaph inscriptions that attest migration disclose origins in the Greek-speaking provinces of Asia Minor closest to the capital.[63] Migration was certainly easiest from nearer regions, and the City had attractive resources. In 370, there was a famine in Phrygia and thousands sought refuge in Constantinople because there was always food there.[64] Evidence for languages other than Greek or Latin is scarce. In the fifth century, a "Syrian" widow Niko inherited a manor in the middle of the City that dated from the days of Constantine, but she was from Antioch and had a Greek name.[65] In 402, the empress Eudoxia led a religious procession in Constantinople of "people speaking different tongues: Latin, Syriac, Greek, and barbaric."[66] But the preacher, John Chrysostom, was belaboring an evangelical point and did not distinguish between residents and visitors (such as sailors), nor did he estimate the size of each group. The empire was multiethnic, but New Rome was largely Greek-speaking.

Languages and cultures

Modern historians routinely call the Roman empire "multiethnic" but rarely name the ethnic groups in question. To be sure, the ancestors of these new Romans came from vastly diverse cultural backgrounds: they had built pyramids, written the Hebrew Bible, sacrificed children to Baal, and fought at Troy, and many once had empires of their own. They had different norms, practices, memories, gods, cults, and languages. They lived in the Nile river valley, in the rocky uplands of Cappadocia, in the fertile coasts of western Asia Minor, on Greek islands, or along the forests of Thrace. Yet this diversity, except for the ecological, was measurably on the wane. A great convergence was taking place toward a set of universal norms, especially in the regions closer to Constantinople. Local languages and cultures were going extinct. Some were large or persistent enough to hang on, but they too would be transformed beyond recognition by Christianity, which was but the next phase of Roman homogenization.

Long before Rome's arrival, a layer of Greek culture had been laid down across the east, in some places only at an elite level while in others it went much deeper, especially in the cities founded by the Hellenistic kings. For pagans such as the emperor Julian, Hellenism stood for a religious-philosophical ideal that all might embrace regardless of their ethnic background (Julian, a member of the Constantinian dynasty, considered himself a Thracian or Illyrian). For both pagan and Christian elites, Hellenism was a universal standard of linguistic and literary excellence. But more than Hellenism, it was Romanization that congealed millions of provincials into a common identity. Roman citizenship was now universal and had replaced local systems of law. At the end of the third century the author of a rhetorical textbook noted that it was "now" useless to praise a city for its excellent laws, since all were governed by the same Roman laws.[67] Distinctive practices may have survived locally as customs, but those that deviated the most were targeted for abolition. Around 295, the emperor Diocletian outlawed the (mostly Egyptian) custom of brother-sister marriage, which offended against "the religion and morality of the Roman laws." It alienated the gods against "the Roman name . . . . All now must remember that they live under Roman laws and institutions." Such marriages are not attested thereafter in the Egyptian papyri, though later bans reveal that they may have survived in Phoenicia.[68]

Emperors were acutely aware that their subjects were all Romans: the world was no longer divided between Romans and their conquered "slaves."[69] As Julian reminded his cousin Constantius, "no matter where they are born, all [subjects of the empire] partake of Rome's constitution, use its laws and customs, and by virtue of this are its citizens."[70] Conversely, subjects were aware that ancient ethnicities had become irrelevant. In the early fifth century a preacher asked, "Who now knows which nations in the Roman empire were which, when all have become Romans and all are called Romans?"[71]

Even so, the Roman name encompassed considerable ethnic, linguistic, and religious diversity. This was not, however, to be found in the pseudo-ethnic names of provinces. In official communications, the authorities referred to the inhabitants of each province as a nation (*ethnos*), an ostensibly natural community defined by common culture and a shared history. "The nation of the Phoenicians," for example, meant the population of the provinces of Phoenicia. Rarely did these artificial provincial divisions map onto actual ethnic groups, but after centuries of official use they had caught on and acquired a life of their own. Local authorities echoed the language of provincial "ethnicity" back to the center in their petitions. It eventually became a standard way of referring to one's origin in literary texts, inscriptions, and daily life: one was a Cappadocian or a Phoenician "by race," or from the Bithynian "nation." In effect, this designated only one's provincial origin. It revealed the power of the administration to create local subjectivities. Provincials internalized governmental labels as personal identity markers, bringing order to the empire's diverse human landscape. For example, the professors in fourth-century Athens divided up their students by *ethnos* i.e., by province.[72]

The people of Asia Minor had little memory of their ancient kings and nations. They were mostly Greek-speaking Romans. But as pseudo-nations, most provinces were associated with stereotypes. For example, Cilicians were quick to anger. Galatians feasted well. Paphlagonians had hairy asses. Cappadocians were vicious roughnecks (when a poisonous snake bit one, the snake died). Cretans were liars (they said so themselves). These silly stereotypes were but variations within an increasingly homogeneous Roman field and may have become more necessary for telling people apart as more meaningful differences slowly disappeared.

Still, both small pockets and large regions of significant difference existed. The pockets were closer to Constantinople and destined for extinction, whereas the large regions lay farther away and would live on after the empire had retreated. To sustain their identities under Roman rule, local cultures had to be large, which gave them the advantage of inertia, or zealous, which required a priesthood. They later survived as separate religious communities under Muslim rule.

The dividing line between speakers of Latin and Greek ran diagonally across the Balkans from modern Albania to the lower Danube, bisecting modern Bulgaria (linguistically, this is known as the Jireček Line). The eastern empire's supply of Latin speakers lay northwest of this line, in the provinces of Dacia and Illyricum, whence came most of the emperors between 268 and 582, including Diocletian, Constantine, and Justinian. If one walked along the military road from Constantinople to Singidunum (modern Belgrade), at the point where it crossed the border from (Greek) Thrace into (Latin) Moesia there was a station appropriately called "Latina."[73] If pockets of the Illyrian language survived then, they would not for long (unless Albanian descends from Illyrian, which is uncertain). Many Illyrians took up service in the army in the third century, indeed they predominated in the officer cadres. A fourth-century senator at Rome wrote that Illyrians might have "lacked culture, but they had been sufficiently schooled by the hardships of the countryside and of military service to be the best men for the state."[74] Illyrians such as Diocletian were staunch Roman traditionalists.

The Thracian language did survive into this period but not beyond it (again, unless Albanian comes from western Thracian). It was called "Bessian" and its last speakers "Bessoi." They were concentrated in the province of Dacia Mediterranea, were noted as skilled miners, and were converted in the late fourth century by a native missionary named Niketas.[75] Their language is attested for the last time in the sixth century in Palestinian monasteries and at St. Catherine's at Sinai.[76] The emperor Leo I (457–474), from the province of Dacia, is called a Bessian, which marks his ethnicity because Bessia was never a geographical or administrative region. Even so, there is no trace of cultural difference in his profile or policies. Yet Bessians insisted on their ethnic identity, for example when two of them enrolled in military units in Egypt in 561, so the name carried affective associations.[77]

In Asia Minor, linguistic diversity was devolving into nothing more than a series of local accents of Greek. Most pre-Roman languages went extinct before the foundation of Constantinople, for example Lydian and Carian. Some still clung to life, but barely. Phrygian ceased producing inscriptions in the third century, and 63 among the last batch of 114 are bilingual (with Greek), the two languages carved by the same hand. Seven or eight of these inscriptions pointedly include the name Aurelius, so these were Romans enfranchised by the Antonine Decree.[78] We hear no more about spoken Phrygian after that.[79] Cappadocian may have survived into the fourth century, but it is tenuously attested then and not thereafter. Basil, bishop of the metropolis Kaisareia, says in a letter that Cappadocia was also home to many Iranians, fire-worshippers who settled there in the time of the ancient Persian empire. They kept to themselves and did not marry outsiders. They are last attested around 460.[80] Cilicia was entirely Greek-speaking. A fifth-century ascetic, who strapped himself into a contraption like a hamster's wheel, is said to have spoken Greek "because he was a Cilician by race."[81]

Galatian was also on life support. This was a form of Celtic introduced to Asia Minor by invading Gauls in the third century BC, but was never used there for writing. In the fourth century, observers noted that the Galatians all spoke Greek but that their "own" language was the same as that of the western Celts.[82] Galatians were called *Gallograikoi* or *Keltograikoi*, i.e., Greek-speaking Gauls. Their own language is last heard in the early sixth century, after a Galatian monk was possessed by a demon: when forced to speak, the demon would allow him to do so only in Galatian.[83] Otherwise, these Galatians had a mainstream Roman profile. This was explained by Themistios in the later fourth century. To justify the policy of allowing Goths to settle within the empire, he argued that they would be assimilated to Roman norms, if treated properly.

> You see these Galatians . . . . The emperors made them a part of the empire. No one would call them barbarians now but only thoroughly Roman. For while their old name has survived, their way of life has merged with ours. They pay the same taxes, enlist in the same armies, receive governors on the same terms as the rest, and obey the same laws.[84]

One place where this transformation was slower was Isauria, in southeast Asia Minor, especially in the mountainous interior. The Isaurians possibly spoke their own language (of the Luwian family), but this is uncertain.[85] They were not untouched by Graeco-Roman culture, but, as a Roman might say, they had not been fully pacified. They periodically burst out of the Tauros mountains in armed bands to plunder neighboring provinces, and the authorities had to respond with force. Eventually a special military governorship was instituted in the mid-fourth century to contain them. They were a unique source of internal insecurity. The dominant image of the Isaurians was of marauders, and a fourth-century list of provinces mentions them among the foreign barbarians, along with the Saxons, Goths, and Persians.[86] Surprisingly, the Isaurians rose to dominate imperial politics in the fifth century, which, as we will see, led to their violent and final pacification by Constantinople. They went out with a bang, not a whimper like the rest.

Beyond the Tauros, "the dividing line between the northern and southern peoples,"[87] we pass into two regions, Syria-Palestine and Egypt, where local cultures took exotic forms ranging from animal-headed gods to men who lived on top of columns to honor a goddess. These two regions had common features. Both contained a majority population in the millions who spoke a language other than Greek, mostly Aramaic and Egyptian. Both had been colonized after the conquests of Alexander the Great by Greeks and Macedonians who established cities from which they ruled the countryside. Greek was the language and culture of the ruling element, concentrated in the cities, though it was picked up by many natives too. Six centuries later, a significant sector of the population could function in both languages. Egyptian and Aramaic cultures were not defined by a rejection of Greek. Instead, as we will see, they were enabled by it.

In Egypt, it is possible that 50–60% of a population of 4–5 million spoke only Egyptian; 10–20% spoke only Greek; and the rest could get by in both in various combinations of proficiency. These estimates are guesses; we will never know for sure. Yet linguistic difference did not impede the flow of information: there was always, it seems, someone at hand to translate.[88] Society was not divided along ethnic or linguistic lines, nor were expressions of ethnic prejudice common. Greek speakers did not discriminate between Hellenic and Egyptian cults in their worship. Members of the same family might have both Greek and Egyptian names. Around 300, a script that we call Coptic was devised for writing Egyptian, a development possibly pioneered by Christians. Coptic used the Greek alphabet, was full of Greek words, and was evidently invented in a bilingual milieu; it did not channel any hostility to Greek. On the other hand, native priests remembered the age of the Pharaohs and national independence, and some could read and write hieroglyphics down to the 390s. Priestly circles had in the recent past disseminated texts decrying the presence of foreigners in Egypt, but not in our period.

Outside perceptions were mixed. Greeks and Romans had long marveled at Egyptian antiquities and oddities. As a novelist of the period put it, "the Greeks find every Egyptian tale delightful." The emperor Julian called Egyptians intelligent and mechanically inclined, thinking perhaps of the pyramids.[89] But there were also negative stereotypes. The Alexandrian Greek accent sounded ridiculous to outsiders, and Egyptians proper elicited fiercer prejudices. The emperor Caracalla empowered the (Greek) authorities of Alexandria to expel native Egyptians who overstayed their welcome. "You will know true Egyptians," he clarified, from their speech, clothes, appearance, and uncouth life, a clear case of ethnic profiling. In 403, a group of Egyptian bishops came to Constantinople to depose its bishop John Chrysostom. One of the latter's supporters denounced them as "bishops with half-barbarian names, derived from Egypt's ancient abominations, whose speech and language were entirely barbaric, and whose character imitated their speech." This was a Christian talking about bishops of the same faith as himself who likely also spoke Greek. The historian Ammianus cast Egyptians as stubborn, litigious, and proud of the scars left by the lash when they failed to pay taxes.[90]

Egyptians did not emigrate to Constantinople in great numbers during the City's initial growth spurt. In the sixth century, Justinian even appointed two units, called the Syrian-Catchers and the Egyptian-Catchers, to arrest Syrians and Egyptians who tarried in the capital and send them packing. The burden was on them to prove that they were *not* Syrian or Egyptian.[91] Universal Romanness had not yet bridged these gaps.

The linguistic breakdown in Syria-Palestine was likely similar to that in Egypt, with Greek dominant in the cities but present also in the countryside. Greek was the language of official business, though the majority of the population spoke Aramaic, while along the fringes of the empire various North Arabian dialects were spoken among people whom the Romans usually called Saracens. Aramaic also had various dialects,[92] and it had long coexisted with Greek and borrowed many words from it. There were enough bilinguals here too that communication was not a major problem. When Rabbula, bishop of Edessa (411–435), preached a homily in Constantinople, he begged the audience to forgive his poor Greek: "I am a man of the countryside, where it is Syriac that we speak mostly."[93]

When texts refer to "Syrians" they often mean anyone from the Syrian provinces regardless of language. Libanios, the arch-Hellenist orator of Antioch, referred to himself as a Syrian from Syria. Syrians were often called effeminate, but this typically referred to the (mostly Greek-speaking) inhabitants of Antioch, who were notorious for their vices.[94] There was thus no Syrian ethnicity and no collective term by which to distinguish Greek speakers from Aramaic speakers. An author writing in Greek had to go the extra mile to explain that he was "a Syrian on both sides, not one of the Greeks who settled in Syria, but a native, speaking the Syrian language and living according to Syrian customs," even if this was likely only the fictional persona of a Greek romance novelist![95]

Unlike Egypt, Syria did not have a unified history, geography, or culture to sustain a common identity among its Aramaic speakers. The Hellenization of the urban elites throughout this region and their entanglement in the workings of the Roman order sidelined or obliterated any residual memory or attachment to the pre-Roman world, and the villages followed the lead of the cities, wherever they could.[96] Exceptions may have included the city of Edessa, the capital of the former kingdom of Osrhoene, which had been annexed recently, in the early third century; Palmyra, much reduced now in importance after its failed bid for empire in 268–272; and distinct religious communities, especially the Jews and Samaritans. Mention of these groups highlights the fact that Aramaic speakers were divided among fiercely antagonistic ethnoreligious communities on the one hand (Jews, Samaritans, Christians), and the majority of the population on the other, which worshipped its traditional gods in non-competitive ways. There could thus be no Aramean identity or solidarity.

Aramaic speakers joined the Roman army, where they learned the military argot of camp Latin or Greek. Members of the Severan dynasty (193–235) spoke Aramaic in addition to Greek and Latin. There were many Roman senators from Syria, but none that we know from the Jews of Judaea (Palestine) or the locals of Arabia province (the former Nabataean kingdom).[97] A Latin graffito from the Sinai reads: "Syrians yield to Latin Romans." While it cannot be dated, it implies that there were non-Latin-speaking Romans, whom the author, a Latin visitor to the region, apparently scorned.[98] But when Syriac Christian literature lifts the veil on Aramaic communities, especially in the sixth century, we will find an uncomplicated identification with Romanía: it was just as possible to be a Roman in Aramaic as in Greek. A forerunner of this trend was the fourth-century Syriac poet Ephrem (d. 373), who strongly identified with the Christian Roman empire.[99]

The prize for resilient refusal to assimilate goes to the Samaritans and the Jewish rabbis. The Samaritans were an ancient offshoot of Judaism, who, of course, considered themselves, not the others, to be the true Chosen People, and whose holy site was not Zion but Mt. Gerizim in Samaria, by the city of Neapolis (modern Nablus). In archaeology and inscriptions they are hard to tell apart from pious Jews, though they were a separate ethnoreligious group. By this time, many lived in and around the metropolis of Palestine, Kaisareia. Some had entered the lower ranks of imperial service, but most were rural. In the later fifth and sixth centuries they repeatedly went to war against the empire to seize Mt. Gerizim. This turned out disastrously for them, but their initial population must have been large for them to muster armies.[100]

As for the Jews of Palestine, their lives had been transformed by the failure of the great wars against Rome (in 66–73, 132–136). Among the survivors, all distinctive institutions of national and religious self-rule had been abolished and replaced with the standard mechanisms of Roman governance: city councils and governors. Jews were excluded from Jerusalem, which was refounded as a colony of Roman veterans and named Aelia Capitolina. Jewish life in the rest of Palestine, e.g., in Galilee, took on a mainstream Roman cultural profile, including all typical displays of civic paganism such as temples to the gods and mythological mosaics. Civic life was dominated by the normal institutions of the Graeco-Roman city, not by synagogues. Most Jews likely maintained only a vague sense of their ethnic background.[101]

A more pious, Torah-oriented mentality survived among a minority, who were led by the rabbis. The rabbis advocated Jewish separation, though they were in no position to implement it. The Mishnah and Talmud show that they rejected many aspects of Graeco-Roman society, from its entertainments and gods to its social values. They were thus countercultural, which came at the cost of marginalization, so they had to find ways to rationalize the fact that many or most Jews had gone mainstream, by treating it as a necessary accommodation. The rabbis had no institutional authority, but through persuasion they appealed to a stricter and more "authentic" Judaism. Unlike most inhabitants of Roman Syria, but like native priests in Egypt, they had access to non-Greek texts that told the history of their own people before Alexander. They could read and write Hebrew, albeit only as a liturgical or academic language. Hebrew was also used for some inscriptions, usually in symbolic ways, as a marker of identity. For the rabbis, Jerusalem remained the symbolic capital of the Jewish nation. It was only among them that one could find determined opposition to the Roman order anywhere in the empire: "Let the Lord inflict revenge on Romans."[102]

From among rabbinical circles a figure arose in the third century with the title of "Patriarch," who acted as a fundraiser-in-chief among the wealthier Jews of the diaspora. The Patriarchs, who belonged to a wealthy dynasty, were local power-brokers and sent out so-called apostles to collect a tithe, which by the fourth century had become a tax on diasporic Jewishness, resented by some. They cultivated relations with powerful Romans, and by the fourth century were given the honorary standing of a senator, the first Jews to be so honored by Rome. However, by the later third century the Patriarch and the rabbis seem to have parted ways.[103] The Patriarchate was ended by the imperial authorities around 425.

In sum, by the fourth century the Roman empire had achieved a level of homogeneity greater than any empire before or since, and was to go further in this direction still. Pockets of unassimilated difference remained that would generate fierce internal warfare, for example with some Isaurians and Samaritans, but they would be crushed. The greatest area of remaining diversity was in religion, though that too was about to be steamrollered by another universal Roman norm. Most local identities did not conflict with universal Romanness but were nested within it. The provinces, which began as administrative arrangements, had become naturalized as regional homelands and had generated pseudo-ethnicities, whose trivial stereotypes were merely variations on a universal norm. That norm was backed by a uniform administration in the areas of taxation, civic governance, military recruitment, and justice. This was not superimposed onto imperial society: it was its very scaffold.

2

Government and the Social Order

Taxation and land

The new Roman empire that emerged from the reforms of Diocletian inaugurated an era of "big government." In the past, emperors demanded a set tribute from each province or city, and local authorities, usually the city councils under loose supervision by imperial officials, allocated the tax burden, often in ways that benefited them. The governors toured the provinces with a small staff to prevent major problems and resolve disputes. The central government was essentially a skeleton staff. But that model came under strain as the defensive needs of the empire mounted after the second century. More armies were needed on more fronts, and the armies were making greater demands. To meet these growing expenses, the emperors devalued the coinage, reducing its precious metal content in order to mint more coins. Apparently, this did not at first lead to inflation, despite the gap between the silver coins' notional and bullion value, but when the emperor Aurelian (270–275) issued a purer gold coin and a new exchange rate, the inflationary dams burst.[1] By the end of the third century, the monetary system was in shambles, and it made more sense for the state to extract resources in kind. This required a larger administrative apparatus, which, in turn, cost more in overhead.

These problems were tackled by Diocletian, who was the founder of the new empire and gave it the form that survived until the seventh century. He set into motion a more rational, uniform, efficient, and even equitable system of national taxation, dispensing with the distinction between Roman conquerors in Italy and conquered non-Romans in the provinces. His system terminated the transfer of wealth from east to west and made the eastern empire a fiscally integral and potentially autonomous unit. When the east acquired Constantinople and then a Senate of its own it became politically distinct too.[2] The groundwork for the separation of the two halves of the Roman empire had been laid well before 395.

The core of the new system was a census of all taxable assets, calculated in notional units of *iuga* (for cultivated lands) and *capita* (for the agricultural workforce). It is unclear how actual acres and people were converted into these notional units, and it probably varied regionally. Yet "fields were measured clod by clod, vines and trees were counted, every kind of animal was registered, and note taken of every member of the population."[3] The tax basis was thus not income or wealth, but land, animals, and people, and the tax rate on them was relatively uniform. This census was periodically revised, because the land changed hands and either came into or fell out of cultivation. Knowing how many taxable units corresponded to each landowner, city, and province, and projecting its own expenses, the state could calculate the taxes that corresponded to each unit, and posted that ratio throughout each province. The burden could be levied in kind or persons (for army recruits and corvées—labor—owed to the state), or commuted to cash. It was common for supplementary levies to be imposed after the first haul. Sometimes the assessment due on each unit was decreased: "we read the letters but did not believe what we were seeing," said a delighted Themistios on one such occasion.[4] Locales struck by a disaster that caused part of the workforce to leave or perish, or that reduced its production, such as a barbarian invasion, plague, or drought, could petition for an ad hoc reassessment. An emperor was at his most generous when he remitted the taxes on an afflicted region. In exceptional cases emperors remitted taxes globally to allow producers to recover.[5] Yet generally it was in the state's interest not to reduce the assessment but to reassign the land so that someone else was responsible for its taxes.

These calculations, along with the census that preceded and redistribution that followed them, were carried out by the office of the praetorian prefect. The prefect emerged as the empire's most important fiscal officer, even as the "second power in the state after the emperor."[6] In the late third century, the prefects had acted as chiefs of staff for itinerant emperors; they were generals, but they were also in charge of requisitions and had administrative functions, such as supervising the provincial governors. Diocletian and Constantine gradually separated military from civilian functions to avoid concentrating too much power into the hands of potential rivals. Thus, the prefects ceased to command armies, but they remained in charge of revenue collection, supplies, and provincial governance. During the fourth century, the empire was gradually divided into regional prefectures, which gave the prefects specific territorial jurisdictions. The eastern empire had two such prefectures: the larger one was Oriens (i.e., "the East"), encompassing Thrace, Asia Minor, Syria, and Egypt (roughly 50 provinces), and the smaller one was Illyricum, encompassing Dacia and Macedonia, including Greece (some 10 provinces).

The civilian governors of the provinces were appointed by the court and rotated out of office after a few years; they reported to the praetorian prefects.[7] Governors, along with all other office-holders in both the civilian and military branches of the administration, were salaried magistrates, not a hereditary nobility. They exercised power based on the impersonal authority conferred by their office, not their personal clout or wealth, though the latter could definitely enhance their standing. There was no fixed aristocracy in Romanía, as its fairly unitary conception of citizenship precluded a caste system. The entire political apparatus consisted of functionaries who worked for the court. Even the Senate, which retained a sense of its corporate identity, was by now an extension of the court. Functionaries could originate in any region and be posted to any other in the empire, serving in many locations throughout their careers. This created opportunities for social mobility, as exemplified by the Balkan peasant Justin who became emperor. Nor was there a regional aristocracy of local "barons" with whom the court had to negotiate to get things done, as happened in the Persian empire and in the later western European kingdoms. In its political organization, Romanía was a proper state, not a coalition of noble families. Moreover, it was second to none among its medieval peers in the density and depth of its bureaucratic organization.

A hostile observer groused that there were more employees in Diocletian's government than there were taxpayers.[8] While exaggerated, this complaint captured the unprecedented scale of the new empire's intrusion into local society. Imperial bureaucracy on such a scale was massive by ancient standards. According to one estimate, the number of the central state's salaried officials rose from fewer than 1,000 to 35,000 or more,[9] roughly half of whom were in the eastern empire. For a population of around 22 million, this is a low ratio by modern standards. Yet many of those officials were aided by attendants and slaves who did much of the actual work but did not show up in the books (or our calculations). The army and Church had their own managers, accountants, lawyers, and staff. Also, the imperial state was assisted by the local apparatus of the city governments, that is the city councilors and their agents and slaves. Moreover, we should not use modern standards to assess how effective this bureaucracy was at surveilling and regimenting the population, as the latter was relatively immobile and economically undiversified compared to its modern counterparts.

The new administration was more efficient at extracting revenue. It had to pay for its own overhead—all those salaries—as well as provide for a large army. Sources from this period also resound with complaints about the oppressiveness of the tax system. It is not clear that the tax burden had risen much. It was, however, more uniformly distributed and possibly more equitably too. The assessment, after all, was calculated on the basis of individual holdings: each *iugum* owed so much grain, wine, cash, etc. This curtailed the discretionary power of city councilors to allocate the tax burden. This equalization was intentional. Constantine declared in 324 that assessments on municipalities had to be based on the schedule published by the governor "so that the multitude of the lower classes may not be subjected to the arbitrariness and subordinated to the interests of the more powerful."[10] This shifted power away from local authorities to surveyors and assessors appointed by the center. The bishop Basil of Kaisareia wrote to an assessor on behalf of a rural district, saying that *other* men in his position might abuse it to "assist their friends, harm enemies, and help themselves to whatever they want," but surely not his correspondent.[11] Councilors likely now paid more and, more importantly, had less say in the process. It is their frustration that we disproportionately hear in our angry sources, because they were among the most literate, eloquent, and whiny people. An increase in their complaining is what we would expect from a fairer system, as outrage is sparked more by lost privileges than oppressive impositions.

Thus, the new empire expended much of its energy on collecting tons of grain and other foods and materials, transporting them, and reissuing them to the armies along the frontiers. We do not know exactly how large the new army was, nor for certain that it *was* larger, but most guesses put it at half a million men, up from 350,000 or so under the Severan emperors. These revenues also supported the administrative and legal bureaucracy necessary to inventory taxable land on the one hand and pay, equip, and feed the soldiers on the other. By paying salaries to its high officials, increasingly in coin, the state thereby constructed a social order in which imperial officials emerged as new elites. The core of the later Roman state was, then, a vast apparatus of redistribution.

The increase of financial transactions happening across more layers of society offered more opportunities for corruption. This generated complaints about the misuse of resources and abuse of power. Modern discussions of late Roman corruption have ranged from the apocalyptic (it caused "the decline") to hand-wringing over whether corruption can be defined at all (an approach that usually focuses on ambiguous cases, such as the sale of offices and fees for service). In reality, official embezzlement and extortion usually operated between those two extremes and well within the levels of operational efficiency. Officials could accept gifts but were advised "not to take everything, or always, or from everyone."[12]

Socioeconomic classes

The largest landowner was the emperor. To the public lands of the Roman people, which he controlled, the centuries had added the personal wealth of the successive emperors along with bequests and the property of convicted traitors and defeated rebels. This extensive and widely dispersed crown land was administered by the office of the *comes* of the *res privata*, who had deputies and branch offices in the provinces. The *res privata* exploited crown land mostly by leasing it, sometimes to the highest bidder. Such land paid both regular taxes and rent, but its renters were free from supplementary levies and compulsory labor. One region in which the emperor owned huge estates, including famous horse farms that supplied the armies, was Cappadocia. The estates there had their own *comes*, with separate estate managers below him.[13] In the mid-fifth century, the city of Kyrros in Syria petitioned the government to have its assessment reduced, revealing in the process that it was assessed at 50,000 *iugera* of private land and 10,000 imperial.[14]

The *res privata* received major additions in the fourth century. Constantine and Constantius confiscated to it most temple lands. In antiquity, the gods owned lands whose revenues paid for the maintenance of their temples and for religious events. These assets had formerly been managed on behalf of the gods and cities by councilors, who often rented them on favorable terms to themselves. Some or most of these lands were now appropriated by the imperial government. It is also possible that emperors confiscated civic lands too, which belonged to the cities and were used to fund their upkeep and other projects; scholars debate whether this confiscation happened and to what extent. Julian restored the temple lands in order to enable local pagan worship, but Valentinian and Valens took them back. Under their arrangement, cities could use a part of the revenue produced by their former endowments in order to carry out basic functions, such as maintain their fortifications, while the rest went to the government.[15] The net result was that less money was available locally and more was redirected to imperial projects.

City councilors were more hemmed in by imperial officials and had access to fewer public assets. They increasingly fell back on their personal resources to do good works. Accordingly, they complained that their cities had been stripped of cultural amenities: the gymnasia were closed, there were no speeches in the forum, temples were empty, and so on. These complaints, which were exaggerated, self-serving, and designed to extract concessions from the center, create an impression that cities declined during this period. The councilor class was having a bad time. Theodosius I even decreed that, if willing tenants could not be found for the temple and city lands added to the *res privata*, their former councilor tenants could be *required* to rent them.[16] The state was interested primarily in productivity and sought to bind people to the land, no matter their rank.

The wealthiest landowners after the crown were senators. Some were colossally rich compared to the majority of the population, though they could never achieve our society's levels of inequality because the basis of their wealth remained land or gold, which were finite, unlike our "fiscal instruments" that conjure digital riches out of the ether. After senators, the city councilors were the wealthiest locally, but great disparities existed between councilors of modest means in a small town and the grandees of a metropolis. When a councilor of Gaza boasted to a Christian teacher that he was "great and among the first men in the city," the latter asked, "And if you go to Kaisareia, what would you be then?" "The poorest of the local big-shots." "And if to Antioch?" "A peasant." "And if to the City of Constantine, and the presence of the emperor?" "There I would be a poor man."[17]

Councilors could refer to themselves as "poor" or "middling" when seeking favorable treatment or comparing themselves to richer peers, but they should not be mistaken for a modern "middle class." Those terms were relative to other elites. Even St. Augustine, a well-educated bishop whose parents were fairly well off, called himself of poor background.[18] In purely economic terms a middle class might have existed among urban craftsmen, merchants, mid-level landowners, and prosperous peasants, who occasionally called themselves "men in the middle," but they never gelled as a self-conscious class.[19] The famous preacher John Chrysostom guessed that a tenth of the population of Antioch was rich, a tenth was abjectly poor, and the rest lay in between.[20] Most people, however, lived in the countryside and so outside John's demographic categories. If we extrapolate from the Egyptian evidence, most land was likely divided into small and medium-sized plots farmed by their owners along with their renters, slaves, and hired labor. The family farm was likely the dominant mode of agriculture, not the vast proto-feudal estate preferred by past scholarship, and this probably remained the case throughout east Roman history.

Diocletian's tax system was long believed to have crushed the peasantry with its exactions, but this bleak picture has been radically revised. There is now mounting archaeological and textual evidence for peasant prosperity in the fourth and fifth centuries. Settlements grew and acquired amenities that were previously limited to cities, and peasant households acquired goods that had previously been beyond reach.[21] Some villages became "urbanized."[22] Far from crushing small farmers, the new tax system may have spurred their economic productivity while shifting some of their prior tax burden to wealthier landowners, leading the latter to construct the familiar complaint of an oppressive state. It is more telling that there were no significant peasant rebellions in the history of the eastern empire.

According to an estimate based on Egyptian evidence, a bit less than half the population owned enough property to provide for itself, while the rest were its dependents, tenants, and slaves.[23] Economic relations among these groups were complex. Landowners could rent land from each other, so a given renter was not necessarily poorer than his landlord or dependent on him. Also, tax declarations to the state listed dependents and sometimes slaves but not renters or hired labor,[24] so we cannot know for sure who exactly, or how many, were working a plot of land. The chief priority of the state in all this was to ensure that lands remained in cultivation so that they could be taxed, and landowners had to pay the poll tax on some of their dependents. To ensure that revenue matched the census schedules, the state issued laws binding some tenants to the fields that they worked. These were the so-called *coloni*, who used to be described in scholarship as proto-serfs, even though the laws made it clear that they were free citizens, albeit bound to the land. The nature of this status has been much debated. The colonate has been seen as an administrative-fiscal arrangement imposed by the state, and not as a new social category of virtual slaves.[25] However, while the status may have originated in such arrangements, the freedom of coloni was increasingly limited and they were bound to the land in a way that constituted them as a distinct legal category between free and slave.[26] In this period, therefore, people belonged to the land as much as the reverse.

But in a growing agricultural economy, owners were in competition over farmers, and this disrupted the tax schedules. When farmers "fled" to farms where they were not registered, their new employers were not liable for their capitation tax and so benefited more from their labor, while their previous landlords were on the hook for the lost productivity. So "flight" was not only an escape from serf-like conditions: positive financial incentives were at work too. Still, while recognizing that coloni were not slaves, the law compared them to slaves and slowly restricted their rights in ways that enabled their exploitation and benefited big landowners who wanted to keep them in place. Preachers railed rhetorically against the abuse of tenants, who were worked night and day, beaten, and weighed down with debt.[27]

Slaves accounted for perhaps 15% of the population, so over 3 million people in the east. This class could likely reproduce itself without infusions of new slaves from wars. As slaves were used both domestically and on farms, their geographical distribution likely matched that of the overall population. Slaves worked the land, manufactured textiles, satisfied their owners' sexual impulses, and bore the brunt of their anger. They also worked in mines, toiling and dying in the dark so that others could have coins and jewelry in addition to food and clothes. Some historians believe that the ancient slave economy continued in force during this period, but others have argued for a relative decline as previously slave professions (such as tutors) were turned over to the free labor market (and became more prestigious) while the colonate edged out large-scale argicultural servitude.[28] The average price of a slave remained relatively constant over the next millennium, at about 17 gold coins.[29]

Women usually had the same socioeconomic status as their men (fathers or husbands), but their political and vocational opportunities were restricted: by both law and custom they could not be soldiers or hold political or Church offices. This was because they were regarded as morally, physically, and intellectually weaker, and were expected to be modest and submissive. The laws sometimes stated as much, and Constantine assumed that women would want to stay in the home "out of consideration of their sex."[30] The point was reinforced from the pulpit: God assigned women to the household and men to public affairs, the marketplace, the armies, and all the rest.[31] Elite women, in particular, were held to higher standards of decorum than others. They were to be "raised outside the public gaze, learn the ways of modesty, and live discreetly."[32] Yet many women were in fact active in public life. They attended the hippodrome, took part in processions, and were prominent in festival dances, which Church writers abhorred but were powerless to stop.[33] Women joined in many protests alongside the men. They were also involved in manufacturing, especially textiles.[34] This was not a society in which women were hidden from view.

Virtually all women married, usually in their teens, and were expected to bear many children. For the population to remain stable given the high levels of infant mortality, they had to have five or six children on average for two or three to survive. Partible inheritance, and the growing insistence of Roman law that daughters receive an equitable (not always equal) share of inheritance, checked the growth of large properties. This was one reason why a hereditary nobility never emerged in Romanía and why its aristocrats were unable to accumulate so much wealth that they could bully the state. A significant number of women at any time were widows who controlled the family assets. Widowhood transformed previously subordinate wives into heads of household, and this was true from peasants all the way up to the court, explaining how some empresses came to power. The law also enabled married women to own and manage property and represent themselves legally, depending on the extent of their legal emancipation from their father's authority and the terms of their marriage. Fully one-fifth of landowners recorded in census inscriptions from Magnesia (western Asia Minor) were women, as were between a fourth and a third of legal petitioners to the imperial court, who were seeking to resolve mostly property issues; the status of these petitioners ranged across the socioeconomic spectrum. In the Egyptian village of Aphrodite, women made up only 14.7% of the taxpayers.[35] Women could wield significant social influence if they were rich or connected. To their credit, the group most convinced of the intellectual equality of women were the Platonists, who remained true to their master. The annals of Platonism boast many women honored for their wisdom, from Sosipatra and Hypatia to Asklepigeneia.

The legal scaffold of society

The social order of the new Roman empire had not "organically" evolved outside the regulatory apparatus of the state, but was in fact its product. The matrix of this order was Roman law and the state's fiscal needs. Who you were in society was defined by your relation to property—whether you owned, rented, worked, or *were* it; by the law's definition of the nature of that property, for example how it might be transferred, used, shared; and by the duties which that property owed to the state. John Chrysostom reminded his congregation in Antioch that "when we take a wife, make a will, are about to buy a slave, house, field, or do anything else at all, we do not do it however we wish but as the laws command." If ever an imperial subject wondered, "What does the emperor have to do with me?", the answer was clear: "It is by imperial law that you own land, a house, a slave."[36]

The impact of imperial law is often understood too narrowly, as a system of punishments assigned to specific crimes or as a set of state impositions, and historians assess the degree of its "enforcement" by trying to understand how the judicial system worked, especially in the area of criminal justice. But that was a small part of what law did. In reality, law provided the basic scaffolding of society, using a small number of variable elements (rights, privileges, and fiscal dues) to define the "status" of each class. These classes included the Senate, the various categories of magistrates, the people of Constantinople, the soldiery, clergy, city councilors, the various guilds (such as the shipmasters who brought grain to the capital), and they ranged down to small landowners, tenants, slaves, and dependents. Not only were they all embedded in the legal order, many of them were created by it and maintained by the state. An increasing volume of legislation specified what each class could do, could own, and owed to the state. That the laws "worked" in this sense is proven by a simple observation: the society that we observe "in motion" in narrative and literary sources corresponds perfectly to the one that is defined in the laws.

The social lattice defined by Roman law left no empty spaces, neither in theory nor in practice. Some groups originated outside it but were later absorbed, for example the Christian clergy, by Constantine, and monks later on. They were thus co-opted and became yet another legally-defined status within the law, with defined rights and responsibilities alongside senators, soldiers, and coloni. To be sure, the laws did not micromanage all aspects of life. In towns and villages across the empire people looked first to local means of solving problems, and the imperial government may have seemed distant.[37] But the categories through which they operated even on a local level—their guilds, systems for tax collection, pressure to produce for the market—were structured by that distant state and its laws. The security that it provided was not perfect, as countless legal complaints attest. Never was being a Roman citizen with access to the courts and a responsive government as important to so many people as in the new empire. In the fourth century, Aurelius Sarapion—whose ancestors were enfranchised in 212—lodged a complaint before a magistrate that a woman had come to his house yesterday and bitterly insulted his wife and daughter "in violation of the laws and of our station in life." He demanded that she be called to account.[38] Another Aurelius in Egypt, making a census declaration before the magistrate on behalf of his family, also named Aurelii, ended with an oath: "I swear the oath customary among the Romans that I have made no false declaration."[39]

It is crucial that complaints were processed through the law and its political networks. Provincials did not have to secure and defend their property through the constant exercise of personal violence, or its threat. This happened, for example, in the west after the fall of the western empire, creating a far more militarized, violent ruling class than the eastern empire would ever have.

When he surveyed the whole of society, the emperor Justinian broke it down into groups defined by their status: senators, state officials, businesspeople, the clergy, soldiers, and farmers, "whose ignorance of civic affairs and desire for nothing but tilling the land is highly desirable and praiseworthy."[40] Some scholars believe that many subjects neither knew nor cared what the emperors decreed, and that the state was so primitive that it could neither communicate nor enforce its laws. But in reality there were no isolated communities that lived in "ignorance" of the bureaucracy. All had to pay three installments per year to the tax collector or a landlord, a necessity that structured their lives as deeply as their culture, language, or religion. The idea of a primitive government is being retired because historians are finding that provincial communities were not only aware of the laws but were exploiting them in court and through petitions to secure concessions from the government. Consider a law passed by Justinian in 533, by which the offspring of a bound colonus man and unbound woman should be considered unbound. So many coloni registered grown children as unbound that Justinian issued supplementary legislation four years later clarifying that this applied only to children born after the law.[41] "The machinery of the state shaped the intimate details of life, even in a remote corner of empire."[42] Justinian complained that too many poor farmers and coloni were coming to Constantinople to press charges against their landlords.[43]

Justinian's interventions show that the state's legal matrix was not static. It was continually revising its own hierarchies, by bestowing privileges on favored classes (such as veterans and Christian priests) and honored professions (such as doctors and teachers), and by granting exemptions from the harsher punishments, supplementary levies, and compulsory labor to both its existing elites (councilors) and the emerging officer class. This was social engineering via the tax code, and it eventually generated the new empire's superelite, who ruled the east through the shiny new marker of Roman status: gold.

The gold economy

Diocletian tried to curb inflation by outlawing it, which failed. He did, however, lay the foundation for a monetary recovery by issuing a stable gold coin, the *solidus*, which was struck at two weights, one at sixty to the Roman pound (0.328 kg) and one at seventy. To obtain the bullion, he requisitioned gold, forcing subjects to sell it to the state in exchange for (notionally overpriced) base metal coins. Constantine minted the solidus at seventy-two to the pound in order to squeeze out a few more, and it remained at or near that weight thereafter (see Plate 1a). The economy of the empire was henceforth dominated by the solidus, which was not seriously devalued until the eleventh century. It was issued in huge quantities after the 340s, flooding the market. By the end of the fourth century it had become the standard unit of value, even in notional or fractional valuations where no actual coins changed hands. Millions of solidi were absorbed by an expanding economy and the commutation of existing transactions from kind or base metal to gold. A military writer was exaggerating when he said that, "starting with Constantine, gold was assigned to petty transactions in place of bronze."[44] But by the sixth century mid-level transactions were taking place in gold.

The same writer also observed that "because of this abundance of gold the houses of the powerful were stuffed full to the detriment of the poor."[45] The gold economy favored the powerful because the alternative to gold coin was low-value bronze. The silver *denarius* had been wiped out during the third century. Silver was still minted thereafter, but its circulation was limited, mostly to soldiers. Gold was instead complemented by a base metal currency, bronze *nummi*, whose value was not fixed in relation to the solidus but fluctuated (as nummi had a silver wash, they were sometimes called denarii). During the fourth century, the value of nummi plummeted, resulting in their massive inflation relative to gold.[46] The emperors' response to their depreciation was to mint more of them, worsening the problem. Provincials began calculating prices in the tens of thousands ("myriads") of nummi and then myriads of myriads. But the solidus held true, so holders of gold, i.e., the new imperial elite, became comparatively richer while those who held bronze lost value. Even rural areas were increasingly monetized in this period, but mostly in bronze.[47] So who exactly were "the powerful" with gold in their hands? How did currency affect the social structure? And where did the state get all this gold?

The cash cycle is well understood. The state minted coins and put them into circulation by paying its soldiers, officers, magistrates, and secretaries; by purchasing materials and carrying out public works; by supporting philanthropic and religious projects; and through its own luxury spending. Recipients spent those coins on consumer goods and food, whence they came into the hands of craftsmen and agricultural producers, and from there they returned to the state via taxes. A tiny amount of coins was lost or hidden away to be found by archaeologists, and some left the empire in foreign trade or as payments to keep barbarians at bay. New bullion entered the empire through war plunder and from mines. We cannot quantify these volumes. Moreover, the state economy was not exclusively or even primarily cash-based, at least not in the fourth century. The state levied a large portion of its taxes, and paid a large part of its salaries, in kind, even if they were calculated in notional solidi. The trend, however, was toward commuting these payments to gold on both ends, a process that was advanced by the early fifth century.[48] This imposed a burden on taxpayers to find gold with which to pay, forcing them to produce for the market and thus stimulating growth. The state was also churning out more coins than it pulled in, because by the later fifth century the general economy was heavily monetized and many coins had circulated for so long that they were visibly worn.[49]

We can identify the classes who benefited from this system and appreciate the pressures it exerted on everyone else. The highest ranked magistrates of the state were paid in gold, along with officials in the secretarial bureaux who were in a position to decide who was paid in gold (and presumably favored themselves), as well as all who were close to them or the emperor. An acerbic historian wrote that "the first to open the maw of his close associates was Constantine, and then Constantius stuffed them with the marrow of the provinces. Under him the top men of every order in the state were inflamed with a desire for riches, just or unjust." He lists specifically the praetorian prefects, generals, chamberlains of the palace, and *quaestors* (the emperors' legal officials).[50] But lower-ranked officers were also clamoring for gold and using devious schemes to get the provincials to pay them in cash rather than kind, such as letting grain rot and then demanding payment in coin in its place. The laws tried to curb this behavior, and by the early fifth century emperors favored commutation.[51]

"Deluged with well-defined privileges," Constantine called the upper cadres.[52] But there were burdens too. A bribe might be necessary to secure an appointment, effectively a pricey "investment." Constantine levied an annual cash tax on senators, the *collatio glebalis*, with rates that varied by wealth, but overall pulled in small sums and was abolished in 455.[53] Another imposition on senators was the *aurum oblaticium*, offered to the emperor upon his accession and at later anniversaries during the reign. The sums mentioned in sources include 1,600 gold lbs (Rome to the western emperor in 384), 3,000 gold lbs (Rome to the eastern emperor in 578), and 3,000 silver lbs (Constantinople to its emperor in 457).[54] These were more serious sums.

The heaviest burdens on senators were the offices of praetor and consul. Between three and five praetors were appointed at a time, who had to subsidize the games or a construction project in the City to the tune of a few hundred lbs silver (each pound of silver was worth about five solidi). The demand was so onerous that praetors were chosen ten years before their term of service to have time to raise the funds. This burden was the greatest obstacle to recruiting men to the new senate. Thus the praetorship funneled provincial wealth to Constantinople. The holder of the consulship—one per year in the east—had to subsidize far more expensive games, capped in the fifth century at 100 gold lbs because some were voluntarily spending more. Consuls gave precious works of art, such as ivory diptychs bearing their name, to their closest associates (see Figure 4).[55]

The imperial aristocracy had a curial background, but now enjoyed advantages over their former peers when it came to buying land, paying taxes in coin, and throwing their weight around in the provinces. Crucially, they were exempt from curial obligations and the "sordid duties" of feeding and billeting soldiers and officials on the move or providing animals and labor for public works. Over time, the empire built up a large cadre of former officials, a new aristocracy of service and gold. It had

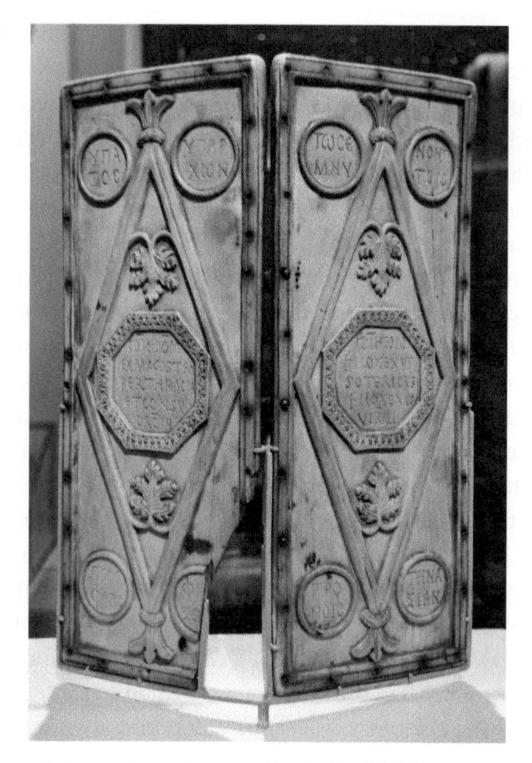

Figure 4 Consular ivory diptych of Philoxenus (525 AD), now at Dumbarton Oaks. It is 33.3 cm x 25.6 cm in size, and bears inscriptions in both Greek and Latin.
Photo by David Hendrix

grown so much by the end of the fourth century that it generated its own internal elite, men who had held the highest offices and bore the prestige rank of *illustris*. The rest, in the fifth century, were no longer required to reside in Constantinople: "we allow them to depart, with no need for permission, to their native land or wherever else they want, and to live there."[56] These senators of lesser grade returned to their cities where they bought up land and eventually displaced the councils politically. That development was still in the future but its seeds were planted by Constantine and Constantius: the first founded the City and its senate and the second created the gold-based elite of the new empire. The City sucked up local councilors and then spat them back, as gold-heavy *honorati*, "men of honor," at the provinces.

In the land census of Magnesia, the largest plot by a wide margin (75 *iuga* to 21 *iuga*, the second largest), belonged to a senator.[57] In his speeches, Libanios of Antioch refers scathingly to the encroachments by current or former imperial officials on the properties of city councilors. Coming in with gold, "they reaped the harvest of imperial service" by buying up distressed properties and loaning money at usurious rates. Libanios saw himself as "waging war" through speeches against such acquisitions.[58] In a pamphlet to Theodosius I, he denounced a nightmarish scam, whereby army officers loaned soldiers to agricultural tenants, who, backed by this hired muscle, refused to pay their taxes and rents. This meant that their landowner, a councilor, was on the hook for the shortfall and the only way he could pay was by selling the land. "And so a councilor is erased from the council." Libanios concludes that "these generals have their eye on one thing only: money, in fact whole mountains of gold and silver."[59] In 386, a law required provincial governors to approve sales of councilor properties "to ensure that the seller was not being overwhelmed by the power of the purchaser."[60]

In regulating the city councils, emperors were caught in a bind. On the one hand, they wanted to recruit the best men to the imperial bureaucracy, army, Senate, and Church, but on the other hand functioning councils were necessary for collecting taxes, underwriting local losses, and managing the cities, which were the feet of the administration. Many laws sought to regulate which councilors could obtain positions that exempted them from curial duties. It was a demographic and fiscal tug of war: there may have been 100,000 councilors in the eastern empire, against a need for some 18,000 salaried officials (not counting the Church). One estimate is 10,000 jobs per generation in the east.[61] The race was on to "escape" into the service, placing a disproportionate burden on those who remained. In the last quarter of the fourth century, emperors began to insist that councilors had to perform curial duties before they could take up higher posts, or leave an heir who could do so, and they limited the plum exemptions to senators of *illustris* rank. But there was still an exodus. Libanios protested that councils were being complacent about allowing their members to leave. "Any excuse is enough: 'This one is a soldier,' and so we keep quiet about him. 'That one is an imperial messenger,' so no one claims him. 'This other one was assessor to a governor,' so he is excused."[62] Councilors were both the beneficiaries and victims of the expanded administration.

Instead of seeing here only the decline of the cities, as historians used to do, we can see it also as the rise of Romanía, a unified state. Councilors wanted to leave because the universal state had opened wider horizons for prestige and profit. Yet the pool of local honor and power did become shallower. For some councilors it did not compensate for the drudgery of their duties. Libanios presents them as less free than their own slaves: "Off they go to a meeting at night, when some have not had the chance to bathe or eat, or have been interrupted at it. Their eyelids drooping with lack of sleep, they are ordered to lay down roads, repair bridges, track down thieves, or collect the grain."[63]

The gold economy exacerbated this imbalance. As tax commutation progressed, councilors owed taxes in gold but were not receiving it directly from the state. And not just taxes: emperors traditionally received a crown of gold (*aurum coronarium*) from each city council upon their accession and at various anniversaries. It went into another imperial treasury, the *sacrae largitiones*, whose *comes* supervised an extensive bureaucracy in the provinces that was in charge of cash revenues, mints, and workshops that clothed imperial officials. This golden crown had to be delivered by councilors personally. Julian, who favored the cities, limited it to 70 solidi, at least for his reign.[64] At that rate it would have pulled in only 2,000 gold lbs across the entire empire.

Councilors therefore *had* to obtain gold, which for most meant producing a surplus and selling it on the market. Taxation thereby stimulated production and monetization. It also created a society that our sources depict as money-crazed. Christian moralists rang the alarm: "You see gold in everything, you fantasize about gold, dreaming of it while you sleep and thinking of it while awake," said Basil to his elite congregation in Kaisareia. "For you, wheat becomes gold, wine turns into gold, and your sheep too are transformed into gold . . . all your thoughts are on gold."[65] What moralists denounced as "greed" an economist might describe as a structural imperative to secure coin, which resulted in a culture of aggressive acquisitiveness: "we spend all of our days scheming how to increase our property, land, slaves; we are insatiable."[66] Some were desperate to position themselves into the cash flow. It became possible to monetize one's public career by treating office as an investment: bribe a higher official to appoint you to a provincial post and then fleece the provincials for cash to recoup your investment. Libanios tells the story of a councilor who sold his lands (technically inalienable); used the money to buy an appointment to high office (either illegal or frowned upon); and then made the money back through misconduct as an official (verging on criminality, depending on what he was doing; for example, he could force people into courts under his jurisdiction). With the money that he fleeced from provincials, he then bought land.[67] This man had fully monetized his land, career, and honor.

Other classes fared differently in the gold stream. Constantine, a surprisingly competent economist, realized that a great deal of gold was flowing to cities and craftsmen, which were effectively tax shelters. He therefore imposed a coin tax, the *collatio lustralis* (or *chrysargyron*, gold and silver tax) on all who made a living by selling goods or services, including sex workers but excluding doctors and teachers, to be paid every four or five years. A startling amount of hatred is directed toward this tax in our sources, both pagan and Christian, which call it a wicked evil and the ruin of the cities.[68] But the tax fell precisely upon the urban classes from which authors came, and on their family businesses. The city of Edessa was paying 140 gold lbs (i.e., 10,080 solidi) when the emperor Anastasius abolished the tax in 498. Upon the news of its abolition, the townspeople rejoiced in public, sang hymns, and processed with lit candles to thank God and the emperor.[69] Edessa was a largish city and a center of trade. If we hypothesize that the average city paid only 40 lbs, that would still bring in, for the eastern empire, 40,000 lbs revenue every four years (or 750,000 solidi per year), a huge sum. But if the sum reported for Edessa represented the haul from its entire province (Osrhoene), then the total revenue would have been significantly lower.

The quadrennial timing was significant, given the rhythm of state expenses. The *chrysargyron* urban tax, along with the donations in gold by senators and councils, were timed to pay for the accessional and quinquennial ("five-year") donative that was given to each regular soldier. The army was the state's largest expense, but data is difficult to come by and the state used mixed means to support and pay its soldiers, including cash, rations, and equipment, though over time the latter were commuted to cash payments. In the fourth century, soldiers received cash primarily upon the accession of a new emperor—five solidi plus a pound of silver, which was itself worth another four solidi in this period—then a five-solidi donative at each five-year anniversary.[70] If there were 250,000 soldiers in the east and they all received the same donative, it worked out to over 17,000 lbs gold, or 1,250,000 solidi, every four years (if officers received more, then add 25%, for 22,000 lbs). Thus, it is possible that between Constantine and Anastasius the urban tax was providing the gold for the state's largest regular expense in coin.

But the donative was only part of the army's cost. There were also the soldiers' rations (*annona*, the same term as the grain supply of the capital), their equipment, and the cavalry's horses. Estimates of the army's overall annual cost vary between 1,250,000 solidi (17,000 lbs gold) and 1,900,000 solidi (26,500 lbs gold) for an eastern imperial army of 250,000 men (adjust up or down for larger or smaller armies). To put that into perspective, the total revenue of the eastern empire has been calculated at between 4 and 6 million solidi.[71] The state also seems to have paid its soldiers a salary in bronze nummi, which was the main way that it put them into circulation, but this did not enrich ordinary soldiers. In one of his exposés, Libanios protested that soldiers were starving because officers embezzled their pay, and what little was left fed soldiers' wives and children.[72]

The taxes on some professions and many small farmers did not rise to the level of a full solidus, so, depending on the extent of commutation, these taxpayers had to convert bronze to gold by combining their payments. In the tax register of the village of Skar in Egypt, long lines of taxpayers contribute myriads of "denarii" each, with only a handful paying in gold, for a grand total—after the conversion—of about three lbs gold.[73] Themistios knew how difficult it was for farmers to scrape together the bronze coins to pay the tax, more so a gold coin, "a sight so dear and scarce for most."[74] Bronze inflation would have disadvantaged them, and they also had to pay the commission charged by the moneychangers.

An archive from the fourth century reveals how this worked in Egypt. The brothers Papnouthis and Dorotheos would borrow gold and use it to buy, from the relevant official, the right to collect taxes from a certain district. They made their profit by converting non-gold payments into gold. It was in their interest, therefore, to stay attuned to even slight fluctuations in the price of gold, though one time a crooked official double-sold the rights to a district, leaving them on the hook for a loan.[75]

We know little about moneychangers. A western law of 445 reveals that they bought bronze from the state in exchange for the gold that they had collected, and were authorized to sell it at a 2.8% markup.[76] Such transactions were ubiquitous in urban areas. John Chrysostom explains how all commerce depended on them, and that people were going in and out of the shops of the moneychangers all day: "the use of money holds our lives together: it is at the heart of all agreements, of buying and selling, everything that we do depends on it."[77]

State expenses rose sharply during the fourth century. The emperors had to pay for the expanded army and bureaucracy of Diocletian and also to build New Rome and satisfy an ambitious new religion. So where did Constantine and Constantius find the gold to issue so many solidi? Possibly new mines were discovered in the Balkans, whence the praise that we hear for Bessian miners. But a chief source of the new gold that was put into circulation were temple treasuries. These were disgorged and melted down as the temples were closed and plundered of precious contents: "Christian men from the palace went around to the temples, intimidated the locals to be quiet, and forced priests to bring out dedications made of precious metal, which were melted down to became public property"—so wrote a satisfied historian of the Church a century later. Others merely noted that Constantine used the temple treasuries to build his City and mint his coinage.[78] These requisitions were likely presented to the pagan public with pragmatic arguments relating to the public good, rather than as a naked sectarian triumph, which is how gloating Christians preferred to see it. Either way, the new empire dug deeply into the guts of the old one to build its new institutions, an investment that paid off.

In the process, the emperors created a new imperial super-elite that was defined by three overlapping attributes. First, it held salaried offices in the state. Second, it benefited from the new economy of gold. And third, it bore the name "Flavius." This was Constantine's family name—his *gentilicium*, in Latin terms—and had been used by him and his father Constantius I as a brand-marker for their dynasty. Diocletian had used the name "Valerius" in this way before them, so that all men in service to the Tetrarchy, down to the reign of Licinius in the east, took the name Valerius. When Constantine acquired the entire empire, Flavius became the name by which one identified with the state. The emperors held it henceforth as a quasi-title, but it was also assumed by virtually all officials, both high and low, soldiers, and many others who were associated with the administration. Exactly how it was bestowed and policed remains unclear, but hundreds of thousands of men across the empire now posed as the "emperor's men," as his kin. In Egyptian papyri and the inscriptions of Aphrodisias in Asia Minor, the Flavii appear as wealthier, more powerful, and more official than the rest, who are mere Aurelii, i.e., Romans enfranchised by Caracalla. The Flavii are often the lessors and creditors in relations with the Aurelii, who are the debtors; likewise, imperial officials tend to be Flavii, whereas city councilors are Aurelii.[79] In the east, Flavius became "the hallmark of the *newly* important."[80]

The personality of government

The government of the new empire has often been mischaracterized as a totalitarian and theocratic-military dictatorship that suppressed the civic culture of the ancient world, eroded political freedom, and subordinated its subjects to a corrupt plutocracy and the intrigues of court eunuchs who encircled a quasi-divine monarch. Diocletian was allegedly the first to adopt a despotic style, adorning his robes and footwear with gems, requiring prostration, and being hailed as *dominus*, "lord." Constantine began to wear a jeweled diadem and issued laws that extended the scope of capital punishment and "judicial savagery," as he fulminated angrily against malefactors and threatened them with the amputation of limbs or pouring molten lead down their throats.[81] This image of oriental despotism was crafted during the Enlightenment, but now its persuasive power has waned. It was a rhetorical construct that served the needs of the Enlightenment, but fails as a description of later Roman government.

The empire's militarism did not deviate from Roman norms. Rome was one of the most militaristic states in history and its imperial monarchy was always a tempered military dictatorship. By establishing a professional army and posting it along the frontiers, Augustus sundered the military and the civic sides of Roman tradition, highlighting urbanity in the regime that operated out of Rome. But this was possible only because of the relative peace of the first centuries, a boon the later empire did not enjoy.[82] After 193, the pendulum swung back to the military and the frontiers. Politics were henceforth defined more by the tension between the emperor and his generals and armies than between the emperor and the Senate. Emperors ceased to reside at Rome and spent their reigns fighting barbarians and rebels. They had to maintain control of the armies just in order to survive, but they were driven also by a duty toward their subjects. There were many years when Diocletian, Constantine, and Constantius could, had they so chosen, idled in the pleasures of Rome rather than slogging through the mud of Danubian campaigns. Even while the emperors marched along the frontiers, their courts and subordinates in the provinces were answering thousands of petitions from their subjects. Emperors were extremely hard-working, micromanaging countless matters out of a sense of purpose. The praise that they received doubled as a subtle reminder of their duties:

> Those services that you have rendered . . . to take upon your shoulders the destiny of the whole world; to forget yourself and live for the people . . . to observe which governors emulate your justice, which commanders maintain the glory of your courage, to receive countless messengers from every quarter, to send out just as many dispatches, to worry about so many cities and nations and provinces, to spend all one's nights and days in perpetual concern for the safety of all.[83]

There was a stock repertoire of virtues for which the emperors were praised, indeed for which they *had* to be praised by those who addressed them on formal occasions: courage, justice, piety, and the like. But the imperial government itself, above and beyond the occupant of the throne, projected personality traits of its own. These included paternal solicitude for the welfare of all its subjects, even for "the common happiness";[84] a striving for the rule of law and for fairness in its dealings with them; and responsiveness to their concerns. If Romanía did not fully embody these values, it was not because the emperors were despotic, cruel, or indifferent. It was because they lacked subtle policy instruments; resorted quickly to threats and punishments when laws were imperfectly enforced; faced large and entrenched inequalities; supported contradictory goals (for example fostering social harmony versus promoting the One True Faith); undercut their bureaucracy in order to not be rendered redundant by it;[85] were suspicious of designs on their throne and desperate to remain popular; and created opportunities for abuse every time they fixed a problem.

Emperors were powerful, frustrated, and insecure, but generally principled and dutiful toward the whole of Romanía. They proclaimed themselves "parents of the human race," "born for the good of the human race," and "liberators of the world." Rome was the "mother of mankind."[86] In this conception, there were no foreigners inside the empire. The provincials were the emperor's "partners" in his concern for the "security of the commonality," and the *res publica* encompassed the entire empire.[87] A state reveals itself best in what it does, but what it says is also important because it reveals the kind of relationship that it wants to establish with its subjects. The emperors were not simply lying to look good.

In the homogenized terrain of the new empire, imperial law impacted everyone more directly, equally, and on a larger scale. Emperors self-consciously legislated for "everyone," "all provincials," and "all citizens." Their interventions had universal scope. This was formerly mistaken as totalitarianism, but it was in fact the rationalism of universal law. Emperors could now order up a universal sacrifice to the gods, produce a census of all lands to be taxed, attempt to cap prices throughout the empire, and demand that all adhere to their preferred theological doctrine. Even in smaller decrees, posted and read out locally, emperors stressed that "our untiring attention and solicitude encompass everything that benefits human society."[88] This trait could be taken to extremes, as when Justinian justified his unceasing interventions in every aspect of life, including the price of vegetables, by invoking the same principles of universal benevolence.

Homogenization and administrative uniformity required considerable buy-in from subjects, which is why the government struggled to ensure fairness, or its appearance. A legal order will fail if it is perceived as unfair, sooner than if it is seen as oppressive. Constantine and Licinius pronounced in 314 that "justice and equity are more important than the strict letter of the law."[89] This was especially true regarding taxation and property, everyone's principal concern. Consider the edict posted by Aristius Optatus, prefect of Egypt in 297, upon the introduction of Diocletian's new tax system. The emperors, he says,

> having learned that the levies of the public taxes were being made capriciously so that some persons were let off lightly while others were overburdened, decided in the interests of the provincials to root out this evil practice and issue a salutary rule to which taxes have to conform. Thus it is possible for all to know the amount levied on each *aroura* . . . from the imperial edict which has been published and the schedule attached thereto . . . . Let the provincials make their contributions with all speed in accordance with the imperial regulations and not wait for collectors to exercise compulsion . . . The collectors of every kind of tax are also reminded to look to their duties to the best of their ability, for if anyone is detected in transgression, he risks capital punishment.[90]

Aristius' official persona was crafted to project the following traits: a recognition of the need for fairness; imperial intervention to guarantee it in the interests of the provincials; a full public disclosure and dissemination of the rules governing the process (it is arbitrary and tyrannical regimes that seek to hide the rules);[91] a preference for voluntary compliance over state coercion; and, just as important, a threat of violence against corrupt officials. In theory, emperors could have squeezed taxpayers simply by raising the tax assessment, a practice that is occasionally attested.[92] But that could be taken only so far before it alienated public opinion and emboldened usurpers. In fact, the immediate effect of Aristius' edict and the new census in Egypt was, possibly, to spark a rebellion. Perhaps the tax burden in 297 was too high, but the principles behind his decree reflected the eagerness of the new regime to be fair and transparent. This was not mere rhetoric. A study of tax records from sixth-century Egypt failed to find that senators enjoyed significant tax privileges.[93]

Thus, imperial rhetoric did not aim to merely to make emperors look good. It communicated the fundamental values which they themselves pledged to follow and expected from their subjects. Emperors regularly promised to work hard, to be fair, and to abide by consensual values, and they expected their subjects to obey the laws and contribute toward the common purpose without delay or deceit. Thus, imperial law not only structured Roman society but articulated the norms of its public sphere.

As money was always everyone's chief concern, emperors strove to explain why taxes were necessary.

> It is by their salaries that soldiers are enabled to resist the enemy, defend citizens from the invasions and cruelty of the barbarians, and protect fields and towns from the attacks of robbers. . . . It is by means of taxation that walls are repaired, cities fortified, public baths warmed, and the theaters intended for the diversion of our subjects supported. Thus the taxes paid by our subjects are used and expended for their own benefit.[94]

The state's paternalism, its claim to be acting in the national interest, was not just rhetorical. This was understood at every level of society, as far down the social ladder as our texts allow us to penetrate. A lowbrow provincial saint's life about a dragon who had occupied the imperial treasury in Constantinople explains how that treasury worked: "the taxes flow into the palace from all over the world and then the emperor uses the money to provide for the common needs of the republic." Provincial authors with even a modest grasp of history understood that the new empire was different from its predecessor: "what Rome once extorted from us at sword-point to satisfy her own extravagance, now she contributes with us for the good of the state we share."[95]

The imperial persona also had an angry side. But the violence threatened by the emperors, which has given them a reputation for "savagery," was directed mostly against their own corrupt officials. In fact, our knowledge of the various crimes that officials committed—including elaborate and inventive scams—comes from laws issued against them, taking up whole sections of the law codes. The empire's subjects, in turn, assumed that their government would be responsive and could be held accountable, which is why they frequently asked the emperors to crack down on sharp practices, even if it was risky to name powerful malefactors. This is extraordinary. Tyrannies typically facilitate the crimes of their officials and do not put so many legal instruments into the hands of citizens so that they may contest official injustices. Whatever was happening on the ground, the government wore a face of sincere accountability. Contrary to the usual custom of military dictatorships, emperors issued many decrees protecting civilians from abuse by the army.[96] They tried to ensure that these laws were enforced and that knowledge of them was not limited to system insiders, who could quietly shelve them. When one emperor realized that protections against abuses by the army were not being followed in a small village in Paphlagonia, he sent special instructions to be carved on a prominent inscription locally.[97] Emperors followed up and followed through. Many laws "put the interests of private citizens above that of the imperial fisc."[98]

Another pillar of imperial ideology was that the emperors should succor the weak and protect them from oppression, "so that the multitude of the lower classes may not be subjected to the arbitrariness and subordinated to the interests of the more powerful," as Constantine declared. It was *humanum* for the emperor to show special consideration for the weaker party.[99] The rich and powerful, then as now, enjoyed enormous advantages in working the system, but they failed to persuade society that they were the better sort, for in legal petitions it is commonly assumed that they were violent and oppressive and that the weaker party merited government protection. It was rhetorically advantageous to be the weaker party before the law.[100] In every city Constantine posted a "protector (*defensor*)" to act as an advocate for the weak. We know about this magistrate from the laws of the brothers Valentinian I and Valens, who especially stood up for peasants, taxpayers, and "the little guy" against abuses by the powerful and state officials.[101] Protecting the weak became such a standard refrain in imperial legislation that an emperor who took it to heart, Justinian, has even been seen as a proto-Marxist class warrior.

It was expected that emperors would respond to subjects' concerns and petitions, provide military protection from barbarians, tax relief for areas struck by drought or invasion, and famine relief. In 322, Constantine ordered his officials to distribute food from the state storehouses to the hungry in North Africa, and later emperors acknowledged that humane rule entailed feeding the poor.[102] But the vast majority of petitions that came to the court, to the tune of many thousands every year, were legal in nature. Subjects from every social class and province as well as officials presiding over cases sought clarification of the law to secure exemptions, resolve pending disputes, or gain some advantage. The chancery responded to all these petitions, creating law and precedent in the process. Some emperors tried to stem the flood of paperwork, by asking local officials to deal with more cases. Still, over time rural populations and the previously disenfranchised gained access to documents, laws, institutions, and concepts of protection before the law that they could use to their own advantage and to constrain the exercise of power by agents of the state. They "made Roman institutions their own."[103] The governor of Edessa in 498 even put a suggestion box outside his office.[104]

In theory, the law and state institutions ensured fair play, but money, influence, and connections certainly perverted or hindered the course of justice.

Contemporaries complained that "if the criminal is rich, it is possible for him to evade punishment, whereas if he is poor he does not know how to work the system and suffers the penalty."[105] People looked to the emperor for solutions. The image of the emperor as champion of the downtrodden against the abuses of the rich is captured in a stock story told about many rulers: the emperor, approached in the street by a distraught and outraged victim, orders the arrest and punishment of an offending official. In these tales, emperors ameliorate the failure of institutions through swift personal justice. Accordingly, they presented themselves "as populist monarchs" concerned not merely about their own elites but all subjects.[106] This fueled a culture of complaint, which was often couched in hyperbolic terms. One had to claim, "we are vexed, oppressed, plundered."[107] We should not take this at face value. There was a competition to be heard over the clamor, not a pervasive rot. Subjects were trying to hold the state accountable to its own standards.

The monarchical republic

What motivated emperors to appear benevolent, fair, and responsive? After all, they commanded armies that could intimidate any dissenters. Their word was law: "whatever pleases the emperor has the force of law."[108] There were no institutions of government that were, either in theory or practice, independent of the monarchy. With no separation of powers, the new Roman empire qualifies as an absolutist monarchy. But in practice it was nothing of the sort. The emperors were desperate to be accepted, to enjoy a broad consensus of support, to be seen as acting within the law, and to exemplify Roman values. Why? The answer is that the basis of their own positions was uncertain, undetermined, always probationary, and not grounded in law. No emperor had a right to the throne or even a right to continue as emperor after his initial accession. All could be replaced, usually violently, if they became unpopular. This is the paradox of east Roman politics: the regime itself—the monarchy—was stable and enduring, but the individual emperors were insecure and often deposed or killed.

The emperor was the nexus of this paradox. On the one hand, he was the *dominus* of the Roman world, to whom all owed obedience and swore oaths of loyalty. He commanded all institutions of government. On the other hand, the imperial position was understood by all, especially by the emperors themselves, as a stewardship of the Roman *res publica*, the impersonal "common affairs" of the Roman people. The *res publica* (*politeia* in Greek) was not a specific type of regime such as a "monarchy," "aristocracy," or "republic" (our definition of that word is a modern twist). Instead, it referred collectively to the government, public affairs, common interests, and society of the Romans independently of the type of regime by which they were ruled, so long as that regime served the interests of the people. It designated the whole of Roman society as a lawful polity grounded in moral consensus about an impersonal common good.

The emperors constantly proclaimed that they were servants of this *res publica Romana* and pledged to promote its welfare. The first words of Diocletian's edict on prices are "the fortune of our *res publica*," which the edict aims to defend against the ravages of greed. Galerius defended the persecution of Christians as one "among the other actions that we are always taking for the benefit and advantage of the *res publica*" (again, the first words of the edict). When Constantius elevated Julian to the rank of Caesar and sent him to Gaul, he told him, before the soldiers, to "hasten, with the united prayers of all, to defend with sleepless care the post assigned to you, as it were, by the *res publica* herself." Valentinian was elected emperor by army officers with an eye "on the good of the *res publica*," and he was advised to take on a colleague, "if you love the *res publica*."[109]

This love was expected to transcend personal interests. When Valentinian refused to break off a campaign against the barbarians and ride to aid his brother Valens, who was embroiled in a war against the usurper Procopius, he justified his decision by saying that Procopius was an enemy only of the dynasty whereas the barbarians threatened the entire Roman world. When Anastasius was elected emperor in 491, he was required to swear an oath to put aside his private disputes and govern the *res publica* to the best of his ability.[110]

While subjects swore to obey emperors, emperors swore to serve their subjects—sleeplessly and tirelessly. What made this relationship tense was that emperors' legitimacy depended entirely on the consent to their rule by the rest of the polity, namely by whatever powerful subsection of it was in proximity to the emperor at any time. Roman tradition admitted no other "right" to the throne, whether by descent, family, experience, divine favor, or personal virtue. All these could be brought forth to support a candidacy,[111] but ultimately emperors were created by popular acclamation: large masses of soldiers or civilians chanting the word "Augustus" followed by the new emperor's name and prayers. Even this conferred no permanent claim. Emperors were acclaimed periodically, and if the chants gave way to grumbles, protests, or open jeers, their acceptance was thereby called into question. An emperor was declared deposed when the Romans—usually the army or the people of Constantinople—elected and acclaimed a rival, resulting in civil war. Rivals popped up whenever a sitting emperor was seen as unpopular or weak. Thus, each reign was a continual referendum, which partly explains the need to be regarded as benevolent, fair, and responsive. The emperors projected a populist persona because they governed a populist polity. Policies were changed, as we will see repeatedly, when the populace took to the streets in large numbers or soldiers threw stones at their officers.

East Roman history features hundreds of coups, plots, and civil wars, instigated mostly by the people of Constantinople, the armies, or palace factions. They often succeeded. Not counting rebels who never took Constantinople (but were regarded as emperors in the provincial domains that they briefly governed),

42 out of 91 emperors between 330 and 1453 came to power through violence. Emperors therefore had to be on their toes, desperate to stay on the good side of public opinion while trying to do what they thought was best for the polity, which was often unpopular. This tension was the driving force of east Roman political history.

Procopius, who fomented a rebellion in Constantinople against Valens in 365–366, "gathered gossip" in the City from "those who were discontented with present conditions" due to the emperor's bad reputation and oppressive officials. To win over the people, he made a stump speech before them, like a candidate running for elected office.[112] Consider also the assumptions regarding imperial power that are reflected in the letter sent by the empress Verina to the people of Antioch in 484 to persuade them to join her in deposing the emperor Zeno and raising up one Leontius in his place.

> "Aelia Verina, perpetual Augusta, to our citizens of Antioch. Know that the imperial authority, after the death of the blessed Leo [d. 474], is ours. We made Strakodisseos emperor, who was afterward called Zeno, to benefit our subjects and all the military units. But now we see the *politeia* and our subjects ruined by his greed, and so we deem it necessary to crown a pious emperor for you who is adorned with justice so that he may save the affairs of the Roman *politeia*, induce our enemies to be at peace, and make secure all the subjects in accordance with the laws. We have crowned Leontius the most pious, who will deem you all worthy of his care and providence." And the entire populace of Antioch immediately rose up as one and cried out, "God is Great! and Lord have mercy, do what is good and best for us."[113]

The reality behind this civil war was a messy conflict of personalities. Politically, however, it could be represented only in terms of high principle: emperors were legitimate only if they benefited the collectivity by safeguarding peace and law, and they could be deposed if they failed. This was the face of power and the persona of the ruler.

The army

Between 193 and 395, the most powerful kingmakers were the armies. Emperors were chosen from among their officers, spent most of their reigns with the soldiers on the frontier, and were often called "fellow soldiers." "It is my duty to ever increase the happiness of my fellow veterans," Constantine declared in a recorded dialogue with former soldiers that he published within an edict.[114] As the dominant element in the Roman polity at this time, the army was imagined as a stand-in and a microcosm of Rome and all its former republican institutions. "The Senate of the camps" it was called by a senator of Rome, an "electoral assembly (*comitia*) chosen from the flower of Roman youth: free men who decided to whom they ought to be subjected" (i.e., the emperor).[115] Theodosius I was praised because he was "chosen ruler in the bosom of the *res publica* by the vote of all the soldiers and with the agreement (*consensus*) of the provinces."[116] A religious writer saw in this a model for the Church: "the presbyters always named as bishop one of their own, chosen by themselves, just as the army elects the emperor." The bishop of Rome was expected to have universal support, not just from his own city. "If it is authority that you seek, then the world (*orbis*) outweighs the city (*urbs*)."[117] In other words, Romanía had surpassed and transcended Rome.

During the third-century crisis, the imperial armies had run amok, elevating countless usurpers to the throne and creating regional Roman states that failed to receive universal recognition. Diocletian restored stability through his collegiate conception of the imperial office and by stamping out remaining challengers. He instituted the use of large military assemblies, summoning representative units and officers from across the empire, to stage important events that called for public confirmation by the armies, such as the acclamation of new co-emperors and the retirement of old ones (including himself). To create a Caesar, an Augustus had to speak before an assembled army, present his request and the reasoning behind it, and then the soldiers, standing in for the *populus Romanus*, approved the choice by acclamation. The army would not refuse the choice presented to it by a sitting Augustus, for that would question *his* legitimacy. But distant armies could elevate their own Augusti, and then sitting emperors had to decide whether to accept them as colleagues or treat them as usurpers. The armies in Gaul, for instance, "were not always obedient to the sitting emperors, viewing themselves as arbiters of the succession."[118] In the fourth century, the western armies elevated Constantine, Magnentius, Julian, Magnus Maximus, and Eugenius. The military acclamation of emperors prevailed until around 400, when accessions began to be staged in and around Constantinople, whose populace thereby inherited this sovereign function.

The early imperial Roman army consisted of some thirty named legions of about 5,500 men each, aided by auxiliary (non-citizen) units of the same size. That structure changed dramatically during the third century and in the reforms of Diocletian and Constantine. The main distinction now was between the mobile field armies (sometimes called the *comitatus* because they accompanied the emperors) and the frontier-defense armies (called *limitanei* or *ripenses*, because they were posted along rivers). The distinction was not firm, as field armies were formed from and continued to draw detachments (*vexillationes*) from the frontier armies. Soldiers were exempt from certain supplementary taxes and labor services to the state, and veterans also received tax exemptions, though soldiers of the *comitatus* received better pay and perks.[119] Overall, this was a more flexible, modular structure made up of a larger number of smaller units.

The military command was separate from the civilian. This made it harder for generals to rebel, for they lacked access to money, supplies, and the necessary political connections. On the plus side for them, it meant that they could rise up through the ranks from obscurity to the top commands, including to the throne. The top generals were the *magister peditum* (i.e., general of the infantry) and *magister equitum* (of cavalry), though later in the fourth century each of these commanded both infantry and cavalry; the armies were still mostly infantry, but with probably more cavalry than before. By 353, Constantius had two generals "in attendance" (*in praesenti*) with others stationed wherever needed, usually Gaul, Illyricum, or Oriens. They in turn commanded subordinate generals with the rank of *comes* and *dux*, who were posted along the frontiers. Provincial governors rarely commanded soldiers.[120]

Feeding, supplying, paying, and equipping the army, even when it was idle, was the main business of government and involved the tax system, levies of labor and goods, state warehouses, imperial horse farms, and strategically-distributed arms factories. Campaigns posed huge logistical challenges for the transportation and storage of food, and incurred campaign costs, so emperors tended to use the smallest force that would do the job. Still, for major wars, civil or foreign, they could muster armies of between 40,000 and 65,000 in size, drawn from both the field armies and *limitanei*.[121] Setting out against Julian in 361, Constantius ordered ahead that 3 million bushels of wheat be stored on the borders of Gaul and another 3 million in the Cottian Alps.[122]

An army of half a million required some 25,000 recruits per year, all young men, taken away mostly from agriculture.[123] Recruitment was a literal burden on the land, for, in addition to volunteers and the sons of veterans, who were expected to serve, conscription was part of the basic land tax, assessed at a notional fraction of its overall obligation. If a property was too small to owe the state a recruit, many of them were bundled together to do so.[124] Some conscripts were unwilling (at least initially) and tried to escape. Pachomios, a founder of Egyptian monasticism, was conscripted when he was twenty and his group were locked up when they reached Thebes en route to the camp in case they tried to escape; they were brought food and water by local charitable Christians.[125] Such measures were (and still are) taken by modern states. There were no serious recruitment problems in this period, and many soldiers were volunteers.[126] The state offered a sign-up bonus, a whopping 30 solidi according to a fourth-century document.[127] Even some city councilors were known to join the army in order to avoid curial duties.[128] Soldiers were provincial Romans who often served near their homes, and fought to protect them.[129] They were well trained. This was no alien occupation force, nor a peasant rabble pressed into service.

The emperors naturally prioritized their personal protection. Constantine had abolished the old praetorian guard of Rome and relied instead on the *scholae palatinae* (five or more units, each of 500 cavalry). The elite corps of *protectores* and *domestici* provided officer training for the army at large. Most *protectores* seem to have been Illyrians, a group that dominated the army and, by extension, also the throne.[130]

Diocletian's reforms tamed the army. The field armies concentrated striking power into the hands of a few co-emperors and generals. Rather than many smaller wars happening all at once, as during the third century, civil wars were henceforth fought on a large scale between rival emperors within the collegiate system, each wielding the armies and resources of a significant part of the empire. The largest military operations tended to be civil wars. This was how Constantine rose to sole power, from his first (unauthorized) acclamation by a provincial army at York in 306, to 324, when he defeated his last remaining colleague, Licinius.

It was these military leaders, then, hardened by civil war, moving tirelessly along the frontiers, and sleeplessly dealing with subjects' business, who created the new empire. The expectations placed on them were weighty, and the decisions that they took were generally sound, placing the empire on solid footing for centuries to come. They sometimes made naïve decisions, as when Diocletian tried to outlaw inflation and Christianity, or when Constantine imagined that bishops could get along. But overall they made good choices, especially about tax equity, stability in the solidus, accountability in government, and, of course, Constantinople as the binding nexus of eastern Romanía. Above all, by casting itself as fair, benevolent, responsive, and bound by its own rules, the state fostered consensual political subjectivities among its subjects. Without them, the eastern empire would not have survived for over a thousand years. East Rome was not a mere agglomeration of territories held together by force, but a unified state. Even authors who complained about it reveal that they had internationalized the principles of rational responsible government. But one experiment remained, to see whether these principles could be extended to a new religion with an unhappy history of persecution at the hands of imperial power.

3

From Christian Nation to Roman Religion

Christianity and the Roman order

A common working figure for the number of Christians in the eastern empire in 300 is 10%, so about 2 million people. But this is only a guess; some put it at half that or lower. Christians were concentrated in Egypt and Syria-Palestine, less so in Asia Minor, and much less in Greece and the Balkans. Christianity was mostly an urban phenomenon, with limited presence in the countryside, where the majority of the population lived. There was only one other type of person that the empire was producing faster than it was making Christians between 30 and 300, namely Romans.

There is no consensus today about why anyone would become a Christian before Constantine. After Constantine, by contrast, it is no mystery why people gradually converted to the new favored religion. A historian of the Church put it well in the mid-fifth century: after Constantine people converted because they saw their ancestral beliefs and practices cast down from a position of privilege and veneration; because they were envious of the honors bestowed by the emperor upon Christians; or because they looked more closely at the new religion and, through opportune dreams and visions, or by speaking with bishops, decided that it was a good time to convert.[1] Even though Christian writers cast conversion as a transformation of the soul and hoped that society would change radically and for the better if everyone accepted Christ, in reality it did not require dramatic changes to one's life. Macroscopically, the empire's conversion changed virtually nothing in the economy, social and political structure, army, tax practices, and political history of the Roman empire. Serious changes were confined to the religious sphere of temples, rituals, beliefs, and priests, with, initially, only minor impact on social values and the law, but far less than we might expect given the commandments of Scripture. It is not clear whether Christianity "triumphed" over the Roman order or was captured by it.

To be sure, references abound to the "triumph" of Christianity under and after Constantine, but it is framed as a victory over pagan cult ("Hellenism"). This, indeed, it vanquished, though the process took centuries. But in the grand scheme of things, that was but a surface struggle. The relationship to watch was instead that between Christianity and the Roman order, which resulted in a less triumphant synthesis: the new faith was co-opted to serve precisely *as* the Roman religion within the framework of the polity. Specifically, what began as a revolutionary attempt to create a new "polity of the Christians" and new "Christian nation" was eventually domesticated as "the religion of the Romans." It was slotted into the Roman order, and so recast that its ambition to create an earthly order of its own was reduced to occasional and usually futile demands by bishops that emperors not dictate the substance of the faith to the Church.

The spokesmen of early Christianity did not regard their movement as a "mere" religion, that is, as a bundle of beliefs, moral precepts, and rituals that could be slotted into an existing social order, political identity, and ethnicity. They had the grander ambition to remake and reorient the soul of each Christian in such a comprehensive way that the Church would effectively become that person's new fatherland, polity, or nation, or at least the "true" one, the "higher" one to which loyalty was given above and beyond the powers of this world. They imagined the Christians as nothing less than a new nation or race of people whose lives were thoroughly remolded and whose worldly commitments were eclipsed. If Christians did not participate in the governance of the Roman empire, argued a theologian in the third century, it was because they held "office" in an "alternative fatherland," the Church.[2]

The leading Christian intellectual of Constantine's time was Eusebios, the bishop of Kaisareia in Palestine. He witnessed the Great Persecution, which lasted on and off between 303 and 313, and then the conversion of Constantine. But the concept of a "Christian emperor" would not have come naturally to him. Before Constantine, Eusebios and other Christian writers did not think of Christianity as a mere set of beliefs, but as an emergent sovereign "polity" in its own right, albeit one that operated within the polities of this world. The Church was the worldly image of the kingdom of God. It had its own sovereign, Christ, was named after a Greek political assembly (*ekklesia*), and its members were "citizens" of heaven.[3] The Christians proclaimed themselves a people apart, or, as their sacred texts put it, "a holy nation," a concept rooted in the Chosen People of the Old Testament.[4] They had their own a polity, "army," and "school." In explaining to the world who they were, Eusebios turned to ethnic or national categories: Christians were neither Greeks nor barbarians but a "new nation (*ethnos*)" that formed a new "polity" named after its founder.[5]

Conversion thereby compromised one's ability to belong to other ethnic groups and hold citizenship in non-Christian polities. Consider Athanasios, the embattled bishop of Alexandria and theologian (d. 373). Pausing in his attacks against other Christians, he wrote a brief book *Against the Pagans* that attacked non-Christian religious beliefs and practices. He focused on those of the Greeks, as they were the most widespread in the eastern empire and the most pressing for the Church to eradicate; indeed, the eastern Church called paganism of all kinds *Hellenism*. But Athanasios attacked the beliefs of other groups as well, including the Phoenicians, Egyptians, Scythians, and Thracians. This was because he, like everyone else, identified religious traditions with specific ethnic groups, and vice versa. Being an Egyptian was inextricably bound up with participating in Egyptian religion. This had serious implications for conversion. There was no conceptual model by which one could take the religion out of being an Egyptian or Greek, replace that content with Christianity, and still carry on as an Egyptian or Greek. As Eusebios explained, "every nation and city is constituted by the worship of its ancestral gods."[6] Its political order would necessarily be dissolved if those gods were repudiated.

Christians took on an identity that conflicted with their prior ethnicities. Ethnically too they became Christians, citizens of a new polity defined in all aspects by Christian law. They would henceforth live only "among"—but not be "of"—the various peoples of the empire. The early Church was not a multicultural institution that embraced diverse ethnic cultures within its fold, albeit stripped of their prior religious commitments. It aspired to overwrite them in their entirety. But if Christians were neither Greeks nor barbarians, they could not be Romans either, at least not good ones. Some Christians had noted that Christ was born under Augustus, meaning that the Christian and imperial orders had come into being simultaneously and that the empire had foreshadowed and smoothed the way for the universal extension of Christianity. But beyond that providential conjunction, which lay in the past, the Roman empire had no place in Eusebios' vision of the future. He did not think that the Church would forever be bound to Rome. The empire was a useful (if dangerous) context that God had provided but it too would inevitably be discarded. A "Christian Roman empire" was, then, not something for which Eusebios was prepared. He had put no thought into how one might be a good Christian and a good Roman. In fact, Eusebios rejected not only the gods, traditions, and foundations of the Roman order, he disputed its core values. He opposed wars, victories, valor, and patriotism and favored the "peaceful wars of the spirit waged for God's polity, and courage for truth over country."[7] By these lights, Rome would be overcome by Christian values. Yet by the end of his life, Eusebios was singing the praises of Constantine's Roman arms,[8] and the Church accepted a seat at the table of Roman power. How did this happen?

For the Romans, religion was a function of specific, juridically defined political communities: each city (*civitas*), tribe, or nation that was recognized by Rome had a religion of its own, including temples and religious rites, as part of its "law" (*lex*). "Every *civitas* has its own religion, just as we have ours."[9] The Romans could, when necessary, distinguish between religious and non-religious matters, but they tended to bundle them together with all other aspects of local citizenship and law. The jurist Ulpian, for example, defined public law as that which relates to the Roman polity, including "religious affairs, the priesthoods, and the offices of the state."[10]

The Romans had their own *religio*, of which they were proud. It had distinctive traditions, rites, priestly orders, lore, and skills, and its public purpose was to ensure good relations between the gods and the Roman people. As the *res publica* was constituted politically, its government had jurisdiction over religious practices, whether to authorize, forbid, or require them, with an eye to the public good. The political leadership regulated the calendar and could forbid all Romans from engaging in certain religious acts, for example human sacrifice, castration, forms of astrology, and specific foreign cults, which were periodically expelled from Rome. There were also obligations, chiefly to participate in ceremonies that invoked the gods in times of peril. Participation in such events was sometimes required of all Roman citizens by law. This was not a religion of "mere" ritual, as it is sometimes represented, but a framework for maintaining the social order and expressing Roman virtues such as patriotism, honesty, reverence, purity, and piety. The Romans boasted that they were the most religious people, by which they certainly meant that they were also the most moral and decent.[11]

Thus Christians and Romans shared the same underlying idea about how "a nation" was constituted, even if Christians based their comprehensive identity on religion while Romans saw religion as only part of a civic or national order. These conceptions of citizenship collided when Christians refused to sacrifice as required by Roman law and were executed as traitors. At such moments, many of which Eusebios narrated, the martyrs talked about having their own emperor, their own laws and heavenly citizenship, and being soldiers in God's army. Some Christian theorists had promised to follow Roman law only when it did not conflict with their own,[12] but this could not reassure Roman authorities because God's law had a lot to say. This concept of the Church as an emerging nation was, to the likes of the emperor Galerius, a cancer eating away at the foundations of the republic, if not a declaration of war. It could be argued that Christianity was by definition disloyal to the Roman order. Galerius, who had persecuted the Church, implied as much in a pronouncement of 311: Christians had made up their own laws (*leges*) and gathered diverse groups of people together—suggesting subversion.[13] *Lex*, as we have seen, was no trivial word in the Roman vocabulary. The Christians, Galerius implied, were setting up a separatist polity.

In 212 AD all free inhabitants of the empire had become Roman citizens. The author of that act, Caracalla, put forward a specifically religious rationale for it, namely to bring the prayers of more Romans to the gods as a thank-offering for his safety, in effect a loyalty oath. By definition, every act of religious devotion in the empire was henceforth made by a Roman. But did this vast and diverse Roman world still have a discrete religion? In becoming all-encompassing, had it lost its religious identity?

The Roman authorities searched for an answer during the third century. In 213, one year after the Divine Gift, Ulpian circulated a handbook for provincial governors that consolidated the current position of Roman law on many matters, including religion and the problem posed by Christians.[14] It was a step toward consistency in policy. In 249, the emperor Decius required that all his subjects perform a public sacrifice and prayer to the gods on behalf of the empire. Decius was not doing anything novel from the standpoint of Roman religion, but the scope of it, in the aftermath of 212, was unprecedented. It was also an innovation on his part that all had to obtain a certificate of compliance, which mobilized the imperial bureaucracy to enforce religious uniformity.[15] By taking the logic of the Divine Gift to the next level and imagining the entire empire as a single city with a religion of its own to be policed by the state, Decius was leaping toward a statal Orthodoxy. Only the specific content of the religion remained indeterminate. Decius did not specify which gods were to receive the sacrifice, though presumably it was the local equivalents of the Roman deities. But the Christians rejected all gods other than their own.

Decius likely did not mean for his decree to instigate a persecution of the Christians. The confrontation between the Roman authorities and the Christian martyrs has nearly always been read from the Christian point of view, as part of a narrative of survival and triumph. But there was a Roman side to it too. These confrontations were part of a Roman effort to understand what religion meant in a more unified, but still diverse social order. The emperor Valerian (253–260) started a persecution by ordering that "those who do not practice Roman religion should recognize Roman rites."[16] But what exactly did that mean in Greece or in Egypt? Anything but Christianity? Judaism was seen as aberrant, but was exempt from such demands as it was the ancestral religion of the Jewish nation, which Rome recognized. Aurelian (270–275) propagated the Sun on his coins as "the god of the empire."[17] A formal structure of religious uniformity was emerging, but its content was still opaque. Diocletian banned astrology along with incestuous marriages as contrary to Roman law and religion; the Manichaean sect as a dangerous Persian import that opposed the older religions—*religiones*—of the Roman people;[18] and Christianity as impious atheism. The emperors were turning their attention to the regulation of religion throughout the empire, just as they had previously done in the city of Rome. Over time, this might have resulted in a homogeneous Roman "religion of empire," just as there was now one law of persons. In fact it did just that, but with an unforeseen twist.

The realignment that is called the triumph of Christianity happened quickly, in just under seventy years. It took place within a Roman structure and had a thoroughly Roman outcome. One might even say the story ended exactly where it began, with a particular religion mandated for the Roman people by their rulers. The first move was made by Galerius, a few days before he died in 311. The Great Persecution that he and Diocletian initiated in 303 had failed to break the Church and had, moreover, generated sympathy for its victims among important sectors of public opinion. It was rare for emperors to admit that a policy had failed, but Galerius did so now, grudgingly. He allowed Christians to pray to their god for the safety of the *res publica*, which effectively admitted Christianity into the fold of Roman religion. Romans could henceforth either be Christians or follow the "ancient laws."[19] It was still only toleration, for Galerius did not like the Christians. Full equality and freedom was granted by Constantine and Licinius two years later, in 313, on the basis of their discussions at Milan. Their subjects could now follow "whatever religion they wished."[20] When Constantine defeated Licinius in 324, he informed his eastern subjects that he favored the Christians, and admitted that some at his court were urging him to eradicate the temples. Yet he would tolerate all for the sake of the common good. Constantine proclaimed that the persecution of the Christians had "stained the Roman nation," and he exhorted that nation to follow the true faith.[21] Liberty and equality had lasted for a decade and had now reverted to toleration, though the poles were reversed.

The Christian emperors of the fourth century placed increasing legal, fiscal, and practical restrictions on what they saw as "paganism," although without yet outright forbidding their subjects from honoring the ancient gods. Interestingly, a term that they used to ban some pagan practices was *superstitio*, which had been used by past Romans to forbid foreign religions, including Christianity.[22] The framework of Roman *religio* was being redeployed now to establish Christianity. The new faith was sometimes called a *lex* ("law"), just as the old one was, and Judaism was still called the *lex* of the Jews, in the old Roman manner.[23] The lines of continuity were so strong that many pagans may not have realized at first that a Christian war against "paganism" was afoot. For example, Constantine allegedly demolished an inaccessible temple of Aphrodite in Phoenicia due to illicit sexual practices that took place there.[24] But one can easily imagine the moralist Diocletian doing the same in an effort to clean up "Roman religion."

To be sure, many Christians were self-consciously engaged in a struggle to abolish paganism. This accelerated during the reign of Constantius II (337–361), the first emperor to be raised a Christian. His successor, Julian (361–363), also raised a Christian, converted back to Hellenism, which he favored while tolerating Christianity. There was a brief lull under Valens (364–378), who was uninterested in the issue. The final step was taken in 380 by Theodosius I, who decreed that "all people ruled by our administration shall practice that *religio* which the divine Peter the Apostle transmitted to the Romans."[25] The circle had closed. After a seventy-year window of toleration, religious choice was no longer a legal option. The emperor, as the supreme authority in religious and all legal matters, had mandated the religion of his subjects. When dissident Christians found themselves persecuted by other Christian Romans, they reasonably complained that this was a revival of the old persecutions by pagan Romans: wrong religion was again being punished by the state. To this, Christians on the state's side could point to St. Paul who said, "Whoever resists authority"—here meaning secular power—"resists the ordinances of God."[26] Christianity had been taken on by the Roman order as its religion, and was now imposed even on other Christians.

In retrospect, it was perhaps the window between 311 and 380 that was aberrant. During it, the main spokesman for toleration had been Themistios, the philosopher-senator who served a succession of Christian rulers. "The Creator," he told the short-lived emperor Jovian in 364, "delights in this diversity. . . . No one had exactly the same beliefs as the next person. So why use force?"[27] Themistios even noted that Christians too were divided into many smaller sects.

Themistios' plea for liberty notwithstanding, after Theodosius the state became increasingly intolerant of religious deviants, who were branded as insane. Roman law swelled with prohibitions and requirements stemming from its new religion, which were many, for Christianity brooked no rivals. But the regulation of religion was not new to the Roman order. The basic structure and concepts remained the same throughout the transition. During the persecutions, for example, Christians were stripped of their civic rights for refusing the religious obligations of Roman citizenship; likewise, after Theodosius members of religious minorities had to convert in order to "enjoy the freedom of Roman citizenship."[28] Full citizen rights were a prerogative of the correct form of worship, and religious dissidents were deemed to live "outside the Roman law."[29] Governors had once demanded that Christians conform to the religion of the emperor; now governors occasionally demanded that subjects, including Jews, conform to the religion of the emperor.[30] The structure of the state religion had not changed. To be sure, the religion of the Romans now had its own name and identity, Christianity, but it was not, as it had once aspired to be, a new nation. Christianity was obsessed with its own name, but it sometimes yielded even on this, accepting the label "religion of the Romans."[31] When the most Christian emperor Justinian pronounced that God had established the polity, he clarified, "I mean that of the Romans."[32] Christian was the adjective, Roman the noun.

In the ancient Roman empire, public prayers were spoken at the games on behalf of the health, fortune, and military success of the Roman people and the "security and eternity of the empire."[33] Likewise, after Constantine the emperors could declare that the Roman state was sustained more by Christian prayers than by toil and sweat.[34] Constantine assumed that Christian priests "servicing their law" would "bring great benefit to the polity."[35] In the early third century, the Christian writer Tertullian had argued that one could not serve two masters, Christ and Caesar. But by the mid-fourth century, Roman soldiers were swearing an oath by Christ to die for the Roman polity.[36] Eventually, Christian priests were blessing and accompanying the imperial armies, and prayers were said in provincial villages to ensure victory.[37] In fact, the first church sermon that survives from the reign of Constantine in the east is an oration celebrating the thirteenth anniversary of his rule. It was preached by none other than Eusebios of Kaisareia. Constantine, he says, prevailed over Licinius through the sign of the Cross, which he has erected in the imperial City "as a talisman to safeguard the empire of the Romans and his imperial rule over all." The ideal of Christian peace had yielded to traditional notions of Roman imperial victory.[38]

With surprising ease, Christianity became an instrument for bolstering loyalty to the empire. In every church, whether in the capital or an insignificant village, worship ended with a prayer on behalf of the empire, the emperor, and his subjects. Bishops prayed for both the Church and "the empire of the Romans."[39] The Liturgy of St. Basil, the one used primarily by the eastern Church after the sixth century, contains a section of prayers (the Anaphora) with the following words: "Remember, Lord, our most religious and faithful emperors . . . strengthen their arm, make their empire prevail, and subject to them all the barbarous people who want war . . . . Remember, Lord, all rule and authority, our brothers in the palace and everyone in the army."[40] They were not only praying for this army but paying for it. Inscriptions placed on government buildings in Kaisareia in Palestine quoted Paul's epistle to the Romans 13:3: "Do you want to not fear power? Then do the right thing!"—presumably by paying taxes.[41]

In later times, at the games in the hippodrome of Constantinople, the people chanted a series of acclamations that sought God's assistance for the emperors, whom they called "the beloved of the Romans" and "the joy of the Romans." It featured this thanksgiving: "We thank you, Christ our God, for breaking up the plots of the foreign nations and crushing our enemies in war."[42]

From a Christian standpoint, a triumph had unfolded between Constantine and Theodosius: "idolatry" was overturned and true religion took its place. But from a Roman standpoint, a single framework had governed that development from Caracalla and Decius to Galerius, Constantine, and Theodosius. This had profound implications for the Christian movement, which its leaders did not at first appreciate. As they reached with both hands for power within the imperial system, their movement was co-opted by the Roman order and processed through Roman concepts. Christianity was henceforth to be regulated by Roman law and institutions. Its clergy became a legal "status" akin to soldiers, city councilors, and coloni. Church governance was modeled even more closely on that of provincial governance. This was not a symmetrical relationship: Christian influence on the Roman order, apart from the regulation of religion itself, was small, and it took centuries to achieve even that.[43] Christianity was taken onboard by the Roman state before it had a chance to think about how it might govern society. It did not generate a new order, as Islam did later, but became an instrument in the regulation of the existing one.

Constantine was a pragmatic ruler and resourceful in extending his appeal to all sectors of society. The bishops were an articulate cadre of social leaders who could provide needed support, and states tend to co-opt dynamic social forces and turn them to their own purposes.[44] It was perhaps no accident that the religion which Constantine chose to unify his empire had the same shape as its universal Roman community. Like Romans, Christians imagined themselves as a nation with members drawn from many different people. Accordingly, Christianity has been praised by historians for its "universalism," which transcended ethnic differences. But Romanía had been built in the same way, as some Christian authors knew. In the early third century, Hippolytos cast the Romans as the Satanic mirror image of Christian nation building. But in reality, Roman universalism had reached its goal earlier than its Christian counterpart and had paved the way for it. It could easily appear that the two were meant for each other. One eastern theologian commented that the universal Roman census in the Gospel of Luke foreshadowed the universal salvation of men promised by Christ, and a Latin Christian, Lactantius, suggested that Christianity was the true law that perfected Cicero's vision of Romanness.[45]

Lactantius' Ciceronian reading of Christianity had a greater impact than historians have realized. Constantine, who had ruled in the west for twenty years and whose native language was Latin, brought to the east a western, Latin Roman approach to religion. Before 324, Greek-speaking Christians such as Eusebios did not factor Rome into their vision of the coming Christian world. It never occurred to them to define the Christian nation in terms of the *res publica Romana*. Yet the only Christian philosophy to which we know Constantine was exposed before 324 was that of Lactantius, a teacher of Latin rhetoric whom the emperor hired as a tutor for his son Crispus. In a magnum opus dedicated to Constantine, the *Divine Institutes*, Lactantius presented Christians not as a new distinct nation but rather as the best kind of Romans: Christianity had come to perfect and fulfill virtues that Rome had long espoused. Lactantius was a new Cicero and put a Christian shine on Cicero's philosophy of the *res publica*.[46]

Christianity is usually seen as an "eastern" influence on the Roman empire. Yet the imperial version of Christianity that prevailed, including in the east, had been recast as traditionalist Roman religion in the west and was brought to the east by Constantine. He thereby laid down another layer of Romanization on the east. Eastern Christians had to adapt to this new imperial model. Eusebios belonged to a generation that had experienced both persecution and Constantine's conversion. Some of his peers had been condemned to the mines, but were now honored guests at the palace, a remarkable turn for which they were unprepared. They were showered with gifts, honors, titles, social power, jaunts at the court, luxury Bibles, gold, and church buildings. At one of those gatherings, Eusebios had a vision that presaged his political conversion: he imagined the imperial palace, where soldiers now mingled with bishops, as "an image of the kingdom of Christ." At the Council of Nicaea (325), Constantine made his entrance in a purple robe adorned with glittering precious gems, "like some heavenly angel of God."[47] Eusebios went on to craft a theory of Christian emperorship, focused on Constantine, in which the emperor was God's image and vicegerent on earth. He also substantially upgraded his view of the Roman empire. The empire was now for him one of the "two blessings for mankind" that God had provided, the other being Christianity.[48] Eusebios had come to love the Roman empire.

Christian dissension

Yet far from changing the Roman order, Christian history became increasingly entangled in it. In the fifth century, Sokrates, Eusebios' continuer as a Church historian, begged his readers' indulgence for the amount of secular history that he had to tell. At least, he wrote, tales of wars and emperors might relieve the tedium caused by incessant Christian infighting and the vicious plots that bishops hatched against each other. Eusebios had once shied away from wars in order to celebrate the peaceful wars of the spirit, but now accounts of wars were a welcome distraction from Christian civil wars. More importantly, Sokrates argued that the disorders of the Church and state had become so intertwined that it was impossible to talk about one without the other.[49] The conversion of the empire had not inaugurated an era of everlasting peace as some had predicted.[50] It had, instead, made the Church more political.

The new religion was flexible enough to attract a diverse following, but inflexible in ways that tore it apart and did lasting damage to imperial society. Let us start with its successes. It stepped into all the places from which its rivals were evicted and operated on different registers to appeal to a diverse constituency. The new faith offered a striking initiation ritual (baptism) and a teaching of personal salvation, like many ancient cults. It also fostered communities of intense loyalty, to which it pledged solidarity and material support. Local congregations had their own saints, leaders, and histories, but still knew that they were fractal versions of a global Christian community, just as local Roman communities were microcosms of Romanía. Christian identity could serve the needs of the individual, village, city, and emperor. It was a pan-Roman religion of empire, an idea toward which emperors had been groping since 212.

To the ambitious, Christianity offered positions of leadership in the clergy. By 400, each city had a bishop, and sometimes more if there were rival Christian communities in it, so there were about a thousand bishops in the eastern empire, a new cadre of civic and pan-imperial leadership. From the fourth century on, bishops came mostly from the ranks of the city councilors, like the priests of the old civic gods, save that bishops held office for life (which, on average, meant for about ten years). Bishops forged Christian analogues for the displaced civic religions, using similar elements such as processions, public prayers, festivals, relics, shrines, and local traditions to honor patron saints and martyrs' relics. Cities thereby acquired new Christian identities. Athens, for example, abandoned its namesake virgin goddess and identified with the Virgin Mary, who moved into the Parthenon; Ephesos switched from Artemis to St. John and the Virgin Mary; and Thessalonike looked to the military martyr-saint Demetrios (see Plate 4b).

Finally, Christianity also invited its most intellectually ambitious adherents to compete with the old philosophical schools in crafting a systematic theory of divinity. They produced a voluminous literature in defense of their faith, defining its doctrines in increasingly specific ways. Thus, Christianity filled up all the spaces of ancient religious practice and thought with its own analogues, which were parts of a unified whole. No other ancient cult had managed to do this.

Yet despite its promise to unify imperial religion, which Constantine was banking on when he made his fateful decision to support it, there never was just one Christianity. At any time, multiple competing groups claimed ownership of the name and fought to exclude their Christian rivals from using it. These conflicts make up most of Christian history. In fact, the events that we can follow in the most detail in the sources are precisely intra-Christian conflicts, leaving political and military history to compete for second place. It was this insistence that one was right and all others were wrong that led official Christianity to self-identify as Orthodoxy, meaning "right belief." But every rival group claimed to be the true Orthodox Church, or the true Catholic (i.e., "universal") Church.

The problem had emerged already during the reign of Constantine, to his dismay. When he realized that Alexandros, the bishop of Alexandria, and his priest Areios (Latin Arius) were quarreling over hair-splitting definitions of the nature of Christ, the emperor urged them to avoid bickering over these "futile points": these are unnecessary exercises, he stated, "trivial, and unworthy of controversy." Such questions should neither have been asked nor answered, for they could lead only to blasphemy or dissension.[51] Constantine was channeling the instincts of Roman government, which, in the words of a second-century governor, warned people to stay away from "hazardous inquisitiveness" when it came to matters divine.[52] Constantine was right, but naïve in thinking that Christian leaders would heed his warning.

Rival Christian communities began to disagree over increasingly arcane theological questions regarding the "substance," "nature," "persona," "will," "energy," and "image" of Christ, fighting viciously and even violently to assert themselves as the one true Christianity and to brand their enemies as heretics. This ensured that the Church, and by extension the empire, was never unified in the way the emperors desired. It was not just intellectuals who took sides in these controversies. Sectors of the populace also protested and clashed in the streets and even inside the churches, spilling blood on behalf of their leaders and theological slogans. Already by 327, Constantine had to intervene to prevent the outbreak of mass violence in Antioch, while by 356 soldiers were no longer just peacekeepers but occasionally joined in the melee, slaughtering worshippers in the "wrong" churches of Alexandria.[53] The transition from a pagan state persecuting Christians to a Christian state persecuting Christians took place astonishingly quickly.

Bishops sometimes expressed the hope that the laity would not get involved in these conflicts. After struggling to explain the Trinity to his congregation, John Chrysostom confessed that "I know that to many this will be incomprehensible. Therefore we avoid agitating these issues, because the rest of the populace is unable to follow them."[54] But partisan bishops, John included, riled up their congregants against the heretics anyway. They should not greet them, touch them, or eat with them. By the sixth century, the legislator had to protect "orthodox" children from their "heretical" parents, when the latter would not feed them or had disinherited them, and intervened when parents disagreed over the faith in which to raise a child.[55] "For fathers are at odds with their children, and children in turn with those who begat them, and a wife with her own spouse."[56] Such hatred was otherwise seen only among the hippodrome fans of the Blue and Green racing teams. These religious divisions amused pagans, who noted that "wild beasts are not so savage to any man as Christians are to each other."[57]

How should we understand this divisive behavior? On one level, theological disputation gave bishops, the new politicians of the Church, an arena in which to compete. Bishops were tied to their sees for life, so their career ambitions beyond that point were limited. A contemporary of Constantine, Alexandros of Lykopolis, proposed that Christian teachers "strive to impress others by the novelty of their doctrines and have turned this formerly simple philosophy into an unspeakable mess" (he himself was a Platonist, a Christian, or both).[58] But this begs the question of why Christian leaders were eager to compete in the first place, and does not explain why the laity got involved or why the arena that they chose was technical theology, as opposed to converting pagans or building hospitals. Bishops did those things too, but not competitively.

During the theological controversies, Christians came to believe that their salvation depended on getting these technical definitions *exactly* right. By the sixth century, the eastern Church had split irrevocably over whether Christ was "in" or only "from" two "natures," a lexical difference that, in Greek, is represented by a single letter (*en* versus *ek*), as a contemporary noted in dismay.[59] It was pointed out occasionally that the New Testament does not use these contentious terms, which were taken from later Greek philosophy. Had Jesus understood salvation in this way, presumably he would have provided the necessary formulas from the start. But this reminder did not stem the acrimony. What caused it? Likely not solely an intellectual passion for theology, as the amount of hostility vented in these controversies was inversely proportional to the general understanding of the issues at stake: most contestants were "fighting in the dark."[60] Nor were ethnicity, language, or economic class the root causes, as Christological differences cut across these categories. Two enemy groups might look exactly the same, until one looked at their formulas. Around 500, for example, a woman realized to her horror that she was in church with people who accepted the creed of Chalcedon, which she did not.[61]

A proper account of the root causes would take us too deep into Christian origins. It suffices to point out elements that were in place by Constantine's time and fueled this behavior. The first is that Christianity proffered not just a set of beliefs and practices but a brand-name identity. To a degree unparalleled by other religious groups in the empire, Christians were devoted to their group name, even obsessed with it. This attachment hardened during the persecutions, when many deduced that they were targeted solely for "the Name." Some martyrs refused to say anything to their tormentors other than "I am a Christian."[62] This identity was taken "not simply to trump, but even to efface all other forms of social belonging: familial, social, and jural-political,"[63] consistent with the ambition to constitute a Christian nation. This required criteria of belonging, boundaries between insiders and outsiders, and ensuring "brand consistency" in practice, ethical comportment, group identity, and belief. It also led perhaps to some of the more extraordinary things that Christians were expected to believe, for group solidarity is established more securely on outlandish claims than obvious ones, which can also be held by outsiders.[64]

As the movement grew, the Church sought to define its "essence." The core message was a promise of salvation through a righteous remaking of the soul; a belonging to God's new Chosen People; a rejection of idolatry; and a new set of values that paradoxically combined humility with strong feelings of superiority over others. The Church elaborated this core message and, anticipating modern corporate branding, sought to articulate its ideals; to cultivate and disseminate its image via logos, symbols (such as the cross and the fish), and diverse promotional media; to foster brand loyalty among an expanding demographic while retaining control of the message; and to counter brand competitors as pagans and heretics. Christians saw themselves as "branded by the sign of the Cross"—some took this literally, or saw crosses in natural shapes all around them. The goal was not only to win over a larger part of the surrounding culture, but "to *be* the culture."[65]

Scholars of early Christianity often situate it in a "marketplace of religions" in the Roman empire, but the metaphor fails as the worshippers of other gods were not competing for souls, nor did they promulgate brand-name identities (with only a few exceptions, such as the followers of Mithras, an exclusive, non-proselytizing club).[66] "Paganism" was not a religious identity, but an amalgamated construct of the Christian imagination. As the worshippers of the ancient gods realized too late, this was a one-sided competition that led ultimately to a monopoly. Of course, in reality Christians mixed and matched beliefs and practices, including both Jewish and pagan elements, but their leadership tried to forbid this or pretended that it was not happening.[67] For them Christian identity was pure and precise.

Thus, Christian groups inevitably became rivals over their differences. Because they all adhered to the Name, they did not split off to form separate brands, as ancient philosophers did, becoming Platonists, Stoics, and the like. The search for the Christian doctrine of God that intensified in the fourth century was both a struggle over the ownership of Christian identity and a contest to define its essence, at a time when its value was increasing due to imperial patronage. But as Alexandros of Lykopolis noted, "there was no law by which disputes could be settled,"[68] in other words no mechanism of adjudication among Christians. The acrimony, then, inevitably became as much about procedure as about substance: through what mechanisms could the various contestants decide who controlled and defined the brand? When Constantine appeared on the scene, they all sought imperial intervention, leading to a chaotic free-for-all among emperors, councils of bishops, individual theologians, communities, urban crowds, zealous monks, and even random holy men with opinions and a following. Sometimes a combination of emperors and councils could prevail over the others and impose a single view—but not always, not on everyone, and not quickly.

Competition over the Name was exacerbated by another unusual aspect of the Christian movement. More than any other group in ancient society, Christians were prone to denounce what was wrong, false, or evil in the beliefs and practices of others, whom they regarded as the willing or unwitting agents of the Devil. The word "against" appears routinely in the titles of their books; "apologetics" was essentially polemical literature. The entire message was premised on Christians being right and everyone else wrong, including worshippers of the ancient gods, Jews, and Christians who held different beliefs. The latter—the so-called heretics—were perceived as more dangerous because they undermined group solidarity and were thus attacked more aggressively. This was a classic case of what Freud called the "narcissism of small differences," where almost indistinguishable groups fought more fiercely against each other in the name of purity than against common foes. Having invested so heavily in crisp group definition, and by insisting on the errors of others, early Christians could not but draw boundaries in confrontational ways. The arena that they chose was that of precise theological formulas.

Most heretics did not start out as troublemakers. They expressed positions about, say, the relationship between the Father and the Son (Arius) or the natures of Christ (Nestorios), presumably in order to articulate or clarify what everyone else implicitly believed, only to find themselves at the heart of a controversy. The instinct to define the doctrine proved an inexhaustible wellspring of controversy. Whatever the origin of each debate, it was not conducted in a spirit of intellectual curiosity. Instead, the stakes—nothing less than salvation or damnation on the spiritual level, and control over the brand and over Church resources on the political level—made them ferocious and relentless. Over time, the doctrine was defined in ever greater detail, even as it moved into questions that Scripture could not answer, indeed that it had never asked. But each issue, no matter how trivial it might appear at first to the likes of Constantine, could split the Church into rival groups that were unable to compromise, assuming they could even talk to each other. Each group believed that "We are the only Christians,"[69] and cast the others as the willing or unwilling agents of Satan. Rival Christians were trying to push their enemies "beyond the very name 'Christian.'"[70]

Such conflicts could not easily be deescalated, as the stakes were always and immediately understood to be all-or-nothing. A position once taken could not be retracted or compromised, because that would imply the possibility of error, and how might someone in error dare to demand that others abandon their ancestral traditions? Thus, the victors in each controversy systematically destroyed the writings of their enemies, something that they did not even do to the writings of the pagans. When Constantine waded into the affairs of the Church, he was attracted to it as the One and Only True Belief but he did not at first understand how damaging this obsession over "monodoxy" could be.[71] It would prove to be a costly division.

PART TWO

DYNASTIC INSECURITIES AND RELIGIOUS PASSIONS

4

The First Christian Emperors (324–361)

Constantine in the east

In 324, for the second time in his career, Constantine vanquished an imperial rival and doubled the extent of his rule. In 312, he had defeated and killed his brother-in-law and former ally Maxentius, and acquired Italy and North Africa. Constantine proclaimed Maxentius a tyrant and annulled most of his official acts. He also appropriated his buildings, converting Maxentius' Rome into Constantine's Rome. Constantine had also come out as a Christian, and stories began to circulate about how the Christian God had helped him to defeat Maxentius at the battle of the Milvian bridge. Now, in 324, Constantine defeated his other brother-in-law and former ally Licinius, and acquired the Roman east. He annulled most of the acts of "that tyrant,"[1] and, by founding Constantinople, obliterated the memory of Licinius' rule.

Licinius' wife was Constantine's sister Constantia and had given him a son, the young Caesar Licinius. Constantine had promised to spare them upon their surrender. Licinius was sent to Thessalonike, but both he and his son were soon executed. Constantine proved to be a capable, diligent, fair, and benevolent ruler. Posterity remembered him as the founder of the Christian Roman empire. But to his family, he was a ruthless killer. Constantine executed more of his relatives than any other emperor, and set a bloody example for his sons.[2]

Constantine the man is hidden from our view behind his carefully crafted, self-promotional images and the pious fictions of Eusebios, bishop of Kaisareia, who wrote the emperor's biography soon after his death. Constantine projected manifold images of himself designed to appeal to different constituencies (see Figure 5). To all Romans he appeared as a champion of freedom, peace (albeit achieved through war), and the rule of law. To Christians he gave clear signals that he was a believer, but his stance toward others was inclusive and conciliatory too. When addressing a Christian audience he mocked Apollo's amours,[3] but in his forum he presided majestically over his City as a heroically nude Apollo. Courting all sides, the emperor sponsored a journey to Egyptian temples by the hierophant of Eleusis, a sacred site in Athens, and issued a bronze medallion in ca. 325 depicting himself as Jupiter holding the Phoenix and his son Crispus, a Caesar, as a new Dionysos with a panther.[4]

Constantine sought consensus and expected his subjects to act in good faith. Yet this stance had its limits. Corrupt officials and arrogant bishops exhausted

Figure 5 Colossal bronze head of Constantine in the Capitoline Museums, Rome. The head itself is over a meter tall, and the full statue would have been 10-12 meters tall.
Shutterstock/Oleg Senkov

his patience and drew forth intemperate language. He also had an Orwellian capacity to rewrite history and expected people to accept fiction in place of what they had witnessed. Contrary to his propaganda, he was the aggressor in his civil wars, and Licinius had not persecuted the Church. Eusebios distorted the truth too, casting Constantine as an unblemished saintly emperor, even a Christian zealot. Eusebios suppressed his hero's questionable acts and pagan overtures, and twisted acts that had no religious import into proof of Christian zeal. Eusebios cannot be trusted regarding Constantine.

Immediately after defeating Licinius in September 324, Constantine founded Constantinople and bound it to his dynasty. At the foundation ceremony on 8 November 324, his son Constantius was also elevated to the rank of Caesar. As Themistios later reminded Constantius, "at one and the same time, the father delineated his City and gave the purple to his son."[5] Constantius thereby joined the rank of his older siblings, the Caesars Crispus and Constantinus II; their youngest brother Constans would be elevated in 333. Constantine's mother Helena and current wife Fausta were granted the rank of Augusta, possibly at the same time in 324 or 325.

Constantine also circulated letters to his new eastern subjects, to be posted publicly or read to them, in which he positioned himself on the religious question. His theology here is vague and convoluted, referring abstractly to a High God. The Christians, Constantine says, practice a good religion and were unjustly persecuted by wicked men, who were presumably now out of the picture. In one place he does distinguish between "those in error" and "the believers," but without specifying their identities; besides, both were to "receive the benefits of peace and quiet." Constantine comes across as a supporter of the Church, but does not mandate or even mention its specific beliefs, goals, and technical terms. He was softly telling his subjects that he was a believer, and therefore that their beliefs were "false" to him, but that he would protect them from Christian hardliners at his court. He did, however, demand the return of property confiscated from Christians during the persecutions, even if it was held by the imperial treasury; keeping it was henceforth a crime.[6] His insistence on this issue reflected the nexus of religion, legal status, and property that structured all of Roman society. Christianity was first recognized through the adjudication of property disputes.

The Arian controversy

The end of persecution meant that religious conflict was more likely to occur among Christians than between them and the pagans. Christianity was a diverse movement ideologically opposed to diversity. It included many groups, such as the Gnostics, Marcionites, and Montanists, each with its own distinctive beliefs. By 324 these were small minorities. A broad consensus had emerged around most matters of practice, organization, and belief, though even this was fractured by splinter groups, including the Novatians and the Donatists, who called for a harsher treatment of Christians who had lapsed during the persecutions. Those groups did not necessarily differ in their theology but they refused to share communion with bishops (probably a majority) who had readmitted the lapsed. The Church in Egypt was splintered between the bishops of Alexandria and the rigorist Church of the Martyrs, or "Melitians" as they were branded by their opponents. Every group, of course, regarded itself as the only true Christianity and branded its enemies by the names of their allegedly discredited human founders.

Constantine's sponsorship of the Church unleashed these forces of division. A minor theological disagreement brewing in Alexandria would explode into a Church-wide controversy about the nature of God that would rage for a century. In retrospect, it would be called the Arian controversy, after a priest, Arius, whose views eventually lost and so were branded with his name. If his views had won, he would have been a Church Father and his enemies would be the "Athanasians" (or the like). Arius taught that Christ the Son was subordinate to God the Father not only in status but also ontologically. This was implied by the very terms "Father" and "Son" and also by Scripture (e.g., John 14:24: "The Father is greater than I"). Father and Son could not both be equally God or be made of the same (divine) substance, for then there would be two gods. Moreover, as the Son was born of the Father, there must have been a time before the Son existed, although this was before the rest of Creation. Moreover, Christ suffered for our sake, but suffering is impossible for the true God, therefore the Word could not have been identical to God. The Trinity therefore exists in three distinct subsistences (*hypostaseis*).

By contrast, Arius' bishop Alexandros argued that the Son was eternally generated by the Father: the Father must always have the Son in order to be the Father. The two have the same "nature" and the Son is his Father's "exact and unchanged image." Alexandros could point to Scripture too (John 10:30: "The Father and I are one"), and argued that Arius posited a high God and a lesser God (indeed, Eusebios of Kaisareia, who helped Arius politically, spoke of Christ as "a second God"). Alexandros wanted Christ to mediate between the Father and the rest of Creation, but lacked the language by which to distinguish between them in a way that did not make them ontologically distinct.[7] All parties agreed on 99% of their beliefs, or more, but focused on the remainder.

The protagonists in the ensuing controversy did not fall into two neat camps but rather along a narrow segment of the spectrum of identification-differentiation of the Son with the Father. The true extremes were not represented in this conflict. These would be the view (at one end) that the Father, Son, and Spirit were just different aspects of God, not distinct persons, which was branded as "Sabellian"; at the other end was the view that God adopted the human being Jesus as his Son, a view that was rejected as "Adoptionism." The protagonists of the fourth-century conflict were packed into the narrower range between "Christ is somehow God but distinct" and "Christ is fully God but somehow distinct." The distinctions were subtle and initially everyone lacked the words with which to express them clearly. They used technical terms in different senses, and sometimes the same theologian varied his usage from one text to the next, so they could not always understand each other. "Cross purposes" is an apt metaphor here. Moreover, philosophical sophistication in Greek was crucial for such God-splitting, so Latin speakers could not keep up. Language itself became a part of the debate, yet most participants set forth definite views *and* insisted on the incomprehensibility of God, especially when logic failed them.[8] It took them a while to realize that they were debating whether the concept "God" admitted of degrees. Also, they often insisted on analogies (e.g., the Son as a fragrance of the

Father; a person and his reason; the brightness of the light; water and vapor), but did not realize that these can at best illustrate, never prove.[9]

Confusion and uncertainty on these issues were already pervasive among Christians in the east, and were not created by the disagreement between Arius and his bishop. Prominent churchmen, such as Eusebios of Kaisareia and Eusebios of Nikomedeia, already held positions closer to Arius' side of the spectrum, but they did not regard themselves as followers of a mere priest, however charismatic he was. It was the trouble at Alexandria that brought all this to Constantine's attention. Arius had been condemned by his bishop Alexandros and had sought support from bishops outside Egypt, notably from the two Eusebioi, who had held local councils acquitting him of heresy and urging Alexandros to readmit him. It became painfully apparent that the Church lacked institutions of governance above the provincial level. When bishops disagreed, how were they to resolve their dispute?

Constantine begged Alexandros and Arius to stop debating what at first he took to be a trivial matter, but he soon realized that the bishops were in earnest. He therefore convened a general Council, to be held at Nikaia in 325 (spelled Nicaea subsequently in reference to the Council only). When they received the invitation and news that their travel expenses would be covered, most bishops "dashed like sprinters from the starting gate, eager to see that miracle": a Christian emperor![10] Approximately 270 attended, mostly from the east (the number of attendees fixed in later tradition was 318, the size of the household of Abraham in Genesis 14:14). Nicaea also established the principle that "Ecumenical" Church Councils could be convened only by emperors. The Roman state was already a structure for global governance and Constantine folded the adjudication of Christian disputes into its mechanisms. Besides, no one else had the resources to pull this off.

In hindsight, the Council of Nicaea would prove to be the most important event of the fourth century after the foundation of Constantinople. But we have no account of its proceedings or politics, and only a partial view of what happened. Constantine, dressed in glittering garments, entered "like some heavenly angel of God." He was praised by a bishop—possibly Eusebios of Nikomedeia—and then addressed the assembly in Latin through a Greek interpreter, expressing the hope that they would settle their disputes peacefully.[11] The Council discussed many issues, including the date of Easter and the integration of the Melitians into the Church of Egypt; it passed 20 canons (rules for the regulation of the Church), mostly regarding clerical ordinations; and celebrated Constantine's *vicennalia* (his twenty-year anniversary) in July. The Council also produced a Creed, a formal statement of faith, to resolve the theological controversy. It proclaimed that the Son was of "the same substance" as the Father (*homoousios*). This was a clear rejection of Arius and those who sympathized with him. This novel and as-yet poorly understood term seems to have been introduced by Constantine himself, who participated in the discussions, or by his closest theological advisor, Ossius, bishop of Cordoba in Spain, who had already represented the emperor at councils in the lead-up to Nicaea. Like most councils to come, Nicaea was run by the court to produce a predetermined outcome, in this case to reject Arius' position. Yet Constantine may have been less interested in the specifics of doctrine than in finding a position around which a viable peace could be built. If so, he was poorly advised to bet on Arius' enemies.

Arius was exiled, along with two Libyan bishops who refused to sign the Creed (Arius was of Libyan origin). So, less than a year after waging a war allegedly to liberate Christians from the persecution of Licinius, Constantine was exiling leaders of the Church in the name of Christian unity. Eusebios of Kaisareia signed the Creed, and sent an embarrassing letter back to his city that explained how it was not inconsistent with his prior theology. It was, of course, but Eusebios was a master dissembler.[12] Eusebios of Nikomedeia and Theognis, bishop of Nikaia, signed the Creed but were soon also exiled by Constantine because they remained on good terms with Arius or the Arians. In fact, the reason was likely political. Eusebios of Nikomedeia had been a powerful member of Licinius' court, representing him in negotiations with Constantine, and was related to his prefect Julius Julianus. After exiling him, Constantine sent a letter to the Church of Nikomedeia, which, following a theological word salad, accused Eusebios of complicity in Licinius' tyranny.[13]

It is even possible that the theology of the *homoousion* that was ratified at Nicaea, which was not part of the tradition of the Church and confused many who signed it, was specifically designed to compromise Eusebios of Nikomedeia, who was on the record as saying that the Son was *not* produced from the Father's substance.[14] Canon 11 of Nicaea on lapsed Christians refers to the "tyranny" of Licinius, which means that discussions of relatively routine administrative matters were overshadowed by the recent war. For the moment, then, Constantine thought that he had brought peace to the Church and simultaneously mopped up the remnants of Licinius' old regime. He would be proven wrong on both counts.

Before Constantine could be disillusioned, his regime was rocked by a scandal so horrific that his court tried to bury it in silence, indicating that his advisors could find no way to exculpate the emperor. In 326, Constantine executed his eldest son, Crispus, a Caesar and hero of the war against Licinius. No one at the time would say why this happened and no one later knew. Soon afterward Constantine also executed his second wife Fausta, some said by cooking her in an overheated bath. Fausta was closer in age to her stepson Crispus, causing later writers to fantasize about an affair between them, or an unrequited infatuation.[15] Later pagans discerned in this crime the guilt that drove Constantine to find a god (Jesus) who would forgive anything, but the chronology of this theory fails: Constantine had declared for Christianity long before 326.[16] Crispus was stricken from official memory, and writers such as Eusebios of Kaisareia who had praised him in the past now pretended that he had never existed.

The construction of Constantinople was in full swing, though no churches in the new capital can securely be attributed to Constantine. The emperor did, by contrast, fund the construction or embellishment of churches elsewhere in the east, for example at Nikomedeia, Antioch (the octagonal Great Church on the Orontes island), and the Holy Land. This activity was linked to a goodwill tour of the east on which he sent his mother Helena in 327. She was authorized to draw from the treasury in order to purchase support for the new regime through gifts to the cities, bribes to well-placed individuals, and charity to the poor. With these funds, Helena embellished shrines at the sites of Christ's birth (Bethlehem) and Ascension (Mount of Olives). Constantine began discussions with Makarios, bishop of Jerusalem, to build a resplendent church of the Holy Sepulcher at the site of Christ's Crucifixion and Resurrection, after a "polluting" temple of Aphrodite had been removed. He authorized Makarios to draw funds and laborers from the governor and to spare no expense: "if you think a coffered ceiling would be appropriate, maybe it can be gilded in gold?," the emperor of the new golden age suggested.[17]

Imperial patronage of the Holy Land enhanced its appeal for Christian pilgrims, who now began to arrive in droves, and showcased imperial piety to them. Helena herself likely had nothing to do with the Holy Sepulcher, though later tradition credited her with discovering the True Cross, allegedly preserved from Jesus' Crucifixion. That relic was first mentioned a generation later, and her alleged discovery of it only at the end of the century.[18] Yet Helena's tour set an example of piety and sponsorship of religion for empresses and east Roman women generally. This was a field in which women could seek public distinction without compromising their decorum.

Subordinationist theology had been routed at Nicaea, but its enemies failed to unite the Church. A war of pamphlets and accusations erupted throughout the east. In 327, Arius petitioned Constantine to be readmitted to the Church, which reveals that Christians already believed that the emperor, who was not even baptized, had the authority to decide such things. Arius knew exactly how to appeal to Constantine. He sent him a statement of faith that, while omitting all reference to the *homoousios*, promised to desist from all unnecessary disputes and, if readmitted, he would "offer prayers for your tranquil reign and your whole family."[19] Dynastic flattery was the path to Constantine's heart, and prayers for peace were all that even Galerius had wanted from the Christians. Around 335, a city in Italy (Hispellum) secured authorization from Constantine to establish a pagan temple and festival in honor of his Flavian dynasty, on condition, replied the emperor, that it not feature "contagious superstition," a vague restriction alluding probably to sacrifice.[20] Pledging support for the dynasty was more efficacious than theological correctness.

In theology, Christian emperors usually preferred consensus over accuracy, even surface consensus. They did not want zeal, intransigence, or for questions to be investigated all the way down until every distinction had been parsed, because they correctly realized that this would lead only to more division.[21] Constantine allowed Arius' evasion regarding doctrine and instructed Alexandros of Alexandria to readmit him: "Make it so that I hear only that you are all at peace and in harmony."[22] But Alexandros died in 328 and was replaced by his protégé Athanasios, albeit in an irregular and contested procedure. Athanasios, who had attended Nicaea as a deacon and would become the leading exponent of the *homoousios*, refused to readmit Arius, frustrating the emperor, who began to threaten him with exile. At the same time, in early 328, a council in Nikomedeia reinstated its former bishop Eusebios, who pledged to abide by Nicaea even though he too was evasive about doctrine. Constantine allowed him to return. Eusebios now added his own pressure on Athanasios to readmit Arius.[23] The balance had quickly shifted to favor the subordinationists, and would stay there for the next half-century.

The messy machinations that ensued need not be recounted in detail. Among eastern bishops who had an opinion on the matter, the majority fell within the subordinationist range of the theological spectrum and Constantine began to realize that they offered a firmer foundation for consensus. In a series of local councils, Eusebios of Kaisareia, Eusebios of Nikomedeia, and their allies began to depose their theological-political opponents. One prominent victim was the anti-Arian bishop Eustathios of Antioch, who was brought down in 330 (or a bit earlier) on a sexual charge; the emperor, it is said, was persuaded to exile him because he spoke badly of Helena.[24] Dynasty was again the clincher.

On the other side, Athanasios was intransigent and uncooperative, had a well-deserved reputation for violence against his Melitian opponents in Egypt, and the legality of his ordination was in doubt. Recent scholarship has cast him as the unscrupulous mob boss of the Alexandrian Church. The Eusebians, acting with the Melitians in an alliance of opportunity, brought a host of accusations against him, from intimidation and bribery to violence and murder. The murder charge was dropped when he dramatically produced the alleged victim alive, a coup that he would never let anyone forget. But by 335, his enemies finally secured his exile on a charge of obstructing grain shipments to Constantinople. When the emperor asked him to explain himself, Athanasios became increasingly exasperated and burst out, "the Lord will judge between me and you."[25] This was not how to talk to emperors. Athanasios was exiled to Trier, in Gaul. His only consolation was that Arius himself died the following year, in a dramatic way. In 336, Constantine ordered the bishop of Constantinople to admit Arius to communion. Arius was on his way to be admitted when he was seized by an urgent call of nature, near the forum of Constantine. Rushing off to the nearest latrine, he burst open and died, or so his enemies gleefully recounted. The exact spot was still remembered and pointed out a century later.[26]

Momentum was on the Eusebians' side. In 336, they secured the exile of Markellos, bishop of Ankyra, who was so anti-subordinationist that he could be cast as a Sabellian (that is, as obliterating any distinction between the Father and Son). The emperor himself had come full circle. In 337, shortly before his death, he was baptized by Eusebios of Nikomedeia, the former accomplice of the "tyrant" Licinius. Eusebios had emerged as Constantine's chief ecclesiastical advisor. He was obviously a capable politician.

Creating the imperial Church

The Church conflicts combined high stakes and sublime principles—nothing less than the Word of God—with methods low and unscrupulous. In sum, they were political. Debates about (literal) substance were derailed into disputes over procedure and points of order, and theological disagreements played out as criminal accusations: Church councils became courts of criminal law and bishops acted as judges over their peers. At the same time, bishops were acquiring real social power. Constantine opened the treasury for Church projects such as buildings, Bibles, and welfare. He ordered fifty deluxe Bibles from Eusebios of Kaisareia. During a famine in the east in 331, Constantine provided the churches with grain from state warehouses to distribute to the hungry. These grants, which were continued by later emperors, gave bishops the ability to appeal to the general population and use charity to sway their religious affiliation.[27]

Through imperial support and private donations of land and money, the churches embarked upon a trajectory that would place them among the largest landowners by the end of the century. But their wealth was not off the charts. Fifty years after Constantine, the revenue of the Church of Antioch was comparable to that of one of the city's richest citizens, but not the richest, and most of it had to go to charity. Bishops were expected, and sometimes audited, to use these resources for the benefit of their congregations, especially the eligible poor and widows, of whom they kept registries. Even so, imperial support enabled bishops to emerge as powerful local patrons, and some had plenty of income left over for pet projects.[28]

Bishops were also expected to divest themselves of land they owned personally in order to not to be distracted from, or conflicted in, the exercise of their duties. They could sell it for cash, which they could then use for episcopal projects; donate it to the Church; or pass it on to an heir, such as a son. This made bishops ineligible for curial duties, though the government tried to ensure that the property itself remained encumbered, even if it passed into other hands. Clergy also enjoyed significant tax breaks and were exempted from "sordid public duties"—a major perk, for which it was almost worth joining the clergy. They had the right to be tried before ecclesiastical courts, just as rabbis and some pagan priests had a similar right to be judged by their peers.[29] A generation after Constantine, there were some who would stop at nothing "for a position in the priesthood, not even flattery, bribery, murder in church, or civic disturbance."[30]

Holding bishops in high moral regard, Constantine also gave them the right to adjudicate local disputes in their episcopal courts, provided both parties agreed. This was a form of binding arbitration for non-criminal matters, but it is poorly attested. In practice, it probably only confirmed the traditional roles that bishops had played in reconciliation and pastoral supervision.[31] This was not an attempt to create a theocracy; if anything, it relieved the burden placed on the state courts by the growing demand for institutional justice, by outsourcing it to the Church. Bishops did not thereby become state officials and they had no say in the workings of the administration.[32] They had no authority, other than moral, to tell anyone what to do. This was no "clericocracy."[33] Bishops did, however, acquire enormous social and moral prestige, which made them powerful players in the game of mutual favors that defined the Roman elite. It was always good to have a few bishops on your side.

Thus, the Christian clergy was integrated into Roman society through the same fiscal-legal mechanisms by which emperors defined and regulated all social classes (curiales, coloni, soldiers, slaves, etc.). This meant that bishops now had to play by Roman rules, which, however, also brought them impressive perks. The converse, however, did not happen: Roman law remained autonomous and was not shaped by Christian priorities, at least not for a while. Historians used to locate the first traces of Christian influence in the marriage laws of Constantine, but this proved to be a mirage. Those laws reflect a conservative Roman mentality trying to define a new imperial elite in times of rapid social change.[34] For example, divorce by mutual consent was not abolished until Justinian did so in 542, though he excepted those who wanted to join monasteries. But this proved so unpopular that it was revoked by his successor Justin II ("many are complaining of the wars that they have to wage at home").[35] Likewise, Constantine decreed that Sunday was to be a day of rest from official business, but, with typical ambiguity, he defined this "day of the Sun" in pagan terms, even though it had been adopted by Christians as *Kyriake*, "the day of the Lord." During his reign, some Christians assumed this provision applied to them too.[36]

Constantine's dynastic and foreign policy

Constantine's shift toward Eusebios of Nikomedeia in ecclesiastical politics coincided with a shift in dynastic plans.[37] After the death of his mother Helena in 329, he began to favor his younger half-brothers, Flavius Dalmatius and Julius Constantius, whom Helena, a "crafty step-mother," had blocked because they were the sons of the woman who replaced her.[38] Julius Constantius was now married to the daughter of Licinius' praetorian prefect Julius Julianus, Basilina, who bore him a son in 331/2: this was the future emperor Julian, the first person we know who was born in Constantinople. Constantine's two half-brothers were given high honors and titles in the 330s, including that of the consulship and patriciate (Constantine revived the rank of "patrician" as a prestigious court title). Dalmatius was given a military command and suppressed a curious but minor revolt by the Keeper of the Imperial Camels on Cyprus, in 334.

Constantine now revamped the succession. After making his youngest son Constans Caesar in 333, to join Constantinus II and Constantius II, he elevated Dalmatius' two sons: Julius Dalmatius was made Caesar in 335 and Hannibalianus was given the striking title King of Kings and the Pontic Peoples. He was likely destined for Armenia and other territories to be conquered in the Persian war that Constantine was contemplating. The emperor's three sons and nephew would thereby form an imperial college, possibly one with two senior and two junior emperors. This was Diocletian's Tetrarchy all over again, but within a single family. Its territorial assignments placed Constantinus II in the west, Constans in Italy and Pannonia, Dalmatius on the lower Danube, and Constantius II in the east. Constantius, a teenager, was dispatched to Antioch under the supervision of Ablabius, the powerful and long-serving praetorian prefect of Oriens (329–337), an ardent Christian from Crete. In 336, in the celebration of the emperor's *tricennalia*, his thirty-year anniversary in power, Eusebios praised Constantine as a charioteer driving a team of four Caesars.[39]

Constantine also secured the Danubian border, with lasting success. Specifically, he built forts along the Danube and a bridge across it from Oescus to Sucidava, which lay on what came to be known as "the Gothic shore."[40] At 2.4 km, it was the longest river bridge of the ancient world. In 332, Constantine sent his son Constantinus II against a group of Goths who were allegedly harassing the Sarmatians (an Iranian-speaking people bordering on Pannonia). Then, in 334 Constantine attacked the Sarmatians for reasons that remain obscure, resettling many of them in Roman territory. Constantine was happy to put a Christian spin on these conventional Roman incursions when he wrote to the bishops at Tyre in 335: "through me, the true servant of God, the barbarians recognized God and learned to worship him."[41] These campaigns, about which we know little, resulted in a peace of thirty years between Romans and Goths, stimulating trade as well as the recruitment of barbarians into the Roman armies. Trade across the border was usually closely monitored and controlled, but now the Goths "were free to buy and sell wherever they wanted."[42] They "were persuaded to love peace."[43]

Along with trade came religion. Christianity had spread among the Goths from Romans captured in raids during the third century. A descendant of these captives from Cappadocia named Ulfila was now consecrated by Eusebios of Nikomedeia as the bishop of all who lived in the lands the Goths, under either Constantine (in 336) or Constantius (in 340). This was one reason why Goths would eventually accept Arian Christianity: Ulfila adamantly opposed the doctrine of the *homoousios*. But his mission was expelled by the Goths in the 340s, and he and his followers were resettled in Moesia by Constantius, who saw in Ulfila a "new Moses." Ulfila translated the Bible into Gothic, apart from the books of Kings, allegedly so as not to further inflame the Goths' warlike spirit.[44] Fragments of his New Testament still survive, from which we know Gothic, the earliest attested Germanic language.

Christianity was spreading elsewhere outside Romanía. Rulers of some neighboring kingdoms followed Constantine in embracing the new faith, namely the client king of Armenia Trdat (or Tiridates, ca. 287–330), who had served in the Roman army and may have converted as early as the 310s; and Mirian III, the king of Georgia (Kartli, called "Iberia" by the Romans), though his chronology is confused. These royal conversions are recounted in later romantic legends that deserve little credence,[45] and their local context and international entanglements are irrecoverable. They were not brought about by missions sent by Rome, and neither Constantine nor any extant source of the period mentions them. Nor is there any proof that Constantine intended them to form a "Christian International Commonwealth" under his direction. Yet these developments were still epochal, being the first steps in the emergence of a Christian periphery around the empire, from Africa and Arabia to the Caucasus and Balkans. Christianity became yet another vector by which the empire projected its might, a form of soft power.

Constantine's death and succession

Having freed his own Christian subjects from the "tyranny" of Licinius, Constantine observed the imperiled condition of Persia's Christians and wrote a remarkable letter to the Persian shah Shapur II (309–379). The emperor proclaimed his devotion to Christianity in typically overwrought prose—"This is the God I profess to honor with undying remembrance," "Him I call upon with bended knee"—and his reference to the Christians of Persia served as a subtle warning to Shapur not to mistreat them.[46] However, by including only this part of the long letter to Shapur in his biography of Constantine, Eusebios twisted the relations between the two monarchs into a testament of his hero's faith. In reality, the two rulers discussed and negotiated many other matters, such as the export of iron to Persia,[47] and Constantine's confessional tone may have been responding to a strident declaration of Zoroastrian principles by Shapur, the sort of posturing that Sasanian Persians relished. By 335, Constantine had decided on war with Persia, for reasons that remain obscure but likely had to do with control over Armenia. His proclamation of Hannibalianus as King of Kings was a provocation to Persia.

A massive expedition was set into motion in 337, but Constantine, who was in his mid-sixties, died en route near Nikomedeia, on 22 May, after being baptized by Eusebios of Nikomedeia. The timing was bad: Constantine had proclaimed none of his sons as Augustus, and Shapur was already moving to meet him.

Constantine was ambiguous in death as in life. His body, placed within a golden sarcophagus wrapped in purple, lay in state in the palace in Constantinople, where military officers, senators, and the people came to pay homage. Meanwhile, Constantius rushed to the capital from Antioch in order to preside over his father's burial in the majestic mausoleum that he had built on the highest of the City's hills. Following Roman tradition, this monument was circular but was conceived, at least in the pious imagination of Eusebios of Kaisareia, as a shrine to the Apostles. Their symbolic presence was represented by twelve "receptacles" (cenotaphs?) along its outer rim, and Constantine was laid to rest in their middle, in a porphyry sarcophagus that may be the one that stands today in the courtyard of St. Eirene (see Figure 6). This arrangement signified either that Constantine was a new Christ or that he was the chief or equal of the Apostles (*isapostolos*).[48] The disturbing implication was neutralized by Constantius, who built a cruciform church of the Holy Apostles adjacent to the mausoleum (finished in 370) and endowed it with the relics of Timothy (in 356) and Luke and Andrew (in 357). This altered the relationship between the emperor and the Apostles. John Chrysostom later said, in apparent ignorance of the switch, that "the emperors in Constantinople

Figure 6 Likely sarcophagus of Constantine in the courtyard of St. Eirene, Istanbul
Photo by David Hendrix

did not choose to deposit their bodies next to the Apostles but outside the doors [of the church], so that the emperors became the doormen of fishermen."[49] Today both monuments are lost, and the Fatih mosque of Mehmet II stands upon their foundations.

Constantine did not rest in peace. In 359, Makedonios, the bishop of his City, moved the emperor's body to the church of Akakios as the mausoleum was in danger of collapsing and visitors were afraid to go in. The move was opposed by a section of the people, and it played into the theological controversies raging at the time, resulting in a battle with much slaughter: "the courtyard of the church was filled with blood and the drains overflowed, so that it ran along the stoa to the public square there."[50]

Like his father, Constantine was regarded by his subjects as deified. He was shown on coins issued by his son Constantius as ascending to heaven in a chariot, and the annual ceremony in his honor evoked the Roman *consecratio*. After all, Constantine was a Roman emperor before he was a Christian emperor.[51] But all this could, with effort, be spun in Christian terms.[52] Later Orthodox Romans gradually stripped Constantine of his pre-Christian associations and layered more Christian fiction over him, turning him into a saint and Orthodox archetype, to the point where he was barely recognizable. His nude Apolline statue in the forum collapsed in a gale in 1106, crushing many people below.[53] It was replaced by a cross atop the column.

Constantine's ruthless pragmatism was dedicated to the pursuit of a grand ambition and carried out with impressive ability. He could switch quickly from subtlety and evasion to brutal decisiveness. His foundation of Constantinople, gold economy, tax policy, and generalship reveal a magnificent vision for the empire's future and an uncommon intelligence. So too did his support for the Church, albeit this was marred by naïveté about bishops. He left his heirs with peace along the Danube but a disastrous war in the east. His murderous ambition to establish his own dynasty destroyed the collegiate system of the Tetrarchy, only to recreate it within his own family. But he could not abolish the bloody precedent that he himself had set. His funeral games would be a round of familial bloodletting.

Popular tradition gave the name Philadelphion ("Place of Brotherly Love") to a square along the Mese of Constantinople because it contained a statue that was interpreted as the three sons of Constantine embracing after their father's death.[54] Perhaps the name was subversively ironic, for in 337, when the eighteen-year-old Constantius rushed back to the capital, he ordered the army to massacre almost all the men of the Constantinian dynasty, except his brothers, of course, who were not there. The victims included his cousins (the Caesar Dalmatius and "King of Kings" Hannibalianus), their fathers (the half-brothers of Constantine), and many others, including the praetorian prefect Ablabius, Constantius' former handler. The "Great Massacre," as Libanios called it, spared only Gallus, a son of Julius Constantius who was thought to be deathly ill, and his half-brother Julian, who was only six (and possibly protected by his relative, Eusebios of Nikomedeia). The official story was that the army acted on its own, but later in Constantius' reign his responsibility began to be acknowledged more openly, and he professed remorse. This was not a mutiny but a targeted family slaughter ordered by a teenager who was in no danger; that it spared the women is proof of planning. Julian later regarded Constantius as the murderer of his family and the author of his misfortunes, including his exile to a state farm in backward Cappadocia.[55] According to the new official line, toed by Eusebios of Kaisareia, Constantine had only ever had three heirs, his sons.

That summer, the brothers met at Sirmium and negotiated hard over how to divide the empire. Constantinus received the west (Spain, Gaul, and Britain), Constans Italy, North Africa, and the western Balkans (Moesia and Illyricum), and Constantius Thrace and the east. With this hammered out, they jointly received the title Augustus from the armies. They were the first third-generation emperors in Roman history. But Constantinus was unhappy with the partition and fell out with Constans. In 340, he invaded Italy and was killed in battle. Constans, the youngest brother, was now the master of two-thirds of the empire and Constantinus II was also stricken from official memory as a "public enemy." In a panegyric of the two surviving sons, Libanios pretended that Constantine had only ever had these two.[56] The relationship between Constans and Constantius was tense, in part because of religious differences. But Constantius was based in Antioch and preoccupied with his father's Persian war.

Sasanian Persia

The Persian empire, ruled by the Sasanian dynasty (224–651 AD), was the only peer state bordering on Romanía. It extended from Mesopotamia to modern Afghanistan, and exercised periodic control over parts of the Caucasus and Arabia. Within this broad domain, it promoted Iranian culture, ideas, religion, and social norms. The Sasanian dynasty adhered to Zoroastrianism and derived from that venerable religion an ideology of imperial kingship, society, and ritual order. Zoroastrians worshipped a supreme God, Ahura Mazda (called Ohrmazd at this time), in ways that verged on monotheism, and disdained or condemned those who sacrificed to non-Zoroastrian gods (called "demons"). Their religion featured a belief in heaven and hell and the judgment of the soul after death, being among the first, if not the first, to hold such notions. The hegemony of Ohrmazd in the empire was monumentalized by the fire altars that the dynasty built and lavishly maintained in strategically-placed complexes. In practice, other religions such as Judaism and Christianity were tolerated, as were aspects of folk Zoroastrianism that did not conform to the doctrines of the mostly hereditary Mazdean priests, the magi, who were also state officials, acting like judges. Throne and altar were more concerned to establish the superiority of their religion than to impose it on others, though sometimes they did persecute groups such as Christians and Buddhists. In the third century, this fertile intersection of traditions gave rise to a compelling and long-lived new religious synthesis, that of Mani. His followers, the Manichaeans, were persecuted by the Mazdeans and by Rome, the latter in the tragically wrong belief that the Manichaeans were Persian infiltrators.

While comparable in wealth, size, and antiquity, Rome and Iran differed in crucial ways. Lacking Rome's unified law of persons, which integrated the population into a single legal and fiscal system, Iran was a true multiethnic empire, treating distinct groups of subjects as collective entities under their own local or religious leaders. There was in Iran no concept or legal practice comparable to Roman citizenship. Also, political power in Iran was not centralized into a single, uniform, and impersonal state system in which a common soldier such as Diocletian could rise to the throne. The monarchy was held exclusively by the Sasanian dynasty, passing power from father to son or at most to an uncle or brother. The dynasty was propped up by a coalition of noble families who lorded it over their home provinces and monopolized the high posts of the court. Whereas a Roman emperor was the commander-in-chief of all his armies and appointed his magistrates for a limited term, the *shah* (or *shahanshah*, "Kings of Kings") ruled through internal diplomacy with his grandees and client kings, who brought their own levies to the shah's campaigns. Another difference was that Romans recorded their laws, literature, and bureaucracy on paper and stone to a far greater degree than the Sasanians, in part because persuasion was a more important factor in Roman society. The city councilor class in particular contained a few hundred thousand people with a shared education and political interests; they lobbied the imperial government, which, in turn, placated them with rhetorical pronouncements of benevolence. More documents survive from any one Roman city than from the whole of the Sasanian realm. This leaves us in miserable ignorance about Sasanian history and society.

For all that they were often at war, Rome and Persia regarded each other as peers—the "two eyes illuminating the world" or "two mountains of the world"—and their rulers sometimes addressed each other as "brothers," recognizing that each was sovereign in his respective sphere.[57] But wars between the two were common in the third and fourth centuries. Upon its foundation in the 220s, the Sasanian empire had taken a more aggressive stance toward Rome than had its Parthian predecessor and had scored notable successes, including multiple defeats of imperial armies, the capture of an emperor (Valerian, in 260), and raids that penetrated deep into Roman territory. These victories were celebrated by reliefs carved on the cliff face at Naqsh-e Rustam in Fars, the burial place of the ancient Achaemenid kings, with whom the Sasanians wanted to be associated. But the tide turned in 298, when Galerius inflicted a crushing defeat on the Persians, allowing Diocletian to dictate terms in the treaty of Nisibis. This granted hegemony over Armenia and Iberia to Rome and transferred to Roman rule a number of districts that were south of Armenia and east of the Tigris (the *regiones transtigritanae*). These Syrian-Arab marcher principalities remained quasi-autonomous under local "satraps," who received their insignia of office from Rome. Their tax status is uncertain, but by 387 at the latest their cities were sending the crown of gold to the emperor.[58] Amida, Nisibis, Singara, and Bezabde in north Mesopotamia became gateways to the Roman east. The treaty held for almost forty years, until Shapur II and Constantine started to itch for a rematch in the 330s.

Constantius' foreign and civil wars

Constantius lacked his father's bold streak and wisely followed a cautious and defensive strategy. Apart from the imperial field armies, the eastern command was led by the *duces* of Mesopotamia and Osrhoene, probably based at Nisibis and Edessa respectively. Their strategy was to fortify major cities and let the Persians wear themselves out in sieges, especially against Nisibis, which was attacked three times in the ensuing conflict, and there was one pitched battle too, at Singara, with bloody but inconclusive results. In fourteen years of war (337–350), Shapur achieved nothing. The Roman sources for this conflict were all written by partisans of Julian or Athanasios of Alexandria and so they are hostile to Constantius: they denigrate him for achieving nothing, but fail to recognize that his strategy was defensive. The Christian poet Ephrem of Nisibis, who lived through the war, did praise Constantius for resisting the Persians (though he did so to score points against Julian). The sieges of those years also gave rise to the first legends of bishops and holy men protecting their cities with miraculous powers.[59] In reality, the east was protected by soldiers and military engineers.

In 350, Shapur was called away to the Central Asian frontier of his empire, which frequently distracted the Sasanians and relieved the pressure on Rome. The respite was timely, for Constantius had just learned that his brother Constans, who had become increasingly unpopular in the west, was dead. In January 350, Magnentius, the general of the western field armies of the Ioviani and Herculiani, rebelled, he was proclaimed emperor by the armies, and Constans was assassinated. In March, Vetranio, the elderly general of Illyricum, was also proclaimed emperor and supported by Constantina, daughter of Constantine I and widow of the murdered Hannibalianus. Her motives are unknown, but likely dynastic: Vetranio pledged loyalty to Constantius and, whether or not this was by design, effectively plugged Constantius' border with Magnentius.[60] Magnentius also sought recognition from Constantius, but was rebuffed.

There were now three emperors again, unsure what to do with each other. The first round of the conflict featured one of the oddest moments of fourth-century politics. Constantius and Vetranio held a conference at Serdica and then met again at Naissus, in December 350: in a ceremony that had been orchestrated in advance, Constantius spoke eloquently before Vetranio's armies and persuaded them to join his side. Vetranio ceremoniously removed the purple, surrendered it to Constantius, and was granted a comfortable retirement in Bithynia. There were now two rivals, as Constantius ruled out a political settlement with Magnentius. The two halves of the empire were again, a generation after Constantine's defeat of Licinius, about to go to war. But to maintain a dynastic presence in the east while he marched west, Constantius recalled his cousin Gallus from his Cappadocian exile and, in March 351, made him Caesar at Sirmium. Gallus was married to the emperor's sister Constantina and dispatched to Antioch. Constantius then waged a long and bitter war against Magnentius, which lasted until August 353, when the usurper committed suicide at Lyon after a series of defeats. This victory earned Constantius the dubious merit of being better at civil wars than foreign ones.[61] The hard-fought battle of Mursa (in Pannonia), in September 351, inflicted massive casualties on both sides, possibly in the tens of thousands. "Vast forces of the Roman empire were destroyed, sufficient for any foreign war," wrote a historian two decades afterward. Both sides knew that "it was not right for Romans to be waging war against Romans."[62]

All the tyrant's legal decisions were annulled, except those that had involved capital punishment, an exception that enabled Constantius to keep the confiscated properties of condemned criminals.[63] Investigations were launched into cases of collaboration with the "tyrant," and the emperor's informants began to implicate an ever-widening circle of traitors on thinner and thinner grounds. Paulus "the Chain" was infamous for linking one person to the charges leveled against another; and Mercurius, a Persian by origin, was called "the Count of Dreams" for his skill at reading treasonous designs into people's dreams. These hated men, who received portions of the condemned's properties as a reward and incentive, instilled fear but made the regime seem paranoid and insecure. They not only uncovered plots: they created them by driving their victims to desperation.[64]

The regime condemned Magnentius not only as an illegitimate usurper but as a barbarian invader (his mother allegedly was a Frank). This was a toothless polemic, for the west had accepted him as a legitimate emperor for three years. Yet it is in Constantius' reign that we first observe the rise to prominence of barbarians in the army. Their recruitment in large numbers likely began under Constantine and would have momentous consequences for the future of the empire, especially in the west. The Roman army had always been supplemented by non-Roman auxiliaries, but these new barbarian recruits of the fourth century, whose legal status is unclear today (and may have been so at the time),[65] came from beyond the borders. They included prisoners. For example, Vadomarius, a king of the Alemanni kidnapped on Julian's orders in 361, turns up as *dux* of Phoenicia later in the decade. Soldiers were sometimes provided by barbarian groups as part of an agreement with the empire, either to enlist in the Roman army or to serve as auxiliaries for specific campaigns (for example, in the war of 324 Constantine's army was supplemented by Franks, Licinius' by Goths, and Constantius II used Goths against the Persians). Recruits were raised among foreign populations that were settled inside the empire (*laeti*), and individuals and groups enlisted because of the social and economic perks and the opportunity to live in the empire.[66]

The separation of military and civilian careers enabled barbarian officers to reach the higher cadres of power in the Roman system, by climbing the ranks of the army. Also, the assimilative powers of Romanía, which had already absorbed so much of the provincial population, easily integrated the sons of these recruits too, as they grew up speaking camp Latin and had known no other homeland. A generation after Constantine, many officers in the Roman army had barbarian names or are known to have been the sons of first-generation recruits. However, we lack reliable statistics about their numbers, because some barbarians took Latin names whereas others, who kept barbarian names, may have been born and raised in the empire as Romans, and were so treated. But their integration could hit roadblocks. Resettlements did not always go smoothly. In 359, some Limigantes, adjacent to Pannonia, petitioned to be admitted to the empire, where they would pay tribute and provide recruits. When Constantius stepped up to address them, he was suddenly attacked, so his army slaughtered and dispersed them.[67] Also, as the denigration of Magnentius reveals, ethnic difference retained its sting when politics required it (though he was probably just a Roman with a foreign mother, not someone who crossed the border as an adult). Some barbarian soldiers played both sides. One Mallobaudes was simultaneously captain of the *domestici* and "king of the Franks" (presumably of those in imperial service). In rare cases, first-generation barbarians were disloyal, betraying the empire at critical moments to their former compatriots.[68] These problems would be exacerbated by the Gothic influx of the 370s, and the polemic directed against Magnentius was an early sign of ethnic tensions.

Having suppressed the tyrant, Constantius now faced the problem of Gallus in Antioch. Gallus had likely not been expected to do much, and was hemmed in by imperial officials who informed the emperor about everything. It was imperial appointees who crushed a minor Jewish rebellion that broke out in Diokaisareia (Sepphoris), Tiberias, and Diospolis (Lod) in 352—the first since the Jewish uprisings of the second century, and a sign of increasing tensions, though neither the patriarch nor the rabbis seem to have been involved in this one. It was also career generals who checked Isaurian marauders in Pamphylia in 354.[69] But Gallus became increasingly erratic, cruel, and murderous, especially toward the leading citizens of Antioch, forcing them to sell their grain at low prices during a shortage. His tyranny, juridical tortures, and executions are recounted in gruesome detail by Ammianus, who was in Antioch at the time and biased in favor of its ruling class, but his testimony is confirmed by Gallus' half-brother Julian, who loved him but admitted that he had a cruel streak, created by childhood traumas.[70] Ties between the cousins had been weakened by the coincident deaths of their wives that year. When Gallus began to kill Constantius' officials, he was summoned under false pretenses, entrapped and misled, and executed in Istria.

Constantius was now sole emperor, a position that he had not sought and could not manage. It was understood that one man could not govern the entire empire, but Constantius had a suspicious nature. A competent general might rebel, whereas an incompetent one would cause problems in the usual way. A relative may not be trustworthy, but Constantius had only one anyway, Julian, a scarcity for which he had only himself to blame. Julian had no political experience and was drawn to Homer and philosophy, which made him seem harmless. In November 355, he was elevated to the rank of Caesar, married to another of the emperor's sisters (Helena), surrounded by watchful officials, and sent to Gaul. Against all expectation, Julian was tremendously successful: a fair judge, a conscientious administrator who managed to reduce taxes, and, far more alarmingly, a good general who defeated the Alamanni at the battle of Strasbourg (357), raided across the Rhine, and inspired devotion in his soldiers. Churchmen were later exasperated by popular praise for Julian: "Must our ears be filled with the praise of his good administration of the public post, relaxation of taxes, good choice of magistrates, and punishment of robbery?"—thus Ambrose of Milan, grudgingly admitting that provincials in the west, Christians included, were still praising Julian thirty years after his death.[71]

Such popularity could have only one outcome. Tensions mounted between Julian and Constantius, who was using his officials to undercut his Caesar. Julian had previously sent to the court separate panegyrics for the emperor and empress, to prove his loyalty, but in 359 he sent a panegyric that begins abruptly, and ominously, with the story of Achilles' wrath against his king Agamemnon.[72] In that year, Constantius was attacked from the east as well, by Shapur, who sent a letter claiming all the territory of his Achaemenid ancestors up to Macedonia, but demanding only Mesopotamia and Armenia. He addressed Constantius merely as "Caesar" while naming himself as "Partner with the Stars, Brother of the Sun and Moon."[73] In 359, after a bitterly-fought siege, recounted in grisly detail by Ammianus, Shapur captured Amida and then, in 360, Singara and Bezabde. He ruined and abandoned the first two, transporting their people back to Persia, and kept only Bezabde. Constantius' defensive strategy was failing. When he demanded reinforcements from his Caesar in early 360, Julian was proclaimed Augustus by his soldiers, who did not want to be sent east. A cold war ensued, as both emperors fought barbarians along their separate frontiers while tensely watching each other. Julian struck first, after the summer of 361, with a lightning march into the Balkans. To his credit, Constantius had prioritized the Persian war, but now mobilized against Julian. Before the two could meet, Constantius died of natural causes on 3 November, 361, in Cilicia, naming Julian as his heir to prevent more civil war. It was a magnanimous decision, and Julian buried Constantius with honor in the dynasty's mausoleum.

Constantius was unloved. A conscientious and hard-working if "mediocre" emperor,[74] he was also pathologically insecure, suspicious, unjust, and murderous, if blameless in his private life. There was now only one Augustus left, Julian, who would appoint no Caesar. An open-hearted and unafraid man, Julian had friends and trusted supporters to whom he could confidently delegate power. He was popular in the west and had no rivals in the east. He was the most educated man to reach the Roman throne in centuries and also had the most impressive imperial pedigree to date, being the great-great-grandson of an emperor, great-grandson of another, nephew of a third, cousin to three Augusti, two Caesars, and a king, and half-brother to a Caesar. Normally in history this is a recipe for mediocrity, but not now: Julian believed that almost all of his imperial kin were bad, and set out to govern differently.[75]

5
Competing Religions of Empire (337–363)

Constantius and the Church

In most respects, Constantius hewed closely to his father's policies and image. He continued to expand Constantinople, its senatorial order, and the gold economy. On the eastern front, he played defense rather than offense, and in Church politics he inherited Constantine's later leanings toward the subordinationist camp. The unity that he sought there eluded him, but he opened new fronts in the dismantling of pagan cult, which led to a backlash under Julian.

In the twenty years after Constantine's death, most of the eastern Church was run by bishops who believed that Athanasios was a thug and unfit for office, and that the Creed of Nicaea did not distinguish sufficiently between the Father and Son. This group was sometimes called "the party of Eusebios of Nikomedeia," and Eusebios was indeed soon elevated to bishop of Constantinople. This loose consensus, consisting of uncoordinated local coalitions, expressed their theological views at the Council of Antioch in 341. The "Dedication Creed" of that Council would become their reference point until the late 350s (it was so named because the bishops had assembled to dedicate the octagonal church begun by Constantine and completed by Constantius, who was present). In contrast to Nicaea, which insisted that the Son was of the same *hypostasis* and *ousia* as the Father, the Dedication Creed states that the members of the Trinity "are three in *hypostasis*" while the Son is "the image" of the Father's substance (*ousia*).[1] By using the term *hypostasis*, the Council captured the Son's distinctiveness and *slight* subordination to the Father. It is useless to call the Dedication Creed heretical in the light of later Orthodoxy. In fact, it was Nicaea's equation of *hypostasis* and *ousia* that would (quietly) be rejected by later formulations of Orthodoxy. Athanasios himself, the champion of Nicaea, held the one-*hypostasis* doctrine until he too (also quietly) changed his mind, around 362, accepted the three *hypostaseis*, and stopped talking about Nicaea's one *hypostasis*.[2]

Later Orthodox tradition and some modern histories cast Athanasios as a lone voice of Nicene Orthodoxy in the dark years of "Arian" rule in the Church. In reality, under Constantius Athanasios was theologically irrelevant, and did not begin to produce his significant work until the end of that reign. Athanasios was unacceptable to his opponents not for his theology (he was never condemned for that) but his criminal and violent behavior, for which he had been condemned by numerous councils, including by bishops who might otherwise have shared his theological stance. To whatever degree Athanasios was associated with Nicaea, he was an albatross around its neck, not its paladin, at least not in the east. It was instead Markellos of Ankyra who was targeted by eastern bishops that disliked Nicaea for veering too close to Sabellianism, for he nearly obliterated the difference between Father and Son.

In the west this played out differently, which brings us to the crux of Church politics under Constantius. Constantine's death in 337 meant that a number of exiled bishops, including Athanasios and Markellos, were allowed to return to their sees. This, in turn, meant that the eastern bishops—"the party of Eusebios"—had to depose them all over again. Athanasios was ejected from Alexandria by imperial forces in 339, with violence on both sides, and fled to Julius in Rome. Julius now appointed himself as the arbiter of all disputes and invited all sides to submit their case to Rome for "a fair verdict." He even invited the Eusebians to a council in Rome on the grounds that episcopal depositions were invalid without the consent of the bishop of Rome.[3] Julius did not know this, but he was opening the first crack in what would become the Schism between the eastern (Greek) and western (Latin) Churches. It is unclear where he got the idea that his see was either a higher or a fairer court of appeals in the Church, but the easterners did not see it that way, not then and not ever. The bishops who met in Antioch in 341 wrote to Julius and conceded that all honor belonged to Rome, but the faith had come from the east. They did not recognize Julius' jurisdiction over them and were appalled that he consorted with the likes of Athanasios.[4]

Julius did more than consort with Athanasios. He held a council in the summer of 341, exonerating Athanasios and Markellos. Julius' use of terms such as "the faction of Eusebios" and "the Arians" shows that he had been successfully propagandized by Athanasios and was probably using this affair to intervene in eastern affairs and establish his jurisdiction over it (a tactic that would have a long future).[5] The easterners' reply was to assert that "we are not followers of Arius. How could we, who are bishops, follow a presbyter?"[6] Athanasios had cleverly cast his criminal convictions as a struggle for the faith, and branded his enemies as "Arians," a category that he invented and then embellished as "Ariomaniacs," to insinuate that they were not Christians: "we are named Christians after Christ, and they are named Arians after Arius."[7] He grasped the potency of the brand name, and kept hammering that message.

In addition to Julius, Athanasios lobbied the western emperor Constans and alienated him from Constantius,[8] a provocation that the latter would not forgive. But Constantius had good reason to be conciliatory. Dislodging Athanasios from Alexandria had met with violent resistance, indicating a measure of support for him there. The two emperors agreed to a joint Council, at Serdica (Sofia) in 343, but this turned into a fiasco. The eastern bishops, who believed that they had already put their house in order and so were reluctant to come, refused to meet with the western ones, who were, after all, accompanied by exiled criminals and heretics and formed a larger bloc that could outvote the east. The two sides never met but did excommunicate each other's leaders (such as Akakios of Kaisareia and Basileios of Ankyra on the eastern side as "Arians," and Julius of Rome and Ossius of Cordoba on the western as "Sabellians"). The westerners passed resolutions that gave Rome the right to review the appeals of deposed bishops, thus retroactively justifying Julius' meddling in the case of Athanasios. But in their manifesto, the easterners specifically rejected "this newfangled rule that the western bishops are trying to establish, that eastern bishops are to be judged by western ones."[9] As the Church historian Sokrates put it a century later, "from that time on the western Church was severed from the eastern."[10] This Schism between east and west would recur periodically, until it became permanent.

On the surface, Church politics in this period were ferocious and unstable, with bishops deposed and exiled left and right, usually for criminal or procedural infractions; with battles fought in the streets between the supporters of rivals for an episcopal throne; and with scandals galore, including sexual ones. The theology continued to be debated fiercely, although defenders of Nicaea remained unable to explain exactly how One is Three (they were increasingly including the Holy Spirit in the consubstantial Trinity). Meanwhile, subordinationists remained unable to define what exactly the Son was if his being was not that of the Father. A loose subordinationist consensus prevailed among eastern bishops between 330 and the late 350s. Its leaders cleared the east of supporters of Markellos and Athanasios and experienced only one setback: in 345, Constans threatened war against Constantius if Athanasios was not restored,[11] so that bishop did return, in 346, to the joy of his supporters in Alexandria. He went on to enjoy the longest stay there of his career, ten years. This also taught emperors a lesson: henceforth exiled bishops were to be sent to remote eastern forts, and not to western capitals where they could meddle in politics.

During the war with Magnentius, Constantius held a council at Sirmium in 351, which reaffirmed the eastern theological consensus. After the rebel's defeat, Constantius systematically enforced this consensus on the west. He required all western bishops, including Ossius of Cordoba and Liberius of Rome, to sign the Creed of Sirmium upon penalty of exile. Some western supporters of Nicaea wrote hysterical denunciations of Constantius as the Antichrist because of this, but the policy worked. The emperor was now able to revisit the matter of Athanasios and tell the world how he really felt about him: "a most vile crook and con man who would deserve every bit of it if he were killed ten times over."[12] Athanasios was ordered to surrender his position in 355, but he resisted violently until 356, when he went into hiding in Egypt. Until 362, he devoted himself to the composition of polemical theological treatises. Finally, Constantius brought the

Creed of Sirmium to Egypt: bishops were required to sign it and decurions were placed under financial pressure to get them to do so.[13]

The eastern consensus, however, which was loose to begin with, gradually splintered and tore itself apart. Granted, the Father and the Son are not of the same substance, but what *exactly* is their relationship? A number of views had emerged by the later 350s, some of which were so alarming that subordinationist bishops reconsidered their position.

Two lowborn but highly educated controversialists, Aetios and his devoted disciple Eunomios, advocated a more robust subordination. In their view, informed by Aristotelian logic, Father and Son were "*unlike* with respect to substance," a doctrine they called *heterousian* (though their enemies labeled them *anhomoians*, as if they taught unlikeness in *all* respects, which Aetios denied). The Son for them was an altogether different entity, a kind of high angel, though akin to God from a human perspective.[14] Rather than rely on analogies, Aetios insisted on a technical understanding of technical terms, and once trounced Basil of Kaisareia in debate, when the latter was still a deacon.[15] This was not an approach that would move the masses, but it gained some traction. It elicited a sharp reaction from those, such as Basileios of Ankyra, who believed that the Son was "similar" (not identical) to the Father in *ousia*—this group is called the *homoiousians*. Basileios argued that if the Son is not at least *like* the Father in substance, he is just a created entity and so unworthy of worship.[16] Basileios and his party persuaded Constantius to exile Aetios and Eunomios in 358, and plans were hatched for twin east-west councils, at Ariminum (Rimini) and Seleukeia (in Cilicia), in 359, to ratify the emerging middle ground.

The only clear resolution reached by the bishops at Ariminum, where some supported the creed of Nicaea and others that of Sirmium, was a formal request to the emperor that they be allowed to go home. Meanwhile, at Seleukeia, a bitter rift opened between the homoiousians and another group who are called *homoians*, because they believed that the Son was "similar to" the Father but were unwilling to specify whether he was similar with respect to *ousia*, a position that, for them, entailed a higher God and a lesser God. Prominent among them were Akakios of Kaisareia in Palestine, the successor of Eusebios and a major player in the eastern consensus since 340, and Eudoxios of Antioch, who favored the heterousians. The majority at Seleukeia was willing to endorse the Dedication Creed of 341, but in the end the two sides just deposed each other and sent delegations to the emperor. Constantius sent the delegations back to their respective councils with a new creed, which the assembled bishops of both councils signed. This creed declared that the Son was "similar to" the Father and "*ousia* was not to be discussed in the future, as it is a non-Scriptural term that has caused much confusion."[17] It appeared that the homoians had won. The next year, Eudoxios secured the see of Constantinople for himself and Akakios held a council there, which was also attended by Ulfila of Gothia, a fellow homoian. This council deposed major homoiousians, though on procedural and criminal, not doctrinal, grounds. As Jerome later said, "the whole world groaned, and learned that it was Arian."[18] One year later, it would learn that it was pagan.

Under Constantius, the Church extended more tendrils into communities outside the empire. Ulfila's (homoian) community had been resettled in Moesia in the 340s, but his translation and missionary work aimed at a wider Gothic audience. The Church in Georgia was also organized by priests who came from the empire. Cappadocian Kaisareia retained jurisdiction over the Armenian Church until the 370s. When Constantius learned that Ezana, the ruler of the formidable kingdom of Aksum (in modern Ethiopia), was interested in Christianity but that his informant Frumentius was a missionary with ties to Athanasios, the emperor wrote to Ezana in 356 recalling Frumentius so that his theological views could be tested. Ezana declined to send him back. Constantius is also reported to have sent a bishop-emissary to the south Arabian kingdom of Himyar, in modern Yemen, but it accomplished little.[19] Foreign policy would henceforth increasingly depend on the projection of such soft power into regions of strategic interest and trade routes, and the cultivation of these ties would become a major responsibility of Roman statesmen and patriarchs. Yet many of the aforementioned connections mentioned would soon be lost or backfired.

If not already under Constantine, then under Constantius the emperor emerged as the de facto head of the Church, a position that was neither explained in theory nor effectively contested. The emperor headed the Church in the same way that he headed everything else: his will was obeyed up to the point where it was not, whereupon a sensible emperor had to weigh the likely consequences of mounting opposition. Whereas powerful bishops could convene local councils and depose each other on their own initiative, in practice these acts were only symbolic unless enforced by the emperor. The emperor, by contrast, could exile a bishop with or without a council, or could arrange for a local council to do his bidding. Also, only the emperor could convoke and pay for an "ecumenical" council that aspired to be binding on the entire Church. Such general councils were prepared in advance and closely orchestrated by imperial officers to produce the desired result, but they did not always do so. The Church had made this deal with the throne, and now had to maneuver within state institutions, as one of them.

From time to time, bishops such as Ossius protested against Constantius' interference in Church affairs, quoting Matthew 22:21: "Render under Caesar the things that are Caesar's, and unto God the things that are God's."[20] However, this rhetorical stance lacked credibility, as those same bishops had invited interventions when proffered by friendly emperors and made full use of imperial power against their opponents. No one opposed imperial intervention when it supported the "right" cause. Acts of the Apostles 5:29 did say that "We must obey God rather than man," but Christian Romans were more inclined to heed St. Paul in Romans 13:1–3: "Every soul should submit to the governing authorities. For there is no authority that is not from God." For John Chrysostom, Paul's words applied to priests and monks too, not just laymen.[21]

Pagans in distress

It was not just Christians who had to adapt to a Christian emperor: pagans also had to do this, and they were still the majority of the population. The emperor had for them always been the highest authority in matters of religion, and this did not change just because he was a Christian. After all, by 337 most "pagans" did not even know that they had a common religious identity. But by 361, many had realized that the Christian-imperial establishment was clumping them together into one category and was increasingly restricting their options. Constantine had likely forbidden state officials from engaging in animal sacrifices (the evidence for this is contradictory), but Constantius and Constans outlawed the practice everywhere: "the madness of sacrifices shall be abolished" upon penalty of death and total loss of property.[22] Sacrifice could also be maliciously misconstrued as divination and "magic," which the state had always regarded as potentially treasonous and which the Church now equated with pagan rituals. Looking at the gods in the sky could be interpreted as sinister astrology. But such bans were not easy to enforce, as most officials locally were pagans and sacrifice could easily be dissimulated as other things. Sacrifice continued, although it required "great courage" even for a praetorian prefect in a city as pagan as Athens.[23] Libanios speaks of a friend's uncle who, "despite the law that banned it and the capital risk that it entailed, went through life in the company of the gods and mocked that evil law and its wicked legislator."[24] Defiance of these edicts became a virtue among pagans.

Moreover, in order to fund New Rome, the Church, and the solidus economy, Constantine and Constantius had confiscated temple land endowments and treasuries, which was a persecution in all but name. Without these funds, shrines could not be repaired, priests could not be paid, and festivals could not be put on. Within a generation, the east was full of temple "ruins" and "remains."[25] Beyond mere neglect, a "ground war" against the temples had been declared under Constantius by many bishops, zealous officials, and empowered lay Christians. Temple demolitions and idol smashing accelerated during his reign, "empowered by the authority given to the Christians in the time of the great Constantius."[26] For the bishops it meant loot but it also burnished their credentials for piety in a time of fierce episcopal competition. It is perhaps no accident that the most insecure bishop of the 350s, Georgios, who was imposed on Alexandria when Athanasios was exiled in 356, indulged in an orgy of temple destructions, "cruelly persecuting the Hellenes."[27] This was one way to unify zealous Christians, who might otherwise turn against him.

Christian polemical treatises "Against the Pagans" continued to proliferate, written even by the likes of Athanasios, only this time their authors had the ears of the emperors. The astrologer-turned-Christian Firmicus Maternus spurred on the sons of Constantine to "eradicate and abolish these practices," these "diseases" that ought to be "purged and amputated."[28] By the time Julian gained the throne, pagans had heard the message. Watching the reign of his cousin, Julian had learned two lessons: restoring freedom to *all* the bishops was the best way to sow discord in the Church; and Hellenic religion had to be defended against Christians bent on its annihilation.

Julian's Hellenism

Julian reigned for only eighteen months, not enough time for his major policies to succeed, especially his effort to revive the ancient religions and stop Christianity. We could bypass his reign with little loss in continuity. Yet more literary sources discuss his reign than that of any previous emperor, and more modern books are written about him than any other, save Augustus and Constantine. Julian was a compelling and polarizing figure. He had a knack for turning the conventional formulas of ancient literature into powerful vehicles of self-expression, making him one of few ancient people whose personality we can glimpse. Moreover, his reign had momentous consequences for Orthodox identity, as his career and the hysterical reactions to it served later as a permanent reminder of the tension between Orthodoxy and Hellenism. In fact, later Romans used him to define and police the boundaries of Orthodoxy. Down to 1453 and beyond, they continued to accuse each other of being "new Julians." Therefore Julian's reign was not, as Athanasios predicted, "a small cloud that will soon pass."[29] He became an obsession that lingered, and still does.

Julian was raised in isolation on an imperial farm in Cappadocia. He was taught to be a proper Christian by building shrines to martyrs and studying under tutors such as Georgios, who later became the anti-Athanasian bishop of Alexandria. During his subsequent studies in the cities of Greece and Asia Minor, Julian converted to Hellenism and came to believe that Christianity was both false and contemptible. He dissembled his faith during his years as a Caesar in Gaul and came out only when Constantius died. In a letter to one of his philosopher-friends, he then reported that "we worship the gods openly, and the army with me is pious too. We sacrifice oxen in public . . . . The gods are ordering me to restore purity, and I obey them gladly."[30] Julian was first attracted to Hellenism through Homer, whom he took as a guide for life;[31] and, second, through late Platonism, to which he contributed hymns and treatises that were treasured by later admirers. Christian theology was an offshoot of Middle Platonism, whose universe generally consisted of a high god and some lesser gods, whereas late or Neoplatonism divided the divine world into a baroque multiplicity of levels, rising from visible lower gods to their "intelligible" counterparts, then to a high god and an ineffable principle behind that. Julian here followed the Syrian-Greek philosopher Iamblichos (d. ca. 325), who had elaborated upon the thought of Plotinos (d. ca. 270) by adding elements of arcane ritual to it (called "theurgy"), to which Julian was uncritically attracted.

Julian was repelled by the paranoid-ceremonial imperial style of his uncle and cousin and, in imitation of Marcus Aurelius, sought to revive a conception of the emperor as the first among equals and as a law-abiding servant of the republic and the gods. He greeted friends informally with a kiss, rather than demanding prostration. He walked before the consuls during their inauguration, considered himself a senator, and asked other senators for advice, allowing them to correct him; and he even fined himself when he carelessly usurped the duties of another magistrate.[32] Julian is one of few emperors who we know had friends, and he laughed off reported conspiracies. He dismantled Constantius' networks of informants, and tried and executed Paulus "the Chain." Julian also abandoned the shaven look of the Constantinian dynasty and adopted the image of a philosopher-king with a full beard (see Figure 7).

Julian's behavior was regarded by some as unbecoming the dignity of his office and at odds with the style of contemporary government.[33] But it was likely an expression of his personality rather than policy. He was spontaneous and impulsive, as well as ascetic and frugal, as even his enemies acknowledged. His personality sometimes showed through at inopportune times. When he and his army were in Antioch preparing for the Persian campaign in the winter of 362–363, straining the resources of the city, the Antiochenes openly mocked him for his idiosyncratic and ascetic behavior. Julian responded by publishing a satire of

Figure 7 Solidus of Julian minted at Antioch (362), praising the "Virtue of the Army of the Romans"

himself, the *Beard-Hater*, that was really an invective against them. It is a subtle text, but a lapse in composure.

For all his "republican" political leanings, Julian did not reform the basic structure of Roman government. He kept the same apparatus in place, including the powers of the new monarchy. He wanted the cities to thrive, regarding them as the basis of classical Graeco-Roman civilization and the matrix of its religions, but he did little more to empower them other than to return their civic and temple lands.[34] His effort to restore Hellenism otherwise fit the mold of a Constantinian emperor, by issuing directives on how priests should behave in order to attract worshippers, by allocating resources from the imperial treasury to his preferred cults, and by playing the part of a king appointed by the gods to guide humanity to the correct form of worship and belief.[35]

Many cities and high-profile individuals responded favorably to Julian's restoration of Hellenism, even enthusiastically. Temples were reopened and Christians billed for damages, sometimes none too gently. Julian was frustrated that the project was coming along too slowly in some places, that pagans were demoralized, or that they were not sacrificing with the same frequency and extravagance as he did ("twice a day if possible").[36] Yet his insistence on sacrifice may have been out of touch with the evolution of pagan cult, if scholars are correct that sacrifice had been declining independently of Christian influence.[37] Julian's friend and fellow theologian Saloustios admitted that "animals are now sacrificed only by the rich, though in the past by everyone." Julian became angry when at the temple of Apollo at Daphne, outside Antioch, he was met by an embarrassed priest who had brought only a goose from his house, as the council of the city had made no arrangements.[38] The temple later burned down, infuriating the emperor, but the investigation into the cause was inconclusive.

Julian deprived bishops of their tax immunities, and enrolled them into the city councils if they had sufficient wealth. Funds that had been earmarked for churches were now transferred to temples.[39] Julian was standing the Constantinian revolution on its head, but using the same tools. His strategy, explicitly identified and denounced by many Christian writers, was not to persecute but to convert people to Hellenism through positive incentives such as gifts, honors, promotions, favors, and persuasion. Gregory of Nazianzos, the Christian theologian who led the charge in blackening the memory of "the Apostate" after his death, was furious that Julian attracted Gregory's own brother Kaisareios, a doctor, with "honors and promises." Kaisareios did not convert, but his presence at the court signaled that imperial service remained safe and even lucrative for Christians.[40] The soldiers had no difficulty in automatically accepting the religion of their emperor, especially one so crowned with victories.[41]

Julian made it explicitly clear that he did not want Christians persecuted or molested, a strategy confirmed by Church writers: "he ordered the people not to commit any act of injustice against the Christians, neither to insult them, nor to force them to offer sacrifice," unless they committed acts of violence upon each other, in which case they were to be lawfully prosecuted. Julian knew that the rival Christian sects were furious at being unable to persecute each other or pagans.[42] Christian polemic against Julian, spearheaded by Gregory, had to adopt a subtle logic: Julian was a persecutor because "he deprived our athletes of the crown of martyrdom . . . he forced with gentleness . . . he persecuted through arguments . . . his very humanity was inhuman."[43] But this level of subtlety was hard to sustain, and subsequent tradition packed the Apostate's reign with dozens of invented martyrs to make his persecution seem less "gentle." Historians should take none of this at face value. In Christian texts, "tyrant" and "persecutor" are technical terms for rulers of a different theological persuasion, regardless of their actions. In many contexts, Christians called it a "persecution" when they were merely expected to tolerate the existence of people who disagreed with them.[44]

Julian recalled all bishops exiled by Constantius and restored their property. Both pagan and Christian authors explain that this was a cynical move, to foster division in the Church, and if they could draw that conclusion, so could he.[45] This effectively favored the Nicene side persecuted by Constantius. In Alexandria, a city with a violent temper, the victims of bishop Georgios rioted and lynched him—possibly the only instance of pagans and Nicenes happily working together. This allowed Athanasios to return and reclaim his position. In 362, he held a council in Alexandria that, bucking Nicaea, conceded that *hypostasis* could be used to denote that which distinguished the members of the Trinity, who were of the same *ousia*. But Julian had been receiving complaints about Athanasios, so he too exiled him from Alexandria and, later, from all of Egypt. The emperor wrote in his own hand under one of these edicts that "this wretch had the audacity to baptize Hellenic women of rank during my reign! Drive him out!"[46]

Raised in the Church, Julian knew well the Christian obsession with their Name, and so he consistently called them "Galilaeans," predictably outraging them. He wrote a wide-ranging refutation of Christianity, *Against the Galilaeans*, which was persuasive enough that it was not preserved among his other works and had to be refuted in the early fifth century by Cyril, the patriarch of Alexandria. Julian also sponsored an initiative to rebuild the Jewish Temple in Jerusalem, which was probably meant as a symbolic blow against Christianity rather than an act of solidarity with Jews. The project would refute Jesus' prophecy about the Temple's destruction (Mark 13:1–2) and should, in theory, have enabled the revival of Jewish animal sacrifice, which could take place only at the Temple. There was enthusiasm for the idea among some Jews.[47] But construction had not advanced when Julian was killed in Persia, after which it made no sense for Jews to advertise the event.

Julian's greatest sin was that he made a robust argument for Hellenism as an autonomous and potentially hegemonic culture with its own gods, literature, history, and values that were at odds with Christianity. Julian's very life embodied this argument, which he articulated in his famous "Edict on Christian Teachers." This barred Christians from holding publicly-funded chairs to teach the Greek classics. The edict's actual impact was minimal—Christians could privately teach whatever they wanted, and there were few public chairs anyway. But its core thesis, which linked the gods to Greek literature and ethics, effectively sided with Christian hardliners who were also arguing that the faithful should steer clear of these demon-polluted texts, and it compromised the efforts of learned Christians to appropriate the classics to their own purposes. They continued to do so anyway, of course, but because of Julian they would do so with a bad conscience for the next millennium and beyond. Too much engagement with Hellenism, or the wrong kind, raised the suspicion of "a new Julian," of "the Greeks" slipping their leash.[48]

Reactions to Julian's Hellenism came from many Christian authors, but the two most enduring were written by his contemporaries Basil, bishop of Kaisareia (370–379), and Gregory of Nazianzos, who was briefly bishop of Constantinople in 381. Both of them had studied with Julian in Athens. Basil wrote a brief treatise on how young men should study the pagan classics, delivering the banal message that they should pick out the good stuff and disregard the bad. This sober text was considered a fundamental treatment of the question by later Romans and early modern Europeans. Gregory, by contrast, wrote two raving denunciations of Julian as soon as his target was safely dead, accusing him, among many other crimes, of sacrificing women and children and hiding their bodies in the cisterns of Antioch.[49] These invectives are a stain on Gregory's reputation. Beyond his personal obsession with Julian, Gregory's main concern was to fashion a sanitized Christian Hellenism that decoupled Greek literature from Greek religion. Gregory went on to produce a huge corpus of speeches, poems, and letters that served as a template for Christian classical literature. Just as Lactantius had argued that Christianity perfected the Roman tradition, Gregory argued, against Julian on the one hand and Christian fundamentalists on the other, that Christianity brought Hellenism to perfection. The pagan classics were literature, not religious texts. The imperial court and other Christians were taking a similar view of the statues that adorned their cities: these were art, or objects of historic and symbolic value, not recipients of pagan cult.[50]

Why was Hellenism such a concern? Part of the answer is that some Christians were attracted to the charms of classical literature, thought, and art, which were different from those of emerging Orthodox culture and dealt with many topics, such as political theory, the virtues of warfare, and eroticism, that the Church avoided. But these Christians did not want their tastes to contradict their faith, so they devised methods of interpreting, rationalizing, and containing their Hellenic culture. There was also a class dynamic. Whereas wealth was the basis of social distinction, classical culture was the main vehicle of its expression. Elites did not identify or interact with each other based on their tax receipts, but by quoting Homer to each other and giving speeches in the Attic style. Hellenism permeated every facet of elite life, from the workplace to the drinking party. This lubricant also smoothed relations between imperial power and local civic elites, providing a common idiom from Britain to Egypt.[51]

Upward mobility, such as that of the theologian Aetios, depended in part on acquiring elements of this culture (in Aetios' case, medical theory and Aristotelian philosophy). Moreover, by the mid-fourth century, Christian theology itself was highly dependent on Greek thought, indeed incomprehensible without it. The Church Fathers needed access to it, but also wanted to feel that they were making only instrumental use of it. They labeled it the "outside" wisdom (*thyrathen*), and accused their rivals (such as Aetios) of straying too far into it. Meanwhile, they pretended that they themselves lived "inside" a world defined exclusively by pure Christian concepts. This was, of course, a fiction: the tastes, social standing, and thinking of men such as Gregory of Nazianzos were embedded in the "outside." Thus, Julian was on solid ground when he insisted that the Hellenic tradition stood on its own and was no one's handmaid. Its texts did not belong to the Christian world of sin, guilt, and humility but projected pride in ancient literary, political, and cultural accomplishments, a Siren call for many Christians. The Fathers were trying to obscure this difference in their appropriation of the Hellenic tradition, and Julian blocked them from doing this quietly. He forced jarring differences out into the open. Orthodoxy and Hellenism were in tension forever after, making "Julian" an ever-lurking danger for learned Christians.

Julian's Persian war

Julian also inherited from Constantius a Persian war that was not going well for the Romans. He fantasized about emulating Alexander the Great and bringing home a Persian victory that would legitimate all his other projects. In the winter of 362–363, he assembled the largest army of that century, 65,000 men or more, larger than any army the empire would muster again. The tale of its expedition into Mesopotamia was told by an eyewitness, Ammianus, and his detailed account cannot be surpassed here. Julian advanced down the Euphrates, while Shapur fell back on the defensive strategy that Constantius had previously used against him: avoid decisive battles and let the invader wear himself out in sieges. Julian captured fort after fort and defeated every Persian army until he arrived at Ktesiphon, the capital, before which he held a round of Homeric athletic games.[52] Unable to take the city or to engage with the enemy, Julian had no choice but to burn his Euphrates fleet and advance back up the Tigris, harassed by the enemy. At one point he rushed into battle without his breastplate and was killed by a lance-blow to the side.

Julian had made no formal plans for the succession, so the high command convened to choose a successor. A messy process produced Jovian, a tall Illyrian captain of the imperial guard of the *domestici*, and he was duly acclaimed. To extricate his huge army from its dangerous predicament and secure supplies, Jovian agreed to a thirty-year treaty with Shapur that gave Persia some rights to Armenia (a source of conflict later on); some of the transtigritane provinces that the Romans had gained in 298; and Nisibis and Singara, whose inhabitants had to be relocated as refugees now to Roman territory. Great nobles from the Persian heartland were brought in to take over the homes and lands of departing Romans. Many Roman writers denounced the treaty as a national humiliation, and expressed their outrage at the Persian banner fluttering atop the city's walls.[53] Among them was a resident of Nisibis, the Syriac Christian poet Ephrem, who cursed Julian and gloated as he watched his corpse escorted past the city: "There I saw the hideous sight, the captor's banner that was stuck on the tower; the persecutor's corpse, that was thrown into the coffin . . . . I stood above it and I mocked his paganism."[54]

Jovian was too ashamed to enter the city when he ordered its evacuation. But Shapur's terms were actually restrained, with good reason: the Roman army had bested him so far in every engagement, and he was running low on supplies too.[55] He asked for just enough to satisfy honor but not so much that his gains would be a constant provocation to future aggression. There had in fact been Romans in the past who argued that Nisibis cost too much, brought little benefit, and caused constant war between "us and the Persians."[56] As it turned out, the new borders held until the later sixth century. Paradoxically, Julian's expedition laid the foundations for peace along the eastern frontier, a crucial factor behind the empire's survival during the fifth century.

Jovian was a Christian, and Julian's army miraculously announced that it too had been Christian all along. Jovian terminated state support for paganism, reconfiscated temple lands, and restored the perks that the Church had enjoyed, but otherwise declared himself for religious toleration. The philosopher-senator Themistios articulated this policy on Jovian's behalf in a speech that is among antiquity's best formulations of toleration. "The treaty secures us peace with the Persians, whereas this policy secures us peace with each other," i.e., between "the two religions (*threskiai*)," Christianity and paganism.[57] Pagans had caught on that they were now a religious group with common interests. Conversely, enough high-placed Christians realized that the persecution of pagans under Constantius had gone too far, producing the blowback under Julian, so they refrained from more attacks on the temples for a generation. Thus Julian's failed pagan reaction, like his Persian war, had paradoxically secured peace on this front too. But peace *within* the Church was beyond reach: Jovian began to receive urgent petitions from many Church factions asking him to banish their theological opponents. He refused to do so, especially regarding Athanasios.[58] This was not for theological reasons, but to prevent violence in Alexandria.

Jovian was mocked in Antioch no less than Julian,[59] proving that religion had little to do with that city's disrespectful behavior toward emperors. On his way to Constantinople, Jovian died in Bithynia from toxic fume inhalation, in February 364, after a reign of less than eight months. He was buried in the Holy Apostles. As for Julian, he was first buried near Tarsos. Toward the end of the century, he too was relocated to the imperial mausoleum in Constantinople, where he was eventually joined by none other than Gregory of Nazianzos and, later, Justinian. His porphyry sarcophagus could still be seen there in the twelfth century, and is today probably standing outside the Istanbul Archaeological Museum (it is the one with rounded sides: see Figure 8).[60] The reviled "Apostate" turned out to be an insider after all. He was the first emperor to be born in Constantinople, spoke Greek as his native language, wrote masterful Attic prose, and never visited Rome even though he was devoted to the idea of Rome and the welfare of his subjects, guided by a sure sense of his divine purpose. Julian was perhaps the first "Byzantine" emperor.

Figure 8 Possible porphyry sarcophagus of Julian, Istanbul Archaeological Museum
Photo by David Hendrix

6

Toward an Independent East (364–395)

At Nikaia in February, 364, the army high command chose a Pannonian officer named Valentinian as the next emperor. He was summoned from Ankyra and acclaimed Augustus by the army. Golden crowns sent by the cities for Jovian reached him instead.[1] Valentinian faced pressure to appoint a colleague, so he chose his brother Valens, whom he made emperor in March at the mustering grounds of the Hebdomon ("Seventh Milestone") outside Constantinople. Valens was the first Augustus to be elevated in the City. He held military office, but had little experience.[2] He was known as a mediocrity, was lacking in charisma, and did not speak Greek. His best qualities were loyalty to Valentinian and competence as a manager of the family's estates.[3] Valens was hard-working and did try to improve the administration, especially its fairness and consistency, but, in the end, he failed in one of his goals, to curb official corruption, which led to a disastrous defeat at Adrianople, his death, and the worst crisis that the empire had faced in over a century.

Valens' wars

At Naissus, where they could recruit more Illyrians and Pannonians to their administration, the brothers divided the armies and the empire, with Valentinian taking the west (including Illyricum) and Valens the east (with Thrace),[4] recreating the division of 340–350 AD. The brothers parted at Sirmium, never to meet again. Valens was the junior partner, while Valentinian was the last and only senior Augustus to prefer the west over the east.

The brothers faced an immediate fiscal problem: Julian had lowered taxes, returned civic and temple lands to the cities, and spent a large sum on his Persian war. His campaign army had to be paid and accession donatives distributed to the soldiers. It helped that they reconfiscated the temple lands, but the new emperors also began to put the squeeze on their subjects for back taxes.[5] This made Valens unpopular, and he was the less secure of the two emperors. He quickly faced a serious challenger for the throne, Procopius, a relative of Julian on his mother's side, whose rebellion lasted for eight months between late 365 and mid-366. Procopius was eventually suppressed and later cast as a buffoonish failure,[6] but the course of events refutes this image. Procopius skillfully leveraged soft assets into hard power, and foreshadowed an emerging model of imperial authority based as much on support in Constantinople as on the army.

Lying low after Julian's death, Procopius monitored Valens' unpopularity, in particular the harshness with which the emperor's father-in-law Petronius was collecting debts to the treasury, and the grievances of Julian's friends and officials who had been purged, fined, or exiled.[7] Using money provided by his supporters, and spreading the rumor that Julian had intended him to succeed to the throne, Procopius suborned the officers of two army units that were passing through the City to deal with Gothic raiders. With their backing, he organized rallies in the City, showcasing his cultural credentials and links to the Constantinian dynasty—he used Constantius' widow and daughter as props—with the result that the soldiers and populace acclaimed him Augustus. Through persuasion, forgery, disinformation, and inventive fundraising, Procopius undermined loyalists and suborned more units away from "the degenerate Pannonian."[8] He used these armies to beat Valens to a standstill in Asia Minor, gaining Thrace and Bithynia. Eventually, he was defeated in battle when some of his generals defected, but Procopius' rebellion had shown how a weak regime could be challenged not though overwhelming military force but by skillful political and economic maneuvering.

Valens never forgave the people of Constantinople and thereafter avoided the City, though he supported its ongoing construction, providing it with a cistern and an aqueduct that still bears his name (see Figure 9), and completing the church of the Holy Apostles. It was also under Valens that the praetorian prefect

Figure 9 Aqueduct of Valens
Photo by David Hendrix

of Oriens (probably Domitius Modestus) began to keep his archives in offices that were located under the hippodrome, indicating that the City was still intended as an imperial capital.[9] The emperor learned one lesson from the ordeal of Procopius' revolt, which was to lighten tax collection, indeed to reduce taxes as much as possible. In order to do this and shore up political support, he and Valentinian implemented a remarkable and far-reaching program of combating corruption among state officials, which did increase the "papyruswork" of government by requiring more receipts, lists, formal declarations, and inventories of everything pertaining to state business, "as if it were a single household."[10] The most detailed inventories of taxable personal properties that survive from this period (on inscriptions from various places in the Aegean) likely stem from these reforms. Along with his brother, Valens cracked down on skimming, scams, extortion, fraud, bribery, and abuses. They punished corrupt officials harshly and frequently expressed a deep concern for "the little guy" and the taxpayer. They also returned a portion of the proceeds of civic lands back to the cities for local use, and increased the purity of the coinage.[11] For this they earned both praise and leaner budgets.

When news of Procopius' rebellion reached him, Valens had been heading to the eastern frontier. He changed tack and devoted the next three seasons (367–369) to attacking the Goths north of the Danube, using as his base Marcianopolis by the Black Sea, a city that had been sacked by Goths in the third century. The Goths had sent a contingent to support Procopius, citing their obligations to the dynasty of Constantine. Valens detained these men, the Gothic king Athanaric demanded them back, and this led to war.[12] Valens cut off trade with the Goths, which caused them hardship, but the emperor failed to bring them to battle in 367 or 368. Themistios led a delegation from the Senate of Constantinople to celebrate the emperor's *quinquennalia* (five-year anniversary) and remind him that "a light hand in taxation is a boon shared by all," whereas war drives up costs and distributes its benefits unequally to soldiers and frontier provinces. Wrap it up quickly, he was telling the emperor.[13]

Only in the third year, 369, did Valens manage to bring the Goths to battle and defeat them, though their casualties were light. Athanaric sued for peace, but would not cross the border to arrange terms, so he and Valens met on ships in the middle of the Danube. The treaty tightened up trade, restricting it to two cities. Valens and Valentinian (in the west) were generally curtailing foreign trade and strengthening river patrols and forts. The number of Roman coins in Gothia (the lands of the Goths) after 370 declined accordingly. Emperors could open and close the borders at their discretion; they were not always permeable and fluid, as much recent scholarship has claimed.[14] If the purpose of the war was to punish the Goths for meddling in Roman affairs, it succeeded, but it did not bring the major victory that Valens wanted. Themistios, who was present at the mid stream meeting, sold the peace to the Senate in early 370, arguing that Valens had mercifully "spared" the barbarians.[15]

The Goths had been lucky, not because of Valens' mercy but because they had enjoyed a thirty-year reprieve from Roman aggression since their treaty with Constantine. The Roman idea of defending a border often entailed regular terror campaigns across the Rhine or Danube, with the army marching through foreign territory, slaughtering and plundering indiscriminately, and taking thousands of captives for sale into slavery. Barbarians rarely posed a serious military threat to the empire: "the real trouble [for the Romans] was in finding the enemy, after that it was leisure-work for the army," wrote one retired officer.[16] Defeated barbarians sometimes had to provide manpower, slaves, and grain to the Romans, hampering their own economies.[17] The Romans sometimes raided *barbaricum* just because an emperor wanted a victory to boost his prestige. In terms of policy, emperors tended to break up emerging coalitions that seemed threatening, even by assassinating or kidnapping their leaders, and propped up more pliable chiefs or kings, whom they supported with cash and gifts (though critics of an emperor could denounce this as "tribute" paid shamefully to barbarians). In their domestic propaganda, emperors were desperate to maintain the ideal of "eternal victory" and unconditional Roman domination over barbarians.[18] The image of captive barbarians was broadcast through coins, speeches, imperial monuments, and floats or painted panels paraded through the hippodrome.

It was precisely from this kind of attention that the Goths had been spared for thirty years, while trade with Rome brought profit and economic development, especially within 100 km of the Danube. Despite being called "Scythians" by the Romans, the Goths were mostly agricultural, not nomadic. They had upgraded their military capabilities through the flow of know-how across the border and by serving with the Roman army. Two main Gothic groups appear in the fourth-century sources: the Tervingi (closer to the border) and Greuthungi (beyond the Dniester). Smaller groups had "kings"—*reiks* in Gothic, which lies behind the *-ric* ending of their names in English—and larger coalitions were ruled by a "judge" (Latin *iudex*), such as Athanaric. The makeup of these groups and their alliances fluctuated, while the territories that they ruled contained many other ethnic groups. The Goths themselves had a common language, which we know from the surviving portions of Ulfila's Bible. They must also have had effective systems of internal authority, judging from how they abided by the terms of the treaty with Rome for thirty years and how they could muster armies to fight an emperor to a standstill.

Even so, the war with Valens destabilized Gothic society. In 369–372, Athanaric persecuted Christians living in Gothia, some of them ethnic Goths, resulting in martyrs and refugees. Athanaric likely viewed Christianity as an instrument of Roman influence, probably correctly. Roman missionaries were operating in his lands (independently of Ulfila) and establishing connections with churches in the empire, such as Kaisareia in Cappadocia. But the persecution created tension between Athanaric's men and local (pagan) community leaders.[19] Also, a civil war broke out between Athanaric and Fritigern, probably in the early 370s. Fritigern asked Valens for help, and he sent an army that defeated Athanaric, again. In gratitude, Fritigern "adopted the emperor's religion, bidding his subjects to do the same."[20]

Valens spent the next eight years based in Antioch, focusing on the east. The Persian shah Shapur had begun to assert what he took to be his rights to Armenia and Iberia, dismantling the establishment of Christianity there. After his Gothic war, Valens was able to shift forces to the east and, following a battle won by his generals in 371, he reclaimed Armenia as a Roman client.[21] The emperor could not control the shifting allegiances of the Armenian noble families, but he could summon, execute, and replace an insufficiently obedient Armenian king (Pap) in 375. Shapur was in his seventies and preoccupied with his Central Asian frontier, and the Armenian nobles were both Christian and pragmatic: "We cannot become servants of the heathen Persians or be hostile to the king of the Greeks. Neither can we carry on hostilities with both of them. We cannot maintain ourselves without the support of one of them," explained an Armenian text of the fifth century.[22]

Valens' religious policies

Valentinian and Valens also declared war on magic, astrology, and various forms of the occult.[23] Valens revealed the extent of his insecurity, greed, and rage when a plot was exposed in 372 to divine, through magical means, the name of his successor. This led to a hunt for magic users in Antioch and Asia Minor, which implicated an ever-expanding circle of former officials and philosophers, leading to many executions and confiscations. Most were pagans and some were intellectuals associated with Julian. Emperors had always been hostile to magic, especially when it was used to influence imperial affairs, but religious bias made Valens' paranoia worse. Many Christians saw no difference between nefarious magic and traditional pagan ritual, or between the occult and Neoplatonism. With his penchant for being in the wrong place at the wrong time, the pagan historian Ammianus lived through the terror of this witch-hunt: people scrambled to burn their libraries, he says, lest incriminating texts be found in them. John Chrysostom, another native of Antioch, recalls that he was walking by the Orontes with a friend at that time and they saw a floating book. Picking it up, they realized that it contained a magical text, which caused them to panic because a soldier was nearby.[24] Corruption made these trials worse: the emperor, his officials, and his informants profited from the property of the condemned. The prefect Domitius Modestus presided over the tribunal. He had been a Christian under Constantius, a pagan under Julian, and a Christian again under Valens.

Valens was not interested in persecuting pagans as such. While sacrifice was banned again and temple properties reconfiscated,[25] the brothers otherwise "granted to everyone the free opportunity to worship that which he had conceived in his soul." This policy was praised by pagans and criticized by Christians.[26] We do not hear of Christian assaults on temples, as had begun under Constantius; the pagan blowback under Julian was all too recent, and no one knew who might come to the throne next.

The brothers were also pragmatic in Church politics, siding with the bishops who seemed to be ascendant in their respective territories. Valentinian was thus officially a Nicene, but in practice indifferent. When bishops began to petition him about doctrine at the start of his reign, he said, "I am but a layman and should not meddle in these matters; let the priests, to whom they pertain, assemble wherever they want."[27] For Valens this approach meant supporting the homoians who had emerged as dominant at the end of the reign of Constantius. Valens' chief advisors in Church politics were Euzoïos of Antioch and Eudoxios of Constantinople, who baptized the emperor in 366 (it is a common error that Theodosius I was the first emperor to be baptized before his deathbed). Valens allegedly decreed that bishops who had been exiled by Constantius, but recalled by Julian, were to be re-exiled. This essentially reaffirmed the Council of Constantinople (360), which targeted homoiousians and heterousians. But Valens allowed so many exceptions that the historicity of this decree has been questioned.[28] Athanasios of Alexandria was one of the exceptions. He had been exiled so many times that it was unclear whether the rule applied to him. Facing Procopius' revolt and desiring peace in Alexandria, Valens allowed him to return, and Athanasios kept his see until his death in 373. Theologically, Athanasios had failed to make the case for identifying Father and Son, for he had been unable to explain how they were to be distinguished. But left alone now in old age, he caused no more trouble.

At this time, proponents of Nicaea (even Athanasios) and homoiousians ("similar in nature") began to find common ground, seeing as they were jointly targeted by the homoians ("similar, but not necessarily in nature"). They began to treat homoians and heterousians jointly as "Arians" (though the latter two groups were at war with each other).[29] The emerging leader of the Nicenes in the 370s, Basil, bishop of Kaisareia (370–379), had a background in homoiousian thought. Basil was a highly educated theologian, gifted diplomat, and capable organizer of charitable and monastic institutions in his city, but his efforts to create a Nicene consensus in Asia Minor were hampered by his aristocratic conceit and tendency to manipulate people for his own ends, including his brilliant brother Gregory of Nyssa and friend Gregory of Nazianzos, who resented being his pawns. These three bishops were lated called the "Cappadocian Fathers" and were celebrated for laying down the foundations of Orthodox doctrine. They also produced a corpus of rhetorical and philosophical works that, to later Orthodox readers, rivaled and surpassed those of classical antiquity. Finally, in their own lives they showed how bishops could combine elite education, asceticism (in their early career), philanthropy, and zeal for Orthodoxy.

Despite his later canonization, Basil was not central to the politics of the 370s, nor was he successful at countering Valens' ecclesiastical policy. Specifically, he tried but failed to create a Nicene axis among Rome, Alexandria, Kaisareia, and Antioch. He failed because Antioch was violently split among two rival Nicene bishops (one of them a former homoian) and one homoian—to say nothing of other minor sects that had their own hierarchies. Athanasios of Alexandria and Damasus of Rome favored the other Nicene bishop, not Basil's choice, and so they did not warm to his advances. Damasus, who had literally walked over dead bodies to mount the papal throne, suspected Basil of heresy. For his part, Basil accused Damasus (behind his back) of "arrogance": he "neither knew the truth nor cared to learn it."[30] Thus, the Nicenes were fatally split. Theologically, Basil had made some progress toward describing how the three members of the Trinity could be distinct while sharing the same indivisible substance, but mere description is not proof. Ultimately, for Basil too it remained a "mystery" how One was also Three. Theologians in the rival camps were just as brilliant, but their works were later destroyed and so we do not know their arguments.

Basil was also careful not to criticize the emperor, and was even co-opted by him. When Valens stopped at Kaisareia in 372, he attended church, brought gifts (which were accepted), and took communion from Basil. Gregory of Nazianzos later tried to write this up as a moral victory for Basil, but there was no getting around what actually happened: a homoian emperor recognized the homoousian Basil as the legitimate bishop of the city and, in turn Basil accepted Valens as a Christian in good standing. Valens even placed Basil in charge of the ecclesiastical organization of Armenia Minor—the western part of Armenia that was under Roman control—thus effectively making him a part of the regime.[31] Formidable though Basil was, he was no threat to Valens and no match for him. Both leaders were flexible in their lifetimes, and were only later recast as tyrant and saint.

Valens was denounced as a cruel persecutor, but that was just Christian code for "emperors with different beliefs than ours." The evidence for persecution is limited and untrustworthy.[32] There was violence in Alexandria again when Athanasios died and Valens sent a pagan general to install the homoian Loukios in 373, ejecting Athanasios' designated successor, Petros. True to his master's form, Petros fled to Rome to stir up trouble.[33] By and large, Valens managed to keep the peace under an homoian hegemony in the Church. It was periodically necessary for him to expel dissident bishops, because they formed rival communities within individual cities and caused civil strife, and even the followers of exiled bishops would still meet and keep the flame alive. There were also smaller groups surviving from the earlier days of the Church. Cyril of Jerusalem (d. 386) had to warn his congregation to ask "Where is the local *Catholic* church?" when traveling, and not "Where is the church?" because Marcionites, Manichees, and others also called their places of worship churches.[34] Ephrem the Syrian (d. 373) complained that in the Roman east there were countless groups (including Marcionites) who called themselves Christians and, frustratingly for him, "call us Palutians."[35] The Name was always paramount. A Melitian (schismatic) Church in Egypt also survived for centuries after Nicaea.

The very idea that there was only one Church was beginning to fray, even among the major players. Aetios and Eunomios, the leaders of the heterousians ("dissimilar nature") failed to win over the imperial Church through theological debate and were persecuted by the homoians. In the 360s they set about creating a separatist Church with its own bishops, which survived to the sixth century.[36] In sum, the homoian hegemony was a thin membrane stretched over a seething mass of factionalism and animosity—and most Romans were still not even nominally Christian.

The gap between ideal and reality in Christianity had never been wider. In attacking pagans, Christian advocates such as John Chrysostom liked to say that Greek doctrines were false because they were based on merely human disputations, doubts, and disagreements, whereas the Christian truth was based on the infallible Word of God.[37] But whose version of it? In a different context, he admitted to his congregation:

> What might we say to the pagans? Suppose that a pagan comes and says, "I want to become a Christian, but I don't know whom to join, for there is much fighting among you, dissension, and turmoil. Which doctrine shall I choose?" Each person says, "I have the truth on my side."[38]

A pagan uninterested in converting might see things differently. With some irony, Themistios told Valens that God would be more glorified and pleased by this diversity of opinion, as it reflected the difficulty of understanding his nature.[39] But God was not pleased, and was about to show it.

The Gothic war

By early 376, Valens had reason to believe that he was the most successful emperor since Constantine. He had asserted himself against the Goths and Persians (at least in Armenia), and the Church was moderately peaceful under homoian rule. Valentinian had died suddenly in 375—while yelling at some barbarian envoys—and was succeeded by his young son Gratian. This now made Valens the senior Augustus. Raids in the mid-370s by Isaurians in central Asia Minor and by Saracens under their queen Mavia in Palestine were repulsed and settled; the latter agreed to supply auxiliary units and accepted a bishop, binding them softly to the imperial core.[40] In 377, Valens went so far as to recall all exiled bishops and released their partisans (many of them monks) from confinement.[41] A bounty of affordable soldiers also appeared suddenly on the empire's doorstep in early 376 in the form of Gothic refugees. The Goths had been attacked by a Central Asian people, the Huns, who were hitherto unknown to the Romans. The Huns practiced terrifying forms of cavalry warfare and devastated the northern Goths (the Greuthungi), whose leader Ermenric would be celebrated in Germanic legend as a fallen hero. The leaders of the Tervingi, including Valens' client king Fritigern, frantically begged for permission to settle in the empire, receiving land in exchange for service. Valens agreed with alacrity.

Valens had been trying to commute military recruitment to cash payments (*adaeratio*). Instead of providing the state with flesh-and-blood recruits, taxpayers could, in proportion to their census assessment, pay cash instead; and he canceled the senatorial exemption from this responsibility.[42] This gave Valens the flexibility to use the cash for non-military purposes. The arrival of the Goths fit right into this policy. They were desperate and so cheap recruits, and it also meant that "the treasury would reap a huge amount of gold each year from the taxes paid by the provinces in place of delivering soldiers."[43] From a managerial standpoint this made sense, but its disastrous consequences would set off a debate over whether defense was merely a managerial issue: shouldn't Romans defend their country themselves rather than outsource the task to foreigners?[44]

Tens of thousands of Goths—warriors, women, and children—were ferried across the river, disarmed, and distributed throughout Thrace. This was standard practice for imperial resettlements, albeit on a larger scale. It could go wrong, as for example with Constantius and the Limigantes in 359. This time, it went catastrophically wrong. The fault lay with officers who began to abuse, exploit, and enslave the vulnerable Goths, feeding them dogs or starving them in exchange for slaves or sex. Valens may have cracked down on his officials' abuse of Roman citizens, but he had not extended such protection to his barbarian guests. More importantly, the provisions prepared for the Goths, or at least those passed on to them by the generals, were inadequate. The figure reported by one source for the total number of Goths who crossed the Danube, 200,000, has found modern defenders and would explain the logistical failure. The Goths, seething already, were set off when the general Lupicinus tried to murder Fritigern after luring him to a banquet, a classic stratagem of Roman assassination.[45] They rebelled and began to plunder the rich districts of Thrace, skirmishing with Roman forces. They were joined by Greuthungi from across the Danube, by Goths who had been previously admitted to the empire but who now rebelled, and by fugitive slaves. In 377, Valens received reports at Antioch describing how his forces in the region, supported by units sent by his nephew Gratian in the west, engaged with scattered bands of marauders but failed to destroy them. The Goths' inability to mount sieges mitigated the damage they were causing, but the disruption was real. Basil of Kaisareia was reluctant to send a letter to a contact in the Balkans lest he be responsible for the courier's death.[46]

In 378, Valens marched to the Balkans from the east, and Gratian planned to join forces with him there. Valens was suddenly under a lot of political pressure: the people in Constantinople mocked him during the games and asked for weapons to defend themselves against the barbarians, if he could not do the job.[47] Gratian was delayed by an Alamanni invasion, which he took longer to wrap up than was necessary, though he did then march to Sirmium. Valens debated with his generals whether to press on or wait for Gratian—the two rulers were apparently not on good terms. In the end he decided to engage with Fritigern's forces using only the eastern field army, which was cobbled together from disparate elements. This was a fateful decision, among the most second-guessed in scholarship. On 9 August, a march of eight miles brought the Romans to the enemy wagon circle. Our only contemporaneous account of the ensuing battle, which was an unmitigated disaster for the Romans, was written by Ammianus. For once he was not present, which makes his report more rhetorical than circumstantial, but at least this meant that he lived to write it. Most of the imperial army was cut down when the Roman cavalry was dispersed and the infantry surrounded. The size of the loss is hard to estimate. If the emperor was leading a force of 30,000 (about one and a half field armies), and two-thirds of it was lost as Ammianus says, then 20,000 Romans died.[48] A large part of the eastern officer class was among them. Widows in Constantinople never learned how their husbands fell.[49] The defeat was instantly understood across the empire as a major disaster. Themistios again found the right image: "Whole armies vanished like shadows."[50]

The emperor was killed in the carnage and his body never recovered. In the course of an afternoon, the eastern Romans lost their field army, their emperor, and the hinterland of their capital. For the first time since the crisis of the third century, a foreign people had overrun an imperial province and there was no army to resist them. The Goths were now ranging freely across the Balkans, "dancing rather than fighting, such contempt did they have for our men."[51] Yet Rome had a tradition of recovering after major defeats, and "one of the kings of the Goths remarked on the audacity of our men, who, while they were easier to kill off than sheep, were still expecting to win."[52] The weakness of the Goths was their inability to conduct sieges, which insulated cities and forts against them, but exposed their inhabitants to starvation.[53]

It was now up to Gratian, the twenty-year-old western emperor, to stabilize the situation, but his own position had been unstable since the death of his father, Valentinian I, in 375. That year, a coterie of generals acting on their own authority had proclaimed Gratian's half-brother, the child Valentinian II, as junior emperor. Intrigues that we cannot penetrate had led to the execution of the capable Spanish general Theodosius in 375/6; both the reasons and the perpetrators remain unknown. Yet by late 378, Theodosius' faction was again powerful enough at the court that Gratian sent the general's son, a thirty-one-year-old officer also named Theodosius, to fight the Goths. At Sirmium on 19 January, 379, Gratian made Theodosius his eastern co-emperor. Much of the eastern army command had been destroyed at Adrianople, allowing a Spaniard to ascend to the eastern throne and breaking the otherwise steady sequence of Illyrians and Thracians. Theodosius was praised for attaining the throne without bribing the army, murdering anyone, or inheriting it dynastically.[54]

In addition to the east, Theodosius was given the prefecture of Illyricum for the duration of the Gothic war. Had Valens controlled Illyricum and its armies to begin with, he might have dealt with the Goths more successfully. In the long run, it would be understood that Thrace and eastern Illyricum were best defended when they were joined together, not when they were split between the two empires. The new emperor, lacking eastern connections, made Thessalonike his headquarters, and most of his top officials were initially westerners. He presented himself as a descendant of the "optimal" emperor Trajan (98–117), also a general from Spain who fought Balkan wars.[55] Theodosius himself remains an opaque figure. He was a staunch Nicene and willing to impose his views on others, but not if it would prove disruptive. In person he was mild, affable, approachable,[56] deliberative, and mediocre, elevating himself not through his qualities but the trappings of office, such as speeches, images, and monuments in Constantinople (see Figure 10). Yet he could move decisively against rivals when necessary. He was a poor general and so relied on subordinates. He was more interested in the west than the east, and barely set foot in Asia Minor. His reign marked several turning points in the empire's history.

As Theodosius was beginning operations, a general appointed to Oriens by Valens, Julius, set a drastic precedent. When the Goths had first been admitted, they surrendered many of their youths to be dispersed in the east as both hostages and soldiers-in-training. After Adrianople, in late 378 or early 379, they rebelled and began to plunder northern Asia Minor, killing locals. Julius was reluctant to approach Theodosius, so he consulted the Senate of Constantinople, which authorized him to do whatever he deemed necessary. Julius sent secret orders to the Roman officers in charge of these Goths that, on the same day in the various cities, they were to assemble them on the pretext of paying them and then kill them. This slaughter was carried out efficiently, by archers overlooking the muster grounds. Ammianus, channeling Roman patriotism, called this "a beneficial deed that saved the east."[57] He ends his history with this very episode, a grim recommendation to his readers. Indeed, in the century to come, eastern Romans would often resort to massacres, pogroms, and ethnic cleansing to destroy barbarians who, they feared, were encroaching on Roman sovereignty. These actions would be taken less by

Figure 10 Silver missorium of Theodosius, a gift to one of his supporters in Spain (Real Academia de la Historia, Madrid). It depicts the imperial court above images of plenty. The dish weighs over 15 kg and is about 75 cm in diameter.
Shutterstock/WH_Pics

the emperors than by the people, and the role played by the Senate in this episode foreshadows the ascendancy to come of the political authorities of Constantinople.

One of Theodosius' priorities was to drum up recruitment, as Adrianople had made enlistment unattractive. Some people even cut off their own thumbs to avoid service.[58] He enlisted barbarian recruits into regular Roman units, but prudently sent some to serve in distant provinces while transferring the soldiers there to his army in Thrace. A unit of such barbarians crossed paths in Lydia with some Roman soldiers from Egypt heading to the emperor. When the barbarians used force on local merchants, the Egyptians called them out, saying that "this was no way to behave for men who wished to live under Roman law." The two groups came to blows and 200 barbarians were killed.[59]

Unfortunately, the Gothic War fought in Illyricum and Thrace during 379–382 is the most important Roman war that we know almost nothing about. In 379 or 380, Theodosius suffered a serious defeat and removed himself from the battlefield, calling on Gratian for aid, which was sent under the generals Bauto and Arbogast in 380/1.[60] Those two prosecuted the war, and Arbogast would later become Theodosius' man in the west.

The Council of Constantinople

While the war was raging, Theodosius removed himself from it and pivoted to religion, seeking a victory in another field. In February 380, he sent a law from Thessalonike to the people of Constantinople stipulating that "all peoples (*cunctos populos*)" under his rule were to adhere to the religion of bishops Damasus of Rome and Petros of Alexandria (the irregularly appointed successor of Athanasios). Only they were to be called Catholic Christians. No others had the right to call their meeting places "churches." They were "demented and insane" and were to be punished in ways that Theodosius promised to specify later. This was not just about The Name, as entities that were no longer recognized as churches ceased to enjoy the status, perks, and privileges that imperial law had reserved for them. The edict's proximate goal was to prepare for the emperor's move to Constantinople, and it appears to have had little impact outside the capital, at first. As late as ca. 390, Libanios did not think that Theodosius had ordered anything regarding the religion of his subjects, but he was being disingenuous for rhetorical purposes.[61] We should not underestimate the radical significance of the edict of Thessalonike: it inaugurated a systematic effort to impose Nicene Orthodoxy on the empire, a program that Theodosius and his dynasty enforced and intensified over the ensuing decades. The law was accordingly placed by Justinian at the start of his own legal code, 150 years later.[62] It had been preceded by a decree stripping heretics of rights, including the name "Christians."[63] The religion and correct doctrine of the empire was henceforth to be decided directly by the state. It left no doubt that the emperor was the head of the Church, and he took it as his responsibility to define the religious affiliation of "all his people."

While at Thessalonike, Theodosius fell ill and was baptized by the Nicene bishop, Acholios. He moved to Constantinople in November 380, entering the City in a triumphal parade (such celebrations no longer presupposed that a victory had actually been won). In January 381, the court orator Themistios delivered a speech stressing the new emperor's civic virtues, for Theodosius wanted to draw attention away from the war, which had gone badly for him.[64] He now sought to organize a Church Council, to be attended only by bishops who agreed with his theology and who would produce a homoousian creed. But homoousians were a minority in the east, especially in the City, whose bishop Demophilos belonged to the homoian consensus that had been dominant since 360. The homoousians had no church and were meeting in a converted house, listening to the seminal theological orations of Gregory of Nazianzos. He had been invited the year before, from his retreat at the shrine of Thekla in Isauria, to rally the tiny community and attack the doctrines of Eunomios. Applying the edict of Thessalonike, the emperor marched from the palace to the church of the Holy Apostles and took it over under armed guard and against the protests of part of the populace. He took Gregory with him, who later recalled that "there was much anger against us . . . it was like a city taken by force and occupied."[65]

The Council of Constantinople (May 381) was attended by around 150 bishops preselected by the emperor to support his position.[66] Unfortunately, our knowledge of its politics depends largely on the self-serving and bitter accounts written later by Gregory, who was confirmed as bishop of Constantinople at the start of the Council. To simplify a great deal of infighting, the Council began under the leadership of Meletios of Antioch, but he died suddenly as it was in progress. The need to find a new bishop for Antioch, given the contentious split among the Nicenes there, posed a delicate problem, and Gregory made a mess of it. He also came under fire from the western and Egyptian bishops, who argued that he, as the bishop of Sasima, a small town in Asia Minor that he had scarcely ever visited, had been uncanonically appointed to Constantinople. The Council of Nicaea forbade episcopal transfers, a provision that had been widely ignored in the east. Hoping for imperial support, Gregory petulantly offered his resignation, which the emperor quickly accepted, relieved to be rid of such a high-maintenance and undiplomatic bishop for his capital. Gregory could not conceal the low opinion that he had of bishops generally and of the populace of the City.[67] Theodosius replaced him with the suave senator Nektarios (381–397), a married and unbaptized but popular layman; he was preferred by the emperor and the people of Constantinople, who were emerging as a powerful force in City politics.[68]

The Creed produced by the Council basically reaffirmed that of Nicaea but modified it on many points, for example by adding a reference to the Holy Spirit, albeit without specifying that it too was consubstantial with the Father and Son.[69] What is today called the Creed of Nicaea is actually the Creed of Constantinople. In its canons, the Council also condemned the heretics anew, forbade bishops from meddling in ecclesiastical affairs outside their jurisdiction, tied their jurisdiction to imperial provinces, and gave to the see of New Rome the highest rank in the Church after that of Rome. This canon is the reason why the Council of 381 was scorned by Rome and not disseminated in the west. Antioch and Alexandria would have protested more but for the fact that their bishops died during the Council and were replaced by it and Theodosius. They were not, then, in a position to protest. Theodosius now had the legal standing to issue edicts requiring that all bishops conform to this Creed through certificates of compliance, otherwise they would be deposed. At the same time, he began to impose legal restrictions and penalties on all who adhered to heretical groups (for the emperor, all heretics were lay, since legally they were not recognized as clergy).

Theodosius did not persecute dissenters systematically, and preferred to use persuasion to bring them over to his point of view.[70] He offered heretical bishops the option of switching to his beliefs in order to keep their sees, which means that he did not regard them as agents of Satan. Still, the irrevocable process of creating the Nicene Orthodox Church had begun. In 388, Theodosius banned public debates of religion.[71]

Constantius and Valens had successfully fostered and entrenched an imperial Church in the east defined by a theological consensus that was on the subordinationist side of Nicaea, while the western empire was mostly Nicene. Had Valens not perished at Adrianople, the ecclesiastical schism between the western and eastern Churches might have occurred now, far earlier than it did eventually.[72] But how did Theodosius manage to overturn this eastern consensus and impose Nicaea, a minority view? His success was, of course, partial and slow. Heretical groups, such as the splinter Church established by Eunomios, continued to exist until the sixth century. Constantinople and other major cities had many bishops simultaneously, each of a different sect. But the trajectory of the smaller groups was one of decline. Theodosius had succeeded by approaching the problem in a new way. Constantius and Valens had removed specific dissident bishops who refused to sign their creeds, but they had not issued a general law stipulating what doctrine they expected their subjects to believe. Theodosius methodically put in place a legal framework that disqualified *all* dissenting bishops and priests. The edict of Thessalonike was not enforced on everyone all at once, nor did it stipulate penalties. But the state withdrew legal and fiscal recognition of their communities as "churches," and over time they were expelled from urban cathedrals by local authorities implementing imperial directives. It became a criminal offense to ordain clergy outside of the framework of the imperial Church.

Moreover, the homoian consensus had been in place since 360, only twenty years before it was dismantled. Subordinationists had split into three factions, the homoiousians, homoians, and heterousians, the first of whom were willing to talk to the homoousians and the other two were fighting each other when the death of Valens delegitimized the homoians. Gregory of Nazianzos lost no time in blaming the Gothic disaster on Valens' theology.[73] Finally, the Theodosian solution had the advantage of not being overturned by later emperors, as his dynasty endured and gradually increased the pressure on all heretics. By the early fifth century, the faith of the westerner Theodosius became the new eastern Orthodoxy. For a second time after Constantine, a western version of imperial Christianity was imposed on the eastern Church.

The Gothic settlement

Theodosius did not contribute to the Gothic war. By late 381 or early 382, Gratian's generals had stabilized Illyricum enough that it was transferred to western control, while the Goths were restricted to Thrace.[74] In October 382, Theodosius agreed to a truce with them that would have momentous consequences, especially for the western empire, which eventually succumbed to them. The Goths technically surrendered but had not been decisively defeated, so they were given generous terms. For the first time in the history of the empire a barbarian group was allowed to settle as a quasi-autonomous community under its own leaders and laws. They were allotted land, though we do not know exactly where it was, or the names of their kings who survived the war, or whether they paid taxes.[75] They did not become Roman citizens and were not allowed to marry Romans. The Gothic general Fravitta, who took up service in the imperial army, needed special permission to marry a Roman woman.[76] According to the agreement, the Goths had to provide auxiliary units, under their own command, to the imperial army. But individual Goths could still enroll in the regular army and thereby were assimilated over time. At least, with Goths to draw upon, the burden of levies was lifted from provincial landowners.[77]

The peace of 382 was unpopular, as Theodosius had promised victory and delivered an accommodation. The task of selling it to the Senate of Constantinople fell to Themistios, who delivered a formal speech on 1 January, 383. In previous speeches he had predicted that the emperor would wipe out the Goths or push them, "the hounds of Hell, across the Danube," but now he had to walk that back. He stressed the blessings of peace, the wisdom of "persuading" and "forgiving" the Goths, and the benefits they would provide as farmers and soldiers.[78] Yet events would show that public opinion did not see this as wise, and things got ugly. The people of Constantinople lynched a prominent Gothic soldier and threw his body into the sea, with minimal repercussions.[79] The garrison commander at Tomis (on the Black Sea coast) in the mid-380s suspected a plot and preemptively slaughtered some of the Goths who were stationed there, enraging the emperor. A large force of Greuthungi tried to cross the Danube in 386, whereupon the general Promotus lured them into a trap and slaughtered them; the survivors were settled as captive-soldiers in Phrygia. This time Theodosius celebrated a triumph.[80]

Domestic troubles and civil wars

Soon after Themistios' speech, Theodosius elevated his four-year-old son Arcadius to the status of Augustus at the Hebdomon mustering grounds outside Constantinople, apparently without seeking Gratian's agreement. Whatever tension this might have caused was preempted by the rebellion of the western general Magnus Maximus, another Spaniard, which, in a replay of the events of 350, resulted in Gratian's murder. Maximus also sought recognition from Valentinian II (in Milan) and Theodosius. Valentinian said no whereas Theodosius waited until 384, at which point he assented. Maximus' portraits were taken to Alexandria by Theodosius' new praetorian prefect of

Oriens, Maternus Cynegius (384–388), a Spaniard and aggressive Christian. Cynegius liked to tour the provinces, but instead of admiring the marvels of ancient art and architecture, he incited violence against pagan temples, statues, and, if they got in the way, their worshippers too.[81] These urges had lain dormant for a generation, since the end of the reign of Constantius, but were now stirred up by zealous bishops, fanatical monks who feared "demons," and local Christian communities, especially in Syria.

Markellos, bishop of Apameia, distinguished himself in this campaign and sought to destroy all the temples in his district. But pagans could fight back. Even with a thousand soldiers on loan from the prefect, Markellos was unable to bring down the temple of Zeus, which was too solidly built; the bishop had to bring in demolition experts. When he later attacked another temple "with soldiers and gladiators," its pagan defenders outflanked him, captured him, and burned him alive. The local authorities decided not to prosecute, piously declaring that he was fortunate to obtain the crown of martyrdom. Incidents like these led the court in 399 to decree that temple demolitions should be carried out "without commotion or disturbance."[82] In response to this violence, Libanios wrote one of his most famous speeches, an impassioned plea to Theodosius to curb the terrorism waged by religious fanatics against pagans and their temples.[83] Theodosius turned a blind eye to these abuses. But by the late 380s he had bigger problems to worry about and did not want pagans, still the majority of his subjects, to be so disaffected. When Cynegius died in 388, he replaced him with the cultivated pagan Tatianus, an experienced official and author of a Homeric poem that had already gone through three editions. He also appointed Tatianus' son Proculus (Proklos), also a pagan, as prefect of Constantinople.[84]

The troubles were in the west and portended another civil war. In 387, Maximus invaded Italy, and the hapless Valentinian II and his court fled to Thessalonike. After consulting the Senate,[85] Theodosius decided to support Valentinian against Maximus. As his first wife, Aelia Flaccilla, had just died, Theodosius married Valentinian's sister Galla. At just this time, Theodosius had concluded negotiations with his Persian counterpart, Shapur III: the two monarchs, both of them distracted by domestic troubles, partitioned Armenia, "splitting it into two parts like a worn-out garment," as a later Armenian source put it. Rome received the smaller portion. When its king Arsak died soon thereafter, he was replaced with a Roman-appointed *comes Armeniae* stationed at Karin.[86] This enabled Theodosius to turn his attention to Maximus. In 388, in a replay of the war between Constantius and Magnentius, Theodosius marched across the Balkans, taking his Goths with him. A speech delivered after his victory praised him for removing this "suspicious" force from a sensitive frontier region and making them into a proper Roman army. Still, in Macedonia he discovered that some of the "barbarians" in his army had been suborned by Maximus, and he had most of them executed. He defeated Maximus in Pannonia, beheaded him, and rescinded his laws.[87] Theodosius now ruled the entire Roman empire and would stay in Italy for three years (388–391), courting the Roman aristocracy. Valentinian was sent to Gaul, to reign under the watch of the general Arbogast.

Those years were marked by urban unrest in the east. In 387, the people of Antioch rose up against new taxes for a military donative. They pulled down and vandalized the statues of the imperial family, an act of treason, and set fire to some imperial buildings. Antiochenes were quick to protest and mock, but were used to abusing their emperors in person. Theodosius was the first in over a century who had not come to their city. The army suppressed the demonstrators, executing some. Theodosius imposed sanctions on the city, closing the baths, hippodrome, and theaters, and stripping Antioch of its municipal status. He dispatched judges to arrest the councilors, pending a verdict about their fate. All forces of persuasion were brought to bear on the authorities to issue a pardon, including speeches by the city orator, Libanios, an embassy to the court by the bishop Flavianos, and pleas by monks who came in from nearby hermitages. They argued that the insurrection had been caused by outside agitators or "the Devil," who hated Antioch because that was where Christians first received their name. Theodosius relented. This disturbance generated many texts, as all sides claimed credit for its resolution.[88]

In 388, the anti-Nicenes in Constantinople, who were still a majority, spread a rumor that Theodosius had been defeated by Maximus and they burned down the house of the bishop Nektarios.[89] A report also reached the emperor in Milan that the Christians and the bishop of Kallinikos, a frontier town on the Euphrates, had destroyed the local synagogue. He ordered that those responsible be punished and that the bishop rebuild the synagogue. At this point, however, the grandstanding bishop of Milan, Ambrose, objected that a Christian emperor could not force Christians to, in effect, support Judaism; moreover, if the bishop refused to comply, Theodosius would effectively have to martyr him. On the basis of this hypothetical threat, to which Christian emperors had not yet found a response, Theodosius lifted the fine. Ambrose then pleaded after a church service that the other Christians be spared too, which Theodosius granted, albeit reluctantly, for Ambrose's argument in effect sanctioned lawless violence against other religions, a position that no emperor at this time could afford to espouse.[90]

By contrast, when Christian agitators in the Persian empire, at roughly the same time, destroyed Zoroastrian fire temples, they were both required to make restitution and executed if they refused to comply on "principled" grounds. Their communities honored them as martyrs, but clearly received the message to refrain from such holy zeal.[91]

The next incident of urban violence in the Roman east took place in 390 and threw both Theodosius and Ambrose into a far more complicated tangle of public relations. The people of Thessalonike rose up and killed the local general, Butheric, when he arrested a popular charioteer for a homosexual advance. Somehow this resulted in an imperial army massacring many thousands of people in the city, an overreaction that stunned the Roman world. Surviving accounts of this atrocity all adopt a moralizing tone and assume that Theodosius ordered the massacre out of "anger," for which he was then bravely censured by Ambrose, who, in a dramatic confrontation, refused to admit him to church. Theodosius had to express remorse and humble himself before the bishop and congregation in order to be readmitted and restored in the eyes of contemporaries; in fact, he came out looking better than before, not least because he had allegedly acknowledged the authority of the clergy in matters of conscience. This tale, however, was a public relations stunt organized by the court with Ambrose's cooperation. In reality, the massacre resulted from a breakdown in the chain of command, and the army may have included more Goths than usual. Rather than admit that he did not control his army—an invitation to be overthrown—Theodosius cleverly converted his incompetence into a morality tale of murderous wrath expiated through rituals that were stage-managed by a bishop eager to be cast in the leading role.[92] The reign of Theodosius was carefully scripted.

Theodosius returned to Constantinople in 391, but his long absence had exacerbated local problems. In Macedonia-Thrace he faced armed resistance by Goths that he eventually suppressed or at least diffused. Among the rebel Goths was the young warrior Alaric, who would change the course of Roman history,[93] though at the moment he was a minor Gothic leader. Soon after the emperor's return, another deadly drama unfolded in Alexandria. In the tradition of that city, its new bishop Theophilos was a dynamic and formidable prelate, called by some the Pharaoh of Alexandria. When he staged a public parade to mock some pagan ritual objects that he found in a former temple, some pagans rose up, killed some bystanders, and took others hostage, and barricaded themselves in the temple of Serapis. This ancient building dominated the city's skyline and contained the empire's largest library, a survivor of the library of the Ptolemies, said to contain over 700,000 books. The imperial prefect of Egypt Euagrius referred the matter to the court, and the reply came back, probably tempered by the pagan prefect Tatianus, that he should grant an amnesty to the pagans—their victims had to be content with earning the title of martyrs—but the temples and idols had to be surrendered. The pagan militants left the Serapeion and the Christians tore it down along with other temples, a victory for them that was widely reported (see Figure 11). Christians fantasized that this wave of temple destruction would radiate out of Alexandria "to every city, fort, village, country district, riverbank, and even the desert." One of the pagans who made it out of the siege was the grammarian Helladios. He moved to Constantinople and boasted to his pupils that he had slain nine men in the fight.[94] Theodosius' default response, at any rate, was yet again to issue pardons and let things quiet down.

Figure 11 Bishop Theophilos of Alexandria standing in triumph over the Serapeion with a Bible in hand (Golenischev Papyrus fragment of the Alexandrian World Chronicle, a Greek text)
Public Domain

The Constantinople to which Theodosius returned in 391 was a notably grander city than the one he had first seen in 380, transformed in the meantime by architects and artists working under the direction of his pagan prefects. On the spine of the hippodrome, the prefect Proculus erected an Egyptian obelisk, with the side featuring Tuthmosis III's cartouche facing the imperial box. It stood upon a huge marble cube, each side of which featured a scene of a majestic Theodosius in his imperial box, presiding over the games and surrounded by his guardsmen, magistrates, and people. Thus, the real Theodosius in his box could look out upon an image of Theodosius in his box—an imperial mirror in marble. The far side of the base, visible to the fans in the opposite stands, featured kneeling Persians and Germans bringing gifts to the emperor. Along the Mese, just beyond the forum of Constantine, a tall tetrapylon was erected with a pyramidal roof featuring images of the winds. It supported a bronze weathervane in the form of a winged woman, which was later called the Anemodoulion, "Servant of

Figure 12 Forum of Theodosius I: the fingers of the giant hand clasping the top of the (broken) column-club can be seen
Photo by Anthony Kaldellis

the Winds."[95] Along with the Milion and its clock, this made Constantinople a symbolic metronome and center of the Roman and natural world.

Farther along the Mese was the new forum of Theodosius, designed to evoke that of his "ancestor" Trajan in Rome. It featured a long basilica along the southern side, a fountain, and a colossal equestrian statue of Theodosius striding upon a marble base that represented the entire world; an inscribed epigram praised him as "the rising sun of the east." The forum's centerpiece was a marble column with a spiral relief depicting the victory over Maximus, only fragments of which survive today. The entrances to the forum were arches with peculiar columns in the form of huge tree trunks grasped at the top by massive hands (see Figure 12). These figurative "columns of Herakles" alluded to Theodosius' homeland, Spain, symbolizing his rule over the entire empire, from the straits of the Bosporos to Gibraltar. A statue of Arcadius stood upon the eastern arch and a statue of Honorius, Theodosius' second son, upon the western one, prefiguring his intended division of the empire. Finally, outside the walls, upon the road to the Hebdomon Theodosius placed a massive freestanding arch to be used in triumphal processions, surmounted by a colossal statue of Theodosius in a chariot drawn by four elephants. This self-styled "Golden Gate" was incorporated into the land walls built by his grandson twenty years later. Perhaps the City's expansion was being foreseen already.[96] A new Theodosian harbor was built along the City's south coast, with granaries to feed the growing population.

With these monuments, built in strategic locations, Theodosius was likely trying to overshadow Constantine as a new founder of the City. It is possible that he abolished the procession of Constantine's statue on 11 May, the anniversary of the City's foundation. His architectural aesthetic, like that of Constantine, was entirely pagan-imperial, except for some small crosses carved in the reliefs (for example, on the shield of a soldier). The concept of a "Christian capital" still lay far in the future. Theodosius also issued instructions about the formal dress and conveyance required of officials in public, and limited the private use of public aqueducts, spaces, and buildings.[97] During his residence in the capital, he endowed it with a new rhythm of celebrations for imperial births, marriages, accessions, consular games, funerals, victories, and their anniversaries.[98] The City began to ease into its rhythm of imperial and religious processions, which were denser than in any other medieval city and brought the people into regular contact with the leaders of Church and state.[99] The City was being prepared for prolonged imperial residence. This, along with the increasingly civilian and pious tenor of court life, called for new modes of imperial self-presentation. When the skull of John the Baptist was "discovered" in 391, Theodosius placed it in his purple robe and carried it in procession to the saint's church at the Hebdomon, outside the City. This "triumph in reverse," the first of its kind, paradoxically exalted the emperor by humbling him before a relic.[100] His first wife, Flaccilla, visited hospitals and personally "brought the pot to the sick and wounded, fed them the soup, gave them their medicine, broke the bread, and washed the bowl, all this without using her servants."[101] Power was being projected by its ostentatious renunciation.

Yet the court was riven by deadly factional strife. In 392, Theodosius replaced Tatianus as praetorian prefect with the *magister officiorum* Rufinus, a Christian from Gaul who had learned Greek late in life. Rufinus brought Tatianus and his son Proculus to trial and had them condemned to death, though on what trumped-up charges is unclear, presumably treason coupled with corruption and packing the administration with personal favorites. Proculus fled but was lured back and executed in front of his father. Tatianus' sentence was commuted by the emperor. He was sent home in disgrace, his vast properties confiscated. Many of his decisions were overturned, his name was methodically chiseled from inscriptions—he had dedicated many statues of the emperor in the provinces—and an extraordinary law was passed banning provincials from Lykia, his province, from serving in the administration.[102] All this was likely inspired by Rufinus, who wielded an unusual degree of influence over Theodosius and had a reputation for brutality.

The western court was even more unstable, as Valentinian II fatally discovered. He tried to assert himself in 392 by dismissing his handler Arbogast, but the latter allegedly tore up the letter in front of him, saying that he had been appointed by Theodosius and could not be fired by Valentinian. The young emperor was later found hanging in his room. What really happened cannot be known.[103] Arbogast waited months for instructions from Theodosius. Receiving none, he chose Eugenius, a former teacher of rhetoric and secretary, and proclaimed him Augustus at Vienne (in Gaul). Arbogast himself was not acceptable as emperor "because of his family background: his father had been a barbarian."[104] Eugenius respectfully sought recognition from Theodosius, but the latter delayed for many more months, until early 393, before deciding to reject Eugenius and elevate his son Honorius as Augustus for the west. So it would be civil war again; for the third time in half a century an eastern emperor would march against a western usurper. It took until 394 for Theodosius to mobilize, but he could have avoided this war had he acted more decisively when he learned of Valentinian II's death.

The events and personalities of the campaign against Arbogast-Eugenius shaped the next generation of Roman history. Arcadius was left in Constantinople under the supervision of Rufinus, acting as a quasi-emperor, while Honorius was waiting to be summoned to the west. Theodosius' top generals were "the Roman" Timasius and Stilicho, who was of half-Vandal origin and married to the emperor's niece Serena. In addition to his regular Roman forces, the emperor called up barbarian auxiliaries commanded by Gaïnas, a Romanized Goth from beyond the Danube who had risen through the ranks of the regular army; Saul, an Alan; and Bacurius, a former Georgian king. As for the auxiliary soldiers, they were mostly Goths from the settlement in Thrace, and a contingent fought under the command of Alaric.[105] In order to make up for the losses of Adrianople, Theodosius had recruited Huns, Armenians, and Georgians.[106]

When the two imperial armies met in the Alps, at the battle of the Frigidus river (Wippach?), on 5–6 September, 394, Theodosius sent his barbarian auxiliaries into battle first, where they suffered terrible casualties. Some Romans saw this as an added benefit of the victory of Theodosius over Arbogast-Eugenius, which he achieved after a predawn surprise attack the next day.[107] Eugenius was captured and executed, whereas Arbogast killed himself. Theodosius summoned Honorius to Italy to become the western emperor. But Theodosius then died unexpectedly at Milan on 17 January, 395. Christian writers quickly mythologized his reign as a Christian utopia and reimagined the war against Eugenius as a struggle against paganism, endowed with miraculous events. This was pure fiction. Theodosius waged two destructive civil wars in order to entrench his dynasty, but his heirs proved to be non-entities, meaning that power was delegated, or taken up, by other political forces that shaped the vastly different trajectories of east and west.

Theodosius was the last emperor to govern the entire Roman empire. As a ruler, he was unobjectionable, patient, and rather opaque. But he did nothing to check the flare-up of Christian violence against Jews and pagans, which would continue under his heirs. He made Constantinople the actual capital of the east by settling his court there. He imposed Nicaea on the eastern Church, a remarkable achievement, but failed to contain the Goths, allowing this foreign army to remain quasi-autonomous right next to his capital. The Goths ceased their violence against the countryside, but, on both occasions when Theodosius marched west, they failed to provide him with soldiers without offering him some kind of violence. Romans of the period wrote about how "we have been made exiles from our homes in Illyricum" and, in 396, "for twenty years Roman blood has been spilled every day between Constantinople and the Alps."[108] The Goths were perceived as a source of instability. No wonder that Theodosius threw them first into the carnage at the Frigidus.

Theodosius died in his late forties. The 390s witnessed the death of older men such as Libanios, Themistios, Ammianus, and Gregory of Nazianzos, men who had come of age in the vastly different world of Constantine and his heirs. After 395, without their living memory to anchor it in that past, eastern Rome embarked on a new phase of history that was defined by the reign of Theodosius and by developments in Christian culture.

7

City and Desert: Cultures Old and New

Pagan cultures

Despite its extraordinary rise to power, Christianity failed to create a total culture around its own institutions, beliefs, and values, as bishops such as Eusebios of Kaisareia had hoped. Instead, it slotted into a preexisting Roman society that was, at first, little changed by it. Even the decline of its chief rival, Hellenism, was caused not only by conversion and Christian persecution but by deeper changes in Roman society. Public sacrifices were apparently in decline already before Constantine, for reasons that remain unclear. The ancient athletic games were also in decline. The last known list of Olympic victors ends in 385 and the network of athletic circuits quietly faded out by the early fifth century; only the Olympic games of Antioch made it to the sixth century.[1] Contrary to a common misconception, the games were not abolished by decree. Instead, interest shifted to the Roman spectacle of chariot racing: the hippodrome replaced the gymnasium. It is not clear that Christian opprobrium had much to do with this. By the fourth century, the games were secular enough that Christians could compete in them, and Church leaders detested hippodrome culture just as much, yet it flourished regardless. More importantly, the old Greek games, festivals, sacrifices, choirs, dramatic performances, and other cultural events had either lost their endowments to inflation or had been stripped of them by the emperors, who used them to fund Constantinople, the solidus, the army, and the Church. This was a persecution, though of an indirect kind. Christians would definitely have seen it that way if it had been done to them.

In addition to waning appeal and lack of funds, the games faced hostility from zealots. For example, in 434 the prefect Leontius announced his intention to hold a version of the Olympic games at Chalkedon, across from Constantinople, as a purely secular event. But Hypatios, the respected abbot of a nearby monastery, announced his intention of going with fellow monks to strike the prefect in the face and prevent this "festival of Satan." The prefect, likely a Christian, canceled his plans because he would have had to arrest and punish anyone who struck him, and he had no desire to make a martyr of Hypatios.[2] Zealots were leveraging their hypothetical martyrdoms to intimidate Christian officials. But while the games in the hippodrome were also regarded as "satanic," they were popular and sponsored by the emperors. The zealots strategically picked fights they could win.

In 400, the empire was probably still majority pagan, or close to half and half. Some cities such as Athens and Gaza remained firmly traditional, most were mixed, and a few were solidly Christian. In 390, John Chrysostom calculated that Antioch, a center of Christian culture, had 100,000 Christians,[3] which might have been half the population, though this is a guess. Christianity had from the start spread faster in cities than in the countryside, where most people lived, so the rural populations, who appear less frequently in our sources, were likely still traditional. Bolder acts of pagan cult such as public sacrifices were performed only in solidly traditional communities or wherever the authorities were sympathetic. By 400, all pagans knew perfectly what Christianity was, and so their rejection of it was self-conscious and stemmed from strong belief and pride in ancestral forms of worship. But pagan religion became increasingly isolated and local as positions of leadership were claimed by Christians and interregional pagan institutions declined. The games, oracles, and festivals stopped drawing pagans together from neighboring regions. The Pythia fell silent, though the town of Delphi continued to prosper.[4]

Christian values and social change

The spokesmen of the Church had always called for a fundamental reorientation of social values. The virtues of the classical world—such as nobility, good birth, good looks, knowledge, courage in war on behalf of the fatherland, victory, pride, wealth, and magnanimity—were recast as vices. Both Jesus in the Sermon on the Mount and St. Paul had taken aim at them, highlighting the fact that a God who allowed his Son to be crucified on behalf of the sins of the powerless would sound absurd to the rulers of the Roman world.

> Not many of you are wise by human standards, not many influential, not many from noble families. No, God chose those who by human standards are fools to shame the wise; he chose those who by human standards are weak to shame the strong, those who by human standards are common and contemptible—indeed those who count for nothing—to reduce to nothing all those who do count for something.[5]

This countercultural message originated in ancient Judaism's rejection of Hellenic cultural values.[6] It was not so much a "message" as an instinct for paradoxical subversion: the foolish would overcome the wise, the weak would overcome the strong, victory (salvation) would emerge from defeat (crucifixion or martyrdom), and exaltation through torture and degradation. Prayer was more powerful than arms. In sum, "when I am weak, then am I strong."[7] God would exalt those who were overaware of being sinful and worthless. Pride was a sin, not a virtue as Aristotle had taught.[8] Pagans were perplexed by this instinct: why would God prefer a penitent sinner over someone who had not sinned to begin with?[9] They had not grasped that henceforth human nature was inherently sinful.

The instinct for paradox allowed Christian writers to retain the language of the classical virtues, albeit in metaphorical and subverted senses. Scripture had already provided a militaristic image of the Christian who "donned the armor of God to stand firm against the Devil." Here truth is a military strap, integrity a coat of armor, salvation a helmet, and God's words a sword. Eusebios of Kaisareia had hoped that Christianity would abolish wars and battles, which he denounced as "the murder of children for the sake of country," and replace them with "the most peaceful wars of the soul on behalf of the truth." Christians with no interest in athletics or soldiering still called their martyrs the "athletes" or the "soldiers" of Christ who won spiritual "trophies" and "crowns."[10] What pagans saw as the execution of contemptible passive victims was recast as the epitome of Christian manliness: martyrs were victors in a war that only they, with truth on their side, could see. Likewise, those who gave up their material wealth stored up invisible credit in heaven. Others renounced their kin to join the family of Christ. Christian writers excelled at metaphorically repurposing traditional values to serve spiritual ends.

The Church produced no better advocate of this message than the preacher John Chrysostom (the "Golden Mouth"), a star speaker at Antioch tapped to serve as bishop of Constantinople (397–404). In hundreds of homilies attended by adoring fans, Chrysostom explored the social and psychological demands of the new message, leaving no doubt in his listeners that it required a reorientation of the soul and a watchfulness against the lingering appeal of old values. The Devil, he reminded them, was always seeking to entrap them through their own desires and countless social conventions. One of his followers recalled how

> he preached ten thousand sermons against avarice, drunkeness, and its daughter, fornication, the mother of death . . . against the fanaticism of the horse races, those who frequented the theaters . . . . He made everyone love the singing of psalms, through which they made the night into day, the market into a church, and the church into heaven.[11]

Chrysostom's vision was to turn the world into one big monastery, and his method was to use the power of persuasion to vivify that ideal before his audience. He preached in a lively, accessible style, sometimes verging on the conversational, using striking images from the daily lives of his parishioners and forcing them to think about the ethical implications of behaviors that may not have worried them much before, for example beating their slaves or wives in anger. His sermons were prized and read out in church for centuries. His vignettes of daily life are priceless records for the modern historian.

But did it all make any difference? Did the values of Roman society change to become more Christian? The answer is mostly no. Christian transvaluation, for all its brilliance, changed little in actual social behavior outside the limited contexts dominated by preachers.

Specifically, Christianization changed nothing in the structure of society, that is in how social classes were defined and related to each other; in the basic social values of land, money, and family; in the institution of slavery; in the economy; the fiscal basis of the state, its operations and goals; in the armies and the military life (except for the symbols on the standards); in the law (except to regulate the Church and ban its rivals); or even in the ideology of the imperial office, which switched allegiance, without skipping a beat, from pagan divine patrons to Christ. Romans had always believed that they were the most religious people and that their empire was favored by the gods to rule the world.[12] Christianity did not change this. The new religion was merely slotted into the place previously occupied by the old, with minimal disruption to the structure of imperial and local society. The military acclamation "Augustus, may the gods preserve you!," was changed to "Augustus, may God preserve you!"[13] That was imperial Christianization in action.

In fact, the influence went mostly in the other direction. Whereas Eusebios had predicted that Christianity would replace Roman wars with spiritual wars, his successor in the early fifth century, the ecclesiastical historian Sokrates, had to admit that Roman wars and politics had instead taken over the affairs of the Church.[14] Rome also colonized the religious imagination. Christian visions of the afterworld cast God's kingdom as the imperial court, with angels dressed like imperial functionaries. The Egyptian monk Theodoros saw an angel "dressed in a shiny tunic adorned with large medallions; his belt was a palm's breadth in width, in bright crimson."[15] John Chrysostom imagined the Second Coming like an imperial procession, though he knew that it would not feature mules and chariots. "Heaven remained a very Roman place."[16]

The armies were indifferent, easily switching their professed religion to please the emperor of the day, from Christian signs and prayers under Constantius to pagan ones under Julian and back again under Jovian. Many officials, such as Modestus, Valens' praetorian prefect, did the same. Insincere conversions for the purpose of gaining favor were denounced already under Constantine, and the problem lingered for centuries.[17] More importantly, elites who did convert, even sincerely, did not change their fundamental values: they remained driven by worldly ambition and love of gold, which was fueled by the empire's unchanged socioeconomic structure. They liked fine things, parties, wine, and to wield power over others; they were acutely status-conscious, boasted of their genealogies, and regularly went to the hippodrome and theater, which in this period specialized in bawdy mime shows, a "Church of Satan" as Chrysostom called it.[18] They had no intention of giving up their classical culture. In this context, fiery sermons were magnificent exercises in moral entertainment. Society's actual pleasures are to be found in precisely what the preachers denounced repeatedly and to no avail.

Christian sources thus present a schizoid picture, torn between the ideals upheld by Christian heroes and the reality around them. When Chrysostom came to the City to be its bishop, he found it, a Christian imperial capital, mired in worldliness, imperial pomp, trade, and gold "unjustly gathered from the tears of the poor," intrigue, and envy.[19] Chrysostom did not reform it, of course, not in the least, and his efforts to do so contributed to his downfall. The City continued to be described that way. Consider, in the sixth century, the debauched society lambasted in Prokopios' *Secret History*.

Some common ground existed between "the world" and the countercultural ideals of the preachers. Christian values partly aligned both with conservative Roman mores, including loyalty to the community, piety, chastity (for women), an abhorrence of deviant sexualities, simplicity of manners, and steadfastness in the face of tyranny, and also with Greek philosophical ethics that prioritized truth, philanthropy, self-control, and a concern for the soul over the body to the point of asceticism. Roman senators once had domestic Greek philosophers to remind them of the fleeting value of worldly things, a role that was now taken up by priests and holy men. Some Christians admitted that they were preaching only a purer version of existing ideals. Chrysostom hoped that his congregation would not fall short of the standards of Hellenic philosophy, and he himself was by no means a stranger to the logic of this world: should they hear a blasphemer, he advised his audience, they were to "slap him in the face, strike him in the mouth, sanctify your hand with the blow." No turning the other cheek, then.[20] Some critics of Christianity found its precepts to be not subversive and dangerous but unoriginal and banal.[21] A smooth, painless, and undemanding conversion was what most new Christians expected, and got.

Christian asceticism

Yet there were always Christians who took the countercultural values of their faith to heart. The Bible clearly states that believers must sell their possessions and give their money to the poor in order to be saved (Mt 19:21), a verse that led St. Antony to do exactly that; to abandon their families (Mt 19:29; cf. Gen. 12:1) and give up their possessions (Lk 14:33); to reject their mothers, fathers, and even their own lives (Lk 14:26); to serve others in order to be "first" among Christians (Mt 20:27); to become eunuchs (Mt 19:12), which some took literally; to abolish marriage, as angels do not marry (Mt 22:30); and that differences in sex and status would, in the end, not matter (Gal 3:28). Some rigorists imitated the example of Jesus' itinerant life or the shared community of goods that was instituted among the first Christians in Jerusalem (Acts 2:44, 4:32), which inspired later monastic communities.[22] Most Christians understood that more was being asked of them even if they could not live up to it. But a minority took up the challenge.

The first celebrated heroes of the orthodox ascetic movement in Egypt were the hermit Antony, who went out into the desert to find solitude, and Pachomios, who organized a franchise of regulated monastic communities. But before them Christians were already practicing ascetic renunciation alone or in groups, in the cities or on the fringes between city and countryside, a lifestyle with a long history among pagan and Jewish groups. These Christians pooled their resources, served the needy, refused to marry (groups of dedicated virgins are attested),[23] or deprived themselves of food, sex, sleep, and material comfort in order to devote themselves to prayer. When Antony, in the late third century, sold his property, he found a "house of virgins" in which to put his sister away and an "old man" to guide him in solitary asceticism. Before Pachomios founded his own community on the site of an abandoned village in Upper Egypt, he had apprenticed for years in a group devoted to asceticism, charity, and discussion.[24] These new communities activated the Christian penchant for metaphor: households were reconstituted with spiritual "brothers," "sisters," and "fathers," and those who abandoned the city to live in the desert became *heremopolitai*, "citizens of the desert."

Already by the mid-fourth century, such lifestyles were not limited to the deserts of Egypt, Palestine, and Syria but were well known in Asia Minor. The homoiousian bishop Basileios of Ankyra wrote a popular treatise *On Virginity* in which he explained that the followers of Christ were renouncing sex, "torturing their bodies" by deprivation, leaving their families, or giving up their property.[25] His colleague Eustathios of Sebasteia was associated with an ascetic movement that aspired to instigate widespread social change. A Church council that met around 340 at Gangra in Paphlagonia condemned his followers for rejecting marriage and sex, abandoning their children "under the pretense of asceticism," urging wives to leave their husbands, inciting slaves to disrespect and abandon their masters "under the pretext of piety," holding that the rich could not be saved, and assembling at homes rather than in churches.[26] In this instance, as in every future instance, the Church sided with the Roman social order; the council was probably headed by the politician-bishop Eusebios of Nikomedeia. Still, the Church could not stop private citizens from living out their fantasy of the perfect Christian life: "Don't conform to this world," St. Paul had said.[27]

According to a distinction that was conventional by the 380s, ascetics were either solitaries (hermits) or lived in service-oriented communities (monasteries).[28] The solitary life was exemplified by Antony as recounted by Athanasios in a text that became wildly successful and inspired thousands more for centuries to come. Hermits lived alone in order to resist the norms and avoid the temptations of social life. Praying continually, they fought off assaults by demons. Sometimes, as with Antony himself, hermits formed loose clusters, called *lavrai*, with masters and disciples who would meet periodically in a common area. The texts highlight their heroes' remoteness, feats of self-denial, lack of concern for worldly values, and ability to confute philosophers despite their own lack of learning. The reality was different. Hermits were never as far from human settlement as the texts imply—at most a day's walk from the centers of agriculture, usually much less. They had to either work or be supported by neighboring communities, in whose politics, needs, and moral dilemmas they were inevitably entangled. Some desert ascetics attracted crowds of suppliants, admirers, would-be followers, tourists, gawkers, and demons looking for a challenge—or hoped to attract them. Thus, a paradox: men who fled to the desert to avoid crowds attracted crowds. One ascetic is said to have dug a long tunnel under Sketis to escape his admirers.[29] But ascetics depended on villages and visitors for both food and reputation. "Gossip management" was essential, but it proved morally exhausting to strike a balance between actual unconcern and the careful cultivation of a reputation for unconcern.[30]

The cells that formed at Nitria, Kellia, and Sketis southeast of Alexandria produced superstar ascetics that drew attention and visitors from all over the empire, including intellectuals such as Euagrios of Pontos and Cassianus, who wrote sophisticated treatises on the theory of the ascetic life. Thus, another paradox: men who supposedly repudiated worldly learning became the models for sophisticated Christian intellectuals educated in ancient philosophy. "Philosophy" here meant "ascetic practice" in opposition to theoretical learning; in fact, it came to mean virginity itself, the furthest that the term has ever come from its primary sense. In reality many ascetics, including Antony, were not as lacking in learning as their hagiographies claimed.[31] And while monks lived in a wide variety of habitats and dwellings, some of their cells that have been excavated resemble "underground atrium-style houses." Others settled in Pharaonic tombs.[32]

"Monasteries" existed under that name (*mone*) already by 334 among the Melitians in Egypt, whose members wore a habit and went by the term *monachos* ("monk"). These enemies of Athanasios were not commemorated in later tradition and we hear of them only through papyri.[33] The first groups that we know well are the federated monasteries founded by the Copt, pagan convert, and former soldier Pachomios, though they were not well known outside of Egypt. His monasteries pooled the properties of their members and lived according to the rules established by the founder. Monks were assigned to specialized administrative positions in their internal hierarchy and engaged in economic production and exchange with surrounding communities to support themselves and their charitable activities. The Pachomian order (*koinonia*) stressed order and obedience to the founder's rule and mature judgment, the point of which was to suppress the individual will, which led away from the love of God. "You are strong men. That is why Pachomios imposed ascetical practices upon you, to soften you."[34]

Pachomios died in 346. His federation eventually encompassed nine monasteries and one convent that was initially directed by his sister and specialized in textile production. If we accept the numbers given in the sources, there were some 7,000 monks under Pachomios' direction, but recent studies would put this figure closer to 4,000. In his portraits of the monks at Nitria, the *Lausiac History*, Palladios says that they numbered 5,000, with 500 more at Sketis, a less accessible site. Our sources give similar figures, such as 2,200 monks and 1,800 nuns for the houses under the direction of the even more rigorous Copt Shenute (who lived to the age of 118). However, recent archaeological study of the economic capacity of his monasteries would reduce those figures by half, to about 2,000.[35] Overall, for the whole of Egypt we might be dealing with a maximum of 20,000 monks by the end of the century, and maybe 50,000 in the eastern empire as a whole. By the sixth century there were a hundred monasteries in and around Constantinople, suggesting a monastic population of 10,000–15,000.[36]

It is not clear that monasticism was a drain on the manpower available for secular labor or military recruitment. Some monks discharged their worldly duties before taking up the habit, and most remained economically active. Valens decreed that men could not skirt their military or curial duties by becoming monks, though this was probably not widely enforced, or not for long.[37] For women, asceticism offered unique opportunities, specifically a way to acquire moral status within a community and even praise for "masculine" virtues, while opting out of the cycle of marriage and childbirth, which was otherwise a social straightjacket. Moreover, ascetic prowess and renown was open to women of all social classes, a rare equalizer.[38]

Monasticism supercharged the Christian genius for paradox. Athanasios famously said that all these ascetics turned the "desert into a city," a city to be understood in a "spiritual" sense, of course. An acerbic pagan poet, Palladas of Alexandria, was more critical: "if they are solitaries (*monachoi*), why are they so many?"[39] Indeed, these "desert cities" soon began to behave like normal cities, amassing property, developing managerial skills, and trading on the market for profit. The theorist Euagrios realized that the "demon of the love of money" could tempt a monastery's steward to accumulate more wealth in order to perform more charitable works, until the means became the ends and the demon revealed itself in its pure form,[40] a remarkable insight, applicable to many modern non-profits. The leaders of the Pachomian communities were alarmed at how quickly their wealth induced worldly modes of thinking.[41] Moreover, as they provided sustenance in addition to forgiveness, the monasteries attracted the desperate and the indigent along with fugitive slaves and criminals, whom they were technically not supposed to admit. For a monk of aristocratic origins, the monastic lifestyle was a step down in comfort, but for others, a former shepherd was reminded, it was a step up.[42] Often social inequalities were merely replicated. One bishop recommended that monks from a poor background should continue to perform manual labor, while the formerly affluent should perform "administrative service."[43] Sex with other monks, especially young apprentices, certainly took place in these communities, judging from the rules' anxiety about all companionship.

The ascetic movement produced a rich store of tales, advice, and theory. This body of literature is fascinating because it grapples with the paradoxes and reverses that one encounters at the limits of human nature, where success, or even sanity, required unusual discernment, compassion and forgiveness, or fanatical strictness. Consider the struggle with demons. There were two ways to understand this. In one sense, demons personified a monk's temptations, such as visions of sensuality and angry thoughts. This directed the struggle inward and tempered the blame that a monk might earn for his failings, as if they were not entirely his own: "a chain of bad thoughts" could be attributed "to the Devil."[44] Treating them as demonic forces was a form of therapy, allowing ascetics to talk frankly about their persistent failure, after decades of effort, to master anger or lust.[45] But demons could also be seen as fully external hostile entities, in which case they were often identified with the pagan gods and their followers, as is hinted already in the *Life of Antony*. Monks who took the fight to this kind of demon, as they did under Theodosius and after, often became violent. When the wrathful abbot Shenute assaulted the house of a prominent pagan and was accused of assault, he defended himself by arguing that "there is no crime for those who have Christ."[46] Not surprisingly, educated pagans considered such monks to be uneducated obscurantists, runaway peasants, parasites, and violent terrorists who plundered sacred places on the pretext of religion.[47]

The ascetic project also produced two contrasting views of human nature. According to one, asceticism aimed to restore the body to its original uncorrupted state, where a purified soul could sustain the body with minimal material support. According to the other, which was more widespread, the ascetic was waging war upon the desires of his or her body, which were fixed aspects of human nature. A sixth-century theorist acknowledged frankly that "chastity is a supernatural denial of nature."[48] Ascetics ran up against nature even at the limits of self-denial. For example, ascetic literature is preoccupied with the problem of moral envy, of monks feeling jealous of the extreme humility of other monks, which could lead them to suspect that those other monks were arrogant in their humility or somehow faking their accomplishments. Indeed, ascetics easily grew proud of their success in abasement, which was itself a sin. Monastic literature was acutely aware of this pitfall, which had been diagnosed about all Christians in the second century ("they take pride in who is the worst sinner").[49] In response, theorists proposed a counterintuitive solution: "the height of humility is to pretend to have vices that you really do not have, so as to be regarded by others as less than you are. Thus, some reach for bread and cheese to avoid being praised."[50]

Ascetics therefore had to carefully modulate others' perception of them in order to escape both the reputation and the sin of pride. The paradox affected the clergy too: an imperial law even stipulated that "he is not worthy of the priesthood who is not ordained against his will."[51] These assumptions created whole rituals of pro forma resistance and even flight: the most ambitious men pretending that they did not want the object of their desire. Thus, many ascetics never escaped the pitfalls and vanities of society, and the pure and simple life turned out to be complicated after all. The fathers advised that, "if you see a young man eager to climb up to heaven on his own, grab his foot and yank him down; it will be better for him."[52] Restraint was perhaps easier in a monastery where the superior could curb excess. Pachomios worried that excessive self-denial led to vainglory, and he restrained his own overachievers by stressing obedience.[53] But "competitive asceticism" emerged among the solitaries of Egypt and Syria, and became absurdly exotic by the fifth century.[54]

Among the pathologies that flourished in these circles was an intense hatred for women as a source of temptation and distraction from prayer. Ascetics advised each other to avoid women, not to touch them, talk to them, or gaze upon them. They told jokes about how men who married would end up being more miserable than the hungriest ascetic. Even in their caves they were tormented by visions of naked seductresses. One monk dug up the grave of a woman whose fond memory haunted him and dipped his cloak in her rotting corpse so that the stench would remind him of the "truth" about her. According to this mentality, still prevalent among religious fundamentalists, the mere presence of a woman was enough to induce a man to rape her.[55] Yet unlike religious societies that respond to this anxiety by sequestering or covering up their women, Roman society took the opposite approach, by requiring such disturbed men to remove themselves, either into the desert or behind walls. Ascetics never dictated or even seriously influenced the gender norms of east Roman society. Women continued to own property, conduct business, walk freely in public, and ignore the bearded zealots if they so desired. In their private lives, they could sleep around (so long as they were not married), drink themselves under the table, and never go to church, and no institution other than their family had the right to restrict or control their behavior. In practice, of course, girls and women likely conformed to gender expectations of modesty, for example by binding their hair up or wearing a head scarf in church.[56] But except for unwanted girls who were deposited in convents as "offerings" to God,[57] asceticism was a voluntary choice and modesty was socially enforced. The state did not enforce these values and the Church could not.

Most Christians wanted to hear about strict morality in sermons and saints' lives, but did not want it imposed on them. John Chrysostom scolded his congregation for "thinking that decency and chastity are appropriate only for the monks." For him, the life of Antony showed "what kind of life was required by Christ's laws."[58] But many Christians preferred to outsource virtue to specialists, or even pushed back against the extremes of what the ascetics were doing: "I am a worldly man, I have a wife and children. Those things are for priests or monks." Chrysostom had to write a treatise *Against the Opponents of the Monastic Life* to address these concerns.[59]

Monks also had a complicated and difficult relationship with the clergy. Unlike in the medieval West, eastern monasticism was a lay phenomenon, i.e., its members were for the most part not ordained and did not want to be ordained because of the responsibilities, distractions, and temptations of the priesthood. Pachomios actively avoided ordination and sought to protect his monks from it too. Not that it was wrong to be a priest, but the *desire* for such a position ruffled one's humility and tranquility. It was demons that put the thought in his monks that they could become bishops. The theorist Cassianus advised monks "to avoid both women and bishops."[60] Moreover, some ascetics sought to recapture the higher moral ground that had been lost when Christianity ceased to be persecuted. Monks were therefore depicted as enduring a daily metaphorical "martyrdom."[61] How else was one to stand out in a Christian world? It was believed by some rigorists that "when a Christian became emperor, Christianity was not honored, but instead deteriorated."[62] Episcopal power and wealth were a manifestation of decline. This put some bishops on the defensive. None other than Athanasios had to argue, to a man whom he was trying to persuade to become a bishop, that he should not believe that the office was just an occasion for sin: "there are bishops who fast, and monks who eat; bishops who don't drink, and monks who do; bishops who work miracles, and monks who don't; bishops who are celibate, and monks who have fathered children."[63] His *Life of Antony* had perhaps been *too* successful.

Ascetics were private citizens making personal choices and so were at first not "visible" to state regulation. After their rampages against pagan temples in the 380s, the pagan prefect Tatianus issued a law that restricted monks to "desolate places," but when the court returned to Constantinople this law was repealed and monks were allowed back into the cities.[64] Until the mid-fifth century, the Church too lacked the institutional means by which to control monasticism. Nevertheless, there was a revolving door between the two, as many bishops had "interned" or apprenticed in ascetic practice before deciding—after a sincere show of reluctance—to accept office, from which they propounded ascetic values. Some bishops, such as Rabbula of Edessa, continued to live like monks and sought to transform their cities into vast monasteries, but in practice they failed to reform even their own clergy.[65] The desert may have become a city, but the Roman city was unwilling to become a desert.

In later tradition, the ideal nexus of episcopal office and asceticism was represented by Basil, the bishop of Kaisareia (370–379), a prominent theologian, ecclesiastical networker, and ascetic theorist. After years of postgraduate study at Athens and a brief stint of teaching at Kaisareia, the young Basil followed other members of his wealthy Christian family who had taken up the ascetic life on their estate of Annisa in the Pontos. He was joined there by Gregory of Nazianzos, and together they neglected the body, studied the Bible, and prayed. Basil describes the place as an Arcadian paradise, and the vast resources of the estate were at hand to bail his group out (moreover, the delicate Gregory liked to keep servants around on his ascetic retreats).[66] As a priest and later the bishop of Kaisareia, Basil became one of the leading theorists of Christian asceticism, writing a number of influential works about its underlying ethical and psychological principles and its Scriptural basis. Basil preferred communal over solitary asceticism. He conceived, and helped to create, a network of brotherhoods and sisterhoods around Cappadocia that practiced moderate asceticism near cities and villages and engaged in charitable works. Basil fantasized that all Christians would eventually become ascetics in this way and, presumably, their properties would be managed by the Church.[67]

On a practical level, Basil was effective at organizing relief for the poor during a food shortage in Cappadocia in 368–369, appealing to the rich through a series of powerful orations.[68] Outside Kaisareia, he built a leprosarium, which was later named the *Basileias* ("Basil's Place"). The emperor Valens granted him tax exemptions and possibly imperial support for the project. Gregory of Nazianzos described this "new city" in the language of Christian paradox: a "common bank vault for the rich, where calamity is deemed a blessing." It was part of a growing movement to endow and institutionalize Christian philanthropy that drew on the many resources of Roman society: monastic care for the weak, imperial financing and administration, and Greek medicine, as doctors were increasingly employed at such centers to treat the ill. The confluence of these factors gave birth to what we can call "the hospital," an institution that turns up in saints' lives and miracle collections with increasing frequency.[69] A hospital dedicated in Syria in 511 was adorned with a mosaic naming, in Greek, the Christian leaders who built it, and below the inscription is an image of the she-wolf suckling Romulus and Remus (see Figure 13).[70] Around the same time, Theodosios the Cenobiarch founded a vast monastery near Bethlehem for 400 monks who prayed in three languages. It featured an impressive array of amenities, including guest-rooms, a hospital, and facilities for monks who were old or demented.[71]

Basil's ascetic arrangements were heavily influenced by his role model, Eustathios of Sebasteia, whose followers had been condemned by the council at

Figure 13 Romulus, Remus, and She-Wolf mosaic laid down in 511 in a Syrian hospital, at Ma'arrat al-Nu'man
ADAM SYLVESTER / SCIENCE PHOTO LIBRARY

Gangra. It is remarkable how small and tightly-knit the circle of ascetic writers was in the fourth-century east. Basil had also emerged from the circle of Basileios of Ankyra, the homoiousian theologian and author of *On Virginity*. In turn, Basil mentored Euagrios of Pontos, the most important of all the ascetic theorists, whom he ordained. Euagrios then studied under Gregory of Nazianzos in Constantinople, at around the time when Jerome, the future translator of the Latin Bible, was with Gregory, and Euagrios later mentored Palladios, the author of the *Lausiac History*. Palladios later met Jerome and detested him. Theirs was a small world.

The culture that emerged from this fascinating fusion of Roman, Greek, and Christian elements was a complex field of overlapping and even competing values, resulting in captivating paradoxes, such as splendid gold mosaics of saints who had renounced all wealth, and trained orators deploying classical rhetoric to convince audiences that they were just homely messengers of a simple truth—professors echoing fishermen. The eunuch chamberlain Lausus, whose magnificent palace stood near the hippodrome, amassed there one of the most stunning collections of ancient Greek art ever, including the Olympian Zeus by Pheidias, the Aphrodite of Knidos by Praxiteles, the Hera of Samos, the Athena of Lindos, and others. Yet Lausus was also the dedicatee of Palladios' *Lausiac History*, which celebrates the ascetic renunciation of vainglory and wealth. This was a culture straining to synthesize conflicting values, both worldly and devout.

PART THREE

THE RETURN OF CIVILIAN GOVERNMENT

8

The Political Class Ascendant (395–441)

In 395, Romanía met a new foe, the Huns, who came pouring through the Dariel pass in the central Caucasus. Splitting into groups, they conducted lightning raids of Armenia, eastern Asia Minor, northern Mesopotamia and Syria, and possibly Palestine. Huns were mounted and relied on speed to surprise their targets and depart before resistance could be mobilized. These raids were destructive, but our sources for them are poor. Some make it seem as if there was no resistance; one says that the Roman defense forces destroyed the Huns; and another says that the general of Oriens, Addaeus, stationed at Edessa, did not allow his "federate" soldiers (i.e., Goths) to fight the Huns because he suspected them of disloyalty, and so they were replaced with Roman soldiers.[1]

The death of Theodosius in 395 left a power vacuum. The reigning emperor in Constantinople was Arcadius, who was eighteen and under the control of the unpopular praetorian prefect Rufinus. Arcadius is described as "led around like a sheep," "dull of mind, with droopy eyes," and "living like a jellyfish."[2] For the next thirteen years, he would reign, but not rule. Weak emperors were handled by politicians, eunuchs, and generals, but "Arcadius' handlers were always at war, fighting each other, not openly, but with deceit and secret malice."[3] His brother Honorius in the west, who was only eleven, was similar in character, but at first he had only one handler, the half-Vandal general Stilicho, so for many years the west had stable leadership. Stilicho employed the pagan Alexandrian poet Claudian as his propagandist. Claudian wrote brilliant Latin poems celebrating his leadership and attacking his eastern rivals, which are often our only source for the events of those years.

The problem of Gothic generals

In 395, Stilicho commanded both the eastern field armies that Theodosius had taken with him to defeat Arbogast and the western armies that he defeated.[4] But he could not keep these forces, nor pay them, for long. The situation was quickly destabilized by Alaric, whom Theodosius had placed in command of some Gothic federates in the 394 campaign. Alaric had returned to the east ahead of the regular armies and, with typical boldness, began to plunder Illyricum and Thrace and threaten Constantinople. His rebellion in 395 kicked off another phase of Gothic wandering that would culminate in the sack of Rome in 410 and the establishment of a Gothic kingdom in Gaul. The core of Alaric's supporters in 395 were almost certainly drawn from the Goths who made the treaty with the empire in 382.[5] Their side of the story is nowhere recorded, so their goals must be inferred from their actions.[6] They included soldiers who did not want to be farmers and perhaps resented their mauling at the Frigidus. They used violence to extract concessions from the Roman state, including salaries and regular supplies, but they did not want to be folded into the regular armies and dispersed. In effect, they wanted the Roman state to support them, a foreign and at times hostile army, within its own territory.

Alaric moved on to Macedonia and then Thessaly, where he was confronted by Stilicho, who had come overland with the combined western and eastern armies—"curly-haired Armenian cavalry and fiery Gauls with golden locks."[7] Claudian's propaganda later claimed that Arcadius, prompted by Rufinus, ordered Stilicho to deliver the eastern armies and depart, and that was why he failed to destroy Alaric. It is more likely that there were dangerous levels of tension between the eastern and western armies, who had just fought a bloody civil war against each other, and Stilicho did not want to deploy them together. Also, the risk of another Adrianople was too high.[8] He sent the eastern armies to Constantinople and returned to the west. At this time, all of Illyricum belonged to the east. Stilicho's propaganda claimed that Theodosius, at a private meeting before his death, had entrusted Stilicho alone with the guardianship of both Honorius and Arcadius, but the east never accepted this claim.[9] Besides, Arcadius was technically an adult and needed no guardian.

The body of Theodosius reached Constantinople on 8 November and was buried in Constantine's imperial mausoleum by the church of the Holy Apostles. The eastern armies arrived under the command of Gaïnas on the 28th, and, when Arcadius went outside the walls to greet them, Gaïnas gave the signal for them to kill Rufinus. The soldiers dismembered him in the emperor's presence. His severed hand was carried around the shops of the City by soldiers calling for "donations for Mr. Greedy," and people tossed them coins.[10] The beneficiary of this regime change was the chief chamberlain of the palace, the eunuch Eutropius, one of Rufinus' main rivals, who now gained ascendancy over the emperor. Rufinus was declared the author of all recent misfortunes and blamed for corruption, so his wealth was confiscated, with much of it going to Eutropius.[11] After Rufinus, no western Roman would ever again rise so high at the eastern court. Conversely, while powerful eunuchs had existed before at Rome, none had ever effectively run the imperial government as Eutropius was now to do, until 399.

Castration was illegal in the empire, so many eunuchs were imported from abroad as slaves, including Eutropius, who was likely from the east. If they were castrated before adolescence, as Eutropius was, eunuchs developed a distinctive physiology: they did not grow facial hair, their voices did not break, their limbs were slightly elongated, and they put on weight differently from other men, for example around the buttocks. Most eunuchs were slaves and used as stewards, managers, or personal agents, which is how they came to dominate the palace staff. They could not aspire to the throne or join the traditional elite, and they often lacked ties to local networks or powerful families, all of which made them useful instruments of imperial governance and survival. Standing outside the structure of power, they could be used to check it. Naturally, many of them were hated by political and military elites, who wrote abusive texts against them. Claudian, for example, wrote vicious invectives against Eutropius on Stilicho's behalf.

As chamberlains of the palace, eunuchs acted like modern chiefs of staff. They controlled the schedule of the court, the emperor's movements, and the flow of information and favors, all of which gave them enormous power. The emperor Constantius was jokingly said to have had much influence over his court eunuch Eusebius.[12] Eunuchs were also a useful scapegoat, as the failures and crimes of a regime could be blamed on them. They were perceived as greedy and corrupt, plotting the downfall of their personal enemies, meddling in people's lives, and unable to control their lusts. But they had also become part of the very logic of the court, a necessary accessory for emperors. Surrounded by these foreign-born, slavish, obsequious, fawning, unmanly, and unscrupulous creatures, emperors automatically looked more Roman, stately, dignified, decent, and masculine.[13]

Eutropius pushed the limits of a court eunuch's power. He arranged for the emperor to marry Eudoxia, daughter of the western general Bauto. He put his own political rivals (two generals) on trial and had them condemned. In 397, he handpicked John Chrysostom, the Antiochene preacher, to be the next archbishop of Constantinople. To prevent the Antiochenes from protesting, Chrysostom was ordered, without explanation, to meet an imperial official outside the gates of his city, whereupon he was virtually abducted and rushed to the capital.[14] In 397 or 398, Eutropius personally led an army against the Huns who had again invaded eastern Asia Minor. He enjoyed some success, for he celebrated a triumph upon his return, was rewarded with the rank of patrician, and was named the eastern consul for 399. The western court did not recognize his consulship, and Claudian heaped scorn on the monstrosity of a eunuch being consul.[15]

Meanwhile, between 395 and 397, Alaric and his army had been ravaging Greece unchecked. They murdered, plundered, and burned their way through Boiotia to Athens, then across the Isthmos and past Corinth into the Peloponnese, leaving a trail of ruin behind them. Archaeological evidence for significant damage dating to the late fourth century has been found in many cities in Greece, and scholars have named it the Alaric Destruction Layer. Archaeologists now tend to reattribute the damages to other causes such as earthquakes, renovations, and Christian vandalism, but there is still much that can be blamed on the Goths, and contemporary sources are explicit about the harm and mayhem that they caused.[16] Greece had not been so wrecked since the Romans had conquered it in the second century BC. An entire generation of Balkan Romans, between 376 and 407, had to cope with the ravages of the Goths, who plundered many provinces. As the Goths were weak in siegecraft, landowners abandoned their country estates and moved into cities. As a result, villa life seems to have declined in that territory (part of what is now Bulgaria). After Alaric, the imperial authorities fortified and garrisoned the Thermopylae pass and built the towering Isthmian Wall, 8 meters tall and 7.5 kilometers long, across the neck of the Peloponnese.[17]

In 397, Stilicho sailed across the Adriatic and landed in the Peloponnese to confront Alaric. There was some indecisive fighting and a standoff, after which Alaric headed north to plunder Epeiros and Stilicho returned to Italy. What happened exactly in Greece remains a mystery, but it was surely a failure on Stilicho's part. The eastern court now yielded to the Goths' demands and granted to Alaric a formal command in Illyricum, probably by giving him a generalship (in this period the most common position was *magister militum*, "master of soldiers"). Our sources are predictably outraged that the destroyer of that land was made its lawful governor, and presumably Alaric was able to draw pay and supplies for his men.[18] But this arrangement did pacify him until 401. Alaric's ambiguous position, which kept crossing the line between leadership of a foreign people and formal Roman office, has divided modern scholars: was he a barbarian invader or a general playing the traditional game of Roman politics? A contemporaneous observer, Synesios of Kyrene, put it graphically in 399 when he imagined Alaric changing "into a toga in order to deliberate with Roman magistrates, and then back into his sheepskin."[19] Alaric and his Goths wanted to be plugged into the Roman system for pay and supplies, but they also did not want to submit to it. They were caught in a bind, both expected to adhere to Roman norms but also regarded as barbaric invaders.[20]

Synesios was one of the most fascinating men of this era, and had more to say about the barbarian problem. He was a landed aristocrat from Kyrene (in modern eastern Libya), who traced his descent, via his city's Spartan founders, to Herakles. He even wrote theological hymns in the Doric dialect of Greek. He was a Platonic philosopher and among the most educated people of his day, having studied in Alexandria under the pagan mathematician and philosopher Hypatia. Yet he was just as capable of calling up cavalry in an emergency and personally chasing after raiders in the desert. On another occasion, he built artillery to throw stones from the city walls. Synesios also had an irrepressible sense of humor, and many of his letters recounting his travels are comedies. Between 406 and 409, the Pharaoh of Alexandria, bishop Theophilos, offered him the episcopal see of Ptolemaïs (Kyrene). After some thought, Synesios agreed, but on three conditions: he would stay married; not pretend that he was not having sex with his wife; and not believe in Christian doctrines such as the Resurrection, which, philosophically, were mere fables. Theophilos agreed.[21]

In 397–400, Synesios was in Constantinople lobbying for a tax break for his native city. Apparently rebuffed by Eutropius, he appealed to a different group of politicians with a speech *On Kingship* that pretends to be addressed to Arcadius but is full of such biting criticism of him—including the "jellyfish" barb—that it can only have been presented to a small group. This speech lays out the virtues of an ideal monarch and inspired many subsequent texts of this kind, in the genre that is sometimes called "Mirrors of Princes." The speech basically expounds an ideology of Roman nationalism. Synesios wanted the emperor to take command of the Roman armies personally, not shut himself up in the palace. He should follow "ancestral Roman tradition" from the era when the Romans won their empire, and cast off jewels and pomp. The soldiers should be home-grown Romans and the polity defended by men nurtured and educated by its own laws. Outsiders should not be given arms. It is a recipe for disaster to rely on barbarians, especially Goths (he meant those of Alaric). "We should win our own victories." Barbarians should not be given offices and power, for they are not loyal to our state and laws, he contended.[22]

The relationship between the two courts of east and west was becoming increasingly ambiguous. In the 380s, the entire empire was still regarded as one state, "a single organism with the same breath and feeling,"[23] even when it had two or more emperors or when its unity was the product of civil war. Laws were still issued under the names of all recognized emperors and were, in theory, valid throughout the empire. However, in practice individual laws were intended for specific regions or were not enforced by an imperial colleague, a divergence that had begun already in the fourth century. For example, Libanios had waited anxiously for Valens to ratify an inheritance law of Valentinian with which Valens disagreed.[24] Moreover, during the fourth century statues depicting the whole imperial college (east and west) ceased to be dedicated in the provinces and were henceforth found only in Rome and Constantinople, and each court issued coins with its own separate designs.[25] The subjects of each half of the empire were increasingly living in separate, sibling states.

In 396, Eutropius had ceded western Illyricum (i.e., Pannonia and likely Dalmatia) to Stilicho, and kept eastern Illyricum (Dacia and Greece) for the east.[26] This division established the boundaries that the eastern empire claimed in the Balkans for the next thousand years, even if at times they were only notional. But in 397, after Stilicho's failed expedition to Greece, Eutropius persuaded the eastern Senate to officially proclaim him a public enemy,[27] and he opened negotiations with the governor of North Africa, Gildo, to transfer his allegiance from Honorius to Arcadius. This was an act of aggression against the west, for Rome depended on North African grain and revenues. Stilicho had to send an army to suppress Gildo. The emperors' handlers were behaving almost like the leaders of rival states, even though the emperors themselves were the sibling rulers of what was in theory a single Roman state. For the next decade the chief sign of this cold war between the courts was the non-recognition of their respective consuls. But the theory remained of "emperors in two bodies having a single empire."[28]

The first eunuch-handler of Constantinople enjoyed a good run, four years, before he was toppled in 399. His fall was part of a dramatic set of events that changed the dynamics of political power in the east, brought the armies under political control, and contributed to the survival of the eastern empire. Specifically, a Roman officer (*comes*) of Gothic descent named Tribigild, a relative of Gaïnas, rebelled in Phrygia with his army of federate Greuthungi, who had been stationed there since 386. Eutropius had apparently refused one of his requests, so Tribigild followed Alaric's model of extorting high office from the court by plundering the provinces, in this case Phrygia, Pamphylia, and Pisidia.[29] Eutropius sent the general Gaïnas to deal with him, but, in a confirmation of what many Romans suspected about barbarians, Gaïnas and his mostly barbarian army joined Tribigild and marched on the capital demanding Eutropius' dismissal. This was immediately granted: a law issued to the new praetorian prefect Aurelianus—Synesios' contact and the winner in a palace revolution—ordered the confiscation of the eunuch's wealth, the destruction of his statues, and the damnation of his memory. Eutropius had other enemies at the court, including the empress Eudoxia. He sought asylum in Hagia Sophia, where, standing over the groveling eunuch, John Chrysostom preached a sermon on the vanity of power to a packed and intensely curious congregation. Eutropius was exiled to Cyprus, but this was not enough for Gaïnas. He was brought back, tried by a court over which Aurelianus presided, and executed.[30]

Gaïnas pressed his advantage. In the spring of 400, he compelled Arcadius to meet him at Chalkedon across the straits and obtained from him the rank of *magister militum* along with the surrender of Aurelianus and other officials who he believed were blocking him.[31] He aspired to the position of Stilicho: a Roman officer of barbarian origin who wielded supreme military authority and managed the affairs of state for a puppet emperor. Gaïnas introduced thousands of Gothic soldiers into the City. He demanded an Arian church for them, though this petition was rejected. Later authors wrote this up as a dramatic face-to-face confrontation between Gaïnas and an uncompromising John Chrysostom, who switched to Latin for the benefit of the general who spoke "in what he thought was the language of the Italians, which he had acquired as a foreign tongue."[32] Gaïnas also failed to occupy the palace, but he had effectively bullied the state into submission, and was consul-designate for 401. Chrysostom evocatively described the mood in the City: "everything was unsettled and in turmoil; no one trusted anyone. We were in state of civil war, but it was all in the shadows, not in the open. Everyone was wearing a mask."[33]

Yet one segment of the body politic had been overlooked: the *populus Romanus*. In mid-July, Gaïnas went to the Hebdomon and, for reasons that remain unknown, began to pull his soldiers out of the City, sparking rumors of impending violence. The populace spontaneously rose up on 12 July and, with the help of the palace guard, shut the City gates and slaughtered 7,000 Goths, including those who sought asylum in a church that was reserved for the orthodox among them, which was burned down. Gaïnas withdrew to Thrace and the emperor proclaimed him a public enemy. The *magister militum* of Oriens, another Romanized Goth named Fravitta, was called up by the Senate and he decisively defeated Gaïnas in a naval battle in the Hellespont. Gaïnas, his ambitions in shambles, marched to the Danube, where he murdered the few remaining Roman soldiers still under his command and crossed the river with his Goths. He was there killed by some Huns who sent his pickled head to the emperor.[34]

Fravitta was criticized for not pursuing Gaïnas to the end, allegedly to spare fellow Goths, but he returned to a hero's welcome and was allowed to celebrate a triumph. When the emperor offered him his choice of reward, he asked that he be allowed to worship openly as a pagan, and this was granted. He was also made consul for 401, then executed amid murky circumstances around 405.[35] The court erected a triumphal column, at the Xerolophos farther down the Mese from the forum of Theodosius, whose spiral relief celebrated the defeat of Gaïnas and the Gothic menace. It was dismantled in 1715, but sketches of the relief were made in time.[36]

In just a few years, the ground had shifted under the establishment of Constantinople, setting the east on a divergent trajectory from the west. The populace of New Rome had asserted itself as a force in imperial politics. They would use this power time and again during the coming millennium, steering the course of history at critical moments, in both secular and religious contexts. Moreover, Gaïnas' effort to dominate the court by leveraging his Gothic soldiers had failed, and power had passed to the political class of Constantinople, where it would stay for fifty years. In the west, by contrast, power was consolidated into the hands of one general. At this time, it was Stilicho, a dynamic defender of the Roman order. But over time the western army consisted increasingly of barbarian mercenaries whose generals were eventually not Romans of barbarian origin but barbarians of barbarian origin. One of them, Odoacer, abolished the rump Roman state in 476, after most of its provinces had been occupied by separatist barbarian armies. Why did this not happen in the east?

The full story will unfold subsequently, but the insecurity of Eutropius, the first eunuch to rule New Rome, is part of the answer. When he came to power, he tried and deposed two generals but apparently did not replace them. During 395–397, it seems that only a *magister militum* of Oriens was appointed, the post most distant from the capital; we do not hear of generals appointed in the Balkans. No generals were sent to fight Alaric, and the problem that he posed was "solved" by dubbing him *magister militum*. In sum, Eutropius under militarized the east, having one general (of Oriens) at a distance and another (Alaric) without access to the court, an arrangement that catered to his insecurity. To fight the Huns in the east in 397 or 398, Eutropius went in person and, it seems, took mostly Gothic soldiers.[37] Roman armies were not being mustered on a large scale, which explains Synesios' call for a national army in 399. But Eutropius was right to be concerned about the threat that military power posed to him, for the first officer who activated the army as a lever of political power, Gaïnas, immediately toppled him. Gaïnas was destroyed by the people of Constantinople and the armies of Fravitta. The ensuing political vacancy was filled by the political classes of the City, who held power for decades and established new norms for its use. Strongmen and half-barbarian generals sometimes appeared, but were suppressed. Thus, Eutropius' undermilitarized approach enabled the political classes of Constantinople to tame the army.

Ethnicity played a role too. Recent scholarship has correctly refuted the idea that there were pro- and anti-barbarian parties in Roman politics at this time and that these events can be understood as the struggle between them. However, this trend has been taken to extremes, with some scholars denying that ethnicity played any role at all and asserting that barbarian armies were not regarded as different from regular Roman armies and were "just as loyal" to the Roman state. This is manifestly incorrect. Our sources exhibit a sharp awareness of ethnic difference and many events—especially massacres and lynchings—were governed by perceptions of ethnicity on the part of the actors involved: Julius' officers in 378 and the people of Constantinople in 400 could identify a Goth when they wanted to kill one. Conversely, Gaïnas knew which of his soldiers were Romans when he murdered them later that year.

Emperors recruited barbarians into their armies because they were cheaper and did not drain the agricultural labor force. Over time these barbarians could be expected to become Romans too. But the period after Adrianople was not normal. The (correct) perception that barbarian armies were not fully under political control led many to distrust their loyalty. When they plundered the provinces and disobeyed orders, even after the treaty of 382, and tried to dominate the capital, they activated murderous reactions. This was not a "color-blind" society. There was a reason why Fravitta, a Goth, was praised so fulsomely for his pro-Roman stance and staunch "loyalty to the Romans."[38] And Gaïnas, who was a Roman citizen, might have succeeded in his coup had he not relied so much on soldiers whom the populace identified as barbarians (Gaïnas recruited his men among the Goths north of the Danube, possibly because he had not been given enough men by Eutropius).[39] Alaric's Goths were treated at all times as a hostile foreign force and accommodated as little as possible until they departed in 401 for Italy. The reason for their move is unknown; a later source says that their subsidies were terminated. Alaric returned to Epeiros in 402–406, but then went back to Italy for good.[40] Thus, by 406 the east was free of major concentrations of barbarian military power, and the politicians in charge, such as Anthemius (404–414), took care not to build up the army or to concentrate it in the hands of one general. The number of officers with barbarian names gradually declined during the fifth century.[41] Eutropius had shown the civilian politicians how to survive.

John Chrysostom

Arcadius' final years were marred by more turmoil, but in the Church. In September 403, the bishop of Constantinople, John Chrysostom, was tried, condemned, and deposed by a Church council held across the Bosporos at a suburb of Chalkedon known as The Oak. Dozens of trumped-up charges were brought against him by priests whom he had suspended and Isaakios, a leader of the monks of Constantinople who was later regarded as the founder of monasticism in the City. The charges included violence, uncanonical depositions and ordinations, creating a hostile environment, arrogance, financial irregularities, improper conduct with women, forgiving sinners lightly, eating alone, and other oddities.[42] The accusations were heard, debated, and amplified by bishops who were politically opposed to John, or just disliked him, and who had been given the green light by the palace to bring him down. John refused to attend on the grounds that the council was being run by his enemies. Their prime mover was Theophilos of Alexandria, who had brought dozens of his client bishops from Egypt with him to pack the council.

The fall of John Chrysostom resulted from a messy tangle of converging background stories. The lead thread was a falling-out between Theophilos and some of his erstwhile clients and agents in Egypt, who removed themselves to the monastic settlements of Nitria. As ascetics they were allegedly appalled by the nature of his fiscal administration and his "lithomania" (passion for building).[43] Unfortunately for them, Theophilos was exceptionally skilled at orchestrating the destruction of his enemies. He went after them on theological grounds, convening a council in Egypt in 400 that condemned the doctrines of Origen, a Platonizing Christian theologian of the third century. Origen's ideas were still popular with many Christian intellectuals and Theophilos knew that his enemies could be tarred by association. Origen had emphasized intellectual rather than bodily salvation, spiritual-allegorical rather than literal readings of Scripture, and a doctrine of universal salvation. Theophilos construed this as a hodgepodge of heresies that were inadmissible by post-Nicene Orthodoxy. Armed with this verdict, he used military force against the Nitrian monks, destroying their cells and books and driving them into exile.[44]

Led by the four Tall Brothers, named after their stature, some fifty of the Nitrian monks traveled to Constantinople and sought John's assistance in 401. He received them cordially but was reluctant to interfere in the business of the see of Alexandria. Yet he wrote to Theophilos about the case,[45] which made Theophilos suspect that the Tall Brothers were being used against him. His political machine swung into motion. He sent agents to the capital to defame the monks, and asked Epiphanios, the bishop of Salamis and a venerable and intolerant heretic-hunter, to hold another council on Cyprus condemning Origen. Epiphanios, who was linked to Chrysostom's enemies in Antioch, even traveled to Constantinople to cause trouble for Chrysostom by publicly snubbing him and branding him, implausibly, as an Origenist. In 402, the Tall Brothers pled their case to the court and, for unclear reasons, the empress Eudoxia pledged to intervene on their behalf. She summoned Theophilos to Constantinople to be tried at a council presided over by John, and she arrested Theophilos' agents in the City, some of whom died in prison. This was the worst-case scenario for both John and Theophilos, as it set them on a collision course. It also revealed the power of the court in Church matters: Eudoxia could casually overrun canonical procedures and institute trials by fiat. The most powerful bishops in the empire now had to follow a procedure misconceived by the court that neither of them wanted.

Theophilos took the overland route and proceeded slowly in order to gather allies along the way and sound out John's enemies. Even John's admirers admitted that he "spoke with excessive license and came across as arrogant," was disliked by many of his own clergy, and had offended powerful people through his caustic rhetoric.[46] He had also come into conflict with the monks of the City, an irony for such a great proponent of asceticism. For him monks had to live quietly in places of solitude, so he "castigated those who went out of doors and spent their time in the city streets," as those in Constantinople did, including their leader, the Syrian Isaakios, who would testify at length at The Oak.[47] John micromanaged Church finances, eliminating some of the perks to which many had become accustomed, and was a stern disciplinarian. Finally, he offended the most powerful player in this drama, the empress Eudoxia, through an ill-timed general invective against women that stressed their vanity, one of his favorite themes. This was reported to Eudoxia as a personal attack against her for hosting Epiphanios of Salamis during his visit.[48] She now turned against John. Thus Theophilos, who had been summoned to be examined at a council *by* John, found himself, after his triumphal entry into the City, orchestrating the trial *of* John. He even reconciled with the surviving Tall Brothers. For Theophilos, the real threat now was the growing power of the see of Constantinople. In 402, John had toured the diocese of Asia and, with the backing of the court and the canons of the Council of 381, had deposed a dozen bishops or more and replaced them with his own appointees. This was Constantinopolitan imperialism in the Church.

John was now tried at The Oak, in absentia, and convicted. Theophilos was a masterful tactician, exploiting the rifts, quarrels, and hatreds that were always simmering within the Church. But the protagonists had again not reckoned with the people of Constantinople, some of whom now protested in defense of their bishop. They barricaded themselves in Hagia Sophia and prevented John's arrest for three days. Finally, John slipped out, surrendered to the authorities, and was conveyed into exile. Violent disturbances broke out in the City, with people railing against the palace. The court recalled him immediately. Monks opposed to John occupied Hagia Sophia, but they were cut down bloodily by soldiers and John's partisans.[49] John was pressured to return to duty even though he had not yet been cleared of his previous deposition. Meanwhile, his partisans, the Johannites, clashed with the Egyptians in the City, with many casualties. Theophilos took this opportunity to leave, citing threats that he would be thrown into the sea.[50] His job was done.

Calm was eventually restored and John resumed his duties, but the underlying problems remained. John's worst enemy was his own mouth. It was understandable that he denounced Theophilos as "the Egyptian Pharaoh" from the pulpit.[51] But weeks later, the City prefect organized a party with dancing and mimes to dedicate a silver statue of the empress on a porphyry column adjacent to Hagia Sophia. It happened to be on a Sunday, and the celebrations could be heard inside the church during the service. John angrily denounced this disruption. When this was reported to the empress she became furious and determined to depose him for good. John then made matters worse by preaching an infamous sermon starting with the words, "Again Herodias is angry, again she wants John's head on a plate" (referring to John the Baptist).[52] He was relieved of his duties and, a few months later, sent into exile for good. Upon his second departure, a fire broke out in Hagia Sophia as his followers were protesting and it destroyed the church itself and the adjacent Senate House. John was held for three years in various remote places in the east—"there is nothing to shop here, but what do I care?"[53] He died in 407 in the Caucasus, possibly after being force-marched to death.

The court had learned its lesson: firebrand preachers eventually resulted in actual fire brands. John's fall proved that stirring rhetoric and an intense personal devotion to the faith were insufficient qualities for a bishop of the capital; in fact, they were liabilities. He was replaced with his predecessor Nektarios' brother, the octogenarian Arsakios—"more speechless than a fish, less active than a frog."[54] The episcopal throne was henceforth controlled by the clerical establishment of the capital; the next time they hired a star preacher from Syria, Nestorios, in 428, they again regretted it. But the messy way in which John Chrysostom was taken down revealed the extraordinary power of the court to convene puppet councils, enforce them and then cancel them at a moment's notice, then reinstate them again, with bishops struggling to adapt to the changing currents of imperial favor. This was not just the empress' doing: the hostility to John ran deep, with factions fighting behind the scenes of our biased sources.[55]

The Johannites tried for years afterward to induce a schism in the Church. They were persecuted but gradually exerted immense pressure that led to John's rehabilitation.[56] John's enemies hated the man himself, whereas his partisans loved what he stood for, which gave them a long-term advantage once he was out of the picture. Thus, both sides got their way. In 438, his remains were returned to the City and received triumphally. The emperor, Theodosius II, knelt before the relics and begged the saint's forgiveness on behalf of his parents Arcadius and Eudoxia. John's remains were placed in the imperial mausoleum of the Holy Apostles, the first non-royal to be interred there. John Chrysostom cut a more attractive figure thirty years after he had been silenced. But still, he had failed to reform New Rome and make it less worldly. His was an austere ideal that society preferred to admire rather than practice.

Another prelate who took an interest in John's deposition was Innocent I, the bishop of Rome. Sixty years before, his predecessor Julius had claimed the right to retry bishops deposed by the party of Eusebios of Nikomedeia. Innocent also decided that John's case had to be reexamined by a joint council of east and west. But no one in the east paid him any attention apart from the Johannites, who were intensely lobbying him to intervene. Even Honorius was recruited to send a letter to Arcadius complaining, among other matters, about the eastern court's interference in Church matters and its refusal to accept Rome's arbitration. In 405, Innocent convened his own synod and dismissed the charges against John, calling for a council at Thessalonike to be attended by John as the lawful bishop of Constantinople. But the delegation conveying the demands of Honorius and Innocent was arrested in Thrace by the eastern government, now headed by the praetorian prefect Anthemius. The western bishops were sent back to Calabria in a rotting barge, and its eastern members were exiled.[57] For some time after that, the Church of Rome was not in communion with Constantinople. This time the schism between east and west was not over doctrine but Rome's self-arrogated right to preside over the entire Church.

Eudoxia died in 404 of a miscarriage or stillbirth. In nine years of marriage, she had given birth to four daughters and one son, and had another miscarriage, which means that she spent much of the reign pregnant. Unlike her husband, she had an imperial temperament, but, as the daughter of a Frankish general, she attracted anti-barbarian prejudice.[58] Arcadius died in 408 and was succeeded by his seven-year-old heir Theodosius II, who had been acclaimed Augustus as an infant in 402, at the military parade grounds of the Hebdomon. The transition was smooth as the government was already in the hands of the capable praetorian prefect Anthemius (405–414), the grandson of Constantius' prefect Phillipus and grandfather of the western Roman emperor Anthemius (467–472).

Civilian government

Theodosius II was a non-entity for the duration of his reign, which was the longest of any Roman emperor yet. Major decisions were made by the top civilian officials, though our sources do not allow us a clear view of the inner workings of the court. These politicians governed capably with an eye toward peace, stability, and prosperity. To this end, they continued Eutropius' policy of preventing the military from dominating the state. The style of imperial government that emerged, centered symbolically on a pious, palace-bound emperor flanked by virgin sisters, represented a sharp break from the military regimes of the past.

The first regent was the prefect Anthemius, who governed by consensus, in particular though the advice of the rhetorician Troïlos, a friend of Synesios.[59] The cold war with the western empire ended in the summer of 408, when Stilicho, who wanted to reclaim all of Illyricum, fell out of favor and was executed. Stilicho had imposed a trade and travel embargo on the eastern empire, which was now lifted. Alaric and his Goths were threatening Italy and Rome, trying in vain to extort concessions from the western empire. Constantinople sent an army of 4,000 to guard Honorius in Ravenna. When Alaric elevated a senator named Attalus to be his own puppet emperor, Ravenna and Constantinople agreed that the east would now impose an embargo on the west: "all naval bases, harbors, shores, and points of departure . . . even remote places and islands, shall be encircled and guarded . . . so that no person may be able to infiltrate the regions of our empire," unless he bore letters from Honorius.[60] Frustrated at every turn, Alaric finally sacked Rome for three days in August 410. While the damage to the city was not extensive, the event shocked the Roman world.

Figure 14 An extensively restored section of the Theodosian Walls, showing the three lines of defense; the moat or ditch before the first line has been filled in.
Photo by David Hendrix

Not coincidentally, at that time Anthemius was fortifying Constantinople and the provinces. It was under his direction that the famous Theodosian land walls of the City were built, a project that lasted nine years (404–413). What he built was the inner (taller) circuit of what eventually became a triple line of defense (a moat and two lines of walls) (see Figure 14). This was 2 km west of its Constantinian predecessor, effectively doubling the area of the City, which had been spilling outside its previous limit since the 380s, when the capital was still "full of builders and architects."[61] The new wall had 96 projecting towers, and the owners of the land on which they were built were allowed to use them but required to maintain them; a later law billeted soldiers on the towers' ground floors.[62] The wall stretched for 6 km from the Sea of Marmara, where it incorporated Theodosius I's Golden Gate, to the Golden Horn. It was beautiful, imposing, and impregnable; for centuries, the enemies of New Rome would fail to breach it. Henceforth, medieval cities would fall into three categories: unwalled, walled, and Constantinople.

Anthemius also provided for the cities of Illyricum that might again find themselves in the path of Goths or Huns. All taxpayers were required to contribute to their fortification, with voluntary contributions being encouraged in the spirit of the public good, while a fleet of 250 ships was created to patrol the Danube. Many cities in Asia Minor built new walls in the later fourth and early fifth centuries, a timely precaution, seeing as Goths had been rampaging in nearby Thrace and then, in 399 under Tribigild and Gaïnas, in Asia Minor.[63] In addition to civic revenues and contributions by decurions, imperial funding for such defense projects was freed up by the regime's reluctance to engage in large-scale military operations. In 409, a Hun named Uldis crossed the Danube and raided Thrace but his followers were simply bribed by the Romans to desert, and he fled. One of his contingents, the Skiroi, were captured and dispersed as agricultural laborers. The court solicited applications from landowners willing to take them on as coloni, so long as they were resettled on the other side of the Bosporos.[64]

The population of Constantinople had by this point surpassed the 150,000 mark, and was possibly much larger, which meant that the food supply also had to be secured. The failure of the grain ships in 409 caused a famine, and the populace burned the house of the City prefect in protest. Two generals went to the protesters and told them, "Go back, and we will order whatever you want." An emergency relief fund was created, and Anthemius issued a law tightening up the cargo runs by requiring more "papyruswork" and making the guild of shipmasters collectively liable for losses, a form of group insurance.[65]

Constantinople began to fill out its urban fabric beyond the core of imperial monuments. As it expanded, the powerful men and women of the Theodosian era left their mark upon its very topography: new neighborhoods were named after the mansions of consuls, generals, senators, and princesses, or after the baths, churches, and other amenities that they built. Oddly, it did not matter whether they had been politically disgraced. Thus, palaces and neighborhoods were named after Gaïnas, Promotus, Anthemius, and Rufinus (the Rufinianae, near The Oak at Chalkedon), in addition to sites named after the emperors and their daughters and sisters.[66] The shrines, churches, and monasteries that they built were not huge, but they endowed the City with a more granular Christian character. The court also staged receptions of holy relics. In 406, Arcadius, Anthemius, and the Senate greeted the remains of the prophet Samuel, "mere pieces of ash" in a box of gold and silk; in 411 these were ceremonially deposited into a dedicated shrine.[67] Such processions, attended by crowds of citizens, shifted the court style from militarism to piety and enhanced the City's topography and attractions.

The new civic culture of the Roman elite opened opportunities for wealthy women, who could fund religious events, support religious personalities, and build churches; there was nothing inherently masculine about prayer, devotion to relics, and virginity.[68] These opportunities were seized by Theodosius II's sister Pulcheria, who, at the age of fourteen in 413, imposed a vow of virginity on herself and her sisters to prevent "ambitious men from entering the palace" and dominating the dynasty. She inscribed the vow on an altar-hanging in Hagia Sophia. It was said that Pulcheria became the de facto ruler and Theodosius' main handler, arranging for him to be trained in proper comportment, horsemanship, and piety. "The palace was converted into something resembling a monastery." The emperor was rumored to wear a hair shirt under his purple robes. He also became an expert calligrapher, and manuscripts that he copied survived to the fourteenth century, including Gospels written in gold lettering.[69]

It is, however, unlikely that Pulcheria called the shots in government, much less so at the age of fourteen. She seems rather to have been in charge of aspects of the regime's public relations, a crucial function now that the populace was just as important as the armies for dynastic survival, if not more so. But decisions were in the hands of the emperor's council, consisting of the leading civilian officials such as the praetorian prefect, the City prefect, and the *magister officiorum*. Later in the reign, Theodosius formally delegated his power to hear appeals to the courts of the praetorian prefect and *quaestor* (his legal advisor), and involved the entire Senate in the process of legislation.[70] Few generals are attested for the first decade of the reign, and even later the court preferred Arian generals of barbarian background, such as Aspar, or pagans, such as the Isaurian Zeno (447–451), a man "dear to Ares," as his wife called him in the floor-mosaic of a bathhouse that she restored in Seleukeia.[71] These men were preferred because they could not hope to muster the political and popular support necessary to make a bid for the throne. For them, the liability of their religion or ethnicity was a career asset.

When the time came for Theodosius to marry, in 421, he or his handlers chose a pretty pagan girl named Athenaïs, the daughter of a professor of rhetoric at Athens. Baptized as Eudokia, she wrote poems in the classical style and engaged in Christian philanthropy. Readers of later chronicles will encounter the traces of a "Romance of Theodosius and Eudokia" recounting their courtship, marriage, and falling out over a big apple, not all of which is to be taken as history. Eudokia was an attractive choice for a nominal emperor and a safe one for the court's movers.[72] Curiously, we have relics of the imperial couple themselves: Theodosius is the only ancient emperor whose handwritten signature survives on a papyrus—ironic for an emperor who allegedly signed papers without reading them—and we have a golden ring of Eudokia, possibly a gift to a favorite.[73]

The generals gradually became more prominent. In 420, Christians fled from Persia to Romanía to escape persecution from the Zoroastrian establishment, and the court refused to hand them back. The two empires fought a brief war in 420–422 over this and some trivial grievances, but it is poorly documented. The war was apparently inconclusive, but the diversion of manpower to the east left the Balkans undefended. Some Huns, possibly under king Rua, took advantage of this opportunity to raid Thrace, reaching as far as Constantinople. The Roman general Procopius, a son-in-law of the prefect Anthemius, was sent to arrange a peace with the Persians, while the Huns agreed to withdraw in exchange for an annual subsidy of 350 lbs of gold. Still, the Persian war allowed two generals of barbarian descent to distinguish themselves: Ardabur, the Alan *magister militum* of Oriens, and Ariobindus, the Goth *comes* of the Gothic federates.[74]

Soon after, in 423, Honorius, the western emperor and Theodosius' uncle, died without designating a successor. The eastern court again delayed its response long enough that a faction at Rome elected its own Augustus, an imperial secretary named Ioannes, who was not recognized by Constantinople. So for the fourth time since 350, an eastern army marched west in 425 to remove a western "usurper" and enforce dynastic control, this time in the form of the six-year-old Valentinian III (425–455), Honorius' nephew, who had been living in exile in Constantinople with his mother Placidia. The army was commanded by Ardabur, but he was captured by Ioannes' forces at Ravenna as he sailed up the Adriatic. Another general, Candidianus, marched overland into northern Italy, but it was Ardabur's young son Aspar, leading the cavalry, who captured Aquileia and then found a path through the marshes to Ravenna, guided, it was said, by an angel. The rebel Ioannes was seized and executed.[75] The rise of Aspar, who was in his twenties, had begun. He would be far subtler than Gaïnas.

The empire was still regarded in Rome and Constantinople as a united state. Between Honorius' death (August 423) and the proclamation of Valentinian III as Augustus in Rome (October 425), Theodosius II was sole Augustus of the entire Roman world, for, in theory, Ioannes did not count.[76] And now that the west was again a junior partner of the east, Constantinople conceived the ambition to codify and streamline Roman law to bring order to the mass of confusing legislation that had accumulated during the past century. As Theodosius put it, the law "was hidden behind a thick cloud of obscurity."[77] In 429, he informed the Senate of Constantinople that he had appointed a committee to codify the law by collecting the most relevant decrees from Constantine onward, and by making a selection of the writings of the best jurists. Only this collection would henceforth be valid in court, and future laws would be valid throughout the empire, though Theodosius reserved the right to change or revoke them.[78] The first component of this project, the *Theodosian Code*, was completed and ratified in 438; the second would not be undertaken until Justinian, a century later. In both conception and execution, the *Theodosian Code* was a landmark of Roman jurisprudence, whose influence would extend for centuries in both east and west. As a historical source, it is a gold mine. We have the minutes of its reception by the Senate of Rome, where Theodosius' letter to the eastern Senate was read out, followed by hundreds of acclamations praising the emperors (e.g., "You are our salvation!"—repeated twenty-six times; "May it please our Augustuses to live forever!"—repeated twenty-two times; and so on).

Unified though the empire was in law, its administrative division had led to two de facto separate states. The embargoes of the first decade of the fifth century had hardened the borders between their territories. Lists were produced of "those provinces and cities that are ruled by the emperor of the Romans whose base is at Constantinople."[79] After 395, the careers of civilian and military officials were normally confined to one of the two empires. Their diplomatic efforts were rarely coordinated, with the result that ambassadors of "the eastern Romans" met ambassadors of "the western Romans" by chance at the same barbarian court.[80] But the west's dependence on the east was increasingly apparent. After 382, the east never asked for western military assistance, but the west's need for help only increased. The east had sent soldiers to protect Honorius from Alaric in 410, and eastern officers swirled around the young Valentinian III. For example, the *eastern* general Ardabur was appointed as the *western* consul for 427. The western empire was now an eastern client state.

When it could, Constantinople helped Rome with its growing barbarian woes. In 429, a joint Vandal-Alan army under the command of the Vandal king Gaizeric crossed over to Africa from Spain. Ardabur's son Aspar was sent with a "large" eastern army in 431 to assist the local general, Bonifatius, in defending North Africa against the Vandals. The Romans were defeated, and one of Aspar's retainers, the future emperor Marcian (450–457), was briefly captured.[81] Aspar was appointed the western consul for 434 while he was based at Carthage. The eastern consul was the Goth Ariobindus, the hero of the Persian war, so both consuls of that year were officers of the eastern army, of barbarian origin, and Arians. Before he departed from North Africa, Aspar concluded a treaty with the Vandals that safeguarded Carthage and its province for Rome. The expedition had helped his career more than it did North Africa.

Religious minorities at Alexandria

While barbarians slowly dismantled the western empire, some bishops were becoming more assertive in the eastern one. The most formidable during this generation was Cyril of Alexandria (Kyrillos, 412–444), the nephew of Theophilos.

Cyril's episcopacy exposed the perilous position of religious minorities, which he repressed at Alexandria. His election in 412 was contested by a rival faction, with fierce fighting in the streets, before the imperial prefect backed his candidacy with force. Cyril then cracked down on the Novatian sect, closing their churches and confiscating the property of their bishop.[82] Two years later, in 414, violence broke out between Christians and Jews over, of all things, dancing performances, and this gave Cyril the opportunity to attack the synagogues, loot them, and expel all the Jews from Alexandria. So our sources say, and indeed there is little evidence for Jews in Alexandria thereafter, though it is hard to imagine how this measure was carried out, or to what extent. These events alarmed the prefect Orestes, who was troubled that "the bishops [of Alexandria] were encroaching on the jurisdiction of imperial officials." Cyril escalated the conflict by bringing in 500 angry monks from Nitria, who publicly confronted Orestes, calling him a pagan. One of them, Ammonios, hit the prefect on the head with a rock and drew blood. Ammonios was arrested and tortured to death, and Cyril attempted to proclaim him a martyr of the faith, but most people knew that was a stretch.[83]

At that point, a fanatical group of Cyril's supporters targeted Hypatia, who belonged to the prefect's social circle. Hypatia was one of the most famous philosophers and mathematicians in the empire, and not just because she was a woman, though contemporaries could not see past that fact, commenting on her beauty and virginity in addition to her intellect. She was also a pagan, unmarried, fiercely independent, and "not ashamed to be out and about among the men."[84] This offended some zealous Christians. A para-ecclesiastical group of hospital orderlies known as the *parabalanoi* who worked under the bishop, often to terrorize his enemies, attacked her in public, tore off her clothes, and murdered her by scraping the flesh from her body with pottery shards. They dragged her remains through the streets and burned them. For this victory over "idolatry," Cyril was acclaimed by his supporters as "a new Theophilos."[85]

The emperor, who was around fifteen in 415, was shocked at this murder, and public opinion at the court turned against Cyril. Laws were issued to mitigate the "terror" caused by the *parabalanoi* by restricting their activities, and Cyril had to bribe court officials to avoid worse.[86] The bishop kept a low profile for the next fourteen years, until he picked the fight with Nestorios. But in just two years he had, through holy terrorism, made the position of Jews, deviant Christians, and pagans precarious. Large-scale violence was no longer the prerogative of the state. It could now be exercised by pious brigades doing God's work, or unleashed by cynical, insecure, or greedy bishops who were willing to call the state's bluff when it came to law and order: would a Christian governor or emperor have the nerve to create Christian martyrs in order to defend Jews and pagans?

Jews

Christianization posed a challenge to the identity of to the empire's Jews. In the aftermath of the great revolts of the first and second centuries, surviving Jews had largely assimilated into the mainstream culture, mixing Graeco-Roman and Jewish elements. But the same was not possible with Christianity. Jews had to decide whether to convert and become Christians, and many did so, or to embrace Judaism as a religious, ethnic, *and* legal identity, which meant that they would be marginalized from the increasingly Christian mainstream. It is not a coincidence that the great age of synagogue construction in Palestine and especially the Galilee commenced in the fifth century. Moreover, villages that obtained a synagogue also tended not to have a church, and vice versa, reflecting a gradual segregation of religious communities. Judaism was coming back as a separate identity and social category.[87]

The category "Jew" was of paramount concern to Christians, and caused anxieties among them in ways that had never been true for pagan Romans, certainly not in the period 138–324, when most Jews were invisible to imperial authorities. Christian texts abound in mostly negative references to Jews and Judaism, but many of them are rhetorical fictions of the theological imagination that were not necessarily reacting to the presence of actual Jews. It was, however, by thinking about Judaism on the one hand and Hellenism on the other that Christians made sense of who they were.[88] As the law began to differentiate groups based on their religious identity, Jews came to be defined as a legal category. The emperor who first began to legislate about "Jews" was Constantine and he did so in relation to Christian concerns: their "nefarious sect" was not to prevent any of their members from becoming Christians. Subsequent emperors were not as abusive toward the Jews as Constantine. However, they defined Judaism by law as a quasi-Christian kind of entity: its "presbyters" and "priests" were to enjoy some fiscal exemptions, just like Christian priests. These Jewish "prelates" were also given the power to decide which Jews were allowed to be members of their sect, and Jewish dissidents were prevented by law from appealing to Roman judges to be reinstated.[89] The emperors were chiefly concerned with three things: to prevent conversions from Christianity to Judaism (on pain of loss of property); to forbid Jews from owning Christian slaves; and to discourage Christian hotheads from attacking synagogues as, after all, "the sect of the Jews is forbidden by no law" (so Theodosius I). These protections were repeated, possibly because Christian attacks were frequent.[90]

By the end of the fourth century, Jews occupied an ambiguous place in the new Roman society. A law of Arcadius (of 398) split their legal status between secular matters, where they fell "under the Roman and common law" and used the secular courts, and matters pertaining to their "superstition," which they could bring before "the elders of their religion." By mutual consent, the parties to a case could use arbitration by these elders even in civil matters, just as Christians could sometimes do with bishops.[91] Jews could not be compelled to engage in official business on the Sabbath, but, after 418, they could not enter the imperial service, though they could be lawyers and decurions.[92] Thus, the requirement introduced by Theodosius I that a full Roman citizen had to be Catholic effectively created a second-class tier of citizenship for Jews. In the early empire, distinctions within the framework of Roman citizenship were based on one's *civitas*, or city of origin; now they were based on one's *religio*. Belonging to a different religion was construed by the imperial authorities as a sign of "hostility to God and the Roman laws."[93]

This legal transformation in effect pushed "the Jews," who might otherwise have been secular Roman subjects, into the hands of their religious leaders, just as it pushed Christians into the hands of bishops. But Jewish religious authorities had a different conception of where the line lay between secular and religious. For example, for Romans marriage was a private, civil matter, and Theodosius I had legislated specifically that Jews could not use their own customs in contracting their marriages.[94] Other areas must have remained ambiguous, leaving individuals with the option of choosing between the two systems. Unfortunately, we have little reliable evidence for Jewish community life. The Mishnah and Palestinian Talmud, compiled around this time, tell many stories but these are not necessarily historical. They are cast as a body of case law illustrating how rabbis interpreted Mosaic Law amid the challenges of Roman society. The rabbis were not yet identified with the synagogues, which continued in many ways to reflect a mainstream Graeco-Roman profile, for example in using figural art. As religious scholars, the rabbis were still a fringe element of Jewish life, limited to Tiberias, Sepphoris, and Kaisareia and the domain of private advice and arbitration.[95]

When the Patriarch ceased to be a recognized office in the imperial system, in 425, the Jews were left with no overarching institutions that could coordinate or unify their communities on an empire-wide scale. This exposed them to violence, for example the destruction of their synagogue at Kallinikos by a Christian mob in 388 and their expulsion from Alexandria in 414 by Cyril. Bishops could call for "the suppression not only of the Origenists but Jews, Samaritans, and pagans."[96] In the fifth century, the emperor banned the construction of new synagogues but set no penalties for breaking this law. Archaeology proves that it was ignored.[97]

Cyril vs. Nestorios

Jews and pagans benefited from the increasingly bitter divisions that distracted the empire's Christian leadership. The inner circle of Theodosius' court did not include the bishop of Constantinople, Attikos (406–425), who was more a manager of the Church than a spiritual leader. He had been an enemy of John Chrysostom, but as bishop he tried to build bridges to the Johannites and eventually ended the schism with Rome over the issue. But Rome remained suspicious of Constantinople, in part because of Illyricum. Whereas the civilian administration of eastern Illyricum belonged to the eastern empire, its ecclesiastical administration formed part of the western Church. In the fourth century, Rome claimed for itself the authority to appoint bishops for Illyricum and delegated it to the bishop of Thessalonike, as the pope's vicar. It is not clear that the bishop of Thessalonike saw himself in this role, and the churches of Illyricum turned to both Rome and Constantinople for advice and oversight, depending on which suited their interest. When a local controversy broke out in 419, some bishops in Greece appealed to Constantinople, which prompted the court to decree in 421 that the bishop of New Rome had supervision over ecclesiastical disputes in Illyricum. This caused a quarrel between Attikos and pope Boniface I, leading to stern letters also between Honorius and Theodosius. The eastern court backed down, but the law remained in the books and Rome rightly suspected that Constantinople would revisit the issue.[98] Illyricum would in fact become a chief cause of the later rupture between the two Churches.

Before those tensions could come to a head, a new theological conflict erupted that would tear the eastern Church apart. A deadlock in the ecclesiastical establishment of the capital led the court to bring in a bishop from outside, one Nestorios (428–431), who was, like John Chrysostom, an able orator from Antioch and zealous reformer. In his first sermon he told the emperor to "give me the earth purged of heretics, and I will give you heaven in exchange; help me to abolish the heretics, and I will help you to destroy the Persians." Nestorios duly cracked down on heretics. The Arians in the capital set fire to their chapel when it was about to be demolished, and the fire destroyed nearby houses as well, earning Nestorios the nickname "Firestarter."[99] Like Chrysostom, he alienated the City's monks by denouncing their roaming and loose living and restricted their movements: "the entire body of the monks fought against him."[100] He seems also to have alienated Pulcheria by restricting her activities and presence in the church and removing her altar-hanging from Hagia Sophia, but our reports about this conflict are unreliable and possibly modeled on the antagonism between Eudoxia and Chrysostom; at any rate, Pulcheria did not play an important role in Nestorios' downfall.[101] These tensions were not the source of the problem, but they proved fatal to Nestorios when, in the moment of crisis, he needed support from the populace and received only hatred.

The problem began when Nestorios mildly objected to the title *Theotokos* that was popularly bestowed on the Virgin Mary. It meant "she who bore or gave birth to God." Technically, Nestorios reasoned, she gave birth not to God but only to the Incarnate Word (Christ). Some priests in his entourage from Antioch were insisting that the term be banned, which outraged many, but Nestorios took a moderate position: the term was permissible so long as it was understood that

Mary did not give birth to God, which was pagan nonsense. Those who wished to be theologically precise could call her *Christotokos*, Bearer of Christ.[102] His enemies quickly distorted this distinction and claimed that he was radically separating the human and the divine within Christ to the point where one could speak of Two Sons, a human and a divine; if the Mother of God had not given birth to God, then Christ was not God but a "mere man." The ecclesiastical establishment of the City, men who had been sidelined when he was made bishop, stirred up popular unrest at his alleged "attacks" on the Virgin Mary. Calls went out for his condemnation as a heretic, which were taken seriously at Rome and Alexandria, whose bishops disliked the growing power of Constantinople in the Church.

Cyril of Alexandria had accompanied his uncle Theophilos to the Synod of The Oak that deposed John Chrysostom. He had seen up close how to destroy a bishop of Constantinople. Alarmed at what he took to be Nestorios' heresy, he began to write defenses of the Theotokos that stressed the unity of Christ, and sent letters to Nestorios correcting him on these points.[103] Nestorios had meanwhile upped the ante by agreeing to review the case of clerics who had been deposed in Alexandria for criminal acts and in Rome for heresy (specifically, the western obsession over Pelagianism).[104] This was perceived as uncanonical meddling in the legal affairs of other sees, as under Chrysostom. Both Rome and Alexandria held councils that condemned Nestorios' heresies. He was sent an ultimatum to recant or be deposed, and Cyril also sent him a list of twelve specific errors (the *Twelve Anathemas*) that he had to condemn if he wanted to remain in communion with Alexandria and Rome. These not only insisted on the term Theotokos but rejected any distinction between the human and divine in Christ, asserting that they were fused together "hypostatically," so that one could not attribute specific aspects of Jesus Christ to one or the other. Because they were fused together, even "the Word of God suffered in the flesh,"[105] a view that ran up against a theological tradition that was entrenched in Antioch. Moreover, the idea that God suffered was anathema to many Christians. Though it was not his intention, Cyril set off a firestorm of his own. In 430, Theodosius decided that the whole matter had to be discussed at an Ecumenical Council, to be held in the summer of 431 at Ephesos. The emperor's action effectively nullified the local councils of Rome and Alexandria. But what exactly was at stake?

The Council of Constantinople had decided in 381 that the Word / the Son was fully God, but had not explained how the human and divine natures interfaced or coexisted in the person of Jesus Christ. Some fourth-century bishops (including Athanasios of Alexandria) imagined that the Word took the place of the human soul within the person of Christ, but this position was later condemned as a heresy associated with Apollinaris of Laodikeia. Apollinaris insisted on the unity of Christ as a person of "one nature" and rejected the distinction between man and Word, which implied that there were "two sons."[106] This position was rejected because it was believed that God became incarnate in order to save the whole human being, both mind and soul; otherwise, God (in the form of the Word) would have been walking around in a zombie body. This heuristic division between the human and the divine in Christ was common among the Nicene theologians of the fourth century and was elaborated by Theodoros, bishop of Mopsouestia (d. 428). He was revered by many Syrian bishops, including Ioannes of Antioch, Nestorios, and Theodoretos of Kyrros. Nestorios' reservations about the title Theotokos stemmed from this precise understanding of the duality of Christ as both man and God. Human failings and limitations could not be attributed to God without blasphemy: "What was conceived in the womb was not in itself God . . . . What was buried in the tomb was not itself God."[107]

All sides in the fifth-century Christological debate agreed that Christ was both a full human being and God, and therefore was of two natures. At the same time, they also agreed that a unified person emerged from this conjunction: it was blasphemous to talk about two minds or two persons coexisting in Jesus Christ as if he were schizophrenic. This was a significant amount of common ground that could be turned into a battlefield only by a strong desire to disagree by distorting each other's position. This desire, however, was in abundant supply. The two sides in the conflict placed a *slightly* different emphasis on the way that they looked at what was otherwise the same conception of Christ. The one side, represented by the Antiochene tradition and Nestorios, stressed that certain aspects of Christ's life on earth (such as his birth, physical weaknesses, and moments of ignorance and passion) could or should be attributed to his human nature, whereas other aspects (such as his miracles and superhuman wisdom) should be attributed to the divine. The other side was represented by Cyril—there was no "Alexandrian tradition" in this matter as is often asserted, there was only Cyril. He stressed the unity of Christ after the Incarnation and saw both natures involved in all aspects of Christ's life. Basically, they were looking at different sides of the same coin. Nestorios accused Cyril of following Apollinaris in collapsing Christ into one nature—in fact, when Cyril produced his controversial formula "one nature of the Word enfleshed," he unwittingly relied on Apollinarian forgeries.[108] Nestorios also believed that Cyril blasphemed with his paradoxical talk about God suffering. For his part, Cyril accused Nestorios of radically separating the human and the divine in a way that yielded two separate sons. Both were uncharitable, polemical, and wrong about each other. Bishops other than the protagonists were confused about the issue and made matters worse when they intervened.

It is impossible to identify a point of substantive difference between the two theological conceptions, and those who insist that it exists are usually writing from within one or the other camp. In fact, it is as easy to find Nestorios categorically rejecting the doctrine of the Two Sons and asserting that Christ was a unified and even "indivisible" entity with one will as it is to find Cyril conceding that Christ did have two natures that remained conceptually distinct, insofar as they had not fused together to form some other, third type of thing: "the difference between the natures was not abolished by their union," he wrote.[109] Cyril did not believe that Nestorios' description of the union of the two natures was robust enough, but his own account tended to rely on analogies ("the fire and the coal") and imprecise language when he reached the crucial point, after which he would say that it was all a mystery or divine paradox anyway. Cyril evaded the implications of Biblical passages that clearly depict Christ as acting in a human way, for example praying. Moreover, the two theologians employed key technical terms in different ways (especially *prosopon*, *physis*, and *hypostasis*), which made it hard for them to agree on what was "real," and yet they were unwilling or unable to define these terms precisely. Cyril was at first unaware that he was taking on not just Nestorios but a powerful school of thought in Antioch. He would beat them at Ephesos, but their approach would prevail in the long run.

The Ecumenical Council of Ephesos was the biggest fiasco that the imperial Church had yet seen, and it happens to be the best documented event from all of antiquity to that point. Theodosius genuinely wanted the bishops to discuss the theological issues without secular interference and reach an agreement in good faith, which shows how badly he misunderstood the character of the ecclesiastical establishment. The metropolitan bishop of each province was invited, in a fatally vague wording, to bring "a few" of his suffragan bishops.[110] Cyril, who understood how councils really worked, brought a huge voting bloc of 50 Egyptian bishops with him. The power of the Alexandrian bishops in Church politics stemmed from their ability to muster large contingents of suffragan Egyptian bishops, whom they personally appointed to office, often through bribes and networks of patronage, and who were loyal to Alexandria. At Ephesos Cyril secured the support of the local bishop Memnon, who brought over to his side many bishops from the host province. Nestorios was isolated and outnumbered from the start, and his habit of stating his positions in provocative terms in private meetings cost him the support of potential allies. The council was set to begin on 7 June, 431, but the contingent of Syrian bishops (who are called "the Easterners" in the sources) was delayed for almost two weeks. Cyril used a pretext to initiate the council without them, on 22 June, and framed it as a trial of his enemy. Nestorios was condemned in absentia as a "new Judas" on the first day by over 150 bishops and the title Theotokos was declared to be orthodox.[111] When the Easterners arrived on 26 June, they convened a counter council on the very same day under the leadership of Ioannes of Antioch and condemned and deposed Cyril and Memnon. As Ioannes had honored the spirit of the invitation, he had limited each metropolitan to two suffragans, and so his council contained only 43 bishops.[112] No doctrinal issues had been settled. There had been no debate. There was no "Council of Ephesos."

The situation in Ephesos was chaotic. Nestorios had attended neither of the two councils and never met with Cyril. The two factions knew that they would win only if they convinced the emperor of their version, and so the court was deluged by partial reports, confusing rumors, and contradictory verdicts, accusations, and counter accusations. Both sides complained of violence: Memnon allegedly incited local mobs and monks to terrorize the Easterners, who were being excluded from the local churches, while Nestorios was accused of using the imperial guard under the *comes* Candidianus to terrorize the Cyrillians.[113] Days passed as the court tried to make sense of it all and salvage something from the mess. The emperor was being pressured by the people and monks of Constantinople, who were celebrating the deposition of the unpopular Nestorios and demanding that it be enforced. The people eventually occupied Hagia Sophia and representatives of the Easterners in the capital reported that they were in danger of being thrown into the sea.[114] The "people of Constantinople" were being treated by the bishops on both sides as a corporate entity with a legitimate stake in the proceedings, as evinced by the formal letters addressed to them, presumably to be read aloud in Hagia Sophia.[115]

Meanwhile, Cyril kept up the pressure at Ephesos by holding more sessions of his council to settle additional Church business. Theodosius at first announced that he would ratify *both* councils and depose Nestorios, Cyril, and Memnon. But this choice overrode the logic of Church procedure, according to which only one of the two councils could be valid, or neither, as the Cyrillians noted in a letter to the emperor.[116] Theodosius invited representatives of the two sides to Constantinople to present their case to him. The venue was then moved to Chalkedon because of unrest in the City, though violent clashes broke out in Chalkedon as well. In the midst of all this, and after months of negotiations, Nestorios resigned and retired to a monastery, leaving the emperor with little choice but to reinstate Cyril and Memnon. As with Chrysostom, the court had felt free to repeatedly invent and then reverse ecclesiastical policy in the wake of a contentious council, and did so under pressure from crowds in the streets. Theodosius then formally dismissed the Council of Ephesos in October, admitting that it had failed "since it turned out to be impossible for you to achieve unity or even to debate the contested issues with each other."[117] The leading theologian of the Easterners, Theodoretos of Kyrros, put it well when he asked about the Council: "What comedian ever wrote a more ridiculous play, and what tragedian a sadder one?"[118]

The Council of Ephesos exacted a heavy toll on the peace of the Church and yet had settled nothing in exchange. Nestorios was condemned, but for views that he never held. The Church was in schism, as the Easterners hosted a series of local councils that again condemned Cyril as a heretic, especially because of his extreme *Twelve Anathemas*. The emperor now brokered a resolution to this crisis through the patient diplomacy of his own agents, and a fragile and tentative agreement was finally achieved by 433. The Easterners accepted the deposition of Nestorios and the title Theotokos, but in exchange Cyril, who had still not understood the basis of Antiochene theology, made what was in effect a far more significant concession, essentially accepting the creed that the Easterners had ratified at Ephesos, namely that Christ was a union of two natures and that it was possible to attribute specific actions reported in Scripture to one or the other nature. The Formulary of Reunion avoided specifying whether Christ was in one or two natures *after* the Incarnation. "Let the heavens rejoice," Cyril proclaimed, but he had laid down the basis of the Easterners' victory at the Council of Chalcedon twenty years later.[119] Moreover, to prevail he had to bribe officials at the court to pressure Ioannes of Antioch to stop defending Nestorios. Cyril was widely accused of drumming up support through outright bribes at Ephesos, and we happen to have a jaw-dropping inventory of the bribes and gifts that he authorized during the negotiations after the Council: "100 lbs of gold to Heleniana, the wife of the praetorian prefect . . . 100 lbs of gold to the palace quaestor . . . four large carpets, four sofa covers, four rugs, six stool covers, two throne covers, six hangings, and two ivory thrones for the *cubicularius* Romanus." Cyril's secretary primly called these bribes—amounting to over 2,580 lbs of gold, not counting gifts and various unspecified sums—"blessings." These blessings nearly bankrupted the Church of Alexandria.[120]

The agreement of 433 was a private one between Cyril and Ioannes, and its enforcement throughout the empire during the 430s, with the help of the imperial authorities, was a messy affair. There were hardliners among the Easterners who had to be deposed. One was condemned to the mines of Egypt, and Nestorios himself was removed first from Antioch to Petra and then to an isolated oasis in southern Egypt, and his works were ordered to be burned in 435.[121] Meanwhile, Cyril was accused by his partisans of selling out to Antiochene two-nature theology. He vigorously denied it, affirming that Christ had one nature that had formed out of the union of two.[122] Cyril was unable to avoid the horns of a theological dilemma that he, more than anyone, had created. Also, his scheming victory at Ephesos made the climate of the eastern Church tense and explosive. When Cyril died in 444, Theodoretos wrote that "the gravediggers must take care to place a huge rock upon this villain's tomb so that he doesn't rise up to plague the Church."[123]

Pagans

Just as Christian authorities constructed a Judaism that reflected their idea of what a religion was, so too did they concoct "paganism," assembling it artificially from a diversity of local cults and beliefs. But whereas Judaism was to be protected even while it was being marginalized, paganism was to be gradually abolished. The Theodosian dynasty warned zealous Christians that pagans and Jews were not to be attacked or have their property plundered, but at the same time it issued many laws forbidding sacrifice and "nefarious rites" before idols on pain of death. It canceled the privileges and exemptions enjoyed by pagan priests; closed the temples; and decreed that pagans could not enter the service.[124] These laws aimed to exterminate paganism through gradual legal discrimination. Yet they were more wishful thinking than social engineering, as pagans, who still made up a significant portion of the population, continued to practice their rites and to serve in the army and administration, and Christians continued to attack them, sporadically but with fierce intent. The problem was too big to be solved by law, and many Christians of the early fifth century preferred to imagine that it just did not exist: "Hellenism has vanished," said one; "the error of idolatry is no more," declared another; and even Theodosius II stated that pagans were to be suppressed, "although we believe that there no longer are any."[125]

The fiction of a monolithically Christian empire would be punctured by reality down to the end of the sixth century. None other than Cyril of Alexandria wrote, after the Council of Ephesos, a long refutation of Julian's anti-Christian treatise, explaining that the work was widely believed to be irrefutable and was still instilling doubts in the faithful. Cyril's opponent at Ephesos, Theodoretos of Kyrros, also wrote a *Therapy for the Hellenic Maladies*, even while claiming that there was really no reason to do so.[126] This contradiction was reflected in the actual history of fifth-century paganism, which presents a highly variable picture. On the one hand, some high officials were openly known to be pagans, such as Zeno, the Isaurian general of Theodosius II, and the poet Pamprepios of Panopolis (Egypt), who rose high at the court of the later emperor Zeno, reaching the consulship even while he "displayed the Hellenism of his religion frankly in Constantinople, where most are Christians."[127] What enabled these men to flourish was the polite fiction that, although they honored the gods, they did not engage in sacrifice or "nefarious rites." While Christian zealots professed that they would not touch pagans or eat in their company, polite society tried to overlook religious difference. Theodoretos of Kyrros invited prominent local pagans to the dedication of a new church. And when a student in Alexandria gloated over the eradication of idols in a funeral oration for a friend, the pagans in the audience complained: "If you wanted to speak against the gods, why on earth did you drag us along to your friend's graveside?"[128] Decorum had been violated.

The Aegean region—the civic centers of Old Greece—remained attached to paganism longer than any other part of the eastern empire. This is shown by the virtual absence of monasticism until later centuries and the failure of this region to produce notable Christian authors, despite being a center of higher education. The schools in Athens remained openly pagan until late, as did many of the city's politicians. Pagan literary activity continued unabated throughout the fifth century. Important historians of this period from Eunapios of Sardeis and Olympiodoros of Thebes (Egypt) to Zosimos of Constantinople (a retired official of the fisc) were pagans, as were poets from Claudian of Alexandria to Nonnos of Panopolis and Christodoros of Koptos (Egypt).[129] It was now that Hellenic Neoplatonism reached its apogee in Proklos of Lykia (412–485). As a young man visiting Constantinople, he was granted a vision of "the goddess," probably Athena, who instructed him to go to Athens.[130] The schools of Athens had gained in importance after the murder of Hypatia in Alexandria. Proklos established a philosophical tradition there that would continue in strength into the sixth century. Through the mysterious forgeries written by "pseudo-Dionysios," Neoplatonism would also infiltrate and take over large swaths of Christian theology. Proklos' successor and biographer was Marinos of Neapolis (Nablus), a Samaritan convert to philosophical Hellenism. These pagan intellectuals, city notables, and imperial officials developed their own networks of friendship and patronage, proud of tradition and disdainfully weary of Christian aggression. They were colorfully described in the early sixth century by the last head of the Platonic Academy in Athens, Damaskios, in his *Philosophical History*.

These Hellenes understood well, especially after the murder of Hypatia, that the Christian empire was unsafe for them, though the violence was random: a mob would be inflamed by a bishop here, some monks would go on a rampage there. Smashing up temples and courting martyrdom were almost job requirements for aspiring saints and bishops. The hermits Rabbula (the future bishop of Edessa and ally of Cyril of Alexandria) and Eusebios (a future bishop of Tella) burst into a temple in Heliopolis (Baalbek) and smashed some statues, whereupon the pagans beat them up and threw them down the stairs. But attacks came from above as well, and one could not simply beat up the authorities. In the mid-fifth century, the philosopher Hierokles gave offense to "those in power" in Constantinople (a code word for Christians) and was flogged, after which he flung his blood at the judge and said, "Cyclops"—another code word—"drink blood now that you have tasted flesh," a reference to the Eucharist. The rhetorician Isokasios was also arrested in 467 in Constantinople and tried for paganism, but he "defused the anger of the crowd" by his noble bearing and consent to be baptized. The pagan professors in Alexandria were targeted toward the end of the century by Christian students, crowds, and imperial inquisitors, and some were arrested and tortured, after which they had to tone down their teachings. Their lectures were monitored by the same para-ecclesiastical groups that had murdered Hypatia.[131]

If they were lucky enough to avoid destruction, temples were converted into art museums, gaming rooms, tax-collection offices, schools, courthouses, homes, and taverns.[132] The temple of Roma and Augustus in Ankyra, which bears the text of the first emperor's *Res Gestae* and still stands, was possibly converted into a monastery.[133] Classical literary culture was also appropriated by the Christian state. In 425, Theodosius II founded what historians sometimes call "the University of Constantinople," endowing three chairs of Latin rhetoric and ten Latin grammarians, five Greek teachers of rhetoric and ten grammarians, one professor of philosophy, and two professors of law, to be housed in facilities provided by the state.[134] We cannot rule out that some of these professors were Hellenes, though the court presumably expected them to be Christian. The state thus salaried Christian scholars of classical studies, Julian's nightmare become real.

In the eastern empire, the term "Hellene" had been given a religious sense. A Hellene was now no longer a member of the Greek people, but rather a pagan of any nation, even a Persian or Saracen, an irony given the word's past. Yet there was also a minor sense in which a Hellene was someone educated in rhetoric and philosophy. When his devotion to Hellenism was questioned by Christian zealots, Synesios explained that "a philosopher should not be evil or boorish, but should be initiated in the Graces and be a Hellene in a most precise sense, namely he should be able to converse with humanity by knowing literature."[135] Christian scholars of the classics would navigate this ambiguity—humanism versus paganism—at their own individual risk. Too much engagement with the Hellenic classics could open one to the suspicion of contamination, of being a "new Julian." So the culture pretended that pagan literature was "external" and Christian texts were "internal," though in reality both were internal; this was just a self-protective pose. Pagan literature, moreover, was not dangerous because of the gods, who had ceased to be a threat in the fourth century. It was dangerous because philosophy could induce Christians to doubt articles of faith and because it praised un-Christian values such as physical beauty, eroticism, valor on the battlefield, and the like. Yet much of it was copied, preserved, and studied regardless, because many Christians too wanted to read and think about precisely such topics. Besides, the pagan material was nowhere near as problematic as anything deemed "heretical," all of which was either destroyed or allowed to lapse, making it difficult to reconstruct what any "heretic" had actually argued.

Given the violence and discrimination that pagans faced in the fifth century, many conversions were shallow or insincere, which created a climate of suspicion among Christians. "It is no wonder that a pagan or a heretic who has no faith is in the church," declared the Coptic abbot Shenute.[136] When Christian students denounced some alleged pagan plots to the prefect of Egypt Entrechius in the 480s, his lukewarm response, and the fact that one of his secretaries was openly a pagan, made them suspect that he too was a pagan. Insufficiently zealous Christians, or those who showed too great an interest in classical culture, could be branded as crypto-pagans. Orthodoxy was easily counterfeited and dissimulated, undermining the idea of a monolithically Christian empire.[137]

Cultures of Christian devotion

The influx of new converts meant that ancient religious practices and habits were imported wholesale into the Church, in some cases unchanged. The pagan roots of Christian forms of worship was a more popular topic of research a century ago than it is today, but it remains the case that early Christianity replicated or absorbed many modes of ancient religion, including dance, song, hymn, prayer, food, feast, the cult of the dead, incubation, oracles, book-divination, healing shrines, processions, and scriptoria. Even animal sacrifices were adapted to Christian worship.[138] Bishops worried that the adoration of the saints and their relics veered too close to the worship of the gods and that pagan-style parties were celebrated beside the tombs of the martyrs.[139] Many festivals of the Roman calendar, such as the kalends, Brumalia, and the nautical festival of Isis continued in Constantinople without much alteration, despite purist griping.[140] Christians instituted prayers, hymns, and processions to celebrate the rising of the Nile, in place of their direct pagan antecedents.[141] In ca. 480, the Parthenon in Athens was rededicated with only superficial architectural changes from the Virgin Athena to the Virgin Mary, who assumed many of the functions of her Olympian predecessor in protecting the city. This conversion was facilitated by forged pagan oracles which predicted that Mary would replace Athena; one of these texts was inscribed by the church's entrance. At that time Athena went to live with Proklos, i.e., his house received her cult statue.[142]

A novel form of Christian asceticism that emerged in the fifth century had roots in Syrian paganism. A chance reference in a second-century text reveals that in the sacred precinct of "the Syrian goddess" at Hierapolis men would climb to the top of tall phallic pillars twice a year and stay there for seven days, "talking with the gods and asking them for blessings on behalf of all of Syria."[143] In the early fifth century, an ascetic named Simeon, who was not satisfied with the rigors of regular monasticism, took to living on a small platform perched at the top of a column (*stylos*) in the vicinity of Beroia (Aleppo). He then moved to progressively taller columns. He lived that way for the better part of four decades until his death in 459. This lifestyle earned him the name "Stylite" and celebrity. Crowds flocked to him for advice, prayer, oracles, healing, gawking, and to arbitrate disputes, and he was honored, at a distance, by the emperors. It is unclear why Simeon and his subsequent imitators chose this way of life—to be symbolically closer to God? —or how he justified it. Even some Christians found it vain and horrifying, "a strange way of life hitherto unknown to mankind."[144] His dependence on others for food and water rules out solitude as a motive. A magnificent church shaped like a cross was later built around his column, which stood in an open-air octagonal courtyard in the middle. It quickly became a destination for pilgrims, though women were not allowed inside. Today it is a UNESCO World Heritage site. As far as Rome, shopkeepers set up small images of Simeon for protection.[145]

As asceticism had become a competitive sport, Simeon found rivals. One Daniel was determined to spend even more years on a pillar, only this time near Constantinople, where the climate is colder. Once he was found with his hair and beard frozen to his chest with ice, and he had to be thawed out with warm water. Emperors and courtiers would go out to visit Daniel. A former prefect, Cyrus of Panopolis, composed an epigram for him, which was carved on his column:

> Standing between earth and heaven a man you see,
> who fears no gales that all about him fret.
> Daniel is his name, great Simeon's rival.
> Upon a double column firm his steps are set,
> ambrosial hunger, bloodless thirst support his frame,
> and thus the Virgin Mother's Son he does proclaim.[146]

In the 440s, Theodoretos of Kyrros wrote, in stilted Attic prose, a portrait gallery of the celebrity ascetics of Syria, most of them hermits. We encounter here and in other texts men and women who wore heavy iron weights, including chains, to restrict their mobility; who stood perpetually, one of them covered head-to-toe in animal hides; who never left the scorching heat of the desert sun (one of them in order to ascertain whether he could withstand the fires of Hell); or who chained themselves to rocks; lived in tiny enclosures where they could not stand up; roamed the fields and grazed with the animals, "no longer human in the way that their minds worked."[147] In the later fourth century, an ascetic in Egypt named Bane is said to have stood continually, while fasting in a dark cell, for eighteen years. The spine of his skeleton, which is extant, reveals that some of the spondyls had fused together so that, if he lay down, he could not then get back up.[148] He had literally turned into a column.

The incredible stories told about these ascetics explore the outer limits of human nature and the Christian counterculture. These men and women excited both admiration and disgust, all the more so when they moved to the cities. The ascetic tradition in Constantinople featured both communal and free-range devotees, but it was the latter who drew suspicion among the clergy as they went around begging for alms and refusing to work. John Chrysostom, who turned against them, complained that their greed was "giving us all a bad name: Christ-Retailers."[149] Jerome explained how the business worked: they sold trinkets at a huge markup that reflected the "value added" by their holiness.[150] In the 420s, the monk Alexandros brought a hundred begging monks to Constantinople from Syria, after they had been expelled from Antioch. They were called the

Sleepless Ones because they maintained a permanent rotation of prayer and hymn singing. They were arrested by the authorities, beaten, and expelled from the capital. They resettled further up the Bosporos, and would become a major force in the coming Christological controversies, as partisans of the Council of Chalcedon.[151]

Monasticism was becoming increasingly disruptive and incompatible with Roman notions of public order. It was also becoming dangerous to minorities and even bishops, when the latter were perceived as heretical by the monks. According to one estimate, there were between 10,000 and 15,000 monks in and around Constantinople in the mid-fifth century.[152] It was the emperor Marcian (450–457) who brought monks under institutional control. He instructed the bishops at the Council of Chalcedon (451), a meeting tightly run by the court, to regulate them. Henceforth, monasteries were to be built only by episcopal permission and monks were to reside in them permanently without meddling in ecclesiastical or political life. The monastic life was now yet another *status* comparable to the many other social orders that were regulated by Roman law. Monks were to be governed by the canons of the Church.[153] This might have worked, had the bishops themselves not subsequently torn the Church and empire apart with theological disputes that fired up the monks' zeal.

The more exotic ascetics did not live in monasteries. Whether they took up their calling in caves, desert tombs, or pillars, they cultivated a certain "look" that was often enhanced by their never bathing, and they made themselves accessible to the general population, for whom they performed countless miracles. Historians shy away from discussing miracles, which require either skepticism or credulity, neither of which are in fashion. An influential thesis has instead shifted attention onto the social roles that these holy men performed as arbiters of local disputes, protectors of the weak, and mediators between higher and lower social classes, being able in some cases to bridge the gap all the way from village communities to the imperial court itself. It is easy to see how these figures, revered by many and seen as obviously above material self-interest, could function as neutral, fearless, and even miraculously potent arbiters. Trade guilds appealed to Simeon the Stylite against new taxes; two young men appealed to him against onerous appointments to the city council; and he held a court of arbitration after prayer at 3 p.m. each day.[154]

Holy men were not sought as arbiters because of an "erosion of classical institutions."[155] This was instead caused by the multiplication of political institutions, their penetration down to the most local social levels, and their fractal reproduction in the Church, army, and fiscal bureaux. In this more complex and intrusive machinery of social negotiation, there were more points of friction into which mediators could insert themselves—or be inserted by others. The primary agency here belonged probably not to the holy men themselves but to common people who sought to leverage them against their perceived oppressors.[156] It was secular elites who had endowed holy men with social capital, outsourcing the more stringent demands of the new religion to these specialists in virtue, and it was then the villagers who spent that capital by recruiting stylites and others to block elite misbehavior, just as they had leveraged Roman law itself to mitigate the burden of other state institutions. Holy men had to choose whether to evade this imposition by "the world" by retreating farther into the desert or, like Simeon and Daniel, to work it into their busy prayer schedule.

Bishops

If holy men occupied the interstices between institutions, bishops were institutional managers. Cities now had three masters-in-residence: their councils, the local representatives of the central government, and their bishops, who mostly came from the curial class but had a different agenda. They claimed to speak for the poor and the humble, and backed that claim by organizing charities (sometimes funded by the imperial government), ransoming prisoners of war, and supporting widows, orphans, and the poor, of whom they kept lists (7,500 in Alexandria, 3,000 in Antioch).[157] "The property of the Church consists of the support of the poor. Let the pagans count how many prisoners their temples have ransomed, what food they have given to the hungry, what prisoners they have supported," one bishop challenged.[158] Bishops sometimes represented their cities or the empire in negotiations with Persia, and even took on military roles if necessary. In a brief Persian war, the bishop of Theodosiopolis directed the operations of a wall-mounted catapult nicknamed "St. Thomas," with which he managed to crush the head of an enemy commander.[159] Bishops apparently brought to their office a variety of skills from their prior careers.

Still, the power of bishops in this period can be (and has been) exaggerated. They had little or no authority to give orders to anyone who did not work for them directly. They could only petition, plead, inspire, bribe, threaten with Hell, or, if they were the bishops of Alexandria or Ephesos, deploy angry mobs. The eastern empire's bishops did not pool their resources to act collectively, so their economic power, unlike that of the state, remained fragmented, local, and earmarked for specific purposes. Some bishops admitted that, "to be honest, we ourselves live from what belongs to the poor."[160] Their finances were sometimes scrutinized and even audited by the state, and the Council of Chalcedon required bishops to employ a fiscal manager (*oikonomos*) "so that the administration of the churches not be without witness."[161] Bishops were respected but beleaguered by busywork. Theodoretos had to lobby the prefect to secure a tax break for his city; he added rather lamely that the famous ascetic Iakobos endorsed his petition "but adheres to his vow of silence and so cannot be brought to write."[162] Individually bishops had little pull at the court, and collectively they presented an unedifying spectacle at many councils, especially at Ephesos in 431 and

449, which not only diminished their moral stature but imperiled many with the charge of heresy. It is no wonder, then, that some men preferred to remain city councilors rather than become bishops, or even used episcopal office as a stepping-stone to an imperial career.[163]

The stakes and risks of episcopal politics were high. The Church modified the Roman practice of *damnatio memoriae*, so that when a bishop was convicted of heresy or other heinous offenses he would not only be deposed and exiled but also stricken from official commemoration, his name literally erased from the lists of a see's former bishops and mentioned elsewhere only with opprobrium and disgust, just like "tyrants" were in the political sphere. When the political winds changed direction, a deposed bishop's name could be reinstated, just like that of a failed emperor whose memory found a later champion.

The Church was internalizing Roman values, but the Roman state was not conversely internalizing Christian values. For the most part, state institutions continued to operate as before. The court made an effort to construct a Christian imperial "style," but it was mostly symbolic, expressed in evocative gestures such as Theodosius II's hair shirt and the virginity of his sisters. He decreed that his retinue would leave their weapons outside when they entered church and that he would remove his crown in deference to God.[164] He received holy men respectfully, such as when the leading abbot in the City, Dalmatios, left his monastery for the first time in forty-eight years to denounce Nestorios.[165] But these symbols were wrapped around a core of Roman pragmatism. A Church historian admitted that Theodosius I "had not always enforced his laws against religious deviants because he did not want to persecute his subjects,"[166] and his son and grandson followed the same policy. Pagans continued to serve in office and synagogues continued to be built, despite the laws. The court also knew that imposing religious uniformity might disrupt provincial tax collection, which it valued more.[167] The devout prefect Florentius cracked down on pimps in the City in 428, but this cost the treasury in revenue, so ten years later the court took him up on his generous offer to make up the deficit personally. Moral campaigns against "disgraceful turpitude" came with a cost.[168]

Sex work had not previously been a serious moral problem, but Christian leaders wanted to overhaul the empire's sexual regime.[169] In the old economy of honor, sexual rights, restrictions, and reputations depended on one's gender and social status: higher-status men were free to exploit the (usually coerced) sexual availability of lower-status women, especially of slaves and sex workers, whereas higher-status women were expected to be strictly chaste. Christian moralists, by contrast, advocated a uniform economy of the conscience, whereby each person, no matter his or her status, was expected to abide by the same rules, authorizing sex only between husband and wife and only for the goal of procreation, the sole reason for which God had sanctified sex; otherwise it was *porneia* ("fornication"), no matter the gender.[170] The prefect Florentius was allegedly concerned that pimps were forcing the sexual conscience of young girls, regardless of their social status (which was probably low). The new sexual ethic, however, wanted to police sexuality more rigorously and to abolish a number of consensual forms, such as homosexuality. Moreover, a double standard for men and women is still reflected in the writings of the Church Fathers and in the lives of Christian aristocrats, and Christian writers balked at the moral redemption of actresses.[171] Old attitudes died hard, and there is no evidence that the new ethic managed to make the leap from the pulpit to society at large, whether in the fifth century or even in the sixth, if we judge by the society depicted in Prokopios' *Secret History*. Imperial legislation was taking only baby steps toward the new Christian values.

The Blues and the Greens

The greatest popular passions of the time, hated by the bishops, were the races in the hippodrome and the theatrical entertainments. The theater in this age included few highbrow plays and featured mostly mime shows (troupes who acted out scurrilous, mythological, and comic skits) and the pantomime (a silent performance by one virtuoso star). Passions among rival fans ran high at these performances and frequently led to violence and even riots.[172] By the mid-fifth century, the old athletic and artistic guilds, troupes, and associations had either gone extinct or were folded by the state into two large umbrella guilds, the Blues and the Greens, which had two smaller subsidiaries, the Whites and the Reds. These were the ancient Roman racing teams, but they were now upgraded to function as empire-wide organizers of spectacles and acclamations. They received horses from the imperial stud farms and state support. An imperial *actuarius*, or paymaster, for the races and theater is first attested in 426. Their activities were supported by local notables, civic endowments, and patrons, the teams' rich fans.

The teams consisted of the staff that organized the events (dancing masters, chorus leaders, animal trainers, and such), though the charioteers were celebrities on short-term contracts. Each team had patrons (some well-placed in the court, or the emperors themselves); fans among the population who cheered for each team and got into brawls with opposing fans; and a club of registered die-hards called "the partisans," about a thousand per team on the sole occasion when we are told their number. The partisans had designated seats in the hippodrome.[173] A moralist of the period took a cynical view of this organization: the authorities had manufactured these sporting rivalries to divert the passions of the youth away from actual civil wars.[174] But soon these passions would spill out in actual civil wars.

This reorganization of the spectacles seems to have taken place during the reign of Theodosius II. For the next two centuries, the fan clubs and their activities defined life in the cities of the eastern empire to a greater degree than monasticism, and they rivaled the impact of the Church on people's daily preoccupations. John Chrysostom complained that many people, instead of knowing passages from Scripture, "know the names, stock, and origin of the horses, how they were reared, how old they are, their performance on the racetrack . . . while others are fanatic when it comes to the theater, its mimes and dancers, and know their families, origins, and training. But if we ask them, 'Which are the epistles of Paul?,' they don't even know the number."[175] Another bishop wrote that spectacles incited people to practice the dark arts in order to give their team an edge. It was all "a plague on the cities, causing division, riots among the people, and families to break up"[176]—but so did doctrinal strife, stirred up by the bishops.

The hippodrome was associated not only with violence but also with paganism. As a monumental space, it continued to evoke a pagan cosmology oriented around the elements, seasons, the sun, and the Dioskouroi as the patron saints of the games (they were ancient hero-gods, the brothers of Helen of Troy). Games and plays were banned on Sundays, but religious zealots still protested the games fervently. In 459, Leo I decreed that no one—*especially* monks—was to carry crosses into public buildings or places of popular entertainment, or to "occupy" such places, "seeing as places of worship are not lacking."[177] In fact, the influence probably ran in the opposite direction, as the hippodrome colonized the religious imagination. The image of the archetypal king, such as Solomon in Jewish literature, was recast to reflect that of the emperor presiding over a people and court marked out by the colors of the racetrack.[178]

Racing-team loyalties inspired the same fanaticism and violence as sectarian Christianity. By the later fifth century, in every city the fans of each team, men and women alike, hated their rivals with a passion verging on "mental disorder." These divisions could override ties of kinship.[179] The emperors were expected to present themselves as men of the people and choose sides, preferring one team over another, while in reality funding both. Paradoxically, this consolidation of the spectacles unified the empire in a common national preoccupation. Blues in one city showed solidarity with Blues in another, and a fan of the Greens in one city was a fan of the Greens "in every place." The leadership of the Blues or Greens in one city could be swapped out, by the authorities, with their counterparts from other cities.[180] Thus, team affiliation was structurally similar to theological affiliation, and the two types of division reinforced each other in the social pathology of the time. Both, after all, were arbitrary: Blues vs. Greens, One-Nature vs. Two-Nature, there was no difference between them other than team colors. Tribal affiliation in both cases was determined by personal narratives and circumstances and often had little to do with reason or self-interest. Both sporting and religious partisans were seen as "willing to die for the cause of their side."[181]

Even so, the hippodrome and theater were protected from the Church and funded by the government. Why did the court support these potentially disruptive entertainments? First, from the start of the Principate, emperors had to be seen as sharing in these popular passions, with a favorite team, in order to maintain their own popularity. Second, emperors were expected to provide bread and circuses to the populace, which was now a global Roman community in every city. But the strongest reason was likely the transition from an itinerant and military style of rulership to a sedentary, civilian, and populist one. Emperors used to be created by military acclamation, and their ongoing legitimacy was confirmed by the presence of thousands of soldiers who periodically shouted their acceptance of a reign—or ended it by violence. Now that emperors rarely left their palace chambers, this vital function could be performed only by the civilian populace, who assembled in the hippodrome, adjacent to the palace. In addition to organizing spectacles, the Blues and the Greens were charged with cheerleading the people to praise God and the emperor at the start of the games.[182] Thus, the games functioned as empire-wide demonstrations of loyalty, taking the place of the defunct imperial cult. The Blues and Greens, hooligans though they were in their sporting rivalries, orchestrated popular demonstrations of legitimacy.

The ceremonies of imperial acceptance shifted gradually during the fifth century from primarily military, with accessions performed at the Hebdomon, to primarily civilian, with accessions performed in the hippodrome. This changed the constituent dynamics of power, for the hippodrome was a more complex space than a mustering field. Confident in its numbers and sometimes agitated by the teams and the partisans, the populace could not only acclaim emperors but vent its grievances, for example against unpopular officials, grain shortages, high prices, or theological matters. This was an old Roman function of the Circus Maximus, but with the people now acting as a pillar of imperial legitimation, their complaints acquired additional urgency.[183] The Blues and Greens helped to keep the people in line.

Cities can be designed to isolate their residents from each other and prevent them from assembling in large numbers. Constantinople was the opposite of that. The ability of its populace to know each other and form common purpose was enabled by the City's social infrastructure. In ancient states with limited or non-existent concepts of public authority, such as Pharaonic Egypt, no architectural provision was made for social gatherings.[184] New Rome, by contrast, was endowed with many open spaces where the populace could congregate: the forums (which also functioned as marketplaces), baths, the hippodrome, porticoed courtyards, assembly courtyards even in the palace (such as the Tribounalios or Delphax), and Hagia Sophia, as well as the boulevard (the Mese) that linked them all together. In Constantinople, when a few hundred people congregated in any one place, a few thousand more showed up to find out why. The Theodosian dynasty forged not only a close but a codependent political relationship with the populace that would last for the rest of east Roman history.

9

Barbarian Terrors and Military Mobilization (441–491)

The rich documentation generated by the Church Councils of this era reveals, in unprecedented detail, the formal mechanisms and procedures by which the court controlled ecclesiastical politics, and the lobbying that unfolded behind the scenes.[1] Yet the inner workings of the court remain opaque after the death or departure of the praetorian prefect Anthemius in 414. There appears to have been no one dominant personality, and somehow all the top officials, the separate branches of the state, and special interests kept peace with each other and maintained a balance of power. This changed in the last decade of the reign.

The eunuch chamberlain Chrysaphius ("Goldy") gained ascendancy over Theodosius and managed to drive out competitors, though how he did this is opaque, shrouded in later romantic fiction. Around 439, Chrysaphius somehow induced the emperor's sister Pulcheria to leave the court and move to a monastery at the Hebdomon.[2] Between 439 and 441, the empress Eudokia had also left the court for the Holy Land, where she was to live until her death in 460, engaged in charitable works and theological politics. The late "Romance of Theodosius and Eudokia" attributed her move to a suspicion of adultery and embellished it with a tale about a large apple. Be that as it may, the imperial couple were definitely at odds. Sober sources tell us that Eudokia murdered an official sent to her from the court, whereupon she was stripped of her retinue, though not her title.[3] Eudokia's departure, and her age, meant that Theodosius would not now produce a male heir. High officials could aspire to the throne, or be accused of doing so.

Extraordinary power was attained by one Cyrus of Panopolis (in Egypt). He was simultaneously prefect of Constantinople, praetorian prefect (of Oriens), and consul for 441. A capable poet, he was popular because he adorned the City with buildings, provided it with night-lighting, and completed the circuit of its sea walls. To make government more accessible, he issued his decrees in Greek rather than Latin. The trend had been in this direction for some time. In 397, Arcadius allowed judges to issue decisions in Greek, and in 439 Theodosius II allowed the wills of Roman citizens to be in Greek. But one day in 441, the people in the hippodrome chanted "Constantine built [the City], Cyrus renewed it! Make room for him, Augustus!"[4] This was too much for Theodosius and Chrysaphius, who removed Cyrus from his positions and confiscated his property. He was accused of paganism and, paradoxically, packed off to be bishop of Kotyaion in Phrygia. The townspeople there had already murdered four of their bishops and were ready for another. But Cyrus won them over by delivering the shortest Christmas sermon on record: "Brothers, let the birth of God, our savior Jesus Christ, be honored with silence, seeing as he was conceived in the Holy Virgin through hearing alone; for he was the Word. To him let there be glory for ever, Amen."[5] After Theodosius' death in 450, Cyrus resigned from his see and returned to private life in the City until his death in ca. 470.

The dynasty was facing extinction. In 439, Theodosius married his daughter Eudoxia to his cousin Valentinian III (425–455), the emperor of the west, but that couple produced only daughters. Moreover, by 440, the western empire was in a bad state, increasingly requiring aid from the east. The fall of the west had begun.

Troubles in the western empire

Decades earlier, the Huns had extended their operations to the Hungarian Plain, which set more migrations into motion, similar to the one that had brought the Goths to the Danube in 376. A different group of Goths invaded Italy in 406 but was defeated by Stilicho. This operation, however, left Gaul defenseless against an invasion later that year by a large group of Vandals, Alans (Iranian speakers), and Suevi. They plundered their way through Gaul and settled in Spain, occupying it by 411. To deal with so many invasions and the civil wars to which they gave rise, the western government abandoned Britain, around 410. Meanwhile, after sacking Rome Alaric's Goths wandered in Italy, Gaul, and Spain before striking a deal with the top western general, Constantius, in 418. They were assigned lands to settle in Aquitaine (in Gaul) and agreed to serve as allies of the Romans, though they remained autonomous and were not reliably loyal. In 429, the Vandal-Alan federation in Spain, under the leadership of the canny Vandal king Gaizeric (428–477), crossed to Mauretania and began to conquer North Africa; they numbered in total 80,000 people (men, women, children, and slaves), including about 15,000 fighters.[6] A joint effort of the western and eastern armies, under Bonifatius and Aspar respectively, failed to destroy the Vandals in the early 430s but did result in a treaty that preserved Carthage and its province of Proconsularis for the western empire. But in 439, the Vandals violated that treaty and seized Carthage, forming their own state in North Africa. The Vandals were Arian Christians and their kings occasionally persecuted the Nicene population. They also started raiding by sea around the Mediterranean, culminating in another sack of Rome in 455. It was likely the Vandal threat that prompted Theodosius and Cyrus to provide Constantinople with formidable sea walls. These would defend the City until 1204.

The western empire was trapped in a vicious circle: its loss of territory and the damage to agriculture caused by invasions resulted in smaller revenues and thus smaller armies, which in turn reduced the government's ability to recover lost territories and defend itself against the next round of invaders. The loss of North Africa in particular, one of the wealthiest provinces and the breadbasket of the city of Rome, which had hitherto required few expenditures for defense, was a game-changer. It had to be recovered if the west was to survive. This called for a joint operation. In light of the danger posed by Gaizeric, Valentinian III issued a law that allowed Romans to bear arms for self-defense and referred to "the imminent arrival of the army of our father, the most invincible emperor Theodosius."[7]

The eastern Romans also had cause to be concerned, for Gaizeric's fleet could now strike anywhere in the Mediterranean. In 440 or 441, in a rare display of gargantuan militarism Theodosius sent a transport fleet of (allegedly) 1,100 ships to Sicily to eliminate the Vandals once and for all. It was to be the first of four such efforts. But before any fighting took place, the fleet was recalled in a hurry and, in 442, Gaizeric made a peace treaty with the emperors that confirmed his possession of North Africa.[8] Two crises had caused the east Romans to turn back: first, the Persians, learning that the armies had been sent west, attacked Roman Armenia. This was quickly resolved when the Romans made (unspecified) concessions.[9] The second, and more important, was a surprise attack across the Danube by Attila the Hun.

Attila and the Huns

The Huns, based in central and eastern Europe, established the first of many nomadic empires that Romanía would face, though geographically speaking the Romans were relatively insulated from the broader steppe, compared that is to other urban empires such as China. The nature of these nomadic empires was fairly consistent, whether they operated on the borders of Rome or China. Mounted warriors, whose economy was commonly pastoral, conquered more sedentary agricultural populations across a wide area, extracting tribute from them along with infantry auxiliaries (if needed) and taxing their trade routes. The people who had fallen under Hun domination included the Goths, Gepids, and Lombards. The Hun cavalry army was able to cover large distances at speed and strike with surprise. Having subjected a core territory, they then raided adjacent empires, sacking cities, plundering the countryside, taking captives, and even fighting their infantry armies, if they could be mobilized in time to offer resistance. The Huns' goals were to plunder and force the Romans to pay regular protection money, which their king distributed to his followers in order to keep them happy; otherwise, he might lose his position and his life to someone who promised to do better.[10] The Huns enjoyed an advantage on the battlefield as they could fire their powerful composite reflex bows from a distance against slower-moving infantry armies. They had a terrifying reputation, which some augmented by practicing cranial deformation, binding the skulls of their infants between two boards so that they grew upward in an oblong shape. This gave them a fierce aspect without, apparently, impairing them.

Nomadic empires were parasitical and extortionate. Attila had no intention of destroying or conquering the Roman empire. He wanted to milk it, which meant that he had to scourge it first. His predecessors had already extracted concessions by raiding. Constantinople had agreed to pay the Huns 350 lbs of gold annually, a sum that was subsequently doubled to 700 lbs. But Attila had now amassed a large following. Before his rise, Huns were easily hired as mercenaries by the Romans. The western general Aetius had been hiring them for decades to suppress Goths and Roman usurpers. But by drawing most Huns into his following, Attila had to expand the scope of his operations in order to keep them happy. In 441–442, he raided Illyricum in a surprise attack, capturing Singidunum, Viminacium, and the major city of Naissus, the latter in an alarming display of sophisticated siege-craft. (Eight years later the historian Priskos passed through Naissus and found it abandoned except for some sick men in the churches, and his party had to look for a place to camp that was not covered in the bones of the men who had fallen in the fighting.)[11] The army in Sicily was recalled as the Balkan provinces were now exposed to Hun attack. Unfortunately, the work of the major historian of that age, Priskos of Panion, survives only in fragments, and so we lack a coherent account. The defense of the Balkans was led by Aspar, but he seems to have been defeated. Aspar was emerging as the eastern empire's leading general and foreign-relations manager, and he arranged the new truce with Attila, with the annual subsidy likely raised to over 1,000 lbs of gold.[12]

Constantinople realized that, with a neighbor such as Attila, the days of relative demilitarization were over. It issued a law in 443 to strengthen border defenses. *Duces* were to ensure that units were up to their full complement and that soldiers were properly trained, a tacit admission that this had not been true before. The *magister officiorum* was to report every year on the state of the army and river patrols.[13] The major reform of this decade was the creation of a new system of five field armies that is codified in an administrative document known as the *Notitia dignitatum*. This lists the major offices of the Roman state, dividing them between the eastern and western empires. It gives to the east five field armies: one for Illyricum, Thrace, and Oriens and two praesental armies for the vicinity of Constantinople, each under the command of its own *magister militum*. Scholars traditionally date the *Notitia* to the 390s, but the system that it describes did not exist before the 440s (only the *magister militum* for Oriens is regularly attested before then). It replaced the far more ad hoc system of appointing generals that had survived from the fourth century. The new armies were created to meet the threat of Attila, but not from scratch. The reform probably rearranged existing units into the *Notitia*-shape, but also entailed additional recruitment. Each of the field armies had up to 20,000 soldiers, so the days of relative demilitarization were over.[14] The Huns, who were formerly a nuisance, had now managed to force the empire to change its strategy. This was understood even by Nestorios in his distant Egyptian exile: the Huns, he pointed out with glee, used to be disunited but were now established in a monarchy that surpassed Rome. The Romans deserved this scourge, of course, because of the injustice done to Nestorios himself at Ephesos.[15]

Attila was distracted in the mid-440s, murdering his co-ruler and brother Bleda and consolidating his rule over the Hun empire. The Romans took this opportunity to stop paying the subsidy, which brought Attila back in force. In late 446, he invaded along the Danube, capturing cities and forts. He defeated and killed the new *magister militum* of Thrace and captured his headquarters, the city of Marcianopolis, and then pressed on to Constantinople. As it happened, the City had suffered a severe earthquake on the night of Sunday, 26 January, which damaged many buildings on the southern branch of the Mese, cracked the land walls, and brought down fifty-seven of the towers. The next day the emperor, barefoot, led a pious procession to the Hebdomon, another "triumph in reverse." Meanwhile, emergency repairs to the walls were organized by the praetorian prefect Constantinus. He set the Blues and Greens to work alongside the regular workforce, and they finished the job in two months. An inscription set up on the Rousiou Gate boasted that "Athena Pallas could not have built stronger walls."[16]

Attila's invasion route brought him to the Thracian Chersonese, where he defeated another Roman army. After that, he allowed his Huns to ravage the Balkan provinces freely, and some reached as far as Thermopylae, in Greece. This was the worst disaster that the eastern empire had suffered since the Gothic War of 378–382. A contemporary lamented that "there was so much bloodshed, it was not possible to count the dead. Even the monks wanted to escape to Jerusalem, and the Huns almost captured Constantinople . . . . They so devastated Thrace that it will never recover."[17] Archaeology confirms this image, for example at Philippopolis.[18] This forced the Roman high command, "gripped with overwhelming fear," to come to terms quickly, which Attila was inclined to do as well, for "a sickness of the bowels" was ravaging his own army. The Romans agreed to cede a strip of territory along the Danube, five days travel in width and extending in length from Pannonia to Novae in Thrace (so effectively surrendering Sirmium and Singidunum as well). The ruins of Naissus would be the border point between the two empires. So much for the defensive arrangements of Anthemius, the law of 443, and the reform of the army high command. This gap gave Attila free access to the Balkan provinces, as the Romans could not resist his river crossings. They agreed not to receive any fugitives from the Huns, and to pay 6,000 lbs of owed back tribute and an annual tribute henceforth of 2,100 lbs (= 151,200 solidi per year).[19] It was the worst humiliation of the eastern empire so far.

With the back pay, the court had to give Attila 583,200 solidi in the first year (or 8,100 lbs), money that could not easily be raised from the ravaged Balkan provinces, shifting the burden disproportionately to the east. Priskos claims that extraordinary levies were imposed, tax exemptions were canceled, and senators had to pay more based on their rank. Some had to pawn off jewelry or furniture, while others committed suicide.[20] This might not be hyperbole. The revenues of the eastern empire have been estimated at between 4 and 6 million solidi, and the annual cost of an army of 250,000 men at roughly 1.5 million.[21] According to these figures, the empire had to turn over to Attila a crippling part of its annual revenue. On top of that, its army had been mauled and had to be brought back to strength.

Even the regular annual payment of 2,100 lbs was a burden in a period of reconstruction and urgent upgrades. It is reported that some western senatorial families had annual incomes of over 4,000 lbs cash plus a third of that in kind,[22] but, even if these reports are accurate, such levels of private wealth are not attested in the eastern empire. To these costs should be added the ransom that the Huns demanded for their prisoners, some of whom individually fetched hundreds of solidi. And the loss of manpower was itself a heavy blow. The Huns marched off a hundred thousand captives or more from the Balkan provinces, reducing state revenues and making the payments sting more.[23] Altogether, this was a significant drain of gold from the empire to the Hungarian Plain, and a shameful humiliation.

It is said that when Attila captured Milan in 452 and saw a painting of the Roman emperor sitting triumphant over slain Scythians, he found an artist to make a painting of Attila enthroned while the emperors poured out gold at his feet from sacks on their shoulders. To disguise the truth about this relationship, one of the two Roman courts bestowed upon Attila the rank of *magister militum* so that the tribute could be cast as provisions for a notional Roman army. For his part, Attila regarded Roman emperors as equivalent in rank to his own generals.[24]

Chrysaphius astutely recognized that Attila's empire was not a real state but a racket that would collapse without its boss. With the emperor's permission, the eunuch bribed one of Attila's associates to assassinate him in 449. The plot failed, but did have a happy side in that the embassy included none other than Priskos the historian, who claims that he was unaware of the plot. Priskos' detailed account of the journey to the court of Attila, his description of how Attila operated, and the debate that he had there about the virtues and flaws of the Roman state with a Roman renegade who preferred living among the Huns is a high point of historical narrative literature. Priskos did not depict the Huns as beasts, as other Romans had done, but as a foreign culture that made sense on its own terms. In his tale, it is the scheming Romans who look worse than the Huns. In 450, Attila even ceded the strip of territory along the Danube back to the empire.[25]

Eutyches and Ephesos II

As if the Huns were not enough, the cold war within the Church between Alexandria and the "Eastern" bishops was heating up. Dioskoros, the new bishop of Alexandria, was every bit as imperious as his predecessors, and his theology rested on Cyril's later formula about the One Nature in Christ. The Antiochene tradition at this time was led by Theodoretos of Kyrros, who was spending much of his time in Antioch and whose Two Nature theology was indistinguishable from that of Nestorios. Both positions were supported by strong arguments but were also vulnerable to devastating critiques, which was inevitable given that they were trying to explain how one component of an indivisible tripartite God could "become Man" in such a way as to retain both human and divine attributes, albeit without mixing them up into some new type of thing or having two personalities. No formula could tie this up without leaving loose ends, and theologians pounced on loose ends like cats on mice. Moreover, the two sides were partially talking at cross-purposes. The Antiochene Two Natures formula referred to the human and divine components of Christ, whereas the conservative Cyrillian One Nature formula insisted that Christ was a single, unified person. The Formulary of Reunion on which Cyril and Ioannes of Antioch had agreed in 433 subtly favored the Antiochene position, but it was not an official position of the Church and had no means of enforcement.

The war of pamphlets and accusations intensified in the 440s.[26] At that point, the regime of Theodosius intervened and, until the emperor's death in 450, did so consistently in favor of conservative Cyrillians and against the Antiochenes. An edict of 448 decreed that clergy who accepted the doctrines of Nestorios should be deposed and that recent theological treatises should be burned if they deviated from the position of Ephesos and Cyril, referring to a new book by Theodoretos, the *Eranistes*. A few months later, Theodoretos was confined to Kyrros on the grounds that "he had been causing trouble to the orthodox" at Antioch.[27] Yet a wrench was thrown into this policy by the Synod of Constantinople in 448. This was a standing committee of bishops and abbots, who assisted the bishop of the capital in managing routine business. Eusebios, the bishop of Dorylaion, accused Eutyches of heresy. He was archimandrite (abbot) at the Hebdomon, about ninety years old and a staunch upholder of the One Nature. It appears from the Synod's minutes that the chairman, Flavianos of Constantinople, helped Eusebios to prosecute Eutyches. Eutyches lacked verbal agility and was duly condemned for believing in the One Nature of Christ after the Incarnation, i.e., the conservative Cyrillian view. Fifty-three bishops and archimandrites signed this condemnation, their verdict based on a Two-Nature reading of Cyril (whom they praised as a standard of orthodoxy) and the Formulary of Reunion of 433 (though the latter was ambiguous on how many Natures there were *after* the Incarnation).[28] This

Synod lit the fuse that detonated the unity of the Church in the east and fissured the Roman empire itself.

The trial of Eutyches blindsided the court, which favored the One Nature formula. While the proceedings were still ongoing, the emperor provided Eutyches with a military escort and sent court officials to attend the trial. One of them, the former prefect and consul Florentius, appears in the minutes to be entrapping Eutyches and sharing Flavianos' view that the One Nature was heretical, but Florentius later denied that and alleged that he had been misquoted.[29] (The acts of the Synod of 448 were entered into the record of the first session of the Council of Ephesos II in 449, which were in turn entered into the acts of the first session of the Council of Chalcedon in 451, which is how we have them, but they are interspersed with comments made at both Ephesos II and Chalcedon, making this dossier a Chinese box.) Eutyches promptly protested his conviction to pope Leo, Dioskoros, and the emperor. Pope Leo, like some of his predecessors, believed that he was the ultimate authority in the Church with the right to retry any case, so he demanded the relevant transcripts. Flavianos sent the minutes and persuaded Leo that Eutyches had been properly condemned. Besides, Leo favored a Two Nature solution, as he explained in a letter that was henceforth known as the Tome of Leo. Catholic tradition sees these events largely through Leo's eyes, but he was a marginal player and did not fully understand the different theological positions.[30]

In contrast to Leo, Theodosius rejected the outcome of the trial. He later stated publicly that in 448 he had "repeatedly" instructed Flavianos to "still the turmoil that he had stirred up" and stop the trial, but Flavianos had gone ahead with it anyway.[31] Accordingly, he broke off communion with Flavianos a week before Easter 449, and punished bishops who had opposed Eutyches by imposing heavier taxes on their churches. Upon Eutyches' appeals, the emperor also ordered no fewer than three reviews of the trial, but these upheld the verdict. Theodosius then summoned a new Church Council to meet in August at Ephesos and review the case. But the outcome was not, this time, left to chance or the bishops. The emperor ensured that this Council would overturn the conviction and find for the One Nature by appointing Dioskoros of Alexandria to be its president. He also barred bishops who had condemned Eutyches in 448 from voting at Ephesos II, and excluded Theodoretos from attending altogether.[32] Theodosius framed the Council as an attack on Nestorianism, which reveals what he thought about the Two Natures position. Theodosius was essentially a One Nature emperor, and the only reason he was not branded as such later was that later tradition had to uphold him as a champion against Nestorios' alleged heresy at Ephesos I.

The Council of Ephesos II, an embarrassment to Orthodox posterity, was orchestrated to yield the results that were desired by the court. Led by Dioskoros of Alexandria, about 140 bishops reviewed the case of Eutyches and overturned his condemnation for heresy. The bishops accepted Eutyches' formula "Two Natures before the Incarnation, and One Nature after it."[33] Dioskoros then went on the offensive, saying that "we should blame not only Nestorios, for there are other Nestorioses."[34] To the shock of many present, he moved to have Flavianos and Eusebios of Dorylaion deposed. Dioskoros brought in guards and would not let some bishops leave until they had signed: "they set soldiers on us with clubs and swords, as well as monks, and in this way made us subscribe."[35] Eusebios fled to Rome, whereas Flavianos was arrested and beaten so badly that he died of his wounds soon afterward. Nestorios wryly observed from exile that Ephesos was a city appointed for the deposition of the bishops of Constantinople.[36] The second session of the Council deposed more "Nestorian" bishops, including Theodoretos, Domnos of Antioch, and Ibas of Edessa. Dioskoros was cleaning house.

Pope Leo had been invited to the Council but had sent delegates instead. They instantly objected to Flavianos' deposition—*contradicitur!* in Latin—after which they fled, allegedly in fear.[37] Many attendee bishops complained later that there was widespread violence and intimidation directed at them from the soldiers detailed to Dioskoros and from the monks who followed bishops allied to him. To be sure, some of these accusations were made by bishops who, two years later when the tide had turned, were explaining why they had gone along with Dioskoros. "What we were to do?," said one, "They were playing in our blood."[38]

Pope Leo was outraged by Ephesos II, which he branded the *Latrocinium*, the Robber Council, a name that stuck.[39] He wrote many letters to Theodosius, protesting the Council and urging the emperor to reconsider and submit the entire matter to himself, as the ultimate Apostolic authority in the Church. Leo wrote to Pulcheria as well as to the people and monks of Constantinople, and he mobilized the entire western court to write to Theodosius, making the same plea. Theodosius ignored this epistolary barrage for over half a year, then blandly responded that Ephesos II had vindicated orthodoxy and that peace could now reign in the Church. He ignored the papal claim of Petrine jurisdiction over the entire Church.[40]

In July 450, Theodosius fell off a horse and died two days later. His long reign was one of prosperity for most of his subjects and had, significantly, not been wracked by civil war. However, the Balkan armies and provinces had been mauled by the Huns and the empire was paying tribute to Attila. Moreover, Theodosius had allowed Dioskoros to polarize opinion between partisans of the One and Two Natures. Narratives began to coalesce around theological slogans, with grievances, villains, heroes, and even martyrs; in other words, beyond the theological issues at stake these positions were becoming *identities*. Because the conflicts played out as trials of prominent bishops and monks and less as strictly intellectual examinations of the theology, people took sides based on feelings about the procedures used in the condemnation of this or that person, about who was unjustly victimized, and who was the bad guy, and theological factions then coalesced around these feelings and narratives.

The Christological division over Natures differed from that of the fourth century about the Father and Son in one more way: in the fourth century, partisans disagreed with the theological positions of their opponents, whereas in the fifth and sixth centuries they disagreed with largely imaginary positions that they only attributed to their opponents, often while the latter were clearly proclaiming that they did *not* hold those positions. Thus, partisans of the One Nature held that "Nestorians" believed in two distinct Sons, one mortal and one divine, while partisans of the Two Natures held that the "Eutychians" believed that Christ did not have a human body or that the divine essence was not immutable. The need to create identities by inventing caricatures and then demonizing those who allegedly believed them proved to be greater than the desire for consensus. Thus, Theodosius left the eastern empire in a state of schism with itself and the western Church, as a tributary to Attila, and with no succession plan. The next regime would have hard decisions to make on all fronts.

The Council of Chalcedon

The accession of Marcian (450–457) was the work of an Arian Alan general (Aspar), a pagan Isaurian general (Zeno), and a virgin princess (Pulcheria). For a month after Theodosius' death, Pulcheria was the reigning Augusta, while the cabal worked out an agreement: Chrysaphius would be executed (this was carried out with satisfaction by Pulcheria); Aspar's aide-de-camp, the fifty-eight-year-old Marcian, a mid-level Thracian officer with no son, would be proclaimed emperor (on 25 August by the armies at the Hebdomon, then by the Senate and people in Constantinople); Pulcheria would become his nominal empress to simulate dynastic continuity; the empire would resist Attila's demands (a point on which Zeno insisted); and Theodosius' One Nature policy would be reversed by a Council that would proclaim Pulcheria's Two Nature beliefs (the two generals were understandably indifferent to this item). One stakeholder who was excluded from this arrangement was, in theory, the most important one: the western emperor Valentinian III, who impotently refused to recognize Marcian until early 452, at which point he gave in.[41] Valentinian's crumbling empire had no armies to impose his will on the east, as Theodosius had imposed his will on the west in 425, and Aspar and Zeno knew it.

When Attila's envoys arrived, Marcian refused to pay the tribute. The gamble paid off: Attila weighed his options and attacked the west instead. Marcian was thus able to forgive his subjects' tax arrears for 437–447 and to eliminate the senatorial tax (*collatio glebalis*), thereby securing good will for his nascent regime.

The emperor even spelled it out: "All men shall know how much Our Piety has benefited them."[42]

The new regime set about erasing Ephesos II, a policy that had popular backing in Constantinople. When Marcian and Pulcheria entered Hagia Sophia, "a massive crowd of clergy, monks, and laity acclaimed them and demanded that Dioskoros and Eutyches be investigated for what they had done to Flavianos."[43] The court was aided in this by the new archbishop of Constantinople, Anatolios. He had been handpicked by Dioskoros from among his closest collaborators to take over the see of Constantinople, but he turned against his master as soon as Marcian and Pulcheria took power. In October, 450, the Synod of Constantinople signed off on Leo's "Tome" and rehabilitated the memory of Flavianos, whose remains were brought back to the City by Pulcheria "upon the request of the clergy and people" and buried in the Holy Apostles. The bishops exiled at Ephesos II were recalled, and Theodoretos wrote to thank Aspar personally for lifting the sentence against him and to lobby for a new Council that would set everything straight. Indeed, what would become the Council of Chalcedon was already in the planning stage (originally intended for Nikaia, then moved).[44] This abrupt change in policy reveals how, without imperial enforcement, Ecumenical Councils had little authority. Emperors could organize Councils to get exactly the results they desired and, conversely, could overturn Councils convened by their predecessors that produced the "wrong" results. To be sure, emperors often insisted that certain matters (such as doctrine) had to be decided by the bishops, but the framework of their deliberations could be manipulated so as to shape the outcome. No one at this time questioned the emperor's presiding authority over the Church. Bishops understood, as one of them said in 449, that "we are under an obligation to obey the Christ-loving emperor, whatever he orders."[45]

Chalcedon was not, however, an attempt to placate the west or pope Leo in particular. Valentinian continued to withhold his recognition from Marcian for months after Chalcedon had concluded its business, and Leo at first opposed the idea of a new Council; then he wanted it to be held in Italy; then, when he heard that it would be held in east, he tried to stop or delay it, before finally yielding, sooner than his emperor, to the inevitable.[46] He had reason to be apprehensive of any Council run by the eastern court, not for reasons of doctrinal integrity but because it marginalized Rome.

Chalcedon was a gargantuan gathering, one of the largest councils in the history of the Church so far. Over 350 bishops attended, though not all of them went to every session. Along with their attendant priests, they totaled a thousand clergy or more. The bishops and secular officials sat in the front facing each other, while the rest stood behind them.[47] The proceedings were controlled tightly by secular court officials, especially the *magister militum praesentalis* Anatolius, who presided over many sessions. Marcian was taking no chances that the bishops would mess this one up too. When the rival factions started insulting each other on the very first day, "the senatorial officials said, 'Such vulgar outbursts are inappropriate for bishops and will not benefit either side.'"[48] There was no violence or rowdy bands of monks. The minutes were recorded by imperial secretaries, not episcopal ones, resulting in the best-documented month-long event of ancient history, better even than Ephesos I.

Dioskoros of Alexandria was duly deposed on the first day, mostly on the grounds of the violence and procedural irregularities of Ephesos II. As it happened, 119 of the bishops at Chalcedon had voted with him at Ephesos II, only two years earlier, so they now had to claim that they had been intimidated: "We all sinned, we all ask for forgiveness."[49] Regular Council attendees were placed in awkward positions: Aitherichos of Smyrna had voted against Eutyches in 448, then denied it at Ephesos II in 449, and now at Chalcedon he had to explain why he had denied it at Ephesos II.[50] Later sessions investigated Dioskoros' financial misconduct and authoritarianism, revealing that he was not universally popular at Alexandria. The bishops approved Leo's Tome among other canonical statements of the faith, and they produced a new creed, on which a subcommittee was working in parallel to the main sessions. The bishops were reluctant to produce a new creed, but the emperor threatened that, if they did not, he would assign the task to pope Leo. It was, then, astute of the organizers to depose Dioskoros on criminal grounds before theology was discussed. The Creed approved in the fifth session hewed closely to Nicaea, treating it and some parts of Cyril as authoritative. Regarding Natures it settled on the following wording:

> one and the same Jesus Christ . . . acknowledged in two natures without confusion, change, division, or separation (the difference of the natures being in no way destroyed by the union, but rather the distinctive character of each nature being preserved and coming together into one person and one hypostasis), not parted or divided into two persons, but one and the same Son.[51]

Using largely Cyrillian language, this definition tried to preserve the Two Natures while insisting on the unity of the person, Christ, that they constituted. It was a compromise in good faith. Of course, it would be rejected by conservative Cyrillians who insisted on the formula "*in* one nature." A sixth-century historian lamented that people were taking sides based on the difference in a single letter: "in" two natures vs. "from" two natures (in Greek, *en* vs. *ek*).[52] The two sides did use the slogans One Nature and Two Natures and so it is appropriate to call them Monophysites and Diphysites, terms that are attested by the early sixth century; we can also call them anti-Chalcedonians and Chalcedonians, respectively. The term "Monophysite" was used by Chalcedonians after the seventh century to condemn those who rejected Chalcedon; before that the most common terms for them were *Aposchistai* (i.e., Separatists or Splitters) or "the Headless Ones."[53] The modern neologism "Miaphysite" is just an ungrammatical version of Monophysite, and offers no advantages over it. Its proponents claim that it avoids the implication that opponents of Chalcedon believed that Christ had only a divine nature, but it is just as easy to clarify that we will not use "Monophysite" in that sense, which is not prominent in the sources anyway.[54]

Both sides claimed allegiance to Cyril, though the Monophysites had better warrant for it. Likewise, Nestorios was condemned by both sides, though the Diphysites essentially held the same position as he did, though certainly not the views for which he was falsely condemned (because hardly anyone had held those views). Writing from exile shortly before Chalcedon, Nestorios took the Diphysite stance of Flavianos of Constantinople and pope Leo as a personal vindication.[55] But his name was irrevocably anathematized. To be restored to the Church at Chalcedon, Theodoretos had to condemn Nestorios, which he did, albeit with extreme reluctance.[56]

Chalcedon passed important canons, including a set that was dictated by the emperor and placed monasticism under episcopal supervision.[57] Canons 9 and 17 gave to Constantinople appellate jurisdiction over other churches. The Council did not recognize (or show any awareness of) Rome's alleged right to hear such appeals. The most controversial canon was the one later called "Canon 28," which confirmed the decision of the Council of Constantinople (381) that Constantinople ranked second after Rome in the hierarchy of Churches, and gave it authority over the bishoprics in Thrace and Asia Minor. Pope Leo's legates attempted to veto this canon, but it passed nonetheless. This put Leo in a bind: the Council vindicated his Tome as a standard of orthodoxy, but also confirmed the rise of New Rome. It did not help that, in their announcement of the Council's decisions to Leo, the bishops of Chalcedon farcically spun the objections of his legates as outrage on the legates' part that Canon 28 was not being attributed to Leo's own initiative, so generous did he desire to be toward Constantinople![58] Such brazen cheekiness stung. Leo refused to ratify Chalcedon because of Canon 28. Even in early 453, Marcian was still writing to Leo, urging him to ratify the Council because his silence was giving comfort to those who opposed it. Leo relented in March, though he kept griping about the "vicious ambition" of the see of Constantinople.[59]

The fallout from Chalcedon

For Marcian, Chalcedon was the final word. He decreed that "no one henceforth was to discuss the Christian faith . . . all will be required to observe the decrees of Chalcedon," and "those who teach prohibited doctrines shall be punished with the ultimate punishment."[60] Marcian's hope that Christians would stop quarreling was, however, badly misplaced. Resistance was immediate, and passions were driven more by narratives, slogans, and identities revolving around talismanic heros, rather than by theology. The Alexandrians in particular were angry that their bishop Dioskoros had lost, and rose up against his replacement Proterios, attacking and routing the soldiers who brought him. But Marcian was not bluffing: he sent 2,000 soldiers by sea from Constantinople and suppressed the insurrection. The prefect of Egypt temporarily canceled the city's grain dole, closed the baths, and suspended the games. This brought the populace to heel, but Egypt would never be won for Chalcedon.[61]

Resistance flared up in Jerusalem as well. Its returning bishop, Iouvenalios (Juvenal), had managed, through canny and treacherous maneuvering, to have his see elevated by the Council to the club of five bishoprics—Rome, Constantinople, Alexandria, Antioch, and now Jerusalem—whose jurisdiction encompassed many provinces; these would later be regarded as the five "patriarchates." Disgusted by Iouvenalios' theological flip-flopping, many monks in Palestine and the people of Jerusalem elected a new bishop, Theodosios, while the Council was still in session. With the support of the resident empress Eudokia, he now set about appointing anti-Chalcedonian bishops throughout the province. His partisans would ask, "Where in the Scripture does it say that Christ is in two natures?"—a methodology that, of course, invalidated almost the whole of theology as it had developed to that point. A leading anti-Chalcedonian agitator in the region was Petros, the bishop of Maiouma, the port of Gaza. He was a prince of the Georgian royal family who had been raised as a hostage at the court of Theodosius until 437, when he fled to pursue the monastic life.[62] From here on, Christian society in the east became increasingly polarized to the point where friends and family had fallings out and people refused to talk to each other, like Blues and Greens at their worst.[63] It is wonderful that we have contrasting perspectives on events, but less so that they consist mostly of vitriol. Christians called each other agents of Satan or precursors of the Antichrist, and saw heart-warming visions of the other side roasting in Hell. "This putrid, gangrenous ulcer" is a taste of our sources' language.[64] The bishops had set the tone, by loudly proclaiming in council sessions that their theological opponents should be thrown into the fire or cut up into bits. In one story, a holy man refuses to worship Satan, whereupon the latter says, "Why not? The bishops at Chalcedon did."[65]

Fortunately, Marcian was a good politician. At Chalcedon he had been acclaimed as "a New Constantine," and in the letters that he wrote to the monks of Jerusalem, Palestine, Sinai, and Alexandria he used Constantinian rhetoric to quiet their tempers. The emperor patiently explained the basis of Chalcedon's Creed, and added:

> [Your violent actions] have revealed your impious purpose, which is opposed to the laws of God and the polity of the Romans. What is right for you is to

> keep quiet, submit to the priests, and follow what they teach you . . . . It is not appropriate for you to meddle in inquiries of this kind, for you do not have the requisite subtlety of mind . . . . You keep saying that we should not turn this into a study of physics, but you are now doing just that, when you ask, How can a virgin give birth and remain a virgin?, or, How can she physically give birth to one who is above the physical world? and the like.[66]

Marcian sent soldiers to install Iouvenalios in Jerusalem in 453. The counter-bishop Theodosios tried to disguise himself as a soldier but was eventually arrested and taken to the capital, where he died in 457, viewed of course as a "martyr" by anti-Chalcedonians.[67]

Even Eudokia relented, though this resulted from international politics. In 451, Attila directed his armies against Gaul where he was defeated, at Châlons, by the western general Aetius and his Visigothic allies. In 452, Attila invaded Italy. Marcian sent soldiers to help Aetius defend Italy and another army to attack Hunnic settlements behind enemy lines. It may have been these actions that finally secured him recognition by the court of Valentinian III. The Scourge of God threatened reprisals, but before he could make good on them he hemorrhaged to death on his wedding night and his empire disintegrated quickly.[68] Marcian had risked Attila's anger, but his gamble paid off. Pulcheria also died in 453, ending the Theodosian dynasty in the east. It would soon end in the west too. Valentinian III personally murdered Aetius in 454, and was himself murdered in 455. The chaos that ensued gave the Vandal king Gaizeric the chance to sail up to Rome and sack the city thoroughly, hauling to Carthage huge cargoes of plunder, artwork, and captives, including Valentinian's widow Eudoxia and her two daughters. They were the daughter and two granddaughters of Theodosius II and Eudokia. To secure their release, Eudokia worked with Constantinople and stood down from her support of Monophysites.[69]

Marcian, heirless husband of a virgin queen, died in January 457 from an illness he contracted while commemorating Theodosius' 447 barefoot march to the Hebdomon. The throne was vacant, but there was no power vacuum. Just as the imperial dynasty was lapsing, Aspar's was entrenching itself, though his was an unconventional shadow-dynasty that, because of religion and ethnicity, could not claim the throne. The son of Ardabur, an Alan general and consul in 427, Aspar was himself a long-serving general and consul of 434, and was related to Plintha, the powerful Arian Gothic general and consul in 417. One of Aspar's sons was Ardabur (consul in 447), whom Marcian appointed *magister militum* of Oriens in 453, while another son (consul of 465) bore the heroic Gothic name Ermaneric. Aspar was the patron of the eastern empire's *foederati*, Gothic soldiers who had been settled peacefully in Thrace and supported financially by the state, possibly since the 420s. Aspar's political position was strengthened by the support of this barbarian army, which, by the 460s, may have been 10,000 strong.

Aspar married the aunt of one of this army's later leaders, Theoderic Strabo, the son of Triarius, and lobbied on behalf of Arian worshippers. The *foederati* were perceived as his quasi-personal followers.[70]

The family of Aspar was wealthy and played the game of Roman politics as consummate insiders, as shown already on Aspar's silver consular missorium of 434, which projects dynastic aspirations (see Figure 15).[71] This shadow-dynasty, however, was possible not in spite of the family's ethnoreligious profile but because of it, for it neutralized them as viable contenders for the throne. Aspar deliberately cultivated this outsiderness. He was polygamous and, at 70, had a pretty and rich Gothic concubine. These were not behaviors that normal Roman senators could flaunt.[72]

Thus, the hegemony of the eunuch Chrysaphius had been replaced by that of a Romanized Arian general, Aspar, the same sequence that had played out under Arcadius. Like Eutropius, Chrysaphius had failed. Aspar was like a new Gaïnas,

Figure 15 Aspar's missorium, commemorating his consulship of 434 AD. It is 42 cm in diameter (Florence). Standing next to Aspar is his son Ardabur, and they are flanked by personifications of Rome and Constantinople. Above are medallions of Ardabur senior and Plinta.
Gainew Gallery / Alamy Stock Photo

but with better manners. His gamble was to avoid Gaïnas' fate. A slightly later historian noted that, whereas "Aspar could not, as an Arian, become emperor, it was easily within his power to place someone else on the throne."[73] His choice fell on a Thracian named Leo (457–474), an officer from one of the armies that Aspar had commanded. Leo, like Marcian, had no son. He was duly acclaimed Augustus at the Hebdomon by the army, magistrates, and people. "Almighty God and your judgment, my most-powerful fellow soldiers," Leo declared, "have elected me to govern the public affairs of the Romans." He promised to the army the traditional accession donative of five gold coins and one pound of silver.[74]

Leo's first test came from Alexandria. Dioskoros' Chalcedonian replacement Proterios had failed to impose his authority on Egypt. Popular demonstrations in the theater chanted "May the bones of Proterios be burned!" and "Drive Judas into exile!" Dissident monks and bishops, including Petros the Iberian, blocked him at every turn and consecrated a rival, anti-Chalcedonian bishop, Timotheos Ailouros ("the Cat"—the Age of Nicknames had begun). As soon as news arrived in Alexandria of Marcian's death, the Alexandrians lynched Proterios, dragging his body through the streets and then setting it on fire.[75] Leo received petitions from both sides in Alexandria, but his response was cautious. He floated the idea of a new council to deal with the situation there, but wisely abandoned it (one bishop in the Pontos complained that he was still paying the bills from his journey to Chalcedon).[76] Another military intervention in Alexandria would probably make matters worse. Leo then hit upon a brilliant mechanism for resolving the situation, which must go down as a high point of Roman national administration: an empire-wide episcopal plebiscite, or "episciscite."

The emperor forwarded the rival petitions from Egypt to every bishop in the empire with instructions that every metropolitan was to convene a synod in order to decide whether Chalcedon was valid and whether Timotheos should stay or go. The emperor's letter was not prejudiced against Timotheos, saying only that there had been disturbances in Alexandria, and he solicited the views of select holy men as well, such as Simeon the Stylite. Each local synod then drafted a response and sent it back, and the court compiled them into the *Codex Encyclius*. All synods decided in favor of Chalcedon and against The Cat except for that of Pamphylia II, which rejected both.[77] The Cat was duly exiled, in 460, and replaced by another Timotheos, a mild man nicknamed Salophakiolos ("Crazy Hat"). The Church of Alexandria was in decline. Never again would it field bishops of the caliber of Athanasios, Theophilos, Cyril, and Dioskoros, even when it was not wracked by internecine strife. The relatively non-violent way—for Alexandria—in which The Cat was replaced can be attributed to the moral weight of the national referendum, which paid large dividends to Leo: the rest of

Leo's wars and Aspar

his reign was relatively untroubled by Church strife. He had successfully deployed a novel instrument of Roman statecraft.

The first half of Leo's reign was peaceful for the eastern empire. In 458, Antioch was struck by a powerful earthquake, which toppled many buildings. Leo provided the city with generous tax relief. Then, in 464 or 465 a great fire broke out in Constantinople. It lasted for four days and swept through large parts of the City, destroying the Senate House of the forum of Constantine, along with many mansions and homes. During the blaze, Aspar carried a water bucket on his shoulders, encouraged the populace to do the same in order to extinguish the fire, and paid everyone who did so one silver coin.[78]

The empire also held its own against the barbarians who were spilling out of the wreckage of Attila's realm. At least three armies crossed the Danube in the mid-to-late 460s, but they were defeated, one by Aspar's son Ardabur; another by Anthemius, who was the grandson of the praetorian prefect of 405–414 and son-in-law of the emperor Marcian; and a third group was led by Attila's son Dengizich, whose head was subsequently displayed in Constantinople.[79] As the Hun threat subsided, a Gothic group later known as the Ostrogoths settled in Pannonia. In ca. 460 they raided Illyricum and were bought off with an annual subsidy of 300 lbs of gold in protection money. Their king's nephew, a child named Theoderic, was sent to be raised in Constantinople, where he would reside for ten years.[80] Later, this Theoderic would preside over a new order in the post-Roman west.

Meanwhile, tensions were building up between Leo and his handler Aspar, and the conflict between them set off two decades of complicated infighting. In the 460s, the two men began to disagree over appointments to the highest offices, as Aspar had grown used to packing them with his allies, relatives, and clients. They were also disagreeing over foreign policy when, in 465, an Isaurian officer named Tarasikodissa produced documents exposing Ardabur's treasonous correspondence with Persia. Ardabur was deposed in disgrace after a dramatic meeting of the Senate, where Aspar distanced himself from his son.[81] Leo quickly promoted this Tarasikodissa, who changed his name to Zeno in honor of the powerful Isaurian general of the previous generation. Leo married him to his daughter Ariadne, who had been desired by Aspar as a bride for one of his own sons. The couple produced a son, the future Leo II, the next year. Moreover, to protect his own person Leo upgraded the palace guard with an elite unit, the *excubitores* ("those outside the bedchamber"), into which he recruited "tall and brawny" men "like massive oaks" with black boots, some from among his own people, Illyrian-Thracians. A young recruit was the future emperor Justin I (518–527), who traveled to Constantinople to join this unit in ca. 468–470.[82]

Leo was trying get out from Aspar's shadow. What he needed was a major success, and a historic opportunity for one was presented by the western empire, which had entered a death spiral of political chaos and military defeat. Like the eastern empire, the west also had a Romanized barbarian kingmaker, the Gothic general Ricimer. At first Ricimer backed the capable emperor Majorian (457–461), who stabilized Italy and restored a fiction of imperial authority in Gaul and Spain. But when Majorian was defeated by Gaizeric in 461 during yet another failed campaign against the Vandals, Ricimer had him executed. By 467, the situation in the west had deteriorated so much that its collapse was imminent without eastern intervention, and so Ricimer allowed Leo to nominate the next western emperor. Leo chose the distinguished senator and general Anthemius (467–472). The relationship between the two halves of the empire had now, in its final days, been fully transformed. Under Theodosius II, the west had become a junior partner of the east; now, under Leo, an eastern senator, called a "Greek" by some in the west, was sent to govern Rome itself. Western Romans were glad for the help: "All hail to you, pillar of sceptered power, the Queen of the East [Constantinople], Rome of your own world, no longer to be venerated by eastern Romans alone, now that you have sent me a prince."[83]

Leo sent more than just a prince: he backed Anthemius with the largest military investment that the eastern empire had made since Julian's expedition to Persia. A massive transport fleet sailed to North Africa to defeat the Vandals under the command of Leo's brother-in-law, Basiliscus. The campaign allegedly involved 1,100 ships at a cost of 7–9 million solidi, or roughly two years' income for the east. Such a surplus was, then, within the empire's ability to generate during the relatively peaceful years that followed Attila's death.[84] This risky gambit was the last chance to rescue the failing western empire, and Aspar was no part of it, either because he (correctly) believed that its success would empower Leo or because he was perceived to be sympathetic toward the Vandals (whose joint kingdom was of the Vandals *and Alans*).[85] But the expedition failed disastrously. Off the coast of North Africa, Gaizeric, the best strategist and canniest politician of the century, lured Basiliscus into a false truce, and then destroyed his fleet with fireships (these were loaded with flammable materials, set on fire, and sent to drift into the enemy fleet). Leo's all-out effort was a complete disaster. When he returned, Basiliscus sought asylum in Hagia Sophia and Leo temporarily abandoned the palace in grief, "haunted by phantoms." This failure bankrupted the east and ensured the doom of the western empire. In less than a decade, Italy too would be ruled by barbarian armies rather than by its native political institutions.[86]

The debacle of 468 tilted the scales back in favor of Aspar, who managed to drive Zeno from the Balkans. Leo appointed Zeno *magister militum* of Oriens, but the emperor was isolated. Aspar now made the play to upgrade his dynasty to a proper imperial one and "did so because he was confident in the force of Goths at his disposal," which, like Gaïnas, he seems to have brought into the City.[87] Aspar demanded and obtained the appointment of his son Patricius as Caesar and Patricius' marriage to Leo's younger daughter. But this move crossed lines that angered the people of Constantinople, whom the powerful often forgot to their detriment. The populace marched to the hippodrome protesting against Patricius' elevation, and Leo had to reassure the people that his conversion to Orthodoxy would be sincere.[88] But to make their bid for the throne, the Asparids were now simultaneously playing both sides of the game, as Gothic-Arian outsiders and Roman-Orthodox insiders, which confused and alienated public opinion.

This situation was untenable for Leo, who cut the Gordian knot in the summer of 471. He ambushed Aspar, Ardabur, and many of their followers in the palace and straight-out massacred them. Patricius was also wounded, and is not heard of again. This massacre earned Leo the name "the Butcher," but did not make him unpopular. This level of political violence had not been seen in the eastern capital in over seventy years, when the people of Constantinople had risen up and destroyed Gaïnas' Gothic army, in 400. Leo also wrote to his colleague Anthemius in Rome to inform him that he had killed Aspar for disobeying orders, and advised him to likewise murder the Goth Ricimer, who had garrisoned Rome with Goths. Ricimer and Anthemius were already at odds, the former supported by barbarian soldiers and the latter by the Roman people. In this standoff, however, the barbarians prevailed and Anthemius was murdered in 472.[89] The different fate of the two emperors nicely symbolized the trajectories of their respective empires.

The cost of Leo's political emancipation was an immediate Gothic war, which revealed the true basis of Aspar's power. The Goths whom he had brought into the capital immediately attacked the palace, but they were defeated by the new palace guard, the excubitors, after heavy fighting. The survivors fled to the Gothic federates in Thrace, who were led by Theoderic, Aspar's in-law, nicknamed Strabo ("the Squinter"). Strabo promptly rebelled. After long negotiations, during which the Goths besieged Philippi and Arcadiopolis, Leo agreed to make Strabo *magister militum praesentalis*, give him sole command of the Gothic federates, and award him a huge stipend of 2,000 lbs of gold. As this sum was to support his men, it means that his federates numbered between 12,000 and 18,000.[90] This was almost as much as the empire was paying to Attila after 447. A deal like this, secured in the course of a single year, had eluded Alaric after decades of fighting in the Balkans. The empire was now readier to pay off quasi-autonomous Gothic armies living on its territory.

The problem was compounded by another Gothic army that arrived in 473. Facing poverty and hardship in Pannonia, the Goths under king Thiudimer of the Amal Gothic dynasty and his son Theoderic, who had returned from his tutelage in Constantinople, emigrated to Illyricum. They captured Naissus and swept down to Thessalonike with an army of over 10,000 men, implying a total population of 50,000 or more (at a later point in its journeys, this group required 2,000 wagons). The court allowed them to settle in Macedonia around the towns of Pella, Pydna, Beroia, and Dion.[91] Unfortunately, we know nothing about the manner of their settlement or its financial aspects. The Amal Goths had been receiving an annual subsidy of 300 lbs since about 460. The empire now hosted two large warlike Gothic populations in close proximity, both of which wanted land, gold, and recognition from the court. Years of warfare were in store for Thrace, which had still not recovered from the ravages of Attila, and these would destabilize imperial politics. But these were problems that Leo would leave to his heir.

Having extinguished Aspar's family, Leo, in failing health, took thought for his own dynasty. He wanted to elevate his son-in-law Zeno to the throne, but "he failed because his subjects refused."[92] It is easy to see why. Even though some Isaurians like Zeno were integrated Roman elites, many others were viewed as the empire's internal barbarians because they mounted regular raids against adjacent provinces and required Asia Minor to be placed on a wartime footing. They were not seen as proper Romans, and were sometimes listed alongside Saracens and Huns as people who left their "own territories" to plunder Roman provinces.[93] In the 460s, some Isaurians on the island of Rhodes engaged in robbery and murder until they were attacked by local soldiers and fled to Zeno-Tarasikodissa in Constantinople. There they harassed some merchants, whereupon the populace assaulted them with stones. It was possibly this incident that led Leo, in 468, to issue a law against private persons keeping armed slaves, private armies, and Isaurians—a revealing use of their name.[94] In 472 or 473, as Leo was pondering the succession, there was a massacre of Isaurians in Constantinople arising from an incident in the hippodrome.[95]

On 17 November, 473, Leo assembled the people, soldiers, and foreign ambassadors from many nations in the hippodrome of Constantinople to acclaim his six-year-old grandson Leo II as Augustus, with the people doing so in Greek and the soldiers in Latin.[96] Leo I then died on 18 January and, soon after, the senate moved that Zeno be elevated to imperial rank "because his son was unable to sign documents"[97] (among other things, surely, that a child emperor could not do). The ceremony of accession took place in the hippodrome, thus completing the transition from a purely military to a mostly civilian mode of accession. Zeno thereby became the first Roman emperor to be elevated to the throne by his son. When this child died of natural causes in November, 474—no foul play is alleged—Zeno ruled alone, or rather with two Augustae, his mother-in-law Verina and his wife Ariadne. It was an inauspicious start to what would become the most turbulent and contested reign since the third-century crisis.

Zeno was the most remarkable emperor of the fifth century. The deck was stacked against him from the start. He enjoyed low levels of acceptance, resulting in many coups to overthrow him and treachery even from his closest associates. He was not a brilliant general and was generally disliked, even viewed as "physically repulsive." He had to cope with two large Gothic armies in the Balkans that attacked him whenever he was vulnerable and a broken Church. He also faced ethnic prejudice from his subjects. A chronicle bluntly states that palace officials hated him "because he was an Isaurian by birth."[98] And yet through wile, deceit, and tenacity he managed to outmaneuver and defeat all his enemies, remove the Goths from the Balkans, leave the empire in a strong position, and die in bed after a turbulent reign of seventeen years.

Basiliscus' coup

The first coup against Zeno tied together the themes of his reign and its cast of double-crossing characters. At its heart was the ambitious Basiliscus, brother of Verina. With the failure of the Vandal expedition on his record, it is remarkable that he still showed his face in public. But his military career before 468 was not undistinguished, and Leo I had sheltered him so that by 475 he had emerged as the "chief of the Senate."[99] Basiliscus and his sister Verina now entered into a conspiracy against Zeno with their nephew Harmatus (*magister militum* of Thrace), and Illus, one of Zeno's Isaurian associates. The previous year, 474, when Theoderic Strabo was ravaging Thrace after murdering a Roman general, it was Illus who had contained the crisis.[100] Zeno was tipped off about the imminent coup and, on 9 January 475, fled to Isauria, taking his wife Ariadne and the treasury with him. The mood in the City was explosive. When Basiliscus was crowned, "an unspeakably horrendous massacre of Isaurians" ensued, another ethnic pogrom. Basiliscus also cut a deal with Theoderic Strabo, who provided the new emperor with Gothic guards.[101]

With the treasury absconded to Isauria, Basiliscus had to squeeze out revenues wherever he could, earning a reputation for avarice. He also undermined his position by rolling back Chalcedon, a decision that he made for unfathomable reasons. Acting on a petition by some Alexandrians, he recalled Timotheos the Cat from his Crimean exile, but the only people who cheered for Timotheos when he entered the capital were sailors of the Alexandrian grain fleet. Upon Timotheos' advice, Basiliscus sent an Encyclical to all bishops in the empire pronouncing, on imperial authority, that Nicaea and Ephesos I were henceforth the only Councils valid for defining the faith; that Chalcedon and Leo's Tome were anathema and should be burned wherever found; and possibly that the relative rank of episcopal sees would be that set at Nicaea, i.e., that Constantinople would not enjoy the episcopal honors of a New Rome. All bishops were required to sign the Encyclical and return it to the court, another novel administrative procedure. Between 500 and 700 apparently did so, many at a gathering held in

Ephesos for that purpose. They bravely declared that they were willing to suffer any consequence for their defense of the true faith—i.e., the faith dictated now by the emperor. If the flip-flop of hundreds of bishops at Chalcedon, a mere two years after Ephesos II, had not proven that most bishops would sign whatever the court required, this toeing of the line now, sixteen years after Leo I's *Codex Encyclicus*, did so.[102]

Bearing the bones of Dioskoros in a silver coffin, Timotheos returned to Alexandria after an absence of fifteen years, replacing the genial and widely loved Timotheos Crazy-Hat, who graciously stepped aside for him. Anti-Chalcedonian bishops were appointed to Antioch and Ephesos, where they apparently enjoyed support despite the official standing of Chalcedon during the past two decades. But in Constantinople Chalcedon enjoyed strong popular support, and its populace and monks intervened again to change the balance of power. They were joined by their bishop Akakios, who feared that he would be deposed. Crowds gathered to protect him in Hagia Sophia and he draped the church as if in mourning. The resistance was boosted by the holy man Daniel the Stylite, who climbed down his column for the first time in decades and, creaking the whole way, walked to Hagia Sophia where, speaking in his native Aramaic through an interpreter, he denounced Basiliscus as a "second Diocletian." He then led a procession to the Hebdomon palace, where the emperor had fled to avoid the tumult, and back again. Basiliscus' popularity was now in shambles, but he needed the support of the populace for the coming confrontation with Zeno, who was marching on the capital. Basiliscus was compelled to go to Hagia Sophia and reconcile with Akakios in Daniel's presence. He then issued a risible Counter-Encyclical that nullified its predecessor, although it did not specify which creed would be valid.[103] This revealed that while an emperor could impose his will on the Church, his policies could be rolled back by the populace, if they came out in force.

Basiliscus' regime was prone to comical levels of infighting. He fell out with Verina by executing her lover, so she began to send aid to Zeno; Theoderic was angry that Harmatus had been made senior *magister militum praesentalis* rather than he; and Illus and Harmatus (who was having an affair with Basiliscus' wife) decided that they would be better off striking deals with Zeno, which is exactly what they did when Basiliscus foolishly sent them with armies against Zeno, in 476.[104] Illus kept Zeno's brother Longinus as a hostage, while Zeno promised to Harmatus the post of senior *magister militum praesentalis* for life and also that his son would be made Caesar. In August, Zeno marched to Constantinople with the forces that he had recruited in Isauria. As Verina, the Senate, and the people were now backing him, he was able to seize the palace and run up the flag for games in the hippodrome before Basiliscus even knew what was happening. For the second time, Basiliscus and his family fled to Hagia Sophia, seeking asylum and abdicating the crown. Zeno pledged that they would not be killed. He then exiled them to Cappadocia, where they were killed. The next year, he executed Harmatus and enrolled his son as a reader in a church.[105] It was equally as unwise to trust Zeno as to oppose him. At least the civil war had not been costly.

Two memorable events occurred in 476. While Basiliscus was emperor, another fire tore through the City, destroying many homes and public places, including tens of thousands of books in the Basilica library (under which Justinian later built the Basilica cistern). The losses included a complete Homer written in gold letters on the intestine of a serpent. Also destroyed was Lausus' fabulous collection of classical statues. Ancient relics and masterpieces vanished in a matter of hours. This was the risk of gathering the best of the best in one place.[106] Zeno issued a detailed law to govern new constructions in the City, in Greek rather than Latin "so that no one would require an interpreter." It stipulated that buildings had to be at least twelve feet apart and could be as tall as desired, but could not block their neighbors' view of the sea, which was deemed a fundamental right; the view from kitchens, privies, and staircases could be blocked.[107]

Zeno and the barbarians

The second memorable event of 476 was the end of the western imperial office. The barbarian general Odoacer, a former associate of Ricimer who had been proclaimed "king" by his army, deposed the emperor Romulus Augustulus and sent a delegation of senators to Constantinople to hand over the western "imperial regalia" and explain his action to Zeno. Odoacer proposed that an eastern emperor sufficed for both halves of the empire and that he, invested with the rank of patrician, should govern the west as Zeno's delegate. Zeno acquiesced, although he noted that Odoacer should rule "in a manner consistent with Roman order" and stipulated that he should recognize as the western emperor one Julius Nepos. Nepos had been proclaimed in Rome in 474, driven out in 475, and had since then ruled the Dalmatian coast. Odoacer recognized Nepos until 480, when Nepos, who never returned to Italy, was murdered. After that Odoacer recognized Zeno as sole emperor.[108] The western empire was thus no longer the junior partner of the eastern one, but a nominal protectorate to be governed by proxy. Zeno had no practical say in how Odoacer ruled, but legal fictions have unintended consequences. Zeno would later send another "delegate" to Italy, Theoderic the Goth, to replace Odoacer; and Justinian would send his armies. The Romans, whose government was now exclusively based in New Rome, never surrendered sovereignty over their western lands.

It is often asserted today that the deposition of Romulus Augustulus was a "non-event" that hardly anyone noticed at the time, and that "476" did not begin to mark something as dramatic as "the end of the western empire" until writers at the court of Justinian began to treat it that way. Thus, ideas about the "fall" of the west have yielded to the notion of its "transformation." However, the alleged lack of contemporaneous reaction to "476" is an argument from silence in a poorly documented period. In fact, there are hints that many in the east saw what happened as a "fall." Almost immediately after 476, anti-Chalcedonian writers argued that God so hated the Tome of pope Leo that "the [western] Roman empire has ended and the city [Rome] that ruled over the entire world is now in the hands of the barbarians."[109]

Zeno could do nothing about the fall of the west. He was still unpopular at home and faced two Gothic armies on his very doorstep in Thrace. The Senate advised him that the treasury could not pay for both groups—"we can barely pay our own soldiers as it is."[110] Seeing as Theoderic Strabo had supported Basiliscus, Zeno stripped him of his praesental command and transferred it to Theoderic the Amal. This military appointment brought with it cash, supplies, prestige, and recognition, but, in this period, it never resulted in a barbarian warlord actually commanding Roman units. The post of *magister militum praesentalis* was treated as a court honor that justified the payment of support funds for barbarian armies. The Amal had moved his followers north from Macedonia to Marcianopolis and Novae in Moesia Inferior, an important military base.[111] There ensued, in 477–478, a complex series of negotiations among the two Gothic leaders and Zeno in which it appears that the emperor was maneuvering them to fight each other while he stood back. The Goths realized this: "while the Romans remain at peace, they want us, the Goths, to wear each other down, so that they can win without having to fight; whichever one of us prevails will then have to face Roman treachery with depleted strength."[112] This was, after all, the centenary of Adrianople: Zeno was right to avoid fighting a pitched battle with Goths in Thrace.

Instead of clashing as intended, the two Gothic leaders joined forces and made joint demands on the emperor. Yet somehow Zeno managed to pry them apart again. In 478, he made Theoderic Strabo *magister militum praesentalis*, pledging to send him pay and supplies for 13,000 men, which indicates the size of his army, whereas Theoderic the Amal was harassed by the imperial armies in 479 and forced to trek westward across the Balkans. Along the way, he sacked Stobi in Macedonia and burned Herakleia in Epeiros. When he approached Thessalonike, the inhabitants became alarmed, fearing that the emperor had promised to give the city to the Goths, and they rose up, destroying Zeno's statues and attacking the prefect of Illyricum. In the more settled days of Theodosius I, such behavior led to a formal inquiry after the insurrection at Antioch, but the incident was now passed by, as the clergy and magistrates managed to calm the crowd. "They took the keys of the gates from the prefect, gave them to the bishop, and manned the walls with locals."[113] Theoderic eventually captured the city of Dyrrachion on the Adriatic coast through the treachery of a local Gothic-Roman officer "who preferred to live in the company of barbarians rather than of Romans."[114] The

Amal settled there, but the situation was unstable as the provincials were paying a high price.

Despite diffusing the Balkan crisis, Zeno's popularity in Constantinople remained low. He had brought Isaurian soldiers with him, though he wisely kept them across the straits, at Chalkedon. Moreover, his relations with Illus, who was now his *magister officiorum*, were deteriorating. In 477–478, Illus was targeted by two assassination attempts that were indirectly linked to the emperor; the second one was blamed on the praetorian prefect Epinicus, whom Illus sent under guard to Isauria. Epinicus implicated Verina, so Zeno surrendered her too, and she joined her accomplice in Isauria.[115] Isauria was becoming a prison for distinguished Romans, while conversely Constantinople was garrisoned by Isaurians.

The inevitable coup came in 479 from one Marcianus, who had the most illustrious pedigree possible at that time: he was the son of the western emperor Anthemius, grandson of the eastern emperor Marcian, and current husband of Leontia, the daughter of Leo I (and thus Zeno's brother-in-law); he had also been western consul in 469 and eastern consul in 472. His soldiers and co-conspirators took the palace by surprise, defeated Zeno, and drove him and his men into a basement. Yet with the throne in his grasp, Marcianus stopped so that his men could eat and sleep, which gave Illus the time to bring his Isaurians over from Chalkedon during the night and bribe Marcianus' men to defect. The rebel was arrested and sent to Cappadocia; when he caused disturbances there too, he and his family were sent to Isauria, the growing prison-colony.[116] Marcianus seems to have had some popular support, which was a cause for concern, but far more alarming was the approach of Theoderic Strabo, who was apparently also a party to the plot. He came, he said, in order to help Zeno, but no one believed this as fugitives from Marcianus' coup had fled to him and he would not surrender them. Strabo, moreover, was an enemy of Zeno from the days of Leo I and the murder of Aspar, which he seems never to have forgiven. It was thought that he wanted to occupy the City "and that the whole populace would side with him out of hatred for the Isaurians." That was a fantasy. Zeno paid him and his army to leave.[117]

Two years later, in 481, Theoderic Strabo made the first-ever assault on the walls of Constantinople, but they were ably defended by Illus. Theoderic moved his assault to the Golden Horn, but failed there too, as also in his attempt to ferry his men across the Bosporos. He withdrew into Greece where he died one morning when he was thrown off his horse onto a spear.[118] The history of the Goths in the Balkans was now rapidly moving toward a resolution. In 482, Theoderic the Amal burst out of Dyrrachion and ravaged Macedonia and Thessaly, capturing the city of Larissa. This was the standard Gothic playbook for obtaining concessions, and it worked: Zeno appointed Theoderic as *magister militum praesentalis* in 483, made him a consul for 484, and allocated land in Dacia Ripensis and Moesia II to his followers. The two men also arranged to murder Strabo's son and successor Recitach in 484, after which the Gothic *foederati* ceased to form a separate group, being mostly absorbed into the Amal's following.[119] The unified Ostrogothic army of 20,000 soldiers or more had come into being.

The* Henotikon *and Acacian Schism

In the midst of this instability, the Church was a low priority, but Zeno could not ignore it. He lacked theological commitments of his own, but he had to depose the bishops elevated by Basiliscus. In other respects, he followed the lead of Akakios, who was an able politician and no fanatic. The fiascos under Basiliscus had revealed that Chalcedon was doomed in Egypt, was unpopular in Antioch, had a mixed reception in Palestine-Syria, was adamantly championed by Rome, and was popular in Constantinople. Akakios sought to steer a middle course through the reefs. Prominent anti-Chalcedonian bishops were declared deposed from their sees, including Paulos of Ephesos, Petros of Antioch (known as "the Fuller"), and (again) Timotheos the Cat of Alexandria. But the bishops of Asia province sent a letter to Akakios, who was their nominal head, begging for mercy, accepting Chalcedon, and swearing that they had been coerced to sign Basiliscus' Encyclical, forgetting that at the time they had sworn to uphold it to the death.[120]

The Churches of Antioch and Alexandria were in disorder. Petros the Fuller's replacements were short-lived. One of them, Stephanos, was stabbed to death with sharp reeds and his body tossed into the river (in 479). The Fuller had also made a change to the Trisagion, a liturgical hymn, which caused a lasting controversy. Specifically, he added the words "who was crucified for us" after "God," reflecting the conservative Cyrillian view that God had experienced human suffering. His successor Kalandion made those words refer to "Christ the King," thereby preserving the Chalcedonian distinction between the Two Natures. But the "Crucified" addition became a Monophysite slogan; one man even taught it to his parrot.[121] In Alexandria, the Cat died in 477 before he could be removed, but his followers, including the Monophysite agitator Petros the Iberian, consecrated Petros Mongos ("Raspy-Voiced") to succeed him. Zeno decreed the return of the genial Timotheos Crazy-Hat, but, despite the Crazy-Hat's efforts at conciliation, this caused a schism in Alexandria between the two bishops. Following the old playbook of Athanasios, Mongos went into hiding, "moving from one house to another."[122]

Akakios had informed pope Simplicius (468–483) about these appointments and had on occasion sought his advice, but, although the two were in theological agreement, Simplicius was becoming alarmed at the extraordinary authority that the bishop of Constantinople was wielding over the eastern Church.[123] This went beyond his jurisdiction, enhanced as that had been by Chalcedon, and contravened claims of papal supremacy. Simplicius was issuing stern instructions about how everything was to be arranged in the east, but no one there seemed to be paying him much attention. In fact, Akakios and Zeno gradually realized that, if they were to bring peace to the Church, they would need a different approach, which would be anathema to the pope, namely they had to come to some arrangement with Petros Mongos in Alexandria and Petros the Fuller in Antioch. These were the horns of the dilemma that now faced Constantinople: alienate the pope by dealing with eastern critics of Chalcedon, or allow chaos to reign in the east by enforcing Chalcedon strictly. In 479, Akakios made his choice and stopped responding to Simplicius altogether. It was the right choice and it lasted for almost forty years. When it was reversed by Justin and Justinian, they tore the eastern Churches apart.

In 482, at the emperor's request Akakios wrote a document, known as Zeno's *Henotikon* ("the Unifier"), to serve as a basis for a return by all parties to mutual recognition and communion. The *Henotikon* recognized the Councils of Nicaea, Constantinople, and Ephesos I along with Cyril's *Twelve Anathemas*—a sop to the Cyrillians; it stressed the need for unity and confessed one Son, not two, who was one being, consubstantial with God in divinity and consubstantial with us in humanity. It did not take an explicit stance on Chalcedon, Leo's Tome, or try to enumerate the Natures, which meant that it would never please hardliners who wanted their specific positions ratified. Many historians see the *Henotikon* as a failed compromise proposed by the court. But extremists are never appeased. The *Henotikon* did create a broad middle ground that marginalized hardliners on both sides and allowed everyone else to read it as a validation of their position. Mongos pitched it as basically anti-Chalcedonian to his Alexandrian followers, winning over most of them, though he had to fend off attacks and persistent accusations by radicals on both sides. The Fuller also accepted it and was restored to Antioch, in 484 (after the war with Illus was over). Most Chalcedonians found the *Henotikon* unobjectionable. A later historian described it as "neither accepting nor rejecting Chalcedon."[124] The *Henotikon* served the majority who wanted peace and were willing to compromise, though history would ultimately be decided by the rest.

Among the zealots were the staunch Chalcedonian monks of the monastery of the Sleepless Ones near Constantinople (the Akoimetoi) and pope Simplicius' successor Felix III (483–492), who formed an axis to undermine the *Henotikon*. Felix sent two legates to Constantinople to depose Mongos and receive Akakios' defense against the charges made against him by Mongos' Chalcedonian opponents. The fact that Felix believed he had such authority indicates the wide gulf that had opened between Rome and the east regarding the governance of the Church. In the event, the papal legates were somehow persuaded to participate in services where Petros Mongos' name was commemorated, and this was taken to signify Rome's confirmation of his standing. When the legates returned to Italy, they were immediately deposed by an Italian synod. Felix and his bishops then excommunicated Akakios in July 484. The person charged to deliver this notice was afraid to do so, and gave it instead to a zealous Sleepless monk. He mingled in the crowd that was entering Hagia Sophia as Akakios was about to officiate and pinned it to his back when no one was looking. In response, Akakios ceased recognizing Felix but took no formal action "and otherwise took no notice of his deposition." Felix also wrote to Zeno, demanding that he choose between Peter the Apostle and his namesake of Alexandria.[125] It was, for Zeno, an easy choice.

The new schism between Rome and New Rome would last for thirty-five years, until 519.[126] Because western historiography often reflects papal biases, it is called the Acacian Schism. Yet already from the days of Constantine the Great, the two Churches were always hovering close to the line of mutual excommunication, and it was *always* Rome that pulled the trigger in protest over its "rights" (whether about Athanasios, John Chrysostom, Ephesos II, or Petros Mongos). Schism was built into the relationship from the start and was not a development of the ninth, eleventh, or thirteenth centuries (as scholars variously pick their starting-points). Its underlying causes piled on over time—for example, the issue of Illyricum added onto that of appellate jurisdiction—making its outbreaks increasingly bitter and eventually permanent.

Illus' rebellion

The year 484 witnessed another dramatic rupture, this time with Illus, a long-overdue settling of scores. After a further assassination attempt in which he lost an ear—this attempt was linked to empress Ariadne, who wanted her mother released—Illus was made *magister militum* of Oriens and dispatched to Antioch. But tensions were mounting, especially as Illus still refused to release the emperor's brother. Illus rebelled in the summer of 484, but had no chance of being accepted as emperor himself "since the Romans hated him on account of his origin and his inflexible mind."[127] Ethnicity was again a factor. Therefore, his captive, the empress Verina, proclaimed the senator Leontius as emperor at Tarsos. Verina noted in a letter to Antioch that Zeno had fallen short of her hopes for the good of the republic. Leontius was accepted in Antioch, but managed to secure little support outside that city and Isauria. In September 484, the rebels were defeated near Antioch by Zeno's new *magister militum* for Oriens, Ioannes the Scythian, after which they held out in the Isaurian fort of Papyrios for four years, until 488. Illus and Leontius were eventually betrayed and executed, and their heads displayed in Constantinople. So many of the generals employed by both sides were Isaurians that the conflict took on the aspect of an Isaurian civil war. Verina died during the siege, and Zeno allowed her to be buried in the Holy Apostles. He had again been fortunate in the ineptness of his opponents.[128]

A curious feature of Illus' rebellion was its pagan aspect. His chief advisor and *magister officiorum* was the outspoken Hellenist Pamprepios of Panopolis, a savvy politician who had lobbied on his patron's behalf and was executed by him as soon as the rebellion failed; his body was hurled off the battlements of Papyrios. We have Pamprepios' horoscope, which accurately predicts his entire career and demise, seeing as it was cast a generation later. Illus' rebellion made no moves or promises to ameliorate the lot of the empire's remaining pagans, yet word spread that he was somehow sympathetic: "the majority hoped for a restoration of the ancient way of life," wrote Damaskios, a later head of the Platonic Academy at Athens. Sacrifices in support of the rebellion were offered in the still-pagan city of Aphrodisias (in Karia).[129] This sudden visibility of pagan hope and power led to a backlash, especially in Alexandria, where radical Christian student groups and monks joined forces to attack prominent pagan intellectuals. The bishop Petros Mongos, balancing precariously on the tightrope of the *Henotikon*, rode the wave of this persecution in the hope of unifying his Church against the common threat allegedly posed by pagans.[130]

Zeno's reign also witnessed outbreaks of mass violence involving the Samaritans. There were two episodes, though neither can be dated, explained, or properly interpreted, nor should we assume that they were linked. The uprisings took place in Palestine, which held most of the empire's Samaritans. At Neapolis (Nablus), many of them attacked some Christians at worship in an effort to occupy their holy mountain, Mt. Gerizim; and a Samaritan named Ioustasas briefly took over Kaisareia where he held games, killing many Christians. Zeno's forces defeated him and sent his head to the emperor to add to his collection. They also captured Mt. Gerizim, where the emperor built a fortified church of the Virgin.[131] These disturbances may have been minor, but were harbingers of worse to come. Religious minorities had grievances against the new Christian order.

Against the odds, Zeno had survived more violent attempts to replace him than any emperor since the third century, and he had ably steered a middle course in Church politics while veiling his personal views, if they existed. There was now only one loose end to wrap up, the Goths of Theoderic the Amal. In small numbers the Goths were willing to be hired by the Romans, but in large numbers they had only one trick: terrorize the countryside and threaten the cities in order to extract concessions from the government. The Amal did this again, ravaging Thrace in 486 and encamping before Constantinople in 487, burning and plundering the suburbs. Zeno prudently chose to offer him money rather than battle.[132] But the situation was untenable for both. Therefore, in the winter of 487–488, Zeno and Theoderic hatched a mutually beneficial plan by thinking outside the box. Theoderic, his army, and his people would leave the Balkans and go to Italy, which he would rule as the representative of the eastern emperor in succession to Odoacer. The plan worked out remarkably well, if not for Odoacer then certainly for both Italy and the empire, as Theoderic turned out to be a capable and wise monarch. Few Goths stayed behind in the east when he left.[133]

Having overcome all his enemies, Zeno died in April, 491, aged around 60 or 65. He left the empire at peace. The schism with Rome was a reasonable price to pay for consensus among the great sees of the eastern Church. The empire was rid of the Goths but angry at Isaurians. Indeed, it seemed at the time that the Roman empire was subject to a foreign power, given the large annual tribute of supplies, called the *Isaurika* and worth 1,500 lbs of gold, that Illus had arranged for Isauria to receive and Zeno had maintained to keep his countrymen happy.[134] This was a huge drain on the treasury, larger than the protection money paid to the Goths and reaching the level of the annual sums paid to Attila.

The turmoil of Zeno's reign must not be mistaken as a systemic crisis in governance. It was caused solely by the emperor's lack of popularity and the resentment that Romans felt toward Isaurians. Zeno survived by manipulative canniness and the ineptness of his enemies. But his position was always weak, and he was unable or unwilling to designate an heir. At least with Zeno the Romans had had a ruler "who understood how to settle any situation to his advantage."[135]

10

Political Consolidation and Religious Polarization (491–518)

The accession of Anastasius

Romanía was not a dynastic state. Unlike the Sasanian Persian and Ottoman empires and the European monarchies, its rulers did not come from one family. In fact, any Roman could become emperor, so long as he was in the right place at the right time to garner the support of key elements of the polity and be put before an army or an assembly of citizens, whose acclamations made him an Augustus. This peculiarity was noted, throughout the empire's long history, by Arab, Chinese, Khazar, and Armenian observers: the Romans "did not [follow the ways] of other peoples whereby the emperor's son succeeds his father."[1] The reason why Romanía was different from other monarchies was that it had been created by a republic, not a specific ruling family, and it had a strong and entrenched concept of the public sphere as something that could be governed but not owned. It was not a "patrimonial state." The emperor no more owned the state than he could sell the Roman forum,[2] and the Romans of this period had a habit of appointing childless older men to the throne, a deliberately anti-dynastic policy. This way the choice of successor would revert to the polity.

The most detailed surviving account of a Roman imperial accession is that of Anastasius.[3] The night after Zeno died, the people and soldiers assembled in the hippodrome where they were addressed by Ariadne, Leo I's daughter and Zeno's widow, who was surrounded by the top magistrates and the archbishop. They acclaimed her—"Ariadne Augusta, may you be victorious!"—and demanded an orthodox emperor for the empire. She replied that she had already authorized the Senate to choose an emperor who was Christian, Roman, and virtuous, and to do so without partisanship. The people now demanded that she expel "the thieving prefect of the City." Ariadne replied that, "anticipating your requests . . . and taking thought for your well-being and all your interests," she had appointed a new prefect. But after long deliberations, the senators could not agree on a new emperor, and it was motioned that Ariadne make the selection. She chose Anastasius, a native of Dyrrachion, who was a *silentiarius*, a mid-level official in charge of palace order. He was acceptable to all. A tall man with eyes of different colors, Anastasius was charismatic, competent, and level-headed; he was also about sixty and childless, so intended as an interim appointment.

Two days later, after Zeno's funeral, Anastasius was "required to swear before the Senate that he would harbor no prior grudges against anyone and would govern the republic with an upright conscience." Allegedly, the bishop Euphemios also required him to sign a statement that he would accept Chalcedon, although this comes from an unreliable partisan source.[4] Anastasius then went up to the imperial box in the hippodrome before the people and soldiers, stood on a shield, and was proclaimed Augustus. He promised the usual donative, five solidi plus a pound of silver, to the soldiers. There ensued ritual chants and exchanges, in the course of which the new emperor acknowledged that "I am not unaware how great a burden of responsibility has been placed upon me for the common safety of all," and "I entreat God the Almighty that you will find me working as hard at public affairs as you had hoped when you universally elected me now." It is likely that these words were spoken in both Latin and Greek, the Greek bearing many Latin grammatical features. As an orator praising the emperor later put it: "some divine decree tilted the vote in your favor: as one, the populace cried out for you; the Senate added its support; the empress approved; the vote was carried."[5]

A month later, Anastasius married Ariadne. Contrary to expectations, he would reign for twenty-seven years, and would actually rule too. Unlike many of his predecessors, Anastasius had no handlers—whether generals, politicians, or eunuchs—whose decisions he rubber-stamped. It is a testament to the institutional power of Roman office-holding that a mid-level palace official could immediately assume command of the empire without having an enormous amount of personal clout. Romanía was an impersonal state. Anastasius, moreover, had his own mind: he rewarded competence and was not swayed by aristocratic prestige.[6] Yet to be obeyed in the long run, an emperor had to be seen to be working for the good of his subjects. As it turned out, Anastasius was among the best Roman emperors.

The Isaurian war

Within months of the transition there was a sporting riot. The people set fire to the area around the hippodrome gates and dragged the emperor's statues off their pedestals. The cause is unclear, but Anastasius promptly replaced the City prefect—the one so recently appointed by Ariadne—with his own brother-in-law Secundinus, pacifying the populace. Suspecting an Isaurian conspiracy behind the riot, Anastasius purged all high-ranking Isaurians, including Zeno's brother Longinus who was *magister militum praesentalis* and had hoped to succeed to the throne. He was banished to Egypt, but other Isaurians regrouped in their homeland, where they joined up with local discontents, including the governor Lilingis (Illus' half-brother) and Konon, the bishop of Apameia who, a true Isaurian, decided now on a second career in the army.[7] They mounted a rebellion and marched on Phrygia in 492, but they were soundly defeated there by the generals Ioannes the Scythian (who had defeated Illus in 484) and Ioannes the

Hunchback. The survivors fled to their homeland, where the war dragged on for six more years in a hard slog of mountain sieges, about which we are poorly informed. But Anastasius was determined to pacify Isauria, a task that the empire had failed to do for over half a millennium, and his generals eventually finished the job, earning consulships. The *Isaurika* fund was terminated, the captured rebels were paraded in the City and hippodrome, and the heads of leaders slain in battle were affixed to poles at Sykai across the Golden Horn, "a pleasing sight for the people of Constantinople, given what they had endured from the Isaurians."[8]

Isauria never troubled the empire again, but continued to provide recruits to the imperial army and skilled masons to the empire. Its pacification formed a cornerstone of Anastasian propaganda. When the people and the empress in the hippodrome, in 491, had declared their preference for a *Roman* emperor, they meant "no more Isaurians." Anastasius was quick to claim descent from Pompey the Great, who had campaigned near his home town of Dyrrachion and was the first Roman to conquer Isauria; the name Pompeius ran in the emperor's family, which was presumably proof enough of descent from the ancient general.[9] The emperor's victory monument for the Isaurian War was the Chalke, or Bronze Gatehouse to the palace, which was actually a vast hall. It bore an epigram that compared the Chalke to six wonders of ancient architecture, all pagan, and then concluded: "After annihilating the Isaurians in his victory, my emperor completed me, the shrine of Dawn, shining in gold and facing on all sides the currents of the four winds."[10]

Anastasius' fiscal policy

Immediately after the war, Anastasius implemented a reform of the empire's monetary economy and tax regime. Urban residents cried out with joy when they learned, in 498, that he was abolishing the tax on trades, the *collatio lustralis* (*chrysargyron*), first imposed by Constantine. The emperor made a great show of collecting all paperwork associated with this tax and burning it publicly, to great acclaim. In Edessa, the people dressed in white and processed to a church singing hymns of thanks.[11] Anastasius compensated the bureau of the *sacrae largitiones* that collected the urban tax by transferring revenue to it from the *res privata*, the bureau that, among other functions, maintained the emperor himself, "a magnificent example of his generosity."[12] The *chrysargyron* had brought in significant revenue but was widely hated. Yet even after abolishing it, Anastasius was able to leave a surplus of 23 million solidi in the treasury.[13] How did he manage this? First, during his reign the empire was, for the first time since the 440s, not paying protection money to Huns, Goths, Persians, or Isaurians. Second, the treasury was probably pulling in record sums from regular taxation, following two centuries of economic and demographic growth. The reign was also free of famine, drought, and outbreaks of disease.[14] Agriculture benefited from favorable climatic conditions and Anastasius nationalized a productive gold mine in Roman Armenia, ending its lease to private contractors.[15]

Anastasius rationalized tax collection by commuting most of it from payments in kind to gold, a conversion that had taken place only in patches and haphazardly before his reign, though he maintained payment in kind to supply army units. With this change, Anastasius was taking advantage of the increased monetization of the economy and reducing waste and inefficiencies. When not enough supplies were brought in for the army, Anastasius authorized compulsory purchases by the state, but at fair market prices and only with his permission. Such purchases were credited toward a region's tax liability or, if they went beyond it, were paid for in cash. Anastasius made a special arrangement for Thrace, "because the farmers are fewer due to the barbarian raids, and what they supply in kind is not sufficient for the soldiers stationed there." Thrace needed this because it hosted many armies. The state always had to purchase additional supplies there and pay its men in kind.[16]

Anastasius also increased the efficiency and probably the fairness of tax collection by removing its oversight from the city councils and entrusting it to an imperial official, the *vindex*, one of whom was appointed per city.[17] The state was now pulling in more cash than before relative to grain, which was better because grain might rot in transport or in a warehouse. Thus, the praetorian prefecture became a gold treasury more than a transporter of goods, reducing its costs. This, in turn, meant that soldiers could be paid more in cash than supplies; Anastasius also seems to have raised their pay. After 511, he folded the quinquennial donative of five solidi into their base pay, which was increasingly paid in gold.[18] But the gold economy stood on feet of bronze. In the fourth century, the value of the base currency had fluctuated greatly relative to the gold, and in the fifth century the bronze coins were so small that thousands of them were required to buy a gold coin. This made life difficult for those who were not paid in gold. Anastasius therefore reformed the bronze coins, in two phases (498, 512). He issued a series of coins whose values (calculated in multiples of notional *nummi*, or *folles*) were fixed against the solidus, "and ordered that they be used throughout the Roman state," which stabilized the system for centuries. "This was pleasing to the people," a chronicle of the period noted.[19] Anastasius did to the bronze, the currency that most people used, what Constantine had done to the gold.

By rationalizing the monetary economy, Anastasius was able to generate surpluses while still spending generously on utilitarian structures throughout the empire, such as baths, aqueducts, harbors, and walls. He rebuilt the Long Wall of Thrace, for example, so that henceforth it was attributed to him alone. He was also able to provide assistance to those in need, such as ransom for captives (1,000 lbs gold in one case) and tax relief or grants of cash for cities devastated by raids or natural disasters.[20] Our sources, however, present a mixed picture of Anastasius, with some praising his prudence and generosity and others condemning him for avarice and stinginess. All verdicts must be treated skeptically. Some of the positive ones were setting him up as an ideal contrast to Justinian, whereas some of the negative ones were angry that he was an efficient tax collector and downgraded the role of the city councils. The most hostile ones were single-issue partisans of Church politics. For them, no matter what an emperor did, he was satanic if he did not support the correct theological formula.[21]

Changes in city life

Changes were also taking place in the empire's cities at this time. Roman culture showcased cities as the "jewels" in the crown of empire, and a large body of research has tried to ascertain their fate in this period by sifting through and combining the archaeological and literary evidence. Yet firm patterns are hard to come by, and one edited volume of papers after another bogs the reader down in a vast amounts of granular detail, in skepticism toward texts, and in contradictory interpretations of the archaeological data. Yet an overview of uncontroversial points may be ventured.[22] While the material changes present a complex picture, the institutional changes have largely been misunderstood.

Some cities in the Balkan provinces were destroyed by the Huns and temporarily abandoned, such as Naissus (a major metropolis) and Nicopolis ad Istrum. When this Nicopolis was later refounded, it was on a much reduced scale, with walls, small churches, and some buildings that were possibly government offices, in other words as a fortified administrative hub and not a population center.[23] By contrast, the damage done by the Goths to cities such as Athens, Corinth, and Stobi can sometimes be traced by archaeologists, but it did not end their history or necessarily touch the sources of their prosperity.

The fate of most cities was shaped by endogenous factors, and in particular by Christianization, rather than by Goths and Huns. In a few cities, monumental temple complexes were converted directly to Christian use, so they retained their familiar classical profile, such as on the Akropolis of Athens. In most, however, pagan temples were either violently destroyed or, more commonly, abandoned and allowed to decay or plundered for their art and building materials. This happened, for example, to the temple of Artemis at Ephesos, one of the Seven Wonders of the ancient world, some of whose elements ended up in Constantinople, including the doors of the Senate House in Constantine's forum.[24] Urban residents grew used to ruins where there had once been monumental architecture. This also happened in Constantinople, where some of the ravages of the fire of 464 were never repaired, for example to the aforementioned Senate House: the intact façade of the building faced the forum, but behind it there was a burned husk. In some cities, such as Corinth, ancient statues were actively destroyed by residents, who broke off their heads and threw them in ditches, and eventually melted down their fragments, tossed them away, or used them to build protective walls and other utilitarian structures.[25]

As cities could tap less of their wealth locally for public works, amenities inherited from the past were often in disrepair, and civic notables were less inclined to spend their money for public purposes, as their finances were more encumbered by the central government. Governors were often the most important patrons of civic buildings in their provinces.[26] Scholarship has focused on the subdivision of elite houses (or at least of their ground floors) into smaller units, especially in the sixth century, and the apparent takeover of public spaces by workshops or small private residences.[27] In many places, people began to reuse the architectural elements of the classical city for other purposes. Were these signs of "decline"? A loss of public spirit and the fall of civic elites? Or did this repurposing reflect population growth and economic vitality? The archaeological evidence can be interpreted in opposite ways. The idea that public spaces were swallowed up by a chaotic encroachment of shops has recently been rejected by a thorough survey, which finds that commercial activities in the eastern cities continued to be regulated by the civic and imperial authorities, and that workshops tended to operate in clearly designated areas.[28]

Some loss, or change, was due to the ongoing religious revolution. The cities had lost their pagan festivals and had less need of temples. The last Olympic games of Antioch were held in the 510s, and the bishop described them as "licentious."[29] In most cities the old festivals were replaced by standardized Roman games and by a Christian cycle of festivals and celebrations, which was recognizably uniform throughout the empire, with variations to emphasize local saints or prized relics. Emperors promoted standardization and the simultaneity of Christian experience across the realm: "it is best for everyone to celebrate Easter everywhere at the same time," Constantine had declared.[30] Thus, even as east Romans were increasingly polarized over theology, their basic national and religious culture was becoming more homogenized and uniform.

The pagan festivals had doubled as market fairs that drew buyers, sellers, and visitors from afar, and these were economically too important to be abolished. They were instead refocused on local saints, while business went on as usual. Local market-fairs (*panegyreis*), which could last up to a month, are attested during the next millennium (and beyond). They tended not to overlap, and so, except for the depths of winter, there was usually one going on in a nearby city or town of a given province. As under the early Roman empire, cities competed over which had the most magnificent Christian festival. We have a lively account of the festival of St. Thekla at Seleukeia in Isauria in the fifth century, whose main rival was the festival of St. Paul at Tarsos. The account tells of some visitors, eating together and comparing what they had liked best. One liked the splendor, another the crowd, a third the assembly of archpriests, or the harmony of the psalms, and so on. But one man said that *he* saw the most beautiful girl under one of the colonnades, and he had prayed that he might have her. Along with such gawkers, these festivals brought in considerable revenue.[31]

Moreover, the neglect and destruction of pagan monuments were offset by the construction of Christian churches and charitable institutions such as hospitals, which changed urban topographies along with the rhythms of daily life.[32] These structures were funded by private donations (sometimes pooling resources for a single project), episcopal initiatives (though Church funds often came from private bequests), and imperial grants. The fifth century saw a boom in the construction of churches, typically three-aisled basilicas, some of them decorated with intricately carved elements and impressive mosaics featuring inscriptions commemorating donors. Bishops also picked up some of the slack in the construction of secular buildings. When Theodoretos of Kyrros was confined to his city after Ephesos I, he noted, in complaining to a court official, that he was not a troublemaker but an upstanding citizen who spent "a large part of Church revenue to build porticos, baths, and bridges."[33] But such expenses could backfire. Theophilos of Alexandria was accused of "lithomania," a passion for building that diverted funds away from charity and betrayed Pharaonic ambitions.[34] Thus, the nature of urban civilization did not change when bishops got involved. Whoever had control of the funds spent them in more or less traditional ways, though bishops introduced an emphasis on charity.

City governance

City governance also changed during the fifth century. In the fourth century, cities were governed by councils (*curiae*) that elected civic magistrates and interfaced with the governor and agents of the imperial bureaux, especially those of the praetorian prefect and *res privata*. Civic administration was supervised by the *curator*, who was still regarded as an imperial official even though he was appointed from among the councilors; the same was true of the *defensor*, a judge of minor cases whose remit was to protect citizens, especially the lower classes, from abuse. In practice, local affairs were managed by an inner circle of powerful councilors called *principales*.[35] Many trades were monopolized by professional guilds, and civic leaders had to negotiate with them. An extraordinary inscription from Sardeis (459) documents an agreement between the guild of builders and the city's *defensor* whereby the guild undertook to insure every order, even if the builder who was contracted was unable to complete the job. This was similar to the scheme of collective insurance that the prefect Anthemius had imposed on the shipping guild that brought grain to the capital. Moreover, the Sardeis agreement hints that the builders' guild may have bargained collectively for their wages.[36]

The curial system changed during the fifth century, when new leadership cadres emerged that took on a major role in local decisions, such as the sale of city land and the appointment of the *defensor*. These parties were the *honorati* (current and former imperial officials), the *possessores* (*ktetores* in Greek, usually rendered "landowners"), and the bishop. The councils continued to exist and perform the basic functions of local governance, and they were still regarded as "the sinews of the republic and vital organs of the cities."[37] Yet they were increasingly marginalized, and some of their functions were taken over by others. For example, many local entertainments fell under the purview of the Blues and the Greens. Anastasius even removed from the councils the supervision of tax collection, transferring it to a new official that he created called the *vindex*. A *vindex* was appointed by the praetorian prefect for "each city of Romanía." The emperor's aim was to "lighten the burden on farmers" by protecting them from "the rapacity of the councils," but authors who viewed this from a curial point of view complained that taxation now became more onerous—which likely means more efficient and fair, perhaps explaining that emperor's surpluses—and they hyperbolically lamented this as the "undoing of the city councils."[38] Indeed, one strain of scholarship views this demotion of the councils as the "decline and fall of the Roman city": once-proud classical traditions of civic politics now yielded to informal factions of rich landowners lording it over the sad ruins of the ancient city.[39] Such pessimism is unwarranted. The councils continued to exist and to function,[40] but they were subsumed within a broader order that was dominated by the more prestigious *honorati* and *possessores*.

In reality what happened in this period was that the history of the councils became entwined with that of the Senate of Constantinople and the creation of an increasingly unified, centralized Roman state. The one process was just the flip side of the other. What scholars call the "flight of the councilors" in discussions of the "plight" of the cities in the fourth century can, if we turn it over, be seen as an expansion of the opportunities available to them to serve in the administration and Senate. Cities were now just one level within a more layered system of centralized governance. By the early fifth century, there were so many thousands of senators that only the highest rank of them, the *illustres*, carried out the functions of that body, while the emperors let the lower ranks (the *spectabiles* and *clarissimi*) go live in their cities; indeed, they encouraged them to do so. These men lost some senatorial privileges and burdens, but retained their rank as *honorati*, which was higher than that of the city councilors, as was the rank of other imperial officials who also retired to their home cities. Meanwhile, some curial *principales* had also received honorary imperial ranks, so that the lowest senatorial ranks and the highest local ones met and fused in the middle to create a new provincial ruling class.[41]

This was no institutional decline. It made sense for cities to be governed by their highest-ranked elements, and these had been drawn upward by the creation of the Senate and the more unified national government of the eastern empire. It would not do for lower-ranked men to govern higher-ranked senators. When the overlap of these elements was still in confusion, Theodosius II gave the example of a councilor of Emesa who usurped the privileges of high senatorial rank in order to bully the governor and tax collectors: "the collection of debts would cease if the collector has to defer to the debtor," the emperor observed.[42] Even a saint—the Monophysite zealot Peter the Iberian—had to stand by quietly while "illustrious men from the city" delayed the liturgy by gossiping about politics.[43] The empire's social hierarchy was not in doubt, unlike its theology.

City government thereby became an extension of imperial government and the gaps between them were closed up. This was not a decline but an integration. The biggest source of ambiguity remains the *possessores* (*ktetores*), a term that is translated as "landowner." In this context, it must have meant something more specific. When our sources refer to the *ktetores* of the city, they refer to a select and identifiable group defined by its political status. Justinian distinguished between *ktetores* and private citizens, and, when an earthquake hit Antioch, Laodikeia, and Seleukeia, he granted to the *ktetores* of those cities the senatorial rank of *illustris*.[44] The new ruling class, therefore, did not represent the triumph of unofficial private men over the official instruments of city governance. After all, the old councilor class had been selected on the basis of its wealth too, so the *ktetores* were likely citizens whose wealth exceeded that of the councilors, an über-council of sorts. A striking scene of their presence on the urban landscape has been proposed for Kaisareia in Palestine: the city's seafront profile was dominated by huge luxury villas that adjoined the palace of the provincial governor.[45]

Some historians believe that this landowning class became so wealthy and powerful that, in a quasi-feudal way, it gobbled up the villages and undermined the emperor's ability to govern. But there is little evidence for this. Such large estates are absent from the daily life of the village of Aphrodite in Egypt, whose financial accounts we know the best. The estates of the elite at Petra (in Jordan), whose sizes we know thanks to papyri, were not all that great.[46] Moreover, there is no good evidence for widespread tax evasion by these elites; its existence is more assumed by historians than proven. Finally, sheer wealth could not enable individuals or institutions to challenge or ignore the emperor. A good example comes from the reign of Anastasius. The poster child for the class of wealthy imperial officials who allegedly became virtually autonomous on their landed estates is the family of the Apiones from Egypt. However, the size of the Apion estates has been significantly downgraded in the calculations of the most recent scholarship.[47] Moreover, Apion lived in Constantinople, not Egypt, and was fully a member of the court. When his performance in the Persian War of 502–505 displeased Anastasius, he was fired and replaced. More dramatically, when he somehow offended the emperor in 510, his property was confiscated and he was forcibly ordained a priest at Nikaia. By the stroke of a pen, Apion was finished—until he was recalled and reinstated by Justin. Emperors had nothing to fear here. At no point in Roman history was there a "feudal" revolution of magnates who undermined the state by taking over whole provinces.

Anastasius' Persian war

Let us turn to the Persian war in which Apion disappointed Anastasius. In 502–504, the empire was given a foretaste of what all-out war with Persia would feel like later, under Justinian. Persia was emerging from a punishing period of its history, during which it had struggled on its northeastern frontier against powerful Central Asian empires ruled by dynasties that are called Huns in our sources, though their relation to the Huns of Attila is obscure. These were the Kidarites (for most of the fifth century) and the Hephthalites (for the later fifth and sixth). The shahs were repeatedly defeated by them in battle and had to pay sizable tributes. Their fortunes had sunk so low that they frequently asked Constantinople for financial and military aid, either as a gift or as a contribution to the joint defense of the Caucasus, probably the Derbent pass by the Caspian Sea that blocked invasions by mutual enemies from the steppe. Some of the emperors had provided aid, but not reliably. The Romans did not want to be maneuvered into conceding that this was a treaty obligation or that they were paying tribute to Persia, which was how the shahs wanted to spin it for domestic consumption. The shah Kavad was in an especially weak position: he had lost his throne, in part due to his support of a Zoroastrian heresy known as Mazdakism, and had regained it with Hephthalite armed support. He was out of money and low on prestige, and looked to Rome for one or the other. He asked Anastasius for money, and received a loan offer instead. He chose war.[48]

The Persian War of 502–504 is exceptionally well documented.[49] Leading a multiethnic army of Saracens, Armenians, Persians, Hephthalite allies, and others, Kavad quickly captured Theodosiopolis in Roman Armenia in 502, swung past Martyropolis, from which he seized two years' worth of taxes—the place had no defenses and did not try to resist[50]—and then marched on Amida. Amida was heavily fortified and resisted his assaults for three months, despite having a small garrison. The city fell when some monks, who were supposed to be guarding a tower, passed out after too much drinking, allowing the Persians to climb the walls. When they took the city, they slaughtered the population until the shah himself entered, riding an elephant. He stripped Amida of all its valuables, even shipping the statues down the Tigris, and the captives were roped together and marched to Persia, to be resettled at a new royal foundation. Two monks who were captured outside Amida were sold to the Huns north of the Caucasus, where they lived for over thirty years, taking wives; they later returned to the empire and told their story. In Amida itself, Kavad installed a garrison of 3,000. Meanwhile, skirmishes were making life hard in the surrounding regions, as Kavad's Saracen raiders clashed with local defense forces and took thousands of captives. Edessa was put on lockdown, though a Roman *dux* did recover Theodosiopolis. Overall, Kavad had caught the Romans "utterly unprepared, for it was a time of peace and prosperity."[51] These regions had not seen real war since the 350s.

Anastasius responded in 503 with what he thought would be overwhelming force. He dispatched the elderly general Patricius with the first praesental army (20,000 men) and his own nephew Hypatius with the second (another 20,000) to retake Amida. Areobindus, a descendant of the consul of 434 and Aspar, led the army of Oriens, numbering 12,000 men, against Nisibis. The praetorian prefect Apion coordinated the supply lines from Edessa. If we add the local forces chasing down Saracen raiders, we can understand why it was believed to be the largest force ever assembled by the Romans against the Persians.[52] But its performance was unimpressive. Areobindus was chased away from Nisibis by the Persians and called for reinforcements. Patricius and Hypatius failed to assist him, perhaps out of spite, and then all were defeated in battle by Kavad at Tell Beshme. The shah and his raiders ravaged Osrhoene again and then departed for their own territory. Yet the Persian garrison at Amida held on, even though famine had led its people to cannibalism (the women conspired together to kill and eat the men). In the summer of 503, Anastasius sent his *magister officiorum* Celer to take over from Hypatius and Apion, who were hostile to Areobindus and were recalled (Hypatius in particular, the emperor's nephew, would turn out to be the most incompetent leader of that era). Celer managed to put the Persians on the defensive through a number of successful smaller operations, and Amida was retaken in 504, when its Persian commander was lured out by a ruse hatched by a local hunter, and killed. Kavad was now ready to make a deal.

Celer bought peace from Kavad in exchange for 1,100 lbs of gold, and more gold flowed from Rome to Persia to ransom prisoners. Anastasius provided generous tax relief and supplies during the war to the affected provinces, Osrhoene and Mesopotamia, and afterward he invested in upgrading their fortifications. He also demanded that his generals explain their pitiful performance. They claimed that they lacked a fortified base in the region, forcing them to roam exposed to enemy attack. After reviewing various proposals, Anastasius fortified the town of Daras by the Persian frontier, across from Nisibis, and turned it into a bunker for Roman operations. Our information about the logistics and budget of this project is detailed, revealing the administrative bureaux of the state in action.[53] Kavad objected strenuously to this construction, but it was he who had ruined the stable relationship between the two empires for a cash grab. Daras was renamed Anastasiopolis, was given a bishop, and became the base of the *dux* of Mesopotamia.

At the time, Anastasius' Persian War could be regarded as a bump in an otherwise peaceful history of coexistence with Persia, like the brief war of 420–422; indeed, the next conflict would not break out for over twenty years. But the war had revealed some of the systematic insecurities within the Persian empire that made its rulers increasingly aggressive. The history of Romanía would, in the long term, become an existential struggle for survival against Persia.

Blues and Greens

Anastasius' reign was pivotal also in the escalation of hatred and conflict between the Blues and the Greens in the hippodromes and streets of many cities, and also between Chalcedonians and anti-Chalcedonians. These parallel outbreaks of tribal violence reveal a society ready to fracture and seizing frivolous pretexts to do so such as mime shows and arcane theological formulas that no one understood. Each arena of conflict is hard to explain on its own. Still, in both cases the imperial state had created institutions that fostered tightly wound team-identities focused on zero-sum competitions, and in the case of the fan clubs the membership consisted largely of idle young men roaming about in the absence of policing. Graffiti from the forum of Aphrodisias (in Asia Minor) express the passion of partisanship: "The fortune of the Blues triumphs!", and similarly for the Greens.[54] Fierce loyalties led to adversarial narratives and then to violence that spilled out into the streets and drew in the authorities. Lives, limbs, and property were lost, and managing this explosive situation caused headaches for the prefect of the City.

In 498, Anastasius deployed the excubitors to suppress the Greens who were protesting in the hippodrome, whereupon one of the fans threw a rock at him, which the emperor narrowly dodged. The man was cut to bits and, in response, the fans set fire to part of the hippodrome, which spread along the Mese. In 502, Anastasius suspended the pantomimes throughout the empire, as their fans were even more violent than those of the races. A recent melee in a theater had claimed 3,000 lives. In Antioch in 507, the celebrity charioteer Porphyrios led a mob to destroy a local synagogue. His team fans, the Greens, rioted on subsequent occasions too, so Anastasius sent officials from the capital to restore order. One of them decapitated a Green who sought refuge in a church, and in retaliation the Greens fought a pitched battle against the combined forces of the emperor's Goths and the Blues. Amazingly, they won, after which they set fire to two basilicas and the prefect's offices, captured and disemboweled the official who had killed their comrade, and hung his body from a statue in the forum.[55]

Repression eventually worked, as the second half of the reign was far less troubled by hooliganism than the first. Anastasius found a constructive way to channel the spirit of competition, by allowing the teams to erect statues in the hippodrome in honor of the most popular charioteer of the age, Porphyrios, when he won for them (like players today, he would contract to race for different teams in turn).[56] The elaborate bases for two of these statues—one by the Blues and one by

Figure 16 Statue base of Porphyrios: the charioteer in his quadriga above, dancing fans in the lower register, the epigrams in between (Istanbul Archaeological Museum)
Photo by Brad Hostetlet.

the Greens—can be seen in the Istanbul Archaeological Museum (see Figure 16). Thirty-two epigrams were written to celebrate his racing achievements, some of them to be carved on the bases. "This Porphyrios was born in Libya but raised in Rome [= Constantinople]. Victory crowned him now for one team, now for another . . . for he often changed teams and horses."[57] He sometimes did this on the same day: winning with one team, then winning again with the team of horses that he had just defeated (this feat was called a *diversium*). Porphyrios was the most famous man in the empire, after the emperor.

Theological polarization

The civil war in the Church heated up just when that between the colors was quieting down. A fragile peace, or cold war, prevailed in the Church during the first twenty years of Anastasius' reign, defined by Zeno's *Henotikon*. By the early 490s, the players for whom the *Henotikon* was crafted—Akakios, Petros Mongos, and Petros the Fuller—had died. Their successors, the patriarchs of Constantinople, Alexandria, Antioch, and Jerusalem, were finding it difficult to endorse the *Henotikon*. In Constantinople they were harried by hardline partisans of Chalcedon, whereas in Alexandria they were harried by its hardline opponents. Soon the patriarchs of Alexandria ceased to pretend that they were not opposed to Chalcedon. Egypt was effectively lost to any Chalcedonian consensus from the late fifth century. Rome, for its part, was staking out the most extreme position of all: not only did it require everyone to recognize Chalcedon, it refused to recognize anyone who did not explicitly recognize its own right to have deposed Akakios of Constantinople and Petros Mongos of Alexandria back in the 480s. As a result, Rome did not even recognize patriarchs who both recognized Rome and agreed with it in accepting Chalcedon, if they did not also see Rome as the ultimate judge in all Church matters. One pope, Gelasius, even proclaimed that Constantinople was really only a subordinate church of its nearby city of Herakleia and that the eastern Romans were really only "Greeks, among whom heresies flourish." This was likely the first instance of the western Christian prejudice that Greek-speaking Christians were prone to heresy. But the easterners largely ignored Rome. Gelasius complained that they regarded him as "proud and arrogant." Rome's claims swelled to fantastic proportions precisely when Rome was being ignored.[58]

In 496, Anastasius deposed Euphemios, patriarch of Constantinople, and exiled him to Euchaïta (in Asia Minor). This was either for intriguing with the Isaurians or for his "Nestorian" sympathies, but the emperor was not rolling out a new policy. He wanted "to make no innovations in the Church."[59] Bishops could be for or against Chalcedon, but so long as they kept to the *Henotikon* the emperor left them alone. Euphemios' replacement, his close associate Makedonios, signed off on the *Henotikon*, as did Flavianos, the new patriarch of Antioch (498–512). Yet beneath the lid of the *Henotikon* there was a boiling cauldron of controversy and disputation, as the factions were always sniping at each other in their efforts to escalate the conflict. One anti-Chalcedonian agitator in Syria was Philoxenos, bishop of Hierapolis (Mabbug), who began a campaign of systematic harassment against Flavianos of Antioch with the goal of deposing him. Philoxenos was a rarity: a native Aramaic speaker from the Persian empire (né Xenaïas), who had climbed the ecclesiastical ladder in Romanía. He produced a new translation of the Bible into Syriac and wrote theological works. The most prominent anti-Chalcedonian agitator of this period was Severos. A pagan from Sozopolis (Pisidia), he studied rhetoric and philosophy in Alexandria and then attended the famous law school of Beirut. During the course of his studies, he fell in with zealous Christian classmates, converted, and took up asceticism under the influence of Petros the Iberian, the chief anti-Chalcedonian of the previous generation. With a convert's zeal, Severos lobbied on behalf of anti-Chalcedonian monastic communities in Palestine, which brought him to the capital in 508 in the company of 200 monks protesting their persecution by Chalcedonian bishops. Anastasius was impressed with Severos and kept him at the court. Soon the emperor began to lean Monophysite.[60]

Tensions were growing between Anastasius and his patriarch Makedonios, who refused to recognize his peers in Antioch and Alexandria.[61] Makedonios and Severos also seem to have engaged in theological debates, during the course of which the text of John 19:34 came into question—Was Jesus "dead" when the soldier pierced him with the lance?—at which point an old Bible "in large letters," which had been found in the tomb of the Apostle Barnabas on Cyprus during the reign of Zeno, was produced from the palace to settle the dispute.[62] Open conflict erupted in 511, when anti-Chalcedonians in Constantinople celebrated the liturgy in the palace and Hagia Sophia by using Petros the Fuller's addition "Crucified on our behalf." This Monophysite slogan provoked the Chalcedonian populace of the City to demonstrate violently. Each side accused the other of starting the violence, and likely both were right. Severos, a witness, graphically described the victims on his side, "who spent many days lying in their beds in excruciating pain, while some among them even shed blood from their places of evacuation, both on the front and back side." The uprising included enough anti-imperial chants for Anastasius to barricade the palace and prepare the fleet in case the court had to leave the City. To defuse tensions he summoned the patriarch, who was being cheered by the populace, and reconciled with him in a show of humility.[63] But humbling an emperor was dangerous business.

Irrespective of any theological differences—assuming they existed between an emperor and patriarch who were both temporizers—Makedonios' position was now untenable: he had become a focal point in a popular disturbance. The court quickly outmaneuvered him. He was lured by the *magister officiorum* Celer into signing a confession of faith that made no mention of Chalcedon and thereby cost him the support of hardline Chalcedonians in the capital. As it was an anniversary year, in July 511 Anastasius distributed his vicennial donative to the army to ensure its loyalty—the palace guardsmen had to swear an oath to defend the faith and the republic and not to plot against the emperor. Anastasius then set forth charges against Makedonios at an emotional meeting of his cabinet. They included disparaging the emperor's faith; subversion of the throne; corrupting the text of Scripture to support "Nestorianism"; and—why not?—pederasty (the patriarch was possibly a eunuch). In early August, the authorities rounded up Makedonios' key supporters. The City was locked down to keep out monastic agitators, and the patriarch was arrested by Celer and exiled to Euchaïta, where he joined his predecessor Euphemios.[64]

The scale of these precautions indicates how seriously Anastasius took the threat of a popular uprising over theological issues. In 494, he had even told pope Gelasius that, for fear of "a tumult by the *plebs Constantinopolitana*," he could not remove the commemoration of Akakios as a rightful bishop of the City.[65]

But elsewhere the Monophysites were gaining ground. The relentless campaign of harassment against Flavianos of Antioch, which Philoxenos of Hierapolis piously called "ten years of resistance," succeeded in 512 when Flavianos withdrew during a battle between the people of Antioch and the monks whom Philoxenos had sent in. With the emperor's approval, Flavianos was declared deposed, and Philoxenos consecrated Severos as bishop of Antioch in his place.[66] Severos' approach was strategic and divisive: upon his elevation, he declared that "we have the venerable bishops of Constantinople and Alexandria on our side, and those who are not are strangers to our communion."[67]

In November 512, Anastasius faced the greatest peril of his reign. So far he had not made explicit pronouncements against Chalcedon, or demanded them from others, and many of the bishops who had been deposed during his reign had been, like him, regarded as temporizers by extremists on either side. But when he allowed the "Crucified" to be added again to the liturgy, it sparked a bloody three-day popular insurrection. Chanting the hymn in its original form, protesters demanded "a new emperor for Romanía," and they pillaged and burned the house of the praetorian prefect Marinus, a Syrian who was seen as a Monophysite influence at the court. They killed an eastern monk and paraded his head around on a pole, calling him "the enemy of the Trinity." From the forum of Constantine, they went to the villa of the general Areobindus and called on him to be made emperor; his wife, Anicia Juliana, had a more illustrious imperial genealogy than anyone else alive at the time, being descended from no fewer than seven emperors. But Areobindus fled, and the protesters heard that the emperor had appeared in his box at the hippodrome. He removed his crown in a gesture of abdication and asked the populace, who now gathered there, to "please stop killing people at random." This performance of humility and moral authority by the eighty-year-old monarch worked, and the insurrection ended. Anastasius was able to arrest some of the perpetrators and punish them.[68]

The consensus of the *Henotikon* had faltered. While it was in force, the patriarchs of Constantinople, Antioch, and Alexandria had managed to weave a subtle course around their own theological preferences, the court's demand for consensus, and the pressure of local hardliners, who were Chalcedonians in Constantinople and Jerusalem, anti-Chalcedonians in Alexandria, and both in Antioch. It is remarkable that the center had held for so long, but the enemies of Chalcedon in the east now moved dynamically to destabilize it. They were more successful at fashioning an anti-Chalcedonian identity of outrage, victimization, and the unity of Patristic thought—indeed, of the unity of Christ—than were the Chalcedonians at defending Chalcedon.[69]

Severos and Philoxenos, who were sophisticated theologians and smart operatives, managed to disrupt and take over the Churches of Constantinople and Antioch, and they pulled Anastasius in their wake. By the end of his reign, aggressive anti-Chalcedonians were winning. The emperor probably did not share their theological zeal. He still did not require any bishop to take a stand vis-à-vis Chalcedon, but he wanted all his patriarchs be in communion with each other, which now meant in communion with Severos of Antioch, who openly condemned Chalcedon. In fact, Severos was acting like the pope, except in reverse: he required bishops to remove from their lists of recognized predecessors any who accepted "the impious deeds of Chalcedon."[70] The other side had no one of comparable stature, apart from the monastic founder Sabas in Palestine and the populace of Constantinople. Yet the coup in Antioch awakened the Chalcedonian community to its peril. Many bishops refused to recognize Severos, and the eastern Churches fractured into competing factions. Some monks in Syria II appealed to the pope directly with charges against Severos.[71] The diocese of Illyricum, which technically belonged to Rome's jurisdiction, was also Chalcedonian, if difficult at times for the pope to govern. The bishop of Thessalonike praised pope Hormisdas as "an infallible pugilist for the true faith."[72]

It was not clear how emperors could resolve such tensions. During the first half of the fifth century, they mastered the art of the Church Council. Ephesos I (431) was an embarrassing debacle because Theodosius II put the bishops in charge, a mistake that his successors avoided. Ephesos II (449) and Chalcedon (451) were tightly controlled and carefully orchestrated to produce exactly the results that emperors wanted regarding which bishops were to be deposed, which canons would be passed, and the thrust of the doctrine that was approved. The vast majority of bishops knew exactly what they were there to do, and did it with alacrity. In the second half of the century, emperors experimented with other instruments for manufacturing consensus, including Leo's referendum (the *Codex Encyclicus*), Basiliscus' fiat (the *Encyclical*), and Zeno's compromise (the *Henotikon*). In all cases, most bishops did exactly what they knew in advance they were expected to do, and signed off even when the positions changed from year to year. The emperors were usually seeking unity, choosing the faction that seemed poised to deliver it, not because they were theologically committed to it. Ever since Constantine, emperors did not want the relevant theological questions to be investigated all the way down, because disagreements popped up at every step. They repeatedly tried to ban theological disputation. Their secular officials, moreover, were theologically flexible or indifferent.[73]

During this initial phase of the conflict over Natures, some bishops were willing to compromise, dissimulate, or change their position in order to maintain the illusion, or create the reality, of consensus. Some changed their mind back and forth while others tried to fuse the two positions ("there is no difference between Two Natures or One Incarnate Nature of the Word").[74] All still believed, or pretended, that they were part of one and the same Church, even if parts of it were corrupt (which parts depended on whom you asked). They all still appealed to the emperor to fix problems, and were not thinking of setting up separate hierarchies. But others, such as all the popes on one side and Severos and Philoxenos on the other, were willing to blow everything up so long as they got their way, and they were buoyed by lay forces. Monastic communities and the people of major cities were willing to riot in theological partisanship. Robust identities were forming around narratives, slogans, grievances, and martyrs, based on "ties of family, friendship, and place, or attachment to a teacher,"[75] but retroactively rationalized in terms of theology or imagined victimization.[76] A murky consensus was still viable so long as the emperors did not join the fray as activists in their own right. Anastasius did not, but his successors fatefully did.

Syriac literature

The anti-Chalcedonian movement lies at the heart of the emerging Syriac literature of this time. Paradoxically, just as the empire was losing linguistic diversity due to the extinction of the tongues of Asia Minor, more of its languages were being written than before. Churches that used Aramaic and Coptic (inside the empire) and Georgian and Armenian (mostly outside) required translations of key documents of the faith, including Scripture, the liturgy and creed, the writings of the Fathers, and hagiography. This development did not reflect provincial hostility to Rome nor did it aim to overthrow the hegemony of Greek culture. To the contrary, the Christian literatures that emerged at this time were written mostly by bilingual scholars and were intimately tied to Greek originals and even extended the latter's reach into non-Greek cultures. Coptic even used the Greek alphabet. Its greatest author, the abbot Shenute (d. 465), was trained in classical Greek, but because he wrote in Coptic later east Romans had no access to his works, indeed they were not even aware of his existence. The scholars who created the Armenian script were preceded by a long tradition of their countrymen studying in the prestigious centers of Greek learning, including Athens, and even teaching there. The first Georgian script was possibly based on the Greek alphabet and devised in Palestine, as its first extant specimen is a mosaic inscription of 430 from Jerusalem (the Bir el Qutt inscriptions).[77]

The most successful new literature in the short term was that in Syriac. Syriac literature should not be fetishized as exotic, subaltern, or more "authentic" than Greek and Latin. It had its own imagery, as all languages do, but its contents hold no surprises for those familiar with Greek patristic texts, and much of its surviving corpus was translated from Greek. Speakers of Aramaic were not thought, either by themselves or by others, to form an ethnic group or nation. They were united and divided by the same passions as other Romans. When the *comes* Chareas entered Edessa in 449, he was greeted by the population with typical acclamations, albeit in Aramaic, including "Victory to the Romans! May the emperor be preserved for Romanía!" (even that vernacular name for the realm had entered Aramaic). The great Syriac poet Ya'qub (Jacob) of Sarug (Batnai) sent a letter to the Christians of Himyar in Arabia claiming that "we Romans admire your way of life." The first secular prose text in Syriac is the *Chronicle* of pseudo-Joshua, which was written by a functionary of the local government in Edessa and reflects a conventional Roman outlook and identification with government, such as can be found in many Greek or Latin texts of the period. The author includes a letter sent to the Church of Edessa by the Church of Zeugma (on the Euphrates) announcing a miracle that pertained to "us, you, and all Romans": a goose had laid an egg on which was written, in embossed Greek letters, "The Romans Will Conquer."[78]

Aramaic speakers were not more likely to be Monophysites. That division in the Church cut across the languages of the Roman east, except in Egypt, where the majority, likely both Greek and Coptic speakers, were Monophysites out of loyalty to their patriarchs Cyril (as he was there interpreted) and Dioskoros. The association of Syriac with the rejection of Chalcedon is a misleading impression caused by the preservation of Syriac texts by the anti-Chalcedonian Syriac Church under Muslim rule, just as the later Chalcedonian Church of Constantinople also filtered out Greek anti-Chalcedonian texts, which also no longer survive. Thus we have the illusion of Chalcedonians as Greek and anti-Chalcedonians as Syriac. But before Islam, language and theology did not align. Many surviving Syriac anti-Chalcedonian texts were translations from the Greek, for example the works of Severos of Antioch, who did not himself write in Syriac. Native Aramaic speakers were also split: bishop Rabbula of Edessa (411–435), a Cyrillian partisan, was succeeded by Ibas (435–457), who hated Cyril. However, the Monophysite cause was vigorously promoted among Aramaic speakers by activist bishops such as Philoxenos, and by the translation of the works of Severos of Antioch, which began already in his own lifetime. As a result, the balance among Aramaic speakers who cared about the issue probably tilted against Chalcedon, especially during the sixth century. There is little evidence for Diphysite Syriac texts, though this may be due to selective transmission.[79]

One-Nature theology made major inroads into Syria, rolling back the so-called Antiochene School of Two-Nature theology that had produced Theodoros of Mopsouestia and Nestorios in the first decades of the fifth century, or at least revealing how thin its support had really been on the ground.[80] In 431, it was the allies of Nestorios from Antioch who were called "the Easterners," but in the insurrection of 512 in Constantinople it was a (supposedly) Monophysite monk who was labeled as an "easterner" and killed. Even so, as late as the 510s Severos encountered lingering devotion to Nestorios at Tarsos and to Theodoretos at Kyrros.[81]

The rebellion of Vitalianus

In 514, Chalcedon found an unlikely champion in the person of Vitalianus, a soldier of Gothic origin from Thrace who had served in the Persian War but did not now hold a high position. He conspired with some "Huns" and managed to suborn the regular Roman units in the frontier provinces of Scythia and Moesia by fanning their grievances against their general. He murdered or corrupted some of their officers and gathered a large army that included many peasant recruits, to whom he made great promises. These farmers may have resented Anastasius' retention for Thrace alone of the system of supplementary levies. Vitalianus never proclaimed himself emperor but marched on Constantinople, demanding justice for his soldiers and a ratification of "orthodox doctrine," i.e., Chalcedon, along with the return of exiled bishops. By this point, the praesental field armies had been mostly redeployed to the east, so Anastasius did not have forces to muster on short notice. He manned the walls of the City and, to secure provincial loyalty, lowered taxes on Bithynia and Asia by one fifth. The emperor quickly agreed to the rebel's terms, after which Vitalianus withdrew to the north. But Anastasius reneged on the deal as soon as he could muster an army, and sent Cyrillus, *magister militum* for Thrace, against the rebel. The fighting was inconclusive, but after it Vitalianus snuck into Odessos, where Cyrillus was based, and slew him with "a Gothic dagger" as he slept between two concubines. At this point the Senate formally proclaimed the rebel "an enemy of the Roman republic." Anastasius sent another army under his nephew Hypatius, but he was decisively defeated and taken captive. Huns (possibly Bulgars) played an important role in these battles, and seized the chance to ravage the provinces.[82]

After his victories, in late 514 or early 515 Vitalianus marched back to Constantinople and secured more concessions: he was appointed *magister militum* for Thrace; he received 2,000 (or 5,000) lbs of gold as ransom for Hypatius; and the emperor promised to convene a Council of the Church at Herakleia that would include the pope. This was the first and last time that a major military revolt aimed not to replace the emperor but to advance a theological cause. In ravaging Thrace with barbarians in order to gain offices and money, Vitalianus was following the playbook of Alaric and Theoderic. Eventually this earned him the fate of Gaïnas and Aspar.

Anastasius did make overtures to pope Hormisdas to bring peace to the Church, but it was a futile gesture. The pope made maximalist demands: the east would have to accept Leo's Tome and the Council of Chalcedon; to condemn Timotheos the Cat, Petros Mongos, Petros the Fuller, and Akakios; and to allow Rome to judge the cases of all deposed eastern bishops. The emperor would also have to agree to "follow the Apostolic See in all things." All eastern bishops would have to sign a profession of faith sent by the pope, and the documents would be forwarded to Rome via Vitalianus, who had taken on the role of armed papal representative in the Balkans. The terms, of course, were deliberately humiliating, with little chance of enforcement even if Anastasius were inclined to try (he was not). It is striking how stuck in the 480s the popes still were. Rome's obsession with control is revealed in the totalitarian set of instructions, the *Indiculus*, that Hormisdas sent with his envoys to Constantinople to govern their every move and utterance.[83] The emperor's response to the pope was measured and correct: he had not condemned Chalcedon, he explained; he *had* asked the Alexandrians to stop condemning it; and it would cause riots and bloodshed if he started enforcing the condemnation of even more bishops. "The living should not suffer on behalf of the dead."[84]

Vitalianus, who maintained separate communications with Rome, watched the negotiations and his Council collapse. He was also stripped by Anastasius of his command. In late 515, he marched on Constantinople again, bringing his Black Sea fleet down the Bosporos. This made him the first agent of papal hegemony to bring an army against the City. But Anastasius was ready this time. His capable praetorian prefect Marinus destroyed the rebel's fleet in a naval engagement by the Golden Horn and then defeated his land forces at Sykai. Marinus was assisted by Justin, who had joined the palace guard as a lad forty years previously and was now *comes* of the excubitors. Vitalianus retreated to Anchialos, where he holed up until the emperor's death.[85] His defeat was celebrated across the empire. In Antioch, Severos composed a hymn "On the rebel Vitalianus and the victory of the Christ-loving emperor Anastasius."[86] Constantinople celebrated one other hero of the war, the charioteer Porphyrios, who, to crown his multifarious career, fought in the battle alongside the fans of his current team, the Greens. Anastasius allowed the Greens to erect a statue in his honor with epigrams that linked his victory on the racetrack to his victory fighting for the emperor: "just as Rome was on the verge of falling, the light of freedom returned . . . for you too took up arms in the battle of the ships."[87]

The empress Ariadne, who had been almost invisible during her second husband's reign, died in 515. Anastasius died in 518, at the age of almost ninety. The fragile peace, or truce, in the Church created around Zeno's *Henotikon* had unraveled during his reign, and Anastasius, whether through conviction or policy, put his finger on the scales to support Severos and the enemies of Chalcedon. Still, he took no overt doctrinal position himself and allowed Chalcedonians to have their victories too, for example, in Jerusalem. He was therefore remembered in ambiguous ways. Anti-Chalcedonians believed he was one of their own, whereas Chalcedonians were confused about him, except for partisans of Makedonios such as the historian Theodoros Anagnostes, who reviled him as a heretic.

Anastasius knew that the Acacian Schism could not be healed without huge disruptions to the eastern Churches, at least not on Rome's terms, which were too imperious. The emperor made another effort after Vitalianus' defeat, but was served by the pope with a list of authoritarian stipulations. Anastasius broke off discussions: "We will stay silent from here on, as it is absurd to show courtesy to those who make threats and refuse to be entreated. We can tolerate being insulted and despised, but we will not be ordered about."[88]

The survival of the eastern empire

Why did the eastern empire not fall in the fifth century as the western empire did? The short answer is that there was no reason for that to happen; it never even came close to facing that prospect. The only loss of territory that it suffered was temporary, a strip along the Danube that was ceded to Attila, and even he seems to have left it as an empty neutral zone. Otherwise, all indications are that the economy and demography of the eastern empire expanded during the fifth century, as did monetization. There were only two moments of fiscal crisis, first when a huge payment had to be made to Attila in 447 and then when years' worth of surplus was lost in the invasion of North Africa in 468. But the surpluses indicate robust revenues. Marcian was able to leave 7 million solidi only ten years after the worst of Attila's extortion, and Anastasius left 23 million, even after he abolished the urban tax in 498.[89] For the eastern empire the fifth century was largely peaceful and prosperous.

The fall of the western empire was caused by two main factors that could, potentially, have toppled the east too but for a combination of luck and policy. In the west, barbarian armies took over many rich provinces, sometimes with the notional consent of the Roman government (e.g., the Visigoths in Gaul) but usually without it (e.g., the Visigoths in Spain, the Vandals in North Africa, the Suebi in Spain, and the Franks in Gaul). Eventually, these formed separate kingdoms that did not answer to Rome. Second, the western imperial armies were increasingly recruited among barbarians who were led by barbarian generals, which eventually ceased to be under Roman political control. The highest office in the Roman state was treated cynically by Ricimer and then abolished by Odoacer, who did not want the nuisance of appointing troublesome puppets, and so Italy too became a post-Roman, barbarian-led state. The concise description of this process by the east Roman historian Prokopios is spot-on:

> In proportion as the barbarian element among them [the western Romans] became strong, just so did the prestige of the Roman soldiers decline, and under the fair name of "alliance" they were increasingly compelled by force to be tyrannized by the intruders, so that the latter ruthlessly forced many other measures upon the Romans against their will and finally demanded that they distribute among them all the lands in Italy.[90]

Regional states emerged in the western provinces where barbarian armies ruled a majority Roman subject population. They retained trace aspects of Roman law and administration for their convenience, but within a few generations the collapse of the unified matrix of Roman law, conscription, and taxation led to a contraction of economies, cities, centralized government, and interregional trading networks.[91]

This did not happen in the east. Only the Balkan provinces had to endure the prolonged residence of barbarian armies, namely of the Goths after Adrianople (376–408), and then of the Ostrogoths under the two Theoderics in 473–488. These caused damage locally but did not destabilize the imperial order, for three reasons. The first was geographic: the straits of the Bosporos and Hellespont, which were heavily guarded, prevented barbarian armies from reaching the more prosperous eastern provinces. When Theoderic the Amal tried to ferry his army across the Bosporos in 487, he was defeated in a naval battle.[92] The City, which was the key to the straits, was awesomely fortified and could be attacked from only one narrow direction, unless the attacker also brought a fleet. This arrangement was deliberate. The land walls of Constantinople were built as Alaric was marching around the Balkans and sacking Rome. Likewise, the sea walls were built as the Vandals were conquering North Africa and about to obtain a fleet. The Romans also built the Long Wall of Thrace about 65 kilometers west of Constantinople, stretching 45 kilometers from the Sea of Marmara to the Black Sea, with towers at about every 150 meters. The wall was rebuilt by Anastasius, but an original construction in the 440s has been proposed. When Theoderic the Amal sent an advance guard against Constantinople in 478, it was stopped by soldiers stationed on the Long Wall.[93] Thus, the Goths' ravages and extortion were limited to the Balkans, where they were essentially penned in. They could not subvert the government or prevent it from collecting taxes or mustering its own armies. Therefore, they had to deal with it from a position of weakness, trying to harass it into making concessions of cash and land. After years of this miserable exercise, all of them chose to emigrate to Italy.

The second reason was fortuitous. East Roman relations with Persia were peaceful between the fourth and sixth centuries, which meant that the eastern empire, compared to the western one, had a much smaller border through which dangerous enemies could enter, basically Pannonia and the lower Danube. It also meant that Constantinople could draw on the ample resources of the east to deal with its Balkan problems, while not having to spend money on wars in the east. This dynamic would change dramatically under Justinian, for the worse.

The third factor was political. In the west, control over the armed forces was concentrated into the hands of a single general (such as Stilicho, Aetius, and Ricimer), who at the end was a barbarian commanding mostly barbarian forces. This eventually led to the liquidation by Odoacer of Roman political authority in the west. In the east, the senatorial political classes of Constantinople managed to retain control of the government, and barbarian generals who tried to take it over, such as Gaïnas and Aspar, were destroyed. Command of the army, which during the course of the fifth century was recruited mostly among Romans, was divided among a number of military commands, so no one generalissimo could take over. A mid-level palace staffer such as Anastasius could take effective command of the machinery of government by virtue of his imperial office and actually rule from the palace, not just reign.

Ethnicity was a major factor. In recent decades, some historians have denied that ethnic difference played a role and that these conflicts, for all that they are described in the sources as between Romans and barbarians, were really only political struggles among rival Roman factions. This thesis must deny that Goths had their own identities and must recast them as regular Roman soldiers. Yet those armies had entered the empire from outside, spoke a separate language, and fought Theodosius I to preserve a quasi-autonomous status as *foederati*, a concession that the emperors would not have made if they had any other choice. Moreover, since our (Roman) sources consistently interpret events in light of ethnic differences between Romans and others, this school has to dismiss the sources for engaging in a purely rhetorical invention of ethnic identity. This strained approach is untenable and unnecessary.[94] Romans were ready to accept barbarians who were resettled on Roman terms. The empire possessed remarkably effective mechanisms for incorporating foreign peoples in this way. But quasi-autonomous armies from across the border that rampaged for decades through the provinces demanding money, land, supplies, and offices were a different matter. The armies of Alaric and the two Theoderics were not treated by the authorities in Constantinople as regular Romans, even when they had to pretend that their barbarian leaders were *magistri militum*. For their part, the Goths had to stick together because the Romans were capable of massacring hostile foreigners who fell into their hands. This was done for example by officers (e.g., Julius in 378, with senatorial approval) and by the people of Constantinople in 400. Perceptions of ethnic difference mattered, and could even be fatal.

Suspicion also attached to Romanized generals of barbarian origin, such as Gaïnas and Aspar, whose standing in the state depended in part on their links to ethnic-barbarian armies. Their careers advanced splendidly so long as they stayed in their lane. Both men knew that they would not be accepted as emperors because they were not perceived as fully Roman and were Arians, a religious identity that deliberately accented their barbarian affiliations. When Gaïnas and Aspar moved to dominate the political scene more overtly, they were both killed. This was not normal in eastern Roman politics of the fifth century, which was remarkably free of bloodshed *except* for the massacres associated with ethnic others. The Isaurians too, for all that they had been subjects of the empire for half a millennium, were viewed negatively as a separate ethnic group. Their history of violent raiding across southern Asia Minor had a lot to do with that. When

Isaurians began to arrive in Constantinople in greater numbers in the 460s, they were specifically targeted by violent attacks and pogroms. Zeno was barely acceptable to the Roman people, and the Isaurian infighting that broke out during his reign left such a bad taste that his successor Anastasius ended the Isaurian problem once and for all and pacified the province, with lasting success. Large-scale Isaurian raids ceased after the 490s.

Constantinople's barbarian clients

The fall of the western empire meant that relations between the two sibling Roman states were replaced with foreign relations between Constantinople and the barbarian kingdoms of the west. This created a more multipolar diplomatic scene. Constantinople had to make treaties with the Vandals in North Africa in a way that it never had with Rome. When he sacked Rome in 455, Gaizeric abducted the daughters of Valentinian III and kept them as diplomatic bargaining chips. He cleverly married one of them, Eudokia, to his son and heir Huneric (477–484), and they had a son, Hilderic, who reigned in 523–530. Thus, members of the east Roman nobility, such as Anicia Juliana, were related to the Vandal ruling family. But since Roman dynasties did not last long, these ties became attenuated quickly when the throne in Constantinople changed hands.

Theoderic (d. 526), ruler of Ostrogothic Italy, used marriage alliances and military interventions to become a power broker among the post-Roman kingdoms of the west, and briefly their de facto hegemon. Theoderic occupied an ambiguous position. He had spent ten formative years of his childhood in Constantinople and had been appointed *magister militum* and even consul, though he was never fully integrated into east Roman political life and was always regarded as a menace. He was sent to govern Italy ostensibly in the emperor's name, yet this corresponded to no known position in the Roman administration; it was an ad hoc invention by Zeno to normalize Theoderic's removal from the Balkans. In Italy, he governed as much as possible according to Roman norms, presented himself to his subjects in an overtly imperial guise (even if only under the lesser title of *rex*), and was praised by his subjects and eastern Roman authors.[95] Yet he never hid the fact that he was an Arian Goth and the leader of a Gothic army that ruled over the Italian-Roman civilians. He was never accepted as emperor of the Romans in the east or, indeed, as a Roman.

There was a brief moment of military tension between the Romans and the Ostrogoths in Italy. In 504, the Goths conquered Sirmium and, the following year, their army there helped to defeat the *magister militum* for Illyricum, who was campaigning between the Danube and Greater Morava river against the Gepid freebooter Mundo. Probably in response, in 508 Anastasius sent a fleet to ravage the coast of Apulia.[96] To normalize relations, Theoderic sent a high-level embassy with a letter to Anastasius that eloquently acknowledged western subordination to the east:

> All other rulers rightfully look up to you with reverence . . . we above all, who by divine help learned in your republic [*res publica*] the art of governing Romans with equity. Our royal realm [*regnum*] is an imitation of yours, a copy of the only *imperium* . . . . Our two republics are declared to have ever formed one body under their ancient princes, and ought to aid one another with all their powers. Let there be always one purpose in the Roman kingdom.[97]

The post-Roman kingdoms in the west recognized the eastern empire as the font of Romanness and of imperial authority, as Anastasius used the instruments of soft power to remind their rulers. He sent to Theoderic the "insignia of the palace" that Odoacer had returned to Zeno when he deposed Romulus Augustulus in 476.[98] He also bestowed titles and honorary office on Sigismund, the king of the Burgundians, causing the latter to gush with gratitude and place himself among

> those whom you have made rich in the most distant parts of the world by granting membership in your court and participation in the venerable Roman name . . . that we are possessed from afar reaffirms the [broad] diffusion of your republic . . . . For my people are yours, we think of ourselves as nothing other than your soldiers . . . our country is your sphere; the light of the East touches Gaul.[99]

In 508, Anastasius bestowed honorary consular rank on king Clovis of the Franks, who had just defeated the Visigoths in Gaul and converted to Nicene Christianity. Clovis shrewdly advertised his association with the empire, probably beyond its intended scope, as quasi-imperial.[100] Constantinople would excel at these forms of soft power, including gifts and tokens of an imperial connection, such as codicils, insignia, and robes of office. The emperor's export control stamps were hammered onto the back of the silver platter known as the Anastasius Dish, found in the Sutton Hoo burial site in Suffolk, UK, bringing a token of imperial bureaucracy to the distant reaches of a society that had reverted back to a heroic state (see Figures 17a–b).[101]

The east Romans could not expect to control the barbarian realms in the west, but at least their kinglets recognized the higher standing of the one surviving Roman empire and were eager to bask in its light. The post-Roman world in the west was still a sub-Roman world. In dealing with them, Constantinople honed the Roman arts of client management, keeping neighboring kings and tribal chiefs bound to it through gifts of titles, honorary offices, and prestige insignia, all wrapped in silk and backed by cash, which the Roman economy continued to

Figure 17a Anastasius Dish (silver), Sutton Hoo burial (British Museum, UK). The dish is 72 cm in diameter and weighs 6.5 kg.

Figure 17b Sutton Hoo control stamps on the Anastasius Dish (detail)

produce in greater quantities than any other. This cultural reach was reinforced by the emperor's leadership in the broader Christian world. For example, the emperor intervened in the succession politics of the Georgian kingdom of the Lazi, and even summoned its king Gobazes to Constantinople. The Romans disliked his Persian attire but were pleased by his Christian insignia. When Gobazes visited Leo I in 465/6, the emperor took him to see Daniel the Stylite, a combination of pilgrimage and tourist visit.[102] Far to the south, a Saracen named Amorkesos (Imru' al-Qays) had seized the island or port of Iotabe (in the Red Sea, but we do not know where). Under Leo, in 474, he wanted to normalize his position, so he was invited to the capital where he was wined and dined, appointed a patrician, loaded with luxury gifts, converted to Christianity (at least nominally), and given the office of *phylarchos* ("tribal leader"), a projection of Roman authority beyond the border. "He went away exalted." In the late 490s, Anastasius brought Iotabe under direct imperial rule. It was settled by Roman merchants and so part of the Indian trade was taxed by the emperor's officials.[103]

Apart from war with Persia, which was rare in this period, the main source of insecurity along the eastern frontier was raids by "the countless tribes of the Saracens."[104] These Arabic-speaking nomads would strike across the desert along the arc from Arabia and Palestine to Syria and Mesopotamia. They could be freelancers, clients of the Persian king, or both. The Romans employed Saracens as mercenaries in their wars, but they were not reliable allies: "they were sometimes our friends and sometimes our enemies,"[105] though the empire's border defenses usually responded effectively to raids.[106] However, Saracens could also destabilize relations between Rome and Persia. As the truce between the two empires was being negotiated in 504, the Saracen allies of both sides conducted unauthorized raids for their own enrichment, and imperial officials had to step in and severely punish "their own" Saracens to stop the chaos from spreading.[107] What emperors needed were tribal leaders who could keep discipline among their own people and defend Romanía against hostile Saracens. Anastasius found his *phylarchos* in the person of Arethas (al-Harith), "after which the provinces knew peace." Arethas' tribal affiliation remains controversial, but this deal created a framework that contained the Saracens for a century.[108] It was onto this increasingly complex international stage that Justinian brought his ambitious agenda of Roman imperial hegemony and Christian uniformity.

PART FOUR

THE STRAIN OF GRAND AMBITIONS

11

Chalcedonian Repression and the Eastern Axis (518–531)

Anastasius died without appointing an heir, and there was no empress to bridge the transition. Possible candidates included his nephew Hypatius, but his record was marred by a pattern of failure and he was absent in the east, serving as its *magister militum* (Anastasius must have known that such a posting kept him away from the throne). Celer had served as *magister officiorum* for fifteen years (503–518) and was widely respected, but was suffering from gout. Patricius had served as *magister militum praesentalis*, possibly for two decades, and was a viable candidate. But in the absence of an heir, the throne tended to go to men of middle rank, such as Marcian, Leo, and Anastasius. When the people assembled in the hippodrome on 9 July, 518, demanding that the Senate choose an emperor, the top court officials deliberated but could not agree. The excubitors acclaimed a tribune named Ioannes, but he was pelted with stones by the Blues. The *scholarii* acclaimed Patricius, but he was attacked by the excubitors and almost killed. Finally, a consensus emerged around the *comes* of the excubitors, Justin, another old, childless man, but with a decent military record. The Senate and people approved this choice, but not before one of the *scholarii* punched Justin in the face, spliting his lip. All the usual ritual acclamations followed, although the process had revealed "a certain lack of order: it was almost improvised."[1]

The enforcement of Chalcedon

It was rumored that the chief palace chamberlain, Amantius, had given a large sum to Justin to bribe the army and people to support the election to the throne of Theocritus, Amantius' staff officer, but that Justin had used the money to canvass for his own election.[2] Justin and Amantius held opposing theological politics. The former was "a fiery partisan" of Chalcedon,[3] whereas the latter was believed to oppose Chalcedon. But after the turmoil of the previous reign, the people of Constantinople wanted no truck with anti-Chalcedonians. Soon before Anastasius' death, the populace had called on the recently-installed patriarch Ioannes, whose views were ambiguous, to denounce Severos of Antioch.[4] On 15–16 July, a few days after Justin's elevation and emboldened by it, the people demonstrated in Hagia Sophia in favor of Justin and against Chalcedon's enemies: "Long live the emperor! Long live New Constantine! Down with Severos! Proclaim Chalcedon! Toss Amantius out! Bring back the relics of Makedonios! Dig up the bones of Nestorios and Eutyches!," and the like. With the doors locked and guarded by the threatening crowd, the patriarch recognized Chalcedon and promised a Synod. The leading monks of the City also sent him a joint resolution advocating the same course.[5] There were at this time almost seventy monasteries in the City and dozens more in its environs.[6]

A few days later, the authorities swiftly delivered what the people and monasteries were demanding. Justin executed Amantius and Theocritus in the palace on a charge of conspiracy. They were later venerated as Monophysite martyrs by the other side. Then, on 20 July, the Synod addressed its findings to the patriarch Ioannes, whose office was here for the first time styled as "Ecumenical Patriarch." Specifically, the former patriarchs Euphemios and Makedonios were to be restored to commemoration; Chalcedon was recognized; pope Leo was to be honored along with Cyril; and Severos was deposed.[7] Never before had political factions and doctrinal affiliations been more tightly entwined and aligned. The people had dictated terms to the palace and the Church, and provided the cover that Justin needed to eliminate his rivals.

In a purge of the previous regime, Justin replaced all of Anastasius' highest officials and generals, though some of them, such as Hypatius, returned to office later, when the new regime was secure. Justin also recalled many officials who had fallen out of favor, such as the Egyptian Apion. He even rehabilitated Vitalianus, who had been declared an enemy of the Roman people and defeated in battle, appointing him a praesental general, patrician, and honorary consul (and, in 520, an actual consul). The basis for this reconciliation was presumably his support for Chalcedon. Justin immediately set out to reverse Anastasius' ecclesiastical policy through a two-pronged approach: mending relations with Rome and deposing bishops who did not accept Chalcedon. The imperial activism of this policy would permanently shatter the unity of the Church.

Justin set in motion the largest-scale persecution of dissident bishops in the empire's history, though it was not an all-out war. It advanced in waves across the empire, but halted when it met passionate opposition and never really reached Egypt. Still, it earned him the names "the Terrible" and "the Schismatic" among his victims.[8] Specifically, the *comes* of Antioch Eirenaeus was ordered to arrest Severos, but he escaped to Egypt, in September 518; it was said that Vitalianus wanted to cut his tongue out.[9] Meanwhile, the patriarch Ioannes immediately sent the acts of the recent Synod to a number of Churches—Jerusalem, Tyre, and Syria II are attested—saying that "he thought it necessary that you know them so that you might be of the same mind as us," which fell short of an order. But local synods there did ratify the acts, and the bishops of Syria II even deposed their metropolitan, Petros of Apameia, the only Monophysite among them.[10]

The rapprochement between Rome and Constantinople escalated the persecution. To persuade pope Hormisdas that he was serious about accepting papal terms, Justin mobilized letters from the papal paladin Vitalianus, the patriarch, and other members of the aristocracy, including the emperor's nephew Justinian, a praesental general in his mid-thirties. Their correspondence forms a thick dossier of pleasantries extolling the imminent peace of the Church and the zeal for Catholic truth by all parties involved. But Hormisdas' terms had not changed since the time of Anastasius: for the east to return to communion with Rome, all its bishops must submit to him; accept Chalcedon and pope Leo as standards of orthodoxy; condemn Akakios, Timotheos the Cat, the two Petroses (the Fuller and Mongos), and all who followed them; sign a written statement to this effect (Hormisdas' *libellus*), and forward it to the pope. Rome had previously condemned Zeno and Akakios for imposing the *Henotikon* by fiat, but this was what it now wanted Justin to do with the *libellus*, without discussion or approval by a Church Council.[11]

On 25 March, 519, the papal legates were greeted as heroes ten miles outside Constantinople by Vitalianus, Justinian, and the Senate, and were escorted to the City and its cheering crowds. In the next few days, they met with the emperor and the patriarch, who was required to sign the *libellus*.[12] The terms accepted by the court to end the Acacian Schism entailed a drastic revision of recent history. Basically, all parishes around the eastern empire had to remove from liturgical commemoration any of their bishops who had been in communion with or recognized Akakios and the others, which meant in effect all bishops since 482, including the patriarchs of Constantinople Euphemios and Makedonios, whose restoration the Chalcedonian crowds of Constantinople had demanded only months earlier. The technical term for such commemorations were the "diptychs," wooden tablets containing the names of saints, bishops, and emperors who defined the history and confession of each Christian community.[13] All these now had to be replaced with a papal view of history. Congregations had to admit that their recent bishops, whom they loved and who had baptized them and their children, were heretics. It did not matter whether they had accepted Chalcedon, but only whether they had submitted to Rome. Even Zeno and Anastasius were removed from the diptychs of Constantinople. The only concession made by the pope was that some names could be removed quietly, without a public humiliation.[14] Secular officials, as always, remained prudent: "We are laity," they said at the meeting between the legates and the emperor, "You tell us that these things are true. Make it so, and we will follow."[15] But it would not go over so easily elsewhere.

During the next two years, every bishop outside of Egypt was required to sign the *libellus* publicly and send a copy to the pope, or else he had to resign or leave his see.[16] The legalistic clarity of the *libellus* made it impossible for the two sides to dissimulate their differences and pretend that they were part of the same Church, and the ensuing wave of expulsions, popular resistance in the street, and the persecution of Monophysite monks fueled more narratives of martyrdom. One Paulos, a priest of the Church of Constantinople, was appointed by the emperor to replace Severos at Antioch, but his methods were so cruel that Justin removed him before May 521, informing the pope that "he had accepted Paulos' resignation" (a euphemism still in use today).[17] Paulos, who was called "the Jew" by the people of Antioch, nevertheless managed to remove many Monophysite bishops, including Philoxenos of Hierapolis, who was exiled to Paphlagonia and then Thrace. Paulos also sent the general Patricius to impose the *libellus* on Edessa, which led to a bloody confrontation with the populace. Justin allowed the Monophysite bishop of Edessa to stay on for a while, but he was replaced in 522 by Paulos' successor at Antioch, Euphrasios, for not signing the *libellus*. Euphrasios was also detested as a persecutor by the Monophysites, who rejoiced when he died in the earthquake that struck Antioch in 526. He was crushed to death by a falling column or obelisk, but the Monophysite version was that, when the episcopal residence collapsed, he fell into a vat of boiling pitch kept by tanners on the ground floor and cooked alive, the flesh melting off his body. But his head was hanging outside, so he was recognized.[18]

Over fifty Monophysite bishops were expelled and it was said that 2,500 bishops and priests signed the *libellum*.[19] This resulted in nominal compliance and conformity, except for Egypt, where the threat of popular violence was too great. But oppression exacted a huge cost. Monophysites began to celebrate the victims of this persecution from the regions of Edessa and Amida and compare them to the martyrs of old. Monks were driven out of their monasteries and forced to camp outside on the rocks in the winter; stylites were forced down from their columns; and a priest was burned alive. One persecutor, the bishop of Amida, introduced lepers into the homes of Monophysite laymen and had them roll around in their sheets and drop pus in their wine jars.[20] In the past, Christians had left their cities to live as monks in the desert; now the deserts were filling up with monks expelled from the cities.

Moreover, the erasure of so many bishops from the diptychs was deemed outrageous by both Chalcedonians and anti-Chalcedonians: "we were being asked to anathematize more or less the entire world."[21] By mid-520, Justin and Justinian were politely but vainly petitioning the pope to show "indulgence" in his inflexible demand for the removal of recent bishops from the diptychs. In some eastern cities, the priests and laity "would prefer death over a life in which they have condemned the dead, no matter the threats and punishments that hang over them."[22] But the pope would not budge: "How can it be more just for an emperor to follow the will of his subjects and thereby go against salvation, than for them to obey him for the sake of salvation?"[23] Hormisdas, who had never lived in a functional Roman state, could not grasp the delicate balance of imperial authority and popular will in Romanía.

When Hormisdas tried to place some of his own clients in key episcopal positions in the east, including Alexandria, the emperor politely refused him.[24] Then, in 520, Vitalianus was massacred in the palace courtyard along with two attendants, allegedly at the instigation of Justinian.[25] A Romanized Goth who had attained the highest court positions, Vitalianus suffered the same fate as Aspar, only he had no army at his back. His revolt had tied him to Chalcedon, and Justin had brought him onside to help smooth relations with Rome. But Vitalianus was sucking up all the Chalcedonian air in the room. It was his name that had been chanted in the Chalcedonian churches,[26] and he was an obstacle in the path of the emperor's ruthless nephew.

The rise of Justinian

Justinian was born around 482 as Petrus, the son of Sabbates, but we know nothing about his education and career until he appears as an officer (*candidatus*) of the *scholarii* in 518. The *scholae* were Constantine the Great's old elite guards, but were now ceremonial units, unfit for combat,[27] so Justinian did not necessarily have a military background. The historian Prokopios, a contemporaneous but hostile witness, claims that Justin was an illiterate, senile, and doddering old man and Justinian was the real power behind the throne.[28] Like much else in Prokopios' scurrilous *Secret History*, this is a caricature. Nevertheless, Justinian, whose name reveals that he had been adopted by his uncle,[29] was Justin's closest collaborator in the negotiations with Rome, and his promotions set him on a track to the throne, outpacing his cousin Germanus, who was made *magister militum* for Thrace. Justinian's elevation from a mere *candidatus* to the highest military office in the empire, *magister militum praesentalis*, in 520, was a mark of unusual favor for a hitherto undistinguished middle-aged man, as was the consulship in 521. His consular games were spectacular, at a cost of 288,000 solidi to the treasury, part of which was thrown to the people and part used to pay for races, twenty lions, and thirty panthers.[30] Vitalianus' assassination was effectively a promotion for Justinian.

Justinian was now a patrician, among no more than a dozen at the court, and living in the palace of Hormisdas, just to the west of the imperial palace. It had been built and named after the son of a Persian prince who fled to the empire in the early fourth century. But two scandals marred Justinian's reputation. One was his fanatical patronage of the Blues. When urban violence spiked in the early 520s, Justin ordered the City prefect, Theodotus "the Pumpkin," to find and punish those responsible, which he did, executing a senator and implicating Justinian. This outraged the court, and Theodotus fled to Jerusalem in fear for his life; he resided in a church seeking asylum.[31] The second scandal was Justinian's mistress, Theodora, a former actress and sex worker. Prokopios later wrote an overblown account of her earlier sexual exploits, casting her, a victim of child abuse and sex trafficking, as a predator who violated Roman social mores. Yet her background is not in doubt, for a Monophysite hagiographer who knew her and viewed her favorably blandly admits that she was "from the brothel."[32]

Justinian wanted to marry Theodora, a desire that reflected two character traits that would define his administration. The first was a remarkable willingness to see beyond conventional markers of status in order to assemble a talented team of strong-minded people. The second trait was a dangerous willingness to push through obstacles to get his way. Regarding Theodora he faced two obstacles, his aunt the empress Euphemia, who opposed the match on moral grounds, and the law, which had forbidden marriages between senators and actresses since the time of Augustus. But Euphemia died in 524, and Justinian immediately pressured Justin to issue a law authorizing the marriage. According to the new law, so long as they "moderate their evil and disgraceful ways," women of the theater could petition the emperor to marry a man of higher rank.[33] Later, as emperor, Justinian would manipulate laws with a similar combination of idealism and cynicism, of principle and advantage.

It was by now obvious that Justinian would succeed Justin, and in 525 he was made Caesar. Our sole notice regarding that promotion says that Justin, who was unwilling, yielded to pressure by the Senate.[34] An adult Caesar had not been created since the reign of Constantius II. Many emperors of the fifth century had died without nominating an heir, leaving the succession open. It seems that the Senate wanted to ensure a smooth succession and avoid scenes like those that occurred in 518. But the designation of an heir locked out potential competitors, including the three nephews of Anastasius and the family of Anicia Juliana, whose imperial pedigree was the most illustrious in the whole of Roman history and whose son Olybrius was a patrician and former child-consul (in 491). Anicia made her imperial pretensions clear when she rebuilt St. Polyeuktos to be the largest and most splendidly adorned church in the City (its remains were discovered in the 1960s). This was a project she began under Anastasius and finished in the mid-520s. The dedicatory epigram in her honor, which was carved onto the building itself, repeatedly refers to her imperial pedigree and her "imperial blood, inherited in the fourth generation" (see Figure 18). It claims that she surpassed Solomon in wisdom and describes the church in cosmic terms, as it reached from the ground to the heavens and from east to west, encompassing the sun, moon, and meadows.[35]

Justinian, a man of peasant background, was not intimidated by the bluebloods. He too used all the arts of elite entrenchment, such as the lavish games of his consulship and the precious ivory diptychs that he gave to aristocratic supporters, to mark his tenure of that office. He even asked the pope to send him relics of Sts. Peter, Paul, and Lawrence for a church that he was building in the

Figure 18 Sculpted arch from Anicia's church of St. Polyeuktos, with inscribed fragment of the dedicatory poem (Istanbul Archaeological Museum)
Photo by David Hendrix

palace of Hormisdas.[36] During the 520s, he and Theodora commissioned and built the church of Sts. Sergios and Bakchos (now the Kücük Ayasofya Camii). It was designed as a dome on top of an octagon on top of a square (see Figures 19–20). This church was a riposte to that of Anicia Juliana, and its dedicatory epigram dismissed the "other emperors" (i.e., Juliana's ancestors) who "honored useless dead men" (i.e., Polyeuktos), whereas Justinian was honoring the glorious martyr Sergios.[37]

In early 526, Constantinople was visited for the first time by a pope, John I. This had nothing to do with Christology. John came on behalf of Theoderic, the Arian king of Italy, to negotiate over the rights of Arians in the empire. The pope was received with honor, and the Latin liturgy was celebrated in Hagia Sophia, with the pope presiding.[38] In the following year, when Justin and Justinian issued a severe law against heretics and pagans, barring them from holding any position in the state, they exempted the empire's Gothic *foederati*, of whom by then there were only a few.[39]

Justin responded quickly and generously when cities experienced natural catastrophes. He sent cash for reconstruction at Dyrrachion, Corinth, and Anazarbos in Cilicia after earthquakes. But two events were horrific enough that they received extended attention by writers of the period. The river that passed through Edessa overflowed one night in 525 and flooded the city. Houses not made of stone were swept away, with great loss of life, and those visiting the baths or living in basements were drowned. The city walls briefly contained the flood,

Figure 19 Church of Sts. Sergios and Bakchos, exterior
Photo by David Hendrix

Figure 20 Church of Sts. Sergios and Bakchos, interior. The decor is all post-Byzantine, apart from the sculpted elements.
Shutterstock/Mikhail Markovskiy

turning the city into a lake, whereupon the walls broke and the countryside was also flooded. Justin promptly began the restoration, officially renaming the city Ioustinopolis. According to Prokopios, a third of its population had died.[40]

The greatest calamity occurred at Antioch, a city that was experiencing fires of a mysterious origin that broke out over a period of sixth months in 525. Then, on 29 May, 526, an earthquake leveled the city, setting off fires that consumed the ruins and those trapped in them. We have an eyewitness account of hellish scenes of destruction, though the figure of 250,000 dead is exaggerated. Survivors were still being brought up from rubble many days afterward, including pregnant women and women who had given birth underground. Justin canceled the games in the City in grief and appeared in church without his crown. He appointed two patricians to supervise the reconstruction and distribution of relief funds, which exceeded 3,500 lbs of gold; one of these patricians was the pagan Phokas, who would later oversee the rebuilding of Hagia Sophia under Justinian.[41] Antioch was struck by another earthquake in 528, undoing the reconstruction that had taken place since 526. This time the victims are reported more credibly at 4,870. The emperor (now Justinian) renamed Antioch as Theoupolis, City of God, to avert divine wrath in the future. But more death was around the corner.[42]

In the spring of 527, Justin's health was failing and the Senate pressured him again to promote Justinian to the rank of Augustus, to prevent any ambiguity about the succession. Justinian was elevated in a sequence of ceremonies, starting with a private coronation by Justin in the palace on 1 April, which Justinian took thereafter as the official date of his accession. There followed, on 4 April, a public coronation by the patriarch in the Delphax, the very place where Vitalianus had been murdered, and an acclamation by the people in the hippodrome. Theodora was proclaimed Augusta at the same time. Justin died on 1 August. A court chronicler portentously noted this as the 197th year of the "royal City," as if a new era had begun.[43]

The axis of war in the east

It was not only in Church policy that Justin and Justinian set the empire on a new and dangerous course. They also militarized the eastern frontier and built up an axis of alliances that prepared the ground for war on an immense new scale, from the Caucasus to Arabia. Roman-Persian relations entered a bellicose phase in the 520s that would eventually escalate to a crescendo of mutual destruction. The fate of Romanía would be decided in the east, and the constellation of forces from which its doom unfolded emerged in the early sixth century. The first step along this trajectory of mutual annihilation was taken by the shah Kavad, who invaded in 502 for opportunistic reasons. Then, as a new international order emerged along the axis from the Black Sea to the Red Sea, both empires were drawn into ever-widening alliances that increased the risk of war. Provocations on both sides created grievances and mutual recriminations that built up over time.

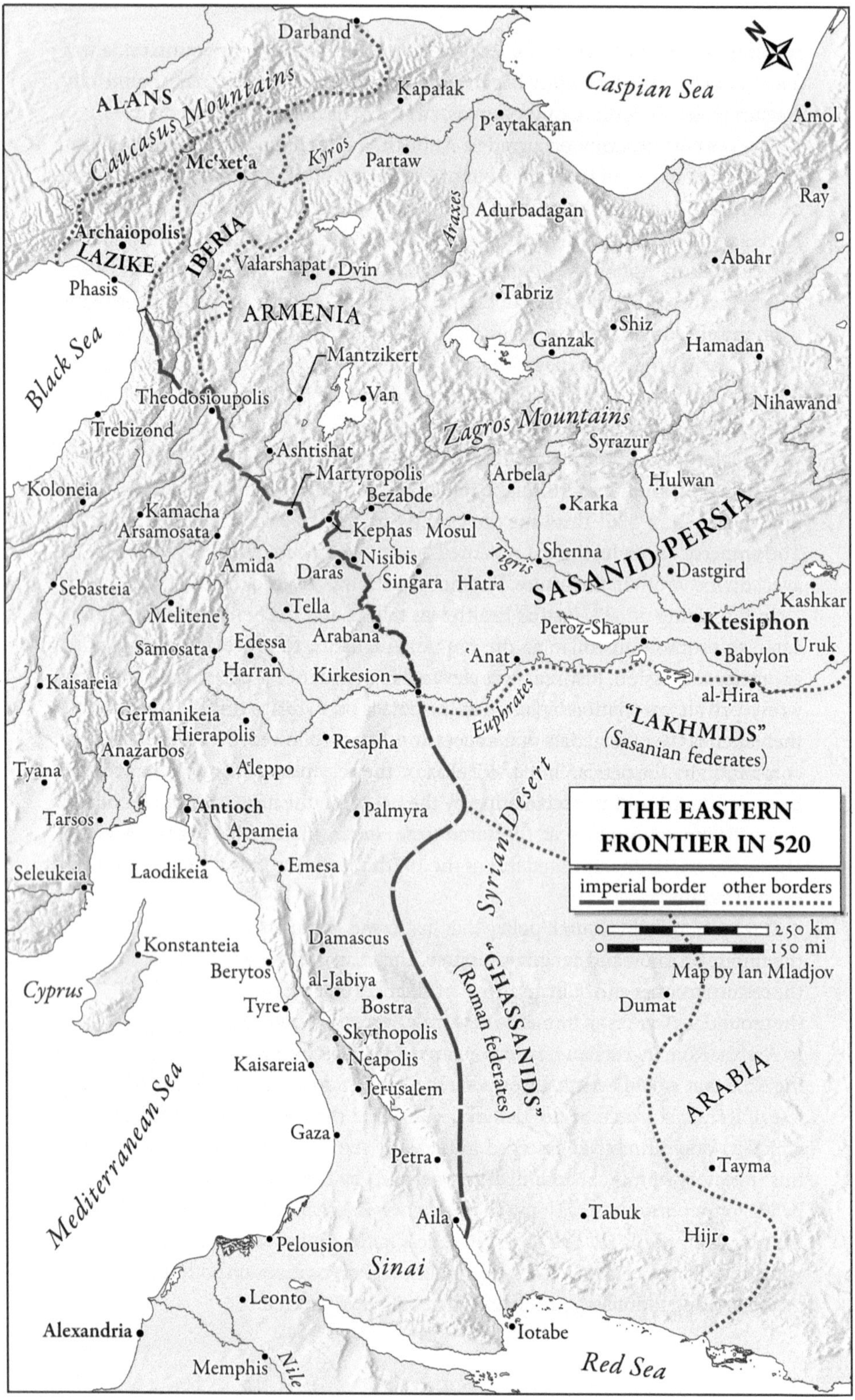

THE EASTERN FRONTIER IN 520

imperial border
other borders
0 250 km
0 150 mi
Map by Ian Mladjov

N
Caspian Sea
Black Sea
Mediterranean Sea
Red Sea
ALANS
Caucasus Mountains
Darband
Kapałak
P'aytakaran
Amol
Ray
Kyros
Partaw
Mc'xet'a
Araxes
Adurbadagan
Archaiopolis
LAZIKE
IBERIA
Vałarshapat
Dvin
Abahr
Phasis
ARMENIA
Tabriz
Shiz
Ganzak
Hamadan
Mantzikert
Van
Theodosioupolis
Trebizond
Nihawand
Zagros Mountains
Syrazur
Ashtishat
Martyropolis
Arbela
Hulwan
Koloneia
Bezabde
Karka
Kamacha
Kephas
Mosul
SASANID PERSIA
Arsamosata
Tigris
Shenna
Amida
Nisibis
Daras
Singara
Hatra
Dastgird
Sebasteia
Kashkar
Tella
Melitene
Arabana
Peroz-Shapur
Ktesiphon
Samosata
Edessa
'Anat
Babylon
Uruk
Harran
Kirkesion
Kaisareia
al-Hira
Euphrates
Germanikeia
"LAKHMIDS"
(Sasanian federates)
Hierapolis
Resapha
Anazarbos
Tyana
Aleppo
Syrian Desert
Antioch
Palmyra
Tarsos
Apameia
Seleukeia
Laodikeia
Emesa
Damascus
Konstanteia
Berytos
"GHASSANIDS"
(Roman federates)
Cyprus
al-Jabiya
Dumat
Tyre
Bostra
Skythopolis
Kaisareia
Neapolis
ARABIA
Jerusalem
Gaza
Petra
Tayma
Tabuk
Aila
Hijr
Pelousion
Sinai
Leonto
Alexandria
Iotabe
Memphis
Nile

The eastern end of the Black Sea was dominated by the Georgian kingdom of Lazica (Lazike in Greek), a client of Persia. In 522, the Laz king Tzath traveled to Constantinople where he was baptized in the Christian faith and married to a noble Roman wife. He was crowned by Justin and given Roman imperial attire, featuring images of the emperor, to replace the Persian garb of his ancestors. The Persian shah Kavad protested that this was a hostile provocation. Justin replied that it was only a religious conversion, to which king Tzath had a right.[44] But the answer was disingenuous, as religious affiliation was not separate from imperial allegiance. The one did not determine the other—the Laz would in fact change sides often during the ensuing wars—but it did shape imperial peripheries and cultural orbits. A few decades later, a Roman historian could claim that "the Laz are not barbarians, for long association with the Romans has made them more civilized and law-abiding."[45] The Laz kingdom had subject peoples with their own leaders. These were appointed or confirmed by the king, who in turn informed the emperor. Constantinople apparently kept detailed lists of the sub-rulers of the Laz realm.[46]

A second source of tension was the kingdom of Iberia, adjacent to the Laz in the Caucasus. This Christian realm was also a Persian client. Perhaps stung by the defection of Lazica, in 525/6 Kavad sought to impose Zoroastrian practices on its king Gourgenes. The king appealed to the empire for help, and he fled to Lazica and then Constantinople when Kavad and Justin sent armies to the region. The Persians overran Iberia while the Romans garrisoned Lazica, removing the native soldiers from two key forts and generally alienating the locals. A Roman army was also sent in 526 or 527 to raid Persian Armenia, under the command of Sittas and Belisarios, officers from Justinian's staff, which indicates that military affairs were in Justinian's hands even before Justin's death. The first raid was successful but the second was defeated. In 528, Belisarios and others were sent to join the fighting in Lazica-Iberia, but they were defeated. The situation was redeemed for Rome when Justinian sent his uncle's former notary Petrus to do the job. The defection of two Persian client kings and the promotion of Christianity in foreign policy by Justin and then Justinian had pushed the empires to the brink of war.[47]

Armenia was still partitioned according to the treaty of 387. The smaller Roman portion had been governed by a *comes Armeniae*, who could be a local. In their portion, called "Persarmenia" by the Romans, the Persians had abolished the Armenian kingship in 428, annexing the region as a province. But in 528, Justinian reorganized Roman Armenia and put it on an aggressive military footing, which provoked Persia. Specifically, he abolished the *comes*, the Armenian "satraps," and their unreliable levies; "satrap" is not a proper Roman office, Justinian sniffed. In their place, he created a new field marshal, the *magister militum* for Armenia, whose soldiers, and those of the *duces* under him, were detached from the existing Roman armies and brought in from the outside, which alienated the Armenians themselves. The first occupant of this post was Sittas, who married Theodora's sister Komito.[48] Then, in 535–536, Justinian divided Roman Armenia into four civil provinces with a regular administration and issued laws requiring "Armenians to conform to Roman laws in all ways," in particular with regard to inheritance: the emperor required that daughters receive a portion. This has been interpreted as a means by which to break up the estates of the Armenian aristocracy and diminish its power. This may well have been the case, though the emperor also valued legal homogenization in its own right ("Armenia should differ in no way from the rest of our realm") and was generally concerned with the status and treatment of women. Disinheriting them he called "a barbaric custom utterly insulting to the female sex."[49] This combination of idealism and calculation was a signature trait of Justinian's reforms.

The majority of Armenians were subject to the Persian empire. Their Church had accepted the Council of Ephesos I (431) and condemned Nestorios, and its theology was deeply influenced by an exposition of the faith sent by Proklos, bishop of Constantinople (434–446), an ally of Cyril of Alexandria.[50] The Armenian Church adopted the Cyrillian formula "One Nature of God the Word Enfleshed," and so at the council of Dvin (in 505–506) it rejected Chalcedon. As the Romans were themselves vacillating over Chalcedon, its rejection by the Armenian Church did not at the time cause a rupture with Constantinople, but when Justin abruptly endorsed Chalcedon in 518 the Armenians found themselves on the wrong side of imperial theology. Still, the rupture would not become clear until the seventh century. In Mesopotamia, by contrast, most Christians belonged to the Church of the East, based at Seleukeia-Ktesiphon. This was the largest Church in Asia and would grow to encompass millions of followers, although its history and even existence remain unknown to most western Christians. It was later called the Nestorian Church, for it accepted the Diphysite tradition of Theodoros of Mopsouestia and embraced the memory of Nestorios as a martyr. Thus, the two Churches of the Persian empire were in communion neither with each other nor with Constantinople, which was just how the shahs wanted it.[51]

The Persian empire was emerging from a period of subordination to the "Huns" and domestic instability. Its Mazdean religious establishment had been challenged by a variant and radical version of Zoroastrianism called Mazdakism, which was alternately endorsed and then suppressed by the shahs. Kavad (488–531) and especially his son and heir Khusrow I (531–579, Chosroes in Greek) tightened their grip on the resources and institutions of their realm. Khusrow instituted reforms that would tax the land in a more standardized and efficient way, centralize command of the army, and create court officers dependent on the shah.[52] The extent to which he succeeded is debatable. It certainly did not attain Roman levels of consolidation and homogenization. The most powerful offices and commands remained in the hands of a few families, a hereditary aristocracy that controlled regional lordships.[53] Still, by 540 these reforms had made the shah into a more formidable adversary.

The two empires' Saracen allies were also being reorganized at this time with an eye toward conflict. Prokopios tell us that in ca. 529 Justinian gave to one al-Harith (Arethas in Greek) the consolidated command of the many Saracen tribes who were allied to the empire, in order to counter raids mounted by the Saracens allied to Persia and led by the energetic al-Mundhir. Al-Harith is called *phylarchos* ("tribal ruler") in the sources, but Prokopios says that he was treated by Justinian as the equivalent of a fellow king. Inscriptions reveal that he and his family took on the Roman imperial name Flavius, which linked them to the court.[54] Modern historians refer to Rome's Saracens as the Ghassanids (a tribal name) led by the Jafnids (the dynastic name of al-Harith's family), and they refer to Persia's Saracens as the Lakhmids (a tribal name) led by the Nasrids (the dynastic name of al-Mundhir's family). But these names do not appear in this way in sources of the period, even in the inscriptions set up by the Roman Saracen leaders themselves. They are taken from later Muslim accounts of the Arab past and applied retroactively to the Roman period. Prokopios implies that al-Harith led a mixed group of warriors, not one tribe. We know little about where or how they lived along the spectrum from nomadic to sedentary; about their relations with provincial populations; or about how deep their reach was into peninsular Arabia.[55] A Saracen tribal leader who defected to the empire in the fifth century set up an "encampment" inside Roman territory that his descendants later moved to a different location.[56] This implies a level of nomadic mobility.

Saracens were deployed to suppress domestic disturbances too. In 529, a massive Samaritan rebellion broke out in Palestine in response to Justinian's repressive legislation. Some Samaritans converted, or pretended to, in order to avoid the legal penalties, "deeming it foolish to suffer on behalf of a stupid doctrine,"[57] but most took up arms. As they had done under Zeno, the rebels created their own counter emperor, one Ioulianos, who held games at Neapolis (Nablus). The local *dux* defeated them in battle with the assistance of the local Saracen phylarch. 20,000 Samaritans were said to have died in battle, and another 20,000 of their children were sold by the Saracens into slavery. This war devastated the agriculture of Palestine. A local abbot, Sabas, traveled to the court and petitioned the emperor for tax relief and money for reconstruction. Mopping-up operations in the hills continued for some time and "the land became destitute of farmers." Many of the survivors "converted out of fear," but under lax officials they dissimulated.[58]

The Saracens allied to Sasanian Persia were based in the Mesopotamian site of al-Hira, near Kufa. The name means "encampment," and its population could pick up and retreat into the desert on short notice.[59] The "house of al-Mundhir" at al-Hira was closely affiliated with the shahs, far more so than the "house of al-Harith" was to the Roman emperors.[60] In 523–524, Justin sent an envoy named Abramios to al-Hira to ransom some captive Roman officers. From al-Hira he had to travel ten days into the desert to find al-Mundhir at a place called Ramla. His party there met pagan Arab tribesmen of the Ma'ad (from central Arabia), who mocked Christianity, and a messenger from Dhu Nuwas, the king of Himyar (aka Yusuf, i.e., Joseph), who announced to al-Mundhir his recent persecution of Christians (in 523 AD). Yusuf was likely seeking an anti-Christian alliance.[61] This remarkable meeting revealed a complex set of religious and regional politics. The states around the Red Sea were becoming increasingly powerful, creating a more multipolar environment for Roman-Persian imperial competition and planting the seeds for major upheavals.

Himyar was an Arabian kingdom in what is modern Yemen (i.e., ancient Arabia Felix). By the fifth century, it had conquered much of peninsular Arabia, including Ma'ad, the large tribal federation at its center. Its ruling class had also converted to a variant of Judaism, or to what scholars call a generic monotheism inspired by Judaism. Many of their subjects were Christians and, for all that later Muslim tradition remembered pre-Islamic Arabia as mostly pagan, there is little or no epigraphic evidence for paganism in the fifth and sixth centuries, though the Ma'ad at the Ramla conference were pagan.[62]

Around 500, Himyar fell under the power of the (Monophysite?) Christian kingdom of Aksum, located across the Red Sea in Ethiopia. The kings of Himyar appear to have become subordinate to and appointed by Aksum, but one of them, Dhu Nuwas / Yusuf, cast off his submission in 522. He killed the Aksumite soldiers in Arabia, proclaimed Judaism as the religion of Himyar, and massacred many of its Christians, especially in the city of Najran. Perhaps in an effort to build an anti-Christian alliance, he advertised this massacre in grisly detail to the conference at Ramla in 524. But Christians also composed horrific accounts of "the martyrs of Najran" and disseminated them in an effort to lobby for an intervention by Aksum and Rome. Possibly with naval support by Justin, the king (*negus*) of Aksum, Ella Asbeha / Kaleb, crossed the Red Sea in 525 and defeated and killed Yusuf. Many Jews were massacred by the Ethiopians in retaliation for Yusuf's persecution of Christians. For fifty years, the kings of Himyar would be tributaries of Aksum, but the greatest among them, Abraha (ca. 535–565), was practically independent.[63]

Thus, the entire axis from the Black to the Red Sea was criss-crossed by a complex network of imperial and religious relationships, many of which could be mobilized in a war. The Laz had nothing to do with the Himyarites, but tension at one end of the axis could pass to the other. This is precisely what happened in 526–531.

Specifically, the defection of the Laz and Iberians from Persia to Rome sparked a small-scale war between the two empires along the border of Lazica and Iberia in ca. 525, which triggered Roman raids into Persarmenia and attacks on Nisibis in 526–527. These were answered by Saracen raids led by al-Mundhir against Emesa, Apameia, and Antioch in 528–529. Al-Mundhir was in the habit of sacrificing his captives to the goddess 'Uzzai (Aphrodite), including, it was said, 400 captured virgins. The wave of war had thus reached Syria. Around this time, Justinian militarized Roman Armenia, consolidated his own Saracens under the phylarch-king al-Harith, and attempted to fortify more places along the frontier.[64] Negotiations failed when Kavad—writing as "the rising sun" to Justinian as "the waning moon"—kept insisting on subsidies from Rome: "since you are pious Christians, spare lives and give gold."[65] Not getting what he wanted, Kavad sent his own armies this time, in 530, to invade the empire. 50,000 Persians were met at Daras by 25,000 Romans under the command of Belisarios, *magister militum* for Oriens, and Hermogenes, *magister officiorum*. The battle is described in detail by Prokopios, Belisarios' secretary. Belisarios' military career had not thus far been marked by success, but his tactics at Daras won the Romans a brilliant victory.[66]

The fighting continued in the Caucasus and Mesopotamia, and negotiations failed after the battle of Daras because Kavad insisted on being paid by Rome for defending the Caspian Gates. Moreover, the shah had been contacted by Samaritan refugees from the uprising of 529, who promised to help him raid or even conquer their homeland, Palestine, and thus that province was swept up into the broader geopolitical maelstrom.[67] Kavad sent an army of 15,000 in 531, accompanied by al-Mundhir with 5,000 of his Saracens, who tried to surprise the Romans by invading along the Euphrates. Belisarios, taking 3,000 Romans and 5,000 Saracens under al-Harith, intercepted them at Chalkis, and the Persians began to withdraw as Belisarios received more reinforcements. At Kallinikos, Belisarios was pressured by his army to give battle against his better judgment, resulting in a defeat, albeit the Persians suffered large casualties too.[68] Negotiations restarted and Belisarios was recalled in quasi-disgrace for an inquiry into the defeat.[69] The Saracens had become indispensable contingents in both imperial armies.

The wave of imperial entanglements reached the Red Sea when Justinian sent envoys to the Aksumites and Himyarites, appealing to their religion. He asked the Aksumites to buy silk in bulk from India, so that the Romans would not have to buy it from Persian middlemen and thereby enrich them, and he asked the Himyarites to send an army of Ma'ad tribesmen against Persia. These plans came to nothing, but they show how, by this point, the entire eastern frontier could be activated from north to south in a way that had once been impossible and likely unthinkable.[70] Georgians, Armenians, Saracens, Ethiopians, and of course

Romans and Persians were now connected through a great mesh of alliances. In the later sixth century, a poet in Constantinople boasted that "no longer is any place inaccessible to me: calm waters are traversed by Italian ships from the northern Black Sea to the far reaches of Ethiopia."[71] But this interconnectivity, which was benign when it came to trade, was also laying the ground for the world wars of the seventh century.

Kavad died in September 531, and his successor Khusrow I, whose position was still insecure, began to negotiate in earnest for peace with Justinian. Neither of the two intended to rule as their predecessors had. Both had plans to transform their respective empires.

12
The Sleepless Emperor (527–540)

In January 532 the people of Constantinople rose up against Justinian. The Nika Insurrection left much of the City a smoking ruin. There were no prior warnings that this would happen, that the people would be backed by most of the Senate, or that, in response, Justinian would order his soldiers to massacre tens of thousands of his own subjects, an atrocity that no other emperor dared commit. It was one thing to assassinate the likes of Vitalianus, but another to slaughter the Roman populace. A month earlier, Justinian had defined emperors, in true republican fashion, as men "who work day and night on the people's behalf."[1]

The **Corpus** *and the laws*

More than any other emperor, Justinian believed that law and imperial authority, wielded autocratically, could produce a uniform, homogeneous, and orderly society whose norms, and ideally whose practices too, admitted of no consequential exceptions, deviations, confusions, or contradictions. His extension of Roman law to the Armenians was part of this project: "Instead of disordered, [it will now be] ordered; properly sorted out and tidy, instead of what was previously disorganized and confused."[2] Other places should follow the law of Rome, i.e., Constantinople, which, history had shown, "had been founded under better auspices" than Elder Rome.[3] As a social engineer, Justinian was therefore both optimistic and a rationalist, though he knew that the world was messy, chaotic, and unpredictable and that "the changing nature of things" called for flexibility and frequent course correction.[4] Indeed, his reign became a tragic contest between his ambitions and the unpredictability of the real world. Fortunately, Justinian had a high tolerance for the human cost—to be paid by others—incurred by his labors "on behalf of the *res publica*."[5]

In the first years of his reign, Justinian brought his love of order to the standardization of the law and the correction of moral depravity and religious deviance. On 13 February, 528, he appointed a committee of officials and legal scholars to produce an updated counterpart of the *Codex Theodosianus*, to be called, of course, the *Codex Iustinianus*. It would collect all imperial law that the commissioners believed should still be valid, smooth out contradictions, and clarify confusions. Among others, the committee included the patrician Phokas, whom Justin had sent to Antioch after the earthquake of 526; the *quaestor* Thomas; Tribonian, who would quickly emerge as the major legal figure of the regime; and Theophilos, a professor of law. The first version of the *Codex* was confirmed a few months later, on 7 April, 529. It does not survive, because it was replaced by the second version that appeared on 16 November 534, featuring—indeed, prominently highlighting—the legislation of Justinian that had appeared in the meantime. Thus "obscurity was eradicated" since "nothing that we undertake should be imperfect."[6]

Meanwhile, on 15 December, 530, Justinian authorized Tribonian to abridge, consolidate, and streamline into fifty volumes the most important works of the authoritative Roman jurists. On 16 December 533—almost two years after the Nika Insurrection—this committee published the *Digest*, which still remains our main source for Roman legal thought. It is worth quoting the opening lines of its authorization:

> Governing our empire under the authority of God . . . we both conduct wars successfully and render peace honorable, and we uphold the condition of the *res publica*. We so lift up our minds toward the help of the omnipotent God that we do not place our trust in weapons, our soldiers, our military leaders, or our own talents,[7] but we rest all our hopes in the providence of the Supreme Trinity. . . . Whereas, then, nothing in any sphere is found so worthy of study as the authority of law, which sets in good order affairs both divine and human and casts out all injustice, yet we have found the whole extent of our laws which has come down from the foundation of the city of Rome and the days of Romulus to be confused.[8]

Justinian and Tribonian also saw the need for a new textbook of Roman law for students, so on 21 November, 533, they unveiled the *Institutes*, which has served its intended purpose ever since. Arms may ensure conquest, Justinian told law students in the preface, but it is only through law that imperial authority can actually govern. Therefore, "study our law. Do your best and apply yourselves keenly to it. Then, you will be able to perform whatever duty is entrusted to you in the government of our *res publica*."[9] Legal education was also restructured. Only the law schools of Constantinople, Rome, and Beirut would henceforth be recognized, not those of Alexandria or Kaisareia, a major power play by the professors on the committee. Henceforth, students in their first year would be known as *Novi Iustiniani* ("Justinianic Freshmen"); in the third the traditional name "Papinianists" would be retained (after the famous jurist); and in their fourth they would be called "Problem Solvers." Abbreviations in legal texts were banned because they caused confusion, and jokes at the expense of the faculty were strictly forbidden.[10]

The *Codex*, *Digest*, and *Institutes* are collectively known today as the *Corpus Iuris Civilis*, or "Body of Civil Law." Already in the sixth century they were being taught in Greek through interlinear translations, summaries, and commentaries written by the law professors, and these formed the basis of all east Roman law in Greek.[11] Justinian intended for the *Corpus*, rebaptized in the name of Jesus Christ, to be the exclusive and eternal source for Roman law. It must have brought tremendous relief to lawyers, judges, and litigants, who previously had to wade through a chaotic mass of edicts, rescripts, and opinions, not all of which were available everywhere. In this goal, Justinian succeeded brilliantly, which is why, after his work was rediscovered in twelfth-century Europe, he was regarded as the archetypal lawgiver (until 1623, when Prokopios' *Secret History* was found, which cast a different light on him). However, the codification created a bottleneck for the transmission of all prior legislation: what we call "Roman law" is, with few exceptions, what Tribonian and his colleagues said it was. They excerpted and discarded according to the needs of their age, which are a filter interposed between us and the Roman past.

Justinian did not only codify prior law. He was busy issuing his own laws between late 527 and the end of 533, many of which were included in the second version of the *Codex*, at the end of their respective sections, thus giving him the final word on many issues. His laws were abridged less severely than those of past emperors, thereby giving the *Codex* a definite Justinianic slant. There was nothing revolutionary about the legislation of those years. For the most part, its concern was to clarify ambiguities in the law that emerged during cases that were referred or appealed to the emperor's court. Justinian was keen to safeguard the integrity of institutions against financial conflicts of interest and immorality; to streamline and clarify procedures such as appeals and arbitration and make them fairer; to resolve tangles in inheritance law caused by the intersection of so many institutions (the state, Church, cities, private individuals); and to curb abuses, especially bribes and "fees."[12] In many cases, he deputized bishops to be his spies on secular officials and on the enforcement of the law in order to circumvent the discretion and likely corruption of secular officials, who chose what to report and what not. This was not necessarily a boon to bishops: they were required to report abuses and could be punished if they did not, which put them in a bind, making it harder for others to confide in them or even have them around.[13] Civil trials were not to last longer than three years, and criminal trials two.[14] Justinian demanded greater fairness in inheritance, especially for women. An amusing problem brought to him was that too many people were designating not a particular church but "Jesus Christ" as their beneficiary in wills. But Jesus was not recognized as a person or legal entity in Roman law. The bequest was henceforth to go to the nearest church.[15]

Moral and religious reforms

Moral reform was an essential component of Justinian's social "correction." He cracked down on dice playing and games of chance that caused players to curse, blaspheme, and go into debt; even priests were known to join in the fun, or so he was told. Gamblers had their hands cut off and were paraded around the City on camels.[16] He also severely punished homosexual activity: offenders had their entire genitals amputated, effectively a death sentence. A bishop punished in this way was paraded around the City. Justinian announced that homosexual acts, being "contrary to nature," caused earthquakes and were a danger to everyone. Natural science of the period could have set him straight on that, had he asked.[17]

There was one vice, pimping and sex work, for which Justinian did have solid insider information through his wife Theodora. His laws cracking down on sex trafficking expose the mechanisms by which girls were lured, through fancy clothes, baubles, and debt, into forced sex work. The pimps then entrapped them through legal contracts. Justinian declared these null and void, and issued a law that came close to banning brothels altogether. Procurers then switched to extracting oaths from their girls, overseen in some cases by imperial officials. Although he was a great believer in the moral validity of oaths, in this case Justinian absolved the girls of any oaths they made to pay back such debts, "sacrificing their chastity in order to keep their word."[18] Theodora converted a palace on the Bosporos into a nunnery for penitent sex workers known as Metanoia (Repentance). But not all women, then as now, ply the trade under duress, and some were unwilling to be rounded up and cloistered.[19]

Religious deviants also stained Justinian's ideal republic. In the early years (527–532), he was obsessed with Manicheans, though it is unlikely that there were enough in his empire to fill a single monastery. But someone dropped a Manichean pamphlet on the City's boulevard—this was a traditional way to start a dispute—causing a moral panic. As under Diocletian, the anxiety was possibly amplified by the Persian war, for Mani was associated with Persia. The penalty for being a Manichean was death.[20]

Justinian also believed that the Christian state had been too "tolerant" of pagans. It was now time for that insanity to end. He renewed existing penalties and demanded that all pagans make themselves known to the authorities so that they could be baptized, along with their households. Nor could they ever go back to their old ways, because the punishment for apostasy was to be death.[21] But this was still an impossible undertaking. If 5% of the population was still pagan—and that might be a low estimate—they would be around a million strong, scattered throughout all the provinces. We know of one campaign to covert the remaining pagans of southwest Asia Minor spearheaded by Monophysite missionaries who, paradoxically, enjoyed the emperor's support. One of the team, the priest and agitator Yuhannan of Amida (whom scholars call "John of Ephesos"), boasts that, over the course of thirty years, 80,000 were converted, "rows of idols were hewn down," and almost 100 churches were built, 55 of them with imperial money. The emperor paid a conversion bonus of 1/3 solidus to each new Christian. Either the missionaries had agreed not to push sectarian interests, or Justinian was co-opting a project that was happening with or without him.[22]

Justinian's own court was apparently infested with pagans pretending to be Christians for the sake of their careers. He had to periodically purge these crypto-pagans, driving some to suicide, in the ancient Roman manner. The purge of 529 implicated the *quaestor* Thomas and the patrician Phokas. Both were exonerated, but Phokas was finally outed in the purge of 545/6, which was instigated by John of Ephesos. John boasted that Phokas took his life with poison, and the emperor ordered that he was not to be buried with ceremony but tossed in a grave at night and alone "like a dead beast. Thus for some time fear seized all the pagans."[23] But piety remained easy to counterfeit. Tribonian is said in a biographical notice to have been a pagan, and we can see that he slipped ideas from Plato, Aristotle, and the Delphic oracle into laws that he wrote for Justinian, probably unbeknownst to the emperor.[24] Pagans were a fact of daily life. An ascetic who dispensed advice in the 520s, The Great Old Man Barsanouphios, was asked, "If a Jew or pagan invites me to a dinner on his festival, or sends me a gift, shall I accept or not?" His answer was, "Do not accept, for it is against the canons of the Holy Church." "But what if the man is important, and a friend of mine, and he is sad because I refuse, what shall I tell him then?"[25]

Justinian also forbade "the teaching of any subject by those who suffer from the insanity of the unholy pagans," who "destroy the souls of their pupils," and he targeted the school of philosophy in Athens, a pagan bastion.[26] This persecution led the seven professors of the Platonic Academy of Athens to shutter their school, between 529 and 531, and move to Persia, which they believed was hospitable to philosophy. The prince Khusrow I, who became shah in 531, was known for his broad intellectual interests. The exiles included the leading philosophers of the age, such as Damaskios the scholarch and Simplikios, the commentator on Aristotle. Their journey to Persia is told in detail by a pagan sympathizer writing fifty years later, likely using Damaskios' own memoirs. He states that they left because "they were being excluded by law from public life, seeing as they would not conform to the dominant religion."[27] Excavations in Athens have brought to light elite houses from this period in which statues of the gods were destroyed or carefully buried so as not to be destroyed, and one whose mosaics were overlaid with crosses. Justinian's command to confiscate the property of recalcitrant pagans seems to have been enforced locally.[28] Whereas Julian had once tried to prevent Christians from teaching Hellenic texts, Justinian was now prohibiting Hellenes from teaching Hellenic thought.

Needless to say, almost every sector of life that Justinian tried to reform carried on as before. Dice playing and sex work did not end, and even the seven philosophers of Athens returned from Persia in 532. The culture was resistant to change. "So what?," a Christian fan of the games told the bishop Yakub of Serugh,

"These are just for fun, and watching them isn't paganism. I'm a Christian and I don't suddenly become a pagan because I watch people dance."[29] What Justinian had so far failed to tackle were the vice and ambition inherent in the money-power racket that structured the the Roman economy. It was this, more than dice playing, that produced un-Christian behavior, as many preachers realized. In the 530s, the emperor would take some steps toward curbing its abuses.

The Nika Insurrection

The year 532 opened with the Nika Insurrection. It appears to have begun as an altercation in the hippodrome between Justinian and the Greens, who complained that they were being oppressed and even killed by a court eunuch, Kalopodios. The exchange became acrimonious. Justinian, who supported the Blues, replied through a herald: "Silence, you Jews, Manichaeans, Samaritans!" The Greens: "Would that Sabbates [Justinian's father] had not been born, so he would not have had a murderer for a son . . . . Farewell justice, you exist no more. I shall turn and become a Jew. Better to be a pagan than a Blue."[30] In the following days, the Blues and the Greens clashed so violently that the City prefect Eudaimon arrested men from both sides and sentenced seven of them to hang, but the execution of one Blue and one Green was botched and they were taken by some monks to a church. Three days later at the games, on Tuesday, 13 January, the partisans of both teams chanted that the emperor should pardon the two men, but he refused. At that point, the two clubs joined forces, left the hippodrome chanting *Nika!* ("Win!"), and went to the prefect's headquarters, the *praitorion*, where the prisoners were held. They sought an audience, but the prefect refused, so they broke in, freed the prisoners, and set fire to the building.

On Wednesday, Justinian hoped that more games would pacify the crowd, but the people set fire to part of the hippodrome and demanded the deposition of the City prefect, the praetorian prefect Ioannes the Cappadocian, and the *quaestor* Tribonian. The emperor promptly fired all three, and appointed Phokas as the new praetorian prefect. By now the riot was no longer a fan-club demonstration: it had become a popular insurrection. The Cappadocian, who was talented at raising revenue for the emperor, had leaned on taxpayers too hard and had abused his position to become personally rich. Some sources claim that he had imposed such high taxes that people were forced to emigrate from the countryside to the City, where they brewed in discontent. Tribonian was also corrupt, selling justice in exchange for cash. Moreover, the populace was upset over the multiplication of crimes for which they were being punished and the severity of law enforcement.[31]

Justinian had capitulated on the key demands, but then made the mistake of sending Belisarios out with some Goths to attack protesters who were mobbing the palace. The populace now looked for a different emperor "for Romanía." They first tried Probus, the nephew of Anastasius, but he had fled the City along with many senators. By Saturday, soldiers had arrived from Thrace who engaged in street battles with the populace, and both sides set fires to smoke or burn the other out. During those days, the fires destroyed Hagia Sophia, St. Eirene, the Chalke Gatehouse of the palace, the Senate, the Sampson hospital along with its patients, and many private homes. On Sunday, Justinian repeated Anastasius' move from 512, appearing in the imperial box with a Gospel book in hand and promising a general amnesty if the crowd stood down. Some acclaimed him, but others called him "an ass." The crowd then acclaimed Hypatius, the nephew of Anastasius, who was taken to the forum of Constantine and, with the support of many senators, proclaimed emperor. Hypatius occupied the hippodrome. It is possible that some senators were discontented with Justinian because he ruled autocratically, without consulting the Senate: "It assembled for the sake of appearances only and because of custom, as it was impossible for any member of that assembly so much as to raise his voice and speak."[32]

Prokopios reports that Justinian planned to escape from the capital, but his resolve to fight back was bolstered by a passionate speech by Theodora, who was unwilling to live at any rank lower than that of empress. Emboldened now to do anything to keep the throne, Justinian sent his guards, whatever units remained loyal to him, and some mercenaries who happened to be in the City, to slaughter the crowd in the hippodrome. They were led by Belisarios, Mundo (a Gepid prince who had once raided the empire and was present with a force of Herul barbarians), and the Persarmenian eunuch Narses. They attacked the hippodrome from three directions and killed between 30,000 and 50,000 people, or almost one tenth of the population of Constantinople. In the past, the populace of the City had risen up to slaughter barbarian soldiers who were threatening the monarchy; now, the monarchy used barbarian soldiers to slaughter its own subjects. A century later, in Palestine, this act was remembered as one of the great calamities of history. In Constantinople it was never forgotten. According to later legend, the bodies were buried under the sand of the racetrack.[33]

The monumental core of Constantinople was now "a smoking ruin, a heap of black, charred mounds, uninhabitable because of the dust, smoke, and stench of materials that had been reduced to ash."[34] On Monday, 19 January, Justinian had Hypatius and his brother Pompeius arrested and executed, and their bodies were thrown into the sea. He confiscated the property of many senators who sided with them and distributed it to his associates, though later he returned whatever was left. And within a year he had restored Ioannes the Cappadocian to his former position and eventually also Tribonian. The emperor sent a report throughout the empire proclaiming his "victory over rebels," and a statue of Theodora appears to have been dedicated in public, with an epigram honoring her role in the "civil war."[35] But this triumph was not easy to celebrate, and Justinian soon suppressed all mention of it in his propaganda. There was, at any rate, no show of remorse for the slaughter of his own people, no matter how "justified" it was from the court's perspective.

Justinian immediately threw himself into many high-stakes projects that defined his reign as much as the codification of the law. He was either desperate to improve his image or taking advantage of the suppression of domestic opposition. He made peace with Persia in 532, and rebuilt the capital, especially Hagia Sophia (532–537). He sought to find a compromise with the Monophysites; conquered North Africa from the Vandals (533–534) and Italy from the Ostrogoths (535–540 for the first phase); and reformed provincial governance (in the 530s). No Roman emperor had ever—or would ever—have so many balls in the air simultaneously.

Specifically, the new praetorian prefect of 532, the pagan Phokas, took up the construction of the new Hagia Sophia, and ground was broken quickly, on 23 February, only a month after the insurrection (see Figure 21). The project would take just under six years to complete, and the new church was inaugurated on 27 December, 537. Phokas managed to collect 4,000 lbs of gold, a sum that would have satisfied Attila but was likely a fraction of the building's total cost, probably a fifth, putting the total cost at over a million solidi. Its architects, Anthemios of Tralleis and Isidoros of Miletos, were products of the pagan schools and likely pagans themselves. They designed Hagia Sophia to reflect Neoplatonic notions

Figure 21 Hagia Sophia, exterior view from the east
Photo by David Hendrix

of divine light, with the golden dome representing the vault of heaven soaring over a marble floor seen as the waters over which the spirit of God drifted at the moment of Creation. It could accommodate 16,000 people and was served by a staff of 500 priests, cantors, and doorkeepers.[36]

The crowning achievement of Roman architecture, Hagia Sophia was the largest interior space that could be designed while keeping its four massive pillars hidden within the walls; anything larger would expose those supports, creating the "elephant legs" effect. The original dome was flatter than the current one, a more ambitious and vulnerable design. Light poured in through the windows along its base, between the ribs, giving the impression that the dome was "floating," or, as Prokopios put it through a Homeric allusion, "suspended from heaven on a golden chain." The light reflected off the ceiling's gold overlay and the marble that lined the interior, bathing the interior in sunlight.[37] Those multicolored marble panels were purposefully imported from provinces all across the Mediterranean, making the interior of Hagia Sophia a symbolic map of Justinian's expanding empire (see Plates 1b–2a).

The liturgical poet Romanos the Melodos composed *hymns* for the new church, one of which was performed while it was under construction. With striking candor, he refers movingly to the grief of those whose relatives were killed in the Nika Insurrection, when the emperor "chastised bad people with the sword." He favorably compares the new church, rising from the ashes, to Solomon's Temple. Thus did Justinian finally answer Anicia Juliana, by "resurrecting" the entire City. Romanos endorsed further aspects of Justinian's agenda, such as reforming sex work and shutting up the mouth of Hellenic philosophy.[38]

War and theology in the 530s

In the summer of 532, the negotiations with the new shah Khusrow resulted in an agreement, the "Endless Peace," which was optimistically intended to last forever. The Romans got Lazica, the Persians Iberia, high-ranking prisoners were exchanged, and Justinian pledged to guarantee the safety and religious freedom of the Athenian philosophers. This clause was likely written by Damaskios himself. The philosophers returned "and lived out the rest of their days in happiness and contentment," though we do not know where. It is an irony that Sasanian Persia had emerged as the patron of Hellenic philosophy (indeed, Christians called Persians "Hellenes," i.e., pagans). But Justinian also reciprocally insisted on the protection of Christians returned to Persia. The deal depended on an immense transfer of cash: Justinian agreed to pay to Khusrow 11,000 lbs gold (792,000 solidi), the biggest payoff in Roman history.[39] Justinian was burning through Anastasius' reserves. As Khusrow's position in Iran was still weak, he was buoyed by an injection of cash amounting to about a seventh of the Roman annual budget. However, Persia's main currency was silver, so Khusrow could not put all that gold into domestic circulation. It was likely used to buy bulk goods from India and China, such as silk, part of which was resold on the Roman market.[40] Justinian, then, had effectively subsidized Persia's long-distance trade with Rome, to Persia's benefit.

At the same time, Justinian was planning another major expense, a naval attack on Vandal North Africa. The last one sent by Constantinople, by Leo I in 468, cost between 7 and 9 million solidi and was a disaster. As the prospect of a new campaign is not mentioned in the sources until it was decided in 532, we do not know whether this was an ambition that Justinian had nursed for years or whether it was devised in the new strategic and political environment of mid-532. Certainly, the eastern Romans had never fully written off the loss of the western empire: this was Roman territory that had been seized by barbarians through what Justinian later called the "neglect" of past emperors.[41] Constantinople had made treaties with the Vandals, but these were pragmatic deals of the moment. Arian kings who ruled over Catholic Romans would never be accepted as fully legitimate. Indeed, some of those kings had persecuted the Catholic Church. Many sources report on the confessors who, under Huneric (477–484), had their tongues cut out and yet were miraculously still able to speak. They traveled to Constantinople to plead for their fellow Catholics back home, and stayed there for decades. Only Prokopios slyly reports that two of them visited brothels in the capital, whereupon they were rendered truly speechless.[42] At any rate, freeing Roman Catholics from Vandal Arian rule was a priority.[43]

A revolution in Carthage gave Justinian a pretext. The Vandal law of succession was that the eldest living descendent of Gaizeric should be king, and in 523–530 this was the elderly Hilderic, the grandson of Valentinian III and great-grandson of Theodosius II. Hilderic allowed Catholics to worship freely and was on good terms with Justinian, but his army was hard pressed by the Moors (aka Berbers), who lived along the periphery of the kingdom and could inflict costly defeats on the Vandals. In 530, Hilderic was deposed by his nephew Gelimer, who was next in the succession but impatient to restore Vandal fortunes.[44] Justinian was lobbied by North African enemies of Gelimer who gave the emperor detailed information about the land, its wealth, its troubles with the Moors, and the treasures that Gaizeric had accumulated on his raids. Gelimer later accused some "eastern merchants" of stirring Justinian to war, possibly by revealing to him the benefits of controlling the east-west trade routes in the Mediterranean.[45] Pottery attests to the survival of long-distance trading routes linking the eastern Mediterranean to Britain, which was likely still a source for tin. The distribution of amphorae reveals that during the Vandal period imports from North Africa to the eastern empire had declined significantly, which enabled internal producers in the east to pick up the slack. There was considerable scope for tapping into African imports and markets.[46] Religious freedom was a prize resting on a heap of cash.

Justinian's first intervention reveals the depth of his cynicism, which he often disguised as principle: he reproached Gelimer for violating the Vandal law of succession. By 532, he was considering military intervention, ostensibly to liberate the Vandals from their "tyrant." But the praetorian prefect Ioannes the Cappadocian was against the risky plan on fiscal grounds. The soldiers too were apprehensive and "every one of the generals, supposing that he himself would command the army, was in terror and dread at the greatness of the danger." The emperor chose Belisarios to command the expedition, a risky choice. Belisarios' record held many defeats, and he had been relieved of his eastern command after the battle of Kallinikos (531). But his one victory, at Daras (530), had shown promise, and Justinian possibly suspected that Belisarios would remain loyal to him no matter how much power he was given or how badly he was treated by the court. Also, Belisarios was devoted to his wife Antonina—some said dominated by her—and she was on close terms with Theodora, for they shared a similar background. The empress likely had a hand in the appointment.[47]

While the armada was being assembled, in 532–533, Justinian turned his attention to the growing problem of Church schism. The reconquest of the west and the Christological controversy in the east were as yet two separate fields of activity, but they eventually intertwined tightly to exacerbate the problems of Church disunion. We will alternate between the two until the connections emerge.

Justin I had demonstrated that most of the eastern Church (except Egypt) could be brought to heel by the court and dissenters could be persecuted. When Justinian came to power in 527, he relaxed the persecution of the monks, possibly influenced by Theodora, who, it was said, leaned toward Monophysitism.[48] But some Monophysites decided that the only way out of their predicament was to create a Church of their own. The step of ordaining separate Monophysite priests by the hundreds was taken by Yuhannan (John) of Tella in or before 530, while he was in hiding in the mountains, and he did so with permission from Severos of Antioch; one of the deacons that he created was the later Monophysite leader and historian John of Ephesos.[49] This move frightened the court. Under guarantees of safe conduct, Justinian summoned to the City five leading anti-Chalcedonians, including Yuhannan of Tella, and put them up for a year in the Hormisdas palace, his prior residence. Here they held confidential, non-binding discussions with five Chalcedonians led by Hypatios of Ephesos, in the hope of finding a way forward for Church union.

We know of discussions that lasted for three days through complementary reports from both sides.[50] Each side believed that it had "won," and there was no real move toward compromise, even on the most basic matters (such as the fact that they were clearly using the word "nature" in different senses). Instead, both sides relitigated the conflicts of the previous century, namely how Dioskoros of Alexandria supported Eutyches at Ephesos II and how Chalcedon admitted Ibas of Edessa's embarrassingly Nestorian letter to Mari. They were all locked in. For both sides, the conditions of union were maximalist: "You have to admit that I am right and you are wrong; you have to rewrite the history of the past century; you have to erase your religious identity and replace it with ours; and then you have to beg forgiveness and, if we are feeling tolerant, we will allow you into the true Church." This politics of maximum humiliation and zero concessions had been established by pope Hormisdas as the standard for "victory" in Church politics. But the emperor needed to prevent the creation of a separate Church and was treating this as a schism, not heresy. He admitted that he did not view anti-Chalcedonians as unorthodox and offered a compromise: Chalcedonians would reject Theodoros of Mopsouestia, Theodoretos, Ibas, and some others along with Nestorios and Eutyches, while anti-Chalcedonians would accept Chalcedon for its rejection of Eutyches, though not its doctrine; both sides could thereafter speak of One or Two Natures in a compromise formula. This was rejected by the anti-Chalcedonians. Compromise was impossible because, through chain reaction, a slight concession would annul one's entire position (if Ibas was out, then so was Chalcedon along with everyone who had ever accepted Chalcedon, and so on).

Incidentally, it was at this meeting that the theological writings of pseudo-Dionysios the Areopagite, among the most important and entertaining forgeries in the history of Christianity, first appear in the historical record, in support of the Monophysite position. Dionysios was supposedly converted by St. Paul in Athens, but the works in question were a transposition into Christian idiom of the pagan philosophy of the Neoplatonist Proklos. The leading Diphysite in attendance in 532, Hypatios of Ephesos, expressed doubts about their authenticity.[51] Even so, they would have a long and distinguished history ahead of them.

Not everyone was locked into the Monophysite-Diphysite echo chamber. For a breath of sanity, we have only to step into the thought-world of the historian Prokopios of Kaisareia. Regarding the theological controversies of the mid-530s, and about Hypatios of Ephesos in particular, he wrote this:

> As for the disputed points, I know them well, but I will by no means mention them for I consider it a sort of insane stupidity to investigate the nature of God, asking what sort it is. For man cannot, I think, accurately understand even human affairs, much less those pertaining to the nature of God. I will therefore maintain a safe silence concerning these matters . . . . I will say nothing whatever about God save that he is altogether good and has all things in his power.[52]

Prokopios accompanied the North African expedition when it sailed from Constantinople in June 533, as Belisarios' secretary, advisor, and, later, historian. It was a smaller fleet than the one Leo had sent in 468, comprising 500 transport vessels accompanied by 92 warships, to convey 10,000 infantry soldiers and 5,000 cavalry, in addition to 400 Heruls and 600 Huns. Belisarios was in command as *magister militum* for Oriens, as the east would not need defending against Persia.[53] The armada sailed across the Mediterranean and caught the Vandals by surprise. Gelimer had even divided his forces by sending an army to Sardinia, whose governor had declared for Justinian. Prokopios has left us a vivid, first-person account of how Belisarios disembarked the army in North Africa and defeated the Vandals at the battle of Ad Decimum (13 September), relying on his cavalry. Belisarios entered Carthage two days later and the Romans ate the banquet prepared for Gelimer.[54] The Vandal king was defeated again at Tricamarum (in mid-December), after which he fled to a mountain fort, eventually to surrender in March, 534.

The military victory, however, was marred by political infighting and bad administration in the province. Belisarios was denounced to the emperor for plotting rebellion, so he quickly returned to Constantinople along with most of the surviving Vandal soldiers (now disarmed) and the treasure of Carthage. The Roman victory had been due to a combination of luck, Belisarios' generalship, and Gelimer's mistakes. The kingdom of the Vandals was no more, its army dispersed, and the fertile province of North Africa restored to the empire. The Vandals themselves disappeared from history. They had always been a small military elite dominating a provincial Roman populace, and were easily swept away after their defeat. Prokopios could hardly believe what he had just witnessed. Surely no "kingdom at the height of its wealth and military strength has been undone in so short a time by five thousand men coming in as invaders and having no place to cast anchor."[55] The first of Rome's barbarian successor-states had fallen to New Rome (see Figure 22).

Justinian did not believe the accusations against Belisarios and allowed him to celebrate a victory in Constantinople. The general processed on foot from his house to the hippodrome, where he and Gelimer both knelt before Justinian, after the Vandal king was ceremoniously stripped of his royal insignia. Among the treasures on display were the spoils from the Temple of Jerusalem built by Herod, including the golden Menorah, which had been looted by the emperor Titus in 70 AD at the end of the Jewish War and taken to Rome. They had been relocated to Carthage in 455 by Gaizeric, after he sacked Rome, and were now taken to New Rome. Someone pointed out to Justinian that these spoils had brought bad luck to every city that held them, so the emperor sent them to Jerusalem, to be kept in churches, which would presumably neutralize their bad energy (Jerusalem was captured by the Persians in 614 and the Temple treasures disappeared). Gelimer was given lands on which to live in Galatia, but would not renounce his Arian faith. Belisarios was made consul for 535 and inaugurated his term by throwing gold and silver from the Vandal treasure to the populace.[56]

Figure 22 Barberini ivory, celebrating the victories of an emperor, likely Justinian, over the barbarians represented by the figure behind the emperor's spear. Christ is on top, exotic tribute-bearers below, and a general on the left. It measures 34.2 x 26.8 cm (Louvre, Paris)
Azoor Photo / Alamy Stock Photo

The eastern empire now had a western outpost, a prosperous territory with a population of about 3 million, most of whom spoke Latin, though Punic still survived. A former Roman diocese, it could easily be slotted into the empire's structure of provincial governance, where it would stay for a century and a half. In April 534, Justinian issued two laws to govern its administration. North Africa (including Corsica and Sardinia) was divided into seven provinces, with a staff of 50 serving under each governor. They would have a praetorian prefect of their own with a staff of 396 men, and a *magister militum*. The emperor specified the salaries of each official, including five physicians, two orators, and two grammarians. *Duces* were stationed along the frontier, warships were to guard the straits of Gibraltar, and Belisarios was to decide where to place each unit. The total cost of the new administration, civilian and military, amounted to about 53,000 solidi, paid out to about 1,250 officials (not counting regular soldiers).

As Justinian liked to name or rename everything after himself, Carthage was given the added name of Iustiniana. The emperor thanked God profusely for this bounty and asked only that "its inhabitants recognize from what most cruel captivity and barbarian yoke they had been freed, and in what great liberty, under our most felicitous reign, they have been found worthy to live."[57]

In addition to its material benefits, victory in North Africa buttressed Justinian's shaky legitimacy. He exploited it to the fullest, boasting in the prefaces of both the *Digest* and the *Institutes* that God had favored him with the defeat of the Vandals, and he assumed the victory titles *Vandalicus* and *Africanus*.[58] But the same problem that had weakened the Vandals in the first place—Moor invasions—immediately assailed Roman North Africa too. These were no mere raiders, but formidable armies that could fight pitched battles. Fortunately, the first general and prefect in command after the conquest was the capable eunuch Solomon, a former retainer of Belisarios. In 535, he defeated a series of invasions by Moors in a campaign that took him into the Aurès mountains. An extensive program of fortification was implemented to safeguard Roman positions, especially in the province of Byzacena, some of which can be positively attributed to Solomon.[59]

Justinian next tested the limits of God's favor by setting his sights on Italy. The opportunity was ripe, for the Ostrogoths too were in dissension. The throne was uneasily shared between two members of the house of Theodoric, his daughter Amalasuintha and his nephew Theodahad, both of whom were separately engaged in secret negotiations with Justinian to sell their share of Italy to him and move east. When Theodahad had Amalasuintha imprisoned and executed, Justinian declared it a casus belli. He sent the Gepid Mundo, now the *magister militum* for Illyricum, to attack Gothic positions in the western Balkans. Mundo quickly captured Salona on the Dalmatian coast. Meanwhile, Justinian sent Belisarios with 4,000 regular soldiers, 3,000 Isaurians, 200 Huns, and 300 Moors to conquer Sicily, which was lightly garrisoned (the centers of Gothic power were in the north of Italy). By the end of his consular year, 535, Belisarios had conquered Sicily. On the last day of the year, he entered Syracuse in triumph and threw coins to the crowds. He was the first Roman consul in centuries to fulfill the duties of the office in the ancient manner.[60] Italy beckoned.

Yet there was no gift from God that Justinian could not mar with religious zeal and fiscal exploitation. What happened next in North Africa was a typical example of Justinianic mismanagement and overreach. The Vandal army had likely never numbered more than 15,000 men. Many were killed in battle with Belisarios; others would have been sufficiently Romanized to fade into the background after their defeat; and thousands were captured and taken to the east, where they were reconstituted within the imperial army as the "Justinianic Vandals" (no group, place, or institution was safe from having Justinian's name slapped upon it).[61] When the Vandals had originally conquered North Africa, they had seized lands to support themselves, which were not taxed; Vandals who held such lands owed the king military service instead. After the conquest, Justinian immediately sent officials to assess taxes on the locals, which caused discontent because these taxes were higher than what they had been paying to the Vandals. In addition, Justinian confiscated the "Vandal lands" to the imperial treasury. He issued a law allowing their former Roman owners to claim them in court, but gave them only five years in which to do so, imposed a high burden of proof on them, and limited claims to their grandparents' generation, which did not reach back to the original Vandal conquest! Moreover, his own soldiers had taken up with the wives and daughters of the deported or killed Vandals, and these women made the persuasive point to them "that it was not right that, while living with the Vandals, they had enjoyed these lands, but after entering into marriage with their conquerors they were then to be deprived of their own possessions." The soldiers did not want to give up the lands to Solomon to register to the crown.[62]

At the same time, the Catholic clergy of North Africa petitioned Justinian to order the restoration of all Church property confiscated by the Vandal Arians and to block Arian priests from converting to Catholicism and carrying on as before.[63] Justinian duly ordered that all Arian Church property be given to the Catholics; that Arian worship be outlawed; and that Jewish synagogues be converted into churches. This edict forced the Vandal Arian clergy into an alliance with the Herul Arian soldiers in Justinian's own army, who numbered about 1,000 and were now barred from practicing their own religion, in violation of prior imperial law, which exempted them.[64] They formed common cause with the new husbands of the Vandal women and mutinied in 536. They tried to assassinate Solomon, but failed, after which they chose Stotzas, a Roman officer, as their leader. At one point, Stotzas led over two-thirds of the imperial army in North Africa, or about 9,000 men.[65] Belisarios had to rush over from Sicily to defeat him in battle, in mid-536, but the rebellion regrouped in Numidia while discontent simmered. Justinian had created greater problems than his fiscal and religious policies were meant to solve in the first place.

Meanwhile, Justinian was putting pressure on Theodahad to abdicate his throne and cede Italy and western Illyricum to him. The emperor was already planning a new organization for Illyricum. In 535, he decreed that the village in which he had been born would be elevated to the rank of an archbishopric under the predictable name Justiniana Prima, i.e., where Justinian *first* appeared. Its archbishop would have jurisdiction over seven surrounding provinces, which were taken out of the jurisdiction of the archbishop of Thessalonike. The emperor said nothing about the more distant rights of the pope over Illyricum, upon which this reform would infringe. Pope Agapetus tentatively accepted this reform, while reserving "all the rights of St. Peter." Justinian also signalled that he would move the seat of the praetorian prefecture of Illyricum from Thessalonike to Justiniana Prima, so that it could be closer to the territories that it governed, but this appears never to have been implemented. Justiniana Prima was endowed with government buildings and churches, but it was more of an administrative center than a thriving metropolis (the site is Caričin Grad in southern Serbia).[66] This was more a statement of intent: Justinian was pushing his authority into the western Balkans.[67]

When Theodahad learned that Mundo had been killed in battle near Salona, in late 535 or early 536, he chose to risk war with the empire, which triggered the invasion of Italy by Belisarios in mid-536. Justinian announced that he would restore the entire empire of the ancient Romans, "from sea to sea."[68] But before the war began, Theodahad sent the newly elected pope Agapetus to plead for peace. Agapetus arrived in Constantinople in the spring of 536. He was the second pope to visit the eastern capital, and he too came at the behest of a Gothic king. But in Constantinople Agapetus encountered an alarming situation: the patriarch Anthimos was unwilling to confess the Two Natures or the Council of Chalcedon and was in communion with none other than Severos of Antioch.

Severos had been invited by Justinian to participate in the conference of 532–533 but had declined for reasons of health and his fear of the City populace. He had been living in hiding in Egypt, changing location frequently and revealing it only to those who brought him food and news; he complained of loneliness.[69] But the court needed a conduit to him, because without him there could be no peace in the Church. Justinian found that conduit in Theodora, who had, or was reputed to have, Monophysite beliefs. She now emerged as the patron of Monophysites in the palace, for which she was praised by some Monophysite writers and, conversely, condemned by some Diphysites. Within a generation, legends sprang up about how she blocked Justinian's Chalcedonian policies in order to favor the Monophysites, for example by sending missionaries to Nubia, south of Egypt. For Prokopios, however, the imperial couple were cynically playing both sides. He saw this as sinister and dishonest, but, if true, it was actually a touch of sanity in a polarized environment. Moreover, Theodora's personal devotion to the anti-Chalcedonian cause is highly doubtful. In late 535, Severos finally agreed to come to the City even though he admitted that "it is pointless: so long as these emperors live, no path toward peace will be found. I will return without accomplishing anything."[70] He made the journey and was hosted with honor in the Hormisdas palace, which had become the Monophysite embassy in Constantinople.

When Agapetus arrived in the spring of 536 he realized that the patriarch of Constantinople, Anthimos, who had been a member of the Chalcedonian team in the conferences of 532–533, was not committed to the cause. Agapetus persuaded Justinian of this and Anthimos was immediately deposed on the pretext that he had been illegally transferred from the see of Trebizond.[71] He did not want trouble, so he went quietly. The pope consecrated a new patriarch, Menas, on 13 March, and died on 22 April, in Constantinople. Severos left the City, and, in May, 536, the emperor convened a Synod that duly anathematized him and Anthimos. At the close of the sessions, the new patriarch Menas declined to take up business that the emperor had not preapproved, "because it is fitting that nothing should happen in the Holy Church that deviates from his will and command." Justinian ratified the acts a few months later, pretending that he was endorsing what the bishops had autonomously decided. He was now finished with dialogue, which had produced the opposite result from what he wanted, a stinging embarrassment for the court. Justinian declared Severos a heretic, forbidding his subjects from owning, copying, or believing Severos' teachings. He and Anthimos were to be exiled from all cities. However, Anthimos retreated into the Hormisdas palace and lived there for ten years under the empress' protection.[72]

The persecution of the Monophysites, on hold since the late 520s, resumed. The pressure was most intense in the east, with "punishments, exile, seizure of possessions, loss of rank and exclusion from all skilled professions." Monks were driven out of their monasteries.[73] Yuhannan of Tella was arrested and died in prison. The Roman state had once persecuted Christians by requiring them to sacrifice before an altar; it now persecuted Christians by requiring them to take Chalcedonian communion. Some Monophysites would spit it out, or regard it as magic or poison.[74] Ironically, many victims of this persecution went to the capital, where they established a thriving monastery in the Hormisdas palace, featuring even stylites and hermits. The Monophysite patriarch of Alexandria, Theodosios, was also summoned to the capital and bottled up in the Hormisdas, from where he unofficially directed the Monophysite movement for thirty years (536–566).[75] The emperor tolerated this because it was one way to contain all these dissidents, and Theodora instructed them not to make ordinations.[76] A Chalcedonian bishop was installed in Alexandria, but lived under military protection. Never one to forget women in his laws, in 541 Justinian stripped female heretics of legal advantages regarding dowries that he had previously granted to all women. In that law, he obsesses again about The Name: these women, he fulminates, "adorn themselves with the name 'Christian.'"[77]

A letter that Severos wrote at this time offers a fascinating glimpse into the stance of the empress. He was informed by a Monophysite contact at the court that she made fun of all bishops named Alexandros, simply because of their name, including the fourth-century enemy of Arius, Alexandros of Alexandria. Severos was "much distressed." Doctrines are "things she does not understand." He had sent her a book explaining his theology, "copied in large letters" for her benefit, but he had not heard back from her, either because she despised it or "was afraid of the emperor's laws against my writings."[78] This image of a disrespectful and ignorant empress, written by the leading Monophysite of the age who had just left the court, is closer to that of Prokopios than to the image of the pious empress we find in the later writings of John of Ephesos, on which the modern rehabilitation of Theodora rests.

Institutionally, the Monophysites were now routed and shut out from all five patriarchates. They were also splitting internally between the followers of Severos and those of Ioulianos (Julian) of Halikarnassos. The latter understood the unity of Christ so robustly that Christ's body was rendered virtually incorruptible by its association with the Word, a view like the one imputed to Eutyches in 448. It came to be called Aphthartodocetism, alluding to Christ's incorruptibility and to the pretense of human passions that he must have put on. Severos and Julian, who formerly were friends and allies, now exchanged polemics, and their followers split into rival factions, especially in Alexandria.

Severos died in February 538, in his early seventies. In an odd way, his life had encapsulated the trajectory of east Roman culture: he began as a pagan Hellene, studied Roman law, converted to an ascetic version of Christianity, and became a theologian and patriarch, and his works survive in Syriac translation, not the original Greek. An anecdote illustrates how far he had come from his roots: shortly before his death, his companions and physicians tried to persuade him to take a bath, but he refused, saying that he had not seen his body naked since he took ascetic vows, almost fifty years before. They had to put him in the bath with his clothes on.[79]

The late 530s witnessed another unusual event. In 536, volcanic eruptions in some other part of the globe, or else a meteorite strike, sent so much ash or dust into the upper atmosphere that it dimmed the sun for eighteen months and caused lower temperatures. This "dust veil event" of 536–537 was recorded in chronicles around the world. The Roman sources exhibit perplexity and wonder at it, but not terror; at most, they treat it as an omen of bad things to come, not as their cause. Its impact on agriculture appears to have been small: the wine tasted bad. Theories that it led to widespread malnourishment or other developments that enabled the plague appear to be entirely conjectural.[80]

Meanwhile, Belisarios was busy in Italy. With a small army, he quickly overran southern Italy, which was lightly garrisoned, and surprised the Goths by entering the city of Rome, on 9 December, 536, a date recorded by Prokopios as marking the return of Roman rule to Rome after a period of sixty years.[81] The Goths had meanwhile killed their king Theodahad and replaced him with Wittigis (536–540), a general, albeit an inadequate one. Belisarios' strategy was to force the Goths to besiege Rome, which they did for over a year, with no success. Wittigis retreated north to Ravenna, which was protected by a swamp, while Belisarios and the other armies that had arrived from the east worked their way up the peninsula in a series of sieges, with every action recorded in admirable clarity by Prokopios. In late 539, Belisarios invested Ravenna, which surrendered to him in 540 when he promised to break from Justinian and establish an empire of his own in Italy. But when the Goths surrendered, he hastened straight back to Constantinople, with yet another king and royal treasury in tow, to pledge his loyalty to Justinian.[82]

There was no public celebration this time, and Belisarios' services were required in the east, where war had broken out again. The year 540 marked the apogee of his success. Prokopios praised him as one of the best generals in history.

> Everyone was talking about Belisarios; to him were attributed two victories such as had never before fallen to the lot of one man to achieve: he had brought two kings captive to Byzantion and, beyond all expectation, had made Roman spoils of the nations and money of Geiseric and Theoderic . . . . The people took delight in watching him as he came out of his house every day and went to the forum . . . he was always escorted by a large number of Vandals, Goths, and Moors. He had a fine figure and was tall and remarkably handsome.[83]

Belisarios had a personal retinue of 7,000 soldiers and officers. Many high officials sported such units at this time, the *bucellarii*, named after biscuits issued with their rations, but no one else had a retinue so large. These were not private armies, for the emperor could reassign them to the regular units, appoint their officers to command in the army, or simply strip them away from an official who had fallen out of favor, as would soon happen to Belisarios. They never posed a danger to the state or the emperors, though they could be used to intimidate people further down the social scale.[84]

The Goths had been defeated by their own bad leadership and by Belisarios' brilliant strategy, which was to force them to disperse and fight in separate sieges across central and northern Italy. By 540, they were scattered and demoralized, but they had not been defeated in a major battle, had lost few men, and felt acutely the indignation of having been tricked. Belisarios' glory masked a dangerous reality on the ground. Italy required careful handling, but unfortunately Justinian lacked the skills to foster political consensus and became his own worst enemy in Italy, just as in Africa. Many of his officials were corrupt and his idea of taxation was strict. Into a situation so volatile, he again sent hated tax assessors and collectors.[85] Italy was not pacified in 540, only subdued and confused. Justinian should have known better. Rapacious taxation by his officials had recently sparked a rebellion in the Armenian provinces, in 538. In 539, this uprising claimed the life of general Sittas, Theodora's brother-in-law, and it drove some Armenian clans to ask the shah to intervene.[86]

Legal and administrative reforms

While his armies were conquering North Africa, Sicily, and Italy, Justinian had embarked upon an ambitious program of legal and administrative reform and church building. By all accounts, he was a workaholic micromanager, who slept and ate little. During the day he switched from military to religious discussions, from budget planning to architecture, and from the price of vegetables to the intricacies of inheritance law. As he involved himself personally in the minutiae of legal cases, and in double-checking and second-guessing the decisions of his officials, throngs of people could always be found in the palace, probably at all hours, waiting on their toes for the moment of their audience. During the night, he would discuss Scripture with old priests, or just continue daytime business, to the distress of his attendants, who were always on call.[87] Theodora, by contrast, took life in the palace at a leisurely pace, sleeping in and enjoying long baths.

Justinian wanted his subjects to know how hard he worked for them. "We lose sleep every night pondering what boon, pleasing to God, we might bestow upon our subjects." "At all times we are sleepless and fasting and undergoing all hardships to benefit our subjects." "Even the smallest matter is worthy of our consideration." "We are concerned with all matters—the high, the low, the in-between."[88] The regime stressed in official communications that it was driven by "universal benevolence toward our subjects."[89] Prokopios, who believed that Justinian was never up to any good, put a negative spin on this. Justinian's nocturnal habits revealed that he was not human but rather something demonic. He cites a monk who claimed that Justinian would walk around at night without his head.[90] Prokopios took the planks of Justinian's self-image and systematically reversed them: "Headless Ones" was a term that the emperor and others used for Monophysites.

Prokopios also caught on to the emperor's megalomania. Not only was he impatient to change everything, he liked to slap his name on it too. In addition to the *Codex*, some military units, and Justiniana Prima, the emperor renamed some twenty cities or forts Ioustinianopolis or appended *Iustiniana* to their name (e.g., to Carthage), and he added his name to magistracies (i.e., *praetor Iustinianus*). It has been well said that, from the start of his reign, Justinian was "conscious of living in the age of Justinian."[91] In 537, he decreed that all official documents should begin by naming the emperor and the year of his reign *before* the year of the tax cycle, the names of the consuls, and any local dating formula.[92] After 541, Justinian ceased appointing consuls altogether, on the spurious grounds that he himself, as emperor, held a "permanent consulship." This was excoriated by traditionalists who called the office "the mother of the Romans' freedom," although it had long been a purely honorific office.[93]

A stream of legislation poured out of the chancery even after the definitive codification of the laws in 534, much of it focusing on property, inheritance, and legal procedure. The technical term for one of these laws is *Novella* (*Novel*), i.e., a "new" enactment. In most of his empire, Justinian issued them in Greek, "not in the ancestral language," as he put it, "but in the common Hellenic one, so that everyone can grasp it."[94] Ioannes the Cappadocian switched the remaining operations of his prefecture into Greek, and the schools of Constantinople and Beirut taught Roman law in Greek. The government had thus made the switch to Greek. From now on, Italian lawyers and administrators who needed Justinian's *Novels* had to translate or crib them from Greek.[95] Roman law was henceforth issued in Greek and translated into Latin only as an afterthought, a reversal of their previous relationship. Likewise, Italy would be governed by mostly Greek-speaking officials sent from the east, another fascinating reversal. Where the court of Constantinople had once operated in Latin over the heads of a Greek-speaking populace, in reconquered Ravenna official business was conducted in Greek over the heads of a Latin-speaking populace.[96]

Also standing over their heads were the grand mosaics of Justinian and Theodora placed in the church of San Vitale in Ravenna, showing the imperial couple bringing as offerings to the church the wine and bread for the Eucharist. The emperor's retinue, with secular and military officials to his right and clergy to his left, are moving in a V formation toward us, whereas the empress' retinue of eunuchs and handmaidens is moving to the right into the gallery (see Plates 3a–b).

In his *Novels*, Justinian aimed at the "simplification of procedure, greater reliance upon documentary proof, and greater concern for the interests of the Church, the state, women, slaves, and children."[97] In the mid-530s, he also issued many laws to reform provincial governance, cracking down on corruption and abuses. A common thread is Justinian's irritation that so many provincials were coming to Constantinople for legal reasons, to complain about abuses or to appeal the verdicts of lesser courts. Provincials were apparently using the legal system in greater numbers, but Justinian, inclined to see everything in moral terms, attributed it to corruption and crime in the provinces. He believed that the problem was due to the sale of governorships, a practice to which emperors resorted, on-and-off, to raise revenue. A prospective governor would purchase his office from, say, the praetorian prefect or the emperor himself and then make good on his investment through low- or medium-grade extortion. This was part of the background noise of the imperial system. But Justinian cast its effects in rhetorically powerful terms: such venal governors left taxpayers destitute, reducing imperial revenue; verdicts were sold, leading to complaints and appeals to the capital; and "that is why there are murders, adulteries, break-ins, beatings, abductions of girls, disorder at public assemblages, and contempt of the laws and of the authorities: everyone regards them as openly venal, like some vile slave."[98]

After consulting with Theodora—and, remarkably, stating in the law that he had done so—Justinian abolished the sale of offices and issued detailed regulations about governors' duties. In a number of provinces of Asia Minor, he consolidated military and civil administration, which had been separate since the days of Diocletian, into the hands of a single governor who was given a higher rank (thereby protecting him from bullying by local notables) and a higher salary (thereby making it harder to bribe him). The provinces in question were not those with the largest armies, so this reform would not empower potential rebels. These enhanced governors, holding offices renamed after Justinian, were charged with law enforcement and collecting taxes in a way that was fair to both the taxpayer and the treasury. They could to push back against grandees who oppressed their weaker neighbors or who shirked paying their own taxes. The emperor saw this as an investment: it would cost money now but "there will be a great improvement for our taxpayers by their being protected from payments to office-holders; and both the sovereignty and the public treasury will be better off from having subjects who are well off."[99] There are places where Justinian admits that his regime was having to spend more money than usual, for example on war (and, we might add, building), which made the efficiency of revenue collection a top concern.[100] Finally, these Justinianic governors would function as a higher court of appeal, reducing the flow of litigants to the capital. This seems to have worked, as we know from Ioannes Lydos, an employee of the legal staff of the prefecture in the capital, who lamented the loss of fees: "the staff perished and, since there were no transactions, an ugly desolation befouled the court of justice; those who retired wept, sinking as they were into an old age of poverty."[101]

Justinian assured his subjects that this reform would result in "a greater flowering, a restoration of the ancient republic, and an honoring of the Roman name."[102] Micromanager that he was, he drafted a set of detailed instructions for governors along with an oath that they were required to swear upon taking office, pledging that they were orthodox Christians, would "work hard on behalf of the monarchy and republic," and had not paid any money to acquire their office. As always, the emperor threatened dire consequences for any who violated his rules, and Prokopios states that those threats were carried out against corrupt officials; he also says that Justinian started selling offices again soon after this reform.[103]

Some historians have argued, on the basis of the reform legislation, that the empire had undergone a tremendous socioeconomic transformation. These laws supposedly reveal that the government had lost control of its own aristocracy and magistrates. The latter had grown so wealthy and had accumulated so much local power that they were operating beyond the state's reach. Local magnates, created by Constantine's gold economy, were now building up quasi-independent local power bases with private armies, dispensing arbitrary justice over subjects who had no recourse, and undermining the imperial state itself by refusing to pay taxes or skimming so much off the top that there was little left for the emperor. The empire was disintegrating into a proto-feudal state. Justinian complained that some people were infringing on the extensive crown lands in Cappadocia, treating them as their own, and that not enough taxes were reaching the court from Egypt.[104] Indeed, the poster child for this revolution is the house of Apion in Egypt, whose finances are known from its archive, partially surviving in papyri. According to some reconstructions, Apion owned a large part of the land in various Egyptian districts, because he was paying most of the taxes that came from them. A few dozen such fabulously rich magnates could, potentially, own most of Egypt. Thus, when combined with this reading of the papyri, the reform legislation points to an imperial authority that had lost most of its local power and was desperately trying to claw it back.

This picture, however, is unpersuasive. The imperial government was never more active or more powerful than in the 530s, fighting multiple wars, codifying the law, imposing its own Chalcedonian bishops in all cities, building churches and fortifications everywhere, including Hagia Sophia, and doing it all successfully and simultaneously. This is not the footprint of a disintegrating state. Moreover, a deep change in the socioeconomic order must appear, at some point, on the surface of the historical record, in the form of provinces splitting away, or grandees refusing to obey direct imperial orders, toppling emperors, forming their own independent foreign policy, or the state being unable to carry out its basic functions. Yet none of that happened. The troubles of the second half of the sixth century had other, more obvious causes, including military defeat, the plague, and the overextension (not the contraction) of state activity. Justinian was already feeling the pinch in the late 530s. Instead of state disintegration, we are dealing with a ruler pushing into the margins in search of greater efficiencies, driven to secure ever more resources by mounting ambitions. The reform legislation thus reflects a state that is seeking to extend its reach even further into the provinces, thereby eroding the marginal corruption that had always been part of the system, if only on the periphery. Of course local landlords had infringed on crown land in Cappadocia, and hired thugs or soldiers to bully their neighbors. This was not new. But Justinian, who wanted "nothing to be overlooked, confused, or ambiguous,"[105] was targeting these previously tolerated abuses and inefficiencies. More than any previous emperor, he deployed law as an instrument of his will on a granular level. This was a high-water mark for Roman law as an instrument of governance, not a sign of collapse.

An inscription from Hadrianopolis (northwest Asia Minor) records a set of instructions sent by the emperor, via an officer of the imperial guard, to the bishop and big landowners of the city. There had, apparently, been some foul play and, after an investigation by imperial agents, the grandees were ordered to disband their "club-wielding cavalry" and limit themselves to ten unarmed retainers apiece. This evidence is usually taken as proof of anarchy in the provinces, but it is likely that such violence was normal and we see it now in detail only because of Justinian's interventions. It is also worth noting the baroque excess of the officer's name, which was common in this era among state officials. Between the "Flavius" and his name (Ioannes) it ran as follows: "*Flavius*, [Who is Loyal to] the Savior, Virgin Mary, [the angels] Michael and Gabriel, [and saints] Ioannes and Theodoros, [A Descendant of] Niketas, Theodoros, Bonos, Eutropios, and Olympios, *Ioannes* the *skribon* of the Great Palace."[106]

As for the house of Apion, recent scholarship has cut it significantly down to size. It turns out that the Apions, who were high officials resident in the capital, were collecting taxes on behalf of the state from many other landowners, large and small, through their agents in the Egyptian nomes, thus the taxes that they paid to the state did not all come from their private holdings. They were now carrying out the duties of tax collectors, but were also paying their fair share of the tax on their personal lands, not less. For all that they were locally powerful, the Apions were not wealthy on a scale to worry an emperor: they were just wealthy enough to be useful. According to one argument, the Apions' liquid assets were generated by the moneychanging operations of tax collecting, which were profitable if carried out on a large scale, though other interpretations have them produce crops in bulk for the market.[107] Emperors were not worried about the Apions, who were servants of the imperial will, fully integrated into the court system of titles and ranks. Indeed, the (hyperbolic) argument in Prokopios' *Secret History* is that the state was fatally oppressing the wealthy, not that Justinian was allowing imperial power to atrophy. No feudalization was happening here.[108]

Justinian's complaints reveal that an increasing number of provincials were expecting imperial institutions to provide and enforce justice. This was a structural feature of the New Roman empire, which was responsive to its subjects' demands for justice. As early as the 450s, the emperor Marcian had noted that "you see long lines of persons who arrive [at New Rome] not only from neighboring provinces but from the farthest borders of the Roman world, coming together and bringing complaints against their adversaries."[109] In 539, Justinian instituted a magistracy for the capital, the *quaesitor* ("inquirer" or "inquisitor"), whose primary job was to interview all new arrivals or non-locals about their business in the City. If it was legal business, the *quaesitor* was to expedite it by pressuring the relevant judges or local parties to resolve the dispute quickly so that these people could be sent off. Meanwhile, some of them were put up in a hostel prepared by the imperial couple for this purpose. Justinian reveals that many of these litigants were farmers and even *coloni* who came to the capital to sue their landlords. This was not a society in which the poor had no recourse.

But many were coming to stay. At this time, Constantinople had reached its capacity of around half a million or more. It was consuming enormous amounts of grain, and over 2,000 tons of salt per year, and burning over 250,000 tons of wood. Justinian was putting the brakes on further growth. Indirect evidence reveals that the *quaesitor* ethnically profiled Aramaic and Coptic speakers to identify non-residents, and Prokopios says that the office also cracked down on heretics and homosexuals.[110] In 535, Justinian had created another new magistracy, "the *praetor* of the people," to deal with crime, including astrology and (again) homosexuality. A deacon of Constantinople was arrested and interrogated by the *praetor* for astrology or apostasy from Christianity.[111]

As with the provincial reforms, the creation of these offices was due not to a sudden explosion of criminality in the capital but rather to Justinian's impatience with deviation and disorder.

Justinian's buildings

Among the duties of the *quaesitor* was to round up beggars. If they were natives of the capital and able-bodied, they were assigned to the "public works engineers, bakery managers, or market gardeners."[112] Justinian needed a workforce for his projects. During his long reign, he rebuilt many churches in the capital, especially Hagia Sophia and St. Eirene, just to the north of Hagia Sophia; the Holy Apostles, rededicated in 550; the Virgin at Blachernai, just outside the walls, which became an important shrine in later centuries; and the hospital of Sampson, situated between Hagia Sophia and St. Eirene.[113] The Holy Apostles was architecturally influential. Its shape was that of a cross with domes on the arms and at the central intersection. While the church is lost today, replaced by the Fatih mosque, the basilica of San Marco in Venice is based on it. Justinian's secular constructions included a new Chalke Gatehouse for the palace. This was no mere gate but a spacious vestibule with a dome whose mosaic depicted Justinian and Theodora in the center, surrounded by senators, and Belisarios fighting Goths and Vandals on either side.[114] Justinian rebuilt the adjacent Senate House, which was also destroyed in the Nika Insurrection. On the other side of the Augoustaion square, he excavated the Basilica Stoa to create the Basilica Cistern, called the Yerebatan Sarayı today (or "Sunken Palace"). It is about 140 meters long and 65 wide, and its roof is supported by twelve rows of 28 columns, for a total of 336 (see Figure 23). Work began in 528, the cistern was finally roofed over in 541, and the Stoa was rebuilt on top.[115]

Justinian also implemented an extensive program of fortification across the frontiers, upgrading the defenses of cities and military installations. We know a few of his military engineers: Victorinos, who worked primarily in the Balkans; and Chryses of Alexandria and Theodoros, at Daras.[116] Theodoros was also sent by Justinian in 531 to Jerusalem to complete the Nea Ekklesia ("New Church") in honor of the Virgin. Its construction, in a prominent location of the city, had

Figure 23 Basilica Cistern (aka Yerebatan Saray, Istanbul)
Shutterstock/Sergey Dzyuba

begun under Anastasius, but had stalled. It was now completed in 543. As the hill on which the church stood was insufficient for the edifice that he was planning, Theodoros changed the urban landscape by building huge underground vaults to support the enlarged design: he made the hill bigger by quarrying blocks from nearby hills. Moreover, the city's boulevard was extended so that the Nea Ekklesia, which dominated Jerusalem's skyline, could be connected to the church of the Holy Sepulcher just to the north. Justinian vanquished Solomon in Solomon's own city. The Nea has mostly disappeared, but it would be historically gratifying if elements from it were used to build the Dome of the Rock, as has been proposed.[117]

The finances of the empire were by now so concentrated that monumental architecture required imperial approval and subvention. "During his reign," wrote Prokopios, "it was not possible for any church to be built or restored without imperial funds, not only in Byzantion but throughout the empire."[118] Justinian thereby gained credit for all major projects, for example the new cruciform basilica of St. John the Theologian that was built outside Ephesos, which was possibly a gift to the leading Chalcedonian theologian and bishop, Hypatios. Monograms of Justinian and Theodora and epigrams in their honor duly adorned the building.[119] The last of the emperor's major new constructions was the fortified monastery of St. Catherine at Sinai, which was likely begun in the 540s and finished after Theodora died in 548, probably in the early 550s. Directly above the apse of the church is a row of medallions of Old Testament figures. The central one is David: his crown bears a cross and the face is that of Justinian.[120]

It was during Justinian's reign that the public spaces of Constantinople were finally oriented around Christian buildings, which now overshadowed the pagan architecture of Constantine and Theodosius I. Cityscapes throughout Romanía received the imprint of Justinian's grandiose Christianity. At Mesembria on the Black Sea, the builders used bricks stamped with the words "Justinian Who Loves to Build."[121] The glaring exception was Egypt, which was punished for dissenting from the emperor's theology and did not receive largesse. Justinian's contribution to Alexandria was a wall to protect the grain supply from protesting citizens.[122]

The decade before 542 was a high point of centralized imperial power. Justinian was the last emperor who had the means to operate on such a scale. But he lived to see his "greater flowering" wither before it could blossom.

13

"Death Has Entered Our Gates" (540–565)

Fortune had smiled on Justinian during the first part of his reign, but would turn against him after 540. Setbacks became the norm, war came to the empire on all fronts, and plague decimated the population. At the end of the decade, Prokopios wrote that "the entire earth was drenched with human blood, a constant stream that was being poured out by almost all the Romans and the barbarians."[1]

The first setback was in motion already as Belisarios was bringing Wittigis and his treasury to Constantinople in 540. The shah Khusrow ended the Endless Peace and invaded the Roman empire, whose eastern provinces, he knew, were defenseless. Khusrow had been lobbied by the Goths in Italy, who wanted him to distract the empire in the east, and by Armenians outraged by the character of Justinian's governors. The main enticement for him was surely the prospect of easy and abundant plunder: the Roman east had not been ravaged by the Persians in almost three centuries. As a pretext, Khusrow alleged that Justinian was trying to suborn the Persian Saracens under al-Mundhir, a charge that, Prokopios says, was true. It was in Justinian's character to break something that was working well enough in the hope of making it better.[2]

In the spring of 540, Khusrow marched up the Euphrates and entered the empire, embarking upon a fairly leisurely tour of plunder and extortion. On his way to Antioch, he sacked Soura and Beroia (Aleppo) while allowing Hierapolis to purchase its safety. The Roman forces could not resist him, as part of the field army had been sent to the west (to North Africa and Italy), while the local defense forces were scattered, overwhelmed, and caught off-guard. In June, Khusrow attacked Antioch and breached a weak point in its wall on the hill overlooking the city. He sacked the city, burned it, and hauled thousands of its citizens away as captives. He then went down to the coast, where he bathed in the Mediterranean and sacrificed to his gods. He returned to Persia via Apameia, where he received another payoff, plundered the churches, and held games in the hippodrome like a Roman emperor, siding with the Greens because Justinian was a Blue. He also extorted money from Chalkis, Edessa, Konstantine, and Daras. The shah performed his religion in the Romans' face, demonstrating that the Christian god was powerless to stop him, and refused to accept ransom from the people of Karrai, even though they offered it, on the grounds that they were "of the old faith."

When the shah returned to Persia, he founded a new city, Khusrow's Better Antioch, where he resettled his captives along with artwork from their city; in the 570s they still numbered about 30,000. He commissioned a mosaic or painting for his palace in Ktesiphon depicting his conquest, which still survived in the ninth century.[3] Through his treachery, and for the sake of a short-term cash-grab, Khusrow had expended the last reserves of goodwill that existed between the two states. His expedition was the greatest humiliation that Rome had suffered since the third century, although it had cost more money than lives. Worse than being defeated, the empire had failed to even mount a defense, a point that Prokopios drove home through the repeated image of bishops groveling for mercy before a cruel heathen king. Prokopios also says that during the peace Justinian had furloughed the frontier soldiers in the east (*limitanei*), possibly only those in Palestine; indeed, some military installations appear to have been abandoned.[4] Justinian's dreams of empire in the west had created a nightmare in the east, as he failed to realize that Khusrow was just as duplicitous, aggressive, and opportunistic as he was.

Khusrow struck another major blow in 541. The Laz too had come to resent the avarice and harshness of Justinian's officials, vices that Prokopios was not afraid to disclose in his public history of the wars. The Laz defected to Persia, and they helped a Persian army reach, attack, and seize the fortress of Petra on the Black Sea. Petra, renamed Petra Iustiniana, was the key to the Roman occupation. This gave the Persians potential access to Asia Minor and, with a fleet, they might even strike against Constantinople itself. Belisarios had meanwhile arrived in the east and raided Persian territory, but accomplished little.[5] It was at this point that Justinian's inner circle began to disintegrate.

The first, "classic" phase of the reign was made possible by a trusted team of talented associates: Ioannes the Cappadocian in finance as prefect, Tribonian in law as *quaestor*, Belisarios in war as general, the scholar and historian Petros the patrician in diplomacy as *magister officiorum*, and Theodora in various aspects of domestic policy. It is fascinating to observe that every single member of Justinian's inner circle was a provincial, except for Theodora. This team now broke apart. Theodora hated Ioannes the Cappadocian—she was not alone in this—because he had bad-mouthed her to the emperor. In May, 541, with the help of Belisarios' wife Antonina, she engineered his downfall, by luring him into a plot and then exposing him. The Cappadocian was ordained as a priest, exiled to Kyzikos and then Egypt, and his considerable properties were confiscated (much as had happened to the prefect Cyrus a century earlier).[6] This came as a relief to many, but something was also going wrong with Belisarios. He was recalled to Constantinople at the end of the 541 campaign, then sent back to the east posthaste when Khusrow returned in 542, then recalled back to the City after a standoff between the two armies. This erratic approach, which undercut the eastern defenses, bespoke distrust. Prokopios tells a lurid tale: Antonina was having an affair and her patron Theodora, in exchange for Antonina's assistance in the prefect's downfall, was harassing Belisarios.[7] He would never again achieve successes like those of the 530s. Then, in 542, Tribonian died and Justinian himself fell seriously ill. The plague had come to Constantinople.

The Justinianic plague

We have many accounts of the contagion known today as the Justinianic Plague—a name that, uniquely, Justinian himself did not claim. The most detailed description of its symptoms and social impact is owed to the scientific precision of Prokopios, who admitted that no pattern could be found behind who lived and who died. An initial fever was followed by the eruption of bubos across the body, which led to a coma, delirium, and death—or recovery. Doctors could devise no remedy, nor could they predict who would succumb. The doctors themselves did not contract it from their patients, meaning that this plague had limited pneumatic transmission (through the air via respiration). Prokopios also observed that the plague traveled: ground zero in the empire was Pelousion, Egypt, in 541, from where it spread to Alexandria, Palestine, and Constantinople by 542. It moved along the coasts and only later penetrated the interior. Prokopios made no further progress toward identifying its vectors.[8]

Today we know that the pathogen behind this outbreak was the bacterium *Yersinia pestis*, whose DNA has been recovered from victims' remains.[9] It lodges in lice or fleas that are carried by rats, which travel on ships or otherwise accompany human mobility. People are infected by the fleas or (more rarely) by consuming infected animals, so transmission was invisible. Its origins are debated: likely Central Asia, but Africa and south Asia have also been proposed. It spread quickly throughout the empire and as far west as England, possibly Ireland. It became endemic to this region, recurring every few years for two centuries, until ca. 750, though its outbreaks were uneven in time and geography. Many centuries later, a relative of this bacterium caused the Black Death.

Sudden mass death disrupted social routines in many ways, for example regarding inheritance and burial. Prokopios says that, at its peak, the plague was killing more than 10,000 people a day in Constantinople, the equivalent of one Nika Insurrection every few days. Justinian also fell ill but recovered, according to the principle enunciated by Prokopios that the plague "picked out the worst people and let them live." The emperor sent out teams to collect and dispose of the bodies, which were so numerous that they were eventually just dumped across the Golden Horn at Sykai, so the odor of death wafted onto the City when the wind blew out of the north. The crisis was so acute that even the Blues and Greens patched up their differences to help with the disposal.[10] Paradoxical as it may sound to us, some called the plague "God's compassion," on the grounds that it punished sin and was thus salutary, as it improved the moral hygiene of the world and spared people from the torments of the afterlife.[11] Some more straightforwardly called it "the wrath of God." In others it induced a crisis of faith. The Church historian Euagrios, who wrote in the early 590s, was infected as a child, during the initial outbreak, but survived. In later outbreaks, he lost his wife, many children, and servants. Euagrios found it hard to understand why this had happened to him and "not to pagans with many children." He was saved from these thoughts by the second St. Symeon the Stylite, who lived near Antioch. The saint's life tells it more bluntly: Euagrios was tempted by blasphemy because his daughter had died while the children of a pagan neighbor had not.[12]

The most terrifying account of "God's mercy" is given by the Monophysite author John of Ephesos. During the initial outbreak he was moving from Syria to the capital. In language laden with horrific Biblical associations, he talks of corpses split open and rotting in the street; houses that became like tombs when everyone inside died; ships of the dead carried adrift on the waves; people throwing up pus; deserted villages; flocks roaming free; and crops rotting in the fields. "Death has come up into our windows, it has entered our gates." John spun his account into an implausible morality tale, wherein everyone who committed a crime during the outbreak was instantly struck down. He says that 16,000 died each day in Constantinople at the peak, and 300,000 corpses were removed (230,000 were counted, beyond that a guess). Business stopped and food became scarce. John was especially distressed at the popular belief that the plague was carried by monks, or by demons dressed like monks, causing people to flee at the sight of them or utter incantations against them.[13] However, society did not scapegoat Jews, heretics, or pagans, and turned grimly to the practical matter of clearing streets and homes of corpses.

Near Gaza, the reclusive ascetic leader Barsanouphios, known as "the Great Old Man," was asked to pray for the world's survival. He replied that the world's existence was guaranteed during this crisis by the prayers of three holy men—Ioannes in Rome, Elias in Corinth, and "one other in the vicinity of Jerusalem" (guess who). Their prayers converged like rays at the "gateway of the spiritual altar of the Father of Lights."[14]

How many people died? And what impact did mass death have on society and the state? The literary sources imply a massive death toll, although they also paradoxically suggest that it had a relatively small impact, as their narratives simply pick up where they left off before digressing on the plague, and carry on as if nothing fundamental had changed. Among modern historians there have been maximalists, who put the loss at 40–60% of the overall population, aligning it with the later Black Death (caused by a related pathogen), and moderates, who argue that the impact was much smaller and that the sources rhetorically exaggerate the death toll. There are no minimalists in this debate.[15] Both have strong arguments, but a more limited demographic impact seems likelier.

A sudden demographic reduction would make labor scarcer and so more expensive; land would be abandoned; rents and taxes would be severely reduced; and military recruitment would become more difficult. There is evidence for all this after 542, but only as limited adjustments to a generally stable system. In March, 542, referring to "the encircling presence of death that has spread to every region," Justinian legislated on the adjudication of disputes between bankers and the heirs of their debtors. However, most of the edict's regulations have nothing to do with the plague and stem from Justinian's ongoing regulation of banking law.[16] Two years later, he legislated against workmen demanding higher wages ("avarice"). But Justinian's officials had previously colluded with trade groups, allowing them to set higher prices, even "monopolies," so the rise in costs that the emperor was now decrying was not due exclusively to the plague.[17] He also made it marginally easier to alienate Church lands that were not producing revenue and allowed lowering rents on them, which is consistent with fewer available tenants. He issued a long edict on tax collection, focusing mostly on his usual concerns—official corruption and making the process transparent—though he pays passing attention to abandoned lands and how to reassign their taxes (and ownership) to neighbors. He does not refer to the plague, and such issues were a standard imperial concern: Justinian had legislated on the reassignment of abandoned land in 535.[18]

Moreover, Prokopios says that the emperor did *not* reduce his tax demands after the plague, expecting neighbors to pick up the slack.[19] This must have been an onerous burden, to be sure, but it could not realistically have exceeded the order of 10%. We cannot believe that half the population started cultivating, and paying taxes on, the lands of the (departed) other half. Moreover, the plague is nearly completely absent from the Egyptian papyri, where agriculture and tax-collecting continued as before, with no evident disruption. The surviving tax schedules show that the city of Aphrodite was paying higher taxes (in absolute numbers) in the late 540s than it had been in the 520s. The tax rate was climbing during the sixth century, and the grain contributions of Egyptian farmers remained steady, which together refute the notion of a widespread depopulation, for example the fantastic claim by John of Ephesos that "the majority of people died in Egypt and it became desolate of inhabitants."[20]

During the contagion, Justinian continued to legislate on divorce, farmer marriages, judges, and litigants, making no reference to plague.[21] Thus, the overwhelming impression from the legal and documentary evidence is business-as-usual, with some tweaks to address a death rate that was higher than usual but not catastrophic. This is not the image of a regime coping with the sudden loss of half its subjects. We have to conclude, then, that the literary sources exaggerated the plague's impact, or that it was much higher in the cities, where their authors lived, and lower in the countryside, which produced the food and taxes. As the plague spread out from the cities, farmers may have feared going into town, which caused urban famines. Constantinople may have been hit harder, but even so the logistical challenge of feeding it did not diminish. In 545/6, the Egyptian harvest was not abundant and grain had to be brought in from Asia Minor and Thrace to feed the City's restless populace.[22]

When first proposed, the moderate position pointed to the lack of mass graves and paucity of inscriptions referring to the plague (one, maybe two). Graves connected to the plague have now been proposed, though it is debatable whether they should be called mass graves.[23] We would expect those under any scenario. A different argument for a lower impact rests on the continued functioning of state institutions and activities that would have ground to a halt by a 50% reduction of revenue and manpower, and would have been crippled by a 30% reduction. When the Black Death wiped out half the people in Europe, everything came to a halt: war, justice, business, trade. The basic infrastructure collapsed. Elites went into hiding until the plague left, and when they returned they had to reconstitute the status quo. This is not what we observe in the sixth century.

In every field, the Roman state continued and even expanded its operations. In the 540s, Justinian was prosecuting *four* theaters of war simultaneously—in North Africa, Italy, the Balkans, and the east—while continuing his program of fortifications and church building across the empire. This was an unprecedented level of engagement for any emperor in the history of the empire, which normally had difficulty waging war on two fronts, much less four. Justinian definitely faced revenue shortfalls. He frequently failed to pay his soldiers on time, which caused them to mutiny, desert, or defect, but this was a problem that existed before the plague. It was exacerbated in the 540s, possibly due to revenue shortfalls caused by plague but also because of the massive war effort. It has been suggested that, in response to budget shortfalls caused by the plague, Justinian issued a gold coin 17% lighter than normal to accompany the regular issue of full-weight solidi, but these lighter coins were first issued before the plague.[24] In the 540s and 550s, the plague changed no ruler's strategy. Khusrow allegedly refrained from invading in late 542 out of fear of the plague, but it did not change his strategy thereafter.[25] Preemptive fear of the plague is not the same as an inability to muster resources because of its effects. In texts, the plague appears as a self-contained digression: cut it out, and nothing seems amiss in the narrative of events after it. Roman society did not buckle under or have to regroup on new terms. It was merely under more strain.

In 543, Justinian appropriated one of the colossal bronze equestrian statues from the forum of Theodosius I and repurposed it as his own, setting it at the top of a tall column encased in brass and erected in the Augoustaion, adjacent to Hagia Sophia. This statue of Justinian was now the highest point in the City and cut to the front of the procession of imperial columns—Constantine's,

Theodosius' (replaced by Anastasius), and Arcadius'—that stretched westward along the Mese. It was intended as a statement of military triumph, at precisely the moment when the empire was in deep trouble. Emperors traditionally ramped up the propaganda of victory after serious defeats. Down to the fifteenth century, this column was the City's main landmark after Hagia Sophia. In his panegyric of Justinian's buildings, Prokopios says that it made the emperor look like Achilles, or "the star of Autumn," an allusion to Achilles' killing spree in the *Iliad*, where that star "is wrought as a sign of evil and brings on a great fever for unfortunate mortals," a clever way to associate the column with plague and the emperor with death.[26]

Justinian's later wars

While Justinian was ill with the plague in 542, Belisarios was denounced to Theodora for saying that he would not accept the court's choice for the succession if the emperor died, which she took as a slight against *her*. With Justinian's approval he was stripped of his retinue and *bucellarii*, who were dispersed among the regular army units, and he lived in disgrace.[27] The Romans and Persians were now fighting on multiple fronts. In late 542—at the height of the plague's initial outbreak—a Roman army of 30,000 invaded Persian Armenia but was defeated in an ambush. Meanwhile, Khusrow was eager to capture Edessa, in part because the city boasted that Christ had pledged that it would never be captured. He besieged Edessa for two months in 543, with elephants and a large siege mound, but without success, and agreed to leave in exchange for 500 lbs of gold. In 545, Justinian and Khusrow agreed on a peace for five years, limited to Mesopotamia, which cost the Romans an additional 2,000 lbs of gold.[28] Meanwhile, the war in Lazica was dragging on, especially after 547, when the Laz defected back to Rome because they were oppressed by the Persians and terrified of the shah's alleged plan to remove them from their homeland and repopulate it with Persian colonists. The war in Lazica, a major and expensive conflict, was recorded in detail by Prokopios and his continuer Agathias (writing around 580). For a full decade (547–557) it was hard fought between large armies numbering 20,000 or more on either side.

In 551, Justinian and Khusrow renewed the armistice for another five years, excluding Lazica; the Romans had to pay 2,600 lbs of gold, which the emperor preferred to hand over in one lump sum so that he would not appear to be paying annual tribute to the Persians. The sum, moreover, cannot have been a great burden on the treasury, as only one supplementary tax called the *aerikon*, or "air tax," pulled in 3,000 lbs gold annually. Even so, paying the Persians anything was unpopular.[29] Meanwhile, the Saracen allies of the Romans and Persians had also been engaged in mutual hostilities, which were apparently sequestered from those between the two empires. In the late 540s, the Persian Saracen leader, al-Mundhir, captured a son of the Roman Saracen leader, al-Harith, and sacrificed him to his goddess "Aphrodite," but in 554 al-Harith defeated and killed al-Mundhir, to the general relief of the Roman east, which he had so often raided and plundered. Finally, the ongoing war in Lazica was brought to an end by another armistice in 557, pending negotiations for a genuine peace.[30]

The truces of 551 and 557 were negotiated by a Persian nobleman named Yazdgushnasp, who came to Constantinople with his family and a full retinue. We have a detailed set of protocols, drawn up by the office of the *magister officiorum* Petros, to arrange for the reception of a senior Persian ambassador. They specify which bureau pays for what expense; how many horses and mules are assigned to his escort; who greets him where; the furnishings of his quarters, and which bureau provides the mattresses and which the pots. This rare glimpse into the workings of the administration reminds us how many moving parts had to be synchronized and how minutely the reception was choreographed, to the point where it resembled an intricate ballet of formal exchanges, with participants decked out in colorful court silks. Prokopios, by contrast, was outraged that the Persians were given free run of the City and its inhabitants, with no handlers to watch them.[31]

During these years, Justinian scored a major victory, but not through arms. He was long irritated that so much Roman gold went to Persian merchants for the purchase of silk. With the assistance of some monks who traveled on his behalf to western China, he managed to obtain silkworms with which to launch his own domestic production. Contrary to a later legend, the worms were not smuggled into the empire in hollow canes. Their ecology is specific, and sericulture, which requires mulberry tree plantations, took years of maturation and expansion before product could be put on the market. This took place in the late 540s, when silk manufacture, weaving, and sale were decreed as imperial monopolies, with capped prices. This was a double windfall for Justinian: his subjects no longer had to pay greatly inflated prices to Persian middlemen, exporting bullion from the empire in the process, and the treasury now made a handsome profit off the need of the imperial elite to bedeck itself in colorful silk garments. This industry probably paid for much of the protection money that the emperor periodically delivered to the shah after 545, if not more.[32] It also positioned Constantinople to dispense prestige to the broader Christian world, as part of its repertoire of soft power, for centuries. The creation of this industry was one of Justinian's greatest successes. The emperor accordingly dedicated to Hagia Sophia a purple and gold altar cloth made of silk that depicted Christ, Peter, and Paul, with scenes of the emperors' deeds along the hem.[33]

The east was free of war after 545, as the brunt of the Roman-Persian war was shifted to the Laz and their neighbors in the Caucasus. By contrast, war was in full swing in Justinian's two new acquisitions, North Africa and Italy. The former had been capably governed by Solomon, who simultaneously filled the offices of *magister militum* and praetorian prefect. The quiet years of his administration came to an end in 544, when his nephew Sergios, who governed Tripolis, invited some leaders of the Leuathai tribe of the Moors to a banquet but, when they raised grievances, he slaughtered them. This led to a war with the Moors in which Solomon was killed. Justinian appointed Sergios in Solomon's place. According to Prokopios, Sergios was stupid, immature, a braggart, and a coward, and he lusted after the wives and money of others, but he was backed by Theodora because he was angling to marry Antonina's granddaughter. Sergios stayed in command for one year before Justinian recalled him, but it was long enough to destabilize the entire prefecture. The Moors began annual raids, plundering and killing on a large scale, and they were abetted by another short-lived Roman mutiny in 545, which briefly took Carthage. The Moors were defeated in 548, after a series of costly battles, by Ioannes Troglita, a career officer who had served under Belisarios. Troglita is famous because his victory was celebrated by an epic poem in Latin, in the style of Vergil, written by Corippus, which also includes a digression on the ravages of the plague in North Africa. For his part, Prokopios ended his account on a grim note: "thus the North Africans who survived, few as they were in number and extremely poor, at long last managed to find a vestige of peace."[34]

Worse was in store for Italy. Stunned but not defeated by the war of 536–540, which saw Belisarios enter Ravenna in triumph, the Goths began to regroup and soon chose a new warrior-king, Totila (aka Baduila). A brilliant strategist, he realized that the eastern Romans were spread thin across the peninsula, were still outnumbered, had not yet established a close relationship with the Italians, and were effectively leaderless. In a series of lightning campaigns, he quickly overran most of Italy and confined the Romans to a number of fortified cities, including Ravenna and Rome. He took Rome in late 546, lost it to Belisarios the following year, and retook it in 550. The Roman command remained divided, undermanned, and underfunded, even when Belisarios was sent back to Italy in 544–549. Having been stripped of his *bucellarii*, with whom he had conquered Italy the first time, he recruited an army of 4,000 in Thrace, allegedly with his own money. Prokopios says that his former boss accomplished nothing in Italy during the next five years. He just sailed from one fort to the next, afraid to face Totila in battle.[35] While we know that the plague reached and "devastated" Italy by 543,[36] and presumably affected both Goths and Romans, it had no discernable impact on the war. In 550, Totila overran Sicily too. By 551 he had a fleet, with which he took Sardinia and Corsica and raided western Greece. Prokopios presents the Gothic king as a noble and heroic leader, who made many peace overtures to the emperor, all of them scornfully rebuffed.[37] For a decade, Justinian refused to consider peace but also failed to end the war.

Theodora's vendettas caused harm here too. Among the most skilled officers in Italy was Ioannes, a nephew of the rebel Vitalianus, but he failed to join up with Belisarios at a critical juncture because he was engaged to a daughter of Justinian's cousin Germanus, whom Theodora hated and had blacklisted. For daring to cross her, she had threatened to kill Ioannes, which made him wary of Belisarios and Antonina (who usually campaigned together).[38] When Theodora died in 548, opportunities opened up for those in her black book. Germanus was appointed to command the Italian war in 550 and given large sums to recruit soldiers in Thrace and Illyricum. He also married Matasuintha, the granddaughter of Theodoric, whose presence on the Roman side might induce some Goths to defect.[39] Germanus died before the expedition could set out, but at least Justinian had found the determination to prosecute the war.

In 551, the emperor appointed Narses to lead the invasion of Italy. Narses was a Persarmenian eunuch and head of the imperial household staff. The choice seems unusual, but over the years Narses had served Justinian and Theodora on a number of sensitive missions, diplomatic, ecclesiastical, and even military. He was loyal to a fault, having led a contingent of soldiers in the massacre that ended the Nika Insurrection. He now refused to lead the Italian expedition unless Justinian provided him with enough men and money to do the job. When those were given, Narses mustered a "huge" force, including units from the armies of Constantinople (i.e., the praesentals), Thrace, and Illyricum; new recruits; 5,500 Lombards; over 3,000 Heruls; many Huns; Persians; 400 Gepids; and other Roman commanders, including one Ioannes "the Eater," who brought their own forces. We do not know the size of the army with which he set out, but at a later point in Italy he led 18,000 men, a figure that does not include all the Romans under arms in Italy.[40] Narses was a superb strategist and tactician. He led his army into Italy and, in late June, 552, crushed Totila in battle at Taginae (Busta Gallorum), near Rome. The Gothic king died of a wound that he suffered while trying to escape. His people continued to resist under new leaders, but were decisively defeated by Narses in the following years. After that, only pockets held out, Verona and Brescia until 562.[41] But the conflict was effectively over by 554. After twenty years of constant war, the kingdom of the Goths was abolished, and so were the Ostrogothic people. The palace eunuch, an old man with a slight build, sharp mind, and even temperament, later came to be known as The Hammer of the Goths.[42]

After twenty years of bitter war, Italy was in shambles. Thousands had perished. Agriculture and trade had been disrupted, causing regional famines, and cities had changed hands many times. The population of Naples was massacred when the Romans took the city in 536, and that of Milan when it was taken by the Goths in 539. Rome was mostly abandoned during the sieges and countersieges of 546–550. Property had changed hands frequently or violently, and ownership titles were contested. Many armies had passed through each area requisitioning supplies from the locals. To top it off, armies of Frankish raiders had invaded Italy, in 539 and 553–554, taking advantage of the war to plunder and, on one occasion, perform mass human sacrifices on a bridge over the Po river. The peninsula's archaeological profile after the war is poorer for all social classes.[43] Italy needed peace to recover, which Narses now provided. In 554, Justinian issued a document to govern the peninsula, which was a compilation of legal decisions that scholars call the "Pragmatic Sanction." It accepted the validity of the acts of the Gothic kings down to Theodahad (d. 536), but nothing after that, and certainly not the grants made by the "utterly abominable tyrant" (i.e., Totila). Justinian's primary concern was to regulate the adjudication of property disputes. Land and flocks had changed hands, and even sections of buildings had been removed, which now had to be returned or paid for. Justinian also imposed his tax system and disseminated his *Corpus* and subsequent legislation as the law of the land.[44] Italy had once been the center of the empire and Thrace a backward province. Now, Italy was a ruined periphery and the center was Constantinople, trying to restore Romanness to its former motherland.

The Romans faced a different strategic challenge in the Balkans, where they were mostly on the defensive, but not against a peer state such as Persia. Here they suffered a series of raids by a variety of uncoordinated and unpredictable groups from north of the Danube, including Huns, Bulgars, and Slavs. These events do not make for a coherent narrative. Until the 540s, when the attacks intensified, the field armies of Thrace and Illyricum generally held their own against the invaders, with occasional losses. Departing from precedent, Justinian frequently appointed recent arrivals from beyond the border, men such as Godila, Askum, Mundo, and Chilboud, to lead Roman armies as *magistri militum*, and they served him well and loyally, even to the death. Such a concession had never been made to, say, Alaric and Theodoric, even when they were appointed *magistri*, but that was because they had their own ethnic armies that they frequently let loose on the Roman provinces. Justinian also spent large sums to fortify the Balkans. In 536, he reformed aspects of the administration to facilitate military logistics. He created a "quaestorship of the army" (*quaestura exercitus*), grouping two Danubian provinces (Moesia and Scythia) with the provinces of the Aegean Islands, Caria, and Cyprus, in order to streamline the provisioning of the former by the latter. Aegean amphorae begin to appear in large numbers along the Danube border, almost certainly linked to this reform.[45]

But the raids worsened. Huns invaded in 539/40 and again in 544, ravaging the Balkans between the Adriatic and Constantinople and seizing captives by the thousands. One group even got past the defenses of Thermopylae to plunder Greece while another got past the wall of the Chersonese—by wading around it in the surf—crossed the Hellespont, and briefly plundered the area around Abydos.[46] The Illyrian field army was distracted at that time by the war against the Goths in Dalmatia and Italy. The later 540s also witnessed an upsurge in raids from across the Danube by pagan Sklavenoi, the first Slavic speakers to appear in the historical record. This was partly because in 545 the emperor had sided with their enemies, the Antai, also Slavic speakers. Justinian was playing a complicated game with the geostrategic situation along the Danubian border.

A complex and fragile network of alliances had emerged there by the late 530s. The Heruls (a Germanic people) had settled in the area around Singidunum (modern Belgrade). Under Anastasius, they had agreed to provide the empire with auxiliary soldiers, of whom they could muster a few thousand.[47] Just beyond them were the Gepids, a more formidable power, able to muster the equivalent of a Roman field army. They had seized Sirmium in 536 and alternately attacked and sided with the Romans. To the west of the Gepids, between the Sava and Drava rivers in Pannonia, settled the Lombards, who were more firmly allied with the empire. In the lower Danube, the lands north of the river were occupied by the Sklavenoi and Antai. Prokopios, who calls their language "utterly barbarous," depicts them as decentralized, almost leaderless groups, but they were able to field large war bands and even to go to war against each other.[48] Farther east, two powers had emerged north of the Black Sea, the Kutrigur Huns between the Dnieper and Don rivers, and the Utigur Huns to their east, north of the Caucasus. In the 540s, Justinian was likely paying subsidies to *all* these groups, but he also took sides in their disputes, helping the Lombards against the Gepids, the Antai against the Sklavenoi, and the Utigurs against the Kutrigurs. In each case, he sided with the more distant people against the nearer ones.[49]

In the late 540s, this precarious balance was destabilized, exposing the empire to attack. It was probably Justinian's alliance with the Antai in 545 that provoked the Sklavenoi to invade most years after that. Their war bands roamed across Illyricum and Thrace, targeting the countryside and vulnerable settlements, killing with abandon, taking captives, and occasionally defeating Roman armies. Prokopios highlights their depredations, probably in order to embarrass Justinian's regime. He describes in graphic detail how they executed their victims by impaling them through the buttocks and intestines on stakes affixed to the ground.[50] Also, because of a leadership dispute, most Heruls renounced their loyalty to the empire around 547 and joined the Gepids, who were at odds with the Lombards. As Justinian supported the Lombards, the Gepids offered to ferry raiders across the Danube to distract the empire, including more Sklavenoi and, in 550/1, an army of 12,000 Kutrigurs. They caused extensive damage until Justinian paid the Utigurs to attack the Kutrigurs' homeland from behind and paid the Kutrigur raiders to leave—or stay on as federate soldiers of the empire on the lower Danube. 2,000 took him up on that.[51] This volatile situation was finally resolved in 552, when the Lombards, with imperial support, defeated the Gepids at the battle of Asfeld. The Gepids returned to their previous alliance with the empire and stopped ferrying raiders.[52] Illyricum and Thrace enjoyed a respite.

With a high tolerance for his subjects' suffering, Justinian had played the game of international *Realpolitik* and had won—in the same year, no less, that Narses crushed Totila in Italy. He had deployed cash, diplomacy, patronage, alliances, and, when necessary, his armies in order to maneuver the peoples who ringed his empire in the north and make them less aggressive. The fact that there now was a game of *Realpolitik* to play at all reveals how much had changed in the empire's geopolitical environment. Foreign relations had become more complex, multipolar, and interconnected. Just as a chain reaction of alliances could trigger war in the east from Lazica to the Red Sea, similar links extended from Pannonia to the Caspian Sea. Emperors would henceforth need more than armies, money, and prestige to steer Romanía through the reefs. As their neighbors became more powerful, they needed more sophisticated skills of diplomacy, complex strategic thinking, alliance building, and contingency planning. Justinian proved himself to be a master of the long game, but his subjects wearied of the short-term losses imposed by this strategy. Some, such as Prokopios, believed the emperor's thinking to be flawed: paying barbarians to refrain from raiding only encouraged others to raid in order to secure the same emoluments; and the ongoing search for barbarian mercenaries to send to overseas wars meant that imperial generals were instructed to spare raiders in order to hire them instead.[53] This bucked traditional notions of Roman supremacy. Nevertheless, these policies were, if not valorous, at least cost-effective—unless you lived in the Balkan countryside.

A further surprise was in store for those who thought that the empire was already overextended. Justinian took advantage of a war among the Visigoths in Spain, in which he was invited to intervene, to establish a Roman presence there along the coast. It reached from Cartagena (the capital of his new province, named Spania) to the straits of Gibraltar. The exact date is unclear, but within the years 552–555. We do not know how far inland the new province extended, but by 589, if not upon its creation, it had its own *magister militum*, whose job was to protect it from "hostile barbarians," i.e., the Goths.[54] This Spanish province is overlooked in the Roman sources and we gain only glimpses of it in western texts. It was endowed with the full complement of legal, fiscal, and military administration as the other parts of Romanía, which is what we would expect from Justinian.[55] His empire now encompassed most of the Mediterranean coastline and its trade routes, which continued to stretch as far as Britain. Justinian may not have restored the ancient empire "from one sea to the other," as he hoped, but at least from one end of the inner sea to the other.[56]

No emperor had ever deployed so many armies on active duty on so many fronts. This imposed severe strains, but it reveals that the empire still had a solid infrastructure and resources. The Romans were at war in Italy (536–554), North Africa (544–548), the Balkans (more intensively in 545–552), Mesopotamia

(540–543), Lazica (541–557), and Spain (after 553), and garrisoning those lands even when not fighting in them. Historians have calculated the size of the individual field armies: 20,000 for Oriens; 24,500 for Thrace; between 15,000 and 17,500 for Illyricum; 21,000 for each of the two praesental armies; 15,000 for Armenia; 15,000 for Africa; and 18,000 for Italy, yielding a total of 150,000. This is exactly the figure that Agathias gives for the overall size of Justinian's armies, a striking independent confirmation. However, it is likely that these armies were operating under strength most of the time, and the two praesental armies were likely ghosts, their units having been dispersed to create the new armies of Armenia, Africa, and Italy. Praesental armies are not attested except as dispersed units after Anastasius' Persian war (502–505).[57] Thus, the total would have been significantly lower. Also, the armies had boosted their ratio of cavalry over infantry in order to cope with Huns and the like, to maybe a third or a fourth, and in the field commanders tended to rely more on mounted units, though this did not amount to a revolution in warfare as is sometimes claimed.[58]

Some historians defend Justinian against criticism that his expansionism weakened the core of the empire, and they blame his heirs for mismanaging his legacy. But this reallocation of military strength indicts Justinian's policies: there was a direct correlation between Justinian's aggression in the west and the weak defense of the Balkans and the east. Even some contemporaries believed that the eastern empire was too exposed to attack because so many of its soldiers had been sent to Italy, Africa, Spain, Lazica, and the east. These priorities seemed lopsided. In the mid-540s, soldiers from the Illyrian army serving in Italy slipped away and returned home without leave because they had not been paid and because the Huns were attacking their families back home.[59]

The Three Chapters

Among the many groups that Justinian victimized, there was only one whose views he actually engaged with—the Monophysites—and this was not only because they made up a large proportion of his subjects. Like the Diphysites, they claimed to represent the position of Cyril of Alexandria, and probably had a better claim to it. They insisted on the unity of Christ, a stance that was hard to beat rhetorically, and on the need for the divine to have experienced humanity directly for salvation to be possible. At the conference of 532–533, Justinian told them that, in his view, they were not heretics but had "excessive scruples over detail and certain names that have been put on the diptychs."[60]

Justinian had already proposed a compromise formula, the "theopaschite confession," according to which "one member of the Trinity had experienced human passions" such as pain and death. This was essentially what the Crucified-for-Us, the Monophysite addition to the Trisagion liturgy, had represented, though Chalcedonians rejected it violently under Anastasius. The theopaschite formula was brought to the capital in 519 by some monks from the province of Scythia as a compromise solution. It was predictably denounced by hardline Diphysites such as the Sleepless Monks, and Justinian too was initially opposed to it but was brought around by, of all people, Vitalianus. Justinian tried to persuade pope Hormisdas to accept it, but failed.[61] The Scythian monks were not welcomed warmly in Rome. But Justinian was undeterred. As emperor, he proposed the theopaschite formula at the conference of 532–533; he included it in an edict on the faith of 533, which did not even mention Chalcedon; and he leaned on two popes to agree to it, John II in 534 and Agapetus in 536. They did not object to it, despite the Sleepless Monks' protests. Rome had previously funded them to agitate against the eastern court, but now that the emperors were listening to Rome the popes quickly abandoned the monks. As for Justinian's interventions in Church matters, Agapetus cautiously noted: "we are not hereby recognizing the authority of a layman [Justinian], but confirming that your faith is consistent with the teachings of the fathers."[62]

Justinian, however, was no ordinary layman. Not only was he an emperor, he was the first Christian theologian among emperors and understood the issues as well as any bishop. In 535, he issued a liturgical hymn, based on a text by Severos of Antioch, that alluded to the theopaschite formula.[63] But this approach to the dispute was futile, as became clear in the debacle of Anthimos and Severos, in 536. Ultimately, what divided Diphysites and Monophysites was not theology. The problem of defining a single person who was made up of two ontologically dissimilar elements was equally unsolvable for both sides. The theopaschite formula should have been theologically acceptable to anyone who accepted the Crucified addition, and yet it was rejected by anti-Chalcedonians for the sole reason that it was proposed by Chalcedonians. In reality, the rupture was maintained by the tribal identities that had hardened around narratives, grievances (real or imagined), legalistic interpretations of past Councils, and talismanic names. "Your Council accepted Eutyches, therefore . . ." "But your Council accepted Ibas, therefore . . ."

At the conference of 532–533, Justinian had almost grasped that the issue was not entirely or primarily theological, but still he was personally committed to the polemics that buttressed Chalcedonian theology. He wrote a treatise for the benefit of some Egyptian monks in which he did refer to his opponents, including Severos, as "heretics."[64] He was particularly stung by the accusation that Chalcedonians were "Nestorians." In order to refute it, he condemned three talismans of the old Antiochene School that lent credence to it, namely Theodoros of Mopsouestia, the anti-Cyrillian texts of Theodoretos of Kyrros, and Ibas of Edessa's letter to Maris, collectively known as the Three Chapters (meaning "Headings"). By rejecting them he tried to fashion a new history of the Church that could be accepted by both sides. His "concession" on the Three Chapters would not induce Monophysites to accept Chalcedon; they had told him as much at the conference of 532–533. But it might persuade them that the imperial Church was not heretical, and thus inhibit their ongoing construction of a separatist Church.

The timing is revealing. Justinian had hosted the theological conference of 532–533 immediately after Yuhannan of Tella began to ordain priests. Likewise, he issued his edict condemning the Three Chapters (in 544/5) immediately after the Monophysites began to ordain bishops again.[65] Their rising star, Yakub (Jacob) Baradaios of Edessa, had just then embarked on his long career of spreading the anti-Chalcedonian message and ordaining priests, including bishops, throughout the Roman east (that Church is called Jacobite after him). Dressed in rags, he would sometimes travel up to forty miles a day, which meant that he was usually alone because no one could keep up with him. There was a bounty on his head, so he never lingered in one place. One of the bishops that he appointed (for Ephesos) was the later Monophysite historian John of Ephesos, who wrote his biography.[66] Another missionary was Yuhannan of Hephaistopolis. One time, at Tralleis, Yuhannan secretly ordained fifty priests in the upper gallery of a church while a Chalcedonian service was being performed downstairs; they would come up to him three at a time while John of Ephesos, astonished at the man's daring, held the sacrament.[67] The nominal head of this anti-Chalcedonian Church was Theodosios, the exiled Monophysite patriarch of Alexandria, living under imperial protection in and around Constantinople. In 566 he would be succeeded by John of Ephesos.

The condemnation of the Three Chapters was hardly concession enough for the Monophysites, who needed a full retraction of Chalcedonian history and identity, no less than what the pope had required of them after the Acacian Schism, only in reverse. But before even reaching that stage, Justinian had to persuade the Chalcedonians to condemn the Three Chapters too, and in trying to do so he broke their unity as well. The solution for disunity created more splinter groups.

The eastern patriarchs signed the condemnation, allegedly under duress.[68] But many bishops in Italy, North Africa, and Illyricum balked. Chalcedon had reinstated Theodoretos and Ibas. The slightest change to its decisions implied that the Council was flawed, and if about that then about anything else as well: thus, "no part of it should be open to criticism."[69] Moreover, it was wrong to condemn bishops (such as Theodoros of Mopsouestia) who had died in communion with the Church before all the trouble began, to which Justinian responded that Judas was also condemned posthumously.[70] The key to securing western compliance was pope Vigilius (537–555), who owed his position to Justinian. Rome now learned that the days when popes could dictate terms to the eastern court behind a wall of Gothic arms were over. There were no barriers now. Vigilius was summoned to the capital in 546 and pressured to support the emperor's policies.

This he did, albeit reluctantly, in a series of documents and promises that he made, retracted, revised, and resubmitted. His invitation turned into a form of captivity, and the pope alternated between living in a palace and seeking refuge from imperial violence in churches. "When we realized that we were under guard, we fled in terror during the middle of the night, passing through a thin wall with pain to our feet." One time, when he was yanked away from the altar, he clung to its supports so that the whole thing toppled over, "for he was a big heavy man."[71] The bishop of Rome was painfully relearning what it meant to live under a Roman emperor of the same faith.

Inevitably, the prospect of a new general Council of the Church was raised during these discussions—it would be the Fifth for those who accepted Chalcedon—but by the time it convened in Constantinople in May, 553 it had little to do with the Monophysites. Its purpose was to ratify Justinian's condemnation of the Three Chapters, which had become a goal unto itself. Only a minority of the 150-plus bishops who participated were westerners, and Vigilius refused to attend. Justinian also did not attend the sessions, but the Council predictably confirmed everything that he asked for, including his theological formulations and the anathemas that went with them. At the opening session, a *silentiarius* from the court read out a document through which Justinian instructed the Council precisely what it was to investigate and what its conclusions would be.[72] The deliberations followed the script of Justinian's theological texts. Never before had an emperor dictated his theological will to a Council so directly, and about an issue so futile and irrelevant; even at Chalcedon there had been some debate and some episcopal will. Vigilius at first refused to ratify the Council in the belief that papal authority in doctrinal matters was greater than that of the Councils.[73] No eastern bishop or dignitary took this position seriously enough to answer it. After a few months, during which he held out against pressure and threats, Vigilius capitulated and signed off on the Council. He was allowed to return to Rome in 555, after almost ten years of captivity in Constantinople, but died on the way.

The western resistance was broken. The few bishops in North Africa and Italy who tried to object were arrested, exiled, or bribed by the authorities, or went into hiding, to write at length but impotently against imperial tyranny. Their long works on the subject constituted the ignominious end of Latin literature in North Africa. In Italy, the next pope, Pelagius (556–561), who was appointed by Justinian, enforced the condemnation of the Three Chapters, even though he too had previously opposed it in writing. He now asked Narses to crack down on bishops who refused to condemn the Chapters.[74] The popes had once required Justin and Justinian to bring eastern bishops into alignment with papal policy; Justinian was now requiring the pope to bring western bishops into alignment with imperial policy.

Justinian had rammed through a painful solution to a problem that he himself had pointlessly created. To convince Chalcedonians that they were not Nestorians—which they did not believe to begin with—he had called Chalcedon unnecessarily into question and alienated western Romans. He was persecuting Christians at both ends of his domain. But opposition to Chalcedon remained a popular force in the east and was forming a separate Church.

Justinian's final years

Under Justinian, Roman imperialism sometimes presented itself as a Christian civilizing mission. Abasgia (modern Abkhazia) was a quasi-independent principality on the Black Sea coast, to the northwest of the Laz. Justinian sent priests to the Abasgoi, instructed them in Christian ways, built them a church, and forbade them from practicing castration (beautiful eunuchs had been their main export). Along with all this came a Roman garrison and the imposition of Roman regulations, which were soon resented and sparked an uprising that had to be suppressed violently in 550.[75] It went similarly with the Tzanoi, who lived in inaccessible mountains behind Trebizond. Like the Isaurians but on a smaller scale, they had raided the empire for centuries, or accepted protection money to stay at home. In 528, they were directly conquered by the imperial armies under Sittas, and Justinian imposed Christianity, garrisons, military recruitment, and roads upon them, "so that they might realize that they were human beings" and give up their savage heathen ways. Justinian celebrated this victory as a "first-time acquisition by Rome." In 558, however, a group of Tzanoi resumed raiding and had to be militarily suppressed, by one of their own, who had made a career in the Roman army. They were henceforth required to pay tribute.[76]

Nature was cruel to the empire in the last years of the reign. The chronicles offer a steady drumbeat of earthquakes and urban fires. The worst earthquake was that of 551, which, among other victims, claimed Beirut, forcing the school of law to relocate temporarily to Sidon. It also caused a tsunami that exposed the seabed for miles. People rushed in to plunder the shipwrecks that were suddenly revealed, but were caught by the returning waters and killed. The tsunami also destroyed the city of Kos. The city was visited by the student and future historian Agathias on his way to Constantinople, and he saw there only "a gigantic heap of rubble, littered with stones and fragments of broken pillars and beams." He could not discern the outline of the streets.[77] Another earthquake in 557 cracked the dome of Hagia Sophia, leading to its collapse in May of the following year. It was rebuilt in a more steepled form, for a second inauguration on the day before Christmas, 562.[78] The second major outbreak of the plague was in 558, and lasted for six months.[79]

The final five years of the reign (560–565) were also marked by significant disorder, with the chronicles recording almost annual riots or violence by the Blues and Greens that started more fires and led to more killing. An entire generation had elapsed since the Nika Insurrection, which, by the early 560s, was an event remembered by parents and grandparents. Even the Samaritans and Jews of Kaisareia rose up in 556 and killed many Christians in an urban uprising, including the governor, leading to severe imperial reprisals. In 551, the emperor had relaxed restrictions on Samaritan wills, acknowledging that they had not been enforced anyway.[80] But they still faced significant legal disadvantages.

Justinian's final years seem to lack a connecting narrative thread and consist of a dismal record of misfortunes. This impression is created by the poorer sources for that period. The early to mid-550s witnessed success in the Italian war, the fortification of the Balkans, invasion of Spain, and Council of Constantinople II. After that Justinian's stance was less proactive, leading later writers to call him old, weak, and apathetic.[81] He was almost eighty by the end of the 550s. The Balkan provinces were mostly at peace after years of suffering, but in 559 an army of Kutrigur Huns and Slavs led by one Zabergan invaded Thrace and split into three raiding parties. One went for Greece, a second for the Chersonese, and a third for Constantinople, crossing the Long Wall, which had been damaged in a recent earthquake. They reached as far as Sykai, across the Golden Horn. The City was gripped by terror, whereupon Belisarios was brought out of retirement. He assembled a ramshackle force of veterans and farmers and, through deception and stratagems, managed to defeat a contingent of Huns. The emperor paid the rest to leave, threatening to close off their route with his Danube fleet. He again incited the (reluctant) Utigurs to attack the Kutrigurs' homeland from behind. To restore confidence, Justinian left the City and resided at Selymbria on the coast for a few months, while the breach in the Long Wall was repaired. When he returned, he prayed at the church of the Holy Apostles and lit candles for Theodora. As he processed back to the palace, the street was so packed with cheering crowds that his horse could barely pass.[82]

Anxiety about the succession mounted. In September, 560, a rumor arose that the emperor had died after his return from Thrace, which led to a run on the bakeries. The senate instructed the prefect of Constantinople to light the lamps throughout the City to show that all was well. It was alleged—falsely, it turned out—that a faction intended to put Theodoros "Short-Arms," the son of the long-serving *magister officiorum* Petros the patrician, on the throne. Then, in November, 562, the "conspiracy of the bankers" was exposed. Among the implicated money-changers were two men from the household of Belisarios, and he now fell under imperial displeasure until July, 563, when his honors were restored. The conspiracy raises the likelihood that the state had been taking out forced loans to cover its expenses. Upon acceding to the throne in 565, Justin II paid back some of these loans from the *res privata*, the emperor's private treasury.[83]

Justinian was wrapping up loose ends. Negotiations between Petros the patrician and the Persian ambassador Yazdgushnasp resulted in a comprehensive peace treaty with Persia, in 561 or 562, whose terms we know in detail because Petros prepared a dossier that was used by the historian Menandros a generation later. The peace was to last for fifty years, and would be binding on both empires' Saracens as well. The Persians accepted the fortification of Daras, but the Romans would not station campaign forces there; the Christians of Persia could worship freely; Lazica was to be Roman and Iberia Persian; and for all this the Romans would pay 30,000 solidi per year, with seven years paid up-front. Petros assured the Persians that they were good for it: "You are making a treaty with *Romans*. It is enough to say 'Romans,' the name says it all."[84]

In October, 563, Justinian, now over eighty, fulfilled a personal vow when he traveled to the shrine of the archangel Michael in Germia, Galatia, the farthest that he had ever gone from the capital during his reign. He was putting his affairs in order, after a fashion. In November, 563, he summoned his Saracen phylarch, al-Harith, to Constantinople for the first time, to discuss the succession to the phylarchy of his son al-Mundhir (569–581).[85] This relationship had lasted since ca. 529. The Saracen dynasty leaned Monophysite, but that did not compromise its utility in the eyes of the court. Few other men had made it through the length of this reign. Khusrow, the shah of Persia, was one of them, as was Narses, now in Italy, and there were also Petros and Belisarios. Belisarios died in March, 565, and his properties were confiscated to an imperial fund.[86]

The greatest mystery of Justinian's reign surrounds an action that he took in late 564. He issued a decree endorsing a theology known as Aphthartodocetism, associated with Julian of Halikarnassos, a former ally and then enemy of Severos of Antioch. Aphthartodocetism was an extreme form of Monophysite theology, in which the human body of Christ was rendered virtually incorruptible through its association with the divine Word. There is no question that Justinian did in fact endorse this position, which was deemed heretical by both Diphysites and Severan Monophysites, but it is impossible to know what the emperor was thinking at this stage. The patriarch of Constantinople, Eutychios, rejected this doctrine and was immediately deposed on trumped-up charges. The patriarch of Antioch also prepared to resist, but was saved by Justinian's death on 14 November, 565.[87]

Like many emperors before him, Justinian died without either producing or publicly designating an heir. A eunuch of the court alleged that the emperor, on his deathbed, had named his nephew Justin as his successor. Justin was duly admitted to the palace by Tiberios, captain of the excubitors. He was acclaimed emperor by the court and crowned by the patriarch Ioannes. He then went to the hippodrome where he was acclaimed by the people, who had gathered there upon the news of Justinian's death. His uncle's body was conveyed in a formal procession to the Holy Apostles, where it was placed in the imperial mausoleum, draped in a funeral pall woven by the new emperor's wife Sophia. It depicted

Justinian's many labors, including the defeat of the Vandal king Gelimer and the liberation of Elder Rome, thirty years earlier.[88]

Justinian had been a strongly institutionalist ruler, working with the existing instruments of Roman governance—especially the law, the armies, and taxation—and pushing them to do more. His predecessors, having the same means, had been more cautious in their use. Justinian had more faith in the power of the law to regulate, improve, and re-engineer society, to standardize it and to reach down to a more granular level. He was guided by the belief that the emperor should intervene in society, directly and at every level, in order to unify and rationalize it, and that problems were fundamentally fixable. His laws appealed to principle, but were often cynically designed to promote his centralizing impulses as well as the corrupt interests of his favorites. In contrast to his predecessors, Justinian did not passively react to the problems brought to him by his subjects, but went out and created his own. Many believed that "he had sown confusion and turmoil."[89]

Using the law, Justinian made life difficult for all the religious minorities of his empire, coercing their conversion or earning their hatred. Here he could display horrific callousness: "To squeeze everyone into a single faith regarding Christ . . . it did not seem to him to be murder if the victim was of a different faith."[90] Justin and Justinian not only failed to work out a compromise with anti-Chalcedonians, they ruined the tenuous compromises that had been carefully crafted by Zeno and Anastasius. Through zeal and intolerance, they permanently split the Church. Most Monophysites regarded Justinian as evil, or, as one Coptic text put it, as "the pit of the abyss" from which "the smoke of a great fire went up, darkening the sun and air."[91] Meanwhile, his condemnation of the Three Chapters made him hateful to many Diphysites in the west, one of whom called him "a new Diocletian." Another critic wrote that, in his efforts to appear learned, Justinian disturbed the Church by inventing problems. His embrace of Aphthartodocetism at the eleventh hour made him suspect to posterity too.[92]

As an imperialist, Justinian used his armies mostly for reclaiming territory that Rome had lost to the barbarians in the west, and he judged the timing of those interventions carefully and cynically, in order to strike against the barbarian kings at their weakest moment. He ended the historical existence of the Vandals and the Ostrogoths. The only new conquest that he made was the small territory of the Tzanoi in the Pontos. He was drawn into the war in Lazica by the Laz and by the broader war with Persia. Justinian was complicit in escalating that war in the late 520s, but the phase of it that began in 540 was mostly forced on him. Persia under Khusrow was the most powerful opponent that Rome had seen in centuries. In the north, where the empire faced off against Lombards, Gepids, Heruls, Slavs, and Huns, Justinian skillfully played the barbarians off against each other, fortified his provinces, and reduced the frequency and the impact of their raids, while finding ways to recruit them for his other wars.

However, Justinian and his inner circle did not adequately explain this complex strategy to their subjects, leaving many of them bewildered in the face of so many simultaneous wars, each with a different strategic objective. It may have seemed that the emperor lost control of the situation, but in reality that happened only in Italy in the 540s, when the empire faced the formidable Totila and was preoccupied on many other fronts and by the effects of the plague. In the end, it turned out that Justinian did know what he was doing. He wrapped up all of the wars during the 550s, leaving his successor with an empire at peace. He never lost his nerve, except perhaps during the Nika Insurrection. This quality was necessary for a ruler juggling so much, but it had a dark side: "With a gentle visage, calm brow, and soft voice he would give orders to destroy tens of thousands of people who had done no wrong, to raze cities, and confiscate all their property to the treasury." The only emotion to which he admitted publicly was erotic passion for Theodora.[93]

Justinian set out to leave his mark on history and succeeded more than any other emperor. His permanent legacy includes the codification of Roman law, the rebuilding of Hagia Sophia and other iconic churches such as the Holy Apostles, and the silk industry. He was also responsible for the emergence of the separatist anti-Chalcedonian Churches of Egypt and Syria, a credit, in this case, that is due to the magnitude of his failure. His reign was among the most prolific in terms of literary production, but he did little to support it, and most of the writers were educated before his time. When they died away in the 550s, the crop that replaced them was meager. Justinian had not nurtured the next generation. His reign also witnessed a horrific sequence of catastrophes, including earthquakes, tsunamis, fires, and the plague. These events damaged cities more than the countryside, and the coasts more than the hinterland. One place that took a pounding, and never fully recovered, was Antioch, whose experiences read like the book of Job: it was struck repeatedly by earthquakes and fires, Persian conquest, and then the plague. Syria generally declined,[94] and so did Italy, because of Justinian's war of choice. But contrary to recent fashion among historians, Justinian showed no interest in the view that The End Was Nigh and no action was taken by him, his officials, or his subjects based on a belief that the Second Coming was imminent. Such ideas were for theological entertainment only and confined to the literary imagination.[95] Justinian had ample opportunity in his hundreds of laws to mention the End Times, if they mattered. He did not.

Justinian was often inflexible in collecting taxes, which may have risen during his reign despite all the hardship, and he was harsh in cracking down on loopholes, evasions, and abuses.[96] He frequently shortchanged his soldiers or did not pay them for years, which caused them to defect or prey on the people they were supposed to be protecting or liberating. These tactics caused disaffection and rebellions in North Africa, Italy, Armenia, Abasgia, and Lazica, with some of those territories defecting to Persia just to be rid of Justinian's officials. In the end, his greatest failure was that he did not know how to cultivate goodwill or generate consensus for his vision of Roman society. It was a mistake on his part not to visit the newly conquered provinces in person, especially Italy, and build up networks of support through personal contacts. He trusted too much in the remote operation of the Roman administrative machinery. This could coerce bodies and money, but not ideals, identities, or loyalties. "Thus did Justinian, after filling everywhere with confusion and turmoil, pass over to the lowest places of punishment"—so wrote a Chalcedonian historian.[97]

14

The Cost of Overextension (565–602)

Justin II

Justin II was the son of Justinian's sister Vigilantia, while his wife Sophia, who was immediately raised to the rank of Augusta, was Theodora's niece; thus the dynasty continued on both sides. Sophia was allegedly a Monophysite who changed sides in 563 to boost her husband's chances for the throne. Our sources mention her and Justin together, as a single source of authority, with uncommon frequency, and she is credited with important decisions. For the first time the emperor and his wife were depicted together on coins. Sophia was the most powerful empress in our history so far. Justin had previously been the palace chief-of-staff (*cura palatii*), not the highest office, but when the moment came he was at the right place and supported by the eunuchs and Tiberios, the captain of the guard.[1]

The beginning of the reign was ugly. Justin had apparently agreed with his namesake cousin, Ioustinos, an experienced general and son of Justinian's cousin Germanus, that, if one of them should become emperor, the other would hold second place in the state. But Justin now arrested his cousin and dispatched him to Alexandria, where he was quickly murdered, allegedly on Sophia's orders. On 3 October, 566, two prominent senators were also executed, Aitherios and Addaios, the second a former praetorian prefect and now prefect of the City, on charges of conspiracy. Aitherios had been implicated in two conspiracies against Justinian, albeit cleared in both, and the two had carried out the arrest of the patriarch Eutychios, when the latter objected to Justinian's Aphthartodocetism. The deeper background of these court factions eludes us.[2]

The new regime took decisive steps to placate wealthy interests and was willing to blame Justinian for the difficulties in which it found itself. "Many things were too much neglected while my father was alive, and as a result the exhausted treasury contracted so many debts, which we propose, moved by pity, to restore to the unfortunate people.... The old man no longer cared: he was altogether cold." For the first time, the treasury was in debt to private interests. Justin paid off those debts and burned the bonds—the reverse of what emperors usually did, which was to burn documentation of *subjects'* debts to the state. Justin did that too, remitting tax arrears back to 560. In 569, Justin made a huge concession to provincial elites, by giving them—the bishops, "landowners," and leading councilors—the right to nominate their own governors; if the court found them acceptable, they would be appointed without paying a fee so that they could govern without having to recoup the cost of their office. This signaled an end to Justinian's micromanagement of provincial affairs, but this method of appointment had been pioneered by him in Italy after the war. A small group of men could now run each province with less oversight. Justin told them that they could no longer complain to him about the quality of local governance, but it is unlikely that much changed in practice.[3]

From the start, Justin signaled his Roman conservatism, by taking on the office as consul upon his accession—in this he would be followed by emperors down to 642—and placing the personification Roma on his coins. He also restored the right to divorce by mutual consent, which Justinian had sought to curtail, noting that petitions had reached him from many couples whose "mutual hatred" had led to "domestic warfare."[4] Justin maintained good relations with the pope (see Figure 24). His regime also signaled that it would be tougher on barbarians. A propaganda poem promised victories over the Persians and Avars linked to Justin's consulship and a new triumphal column in "Byzantine Rome."[5] At his

Figure 24 Silver-gilt cross reliquary sent to Rome by Justin II and Sophia. The Lamb of God is in the middle, with medallions of the emperor and empress to the left and right. It is 40 cm tall and 30 cm wide (Vatican).
White Images/ Scala/ Art Resource, NY

accession, Justin pointedly rebuffed an Avar embassy, scornfully rejecting its demand for a subsidy. Justin wanted to make "peoples and kingdoms tremble" with his "stiff determination": "You dare match strength against me?"[6] He is frequently accused of stirring up unnecessary wars that brought ruin to the empire. It would probably have been better to pay for peace. Justinian had only recently, and barely, managed to wrap up his wars and establish peace on all sides, and paying barbarians was his standard practice. But Justin was politically weak and needed to put on a show of strength.

Justin's confrontational stance was successful, at first. But the international scene was becoming more complex and interconnected, so that no emperor could control it. Specifically, in the 550s and 560s, the Hephthalites were defeated and replaced as the dominant power in Central Asia by the Turks, who then expanded westward. The group whom the Romans called the Avars was an army, 20,000 strong—so about the size of an imperial field army—that had fled from the Turks and traveled west to the Caucasus (ca. 557) and the Danube (ca. 561). When they first appeared north of the Caucasus, in 557 or 558, they sent envoys to the court of Justinian via the general Ioustinos, the son of Germanus. These steppe warriors made an impression on the Romans with their braided hair and "snaky" pigtails. Justinian had given them expensive gifts, which was later seen as the action of "an old and weak man, who had lost his warlike spirit."[7] They petitioned Justinian to be allowed to settle by the Lower Danube, but were instead offered Pannonia II, the land formerly occupied by the Heruls. The Avar khagan Baian rejected this offer and set about subjugating peoples north of the Black Sea and Danube.[8] He did not move against Romanía, even when insulted by Justin II, but instead raided the Franks.

Baian was drawn into the ongoing conflict between the Lombards and the Gepids, which was sparked by the Lombard king Alboin's desire to marry the Gepid king's daughter, Rosamund. In 566, the Romans intervened decisively in that struggle on the Gepid side after being promised Sirmium in exchange, but the Gepids had then reneged on the deal. In 567, Alboin bought Avar assistance at great cost (one tenth of Lombard livestock and half the expected Gepid booty), but he then defeated the Gepids in battle without Avar help. He married Rosamund and, according to legend, turned her father's skull into a drinking cup. But others rushed in to benefit from Alboin's victory. The Avars seized most Gepid lands in the Carpathian Basin. The Romans had also not fought in the battle but picked up Sirmium and the Gepid royal treasury for themselves. These were major gains for the Avars and Romans, who had not fought. It was a disaster for the Gepids, who were absorbed into the Avar empire. However, it was a victory with few gains for the Lombard Alboin. The Avars immediately besieged Roman-occupied Sirmium, though the khagan candidly asked for a token concession "so I am not dishonored before the tribes that follow me if I leave with no profit." He got nothing. Years of acrimonious negotiations ensued, but Justin's approach was paying off: Sirmium, lost to Rome since the 440s, was now restored to the empire.[9]

Justin was also cultivating close relations with the Turks, to use them as a counterweight to the Persians and Avars, whom the Turks viewed as their runaway "slaves." He also wanted to access alternative trade routes through Central Asia, especially for raw silk. The Turks established a large delegation in Constantinople, hundreds strong, and Justin sent Zemarchos, *magister militum* for Oriens, on a two-year mission to the Turk khagan in Central Asia (569–571). In addition to military and trade agreements, this journey resulted in a narrative of the embassy's travels through foreign lands.[10] A Roman-Turkish alliance was forming.

In the meantime, a disaster struck Roman Italy, which altered the history of the peninsula forever. In 568, Alboin gathered his followers, Lombards and others, and, like Theoderic before him, trekked across the mountains to find a new home in Italy. It had been only seven years since northern Italy had finally been cleared of Frankish raiders, and it had not recovered. As late as 565 or 566, a Herul in Roman service rebelled in the north and was proclaimed king by his followers. He was suppressed by Narses, but the event demonstrates that imperial authority there was tenuous.[11] Narses was likely recalled to Constantinople before the Lombard invasion, but within a few years legends began to circulate that he had invited the Lombards into Italy to spite the empress Sophia, who had allegedly insulted him as a eunuch.[12]

In any case, Alboin quickly overran the Po valley, leaving garrisons in key locations under his *duces*—a Roman military office that later gave rise to medieval "dukes." Ticinum (later Pavia) withstood him for a full three years (569–572) and pockets of imperial control survived in the north until ca. 601, including Cremona and Mantua. But breakout groups of Lombards captured Spoleto and Benevento in the south, under their own *duces*, Faroald and Zotto, respectively. Imperial control over Italy was now fragmented. It included Genoa, various discontinuous coastal zones, and the area around Ravenna, including the Pentapolis along the Adriatic coast. It also included Rome, which was linked to Ravenna via a narrow corridor, as well as the far south of the peninsula. Ravenna was the seat of imperial power and the exarch (the governor), but Rome was a far larger city: their populations are estimated at 12,000 and 100,000 respectively. The swift collapse of the imperial defenses is not easy to explain; later sources attribute it to the ravages of plague and a famine in 568. But before the conquest could be consolidated, Alboin was murdered, allegedly at the instigation of his wife Rosamund, whom he had toasted with the goblet-skull of her father. Rosamund fled to Ravenna with the royal treasury, which was forwarded to Constantinople. The momentum of the Lombard invasion stalled in the 570s, as imperial gold sowed dissension among the *duces*.[13]

Our sources for these events are poor, so we do not know what induced, or enticed, Alboin and his followers to migrate to Italy, whether it was apprehension at being squeezed between the Romans and the Avars or the opportunities that it offered. Nor can we reconstruct a coherent narrative of the imperial response to this invasion, or explain its failure. Eastern writers after the age of Justinian paid little attention to Italy, a theater of war that would always rank third (or less) in the priorities of Constantinople after the Balkans and the east. And yet, before 572, the empire was not preoccupied with major warfare on other fronts. We cannot explain why significant reinforcements under experienced generals were not sent to Italy before 575.

Justin II was an "avid builder" of churches and palaces.[14] He also had a go at Church union, holding talks with leading Monophysites over a new compromise Cyrillian formula, which was promulgated in 571. This had a predictable fate: as it did not explicitly condemn Chalcedon (or mention it at all), but implicitly allowed Chalcedonians to abide by the Council, it was unacceptable to anti-Chalcedonians. The disagreement, in other words, was again not primarily theological, as a joint formula could have been worked out. According to the leading Monophysite John of Ephesos, who was in the capital, the discussions were conducted under duress, and matters were complicated by splits within the anti-Chalcedonian community. In the end, each side accused the other of "obstinacy" (today they might say that their "identities" were at stake). With consensus beyond reach, the patriarch of Constantinople Ioannes Scholastikos began to persecute the anti-Chalcedonians, especially in the City, ending the toleration of their communities, which dated back to the 530s. Congregations were broken up, churches and monasteries taken over, and priests imprisoned in harsh conditions. The patriarch forced many of them to take communion with the imperial Church, even with violence, and implemented a novel policy of re-ordaining their bishops as if they were laymen. This had no basis in canon law and made even the emperor uncomfortable. John of Ephesos wrote an account of these travails while in prison and smuggled it out piecemeal, which explains why it is so disjointed. It is a rare specimen of prison literature, whose author complains that mice had made a nest in his pillow and kept him up all night with their squeaking.[15] Chalcedonian sources suppress mention of this persecution.

The divide over Chalcedon was growing ever wider and harder to ignore. In the later sixth century, one Epiphanios founded a monastery in a Pharaonic tomb near Thebes, in Upper Egypt. Its walls were painted with doctrinal texts, in both Greek and Coptic, illustrating beliefs Chalcedonian (identified as bad) and anti-Chalcedonian (good), so the visitor knew exactly where he stood.[16]

Still, Church affairs were no reason to neglect Italy. The three-year window for intervention in Italy that was afforded by the siege of Ticinum (Pavia) was squandered, while the east drifted into crisis too. Specifically, Justin is blamed for irresponsibly starting a war with Persia that ruined Justinian's hard-won peace and set the empire on a destructive path. This reproach was begun by contemporaries and drew support from the emperor's lapse into madness. But it overlooks the increasingly interconnected stage of Great Power politics.

The following alignments were falling into place simultaneously. In 569–571, Constantinople was reaching an overtly anti-Persian agreement with the Turks in Central Asia, which alarmed the Persians. In retaliation, in ca. 570 the shah sent a general to Arabia who deposed the Christian king of Himyar and subjected much of Arabia to the Persian empire. The deposed king, the son of the great Abraha, was perceived by Aksum and Rome as a distant client of their own, and so his fall "angered the Romans."[17] Persia's move was not without economic advantage, as it could now tax the silk trade from India. In 570–571, the Roman and Persian Saracens also came to blows, for their own reasons, and the Roman Saracens prevailed.[18] Also in 571, many Armenians rebelled against Persia, objecting to the shah's plan to build a Zoroastrian fire complex in their land. The rebels, led by Vardan Mamikonean, secured a secret offer of assistance from the Romans. When they defeated the Persians, their leaders went to Constantinople to obtain actual support. The shah blamed the Romans for his own mess, and Justin now refused to send the peace payment to Persia, which was effectively a declaration of war.[19] Thus, the arc of war now stretched, not just from the Black Sea to the Red Sea, as it had in the 520s, but from Central Asia to Italy on the one hand and to Arabia on the other. It included many empires, tribes, and armies that could individually do great harm to the two old contenders, Rome and Persia. This was no longer the bipolar world of Constantine and Shapur, but a tinderbox of world war, in which the great players were alarmingly vulnerable.

The Romans struck first and enjoyed some initial successes. The Armenian rebel Vardan, aided by a Roman army, defeated the Persians twice and captured Dvin in 572. The empire had rarely before established an army so far to the east.[20] In 573, another Roman army defeated the Persians near Nisibis and put the city under siege, hoping to reverse its humiliating concession by Jovian in 363. But then the tide turned. The siege failed, and two Persian armies invaded the empire. One captured the rich city of Apameia, plundering it and taking its population away into captivity. This city, a jewel of the province of Syria, suffered such extensive damage—some of it attested archaeologically—that it was afterward only a "shadow" of its former self. The other army, commanded by Khusrow himself, captured Daras, the bulwark of Roman defenses in the east, after a six-month siege. The shah plundered it and took its population captive. Khusrow had not enjoyed such victories since his grand tour of the Roman east and capture of Antioch in 540, over thirty years before. It is reported that he sent 2,000 virgins from Daras to the Turks, as gifts and to display his humiliation of their new allies, the Romans.[21]

This defeat was so shocking that it drove Justin over the precipice into madness. At least that was how some contemporaries explained why the emperor began to suffer from a debilitating mental illness. According to one account, Justin would imitate the sounds of animals; was prone to extreme anxiety attacks; had to be wheeled around the palace on a throne on wheels in order to be calmed down, or have an organ playing continually in the background; bit his nurses; and tried to leap from the windows.[22] Meanwhile, the military situation was deteriorating. Relations with the Avars too had worsened, and the general Tiberios—the emperor's confidant and *comes* of the excubitors—was defeated by them in 574.[23] The empire was now at war on three fronts—with the Lombards, Avars, and Persians—and the emperor was incapacitated. Yet Justin had moments of lucidity. During one of them, after conferring with Sophia he appointed Tiberios as Caesar. This took place in an emotional ceremony in the palace courtyard, before a crowd of thousands, on 7 December, 574. Tiberios was given the name Konstantinos.

Tiberios II Konstantinos

Tiberios immediately made peace with the Avars, that "ugly nation of hairy barbarians," for an annual payment of 80,000 solidi (1,111 lbs). Persia too proved unexpectedly amenable, especially when Sophia appealed to Khusrow not to wage war on a woman with a sick husband. He agreed to a one-year truce in exchange for 45,000 solidi and then three years (575–578) for 30,000 annually. These deals always excluded Armenia, where the war continued. So far the Turkish alliance had yielded no benefits; in fact, the Turks were angry that the Romans had made peace with their former slaves, the Avars. The Roman ambassadors were forced to participate in the funeral rites of the late Turkish khagan (Istemi) and slash their faces in mourning. A Turkish inscription from Mongolia records that this funeral was attended by ambassadors from China, Tibet, the Avars, Romans, Kyrgiz, and others, a striking assembly of this increasingly multipolar and interconnected world. The Turks then attacked the Crimean Bosporos, a Roman client.[24] But at least Constantinople did manage to send forces to Italy. The general Baduarius, Justin's son-in-law, was dispatched there but suffered a crushing defeat by the Lombards in ca. 576 and died soon afterward. It is likely that he had not taken an army. The Persian war prevented Tiberios from diverting soldiers "as he did not believe that he could fight in both the east and the west." He therefore sent a notable from Old Rome with 3,000 lbs to bribe Lombards to defect or, failing that, to hire Franks to attack them.[25]

The state finances present a contradictory picture under Tiberios. In 575, the new Caesar forgave tax arrears down to 571 and reduced taxes by a fourth for four years, noting that visitations of the plague had made it difficult for subjects to pay but also that he was having to spend more on military campaigns. He was also lavishly generous, so that Justin and Sophia restricted his access to the treasury, lest he undo their earlier savings. It appears, then, that the first years of Justin II had yielded a surplus. Sophia would also not let Tiberios bring his wife and children into the Great Palace—like her aunt, she could not bear the thought of any woman taking her place—so he had to visit them after hours at the Hormisdas. Tiberios was indifferent to religious controversies and halted the persecution of Monophysites. When the patriarch pushed back, Tiberios asked him, "Are these Christians?" "Yes, they are." "Then go sit in your church, and be quiet, and do not trouble me about this again." Attacks henceforth targeted only top leadership, such as John of Ephesos.[26]

The lull in hostilities was temporary and the Romans soon found themselves fighting on *seven* fronts. The Goths in Spain were chipping away at the imperial province, and the Romans there presumably had to fend for themselves, without aid from Constantinople. A Moorish king called Garmul made life difficult for the North African provinces by his invasions, in the course of which he killed one prefect and two *magistri militum*. The war there is poorly attested but seems to have lasted for a decade after ca. 569. The *magister militum* Gennadios defeated this rebellion in 578 and killed Garmul, but monks, priests, and presumably laymen too were emigrating from North Africa to Spain.[27] Italy was in chaos, as the imperial strategy appears to have been to bribe Lombard chiefs. The war with Persia resumed in earnest in 576, now on both the Caucasian and Mesopotamian fronts, and it would last, paused by negotiations, until 591, when it was resolved in the most unexpected way. But until then, it remained the empire's chief military preoccupation, to which most resources were devoted. The Romans' position was not bad, as they held Persian Armenia and could venture as far as Azerbaijan and the Caspian Sea. However, they had lost Daras and repeated Persian invasions had ruined many cities, including Sebasteia and Melitene. Roman morale was boosted in 576, when Ioustinianos, another son of Germanus, defeated the shah and sent him fleeing for safety. The Romans even captured his tent and fire altar. In sum, both empires ground each other down without making significant gains.[28]

Tiberios II Konstantinos was proclaimed Augustus a few days before Justin died on 5 October, 578. He strengthened his position by the outlay of generous gifts to domestic supporters, up to 7,200 lbs of gold in addition to silk and other precious goods. Sophia reproached him for wasting her savings and refused to vacate the palace, so Tiberios had to build an annex to house his own family. Eventually Sophia was forced out.[29] The emperor's greatest concern, however, was finding enough soldiers for all the wars. These worries "gave him neither rest nor breathing time, but wars and rumors of war multiplied around him . . . . he is full of care how best to gather soldiers."[30] 15,000 barbarians were recruited beyond the Alps and the Danube, named *Tiberianoi*, and sent east, under a new *magister militum* for Oriens, Maurikios.[31] But the situation deteriorated further, as the sixth front, in the eastern Balkans, opened up.

Slavic forces, up to 100,000 strong, began to cross the Danube in ca. 577–581 and raid Roman territory, roaming as far south as central Greece. This time they began to linger in imperial territory and could not be dislodged "because the emperor is preoccupied with the war against Persia," as contemporaries noted. They settled near Thessalonike. In the next century, this migration would begin to alter the ethnic profile of the Balkans. These Slavs were in theory subject to the Avars, but khagan Baian could not control them. Tiberios asked Baian to attack the Slavic lands in the lower Danube in order to force the others to return home, and he even sent officials in 578 to ferry an Avar cavalry army across the Danube in Pannonia, escort it across Illyricum, and ferry it back again in Scythia, where they laid waste to the Slavic homes. But this did not solve the problem, and possibly induced more Slavs to emigrate south.[32]

The seventh front opened in 578 in the western Balkans when the Avars suddenly broke the treaty and again besieged Sirmium, which they believed was rightfully theirs, as a part of their Gepid inheritance. The emperor had no army to send against them, "not even a tiny force." The city held out for over two years but was in the end reduced to starvation. One inhabitant carved a poignant prayer on a brick: "Lord, help the city, stop the Avar, and protect Romanía and me." In 582, Sirmium was surrendered to the khagan, though its inhabitants were allowed to depart to the empire. A year later, a fire broke out and destroyed the city. Sirmium would be lost to the Romans for the next five centuries. In order to secure peace, Tiberios resumed the payments, including, most humiliating of all, back payments for the years of the siege.[33]

Unlike most of his predecessors, Tiberios planned for the succession. On 5 August, 582, he proclaimed as Caesars his generals Maurikios, a forty-three-year-old Cappadocian, and Germanos, who was then in North Africa, and betrothed them to his daughters Charito and Konstantina, respectively. Sensing his imminent demise, Tiberios elevated Maurikios to the rank of Augustus on 13 August and died the next day.[34]

Maurikios' wars

Maurikios (582–602) faced three challenges: how to fight concurrent wars with limited manpower; how to do so cheaply, as he found the treasury empty and revenues fell short of expenses; and how to raise money and cut expenses without alienating core constituencies. It was a delicate balance, and he managed it for twenty years. But when he failed, he failed so spectacularly that it not only toppled his regime, it destabilized the empire.

The first half of the reign was the most difficult, as the empire was fighting the Avars and the Persians simultaneously. Maurikios tended to rely on a small group of generals, whom he rotated in and out of command, recalling them when they were defeated or did not carry out his orders precisely. These recalls did not end careers: Maurikios just benched them for a while, then sent them out again. They included Ioannes Mystakon ("the Mustache"), the emperor's brother-in-law Philippikos (who was also appointed to be *comes* of the excubitors), Priskos, Komentiolos, and, in the 590s, the emperor's brother Petros. They were all, on the whole, competent, but our main historian, Theophylaktos Simokattes, writing in the 620s or 630s, reflects a tradition that favored Priskos and disparaged the others.[35] Maurikios' regime was centered on his family, and he lavished honors, titles, and properties on many relatives, which hurt his image. His advisor was his cousin or nephew Domitianos, whom Maurikios, back when he was general in the east, had made the bishop of Melitene. Maurikios' wife also immediately produced a son, on 4 August, 583, the first to be born to a reigning emperor since Theodosius II and so named after him. The imperial couple went on to produce five more sons and three daughters. There had never been such a bounty of heirs in the history of the empire, but it was all for nothing when their executioner came in 602.[36]

The war in the east dragged on as the two sides attacked each other's border forts and fought occasional battles. The Romans usually prevailed, but gained no strategic advantage. It is possible that the Persians, under shah Hormizd IV (579–590), the son of Khusrow I, regained partial control of Persian Armenia. Hormizd abolished the crown of Iberia and sent his son, the future shah Khusrow II, to govern the eastern Caucasus.[37] In 582, the Romans changed their approach to the southern marches by abolishing the Saracen phylarchate. Maurikios began to suspect al-Mundhir when the two had campaigned together in 581. The phylarch was now arrested and taken to Constantinople, where he was put on trial in 582 and exiled to Sicily. The emperor withdrew subsidies from the Saracens, thereby removing the patronage network that held them together and disbanding their organization. Relations between the Romans and the Saracen dynasty had often been tense, especially given Roman stereotypes about Saracen disloyalty, and it did not help that the phylarchs were Monophysites (whence John of Ephesos presents al-Mundhir as a hero done in by imperial perfidy).[38] The dynasty had made powerful enemies at the court, but had never integrated itself well enough to play the system from the inside. Phylarchs served, indeed existed, at the pleasure of the emperor, and al-Mundhir had crossed a general who then became emperor. As the war with Persia had shifted to the north, where the Saracens were less relevant, this change in policy had little immediate strategic impact, but would have graver long-term consequences. For now, Saracen units still assisted the Roman armies.[39]

The conflict with the Avars was also not an all-out war. The khagan was following the same playbook as Attila: raid along the Danube, and occasionally into Thrace, in order to force the empire to pay protection money, then raid again in order to raise his price. A few cities had to be destroyed to drive the point home (such as Singidunum in 583 and Anchialos on the Black Sea in 588), though major cities in the interior managed to repel Avar and Slav attacks by relying on their walls and artillery (such as Thessalonike in 586 and Philippopolis and Adrianople in 587). The khagan used the gold and gifts that he extracted from the empire to solidify his standing among his chiefs, and they, in turn, held down his subjects and wide territories north of the Danube and in the Carpathian basin. The khagan needed the empire, and negotiated with it as a peer. He could not afford to destroy it, at least not without radically revamping his own political economy. In 584, he managed to raise his fee from 80,000 to 100,000 solidi, and in 598 to 120,000 solidi. This was far more than Persia had ever received from the empire. During Maurikios' reign, the khagan received about 3 million solidi, to say nothing of precious gifts, ransom for captives, slaves, and direct plunder. The Avar treasury was eventually captured by Charlemagne in 796, who distributed it to his clients and followers. The only part of it that can be identified today is a silver box cover with the image of an east Roman emperor.[40] These payments caused anxiety on both sides, as the emperor could not be seen to be paying tribute to a barbarian, while in Avar culture it was the superior chief who gave the greatest gifts to his subordinates. But they made it work with bluster and dissimulation.[41]

Strained revenues

The empire could not bring overwhelming force against the Avars and crush them once and for all. When credible numbers are given in the sources, the operational armies of this period—in the east and the west—rarely exceeded 10,000 men.[42] Justinian had dispersed the two praesental armies to his new conquests, so they no longer existed. But the field armies of Illyricum and Thrace had a paper strength of ca. 20,000 each. Where were the missing men?

It is possible that there were more operations going on than our source, Theophylaktos, knew about, focused as he was on a tight cast of characters (Priskos, Komentiolos, and Philippikos). He says nothing, for example, about the siege of Thessalonike by the Slavs in 586, which we know about from the sermons preached by the bishop in the 610s to honor the city's saint, Demetrios, for coming to the rescue (see Plate 4b). The bishop reveals that the city's prefect and his soldiers were absent during the siege, dealing with a matter in Greece, which is also not specified here or in Theophylaktos; this may have been another Slav attack.[43] But the praetorian prefect of Illyricum in Thessalonike was not a *magister militum*, and his men were probably a small retinue. Where were the main armies?

The answer must be fiscal: Maurikios could simply not afford to hire more soldiers. Allegedly he found the treasury depleted by Tiberios' generosity, "swept clean as if with a broom." He therefore had to become parsimonious, which was resented in itself but his unpopularity was compounded by the favors that he bestowed on his relatives and the vanity project of building up his home town of Arabissos in Cappadocia, where his constructions were destroyed by earthquakes in 586–588.[44] Given that the army was the state's greatest expense, it made sense that emperors would reduce the number of active soldiers in order to cope with deficits, as Justinian had done.[45] Paying the enemy to remain at peace, even with 100,000 solidi, cost less than the maintenance of a field army at full strength, so this made fiscal sense, provided the subsidy *did* keep the Avars at bay. Their raids were in fact intermittent, which means that the payments were buying years of peace. Thus, whereas in the early fifth century the empire had demilitarized in order to protect the court from its own generals, in the later sixth it demilitarized due to fiscal constraints.

Moreover, Maurikios' limited forces had to be divided between two active theaters, the Balkans and the east, which meant that neither could be prosecuted fully. Other theaters (Spain, North Africa, and Italy) had to fend for themselves. As soon as the Persian war ended in 591, units were transferred to the Balkans and decisively changed the balance of power; and when the Persian war restarted in 602, those units were sent east, exposing the Balkans to Avar and Slav predation. In sum, the Roman army in this period could deal properly with only one major enemy at a time.

Why was there not enough money? The empire bequeathed by Justinian to his successors was overextended and more expensive. Justinian himself had been unable to cover expenses and had to cut corners. Also, recurring outbreaks of the plague—every fifteen years in the City, for example—had further eroded the tax base, as Tiberios II had noted in his tax-relief law of 575.[46] Moreover, the disruptions of the sixth century were having a cumulative effect, including Avar and Slavic raids, deportations of urban populations from Antioch, Apameia, and other cities into Persia, and the earthquakes, fires, and plague. If you lose a city here, a city there, eventually state revenues will diminish appreciably. During the second half of the sixth century, many towns in the Danubian province of Scythia Minor had become fortified settlements, after which, by ca. 600, they were either abandoned or ruralized, with slight circulation of coins.[47] It seems that emperors had raised taxes after 540, with rates peaking around 570, which made it likelier that taxpayers would default and require relief. The city of Aphrodite appears to have been paying almost three times more tax in solidi by the end of that period. However, this may reflect increasing commutation to cash payment of all dues, rather than only a tax hike.[48] In the 590s Maurikios withdrew Justinian's heavier bronze coins from circulation and reissued a greater quantity of lighter-weight coins, a policy of marginal savings.[49]

The emperor also tried to impose austerity-driven cuts, which made him unpopular with the army. In 588, he proposed a pay reduction of 25%, possibly to be offset by the provision of equipment that the soldiers were still being expected to buy themselves, and by improved terms of service. This caused the field army of Oriens to mutiny during Easter. The general Priskos tried to calm the soldiers by parading an image of Christ, but they threw stones at it—so much for piety when salaries were at stake—and Priskos fled. Later they also tore down images of the emperor and reviled him as a "shopkeeper's accountant." The Persians took advantage of the mutiny to invade, but the rebel army marched against them and defeated them soundly. The emperor sent bishops to plead with the army, mostly to no avail, though one Church writer says that his boss, Gregorios, the bishop of Antioch, moved the soldiers with an intensely nationalistic speech that referenced the heroes of the old Republic. The pay cut was canceled and the army returned to obedience in 589. In 594, Maurikios tried to impose a similar measure, which also sparked a mutiny, this time in Thrace with more insults directed against him, so it too was not implemented.[50]

Italy and the west

Within these constraints, Maurikios was a conscientious ruler who strove to improve the empire's position. In the late 580s, one of his generals, Comenciolus (probably not the same as Komentiolos) was shoring up the defenses of Spania, as we know from an inscription at Cartagena. The Gothic king Reccared (586–601) had recently converted from Arianism to Roman Christianity, so the imperial line was now that Spania had to be defended from "barbarians" instead of from heretics. The empire meddled in internecine Visigothic quarrels, playing one side against the other.[51] Meanwhile, in North Africa and Italy the emperor united the top civilian and military commands and created the position of exarch, based in Carthage and Ravenna respectively. This effectively replicated the power that had been wielded by the eunuchs Solomon and Narses immediately after the conquest. The exarchs became quasi-autonomous commands that likely did not receive significant military reinforcements from the imperial core. The exarch of Carthage Gennadios defeated Moorish attacks in ca. 589 and 595; this province had another century of life in it.[52]

As for Italy, Maurikios made an alliance with the Frankish king Childebert II of Austrasia and induced him, in the mid-580s, to invade Italy a number of times in order to weaken the Lombards, but the result of these expeditions was instead to strengthen the Lombard monarchy in northern Italy under king Authari. Maurikios had subsidized the Franks to the tune of 50,000 solidi, but they failed to assist the empire. The emperor complained that he wanted his money back until, in 590, he decided to do the job properly. The dynamic exarch Romanos was sent to open an offensive against the Lombards along the Po river. He made significant gains, but then another Frankish army arrived, sent by Childebert, whose aims were unclear. In correspondence that survives, Romanos tried to ascertain whether the Franks were there to assist him to end the Lombard monarchy. They pretended to be true to the alliance, but left after securing the allegiance of the Lombards to their own king.[53] Ultimately, the Romans made limited gains. Their position was hampered by constant warfare along multiple fronts in Italy. It was difficult to strike a comprehensive deal with the Lombards, who were often themselves disunited. Pope Gregory I (590–604) was trying to make side deals to protect the city of Rome from the barbarians, but these interfered with Romanos' plans. The pope complained that the exarch "is pretending to fight against our enemies, while he forbids us from making peace." The two men did not get along.[54]

In Catholic tradition, Gregory "the Great" is a towering figure in the history of the Church and an inspired exponent of its pastoral philosophy. His extensive corpus of letters reveals that the Church of Rome was the most powerful institution that still survived in the former capital. The city's Senate as a functional body did not outlive the sixth century. The pope was in many ways the city's chief administrator, and we catch glimpses of his future in the independent deals that Gregory was making with the Lombards in Rome's vicinity and the international diplomacy in which he engaged via correspondence. But when all is said and done, the pope remained the bishop of a provincial city in a low-priority region of the empire, "suffering in the midst of Lombard swords." He probably administered more land than any other Church in the empire possessed, but his revenues had likely diminished. His predecessor Pelagius I had complained that income from Church lands in Picenum was down from 2,160 solidi in ca. 500 to 500 solidi. Moreover, Gregory lacked the authority to make major policy decisions, and had to petition, beg, and complain to imperial officials in order to get things done, even in areas of Church governance. He was anxious not to do anything "detrimental to the interests of the *res publica*." In 598, Maurikios sent an official, Leontios, with a staff to scrutinize the finances of Sicily and Italy, and the investigations roped in some of the pope's favorites, without him being able to do anything about it other than protest.[55]

In the first years of the seventh century, the Lombard king Agilulf (590–616) was able to take Padua, Cremona, and Mantua, using Slavic soldiers that were loaned to him by his ally, the Avar khagan. In 605, the new exarch Smaragdos ended the war by making a treaty with Agilulf. This entailed a (one-time?) payment of 12,000 solidi and effectively conceded two-thirds of the Italian peninsula to the barbarians.[56] The war had produced some fascinating careers. There was, for example, Droctulf, a Suebian by birth who was raised by the Lombards, and even became a duke, but switched over to the empire and fought against its enemies in every theater: the Balkans, Italy, and North Africa. A fierce warrior, fighting under the banner of St. Vitalis, he became a champion of Ravenna and a terror to his former people. When he died, in ca. 606, the bishop allowed him to be buried in the church of San Vitale, under the gaze of Justinian and

Theodora, celebrated by an epitaph: "long was the beard that grew down on his vigorous breast / loving the standards of Rome and the emblems of the *res publica* / aid unto them he brought, crushing the power of his race . . . . He deemed Ravenna his own fatherland, dear to his heart."[57] The body of another warrior was excavated recently in a Lombard necropolis in the north, who had replaced his amputated hand with a prosthetic blade, which he tightened by pulling on the leather straps with his teeth.[58]

The Persian civil war

Maurikios' big break came in 590. The shah Hormizd was unpopular among his subjects, and had in particular given offense to one Bahram Chobin, who had just been defeated by the Romans in the Caucasus. Bahram belonged to the noble house of Mihran, a Parthian family that ruled in northern Iran. He now rebelled against Hormizd and gained significant support, as he was a hero of the Persian-Turkish wars in the northeast (indeed, his memory would be celebrated in Persian tradition for centuries thereafter).[59] Bahram defeated a force that was sent against him by the court, and Hormizd was deposed in a coup and blinded. His son Khusrow II (590–628) was appointed to rule in his place, probably as the puppet of a court faction that then executed Hormizd. But in February, 590, Bahram defeated Khusrow II in battle and claimed the throne, in effect a dynastic revolution. Khusrow fled to the Roman empire. He was not the first member of his house to seek foreign help in order to regain his throne. Kavad had fled to the Hephthalites in the fifth century and was reinstalled by their army, and plenty of Persian princes had fled to Constantinople.

From the eastern border, Khusrow sent an appeal to Maurikios, calling Rome and Persia "the two eyes of the world" and asking for help in exchange for everlasting gratitude. He sent ambassadors offering to cede Daras, Armenia up to Dvin, and Iberia up to Tiflis to Rome. Maurikios agreed. According to later sources, he did so against the objections of those who believed that Khusrow was not trustworthy and preferred to let the Persians wear themselves out in civil war, but these reports were written in hindsight.[60] Khusrow, who spent the winter at Hierapolis with his many wives and two infant children, put on a Christian face, sponsoring the shrine of St. Sergios at Sergiopolis (Resafa) and promising to endow it with wealth and relics. In 591, two Roman field armies marched deep into the Persian empire from different directions. These were the armies of Oriens under one Narses, escorting Khusrow, and of Armenia under The Mustache. Along with the Persian allies recruited along the way, they managed, through a coordinated movement, to converge on Bahram in the Zagros mountains and crush him at the battle of the Blarathon river, near lake Urmia. Bahram fled to his old enemies, the Turks, where he was later assassinated by agents of the shah.

Theophylaktos reports that the Roman side had 60,000 men at the battle—the total size of Julian's expeditionary force in 363—and Bahram 40,000. These numbers are high, but nothing less than control of the Persian empire hung in the balance, and both sides would have mustered their full strength. An eastern source says that each Roman field army in this campaign had 20,000 men, which matches their nominal strength, and they were joined by 10,000 Persian allies, a plausible figure.[61] So the empire still had the resources and skill to wage war on a vast scale when it came to decisive confrontations. The payoff of this gamble was significant, for Khusrow fulfilled his pledges.

The zone of Roman control now extended farther into the Caucasus than ever before. As the gains were soon lost, we know little about their administration. An Armenian mathematical text from the seventh century offers a glimpse of the fiscal mentalities that Romans brought to these lands: students are asked to calculate how much money was once in the treasury of Constantinople if thieves stole three quarters of it, given the amount left; and to calculate the salaries of the priests of Hagia Sophia (it works out to 230,400 solidi, an impossible figure).[62] Maurikios was the first emperor to use Armenia primarily for recruiting, a policy that would have a long future. He also pressured the Armenian Church to accept Chalcedon, but its head, or *katholikos*, was located at Dvin within the Persian zone and so "refused to eat the baked bread or drink the warm water of the Greeks." This referred to differences in the celebration of the Eucharist by Romans and Armenians. In response, the emperor established a rival Chalcedonian Armenian Church with its own *katholikos*. The Iberian Church by contrast sided with the Chalcedonians, and so with the empire.[63]

In the 580s, Maurikios had declined to intervene in the domestic split between Chalcedonians and anti-Chalcedonians: "We have enough to do with the foreign wars, don't bring domestic wars upon us too!" he said to churchmen who urged him to persecute. But after his Persian victory, along with the pressure that he put on Armenia he authorized bishops to go after Roman Monophysites. Monophysite sources likely exaggerate when they depict this as a brutal persecution. Our sole Chalcedonian source euphemistically says that "many were brought into union with the Church," a bland statement that likely covered up much violence.[64]

For his part, Khusrow was preoccupied during the 590s with establishing his authority in Persia. He did, however, made good on his promises to St. Sergios by sending gifts and dedications to thank the saint for victory and for the pregnancy of his Christian wife Shirin. In a letter that accompanied one of his dedications, Khusrow states that his wife was a Christian and he a "Hellene," i.e., a pagan. He also refers to the proper name—Romanía—of the state that helped him.[65] Pope Gregory I wrote a letter to console bishop Domitianos of Melitene, who accompanied the expedition of 591, for not managing to convert Khusrow: "the Ethiopian is black when he enters the baths, and black when he leaves" (according to later legends, the shah did convert).[66] At some point in the 590s,

Khusrow executed al-Nuʿman, the leader of the Persian Saracens at al-Hira, who had himself converted to (Nestorian) Christianity. Nuʿman earned this more by his failure to support the shah in 590 than his conversion. Thus, within a decade, both empires dismantled the leadership structures of their Saracen clients and replaced them with decentralized groupings.[67] This likely facilitated the Arab conquests of the 630s.

Containing the Avars

The end of the Persian war allowed Maurikios to transfer armies from the east to the Balkans, where, during the next ten years (592–602), they gradually contained the Avar threat, refortified defenses, and took the fight to the enemy, striking out into the Avar and Slav homelands across the Danube. The Avars and Slavs were both dangerous opponents, but for different reasons. Their military ethnographies are laid out in a clear and informative treatise on strategy attributed to the emperor himself, the *Strategikon*. Avar armies were a combination of armored heavy cavalry and mounted archers, and relied on speed to outmaneuver their opponents and on ruthless pursuit in victory. They had the advantage of the stirrup, which they brought to Europe, where it was quickly adopted by the Romans. Avars fought arrayed by "tribe and clan," but we know nothing about internal Avar ethnic distinctions. The emperor could negotiate with the khagan and treat the khaganate as a unified entity.[68]

Slavs, on the other hand, operated in decentralized bands that were good at ambushes, guerilla warfare, and melting into the terrain, especially in mountains and marshes. They distantly acknowledged the khagan as an overlord, though he often found it difficult to control them, and they had no leaders with whom the empire could negotiate deals that were binding on large groups. Whereas Avars attacked cities and armies, and had destroyed many forts and communities along the Danube, Slavs mostly disrupted the countryside and imperiled agriculture, tax collection, and the movement of goods and people. But Slavs could besiege cities too, such as Thessalonike in 586. An eyewitness recounts how they surrounded it, consumed the harvest and fruits, and set fires along the walls before launching a week-long attack with siege engines. With some Avars, Slavs raided as far south as Corinth and Athens in the 580s. In 2004, over thirty skeletons from the later sixth century, mostly of women and children, were found in a cave in the Argolid, where they had sought refuge with provisions and, eventually, perished.[69]

Khagan Baian was succeeded soon after 583 by a son, and the latter by a brother. We do not know their names, but between them they ruled until at least 626.[70] Their raids had done extensive damage to the Roman provinces, especially along the Danube plain, but had not claimed more territory since the capture of Sirmium. The Roman counteroffensive of the 590s gradually restored imperial control along the Danube, imperfectly to be sure, as intermittent raids continued. Coin finds and archaeology suggest that the border forts remained in imperial hands and were in use.[71] In 593 Priskos led a punitive campaign against the Slavs north of the lower Danube, operating in territory that had not seen a Roman army since Valens' campaigns of the 360s. In line with the advice given in the *Strategikon*, Maurikios asked Priskos to spend the winter there and continue his bloody operations, because it was harder for the Slavs to seek cover in that season. But the army refused and returned to the empire. The soldiers were also unhappy that their plunder was sent to the emperor, and part of it was used to appease the khagan for this attack on his nominal Slavic subjects.[72]

Subsequent campaigns aimed to restore imperial control westward along the river. In 597–598, the khagan invaded Thrace again, but he accomplished little and his army was decimated by plague, which killed seven of his sons, so he withdrew in exchange for an increase in his annual payment. He also formally recognized the Danube as the border between his realm and the empire, with the provision that the Romans could cross to attack hostile Slavs. But in 599, it was the emperor who broke the treaty and sent armies under Komentiolos and Priskos to attack the Avar homeland north of Singidunum and Sirmium. The Romans scored notable victories, causing a number of the khagan's followers to defect to the emperor.[73] In 602, Petros was sent to ravage the Slav lands, and was again ordered to spend the winter there. The soldiers again refused, perhaps in the belief that they would not be supplied from the empire but would have to forage in order to survive, a belief that jibed with Maurikios' penny-pinching reputation. This time matters went badly awry, because Petros refused to disobey his brother's order. Thereupon the army mutinied, elected their officer Phokas as their leader, proclaimed him as their emperor, and marched on Constantinople. Suddenly, regime change was in the air.[74]

Maurikios had capably managed the empire's conflicts. He had concluded the war with Persia with a victory that put the shah in his debt, and he was gradually rolling back the Avar-Slavic advance, all within the limited means at his disposal and without raising taxes. But he had also alienated key constituencies. His failed attempts to reduce army pay and strip soldiers of their booty had taught the army how to mutiny and get what it wanted. Too much damning "fake news" circulated about the emperor, who failed to cultivate popularity. It was alleged that he had secretly instructed Komentiolos to throw a battle in 600 to the khagan in order to punish the army, and then refused to ransom the prisoners. The army sent a delegation to the court, which included Phokas, but it was treated scornfully. The accusation was, of course, preposterous, but it was a bad idea to humiliate those who thought it was plausible.[75] The emperor was also unpopular in the City, in part because of his partiality toward his own relatives. The populace protested during a food shortage earlier in 602, throwing stones at the imperial family and chanting an insulting song about him:

> He found his heifer tender and soft, and he fucked her like the proverbial young cock, and fathered children like chips off the block. Now no one dares speak; he's muzzled us all. My Lord, my holy Lord, fearful and mighty, let him have it on the skull for his conceit, and I'll bring you the great bull in thanksgiving![76]

When he heard that a mutinous army was approaching, Maurikios tried to draft the hippodrome fan club members as a makeshift defense force. As various factions jockeyed over the succession, the populace abused Maurikios with chants and burned down the house of the praetorian prefect Konstantinos, nicknamed "Lardy." Maurikios fled across the Bosporos on 22 November, 602, dressed as a commoner, his authority in shambles and, likely, deserted by the excubitors. On the 23rd, Phokas was crowned by the patriarch in the church of St. John at the Hebdomon. Two days later, Phokas entered the City and was unanimously acclaimed Augustus by the people. Two days after that, Maurikios and his family were arrested and taken to Chalkedon. With undeserved cruelty, his sons were executed before his eyes, and he then shared their fate; their heads were displayed at the Hebdomon. Phokas purged the administration of the men who were deemed most responsible for the financial and military misery of the soldiers on the Danube, executing the praetorian prefect and the generals Petros and Komentiolos. Philippikos and Maurikios' daughters survived by joining monasteries. The general Priskos, by contrast, was made *comes* of the excubitors and later, in 605, married the new emperor's daughter.[77] Phokas left everyone else in place.

The eastern empire had not experienced such a political convulsion in its entire history, and emperors had not been directly overthrown by the army since the third century. A Church historian writing in the 590s commented that after Constantine, only a pagan (Julian) and heretic (Valens) had been killed, because God supported Christian emperors.[78] Maurikios' successes notwithstanding, he had failed, in an age of fiscal austerity, to keep public opinion on his side. Yet the Romans soon found out how much depended on that one man's life. Maurikios' death would unleash the Furies and change the face of the world. At a monastery in Asia Minor, a holy man told his monks that he had seen a vision of the emperor's death. They replied that it served him right for all the things that he had done badly. "Children," he responded, "this man will soon be removed, but after him such terrible things will occur as this generation cannot possibly imagine."[79]

Broader horizons, shallower culture

As recently as the fourth century, Rome had one true peer—Persia—and was surrounded elsewhere by barbarians with rudimentary states and armies that were generally no match for its own. By contrast, the world of the sixth century was more multipolar. The Visigoths, Franks, and Lombards developed quasi-Roman courts, laws, and armies, and an arc of Great Power politics extended from the Avars to the Turks and Persians, and in the south to Himyar and Aksum. The conquests of Justinian had entangled Romanía more deeply in this wider world. The emperors were now holding hostage the daughter of a Visigothic queen to leverage the Franks to attack the Lombards in Italy; they were sending embassies to the Turks in Central Asia and hosting a delegation of hundreds of Turks in Constantinople; and they were fighting battles in Azerbaijan to reinstall a Persian shah on his throne. This was no longer a world with Roman horizons.

The antennas of Roman information gathering were attuned to ever more distant signals. The sixth century was a golden age of diplomatic-travel literature, as ambassadors wrote accounts of their travels to Aksum and Central Asia, which were quickly devoured by the reading public. The ethnographies and foreign histories in Prokopios range from Scandinavia to Central Asia and the Red Sea. For the first time, through the mediation of their Turkish allies, the Romans received detailed knowledge of northern China, with references even to Korea, and through the overseas trade route they learned about India, Sri Lanka, and southern China. Never had there been such knowledge of the broader world. The historian Agathias (ca. 580) obtained a chronicle of the shahs and authentic Zoroastrian lore from inside the Sasanian court.[80]

This extension of contacts and information also enabled Constantinople to project its prestige on a broader canvas. Among the post-Roman kingdoms in the west, the eastern empire remained the one and only *res publica Romana* and was still the gold standard for political authority, or regal pretense. In the poem that she commissioned for Sophia, the Frankish nun (and retired queen) Radegund of Poitiers praised the eastern empress for ruling over "the kingdom of Romulus." As far north as East Anglia, a Byzantine silver dish with export stamps was included in the royal burial at Sutton Hoo (see Figure 17a–b on page 248). In the east, Roman ambassadors persuaded the Turks that Rome was superior to Persia by referencing a statue of Trajan that still stood in Persia, a legacy of his conquests, which the shah promptly tore down to erase the lingering humiliation. A Nestorian author of a Christian geography cited Roman coins as proof that Romanía was superior to other nations, as the solidus was valid currency throughout the world. One of his contacts, a merchant named Sopatros, claimed that he had humiliated a Persian rival by asking the king of Sri Lanka to compare a golden solidus to a silver Persian drachma and then decide for himself which king, depicted on his respective coin, was greater.[81]

Domestically, Roman culture remained capable of extraordinary feats and creative work, including the compilation of the *Corpus* by the jurist Tribonian and his committee; the building of Hagia Sophia by the architects Anthemios and Isidoros; and the commentaries on Plato and Aristotle by Simplikios, Olympiodoros, and Ioannes Philoponos. The latter even performed experiments to disprove Aristotle's theory of gravity, a thousand years before Galileo.[82] This was also the culture that produced the magnificent forgeries of pseudo-Dionysios and Prokopios' *Wars* and *Secret History*. However, all of these men were educated before Justinian repressed Hellenism and diverted funds away from culture and schools to wars, walls, and churches.[83] These policies had palpable consequences a generation later, as the end of the century was a wasteland by comparison. The schools of Athens (philosophy) and Beirut (law) disappeared. Those of Alexandria survived, but philosophy as an autonomous discipline and way of life died out, and so did the thriving legal culture that had produced the *Corpus* and its scholia.[84] There were to be no more great jurists and architects. The production of secular books plummeted after Justinian and the book market generally collapsed after 600.[85] No interesting theologians emerged during the second half of the sixth century, not on any side of the many divides in the Church.

The opposite choices, with the opposite effects, were being made in Persia. Khusrow I was an amateur intellectual who attracted scholars from many cultures, even from outside his empire, including the philosophers of Athens. Persia became a center of philosophy and translation, including from Greek into Syriac and Syriac into Pahlavi (Middle Persian). This laid the groundwork for later Arabic thought, an even more significant chapter in the history of thought.[86] Romanía had opted out of that trajectory.

Latin literature also ceased to be written in the empire after the 560s. Both laws and military manuals, such as the *Strategikon*, were henceforth in Greek. In North Africa and Italy ancient literary culture had survived under the Vandals and the Goths, but after Justinian it collapsed there too, after a futile protest in defense of the Three Chapters; it had long since been extinct in Spain. Thus, higher culture was being run down by war, plague, repression, and austerity in both Romanía and its overseas territories.

Many scholars believe that during the sixth century Roman society became—or already was—"monolithically Christian." This is difficult to measure. Overt pagan worship had been systematically targeted by the state and, even though the laws could not always be enforced, after centuries of discrimination and violence the worship of the gods had been finally uprooted by the end of the sixth century. People were arrested, tried, or killed by angry mobs in Constantinople simply on the suspicion of being pagans, and the authorities allowed it. Even patriarchs of the Church could be denounced as crypto-pagans and had to rush to Constantinople to clear their name. When a patriarch of Jerusalem was accused of various crimes, it was suspected that he was being framed by pagans whom he had outed, and that the judges were also pagans in disguise.[87] Paranoia about secret religious beliefs and occult networks had set in, and would never fully go away.

The cultural framework of Roman society had also shifted from pagan common reference points to Christian ones, or rather it had expanded to include them. Cities identified with their saints and famous bishops as well as with their ancient founders and patron gods. In the late sixth century, an imperial monument in Alexandria was ascribed to Alexander the Great and said to contain the relics of the prophet Jeremiah, brought there by Alexander himself. Even the early history of Constantinople was retroactively Christianized. Its original adornment relied on thoroughly pagan referents, but, in the later historical imagination, Constantine was associated with churches and holy relics. The symbolic language through which people interpreted their own experiences was that of Scripture, which displaced the world of Homer and tragedy. While the stories of the Bible were recounted in the churches, no institution disseminated the rudiments of ancient culture to the people at large.[88]

On the other hand, *literary* paganism was unaffected. Christian authors moved enthusiastically into the spaces vacated by their pagan counterparts, and crammed their works with florid mythological references. A Church historian of the 590s digressed to compose a rhetorical description of the personified deity of Opportune Moment (*kairos*), probably describing a statue of the god. Likewise, a secular but pious historian of the 630s, addressing the patriarch of Constantinople, crammed dozens of classical and mythological comparisons into his dedicatory preface. The feats of the emperor Herakleios would naturally be compared by his court orator, a deacon of Hagia Sophia, to those of Herakles.[89] All this had counterparts in the arts. A sixth- or seventh-century treasure from Lampsakos (on the Hellespont, not far from Troy) contains a number of silver spoons, some of them inscribed with the names of the Apostles but most with the sayings of the Seven Sages of ancient Greece, and some with verses of Vergil's *Eclogues*, in Latin. The archetypes of elite culture had expanded to include Christian referents, but had not shifted over to them exclusively.[90]

Imperial authority continued to be framed in traditional ways and took no more than baby steps toward overtly Christian forms. Christian images were pervasive at this time, as they had simply taken over the spaces, and many of the functions, of pagan images. But imperial use of Christian images was still vestigial. The saints appeared only on the hangings in Hagia Sophia, not the fixtures, walls, or dome. Justin II placed images of the Virgin on his seals, but not on coins. The Latin epic poem celebrating his accession invents a vision of

Christ and the Virgin authorizing the emperor to rule.[91] Yet, overall, imperial self-representation had changed little.

The legal system had barely budged in a Christian direction. Even to the extent that it regulated the Church, it brought the latter into the orbit of Roman law rather than vice versa. It is possible that villagers increasingly brought their disputes to the arbitration of religious men instead of the secular courts, but this development had been encouraged by the imperial legal system itself, which was eager to slough off low-stakes busywork.[92] On a more fundamental level, Christianity had still brought no changes to the economic, social, and political structures of the empire or—and this is perhaps more important—to the social values that underpinned them, other than to become more deeply integrated into them.

Justinian had tried to go deeper and crack down on behaviors that he deemed un-Christian and immoral, from adultery and homosexuality to dice playing. But this effort did not strike at the heart of the worldly values that preachers regularly denounced, and even there he failed. People still attended church to gossip, ogle the women, strike business deals, make fun of the priest, and leave early. Few understood Christian theology.[93] Meanwhile, erotic poetry rose to a high standard, among pagans and Christians, and remained vibrant until the 580s, when secular culture generally declined. This circle of poets included Paulos the *silentiarios* (who also wrote an edifying poetic description of Hagia Sophia for Justinian's court) and the lawyer and historian Agathias. They delighted in poetic transgressions against Christian sexual norms.

> When I saw Melite, I grew pale, for her husband
> was with her. Here is what I said, trembling:
> "May I push open the bolts on your door,
> loosening the peg of your folding entrance,
> and, penetrating the wet bottom of your front-doors,
> plant the tip of my key right in the middle?"
> She laughed and said, looking at him sideways,
> "You'd better stay away from the doors, or the dog will get you."[94]

For the survival of sixth-century literature, we are at the mercy of its later transmission, which was deliberately selective. Latin texts survived if they piqued western medieval interests; Syriac texts if they were anti-Chalcedonian; and Greek texts if they were Chalcedonian or appealed to the later literary tastes of Constantinople. Only rarely may we circumvent this filter. The lawyer and poet Dioskoros (ca. 525–585), a chief citizen of Aphrodite in middle Egypt, is one such case. He would be utterly unknown had his papyrus archive and library not been found in a jar. Dioskoros was bilingual in Coptic and Greek, and wrote petitions and legal documents on behalf of his fellow citizens and city, as well as poems (in Greek) praising various officials. He was trained in Roman law, educated in the Greek classics, and immersed in the Christian culture of his time; his father had founded a monastery, and Dioskoros was its legal patron. His diction is drenched in mythological allusions and shaped by Scripture and the liturgy. It is also because of him that we have long passages from the comic playwright Menandros, which would otherwise be lost. Dioskoros thus represents a remarkable nexus of sixth-century Roman culture, combining elements that were Egyptian vernacular, classical Greek, local and pan-imperial, as well as Christian, both monastic and lay, into his complex profile. He maneuvered skillfully within the legal system and the imperial bureaucracy, even traveling to Constantinople to defend his city from an administrator who wanted to take over its tax collection. However, no cultural or religious tradition had any interest later in preserving his memory, because he was too much of all of them at once, and not enough of one. His poetry has been called the worst ever. But we are lucky to have him as a corrective to later filters.[95]

Roman culture did not change dramatically in the sixth century. However, it had wasted tremendous energies in the conflict over Chalcedon, an obsession that proved intellectually sterile, culturally stultifying, and socially divisive. This dispute kept the culture in stasis, as each faction clung fast to its fifth-century coordinates, relitigating the decisions of all the Councils. The eastern empire was meanwhile battered by wars, was decimated by recurrences of the plague, and was unable to generate prior levels of revenue. Still, it had ended the Persian war to its advantage and was pushing the Avars out of the Balkans. A trajectory of recovery could be foreseen in early 602—until Phokas' coup.

PART FIVE
TO THE BRINK OF DESPAIR

15
The Great War with Persia (602–630)

Phokas

The portraits of Phokas and his wife Leontia were received at Rome with acclamations on 25 April, 603, as noted in a brief report that awkwardly also lists Phokas' slaughtered victims. Pope Gregory I, who was a friend of Maurikios from his time as papal representative in Constantinople and had baptized his son and designated successor Theodosios, wrote a fulsome letter to their murderer Phokas that proclaimed, "*Gloria in excelsis Deo!* We rejoice that the kindness of your Piety has come to the imperial throne." The letter has long embarrassed the pope's admirers, and perhaps his praise of the new regime was meant as indirect advice on how to govern properly. There was not much that a bishop of a provincial city could do about the politics of the center. He frames the distinction between Romanía and the barbarian kingdoms in an interesting way: "The kings of the various tribes [*reges gentium*] are masters of slaves, yet the emperors of a republic [*imperatores rei publicae*] are masters of free men."[1]

After his fall, Phokas was demonized as a tyrant who oppressed his subjects and lost the eastern provinces to the Persians. This image was created in part by duplicating entries on domestic scandals, so that one execution became three, or splitting up single events and distributing their fragments across different years, and by backdating the Persian conquests of the 610s to the 600s.[2] There were in reality only two main bouts of violence in the City. The first was in 603. Phokas appeared late to the games because he was drunk and the Greens mocked him: "You're drunk again and out of your mind." Phokas ordered many of them to be mutilated or executed, and in response they protested and again burned down the *praitorion* and prison, traditional targets of popular protest.[3]

Phokas made few changes to administration and to foreign policy. The Avars seem to have kept the peace after the Roman resurgence of the 590s. However, Khusrow II cynically decided to avenge the murder of his "father" Maurikios by invading the Roman empire. Accompanying his armies was a person claiming to be Maurikios' son Theodosios, who had escaped the massacres of 602; the truth of this was as obscure then as it is now. This war with Persia was aggravated by the rebellion against Phokas of the general Narses, the one who had restored Khusrow in 591. Narses now seized Edessa. He was likely not collaborating with the shah, but he forced the empire to fight a civil war on top of the Persian one. Phokas transferred armies from the Balkans to Asia, increasing the peace payment to the khagan—so to more than 120,000 per year.[4] The chronology of these years is muddled because we have only later chronicles. The Romans were decisively defeated by the Persians in battle, and after a siege of between nine and eighteen months mounted by Khusrow in person, the bunker of Daras fell again to the Persians in 604 or 605. Its inhabitants were slaughtered and its wealth taken to Ktesiphon by the shah.[5] Khusrow entrusted the war to his general Farrukhan of the house of Mihran. He was also known as Rasmiozan, Khoream, and Shahrbaraz ("Boar of Empire"). He would become the most fearsome enemy Rome had known since Hannibal.

Phokas' legitimacy remained tenuous. The rebel Narses was lured to Constantinople under assurances of safety, and then burned alive.[6] A conspiracy was uncovered in 605, involving Maurikios' widow Konstantina (a daughter of Tiberios II), the patrician Germanos, the praetorian prefect Theodoros, and lesser figures of the court, holdovers from the previous regime. They were all arrested and executed. Along with the executions of 602, this was the greatest slaughter of royals since the summer of 337. The conspirators may have been planning to support the pretender Theodosios and thereby end the Persian war.[7] Phokas had now eliminated the previous imperial family and the upper echelons of its court. In need of political support, he married his daughter to Maurikios' general Priskos. But the manner of Phokas' own ascent had weakened the security of the imperial office.

The Persian war followed the usual pattern, splitting between Armenia and Mesopotamia. The difference was that the Persians now began to occupy the cities and territories that they won, which had not happened before. Specifically, they managed, against heavy resistance, to expel the Romans from Persarmenia, the prize of Maurikios' settlement of 591. By ca. 606, they were pushing into Roman Armenia too and in ca. 607 they took Theodosiopolis (Karin) along with other cities and forts. They dismantled the Chalcedonian hierarchy of Maurikios and gave the region to the anti-Chalcedonian Armenian *katholikos*.[8] The road into Asia Minor was open. Meanwhile, Persian forces were also advancing in Mesopotamia, though the sources are poor and the chronology muddled. It is not clear whether they were resisted by Roman field armies or only by city garrisons, but the enemy advance was contested every step of the way, making it a brutal slog. By ca. 608, they had taken Amida and other fortified towns, and allowed anti-Chalcedonian bishops to return. The Romans abandoned everything east of the Euphrates, and were unable to mount counterraids.[9]

Unsurprisingly, a rebellion broke out in 608, but in an unexpected place: North Africa. It was launched by the exarch of the province, Herakleios, a veteran of Maurikios' wars in Armenia. He was supported by his son, also Herakleios, whom the conspirators intended for the throne, as well as by the exarch's brother Gregorios and his son, Niketas. The two Herakleioi assumed the office of consul, which was an imperial prerogative in this period, and began to strike their own coins.[10] The civil war that they set into motion was the most destructive that the eastern empire had yet suffered. It ravaged Egypt, a productive province, and distracted the court, allowing the empire's foreign enemies to make large territorial gains. The empire's collapse was precipitated by this war.

The rebels sent an advance army of 3,000 under one "Bonakis" to Egypt (he is so named in the Ethiopic translation of our source, the chronicle of Ioannes of Nikiou). They hired barbarian auxiliaries, mostly Moors, and suborned imperial officers in Libya and Egypt through bribes and promises. In mid-608, Niketas and Bonakis defeated the governor of Alexandria and took possession of the city. Egypt was splitting violently between partisans of the two sides, and so were many cities throughout the empire, especially in Syria and Palestine. The Greens supported the rebels, whereas the Blues tended to be Phokas loyalists. Many sources describe the ensuing civil strife and lament the lives that it claimed. "In all regions, they took up the sword and slaughtered each other." The *Miracles of Demetrios*, written ten years later, praises the saint for preserving his city Thessalonike from the madness, sent by Satan, that raged across the empire for two years (608–610). The fan clubs had effectively become political factions. Throughout the empire, from Egypt to Ephesos, the Blues set up inscriptions for Phokas and the Greens for Herakleios. Phokas sent Bonosos, *comes* of Oriens, to suppress the disorders in Syria and Palestine, from Antioch to Kaisareia, and he did so with extraordinary violence.[11] Bonosos was widely reviled as "horrific," "inhuman," and "a hyena." A monk later claimed to have seen his soul escorted to a special pit in Hell, whose demonic sentinel had not opened it to admit anyone since Julian the Apostate.[12]

After butchering his way from Antioch to Kaisareia, Bonosos mustered the eastern armies to confront the rebels. The fighting in Egypt in 609 was protracted and fierce. Bonosos defeated and killed Bonakis, and began to imprison or kill the "traitors." Meanwhile, Niketas held Alexandria with a force of "soldiers, barbarians, local citizens, Greens, sailors, and archers." After many engagements, Niketas prevailed and drove Bonosos from Egypt, and then set about pacifying the province, which was tearing itself apart in recriminations and reprisals. He issued a grant of tax relief for three years. By mid-610, Phokas' name disappears from the papyri.[13] The rebels had achieved important strategic goals: they had removed about 30% of Phokas' revenue, while most of his forces were tied down fighting the Persians. The rebels' control of the grain fleet was also a sword of Damocles hanging over Constantinople. It is also striking how, in this war, mere generals were appointing patriarchs to serve partisan interests. Bonosos appointed Zacharias to Jerusalem, deposing the incumbent, while Niketas appointed Ioannes (later known as the Almsgiver) to Alexandria, a man to whom he was bound by ties of ritual brotherhood. Controlling the see of Alexandria was necessary after the remission of Egyptian taxes, because the Church of Alexandria held 8,000 lbs of gold in cash, in addition to its real estate and trading fleet.[14]

Herakleios junior does not appear in the fighting of those years. In 610, he sailed to Constantinople to seize his prize, stopping along the way to rally his Green supporters. He had with him both regular soldiers and many Moors. An inscription from Constantinople records the death of a soldier serving in such a unit, led by one Zar. Meanwhile, the regime was imploding, as Phokas did not know whom to trust. Many of his enemies went over to Herakleios at Abydos, in the Hellespont, after which the rebel moved his ships to within sight of the capital. Phokas tried to organize the City's defenses, but he was betrayed by the Greens and by Priskos, a nimble survivor, who withdrew the excubitors at a critical moment. Resistance collapsed and the hated Bonosos was killed trying to escape. Phokas was arrested on 5 or 6 October and brought before Herakleios. "So this is how you have governed the state?," he was asked. "Let's see if you can do better," Phokas replied before he was executed. His brother, a general, and the regime's chief accountant were also executed, their bodies mutilated and set on fire. Herakleios, thirty-five years old, was "proclaimed emperor by the Senate and people" and crowned by the patriarch Sergios in the palace. At the races the next day, images of Phokas were burned along with the flags of the Blues. The Blues themselves fled for asylum to Hagia Sophia.[15]

It was a desperate gamble for Carthage to launch a regime change against Constantinople, but the rebels' two-pronged strategy—army and navy—had paid off. Phokas was duly condemned as a "Gorgon-face," "Cyclops," and "Hydra," and the defeats that were yet to come were retroactively blamed on him.[16] Yet Herakleios' coup inflicted far more direct damage to the already weakened Roman state than Phokas'. Worse, Herakleios had forced Phokas to divert scarce assets away from the defense against Persia to fight a civil war in Egypt. It was the opening that Khusrow needed. In 609/10, the shah transplanted the populace of Theodosiopolis to Hamadan in Iran, and Shahrbaraz took Edessa, Karrai, Kallinikos, Tella, and Kirkesion, through either assault or surrender. Then, in August, 610, Zenobia was "the first city west of the Euphrates to be taken."[17] The east was falling, and the shah was thinking beyond the traditional rhythm of raid, siege, and counterraid. He had embarked on conquest.

The conquests of Khusrow II

Khusrow II was an insecure ruler. When he was twenty, in 590, his uncles Vistahm and Vinduyih, of house Ispahbudhan, conspired to overthrow his father, Hormizd IV, and elevate him to the throne. Khusrow was immediately overthrown by Bahram Chobin, of house Mihran, and had to be restored by the Romans. These events broadcast the dynasty's weakness, and it was all the more humiliating that the young shah had lacked agency in both of his accessions. For much of the 590s, he struggled to suppress a rebellion by Vistahm, who carved out an independent realm in the north. Following the reforms of Khusrow I, the high command of the army was divided among four districts, those of the East, South, West, and Azerbaijan, each under a general from a noble house called a *spahbed*. Vistahm now controlled the East (Khorasan) and Azerbaijan. In order to suppress him, Khusrow had to rely on assistance from the Armenian noble Smbat Bagratuni, whom he then put in command of Khorasan (though Armenian sources, on which we rely, exaggerate the role that Armenian nobles played in the affairs of Rome and Persia).[18] By 601, Khusrow regained control of his empire, but relations with key noble houses were precarious and his reliance on Christians and Romans, at the cost of territorial concessions, had tarnished his authority. The eastern Roman provinces were now made to suffer so that the shah could shore up his regime.

Maurikios' murder in 602 gave Khusrow the chance to symbolically pay off one of his debts and profit in the process. As he had been proclaimed Maurikios' "son," he could now avenge his "father" by attacking the latter's murderer, which in practice meant attacking the Roman empire. This was legitimated by the cynical use of the pretender Theodosios to restore Maurikios' dynasty just as Maurikios had restored his, and also by extravagant displays of grief for Maurikios, widely regarded as insincere: Khusrow and his entire court dressed in black and lamented the murdered emperor for days.[19] In the 600s, the Persian attack swept through Armenia (both Persian and Roman) and conquered all Roman territory east of the Euphrates. The war thereby kept the Persian nobles occupied in a project that would simultaneously enrich them and restore the shah's prestige. It is possible that he was fired up by the dream of restoring the empire of the Achaemenids. Proof of this ambition is hard to find, but that was how the Romans traditionally viewed Sasanian aggression. The Sasanians did link themselves to the Achaemenids by placing their triumphant rock reliefs adjacent to the tombs of Dareios and Xerxes.

What enabled Khusrow's armies to succeed was the absence of the Roman field armies. The army in Armenia was defeated and fell back to Asia Minor, but its counterpart in Oriens was absent from Syria, possibly because the Roman civil war had drawn it to fight in Egypt against the armies of North Africa, mauling both. Moreover, the Roman military command was divided. Phokas' brother Komentiolos, who was probably *magister militum* of Oriens but had withdrawn to Ankyra, refused to recognize Herakleios in 610–611 and had to be assassinated by Ioustinos, who was likely the *magister militum* for Armenia.[20] The armies, then, were disunited, disordered, and out of place. They were surely also undermanned.

The Persians struck in two directions. One army, under Shahin, invaded central Asia Minor, capturing and sacking Kaisareia in Cappadocia. Asia

Minor had not seen military operations since Anastasius' Isaurian campaign of the 490s, and the "terror" of this attack spread far and wide. Allegedly, the Christians fled while the Jews submitted. This may be anti-Jewish slander, though events would reveal that many Jews of the empire favored the Persians (just as Samaritans had solicited Persian intervention after their revolt in 529). Shahin was blockaded at Kaisareia for a year by Priskos, who was still *comes* of the excubitors, but the Persians managed to defeat him in battle and withdraw to Armenia, taking many captives with them. Herakleios personally visited the camp in Cappadocia during the blockade, after which he deposed Priskos and forced him to become a monk, ending his long career. In 613, Shahin captured Melitene.[21]

Meanwhile, the second force under Shahrbaraz, the "Boar of Empire," overran Syria in 611–612, capturing Apameia, Antioch, and Emesa. He there found refugees from the territories that the Persians had previously conquered, and expelled them. Shahrbaraz killed Roman soldiers "wherever he caught up with them, at their heels all the way." These events were momentous for those who lived through them—traumatic for the Romans and triumphant for the Persians—but we glimpse them mostly through brief chronicle entries. In 613, Herakleios, his brother Theodoros (who bore the high court title of *curopalates*), and his cousin Niketas (the new *comes* of the excubitors and now a patrician), joined forces in Syria to repel the invaders. They were defeated near Antioch by the combined armies of Shahin and Shahrbaraz in a battle that was costly to both sides. The Romans withdrew to Cilicia, where the Persians won another Pyrrhic victory. The emperor pulled back to Asia Minor, while Tarsos and Cilicia fell to the Persians.[22] The empire was already taking on the geographical contours of its middle-period phase.

The Roman army had fought desperately but was now too depleted to offer serious resistance. While the Persians consolidated their occupation of Syria, Shahrbaraz went on to take Damascus in 613 and then Palestinian Kaisareia and Jerusalem in 614. The cities "begged for peace, bowed their necks in submission," and accepted garrisons.[23] But at Jerusalem, the Blues and the Greens pressured the citizens and the patriarch Zacharias to murder the Persian garrison and resist. It appears that the fan clubs had been taking on a greater responsibility for civic defense ever since 602, if not earlier. The Persians duly returned and invested the city in April. Zacharias dispatched the abbot Modestos to bring in reinforcements from Jericho, but they were defeated. We have an eyewitness account of the city's fall after a twenty-day siege and the massacre of its residents that ensued. This was written in Greek by Strategios, a monk at St. Sabas (Mar Saba), but survives in Georgian and Arabic translations. It channels powerful Biblical parallels to recount the slaughter and deportation of the faithful to "Babylon," i.e., Ktesiphon, and is meant to inflame Christian opinion: "By the rivers of Babylon we sat down and wept." The exiles included the author himself, who later escaped and returned, the patriarch, and many craftsmen. The Persians, "that impure race," valued skilled workers above other captives.[24]

The conventional explanation of these misfortunes among pious Romans was that God was punishing them for their sins, and that suffering was a form of atonement and purification. We have a pastoral letter written by Zacharias in captivity in which he admonishes the churches back home to "behold, be afraid, and guard yourselves"—in a spiritual sense, of course. Exile was in fact a blessing sent by Christ because it prevented the captives from engaging in their usual sins: "Don't you see how many diabolical sexual acts it has prevented?"[25]

The fall of Jerusalem attracted much attention at the time and even became the subject of a poem by Sophronios, later the city's bishop. This was due to Jerusalem's religious importance and the capture by the Persians of the True Cross, which was also taken to Ktesiphon. The Christian captives were made to trample upon this sacred object. It was also a noteworthy event because of the extent of the slaughter. Contemporary estimates ranged between 17,000 and 90,000 casualties, plus tens of thousands of captives taken to Persia, though only the lowest of these figures would be compatible with the highest modern estimate for the population of the city (ca. 50,000). Strategios appends to his report tallies of the bodies that were later found at thirty-five locations by the official Thomas, who made the gruesome inventory. Archaeologists have discovered mass graves from this period in some of those exact locations, some with hundreds of bodies, in which women and children predominate. These can be securely linked to the events of 614. By contrast, the physical damage to the city appears to have been minimal, or quickly repaired, except for one official building that was destroyed and never rebuilt. Inside were found 264 gold solidi of Herakleios in mint condition and struck from the same die, a unique find. Contemporaries also noted that many of the region's Jews sided with the Persians and seized the chance to vent their pent-up hatred. Christian authors elaborated on this theme with relish, and Strategios claimed that Jews ransomed Christian prisoners in order to then murder them.[26]

However, to properly annex his new provinces, Khusrow found that he had to adopt a more Christian-friendly approach. The shah ordered Shahrbaraz to repair the damage done to Jerusalem and expel the Jews. Modestos was appointed as acting patriarch, and he quickly began to fundraise. Assistance to rebuild the damaged churches came from the Churches of Armenia and Alexandria (contributing 1,000 solidi, food, and workmen), and from Yazdin, an official at the shah's court. Khusrow was already behaving like a Christian Roman emperor.[27] But his army in the occupied territories was still plundering and killing. The Persians and their Saracen allies hunted monks and hermits in the hills of Palestine, enslaving some and killing others, including one who was over a century old. Monastic life was severely disrupted and the monks later distinguished between the good times "before the Persians came" and the bad times afterward. The Romans, by contrast, desperately tried to cope with this cascading disaster. The patriarch of Alexandria, Niketas' appointee Ioannes the Almsgiver, earned his moniker by taking in refugees from Syria-Palestine and ransoming captives, among them a thousand enslaved nuns.[28]

In 615, Shahin brazenly demonstrated the extent of Persian superiority. He marched across Asia Minor and besieged Chalkedon, in full view of Constantinople. His choice of target was possibly meant to send a message back to Syria, as the Persians were trying to win over their new anti-Chalcedonian subjects. Herakleios sailed across the straits, personally presented Shahin with gifts, and attempted a diplomatic resolution. Shahin agreed to take a message back to the shah, specifically a letter from the Senate to be delivered by the praetorian prefect Olympios, the City prefect Leontios, and the patriarch's deputy Anastasios. This missive, which survives, fawns over Khusrow, begs him to forgive Herakleios for not announcing his accession, and obsequiously begs for peace. Herakleios offered to become Khusrow's "son." Shahin departed, but the Roman envoys who went with him, three of the highest-ranked men in the state, never returned from Persia. By this violation of diplomatic immunity Khusrow signaled that this was to be a war to the finish.[29]

Shahin did not capture Chalkedon, contrary to a later belief.[30] It also used to be believed that for the next decade (ca. 615–626) the Persians conducted raids throughout Asia Minor and destroyed many cities, effectively ending urban culture in this part of the Roman world. This conclusion was based on scattered references to raids in chronicles, on the scarcity of coins after ca. 615, and on archaeological evidence of destruction at Sardeis, Ephesos, and other sites. Yet the archaeological evidence turns out to be ambiguous, and the collapse of the monetary economy could have had causes other than the destruction of cities.[31] The Persians were not primarily interested in destroying bathhouses and gymnasia, though arson was a standard part of their panoply. They wanted captives, plunder, and to degrade the enemy's operational capacity through attrition. After the attack on Kaisareia (611) and the attempt on Chalkedon (615), they captured Ankyra in 620 or 622, a major city and military base on the main road across Asia Minor, killing and enslaving its inhabitants and burning the city. The event is well attested, with references to monks who became refugees or were hunted down and killed.[32]

In 622/3, the Persians allegedly attacked the island of Rhodes, taking captives, including the governor. How they got there is a mystery, as at no other time during this war did they have a fleet. It is possible that this was carried out instead by Slavs, who were raiding the islands at exactly this time.[33] Certainly the Persians ranged widely across Asia Minor during those years, but they did not "conquer" it. Instead, they spread fear. Many coin hoards and buried treasures from those years have been excavated, including a magnificent collection of silver utensils and gold jewelry from Kratigos near Mytilene on the island of Lesbos. It is currently on display in the Byzantine and Christian Museum of Athens. On Samos, the kilometer-long tunnel of Eupalinos, an aqueduct of the sixth century BC, was transformed into a huge refuge for a large number of people prepared for a lengthy stay. A wealthy woman of Edessa buried all her gold and silver in anticipation of being arrested by the Persians. She had hosted Khusrow when he passed through as a fugitive in 591 and he knew her wealth.[34]

With the Romans on the defensive in Asia Minor, Khusrow moved to seize the greatest prize of all, Egypt, which generated up to 30% of the eastern Roman empire's revenue. His armies invaded in 619 and captured Alexandria easily, as the patrician Niketas and patriarch Ioannes the Almsgiver had already fled, the former to Constantinople and the latter to his native Cyprus.[35] The Romans probably had no army with which to resist. The Persians advanced southward alongside the Nile, spreading panic "with much bloodshed," until they secured all of Egypt by 621. Their general was probably Shahrbaraz, but there is uncertainty on this point.

The Persian occupation

Many papyri and other texts survive from the Persian occupation of Egypt (619–629), in Greek, Coptic, and Pahlavi (which few can read), and they reveal manifold aspects of daily life as well as the initial fear caused by the invasion. A monk from Cyprus happened to be on a pilgrimage in Alexandria at the time of the invasion, and he commented on the "commotion and confusion" that it caused. Coptic sources talk of massacres of monks and the pillaging of monasteries. Archaeological evidence of destruction has also been found, though this is ambiguous.[36] Women in Upper Egypt wrote frantically to nearby monastic figures asking what to do "in the matter of the Persians, for they will be coming south." When he heard that the Persians were coming, Pesenthios, the bishop of Koptos and a saint of the Coptic Church, told his flock that God had "abandoned them to the nations without mercy," and fled south to some ancient tombs. One of the mummies there rose up before him and asked to be forgiven for having lived as a pagan.[37]

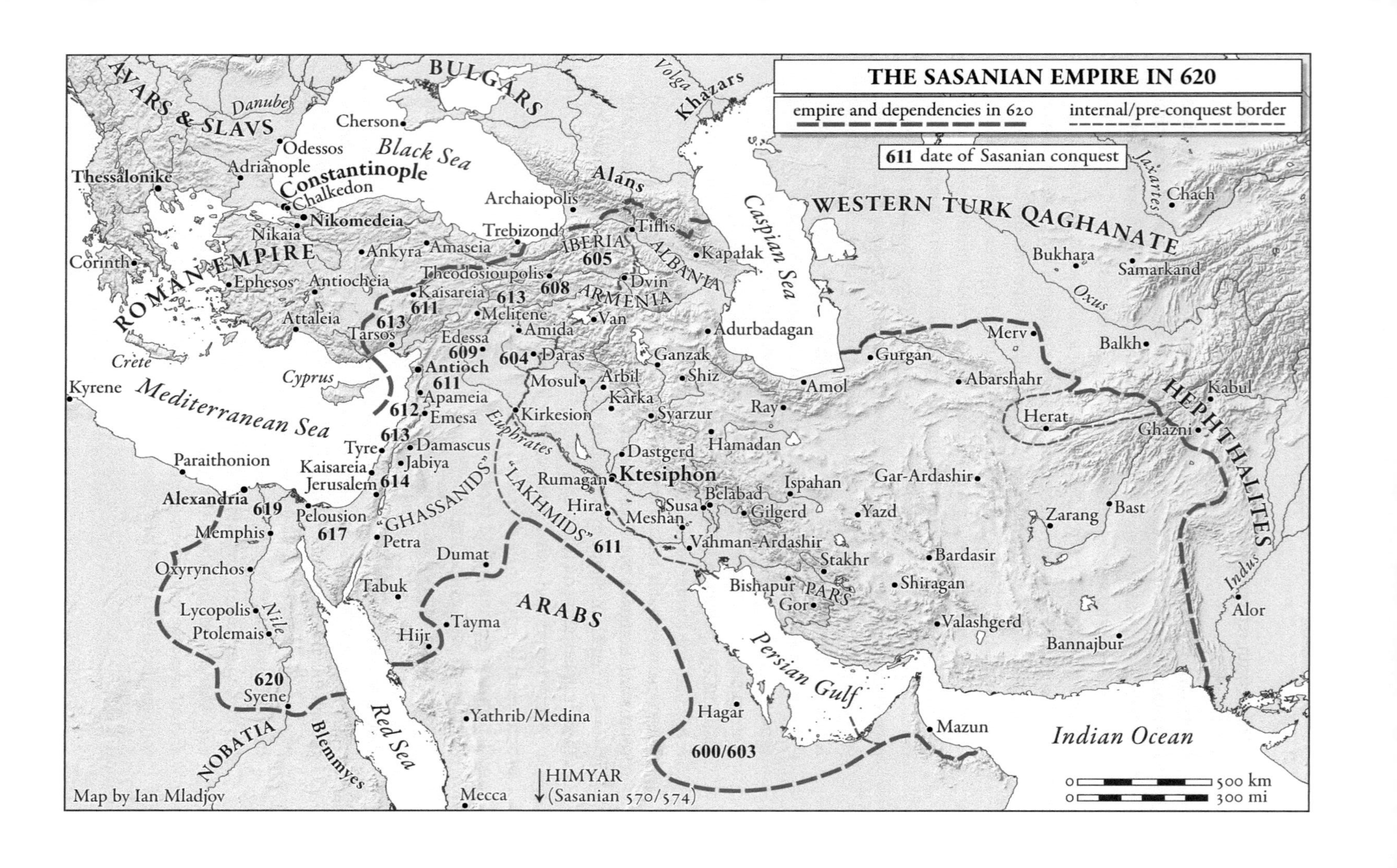
THE SASANIAN EMPIRE IN 620
empire and dependencies in 620
internal/pre-conquest border
611 date of Sasanian conquest
AVARS & SLAVS
BULGARS
Khazars
Volga
Danube
Cherson
Odessos
Black Sea
Adrianople
Thessalonike
Constantinople
Chalkedon
Nikomedeia
Nikaia
Corinth
ROMAN EMPIRE
Ephesos
Antiocheia
Ankyra
Amaseia
Trebizond
Archaiopolis
Alans
Tiflis
IBERIA
605
ALBANIA
Kapalak
Caspian Sea
WESTERN TURK QAGHANATE
Jaxartes
Chach
Bukhara
Samarkand
Oxus
Theodosioupolis
608
Dvin
ARMENIA
Kaisareia
611
613
Melitene
Van
Attaleia
Tarsos
Crete
Cyprus
Edessa
609
Amida
604
Daras
Antioch
Apameia
612
Emesa
Kyrene
Mediterranean Sea
Adurbadagan
Ganzak
Shiz
Arbil
Mosul
Karka
Kirkesion
Euphrates
Syarzur
Gurgan
Amol
Ray
Merv
Abarshahr
Balkh
Kabul
HEPHTHALITES
Herat
Ghazni
Hamadan
Dastgerd
Tyre
Damascus
Jabiya
Paraithonion
Kaisareia
Jerusalem
614
Alexandria
619
Pelousion
617
"GHASSANIDS"
Petra
Ktesiphon
Rumagan
Hira
"LAKHMIDS"
Belabad
Susa
Meshan
Gilgerd
Ispahan
Gar-Ardashir
Yazd
Zarang
Bast
Vahman-Ardashir
Stakhr
Bardasir
Memphis
Oxyrynchos
Dumat
Tabuk
ARABS
Tayma
Hijr
Lycopolis
Nile
Ptolemais
620
Syene
NOBATIA
Blemmyes
Red Sea
Yathrib/Medina
Bishapur
PARS
Gor
Shiragan
Valashgerd
Indus
Alor
Bannajbur
Persian Gulf
Hagar
Mazun
600/603
Indian Ocean
HIMYAR
(Sasanian 570/574)
Mecca
0 500 km
0 300 mi
Map by Ian Mladjov

The Persian occupation lasted for twenty years in northern Mesopotamia, such as at Edessa, and in Egypt for ten. Recent scholarship has tried to downplay its severity by arguing that after the initial "jolt" of conquest life went back to its usual rhythms and that the Persians maintained a quiet and discreet presence.[38] Indeed, in the papyri we see people conducting routine transactions. Archaeology does not reveal significant damage to buildings in Syria, Palestine, or Egypt. After all, the Persians did not want to ruin their profitable new provinces. They retained in place the previous system of administration and so, we are told, most people might not have noticed much of a difference. But this rosy picture is unconvincing.

Routine transactions would have continued even under a highly repressive occupation. That people were alive, had property, and carried on proves little. Archaeology can reveal damage to monuments but rarely to people, demography, psychology, social values and attitudes, or quality of life, at least not in such a compressed time frame. That the Persian military governor (*marzban*) of Kaisareia in Palestine governed from the Roman *praitorion* establishes only a surface continuity. Proponents of a "soft" occupation focus on routine transactions and negative archaeology, while failing to consider the impact, both immediate and long-term, of the mass slaughters with which the occupation began, the widespread anxiety and terror, "countless captives," enslavement and mass deportation to Mesopotamia, waves of panicked and indigent refugees fleeing west, the presence of a foreign army and its loathed religion, arbitrary oppression and exactions by the occupation authorities, and onerous taxation that was used to fund an ongoing war against other Christians. Apart from all that, yes, life carried on as usual.[39]

Hundreds of thousands of Roman captives were deported to Mesopotamia or farther east. The lords of Iran were always in need of agricultural labor and skilled craftsmen, and had deported it from Romanía when they captured Antioch in 540 and Apameia in 573. Sometimes they resettled them as a discrete population unit, as at Khusrow's Better Antioch, whose survivors and descendants formed a Roman ethnic enclave still in 590. When Herakleios later invaded Mesopotamia, many captives who had been marched away from Edessa, Alexandria, and other Roman cities flocked to his army.[40] Alternatively, the shah divided his captives into smaller groups in order to force them to assimilate faster, as a hagiographic text from ca. 500 states: "From all the peoples [under] his jurisdiction, he brought more or less thirty families and settled them among one another, so that through the mixture of peoples the captives would be bound by their families and affection, and it would not be easy for them to depart in flight gradually to the lands from which they were seized."[41]

As for those who were not deported, they now lived under an occupation authority to which they had no political relationship and no established means for resolving disputes and checking its abuse of power. Most testimonies come from Egypt. An estate agent explains that he cannot carry out his functions because he fell "into the hands of the Persians"; another person notes that the Persians beat him up, threw him in a ditch, and took away his children; a woman named Maria says that "the barbarians have carried off the father and the son and have slain [. . .]"; a widow writes that the Persians killed her husband, beat up her son, and took their cattle, except for one pair, but that was then taken as payment by the tax collector. Similar abuses had occurred in the Roman empire. But in the past, victims could and did appeal to the Roman authorities, which is how we know about them. Roman society consisted of multiple networks of mutual support and patronage, which limited each other's ability to abuse. But now, under foreign occupation, those networks did not reach to the very top. Victims could only turn pathetically to bishops for support. Movement was also restricted, and travel along the Nile was by permit only, causing additional hardship.[42]

In Palestine, hermits abandoned their cells and sought safety in monasteries, left the province, or fled far into the wilderness. It was harder to forage for food and instead of holy men one now ran into murderers and thieves. Saracens took advantage of the collapse of imperial defenses in order to raid again. In some cases, they seized provincials and tortured them for days to reveal where they hid their wealth.[43] The number of dedicatory inscriptions plummeted, except in Arabia province, east of the Jordan, which was situated off the Persians' main transit and supply routes.[44]

The finances of the occupation also repay closer study. The economy remained monetized because of the continued circulation of preexisting Roman coins, the introduction of silver coins (presumably to pay the Persians themselves), and the issue, by the occupation authorities, of imitation Roman coins, some of them with ungrammatical or gibberish labels. These mistakes are usually attributed to a lack of skilled craftsmen, but we should not rule out deliberate insult.[45] The Roman provinces were plundered and squeezed dry. The *marzban* of Edessa stripped 112,000 lbs of silver from the city's churches, some of it literally scraped off the columns and altar of the main church, because the townspeople had the effrontery to complain to Khusrow about him. If converted into gold currency, this would be more than half a million solidi. It was perhaps an exaggerated figure, but the sanctuary of Hagia Sophia was adorned by Justinian with 40,000 lbs of silver, and in 610 the Church of Alexandria held over half a million solidi just in cash, a sum that, while meticulously counted, was said to "surpass human accounting."[46]

The tax sums collected in Egypt, in solidi paid to "the King of Kings," seem large in comparison to the highest sums previously due to the Roman treasury.[47] A striking papyrus lists all the animals that were requisitioned for the "kitchen" of the Persian governor, Shahralanyozan, including one camel on each Tuesday.

The occupation forces also purchased goods from the locals, which is sometimes taken as proof for business as usual, but the prices that they paid were below their usual Roman levels, which is indicative of an exploitative military occupation.[48] A later, but well-informed Muslim geographer had data which showed that Khusrow's revenues increased by 42% between 608 and the end of his reign. In the Arabic tradition, Khusrow was remembered as an avaricious monarch who indulged in decadent luxury, with thousands of women for sex and his palaces stuffed full of luxury goods, the fruits of his conquests, making "his rule hateful to his subjects." This massive transfer of wealth from Rome to Persia may explain the extravagant luxury that the Arab conquerors found in Mesopotamia, though, to be sure, the Arabs liked to contrast their enemies' wealth to their own rugged poverty. But when Herakleios opened up Khusrow's palace at Dastagerd, his men found huge quantities of aloe, pepper, silk, linen, sugar, ginger, silver, woolen rugs, and woven carpets. They burned it all.[49]

Khusrow and the Churches

Khusrow had conquered more lands than any of his predecessors save the founder of the Sasanian dynasty in the third century. He had gone from being the weakest Sasanian monarch to the most powerful. Accordingly, he took on the title Abarwez, "The Victorious" (Parviz in New Persian).[50] A worshipper of Ahura Mazda, he now ruled more Christians than did Herakleios, and as many Romans. Ethnoreligious diversity was less of a problem for a Persian ruler than a Christian Roman one. The Zoroastrian establishment was accommodating to most other religions, so long as they did not question its superiority or disrupt its social order. Christian zealots in the Sasanian realm sometimes did just that, for which they were punished, but these so-called persecutions were not efforts by the state to eliminate or check Christianity. The leadership of the Church of the East was well integrated into the Sasanian political and social system.[51] But Khusrow's conquests now tilted his empire even further in a Christian direction. His prestige and power were greatly increased, but came with more Christian headaches.

Khusrow now had three rival Churches to deal with, namely the Church of the East (Diphysite and "Nestorian") with which he was already familiar—his wife Shirin belonged to it—as well as the Chalcedonians and anti-Chalcedonians. In the conquered territories it made sense to favor the latter, who were the victims, and might be seen as the potential enemies, of Constantinople. However, he allowed places that were solidly Chalcedonian, such as Jerusalem, to keep bishops of their own persuasion. This reversal of imperial patronage allowed the Monophysites in the Roman provinces to organize again. For example, the Monophysite bishop of Antioch Athanasios "the Camel Driver" sent envoys to Alexandria where they met with his Coptic counterpart Anastasios (not the Chalcedonian patriarch Ioannes the Almsgiver) and agreed to a union, in 616 or 617. For reasons that we cannot fathom, this was brokered by the emperor's brother Niketas. The Monophysite West Syrians and Nestorian East Syrians were already bitter enemies, leading the shah to convene conferences of the two groups at his court, where he tried, and failed, to broker agreement. Khusrow II was now truly behaving like a Roman emperor, and failing like one too. He too appointed secular officials to preside over theological meetings, and even ordered captive philosophers from Alexandria to clarify the contentious issues.[52]

Khusrow believed that he had standing to arbitrate Christian theological debates. He did rule over a plurality of Christians in the world, and his authority was enhanced by his possession of the True Cross, which he entrusted to his wife Shirin. It was showcased in a special treasury and rolled out for special occasions. For the East Syrians, loyal subjects of the Persian crown, it was God who had "broken the Romans in the presence of the Persians, because they had shed the pure blood of the emperor Maurikios and his sons." Thus the Cross had, by right and by divine power, come to Khusrow.[53]

Historians sometimes suggest that the Roman Monophysites sided with the Persians and welcomed their liberation from Constantinople. This appears to be wrong. The Monophysite "shadow patriarch" of Alexandria, Anastasius, stated to his counterpart in Antioch, Athanasios, that "we pray for the victory of our emperor to assist Niketas." Athanasios' response says nothing about the shah who had restored him to his position. In a century of Roman-Persian warfare, from the 520s to the 620s, Roman Monophysites had shown zero inclination to side with the Persians. The Syrian Jacobite tradition later remembered Khusrow as bringing "tribulations, pillage, captives, and killing." The Coptic Church exhibited no preference for, or allegiance to, the Persians, and saw them in negative terms as infidels. By contrast, they attributed the eventual Roman victory, won by a Chalcedonian emperor, to "the grace of Christ."[54] A semi-Greek semi-Coptic papyrus from the early seventh century preserves a liturgical prayer that is usually linked to the Arab invasions, but works just as well for the Persian war. We pray, it declares, "for our benefit, in order to wage war together against them, and for them to subdue all that belongs to the enemy host. We pray on behalf of the citizens living in faith among them. For our city and all the cities, and our land and the villages and our common faith."[55]

The shah had reason to worry about his Roman subjects' enduring loyalty to the emperor, and even more so about the emperor himself and his remaining armies. No Roman officers or imperial magistrates went over to the Persian side during the war, and it does not appear that the Persians ever invited them to do so, even the ones they captured. The occupation was about conquest and exploitation, not co-optation and integration. The war would not end unless the Persians could eliminate the Roman state altogether.

Herakleios' counteroffensive

Constantinople never lost control of Asia Minor during these trying times; it was raided, not occupied. What happened in the Balkans is less clear, as the Avars and Slavs began to raid again, and possibly to settle, south of Danube. They were enabled to do so by the withdrawal of the armies to the east and the civil war of 608–610.[56] Eventually most of the Balkan provinces would be lost, but there is no way to date the pace of this loss. The *Miracles of Demetrios* thanks the saint for protecting Thessalonike during two more sieges, which are dated approximately to ca. 616–618. The author of the second collection sets the stage by recounting how the Slavs—he knows their individual tribal names now, such as Drogoubites, Sagoudates, and Belegezites, and their leader, Hatzo—had dugout ships with which they had reached Thessaly, Greece, the islands, Epeiros, and the whole of Illyricum. They now wanted to conquer Thessalonike and relocate their families to it. These Slavs had come from relatively nearby, not from across the Danube, and Thessalonike now hosted Christian refugees from other cities.[57] The Roman order in the interior was collapsing.

Failing to take the city on their own, the Slavs asked the Avar khagan for help, and he came to Thessalonike with his army two years later. The refugees from Naissus and Serdica were distraught because they had already experienced Avar siege warfare: "One of their rocks is enough to demolish your walls." (Does this mean that their cities had already fallen?) At any rate, Thessalonike withstood the assault, and the khagan was bought off thirty-three days into it.[58] From a revenue perspective, the Balkans were by this point contributing little to the treasury, and had to fend for themselves with little imperial support. However, shipments of food were sent to Thessalonike during the siege. The Roman military organization also seems to have collapsed, except in Thrace nearest to the capital. Coupled with the loss of Syria-Palestine in the 610s and Egypt in 619, Herakleios was presiding over a rapidly failing state that was being dismembered by "grasping wolves."[59]

In 615, Herakleios issued a new silver coin, the hexagram, which was worth a twelfth of a solidus, a notional value that was probably higher than its bullion value. It featured a cross on the reverse with the remarkable legend *Deus adiuta Romanis*, "God help the Romans," the battle cry of the imperial army (see Figure 25). He also cut all state salaries in half and reduced the weight of the bronze follis from eleven to eight grams, and then in 624 to five grams. Two mints that operated briefly in Cilicia (616–617) and Isauria (618) were possibly meant to support units defending the passes into Asia Minor.[60] At Alexandria, Niketas had to (politely) confiscate funds from the Church because "the empire is in dire straits and needs money." Herakleios was running out of cash, soldiers, and provinces all at once. Then, in 619, when the Persians conquered Egypt, he ran out of food. The City authorities began to charge a modest fee of 3 folles per

Figure 25 Coin of Herakleios with the legend "God help the Romans!"

loaf in early 618, but now they had to suspend bread distribution altogether. This led to a famine that was accompanied by an outbreak of plague. For centuries, the grain fleet had kept Constantinople alive. Without it, its population was liable to contract dramatically. It was later said that Herakleios thought of abandoning the City and returning to Carthage, but he was dissuaded by the patriarch Sergios and the people of Constantinople.[61] Carthage was spared the irony of becoming the Third Rome. Yet it has been argued, based on the seals of certain officials, that grain from North Africa and especially Sicily was diverted to the capital to compensate partially for the loss of Egypt.[62]

Had Herakleios been of a defensive mindset and hunkered down in Asia Minor, the next phase of Roman history would have begun right then, albeit with the Persians, rather than the Arabs, as the chief opponent. But his daring coup in 608 had shown a strategic brilliance. While Niketas pinned the enemy down in Egypt, Herakleios had sailed to the capital. Yet the emperor's options after 619 were limited. He could not realistically slog his way through Syria and Palestine to reconquer the east. He would have been exposed to too many entrenched Persian armies. Besides, he had tried that approach, and failed, in 613. He now thought outside the box. He would personally take command of the campaign, leave the empire, slip around the leviathan's tentacles, and, with the help of unconventional allies, strike at its heart. But to do that he needed an army, and for an army he needed money.

The plan was put in motion in 622, when Herakleios borrowed the silver and gold stored in the churches of Constantinople, possibly including the churches of Asia Minor as well. If the churches of Edessa had amassed 112,000 lbs of silver, and that of Alexandria 8,000 lbs of gold in cash alone, the brimming sacristies of

New Rome could conceivably fund this desperate gambit.[63] The emperor trained a new army, which he marched to Armenia and then "Persia." Unfortunately, our knowledge of this campaign derives solely from a pompous panegyric written by the court poet, Georgios of Pisidia. It suggests that Herakleios defeated a Persian army in battle somewhere in the east, after which he returned to the capital.[64]

Herakleios also had to secure his rear, which meant reaching an agreement with the Avar khagan, the younger son of Baian. A meeting between the two was arranged in 623, to be marked by chariot games and imperial pomp at Herakleia, just outside the Long Wall of Thrace. But the khagan tried to ambush Herakleios before he reached the city. The emperor escaped by dressing like a commoner and racing his horse back to the capital, with his crown held under his arm. The Avars then ravaged Thrace as far as Constantinople, plundered the churches outside the walls in view of the citizens, and took away 70,000 captives. It was a bitter humiliation, but a peace agreement was eventually reached. The annual tribute was raised to 200,000 solidi, and Herakleios gave as hostages his nephew, a natural son (Ioannes Athalarichos, born to a Gothic concubine?), and a natural son of the patrician and *magister militum* Bonos. If the Avars had indeed been receiving their annual tribute all these years, they would have obtained over 2,500,000 solidi since 602.[65]

Finally, in 624, the Roman state showed its teeth. Instead of invading Syria or Mesopotamia, Herakleios caught the Persians by surprise when he marched, from Kaisareia, to the northeast, up the Euphrates to Theodosiopolis, then down the Araxes to Dvin, which he destroyed. Leaving a swath of destruction in his wake, the emperor proceeded directly south to Ganzak, where the shah was residing. Khusrow fled into the Zagros mountains, leaving the city to be plundered. Herakleios won an even greater symbolic victory when he captured and destroyed the Zoroastrian temple complex of Azar Goshnasp (at Takht-e Soleyman in west Azerbaijan). He extinguished its sacred fire and polluted the lake with corpses, a grave offense for Zoroastrians. This avenged the capture of Jerusalem in 614, especially as, among all the fire altars, this was the one closely associated with the shah himself. The Roman army then moved to Caucasian Albania, adjacent to the Caspian Sea, where the emperor recruited Laz, Abasgians, and Iberians to his banners. Armenians are never mentioned as fighting for him in the east, further refuting the modern fiction that Herakleios was an emperor of Armenian origin who drew his support from Armenia.[66]

In Caucasian Albania, Herakleios was quickly surrounded by two Persian armies, under Shahrbaraz and Shahraplakan (the "Panther of Empire"), with another army under Shahin on the way. Khusrow was eager to eliminate his rival and now had him trapped. Yet during the winter of 624–625, Herakleios managed to outmaneuver and defeat all three armies in numerous battles, both singly and in combination, confusing them with his seemingly erratic movements west to Siwnik', south across Siwnik', west to north of lake Van, then east to Amida and Samosata. Herakleios' performance was virtuosic. The fate of Rome rested on this one last army, and a single defeat in these lands, so far from Roman territory, would have spelled doom. Yet Herakleios managed to prevail in every encounter, even to sack Shahrbaraz's camp, seizing his wives and slaughtering his bodyguard. The Boar fled and survived. Herakleios retired to Asia Minor, deserted by his Caucasian allies during the frantic pursuits. It was one of the most extraordinary years in the annals of Roman warfare, and it is a pity that we have only condensed accounts.[67] Herakleios had embarrassed Khusrow and Shahrbaraz, but he had not made solid strategic gains. Ultimately he was driven out of Transcaucasia.

Unfortunately, we do not have reliable figures for the size of these armies. It is unlikely that Herakleios led more than the equivalent of one "classic" field army (20,000 men). He displayed an astute sensitivity to morale and propaganda. Before leaving Constantinople in 624, he read aloud to the patriarch and the Senate an insulting letter ostensibly sent by Khusrow that taunted him, rebuked him for not surrendering ("bring your wife and I will give you an olive grove to make a living"), and threatened to destroy him as easily as the Jews had killed Christ. Before giving battle, Herakleios encouraged his men to fight for God and "the sovereign state of the Romans," and allowed them to believe that death in battle was tantamount to religious "martyrdom." Finally, he sent dispatches back to the City recounting his heroic victories.[68]

Khusrow decided that, if he could not destroy the emperor in the field, he would strike at his capital, which would also be an effective way to end Romanía. In 625, the two monarchs turned the conflict into a "world" war. Khusrow coordinated a joint attack on Constantinople with the Avars, while Herakleios sent an envoy to seek Turkish help against Persia. Thus the war, which already raged from the Caspian Sea to Upper Egypt, drew in participants from Central Europe and Central Asia. In 626, Khusrow sent two armies across Asia Minor, under Shahin and Shahrbaraz, against Constantinople. Herakleios' response is garbled in the sources. He is said to have divided his army into three parts. One part, allegedly 12,000 men but probably much smaller, he sent ahead to reinforce the defense of the City; a second part he kept with himself while he coordinated with the Turks; and the third he entrusted to his brother Theodoros, who engaged with Shahin and resoundingly defeated him. Shahin's pickled body was sent back to the shah, who mutilated it.[69]

The siege of Constantinople, for which we have three eyewitness accounts, was the first sustained attack on the City by a foreign enemy, and put the empire's defenses to the test. They held, but the trauma and jubilation of the ordeal were indelibly imprinted on Roman memory. The defense was organized by the general Bonos, as regent for the emperor's teenage son and heir Herakleios

Konstantinos (he had been born in 612 and crowned Augustus in 613). Shahrbaraz occupied Chalkedon and made his presence visible from across the straits by burning the churches and suburbs. The vanguard of the Avar army arrived at the Long Wall of Thrace on 29 June, preventing the people of the City from harvesting their crops. We are told that the vanguard was 30,000 strong and the khagan's total army was 80,000, figures that are not impossible, considering that they included thousands of Slavs with their dugouts for a naval assault, and that the khagan's supplies ran out a week after he arrived on Tuesday, 29 July, forcing his departure. The Avars and Persians communicated with fire signals across the Bosporos.[70]

The khagan paraded his army to intimidate the defenders. In response, the patriarch Sergios processed along the walls with an image of Christ, one of the so-called *acheiropoietos* images that was miraculously "not made by human hands." He positioned icons of the Virgin on the gates to force the enemy to attack them and thereby incur divine wrath. The Avar attack on the Theodosian Walls began on Wednesday, 30 July, and continued for a week until 7 August. It concentrated on the middle, hilly, section around the Fifth Gate, but otherwise extended along their entire length. By Friday, the khagan had deployed twelve siege towers against this central section of the walls, and his Slavs had launched their canoes in the Golden Horn, in the shallows where they could not be attacked by the Roman fleet. On Saturday, 2 August, the khagan requested a parley. Three high officials and the patriarch's second-in-command went out and found him in the company of three Persians, dressed in silk, sent by Shahrbaraz. The khagan proposed that the people abandon the City with only their clothes and entrust themselves to the Persians, who would presumably deport them. It appears that he was planning to destroy Constantinople, not occupy it. The terms were a non-starter, and the three Persians were arrested as they secretly tried to recross the Bosporos. One was sent back to the khagan without his hands, but with the head of the second tied around his neck, while the third was executed on a boat in sight of the Persian camp.

On Monday morning, at dawn, the Slavic canoes managed to slip past the Roman naval patrols and reach the Asian shore, where they picked up 3,000 or 4,000 Persians. But these ships were sunk by the Romans during their return. The attack on the land walls continued and intensified on 6–7 August, when the Slavs were ordered to bring soldiers against the sea walls in the Golden Horn. But the Romans were prepared and lured the Slavs into a trap; their slaughter turned the waters red. On 8 August, the khagan ended the attack, dismantled and burned his siege engines, and marched off to his own lands. He had been foiled by the Theodosian Walls, the Bosporos, the irrelevance of his strongest asset (his heavy cavalry), the logistical nightmare of feeding a huge army, and the determination of the Romans. The blow to his prestige weakened his position, forcing the Avars to spend years suppressing revolts among their subjects. Shahrbaraz departed empty-handed to Alexandria.

For the Constantinopolitans, the experience had been terrifying but also, in the end, triumphant. The patriarch Sergios crafted its dominant interpretation, by attributing the Roman victory to the intercession of the Virgin Mary. This was possible only because the emperor was absent, otherwise he would have received the credit. Writers close to the patriarch composed sermons, poems, and dispatches that highlighted the Virgin's concern for her chosen people, which she showed by pleading before Christ with her "weaponized tears" on behalf of the Romans or by personally sinking Slavic ships in the thick of battle.[71] The Virgin now became the chief military protector and patron of Constantinople. The patriarch wrote the verses honoring her that now open the Akathistos Hymn (so named because the congregation stands): "To you, our Champion General, your City gives thanks for victory and delivering us from suffering." It was a refinement of the Christian paradox to treat the humble figure of Maria as a "general" who prevailed on the battlefield, just as the Akathistos itself dwells on the paradox of a powerless mortal woman delivering eternal salvation to mankind and prevailing over death.

We do not know where Herakleios was during the siege of his capital, but he failed to meet up with his new allies, the Turks, when they arrived in Albania in 626. They raided Persian-controlled territory and departed.[72] Herakleios did join up with them in the summer of 627, before Tiflis in Iberia, which they were besieging. They were led by the jebu khagan, a subordinate of the great king of the Turks in Central Asia. It is said that he had an army of 40,000 with him, which, if true, means that the ensuing campaign, which finally broke the back of Khusrow's regime, was more a Turkish than a Roman operation. Nevertheless, it was also the outcome of astute Roman diplomacy that had begun long before, under Justin II, and aimed to encircle Persia. Now it finally paid off. In a staged ceremony before their armies, Herakleios and Ziebel, brother of the khagan of the Western Turks, embraced and exchanged gestures of mutual respect and esteem, with the emperor putting his crown on Ziebel's head, calling him his son, bestowing expensive gifts on his nobles, and even offering him his daughter Epiphania-Eudokia, a crowned Augusta, in marriage, a concession unprecedented in Roman history. But what Herakleios received in return was priceless: the survival of Romanía.[73]

Tiflis fell two months later and the joint Roman-Turkish army surprised the Persians by marching south, even though winter was coming. The invaders crossed the Zagros and approached Nineveh, near which they destroyed a Persian army commanded by Rahzadh, on 12 December. Most Persian armies were occupying the Roman provinces and the forces that Khusrow could scrape together were too small to defeat this invader. Yet the shah sent them in anyway, which the Persian officers regarded as suicide missions. The Romans marched down the Tigris, plundering palaces along the way. The shah was forced to flee to Ktesiphon from his favorite palace at Dastagerd, only 100 km north of the capital. Nine days later, in early January 628, the Romans sacked Dastagerd, freeing the captives that they found. They now rampaged freely through the Persian empire's agricultural base, destroying the palaces of the aristocracy and hunting and eating the exotic animals roaming in their parks. The weakness of Khusrow's regime had been disguised by the war, which had lasted for almost thirty years, but the pressure on it now proved too much. A conspiracy was hatched by some leading officers and the shah's son Kavad-Siroe. Herakleios was personally brought into it by one of the leading conspirators, a son of Rahzadh who probably blamed his father's death on the shah. With the coup in motion, the Romans and their allies withdrew north to Azerbaijan, settling in on 15 March. Two weeks later, it was announced that Khusrow was deposed. His son Siroe had been crowned shah as Kavad II and then ordered the execution of "that foul tyrant," his father, along with dozens of his own brothers and half-brothers.

In the past, the Romans had suffered at the hands of nomadic armies. Now they had the pleasure of accompanying one into Persia. The victory also vindicated their faith: the Son of God had triumphed over the God of the Sun.[74] Herakleios had been sending dispatches to Constantinople to inform his subjects about the campaign. In these he minimized the role of the Turks and showcased his own heroic exploits. On 15 May, the dispatch that was read aloud in Hagia Sophia was exultant: "Let the heavens rejoice!" It went on to explain that Kavad II Siroe was now shah and had agreed to withdraw from Roman territory. After a detailed narrative, Herakleios appended the letter that he had received from Kavad II, which called him "brother" and pledged to free all Roman captives. In response, the emperor called the new shah his "son" and demanded the return of the True Cross and the envoys of 615. Kavad-Siroe said that he would look for the True Cross; as for the envoys, one had died and the others were murdered by Khusrow when Herakleios invaded Persia.[75]

The postwar settlement

Herakleios and his brother Theodoros set about liberating the Roman cities of Mesopotamia and Syria. We can only imagine the scenes that played out as the Persian garrisons departed. Only at Edessa did the Persians resist, aided by the city's Jews, but Theodoros forced their surrender with catapults. He began to execute the ringleaders of the Jewish opposition, when orders arrived from Herakleios to spare them. When the emperor arrived at Edessa and went to receive communion, the bishop refused him unless he first renounced Chalcedon. Even our Monophysite source calls this bishop "an uneducated fool." In anger, Herakleios replaced him with a Chalcedonian. But while Syria and Palestine were returning to Roman order, one major player remained in place: Shahrbaraz, in Egypt.[76] He was ready to switch sides. In the fall of 628 Kavad II died and was succeeded by his son, the child Ardashir III. Shahrbaraz refused to accept Ardashir and somehow came to an agreement with Herakleios. In exchange for the evacuation of Egypt, the emperor would provide him with military assistance in his bid for the throne in Ktesiphon. It was 590 all over again, except that the emperor was now supporting the rival of the Sasanian dynasty rather than its heir.

It was a dizzying reversal. Herakleios and Shahrbaraz had crossed swords many times in the past two decades—near Antioch in 613 and in the Caucasus in 624–625. The Boar of Empire was the most formidable enemy the Romans had encountered in the whole of their history, greater than Hannibal or Mithridates. Now the two men met in July, 629, at Arabissos of Cappadocia, the birthplace of the emperor Maurikios, to become allies and kinsmen. Shahrbaraz's daughter was appropriately renamed Nike and betrothed to Herakleios' mute son Theodosios (born to the emperor's second wife, and niece, Martina), while Shahrbaraz's son was made patrician and baptized as Niketas.[77] The name referred to the Romans' recent victory but also honored Herakleios' loyal cousin, who had died after 619. Bound now to the emperor, and with the help of a Roman army, Shahrbaraz was able to march to Ktesiphon and become shah in April 630, after killing Ardashir.

Shortly before the meeting at Arabissos in 629, Herakleios had personally restored the True Cross to the Holy Sepulcher church at Jerusalem, on 21 March. A pious fiction was concocted that the relic had been kept "locked" during its captivity and that its container was only now opened with a key held by Modestos, the acting bishop of Jerusalem. The tale is refuted by much independent testimony about the use (and abuse) of the Cross by the Persians. Suspicions are also aroused by the likelihood that this cross came to Herakleios from Shahrbaraz, when he was in Egypt planning revolt, long before he reached Ktesiphon. Be that as it may, the restitution of the Cross to Jerusalem captured the imagination of contemporaries, who treated it as the key symbolic moment of victory for the Christians. In addition to the many texts that celebrated the occasion, ten years later the scene was depicted in a sculpted relief over the north entrance of the Armenian church at Mren.[78]

After its display in Jerusalem, the Cross was sent on to Constantinople, where it was formally received by the patriarch Sergios. Herakleios himself then returned to Constantinople in September, 629, six years after his departure in 624 and soon after his conference with Shahrbaraz. The triumphant hero was greeted by the populace with effusions of joy. One wit even compared his six-year labor to the six days in which God created the world. No triumph had been more amply deserved. The emperor brought four elephants and celebrated many days of games in the hippodrome. He now sported a large mustache and long beard, inaugurating a lasting trend in imperial self-presentation (see Figure 26).

Figure 26 Coin of Herakleios with beard and mustache

As per his agreement, he dispatched his daughter Epiphania-Eudokia to marry the western Turkish khagan, but when news arrived that he had been killed, she was recalled.[79]

Reconstruction presented a daunting challenge. Hundreds of thousands had been displaced, deported, or killed. Many cities had been systematically plundered and loads of provincial wealth had been transported to the east, where it could not be recovered (the Arabs found it waiting for them a few years later). The Roman armies had been ground down; probably only one or two functional field armies remained. State revenues had collapsed. Refugees began to return, "seeing as," one of them stated in advance from North Africa, "the fear of the barbarians has been lifted, due to which I made such a long journey across the seas, for I love my own life" (this was the monk and philosopher Maximos).[80] A whole generation had come of age, especially in Syria and Palestine, under Persian domination. The anti-Chalcedonians had tasted power when Khusrow turned over key bishoprics to them. In the far-west, in Spain, the Visigoths had seized the opportunity to conquer Malaga in ca. 615 and to terminate the Roman province of Spania altogether in ca. 624 by taking Cartagena.[81] And few knew what was even going on in the Balkan hinterlands beyond the walls of Thessalonike.

In 630, Herakleios began another tour of the east. He took the Cross back to Jerusalem: "none of the Christian emperors are said to have visited Jerusalem," noted a contemporary, "but only this most serene and all-pious emperor did come, with the life-giving Cross of the Savior."[82] From there he traveled via Konstantina (Tella) to Beroia (Aleppo), where he received a delegation from the Persian court, no less than the *katholikos* of the Church of the East, Ishoyahb.

Shahrbaraz's career had come to an end when he was murdered after only forty days on the throne. He had been replaced by Boran, a daughter of Khusrow. According to one source, she agreed that the borders between the two empires would be those of 591, i.e., the maximum in terms of Roman gains.[83]

Around this point in the reign, much scholarship on Herakleios goes off the rails of history and plunges into apocalyptic fantasy. It is commonly said that the emperor, his court, and his subjects interpreted the Persian war and the events surrounding the Cross and Jerusalem in terms of millenarian scenarios, that is, as heralding the End Times, and that this interpretation shaped the emperor's policies and image. The latter included the emperor's personal visits to Jerusalem, an order to convert all the Jews in the empire, and the official adoption in 629 of the title "*basileus* of the Romans, faithful in Christ."[84] This title is cited by historians as proof that the empire was henceforth Christian rather than Roman, or, depending on one's ideology, that it was Greek rather than Roman. But none of this holds up.

The reign did not witness the production of more eschatological literature than usual. End Times speculation was a background hum in the Christian empire, usually in hagiography, and it probably dips rather than peaks in this period. No source links Herakleios' policies to eschatological ideas about the Last Emperor, Antichrist, and Second Coming, and the court itself encouraged no such link. We have a number of contemporaneous accounts of the restoration of the Cross and not one of them so much as alludes to eschatological scenarios. One even invokes the traditional Roman idea of the "restoration of the republic." The emperor's chief propagandist, Georgios of Pisidia, presented his victories in the traditional terms of renewal and rebirth, not as heralding The End.[85] Instead, it was *Jewish* texts that saw the events at Jerusalem in apocalyptic terms.[86]

As for the title *basileus*, that was what the inhabitants of the eastern empire had called their ruler for centuries, even on formal occasions. The emperors had also used it before Herakleios, for example in their correspondence, monograms, and as the term for their "reign" (*basileia*). It was present everywhere but in the official title used in laws and on coins, so in adopting the Greek title Herakleios was merely acknowledging a linguistic fait accompli, as Justinian had done in 535 when he began to issue laws in Greek. The association of the imperial title with Christ—"*basileus* faithful in Christ"—was also not a novelty.[87]

The forced conversion of all Jews is a complex problem, in part because the sources are contradictory, late, or written far from the events, and in part because Jews obviously survived in the empire. The more credible sources recount a number of unconnected episodes that are unrelated to eschatology. Herakleios allegedly forbade Jews from living within three miles of Jerusalem. But Khusrow II had already expelled Jews from the city during the occupation, and Herakleios' act is not consistent with a policy of forced conversion anyway. Another source says that the Jews of Edessa were expelled after they refused to surrender the city in 628, which is certainly possible. Many Jews had sided with the Persians during the war, but the evidence for reprisals against them is late and unreliable.[88] Only in one province is forced conversion unequivocally attested, and it was oddly far from the war itself: North Africa. The theologian Maximos was there and reported that the governor had just returned from Constantinople with orders to baptize all Samaritans and Jews. Maximos disapproved, adding, "I hear that this has happened across the entire empire of the Romans." Later sources also say that it did, but contemporaneous evidence beyond what Maximos heard is lacking. Our other seventh-century source for the events in North Africa reveals that one could be a Jew openly in Constantinople itself, but not in Carthage.[89] It is, perhaps, an unsolvable problem, but eschatology does not hold the key.

The war and occupation had ruined the empire, yet Herakleios' spectacular victory against all odds endowed him with extraordinary authority as a Christian ruler favored by God. This was marred only by his marriage to his niece Martina, of which some Christian moralists disapproved. Herakleios immediately began to spend his moral capital to achieve Church unity, by advocating a compromise theological formula endorsed by the patriarch Sergios of Constantinople. This new approach sidestepped the thorny question of Christ's Natures to stress the unity of his "activities" or "operations" (*energeiai*), whence it is called Monoenergism. It was not an issue on which either side had a settled view.

In 629, at Antioch and Hierapolis (Mabbug) Herakleios tried to win over the anti-Chalcedonian bishops of Syria, but our sources disagree on whether he succeeded. It is possible that Athanasios the Camel Driver, the anti-Chalcedonian patriarch of Antioch, was willing but could not persuade his bishops. The Syriac sources admit that many of their monasteries accepted Chalcedon on the basis of this formula. In 630, Herakleios met at Beroia (Aleppo) with the new Persian queen's envoy, the *katholikos* of the Church of the East, Ishoyahb, and asked him for a profession of his faith. Finding that he was in agreement with it, the emperor celebrated mass with him. Ishoyahb's one condition was that he could not commemorate Cyril of Alexandria, to which the emperor agreed. The two men parted in the expectation of union premised on Monoenergism, though Ishoyahb was criticized for this by his bishops when he returned home. The emperor also pressured the Church of Armenia to accept Chalcedon in its Monoenergist version, which it did at the Council of Theodosiopolis (Erzurum), dated between 631 and 633 and possibly attended by Herakleios himself. During the Persian occupation, the Armenians had been pressured by the shah to reject Chalcedon, though some dissidents continued to accept it; now that they had to accept it, some dissidents continued to reject it.[90]

The hardest nut to crack was Egypt. Herakleios assigned the task to Kyros, the capable bishop of Phasis in Lazica, whom he had met during the war. In 631,

Kyros was appointed to be simultaneously the prefect and acting patriarch of Alexandria, an unprecedented combination of secular and religious high offices. Although his anti-Chalcedonian counterpart Benjamin refused to meet with him, by wielding the compromise of Monoenergism Kyros managed to win over many members of the anti-Chalcedonian Church, including monasteries. A Council in 633 produced a Pact of Union, which Kyros reported to Sergios as a great success: "All the clerics of the so-called 'Theodosian' sect [Severan anti-Chalcedonians], along with those who shine in the civilian and military offices, as well as the people of Alexandria, stretching into the thousands, celebrated the liturgy with us on the third of June, uniting with our Holy and Catholic Church." Not everyone was won over, of course, and the Monophysite tradition later recounted, with the usual hyperbole, that Kyros had viciously persecuted the holdouts. Still, the emperor's push for union was gaining momentum. In just a few years, he had made more progress in that direction than any previous emperor.[91]

But Church union was destined to remain beyond reach. Some principled objector always appeared to throw up the barricades, sow suspicion, and raise the cost of compromise. Efforts at union thereby tended to produce a third faction, the unionists, who fought against the other two preexisting factions. This was to be the fate of Monoenergism and its offshoot Monotheletism. The objector in this case was the Chalcedonian monk and author Sophronios of Damascus, who had fled to North Africa during the war. He had attended the deliberations of 633 in Alexandria and pleaded with Kyros not to promote the doctrine of One Activity. Possibly he saw it as a victory for the anti-Chalcedonians, who were allegedly celebrating that "we have not now come into communion with Chalcedon, but it with us." Kyros asked him to compromise for the sake of saving souls. Sophronios then went to the capital to plead his case to Sergios, who, like Constantine the Great before Nicaea, realized that this was turning into "a pointless war about words" and that further discussion of *energeia* would be counterproductive. Yet the seeds of Chalcedonian dissent had been planted, and Sergios failed to win over Honorius of Rome to the new formula, though the pope did not condemn it either. Sophronios became patriarch of Jerusalem in 634, which raised the possibility of another anti-Constantinopolitan alliance between Chalcedonian dissidents and Rome.[92]

That alliance would indeed come to pass. No sooner did Sophronios ascend the patriarchal throne than he sent out an encyclical repudiating Monoenergism—two Natures, after all, required two modes of activity, not one. He dispatched one of his associates to seek a papal alliance.[93] For now, Herakleios was still riding high after his victory, although in just a few years he would lose that advantage along with most of his empire.

16

Commanders of the Faithful (632–644)

The origins of Islam

The origins of Islam and the Arab empire lay in the western part of the Arabian peninsula, in a mountainous region along the Red Sea called the Hijaz. The Romans had paid little attention to it, and their interactions with Arabic speakers had so far been limited to the desert arc spanning from Jordan along the Syrian *limes* to Mesopotamia, and secondarily to Himyar (Yemen), which had long been contested between Christianity and Judaism as well as by its neighbors Aksum, Rome, and Persia. At times, Himyar was a unified state, capable of projecting its power across large parts of the Arabian peninsula. By contrast, the society of the Hijaz was structured around clan and tribal affiliations, and its wealth came from pastoralism and trade, supplemented by raiding. The values of this society are partly reflected in the corpus of pre-Islamic Arabian poetry that was preserved by later scholars, which sings of tribal politics, loyalty, love, loss, and battle. The Hijaz was religiously mixed: Jews, Christians, and polytheists populated the formative background of Islam. A number of prophets are attested in the early seventh century, but they were eclipsed by Muhammad (ca. 575–632), of the Quraysh tribe of Mecca (Makka). Inspired by a series of divine revelations, he preached a revolutionary message of strict loyalty to one God, Allah, and obedience to a new set of religious strictures, coupled with dire but typically vague warnings about the imminent end of the world.

Muhammad's pronouncements were later collected by his followers and compiled into a sacred text, the Quran (meaning "Recitation"), though we do not understand the editorial process itself. Certainly, the Quran contains many of the Messenger's authentic pronouncements, but we cannot reliably distinguish them from later interventions. It criticizes Jews, Christians, and Arabian pagans, and thereby calls a new religious identity into being, although it does so in the name of restoring the primordial state of a true religion that had been corrupted by Jews and Christians. Muhammad's followers were originally called the "Faithful" or "Believers" (*mu'minun*), or the "Emigrants" (*muhajirun*)—because they left their previous abodes to follow the Messenger to Yathrib (Medina) and to participate in the wars of conquest that ensued. They were also known as the *Muslimun*, "those who submit to God," a term that was not used much at first, though it is in the Quran (22:78); by the end of the century, it had become the established name for the new community. The Quran presupposes knowledge of many traditions of the Bible as well as the Christian tale of the Seven Sleepers of Ephesos and versions of the Alexander Romance. But it is also enmeshed in Arabian paganism, both by attacking it and because much of its lore and vocabulary for ritual, prayer, and theology are drawn from it and repurposed. Allah, literally "the God," had been one of the Quraysh gods, whose shrine was the Kaaba rock in Mecca. According to one tradition, the shrine had been rebuilt during Muhammad's youth with beams from a Roman shipwreck.[1]

While Muhammad was at Mecca, among his early converts were his fellow Quraysh Abu Bakr and ʿUmar (who was originally an enemy). In 622—so just as Herakleios was beginning his counteroffensive against Persia—Muhammad and many of his followers were forced by opposition in Mecca to depart for Yathrib (later called Medina, i.e., "the city," short for "the city of the Prophet"). This emigration was called the *hijra* and soon after Muhammad's death in 632 it was taken to mark Year One of Muslim chronology (which uses a lunar calendar). The earliest use of this system is attested on a papyrus from 643 (i.e., year 22 of the *hijra*), so immediately after the conquest of Egypt.[2] In the conflict that ensued between Mecca and Medina, the Faithful eventually prevailed, especially after the conversion of the Quraysh leaders Khalid ibn al-Walid (a fierce warrior who became known as the Sword of God) and ʿAmr ibn al-ʿAs (the later conqueror of Egypt). When Muhammad died in 632, his companion Abu Bakr (632–634) was chosen to lead the army, and thereby the movement as a whole, as "Commander of the Faithful" and "Deputy (*khalifa*) of God," or caliph.[3] There were no rules for the succession, which was always arranged in an ad hoc fashion, nor was there a consensus about what the powers and responsibilities of these leaders were. These questions were left unanswered at this time, but they would eventually undermine the unity of the Faithful and, ultimately, the stability of the caliphate.

During his short reign, Abu Bakr launched a series of campaigns across the peninsula, in which the military commander Khalid ibn al-Walid won the most important victories. These were later called the Ridda Wars, or Wars of Apostasy, on the fiction that their targets had apostatized from the Message. In reality, Abu Bakr conquered Arabia and placed it under his leadership, from Yemen and Oman in the south to Bahrain in the east and the Syrian and Mesopotamian frontiers to the north. His success was due to several factors, including the new religion, which had enabled the formation of an alliance larger than that of its merely regional or tribal enemies; the disunity of those enemies; and the decline of all previous Arabian powers, especially of Kinda (in central Arabia), Himyar in the south under its sub-Sasanian leaders, and of the Saracen phylarchies in the north. The Romans and Sasanians had eliminated their Saracen client kings in the later sixth century, leaving both empires without buffers to the south and with little sway through proxies in Arabian tribal politics.

The Arab conquests

What happened next is exactly what we would expect of a newly created military power, riding a wave of victories and convinced of its religious superiority. It expanded its operations to include the territories of neighboring empires, Rome and Persia, who happened to be worn out by decades of war. The Faithful now set about creating an empire of their own, not to spread their faith but to demonstrate its superiority and to benefit materially. Our sources for these events are both abundant and meager at the same time. They are abundant because later Muslim authors wrote extended accounts of the life of Muhammad and the early Islamic conquests, featuring epic battles, curious anecdotes, impressive details, miracles, speeches and dialogue, and (for Muslims) edification. They are meager because little in this huge mass of narrative can be treated as actual history. Most of it was designed to make Muslims look good in ways that mattered later, or to make some Muslims look better than others. These accounts were written long after the events in question, and then rewritten and embellished before reaching the form in which we have them, two or three centuries after the conquests. They contradict each other frequently; project later developments, concerns, interests, ideologies, and institutions onto the seventh century; exaggerate minor skirmishes into major battles; and lack a reliable chronology. The best among them agree on the outline of events and undoubtedly contain much historical material, but it is hard to know which ones they are. Each potential nugget of information has to clear multiple tests in order to be accepted as *possibly* historical.[4] On the other hand, we also have contemporary comments made about the conquests by non-Muslims. These are meager in the usual way, but have the advantage of proximity.

The simultaneous conquests of Palestine, Syria, and Egypt (on the one hand) and Sasanian Iraq (on the other) were planned and directed from Medina and carried out by disciplined armies that operated with relative independence on their various fronts. The image of uncoordinated freewheeling raiders toppling the two greatest empires of antiquity is a fiction.[5] It is not clear whether Abu Bakr sent his armies out with the aim of conquering Roman and Persian provinces, or, as an extension of the Ridda wars, to bring under his control only the Arabic-speaking tribes that lived between the two empires and his own, a more limited objective, albeit one that inevitably drew him into broader conflicts.[6] Like Attila and the Avar khagans, who led armies-on-the-move rather than settled states, Abu Bakr had no choice but to use his army and reward it from the spoils, or watch it turn against itself, or against him. The Faithful were forbidden from fighting each other, but fighting was ingrained in their culture and was the means of their all-too-recent unification. In attacking the two exhausted empires, early Muslims found a fight that could keep them united.

Intra-Saracen fighting along the border would not have alarmed the Roman authorities and provincials. But the raids soon entered the provinces and, in 634, led to clashes with imperial forces. It took the Muslims less than three years (634–636) to defeat the Roman armies in Palestine and Syria, and four years more to establish control over every major city from Gaza to Edessa. Their armies moved separately under the command of Abu 'Ubayda, 'Amr ibn al-'As, Shurahbil, Khalid ibn al-Walid, and Yazid of the Umayya clan of Quraysh, though the sources frequently contradict each other as to who was commanding which operation, and, besides, they often joined forces for major battles and sieges. All together they probably totaled 24,000 men, a bit larger than a full Roman field army.[7] The course of events is hard to establish. The first major Muslim victory appears to have been in February, 634 at Dathin, twelve miles from Gaza, where the governor of nearby Kaisareia, Sergios, was defeated and killed. A later Roman chronicle reports that the Muslims had been brought in by "Arab" border guards of the empire who were angry at not being paid and turned for help "to the men of their own race."[8] But this version may have been a later, ethnically-charged ascription of blame.

While Muslim armies were operating in the Palestinian countryside, Khalid performed a legendary feat, a march across the desert from the Persian front in southern Iraq to the edge of Syria. This we know only from later Muslim sources, which disagree on both its route and chronology. Khalid then attacked the Christian Saracens who lived near Damascus—they are identified in the Arabic sources as Ghassanids—and raided the city's hinterland. The Muslims converged on the city of Bostra, which they forced to surrender and pay tribute. Next—we are still in 634—they defeated a number of Roman armies sent against them, in hard-fought battles that are variously recounted. The cities of Pella (Fahl) and Skythopolis (Beth Shan) submitted as well. We have contemporary confirmation of this disruption in provincial life. In September, 634, Sophronios wanted to travel from Askalon to the Sinai for a funeral, but was hindered by the disorders caused by the "Hagarenes" (another Roman name for the Saracens). Sophronios was then made patriarch of Jerusalem, and his Christmas homily for 634 refers repeatedly to the "godless Saracens" who were blocking the roads to Bethlehem and spreading murder and fear throughout the region. If only Christians reform their own lives, he promises, this enemy will be defeated.[9]

The caliph Abu Bakr died in the summer of 634 and was succeeded by his associate 'Umar (634–644), and the war in Syria and Palestine continued without interruption. The Muslim armies converged on Damascus, which they surrounded, besieged, and allegedly captured, whether by force or negotiation, after which they took Emesa (Homs)—all this by 635 or 636. Only now did the Roman counteroffensive began. The forces that the Muslims had defeated so far were likely small, unprepared, and unaware of the nature and goals of the enemy. It would have taken months for it to sink in that these were not regular Saracen raids. Herakleios instructed his brother Theodoros to take the armies of northern Mesopotamia and attack the enemy at Emesa, but he was defeated and returned to Constantinople in disgrace. In a homily delivered on 6 January, 635 or 636, Sophronios of Jerusalem referred rhetorically to many battles taking place between the Romans and "the God-hating Saracens," and he equates all this bloodshed with "the abomination of desolation" that the prophet Daniel had foretold.[10]

Many Roman units had already been defeated piecemeal in scattered battles, an indication of how overstretched the army was in these provinces six years after its life-or-death struggle with Persia. Even in the best of times, Roman defenses were stronger in the north, to face the Sasanians. There had never been a strategic need to protect against an invader coming from the southeast, and so there was no defensive system aimed in that direction. These early defeats at the hands of the Muslims cost the Romans precious resources and limited Herakleios' options. The emperor had come to the east and established his headquarters at Antioch. By this point, he had resources for only one push. He assembled a field army and placed it under the command of the Roman general Vahan (or Vaanes) and the treasurer (*sakellarios*) Theodoros Trithourios, and they began to defeat smaller Muslim contingents and push them to the south. In the face of this counteroffensive, the Muslims abandoned Damascus and Emesa, and then regrouped and joined forces. The two sides faced off in the valley of the Yarmuk river, east of the Sea of Galilee, in the summer of 636. Their maneuvers and operations seem to have lasted over a month and ended in a decisive Muslim victory. It is impossible to reconstruct the battle as the sources are late, garbled, and embellished. Something about infantry, then cavalry; confusion and miscommunication; units are isolated; suspicion of treason; an ambush; then defeat leads to flight and a slaughter in the ravines. When the dust settled, it was clear that Palestine, Syria, and Mesopotamia could not be defended. There was, for now, no possibility of recovery from this disaster, as the emperor had bet all his remaining resources on that one throw.

The Muslims pursued the fleeing Roman units north, and retook Damascus and Emesa by early 637. They then dispersed again to reduce the remaining cities of Syria and Palestine, including Jerusalem and Gaza (637 or 638). Only Kaisareia and Tripolis, which could be supplied and reinforced by sea, managed to resist for long. Herakleios retreated into Asia Minor in order to organize its defenses, just as he had done twenty years ago when the Persians came. Romantic traditions have him bidding farewell to the Roman east with the words "Save yourself, Syria" or "What a rich land this is for the enemy,"[11] but that was imagined in hindsight. At the time, the Romans were regrouping. They had recovered from worse at the hands of Persia. One way to staunch the bleeding was the tested method of paying the invader off. The initiative was taken by local commanders. At Chalkis, the governor of Edessa Ioannes Kataias arranged a truce with the Muslims in ca. 637, by which they agreed not to cross the Euphrates in exchange for 100,000 solidi; and Kyros, the governor-patriarch of Alexandria, paid them 200,000 solidi a year to keep them out of Egypt, an agreement that held for three years (ca. 636–639). It is likely that Kyros did this because Egypt had been attacked and its general defeated and killed. These sums are plausible, and comparable to what the Romans had formerly been paying the Avars.[12]

In spite of their momentum, the Muslims agreed to these terms because they too needed breathing space to consolidate their gains and make basic arrangements for their empire. The Muslim sources also report a plague that carried away many of the soldiers and leaders of the invading armies. It was at exactly this time (ca. 637–638) that ʿUmar is said to have visited Palestine in person. While the historicity of this visit can be doubted, the caliph did make fundamental decisions that shaped the course of Islamic and world history. One was that his soldiers would be supported by stipends paid from the proceeds of the conquests, as opposed to being given land and encouraged to settle among the provincials as their landlords. This, for now, preserved the Faithful as a distinct (military) class and prevented their assimilation. At the same time, the stipend system encoded differences of rank and prestige among the Faithful, as those who had been with the movement the longest were given preference over more recent converts. The Quraysh had been given more prestigious command positions than other followers of Muhammad, especially the natives of Medina, and the bedouin were generally viewed as inferior by the Hijazis. These and other tensions would come to a head during the career of Muʿawiya, a Qurashi of clan Umayya, whom ʿUmar now appointed the governor of Syria-Palestine in ca. 640. Muʿawiya made Damascus his headquarters and, when he later became caliph, his capital. Muʿawiya would be a more important figure for Roman history than any Roman emperor of the time.

In his alleged visit to Jerusalem, it is said that ʿUmar was received by none other than Sophronios, an occasion that fueled much subsequent fantasy, literary elaboration, and religious polemic. In reality, Jerusalem was low on the invaders' agenda, which was primarily strategic and economic and not symbolic-religious. Jerusalem is not even mentioned in the Quran. It was, however, a symbolic focal point for later writers. What happened during ʿUmar's visit is beyond our reach. More important were the decisions that ʿUmar made regarding the lives and rights of the conquered and their relations with Muslims. Most cities had surrendered and agreed to pay the tribute on condition that their lives, property, and religion be safeguarded, and these agreements became the basis for the new empire. In later centuries they were elaborated into the so-called Pact of ʿUmar that highlighted the superior status of the Muslims but codified the right of others to exist. At the time of the conquest, the Faithful had little or no interest in converting others to their faith, especially those who did not speak Arabic. Yuhannan bar Penkaye, a monk writing in Syriac in the 680s, explicitly said that they wanted only tribute and "allowed each person to remain in whatever faith he wanted . . . there was no distinction between pagan and Christian."[13] 'Umar also allowed Romans to leave the conquered territories freely. One of the goals of the truce was presumably to ensure safe passage to Roman refugees, of which there were thousands, possibly tens of thousands, as when the Persians came. Many people lived through both conquests.[14]

By 638 or 639, Herakleios was ready for another offensive and canceled the truces, possibly alleging that they were made without his agreement. He dismissed Ioannes Kataios from Edessa. Two Roman armies then converged on the Muslims in Syria, especially at Emesa, one from the west under Valentinos (possibly ferried to the coast by the fleet, for example to Tripolis) and another from Mesopotamia under David the Armenian. But they too were defeated and repelled.[15] While the chronology is confused, the Muslims took over the rest of Syria, including Antioch, and advanced into Mesopotamia, taking Edessa, Amida, and Daras and joining up with the Muslim armies that were simultaneously reducing the Sasanian empire. The Roman empire had lost all its Syriac-speaking subjects.

As part of his counteroffensive, Herakleios also terminated the truce in Egypt that had been arranged in ca. 636 by Kyros, the patriarch of Alexandria. The emperor recalled Kyros to Constantinople in ca. 639, where he was accused of financial irregularities and exiled. Kyros was replaced by a series of generals who were sent to fight the enemy, all of whom were defeated when the Muslims invaded properly, in late 639. Muslim tradition has Egypt fall to 'Amr, who invaded in late 639 and marched along the eastern edge of the Nile Delta to the huge Trajanic fortress of Babylon at its apex (where Cairo would later be built). But a new reading of our main Christian source, John of Nikiou, has revealed that another Muslim army was simultaneously heading north from Middle Egypt. How it got there is a mystery, because John's text has a lacuna covering the entire reign of Herakleios down to this point. This reading highlights the unreliability of the later Muslim versions.[16]

'Amr and his colleagues subdued Middle Egypt when they converged on Babylon in the summer of 640. They were reinforced by 'Umar with another army, and received supplies and other assistance from the provincials whom they had already conquered in the south. The Muslims were not liberators: 'Amr confiscated the property of Roman magistrates, "doubled the taxes on the peasants, forced them to carry fodder for the horses, and perpetrated innumerable acts of violence."[17] The Muslims invested Babylon and forced its evacuation by Easter 641. John of Nikou's detailed account reveals the chaos that prevailed in Egypt at that time, as Muslim contingents struck out across the Delta, attacking the cities, slaughtering civilians, and making the countryside unsafe. Meanwhile, the Roman command collapsed as the notables fled to Alexandria and rival Roman factions, including the Blues and the Greens, were quarreling over a tangle of fiscal, military, and doctrinal issues. There are archaeological indications that parts of Alexandria were in a bad state, abandoned or buried under debris.[18]

The leadership in Constantinople also lapsed during the crucial months of early 641, for Herakleios died in January, 641 and his complex family situation resulted in rivalry between two factions. Kyros was recalled from exile by the faction that wanted peace and sent to Alexandria in the fall of 641 to strike a deal with ʿAmr. The patriarch purchased eleven months of peace during which any Romans who wished could evacuate Alexandria. After that, the Muslims would respect the Christians' freedom of worship. The people of Alexandria rose up against Kyros when they heard this, but he said, "I have done this to save you and your children."[19]

Thousands must have fled from Alexandria to Constantinople, especially the most prominent Egyptian families. A Muslim historian records that 30,000 of the wealthiest people loaded their possessions on huge ships and left. The great households of Roman Egypt suddenly disappear in the papyrus record after that.[20] Kyros died before Easter of 642, as the city was about to be handed over. He had presided over the end of Roman rule in Egypt, which began seven centuries before. His role in that story was a decent one. The empire would have lost Egypt anyway, along with all its Coptic speakers and Monophysites. Kyros ensured that more of them would survive the transition. The alternative had been painfully exhibited in 641 by "the horrors committed in Kaisareia" when the city fell after a bitter siege to (probably) Muʿawiya. Thousands were slaughtered or enslaved, taken to the Hijaz to work as clerks or manual laborers. When Tripolis was besieged in 644, Roman ships evacuated the population overnight.[21]

In that year, ʿUmar was assassinated. His death and that of Herakleios marked the end of an era not just for a generation that had witnessed the most remarkable revolutions of fortune, but for world history. The Persian empire was on the verge of extinction, the Roman one had been significantly and irrevocably reduced, and an Arab Muslim empire had just been born. Roman writers noted that their empire used to extend from Scotland to Persia, but "now we see Romanía brought low . . . truly diminished." Later Arab writers remembered how some Romans of Syria used to view them "as more contemptible than the lice which inhabit the buttocks of camels," but now they had to obey the Muslims' orders.[22] ʿUmar's assassin had, strangely enough, experienced all the vicissitudes of that turbulent era: Abu Lu'lu'a Fayruz al-Nihawandi (i.e., Peroz of Nihawand) was a Christian

Persian carpenter who had been captured by the Romans in Herakleios' war against Persia and then by the Muslims when they invaded Romanía.[23]

Why did the Romans lose?

It is easy to explain why the Romans lost this war. The prolonged conflict with Persia had downgraded the empire's operational capabilities, including its organization, manpower, and wealth. The Muslims invaded provinces that had been stripped of all Roman military presence for fifteen years. The empire was facing severe hardships after the devastations of the Persian occupation and was in no position to reconstitute itself quickly. It is unlikely that the defenses of Palestine and southern Syria had been built up in the three years (630–633) that Herakleios controlled them, nor were they a strategic priority. The defense of those provinces was never designed to counter a sustained invasion by a coordinated enemy, only Saracen raids that looted and quickly left. Therefore, the Muslims struck with surprise against a weak point in the empire's defenses at its weakest moment. They knew these facts in advance and exploited them, whereas the empire knew nothing about them, their goals, or the extent of their capabilities. It probably took some time for the Roman command to realize that the new enemy were conquerors, not mere raiders, and that losing battles meant losing provinces. It is also possible that the invaders outnumbered the Romans in every battle that they fought, in spite of the exaggeration of the size of the Roman armies in Muslim sources. Thus, "the bloodshed at the Yarmuk was followed by the conquest and conflagration of Palestine, Kaisareia, and Jerusalem, the undoing of Egypt, and, in turn, the enslavement and incurable desolation of the mainland, the islands, and the whole of Romanía."[24]

Ultimately, it did come down to winning battles, though unfortunately we know almost nothing about early Muslim tactics and fighting styles. Their new religion was a decisive factor too, as it united the previously warring peoples of Arabia into a single, centralized force. This had never happened before, and so the potential of Arabia to create an external empire had never yet been realized. But that moment of unity passed quickly: the conquerors would soon turn back to fighting each other, only on a larger scale, giving their enemies breathing room. Moreover, when they encountered enemies who had not been worn down by war, or who were well coordinated, such as the Romans after they regrouped in Asia Minor, Arab expansion would slow to a crawl, stop, and then be reversed.

It is likely that the imperial government and other secular-minded Romans understood many or all of these factors at the time, or soon after. Unfortunately, their thoughts have not been preserved for us, as secular literature was a casualty of the wars and disruptions of that period. Only a thinning trail of mostly religious literature survives. The best that this could muster was partisan polemic or vapid moralizing. The Monophysites interpreted Roman defeat as a divine punishment for the sin of supporting Chalcedon, whereas Chalcedonians saw it as punishment for the sin of Monoenergism, or of not persecuting Monophysites more harshly, or just for sin generally. These were lazy but predictable responses from the toolkit of partisan thinking. One could always salvage some consolation from the wreckage: "Don't tell me that Christians are oppressed and enslaved today. What matters is that, despite this persecution, our faith still stands and so does our kingdom, and our churches are not closed, even surrounded by all these nations who rule over us and persecute us."[25]

It is often assumed that the empire had so alienated its religious minorities that they embraced the Muslim invaders and either helped them or at least did not resist them as strenuously as they might have. This has a fitting moral ring to it and provides narrative closure to the history of theological dispute that had wracked the empire for centuries. However, the evidence does not support it. Monophysite partisans continued to uphold the legitimacy and divine mission of the Roman empire all the way down to the Muslim conquest and, in some cases, beyond it, even if they disagreed with the doctrinal stance of the emperor and sought to bring him around to the truth. Many had been won over by Herakleios' Monoenergism in the years immediately preceding the Muslim invasions. Conversely, most found Islam to be repugnant, and hated the fact that they were now second-class citizens in a Muslim empire. However, in the centuries to come they had to wear an ingratiating face to please their new masters. In particular, Islamic law distinguished between those who had resisted Muslim rule, who were allotted the fewest rights in the new order, and those who had surrendered or supported the conquests, who were given the most privileges. Therefore, over time cities and religious communities had an interest in rewriting their histories to make it seem as if they had accepted the Muslims with open arms, which brought them benefits in the present. For this reason, later accounts, such as those produced by the Coptic Church under Islamic rule, are suspect.[26]

After all, civilian populations in the Roman empire, which were barred by law from keeping arms, did not regularly resist militant invaders unless their own lives were at risk or they could expect imminent assistance from the imperial armies. Otherwise, the expectation was that they would keep their heads down, pay the ransom or tribute, and try to survive the ordeal. It was the emperor's responsibility to then deal with the problem. "Struggles to the death" were not part of the Roman repertoire, and historians are wrong to expect them. Passivity on the part of Monophysites is therefore not noteworthy. What matters is that there is little proof from that time that Monophysites assisted the Muslims during the conquests *because* they were disaffected. John of Nikiou, a Monophysite writing a few generations later, did note that, during the conquest, the Egyptians hated Herakleios because of the persecution and that this emboldened the Muslims, but at no point in his narrative does this actually help the conquerors. To give a striking example, right after John says this, ʿAmr sends some of his soldiers against the city of Antinoe, but the townspeople are eager to resist them—it is the imperial officer who flees to Alexandria![27] Many Egyptians were forced by the conquerors to provide supplies and support, but this had nothing to do with their religious identity. Unlike Khusrow II, the Muslims were indifferent during the conquest to the distinction between the rival Churches.

Ethnic and religious perceptions of the conquests

Few or no Romans had so strong a sectarian identity that they would have preferred to be ruled by Saracen barbarians who had just invaded across the desert frontier, plundering and killing, rather than by other Romans, simply because the latter accepted Chalcedon. There was an ethnic aspect too. The Romans did not primarily identify the invaders by their new religion, but as ethnic Saracens, no different from the Saracens who had lived along the empire's periphery for centuries; in fact, they sometimes confused the two.[28] In 634, Sophronios identified the invaders as the "godless Saracens." Perhaps he did not yet know about the Message, or thought it was essentially godless. One of the earliest (indirect) references to Muhammad can be found in an anti-Jewish text purporting to be the tale of a Jew who was thrilled to have been forcibly converted to Christianity under Herakleios. The text, written between the 630s and the 670s, refers to the "false prophet who has appeared among the Saracens."[29] This ethnic identification of the conquerors is found in Greek, Syriac, Chalcedonian, and anti-Chalcedonian texts.[30] John of Nikiou presents them in religious terms ("the enemies of God") and as "a faithless barbarian race."[31]

Despite their internal diversity, the first Believers presented a coherent ethnic profile to Roman observers, which is why they immediately labeled them as Saracens, *Tayyaye* in Syriac, and understood them primarily in ethnic rather than religious terms; thus, their "atheism" was seen as a function of their barbarism, and not as a new religious message, at least not initially. After all, the invaders spoke mutually intelligible varieties of Arabic, and their subgroups shared cultural norms that were encoded in an Arabian poetic tradition and made sense only to people from Arabia. Another ethnic marker was the clan and tribal affiliations that structured Arabian life but did not extend to those who did not speak Arabic. Immediately after the conquests, the victors began to record tribal genealogies that were later compiled in written form into an overarching Arab ethnicity. Papyri from the later seventh century reveal that the conquerors had their own bureaucratic formulas, exported from Arabia, which differed from those used within the empire.[32]

While the conquerors were (in their own mind) defined by a new religion, this was not initially very inclusive. The Quran calls Muhammad "an apostle to all mankind," even though it repeatedly stresses that it is delivering an "Arabic" message precisely in order to be understood by its intended audience.[33] The Quran says nothing about the management of empire or about the relations between Believers and those who could not understand the Quran. Empire was not an eventuality for which Muhammad had prepared his followers. Moreover, many ideologies refer to "mankind" when in practice they have a limited group in mind. For example, in the Roman empire, "ecumenical" meant "throughout the Roman empire," not what the term literally means. The conquerors showed little interest in converting Romans. They did not offer a choice between conversion or tribute, as is often claimed, but between tribute and more attacks until they agreed to tribute. A text probably written in the 660s has Muʿawiya say, "If the Romans want peace, let them surrender their weapons and pay the tax."[34] Conversion was not the goal: Islam was reserved for the conquerors, along with the proceeds of victory.[35]

The Muslims did not proclaim the tenets of their faith in media that their subjects could understand. Certainly, they found Christian allies, auxiliaries, collaborators, servants, and even some people who wanted to convert. But for the first century of Muslim history, the Believers remained a tiny "Saracen" minority within their empire, an occupation army settled in self-segregated garrisons. For Muʿawiya, Islam belonged to the conquerors, and he pursued no policy of conversion.[36] For the Romans, therefore, the new message was simply that Saracens ruled.

Speakers of Arabic, however, were treated differently by the conquerors. They *were* expected to convert and were specifically targeted for proselytization.[37] Indeed, that is what the Ridda (Apostasy) wars were all about, and they contrast in this respect to the conquest of the Roman provinces. "Christian Arabs" became a problematic category that required special treatment, or termination, whereas other Christians did not. In short, Islam operated from the start with an implicit ethnic framework. Although the idea of "Arab" ethnicity evolved gradually and later in Muslim literature, it was implicit from the start. A famous papyrus from Herakleopolis (Ahnas), in Egypt, contains the first attestation of the *hijra* dating system (22 AH = 643 AD). It is a receipt for sixty-five sheep handed over to the Muslim emir ʿAbdallah ibn Jabir by the city notables, and it is written in Greek by the notary Ioannes and in Arabic by one Ibn Hadid. Egypt may have been under occupation, but Romans would have their receipts! On the back of the document, Ioannes noted that the receipt was for a down payment on the taxes owed to the Magaritai, i.e., the *muhajirun* (Emigrants), which is what early documents called the Muslims, using their terminology. But in the section of the text that Ioannes wrote as if from the mouth of ʿAbdallah, and countersigned in Arabic by ʿAbdallah himself, he makes the emir say that the sheep were "for the Saracens with me." Was this an act of ventriloquism by Ioannes, or did the emir consent to an ethnic identity that, for all intents and purposes, meant "Arab"? Starting in the 660s, inscriptions and papyri in Greek start referring to the "Arabs."[38]

This switch from "Saracen" to "Arab" could have been instigated only by the rulers themselves. At home, the conquerors may have been Kinda or Maʿad, but in the context of empire they became homogenized as Arabs. Conversely, their new Christian subjects began to lose their Roman identity. For the new rulers, the *Rum* were the people of the surviving Roman state beyond the Tauros mountains. Over time, this created a disincentive for Christians in the east to continue identifying as Romans, leading them to identify primarily with their Churches and languages. Romanness eventually went extinct in the Near East in parallel to the growth of Arab and Muslim identity.

17
Holding the Line (641–685)

Herakleios' dynastic arrangements proved unstable. His first wife Eudokia had given him an heir in May 612, but then she died in August of that year. Her son, also named Herakleios, was crowned co-emperor in the first year of his life as Neos Konstantinos III ("the New Constantine"). In 630, at the age of eighteen, he produced an heir of his own, also named Herakleios. However, by the 620s at the latest, Herakleios Senior had married his niece Martina. This was an unpopular match because the Church forbade such unions, and some regarded it as an abomination. This marriage produced numerous children, including Herakleios II (ca. 626), who was commonly called by the diminutive "Heraklonas" and was also made emperor before his father died in 641; it also produced David and Martinos, who were Caesars. When Herakleios Senior died, Konstantinos III and Herakleios II (Heraklonas) were supposed to rule jointly, although the latter, as a minor, was represented by his mother, Martina. Konstantinos III elevated his son Herakleios to the rank of Caesar.

Factions formed around these two dynastic lines. Konstantinos III had the support of the general Valentinos and the treasurer Philagrios, while Martina was backed by the patriarch Pyrros (638–641) and his allies in the Church. It appears that the people favored the eldest son, Konstantinos III, but he died suddenly in the spring of 641, possibly in April. This left the faction of Martina in power, and it was they who sent Kyros back to Alexandria to negotiate the surrender of Egypt to the Arabs. They also removed the young Herakleios from the imperial college. But Valentinos favored a more aggressive stance toward the Arabs and had been given most of the money in the treasury by Konstantinos III right before the latter died. Valentinos marched to Chalkedon and destabilized the regime. In September, 641, the people of the City demanded that the court accept the young Herakleios (son of Konstantinos III) as co-Augustus, and this was duly done; he also took the name Konstantinos, though he was commonly called Konstas (i.e., Constans). But Martina's child David was also made Augustus with the name Tiberios. This game of thrones was an untenable standoff. In the fall of 641, the patriarch Pyrros was forced to resign and soon afterward, possibly in November, the Senate, under pressure from the people and army units, deposed Heraklonas, Martina, David-Tiberios, and Martinos. Their faces were mutilated and they were exiled to Rhodes. A younger son of Martina was castrated "for fear that he would one day become emperor." This was the first time that castration was used to disqualify an heir, though he died soon after the operation. Valentinos had secured his ascendancy over the child-emperor Konstas, while the Arabs were consolidating their hold on the east.[1]

Arab raids begin

Romanía was in shambles. It had lost control of most of its Balkan territories, excluding some strips of the Aegean coast. It had lost the whole of the east to the Arabs. The population of Asia Minor was roughly the size of that of Syria and Egypt, but Egypt's agricultural surpluses were irreplaceable, especially for provisioning Constantinople. Its new masters now diverted them to the Hijaz. Compared to its heyday a century before, it is likely that the empire had lost 75% of its revenue. Thousands of people from the eastern provinces, including military units, were evacuated from the areas of the conquest to Asia Minor. While they were assets, they also had to be fed and settled in short order, during an unfolding crisis. Unfortunately, our documentary sources dry up at this time too, so we cannot directly see the chaos and confusion that this caused, but we can imagine it. In 641, Konstas' accession donative to the army was only three solidi, half the usual, and was probably paid to fewer soldiers than ever before in imperial history.[2]

The Arabs did not give the Romans the opportunity to regroup. They began to raid into Asia Minor almost immediately, plundering, killing, destroying villages and, when possible, cities too, and taking thousands of captives and livestock back with them. The chronology and targets of these raids is poorly known. The Roman sources are meager, and the Arabic sources pay less attention to these raids, as they resulted in neither conquest nor great glory, and eventually became routine. One of the first raids is said to have been led by Muʿawiya in the early 640s, and reached Euchaïta, in the Pontos near the Black Sea. He sacked it, taking captives and torturing the locals to reveal where they had hidden their valuables.[3] Over time, these attacks destabilized both urban and agricultural life in Asia Minor, leading to a contraction of cities around their fortified cores and hampering any economic recovery. But the Arabs' reluctance or inability to occupy territory north of the Tauros, and their failure to take Constantinople later on, ensured the survival of the rump Roman state. Roman counterattacks were ineffectual at this time, and we know little about them. It is possible that the general Valentinos led an attack against the Arabs in ca. 643, but retreated when they approached. Upon his return, he brought 3,000 soldiers into the City and tried to bully the court and patriarch, much as Gaïnas had done in 399–400, with similar results. The populace rose up, dragged him out of his house, cut off his head, and burned his remains.[4]

For the next century, we have only snippets of information about Roman history, excepting only the religious controversies. In fact, it is possible that no native Roman account of the reign of Konstas II (641–668) was ever produced. It remained a gap in the historical tradition, filled in only by translations of later foreign sources. But even from those snippets it is clear that the empire in the 640s and 650s was continuing to lose ground and had not yet hit rock bottom. The raids by Muʿawiya and his deputies continued, striking into Cilicia, Isauria, and Cappadocia. Kaisareia and Amorion were specifically targeted. Muʿawiya was a shrewd and forward-thinking leader. He realized that war with the Romans could not be won in the long term unless the Arabs had a large fleet, which he proceeded to assemble in order to strike at the islands and coasts. His first target was Cyprus, which was a rich prize in itself, as it had largely escaped the great wars of that era. Herakleios had reconstructed an aqueduct there in 631, and building inscriptions continued to appear even after the Romans had faltered in Syria.[5] It was strategically located and used by the Romans to regroup and counterattack in the 630s and to support nearby coastal cities that were holding out, such as Kaisareia.

The Arabs raided Cyprus in ca. 649. The Romans then defeated an Arab fleet—we do not know where—that was headed to Constantinople, and they did so by using Greek fire, the first reliable attestation of this terrifying weapon. It was a highly flammable substance like napalm that was hurled at enemy ships through siphons and set on fire to create an arc of liquid flame that could burn even on the surface of the water. Its composition and use were carefully guarded state secrets. Despite this victory, the Roman command made peace with Muʿawiya and paid him tribute for it. The emperor gave Gregorios, the son of Herakleios Senior's brother Theodoros, as a hostage. During this truce, Konstas tried to regain the ground that the empire had been losing in Armenia. The end of the great war with Persia had given the Romans jurisdiction over Persian Armenia—according to the borders of 591—but it was difficult to maintain a solid hold on it. The Armenian nobles were fractious and uncontrollable, and the Arabs began to raid Armenia in the 640s. Constantinople gave titles and offices to local lords in order to keep them loyal, but the Armenian Church refused to accept Chalcedon in 649. Also, the empire's local client in the region, the patrician Tʿeodoros Rshtuni, capitulated to the Arabs in ca. 652, after the Romans suffered a defeat. In response, Konstas marched to Theodosiopolis (Karin) and then on to Dvin, where he spent the winter of 652–653, pressuring the Armenian lords and clergy into obedience. But then he hurried back to Constantinople when he learned that Muʿawiya was breaking the truce.[6] He left behind a general, Maurianos, to hold Armenia, but in 654–655 an Arab army defeated him too, annexing Persian Armenia as well as Theodosiopolis to the caliphate. The Romans had been pushed out of the Caucasus, farther west than even the treaty of 387 had stipulated.[7]

Muʿawiya broke the truce because he had resolved to terminate the Roman empire for good. He launched a series of determined attacks against it, though they are hard to date.[8] He attacked Cyprus again in ca. 653. As in the first attack, the invaders engaged in killing, pillaging, burning of cities, taking captives, and possibly leaving garrisons for limited periods. In 654/5, Ioannes, the bishop of Soloi on Cyprus, renovated a church and noted in his inscription, with probable exaggeration, that 120,000 captives had been taken in the first attack (in ca. 649) and 50,000 in the second. Decades later, some of them resided near the Dead Sea, forced to work on unhealthy farms. Cypriot archaeology is typically inconclusive about these attacks, with evidence for destruction sitting next to that for survival and continuity, so that scholars can emphasize whichever they want.[9] It was later believed that one of the earliest female followers of the Prophet, Umm Haram, died on Cyprus in the first attack, albeit by falling off a mule, not in battle. Her shrine outside Larnaka, which still attracts pilgrims, was known to the emperor Konstantinos VII Porphyrogennetos (d. 959).[10]

The next targets were Crete, Kos, and Rhodes, along the approach to Constantinople. A century later, a tale was circulating that the Arabs pulled down the colossal statue of Helios that stood at the harbor of Rhodes and sold its remains as scrap to a Jew of Emesa. It is unlikely that any part of the Colossus still survived, much less stood, but the tale nicely encapsulated the passing of an era.[11] In ca. 654, Mu'awiya was ready to strike at Constantinople. He himself marched to Kaisareia in Cappadocia, while his fleet, under Abu l-A'war, sailed along the southern coast of Asia Minor. At Phoinix, off the coast of Lykia, it was met by the Roman fleet under the emperor Konstas himself, who was now twenty-five, the only Roman emperor to command a naval battle in person. The Romans lost the ensuing Battle of the Masts, and it was reported that the emperor fled in disguise, though it was a costly victory for the Arabs too. The Armenian history attributed to Sebeos, which was likely written in the later seventh century, does not recount the Battle of the Masts, but does claim that Mu'awiya marched to Chalkedon and his fleet reached Constantinople but was destroyed by a storm within sight of the walls. The survivors returned home.[12] If true, this would be the first Arab attack on the City. The noose was tightening, and the Arabs now had the fleet that the Persians had lacked.

The assassination of the caliph 'Uthman in 656 temporarily halted the push to destroy Rome and led to the first Muslim civil war, a tangle of tribal, regional, religious, and personal rivalries that had been simmering beneath the surface of the conquests. They burst out now, altering the course of Muslim history. Mu'awiya, the craftiest of the contestants, backed by the resources and armies of Syria and Palestine, emerged as the victor in 661 to claim the caliphal title. But the conflict occupied all his attention after 656. In ca. 659, he even purchased a truce from the Romans by paying *them* 365,000 solidi per year plus one horse and one slave per day (as a hostage, he even sent his general 'Abd al-Rahman, none other than the son of Khalid ibn al-Walid).[13] This peace gave the Romans five years to regroup and an injection of cash. As events proved, they used both wisely.

Anti-Monotheletism

One challenge that the court had already resolved decisively was a node of resistance, in the west, to its ecclesiastical policy. In the 630s, in the flush of his victory over the Persians, Herakleios began forging a compromise with leading Monophysites by using the formula of Christ's Single Operation or Activity (*energeia*), which was backed by the patriarchs Sergios of Constantinople and Kyros of Alexandria. But in 636 or 638, as the Arab war was raging, and possibly in response to opposition by Chalcedonian hardliners such as Sophronios of Jerusalem, for whom Two Natures called for Two Activities, the court backed away from this approach. Herakleios issued an *Ekthesis* (*Exposition*) that reiterated the creeds of the five Ecumenical Councils and banned anyone from using either phrase, namely One or Two Activities, because each was offensive to some. The phrase Two Activities, the *Ekthesis* notes, could be taken to imply that Christ had two wills that were potentially opposed to each other, which is impious. This reiterated a position taken by pope Honorius.[14] Herakleios had other problems to worry about, and was finished with this business. Neither he nor his successors tried to impose a new formula.

However, some Diphysites decided, based on the wording of the *Ekthesis*, that the court was pushing a doctrine of the One Will. Intellectually, they were led by Maximos, a disciple of Sophronios who was one of the greatest theologians in the history of the Church and was adept at using ancient philosophical concepts to clarify Christian doctrine. He too had used the notion of the "one will" of Christ in the past, but now, for reasons that remain unclear, he decided that the *Ekthesis* was promulgating a heresy. He went to war against Constantinople at precisely the time when the empire could least afford more division. Maximos was among many monks and other refugees who fled before the Arab conquests to North Africa and Italy; among them was also Theodoros of Tarsos, later the archbishop of Canterbury in England (668–690). Rome now became a center of resistance to Constantinople. In the later sixth century, pope Gregory had little access to Greek learning, but in the mid-seventh, in part due to this migration, Rome had become a center of eastern thought. Eastern refugees formed a powerful monastic lobby that agitated against Constantinople's alleged "Monotheletism." In Carthage in 645/6, they humiliated Pyrros, the ex-patriarch of Constantinople, in a public debate with Maximos. The transcripts of this debate, however, were a later literary concoction by the anti-Monotheletes, who were adept and unscrupulous propagandists. Pyrros allegedly went to Rome to recant his heresy and seek forgiveness. It is reported that pope Theodore (642–649) confirmed him as patriarch of Constantinople, which, if true, constituted a rejection of the political order in the capital. The bishop of Rome had no authority to appoint a bishop for Constantinople.[15]

This eastern element co-opted the authority of the Church of Rome in its feud with Constantinople. Pope Theodore, who, like Maximos, agitated to expand and exacerbate the rift with Constantinople, was from Palestine, the first among a number of Greek-speaking popes in this and the next century. Now that Rome was theirs to wield, these easterners exalted it as supreme among the Churches of the world, granting it "the *imperium*, the authority, and the power to bind and to loose throughout the entire world." Christian dissidents in the east had in the past flattered the see of Rome when they sought its help against their own bishops. This was always a tactical move, not an unconditional acceptance of papal supremacy. But now the anti-Monotheletes gave the most full-throated endorsement of Rome's preeminence ever offered by easterners. They attacked Paulos, the patriarch of Constantinople, for his "heresy"; in response, he maintained a dignified silence. But Rome also had to awkwardly explain away pope Honorius' prior affirmation of the One Will, a thorn in its side to this day. By "One Will," the easterners argued, Honorius had meant "Two Wills."[16]

In the context of a collapsing Roman empire, anti-Monotheletism became a seditious movement, and not only by opposing Constantinople's demand for a moratorium on theological precision. Gregorios, the exarch of North Africa, who had presided over the disputation between Maximos and Pyrros, rebelled against the emperor in the same year. The revolt was over quickly: he was defeated in 647 at a battle near Sufetula (Sbeitla) by Arab raiders, who periodically ranged this far along the African coast, and he likely died in the battle. The provincials had to pay protection money to the Arabs to be spared further raids. Gregorios' motives and goals are unknown, but Constantinople suspected that he received moral support from the anti-Monotheletes.[17]

The court sought to keep the theological peace by issuing the *Typos* (*Formula*), in 647/8, which reaffirmed the five Ecumenical Councils and banned all discussion of Operations and Wills, on pain of punishment. Constantinople had no interest in the One Will; there were at this point no "Monotheletes." However, the anti-Monotheletes needed "Monotheletism" in order to pin it on Constantinople. Theodore convened a Synod of mostly Italian bishops at the Lateran palace in Rome to condemn Monotheletism and all the recent patriarchs of Constantinople, declaring Paulos deposed. The Synod met in October, 649, though Theodore died shortly before it convened. Its president was his successor Martin I (649–655), whose accession, however, had not been ratified by the imperial court, and the Synod itself was in direct violation of the prohibition in the *Typos* of precisely such discussions. The Acts that we have are not exactly a transcript of the proceedings but yet another literary confection of the easterners at Rome. They were written in Greek before the Council, pretending to be a translation of the Latin proceedings, and then translated into Latin. The Council basically ratified its own preexisting Acts. They were crammed full of Maximos' theological views and posed as the record of an "Ecumenical Council," although so far only an emperor could convene such a thing. Maximos called it the Sixth Ecumenical Council. The Synod posed a direct challenge to the authority of the emperor in the Church, and set up the bishop of Rome in his place as the guardian of orthodoxy. Martin went so far as to depose "irregular" bishops in Palestine and replace them with his appointees, an extraordinary usurpation.[18]

Rome demanded that the entire Church accept its decisions. Thessalonike, for example, was regarded by the pope as subject to Rome, but when Paulos, its bishop, was informed about the Synod, he refused to condemn the Monotheletes. Martin duly excommunicated him and informed the people of Thessalonike that their bishop was deposed. They ignored the pope.[19]

"Monotheletism" did not really exist. To be sure, the anti-Monotheletes were sincere that such a heresy was a major threat to the Church. It was precisely such sincerity that had split the Church many times before, even absent an actual difference of theological opinion. The court was not backing a particular formula at this time, but the anti-Monotheletes were condemning all recent patriarchs of Constantinople as heretics, which meant that the capital could not but view the faction around Maximos as a dissident threat. Maximos was theologically more sophisticated than his imagined opponents but even so, no party to the dispute managed to offer a convincing theory of the "will" that could justify the heated polemics. Even Maximos was initially tripped up by the possibility that Christ might have *three* wills, one for each of his Natures and one for the unified Christ-person (he later repudiated this position). The patriarchs of Constantinople and pope Honorius had merely been insisting that Christ was not a split, schizoid personality when they affirmed the One Will, and they had wanted to tamp down theological acrimony by allowing everyone to believe freely regarding Activities. But Maximos and his faction were in principle opposed to compromise, ambiguity, and accommodation, and hated to let sleeping dogs lie. But sleeping dogs, when provoked, can bite.[20]

In ca. 651, Martin was implicated in a rebellion by the exarch of Italy Olympios, who then died fighting Arabs in Sicily. This was the tipping point for Constantinopolitan forbearance—two rebellions too many associated with the self-proclaimed anti-Monotheletes. In 653, Konstas sent a new exarch, Theodoros Kalliopas, who promptly arrested Martin, Maximos, and their troublemaking associates. Martin was hauled to Constantinople and tried before the Senate on charges of sedition and usurping the papal throne. He was not allowed to turn the discussion to theological matters. Found guilty, he was sentenced to death, which was commuted to exile at Cherson, in the Crimea, where he died in 655/6. This was the worst treatment that a pope had ever received at the hands of an emperor, and yet no pope had yet acted with such reckless impudence and treasonous intent toward the imperial capital. It appears that Rome was not displeased at Martin's removal: he received no Italian support during the days of his tribulations. Konstas kept the papal throne in Rome vacant for over a year and suspended many of the rights of the Roman Church. By 657, pope Vitalian had snapped back to obedience and communion with Constantinople.[21]

Maximos was held for two years in detention and then charged with many acts of sedition in 655, the year after the first Arab attack on Constantinople. His trial posed loftier issues, though the account of it that we have is another piece of anti-Monothelete hagiography. Among other crimes, he was accused of hating the emperor and hindering the war effort against the Saracens; giving moral support to the rebel Gregorios in North Africa, which Maximos did not deny; gainsaying that the emperor was also a quasi-priest; dividing the Church; rejecting the *Typos*; and being biased in favor of the Latin over the Greek Church. In his defense, Maximos elevated intransigence to a virtue, and refused to be reconciled with Constantinople even if the emperor repealed the *Typos*. Nor was that enough: to be accepted by him, the emperor would also have to condemn all who were anathematized by the Lateran Synod, in other words to capitulate unconditionally to anti-Monothelete demands. Anyone who had opposed Maximos' faction would have to confess that he had been an instrument of evil and consent to have Maximos (or his like) dictate his beliefs and identity to him. Like many zealots before him, Maximos understood Orthodoxy as a maximalist victory over others. This attitude enraged his prosecutors: "You utter villain, you consider us and our City and the emperor as heretics? In reality, we are more Christian and orthodox than you."[22]

The court's priority was not to punish Maximos but to entice him to enter into communion with Constantinople. Konstas did not want to alienate the learned monk's supporters. In order to win him over, the emperor was prepared to let Maximos define the terms of a theological compromise. He could parse the One Will and Two Wills however he wanted—the court even suggested the formula "One and Two"—but condemning the patriarchs was ruled out. In other words, Maximos had to find a way to accept the *Typos*, or at least not reject it. While this dragged on, the Arab civil war in 656 gave Konstas the opportunity to regroup his forces and put Romanía on a sound defensive footing.

The Romans regroup

Roman strategy had to adjust to a new reality. The army of Illyricum had basically disappeared during the first decades of the seventh century, as Illyricum itself was lost. The remains of the field armies of Oriens and Armenia had, in the late 630s, been pulled back to defend Asia Minor. The field army of Thrace had partially survived, but we do not know where it was stationed in the mid-seventh century. A new field army known as Opsikion (from Latin *obsequium*, meaning in attendance upon the emperor) is attested by ca. 660. The fleet, more important than ever, was reconstituted as the command of Karabisianoi (literally, "shipmen"), based probably in the Aegean. It is possible that the naval command of the Kibyraiotai, responsible for the southern coast of Asia Minor, was also created at this time, though it is not attested until the eighth century. This was an unprecedented level of interest in the navy, a response to Muʿawiya's investment in fleets. A letter of the emperor Justinian II in 687 attests that these named forces, along with those of Italy and North Africa, constituted the basic framework of imperial defense. It must have come into being under Konstas II. But we do not know the size of these forces in the mid-seventh century.[23]

Konstas took advantage of the truce with Muʿawiya to energetically restore his authority in many trouble spots. A meager chronicle entry informs us that in 657/8 he campaigned against the Slavs, but we are not told how far into the former Balkan provinces he reached. In 655, imperial control did not extend farther than Perberis, near Bizye in Thrace, so Konstas likely concentrated on pacifying Thrace. He took many captives and possibly expanded the zone of imperial control. One group of Slavs, the Belegezites, had settled in Thessaly and had joined in an attack on Thessalonike in the 610s. But in the 670s, when other Slavs attacked the city, the Belegezites were friendly and supplied it with food during the siege. Thus, the process by which they were absorbed into the empire appears to have begun under Konstas.[24]

The extent and nature of Slavic settlement in the Balkan provinces is hotly debated, because we lack documentary evidence; the archaeological evidence is ambiguous and inconclusive; and the topic impinges on the national ideologies of several modern states. Clearly, the empire lost control of its Balkan hinterland, which implies that the Avars and Slavs made their presence felt everywhere. But loss of control does not require demographic change. Imperial governance required stability and a measure of compliance from its subjects. A group of well-ensconced newcomers, marauding throughout a region or forcing their own protection racket on provincials, could disrupt the administration. For their own part, provincials, especially slaves, could seize this opportunity to get out from under the authorities' thumb. As early as 600, a military treatise discussing Slavs warned that "even some Romans have given in to the times, forget their own people, and prefer to gain the goodwill of the enemy." Considering how the southern Balkans were gradually reabsorbed by the empire in the eighth and ninth centuries, and their population linguistically Hellenized, the enduring presence of Roman provincials can be assumed. However, many relocated to mountains or fortified coastal settlements, abandoning lowland valleys.[25] Cities contracted. The monetary economy largely disappeared, except in the cities that remained under imperial control, such as Thessalonike, Athens, Thebes, and Corinth, and the complexity and quality of material culture plunged more or less everywhere. The lights basically went out in Greece between the late sixth and mid-seventh century.[26] Moreover, just as many Romans had fled from Palestine to North Africa and Rome, many fled from Greece to Sicily and southern Italy, thereby reintroducing the Greek language into Magna Graecia.[27]

The domestic history of Konstas' regime remains opaque to us because of the lack of Roman sources and the indifference of the foreign ones. He made his infant son Konstantinos co-emperor in 654, and awarded the rank of Augustus to his two other sons, Herakleios and Tiberios, in 659. It appears that an Augustus was now regarded as inferior to a *basileus*.[28] In 659, Konstas also executed his brother Theodosios, for unknown reasons.[29]

In 659–660 or 660–661, the emperor took advantage of the Arab civil war, which was then at its peak, to reestablish his hegemony over the principalities of the Caucasus. He traveled to Armenia and Azerbaijan, summoning the local lords, giving them titles and gifts, including fragments of the True Cross, and winning back their allegiance. He reinstalled Narses, the Chalcedonian *katholikos* of the Armenian Church, and personally attended the inauguration of a new cathedral at Vagharshapat. Its piers feature sculpted eagles, and the column capitals display the *katholikos'* monogram in Greek, both signs of his Roman allegiance.[30] For the next two centuries and more, these principalities would oscillate in their allegiance between Rome and the Muslims. The local lords sought to protect themselves, preserve their independence, and extract concessions. Their lands would not be governed directly by the Roman administration, as Justinian and Maurikios had attempted, until the tenth century. In the meantime, emperors were usually limited to soft power and loose assertions of hegemony that rarely verged on sovereignty.

The empire was finding its footing again. Perhaps this emboldened Konstas to finish off the challenge to his authority posed by the anti-Monothelete agitators. In 662, Maximos and his follower Anastasios were given their last opportunity to compromise. When they refused, they were tried and condemned. Specifically, an assembly of bishops, including the patriarchs of Constantinople and Antioch and a representative of the patriarch of Alexandria, condemned Maximos as a heretic. The Senate then decreed that their tongues and right hands were to be cut off, after which they were exiled to Lazica. Maximos, "who was an extremely short man and frail of body," died within months of his arrival there.[31]

The Arab civil war was over by 661 and Rome's old enemy Muʿawiya, who emerged as the new caliph, was certain to restart hostilities. Even so, in 662 the emperor embarked on his longest journey yet, this time to Italy, where no eastern emperor had traveled since Theodosius I, three centuries earlier. In the aftermath of the Lombard invasion, Italy had evolved a unique territorial configuration. It was fragmented between imperial and Lombard zones of control, in both the north and south. Italy had been a war zone ever since 535, knowing only brief interludes of peace. Raiding, plague, famine, and the breakup of the peninsula into rival Lombard and imperial zones disrupted its ancient trade networks and ravaged its former prosperity. The population declined and so did surplus production, the scope for state extraction, the volume of goods marketed, and interregional trade. It was thus more difficult to mobilize resources for large-scale projects, and even the elites present a materially diminished profile. The old buildings were ransacked as quarries and cities exhibited empty spaces, or were ruralized. With the switch from stone and tiles for housing to more perishable materials such as wood and thatch, it is harder to find the people in the archaeology of post-invasion Italy. By ca. 600, pope Gregory lamented that because of the Lombards "cities have been depopulated, fortresses razed, churches burned down, monasteries and nunneries destroyed, the fields abandoned by mankind, and, destitute of any cultivator, the land lies empty and solitary."[32]

A social transformation was taking place in imperial Italy. As city councils went extinct (by ca. 600), the Roman army and its officers became the matrix of a new social and landowning elite. In many ways, the rulers of central medieval Italy emerged out of the empire's military administration. That was still in the future.[33] In the mid-seventh century, the imperial corridor across the center of the peninsula was riven by tensions between the exarch at Ravenna and the city of Rome, which was developing its own institutions of self-governance, in which the popes played an increasingly leading role. But the exarchs, and by extension the emperors, were still the most powerful players. A dynamic Armenian, Isaakios, who served as exarch for eighteen years (625–643), was able to confiscate the treasures of the Lateran palace, send a portion of them to Herakleios in ca. 638–640, and expel the clergy who opposed him. It was his intervention that may have tipped the papacy into opposing Constantinople over the issue of Wills. The lid of his sarcophagus survives at Ravenna, with a poetic epitaph in Greek: He "preserved Rome and the West intact for his serene sovereigns, Isaakios, the ally of the emperors, the great ornament of the whole of Armenia—for he was an Armenian, from a noble family. Now that he has died with honor, his wife, chaste Sosanna, sorely wails."[34]

Isaakios' main opponent toward the end of his tenure was the Lombard king Rothari (636–652), who conquered Genoa and the rest of Liguria from the Romans in the early 640s, causing great destruction, and it was possibly he who killed Isaakios.[35] But the exarchate was stable, and the Lombards were mostly preoccupied with killing each other. In 653, the exarch Theodoros Kalliopas easily arrested pope Martin and his coterie, and packed them off to Constantinople.

Konstas took an army with him to Italy, including the Opsikion, and a fleet. His itinerary—reaching Taranto via Athens and Corinth—is known from western sources and a wave of coin finds along his route.[36] The emperor made Naples his initial headquarters and reduced some of the territories of the Lombard dukedoms in the south. He tried to capture the city of Benevento, but failed. He arrived at Rome on 5 July, 663, and took up residence on the Palatine hill, which, after all, he owned, as he did most of the old city's monuments. Konstas spent twelve days in Rome engaged in cordial, but carefully choreographed, celebrations with pope Vitalian. He also stripped the bronze from churches and monuments, using it to pay soldiers and sending part of it back to Constantinople. As for the *Typos*, all sides maintained a stance of "don't ask, don't tell," which is after all what the *Typos* required. Konstas then crossed over to Sicily toward the end of the year and used Syracuse as his headquarters until the end of his life in 668. In 666, he was lobbied successfully by the bishop of Ravenna to make his see autocephalous from Rome. Ravenna's bishop was to be appointed locally with no interference from the pope. This may have been lingering payback for the troubles caused by papal overreach over "Monotheletism."[37]

Our knowledge of Konstas' activities at Syracuse comes from a hostile western source, which rhetorically denounces the taxes that he imposed on the people of Calabria, Sicily, Africa, and Sardinia.[38] Historians have speculated about his goals in this unconventional venture in Italy: they were likely to confirm the loyalty of the Italians, and especially of Rome; extract resources, especially grain with which to feed Constantinople; organize the defenses of North Africa and Sicily against the growing Arab threat in the central Mediterranean; and subject the Lombards in the south.

The Arab raids into Asia Minor resumed as soon as Mu'awiya prevailed over his enemies and became the first Umayyad caliph (661–680). The raids cannot always be dated precisely, but experienced generals, including 'Adb al-Rahman, the son of Khalid ibd al-Walid, ranged throughout Asia Minor, from Isauria to the Pontos and as far west as Bithynia, taking thousands of captives. The raiders also began to spend the winter on Roman territory, keeping the locals terrorized and cooped up for months at a time. Eastern chronicles pay little attention to the raids, in part because they did not result in conquests but also because the later Abbasid tradition, which compiled this information, was not interested in highlighting the deeds of the Umayyads. But occasionally the victims recorded their experiences. Euchaïta was invested for seven months and attributed its salvation to the military saint Theodoros. The collection of his miracles recounts how the populace sought refuge in the upper fortifications while the Arabs occupied the lower city. The invaders demolished the saint's shrine and gathered many captives from nearby provinces, but eventually departed because of the odor of the dead bodies. When the people came down, "they beheld the stench and desolation of the city and wished to move away from their home to other cities," although the saint prevented that. Yet the danger was always present: "because of the yearly attack of the enemy, we were all staying close to the stronghold."[39] Economic life was disrupted by these precarious conditions throughout most of Asia Minor.

Many would have wondered why their emperor was in Syracuse during all this. A critical point came in 666/7, when the general of the army of Armenia, a man of Persian background named Saporios (Shapur), rebelled. We do not know his goals or grievances, but he quickly made an alliance with Muʿawiya, who sent him an army under one Fadala. Constantinople sent an army to confront Saporios, but he died in a freak accident (striking his head on a gate when his horse reared up).[40] Rather than recall Fadala, Muʿawiya made another push to end the empire. He dispatched his son Yazid, the future caliph, with another army to join Fadala. Our reports of this campaign, including another siege of Constantinople that historians traditionally placed in the 670s, were mangled in the chronicle tradition, but the problems of their chronology have now been brilliantly resolved. Yazid and Fadala marched to Constantinople in 667 and occupied Chalkedon, where they were joined by a fleet from Syria and Egypt. In Islamic tradition, this expedition was remembered primarily because it was accompanied by four Companions of the Prophet from his days at Medina, one of whom, Abu Ayyub, died during its course (he is honored today at the shrine of Eyüp, in Istanbul). The attackers spent the winter of 667–668 besieging the capital. For the Arabs, this was one invasion among many; for the Romans, it was an existential threat. Some believed that the enemy was aided by demons, who temporarily left the men they were possessing in order "to help their companions, the Saracens."[41]

The fear in Constantinople is easy to imagine. Elders could recall the siege of 626, and most of the populace remembered the aborted naval attack of 654. The emperor and a significant part of the army were absent in Sicily. It is not clear who was in charge in Constantinople at this time, possibly Theodoros of Koloneia and the *cubicularius* (eunuch chamberlain) Andreas. Yazid assaulted the walls of the City from both the land and the sea in the spring of 668, but failed to breach them. Hunger and disease eventually forced the Arabs to fall back, but they still blockaded the capital. For two years (667–669), the patriarch Thomas was cut off from official communication with the pope "because of the persistent attack by the godless Saracens."[42]

At that lowest point in Roman fortunes, the most alarming news arrived in the fall of 668. The emperor Konstas had been murdered in his bath in Syracuse, either with a sword or a soap bucket, and the army there had proclaimed Mizizios, the *comes* of the Opsikion, as emperor. He was of Armenian origin and, apparently, handsome.[43] The empire was now split in two.

Stabilization

This moment should have been the end of the eastern Roman empire. The emperor in Constantinople, Konstantinos IV, was only sixteen and his City was invested by an ensconced Arab army that was raiding its hinterland with impunity. The flower of Romanía's military was in rebellion in a faraway province. For sixty years, the empire had been on the defensive, fighting for its life against Persia and the Arabs.

In the past three decades the Romans had been consistently losing battles and territory, much of which they would never recover. The regime was out of money, and the population of its capital, after decades of plague and the loss of Egyptian grain, had dwindled to under 100,000, possibly to as low as 40,000.[44] But at this very point, the Romans began to win battles again and embarked on a gradual trajectory of long-term revival and even expansion.

We understand little about Konstas' murder, or who was behind it. Nor do we know how the regime of Mezizios was terminated or when. According to one tradition, Konstantinos IV sailed to Sicily and put Mizizios to death; according to another, this was done by the army in Italy. Either way, Italy ceased to be the court's focus of attention. The emperor's presence there had served a purpose. Soon after the army returned home, an Arab fleet from Egypt raided Sicily, which had so far been untouched by war, killing thousands and taking away many captives along with the bronze that Konstas had stripped from the monuments of Rome.[45]

Yazid ibn Muʿawiya had already left the blockade of Constantinople and returned to the caliphate in late 668 or 670, which we know because in late 670 he led the hajj to Mecca. But the Arabs had positioned garrisons in Roman territory, including a significant one at Amorion, in central Asia Minor. It seems that Fadala spent the winter of 670–671 at Kyzikos, on the Sea of Marmara, after which he too departed from Romanía. The *cubicularius* Andreas took Amorion back during the winter of 669–670 or 670–671: during a snowy night, he and his soldiers stealthily scaled the walls and slew the garrison, allegedly 5,000 men.[46]

The momentum was still on the Arab side, but the tide turned during the 670s. There are hints that a Roman fleet attacked Egypt in 671/2. And in the period 672–674, the Romans inflicted two significant defeats on the Arabs, one on land and one at sea. Our sources are late and garbled but suggest that in 672 Muʿawiya made another major push to destroy the empire with a joint sea and land operation. His fleet was commanded by Muhammad ibn ʿAbdallah and ʿAbdallah ibn Qays, while the army was led by Sufyan ibd ʿAwf. These forces wintered along the southern coast of Asia Minor, in Cilicia and Lykia, with one contingent wintering as far as west as Smyrna. In ca. 673, the Romans decisively defeated the land army at a battle that possibly took place at Syllaion, in southern Asia Minor. Their generals were Floros, Petronas, and Kyprianos, who are said to have killed 30,000 Arabs. The Arab fleet was then destroyed either by a storm or an attack of the Roman navy, or both. The Romans again used Greek fire.[47] This was the first major check that the expanding caliphate received, the first counteroffensive that any of its targets around the world was able to launch.

Arab raids continued during the 670s, but their objectives were distant from Constantinople, such as Crete and Rhodes.[48] It became increasingly common for the raiders themselves to be attacked, blockaded, and sometimes destroyed. The Romans had finally adjusted their strategy to the defense of Asia Minor. They even went on the offensive. In 677, a Roman fleet sailed to the coast of Phoenicia and disembarked an army that took over Mount Lebanon. Ensconced in difficult terrain, this force of marines engaged in guerilla warfare against the Arabs, coordinating its attacks with the imperial command in Asia Minor in order to assist Roman raids and hinder Arab ones. It quickly grew to many thousands by attracting runaway slaves and natives from all around. They raided the territory of Antioch and eventually as far south as Galilee. This group came to be called Mardaïtes in Greek and Jarajima in Arabic, names of unknown etymology. Modern scholars treat it as an ethnic group that may have preexisted the Arab conquests. However, our earliest source links their origin to the Roman military intervention of 677. The Mardaïtes severely disrupted Arab operations along the eastern border. Arab raids into Asia Minor diminished in frequency after 677.[49]

The Slavic wave in Macedonia broke against the walls of Thessalonike at exactly the same time. Slavic-Roman relations had been normalizing in some respects. Trading relations were established between the city and the Belegezites in Thessaly, and the *rex* of the Rynchinoi, Perboundos, lived in Thessalonike, wore Roman clothing, and spoke Greek. However, he was denounced to the emperor for plotting against Thessalonike and, to make a long and dramatic story short, he was arrested and executed. In response, the Slavs of the Strymon river valley, along with the tribes of the Rynchinoi and the Sagoudates, blockaded Thessalonike by land for two years, 676–678. The city was gripped by famine, described movingly by an eyewitness in the collection of St. Demetrios' miracles. The emperor could send only ten cargo ships with supplies, "because he was busy with another war," probably the operations taking place at that moment in the Lebanon mountains. The attackers made a determined but unsuccessful effort to capture Thessalonike by force in July, 677, after which they raided far and wide in their ships, reaching the Sea of Marmara and disrupting the provisioning of the capital itself. Eventually the emperor was able to send an imperial army that dispersed the Slavic host, and he sent more grain ships to feed the Thessalonians.[50]

The Sixth Ecumenical Council

Konstantinos' regime had successfully stopped the bleeding on many fronts. There was one more open wound, however: Rome. For reasons that remain obscure, Rome was again refusing to recognize the patriarchs of Constantinople in the 670s, possibly because of the treatment of pope Martin, the theological issues left open from the Lateran Synod of 649, and the removal of Ravenna from papal jurisdiction. In 678, the emperor wrote to pope Donus and invited him to initiate a series of local councils that would resolve the question of the One or the Two Wills, and to send delegates to Constantinople to discuss the issue in order to heal the "schism" that had emerged between the Churches. Konstantinos professed that he did not know the causes of this schism. These initiatives eventually led to the convocation of an Ecumenical Council, the Sixth, in November, 680. By that time, all the major decisions had been made in advance. Rome, now led by pope Agatho, had insisted on the condemnation of the patriarchs Sergios, Paulos, Pyrros, and Petros of Constantinople and Kyros of Alexandria. Agatho got what he wanted, which means that Konstantinos sacrificed the pride of his capital in order to secure union with Rome. By this point, however, those patriarchs were half a century in the past. At least there was no doctrinal obstacle, since Monotheletes, as defined by Maximos and the Lateran Synod, did not exist. There were only those who balked at condemning a series of legitimate patriarchs of Constantinople on a made-up charge of heresy—a question of politics and pride, not doctrine. The only dissenter at the Council who upheld the teaching of the One Will was Makarios of Antioch, who was duly deposed. But the Council was not a clear win for the pope, who got more than he bargained for. Makarios pointedly reminded the assembled bishops that pope Honorius had also agreed with Sergios on the matter of Wills, so pope Honorius was formally condemned as well.[51] This disrupted the papal narrative of Rome's unerring orthodoxy.

The Council's high point was when Polychronios, a monk who opposed what Rome and Constantinople were trying to do, pledged to resurrect a dead man by placing his profession of faith on the body; if he failed, he would submit to the emperor and Council. The assembly went over to the Zeuxippos baths where Polychronios placed his profession on a corpse that had been laid out there for that purpose and whispered in his ear for a long time, but to no avail. "I am unable to raise the dead," he admitted, but refused to change his beliefs.[52] This episode was likely embellished, or invented, in the subsequent elaboration of the Council's Acts. It is an example less of credulity and more of literary ridicule and polemic. These Acts probably disguise the Council's back-room dealings, as the emperor pressured his Church to accept Rome's position.

Pope Martin and Maximos the Confessor were also not rehabilitated at the Council. For all that they had dedicated and given their lives to the struggle against the One Will, they were not even cited at the Council as authorities on that issue. They had been condemned for treason, and condemned they would remain. Nor was the Council shaped by Maximos' theology. The assembly read passages from past theologians and Councils in order to declare them authentic or forged, making the Council into a vast exercise in patristic philology. This was necessary because the question of Wills had not been treated by the Fathers in a systematic way, and so the Council had to track down and scrutinize hints found in authoritative texts. In the end, Rome and Constantinople agreed on a mutually advantageous union. In 681, the emperor lightened taxes on the papal estates in Sicily and Calabria, and in 682/3, he restored Ravenna to Rome's ecclesiastical jurisdiction. Ravenna lost out in this struggle, even though in the 670s a grand mosaic had been erected in the church of Sant'Apollinare of Classe, evoking the famous mosaics of Justinian and Theodora, which depicted Konstantinos IV and his sons handing over a privilege to the bishop of Ravenna (see Plate 4a). In 684/5, the emperor allowed the bishops of Rome to take office immediately upon their election, without waiting for imperial ratification.[53]

Thus, in exchange for sacrificing four of its own patriarchs, Constantinople secured its position in Italy, which had become increasingly precarious. Italy, Sicily, and North Africa were now more important for the empire than the entire east, which had been lost. Compromise with the Monophysites was, by 680, a moot point. Rome was an increasingly valuable ally, as it was beginning to project ecclesiastical power into the territories of the former western empire. Even Gothic Spain was now Catholic, and the Church of Britain, which had become England, was led by Theodoros of Tarsos, an eastern prelate with close ties to Rome.

Makarios of Antioch's passionate defense of the One Will at the Council reveals that actual Monotheletes now did exist, especially in Syria (and they would survive for many centuries, sometimes under the name "Maronites").[54] Like all Christian groups, they regarded themselves as the legitimate heirs of a continuous orthodox and Chalcedonian tradition, and everyone else as a deviation from it. Indeed, they found ample support in patristic tradition for their view of Christ's Will, which their Dithelete opponents struggled to explain away (and vice versa). This was because no one had previously thought that this was a pressing problem. In reality, both groups were *created* by the controversy of the seventh century; the latter was not a response to their prior existence. It was by picking fights that splinter groups were created in the Church, not the other way around.

The Sixth Ecumenical Council effectively closed the cycle of theological controversies that had preoccupied the Roman empire and Church since the early fourth century. "Substances" had led to "Natures" and then to "Activities" and "Wills." The first controversy was resolved by the death of Valens and the policies of Theodosius; the second was not resolved but was now of little concern to the Chalcedonian empire that survived the Arab conquests; and the third had never existed in the first place, and so was easier to resolve. The era of the theological controversies was over, at an incalculable cost to the empire and the unity of the Church.

The empire's reduction in size was painfully apparent at the Council. The emperor had asked the patriarch to bring all his bishops to it, but only 42 attended the first eight sessions, the lowest number in the history of Ecumenical Councils. By the end, ten months later, the number had risen to 166, 135 of them from the patriarchate of Constantinople. But almost no bishops attended from Thrace and few from southwestern Asia Minor compared to northern Asia Minor, which has plausibly been attributed to the damage done to the cities there by Arab raids.

The cities either no longer existed or had no bishops.[55] The Roman empire was in shambles. Moreover, the Council was conducted against a backdrop of dynastic strife, which peaked in late 681. Some officers of the army of Oriens agitated on behalf of the emperor's brothers Herakleios and Tiberios, who held a lesser imperial rank. Apparently, their slogan was that there should be three emperors to match the Trinity within God. Theodoros of Koloneia, the *comes* of Opsikion and power behind the thrones of Konstas and Konstantinos, arrested the ringleaders. The emperor impaled twelve of them, mutilated his brothers by cutting off their noses, and also exiled his mother Fausta, the daughter of the rebel general Valentinos, for speaking up on their behalf. We know nothing more about this disturbance, or if it was linked to the Council. Konstantinos had two young sons, Ioustinianos (the later Justinian II) and Herakleios, but it seems that he did not elevate them to imperial rank at this time.[56]

The empire was to suffer one more blow before it could settle into its new rhythms. A group of Bulgar warriors migrated from north of the Black Sea to the Danube delta, from where, under the leadership of Asparouch, they raided Thrace. In 681, Konstantinos campaigned against them north of the Danube, with both a fleet and an army, and managed to put them on the defensive. Allegedly, however, when the emperor left the front due to his gout, this was misinterpreted by his men as a retreat. The Romans fled and the Bulgars pursued them south of the Danube, where the invaders subjugated many Slavic tribes and "captured many forts and villages that belonged to the Roman state." The area settled by the Bulgars lay between Varna (on the Black Sea coast) and Dorostolon (on the Danube), a conclusion based on the distribution of new burial assemblages. The emperor made peace with the Bulgars by paying them an annual tribute, although its size is unspecified. If the field army of Thrace had not already been relocated to western Asia Minor, to what would eventually become the theme of Thrakesion, it was now. The Bulgars had a long way to go before becoming a regional power, but Romanía was now hemmed in by the Bulgars in Thrace and the Arabs in the east.[57]

Despite the retreat before the Bulgars, Konstantinos' regime had staunched the bleeding and secured a defensible position for the empire. His final years were relatively peaceful, while the caliphate was destabilized and cascaded into civil war after the death in 680 of Muʿawiya, one of Rome's greatest enemies. To secure his northern frontier during this struggle, the caliph ʿAbd al-Malik (685–705) agreed to a peace with the Romans, just as his grandfather Muʿawiya had done in the late 650s, paying them 1,000 solidi, one slave, and one horse per day. The revenues of Cyprus would be shared between the two empires, and the Romans would remove their guerilla forces, the Mardaïtes, from the Lebanon. These commitments were undertaken by Justinian II, who ascended the throne when his father Konstantinos IV died in July, 685.[58]

Justinian II was taking over a battered empire. In the mid sixth century, a Biblical geographer had confidently predicted that "the empire of the Romans partakes of the dignity of the kingdom of Lord Christ and so it will last undefeated until the end of time." By the early seventh century, when Andreas, the bishop of Kaisareia in Cappadocia, wrote a commentary on the book of Revelation, that confidence had diminished. When he came to the question of the Babylon whose destruction was prophesied in that text, he was uncertain whether it was Persia or, as many claimed, Rome. He feared it was the latter, but prayed that "we be delivered from the prophesied trials and not see the arrival of the Antichrist or the movement of those nations." But by the end of the seventh century, the author of an apocalyptic text had seen the truth: "the sons of Ismael, son of Hagar, will rise up against the empire of the Romans . . . seeing as the End has come and there is no more time left."[59] But he was wrong. Romanía still had a long life ahead of it.

PART SIX
RESILIENCE AND RECOVERY

18
Life and Taxes among the Ruins

In the late seventh century, a Gallic bishop named Arculf, who may or may not have existed, visited Constantinople on his return from a pilgrimage to Jerusalem. He later recounted his experiences to Adamnán, the Irish abbot of the monastery of Iona, telling him about attractions in Constantinople such as the church that held the True Cross, an image of the Virgin, and tales about the veneration of St. George. Adamnán wrote that Constantinople was "assuredly the metropolis of the Roman empire" with domiciles of "wondrous magnitude, like the houses in Rome."[1]

At this time, Christians who lived in the former provinces of the western empire, from Spain and Italy to Britain, recognized Romanía as the one and only Roman empire. They sometimes called its inhabitants "Greeks," mostly because of their language, but they did not deny that it was *the* Roman empire. They also recognized Constantinople as a Christian city full of holy relics and a trendsetter in the veneration of saints and images. The barbarian kingdoms of Europe looked less to classical antiquity and more to this eastern empire as the gold standard for Roman imperial identity. When Isidore of Seville (d. 636) tried to explain what a "triumph" was, he drew on the Greek vocabulary used then in Constantinople. He declared that "Constantinople is now the seat of the Roman empire and head of the entire East, as Rome is of the West." Rome, in reality, was only a provincial city in the eastern empire's Italian territories, and had no imperial pretensions. In 680, pope Agatho pledged his obedience to emperor Konstantinos IV as the lord of "all Christians" who would "prevail over the foreign nations who resist."[2]

Arculf was understandably impressed by Constantinople's buildings. The City was adorned with a panoply of imperial monuments, including triumphal arches, paved and colonnaded streets, tall columns bearing statues of the emperors, countless classical works of art, and a massive hippodrome and palace complex. It featured the most impressive fortifications in the world, the Theodosian Walls, and the grandest church, Hagia Sophia. There was nothing like it in all of Christendom, except perhaps Rome itself, but Rome had not functioned as an imperial capital in over two centuries. Western visitors would gape and rave about the wonders of Constantinople for the next six centuries. Even so, Arculf could not have failed to noticed that the City was a ghost town. By the late seventh century its population, between 40,000 and 100,000, had declined to a fraction of its peak of about half a million in 541 AD.[3] This meant that four out of every five apartments, homes, and neighborhoods were abandoned or in ruins. It was a city of empty spaces. It was no longer supplied with grain from Egypt but from Thrace, Sicily, and Bithynia, in addition to its own local production. The City's decline was but one aspect of a catastrophic downturn in the fortunes of Romanía that had taken place during the seventh century.

One person whose life overlapped with that catastrophe was Theodoros of Tarsos, archbishop of Canterbury in Britain (602–690). He was an east Roman, born in Cilicia at a time when the empire was still dominant in the Balkans and the Near East. He experienced firsthand the Persian occupation of the east in the 610s and 620s, and eventually traveled to Constantinople. More waves of refugees streamed out of the east to North Africa and Italy when the Arabs subjugated Syria, Palestine, and Egypt in the 630s and early 640s. A learned monk, Theodoros was living in Rome in 667 when he was appointed archbishop of Canterbury, a position that he held until his death in 690. He lived long enough to see the Romans regain their footing in the 670s, after the momentum of Arab expansion stalled. When Pope Agatho wrote to the emperor in 680, he said that there was only one man who understood the complexities of the theological issue of Christ's Wills, namely Theodoros, "the archbishop of the great island of Britain and a philosopher."[4] Age and infirmity prevented Theodoros from traveling to Constantinople for the Sixth Ecumenical Council of 680. Had he done so, he would have returned to a changed land.

Romanía had lost the Balkans to the Avars and Slavs and the east to the Arabs. As a result, state revenue was at least three quarters smaller than before, about one million *nomismata* (solidi), down from 4–6 million in the mid-sixth century.[5] This shock was immediately followed by a barrage of Arab raids into Asia Minor and naval raids across the eastern and central Mediterranean. It was only during the 670s that the Romans managed to organize their defenses and defeat the Arabs on land and at sea. But the damage had been done. Some feared "that the empire would fall."[6]

Had Theodoros returned to Romanía in 680, his Anglo-Saxon companions, who could build only with wood and thatch and believed that the Roman ruins of their native land had been built by Giants, would have been amazed by almost any city in Asia Minor, given their monumental amenities. But Theodoros would have noticed the changes, as do modern archaeologists. To be sure, not all cities declined in the same way or to the same extent, and the modern debate is carried out on a site-by-site basis. Yet the trends are clear. The central Balkan provinces exhibit an archaeological profile of almost complete abandonment and demographic collapse. The empire clung on to the coastal edges, where settlements and stray coins are found.[7]

In most cities in Asia Minor, the inhabited area contracted dramatically to the fortified citadel at their center. Monumental construction ceased altogether, as had upkeep on existing structures apart from defensive walls. Some cities, such as Nikaia and Ankyra, dismantled their theaters in order to repair their walls.[8] Other towns were abandoned, or relocated to more defensible positions, while the rest shrank in size. There was less money available to rebuild after natural disasters such as earthquakes. It is telling that, after ca. 700, Roman towns were often called *kastra*, i.e., "forts," rather than *poleis*, "cities." There were times when residents, or only the women and children, had to evacuate and flee into the mountains when raiders approached.[9] Roman generals were advised to avoid open combat with the enemy and resort instead to guerilla warfare, stalking and ambushing the Arabs as they returned home.[10] The extent of dislocation was staggering. Many priests fled from their cities "on the pretext of a barbarian invasion." Whoever could fled to the capital, which the authorities discouraged. Yet when bishops were summoned to the Council of 680–681, many cities in Asia Minor had none to send, or lacked the resources to send them.[11] The question was only how much, not whether, each city and district had declined, and the destruction was possibly worse in Greece, Macedonia, and Italy than in Asia Minor. The author of a religious-apocalyptic drama, surveying the wreckage of the seventh century, inferred that it must have been caused by levels of sin "the likes of which no generation of the earth had seen before."[12]

The institutions of local governance also declined, except for the Church and the army, which were managed from the capital. The city councils, which had performed the routine labor of local administration, had largely disappeared, as had the senatorial elites and big landowners who governed civic affairs between the mid-fifth and early seventh centuries. In the later ninth century, Leon VI formally abolished these bodies long after they had ceased to function in practice: "political affairs have a different shape in our day, as everything depends exclusively on the forethought and governance of the emperor."[13]

The economy had contracted. Evidence from the botanical analysis of core samples suggests a decline in agricultural production to levels unseen since the second millennium BC and an expansion of wild forests. Around lake Nar in south-central Asia Minor, agriculture collapsed and did not resume again until the tenth century.[14] Olive tree cultivation, geared to market production, also declined as peasants turned to more pressing needs, and the trees went feral. Pastoralism likely expanded in relation to agriculture.[15]

Long-distance trade across the Mediterranean diminished to its lowest levels in history, and networks of exchange became more local. Historians reconstruct these fluctuations by tracking the types and origin of the pottery containers, such as amphorae, in which goods were transported. Networks that had flourished in the fourth–sixth centuries, especially that represented by African Red Slip ware, began to decline in the later sixth century and had mostly disappeared by the end of the seventh. In the fifth and sixth centuries, eastern merchants were a familiar presence throughout the western Mediterranean, even as far as Britain, where they traded wine in exchange for (possibly) tin. The Church of Alexandria was invested in this long-distance trade in the first decades of the seventh century, as were shipowners in Constantinople. But such ventures lapsed during that century.[16] Denser networks of exchange survived locally, within provinces if they were inland, or around the Aegean coastlands and islands if by sea. Another network continued to link Cyprus (which was now "neutral" territory), southern Asia Minor, Syria, and Egypt.[17] Only the state could now ensure bulk transport across the longer distances, for example if it was hauling grain from Sicily to feed Constantinople.[18]

Part of this decline may be illusory, due instead to a switch to perishable containers such as wooden barrels or leather skins that were better for overland transport, but leave no traces. Candles, which also leave no trace, replaced clay lamps in this period. Housing likely switched from stone-and-tile to wood-and-thatch, a decline in living standards to be sure, but because those materials do not survive, they leave a wrong impression of desolation and abandonment. However, the creation of a militarized border hindered movement and the transportation of goods between Asia Minor and Syria.[19] This affected the history of the Church too, as something like an Iron Curtain dropped between the empire and the areas under Muslim rule. Debates in Constantinople did not spill over into the east, as they once had, and few eastern clergy participated in the controversy over Wills after 640.

The Roman economy became less monetized. The state continued to mint both gold and bronze coins, though the former were slightly debased and the latter became lighter. However, as the state's revenues had been slashed, it pumped out fewer coins than before. In fact, the 365,000 solidi pledged by 'Abd al-Malik in the treaty of 685 may have been its single largest source of income. As a result, the archaeology of some regions, especially in Asia Minor, gives the impression of a largely demonetized economy. In some places this happened to a lesser extent, including Constantinople (naturally), eastern Sicily, Calabria, Athens and Corinth, Mesembria (a naval base on the Black Sea), and Amorion. These places hosted the imperial court or had a military presence, which explains why money was spent there by the government. Amorion, for example, became the new base of the army of Oriens (Anatolikon, in Greek), and even its bathhouse continued to operate, albeit filled with buckets from a well, not via pipes.[20] In 668, the coinage abruptly drops off in most of the empire. Konstantinos IV then reformed the bronze follis, by issuing it at four times its prior weight and value. Presumably this was an effort to create a prestige bronze coin to take the place of payments in gold, of which there was a shortage, but this reform did not long outlast his reign.[21]

As for how the state paid its soldiers when they were pulled back into Asia Minor, the likeliest explanation is that provincial taxes were collected in kind and delivered to the soldiers stationed in each province, just as had been done in the later third and fourth centuries, only the distances involved were now smaller. Our lack of sources makes this hard to prove, but it remains the likeliest scenario.

The cities' classical profile receded, and they stressed instead their devotion to patron saints. The most famous were the military martyrs, for example Sts. Demetrios (see Plate 4b) at Thessalonike and Theodoros the Recruit at Euchaïta, and they were thanked for protecting their cities from barbarian attacks. Constantinople was protected by the Virgin, who was now seen as a militarized figure, a "general" who destroyed Romanía's enemies from above, starting with the Avaro-Slavic siege of the City in 626. St. with specialized functions emerged too. Saint Artemios had a shrine in the City, in a church of John the Baptist, specializing in hernias and testicular disorders. His miracles, compiled in the 660s, catalogue these afflictions with a sense of humor. The saint stepped in to help where secular medicine failed, often by painfully crushing or lancing the patient's organs in a vision or dream.[22]

Saints were good for local economies. Festivals with lucrative markets coalesced around the celebration of their feast day. Ephesos boasted of the church and pilgrimage site of St. John the Theologian. In the late eighth century, the annual festival of the saint was allegedly generating 100 lbs of gold in tax for the treasury, which sounds excessively high, if indeed the tax represented 10% of total revenue. Athens had converted the Parthenon into a church of the Virgin, who took on many of the attributes of the city's former goddess. The Parthenon, with its pediment sculptures intact, became a major attraction for pilgrims from as far as Italy and the Caucasus. These were now the main coordinates of civic life and identity. Cities that were formerly named after Zeus, Apollo, and Aphrodite were rebaptized as the City of Christ, City of the Theotokos, and City of the Cross—but not Athens, which always bore its classical past with pride.[23]

Asia Minor acquired a new strategic reorientation as it became the core of the remaining Roman state. Before the seventh century, it did not need defending and it supplied food, horses, and equipment to armies stationed elsewhere. Now the armies were distributed across its vast territory, which had to be reconfigured for front-line defense. Thus important sites emerged that did not descend from ancient cities. A classical historian might not recognize names such as Malagina, Dazimon, Charsianon, Podandos, and Loulon. These were fortresses, mustering grounds, administrative centers, depots, warehouses, refuges, and new control nodes for resources and mountain passes in a transformed strategic environment. In Cappadocia, there was an ancient tradition of carving villages and towns out of the soft rock of that region; these are sometimes called "troglodytic." They could be subterranean, carved into the face of a cliff, or a hollowed-out rock cone. In the centuries to come, they were expanded to sixteen towns that could accommodate at least a thousand people each. Malakope (modern Derinkuyu) could hold 20,000, supplied by an underground river that also carried away the waste. These towns and villages featured rock-cut churches, cisterns, heavy millstone doors to seal off compartments, and other amenities such as rock-cut toilets from the early imperial period. Troglodytic habitation afforded concealment from the enemy, protection from the elements, and a stable temperature year-round (see Figure 27). They are rarely mentioned in the sources, however, so we have no descriptions of life within them. We have one reference in a tenth-century historian to the Cappadocians as a people "who formerly used to be called Troglodytes because they lived in holes, hollows, and labyrinths, as if in nests, dens, or lairs."[24]

Rome, Constantinople, and Thessalonike declined relative to their earlier apogees, but they remained major population centers. Some of the larger cities in Asia Minor seem to have made it through the transition with minimal damage, apart from demographic decline, including Nikaia, Nikomedeia, Smyrna, and Trebizond. Sicily was a significant and productive province that had largely been spared the horrors of war. Its economy remained monetized above the norm elsewhere.[25] Ravenna, headquarters of the Italian exarchate, continued to import Aegean wine.[26] The empire's silk industry also survived, producing luxury textiles for both sale and diplomacy. Catalogues of Byzantine silks that survive

Figure 27 Cappadocian carved-out cities (here Guzelyurt)
Shutterstock/matias planas

in Europe, often as prestige fabrics used to bury kings, bishops, and saints, include dozens of items that are tentatively dated between the seventh and ninth centuries. However, we do not know the industry's volume, and Romanía was likely still importing silk too.[27] Thus, despite major losses, the foundations for a revival were there.

Literary production collapsed, especially genres that required engagement with the ancient tradition (such as classical historiography, rhetoric, philosophy, and theology), as did most narrative writing, including hagiography. Thus, we have few sources for this period. Essentially, the whole elite stratum of cultural production was decapitated, exposing substrata of vernacular culture that had been there previously but now came to the fore. Its concerns are reflected in the works of the prolific author Anastasios, a monk who had moved from his native Cyprus to Sinai. Among his works, which became popular later on, was a set of answers to questions that Christians were frequently asking around 700 AD. These included "What is a true Christian?" (1) "Why would Christ love us more than he does the angels?" (5) "Can one be saved on account of one good deed?" (10: Yes.) "Does day come before night, or the reverse?" (15) "What is the soul?" (19) "Why do Christians suffer more from gout, leprosy, and epilepsy than the infidel nations?" (26) "May I go to church after sex with my wife, or a wet dream, provided I wash first?" (38: Yes).

One of the burning questions of the day was why the "faithless Saracens" had prevailed over the Christians, which violated the latter's core belief that their faith was destined to expand and reign supreme. The easiest and most common answer was that God was punishing them for their sins. As Christians were divided into rival groups, each blamed its rivals for promoting beliefs that angered God. Thus, supporters of the Council of Chalcedon blamed its opponents, and vice versa; and anti-Monotheletes, including Anastasios, blamed Monotheletes. But this facile explanation could not withstand scrutiny. Anastasios noted that yes, we have been given over to "tyrants" because of our sins. But even if the Saracens were removed, we would quickly turn against each other. More troublingly, did the conventional answer mean that the Arabs' actions were approved by God and therefore perhaps should not be criticized? Not at all, he replied. Their crimes—forcing virgin nuns to marry, etc.—are hateful to God, just like those of the ancient Assyrians against the Jews. God gave them "leeway" to punish his Chosen People, but then destroyed them. There was still hope that the Arabs would face God's wrath.[28]

Roman Orthodox authors wrote many polemics during the seventh century, mostly against heretics, pagans, and Jews, and one even swiped at the Buddha and Mani for good measure. The intensified attacks against Judaism can be explained by the prominent role that many Jews played in facilitating the Persian invasion of the 610s, though it has been proposed that Jews were surrogate targets for similar practices within Islam (avoidance of pork, circumcision, aniconism). A polemical literature specifically devoted to Islam had not yet emerged.[29]

The Council in Troullo

This ideologically unsettled world called for a new path forward. The emperor Justinian II responded to this challenge, with both words and actions. In 692, he convened his own Ecumenical Council in the domed hall of the palace, whence it acquired its name "in Troullo" (by the twelfth century it was also being called the "Quinisext" Council, i.e., a supplement to the Fifth and Sixth Councils of 553 and 680–681). It was attended by 220 bishops, including some from Syria, Palestine, and Egypt, as the 685 truce with the Arabs enabled them to attend. This Council was unique in several ways. Unlike its predecessors, it was not convened to resolve a doctrinal controversy. It was not attended by rival theological factions and did not put heretics on trial. Such disputes had already been resolved to the satisfaction of the imperial authorities. What Troullo did was approve a set of 102 canons, or rules for the regulation of Christian life, including clergy, monks, and laity. Many were recycled from the Church's existing conciliar tradition. They regulate marriage and behavior in church, and attempt to reform Christian life mainly through prohibitions, with a recurring anxiety over Judaism and paganism. Priests are not to operate taverns on the side nor have contact with Jews, not even to receive medical care. No one is to play dice, attend mime shows, pretend to be demonically possessed, marry a heretic, celebrate the ancient pagan festivals, set an image of the cross into the floor, or own "images that incite lust." But many pagan customs rejected by the Council were folk traditions embedded in the rhythms of Christian life; some survive to this day.[30]

Its canons were a hodgepodge, but Troullo enabled Justinian II to send a political message that he was reforming the lives of his subjects in order to promote their spiritual salvation. Troullo was like other Councils in that it was conceived, convened, and directed by the court. In the final text, the canons are preceded by a formal address by the Council to the emperor, praising him as the "eye of the world" to whom God has entrusted the management of the Church. Like a new Phinehas—a Biblical figure who slaughtered fellow Jews for marrying foreigners and practicing idolatry—the emperor was uprooting paganism and Judaism in order to protect his "flock," God's "Chosen People," from their own propensity to sin. The emperor signed the acts first, as "Emperor of the Romans, Faithful in the God Jesus Christ."[31]

Justinian I had legislated on some of the issues touched on by the Troullan canons, but his instrument had been the civil law. Justinian II was now taking on the guise of an Old Testament reformer, heralding a Scriptural turn in the imperial image that marked the eighth century. "The people are to seek their salvation in fear of punishment, and reform their lives for the better."[32] Justinian II's instrument was canon law and its penalties were spiritual (excommunication or penance), not bodily or financial. Troullo consolidated the Church's canonical tradition and set a new pietistic tone for the beleaguered empire by stressing "popular morality and correct practice."[33] Justinian aspired to redefine Roman society on a Christian basis and draw stark lines between his empire and the Islamic caliphate.

Justinian II and ʿAbd al-Malik

Not by coincidence, the Umayyad caliph ʿAbd al-Malik (685–705) was also sharpening the definition of Arab Muslim identity over and against the religions of the majority of his subjects. It was during his reign that the official paperwork of the caliphate began its gradual switch from Greek to Arabic, which incentivized scribes and administrators to learn the new language. The Prophet Muhammad's name began to be showcased prominently on public documents. In 692, ʿAbd al-Malik completed the Dome of the Rock in Jerusalem. Its triumphal inscription used Quranic language to reject the Trinity and downgrade Jesus from the Son to only a Messenger of God (the Dome was not a mosque and its original function remains a mystery). ʿAbd al-Malik also stopped issuing Roman and Persian-style coins and replaced them with a different, unified currency that eschewed images and was inscribed with Arabic legends. It was also roughly during his reign that the Prophet's religion came to be known definitively as Islam and his followers as Muslims.[34] These developments occurred in part because of the Muslim civil war in which ʿAbd al-Malik prevailed in 692. But they were also due to rivalry with the Christian empire.

ʿAbd al-Malik was in a weak position when he came to power in 685, and made peace with Constantinople to secure his northern border, agreeing to pay 365,000 coins per year. Various reasons were alleged for why the treaty failed in the early 690s, with each side blaming the other, but it was likely broken by ʿAbd al-Malik, as it coincided with his victory in civil war. Had Justinian intended to strike, he would have done so while the caliph was engaged in the south. The Arabs invaded Asia Minor in 692/3 and defeated the Romans at Sebastopolis, north of Kaisareia. The empire's Slavic auxiliaries allegedly defected to the enemy during the battle. After this, the Arabs resumed raiding again and the payments ceased.[35]

Coins also became a medium of ideological confrontation. In 690, Justinian introduced a striking innovation, placing Christ on the front of his coins, which no past emperor had done, and he moved his own imperial image, labeled as "the servant of Christ," to the reverse (see Figure 28). The Council of Troullo had just decreed that Christ was not to be shown symbolically as a lamb but only in human form. The emperor was literally declaring that Christ and he were two sides of the same coin. Meanwhile, before his thorough overhaul of Islamic coinage ʿAbd al-Malik began to issue Roman-style coins that lacked the transverse bar on the cross, which was a desecration of their traditional Christian

Figure 28 Coin of Justinian II showing Jesus Christ; the latter is identified as King of Kings and the former as the Slave of Christ.

symbolism. In 693/4, after the battle of Sebastopolis, he issued a gold coin with the image of a man holding a sword and a Muslim legend in Arabic. The figure is usually understood to be the caliph, but it may instead have represented the Prophet. This run lasted for three years, to be replaced thereafter with purely aniconic coins bearing Arabic legends.[36]

The lines of distinction were being drawn as warfare was erupting again between the two states. It is customary to stress how unequal this struggle was, considering the extensive size and resources of the caliphate compared to those of the "rump" Roman state. Even a Roman military strategist admitted that his empire was facing enemies who were "vastly superior to us in the size of their armies."[37] Arabic culture was also to attain superiority in science and philosophy too, though no Roman seems to have admitted this before the eleventh century. ʿAbd al-Malik's move to a purely aniconic currency and non-Roman coinage was less a gesture of triumph over the Romans than a sign of their fading relevance: he was no longer playing their game. The Islamic world was large enough to set its own agenda independently of the Roman past. The center of this world's gravity shifted away from Constantinople to Damascus and later to Baghdad.

Yet Romanía not only survived the Arabs' determined assaults: it gradually even regained ground at their expense. Barely two centuries after its creation, the caliphate was spiraling into disarray while Romanía was becoming stronger. By the eleventh century, the Romans were dominant in the Balkans, the Caucasus, and northern Mesopotamia and Syria. The Roman empire outlived the caliphate, which had ostensibly supplanted it.

One reason for this was that identity and power were not aligned in the caliphate as they were in Romanía. The latter was, and understood itself to be, "the polity of the Romans." By 700, nearly all of its citizens spoke Greek, belonged to the same (Chalcedonian) Church, and were ethnic Romans. They had a single state, whose avowed purpose was to protect them and promote their welfare, both material and spiritual. The government preferred to use persuasion and consensus building with its subjects rather than force; it valued buy-in, not just compliance. The Romans had a single, unified military command that pooled all the provinces' resources in order to protect the whole Roman territory. Their army was supported by a unified system of administration and law. There were no agrarian revolts and no efforts to form splinter states at this time. Rebellions in the provinces aimed to secure the capital, Constantinople, and renew the government, i.e., they were coups d'état. Romanía was less an empire and more a national state.

By contrast, the biggest challenge facing the caliphate, one that proved fatal to it, is that it never developed a consensual governing ideology. A small number of Arab warriors, temporarily unified by a new religious message, took advantage of the ruin left by the war between Rome and Persia to carve out an empire for themselves. The populations they conquered were forced to pay taxes in order to support this army of conquest. But what then? To whom did this power belong and what was its purpose? At first, the conquerors were uninterested in converting others; in fact, they had a disincentive to do so, because that would diminish their tribute. But what did the rulers owe to the ruled, if anything, other than not to kill them? The conquered Christians, Jews, and Zoroastrians did not identify with the project of the caliphate, which imposed foreign rule on them along with higher taxes. For the first time in centuries, there were agrarian revolts again in Egypt.[38]

Moreover, what happened when the conquered began to convert to Islam and learn Arabic? Did they owe taxes? Did they too become Arabs and were they entitled to a share in the proceeds of empire? These pressing questions were soon complicated by another development: the conquerors settled down in cities and hired non-Arab mercenaries, especially Turks, to do their fighting for them. How were the lines of identity and power to be drawn then? Whose benefit was the whole edifice supposed to serve? More importantly, how were rulers to be chosen? No consensus emerged regarding these critical issues, and so loyalties formed around competing dynasties, families, and tribes. These factions regarded each other with suspicion from the start and periodically fought civil wars. The political unity of the Muslims, enjoined in the Quran, was a pious fiction. Infighting began almost immediately and eventually the caliphate disintegrated as regional dynasties broke away from the center. The various factions held widely divergent beliefs about identity and purpose, about who should be ruling whom, why, and how.[39] The Romans had long since resolved such questions.

The new administration

Justinian II was sixteen when he ascended the throne in 685 and twenty-three when he convened Troullo, where the bishops proclaimed him their shepherd and Christ's vice-gerent. He was an energetic emperor, sending armies to secure Roman interests in the Caucasus and Balkans, though he did suffer setbacks, such as at Sebastopolis. Moreover, he had inherited prestige. His dynasty was the first in Roman history to reach the fifth generation in father-to-son succession. Its founder Herakleios (610–641), who had defeated the Persian empire, was becoming a legend. Justinian's father Konstantinos IV had stemmed the Arab tide and convened the Sixth Council against Monotheletism. Before he ascended the throne, locks of Justinian's hair were sent to the armies and the pope.[40] As a child, he had been depicted next to his father in a grand mosaic in the church of Sant'Apollinare of Classe in Ravenna (see Plate 4a). Yet none of this protected him from his personal unpopularity, caused by his cruelty and paranoia. His fall followed a familiar script.

In 695, Justinian appointed Leontios to be general (*strategos*) of Greece. Leontios had formerly commanded the army of the East (Anatolikon) and had led a major incursion into Armenia and Georgia in 685/6. But he had spent the past three years in prison, possibly for losing the battle of Sebastopolis. Fearing that his new appointment was a ruse to kill him, he and his accomplices incited a revolution. Retracing the steps of many popular uprisings of the past, they went to the *praitorion*—the headquarters of the City prefecture—where they arrested the prefect and freed the prisoners, a gesture that signaled the regime's illegality. They sent heralds to summon the populace to Hagia Sophia, where they called on it to depose the emperor. This was a decisive moment: if the people supported the emperor, they would not turn out and the rebellion would fizzle. But this time they came chanting "Dig up Justinian's bones!," a traditional curse for disavowing an emperor, and occupied the hippodrome. Justinian was hauled out, his nose and the tip of his tongue were cut off, and he was exiled to Cherson, in the Crimea. His financial officials, the *logothetes* of the *genikon* Theodotos, a former monk, and Stephanos the Persian, a eunuch, were hated and were burned alive. "Leontios was then acclaimed emperor by the crowd."[41] But who were these officials and what did they do?

The new state administration had emerged directly from its predecessor. A *strategos* was just the Greek translation of *magister militum*. As the government stopped using Latin, it switched over to Greek equivalents, but the military structure remained recognizable, with the difference that the main armies had been pulled back into Asia Minor. They still had only one function: "to fight the enemy on behalf of the republic."[42]

On the civilian side, the prefecture of the City, an office descended from the urban prefect of ancient Rome, remained in place until the thirteenth century.

But this was not true of the praetorian prefectures and other palatine bureaux such as the *res privata*, *sacrae largitiones*, and, in part, the portfolio of the *magister officiorum*. Starting in the later sixth century, their fiscal departments were hived off into separate bureaux called *logothesia* or *sekreta* (from Latin *secretarium*), each under the direction of a *logothetes* ("accountant"). The logothetes had been lower-ranking fiscal controllers, possibly those who did the actual work under the prefects' supervision, but now they rose to the top. By 700, three main *logothesia* had emerged: the *genikon* ("General Bureau"); *eidikon* ("Special Bureau"); and *stratiotikon* ("Military Bureau"). The hierarchy had essentially been decapitated, leaving the lower layers to carry on with the work. Unfortunately, this period produced few written sources, so these changes have to be reconstructed from the officials' seals, with which they certified documents. These are supplemented by stray references in the sources and inferences drawn from ninth- and tenth-century reports about their activities.

Among the first known logothetes of the *genikon* was the former monk Theodotos, who was burned by the people of Constantinople in 695. His office was responsible for collecting the basic land tax. This entailed maintaining and updating the census of taxable properties. A ninth-century military theorist wrote that "those who assess the taxes must be just in the way that they go about it; they should have some knowledge of surveying, agricultural methods, and accounting. For the amounts assessed for tax purposes are based upon the area of land, and upon its quality as well. . . . They must be able to estimate the effects of climate and topography." To carry out this work, their agents consulted manuals of land measurement (the literal origin of the word "geometry").[43]

As the distinction between cities and their hinterlands had been eroded, when it came to taxation the central government dealt directly with the villages and agricultural districts, which became the main units of account and collection. There were two main taxes, the land tax and the poll tax (i.e., per head), though it is unclear how the latter was assessed. Each fiscal district was collectively responsible for its dues, so neighbors had to pay the taxes for abandoned lands (unless, of course, an adjustment was made to the census).[44] This fostered both solidarity and mutual suspicion among the villagers, which are typical for village life anyway. Most districts were subject to supplemental requisitions depending on their assets or designation. These ranged from specialized goods and labor (e.g., to maintain the roads) to animals and recruits for the army, and from levies to meet an emergency to compulsory purchases at prices set by the state. Presumably, liability to one type of corvée or requisition conferred an exemption from the rest, so that the burden was distributed evenly, though the system could be abused, which led to protests and sooner or later someone was thrown onto a bonfire in the forum.

The state's focus had shifted from the great landowners and local notables, who had mediated in previous centuries between the imperial government and the world of small farmers, directly to the farmers themselves. There is little evidence for large estates in the later seventh and eighth centuries, apart from those of the Church. The *Farmer's Law* is a collection of regulations assembled in this period that deals almost entirely with the concerns and legal issues that arose among small producers. Most of its provisions stem from later Roman law and it fleshes out some of the gaps in its regulation of agricultural life: "if a man is cutting a branch and accidentally drops his axe from above and kills another man's beast," and so on.[45] This was a popular text, as indicated by its many copies. After all, it was not just the tax base that was now rooted in the world of small producers: the soldiery too was settled among, recruited from, and supported by agricultural families. This made the state especially sensitive to the concerns of the countryside and keen to protect and regulate small landowners.

As the circulation of coins in Asia Minor had collapsed, most tax collection between ca. 660 and ca. 750 took place in kind. The emperors gradually increased the money supply so that by the 760s Konstantinos V could demand that more taxes be paid in gold. The tradition is hostile to him for religious reasons and distorts his every action. It was thus said that, in order to obtain the scarce coin with which to pay, farmers were forced to sell their produce for prices so low that they had to liquidate their lands and hang themselves. This is standard exaggeration in Roman polemic. In the early ninth century, the supply of coin increased sharply and economic transactions, both private and with the state, steadily became more monetized. Either way, this was still the most efficient tax system in the medieval world.[46]

"The most splendid building in which the *genikon* was housed," near the Great Palace, was demolished by an emperor in the later twelfth century.[47] In the five centuries of its existence, its work was complemented by the other *logothesia*. The bureau of the *eidikon* managed the state's stockpile of bulk goods, such as silk, clothing, furniture, tackle, and other equipment, along with most state workshops, such as arms factories. It even had Arabic clothes for use by Roman spies.[48] The logothete of the *stratiotikon* was in charge of recruitment, military supplies, and pay. A fourth important *logothesion* is attested by the mid-eighth century: the *dromos*, i.e., the *cursus* or public post. Its logothete was in charge of internal transport and communications, and so of animal stocks and supplies. Eventually he took over key aspects of imperial diplomacy and was a major political figure, not just a bureaucrat. The logothete of the *dromos* was often the emperor's deputy and prime minister.

By 700 two overlapping grids of administration lay upon Asia Minor. The first was that of the ancient provinces (such as Bithynia and Paphlagonia), which formed the basis of the fiscal, civilian, judicial, and ecclesiastical administration. The provinces still received individual governors (called *praitores*, from the Latin *praetor*). The Church retained this provincial organization, according to the rule reaffirmed at Troullo that "the order of ecclesiastical affairs will follow the form of the civilian political order" (canon 38). The second grid was that of the armies that were withdrawn into Asia Minor: the Anatolikon, Armeniakon, Thrakesion, and Opsikion, plus the navies in the south and west. In the eighth century, the districts in which these armies were settled were called "military commands" (*strategides*).[49] Now, these two administrative grids had to coordinate with each other and with the *logothesia* in Constantinople so that the soldiers could be equipped, fed, and, ideally, paid. The ninth-century military theorist quoted previously also wrote that "the financial system was set up to take care of matters of public importance, such as the building of ships and of walls. But it is principally concerned with paying the soldiers. Each year most of the public revenues are spent for this purpose."[50]

The officials responsible for this coordination between 650 and 800 are known mostly from their seals, and reconstructing their history and bailiwicks requires patience, ingenuity, and guesswork. There is no reason to rehearse here all the problems.[51] The most important concerns the *kommerkiarioi*. They descended from the *commerciarii*, who had collected taxes on trade at the border. They were now associated with *apothekai* (state "warehouses") in the provinces, including inland provinces far from the border. It was likely their new task to provision the armies and capital, not just tax trade, which had dramatically declined anyway.[52] Moreover, during the eighth century the *kommerkiarioi* and other officials are associated on their seals less with the old civic provinces and increasingly with the regional military commands. The latter (Anatolikon, Armeniakon, etc.) eventually became the basic units of provincial administration and acquired geographical identities. At the start of the ninth century, they became the "themes" (*themata*), but before then the term is, strictly speaking, anachronistic.

We have no idea how these "warehouses" worked. And there is one more problem. Eighth-century sources suggest that the state expected soldiers to acquire part of their own equipment for themselves, and in the tenth century the emperors began to issue laws protecting the (privately owned) lands that were earmarked for the maintenance of their soldiers, claiming that this protection had previously been a matter of custom and not law.[53] But how did soldiers acquire lands in the first place, when they were relocated to Asia Minor in the seventh century? Also, beyond the issue of ownership, where were they housed, given that most of them would not have previously owned land in Asia Minor? There are two schools of thought, neither of which is supported by much evidence (because there isn't any either way). One theory is that the state resettled the soldiery on imperial estates, an option that was used in the past with barbarian groups that it intended to recruit into the armies, and there probably were enough imperial estates in Asia Minor to make this feasible. Another theory is that it billeted those soldiers on the civilian population, which was also standard practice (albeit not on a permanent basis), and that the soldiers then somehow acquired their own lands. The soldiers in Italy did that at roughly the same time. The problem remains open.[54]

Leon VI instructed his armies to protect farmers above all others because "these two professions are necessary for national survival: farming feeds soldiers, while soldiering guards farmers."[55] These two groups were now more closely linked than ever. Soldiers were settled among village communities and eventually owned lands themselves, though these were liable to the basic tax only, not supplemental levies. Moreover, it appears that soldiers' families (including parents, widows, etc.) were required to either provide and support that soldier or, if they could not, to pay the state a supplemental tax so that it could support a soldier elsewhere. Thus, supporting the army was woven into the tax system. It is not clear whether this burden fell on families or on their properties, as we know of no cases where such a family sold its land (would the duty pass to the new owners?). In addition, the state supported soldiers with supplies in kind and coin payments called *rogai*. In later times those payments, of five *nomismata* (gold *solidi*) per soldier, were made to each of the four main armies (Anatolikon, Armeniakon, Thrakesion, and Opsikion) on a four-year rotation.[56]

Elites and ideologies

If each of those armies had 10,000 soldiers, and their average household comprised six people—both of which are conservative estimates—then the social status, personal finances, and identity of at least a quarter of a million people distributed across Asia Minor were linked directly to the state, its institutions, and its ideology. Moreover, those soldiers were fighting not just because of a distant paymaster but in defense of their lands, communities, faith, and national identity as Romans. The emperors themselves encouraged this. Heralds were to remind the soldiers before battle that "the struggle is on behalf of God and the entire nation . . . on behalf of brothers who share the same the faith, and women, children, and the fatherland." The "fatherland" (*patris*) was not understood narrowly as one's village or district, but Romanía as a whole. Romanía was often imagined as a vast kinship structure, whose father was the emperor.[57]

The Church was enmeshed in the same ideology. The liturgies in use at the time contained prayers for the emperor and the army.[58] A military service of the tenth century prayed to the Lord to "save your people . . . grant victories to the emperors against the barbarians, and guard your polity through the cross."[59] Moreover, the Church was thoroughly structured by state institutions, ranging from its tax status and the rights and duties of priests, which were regulated by both civil and canon law, to its organization, which was explicitly modeled on the state's provincial administration. It is often seen as a national or state Church.

Provincial society in this period was oriented around self-defense, meaning the army and its needs, and local piety. The army and the Church were the main avenues for social advancement. As the law did not grant special rights based on family or place of origin, there were no castes or feudal families in Roman society. Thus talented men could rise from humble origins in the provinces to positions of great power. At any time, the elite in the capital consisted of both City natives and provincials who had risen through the ranks or emigrated. For instance, Justinian was overthrown in 695 by Leontios, a general from Isauria, whose accomplice was Gregorios, an officer from Cappadocia turned monk. His top fiscal officials were Theodotos, formerly a hermit in Thrace, and Stephanos "the Persian," likely a second-generation immigrant. To be sure, the wealthy and well-connected enjoyed advantages when it came to advancement, but social mobility was not uncommon. A mural in a public bathhouse in the capital reminded everyone that the emperor Justin I (518–527) had risen up from poverty: "God can raise the unfortunate man from the dung pile and place him at the head of the people."[60] Many emperors feared being replaced, so they looked for talented men of humble origin to place in sensitive positions, because such men would be more dependent on the throne and less on their own networks. Constantinople was not reserved for an exclusive elite. It was, as the emperor Herakleios called it, "a common fatherland" for all imperial citizens.[61]

In this political system, then, there was no true aristocracy, meaning families whose right to hold titles or offices was enshrined in custom or law. There were only families who played the political game well enough to stay in the spotlight for a while. With the collapse of the civic elites, that hierarchy was now tightly concentrated around the imperial court, which became the arbiter of power and prestige. Titles and offices were bestowed at the discretion of the court, which preferred to rotate men through the ranks in order to satisfy as many as it could and to prevent any from becoming too powerful. These men wrapped themselves in the rhetoric of aristocracy, being flattered as "well born," "noble in character," and "virtuous," but this could be said about any powerful or wealthy public figure, even someone of middling status who aspired to social respectability, regardless of who his ancestors were. No one looked closely. Crucially, it was also possible to be praised for the exact opposite: "he attained his rank not because of his ancestors or anyone's lobbying, but based on his personal accomplishments."[62] The principle of equality was, moreover, enshrined in the legal system. In the law code that he issued in 741, the *Ekloge* (*Selection of Laws*), Leon III commanded his judges "not to disdain the poor man or to permit the powerful man to commit injustice with impunity"; in sum, "to honor justice and equality."[63] Thus, even the social ethos was only partly aristocratic. Compared to Persia and Armenia, which, like western medieval Europe, had entrenched, family-based aristocracies, Romanía has even been called "anti-nobiliary." In 996, the emperor Basil II estimated that powerful families stayed on the scene for about "seventy or a hundred years." This was an underestimate, but their power did depend on court politics, not aristocratic right.[64]

Romanía was not a aristocracy in another sense too, namely that wealth, status, and power were generated far more by holding state office than through landownership. There were no private castles, armies, or feudal subrealms in the polity of the Romans, and no subject of the emperor was ever able to challenge Constantinople based on his private resources. Rebels always sought to mobilize the state apparatus, either of the court or the army, in their bids to dethrone the emperor, and they could do so only if they were already members of the system that they were trying to leverage. Until the late twelfth century, they aimed to take over the power of the state and wield it as emperors themselves, not to curtail it by securing regional baronial privileges or break away from it altogether. There were good reasons for this. First, no one could compete with the resources of the Roman state. Thus, even local elites aspired to positions in the state and wrapped their ambitions tightly around it, constituting an aristocracy of service. As a result, they were also less inclined to seek their fortunes in trade.[65]

Elites of this period literally invested *in* the state. In addition to offices, which entailed military or civilian functions, the court also operated a hierarchy of honorific titles that did not carry specific duties other than ceremonial attendance but that conferred social prestige, clout, and access. Some were bestowed on members of the imperial family or people whom the court wanted to affiliate with itself, such as *kaisar* (Caesar), *nobelissimos*, and *kouropalates*; others were reserved for a small circle of favorites, such as *magistros* and *patrikios*; and below them, starting from the *protospatharios*, was a descending list of titles whose names derived from functions of the palace such as *mandator* (herald) and *silentiarios* (usher) and the offices of the Republic such as *hypatos* (consul), which had been absorbed by the palace and turned into honorifics. This social hierarchy was centralized, and consolidated, and emanated from the palace, reaching down into the provinces. Offices and titles were usually combined; thus, generals (*strategoi*) were often *patrikioi*, and women shared in their husbands' rank. Many titles came with a salary (*roga*) that was paid by the emperor personally to the highest ranks at a special ceremony. By the tenth century, and likely earlier, it was possible to purchase a title from the court, a non-hereditary privilege granted by permission. Depending on the size of one's initial investment, the annual return could be as high as 9.72%, so it would have taken eleven years to break even. As titles were awarded to mature adults and life expectancy was low, this was a major source of revenue for the court. The aristocracy was literally investing its capital in the state system.[66]

Another reason why private or local interests were not at odds with the state was ideological. Romanía was held together by a robust conception of the public good. The apparatus of government was regarded as public property that did not belong personally to the men who staffed it. This concept of the *res publica* was fundamental to the Roman tradition and had not lost its vitality in later times. Imperial pronouncements often reassured their audiences that "none of this belongs to us personally, we are managing it on trust" (whether from God or the people). In the preface to his *Ekloge*, Leon III referred to his position as "entrusted to him by God" on condition that he spend sleepless nights promoting "the common interest." An appendix contained excerpts from ancient law explaining the distinction between private and public property, the latter including "rivers, harbors, theaters, and the like, which are owned by the public (*demosion*) but used by all in common." This idea was not beyond the average Roman's grasp, as it governed daily life. The *Farmer's Law* contained a provision about workshops built illegally on a village's "common land." One sixth of the spoils won in battle had to be set aside for the public treasury. Soldiers swore oaths to the emperor *and* the polity, combining personal with impersonal forms of loyalty. Finally, the main meaning of *demosion* was "state taxation." This, then, was the opposite of what political theorists call a patrimonial state. Roman magistrates were acutely aware of the public function they were expected to discharge.[67]

These ideas about the public good, the executive and public function of the monarchy, and the distinction between private and public property were still robust around the turn of the millennium, when the dictionary *Souda* encoded them in its definition of kingship (*basileia*): it "is a public good, but the resources of the state (*demosia*) do not, conversely, belong to the *basileia* . . . . The reasoned collection of taxes is a function of stewardship."[68]

Romanness in this period was both a political identity—being a member of the Roman polity, embedded in its complex web of reciprocal expectations—and an ethnic one, identifiable by markers of language, religion, custom, dress, and the like. Yet true to the founding myth of ancient Rome, New Rome was open to foreigners willing to adopt its ways. Individuals were fairly easily assimilated, but so were groups over the course of two or three generations, depending on their size, especially when their leaders were given titles and offices as incentives. By learning Greek, converting to Orthodoxy, and taking on Roman names, outsiders could become indistinguishable members of the polity, though the memory of their ethnic origins followed them for a generation or two. Stephanos, Justinian II's fiscal official who was burned alive in 695, was known as "the Persian," which probably did not help his public image. The patriarch of Constantinople Niketas (776–780) was a eunuch of Slavic origin: not "a Slav" but "from among the Slavs." He had an accent and could not pronounce Greek diphthongs, firing back at anyone who corrected him: "I hate your diphthongs and triphthongs."[69]

The emperors promoted cultural assimilation on the level of policy. Leon VI claimed that his father Basileios I (867–886) had persuaded the Slavs of Greece "to change their ancient customs: he made them into Greek speakers, subjected them to rulers according to the Roman way, honored them with baptism, freed them from slavery to their own rulers, and trained them to take the field against the nations that make war on the Romans."[70] This attributed to a single emperor what had been a generations-long policy. When Theophilos (829–842) admitted a large group of Khurramite (Iranian) warriors into Romanía, he used conversion, dispersal, marriage with provincial Roman women, and registration in the army to assimilate them, for which he earned the label "foreigner-loving."[71]

The army was the most efficient engine of Romanization, and in this period it absorbed many Armenians and Slavs. Many of these immigrants took on Roman names, making them difficult to identify. Conversely, Armenian-Iranian names, especially Bardas and Bardanes, became popular in the Roman army and so ceased to signify ethnic origin. Contrary to a common error, the Armeniakon army was not named after the ethnic composition of its soldiers but because it had originally been formed to defend the Armenian provinces created by Justinian I. When it was pulled back into Asia Minor, it kept its name. Sources distinguish between the Roman soldiers of Armeniakon and their ethnic Armenian allies. Following Roman tradition, military units often bore barbarian names that did not necessarily reflect their current ethnic makeup.[72] A unit of *Gotthograikoi* ("Greek-speaking Goths") was stationed in Bithynia in the seventh and eighth centuries, possibly as part of the elite Opsikion army. But the Goths from whom it originally took its name had likely long since been replaced by native recruits, who kept the old unit-name.[73] Some immigrants did retain their names: one Yazid, for example, known only by his seals, rose through the ranks of the army in the eighth century to become *comes* of the imperial stables, with the title imperial *spatharios*.[74]

Romans of ethnic background could even rise to the throne. The emperor Philippikos Bardanes (711–713) did have some Armenian or Persian ancestry, but it was likely distant. His father Nikephoros had held Roman offices in the 660s, and Philippikos was raised in Romanía and educated in Greek literature. His cultural profile was entirely Roman.[75]

19

An Empire of Outposts (685–717)

The core of Romanía was now Asia Minor, home to an estimated 7–9 million people, down from about 9–10 million in the earlier period.[1] The empire's territory was otherwise a discontinuous series of outposts, bunkers, islands, fortified coastal cities, imperiled territories, loosely affiliated client tribes and polities, basically a series of fragments strung out along the Mediterranean. "Its head was Asia Minor; the rest, in Europe, the tail."[2] In fact, Constantinople itself was a highly fortified bunker in the corner of Thrace that the Romans still controlled.

In 685, the Romans still held two major commands, or exarchates, in the west: North Africa, which included Sardinia and Corsica and was governed from Carthage; and Italy, which consisted of Ravenna, Rome, Apulia, and Calabria. Sicily was an independent command. The first of these to fall was North Africa.

North Africa

Our sources for the Arab conquest are late and include no local perspectives. After making three major incursions overland from Libya (in 647, 665/6, and 666/7), the Arabs took advantage of the Roman civil war that followed the murder of Konstas II in Sicily in 668 and, in the early 670s, founded the forward base of Kairouan in the province of Byzacena, not far from Carthage. This project was spearheaded by ʿUqba, a nephew of the conqueror of Egypt ʿAmr ibn al-ʿAs. In 678/9, Romans and Arabs fought to a standstill outside Carthage itself. This resulted in a peace treaty, though raiding continued.[3] In 682/3, ʿUqba raided deep into Numidia. According to later sources, he reached the Atlantic, though this cannot be verified. Along his return, he was ambushed and killed on the edge of the Sahara by the Moor leader Kasila. Kasila was presumably an ally of the Romans because, when he went on to take Kairouan, it was said that, in 685, "Africa was subdued and brought back into the Roman empire."[4]

The reprieve was short-lived. Town by town the Muslims regained ground. After his victory in the Muslim civil war and defeat of Justinian II at Sebastopolis in 692/3, the caliph ʿAbd al-Malik sent an army under Hassan ibn al-Numan to finish off Roman North Africa. Hassan captured Carthage in 695 and began to suppress the Moors. So far Constantinople had left the province to fend for itself, but now it responded in force. The new emperor Leontios (695–698) dispatched a large fleet that retook Carthage and the surrounding territory in 697. But this fleet withdrew when it heard that ʿAbd al-Malik had dispatched his own navy in response. The Romans withdrew to Crete, where they were embroiled in another civil war. The Arabs retook Carthage and began to raid Sicily, Sardinia, and beyond.[5] Carthage was lost forever, and not just to the Romans. Hassan dismantled the city and used its materials to found Tunis nearby. Carthage was rediscovered much later by antiquarians and archaeologists.

The fall of the exarchate of Africa orphaned a number of the empire's other overseas possessions. It is unclear whether the Romans still held Septem (Ceuta), at the straits of Gibraltar, or Tingis (Tangier). Justinian I had installed a garrison at Septem immediately after his conquest of North Africa in 534, and its last mention as an imperial possession is in 641 as a place of political exile. In 687, the emperor Justinian II mentioned the army of Septem in a letter to the pope, but was that unit still based there or only keeping the name? When the Muslims invaded Spain in 711, Septem was held by a "count Julian" who apparently recognized the Gothic kings of Spain, not the emperor. The Balearic islands (Mallorca, Menorca, Ibiza) also belonged to the empire, and began to be raided by the Arabs in 708. It is unknown when the empire lost them, possibly not until ca. 800 or later. It is likely that the Romans governed there through an *archon*. The court typically bestowed this title upon local leaders who interfaced between an imperial outpost and the central administration; the same title was used also on Malta, Crete, Cyprus, and central Greece.[6]

Sardinia and Corsica

On Sardinia, the empire maintained a regular army under the command of a general (*doux*), along with administrative staff and tax collectors. Many seals have been found documenting their work. Sardinia was not a distant, quasi-autonomous possession: it was a well-integrated province, though the mountainous interior was inhabited by raiders known as "Barbaricini"—Moors, according to Prokopios—who troubled the *doux*. The Greek language had a strong presence and influenced the local vernacular. The island had likely received refugees from the east, and a community of Greek-speaking monks is attested after 658. A Greek inscription was set up in the north of the island (at Porto Torres), in the seventh or eighth century, to celebrate the defeat of Lombard raiders by the *doux* Konstantinos. It succinctly formulates imperial ideology:

> May the Fortune of the emperor and of the Romans prevail! You, Konstantinos [the emperor], sole victor, lord of the entire earth, and destroyer of the Lombard enemies and other barbarians: while a double storm shook the republic and while barbarian ships and weapons were directed against the Romans, you . . . proclaimed to your subjects the Divine Word . . . so that Konstantinos, the most glorious consul and *doux*, could offer to you . . . the defeat of the barbarians.

The most famous resident of Byzantine Sardinia at this time was the body of St. Augustine (d. 430), which had been moved to Cagliari during the period of Vandal rule in North Africa (439–534).[7]

In the late sixth century, Corsica was also subject to the exarch at Carthage, but it dropped out of the empire at a later, unknown point. From its bases on Sardinia, Sicily, and the Balearic islands the empire could project naval power into the western Mediterranean. An imperial attack on Spain is attested in the period 694–702, possibly in 696 in conjunction with the temporary reclamation of Carthage, but it was defeated by a Gothic general.[8] Imperial fleets would remain active in the western Mediterranean down to the tenth century. An emperor at that time even boasted that "the emperor of Constantinople rules the seas as far as the Pillars of Herakles."[9]

Italy

Sicily was solidly integrated into the empire, both administratively and culturally. Many Sicilians were Greek-speaking and shared the same culture with the Romans of Asia Minor. For five years (663–668), Syracuse had functioned as the capital of Konstas II. By 700, the emperors had begun to appoint *strategoi* there. Ecclesiastically, Sicily was subordinate to Rome, though the emperors could intervene in all aspects of Church administration, including rent and tax collection. Malta was governed by a *doux*, subordinate to the Sicilian general, who liaised with local *archons*; it too was used as a place of exile. The empire lost Malta to the Muslims in 870, by which time most of Sicily had fallen.[10]

In Italy, the empire controlled a patchwork of territories, the wreckage from a century of warfare against the Lombards, and its control over those territories was increasingly tenuous. In the south, Calabria and Naples belonged to the Sicilian command, though most of Apulia had been occupied by the Lombard duke of Benevento. In the north of the peninsula, the imperial forces were led by the exarch at Ravenna, who commanded militias stationed there as well as in Venetia, the Pentapolis (along the Adriatic coast), Perugia, and Rome. Ravenna was linked to Rome through a narrow corridor that cut between the Lombard kingdom in the north and the Lombard duchy of Spoleto. Ravenna had functioned as an outpost of the eastern capital for so long that it had acquired some distinctively eastern Roman features; in some respects it was a "Constantinople of the West."[11] Yet the exarch's dispersed forces were increasingly local in origin, outlook, and ambition. Their officer class, many of them descended from soldiers and secretaries from the east, had gradually acquired lands and became the leading social class in their locales. They became the ancestors of the nobility of many Italian towns, including Rome, and even later they continued to bear eastern names. Italy was too big and too enmeshed in broader European politics for the fragmented imperial forces to maintain a discrete identity so far from Constantinople. They were pulled into and absorbed by the peninsula's increasingly separate history. This happened especially at Rome, whose most powerful institution was the Church. The Church of Rome was the largest landowner in Italy, possibly in the entire empire, and was often at odds with Constantinople.[12]

The bishops of Rome had clashed with Constantinople over a number of issues that multiplied and compounded over time. These included Rome's view of itself as the supreme head of the Church and its self-appointed right to adjudicate all disputes with finality; the title of "ecumenical patriarch" claimed by the bishop of Constantinople; and the jurisdiction of the churches in the former prefecture of Illyricum. Rome and Constantinople were frequently in schism. It is commonly believed that this did not emerge until later, whether in the ninth, eleventh, or thirteenth century, depending on how one defines it. But its foundations are visible already in this period. East and west were not in communion for most of the fourth century over the question of divine substance and the controversy over the criminal convictions of Athanasios of Alexandria. They were in schism over the deposition of John Chrysostom at the beginning of the fifth century, then again during the Acacian Schism in the late fifth and early sixth century, over Monotheletism in the seventh, and in the 670s for unknown reasons.

A distinction between "eastern" and "western" bishops was already established in the fourth century, primarily on the ground of language, and it often took on adversarial overtones. Justinian I had pushed back against it by arguing that one should not think about the Church in those terms. But it was already entrenched. Given how frequently the two Churches were in schism, the anguished refrain of "seeking Union" between them was frequently invoked, and it would echo down the centuries to our day.[13] However, there was still a major difference between these early ruptures and what began to happen by the twelfth century, namely that they concerned largely the top leadership of the two Churches and not the majority of their flocks, who probably did not yet believe that they belonged to separate Churches, unless they were unusually scrupulous about following their respective prelate's politics. So these were schisms among the leadership, not yet among the faithful. Separate identities, which we call "Catholic" and "Orthodox," had not yet emerged.

Justinian II invited pope Sergius (687–701) to attend the Council of Troullo in 692, but the pope, a Greek speaker born in Sicily to parents who were refugees or emigrants from Antioch, declined. Moreover, Sergius then refused to ratify its decisions because some of them apparently contravened Roman practice, though a space had been left vacant for him to sign directly after the emperor and above the patriarchs of Constantinople and Alexandria, a space that remains vacant in the modern edition. For these events and what followed, we depend entirely on the *Book of Pontiffs*, a series of brief papal biographies. This work promotes a papal view of history and yet is evasive when it comes to the controversy over Troullo. It says that Justinian sent a court official, Zacharias, allegedly to bring the pope to Constantinople, but Zacharias was opposed by the armies of Rome *and* Ravenna, as well as the people of Rome, and he hid under the pope's bed in terror. If this really happened, it indicates a realignment of the local militias and

Roman people away from Constantinople and toward a new structure of power oriented around the papal court.[14] But the book is untrustworthy.

Between 701 and 705, the exarch of Italy Theophylaktos, a court eunuch, faced another mutiny by the Italian armies when he visited Rome, and the pope, John VI, again had to pacify the mutineers. We do not know why the exarch went to Rome, but the fact that he came from Sicily indicates that perhaps he lacked confidence in the armies of Italy. Indeed, when Justinian II regained the throne (705–711), he sent the general of Sicily, Theodoros, to capture Ravenna, arrest its bishop Felix and other "rebels," and bring them to Constantinople, where Felix was blinded. The *Book of Pontiffs* claims that this was a fitting punishment for some mild disobedience that the bishop of Ravenna had shown to the pope, but such petty quarrels were likely far from the emperor's mind; he was sensing instead that Italy was slipping out of the empire's grasp. But his actions precipitated what he feared. The Ravennates formed a local defense force to protect their city against similar attacks. "We have all drunk foul poison from the mouth of the serpent, brought from the Byzantine sea."[15] The exarchs continued to be based at Ravenna, but the city, like Rome, was developing autonomous institutions.

Justinian then asked pope John VII (705–707) to convene his own synod of bishops to approve as many of the canons of Troullo as they saw fit, but this offer was also rejected. As if these refusals were not mysterious enough, papal policy then swung inexplicably to the opposite extreme. Pope Constantine I (708–715), a Syrian, accepted the emperor's invitation to travel east (he would be the last pope to do so before the twentieth century). The *Book of Pontiffs* highlights the honors that he received on the way. Pope and emperor met at Nikomedeia in 710: "They rushed together in mutual embrace and there was great joy among the people." But the text does not reveal the purpose of this journey, which certainly concluded with Constantine recognizing Troullo in some fashion, perhaps only verbally, a concession that the *Book of Pontiffs* conceals. There was no sign so far that Rome was seeking its independence from the empire or even of the idea of a papal state.[16]

It is still unclear why Rome so disliked Troullo. It was probably not because of its canons but because the court had organized an Ecumenical Council without papal input and participation, and then listed the churches of eastern Illyricum under the patriarchate of Constantinople.[17] The churches of Illyricum technically belonged to Rome's jurisdiction but had looked to Constantinople since the fifth century. It was an established principle that the organization of the Church should follow that of the state. By this standard, articulated at many Councils, the Illyrian churches (especially those of Greece) belonged to Constantinople.[18]

The empire still maintained a foothold in Istria, at the head of the Adriatic Sea. Its inhabitants were understood in western Europe to be "Latin subjects of the Greeks."[19] This enclave fell periodically into Lombard hands after the mid-eighth century and was annexed by the Franks in 788. In 804, the locals complained about the rapacity of their Frankish governors, which they contrasted to the good old days of the "Greeks." This led to an investigation by Charlemagne's officials, the *Plea of Rižana* (modern Slovenia), where the locals itemize the perks of their former life under Constantinople, such as low taxes and rents; a reliable system of justice; restraint in the use of official violence; the grant of imperial titles to worthy locals; and a stable hierarchy, reflected at official functions, that integrated locals and imperial magistrates.[20] This rosy picture was self-serving, to be sure, but many locals continued to bear eastern names, revealing affective ties to their former polity. The imperial administration had had an interest in keeping them loyal, and the *Plea* reveals that it had applied a light touch, coupled with social and political integration. A system emanating from Constantinople structured local society on a granular level in this corner of the Adriatic.[21] But now it was being impoverished by rapacious Franks. As the *Plea* notes, "our relatives and neighbors in Venetia and Dalmatia, and even the Greeks under whom we formerly lived, ridicule us."

Illyricum and Greece

The empire had long since lost control over the interior of Illyricum, a loss that extended into the mountainous core of western Greece and the Peloponnese. These regions were now inhabited by a mix of former Roman provincials (Latin-speaking in the north, Greek-speaking in the south) and Avar and Slav settlers. We have no narrative or documentary evidence for what happened in the north before the legends recounted by the emperor Konstantinos VII Porphyrogennetos (d. 959) about the coming of the Croats and Serbs. It is possible, though not certain, that the empire exercised a distant suzerainty over some of the coastal, Latin-speaking towns of Dalmatia, such as Zadar, Dubrovnik (Ragusa), and Split. It certainly claimed them as possessions and needed them to keep the routes open to Ravenna, Venetia, and Istria. Konstantinos VII affirms this suzerainty but gives confusing accounts about how these cities fell out of, and were then restored to, imperial control. In the treaty of Aachen between Romanía and Francia in the early ninth century, they were recognized as possessions of the eastern empire.[22]

Most of mainland Greece had fallen out of imperial control but was ringed around by islands and fortified coastal cities from which the administration would gradually be restored to the interior. These included Dyrrachion and the Ionian islands in the west; the coastal forts of Methone and Monembasia and the cities of Argos and Corinth in the Peloponnese; Athens and Thebes in central Greece; and Thessalonike in the northern Aegean. By 695, Hellas (Greece) formed a military command, though we do not know where it was based or what its local presence was. A naval command called Karabisianoi ("shipmen") operated in the Aegean since at least ca. 680, but references to it cease after ca. 730. The Aegean navy certainly continued to exist, but its organizational structure during the eighth century remains obscure. Thessalonike was governed by a prefect (*eparchos*). He likely descended from the former praetorian prefect of Illyricum, who had retreated to the largest remaining city of his crumbling prefecture.[23]

The ring of imperial enclaves around Greece looked out onto a hinterland dominated by Slavic tribes. Thessalonike had barely survived a blockade by Slavs in 676–678 and, when the Anglo-Saxon pilgrim Willibald sailed from Sicily to Monembasia in 723, his biographer placed the latter "in the land of Slavinia." But at the same time, many Slavs were also integrating into the empire by establishing trading relations with the coastal cities, assimilating to their culture, and taking up residence in them. Some of their leaders began to receive titles from the court in Constantinople, which recognized them as *archons* of their people. Presumably, these coveted titles came with salaries and required the chiefs to at least pretend to be Christian.[24]

The reclamation of Greece was an imperial priority. In the late 680s, during the truce with ʿAbd al-Malik, Justinian II opened the corridor between the capital and Thessalonike, fighting Bulgars along the way. He resettled some "Scythians" (Slavs?) along the Strymon river, between Thrace and Macedonia, to defend the gorges. Subsequent emperors did the same, relocating large groups in order to change realities on the ground in Thrace and Greece. Justinian also removed many Slavs from Thrace and took them to Asia Minor, calling them his "Chosen People" and training them to fight against the Arabs. Unfortunately, in their first encounter with the enemy, at the battle of Sebastopolis in 692/3, they defected to the enemy. Justinian allegedly massacred or enslaved the rest. As the tradition is hostile about him, we cannot believe every atrocity report.[25]

Cherson

The empire's outpost in the far north was the heavily fortified ancient city of Cherson, located in the south of the Crimea (a rhomboid peninsula slightly larger than Sicily). Cherson was a remnant of earlier times in another sense too. Its seals reveal that it was governed by an *archon* who was also an imperial official bearing court titles, but he interfaced locally with the "fathers" of the city, its "first men," and "defenders." These magistracies were common in earlier times (fourth–sixth centuries), but had disappeared elsewhere. The steppe empire of the Khazars, a Turkic people who ruled the lands north of the Black Sea and the Caucasus, also had a foothold in the Crimea, though the terms of their entente with the Romans are unknown. Cherson was used by the court as a place of exile, for pope Martinus in 653 and the deposed Justinian II in 695.[26]

Justinian, minus his nose, spent ten years in exile in the Crimea. A hostile historian later wrote up a detailed account of his return to power. The deposed emperor aroused suspicion when he began to plot his return, so he escaped from

Cherson and sought protection with the Khazar khagan, whose sister he married after giving her the Christian (and imperial) name Theodora. Justinian eventually made an alliance with the Bulgar leader Tervel and marched with a Bulgar army on Constantinople. Its citizens would not allow him in so he crawled through an aqueduct. He raised the cry of "Dig up his bones!" against the emperor Tiberios III (698–705) and managed to regain his throne, keeping it for six years (705–711). A western source says that Justinian sported a prosthetic golden nose at this time. He allegedly sent many fleets to massacre the people of Cherson in revenge, but the Chersonites and Roman fleet eventually joined forces and proclaimed as emperor one Philippikos Bardanes (711–713), another political exile. Philippikos sailed to Constantinople, taking it without a fight while Justinian was in Asia Minor. The rebels slaughtered Justinian, his child with Theodora, and his leading officials. His first reign had been ended by the people of Constantinople, and the second by the Chersonites and the fleet. The Heraklian dynasty was both established and undone by a fleet that sailed to the capital from a regional control center (Carthage in 610, Cherson in 711). Justinian was by this point so unpopular that people stopped giving that name to their children; it disappears from seals in the eighth century.[27]

After his restoration to the throne in 705, Justinian bestowed the junior imperial title of *kaisar* on the Bulgar ruler Tervel and invited him to the City, where all were expected to show him proper deference. This title is indeed attested on one of Tervel's seals, accompanied by a prayer to the Mother of God, which means that, like various Slavic *archons* of that time, Tervel at least pretended to be a Christian. The emperor was co-opting the khan into the court system. Tervel is mentioned in a Greek inscription carved on the face of a sheer cliff at Madara in northeastern Bulgaria. It calls him an *archon* and records his agreement with "the emperor whose nose had been cut off." There is a debate about how well the text can be read, and it may have been set up a century later, under khan Krum. We have a contemporary description of the ceremony in which Tervel handed out gold, silver, and silk to his followers, goods that he was given by the emperor. But Bulgaria was not part of the empire. In 716, the emperor Theodosios III and the Bulgar khan drew up a detailed treaty that defined the border between the two states and stipulated terms for refugees and the certification of merchants. This agreement secured peace between the two polities until the 750s.[28]

The eastern frontier

Romanía's longest continuous land border stretched from the Caucasus diagonally across Asia Minor to the Mediterranean, and it was defined for much of its length by the Tauros and Anti-Tauros mountains. Iberia (eastern Georgia, or Kartli) and most of Armenia had been subjected by the Arabs, who ruled there through quasi-autonomous local principalities. In 697, even Sergios, the Roman-appointed ruler of Lazica (western Georgia on the Black Sea), ceded his realm to the Arabs.[29] The loss of Caucasia was a blow to Rome's imperial pretensions. In the sixth and early seventh centuries, Constantinople had dominated Georgia and annexed large parts of Armenia. These gains were now lost, but their memory remained. For the next three centuries, the empire would periodically intervene in Armenian affairs by invading when the Arabs were weak or distracted and also by making anti-Arab alliances with the Khazars, who could raid across the Caucasus. Constantinople also cultivated pro-Roman factions in Armenia by deploying the tools of soft power, especially by awarding court titles to loyal proxies along with gifts and cash. Religion was a problem, however, as the Armenian Church, when left to its own devices, tended to reject the Council of Chalcedon. But pro-Chalcedonian Armenians could be found and won over. This multipronged approach eventually paid off: in the tenth and eleventh centuries, most of Armenia would fall under Roman rule again. By 700, the only outpost of empire in Transcaucasia was the fortified city of Phasis on the Black Sea coast.[30]

Fortunately for the empire, the loss of Transcaucasia did not mean that it had to fear attack from that direction. The Arabs did not settle their own armies there in great numbers and the local client rulers whom they appointed were not inclined to attack the Roman empire, preferring to feud against each other. For the Romans, the most dangerous border was in the southeast, facing onto northern Mesopotamia and Syria. It was from here that the Arabs raided into Asia Minor, and it was this part of the border that the Romans heavily fortified, garrisoned, and patrolled. The empire continued to hold the Cilician plain, south of the Tauros mountains, including the cities of Tarsos and Mopsouestia, until the 710s, when that region too was lost. Yet the Arabs were unable or unwilling to establish any permanent presence in the interior of Asia Minor during their raids. The mountain passes, hostile population, cold winters, Roman defenses, and unreliable supply lines discouraged occupation.[31] Moreover, the interests of the population of Asia Minor and Constantinople were aligned: to protect the "fatherland" from Arab conquest.

Peace treaties with the Muslims could be only for a limited time, allegedly because nothing more was permitted by the Quran: the caliphate and its successor states were ideologically committed to the long-term goal of conquering the infidel Romans.[32] In the eighth century, both Romans and Arabs resettled populations away from the border, turning it into a depopulated no-man's land that was hard to cross, except for determined forces. Arab attacks came from two directions, which the Arabs, thinking of them as a boxing match, labeled "the left" (i.e., Syria and Cilicia, with Tarsos as the main expeditionary base) and "the right" (i.e., Jazira, northern Mesopotamia, from Melitene). The only outpost maintained by the Romans behind enemy lines consisted of the Madraïtes, a military unit installed there in an amphibious operation in 677. It was their attacks that pressured 'Abd al-Malik to sue for peace in 685 and make extraordinary payments to the Romans, but he also demanded that the Mardaïtes be withdrawn. Justinian II complied. The corps, withdrawn to Romanía, retained its unit identity until the tenth century. Justinian was criticized for removing this bulwark of Roman power from Syria.[33]

Cyprus

An unusual situation prevailed on Cyprus, which had twice been attacked by the Arabs in the mid-seventh century and partially depopulated. The agreement between Justinian II and ʿAbd al-Malik created a unique regime for the island that, by and large, exempted it from the broader conflict for almost three centuries. Specifically, Cyprus was demilitarized and its taxes were shared between the two sides. This arrangement is traditionally called the "condominium," though sovereignty over Cyprus was not divided: it remained with Rome. Later Muslim jurists were not sure what to make of it. Was Cyprus subject to Muslim authority (because it paid tribute) or not (because it was not)? The arrangement got off to a rocky start. In ca. 691, Justinian relocated the bishop of Konstantia along with many Cypriots to the province of the Hellespont, where he founded a city, New Justinianopolis. This was situated at Artake near Kyzikos on the Sea of Marmara, possibly to guard the approach to Constantinople and diminish the revenue paid to the Arabs from Cyprus (also, the crown offered to his ancestor Herakleios, when he sailed to Constantinople in 610, had come from Artake). As the Church of Cyprus was autonomous of Constantinople, the Council in Troullo extended this privilege to its new location, giving the bishop rights over the province of Hellespont. But this relocation was taken by ʿAbd al-Malik as a breach of treaty, allegedly leading him to resume hostilities. New Justinianopolis did not last long; its citizens were returned to Cyprus only a few years later.[34]

The Romans maintained a small staff on the island, mostly fiscal officials, and it is not until the tenth century that we hear of a Muslim minority living there with its own officials. The monetary economy had collapsed by 700, which was only to be expected since there were no soldiers to pay, and the repeated deportations cannot have helped. In addition to those carried off by the Arabs in 649 and 653, and then by Justinian in 691, the caliph al-Walid carried out another one in 743 "because of some suspicion," but in reality because the Romans were distracted by a civil war; he later allowed his captives to return in exchange for higher tribute. Archaeologically, Cyprus presents a similar picture to much of Asia Minor: urban contraction and abandonment, a decline in living standards, a lack of new buildings, and likely demographic shrinkage. Yet the island was still connected to networks of interregional trade with Asia Minor, Syria, and Egypt, both importing and exporting. At the Council of Nicaea II in 787, the bishop of Konstantia told a story regarding thirty-two Cypriots who had sailed to Syria in two ships, presumably for trade. One of the Arab soldiers who was assigned to escort them there did not believe that holy icons had any power, so he scratched out the right eye of an icon with his spear to test it, whereupon his own eyeball popped out onto the floor.[35]

The caliphate

The Romans held no territorial outposts within the caliphate, but they did possess cultural affinities with many of its subjects. Muslims were a tiny minority in 700. To be sure, the Christians of the caliphate were divided over Chalcedon, and many spoke Syriac and Coptic, not Greek. However, there is no reliable evidence that they preferred Arab to Roman rule, although they adjusted as best they could. They are often treated by historians as passively indifferent to who ruled them, as if they swapped one interchangeably oppressive master for another. In reality, they probably preferred to be part of the Christian empire, even if its rulers were (for now) Chalcedonians. Arab taxation seems to have been more onerous than its Roman predecessor and was extracted to benefit a small minority who were a foreign occupation army. It was even more centralized, obsessively micromanaging, intrusive, and extractive than Roman taxation, and reinforced with threats and insults, not appeals to common values. Conversion to Islam was driven in part by a desire to escape the additional burdens brought by the conquest. Moreover, many Egyptians were required to serve as rowers in the navy and were sent overseas to drown in battles fought against other Christians. These conditions sparked agrarian revolts, which were unheard of in Romanía.[36]

The contrast was well illustrated in a treatise written by a Muslim scholar of the tenth century, who recounts a dialogue between a Roman ambassador and a caliphal official. When the latter ridiculed the small size of the emperor's revenues, the Roman replied:

> We are more prudent and wise than you concerning taxes. You take properties from people, you make them your enemies and make their blood boil . . . . But we set it in the amount I mentioned so that it is taken seriously. In this way we are sure of not antagonizing the people, while at the same time securing our revenue and saving ourselves from the problems you have.[37]

The Christian group most suspected by the Muslim authorities as a likely Roman fifth column were the Chalcedonians, later known as the Melkite Church (from *malik*, "king," because they took the emperor's side in theology). They were sometimes arrested and punished on suspicion of being spies, not without cause. The Roman navy continued to attack coastal cities, from Laodikeia and Tripolis to Egypt, and the Muslims feared that the local population might be complicit. The Muslim shipyards were accordingly moved from Alexandria to Fustat (where Cairo was later built).[38] But little came of military collaboration between Romans and ex-Romans. In the long run, the Greek-speaking population of the caliphate proved to be a different kind of asset to the Roman empire. As they immigrated to the empire in the eighth and ninth centuries, they brought with them their learning, books, labor, and skills, infusing new life, from its former lands, into a devastated culture.

Consider Andreas, a monk in Jerusalem, who was born in Damascus ca. 660. In 695, he was sent by his bishop on an embassy to Constantinople, where Justinian II persuaded him to stay and direct an orphanage. Later he became a bishop on Crete and one of the leading hymnographers of the Orthodox Church and a saint. The land of his birth, Syria, had been lost so recently that, had he been born a generation earlier, he would have started life an imperial subject. But his Roman biographer referred to it now as "the land of our enemies." Yet Syria and Palestine still produced important Greek writers, including Andreas himself and, in the eighth century, the great theologian John of Damascus.[39]

Political instability

Justinian II visited many of the lands of his far-flung domain. He opened the corridor between Constantinople and Thessalonike and traveled to the Armenian marches in the east. He had been exiled to the Crimea, dealt with the khagan of the Khazars, marrying his daughter, and befriended the ruler of the Bulgars. In death, he also visited his empire's Italian provinces. His severed head, with or without its prosthetic nose, was sent to Rome, where it was brought before his erstwhile guest, pope Constantinus, who had just returned from his meeting with Justinian in the east. Along the way it had stopped at Ravenna, "led through the streets, fixed on the point of a lance."[40]

Justinian's grim fate reflected that era of political instability. The period between his first fall from power, in 695, and the 720s, when Leon III secured himself on the throne, was turbulent, but it was not an "age of anarchy." State institutions functioned well, there was little social unrest, and the Romans held their own against the Arabs; in fact, they emerged from that era victorious, guaranteeing their survival and setting the empire on a trajectory of revival. Instability was limited to the throne. As the polity transited between dynasties, various constituencies jostled for power. Each new emperor was insecure chiefly before the people of Constantinople and the army, and it was only Leon III who tamed, or appeased, both by saving the polity from Arab conquest during the great siege of the capital.

Unfortunately, the events of this period are known mostly from one source, a contemporaneous history written probably by the patrician Traïanos, which survives only through its independent reuse by later writers.[41] Traïanos had inside knowledge, but was fiercely biased against Justinian II. That emperor, as we saw, was deposed in 695 by the people of the City who were called out to a revolution by the general Leontios. As emperor, Leontios sent the fleet to reclaim Carthage but when the expedition failed, its leaders rebelled on the way back, at Crete in 698, possibly fearing punishment. They elected an officer, Apsimar, as the new emperor and renamed him Tiberios III, thus linking him to the Heraklian dynasty. After a standoff at Constantinople that lasted for months, Tiberios was able to enter the City and depose Leontios, who was confined to a monastery, minus his nose. We saw earlier how Justinian regained his throne in 705, and lost it in 711 to Philippikos Bardanes, as coup was followed by counter coup.

Philippikos reigned for almost two years (late 711 to mid-713) and enacted two major, and equally strange, measures. One was to expel all Armenians from Romanía into the caliphate. The other was to repeal the Sixth Ecumenical Council of 680–681, which condemned the doctrine of Christ's One Will. Procedurally, he did this not by convening a Council but at a meeting of the Senate and top clergy. All signed his decree, including bishops such as Andreas of Crete and Germanos of Kyzikos (later patriarch). They later claimed that they signed under duress (but of course they would claim that). It was strange not only that the emperor would reverse direction in a matter that was settled but that so many would go along with him. Changes in Church policy usually required careful planning and generated heated polemic. But this time, in a matter that had literally sparked wars in the seventh century, almost everyone complied with the emperor's request, and then switched back again the next year when his successor repealed the repeal. Philippikos also destroyed the records of the Sixth Ecumenical Council and removed its image from the Milion, the domed tetrapylon that marked the empire's symbolic center, which had been adorned with mosaics depicting all the Ecumenical Councils. Rome repudiated his policy, and possibly Philippikos himself too, but the exarch of Ravenna traveled to Rome to reassure everyone that nothing had changed, as Philippikos had himself been deposed in the meantime.[42]

In mid-713, the general of Opsikion in Thrace, Georgios Bouraphos, sent a squad to infiltrate the palace and blind Philippikos. He retired to the monastery of Dalmatou, as had Leontios before him. According to one source, what agitated Bouraphos was an invasion of Thrace by Bulgars, who were angry that Philippikos had suspended their annual payments and were possibly using the execution of their patron Justinian II as a pretext. They had plundered widely and reached Constantinople itself, assaulting celebrity weddings in the countryside. On the day after Philippikos was blinded, which happened to be Pentecost, the Senate, clergy, soldiers in the City, and the populace gathered in Hagia Sophia where they appointed as emperor Artemios, Philippikos' secretary (*protasekretis*), giving him the name Anastasios. The rapidity of the transition implies a planned conspiracy, but within days Anastasios blinded Bouraphos too. With our meager information, it is impossible to discern the politics of these factions.[43]

The siege of Constantinople

Anastasios II restored the Sixth Ecumenical Council, a move endorsed by everyone who had signed off on its condemnation the previous year. Meanwhile, a real issue was calling for attention. The Arabs were raiding deeply into Asia Minor on a regular basis, and they had finally established control over Cilicia, destroying Tyana and fortifying Mopsouestia as a base for launching more attacks. Roman raids into the caliphate were far rarer, although the Romans had developed effective tactics for intercepting and defeating raiding parties.[44] The caliphs, observing the Romans' political instability, made another all-out push to conquer Constantinople. This would be their third attempt to take the City (after ca. 654 and 667–668), and coincided with the entry of Islamic arms into Spain, at the opposite end of the Mediterranean. Roman intelligence reported the construction of a large fleet and extensive preparations. Anastasios repaired the walls of the capital, replenished its stockpiles, and told its residents to store up provisions for three years or leave. In 715, he sent a fleet to attack an Arab forward-base, but at Rhodes the Opsikion army, which probably felt unfairly cut out of the succession in 713, mutinied and killed its admiral. It then moved on Constantinople, proclaiming an emperor of its own along the way, a tax collector named Theodosios. Anastasios left the capital for Nikaia, possibly distrusting the populace, and the war in the Sea of Marmara between the two sides lasted for months. Eventually, Theodosios III was crowned in Constantinople and Anastasios II retired to Thessalonike as a monk.[45]

The Umayyad general prosecuting the war was Maslama, a son of the caliph ʿAbd al-Malik (685–705), half-brother of caliphs al-Walid I (705–715), Sulayman (715–717), Yazid II (720–724), and Hisham (724–743), and nephew of ʿUmar II (717–720). After extensive preparations, he entered Asia Minor with a large army in 716, planning to make Amorion his summer base. That city had declared for Theodosios III, but Leon, the general of Anatolikon, was posing as a champion of Anastasios II and was allied to Artabasdos, the general of Armeniakon. Maslama lost Amorion to the trickery of Leon, who pretended to join the Arabs but then entered the city, where he was proclaimed emperor in the summer. Maslama marched west and spent the winter of 716–717 in Asia province (i.e., the Thrakesion command), preparing his assault on the capital. His armies "slaughtered the men and sent the women and children back home as slaves," while his fleet wintered in the Aegean, where they scrawled graffiti in Arabic at Knidos and elsewhere. Meanwhile, Leon marched to Nikomedeia, where he captured Theodosios' son. In anticipation of the Arab siege, Theodosios was pressured by the military and civilian leadership to abdicate in Leon's favor, which he did in the spring of 717. Leon entered the City and was crowned in Hagia Sophia on 25 March. Constantinople was prepared for the assault, but it would be put to the test.[46]

In the summer of 717, Maslama's army crossed the Hellespont at Abydos and marched overland to Constantinople, which it invested with a palisade and siege engines. An Arab fleet of allegedly 1,800 vessels arrived soon thereafter, but when twenty of its transport ships were stalled by the wind as they sailed past the City, Leon sent out warships to destroy them. The rest of the fleet anchored along the

Bosporos, so Leon drew a heavy chain across the entrance to the Golden Horn, barring them from that strategic inlet (this is the first historical reference to that device). Leon had also made an alliance with the Bulgars, who attacked the Arab encampment and inflicted heavy casualties. Thus, the Arabs were hemmed in too. The ensuing stalemate lasted into the winter, which was so severe that many Arabs and their animals perished.

In the spring of 718, the Arab army was reinforced by two more fleets, amounting allegedly to another 760 ships, so that the water, from the City to the Asian shore, "appeared to be a sea of timber." But many Egyptian sailors, who were Christians, defected to the emperor, and Leon sent his ships to incinerate the enemy fleet with flamethrowers spewing Greek fire. To avoid that horror, the Arabs stationed their fleet on the Asian side, but here they were blockaded by the Roman land forces, leading to a famine in the Arab camps. They began to eat animals and dead comrades, and eventually illness set in, while the Bulgarians were attacking them in Thrace. The expedition became a debacle. In the summer of 718, the Arabs withdrew, and more of them perished in fierce storms on the way back. A grammarian composed a hymn to celebrate the victory over "the haughty spirit of hostile Ismael," inviting his audience to join in the clapping as he recited the hymn "What Great God." The patriarch Germanos attributed the victory to the Mother of God, who was regarded as the City's protector ever since the Avar siege of 626. Later Romans who were hostile to Leon for religious reasons did the same, but at the time he was the real winner. His strategy had been brilliant.[47]

During the siege, the general of Sicily Sergios came to believe that the capital had fallen and so he reconstituted it at Syracuse. He proclaimed one Basileios as emperor and the latter appointed magistrates, as if the capital had been relocated to Sicily. This provides a fascinating glimpse of an alternative future history of the Roman state, had Constantinople fallen. But when Leon's envoys announced the emperor's victory, the Sicilians returned to obedience with rejoicing: they had, after all, aimed to continue Romanía, not break from it. Sergios fled to the Lombards and was later pardoned, but the magistrates of his court-in-exile were arrested, and some were executed. Leon faced two more domestic challenges to his reign. The deposed emperor Anastasios, now a resident of Thessalonike, tried to reclaim his throne in 718/9 by calling in old favors from his former officers and asking the Bulgars for help. With them he marched on the capital. But Leon arrested those officers in Constantinople and asked the Bulgars to desist, which they did, with apologies. Anastasios, the bishop of Thessalonike, and some chief ringleaders were executed, while others were exiled or fined. The final rebellion that Leon faced came from the army of Greece in 727. It proclaimed one Kosmas as emperor and sailed against the capital, but was defeated by Greek fire and surrendered.[48]

The siege of Constantinople paradoxically stabilized the Roman polity and enabled a new dynasty to emerge. Fittingly, Leon's son and successor Konstantinos V was born during the siege. Success had secured Leon's position and ended the cycle of instability that had lasted an entire generation, since 695. The threat of military coups reverted back to its seventh-century frequency of one every fifteen or twenty years. This was more frequent than in the preceding centuries (fourth–sixth), but the armies were now positioned closer to the capital and more deeply enmeshed in its politics.

Conversely, the defeat at Constantinople was a major blow to the finances and prestige of the Umayyad caliphate, and the loss of the fleet ended Arab naval hegemony. Indeed, Leon was able to mount naval raids against Syria in 719 and Egypt in 720. The caliph 'Umar II (717–720) paused the policy of expansion, and even considered pulling back from Spain, Cilicia, and Central Asia, though he was dissuaded from going that far. The annual raids against Romanía continued, and discriminatory laws were imposed on Christians in the caliphate possibly because of the defeat.[49] Constantinople and the caliphate continued to exchange embassies to protest and negotiate, and to exchange pleasantries and occasionally prisoners. Both sides were well informed about the other. But it was war that created the framework for diplomacy. The defense of Constantinople blocked the Arabs from expanding into the Balkans and Europe. A few years later, at the battle of Poitiers in 732, the Franks likewise defeated an invading Muslim army from Spain. The Muslim dream of conquering "Rum" was deferred to an indefinite apocalyptic future. "The Romans," declared one of their prophesies in resignation, "are people of sea and rock: whenever one generation goes, another replaces it. Alas, they will be with you to the end of time."[50]

20

The Lion and the Dragon (717–775)

Leon III (717–741) and his son Konstantinos V (741–775) were among the most capable and successful emperors of the Romans. However, we know little about them, and even that is filtered through the lens of intense partisan hatred and then warped by lies. This distortion, unlike any other in Roman history, was perpetrated by later authors obsessed over the issue of religious icons. Leon and Konstantinos had increasingly questioned and then tried to stop the use of icons in worship, whereas the surviving sources were written by authors who were strongly pro-icon. This issue was socially marginal. Most people, including most bishops, monks, and soldiers, went along with what the emperors wanted, but a minority was intensely invested in this issue and they eventually prevailed. They suppressed information, concocted fictions to make the enemies of icons look bad, plagiarized texts, inserted passages into past texts in order to make them more supportive of their view, and engaged in hysterical denunciations. For example, they claimed that Leon and Konstantinos were forerunners of the Antichrist, dragons, or just Satan in human form, who consorted with wizards and Jews and sacrificed children in their dungeons.

Leon's dynasty was later called "Isaurian," a name that stuck because Isaurians had a bad reputation in Roman eyes, but he was really from Germanikeia (Marash) on the northern Syrian border. He was born ca. 685, when that city was changing hands between Romans and Arabs. An Arabic source says that he could speak "both Arabic and Roman [i.e., Greek]," but this cannot be confirmed.[1] His family moved to Thrace where he joined the army and rose through the ranks.[2] His son Konstantinos, born during the siege, was made co-emperor in 720 and married in 733 to Tzitzak (renamed Eirene), a daughter of a Khazar khagan. Leon gave his own daughter Anna in marriage to his supporter Artabasdos, who became *kouropalates*, a high imperial title.

Under Leon, Romanía was secure though not safe. It was at peace with the Bulgars, but the Arabs continued to raid in Asia Minor and attack Sicily. A major attack against Gortyn on Crete in the 720s is mentioned in the life of Andreas of Crete. The bishop and populace sought refuge in a citadel besieged "by the wicked sons of Hagar," but the attackers were beaten off. Hagiographic texts typically omit the soldiers and officials who did the work and concentrate instead on the saint's prayers, a focus that generally distorts the history of this period.[3]

The main target of Arab raids was Asia Minor, which was attacked on an almost annual basis and to devastating effect. Some of the raids were led by al-Battal, who became legendary in later Arabic and Turkish epics and even films. Many towns were sacked, including Ikonion, Neokaisareia, Gangra, Charsianon, and Ankyra, and thousands of prisoners and much loot were hauled away. Usually the inhabitants of Roman towns sought refuge elsewhere until the invader had departed. The Roman defenses were struggling to keep up. One success came in 727, when an Arab army made a determined effort to take Nikaia. The defenders, led by Artabasdos, resisted a forty-day siege, though the city suffered extensive damage. Later pro-icon sources attributed the victory to the prayers of the Fathers of the Council of Nicaea (of 325), whose icons adorned the church there. Two years later, the Saxon pilgrim Willibald went to Nikaia to see this church, and does indeed record that it was adorned with images of the Council Fathers. Artabasdos rebuilt the walls, in part by reusing stones from the ancient theater. An inscription was set up that, like the inscription set up by the *dux* of Sardinia a thousand miles away, honored the "Christ-loving emperors Leon and Konstantinos," and then Artabasdos himself, who led the work on site.[4]

The Ekloge

Leon's greatest monument was not physical: it was his law code, the *Ekloge* ("Selection") of laws from the Justinianic *Corpus*, as its long subtitle declares. It was issued in March 741, shortly before Leon died, in his name and his son's. It would exert enormous influence over the subsequent history of Roman law, even outside Romanía. The *Ekloge* is a practical handbook designed to be accessible, concise, and clear. It reflects a simpler and less stratified society than did Justinianic law, a society of soldiers and farmers and not of senators and city councilors. It defers to canon law for the supervision of priests and monks. It makes some innovations, for example by treating marriage as a Christian institution and not, as in ancient Roman law, a private contract. Divorce was restricted tightly. Unmarried men caught fornicating were to receive six lashes, and homosexual acts were a capital crime.[5] Otherwise, the *Ekloge* replaced capital punishment with the amputation of extremities, often those extremities supposed to be chiefly involved in the commission of the offense or symbolic of it. The claim in the subtitle that the *Ekloge* moderates the laws "in the direction of greater humaneness" probably refers to this change. It may have been inspired by Jesus' claim in Matthew 5:30: "if your right hand is tempting you to sin, cut it off and throw it away; for it is in your interest to lose a limb rather than for your entire body to fall into Hell." Indeed, the *Ekloge's* preface declares the lawgiver's intention to promote his subjects' "salvation." This is not just a penal code, but an effort to help Christians attain salvation by discouraging sin.[6]

An Old Testament spirit looms over the preface of the *Ekloge*. It is a homily on justice that relies on Biblical quotations and avoids classical images and motifs.

Law was given by God so that people could attain salvation, and the emperors refer twice to Solomon by name as their model. It was no accident that, within a few generations, a scholar produced the *Mosaic Law*, a rearrangement of Old Testament law according to the tables of the *Ekloge*, and the two texts were later bundled and transmitted together. But Leon's Old Testament conception of law channels an essentially Justinianic content and is entwined with Roman imperial notions. Judges must be impartial between poor and rich and must dispense justice equally, while the emperors "are preoccupied by great concerns: with sleepless minds we search for what pleases God and benefits the common good . . . hoping to restore the ancient jurisdiction of the *res publica*."[7] Emperors were still "restoring the republic."

The veneration of icons

The *Ekloge* does not mention icons, which contradicts the later image of Leon III as their fanatical enemy. According to one of those texts, Leon had usurped the throne with the skills of a fox, but later roared like a lion against the Church.[8] In reality, icons were marginal to his concerns.

Icons were two-dimensional representations of Christ, Mary, and the saints, whether paintings on walls, freestanding panels, mosaics, or low-relief sculptures. In the overall visual environment, these Christian images took their place among thousands of representations of the ancient gods that still survived in the public spaces of Constantinople and other cities, such as Ephesos and Athens, along with the statues, mosaics, and paintings of emperors, statesmen, heroes, and charioteers. In almost all the cultures of the ancient Roman empire, figural representation was an intuitive way to posit the presence of someone who was physically absent (such as an emperor) or invisible (such as a god). Christians were part of this world and had internalized its logic, often carrying it over from their pre-Christian lives. Thus, starting in the fourth century, Jesus and his disciples were carved on the sides of sarcophagi, depicted in glorious color in church mosaics (as can still be seen in Ravenna), and painted on panel icons, which relied on the same techniques as had once fashioned images of the gods. These panels, placed in churches, homes, or in public, were often "votive" offerings, that is they were dedicated to the god or saint in gratitude for assistance, usually healing.[9]

These practices were taken for granted and generated little controversy and little theory. Images were part of the wallpaper of Christian devotion. They were not dragged into the great theological controversies of the fourth through seventh centuries, and were mentioned only in passing. By the sixth century they were still incidental, but appear in prominent locations. It is possible that portrait icons in stone of Christ, Mary, and the Apostles were set atop the *templon* (an architrave barrier separating the nave from the sanctuary) of the church of St. Polyeuktos in Constantinople, build by the aristocrat Anicia

Juliana in the 520s (however, it has also been suggested that these images, found defaced in the debris of the church's foundations, did not belong to it originally and were later creations). The *templon* of Hagia Sophia certainly featured silver icons, and its altar was draped with a silk depicting Christ, Peter, and Paul, with scenes of Justinian's accomplishments along the hem.[10] The patriarchal palace and many churches featured images of the Church Fathers, some of whom were saints. Dissident Christian groups kept images of their own Fathers. In the seventh century, churches were decorated with spectacular mosaic images of their saints, such as Demetrios in Thessalonike (see Plate 4b). By 700, the Milion—the City's most central monument—sported mosaic images of the six Ecumenical Councils.[11]

Images shaped the logic of religious experience. They could, for example, elicit emotional reactions (an image of the sacrifice of Isaac drove a bishop to tears), or inspire one to a better life. They were used by preachers to illustrate points of theology and Biblical lore, and considered as one among many ways to "honor" the saints.[12] Images of the saints were acquired at pilgrimage sites, for example of St. Menas in Egypt, and taken home by pilgrims. In the later sixth century, a pagan set up an image of Christ in his house to persuade people that he was really a Christian, and he invited them to come see it. A contemporary Platonist sympathizer explained, in a playful epigram, how an image of the angel Michael elevates the mind to its invisible subject, and this act of "reverence" causes the beholder to tremble as if in the angel's presence.[13] In the seventh century, icons performed healing miracles; were used for oath taking; helped people to recognize a saint when they saw him in a vision; and were used as conduits for people to address the saints in church. In the late seventh century, our Gallic visitor to Constantinople, Arculf, documents a fully developed cult of images, with icons that performed miracles, were venerated, and were spoken to "as if it were St. George present in person."[14] Icons also acquired military functions. When Herakleios sailed against Phokas in 610 to seize the throne, he used an icon of the Virgin as a kind of banner, and when the Avars attacked Constantinople in 626, the patriarch placed icons of the Virgin on the gates in order to bring down her wrath on anyone who attacked them, an ancient talismanic practice.[15] Justinian II associated Christ prominently with imperial power—or vice versa—when he put Christ's image on the nomisma.

The cult of icons thus appears to us as a set of disconnected datapoints that were not organized according to any Christian "theory" of images. Some scholars take an evolutionist approach and postulate that icons gradually accumulated functions and cultural prominence until the later seventh century, when they finally received "veneration" and theological justification (the Council in Troullo decreed that Christ should be depicted in human form and not only symbolically as a lamb, to remind us that God became a man, as the essence of God cannot be depicted). The holy grail of these discussions are images that appear to have been situated directly in the path of Christian worship, such as in the apse of the church, because it was these that most troubled the "iconoclasts." A major new interpretation of the material evidence suggests that churches in Constantinople and Asia Minor, the core regions of the empire, had always tended to showcase the cross most prominently, whereas figural images were more common in other regions, such as Italy and Egypt. This geographical differentiation suggests that the promotion of the cross by the iconoclasts was merely an emphasis on received tradition in those regions, and nothing new or distinctive.[16] Still, icons may have received veneration even if they were not in the apse or dome of a church, and many of their uses did not fall neatly into the categories of "ex voto" or "veneration." A recently-edited text, tentatively dated to the fifth century, contains a dialogue between a Christian defender of the veneration of icons and a critic who clings to Old Testament prohibitions; this might anchor later practices in earlier thinking.[17]

A more skeptical approach has indicted most of our sources as forgeries or interpolations made by later defenders of icons who wanted to prove the antiquity of their views and practices. While such falsification did take place, this argument goes too far and becomes circular when it rejects early texts just because they show icons working miracles and receiving veneration. Most of the aforementioned texts can be defended against such skepticism, or were never impugned.[18] A problem for the ultra-skeptical view is that Latin and Syriac texts attest to the cult of icons in the fifth and sixth centuries, and they could not have been tampered with by later iconophiles.[19]

Leon III and icons

Unfortunately, we do not know what Leon III did regarding icons. Whatever it was, it had a minimal impact and resulted in almost no concrete actions. He did not convene a Church Council but rather, in 730, a meeting of the Senate and Church leadership, where he expressed his position and required the others to subscribe to it. Its contents are not reliably reported. The contemporary life of pope Gregory II says that the emperor instructed the pope "that no church image of any saint, martyr, or angel should be kept, as he declared them all accursed." Gregory refused to comply, but his biography is so biased that it may well be twisting an order to not add *new* images to the churches of Rome, or to ensure that veneration was not veering into the *worship* of icons. Iconophile polemic gives the impression that the emperor wanted to destroy icons. This is what "iconoclasm" literally means, though iconophiles more commonly used the term "iconomachy," or "fighting against images," for their opponents.[20] But is not clear there was an actual decree, and there is no sign of its enforcement. The story that Leon III removed the image of Christ from the Chalke Gatehouse has been shown to be a later legend (that image was set up by Eirene later on, prompting a retroactive fiction that it had been taken down by Leon III). The patriarch Germanos (715–730), who had supported Monotheletism in 712, was pressured to resign, possibly because of his opposition to Leon's policy, whatever that was. He was succeeded in an orderly way by his deputy (*synkellos*) Anastasios.[21]

Leon was clearly critical or skeptical of icons in some way, and his son Konstantinos V (741–775) would take this further. But what prompted Leon to do anything regarding icons? We can disregard later tales that he was terrified by a volcanic eruption in the Aegean or bamboozled by a Jewish wizard. Some scholars argue that Leon was trying to recapture the favor of God after the great defeats of the seventh century, but that is a truism: all emperors hoped to gain God's favor. Others point to the Arabs, assuming that any new initiatives must have been related to the Roman state's most important foreign challenge. But this works better for Justinian II, who put Christ on his coins, knowing that it would irritate Muslims. The simplest explanation is that Leon believed that something was wrong in how Christians were treating icons and that he took the prohibition against graven images by the Second Commandment seriously. The *Ekloge* reveals that he was inclined to Old Testament models of piety.

As it happens, icons were being debated elsewhere as well. Pope Gregory protested the actions of a bishop of Marseilles who smashed some icons in his church because congregants were worshipping them. There is evidence, albeit unreliably transmitted, of a seventh-century reaction against icons in Armenia, and then a pro-icon response.[22] The caliphs were also taking a stand. The adornment of ʿAbd al-Malik's Dome of the Rock, an overtly anti-Christian monument, is aniconic, and that caliph also removed figures from his coins. His son Yazid II (720–724) banned figural representations throughout his domain, even for his Christian subjects, though it was unevenly enforced and soon overturned. A large number of mosaic floors in churches in Palestine and Jordan were modified to comply with this ban, but the timing suggests that local Christian communities had their own reasons for taking a similar position.[23] Yazid targeted all images of human beings and animals, so his edict could not have inspired the east Roman iconoclasts, who targeted primarily images of the divine in the context of worship (and secondarily those of saints), but otherwise sponsored representational art.

Images had been debated in Romanía too, but this took the form of debates between Christians and "Jews," in which the latter, at least as they were imagined by Christians, argued that the former were idolators for worshipping created things rather than the Creator. These debates had antecedents in the fifth century and peaked in the seventh, when Christian Romans wrote many anti-Jewish texts that assuaged anxieties about images. One can easily imagine that Christians engaged in forms of image veneration that smacked of idolatry and superstition. The letters of the patriarch Germanos reveal that bishops and congregations in Asia Minor were having doubts before 730: were worshippers showing too much reverence for material objects rather than their Creator?[24] Leon III probably doubted that most Christians could grasp the subtleties of "relative veneration" and not cross the line into idolatry.[25] He may have been spurred by the broader international debate over images, but his position was internal to Roman culture. Possibly, it reflected a split between the aniconic traditions of Asia Minor and the established use of religious images in other parts of the Christian world, such as Italy and Egypt.[26] There is no proof, however, that Leon attributed the Roman defeats in the seventh century to icon worship. Modern scholarship has invented that link, and later iconophiles would have pounced on such an argument, had it been advanced.

The rift with the pope over icons was only one factor that shaped the imperial position in Italy, and not the most important one. The *Book of Pontiffs* explains that, before icons became an issue, pope Gregory II was already in rebellion against Constantinople by preventing tax collection, and this allegedly led to attempts on his life by imperial officials. The information that we have from Greek texts (specifically, the chronicle of Theophanes) is chronologically garbled but it says that Leon had imposed a poll tax on one-third of the farmers in Sicily and Calabria and then confiscated the revenue of papal lands (*patrimonium*) in those provinces, a sum of 25,200 nomismata per year (many of these were likely imperial lands entrusted in the past to the Church). It is likely that the poll tax was imposed on the farmers of the papal lands, and this was probably what the pope was obstructing. In response, Leon confiscated the lands in question. This move, which took place in the late 720s, was a major blow to papal finances, but it bolstered imperial food security, especially after the loss of North Africa in the late 690s. Leon then sent his letters about icons, which generalized the rebellion against him to the rest of Italy, and the exarch Paulos was murdered. While the empire had strengthened its position in the south, Rome, Ravenna, and the Pentapolis were slipping out of its grasp as pro- and anti-imperial factions fought it out.[27]

Gregory II refused to recognize the emperor in his official correspondence after late 726. Although Ravenna returned to imperial control by January, 731, the next pope, Gregory III (731–741), convened a synod in November 731 to reject the new policy on icons. Rome was now asserting itself as an independent player. Two popes (Theodore and Martin) had done this already in the mid-seventh century over Monotheletism but imperial arms had suppressed their movement. Yet the current situation was different. The loss of the patrimonial estates in the south diminished the flow of cash and goods into Rome, affecting a large part of the population and turning it against Constantinople; also, Rome now had its own militia, which was increasingly loyal to the pope. Families of imperial officials at Rome were gradually switching from an imperial allegiance to a papal one, and from Greek to Latin. This trend is exemplified by the career of Theodotus, who commissioned a chapel in the church of Santa Maria Antiqua and donated many lands to the Church of Rome.[28]

In the 730s, papal Rome had to navigate a complex political landscape that included the exarch, the powerful Lombard king Liudprand (712–744), and the Lombard dukes, who often acted independently of their king. During that decade, these groups formed all possible alliances with and against each other, until the Lombards took Ravenna in 739. By this point the pope had decided that Rome was more vulnerable to the Lombards than to the weak imperial regime, and so he reversed his stance. To restore Ravenna to the emperor, he brokered an alliance with the Venetians. In his letter to them, Gregory III expresses his (rediscovered) loyalty "to the great emperors, our sons, Leo and Constantinus."[29] Rome and Ravenna were restored to the empire, though the first was de facto autonomous and the second was hanging on by a thread. Even so, geopolitics drove the pope to overlook the matter of icons, just as Gregory II had originally broken with Leon not over icons but lands.

Leon's reign ended as it began, with a major victory over the Arabs. In 740, the Umayyads launched an unusually large expedition into Asia Minor, consisting of three separate armies. Two of them accomplished little and returned home, but at Akroinon in Phrygia (near modern Afyon), Leon and Konstantinos destroyed an army of 20,000; among the dead was the hero of later legend, al-Battal. This was one of many Arab defeats taking place around the world at that very time, precipitating the disintegration of the Umayyad caliphate, its replacement by the Abbasids, and a new balance of power.[30] For the past century, the Romans had been fighting to defend their homeland. In the next century, the rhythm of raid and counterraids was more balanced and relative safety was gradually restored to Asia Minor.

Konstantinos V

Leon died on 18 June, 741, in his mid-fifties, and was buried in the imperial mausoleum of the Holy Apostles. He was succeeded by his son Konstantinos, who was twenty-two, but the succession was quickly contested by Artabasdos, the new emperor's older brother-in-law and general of Opsikion. This precipitated the first true civil war of this period, in which all the armies picked sides (as opposed to a strike by one army against a sitting emperor, which was the trend in the period 698–717). Unfortunately, our sources are poor and so we cannot reconstruct the politics of this war. Konstantinos would later allude to the slanders brought against him by his relatives during it, including perhaps the accusation that he was "alienated from God." Nor can we date the war precisely: it lasted for just over two years, either 741–743 or 742–744. Artabasdos sprang his rebellion at the beginning of a joint expedition against the Arabs. Konstantinos was taken by surprise but fled to Amorion and won over the Anatolikon army; he was later joined by the Thrakesion. But Constantinople was betrayed to Artabasdos, whose son Nikephoros commanded the armies in Thrace. From the capital, the rebel issued coins and received embassies. Our pro-icon sources also say that he "restored icons," but it is unclear what that means or if it is true (the enemy of any "iconomach" was automatically taken to be pro-icon). Artabasdos won over the army of Armeniakon, placing it under his son Niketas.[31]

Konstantinos was the better strategist. When Artabasdos and the Opsikion attacked western Asia Minor in the second year of the war, Konstantinos defeated him near Sardeis and then defeated his son Niketas and the Armeniakon near Nikaia. With the fleet now on his side, Konstantinos blockaded the capital, and defeated Artabasdos again when the latter came out and offered battle. The blockade lasted for over a year and caused famine. In the third year, Konstantinos defeated Niketas again near Nikomedeia and took Constantinople. Artabasdos fled but was captured near Nikaia. With the flair for theatrical display that would mark his reign, Konstantinos paraded his captives in the hippodrome during the games, then blinded and exiled them, along with their chief supporters.

Konstantinos V had displayed extraordinary military talent and leadership. He would go on to reign for another thirty years as one of the most dynamic rulers in Roman history. He secured Romanía's safety, reformed its armed forces in ways that set the tone for the next two centuries, and placed Constantinople on a long-term trajectory of growth. He liked music, dancing, banquets, and handsome men, and was not defensive about these non-ascetic tastes. He also set up images of hunting and chariot racing. Had any sources survived that were favorable to him, we might find in them a larger-than-life figure, one who was later reported to have slain a dragon. As it is, we can barely glimpse the events of his reign through the meager reports of later writers, or understand his policies through the hatred and vitriol that were heaped on him by the partisans of icons ("this pernicious, crazed, bloodthirsty, and most savage beast . . . led astray by magic," "this dragon that has us in his power," etc.). Their quality is summed up by the tale that he defecated during his baptism, earning the moniker Kopronymos, "Shit-Name." But the bishops who assembled at the Council of Hiereia in 754 rightly hailed him as a "New Constantine."[32]

Konstantinos had much to rebuild. A series of powerful earthquakes had destroyed many buildings and parts of the walls of Constantinople in 740. Leon and Konstantinos had begun the repairs, as attested by many inscriptions placed on the towers that they rebuilt, which are still there. Another victim of the quakes was the church of St. Eirene, which Konstantinos rebuilt in the later 750s, giving us the large version that we have today. The apse mosaic consisted simply of a large black cross (see Figure 29). This used to be taken as a declaration of iconoclasm but it may have been a banal continuation of local tradition. A recent argument attributes the renovation to Eirene *after* she had

Figure 29 Nave and cross in the apse of the church of St. Eirene (Istanbul).
Shutterstock/MehmetO

restored icons, further proving that the cross was not part of the culture war over icons.[33]

In the late 740s, bubonic plague swept through the eastern Mediterranean, the last outbreak of the Justinianic plague that had first visited Constantinople in 542. This time it ravaged the City for about a year, 747–748. We have a graphic description of mass death, the hallucinations seen by the ill, and a method that was improvised to cart away so many bodies by laying planks across yoked beasts of burden. To avoid the contagion, the emperor left the City and governed from Nikomedeia via correspondence. While it was an exaggeration to say that "the City was left almost uninhabited" after this, the emperor brought many families from Greece and the islands to replenish its population. In 766/7, Constantinople suffered a severe drought, so Konstantinos imported thousands of craftsmen from Asia Minor and Thrace and they repaired the aqueduct of Valens, which had been out of commission since the early seventh century (see Figure 9). Both water and people began to flow again into the capital.[34]

The emperor was laying the foundations for sustained growth, and he took advantage of the decline of the Umayyad caliphate. By the 740s, Muslim expansion had been stretched too thin and stalled on all fronts, and the caliphate's neighbors had learned how to fight back. The caliphs were finding it harder to reward their close supporters with plunder and the proceeds of new conquest. At the same time, the uncertainty about political legitimacy that was inherent in the Muslim Arab empire was producing multiple concurrent rebellions against the dynasty's authority. One of the most well-executed came from the Abbasids, who, despite being ethnically Arab, rallied support among non-Arab Muslim converts, who had been marginalized in the Umayyad system, as well as among the Shia. They carefully built a secret network of opposition to the Umayyads, which then rebelled openly from its bases in northeastern Persia in the late 740s. By 750, the Umayyads were defeated and massacred, even in violation of assurances of their safety if they surrendered. The Abbasids now took over, allowing more room for non-Arab Muslims and even non-Muslims in the administration of the empire. The new dynasty presided over a flourishing civilization, distinguished by its wealth, literature, and philosophy. However, Muslim political authority remained tenuous under them as well, and their caliphate began to disintegate within a century under the pressure of centrifugal forces. For now, the base of the new dynasty was in Iraq and Iran, not Syria, which shifted attention away from the Roman border, especially after the foundation of Baghdad in the 760s.

Raids into Asia Minor became rarer after 741, and the Romans took advantage of this. Konstantinos sent raids of his own into the caliphate and personally led two major incursions, one in ca. 745 against the region of Germanikeia, and another in ca. 751 against Theodosiopolis and Melitene. He carried away thousands from those cities and their territories, possibly even hundreds of thousands, including Armenians and Syriac-speaking Monophysite Christians, and resettled them in fortified settlements in Thrace. By depopulating the eastern frontier zone, he made it harder for Arabs to mount raids from those cities, and by repopulating the frontier in Thrace he created a bulwark against the Bulgars.[35] It is indicative of ethnic perceptions that Constantinople was repopulated by people from Greece but not from Syria and Armenia.

The Bulgars, however, objected to the settlements. Breaking a long-standing peace in ca. 756, they raided Thrace and reached the environs of Constantinople, demanding payment in order to tolerate the new forts (seeing the latter, perhaps, as violations of the treaty of 716). This raid ignited hostilities between the two allied powers that would last for over sixty years. For the rest of his reign, Konstantinos used the Bulgars as his punching bag, launching about ten campaigns against them, some involving coordinated land-and-sea operations, with the army marching against Bulgaria from the south and the fleet entering the river and attacking the Bulgars from the north. The brief notices we have about these wars suggest that Konstantinos usually emerged victorious. A lover of spectacle, he celebrated two triumphs in Constantinople, the first on record since the days of Herakleios. They featured parades of spoils and captives bound by wooden shackles. The City was adorned with "images on walls commemorating his victories in war and rout of the barbarians." But he also used diplomacy to negotiate truces, plant agents among the Bulgars, and destabilize their leadership.[36] The Bulgar state appears to have been weak and unstable, but it would not long remain so.

At the same time, in the early 760s, Konstantinos reformed the imperial army. The revolt of Artabasdos had shown how dangerous the Opsikion was. It had repeatedly demonstrated its willingness to make and unmake emperors, and was stationed too close to the capital. Konstantinos entrusted it to men who held lower court titles, thereby making its command less prestigious, and by the early 760s he had revamped the old palace guards, the *scholai* and excubitors, to be elite fighting forces and enforcers of the imperial will; they were attached to the emperor under the command of the *domestikos* of the *scholai*. The army thus acquired two tiers: the fully professional soldiers of these new battalions (*tagmata*), who were better paid and stationed in Constantinople, and the provincial armies of Asia Minor, which were descended from the field armies of the fourth–seventh centuries and were now increasingly being called *themata*. Subsequent emperors added more *tagmata*, whose leaders often functioned as overall commanders of the imperial army. Then, after a great plot in 765/6, in which the *komes* of Opsikion was implicated, the emperor broke that army into three parts, detaching from it the Boukellarion and Optimaton (the latter used as a support, supply, and transport unit for other forces). The three resulting armies were smaller and so individually less of a threat to the throne, for they were now under separate commanders and geographically discrete. This subdivision of the old field armies was continued by subsequent emperors. The major conquests to come would be carried out by this army of territorially smaller provincial *themata* wrapped around a core of elite *tagmata*.[37]

Konstantinos V and icons

As for icons, just as Leon III had taken no (documented) action in the decade after announcing his policy in 730, so too Konstantinos did nothing during the first decade of his reign. As late as ca. 768, during renovations to Hagia Sophia, the patriarch Niketas altered the mosaics in an upper-level conference room so that they depicted crosses instead of images of Christ and the saints, and he plastered over similar images in another room. The changes can be seen today, and were made with great care; this was not a violent act of destruction. In other words, images of Christ remained prominent in busy rooms of Hagia Sophia for decades during the reign of this "iconoclast" and his handpicked patriarchs.[38] What did iconoclasm mean for them, then?

It was only in the 750s that Konstantinos began to propagate his views on icons through speeches and a pamphlet of *Inquiries* (*Peuseis*) addressed to bishops. A major plank of his argument was to marshal quotations from previous Church writers that supported his view of icons and thereby proved the orthodoxy of his position (the iconophiles would later become obsessed with arguing that these testimonies were forged or written by heretics). Konstantinos' original works have not survived, though we can partially glimpse the *Peuseis* from its refutation by the pro-icon patriarch Nikephoros (in office 806–815). Two of its arguments proved to be consequential. The first was based on the Chalcedonian understanding of the union of the divine and human in Christ: an icon cannot depict the divine, and so it must split off the human alone in a manner reminiscent of "Nestorios." This was effectively a response to the Council in Troullo, which argued that Christ not only can but should be depicted in human form because God chose to be incarnated as a man. Konstantinos' second argument was that the true "image" of Christ is the Eucharist, as Christ himself had intended.[39]

Konstantinos convened a Council to ratify these views in 754. It was held at the palace of Hiereia, on the Asian coast of the Sea of Marmara near Chalkedon, between February and August. It was attended by 338 bishops, almost all of them from the patriarchate of Constantinople, yet the patriarch himself had just died so the Council was chaired by the bishop Theodosios of Ephesos, son of the emperor Apsimar-Tiberios. The final session of the Council, which declared itself to be the Seventh Ecumenical Council, was held in the church of the Virgin at Blachernai in Constantinople. We have its *Horos*, or *Decree*, from the Acts of the Council of Nicaea II (787), which convened to overturn it. This *Horos* explains the arguments against icons and frames them within a narrative of creeping idolatry, introduced by Lucifer and countered first by Jesus (relating to ancient paganism) and then by the current emperors (Konstantinos V and his crowned son Leon IV, who was four at the time of the Council). The *Horos* ends with prohibitions and anathemas, including against anyone who makes a religious image or venerates it, though, the bishops warn, no one is to lay hands on valuable vessels, cloths, or anything that has actual *use* in a church simply because it has images on it; the emperor and the patriarch had to give approval for that. The Council condemned the ex-patriarch Germanos, a certain Georgios (otherwise unknown), and Mansour, which was the Arabic patronymic of John of Damascus, who had been writing works in defense of icons from inside the caliphate. After appointing a new patriarch, on 27 August the assembly gathered the people of Constantinople in the forum of Constantine and publicly proclaimed the Council's findings.[40]

The *Horos* is a frustrating document. It bans the manufacture and worship of religious images, but does not call for the destruction of existing ones. Does this mean that existing images could stay in place so long as they were not venerated? Was it the attitude of the viewer that mattered, rather than the image itself? The *Horos* also rejected images of the Virgin and the saints, which clearly did not face the same theological problems as those of Jesus, but it offered a lame argument for this rejection: holy figures should not be honored with the pagan arts of painting. But why did this not also apply to images of the emperor?

Finally, the *Horos* does not seem to have been enforced. We know of almost no icon destruction taking place under Konstantinos V. The rhetorical denunciations by later iconophiles do not provide good evidence to the contrary, because they are vague, hysterical, and untrustworthy. For example, they often claim that Konstantinos scorned the Virgin (along with the saints and their relics). But this is mere slander, amply refuted by the reverential tone in which he and Hiereia speak of the Virgin and saints. After all, the Council's final session took place in her church at Blachernai, and it was likely this emperor who built the church of the Virgin of the Pharos in the Great Palace; he betrothed his son Leon to Eirene of Athens in that church in 769.[41]

The production of new images was probably curtailed. The images in the upstairs rooms of Hagia Sophia were replaced with crosses, but that was over ten years after Hiereia and done during the course of renovations. The apse mosaic in the church of the Dormition at Nikaia was also replaced with a cross (see Figure 30), and it is possible that the church of the Virgin at Blachernai, where the last session of the Council took place, was whitewashed or painted with floral motifs. There is a debate over whether some small provincial churches from this period were adorned with floral motifs rather than religious images, though this too may have simply continued older traditions and not been due to a concern over icons. That concern, moreover, was not over icons per se but their veneration, so removal or destruction would have targeted only the most prominent ones. It is possible that the sculpted icons on the templon of the church of St. Polyeuktos were defaced and taken to the basement (which is how they survived), but we do not know when this occurred; it could have been during the "Second Iconoclasm" of the ninth century or even in Ottoman times (see Figure 31).[42] On the other hand, few images survive in the empire that were made before the eighth century, unlike at Rome and Sinai. Some scholars attribute this to iconoclasm, whereas others attribute it to the ravages of history, which affected Romanía far more than Rome and Sinai, or to the fact that images were not part of the traditional repertoire of churches in Asia Minor. The images of St. Demetrios in his church at Thessalonike were left alone even though they were well within the emperor's reach (see Plate 4b).

There is no reliable evidence for repression or opposition to Konstantinos' position. No bishops are said to have dissented from the new policy or to have been deposed because of it. Apparently, the emperor required state officials and soldiers to swear that they would not venerate icons.[43] Iconoskepticism was likely used as a badge of loyalty to the regime, not a policy to be implemented universally. Later iconophiles insinuated that the great plot of 765/6 had something to do with icons, but even their accounts, stripped of political context as they are, do not support this. The conspirators included many top officials: two ex-logothetes of the *dromos* (one currently the general of Sicily), the *domestikos* of the excubitors, and the *komes* of Opsikion. Many were executed. The patriarch Konstantinos, who had been appointed at the Council of Hiereia, was implicated

Figure 30 Image of the Virgin and Christ that replaced a cross (whose outline can still be seen in the background) in the apse of the Koimesis church of Nikaia.
Photo by David Hendrix

too. At first he was exiled, but a year later he was brought back and made to endure a horrifying series of public tortures and humiliations before being beheaded, and his head was hung from the Milion for three days. These events represented a major upheaval in Constantinopolitan society that lasted for years, as the circle of suspects widened. But it was likely only political. Not even the later iconophile sources claimed that the conspirators were interested in icons.

The emperor was also concerned about seditious monks independently of the issue of icons. One of the threads that unraveled during the great plot involved monks who were "encouraging many people to take up the monastic life and

Figure 31 Defaced images of holy figures from St. Polyeuktos, found in the church's excavated basement. Their original location is unknown, as is the date and purpose of their mutilation.
Photo by David Hendrix

scorn imperial dignities and money." The ascetic leader Stephanos was executed over this during that tense year. His highly embellished biography was written forty years later and implausibly links his execution to his defense of icons because, in the changed environment of the early ninth century, that was becoming a passport to sainthood. The text describes the popular assemblies convened by the emperor, who interacted with the crowd in operatic style and staged plays of redemption for officials who had lapsed and become monks.[44] Even if these are fictional accounts, it is likely that Konstantinos, a worldly man, *was* offended by the conversion of his officials to monasticism and the disparagement of secular pursuits by religious activists. Allegedly, he forced some monks to renounce their vows and parade in the hippodrome holding the hand of a woman and being spat on by the people. Other monks were "forced or tricked into accepting money, imperial offices, and marriages." This all sounds strange, and smacks of distortion. The reality was likely that Konstantinos had barred secular officials from becoming monks, which previous emperors had decreed too, and this was how he now publicly nullified their monastic vows.[45]

Konstantinos is said to have secularized one monastery, turning it into a barracks (for the newly formed *tagmata*?), and to have destroyed others. These acts can be given perfectly banal explanations in light of his renovation of the City.[46] But his general Michael Lachanodrakon, of Thrakesion, is said to have persecuted monks in Ephesos around 770, a policy for which no explanation is given in the sources, not even icons.[47] The regime was not waging a war against monks in general—plenty of monasteries accepted the new policy on icons, whatever that was exactly—nor is it even clear that it was attacking monks who were vocally pro-icon. By stripping out context, our sources made it hard to understand these events, which occurred within a tight time frame.[48]

Some scholars have argued that iconoclasm was an attempt by the imperial Church to control the wild power of charismatic saints, holy men, and monks, and tighten up the profusion of sacred power that icons represented. The evidence, however, suggests that the policy was precisely about icons and the seemingly idolatrous forms of worship that they enabled. It was not an attack on the idea of intercession either: the *Horos* of 754 stipulates that saints and the Virgin can intercede on our behalf but they must be addressed through prayer rather than painted wood. Iconophile writers say that toward the end of his reign Konstantinos questioned the intercessory power of saints, though this cannot be verified.[49]

The loss of Ravenna

Where Konstantinos V failed, or made little effort, was Italy. By the early 740s, the imperial presence in the center and north of the peninsula was nominal. The two main powers were the Lombard king Liudprand (712–744), who was trying to annex as much of the exarchate and duchy of Rome as he could, and the pope, who was trying to block Liudprand and wanted to claim Ravenna as a papal protectorate, and the balance of power between pope and exarch had now tilted in favor of Rome. The pope at this time was Zacharias (741–752), the last of the Greek popes (possibly an Athenian), who had translated into Greek the *Dialogues* of pope Gregory I, after which that work entered Greek intellectual life. Zacharias managed to shield Ravenna for a while, but the city fell to the Lombard king Aistulf in 751. Konstantinos V sent envoys but they were unable to persuade Aistulf to return it. The new pope, Stephen II (752–757), invited the emperor to come with an army and deliver Italy from the Lombards, but no army arrived from Constantinople. Throughout these events, the popes were acting as loyal subjects of the emperor and the issue of images never came up.[50]

Lombard power threatened Rome's security and papal ambitions. As the empire was no longer balancing out the Italian triangle of power, pope Stephen turned to the Franks. He traveled across the Alps in 753 and met king Pippin (751–768), inviting him to intervene in Italy. Present at the meeting was Pippin's eleven-year-old son and eventual successor Charles, the future Charlemagne. Pippin was the first of the Carolingian kings and had only recently secured his elevation to the throne with papal support. He marched into Italy twice, forced the Lombards out of Ravenna and the Pentapolis, and gave the exarchate to the pope. Konstantinos V sent envoys to persuade Pippin with promises of gifts to restore the exarchate to Constantinople, but Pippin was too "devoted to St. Peter."[51]

Thus, Ravenna and the exarchate were forever lost to Constantinople. This had significant consequences. The empire lost a major stake in Italian politics and was henceforth confined to the south, though it retained a loose hegemony over Istria and Venetia. Italian history embarked on a different trajectory. A papal state had effectively replaced the exarchate in central and northern Italy, though the popes too, like the exarchs before them, struggled to hold it together. Still, a later emperor in Constantinople acknowledged that Rome "was no longer part of the empire" and had its "own self-rule, under the pope of the day."[52] In the new papal view the *res publica* was henceforth that of St. Peter, not the eastern empire. In fact, as this new Republic leaned heavily on its Roman identity, it began to deny the Romanness of the eastern empire, tacitly at first but later openly. In the second half of the century, papal correspondence began to call the easterners and their empire "Greek" instead of Roman. This label was pejorative. In writing to Pippin, pope Stephen referred to the "pestiferous malice" of the Greeks.[53] Then, when little Charles grew up and claimed the title "emperor of the Romans"—even though there were no Romans of whom he was the emperor—the Frankish realm developed its own ways of denying eastern Romanness. These ideological moves still shape western perceptions of "Byzantium."

More ominously for the long-term, in writing to Pippin the pope explained that war against the enemies of the Church of Rome was now a religious obligation.[54] Rome was authorizing its armed "sons" to attack its enemies. Anyone who did not accept Rome's ecclesiastical sovereignty was eventually labeled an enemy of the Church, with dire consequences for Romanía.

The empire did, however, maintain a presence in the south, and not only in the lands that it directly controlled. The duchy of Naples was de facto autonomous but often sided with Constantinople and remained a center of Greek culture. Even the Lombard dukes of Benevento could be drawn into the empire's orbit. Arechis II (758–787) built his own cathedral of Hagia Sophia and, when he feared Frankish aggression, offered to submit to Constantinople, pledging to dress and cut his hair in the eastern fashion.[55] Moreover, local hierarchies and social structures emerged from the administrative and legal matrix that the eastern empire had brought to Italy, as shown by titles, personal names, and the language of power, which used the Greek version for the names of Roman offices (even when those had originally come from Latin). When Rome and the Lombards looked to the Roman past for validation, they were really looking sideways to the east Roman present, albeit without acknowledgement. Popes quietly appropriated the symbols and prestige of eastern Romanness, even while they openly attacked Constantinople as un-Roman.[56]

Having lost central Italy, Constantinople strengthened its hold on the south. At some point in the eighth century, the churches of Sicily and Calabria were removed from the jurisdiction of the Church of Rome and transferred to that of

Constantinople. It used to be believed that this was done by Leon III in order to punish the papacy for not accepting iconoclasm, and that he also transferred the churches of Illyricum to Constantinople. But no such action by Leon is attested. As we saw, the churches of Illyricum were functionally under Constantinople since the seventh century. The transfer of Sicily likely took place in the 750s (and is attested in 785).[57] The detached sees, from Reggio and Syracuse to Athens, Thessalonike, and Crete, were mostly Greek-speaking, so this transfer consolidated Romanía as a primarily ethnic Roman state with a unified government and Church.

In August, 775, Konstantinos set out on campaign against the Bulgars, but fell ill and had to be carried back. He died on 14 September, and was buried in the imperial mausoleum. He had managed to stabilize Romanía and set it on a path of growth and revival. In this he was aided by the collapse of the Umayyad caliphate. Still, he had faithfully played the role of a New Constantine, refounding the City, creating mobile armies for campaigns, and convening a Council that in his mind had cleansed Christianity of idolatry. He had also planned for the succession. Little could he have known at the time of his death that his legacy would be undone by a girl from Athens.

21

Reform and Consolidation (775–814)

The rise of Eirene

Eirene was not the court's first choice of bride for the young prince Leon. That was king Pippin's daughter, Gisela. Konstantinos V tried to woo the Franks away from a papal alliance and align them with Constantinople. He sent them gifts, including, in 757, an organ, an instrument unknown in the west.[1] At Constantinople it had been used since antiquity to accompany court ceremonies and hippodrome games (where it is depicted on the base of the Egyptian obelisk). It was an accessory of imperial power, not used in churches. In 765, Konstantinos proposed a marriage between Leon and Gisela.[2] Leon, who was half-Khazar on his mother's side, was born in 750 and made co-emperor a year later. He was the first prince to be born in a chamber of the palace that was covered in porphyry marble or hangings, after which he was called "Born in the Purple" (*porphyrogennetos*).[3] The court was investing in boosting the prestige of its brand. In proposing the match, Konstantinos was perhaps hoping for the return of Ravenna. But Pippin stuck with Rome. In 767, he convened a council at Gentilly to investigate the matter of icons. After a debate between Roman and Constantinopolitan advocates, it found for Rome. In 769, a Lateran synod at Rome condemned the Council of Hiereia as heretical.[4]

Constantinople was also investing in Greece, which may explain the choice of Eirene, though we know little about her background. The Parthenon, now a church of the Virgin, was becoming a major site of Christian pilgrimage. Imperial control was solid in Attica and most of Boiotia but beyond that, in Thessaly and the Peloponnese, lay a fuzzy frontier of territories controlled by Slavic chiefs who were being gradually absorbed into the imperial system. Greece was ringed about by bishoprics, from Aigina and Monembasia in the east to Zakynthos and Kephalonia in the west. These were loyal to the capital and could spread the faith to the interior—a second Christianization.[5] Konstantinos had relocated thousands of people from Greece and the islands to Constantinople, and Eirene strengthened these ties.

The teenage bride was brought to the capital by ship and was likely escorted by eunuchs who instructed her in court protocol. Her life was henceforth dominated by ceremonies, in which she was required to do little but pose regally as the dance of courtesies and acclamations swirled around her. She was brought to the City from the palace of Hiereia by an imperial ship on 1 November, 769, and there received by senators and their wives. Two days later, the patriarch celebrated her betrothal to Leon in the church of the Pharos. On 17 December, she was crowned empress in the Augousteas hall of the palace before processing to the church of St. Stephen, where she was married to Leon. We have detailed protocols for these ceremonies, which involved a long series of gestures, movements, prayers, changes of attire, and acclamations. At many points, the highest court dignitaries bowed before the new empress, reciting lines in Latin ("Bene, bene, Augusta!") and Greek ("Many years!).[6] A year later, on 14 January, 771, in the Porphyra room Eirene gave birth to Konstantinos VI, named after his grandfather. This triggered another round of receptions in the palace, with acclamations and blessings, and an assembly of the people in the hippodrome, with antiphonal chanting led by the racing teams ("A good day for victories!"). The court treated the entire City to *lochozema*, a drink special to such occasions, set out in large quantities along the boulevards. The infant was baptized in Hagia Sophia.[7] These ceremonies were the rhythm of life of the capital. They communicated intent, marked continuities and changes, and ratified popular support for the regime.

Another round of ceremonies was triggered by the death of Konstantinos V in 775. His body was conveyed from the palace to the imperial mausoleum along the Mese, accompanied by a military procession and chants ("Go forth emperor, the King of Kings summons you!").[8] Eirene also attended political ceremonies. A few months before she was brought to Constantinople, her father-in-law had elevated two of his sons by his third wife, Christophoros and Nikephoros, to the rank of Caesar.[9] Leon IV was the senior emperor, but they were potential rivals within the extended family. Eirene now saw how that problem could be solved. Leon used the money that his father had saved up to win over the people, senators, and soldiers in the City. Then, the military commanders demanded that he crown his son emperor too. To overcome his (ritual) reluctance, Leon asked in return that everyone swear an oath to accept his son as emperor if he himself should die. This popular oath was sworn at a ceremony in the hippodrome and signed in document form by all parties. On Easter Sunday, 776, Konstantinos VI was made co-emperor in the hippodrome. One month later, the Caesar Nikephoros and possibly his brother Christophoros as well were accused of plotting a revolution; the conspirators were whipped and exiled to the Crimea.[10]

Leon IV died after five years on the throne (775–780). He does not appear to have taken any "iconoclastic" action, but then again neither did his father for most of his reign. The only reported incident is the expulsion of some high-ranking eunuchs from the palace for icon worship, after a whipping, which is both trivial and likely distorted in the telling.[11] Arab raiding continued, though the Romans held their own. A large expedition in 777/8, under the formidable Michael Lachanodrakon and a number of Armenian generals, attacked Germanikeia and rounded up more Syrians, who were resettled in Thrace. A retaliatory Arab attack the next year reached Dorylaion, but Roman strategy proved its worth: the emperor ordered his generals to avoid battle, fortify all places with garrisons, harass the Arabs from behind if they sent out raiding parties, and burn the horse pastures ahead of them. The Arabs and their horses grew hungry after two weeks, and they left. They tested the defenses of Amorion on the way back, but found them too strong.[12] This was textbook "defense-in-depth."

When Leon died on 8 September, 780, Eirene was in her twenties and their son Konstantinos VI was ten. There is no evidence of a regency committee or male supervisors for the young heir. Mother and son jointly held the rank of Augusta and Augustus. While only Konstantinos appeared on the front of the gold coins (with Leon III, Konstantinos V, and Leon IV on the back), Eirene was determined to make her own decisions as the adult co-emperor. One month into their joint reign, suspicion of a plot fell on a host of top officials, including the logothete of the *dromos*, a former general of the Armeniakon, the *domestikos* of the excubitors, the *droungarios* (i.e., admiral) of the Dodecanese, and others. They were whipped, tonsured, and exiled. Also implicated were the former Caesars, Leon IV's half-brothers. Eirene forced them to become priests and to publicly give communion at the Christmas service, 780, while she watched. Eirene had acquired the dynasty's flair for powerful theater. Her rise reveals the extent of power that a woman could wield in the court system if she were as ruthless as her male counterparts.[13]

Eirene also realized that military men were the greatest threat to her, and so she relied heavily on palace eunuchs. They could not claim the throne, depended absolutely on her favor, and lacked families to divide their loyalties. Moreover, she could meet with them privately without violating gender norms of female modesty. After all, it was eunuchs who had taught her how to survive at the court from the moment of her arrival. They were experts at choreographing her ceremonies and formal appearances to project power. Her chief eunuchs were the *sakellarios* (fiscal official) Ioannes, whom she also put in charge of the armies of Asia Minor; the patrician Staurakios, who became logothete of the *dromos*; and the patrician Theodoros, whom she sent with a large fleet to Sicily to suppress the general Elpidios, who was implicated in the conspiracy. Elpidios fled to the Arabs in North Africa, and Eirene, with striking vindictiveness, had his wife and sons flogged and tonsured.[14]

Eirene sought good relations with the Franks. Charlemagne had conquered the Lombard kingdom in Italy in 774 and so now ruled Constantinople's former territories around Ravenna. He had close ties with the papacy and was encroaching on the south, potentially threatening the imperial provinces there. An alliance was therefore advantageous. Eirene sent envoys to Aachen, where Charlemagne often resided, proposing a match between his daughter Rotrud and Konstantinos VI, and the proposal was accepted. A palace eunuch was left behind to instruct the girl "in Greek language and literature and the customs of the Roman empire."[15]

On the international stage, Eirene and her underage son were overshadowed in the west by the spectacular expansion of the empire of Charlemagne and in the east by the apogee of the Abbasid caliphate, which was about to receive its greatest caliph, Harun al-Rashid (786–809). In 782, Harun was a dashing teenage prince and his coming-out party, a gift from his father, the caliph al-Mahdi, was a full-scale invasion of Asia Minor to be led by the prince. The main column reached Chrysopolis, across from the capital, while other units attacked Phrygia and Asia, defeating Lachanodrakon. But the Romans responded strategically and the Arabs found themselves surrounded, whereupon they offered to negotiate a withdrawal. However, Staurakios and the *domestikos* of the *tagmata* went to the meeting without precautions and were captured. Eirene had to agree to a three-year annual tribute to get them back—90,000 nomismata—whereupon the Arabs departed with vast plunder.[16] Harun developed a taste for invading Romanía.

After that humiliation, Staurakios needed a win. In 783, Eirene sent him with an army against the Slavs. He marched past Thessalonike, down into Greece, and entered the Peloponnese. His was the first imperial army to reach this region in over a century. Our chronicle entry says only that he "subjugated all the Slavs and made them tributaries to the polity." The process of absorbing the Peloponnese back into imperial administration had begun, although it had a long way to go. Staurakios returned in January, 784, to celebrate his victory in the hippodrome. In May, the emperors paraded through Thrace, to the accompaniment of an organ and band. Eirene refounded Beroe (Stara Zagora), a city that had been abandoned since ca. 700, as Eirenopolis, a bold declaration of her imperial standing. An inscription found in 2005 confirms the rebuilding of the town by "Konstantinos and Eirene, the all-wise rulers of the Romans." The pair also entered Philippopolis and repaired the walls at Anchialos. This jaunt was likely only the celebrity aspect of a deeper extension of administrative control over Thrace, whose mundane aspects are not recorded. It significantly extended the empire's control in the Balkans.[17]

The restoration of icons

By late 784, if not sooner, Eirene had decided to overturn Hiereia and restore the veneration of icons. Her reasoning is unknown. It does not appear that large segments of society held strong views about icons, either way. The bishops largely went along with imperial policy. They had signed off on Monotheletism in 712, and condemned it the next year. Likewise, they signed off on Hiereia in 754, and then embraced Nicaea II in 787, with little dissent. They embraced iconoskepticism again after 815, only to revert to iconophilia in 843, always dancing to the court's tune. There is little evidence for widespread monastic

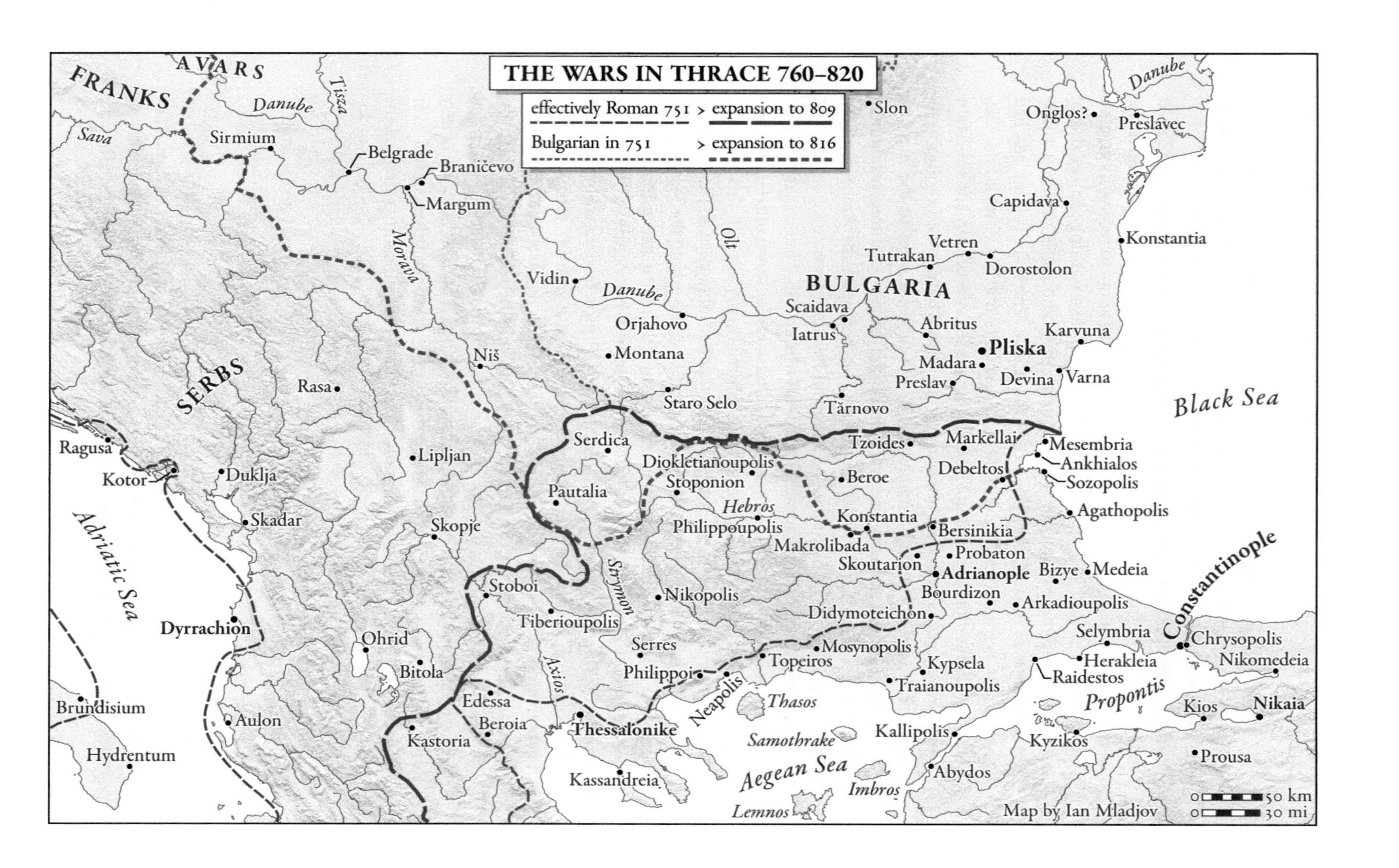
THE WARS IN THRACE 760–820
effectively Roman 751
> expansion to 809
Bulgarian in 751
> expansion to 816
FRANKS
AVARS
Sava
Danube
Tisza
Sirmium
Belgrade
Braničevo
Margum
Morava
Vidin
Danube
Olt
Slon
Onglos?
Preslavec
Danube
Capidava
Konstantia
Tutrakan
Vetren
Dorostolon
BULGARIA
Scaidava
Iatrus
Orjahovo
Montana
Abritus
Pliska
Karvuna
Madara
Devina
Varna
Preslav
Niš
Staro Selo
Tărnovo
Black Sea
SERBS
Rasa
Ragusa
Kotor
Duklja
Lipljan
Serdica
Tzoides
Markellai
Mesembria
Ankhialos
Sozopolis
Debeltos
Diokletianoupolis
Stoponion
Beroe
Pautalia
Hebros
Skadar
Adriatic Sea
Skopje
Philippoupolis
Konstantia
Makrolibada
Bersinikia
Agathopolis
Probaton
Skoutarion
Adrianople
Bizye
Medeia
Constantinople
Stoboi
Strymon
Nikopolis
Bourdizon
Arkadioupolis
Tiberioupolis
Didymoteichon
Dyrrachion
Ohrid
Serres
Mosynopolis
Selymbria
Chrysopolis
Bitola
Axios
Philippoi
Topeiros
Kypsela
Herakleia
Nikomedeia
Raidestos
Traianoupolis
Edessa
Neapolis
Thasos
Proponti
Brundisium
Aulon
Beroia
Thessalonike
Kallipolis
Kios
Nikaia
Kastoria
Samothrake
Kyzikos
Hydrentum
Aegean Sea
Prousa
Kassandreia
Abydos
Imbros
Lemnos
Map by Ian Mladjov
0 50 km
0 30 mi

opposition to Leon III and Konstantinos V, such as would develop against "Second Iconoclasm" in the ninth century. Conversely, there is also little evidence that iconoclasm was enforced, and certainly there was no "persecution." Moreover, the theological needle had not moved since Hiereia. The Council that Eirene convened revealed no knowledge of the works of John of Damascus defending icons, and theologically it was less sophisticated than Hiereia. However, one rationale that Eirene gave to the Council for reversing Hiereia was convincing: the Church of Constantinople was now alienated from all other Chalcedonian Churches, both of the east and the west, and it was time to repair that rift.[18]

The armies also adopted whatever position the emperors demanded, with one exception. Certain elements of the *tagmata* were fiercely loyal to the memory of Konstantinos V and to the oaths that they had taken to uphold his position on icons. Eirene may have been aiming to appropriate the dynasty's use of oaths for her own benefit (and that of her son). If she could disrupt the scene with another Council, and link loyalty to her with a new official policy on icons, she could then require critical stakeholders to invest in her success. It would also draw out any potentially disloyal elements.

Eirene appointed a layman, Tarasios, to the patriarchate, on Christmas 784. He was the chief imperial secretary (*protasekretis*) and knew how to follow orders. Letters were sent to pope Hadrian inviting him to come to the planned Council or send delegates, as well as to the eastern patriarchs, to ensure that the Council was properly Ecumenical, unlike Hiereia. Hadrian sent delegates, but his response to the emperors demanded that formerly papal lands in southern Italy be restored to him; that the jurisdiction over the churches of Calabria, Sicily, and Illyricum return to Rome; and that the patriarch stop referring to himself as "ecumenical," which was "heretical." The Council ignored these demands, although Hadrian's letter was read aloud, and they were later omitted from the Greek version of the *Acts*. As for the eastern patriarchs, it is not clear whether they sent delegates or even consented to the Council. But two eastern churchmen were nonetheless produced who acted as if they were delegates.[19]

The Council got off to a rocky start. It convened in the Holy Apostles church of Constantinople on 1 August, 786, but the meeting was disrupted by several bishops, perhaps ten in all, and the soldiers of the *tagmata*, who entered the church with a commotion, objecting to the proceedings (iconophile texts later embellished them with drawn swords and threats of violence). Eirene postponed the Council, but planned her moves carefully. On the pretext of an Arab campaign, she sent the *tagmata* to Asia Minor, replacing them in the City with units from Thrace under generals loyal to her. It was probably at this time that she created the *tagma* of the *vigla* or *arithmos*, and recruited soldiers into all the *tagmata* that would be loyal to her. She then disbanded the leading elements of the military opposition, and transferred them and their families—6,000 people—to provincial posts.[20]

A year later, in late 787, Eirene was ready to try again, this time at Nikaia, without military interference. Around 340 bishops and 132 monks met in the local church of Hagia Sophia between 24 September and 13 October (see Figure 32). They proclaimed Hiereia heretical and branded iconoclasts as "those who accuse the Christians" (i.e., of idolatry), but the Council did not name these iconoclasts, and certainly did not repudiate Leon III or Konstantinos V, the ancestors of the current emperor. The Council's iconophile position was a foregone conclusion, decided in advance by the court. The Seventh Ecumenical Council was now to be Nicaea II, and not Hiereia. Like the Sixth a century earlier, it too was a mostly philological exercise, producing many testimonia for the veneration of icons, defending the authenticity of those texts, and proving that iconoclastic proof texts were either forgeries or heretical.

The Council's theology did not go much beyond the idea of Troullo that images of Christ remind us that God became incarnate for our salvation. It drew a distinction between worship, which is due to God only, and veneration, which passes through an image to its prototype. This idea picked up St. Basil the Great's theory (in the fourth century) about how imperial images worked, and extended it into the religious sphere. The Second Commandment was not an obstacle because God himself had ordered Moses to decorate the tabernacle. Iconoclasm was put down to foreign influence or heresy, though repentant iconoclast bishops were allowed to keep their positions. Thus, "we decree . . . that venerable and holy images, made in colors or mosaic or other fitting materials . . . are to be dedicated in the holy churches of God, on sacred vessels and vestments, on walls and panels, in houses and in the streets . . . . In their honor an offering of incense and lights is to be made, in accordance with the pious custom of the men of old."[21]

The assembly then sailed to Constantinople, where, in the Magnaura hall, they presented their *Horos* to "the emperors New Constantine and Eirene the New Helena," referring to the first Christian emperor, who had convened the First Ecumenical Council of Nicaea, and his mother. The emperors signed the *Horos*—the first time an empress ever did this. Eirene had successfully linked the Church's profession of faith to loyalty to her and her son. Soon after the Council, she began to appear on the regime's coins, to the right of her son (the left position was that of greater honor). Even though Konstantinos was seventeen, he was still being shown as a beardless child (see Figure 33).[22]

Religious icons were restored in theory, but there was no rush to place them everywhere. The only image that we know Eirene set up was that of Christ on the Chalke Gatehouse of the palace, which was significant but symbolic, as it was not used in worship. (When Leon V removed it later, the myth developed that Leon III had also taken it down in 730.) Otherwise, the apse mosaic of the church of Hagia Sophia in Thessalonike, which celebrates Eirene and Konstantinos, featured a cross, in the usual style of the dynasty (though we do not know if the

Figure 32 Church of Hagia Sophia at Nikaia where the Council of Nicaea II met
Photo by David Hendrix

Figure 33 Joint coin of Konstantinos VI and Eirene, with prior rulers of the dynasty on the reverse

mosaic was made before or after 787). The patriarch Tarasios is said to have commissioned a series of images celebrating the martyrs, but his biography was written in ca. 845, after the second restoration of icons, and is untrustworthy on such points.[23]

Eirene vs. Konstantinos VI

Unfortunately for Eirene, the Council was immediately followed by military defeat on three fronts. In 788, an Arab army defeated the Romans at Podandos in Anatolikon, killing many soldiers and officers; a Bulgar raid killed the general of Thrace at Strymon; and an expedition against Benevento in southern Italy was defeated and Eirene's military logethete, the eunuch Ioannes, was killed.[24] It was the worst way to kick off a new era, and the restoration of the icons, rolled out to great fanfare at home, did not noticeably improve the empire's relations with other Christians. These failures eroded Eirene's credibility.

The decade after the Council was politically turbulent, as tensions between Eirene and her son, and their respective supporters, destabilized the polity. We do not know the reasons behind this animosity, nor can we clearly discern the factions or their motivations, because all we have for those years are the annalistic entries of Theophanes, which contain valuable information but are disjointed and leave many gaps. In 790, Eirene arrested and flogged her son and his supporters, and put him under house arrest. She then demanded that the armies swear to obey only her, not him. The Armeniakon objected, leading to a widespread mutiny against Eirene. The armies demanded Konstantinos, and got him. After he was acclaimed as sole emperor in the forum of Constantine, he flogged and exiled Eirene's eunuchs, including Staurakios and Aetios, and confined Eirene to the Eleutherios palace, which she had built in the south-central part of the City. But then early in 791, she was inexplicably restored to her rank as empress, with her eunuchs. She had not been removed from the coins in the meantime.[25]

In those years, Konstantinos campaigned against Bulgar and Arab raiders, but achieved little. In the summer of 792, he marched against the Bulgars, but was badly defeated at Markellai, where he lost many men and officers, including the redoubtable Lachanodrakon, who had served all emperors loyally regardless of their stance on icons (his career never had anything to do with icons). A soldier who fought in this battle was the later monk Ioannikios, whose biography credits him with saving the emperor's life during the chaotic flight back to the City. The experience left Ioannikios with such emotional trauma that he deserted the army and became an ascetic.[26] Back in Constantinople, Konstantinos faced down yet another plot by the *tagmata* to put his uncles, the sons of Konstantinos V, on the throne. He blinded Nikephoros and cut the tongues out of the rest. In 793, he had to march east to suppress the Armeniakon, an army that was often discontent during those years. The emperor brought a thousand of its men in chains back to the City, tattooed their faces with the words "Armeniakos rebel," and dispersed them among the islands. That year, the coins changed, putting Eirene on the front and Konstantinos (still beardless!) on the reverse. We cannot see what was happening at the court that caused these changes.

Figure 34 Sole coin of Eirene, showing the empress on both sides

In 795–796, Konstantinos made progress against the Bulgars and Arabs. But by the summer of 797, the deck was reshuffled: Eirene had managed to subvert the *tagmata* and plant her agents in Konstantinos' retinue. Acting on her orders, they arrested him and blinded him cruelly in the room in which he had been born, the Porphyra chamber of the palace. It is not clear how long he survived after that, but he was out of the picture. Eirene stepped forward as sole emperor (797–802). The gold nomisma now featured only her, as *basilissa*, both front and back, severing her ties to the rest of the dynasty (see Figure 34), and she issued laws as a *basileus*, using the masculine form of the title. Later tradition struggled to reconcile the saint who restored icons and performed miracles after death—for so she was regarded by some iconophiles—with the mother who blinded her own son.[27] But there was apparently no reluctance among the Romans to finally accept a woman as their sole ruler, one who was not merely standing in for a younger man. By 797, Eirene had been Augusta for almost thirty years.

The struggle between mother and son was over, but this did not end the state's instability. Eirene's chief eunuchs, Staurakios and Aetios, hated each other, and Aetios managed to undermine his rival, who died in 800. There were also *two more* alleged attempts to proclaim the sons of Konstantinos V, who had already been whipped, ordained, and blinded or mutilated for prior coups in their favor. They were now sent to Athens, Eirene's home town, where all of them were blinded and placed under the guard of the empress' kinsmen. Their very bodies had become a grisly record of recent domestic turmoil. Meanwhile, Aetios consolidated his power, placing the Opsikion and Anatolikon armies under his own command, entrusting Thrace to his brother Leon, and making an alliance with the *domestikos* of the *scholai*. Aetios now held the capital in his grip.

To shore up her popularity, Eirene organized a memorable religious procession to celebrate Easter in 799. She rode along the Mese from the Holy Apostles in a golden chariot pulled by white horses and accompanied by patricians and top generals, while she flung coins to the crowd. She also reduced or abolished dues and taxes on travel and trade in and around Constantinople. The abbot of the monastery of Stoudios wrote an ecstatic letter of thanks to her: "angels from your holy palace appeared and announced to us what you had done . . . . That lawless yoke that lay upon our people has been lifted!" All this over a tax break! But he, Theodoros of Stoudios, was greatly in her debt, as she had just appointed him to lead that prestigious monastery.[28]

Eirene had fully deconstructed the dynasty. She had abolished its signature cause at Nicaea II, albeit without condemning Leon III and Konstantinos V. In the 790s, she stopped putting them on the nomisma. By blinding her son, she ensured that their dynasty would end. And, as sole empress, she passed two laws that took aim at them again. One limited the use of oaths—the dynasty's chief instrument for securing loyalty—and criticized the Old Testament as an "imperfect shadow" of Christianity. The other banned third marriages as "unlawful and bestial." Konstantinos V had married three times, and his younger sons who had sparked so many plots were born of that third union.[29]

Arab raiding became more aggressive during this period. In the late 790s, their attacks reached Ankyra and Ephesos and defeated Roman armies, such as the Opsikion. These successes were in part due to the militarization of the Cilician frontier by the Abbasid caliphs, which was completed by Harun al-Rashid. He viewed the Romans as the caliphate's greatest remaining rival. Many towns in Cilicia and northern Syria, such as Mopsouestia, Adana, Anazarbos, Adata (Hadath), and Germanikeia (Marash), were built up as defensive bulwarks for the caliphate and forward bases from which to raid Romanía. In addition to their regular garrisons, they also attracted volunteer fighters, who were given lands and subsidized by the rest of the Islamic world through donations. These outposts of military-religious zeal were known as the *thughur*, and annual raids were their main occupation. To stem their depredations, it is possible that Eirene paid for yet another temporary truce with the caliph.[30]

As Harun al-Rashid was eroding the physical security of Asia Minor, the papacy and the Franks took another step toward undermining the standing and prestige of the eastern empire among Christian states. On Christmas Day, 800, in Rome, pope Leo III crowned Charlemagne *Augustus* and *imperator Romanorum* (emperor of the Romans).[31] It was perhaps inevitable. After decades of war and conquest, the king of the Franks had amassed more domains, titles, and subjects than any of his peers. It was ultimately only a Roman imperial title that could express and satisfy his increasingly hegemonic position, which was no longer that of a mere king. His capital at Aachen was sometimes called a "New Rome," while its adornment, ceremonies, and trappings borrowed heavily from those of the City that already bore that name. His dynasty had already been awarded neo-Roman titles by past popes. Charlemagne had been a "patrician of the Romans" since childhood, and pope Hadrian had addressed him as a "New Constantine."[32]

Charlemagne's court had even objected to the Council of Nicaea II on the grounds that the Franks had not been consulted, as if they had standing comparable to the emperor and the five patriarchs of the Church. His leading theologians, Theodulf and Alcuin, had, in rejecting Nicaea II, even pointed to the reduced authority of the eastern empire.[33] Charlemagne and his court were struggling to articulate their own conception of Frankish empire, and it appears that the king was not happy with pope Leo for springing the imperial title on him that Christmas Day. Charlemagne did not want to be beholden to the pope, whom *he* had just restored to Rome, defeating his enemies who had driven him out; and he did not want to be bound to the city of Rome. There were no actual "Romans" in his domain proper of whom he was the emperor, which is why he avoided stressing the Roman part of the title.[34] But the pope and some of Charlemagne's subjects saw in his coronation a displacement of Constantinople's rights. In fact, a chronicle written soon after argued that the imperial title had lapsed in the east because a *woman* sat on the throne.[35]

It is not recorded how the Romans reacted to a Frank being proclaimed as a (or the?) emperor of the Romans in 800. His daughter's engagement to Eirene's son had been broken off during the mid-780s for unknown reasons, but Eirene tried to restore good relations with Aachen. Historians have speculated too much about a brief chronicle entry which says that Charlemagne, a recent widower, offered to marry Eirene.[36] But Eirene's time was up. Many patricians, including the general logothete Nikephoros, the *domestikos* of the *scholai*, the *quaestor*, the officers of the *tagmata*, and others, went to the Great Palace on 31 October, 802, while she was at the Eleutherios palace. There they proclaimed Nikephoros as emperor and sent soldiers to arrest Eirene. Heralds proclaimed the new regime throughout the City, and Nikephoros was crowned in Hagia Sophia the next day. All this took place before the eyes of Charlemagne's envoys, though there was no resistance, indicating that Eirene had lost credibility among the populace. She was exiled to the Prinkipos island in the Sea of Marmara, and then to Lesbos.[37]

The next summer, Nikephoros was challenged by Bardanes (later called "the Turk"), a career officer who led the Anatolikon. He was one of the four patricians who had escorted Eirene's chariot in 799. Bardanes marched to Chrysopolis, but then abandoned his revolt, either because he had no hope of acceptance by Constantinople or his officers deserted him. Possibly it was because the news of Eirene's death on 9 August, 803, reached him; it was said that he was rebelling in her favor. The emperor sent him a signed pledge that he would not be harmed, and Bardanes retired to a monastery on the island of Prote. He was later blinded by some soldiers, though the emperor denied responsibility. Nikephoros crowned his son Staurakios as co-emperor in December 803.[38]

The reign of Nikephoros (802–811) was pivotal. He reformed the provincial and fiscal administration, setting the stage for the next two centuries; expanded imperial power in Greece; and witnessed the rise of Bulgaria as a major rival in the Balkans. It was also now that iconophile groups began to deploy the rhetoric of martyrdom, instigated a culture war, and invented "iconoclasm" after the fact.

The rise of the iconophiles

The new iconophiles defined themselves during this period in ways that set the stage for Second Iconoclasm. The latter was an entirely different phenomenon from First Iconoclasm, in fact it retroactively reinvented First Iconoclasm, promulgating a myth that still holds sway today. We now know that Leon III and Konstantinos V hardly enforced a thoroughgoing "breaking" or removal of images; that there was no "persecution"; and that nearly the whole of Roman society (lay, clerical, monastic, and military) went along with imperial policy. But if First Iconoclasm was so inconsequential, why all the sound and fury? Well, where there is smoke, there is often a smoke-making machine.

We have no reliable record of domestic opposition to First Iconoclasm. Resistance to it came instead from Palestine and Rome. John of Damascus, an impressive theologian who has been considered the last of the Church Fathers, was active in Palestine and wrote treatises in defense of icon veneration, to which were attached florilegia (i.e., anthologies) of supporting patristic texts. His main argument is a defense against idolatry: Christians do not actually worship the material images, but give honor to God by venerating them. John descended from a family that had served the caliphs as top administrators, but his own biography is unknown. He may have been a monk at the monastery of St. Sabas outside Jerusalem, but that is known from a later source. The date of his death is also unknown, and may have been as late as the 760s.[39] He had little influence on the debate inside the empire, at least at first. His writings were not used at Nicaea II, though that Council reversed his excommunication by Hiereia.[40]

The other center of iconophilic activity was Rome, and in particular the mostly Greek-speaking monastery of St. Sabas, a branch office of the one in Palestine founded in the mid-seventh century. Rome had rejected iconoclasm in two councils (731, 769), which had produced florilegia of texts from the Fathers that were related to those of John of Damascus. The monastery of St. Sabas was the force behind iconophilia at Rome, and when pope Hadrian sent his legates to Nicaea II, one of them was Petrus, the abbot of that monastery. Petrus brought the Roman florilegium along with other anti-iconoclastic texts that were used at the Council. One contained an attack on Leon III and Konstantinos V, including the story of his baptismal defecation. Then, at the Council itself, one of the two oriental monks present supplied the story of Leon III's inspiration by the Jewish wizard who had previously advised caliph Yazid.[41] The myth of iconoclasm was coalescing. It was taken to the next level in 807 by a deacon of Hagia Sophia (under the patriarch Tarasios) who, after consulting those texts, composed a mostly fictional biography of the ascetic Stephanos the Younger. Stephanos had been executed by Konstantinos V for political subversion, but the *Life*, reviving narrative tropes from ancient Christian martyrology, recast him as a martyr of the dragon-emperor's "persecution." This text made a quantum leap by marrying hagiography to anti-iconoclasm.[42] The author of this text was interestingly linked to Palestinian circles, and wrote a text for one of their martyrs too, who was killed by the Muslims for apostasy.[43] The capstone of the anti-iconoclast narrative was then put in place by the chronicler Theophanes, who, in ca. 814, relying on these tendentious texts and little else, transformed them into a "history" that has been retold ever since.

The revival of monasticism

Another culture war was brewing in parallel to iconoclasm, and soon intersected with it. Monasticism had declined during the seventh and early eighth centuries, but began to recover around 770. A number of communities were founded then, especially in Bithynia, a gorgeous land near the capital. Many of their founders had a background in imperial service, which means that they had loyally served under, and benefited from, the regimes of iconoclastic emperors, a fact that later had to be covered up through invented narratives of persecution. Some of them were educated and their families participated in the new foundations, which were often on private land. The best known is Platon, who founded Sakkoudion in Bithynia with the help of his nephew Theodoros (later the abbot of Stoudios).[44] The Church was at first apprehensive about the moral standards followed in these new monasteries, especially about the mixing of genders, and canons were passed at Nicaea II to regulate them.

Platon of Sakkoudion attended Nicaea II, but the most vocal monk there was Sabas, abbot of the monastery of Stoudios in Constantinople (a foundation of the fifth century) and a relative of Platon's nephew Theodoros. Sabas wanted to take a hard line against iconoclast bishops and expel them from their positions, in part because his group wanted to fill them. The patriarch Tarasios, who led the Council and had also founded his own monastery just outside Constantinople, "praised [them] as zealots on behalf of the canons and Gospel ordinances," but steered the Council toward forgiveness, otherwise huge swaths of the episcopate would have to be deposed. The restoration of icons did not aim to overhaul the Church leadership.[45]

Only a few years later, it was Platon and Theodoros' turn to be "zealots for the canons." The empress Eirene arranged in 788 for her son Konstantinos VI to marry Maria, a girl from Paphlagonia, who gave him two daughters. But in 795 Konstantinos divorced Maria, sent her to a convent, and married Theodote, one of his mother's ladies-in-waiting and a cousin of Theodoros. This marriage violated Church canons, though dispensation was not uncommon and emperors were often treated indulgently. Tarasios found a halfway solution: he did not officiate at the second wedding but allowed an abbot, Ioseph, to do so. Yet Platon and his nephews broke off communion with the patriarch in protest, for which they were arrested and exiled. They regarded it not as a marriage but as adultery (*moicheia*), whence it came to be called the "Moechian Scandal." After Eirene blinded her son, she freed Platon and Theodoros and appointed the latter to lead Stoudios, in succession to his relative Sabas, who had held the floor at Nicaea II. In lockstep with changes in imperial policy, Tarasios now deposed and defrocked the abbot Ioseph (code-named "The Scandal").[46]

In the following years, Theodoros massively expanded the membership of the Stoudios monastery, possibly to 700 by 807 and 1,000 by 815, though some were in the subsidiary monasteries that his federation acquired in Bithynia. During his long career as abbot first of Sakkoudion and then of Stoudios (794–826), Theodoros devised new rules that would reform monastic life and make it more organized, disciplined, rigorous, and accepting of members from all social classes. In this respect he was at the forefront of a general reform of monasticism toward more communal and egalitarian forms, and away from private foundations that perpetuated class privilege. Theodoros wanted his monks to be equal, to check their class prejudices at the door, and to take on duties assigned to them by their superiors. His strict regiments of prayer and work were designed to break down the personality and make it unquestioningly obedient to one's superiors and God. The monks even had to swap their underwear every week, regardless of size and cleanliness, to drive home the virtues of humility and interchangeability. The rules were written down and the complex institutional hierarchy of the house spelled out. Ideally, monks of Stoudios were taught to read. At this time Greek developed its lowercase letters (minuscule). We do not know exactly who invented them or where, but Platon of Sakkoudion is possibly the first person recorded as using them, and some of our first minuscule manuscripts are associated with the Stoudios scriptorium.[47] Stoudios was also connected to the monastery of St. Sabas near Jerusalem. In addition to their common struggle against iconoclasm, the monks at Stoudios devised a new form of liturgical prayer that mixed elements of the Sabbaite tradition with that of Constantinople. It spread and would ultimately dominate Orthodox practice.[48]

From then on, monasteries became an important part of social life. They were feeder institutions to the Church, as many monks subsequently served as bishops, especially from the "Ivy League" monasteries of the capital. They also interfaced with the court, as many emperors used monks as advisors or showpieces for the piety of their regime. Monasteries provided a range of services to the public too, through their charitable wings (such as orphanages and homes for the elderly), prayers, and spiritual advice. Non-monks sometimes rented rooms in monasteries or retired there in old age to be cared for by the community, usually in exchange for a bequest. Intellectual life was never dominated by monasteries as happened in western medieval Europe, but they made important contributions and some had serious libraries that functioned as research centers.

Over time, Orthodox monasticism adopted Theodoros' model, which he promulgated in many texts. But the reformer's own life was anything but orderly and quiet, as his ideal monk was expected to be. When patriarch Tarasios died in 806, Platon and the Stoudites lobbied for Theodoros to replace him,[49] but the emperor Nikephoros opted for another layman, also named Nikephoros (806–815), a former secular official who had written an imperial history back in ca. 790 and had since directed charitable institutions. The emperor took the precaution of locking up Theodoros and Platon for twenty-four days so that the investiture could take place without trouble.[50] Relations between the court and Stoudios worsened when the emperor then pressed his new patriarch to rehabilitate the former abbot Ioseph "The Scandal," because he had played a critical role in defusing the revolt of Bardanes the Turk in 803. The patriarch duly convened a synod that restored Ioseph to the priesthood. In response, the Stoudites shunned liturgical communion with anyone who was in communion with The Scandal, including the patriarch. This was especially problematic because Theodoros' brother and ally Ioseph had just been made bishop of Thessalonike.

Zealous adherence to the canons could create a chain reaction of nonrecognition that effectively split the Church (I don't recognize him, but if you do, then I don't recognize you either, and so on). Few sided with the Stoudites in their inflexible stance that "the laws of God hold sway over everyone . . . otherwise we can all do as we please and the Gospel is refuted."[51] Some monks said that the Stoudites "were addicted to finding scandals everywhere, and thought themselves better than others."[52] Most preferred to invoke the concept of *oikonomia*, which held that in some circumstances an otherwise fixed order can bend for the purpose of securing a greater good, such as peace within the Church and harmony between it and the state. A severely strict application of the law can have bad outcomes. *Oikonomia* was not just for opportunistic exceptions. It could be argued that the Incarnation itself was such a "special dispensation," a concession by God for the salvation of mankind.[53]

The Stoudites had instigated a culture war by taking an inflexible stand on a matter of principle. Matters eventually came to a head. Stoudios was surrounded by soldiers and the zealots were brought before a Church synod in January, 809. Theodoros and his brother Ioseph, the bishop of Thessalonike, were deposed, and they, along with Platon and other monks, were exiled again, though for only two years at most. Few sided with them in all this, not even Theophanes, Theodoros' own monastic sponsor from way back. This Theophanes of Sigriane was another former courtier who had founded a monastery, Megas Agros, on his estates. He is almost universally identified with the chronicler Theophanes, but there are good reasons to doubt that.[54]

This rift, whose protagonists were all nominally iconophiles, brought two problems to the fore that would shape reactions to Second Iconoclasm after 815. The first was an anxiety over the degree to which the emperor could dictate terms to the Church. Theodoros here found common cause with the Church of Rome, which had its own reasons for insisting on the separation of spiritual and worldly authority. Theodoros even appealed to pope Leo III, arguing that "there is no special Gospel for emperors" and calling for a new synod at Rome that would overturn the verdict against him. He did not get his wish, but his protests resonated with anti-iconoclast thinking. Around the same time (early ninth century), someone forged letters ostensibly by pope Gregory II to emperor Leon III, blasting the latter for his iconoclasm and making him boast that "I am both emperor and priest."[55] Thus, the two issues were increasingly fused together.

The second was Theodoros' martyrdom complex. More than anyone in this period, he used the image of the ancient martyrs of the Church to describe nearly everything that was dear to him. Ascetics were martyrs because of the trials that their bodies endured in self-deprivation; iconophiles were persecuted martyrs under iconoclast emperors; Christian captives killed by the Bulgars were martyrs; and, of course, the experience of the Stoudites themselves at the hands of Konstantinos VI and Nikephoros was tantamount to martyrdom. He used literary hagiography as a vehicle to promote the righteousness of his group, and cast them as saints during their lifetimes. He began with his mother Theoktiste, who died ca. 797 (an ascetic, hence a martyr) and his uncle Platon, who died in 814 (obviously a martyr).[56] This obsession further promoted the false idea, which was advocated for example by the *Life of Stephanos the Younger*, that iconoclast emperors were persecutors. This idea shaped reactions to Second Iconoclasm.

The reforms of Nikephoros I

While Theodoros reformed monasticism and quarreled with emperors, the emperor Nikephoros was reforming the imperial administration and fighting Arabs and Bulgars.

Asia Minor had two overlapping matrices of administration, the old civilian and ecclesiastical provinces, governed by *praitores*, and the military districts with the armies (called *strategides* or *themata*). During the eighth century, managerial emphasis had drifted gradually toward the latter, which now, in the early ninth century, absorbed the former provinces, yielding a single, streamlined framework for provincial governance. The new governors were henceforth the generals (or *strategoi*) of the *themata* of Anatolikon, Armeniakon, Thrakesion, Opsikion, Boukellarioi, and Kibyrraiotai. The *praitores* were assigned to the themes as judges, while other officials, answering to the general logothete, increasingly supervised fiscal matters, including provisioning the army. The fiscal apparatus of the state had long since stabilized and, as the economy gradually recovered, was increasingly monetized. The *kommerkiarioi* had, since ca. 730, gone back to collecting taxes on trade on behalf of the general logothete. Thus the "theme system" finally emerged as a unified framework for provincial and military administration. The themes were now both armies and administrative units, and the term is used in this dual way from the 810s onward. In tracing these reforms, we are aided by a hierarchically-arranged list of offices (or *Taktikon*) that was produced in the mid-850s, when the process was complete. Nikephoros' reign emerges as pivotal. He was, after all, the first emperor in Roman history whose previous post was in high-level fiscal administration.[57]

The emperors created new themes during the ninth and tenth centuries, both by subdividing large ones (as Konstantinos V had done to the Opsikion) and annexing territory, especially in the Balkans. Themes of Macedonia, Strymon, Thessalonike (previously governed by a prefect), Peloponnese, and Zakynthos appeared around 790–810. Staurakios' campaign in 783 had laid the foundations for some of these commands.[58] Nikephoros was especially active in consolidating Roman rule in the Peloponnese. Unfortunately, our sources come from the tenth century and are unreliable. One is the *Chronicle of Monembasia*, which is really a propagandistic text on behalf of the Church of Patras. According to it, the western Peloponnese was overrun by Slavs, but Nikephoros' armies pacified and converted them, allowing the original inhabitants to return. The emperor then refounded the city of Sparta with a multiethnic mix of eastern settlers. Another text recounts oral traditions about how Nikephoros' resolved a violent dispute between the city of Patras and Slavs in its vicinity who had "rebelled" in 805, a term which implies that the state considered them as its subjects.[59]

What really happened is hinted at by the chronicler Theophanes, who was writing in the 810s but hated Nikephoros with a passion because the emperor's reforms harmed the financial interests of his class. He attributes to Nikephoros ten "Vexations," or evil deeds. The first of them is that emperor ordered many of his subjects in Asia Minor to sell their lands in late 809 and move to "the Sklavinias," i.e., to areas around Thessalonike and Greece. So a policy of mass resettlement, a huge logistical operation, was used to reinforce imperial control over Greece. This was likely linked to the second Vexation, which entailed the military registration of many people, including the poor, while the cost of their equipment was to be borne not only by their families, as heretofore, but by a designated community (e.g., a group of farms or village district). It is not clear how many additional people were drafted in this way and how much land (of non-soldiers) was encumbered. But this funding structure tightened the link between military obligations and the land, and not just the land owned by soldiers' families.[60] Meanwhile, each thematic army developed a smaller core of first-grade soldiers, who were better trained and paid and available for full-time duty, as opposed to the rest, who were called up only for specific campaigns. The first-grade soldiers were perhaps on a par with those of the *tagmata*. Nikephoros created a tagmatic unit in 809, the *Hikanatoi*, for cadets. Its first commander was the emperor's ten-year-old grandson Niketas, the future patriarch Ignatios.[61]

These reforms would be incomplete without a new census, which was duly carried out with a processing fee of 1/12 nomisma per taxpayer. The emperor also canceled a number of tax exemptions, probably those granted by Eirene; raised the taxes on lands earmarked for Church charities; and passed other measures to benefit the fisc. These reforms were seen by Theophanes as Vexations designed to ruin subjects. That certainly was not their intent and, given this author's prejudice, it was likely not their outcome either. Writers such as Theophanes reflected the interests of propertied classes who howled with outrage when their perks were mildly scaled back. Other texts call Nikephoros "an orthodox emperor who loved the poor."[62]

Yet the Arabs continued to raid into Asia Minor for plunder and captives, for Harun al-Rashid prioritized war with Rome. Roman counterraids were smaller and less frequent (probably at a ratio of 3:1). Harun invaded in the summer of 806 with a huge army, but captured only some border forts. Nikephoros bought him off with 30,000 or 50,000 nomismata. This campaign is written up in our sources as a big deal, probably because of the caliph's personal attendance, but it did not amount to much. At the same time, his fleet attacked Cyprus and carried away 16,000 captives who were sold into slavery or ransomed (the bishop fetched 2,000 nomismata); and in 807 his fleet attacked Rhodes. The Arabic tradition records romantic tales and poems about Harun, and it quotes his colorful but fictitious correspondence with Nikephoros.[63] At the time, it seemed as though the caliphate could bludgeon Romanía indefinitely. But the latter was far better organized and strengthening its infrastructural base, whereas the caliphate, despite its superiority in resources, was a ramshackle operation on the verge of falling apart. It was only the glamor of Harun's reign that masked that reality.

The same was true of Charlemagne's empire. Its institutions were shallow and its common purpose weak. It had a part-time army, was ethnically disunited, and held together not by a shared identity but the person of the king. To hold it together, Charlemagne rewarded his nobles with lands in conquered territories, which gave them the power bases from which they later resisted royal authority. When Frankish imperialism ran out of steam, these nobles turned against each other and the edifice collapsed. By contrast, Nikephoros relied on professional armies, a uniform administration, and salaried officials who worked for the state. The vast majority of his subjects were—ethnically, politically, and legally—Romans.

Krum and the Bulgar wars

The Arab raids distracted Nikephoros from his Balkan priorities. He had paid special attention to strengthening Romanía's position there, and the Bulgars were a growing threat to it, albeit one that could be defeated. Konstantinos V had consistently beaten them and, despite setbacks (such as the battle of Markellai in 792), the Roman conquest of the khanate was not an impossible dream. Eirene had pushed the border to Beroe and Philippopolis. Roman settlers had been moved into Thrace and Macedonia in large numbers, and new bishoprics were founded there.[64] By 809, Roman arms had advanced to Serdica (Sofia). This city had been lost for two centuries, and we know of its capture because the Bulgar khan Krum took it that year and massacred the garrison, though he then left. Theophanes, hostile to Nikephoros as ever, omits to record the city's original capture by the Romans.[65] The noose was tightening around the khanate and Nikephoros decided to deliver the final blow.

In the summer of 811, Nikephoros assembled a large army, including the *tagmata* and units from most of the themes. His son Staurakios commanded the *Hikanatoi*, with cadets fifteen and older. At this time the empire could probably not field an army larger than 20,000. The Romans defeated the Bulgars twice along their march and occupied the khan's capital, Pliska. Nikephoros distributed the khan's treasure to his soldiers and they drank his wine. Before departing, the Romans burned the khan's palace (there is a debate about whether this can be confirmed archaeologically). The Romans then marched west toward Serdica, plundering and burning the fields along the way, as one of Krum's inscriptions verifies: "that old bald emperor came with his entire army and burned our villages, and took everything." In late July, the Romans encamped in a valley in the Haimos foothills, and found that one end of it had been blocked by a palisade. Nikephoros failed to reconnoiter the area or post enough guards at night. At dawn on 26 July, Krum rushed the tents of the emperor and the *tagmata* while most of the Romans were sleeping, and massacred thousands. In their panicked rout, some Romans fell into the river and drowned, or were trampled by those who came behind them, who crossed over the bodies. Others rushed to the palisade and climbed it, but they did not know that there was a chasm on the other side, and they fell to their deaths or broke their limbs. Some set fire to the logs, which then fell on those below and burned them.[66] "A terrible tragedy, wrapped in an even greater comedy."[67]

It was the worst military disaster suffered by the Romans in centuries. The emperor himself was killed, along with the generals of Thrace and Anatolikon, the commanders of two *tagmata*, and many patricians, including the prefect of Constantinople and Aetios (Eirene's eunuch), along with thousands of soldiers and officers. The emperor's son Staurakios escaped but received a mortal wound to the spine. The *Hikanatoi* were cut down. Theophanes reports that Krum turned the emperor's skull into a drinking vessel, coating it with silver. The disaster was traumatic, and many mourned for "our departed brothers and fathers."[68]

The Roman position in the Balkans, so methodically built up, collapsed after this defeat, and events moved quickly. Staurakios clung to the throne and to life, but in October, 811, he was replaced by Michael I Rangabe, his brother-in-law, and retired to a monastery, where he died in January, 812. Michael distributed 500 lbs gold (36,000 coins) to the widows of soldiers who fell in Bulgaria. He was a pious emperor who consulted bishops and monks (especially Theodoros of Stoudios) on matters of state, and lavished endowments and expensive gifts on the churches, "scattering all the funds that Nikephoros had carefully saved up." Michael also asked the patriarch Nikephoros to cancel the rehabilitation of Ioseph "The Scandal," and the patriarch saved face by asking the opinion of pope Leo, who concurred with the new emperor and the Stoudites.[69]

Meanwhile, the Bulgars were rolling back Roman gains in Thrace and Macedonia. Settlers streamed back from Anchialos, Beroia, Philippopolis, and Strymon. Krum boasted in an inscription that "God instilled fear in the Romans and they deserted [those places] and fled."[70] The project of a generation was undone. When Michael tried to march out against the Bulgars in the summer of 812, his army refused. He was also busy resettling the refugees, including Bulgars who fled from Krum. The khan was demanding them back in exchange for peace, but the emperor's advisors were split: the patriarch and many bishops favored returning the Bulgar refugees in order to secure peace, as Roman lives were worth more, whereas the Stoudites were against it, as God demands the protection of all suppliants. In the end, the offer was rejected, probably because Michael's regime was not secure enough to withstand the political fallout of humiliating concessions. Meanwhile Krum, who learned to build siege engines, captured Mesembria and Debeltos in November, 812. Debeltos contained stores of Greek fire and thirty-six flamethrowers. Krum advanced into southern Thrace, and Michael marched against him with a large army drawn from all the themes. The battle took place on 22 June, 813, at Bersinikia near Adrianople. The Romans were roundly defeated and fled in panic.[71]

In the chaos of the rout, a consensus emerged among the leadership that Michael had to be replaced with Leon, general of the Anatolikon, a capable officer of Armenian descent. He was proclaimed at the Hebdomon, the parade grounds seven miles from the City, from where he entered Constantinople and the palace and was crowned in Hagia Sophia on 12 July, 813. Michael and his family sought refuge in the Pharos church and became monks. Michael would live on for thirty-two more years, though Leon V castrated all his sons (one was Niketas, the future patriarch Ignatios).[72] Meanwhile, Krum left a force to invest Adrianople and arrived before the walls of Constantinople only a week after Leon's accession. He ostentatiously performed animal and human sacrifices outside the Golden

Gate, possibly to his god Tangra. The khan had no chance of taking the City, so he offered to negotiate. Leon tried to ambush him at a meeting, but the khan escaped, possibly wounded. In retaliation, he plundered and burned the palace of St. Mamas at the mouth of the Golden Horn along with many churches outside the City. He then destroyed towns throughout Thrace, even in the Chersonese (Gallipoli), and seized Adrianople on the way back, taking thousands of captives with him.[73] Thrace was ruined.

Had Nikephoros' project succeeded, the Bulgars would have been pushed up to the Danube plain. Instead, it was the Romans who were pushed back to a narrow ring of Thrace around their capital. The Bulgars, a former ally, had become a credible adversary, just as Arab power was waning in the east. Krum had simultaneously expanded his reach into the middle Danube region, taking advantage of the fall of the Avars to Charlemagne, and also to lands north of the river. The Bulgars were establishing their own empire and dealing with the Franks and Romans as near-equals.

There was, at least, some good news on the Frankish front. The empire and Charlemagne had, in the past decade, been engaged in a struggle over Venetia and the Dalmatian islands. The Franks considered those territories as belonging to the crown of Italy, which was worn by Charlemagne's son Pippin. Nikephoros had sent two fleets from the naval theme of Kephalonia to enforce imperial hegemony, and the Franks conceded them to Constantinople. In exchange, Charlemagne asked to be recognized as emperor. Michael I consented, and so the Roman ambassadors in 812 acclaimed Charlemagne as emperor in Greek and Latin (i.e., "*basileus* and *imperator*"), but not "of the Romans." He was just emperor-at-large, a concession that the Romans probably made to him personally, not to his dynasty. Letters sent by later emperors to his heirs called them "kings of the Franks and Lombards, their so-called emperors"—one can hear the quotation marks.[74] A detailed treaty was worked out over Venetia, called today the Treaty of Aachen. Venetia would be nominally subject to Constantinople, but in practice autonomous. It was at this time that the Venetians began to build up the Rialto as their principal settlement. Without a hinterland to exploit, they invested in trade. Constantinople treated Venice as an overseas base for its operations. In 840, a patrician from the court oversaw the construction there of warships in the "Greek" style to assist with operations in Italy.[75] So just as the imperial pretensions of Charlemagne were formally confirmed by the actual empire of the Romans, whose emissaries used Greek to do so, the Venetians were also building up their own "Roman" credentials by looking sideways at "Greek" Constantinople.[76]

In 814, Krum was preparing for an assault on Constantinople, including 5,000 armored carts, catapults, and rams, and he sent raiding armies to ravage Thrace. Leon V strengthened the walls, especially around Blachernai (close to the Golden

Horn), and he sent envoys to Aachen to seek an anti-Bulgar alliance. They found that Charlemagne had died in February. When they returned, they found that Krum had died too, in April, of a cerebral hemorrhage ("streams of blood had poured out of his mouth, nose, and ears"). Leon circulated a notice throughout the realm claiming that the khan had died of the wound he received during the ambush of the previous year.[77] Harun al-Rashid had died in 809 and his heirs had already begun to fight among themselves. The three great rivals to the Roman emperor had all died within a few years. Despite recent defeats on the battlefield, Romanía was well positioned to come out ahead.

22
Growing Confidence (815–867)

Iconoclasm, again

Leon V (813–820) was the first emperor since Leon III who rose up through the army. Impressively, he faced no rebellions, mutinies, or plots—except the one that claimed his life. Our sources agree that he was an able, clever, and efficient ruler, incorruptible, just, and intimidating. "He trained the soldiers in person."[1] Early in his reign he began to make iconophiles nervous by asking questions about icons and crowning his son Symbatios co-emperor with the name Konstantinos. The sequence Leon-Konstantinos was a red flag. Leon was drifting into iconoskepticism.

The restoration of icons had not helped Romanía. Thrace was a ravaged land all the way to the suburbs of Constantinople. The project of expansion had failed and all emperors who had accepted the veneration of icons had ended badly. Many, especially in the army, could see that iconoclast emperors were consistently victorious, whereas icons had brought only defeat. In 812, soldiers *again* began to call for the (blinded) sons of Konstantinos V, and in 813, just as Michael I was about to be defeated at Bersinikia, some people opened Konstantinos V's tomb and called on him to "Come forth and save the republic!," echoing the words of his funeral. Soldiers from the *tagmata* were discharged for expressing such views. They had, after all, been the chief target of Konstantinos V's propaganda and, apparently they could be recognized by their close shaves. But there were monks too who were agitating against icons in the City. One had his tongue cut out for scraping off an icon; he was likely regarded as a confessor by those who shared his views.[2]

Leon proceeded cautiously and methodically. In the second half of 814, he appointed two commissions to look into the question of icons. The first one was headed by Ioannes, the abbot of the prestigious imperial monastery of Sts. Sergios and Bakchos, whose church had been built by Justinian (Ioannes was also called "the Grammarian," likely because he had once been a teacher). The commissions scoured Christian literature and assembled passages from the works of the Fathers that were critical of icons. In December, Leon summoned the patriarch Nikephoros and told him that the soldiers were blaming icons for the victories of the Arabs and Bulgars. "Can you make a small compromise, an *oikonomia* for the sake of these people, and remove the low-hanging icons? If not, can you explain to me why you venerate them, seeing as Scripture nowhere requires it?"

The patriarch replied that the practice had been passed down through unwritten tradition, like many other things that Christians do, and the matter was settled and need not be investigated. "Can you then debate with my team, who claim to have found many passages that refute the veneration of icons?" The patriarch sent bishops and abbots to explain the issue to the emperor, but they refused to debate his commissioners. At that point, some soldiers threw rocks at the image of Christ on the Chalke Gatehouse of the palace, the image that Eirene had set up, and Leon took it down so that it would not be further insulted. Some suspected the incident was staged.[3]

In response, the patriarch assembled many bishops and monks to his palace and asked them whether they agreed with the commission. They proclaimed their Orthodoxy and pledged in writing to resist iconoclasm to the death. They met with Leon in the palace and some, including Theodoros of Stoudios, told the emperor to his face to stop meddling in Church matters and stick to governing the state. "But I too am a child of the Church," Leon replied, "and will arbitrate between the two sides to discover the truth." More explicitly than before, this had become a debate over the emperor's power to decide religious matters. Our sources highlight the brave stances of a few iconophile stars: Euthymios of Sardeis, Michael of Synnada, Theophylaktos of Nikomedeia, the "zealous" Theodoros of Stoudios, and the patriarch—old rivals who were now presenting a united front. Yet most others eventually fell in line behind the emperor. Leon was smooth and crafty, "a wolf in sheep's clothing." After many meetings, he managed to lure most of Nikephoros' support away. The patriarch was isolated, ill, harassed by soldiers, and unwilling to debate any more. Crowds outside were shouting, "Down with icons! Dig up their bones!," a slogan used to depose emperors. Nikephoros abdicated and was confined to an island monastery.[4]

A new patriarch, Theodotos Kassiteras, was invested on 1 April, 815, and a Church Council convened after Easter in Hagia Sophia. It restored Hiereia (754) as the Seventh Ecumenical Council and annulled Nicaea II (787). The bishops of 815 attributed Nicaea II to "the naïveté of a woman." They forbade the making and veneration of icons, albeit without calling for their destruction: "We refrain from calling them 'idols,' for some evils are worse than others." The bishops relied on the arguments of Hiereia, although their florilegium strengthened the case against icons of saints: the true image of a saint is the Christian who imitates their virtue. Several bishops who refused to sign the decree were anathematized and deposed, though, as the former patriarch bitterly noted in his writings from exile, many of those who did sign had also, just a few months earlier, signed Nikephoros' pledge to resist iconoclasm to the death.[5]

Several bishops were removed from their sees and replaced, as were abbots from their monasteries, such as Theodoros of Stoudios. He set about writing his treatises in defense of icons and organizing the resistance from the various places where he was detained in Asia Minor. That underground resistance is worthy of further study, as it involved code words, surreptitious correspondence, and a cell-like structure. A few years before, when iconoclasm was not a live issue, Theodoros was willing to treat the error of iconoclasts as "not an essential matter." But now, eager for a fight, iconoclasts became the worst kind of heretic for him. The main problem that he faced as an organizer was where to draw the line between his community and the fatally compromised heretics beyond it. It was apparently acceptable *oikonomia* to greet a heretic and share a drink with him, but not to eat with him.[6]

Leon needed a military victory to bolster the case against icons. Krum's son Omurtag, having assumed the Bulgar throne, was sending raids into Thrace. In 816, Leon marched up to Mesembria and, using a stratagem, ambushed a Bulgar army at night, annihilating them in their sleep. After that, Omurtag and Leon negotiated a far-reaching treaty. Its terms are known from Bulgar inscriptions (written, as most were, in Greek). Constantinople surrendered its claims to a broad zone that stretched from Mesembria to Serdica between the Haimos range and the Hebros (Marica) river, and captives were exchanged one-for-one. With peace established, the emperor was able to start rebuilding the ruined towns of Thrace. For their part, the Bulgars dug a massive earthen trench, the Erkesija Dyke, 131 km long, 3 m tall, and 15 m wide on top, running between the Hebros river and the Black Sea. Ratifying the treaty required each side to participate in the religious rituals of the other, and *oikonomia* presumably enabled Christian Romans to engage in pagan rituals for the sake of peace. But the treaty held for thirty years. Good dikes made good neighbors.[7]

Leon was also lucky in having little trouble from the Arabs. The caliphate was preoccupied with its internal conflicts and its incipient implosion. The focus of our sources is instead on his persecution of iconophiles. Some bishops and monks—a few dozen at most—were detained, pressured to declare for iconoclasm, possibly beaten and whipped if they reacted with obstinacy or impudence, exiled, relocated, and then hauled back for more re-education. But was this a "persecution"? These priests and monks were refusing to follow the orders of their Church superiors and to take communion with the patriarch, and their behavior was frequently offensive and self-righteous. The Church canons prescribed punishments for such behavior. Moreover, their trials and tribulations were recorded in hagiographical texts by partisan authors, who were often their allies and personal friends and modeled their exaggerated accounts on the suffering of the ancient martyrs. Even before Leon, these men were primed and ready to interpret their experiences as martyric. Theodoros of Stoudios finally got to live out his dream of being persecuted by a "heretical" emperor. It was good for the soul, he wrote.[8]

It is clear even from these partisan accounts that the goal of Leon and his agents, especially Ioannes the Grammarian, was not to hurt the opposition but win them over in order to unify the Church. They preferred to use persuasion and bribes and were content with mere outward consent. There was no requirement to destroy icons, only to take communion with the patriarch. Violence was the last resort and few died of it, such as the Stoudite monk Thaddaios, who was of Bulgar origin. He spoke with an accent and may have aroused ethnic prejudice. Overall, Leon's campaign was successful. There were no mass protests and, as Theodoros admitted, almost all bishops, monks, and state officials conformed. Most people were just not interested enough in the issue to suffer for it.[9]

There was no conflict between the emperor and "the monks." That is another false impression created by the polarizing rhetoric of dissident hagiography and the letters of Theodoros. For him only fanatical iconophiles were true monks, and so by definition the emperor was at war with "the monks." It is likely that letters of his that referred to iconoclast monks were later expunged. Moreover, the martyrological hagiographies that his group wrote to praise itself falsely projected that polarization back onto First Iconoclasm, retroactively distorting it too. As iconoclast texts were later purged, iconophile hagiography became the sole record for both phases of the controversy. The iconoclasts surely had "confessors" of their own in the period of icon ascendancy (787–815), but they were scrubbed from the record too. Thus was "Byzantine Iconoclasm" invented.[10]

Michael II

Back when he was an officer, Leon had benefited from the patronage of Bardanes the Turk, the rebel of 803, as had two other men, Thomas and Michael of Amorion. Leon regarded Michael as a friend and, when he became emperor, appointed him to command the excubitors. But in 820, Leon arrested Michael and imprisoned him in the palace dungeon. On Christmas Day, some men infiltrated the palace and murdered Leon in church. They brought Michael out of his cell and placed him on the throne, where he was acclaimed emperor. It was later said that he was still in chains, but that is probably wrong. Leon's four sons were castrated (one did not survive) and exiled. The ex-patriarch Nikephoros is said to have remarked that, "even though Leon had been a persecutor, the City had lost a man who knew how to handle public affairs."[11]

No sooner had Michael II taken the throne than his old comrade Thomas rebelled in Asia Minor, resulting in a vicious, three-year civil war, much like that between Konstantinos V and Artabasdos a century earlier. These were essentially rival bids from within the army to replace Leon. Thomas won over the Anatolikon and Kibyrraiotai, and sought an alliance with the caliph, while the Opsikion and Armeniakon sided with Michael. Thomas ferried his soldiers to Thrace, where they invested Constantinople in 821. The siege lasted for two years and featured fierce fighting along the walls and the use of Greek fire in naval warfare. Michael called on the Bulgar khan Omurtag (814–831), who harassed the besiegers. Eventually, Thomas' units abandoned the siege and holed up in various cities of Thrace, which Michael reduced piecemeal by the end of 823. Thomas was eventually surrendered by his supporters. Michael placed his foot on his enemy's neck, the old Roman ritual of *calcatio*, and then dismembered Thomas and impaled his torso.[12]

Our sources for the rebellion are chronologically garbled and rhetorically embellished. This is a rare case where both sides are presented negatively, Thomas as an old Slav, lame of leg, who sold out to the Arabs and led an ethnically mixed army, and Michael as having a speech impairment and alleged link to a heretical group in central Asia Minor, the Athinganoi (whose beliefs remain elusive). The negative image of Thomas came from Michael's propaganda, and Michael was tarnished in subsequent tradition because, even though he relaxed Leon's "persecution" of zealous iconophiles, he did not overturn the Council of 815. He was petitioned to restore the icons, but replied that he would make no changes to the established order of the Church. Therefore, he was cast as an evil heretic who doubted the Resurrection, spat on scholarship, and liked sex.[13]

As soon as Leon V's murder was announced, Theodoros of Stoudios rejoiced—in fact, he claimed that "the heavens and the earth are ringing with joy, now that our persecutor has been crushed," and "the manner of his death is fit for a comedy." But Michael II proved to be a disappointment and would not restore the icons, despite repeated iconophile appeals: "the winter has passed, but spring is not yet upon us."[14] Nor would the iconophiles participate in "debates" with their enemies, which could result only in "victories" for the organizers. Theodoros kept insisting that the issue could be resolved only by the Church and only if the pope was involved, not because he believed in papal supremacy, but opportunistically because he knew that the pope supported his view. In another controversy, when Rome did not support his position, Theodoros' stance had been different: "what do we care whether the pope does this or that?"[15]

In 824, Michael and his son and co-emperor Theophilos wrote to Louis the Pious, Charlemagne's heir, to announce their victory over Thomas, give their side of the story, and explain their policy on icons. This document survived in the west, in Latin translation, and so could not be destroyed by the iconophiles. It gives us a rare self-presentation of an "iconoclast" regime. It criticizes those who removed crosses from the churches and replaced them with icons. Such people pray to these images and even appoint them as godparents to their children (a practice attested and approved by Theodoros of Stoudios, no less). They scrape paint from the icons and mix it into the Eucharist wine. What then was to be done? Images around eye-level are to be removed, Michael II says, to prevent superstition, but those that are higher up may stay, to be seen from below as a kind of visual Scripture. This, then, was a moderate position, which iconophile hysteria had distorted.[16] Leon V and Michael II professed a concern about images "down low,"[17] those that were squarely in the visual path of worship. Yet this was perhaps disingenuous, as the Council of 815 had rejected all icons.

The Franks at the time were forging their own, idiosyncratic approach to religious icons that rejected both Hiereia and Nicaea II, as well as whatever Rome was telling them—but that is not our story. Michael sent another item to Paris that had a profound impact on western medieval culture: a manuscript of pseudo-Dionysios the Areopagite, gifted to the abbey of St. Denis on the fiction that the author of those texts was the same as St. Paul's convert in Athens *and* the patron saint of Paris. Michael could not have foreseen how much this text, once translated into Latin by John Scottus Eriugena, the most important Latin philosopher of the ninth century and reviver of Neoplatonism, would impact western intellectual history. That same book was possibly seen six centuries later by the emperor Manuel II Palaiologos when he visited Paris in 1400.[18]

During the civil war, the southern fleet had sided with Thomas and had suffered heavily from the Greek fire of the imperial fleet at Constantinople. This exposed outlying islands, such as Crete and Sicily, to attack. The attack on them came from a new threat that would grow over the next century: Muslim warlords acting independently of the caliphate. Freebooters under one Abu Hafs, who had been expelled from Andalusia by the Umayyad emir for being a nuisance, and then also from Alexandria, raided Crete and other islands during the civil war. Realizing that they were vulnerable targets, around 826 they overran Crete, which had only a tiny garrison, and established their headquarters at the site of later Herakleion, which was strategically located for controlling the island. Michael sent two expeditions against them—the second including the Kibbyraiotai fleet—but they were defeated. A third campaign expelled the raiders from other islands. But the loss of Crete was a disaster. Just when the eastern frontier was stabilizing, the entire Aegean coastline and the islands were exposed to Muslim raiding.[19]

An even worse disaster was unfolding in the west that distracted Michael from the recovery of Crete. In 827, a large and ethnically mixed army from the Aghlabid emirate of North Africa invaded Sicily. The origin of this campaign was later woven together with tales about a Roman officer on the island, Euphemios, who rebelled, was expelled, and sought Aghlabid help. His story is irrelevant. In reality, a Muslim army invaded Sicily, marched across the island, and besieged Syracuse. This set off a fierce war that raged for four years over the entire island, as both sides received large reinforcements from Spain and Constantinople. There were moments when each side seemed close to expelling the other from the island, but by 831 the war resulted in a division, with the Muslims ensconced at Palermo and the Romans at Syracuse. Both cities suffered during the war. For the Romans this outcome was effectively a defeat, for Sicily was one of their most prosperous, fertile, and, so far, undamaged provinces, and it now became a war zone yielding diminished revenues.[20]

Theophilos

Michael died on 2 October, 829. He was buried in the imperial mausoleum and succeeded by his son Theophilos (829–842). Theophilos was sixteen and had been crowned co-emperor back in 821.[21] He was to be the last iconoclast emperor and the most dedicated to the cause. His tutor had been Ioannes the Grammarian, whom he now made *synkellos*, his own representative to the patriarchate. Yet despite his position on icons, a glamor later attached to his memory. This was due to his personal qualities and to his widow Theodora, the second empress (and saint) to restore icons. She ensured that Theophilos would be remembered favorably even as she dismantled his policy.

Theodora had been selected in a bridal pageant, a fascinating method for finding the next empress that was occasionally used by the court in this period. Scouts would be sent out throughout the Roman lands with a portrait of the ideal bride, and they selected the most promising candidates based on beauty, decorum, and reputation. The girls would be interviewed at the court; rated for modesty and skill at feminine tasks; scrutinized by the emperor's mother; and even inspected nude from head to toe for blemishes. Some scholars have argued that all this was a fiction, because most of our accounts of them are shot through with fictional and novelistic elements. But the practice is too well attested to dismiss in its entirety, even if legends did form around it, such as about the bride show for Theophilos. He was allegedly smitten by the beautiful but smart Kasia (or Kasiane), and tested her by saying, "The worst evil came into the world through woman," referring to the temptation of Eve. She replied, "And so did the best of the best," referring to Jesus, born of Mary. Theophilos didn't like the riposte and gave the golden apple to Theodora. Kasia joined a monastery and became a famous hymnographer.[22]

Theophilos benefited from the onset of long-term growth in the economy and demography of the empire. By the later eighth century, the state was collecting most of its taxes in cash, so its need to move goods around in bulk diminished. A greater portion of the overall, non-state economy was monetized as well, perhaps 20%. With the state spending more money on the army and other sectors, coin finds increase, especially in southern Greece.[23] Moreover, revenues were growing. Estimates of Theophilos' annual budget, which are conjectural, range between 1.5 and (implausibly) 2.8 million nomismata, up from one million in 700. Theophilos is said to have amassed a reserve of almost 7 million (an unlikely figure that occurs in a polemical context, to show how much money his son wasted).[24] At any rate, the court had cash, and the young emperor took to building with a passion. He sensibly restored the sea walls of the capital, as there was now a hostile fleet within striking distance, on Crete. He expanded the palace with sparkling halls, domes, colonnades, mosaics, chapels, pavilions, and terraces. 1.5 million nomismata were literally poured into the form of a plane tree, two lions, two griffons, and two organs. The birds perched on the tree could be made to warble musically and the lions to roar.[25]

Theophilos was also keen to project his wealth abroad. In 829, he sent Ioannes the Grammarian on an embassy to Baghdad whose goal was to astound the Arab court with luxury gifts, almost 30,000 in cash, and the envoy's learning, to earn the emperor a reputation for "magnificence." Theophilos built a palace, the Bryas, "in the Saracen style," based on descriptions that Ioannes brought back. The Romans had caught on to Muslim cultural sophistication, and did not want to lag behind, at least in their own eyes. Now they finally had the resources to make a credible showing. Theophilos found the most learned man in the realm, Leon the Philosopher (the Grammarian's nephew), and gave him a teaching job. Later, in 837–842, Leon was archbishop of Thessalonike. He was an excellent philologist, poet, and inventor. The Romans concocted a tale according to which the caliph al-Ma'mun (d. 833) had wanted to hire him so badly that he entered into a bidding war for his services with Theophilos. The story is absurd, but reveals Roman insecurities.[26]

Theophilos attended the courts of justice to ensure that verdicts were fair and impartial, a virtue for which he was later praised (around 1100, a satirical text made him a judge in the underworld). At the start of his reign, Theophilos even executed the men who assassinated Leon V, his godfather, although that murder had brought his own father to power. Theophilos would also visit the markets of Constantinople and personally inquire about the prices of all products. Perhaps he was worried about inflation, given his spending. By this point the City had well over 100,000 people.[27] Mediterranean trade was generally on the rebound, though we hear little of Roman merchants, not because they did not exist but because the elite preferred to make their fortunes through state service and our sources focus on them. One of Nikephoros' "Vexations" forced the "distinguished" shipowners of the City to accept a government loan of 864 nomismata and pay it back at ca. 16% interest. This effectively required them to expand their operations, probably to supply the growing capital. For his part, Theophilos allegedly burned a large cargo ship owned by his wife Theodora. "Who has ever seen a merchant-emperor of the Romans?" he asked. The story has been interpreted as revealing both disdain for trade and its opposite, seeing as even the empress was involved.[28] Interestingly, miracles of an economic nature saw an uptick in ninth-century saints' lives.[29]

Constantinopolitan shipping has been illuminated in recent years by the discovery of 37 well preserved shipwrecks at Yenikapı (the Theodosian harbor on the south side of the City). They date between the fifth and eleventh centuries, with a concentration in our period, and are being studied by an interdisciplinary team. Most were used for local traffic and for supplying the City, but a number of light warships (*galeai*) were also found among them, about 30 m long. These were built to be sturdier and with better materials, indicating that the state spared no expense in outfitting its ships. These finds have shed light on the gradual transition in Mediterranean shipbuilding from a shell-first to a skeleton-first approach.[30] The bones that were found in the ships suggest that horses, donkeys, bears, and ostrich legs were consumed as food. Bear skulls showed signs of abuse, possibly in training for the circus, and some had marks from muzzles. A dog had its leg set after it had been broken.[31]

Theophilos and the army

The greatest state expense was the army. In the 770s, the total strength of the Roman army may have been around 80,000. For the reign of Theophilos we are fortunate to possess a detailed inventory of the themes, their soldiers, and costs written by al-Jarmi, an Arab captive who returned home in 845. Themes were being subdivided (Cappadocia was spun out from Anatolikon; Chaldia, in the far northeast, and Paphlagonia from Armeniakon; and so on), and new ones created along the empire's fringes (Cherson and Dyrrachion). The old themes still had the larger armies, the new ones between 2,000 and 4,000 (at least on paper). The total strength of the thematic armies at the end of Theophilos' reign has been estimated at 96,000 in the themes, plus another 24,000 in the *tagmata* (which seems too high), for a total of 120,000, so a 50% increase since Konstantinos V. Between a fourth and a fifth of these forces were cavalry.[32]

In practice, the army was not always kept up to strength, and campaigns were fought with smaller forces. Even in the tenth century after more growth, an army of 5,000 or 6,000 cavalry was deemed sufficient to ward off a routine enemy attack. The emperor Leon VI planned for campaign armies of 4,000, 8,000, and 12,000 men.[33] It was a feat of logistics to field an army of 15,000 or more. Such a force, for example, would require almost 30,000 horses and mules, for the cavalry (mounts and remounts) and the baggage train. This, in turn, depended on a vast infrastructure of horse farms, grazing lands, supply stations, muster and training grounds, and roads, to say nothing of the villages' collective responsibility for maintaining the soldiers. The government's footprint on local society was massive. One calculation for the overall annual cost of this army (just the salaries, at full strength) puts it at almost 1.5 million nomismata.[34]

After the death of Harun al-Rashid, the caliphate became increasingly unstable, but in the 830s his sons al-Ma'mum (813–833) and al-Mu'tasim (833–842) revived Harun's tradition of attacking the Romans. Al-Ma'mum personally led an invasion of Cappadocia in 830, which provoked a fierce retaliation by Theophilos, who rampaged through Cilicia, plundering the cities after trouncing their armies and taking thousands of prisoners. The emperor then celebrated a triumph in Constantinople. The procession went from the Golden Gate to Hagia Sophia and then to a platform raised before the Chalke Gatehouse, on which stood an organ, cross, and throne for the emperor. After receiving golden armbands from the people, Theophilos spoke about the war's success. In response, al-Ma'mum invaded one or two more times, but did not accomplish much and fell ill and died during the invasion of 833.[35] It took his brother al-Mu'tasim a few years to consolidate his rule, and some of his rivals even defected to the Romans.

The caliphate had for years been trying to suppress the Khurramites, a group of rebels based in Azerbaijan. They were Iranians (hence the Romans called them "Persians") and their religion was a mix of folk Zoroastrianism and Islam. By the early 830s, the Khurramites were losing the war against the caliphate and, in 834, thousands of them, under their leader Nasr, emigrated to Romanía and were taken on as auxiliaries in the imperial army. In 837, when the main body of Khurramites under Babak was defeated, thousands more arrived. The highest figure that we have for the combined strength of these battle-hardened refugees is 30,000. The Roman state was eager for manpower, especially for men who were motivated to fight the caliphate. Some Romans even imagined their polity "as an altar of refuge for those fleeing from savagery."[36]

With his new allies, in 837, Theophilos raided regions that had not been visited by Roman armies since the time of Konstantinos V. His army took Sozopetra, then marched through the territory of Melitene to Asmosaton, which they sacked and burned. Along the way, they defeated the Arab armies that challenged them and took thousands of prisoners. The eastern sources, both Christian and Muslim, highlight the atrocities committed by the joint Roman-Persian army against the locals—slaughters, disembowelments, mutilations, and rapes—but at home this was cause for a second triumph. The emperor was met by the children of the City wearing "crowns made from flowers."[37]

Al-Mu'tasim was infuriated by the attack and mounted a huge punitive expedition, targeting Ankyra first and then the most important military city: Amorion, the capital of Anatolikon theme and origin of Theophilos' dynasty (later sources wrongly imagined that the caliph's birthplace was Sozopetra, making his response personally motivated). In late 837, his general Afshin had crushed the remaining Khurramite forces under Babak in Azerbaijan, and so the caliph was able to deploy his full forces in 838. The historian al-Tabari preserves a detailed and reliable narrative of the expedition, written likely by a participant and worth reading, especially for its accounts of how information was gathered about enemy movements during a campaign; the Roman sources, by contrast, are confused.[38] Al-Mu'tasim entered through the Cilician Gates and marched north to Ankyra, while Theophilos encamped north of the Halys river to intercept him. But then news reached the emperor that another Arab army under Afshin had invaded from the east and was marching toward him via Armeniakon. Theophilos took a detachment of his army and fought with Afshin at Anzes, in the plain of

Dazimon, on 22 July. The Romans were initially successful, defeating the enemy infantry, but in the pursuit they were attacked and routed by the Turkish cavalry archers. The Romans fled in panic, and the emperor barely escaped with his life. Upon news of the defeat, the soldiers in the main camp by the Halys dispersed, and the emperor, positioned further north in Paphlagonia, desperately tried to rally his soldiers and organize a resistance.

The inhabitants of Ankyra abandoned their town and took to the hills, so when al-Muʿtasim and Afshin rendezvoused there, as per their original plan, there was little for them to do other than destroy the walls—heavy labor with no profit. Theophilos sent reinforcements to Amorion, including Aetios, the general of Anatolikon, before the united Arab host converged on the city and besieged it on 1 August. But part of the walls had been undermined by a heavy rainfall and had not been properly repaired, despite the emperor's instructions. A deserter, a former Muslim, revealed this to the caliph. The latter used mangonels to breach the walls at that point and concentrated his attack there. After days of heavy fighting, a Roman soldier (Boïditzes) in charge of that section felt inadequately supported by his general, Aetios, and surrendered to the Arabs in exchange for the safety of his men. The Arabs entered the city and, when the slaughter was done, they took all its surviving residents and soldiers captive, including Aetios and a large number of patricians and officers. Theophilos offered huge sums as ransom, but al-Muʿtasim demanded the return of the Persian leaders who had sought refuge in Romanía, a demand that was rejected. So the caliph burned the city and hastened back to Syria because news of a rebellion had reached him. But some of his captives walked too slowly while others were killing their captors, and the army began to suffer from a lack of water. The caliph therefore kept the Roman officers but massacred the rest, a total of 6,000.

The campaign came at a huge cost for the caliph, and paid few dividends. He was soon embroiled in suppressing another rebellion at home, and the caliphate gradually disengaged from the Roman front. The destruction of Amorion may be seen as the culmination of two centuries of raiding. The tide of war would soon be reversed; in fact, it already had. But at the time the campaign was a disaster for Theophilos. He had to race back to Constantinople to quash rumors of his death and suppress a plot. Amorion, a strategic hub and the most bustling city in central Asia Minor, was destroyed and abandoned for a generation, as confirmed by excavations. These poignantly turned up, among the ruins, a coin celebrating Theophilos' prior triumph.[39] The Romans coped with this disaster in the way that made most sense to them: they sanctified as martyrs the officers who were taken away and executed in 845, alleging that they had steadfastly refused to embrace Islam. They became the famous Forty-Two Martyrs of Amorion. This diverted attention away from the strategic failure of the campaign. And of course nothing was said about the victims of the Roman attack on Sozopetra in 837, who included both Christians and Muslims. On the Muslim side, the capture of Amorion was celebrated in a poem by Abu Tammam, which became one of the most quoted poems in Arabic literature. He compared the city to a wild woman tamed by the caliph's force.[40]

During the chaos of the Roman defeat in 838, the Persians had staged some kind of revolt, withdrawing north to Sinope or Amastris on the Black Sea. The causes and nature of this revolt are obscure, and it ended quickly when Theophilos made a show of force. The Persians' leader at this time was Theophobos, a young man who had been raised as a Roman. He was confined to the City and executed in 842 after Theophilos' death, allegedly on his orders. Meanwhile, rank-and-file Persians were dispersed into smaller units of 2,000 and resettled throughout the themes, in order to assimilate them to Roman society. The emperor even ordered that Roman women in the provinces had to marry them, and we know of at least one such wife, the later St. Athanasia of Aigina. For this action, Theophilos' critics accused him of being "a barbarian-lover," but the policy worked. A few generations later the Persians were "extinct" as a distinct group.[41]

The end of iconoclasm

Another group that was going extinct were the iconophile celebrities. Theodoros of Stoudios had died back in 826 and the ex-patriarch Nikephoros in 828, under Michael II, though they left behind a significant corpus of works defending the veneration of icons. Theodoros' brother Ioseph (the ex-archbishop of Thessalonike) and the septuagenarian Euthymios (the ex-bishop of Sardeis) were arrested in late 831 for circulating prophesies that predicted the emperor's death. Euthymios died after a whipping.[42] Those prophetic texts were written by a learned abbot from Syracuse, Methodios (a name evoking associations like those of Nostradamus today). He had arrived in Constantinople in 821 as a papal envoy and tried to convince Michael II to reverse his stance on icons, and for this he was confined to an island. He was, after all, an imperial subject plotting with a foreign power (the pope) to undermine state policy. While in confinement, he wrote the *Vision of the Prophet Daniel*, which survives in Slavonic translation. It recasts contemporary events in apocalyptic terms and predicts Michael II's death (a different text that he wrote about Theophilos a few years later resulted in the arrest of Euthymios). Methodios himself, however, was treated indulgently. He was invited to the palace and apparently held in high esteem by Theophilos on account of his occult learning. Our sources about this are confusing; some say that he was imprisoned in the palace.[43]

Theophilos cracked down more harshly on iconophile resistance than had his father or even Leon V, but apparently it was only opposition to imperial policy that was targeted, not the veneration of icons or pro-icon convictions. One icon painter, Lazaros, is said to have been tortured: he had red-hot iron plates pressed to his hands, but was miraculously still able to paint afterward. The artist himself was a historical figure who went on an embassy to Rome in 857, but the tale of his torments appears only in the mid-tenth century and is untrustworthy. Otherwise, only those who publicly opposed the authority of the court and the position of the Church were arrested, or who refused to take communion with their bishop. They were a small group. Some went into hiding. There were no popular demonstrations in their favor.[44]

As the older generation of iconophiles died out, new faces from Palestine appeared. Around 800, many Chalcedonians from the caliphate, especially those who could speak Greek, emigrated to Romanía, perhaps in order to escape the worsening conditions of Christians under Muslim rule and the adoption of the Arabic language by the Melkite Church. Three monks from the monastery of St. Sabas came to Constantinople in the mid-810s and were arrested, imprisoned, and tortured for agitating in favor of icons. They were Michael, *synkellos* of the patriarch of Jerusalem, and two brothers, Theodoros and Theophanes; all were in touch with the Sicilian Methodios. In 836, the emperor Theophilos had a longish poem tattooed on the faces of the two brothers accusing them of "twisted heresy," after which they were known as the Graptoi, or "Inscribed Ones." The low quality of the verses was presumably part of the punishment.[45]

Thus, Theophilos' iconoclasm did not arouse much opposition, except from a minority of dissidents, who were effectively suppressed. The prime mover of this Second Iconoclasm, Ioannes the Grammarian, was duly appointed patriarch in 837 or 838, when the post opened. He was a "skilled debater and subtle politician,"[46] but was so demonized by iconophile polemic as a sorcerer (and worse) that his accomplishments are hard to appreciate. His nephew Leon the Philosopher (and Mathematician) became archbishop of Thessalonike around the same time. Leon wrote interesting epigrams on Epicurus, geometry, and the ancient erotic novels. He was accused by a former student of abandoning Christianity for Hellenism. His surviving homily from Thessalonike starts out with an excursus on number theory and Neoplatonic readings of Christianity, and then oddly recounts a miracle tale in which an icon of the Virgin plays a positive role. Leon then argues that our present reality is an icon, or riddle, foreshadowing the future. Whatever his agenda was, it was his own.[47]

The succession remained uncertain in the 830s, as the imperial couple produced five daughters but no son who survived. Theophilos bestowed the rank of *kaisar* on the patrician Alexios Mosele and engaged him to his youngest daughter, Maria. Scholars assume that this marked Mosele as the presumptive heir, but the rank of *kaisar* did not necessarily mean that (Justinian II had bestowed it on the Bulgar ruler Tervel). Mosele was dispatched to suppress Slavs in the corridor between Constantinople and Thessalonike and fight against the Muslims in Sicily in 838. But Maria died and Mosele lost the emperor's favor and retired to a monastery.[48] In January, 840, Theodora gave birth to a son,

Michael III, who was crowned co-emperor. Theophilos died two years later, on 20 January, 842, meaning that another empress would rule on behalf of an underage heir, sixty years after Eirene had done the same.

Theodora's regime immediately set about restoring the veneration of icons. This "Triumph of Orthodoxy" is known through later sources that conflict on the details and claim credit for different parties. We have no official documentation, which is odd for an event that, in retrospect, was regarded as so important. The prime movers appear to have been Theodora herself; Theoktistos, the logothete of the *dromos* and (probably) a eunuch, on whom Theodora, much like Eirene, relied to govern the state (he had also been party to the assassination of Leon V); and Theodora's brothers Bardas and Petronas, both patricians and military officers. The restoration of the icons was, then, a coup in the Church orchestrated by politicians who were previously loyal to Theophilos and his iconoclastic agenda. The conspiracy included the abbot-prophet Methodios, who had also lived in the palace under Theophilos.

The simplest explanation for this change in policy is that Theodora was personally an iconophile. This idea was promoted in a number of texts hailing her as a saint for restoring the icons. To be sure, the back-and-forth of the controversy over icons, from beginning to end, depended on the preferences of the rulers and not on swings in public opinion, which remained, as Theodoros of Stoudios had put it, "untroubled and indifferent" to the whole matter.[49] We need not believe the tales that circulated later according to which Theodora, her mother, and her daughters venerated icons clandestinely under Theophilos. These stories had a gendered logic. Iconophiles noticed that iconoclasm was initiated by two military emperors named Leon and terminated twice by empresses who were regents for underage heirs. In response to the militarism of iconoclasm, the veneration of icons acquired a feminine aspect, and the ongoing invention of its history populated the families of the iconoclast emperors with female relatives who secretly venerated icons, such as a daughter of Konstantinos V, Eirene, the second wife of Michael II, Theodora, and others.[50] It was easier to tell stories of feminine piety than of women cleverly navigating the corridors of power.

The more pragmatic factors are obscure. Theodora may have reasoned that support for iconoclasm was perfunctory, a matter of obedience to official policy, whereas the iconophiles had produced a small but vocal group of activists who claimed the moral high ground and histrionically linked their cause to the ideals of martyrdom and resistance to heresy. The iconoclasts lacked such a voice. Unlike 786, there was now no longer an anti-icon lobby in the army. Also, after Amorion iconoclasm was no guarantee of victory.[51] Therefore, as Theodora's nascent regime was more vulnerable to disruption from iconophiles, she moved to co-opt them. Repressing them was more trouble than it was worth, whereas their support would bolster her regime and smooth relations with other Christian states and Churches. And if her regime calculated that iconoclasts would offer little resistance, they were right.

The movers in the palace canvassed for iconophile support among the hermits of Bithynia, not the Stoudites. Theodora recalled the exiles to the capital and many meetings ensued in the palace and Theoktistos' house, where a plan of action was worked out and "debates" planned between Methodios (the intended new patriarch) and whoever took up the challenge on the other side. This was exactly how Leon V had proceeded in 815. Theodora also struck a deal with her new iconophile allies. She insisted that Theophilos' reputation not be tarnished in the process, and she told a tale of her husband's deathbed repentance. At one meeting, she sweetened the deal by casually mentioning that Theophilos had even left some money for the ascetics in his will. "To Hell with him and his money!", one of the hermits burst out, but eventually they all saw reason. By March, 843 the pieces were in place. A synod of some kind was held on 3 March—though it is barely attested—where Nicaea II was reaffirmed, canceling both Hiereia and the Council of 815; Methodios was elected patriarch; and the patriarch Ioannes the Grammarian, who did not attend, was deposed. On 10 March, Methodios held an all-night vigil at the Blachernai church, after which, on 11 March, the first Sunday of Lent, he and all the priests who were now on his side processed to Hagia Sophia with an icon of Christ and the Virgin held high. There they were joined by Theodora, Michael III, and the court, and a new liturgy composed by Methodios was performed. The procession was repeated annually thereafter and the Feast of Orthodoxy has been celebrated on the first Sunday of Lent ever since.[52]

The restoration had winners and losers. The remains of the patriarch Nikephoros were brought back to the City and, in a solemn procession, buried in the church of the Holy Apostles. Ioannes the Grammarian was, according to one version, confined to a monastery cell whose ceiling had an image of Christ "that stared at him sharply." Ioannes, whose behavior throughout had been, as far as we know, proper, was subsequently demonized as a sorcerer and harbinger of the Antichrist. These polemics also took the form of manuscript images, where Ioannes is compared to the men who gave Jesus vinegar, to Simon Magus, or he is instructed by king David on the true meaning of Psalm 113 that condemned idolatry (see Figure 35).[53] It is unclear how many priests and bishops were deposed with him. Some historians speak of a great purge of the Church, targeting all those who were ordained by iconoclast bishops as well as those who were ordained by Nikephoros but who had gone iconoclast after 815. But we hear little of the massive disruption this would have caused. There were "iconoclast" priests who "repented" and were allowed to join the winning team.[54]

Prestigious monasteries were turned over to supporters of the new regime. Michael, the *synkellos* from Jerusalem, was appointed *synkellos* to Methodios and

Figure 35 The famous anti-iconoclast page in the Khludow Psalter, where iconoclasts who paint over Jesus' image are compared to the soldiers who pierced his side on the Cross.
Public Domain

abbot of the monastery of the Chora. Theophanes, one of the Graptoi, became the bishop of Nikaia, against objections that he was unsuitable. The most unexpected winner was the emperor Theophilos, whose last-minute conversion was

Figure 36 Apse mosaic of the Virgin and Child in Hagia Sophia (ninth century)
Photo by David Hendrix

broadcast by the court and made its way into a number of texts. His own iconoclast officials and in-laws, who masterminded the restoration of icons and never expressed any contrition for their past, were likewise rehabilitated in subsequent hagiography. Thus, posterity ended up with a mixed view of Theophilos, even though he had been the most fervent iconoclast emperor.[55]

The restoration of icons was a political settlement of a dispute within the Church, and it was brought about by former "iconoclasts." It was not primarily about icons as such or their theology. Icons did not start going up everywhere after 843, only on the much-contested façade of the Chalke Gatehouse. It was not until 867, a whole generation later, that the cross in the apse of Hagia Sophia was replaced with a mosaic of the Virgin and Child (see Figure 36). It was accompanied by an epigram that presented it as a "restoration by the pious emperors" of an original figural mosaic, but this was likely a fiction: it was the first figural mosaic in that space, posing as a restoration. In the tenth century, this epigram was placed at the start of the *Greek Anthology*, an important poetic collection.[56]

The synod that restored icons in March, 843 made no theological advances on Nicaea II. Many treatises had by now been written on religious imagery, by John of Damascus (which were still unknown), Nikephoros, and Theodoros of Stoudios. These are sometimes hailed as great achievements, but there is no sign that they influenced the course of the dispute. In this respect, the struggle over icons was fundamentally different from the theological conflicts of the fourth through seventh centuries. Those were about verbal formulas that became slogans and the rallying cries of competing identities, with no observable difference in Christian practice or material culture. "Iconoclasm" was about the use and placement of icons, and it was debated primarily through rudimentary theories buttressed by the compilation of citations to prior Christian literature. The sophisticated arguments of a Nikephoros or Theodoros were largely irrelevant to the *history* of the debate.

Yet, like the theological controversies of the past, iconoclasm created that which it opposed. Before it, icons had not been a pervasive, extensively theorized, and indeed almost necessary part of Christian worship. It was during this struggle that iconophiles came to see icons as a core component of Orthodox worship, in the same way that previous theological controversies treated doctrines created during the controversy as eternal truths of Christian belief. It was "Iconoclasm" that established the veneration of icons.

The regime of Theodora

The Romans finally began to benefit from an improved geostrategic situation. Al-Mu'tasim's invasion of 838 was the caliphate's last direct attack before it began to disintegrate. Many of its regional governors became autonomous or founded separatist dynasties. The caliphs faced rebellions even in territories close to Iraq. Agricultural productivity declined, while social inequality and exploitation began to make even Iraq itself ungovernable. Most importantly, the caliphs became increasingly beholden to their Turkish mercenaries, disrupting their ability to implement coherent, centralized rule. From now on, the threats faced by Romanía came from smaller and more regional Muslim powers along the periphery, though these too were capable of striking hard.

Aghlabid forces were firmly established in the west of Sicily and continued to expand their holdings, albeit slowly, after heavy fighting. In 843, they took Messina, which gave them control of the straits and limited the empire's access to the western Mediterranean. Romans emigrated from Sicily to the Italian mainland or farther east. But the Aghlabids expanded operations into southern Italy too. They raided Calabria and intervened in the conflicts of the Lombard duchies. Mercenary armies of "Saracens" or "Moors" (in reality, ethnically mixed Muslims) were hired first by one side and then the other, which gave them the opportunity to become ensconced in the mainland. Muslim forces briefly occupied Taranto (840) and Bari (841), and raided in the Adriatic as far as Istria. Constantinople called on Venice for help, but the Muslims prevailed in the naval fighting. The Saracens were leapfrogging over the empire's holdings in Sicily and Calabria. They occupied the islands off the Italian coast and, in 846, landed at Ostia, marched up the Tiber, and plundered the suburbs of Rome itself, including the churches of St. Peter and St. Paul-Outside-the-Walls. As New Rome now lay beyond the Muslims' reach, Old Rome was becoming more accessible. The event was traumatic for the papacy. Interestingly, among the treasures in St. Peter's was a silver table with an image of Constantinople on the top, a gift by Charlemagne. Even in Old Rome, the Muslims were finding images of New Rome.[57]

Attacks came also from Crete. This was no den of pirates, but a full-blown emirate with its own army, navy, intellectual and religious life, and treaties with other Muslim powers. The Romans in the Aegean experienced it primarily as a predator. Some Greek islands, such as Aigina, were abandoned as their residents sought the safety of the mainland. Even coastal settlements moved further inland, or behind mountain slopes so as not to be visible to pirates. The imperial navy conducted regular patrols armed with Greek fire, and chains of watchtowers and fire signals warned inhabitants of impending attacks. On one occasion under Theophilos, the Cretans even marched into the hinterland of the Thrakesion theme, although they were soundly defeated by the local general.[58] But for the Roman high command, these precarious conditions, which disrupted both the economy and communications, were unacceptable, and the reconquest of Crete became a top priority. Theoktistos, the logothete of the *dromos*, undertook this personally in 843. He sailed to Crete and besieged some cities but, for reasons that remain unclear, abandoned the campaign. A contemporary lamented that "Crete and Cyprus, Euboia, Lesbos, Sardinia, and Sicily are no more . . . they are in danger of not belonging to the Christians."[59]

In the east, Romanía's main opponent was 'Amr al-Aqta, the quasi-autonomous emir of Melitene and veteran of the 838 campaign against Amorion. In 844, he raided Asia Minor as far as Malagina, the military depot in Bithynia. Theoktistos again personally took the field against him but was badly defeated. He blamed the defeat on Theodora's brother Bardas, who was expelled from the City.[60] 'Amr became an even greater danger when he was joined by members of the Paulician sect who were fleeing from Romanía. The origins and beliefs of the Paulicians are obscure and controversial. The sect originated in the borderlands between Armenia, Asia Minor, and Syria, though it came to the attention of the Roman authorities only in the ninth century. They were seen as "Manichaean" dualists, that is as believers in a cosmic struggle between a good and an evil god. This was probably an erroneous characterization of their beliefs, which took their cue from St. Paul; Paulician leaders even took on the names of the Apostle's companions. Roman law, however, punished Manichaeanism with death. In 812, the patriarch Nikephoros advocated the death penalty for them but was opposed by Theodoros of Stoudios, who argued that everyone should be allowed to repent. The emperor Michael I heeded the abbot over the patriarch, yet some Paulicians were executed nonetheless.[61]

In the mid-840s, Theodora cracked down on the Paulicians in Asia Minor. Many were executed (though not 100,000, as our sole source claims), and their properties were confiscated to the imperial treasury. In distress, a Paulician named Karbeas, who was an officer in the imperial army, led 5,000 of his co-believers (a more plausible figure) to ʿAmr at Melitene, where they were organized as an anti-Roman cohort settled at the fort of Tephrike, located between Romanía and Armenia. A later Roman ambassador to Tephrike reported that "they regard themselves as Christians, and call us instead 'Romans,' as if that were our religious identity, whereas in fact it is our national identity." The Paulicians then joined the Muslims in raiding Asia Minor, or did so on their own.[62] They are unusual among Christian sects in quickly transforming their religious identity into a political one, and then in forming armies to attack their former polity.

Despite his failures against Crete and ʿAmr, Theoktistos managed to remain in charge of the administration and sideline his rivals until 855. Apart from the aforementioned events, those were quiet years. Romanía was entering a phase of relative security and cultural consensus. The issue of icons was settled, never to be reopened. The Romans were increasingly bringing the fight to the enemy. In May, 853, a Roman fleet attacked Damietta, an important port and military depot in the Nile delta. Its defense force had been withdrawn to Fustat to police a festival, so Damietta was unguarded. 5,000 Roman marines captured and destroyed it, seizing shipments of weapons intended for the Arabs in Crete. Six years later, in 859, the Romans raided Damietta again.[63]

The regime of Bardas and Michael III

In the 850s, politics at the court took a strange turn and began to resemble a murderous soap opera. The events, which resulted in a change of dynasty, need only be summarized. Theodora and Theoktistos arranged for the teenager Michael III to marry Eudokia Dekapolitissa, because they detested his girlfriend, Eudokia Ingerina (though Michael allegedly continued his affair with her). Then Theodora's brother Bardas gained influence over Michael, stoked his resentment, and the two of them ambushed Theoktistos in the palace on 20 November, 855, and killed him as he was carrying paperwork from the office. After a family standoff, Bardas and Michael expelled Theodora and her daughters from the palace and confined them to the convent of Gastria, which became the place to offload unwanted imperial women. Bardas governed for a decade on his nephew's behalf, as *kaisar* after 862. During that time, Michael took up with an older, muscle-bound peasant from Macedonia named Basileios, whom he made his chamberlain (*parakoimomenos*, a post normally held by eunuchs), and a patrician. The two men eventually ganged up on Bardas and murdered him on 21 April, 866, during another (aborted) expedition against Crete. Michael adopted Basileios and proclaimed him co-emperor in Hagia Sophia on 26 May. He also gave him his former girlfriend, Eudokia Ingerina, to have as his wife. On 24 September, 867, the farce ran its course when Basileios murdered Michael and established his own dynasty—unless of course one believes, as some did at the time, that Michael was sleeping with Ingerina all along, making Leon VI, who was born in late 866, the son of Michael and not Basileios. In return for the use of Ingerina, Michael gave his own eldest sister Thekla to Basileios as a mistress.[64]

Little of this is serious history. Parts of it were written to expose the sordid origins of the Macedonian dynasty (the sexual arrangements), whereas other parts (Michael's dissolute lifestyle) were concocted to justify his murder by Basileios. Theodora, the restorer of icons, had to be presented as blameless, passive, pious, and long-suffering, and even as predicting that Basileios would displace her own son. Yet one chronicle tells of a plot by Theodora against Bardas (her brother) after she had been expelled from the palace, so maybe she was not passive.[65] The Macedonians also had to blacken the memories of both Bardas and Michael III, Basileios' victims. Bardas, whom even his enemies called "a dedicated and energetic manager of the republic,"[66] was slandered as sleeping with his own daughter-in-law. Meanwhile, Michael's image was modeled on the likes of Nero, with all the requisite crimes and follies, to justify his murder in the name of the common good. The logothete Theoktistos—who had tortured iconophiles under Theophilos, only to become a saint later on—had to be cast as a victim of Bardas' lust for power. Basileios was then the capstone of this drama, a figure of massively heroic stature and unrivaled royal pedigree, chosen by God and destiny to restore the republic, acting always for the common good and in self-defense as he murdered his way to the top. No one was fooled. As soon as the dynasty had expired, Michael Psellos wondered how it became so great in light of "the lawless way in which its roots were planted with murder and bloodshed."[67]

In reality, Michael III emerges as a fun-loving young man who wronged no one, and under him Romanía prospered. His reign was stable and successful. There are hints that his building program in the capital was extensive. He rebuilt the Church of the Pharos in the palace, and inscriptions attest to work in provincial cities, especially Nikaia and Ankyra.[68] The regime, whether led by Bardas or Michael himself, was successful in fighting the empire's enemies in the east, which later Macedonian writers suppressed or buried under invented defeats. In reality, when it came to raiding the balance tipped in favor of the Romans, who rampaged through Cilicia in 855, and attacked Asamosaton, Amida, and Tephrike in 856 (under the lead of Petronas, Michael's other uncle) and Samosata in 859 (jointly by Michael and Bardas).[69] 'Amr of Melitene and the Paulicians raided too, but to lesser effect. 'Amr scored his greatest success in 863, when he penetrated deep into Asia Minor and sacked Amisos on the Black Sea coast, but he was then destroyed at Poson, on 3 September. His conqueror Petronas led the *tagmata* and most thematic armies, and prevailed through a brilliant tactical encirclement. The Arabic historian al-Tabari says that Michael participated in the campaign (the Roman sources are silent about that), and it is possible that the

Paulician Karbeas fell there too. Petronas celebrated a triumph in Constantinople, parading ʿAmr's head on a stick. "After that, there was deep peace in the east."[70]

The regime was less successful in the west, where the Muslims chipped away at Sicily, defeating another fleet sent from the capital. In 859, they captured Enna (Castrogiovanni) at the center of the island, which the Romans had been using as their military headquarters. Henceforth, the Romans were confined to the eastern part of Sicily, with Syracuse as their base.[71] But the most alarming event of the reign occurred in the following year, on 18 June, 860, when Constantinople was suddenly attacked by a Viking fleet of 200 ships. The emperor was in Asia Minor preparing for a campaign (this was before Poson), and the City had to fend for itself. The Vikings plundered the suburbs and coasts, terrifying the Romans with their willingness to slaughter for its own sake. Then they abruptly left, though possibly many of them perished in a sudden storm. The patriarch Photios delivered two emergency sermons at the time, in which he called the attack "a bolt from the farthest north, a hail-storm of barbarians," sent as a punishment for the Romans' sins. He claims that the Virgin drove them away after he and the citizens processed on the walls with her garment, the sacred *maphorion*. That previously "unknown nation, which is now famous," were the Rus'.[72]

Photios, Nicholas, and Bulgaria

Whether Photios had heard of the Rus' before 860 or not, by 867 he knew their name and could claim, in an encyclical letter to the patriarchs of the east, that both the Rus' and Bulgars had abandoned their "Hellenic atheism" (i.e., paganism) and accepted Christianity from his hands.[73] About this conversion of the Rus' we hear nothing more, but the conversion of Bulgaria was a complicated affair that drew in the Franks, the pope, and Constantinople, and Photios found himself at the middle of it. His career was dogged by controversies that caused dissension within Roman society and further widened the "significant rift" that already existed between the eastern and western Churches.[74]

When the patriarch Methodios died in 847, Theodora replaced him with Ignatios, son of the emperor Michael I and grandson of Nikephoros I, who had survived the ill-fated expedition to Pliska in 811. He had been castrated by Leon V, and became abbot of a monastery that had not resisted Theophilos' iconoclasm. Theodora seems to have appointed him without the convocation of a synod, so his election could be challenged as uncanonical. After Theodora's downfall, Ignatios fell afoul of Michael III's regime. He was formally deposed; it appears also that he resigned, possibly under pressure.[75]

A synod then elected Photios, the head of the chancery (*protasekretis*), as the new patriarch, and he was presumably the court's choice. Photios was a great-nephew of the patriarch Tarasios and his parents had suffered under Theophilos because of icons, or so Photios claimed. One of his uncles had married

Theodora's sister and another was the ex-patriarch Ioannes the Grammarian (who died around this time, in the early 860s). Photios was a learned scholar, unlike Ignatios, who despised secular learning. His lexicon and reviews of ancient books (*Bibliotheca* or *Myriobiblon*, i.e., "Ten Thousand Books," in reality just under 300) are still used by classicists today. A layman when he was elected, he had to be rushed through the grades of the priesthood in a week to be made patriarch on Christmas, 858.[76] During his first patriarchate (858–867), Photios made the defeat of iconoclasm his signature issue, whether because of his background or as a safe issue on which to grandstand. At most of the Councils that are about to be mentioned, he insisted on repeatedly condemning iconoclasm. It was also during these years that religious images appeared in prominent churches of the capital, such as the Pharos and Hagia Sophia, and Photios harped on these images in his homilies from the 860s.[77] A whole generation had elapsed between the triumph of the icons and their appearance in churches in the capital.

However, the manner of Photios' election created a schism in the Church, as some bishops refused to accept Ignatios' deposition. A detailed account of the ensuing conflict is not necessary here, as it would take us into the weeds of Church procedure. The issue was supercharged, however, when pope Nicholas I (858–867) exploited this opportunity to intervene in the affairs of Constantinople. Popes had in the past asserted the right to review and confirm or overturn the deposition of eastern prelates, though they had recently declined to involve themselves when eastern priests appealed to them (e.g., Theodoros of Stoudios during the Moechian controversy). But Constantinople had never recognized this Roman right. Appeals to Rome had supposedly been authorized by the canons of the Council of Serdica (342), but that had been an ad hoc decision to allow pope Julius to intervene in the case of Athanasios. Serdica was a split council, whose canons lacked legal validity in the east. A later Orthodox scribe noted that "this canon is clearly about bishops in the west . . . until now, such a custom has not taken hold anywhere [in the east]." Besides, whatever Serdica may have decided, it was superseded by the Ecumenical Council of Chalcedon, which gave the right of appeal to Constantinople. Finally, not even Serdica had authorized what Nicholas demanded after his disquisition on Roman supremacy: namely, that "the emperor of the Greeks" should hold a council before the pope's legates to reexamine the case of Ignatios, and then the legates would report back to Nicholas so that he could make the final decision. He also demanded the return of Illyricum to the Church of Rome along with the old papal patrimonies in Calabria and Sicily.[78]

Constantinople must have wondered where the pope was deriving these newfound powers to *personally* arbitrate all disputes in the Christian world. The eastern Romans knew by now that Old Rome had an exalted sense of its place in the world and sometimes tended to act imperiously, but the procedure proposed by the pope was radically new. Little did they know that Nicholas' conception of his powers was based on a set of forged documents, the *Pseudo-Isidoran Decretals*.[79] Still, for the sake of good relations they indulged him, as the bishop of Kaisareia put it, "for the sake of the honor of St. Peter."[80] Yet Constantinople insisted that the verdict be pronounced there and then, and not referred back to Rome, and discussion of Sicily, Calabria, and Illyricum was out of the question. The council was held in 861 in Constantinople, with the emperor in attendance, though its acts were suppressed by the Ignatians later. Photios and the court treated this council as yet another opportunity to condemn iconoclasm, with the matter of Ignatios as secondary. Still, the legates duly ratified Ignatios' deposition.

This news was brought back to Nicholas along with a deferential letter by Photios. But the pope, after a long deliberation, announced in 862 that he did not accept the council, and he deposed his own legates for violating his instructions. In 863, after he had been lobbied intensely by partisans of Ignatios who had come to Rome, Nicholas convened a synod in Rome that found in favor of Ignatios and deposed and excommunicated Photios. It is possible that Nicholas had come to an agreement with the followers of Ignatios, that their man would restore Illyricum to the papacy in exchange for his reinstatement, or at least so claimed pope John VIII in 874. But, as Constantinople saw it, Nicholas was trying to depose a patriarch on his own authority, citing not a heresy but newfangled procedural rules amplified by a fantastic theory of papal supremacy. Vicious abuse against Photios was aired at the Roman council and communicated to Constantinople.[81]

There was a pressing reason why Nicholas had his eye on Illyricum at this time. He knew that king Boris of Bulgaria was preparing to convert to Christianity, and Bulgaria overlapped with much of the former diocese. It is unclear why Boris wanted to convert. It may have been a personal decision, though we can dispense with the fanciful tales of the sources, including that he was forced to convert when Michael and Bardas menaced him with an army and fleet in a time of famine.[82] Bulgaria had always had a large Christian population, and they may have shifted the culture internally. The two major powers flanking the kingdom, Francia and Romanía, were Christian, and Boris wanted to be seen as a peer and not a savage, like the pagan Magyars (Hungarians) and Varangians (Rus') who were causing him such trouble further north. Churches also enabled kings to organize and manage their realms in more centralized ways.

Contrary to a popular myth, Constantinople had no master plan to convert foreign nations. For all that "the conversion of the Slavs" is regarded as a great accomplishment, the Romans took little or no active interest in the conversion of any Slavs who did not live within the empire. They responded passively, and with more duty than enthusiasm, to petitions from foreign kings asking for help to convert their realms. The Romans never viewed converted barbarians as equals. Conversion could at best "tame" the savages, but they remained barbarians.[83]

The most famous missionaries of this era were two brothers from Thessalonike, Constantine and Methodios, who were dispatched to Moravia when its king Rastislav asked Michael III for experts who could teach in the Slavic language. Constantine had allegedly studied under Leon the Philosopher and Photios, and was a friend of the latter. He devised Glagolitic, the earliest script for Slavic, and translated many Christian texts into it. The script that evolved from it, Cyrilic, was named after the monastic name that he assumed before his death in 869. The two brothers believed that people could celebrate the liturgy in their own vernacular tongues and not only Greek and Latin, as some in the west believed. In Venice, Constantine reminded the skeptics that Armenians, Syrians, Persians, Georgians, Goths, and others already worshipped God in their own languages.[84] Yet Constantine-Cyril and Methodios are not mentioned in east Roman texts. They remained unknown in their native land until references to them seeped in from much later Bulgarian sources.

In 864, Boris and many of his boyars were baptized by east Roman bishops. The king took the name Michael, after the emperor who sponsored him. Yet Boris was keeping his options open and seeking advice and missionaries from the Franks and Rome too. Meanwhile, the tensions between Rome and Constantinople were rising. In a letter that likely used severe language, Michael III protested the papal synod of 863 and reminded the pope that the retrial of Ignatios in 861 had been a courtesy to Rome. However, we know about this letter only through Nicholas' long response to it in 865, which was written by a native of Rome, Anastasius the Librarian, as the pope was ill. Anastasius did more than anyone else to poison the west's view of the eastern empire, for this polemical letter proved to be influential. It contains a long defense of papal supremacy, and tries to score points against "the Greeks" along the way. "Nicholas" claims that Michael insulted Latin as a "barbarous and Scythian tongue," which has been taken by modern scholars as a sign that Constantinople was leaving its Latin past behind, but the emperor was probably referring only to the vulgarization of contemporary Roman Latin, which made it difficult to translate in Constantinople. Anastasius distorted the text to wax indignant, and demanded that Michael cease calling himself "the emperor of the Romans," as the "Greeks" spoke no Latin at all. He rubs it in that the Greeks had lost Crete, Sicily, and other provinces. Above all, he avers, the power of Rome over all the Churches is rooted in Christ, not in any Council, so the emperor has no authority to resist it. The pope was "the ruler of the entire world."[85]

The conversion of Bulgaria threw fuel onto this fire. In later 866, Nicholas sent to Boris a text with 106 chapters, each of which answered a question about the ethical consequences of conversion, from food and clothing to sexual practices and war. It is a gold mine of information about pagan Bulgar life, at least the version of it that the pope struggled to understand from the questions put to him by Boris. The Bulgarians—which is what we call Bulgars after their conversion—set about implementing the basic requirements of Christian life. Cremations, for example, virtually disappear from their cemeteries at this time. The boyars had to give up all their wives but one (this has not left an archaeological record). But in some of his answers, the pope rejects what "the Greeks" were allegedly telling Boris about minor aspects of Christian life (e.g., clothes and washing). Nicholas also wrote "to the man Photios" and called him a viper and a Jew. He called on theologians in western Europe to condemn the "Greek heresy." Writing against the "errors of the Greeks" now became a genre of Latin theological polemic, and "Greece" was regarded as a breeding ground of heresy.[86]

A similar realization of religious difference was dawning on Constantinople too, with grave consequences. East Roman missionaries in Bulgaria reported that their Frankish counterparts advocated clerical celibacy and other practices that deviated from Orthodoxy. "The crown of these evils," as Photios characterized it, was the addition of a word, *filioque*, to the Creed of Nicaea, which made the Holy Spirit proceed not just from the Father (as in the original text) but from the Father *and* the Son. This arbitrary tampering with the Creed—no matter its theological import—was a serious offense.[87] The papacy had not yet adopted this formula; for now it was a Frankish error. But Bulgaria had become a battle-ground for three conceptions of Christianity linked to three rival states.

In the summer of 867, Photios convened a council in Constantinople. It is tenuously attested because its acts were systematically destroyed by the Ignatians and the popes. Yet it billed itself as an Ecumenical Council for the condemnation of all heresies, especially iconoclasm. It also anathematized Nicholas and conferred the title "emperor" on Louis II of Italy, probably in the hope that he would move against Nicholas, as he had done in the past for his own reasons. However, the pope died on 13 November, before he could learn of this council.[88] And events were moving quickly in Constantinople too. Bardas had already been assassinated by Basileios in 866, while on a campaign against Crete. The official story was that he was plotting to kill Michael.[89] Basileios was proclaimed co-emperor on 26 May, 867 (thus, his signature was also on the Acts of the Council of 867, which is why he too later wanted them to be destroyed). Then, on 24 September, Michael was murdered and Basileios became sole emperor.

On the cusp of empire

By 867, the Roman empire had pulled ahead of the competition, leaving its own "successors" behind in both west and east. A few generations earlier, it was not obvious that this would happen. In 800, Romanía was overshadowed by the Frankish empire of Charlemagne and the high point of the Abbasid caliphate. Charlemagne conquered the kingdom of the Lombards, territory that had once belonged to Constantinople, and forged a more constructive relationship with the papal state than Constantinople ever had. Harun al-Rashid sent an elephant to Charlemagne and received Spanish horses in return, exchanges that bypassed the Romans.[90]

Yet by mid-century both Francia and the caliphate were in terminal decline. Both had feet of clay and collapsed under their own weight. Neither was unified in culture, ethnicity, institutions, or political purpose, and their regional nobilities and provincial populations saw no reason to remain loyal when the center revealed its weakness. The polity of the Romans was on the opposite trajectory. It had finally aligned the emergency measures of the crisis years with institutions inherited from antiquity, creating a streamlined and efficient administration. It remonetized its economy with its own national currency and struck the right balance between efficient taxation (enough for the state to now be rich) and provincial loyalty. It was possible to imagine the polity as a "human body, in which every part plays a role that contributes to the good of the whole.... State officials should not be more concerned about themselves than their subjects, and should strike a balance so that neither the treasury nor landowners suffer injustice."[91]

The international scene in which Romanía operated had also stabilized. The extent to which the Romans had a Grand Strategy is debatable. But ambassadors were coming and going in all directions, bearing gifts, information, and proposals. Constantinople often sought marriage alliances with the Frankish kings, though none of them had yet worked out. The important thing was that the courts were in frequent communication. The two empires were distant enough that they touched only in Venetia, and rarely in southern Italy, which eased relations. "If you have a Frank for a friend, he is clearly not your neighbor," said a Greek proverb from this time.[92] Despite growing prejudice against the "Greeks," Constantinople remained a gold standard of imperial Romanness in the west, though it was copied tacitly more than recognized explicitly. When western Europeans of this age looked back to the ancient Roman empire, in reality they were often looking sideways to the current Roman empire.

Roman embassies to the caliphate sought to secure the ransom or exchange of prisoners, and tried to make sense of the Muslims' cultural achievements. But as the Muslim world broke up, Roman diplomacy exploited the rifts. For example, the emperors sought an alliance with the Umayyads in Spain against the Aghlabids in Sicily. While this did not result in joint action (for now), we have a fascinating account of the court of Theophilos written by a Spanish envoy, a poet who told the emperor that "I am so captivated by the charms of the queen [i.e., Theodora], that I can't listen to the conversation."[93] A military manual of that era advised that, if envoys come from a distant land, they may be shown anything, but, "if they come from strong nations nearby, we should not show them our wealth or the beauty of our women, only the number of our men and the polish of their weapons."[94]

As for the north, it is doubtful that the emperors had a grand policy for the steppe, even though scholars often depict them as trying to maneuver the Khazars, Rus', Pechenegs, and Magyars like pieces on a board, as Justinian I had done with his northern neighbors. This illusion emerges from a dossier compiled in the tenth century by Konstantinos VII, the *De administrando imperio*, but its stories are not reliable.[95] Imperial diplomacy usually just tried to keep tribal lords happy with precious gifts, silk, and cash. There were Roman spies everywhere and mission reports were filed in the imperial archives. These operations, like the manufacture of Greek fire, were secret enough that we know little more about them than their existence.[96]

Contrary to another myth, the empire did not have an "ecumenical" or "universal" ideology. Ever since antiquity, the Romans viewed the *oikoumene* as coterminous with their polity and its dependencies and not as an abstract ideal transcending state, cultural, ethnic, or religious boundaries, which is the modern sense of the word. Much confusion has been caused by slippage between these two meanings. Moreover, the Romans had no ambitions to conquer the world or even all the territories that they had lost since the fourth century, except in the Balkans and along the eastern frontier, in which they succeeded in the tenth and eleventh centuries. They did not anticipate, plan for, or work toward the conversion of all people to Christianity. There was no bureau for missionary activity, and no state operations can be linked to apocalyptic End Times scenarios.[97] To be sure, the emperors believed that they were the most prestigious monarchs in the known world and that only their state was fully legitimate in both Roman and Christian terms. They expected others to look up to them as "fathers."[98] They were not surprised when foreign people, from Italy to Kiev, erected their own versions of Hagia Sophia in their cities and generally imitated Roman ways. But they knew where the boundaries of Romanía ended and where *barbaricum* began.

In this period, Romanía was not an "empire," at least not in the sense that this word has acquired in English, namely a state constituted through the conquest by one ethnic or ethnoreligious group of a number of others, who are maintained in a state of subjection to the metropolis. The polity of the Romans had ceased to be that a long time ago. The vast majority of its population, in both the capital and the provinces, were ethnic Romans with the same legal standing. In fact, there was no word in medieval Greek that corresponds to our "empire." Historians use that term through a double inertia: first, because Romanía was the direct continuation of the ancient *imperium* and, second, because medieval Latin protocols translated *basileus* as *imperator*. Yet despite these philological facts, the Roman state in this period was not sociologically an empire. It was the kingdom or polity of the Roman people, which is what it consistently called itself. It was more like a national state than an empire, though it was on a path toward empire.[99]

The ninth century was a brief moment of equilibrium between Romanía and its main rivals, the papacy in the religious sphere, the Franks in claiming the legacy of Roman empire, and the Muslims in offering an alternative to the Christian Roman order. It is no accident that this was when Constantinople and the Frankish kings began to spar over the imperial title; when Rome and New Rome began to spar over Latin and its relation to Romanness; and when one Niketas of Byzantion, using a Greek translation of the Quran, wrote the first refutations of both Islam and Armenian Christianity.[100] The lines of difference were being drawn more sharply.

Iconoclasm had driven a wedge between the Church of Constantinople and the Chalcedonian Churches outside the empire. But the Triumph of Orthodoxy in 843 did not result in a harmonious reunion. The Triumph was limited to Romanía and its Church; no other part of Christendom had gone through the convulsions of "Iconoclasm." Thus, Romanía bore the imprint of a unique historical experience. This included a powerful narrative of evil heretical emperors persecuting icon-venerating confessor-monks. The Triumph did not open channels to the eastern Churches, which had already embarked upon a different historical trajectory under Muslim rule. Some adopted the Arabic language, which took them further away from the common ground that they shared with Romanía. Nor did it ease relations with Rome, which immediately became more aggressive than ever under Nicholas, who pressed Rome's demand to rule the Church in a monarchical way. Photios and Michael III pushed back against that claim, leading to what scholarship, given its western bias, calls the "Photian Schism," although it was the pope who first excommunicated the patriarch. Photios had, up to then, been accommodating and deferential to Rome.

The conflict between Rome and Constantinople was for now limited to the leadership of the Church and the court. There was, as yet, no clash of identities on the ground, no "us" versus "them," at least not on the eastern side. Many eastern Romans thought highly of the Church of Rome, which had been on the right side of most theological controversies. Pope Nicholas, by contrast, had fully developed an outlook of us versus them, "they" being the heretical, faithless Greek. It would take a long time for the easterners to develop an equivalent polemical outlook, but when they did it would become a constitutive element of their Orthodox identity. From an esteemed and prestigious source of religious authority, Rome would, for many, become the Great Enemy. But those battle lines had not yet been drawn. At any rate, the papal state was quickly enmeshed in the sordid politics of the city of Rome and declined dramatically after the 870s. For two centuries, it was in no position to make demands. The apogee of east Roman power (930–1050) coincided with weakness among the Franks, popes, and caliphs.

The Greek literary tradition was another common patrimony over which these heirs of the ancient world contended. Arabic science and philosophy had shot ahead of their Roman counterparts, but continued to rely heavily on foundational ancient texts, which had to be translated from ancient Greek into Arabic, often via Syriac. This was an act of cultural appropriation, and the Muslim world imagined that its leading scholars were traveling to "Rum" in order to find manuscripts and teachers of Greek (though it is debatable whether they were actually doing so). The Arab essayist al-Jahiz (d. 869) polemicized against Romans who lay claim to the ancient Greek patrimony. Ancient texts, he says, were written by pagan Greeks, whereas the "Rum" were Christians and Romans. Some Muslim scholars claimed that contemporary Greek, which they called "the language of the Romans," was a separate language from "Ionian," which is what they called ancient Greek.[101] On the papal side, pope Nicholas' ghostwriter, Anastasius the Librarian, who knew Greek, translated a number of works into Latin, focusing on Christian literature. He saw this as an act of reclamation, of bringing Christian texts "back" into the Latin fold where they belonged, taking them away from the heretical and deceitful "Greeks" of the east.[102] Thus, while the Arabs were appropriating Greek culture from the "Romans" (who were definitely *not* Greeks), Latins were appropriating Christian and Roman culture from "the Greeks" (who were definitely *not* Romans). That is what it looks like to be caught in the middle.

The revival of learning

The east Romans alone did not need translations to access the literature of the ancient Greeks and the Church Fathers. We have that literature today because they preserved it in its original language, which was still the language of their formal education. More than just preserving it, they shaped the classical canon by deciding which texts to copy into the new minuscule and which not. Our canon is thus an east Roman artifact, focusing on genres, authors, and texts that they liked or needed, while the rest was allowed to fall away.[103] They took little interest in foreign intellectual developments, deeming their own classical and Christian heritage to be sufficient for higher learning, enjoyment, and piety. From the Arabs they took some astronomical and occult knowledge, whereas from the contemporary Latin west they took almost nothing. They already had all the Latin they needed in the form of Greek versions of Justinian's *Corpus*, which was about to be reissued formally by Leon VI at the end of the century.[104]

According to an influential thesis, the end of iconoclasm in 843 inaugurated a phase of humanism in literature and a closer engagement with ancient models.[105] This probably puts it too late. The first wave of authors to experiment with both old and new literary genres were educated in the second half of the eighth century. They included the historian and patriarch Nikephoros; the chronicler Theophanes; the hagiographer Stephanos the deacon, who had a talent for dramatic narrative and invective; and of course Theodoros of Stoudios, a vivid writer who, moreover, used Aristotelian logic to defend the veneration of images. The second wave was educated around the turn of the ninth century, along with the invention of the new script. These included the patriarchs Ioannes the Grammarian (whose thought was later suppressed), Methodios, and many hagiographers, including Ignatios the deacon, who aimed to write in a difficult, hyper-classical register (a style that fails even when it succeeds). The star of that generation was Leon the Philosopher. After he had been dismissed as bishop of Thessalonike in 843, he went back to teaching. A special school was set up in the Magnaura wing of the palace for him and his associates to lecture on philosophy, geometry, astronomy, and grammar. This was sponsored by the *kaisar* Bardas and is often called a "university" by scholars. The teachers were paid by the state and students attended for free.[106]

Leon also devised the optical telegraph, an "early warning" system of fire beacons that connected the eastern frontier to Constantinople. At the beginning and end of the line were two synchronized clocks divided into twelve hours, so that a signal lit at a particular time corresponded to a specific message, e.g., warning of an Arab invasion. Thus, word could be sent to the capital across the whole of Asia Minor in less than an hour. Scholars are uncertain whether to believe in its existence: did these Romans have telecommunication systems in addition to flamethrowers? But local versions of this system are also attested, including in the southern Italian provinces, that linked together the "furnace watchposts" and mountain passes along the frontier.[107]

The third generation, educated before 843 but emerging after it, was that of Photios, a man immensely educated by any standard, and his associates, such as Constantine, who was sent to Moravia and invented the first script for Slavonic. And there was certainly more intellectual activity going on than is mentioned in our (relatively thin) narrative sources. We have, for example, the "Philosophical Collection," a group of eighteen manuscripts containing mostly philosophical works in minuscule script, copied by nine scribes, some of whom collaborated, during the years ca. 850–875. This collection contains our oldest manuscripts of Plato and the Neoplatonists.[108] It has been proposed that this interest in ancient thought was a defensive and belated reaction to the rise of Arabic philosophy, which was encroaching on domains that the Romans regarded as the hallmarks of their own, ostensibly superior civilization.[109] The biography of Constantine, the missionary to Moravia, recounts that saint's (fictional) sparring with Muslim scholars during his journey to the caliphate. When it came to secular learning, he told them that they were like men who boasted of owning the sea after they had dipped their buckets into it. "In reality, all the sciences come from us," he told them. In Constantinople, higher learning could be imagined as "an asset of the nation of the Romans that should not be revealed to foreigners."[110]

PART SEVEN

THE PATH TOWARD EMPIRE

23
A New David and Solomon (867–912)

The rise of Basileios I

Constantinople was growing again, largely through internal migration from the provinces. A glimpse of it is offered by the young Basileios, who set out from poverty in Macedonia for "he knew that in large cities people of talent can prosper and advance to a higher station in life."[1] His ascent to the throne is obscured by the extravagant myths that his dynasty concocted about him later. Certainly, by the time that he was crowned co-emperor in 867 he must have been regarded widely as a suitable leader. He had climbed the ladder of patronage into the court, then rose up through the hierarchy by making allies, gaining offices, and murdering the opposition. The opportunity for such mobility was a characteristic of Roman society, which was not legally stratified into castes, classes, or clans. Basileios exemplified how open the political establishment could be to men of low provincial origin. A poem praised him as "a new David" who "rose up from the sheepfold to rule the state, coming from a family of humble private citizens."[2]

Basileios' ascent also highlights the weakness of the dynastic principle. This aspect of the Roman system drew surprised reactions from foreigners, including Arabs, who commented that there was no hereditary right among the Romans or a set rule for the succession ("it is open to anyone, even women; only strength counts"); a Chinese traveler, who noted that the Romans chose the most capable man as their king but then deposed him if he failed; and a Khazar, who wondered why the Romans chose emperors from different families: "We do it by family," he explained. Constantine-Cyril replied to this by pointing to the example of David, who rose up because he was chosen by God.[3]

Yet the new David ruled over a polity with an emerging aristocracy, where office-holders increasingly tended to have the same family names. The senatorial class of the earlier period—men who bore the name Flavius and owned estates in many provinces—had lapsed during the upheavals of the seventh century. After that, the upper echelons of the state and Church were occupied by men who bore only a Christian name, perhaps accompanied by a nickname, ethnic marker, or place of origin. The career of Photios demonstrates how family networks and inherited wealth could propel men to power, but it was only in the ninth century that some families began to assert their identities by taking on surnames. These became common on seals by the later tenth century and standard by ca. 1030. Many of these families had risen through service in the sparsely-populated frontier districts of Asia Minor, such as Cappadocia and Charsianon.[4] Maleïnos, Kourkouas, and Phokas, names that would be so prominent in the tenth century, took center stage during the reign of Basileios I, joining those of Argyros, Skleros, and Doukas. They were not quasi-independent feudal lords, but army officers who cultivated family traditions of military service. Their status stemmed from offices, salaries, and titles, and they served at the pleasure of the emperors. The emperors needed such leaders, but also had to protect themselves from them, so they played them off against each other and rotated them in office. They also balanced them out with new men and eunuchs, who owed all to the court and lacked prestige.[5] Thus, the Macedonian dynasty, which had no family name, was gradually flanked on one side by generals who did and on the other by eunuchs, clergy, and aspiring newcomers.

The Council of 869–870

The emperors could divide and conquer the Church too. Immediately after the murder of Michael III, Basileios fired Photios, confining him to the monastery of Skepe on the Bosporos, and reinstated Ignatios, recalling him from his island exile. The emperor also scrambled to recall the envoys traveling to Rome with the Acts of the anti-papal Council of 867.[6] Basileios then initiated a complex procedure for unraveling the recent history of the Church and reinstating the dissident Ignatians, effectively turning the clock back to 858. In 868, he sent envoys to pope Hadrian II announcing the change in policy and asking Rome to ratify it. Meanwhile, he organized a Council in Constantinople, to be held with papal sanction, to annul Photios' patriarchate. In doing this, Basileios was dismantling another part of the regime of Bardas and Michael. But he was crafty as well as brawny: by overturning the Church establishment and bringing a rival party to power, and then getting Rome to ratify the results, he was embedding his own legitimacy into the heart of a new order. Many people's interests would then depend on him being the lawful emperor. But he did not destroy Photios; in fact, he kept him in reserve.

Rome was happy to take the lead. Hadrian held a synod in St. Peter's in 869 condemning Photios in the strongest terms. Basileios was recognized as a pious emperor and his signature on the Acts of 867 proclaimed a forgery (some were even pretending that the whole Council was a literary confection by "the Devil's servant," Photios). The "Acts" were then publicly tramped upon and burned. A sudden rainstorm failed to quench the fire, or so claimed the pope's biographer.[7] But the pope also laid down strict terms for Constantinople, going beyond what the emperor wanted: all priests consecrated by the non-patriarch Photios had to be deposed; the pope's legates were to preside over the Council in Constantinople; and, most humiliating, merely in order to participate in the Council bishops had to write out by hand and sign a *libellus satisfactionis*, a legal document that laid out the terms of Photios' condemnation and affirmed Rome's supremacy over the Church: "we follow the Apostolic See in all things and observe all its decrees" for there lies "the complete and true integrity of Christian religion," i.e., in obedience to "the supreme pontiff and universal pope." This totalitarian text was based on the *libellus* that Hormisdas had required eastern bishops to sign in 519 in order to end the so-called Acacian Schism, which forever shattered the fragile unity of the eastern Church. The idea may have been suggested by Anastasius the Librarian, an inveterate enemy of New Rome. Basileios and Ignatios protested and called this "a new and unheard-of procedure."[8]

The Council did, nevertheless, meet as planned, between 5 October, 869, and 28 February, 870, in Hagia Sophia. It duly condemned Photios (who declined to answer accusations against him) and reinstated Ignatios. But in other ways it did not go as the pope desired. The honor of presiding was given not to his legates but to a court patrician. The eastern bishops showed their disdain for the proceedings by boycotting them. Only twelve were present at the first session, hard-line Ignatians, and the number of those who signed the *libellus* by the end had risen to only 102 (compare 318 at the Photian Council of 861 and 383 at the Photian Council of 879–880). This was, in other words, a "minority Council." Even Anastasius the Librarian, who attended the end of the Council and on whose Latin translation of the Acts we depend, commented on how few bishops turned out.[9] Some of those who signed complained to the emperor that "the Church of Constantinople was being subjected to the power of Rome . . . like a servant to her mistress."[10] The bishops refused to ratify the canons that asserted Rome's supremacy in the Church and insisted instead on the pentarchy, that is the five patriarchates acting together, with Constantinople ranked second after Rome and not last after Jerusalem, as the pope wanted.[11]

Rome's greatest defeat at the Council came in the last session, when the Bulgarian envoys arrived. Frustrated with Rome, Boris-Michael wanted to settle the question regarding the status of the Bulgarian Church, and finally he turned to Constantinople for a solution. The papal legates insisted that Bulgaria belonged to St. Peter, and that no one else had a right to change that "because you too are all subject to Rome." But the representatives of Alexandria, Antioch, and Jerusalem observed that the bishops of the territory conquered by the Bulgars in the 680s had spoken Greek, and thus that territory fell under Constantinople's jurisdiction. The legates protested vehemently, and produced a secret papal letter to Ignatios, which declared that his reinstatement was conditional on his not interfering with Rome's plans in Bulgaria. But Ignatios declined to read it, and appointed an archbishop for Bulgaria. Rome's missionaries there were expelled. While the papacy accepted the Council (and, in later centuries, even ranked it as the Eighth Ecumenical), pope Hadrian wrote to Basileios in 871 to express his great disappointment, and ordered the emperor to withdraw from Bulgaria. It is likely that Rome had backed Ignatios all along on condition that he not interfere in Bulgaria, but Ignatios followed the same policy there as Photios, and Basileios the same policy as Michael III.[12] Only the dynasty had changed, not imperial policy.

The return to Italy

Basileios was meanwhile entrenching his dynasty. In late 867 or early 868, he proclaimed his son Konstantinos co-emperor, and then Leon on 6 January, 870, while the Council was in session. In fact, Anastasius the Librarian came to the Council not only to promote a papal agenda but to broker the engagement of Konstantinos to Irmengard, daughter of the western Augustus Louis II of Italy.[13] This union was part of a planned alliance for a joint east-west campaign against the Saracen emirate of Bari, created in 847. Muslim armies were gradually putting down roots in Italy, having taken Taranto too, and were raiding widely across southern Italy. It was Louis' life goal to eradicate them, but after years of failure he sought help from the east. For its part, Constantinople wanted secure access to the Dalmatian coast, which was also under Saracen attack, and possibly to relieve Sicily, where the fighting remained fierce and the Romans were reduced to Syracuse and Taormina; Malta was lost in 870. Without a base in mainland Italy, a recovery in Sicily appeared unlikely.[14]

In 868, the *droungarios* (admiral) of the imperial fleet, Niketas Ooryphas, with a hundred ships, relieved the pressure on Dalmatia.[15] In 869, with a fleet of (allegedly) 400 ships Ooryphas sailed to a rendezvous with Louis at Bari, but the two forces failed to connect, or to get along, and he returned to Corinth. In 870, Ooryphas continued to subject Slavic forts on the Dalmatian coast to imperial control.[16] Meanwhile, Louis freed parts of northern Calabria from attack, and that region, an imperial province, declared for him, which infringed on imperial rights. Louis finally took Bari in 871, without eastern assistance. At that high point of his success, Louis sent his famous letter to Basileios, which was also written by none other than Anastasius the Librarian. The letter justified Louis' encroachments on imperial territory in the south as necessary to repel the Saracens. But the letter also digressed at length on matters of imperial ideology. Apparently Basileios had reproached Louis for using the title *basileus*. In response, the self-styled "emperor Augustus of the Romans" explained in detail to the "emperor of New Rome" why neither he nor his people were Romans, as they were only "Greeks." The empire of the Romans now belongs with the Franks, who are orthodox, whereas the Greeks have lost it because of their heresies. Anastasius, a masterful propagandist, was the most virulent ideological opponent to date of the eastern empire, and his polemics, which were disseminated widely, have shaped western perceptions to this day.[17]

Yet Basileios would have the last laugh in Italy. Louis was imprisoned by the people of Benevento, which he had used as his base, and released on condition that he never return. This gave Basileios an opening. The imperial fleet captured Otranto in 873, Bari in 876, and Taranto in 880, forming the nucleus of a new theme in Apulia. The Romans had returned in force to Italy and set about clearing it of Saracens and Lombard rulers. In 877 and 879, pope John VIII (872–882), who was building an anti-Muslim coalition in the south and had failed to obtain aid from the Frankish kings, requested ten ships from the imperial governor in Italy for the defense of Rome. Imperial ships began to patrol the Tyrrhenian Sea again.[18]

These gains, however, were counterbalanced by the fall of Syracuse, on 21 May, 878, after a nine-month siege and intense fighting. We have an eyewitness account by Theodosios the Monk of the hunger suffered by the defenders, the last days of the fighting, and the slaughter that ensued when the "barbarians" broke in. Theodosios and other prisoners were marched to Palermo by "Ethiopian" soldiers, and enslaved along with many captives from around the Mediterranean, including the bishop of Malta. An imperial fleet under admiral Adrianos was sent to relieve the city, but never made it past Monembasia, allegedly because of the winds; the admiral sought asylum in Hagia Sophia. The fall of Syracuse was a major blow and Basileios took heat for it in public opinion. A story was circulated by his critics that no relief fleet was sent because the sailors were busy building the emperor's vanity project, the huge New Church (Nea Ekklesia) near the palace.[19]

Imperial strategy in the west had pivoted from Sicily to southern Italy. This was not because Constantinople lost interest in Sicily. Many fleets had been sent to reclaim the island, and they had failed, and many more would be sent until the eleventh century. The Aghlabids were too entrenched, in part because they could easily send reinforcements to Sicily from Tunis. But the empire needed a territorial base in the central Mediterranean to protect Calabria (whose Greek-speaking population had swollen with refugees from Sicily); to project imperial power in the western Mediterranean; to patrol and defend the Adriatic; and to intercept Saracen raids on western Greece.[20] Moreover, southern Italy held intrinsic interest and was a former imperial province. It had a significant Greek-speaking population (more in Calabria than Apulia) and it gave the empire a foothold in Italian affairs, which, since the time of Charlemagne, involved both the papacy and the Frankish realms. Constantinople wanted a say in Italy.

Basileios I and the east

Basileios pursued an aggressive strategy in the east too, with great success. After the defeat of ʿAmr of Melitene in 863, his allies the Paulicians of Tephrike became the Romans main adversary. Their leader was Chreisocheir, "Golden Hand," who raided across the length of Asia Minor, one time reaching as far as Ephesos, where he entered the church of St. John the Theologian on his horse. Basileios sent an envoy to Tephrike in 869–870, Petros of Sicily, who wrote an account of the history and beliefs of that sect. This survives only in later versions that pose a tangle of interpretive problems, and was biased to begin with.[21] Basileios took the field in person against the Paulicians in 871, but was defeated. In 872, he sent his son-in-law, the *domestikos* of *scholai* Christophoros, to confront the Golden Hand, who was near Ankyra. Flanking the enemy with the armies of Armeniakon and Charsianon, Christophoros hemmed the Paulicians in and stalked them as they withdrew eastward. At Bathys Ryax, the Romans attacked at dawn and destroyed them. Chreisocheir's head was sent to the emperor, who used it for target practice with his bow.[22]

Tephrike itself fell soon after, no later than 878, though we lack a detailed account. According to Petros of Sicily, many of its inhabitants were Orthodox to begin with. The Paulician leadership fled to Muslim lands or Armenia, so the territory was easily annexed.[23] As for the Arab frontier to the southeast, the balance of raiding had decisively shifted in favor of the Romans. In the 870s, they captured key forts along the invasion route through the Tauros and Anti-Tauros mountains, which greatly strengthened the empire's defenses. The emperor himself led raids in 873, which took and plundered Sozopetra and Samosata but failed to take Melitene, and in 878, which raided the territories of Germanikeia and Adata. This was likely the expedition that then went on to capture Tephrike. During the return, Basileios coolly ordered the execution of thousands of prisoners, including many Kurds, "because they were useless and a burden in difficult terrain." These two campaigns culminated in triumphs in the capital, a much-needed boost to the emperor's legitimacy.[24]

But as overland attacks against the empire tapered off, its coastlines became increasingly vulnerable to naval attack. These came from three directions: western Greece was attacked by Muslim fleets from North Africa, Sicily, and Italy, whereas the Aegean was raided from Crete and Tarsos. Thousands of provincials were captured and led away to the slave markets of the Mediterranean and the east, and the raids also disrupted trade and communications. The biography of Basileios I recounts several episodes of the Roman navy repeatedly defeating raiders with Greek fire to protect the provincials.[25] Saints' lives of that era confirm that the fleet was regarded by many provincials as a protective force. They too worked in and for the fleet, further binding their interests to those of the capital.[26] The emperors viewed military deployment as a duty toward their subjects and "the republic of the Romans." The struggle was on behalf of God and "the entire nation," for our brothers of the same faith and "the fatherland."[27]

The return of Photios

Basileios was also eager to cultivate his royal image. King David, who rose to the throne from the sheepfold, was an obvious comparison. A new wing of the palace featured a mosaic of his family in which his children thanked God "for raising our father up from Davidic poverty." The ex-patriarch Photios helped to fashion the regime's propaganda. Basileios had released him from confinement.

A large part of the Church hierarchy and many secular officials remained loyal to Photios, and his extensive correspondence reveals that he maintained his network. Soon enough he was honored in the palace and appointed to tutor the princes. He wrote hymns for Basileios, comparing him to David.[28] He was also accused by his enemies of concocting an elaborate forgery, accompanied by a prophecy, according to which Basileios was descended from the ancient Armenian king Trdat the Great. If Photios was involved, he was a willing tool of the court. In 888, Leon VI delivered a funeral oration for his parents, in which he claimed that his father was descended from the Persian Achaemenid dynasty, of whom the Armenian Arsacids were, he argued, an offshoot. Scholars have taken Basileios' Armenian ancestry at face value (though, tellingly, not the Persian one). Yet this entire genealogy was likely forged to bolster the court's diplomacy with the newly revived Armenian kingship under Ashot I Bagratuni, a subject of the caliph. Basileios treated Ashot as his "beloved son," and an Arsacid connection gave him an edge.[29]

When Ignatios died on 23 October, 877, he was immediately replaced with Photios, who had the full backing of the court and the vast majority of the clergy. The emperor wanted Rome's consent and, after an exchange of embassies, another synod was held in Constantinople, from November, 869 to March, 880, with 383 bishops attending, to make it official. The pope, John VIII, was amenable to Photios' return given that the imperial fleet was defending Rome, but he required Photios to apologize for his past misdeeds and give Bulgaria to Rome. Moreover, John and his legates insisted on Roman supremacy in the Church at every turn. But this time the papacy needed imperial goodwill.

Photios presided at the Council, while the emperor and his officials stayed away, allowing the bishops to reach their foregone decisions without "offensive" interference; the emperor was, moreover, mourning the recent death of his eldest son Konstantinos.[30] This Council annulled the decisions of that of 869–870 (and Photios ensured that its Greek acts were suppressed). The patriarch did not apologize, and the demand that he do so was quietly dropped at the meeting. He claimed to have been reconciled to Ignatios and asked for the restoration of the bishops whom he had consecrated during his first patriarchate and who had been deposed after 870 (a couple dozen have been identified).[31] Rome and the eastern bishops had different ideas about what was happening. The former saw the pope as creating peace in the Church and deciding the issues at hand, whereas the latter believed that peace had already been created by them and the legates were there only to declare that Rome now recognized Photios. But both sides were willing to tolerate each other's viewpoint. The pope duly ratified the decisions and thanked Basileios "for the fleet that was defending St. Peter."[32]

At the Council, Photios actually yielded on Bulgaria, but asserted that the emperor had the final word. One bishop, Prokopios of Kaisareia, had wild ideas about that. "When all nations come under the power of our emperor, then he will give to each his own." And another added, "since the pope and Photios love each other so much that they effectively have the same soul, they basically have the same jurisdiction and benefit from each other's things." Still, the pope believed that the Council had given him Bulgaria.[33] Both sides failed to account for Boris-Michael himself. He stopped answering the pope's mail in the 880s, and the papacy soon fell into disarray and was unable to capitalize on Photios' concession. Also, Boris-Michael began to sponsor Slavic-speaking preachers, who continued there the work that Constantine-Cyril and Methodios had begun in Moravia. The Bulgarian Church kept close ties with Constantinople and initiated a project of translating Greek Christian texts, but it was also its own entity, not inclined to take orders from a foreign court.[34]

Leon VI

Basileios' final years were politically turbulent, though reported in suspect and unreliable ways. In 883, he was persuaded that Leon, his eldest surviving heir, was plotting against him. The conspirators allegedly told Leon, who was sixteen, to carry a dagger with him on hunts to protect his father, and then told Basileios that Leon was carrying a dagger to kill him. Leon, with his wife Theophano, spent three years confined to the Pearl wing of the palace, built by Theophilos. In 885/6, another conspiracy was uncovered. This was led by Ioannes Kourkouas, captain of one of the *tagmata*, and included 66 other offices and court functionaries. Their hair was singed off, they were paraded naked to the forum of Constantine, and then exiled. For reasons that remain opaque, and surely did not involve a talking parrot, Leon was released from confinement in July, 886. Basileios then died on 29 August in a freak accident on a hunting trip, after a stag allegedly dragged him on the ground for miles, straining our credulity. But Leon did become emperor, along with his younger brother Alexandros, also a teenager, who had been crowned in ca. 879. Basileios was buried in the imperial mausoleum but at the same time Leon transferred the body of Michael III from the monastery across the Bosporos where he had been buried and laid him to rest also with great pomp in the same mausoleum, fueling the suspicion that Michael was his father. But it may have been only an act of dynastic reconciliation; after all, Michael III had adopted Basileios in 866, so there were spiritual ties to be honored as well.[35]

Leon immediately deposed Photios and put him on trial, though we do not know the charges. Presumably they revolved around the intrigues that had led to Leon's confinement in 883–886. Photios was, it seems, not convicted, but confined to a monastery regardless, as were many of his friends and family. One of Photios' associates, Theodoros Santabarenos, whom the sources depict as a kind of bishop-wizard, was exiled to Athens and blinded. Leon appointed as patriarch his own brother Stephanos (886–893), at the uncanonical age of nineteen. Remarkably, that went smoothly. Basileios had appointed Stephanos to be Photios' *synkellos*, so he had likely intended this succession. Leon delivered a homily in Hagia Sophia to mark his brother's accession.[36] After Stephanos' death in 893, Leon's patriarchs were all from Asia Minor or southern Italy, not the capital. In secular matters, Leon initially relied on one of his father's generals, Andreas "the Skythian" (i.e., Slav), and during the 890s his chief administrator (as logothete of the *dromos*) was Stylianos Zaoutzes, whom a hostile source calls an Armenian. After Zaoutzes' death in 899, his relatives plotted against the emperor and were purged.[37] During the years 900–908, Leon relied on an Arab eunuch, Samonas, whom he eventually promoted to chamberlain (*parakoimomenos*). The regime's leading generals were provincials, such as Phokas and Doukas. Thus, the emperor's inner circle, just like that of his model Justinian, consisted of provincials and men with an ethnic background. Leon was himself the son of a Balkan peasant, though raised in the palace, and his first wife Theophano was a native Constantinopolitan.

Imperial Italy

Leon inherited a state that was gradually becoming more imperial, in the sense that it was acquiring and ruling over territories that may have belonged to it in the past but were now inhabited by non-Romans. The largest addition at this time was Apulia in southern Italy. What pulled the Romans into this region was dissension among the Lombard states (Benevento, Salerno, Capua) and the free cities (Naples, Amalfi, and Gaeta), along with the rapid expansion of the Muslims, who were operating in separate groups. Louis II had failed to impose his authority, while the popes, struggling to organize a proto-crusade, had failed to assemble an effective anti-Muslim alliance. But Basileios could spot an opportunity. His forces had taken Bari in 876. Between 880 and 891, he and then Leon VI focused their attention on Italy, sending many large fleets and armies that at one point included the generals of Thrace, Macedonia, Kephalonia, Dyrrachion, Hellas, and Sicily (or what was left of it, i.e., Catana and Taormina). A succession of commanders, including Nikephoros Phokas in 886, defeated the fleet of Muslim Sicily, patrolled the Tyrrhenian Sea, and cleared most of Apulia and Calabria of Muslim strongholds. They established imperial control, though they failed to make headway on Sicily. The new territories were placed under the theme of Kephalonia, but around 900 a new theme of "Longobardia" (Apulia) was created, named after the Lombard majority who lived there. An Arab historian specified that the population of Bari was Christian but not Roman.[38] What Louis II had labored his entire life to sow, Constantinople now reaped.

The difficulties under which the Greek-speaking Orthodox communities of the south had been living because of the Muslim raids are revealed by Photios in a letter to Leon, the bishop of Reggio, who had asked him for advice. Photios opined that laymen could baptize infants if there were no priests available;

husbands could take back wives who had been raped by Muslims; and Christian children raised Muslim could be forgiven and allowed to take communion.[39]

Benevento, Salerno, and the free cities now became satellites of the imperial presence in the south. The emperor was again recognized on some local coins and in the dating formulas of Gaeta and Naples, where Greek was a prestige language. In 882, Gaideris, the deposed ruler of Benevento, went to Constantinople and was given the town of Oria to govern as a guest ruler. Guaimar, the ruler of Salerno, also went to Constantinople in 887 where he received the title of patrician, which he sported in his official documents. He also accepted money and soldiers to use against the Muslims, as did Guido of Spoleto. Naples received military assistance for its struggle against Capua. In 891, the imperial general Symbatikios occupied Benevento, which served as the base of the theme of Longobardia for almost four years, at which point the imperial forces were driven out and relocated to Bari. An imperial attack on Capua and Salerno in 892 was repulsed.[40] Direct occupation of the Lombard duchies was, then, a step too far. Even so, Constantinople had swiftly transformed the Italian south. Its hegemony there would last until the mid-eleventh century.

The empire henceforth had easier access to the Adriatic Sea and to central Italian affairs, and it had a secure staging-ground for attacking Sicily. It also took on more Lombard and Jewish subjects, especially in Apulia, where Greek speakers were a minority. This called for flexible strategies of governance. Authors from the heartlands of Romanía paid little attention to southern Italy, and yet we have more documentary evidence from there in the form of contracts, wills, and deeds than from any other part of the empire, and they are mostly in Latin. They reveal that these new Lombard subjects were allowed to live partially under their own laws, an arrangement with few parallels elsewhere in the empire. They also had their own notables, who sometimes bore the non-Roman title *gastald*, and they followed the Latin rite in their churches. Calabria was under the metropolitan bishop of Reggio, subject to Constantinople; Otranto was an archbishopric, also under the patriarch. But the mostly Latin sees of Longobardia were subject to Rome, and pope Stephen V complained when a governor tried to install a bishop at Taranto who would subject that city to Constantinople. The mixed and religiously peaceful situation in Italy reveals how irrelevant the disputes of high Church politics were to people on the ground.[41] The emperors emphasized that these Lombards had been "restored" to the Roman polity by the campaigns of the 880s and that, because the general Nikephoros Phokas had treated them generously, they were now "free." Yet they were not allowed to govern Longobardia or command its armies; those functions were reserved for appointees from the capital. And Leon wrote that the Lombards were "greedy, as we know from experience, when some of them come here on business."[42]

The Jews of southern Italy were, like those elsewhere in the empire, subject to their own laws and leaders when it came to religious matters. But Romans and Jews marked the boundaries of religion differently. Thus, Jewish women in the empire were able, over time, to secure a number of rights from the secular courts regarding divorce and control over property that Jewish women elsewhere did not enjoy. This development embarrassed the rabbis, but there was nothing that they could do about it.[43] The Jewish communities of imperial Italy produced learned men such as Shabbatai Donnolo, who knew Latin, Greek, and Hebrew, and it is likely that the *Sefer Yosippon*, a Hebrew version of Josephos that became popular among medieval Jews, emerged from this milieu too. Scholars sometimes claim that Basileios initiated a "violent persecution" of Jews throughout the empire and tried to force them to convert to Christianity, but the most reliable sources say only that he tried to bribe many of them to do so with cash and titles. Christian sources had no reason to hide coercion against Jews, had it occurred. Some praised his policy of converting Jews through persuasion and even went so far as to pretend that it had worked universally, whereas others critiqued it for creating insincere Christians. Most Jews likely just ignored it.[44] But their communities remained vulnerable to social violence. In the later tenth century, the wandering holy man Nikon told the people of Sparta to expel their Jews in order to lift a pestilence. Allegedly they did so, though at least one prominent Christian notable protested the injustice of that act, and he was promptly killed by God for resisting the saint.[45]

Laws and literature

Christians regarded the Hebrew Bible as a proto-Christian and even anti-Jewish text. Nikon quoted Jeremiah in his denunciations of Jews. Basileios himself had taken David as his model and, in a moralizing text that he had Photios prepare for Leon, exhorted his heir to emulate Solomon "above all."[46] Acting in a more Solomonic mode, the dynasty initiated a "cleansing of the laws" that would replace the *Ekloge* of the now-hated Isaurians. The first book to appear, in the 870s, was a textbook, the *Manual of Law* (*Procheiros Nomos*), whose preface draws its moral force from the Old Testament and quotes Solomon on the virtue of justice. The second, in the 880s, was an *Introduction* (*Eisagoge*), a summary of Justinianic law in forty headings. Its preface and the first few headings were likely written by Photios. He avoids the Old Testament, and makes instead a Platonic-philosophical argument for Christian law. This text has generated much interest because the first headings contain the only quasi-constitutional attempt to define the imperial position, subjecting it to the laws and defining its function in terms of its service. It then does the same with the office of patriarch, defining it as the spiritual counterpart to the throne. This was a theoretical exercise lacking any means of enforcement, but it may reflect a heightened urgency in the aftermath of iconoclasm to limit imperial interference in Church matters. By this point, many orthodox writers believed that "heretical" emperors, especially the iconoclasts, had arrogantly presumed to be "priests" who could dictate doctrine to the Church. Yet this claim is made only in forgeries or polemical texts. No emperor of this period asserted such a thing, though some flirted with the idea. At any rate, the *Eisagoge* tried to define proper boundaries, but in vain: the power of the emperor could not be contained by constitutional formulas.[47]

Finally, on Christmas Day, 888, Leon released a sixty-book edition in Greek of Justinian's *Corpus Iuris Civilis*, the *Basilika*, a project set in motion by Basileios. The text was based on Greek translations of the *Corpus* made in the sixth century for teaching, so the link between the Macedonians and Justinian was direct. The preface of the *Basilika* stresses the Roman context of Justinian's laws. Thus, the prefaces of the three legal texts of the Macedonian dynasty had effectively cycled through the three foundations of the culture: Biblical, Greek, and Roman.[48]

Leon then went on to issue over a hundred laws (*Novels*) of his own, in which he both emulated and criticized Justinian, aspiring to purify, correct, and update his legislation. Many of these are addressed to Stylianos Zaoutzes and they range widely in subject matter, from whether eunuchs and women can adopt children (yes) to building codes and regulations. The most important of these laws required a religious celebration for the validity of marriage, which, before then, had continued to be a private contract, as per ancient Roman law. In many of his laws, Leon was "elevating certain practices from the rank of silent custom to the normative honor of law," for he viewed formal law as emerging from a dialectical exchange between the polity and the lawgiver, as well as between himself and past Roman legislators.[49] Leon, an emperor who never went on campaign, also issued a vast military manual, the *Taktika*, in the form of an imperial law, though at times it reads like a sermon addressed to his generals. It reworked and elaborated the *Strategikon* of Maurikios (582–602).

Some historians believe that this programmatic return to the Roman past was an anxious response to western challenges to eastern Romanness. The court was burnishing its Roman credentials in the face of ideological aggression from the popes and Franks. However, there is no trace of such insecurity in these texts or any reference to the west as a potential peer. It is modern scholars, not the east Romans, who view eastern Romanness as tenuous and in need of validation. Not for a second did Constantinople regard the Frankish kings and popes of the ninth century as viable contenders for the Roman legacy. Moreover, Justinianic law was still almost unknown in the west, so this was not an arena in which the west could even compete. Rather, what we have here is an upstart dynasty that was making a strenuous effort to entrench itself by burying the Isaurians, their iconoclasm, and their Mosaic predilections. East Roman culture was returning to its older matrices and eventually to its classical Hellenic patrimony too. The Old Testament was too narrow a framework for this complex emerging culture.

Leon was the recipient of an allusive poem on Xenophon's *Anabasis* that made subtle comparison between the characters in the text and the personages of his court.[50] He cultivated an image as "the Wise," and was the most learned emperor since Julian (361–363). A holy man passing through the palace once spied him through the door practicing calligraphy and asked him if he knew where the emperor was, whereupon Leon revealed his red slippers.[51] The emperor was also an accomplished homilist, who regularly spoke in churches on feast days. In these addresses, he and others would sometimes drop references to ancient mythology, not often in a positive way, but with intent to display their esoteric knowledge of classical literature.[52] The court was also attended by Arethas, a native of Patras in the Peloponnese who was tried, and cleared, on a charge of atheism around 900. After that, he served as court orator and in ca. 903 became bishop of Kaisareia, a highly prestigious position. Arethas wrote acerbic and combative works in turgid Greek laced with classical references. He was a bibliophile and commissioned deluxe copies of many classical authors, including Euclid (for 14 nomismata) and Plato (for 21). He marked up his copies of Lucian, Aristeides, and others with notes. In one of these marginal comments, for the first time in recorded history he used the term "lesbian" in its modern sense (alongside the ancient *tribas*, "rubbing women").[53]

Higher education was still primarily philological, that is it aimed to impart skill in the use of ancient Greek, following the rules of the rhetorical tradition. Most authors of this time were preoccupied with orthodox themes, despite their classical training, but some probed more deeply into ancient ways of thought. If, in the ninth century, non-orthodox modes of thought were advanced by Leon the Philosopher, around the turn of the tenth century they were continued by Leon Choirosphaktes, who even wrote an epigram for the Philosopher. Choirosphaktes was one of Leon VI's ambassadors, traveling on missions to Bulgaria after the war of the 890s and to Baghdad and the eastern patriarchates ten years later. His correspondence offers us a rare glimpse into the perspective of an imperial envoy, including his personal feuds (against Arethas) and his brief exile after 907 for failing on an eastern mission. His *Theology in A Thousand Verses* is a philosophically subversive text that injects astrology into orthodoxy. Arethas viciously accused Choirosphaktes of secretly forsaking Christianity like a new Julian.[54]

Literary classicism was reaching the provinces too. In 873/4, a certain Leon, with the court rank of *protospatharios*, built an impressive church in honor of the Virgin at Skripou, i.e., Orchomenos in Boiotia, right in the midst of city's ancient monuments, blocks of which were reused in his church. One of the inscriptions on it is a poem in Homeric hexameters that praises him, the Virgin, and Orchomenos, making subtle allusions to Homer's text (see Figure 37). This Leon was likely a student of Photios, from whom he received a letter dense in classical references urging him to avoid classical references and stick with Christian ones.[55]

Figure 37 Dedicatory inscription of the Skripou church in Boiotia (ninth century)
Photo by Schuppi.

Leon VI was also interested in regulating trade. The Romans had a long-standing trade treaty with the Bulgarians, first drawn up in 716, renewed in 816, and apparently still in effect. He also made an alliance with Ashot I Bagratuni (d. 890), the king of Armenia, which included provisions for trade, and he renewed it with the latter's son and heir Smbat I (d. ca. 914). Unfortunately, we do not know its terms, but apparently it gave to merchants of the emirate of Azerbaijan access, via Armenia, to the Roman market.[56] At the end of his reign, Leon also made a treaty with Oleg, the ruler of Rus'. It stipulated penalties for violence and theft committed by members of each nation; the return of prisoners and property of deceased ex-pats; and the protection of merchant vessels. Rus' visitors had to stay in the St. Mamas quarter outside the City and could enter fifty at a time, unarmed and escorted, and their names were recorded. The treaty was renewed in 945, with clauses requiring the prior certification of merchants by their rulers and limiting how much silk they could buy. Leon renewed the ancient ban on the export of weapons to barbarians, a capital offense.[57]

In the last year of his reign, 911–912, Leon also compiled the *Book of the Eparch*, a set of regulations for the City guilds. The "eparch" was the Greek name of the City prefect, an office that performed the same functions as it had in ancient

Rome: maintaining order in the capital up to a 100-mile radius, supervising its provisioning, and surveilling foreign residents. Based in the *praitorion*, the prefect was easily identifiable by his distinctive black-and-white robe, white horse, and large staff. The guilds that he supervised ranged from notaries, silver and gold dealers and moneychangers, and the silk business, to candle and soap makers, butchers, and humble craftsmen. The book defined the criteria for membership in each guild, the economic domain of each, and penalties for price gouging and hoarding. One chapter is dedicated to an official who monitored foreign traders in the City and stipulated where and for how long they could do business (never more than three months). Their purchases were recorded so no forbidden items would be exported from Constantinople. A special guild imported and sold garments from Syria.[58]

Romanía was therefore open for business, but trade was closely regulated by the state. Foreign cargoes (including slaves) had to stop at designated ports of entry and pay an import tax (*kommerkion*) to customs officials, normally 10% of their value. The Arab geographer Ibn Hawqal records that, in the later tenth century, the annual revenue of the *kommerkion* at Trebizond was 72,000 nomismata per year and at Attaleia between 21,600 and 30,000. For ships approaching the City, the *kommerkia* were at Hieron (in the Bosporos) and Abydos (in the Hellespont).[59] It was not only cargo but travelers who were sometimes stopped at checkpoints or by patrols, especially if they were wore foreign garb. The protagonists of some saints' lives, both real and fictitious, were detained, interrogated, and even arrested for suspicious behavior or their looks.[60]

Leon VI's wars

It was a trade dispute that sparked a brief war with Bulgaria, or at least that provided its ruler Simeon with the pretext for one. Leon had apparently moved the designated depot for Bulgarian-Roman trade from Constantinople to Thessalonike in order to please Zaoutzes, who wanted to benefit one of his clients, and the terms disadvantaged the Bulgarians. Simeon protested, received no redress, and so in 894 he invaded.[61] He had a fascinating background. Simeon was Boris' third son and had spent part of his youth in Constantinople, in the 870s or 880s, receiving a Greek education. He was known as a "half-Greek" and could speak the language, although hostile Romans mocked his accent. Still, he could be counted on to know his Homer.[62] Boris abdicated in 889 in favor of his eldest son, Vladimir, but when Vladimir backed a pagan revival, Boris came back and imprisoned him in 893, replacing him with Simeon. At the time, Simeon was a monk and likely engaged in translating patristic texts into Slavonic. As king, he sponsored this literary activity in order to endow his realm with these accessories of Roman-Christian statehood, and he founded many churches and monasteries.[63] But one of his first actions as king was to attack the Romans, possibly to assert his independence.

Simeon won an initial victory in 894, so Leon persuaded the Magyars to attack the Bulgarians from behind. The Magyars were the latest army of nomadic horsemen to invade eastern Europe and settle north of the Danube. The Romans called them Turks, "a people we had not heard of before they became useful."[64] They were ferried across the Danube by the imperial fleet under Eustathios, while the army under Nikephoros Phokas attacked Bulgaria directly. This strategy brought Simeon to his knees in 895, resulting in a favorable peace agreement. But the Magyars departed after selling their Bulgarian captives to the emperor, and Simeon persuaded the Pechenegs, another people of the steppe, to attack *them* and their lands from behind. Subsequently, the Magyars, terrified of the Pechenegs, "emigrated to the land where they currently live." This eventually became the kingdom of Hungary, but only after the Magyars had visited their "ferocity, crueler than wild beasts," on central Europe. Moreover, Leon had withdrawn Nikephoros and Eustathios, which perhaps made sense when the war seemed over, but it unwisely removed all the pressure on Simeon. He attacked again in 896 and crushed the combined thematic armies at Boulgarophygon in Thrace, not far from Constantinople. In the revised agreement that ensued, the emperor had to ransom thousands of prisoners and agreed to pay an annual subsidy (of unknown size) to Simeon.[65]

Muslim attacks now came from the sea and became a devastating threat again, just when the Romans had finally dominated the eastern land frontier. This naval threat spanned the southern arc from Sicily and Crete to the Cilician and Syrian *thughur*. In 901, the Aghlabids of Sicily sacked Reggio in Calabria, slaughtering the inhabitants and enslaving the survivors, though a Roman fleet managed to defeat them and free the prisoners. In 902, the Aghlabids attacked Taormina, the remaining outpost of Roman Sicily, and captured it after two weeks. There ensued another slaughter—"a flood of blood"—and recriminations in Constantinople about the terminal loss of a once prosperous province.[66] In the Aegean, the Romans had to contend not only with the emirate of Crete but also with the fleets of Tarsos and Tripoli, the former led by Damianos, a convert to Islam, and the latter by Leon, an ex-Roman from Attaleia who had converted in captivity. Attaleia was one of the empire's main naval bases, so Leon of Tripoli knew his targets well. Leon VI was unlucky in that his main opponents, especially Simeon and Leon of Tripoli, knew Romanía from the inside, including its weaknesses. These Muslim fleets attacked Samos ca. 892, capturing its governor; they took Demetrias in Thessaly (ca. 901) and Lemnos (ca. 902), and they terrorized and raided other coastal settlements. Refugees fled to Thessalonike, while the Arabs of Crete subjected some islands (such as Naxos) to their power and even collected taxes from them.[67]

Leon of Tripoli's greatest success came in 904. The emperor was informed that the enemy fleet was approaching Constantinople and he sent the imperial navy under Eustathios to intercept it, but the Muslims chased the Romans back into the Hellespont. Leon of Tripoli then sailed back across the Aegean to Thessalonike, which he besieged and captured on 31 July. He was stalked, but not hindered, by the imperial fleet. The siege, the fall of the city, and the wretched fate of those killed or taken to the slave markets of Crete and the east are recounted in detail by an eyewitness, Ioannes Kaminiates, in his *Capture of Thessalonike*. He evocatively describes a civilian's helplessness in the face of such random violence, his terror at the enemy's Sudanese soldiers, and the despair experienced during that age by so many thousands of men and women from Syracuse, Reggio, Demetrias, and other targets of Saracen attack. Thessalonike had been assaulted before but had never been taken, attributing its salvation to St. Demetrios. But the saint's reputation came through this intact, for the blame could always be shifted onto the emperor and the sins of the Christians: "that is why the saint allowed the slaughter of his people and profanation of the shrines."[68]

It is unclear why the imperial navy did not assist the city. Immediately after the retreat into the Hellespont, the emperor had replaced Eustathios with Himerios in command. It is possible that the fleet refrained from engaging at Thessalonike to minimize possible losses, while imperial agents negotiated and obtained the release of prisoners.[69] Nor was the emperor dithering. In his *Taktika*, Leon advised that, "when the Saracens come by sea, you go by land and, if possible, attack them at home." The Romans did now enjoy the upper hand on land, so, in 904, the generals Andronikos Doukas and Eustathios Argyros attacked Germanikeia where they also defeated the forces of Mopsouestia and Tarsos.[70] Meanwhile, Himerios, a capable admiral, sought to turn the tide of the war at sea. In 906, he scored a big naval victory, though its location is unknown. Andronikos Doukas was ordered to support this operation by land, but fell afoul of court intrigue, caused possibly by a feud between the Doukes and the emperor's chief eunuch, Samonas. Doukas was tipped off that it was a trap to arrest and blind him, which may itself have been a trick to induce him to refuse to follow orders. Around 907 he fled to the caliphate, where "he was required to convert to Islam."[71]

Never in the history of the empire had naval warfare played so prominent a role as under Leon VI, who even prepared a naval complement to the *Taktika*, the *Naumachika*. Himerios kept up the fight. The imperial navy raided Syria and took the city of Laodikeia in 909/10. At some point Himerios also attacked the Muslims on Cyprus, perhaps because their navies were assembling there. But his attack was seen as a violation of the agreement regarding the island and elicited a fierce assault on the Christians on Cyprus by Damianos of Tarsos in 911 or 912. One of the bishops of Cyprus, Demetrianos of Chytrion, traveled to Baghdad to ransom prisoners, and the patriarch Nikolaos Mystikos wrote a letter, probably to the caliph, protesting the injustice done to the civilians who were not responsible for Himerios' actions. The patriarch opened by saying that "there are two powers in the world, those of the Saracens and the Romans, which are like two great beacons in the sky." They should keep open channels, "despite the differences in our way of life, habits, and religion."[72]

We have an inventory of ships, men, equipment, and expenses for a large expedition against Crete or Syria under Leon VI, which historians usually place in 911, though there is no record of it taking place. The document offers a fascinating glimpse into the accounting systems used by the various *logothesia*. Provision is made for a fleet of almost 180 ships, around 7,000 soldiers (in addition to sailors), and a cost of almost 250,000 nomismata. But the figures are often ambiguous and possibly corrupt, and all who tally them arrive at different results, including the secretary who drew up the text. Highlights include 700 Rus' auxiliaries to be paid 100 lbs of gold, fulfilling the terms of the treaty with Oleg, and a provision for spies to be sent to Tarsos and Syria ahead of the campaign. Whether that took place or not, Himerios was badly defeated off Chios by Leon of Tripoli in 912.[73]

The most distinctive experiences of the age, then, were sea raids and naval warfare. As the Romans were gaining the upper hand on land in the east, Muslim fleets threatened coastal populations with violence and captivity. The fear of raids, whether by land or by sea, shaped the daily life of the Romans between the seventh and tenth centuries far more deeply than did iconoclasm or the controversies over Leon VI's marriages, though scholars have devoted far more attention to the latter topics. Yet defending the core territories of Romanía was the major preoccupation of the state. It pooled resources from the national territory in a collective effort to provide safety. As far as we can tell, there was near-total buy-in from provincial Romans to this project and no resistance to either its fiscal aspects or pragmatic purpose—the defense of the fatherland—as articulated by Leon VI in his military manual.[74] In this, Roman strategy succeeded. The state managed not only to curtail the incidence of raiding, but eventually annihilated all the hostile states on its periphery and gave Asia Minor over a century of peace and prosperity.

The state and the Church also provided funds with which to ransom citizens who had been taken captive, and engaged in regular prisoner exchanges with the Arabs. This made taking captives a competition for profit, and reinforced the cycle, as neither side wanted to face a shortfall at the next exchange. In fact, captives had become financial instruments in their own right: a raider might spare people's lives in return for paperwork crediting him for their number at the next exchange; or you could purchase prisoners from raiders knowing that you would profit by selling them back to the empire. Credit systems and investments sprouted around people's bodies.[75]

The Tetragamy scandal

The most notorious chapter of Leon's reign was the Tetragamy, the scandal caused by his four marriages. This concerned a tiny group of people but attracts disproportionate attention because many texts were written about it, opening the question of whether the emperor was subject to the laws and when *oikonomia* (discretionary exemption) could be afforded to him. But that description makes the dispute seem more principled than it was. In reality, it was a drama of conflicting personalities.

Leon's first marriage, to Theophano Martinakia, was arranged for him by his parents when he was fifteen. She was pious and the couple drifted apart after the birth of a daughter. Theophano died in 895/6 and was subsequently regarded as a saint. In 898, Leon married his girlfriend, Zoe, the daughter of his minister Zaoutzes. Second marriages were allowed, but not in order to legalize a preexisting affair. The patriarch Antonios Kauleas refused to perform the service and deposed the palace priest who did.[76] But Zoe died within two years (899/900), leaving Leon, who wanted a male heir, with yet another daughter. He quickly married again, in 900, even though third marriages were severely frowned upon in canon law and Leon himself had issued a law that required strict penance for them. It does not appear, however, that Leon performed any penance for this marriage to the beautiful Eudokia Baiane from Opsikion, nor was it controversial.[77] A year later Eudokia gave birth to a son, Basileios, but she died in childbirth, followed by the infant. Leon was now in an unprecedented situation. Through no fault of his own, his marriages had failed to produce an heir, and fourth marriages were so far beyond the pale that canon law had not even deigned to condemn them explicitly.

Leon now flipped the problem around: *first* he would produce an heir and *then* see if he could leverage the heir to justify another marriage. Even though he had outlawed concubinage,[78] he took up with Zoe Karbonopsina ("Coal-Eyes"). In 905, she gave birth to a son, Konstantinos VII. Given the circumstances of his birth, it is no wonder that he later insisted on the term *Porphyrogennetos*, Born in the Purple. The next step was to legitimate the child. The patriarch, Nikolaos Mystikos, agreed to a baptism in Hagia Sophia but only on condition that Leon repudiate Zoe. Leon swore an oath to it and the baptism took place on 6 January, 906, the feast of Epiphany, with a crowd of prominent godfathers, including the co-emperor Alexandros and eunuch Samonas. But three days later Zoe was back in the palace and within a few months she was married to Leon and proclaimed Augusta.[79] Leon had called the patriarch's bluff.

There was no overt opposition from the Senate or populace, which should be taken as tacit approval or indifference. Resistance came from a small number of prominent bishops, including Arethas of Kaisareia, who urged the emperor to put Zoe away in order to preserve the moral order on which the Church and society rested; or, in his words, "thank her for her service and turn her out, just as we throw away the husk after it has brought forth the fruit." The patriarch Nikolaos sided with the opposition officially, but was simultaneously advising Leon how to extricate himself from this impasse, namely by asking the pope and patriarchs of the east for a writ of *oikonomia* and trying to change the dissenters' mind, which earned Nikolaos, from one hardliner, the insult "rapist of the bride of Christ" (i.e., of the Church).[80]

When Leon tested the waters by attending Hagia Sophia with the Senate on Christmas, 906, the patriarch did not allow him to enter through the imperial doors, a drama that was repeated on Epiphany two weeks later. "You can force your way in," he told Leon, "but the bishops and I will leave." Leon allegedly fell to the floor and wept, and did not press the issue. Instead, he organized a charm offensive. He invited Nikolaos and the leading bishops to dinner at the palace—Arethas refused to attend—to persuade them to grant *oikonomia*, especially now that he knew that the foreign patriarchs had agreed to it. In his private apartments, he had them hold little Konstantinos and bless him. But Nikolaos afterwards summoned the bishops to the patriarchate and required them to swear in writing that they would never yield, "to the point of death."[81]

Leon's counter attack was immediate. He exiled Nikolaos to a monastery near Constantinople on the charge of collaborating with the rebel Andronikos Doukas (the latter had just disobeyed the order to assist the admiral Himerios), and exiled his bishops too, though he was still trying to win them over. Leon then pressured the *synkellos* Euthymios, an ascetic and his own spiritual father, to take over as patriarch, threatening that otherwise he would pass a law allowing third and fourth marriages. Euthymios accepted the post on condition that the emperor legislate explicitly *against* (future) such marriages, which he did.[82] Soon thereafter Arethas accepted the *oikonomia* too and returned to the capital, where he wrote speeches and letters explaining his about-face to colleagues and former allies. Thus, during the course of the controversy Nikolaos and Arethas had flipped positions.[83] The patriarch Euthymios crowned Konstantinos VII co-emperor in Hagia Sophia on 15 May, 908, but refused to follow the Senate in recognizing Zoe as Augusta. As for Leon, for the rest of his life he would be admitted to the church only as a penitent; he lost his imperial right to stand inside the sanctuary and sit during the service.[84]

The Tetragamy affair raised questions of grave "constitutional" import regarding the power of the emperor, though these preoccupied only a tightly-knit circle of people of similar religious and educational background. Nikolaos was a relative of Photios and a "fellow pupil" of his along with Leon (although a much older one); he was also the emperor's "brother by adoption" (referring to a baptismal link); and his ex-secretary (whence the name "mystikos"). For his part,

Arethas was influenced by Photios' writings and, during the years 900–903, had given speeches praising Leon and Nikolaos. Euthymios was Leon's "spiritual father." One Niketas David was an implacable enemy of *oikonomia*, but he was a protégé of Arethas and rabid anti-Photian. The Tetragamy scandal, then, was a scrap among men who knew each other well and may have grown too familiar with their younger patron Leon, treating him as a peer until they realized that he wielded the power of the throne. In reality, Leon was not more autocratic than other recent emperors, many of whom had deposed patriarchs and acted in ways that contravened the canons. But he was surrounded by learned churchmen who felt free to address him in familiar terms. In the end, the Tetragamy proved nothing: *yes*, bishops could resist emperors on principle, even though their behavior was not always principled; and *yes*, emperors did ultimately have their way, even if they used secular power to do it and came out with a tarnished image.

24
A Game of Crowns (912–950)

Leon VI died on 11 May, 912, and his funeral lament was sung "to the tune of the 'Ruler of the World.'"[1] He left behind two co-emperors: his childless brother Alexandros, who was in his early forties, and his son Konstantinos VII. During Leon's reign, Alexandros had been sidelined to mainly ceremonial functions. Our sources claim that Leon suspected him of plotting, but this cannot be verified. He now became the senior emperor, but died of an illness on 6 June, 913. The sources are hostile to him, depicting him as a sexually debauched hedonist who practiced magical arts.[2] But he did not commit crimes of which we are aware. He removed Leon's widow, Zoe "Coal-Eyes" from the palace, purged some of his brother's men, and placed the admiral Himerios in prison, where he died six months later. Himerios was married to Zoe's sister and had just lost a naval battle to Leon of Tripoli in early 912.[3] Alexandros also deposed the patriarch Euthymios and reinstalled Nikolaos, but every regime since 843 had changed patriarchs upon its accession, and we have (unverifiable) reports that Leon wanted Nikolaos to be restored. Euthymios was beaten violently when he was deposed and exiled along with four other bishops, but that may have been Nikolaos' doing: "Do with them as you will," the emperor had told him. Nikolaos set up a mosaic image of Alexandros inside Hagia Sophia, which is still there. Above the imperial gateway, where Leon VI had been turned away in 907, he placed a mosaic of an emperor prostrating himself before Christ (see Plate 5a).[4]

The regency and Zoe

Before he died, Alexandros appointed a regency committee to manage affairs during the minority of Konstantinos VII, consisting of Nikolaos and four courtiers. But the regency was seen as weak. A mere three days later, the palace was attacked by Konstantinos Doukas, the son of Andronikos (the rebel and apostate of 906–907). He had escaped from Baghdad via Armenia and been reappointed to a thematic command by Leon VI. Apparently, he cultivated a mystic aura about his destiny, which was to govern the Roman state. Now he was *domestikos* of the *scholai*, a top military post. Some sources say that the patriarch Nikolaos was among those who invited Doukas to seize the throne, though this is unlikely. Doukas' followers gathered at night by the entrance of the hippodrome and acclaimed him emperor, after which they tried to force the Chalke Gatehouse, but they were repelled by the palace guard. After his son and cousin fell fighting, Doukas retreated, but his horse slipped on the pavement. He was identified and decapitated. Some 800 men fell in the battle, and there ensued a purge of Doukas' supporters, including Leon Choirosphaktes, who became a monk in the Stoudios. Many others were exiled, mutilated, or executed until some judges ordered an end to it, on the grounds that it was staining the reign of a child emperor: "How dare you do such things in his name?" Doukas' head was paraded through the City and thrown into the sea.[5]

If the first challenger was a Roman who had spent time in Baghdad, the second was a Bulgarian who had spent time in Constantinople. This was Simeon, the king of Bulgaria. Back in 903/4, he had set up boundary markers in Greek between his state and that of the Romans, some 20–30 km north of Thessalonike. He there named the Romans first and called himself generically the *archon* (ruler) of the Bulgarians, a title that was acceptable to Constantinople and even implied some subordination to it.[6] But now, in August, 913, he marched to the walls of Constantinople, in part because Alexandros had refused the tribute pledged at the end of the war of 894–896, and in part because he had upgraded his title to that of *basileus* and wanted Constantinople to recognize him as a peer and not as the "son" of a child emperor. When he reached the City, Simeon did what Bulgarian rulers loved most: he dug a long ditch, this one from Blachernai to the Golden Gate, and made his headquarters at the Hebdomon, a site associated with the acclamation of new emperors.

The regency was eager to negotiate. Simeon's sons were invited to a banquet with Konstantinos VII at the Blachernai palace, and the patriarch Nikolaos met Simeon at the Hebdomon where . . . well, here we enter a quagmire of evasive texts and divided scholarship. What happened between Simeon and Nikolaos? The king knelt before the patriarch, who blessed him and placed his own cowl on him in lieu of a crown. This was a valid coronation of sorts, but when Simeon asked the senators in attendance to do him obeisance Nikolaos said that "it is abominable for Romans to do obeisance to an emperor unless he is a Roman." Romanía was a national monarchy and, in his letters to Simeon, the patriarch consistently referred to Romans and Bulgarians as two "peoples," not just separate crowns. As Simeon departed peacefully, the tribute was probably restored and he must have agreed to a compromise: Constantinople would recognize him as *basileus* (of the Bulgarians) and "brother" to the emperor of the Romans. Simeon had come not to attack, but to upgrade his status by bullying the weak regency.[7]

These concessions further weakened the regency. The third challenge came from Zoe, who succeeded where the men failed. Zoe peeled one of the regents, the *magistros* Ioannes Eladas, away from the rest, and occupied the palace in October, 913. She abolished the regency, installed her own men in key posts, and ruled as co-empress with her underage son, as Eirene had done after 780 and Theodora after 842. Zoe also confined Nikolaos to his patriarchal duties and prevailed on him to recognize her as Augusta.[8]

Zoe's administration was capable and successful. Simeon attacked again in 914, raiding Thrace and occupying Adrianople for a few days in September, but he was persuaded with costly "gifts" to depart. His actions are not explained in the sources. Perhaps Zoe had again suspended the tribute to show that she was tough on barbarians, or Simeon wanted Konstantinos VII to marry his daughter.[9] In the same year, the court was visited by Ashot II of Armenia, a man who could bend a steel bar into the shape of a circle. Yet he could not assert his authority at home because he was harried by the Muslim emir of Azerbaijan. His visit and alliance with the empire was arranged via correspondence between the patriarch Nikolaos and the *katholikos* of the Armenian Church (and historian) Yovhannes Drasxanakertc'i. Ashot II was loaded down with titles and gifts and escorted back by a Roman army that pacified the Armenian realm of Taron and marched almost to Dvin. The *katholikos*, who favored the alliance, made himself scarce lest he give the impression of condoning the Council of Chalcedon. At the same time, Roman armies attacked Tarsos, Germanikeia, and Samosata, taking prisoners. Thus Taron was flipped from a caliphal client to a Constantinopolitan one, and the Romans solidified their advantage on the eastern frontier. Their position improved at sea too. Damianos of Tarsos fell ill during a raid in 914 and died.[10]

Finally, in 915, the empire demonstrated its leadership in southern Italy. Imperial agents played a key role in organizing an alliance of all Christian powers to destroy the Muslim base of Garigliano, located between Latium and Campania and supported by Gaeta. It had terrorized central Italy for a generation and even attacked the monastery of Monte Cassino. The empire's military contribution to this effort was a blockading fleet and camp on the seaward side, while pope John X, the cities, and Lombard dukes led their own armies on the landward side. This proto-crusade was a military success, and all the local players rushed to take credit for it. It is not even mentioned in Greek sources.[11]

The Muslims in Sicily had been preoccupied with a civil war, but were now firmly under the control of the Fatimids in North Africa. The imperial authorities made a treaty with them in ca. 914–918 to pay 22,000 nomismata annually in exchange for peace. However, their raids intensified, probably because the tribute was periodically withheld. In the years that followed, the Saracens captured and sacked Reggio in Calabria, then Oria and Taranto in the late 920s. At Oria, one of their captives was the Jewish scholar Shabbatai Donnolo, who was then twelve years old. He was ransomed but his parents were enslaved at Palermo and North Africa. After ca. 930, these raids became rarer and peaceful trading relations developed between Sicily and southern Italy.[12]

Zoe then pressed her luck too far. She initiated hostilities against Bulgaria, alleging Bulgarian attacks on Dyrrachion and Thessalonike. The Romans followed the same strategic playbook as before. Allied Pechenegs would attack

Simeon from behind in concert with the imperial fleet, while the Roman *tagmata* and themes under the *domestikos* Leon Phokas would attack frontally. This was probably an unprovoked attack that aimed to "obliterate" Simeon. However, on 20 August, 917, the Roman army was defeated near Anchialos (aka Acheloos). The fleet, under the *droungarios* Romanos, was supposed to ferry the Pechenegs across the Danube, but this mission had failed, and, for that and for not rescuing the fleeing Romans, Romanos narrowly escaped being blinded by Zoe. Simeon defeated Phokas again in Thrace, closer to the capital, but pulled back, possibly to deal with the Serbs, who were being incited by Constantinople to attack him from behind. Nikolaos tried to defuse the situation through diplomacy. He reminded Simeon that Avars and Persians had also once stood before the walls of the City, "but now they are nothing but a memory, while the Roman empire still stands firm." He begged Simeon to show gratitude to the Romans, who had saved his people from heathenism. But he could not disguise the fact that it was the Romans, this time, who were the aggressors. Their defeat, moreover, kicked off a series of intrigues at the court as rival factions backing the patriarch, Phokas, and Romanos struggled over control of the young Konstantinos. In the end, the admiral Romanos prevailed: on 25 March, 919, the fleet sailed into the Boukoleon harbor and Romanos entered the palace under arms.[13]

The rise of Romanos I

Of humble origin and about fifty years old, Romanos came from Lakape in the eastern marches of the Armeniakon theme that had been settled by Romans under Basileios I (the surname "Lakapenos" is not attested until the late eleventh century). Romanos methodically entrenched himself in the palace and wrapped his family tightly around the dynasty. He appointed Nikolaos as his advisor and, in May, 919, married his daughter Helene to Konstantinos VII. When Leon Phokas rebelled and occupied Chrysopolis, a letter was sent to his forces in the name of the emperor expressing full confidence in Romanos, and they melted away. Phokas fled but was arrested and blinded. In July, 920, Romanos and Nikolaos convened a Church Council that issued a Writ of Union regarding third marriages, which were to be allowed in special cases and followed by penance, while fourth marriages were "denounced as foreign to the Christian life." This reconciled the followers of Nikolaos and Euthymios, apart from a few hardliners. The Writ of Union was henceforth read out in church every year on the second Sunday in July, a personal humiliation for Konstantinos and a stain on his dynasty. A month later, Zoe was confined to a convent on suspicion of plotting against Romanos, never to return. Further purges isolated the heir from his eunuchs, tutors, and other supporters. Yet, as one scholar wrote, he was "lucky to have lived in the tenth rather than the ninth century. He was neither murdered nor mutilated, only married."[14]

Romanos brought in his own men, such as the general Ioannes Kourkouas and the patrician (soon-to-be *magistros*) Niketas Helladikos, who hailed from

Athens and Sparta and was the author of classicizing letters and other works. By September, 920, Romanos was secure enough to have himself proclaimed as *kaisar* and, on 17 December, 920, as a full co-emperor; his wife Theodora was next proclaimed Augusta. If ever in the history of the empire an admiral could become emperor, it was in this age of naval warfare. On 17 May, his son Christophoros, who was married to Niketas' daughter, was made co-emperor. Konstantinos was being marginalized by degrees. Romanos faced many plots and conspiracies during his reign, whether real or alleged. None threatened the stability of his rule or led to widespread tumult, but all led to purges. After another round of such purges at the end of 921, Romanos was promoted ahead of Konstantinos to become the senior emperor. The shifting balance of power and relative standing within this growing imperial college was proclaimed in nuanced ways on the coinage. Konstantinos was subordinated symbolically by being kept beardless long after he would have physically grown a beard, and the relative placement of co-emperors on the coins also signaled their status. The game of crowns was played out on the coinage itself.[15]

The jilted included not only Konstantinos but Simeon of Bulgaria, who also wanted to marry into the dynasty and aspired to an imperial rank recognized by, and possibly even at, Constantinople. The rise of Romanos complicated those ambitions but Simeon was determined to push the issue. His goals and strategy in 918–923 are hard to understand. He raided central and southern Greece, forcing people to flee to the islands or the Peloponnese, and he may have occupied Thebes. The Peloponnese faced unrest from the local Slavs too, especially the Melingoi around Mt. Taygetos, though there is no evidence that they were working with the Bulgarians. They were suppressed by direct imperial action.[16] Simeon's armies defeated the Romans once in Thrace, and then, on two occasions in 920–922, directly outside Constantinople, after which they burned a palace and suburb. Simeon occupied Adrianople after a bitter siege, yet left it again. Our main source for these events implies that the Bulgarians left after each victory.[17] But the *Life of Maria the Younger* claims that the Bulgarians occupied cities in Thrace that were abandoned by their Roman inhabitants during the war. Maria was the daughter of an Armenian who had immigrated to the empire under Basileios I. She was born in Constantinople and married a captain in the Roman army who was stationed at Bizye in Thrace and who later beat her to death. One of her sons, Baanes, commanded the defenses of Selymbria against the Bulgarians. This text presents the Bulgarians as barbarians, but potentially tamable through miracles. Simeon comes across as a savage.[18]

The patriarch wrote numerous preachy letters to Simeon, exhorting him to seek peace rather than war and blaming the Devil for inciting warfare between two Christian peoples, the Romans and Bulgarians. But Nikolaos refers to no specific events other than the battle of 917 near Anchialos, and repetitively recites a stock list of atrocities (murder, the plundering of churches, and rape of virgins). He also reveals that Simeon was demanding, if not to govern the empire, at least to be recognized as "emperor of the Romans." In fact, on some of his seals Simeon was calling himself exactly that, and at one point he refused to recognize Romanos as emperor, as if he had a say in the matter. Nikolaos kept insisting that the Romans would never accept him as emperor, allow him into Constantinople, or make him "emperor of the West," whatever that meant. Would he not rather have some cash, fancy clothes, or territories instead? Clearly, he had no friends or supporters inside Constantinople.[19]

In September, 923, Simeon marched to Constantinople again and met with the patriarch, after which he agreed to meet with Romanos, on 11 November; this was probably in 924. The emperor built an elaborate pier in the Golden Horn for the imperial barge to dock, while Simeon approached by land after his soldiers had "acclaimed him emperor in the language of the Romans" (Greek or Latin?). Our chronicler favors Romanos in his account of the event. He says that the emperor took a relic of the Virgin with him whereas Simeon burned the church of the Virgin at Pege. The two monarchs embraced and agreed to a peace, though we know nothing about its terms, if there were any apart from some promised garments.[20] And thus this odd "war" ended. Simeon still called himself "emperor of the Romans" or "of the Bulgarians and the Romans," depicting himself on seals in the garb of a Roman emperor. Romanos subsequently scolded him for this ridiculous affectation:

> If you want to call yourself that, what's to stop you from calling yourself lord of the entire earth? Why not caliph of the Arabs, for that matter? . . . Thousands of Bulgarians have fled to our realm: does this entitle us to call ourselves emperors of the Romans and the Bulgarians? Of which Romans exactly do you claim to be the emperor? Those whom you have taken prisoner?[21]

But at least the fighting had stopped.

Nikolaos died in 925 and Simeon in 927. Simeon had extended Bulgarian power to its maximum extent, dominating Serbia but failing, in his last year, to subjugate Croatia. Simeon's son and heir Petar (927–969) inherited an unstable situation. Petar, allegedly without provocation, invaded Roman Macedonia only to change course and seek a Roman alliance. It is possible that he was constrained by a war party within Bulgaria, and had to move with discretion to establish peace. The events are obscure. After some secret diplomacy, he personally came to Constantinople to sign a treaty. On 8 October, 927, in the church of the Virgin of Pege outside the walls, he was married to Maria, the daughter of the co-emperor Christophoros and so the granddaughter of Romanos and the *magistros* Niketas. The chronicler includes a moving description of her bittersweet sorrow at leaving her family and departing to reign in a foreign land. The Bulgarians demanded that her father Christophoros be acclaimed before Konstantinos VII, so Romanos took this opportunity to promote his son ahead of the Macedonian heir, who was again demoted. For his part, Petar contented himself with the title *basileus* of the Bulgarians, which Constantinople accepted. Petar preferred peace to war and was later regarded as a saint by the Bulgarians.[22]

The history of Roman-Bulgarian relations presents a curious image. The Bulgars, an invading army that conquered the empire's Danubian provinces in the later seventh century, quickly became an ally who helped defeat the Arabs and kept peace with Constantinople for the first half of the eighth century. There followed sixty years of increasingly bitter warfare that benefited no one (750s-816), and then a century of peace during which the Bulgars built a resilient Christian state, drawing much of their culture and institutions from their Roman neighbors. That peace would last until 971, excepting the on-again, off-again wars of Simeon. Thus, between 700 and 971, there were approximately 55 years of war versus 220 of peace, trade, and collaboration based on treaties and clearly demarcated borders. Leon VI claimed that "the Bulgarians have embraced the faith of the Christians and gradually acquired Roman traits, casting off their wild and nomadic way of life."[23] Simeon, who presented himself as a Roman emperor and had the requisite education, promoted the translation of the Orthodox classics into Slavonic, a project that was continued by Petar. Yet despite these growing cultural affinities, the two states would eventually fight a war to the finish. The Romans had already tried to obliterate the Bulgarians three times (under Konstantinos V, Nikephoros I, and Zoe). In the end, imperial rivalries and ethnic differences overcame a history of coexistence and a shared faith.

Conquests in the east

Peace with Bulgaria enabled the Romans to expand in the east, creating a new imperialist paradigm for the frontier. To be sure, the familiar rhythms of that frontier—raiding, counterraiding, and the exchange of prisoners across a militarized border—continued, but the scales were tilting heavily in the Romans' favor. Their state was growing stronger and wealthier, whereas the disintegrating caliphate was no longer capable of unified action, and its *jihad* against the infidel was now carried on by a constellation of frontier emirates. Tarsos was preeminent over the cities of the Cilician *thughur*. To the northeast, Adata, Samosata, and Germanikeia lay on the other side of the pass of Hadath from the empire. Next, the emir of Melitene was the most formidable foe near the pass of Melitene. And then, in broader Armenia north of lake Van, a cluster of towns such as Mantzikert, Khliat, Berkri (Perkri), and Arčeš were governed by the Arab Qaysid dynasty. To their east lay the formidable power of Azerbaijan, ruled by the Iranian Sajid dynasty, which the Romans called "Persia." A Muslim bureaucrat in Baghdad at this time described the caliphate's stance as defensive toward the Romans, who were the greatest foe of the Muslim world. He mentioned neither *jihad* nor dreams of conquering Constantinople.[24] Those days had passed.

Muslim raids now rarely threatened the core of Asia Minor and its major cities, whereas Roman raids regularly targeted Melitene, Germanikeia, and the bunker-towns of Cilicia. Roman envoys were given lavish receptions in Baghdad and, at the exchange of 917, the Romans had so many more Muslims to ransom that they profited by 170,000 gold coins.[25]

The empire was also making incremental territorial gains in the east by offering titles and formal commands to foreign notables and adventurers in the borderlands. These new militarized districts and themes carved some territory out of the old themes and joined it to newly annexed territory. Thus, along the middle stretches of the border, Leon VI created the themes of Mesopotamia and Sebasteia. The former included the lands of Tekes, a minor Armenian principality whose ruling family were given military commands elsewhere in the empire. This pattern of exchange (lands for offices) would drive expansion in the Caucasus region for the next century and a half. Toward the south, Leon established the *kleisoura* (or quasi-independent militarized district) of Lykandos, which later became a theme in its own right. It was spearheaded by the Armenian nobleman Mleh (Melias), who was authorized to settle his men in "land that was empty and uninhabited." Melias was charged with defending Romanía from Muslim attacks, counter attacking into Muslim lands, and bringing men to imperial expeditions, for example the attack on Bulgaria in 917. For all this he was honored with the rank of *magistros*.[26] In the mid-tenth century, a number of smaller militarized commands were created along the middle stretches of the eastern frontier, between Melitene and Theodosiopolis, including Derzene, Asmosaton, Charpezikion, and Chozanon. These were collectively known as "Armenian themes," in contrast to the old "Roman themes." Their creation encouraged the immigration of Armenian soldiers, increasing their presence in the imperial armies of the conquests to come.[27]

Constantinople was also trying to capture the allegiance of the major Armenian and Georgian principalities. The king of Abasgia along the Black Sea coast was given the title of *exousiastes*. The rulers of Taron (west of lake Van, bordering on the empire) were given a manor in the City and a stipend, while the king of the Iberians (Georgians) traditionally held the title of *kouropalates*. Ashot II of the Iberians came to the City in ca. 923 to obtain that title in person. He was received with pomp and awed by Hagia Sophia, declaring that "this sacred place is truly where God dwells."[28]

This frontier paradigm was transformed by two intense bouts of Roman aggression, the first in 927–934 led by the *domestikos* of the *scholai* Ioannes Kourkouas, who conquered Melitene, and the second in 954–969 by the *domestikos* and then emperor Nikephoros Phokas, who followed the same playbook as Kourkouas in conquering Cilicia and Antioch and subjugating Aleppo. The gap between these two phases of conquest was due to the brief resurgence of Arab power under the Hamdanid ruler of Aleppo, Sayf al-Dawla, and the incompetence of Nikephoros' father, the *domestikos* Bardas Phokas (brother of the failed rebel Leon), who led Roman operations in 944–954.

Kourkouas' approach—move fast, break things, and see what shakes loose—was a radical departure from previous strategy, which had stressed defense. It was instead a supercharged and systematic version of the raids that the empire had been sending occasionally against the Muslim cities. In 927–934, Kourkouas, aided by his brother Theophilos (general of Chaldia) and Melias the Armenian, ranged from Samosata and Melitene in the south to lake Van and as far as Dvin in the east, and Theodosiopolis (Karin or Erzurum) in the north. The Romans ravaged those territories in order to break their resistance, and did not spare civilians. They occupied and sacked major cities, only to move on or be driven out a few days later, taking captives. Dvin, ruled by the emir of Azerbaijan, had not seen a Roman army since Konstas II in 652. In 927/8, Kourkouas introduced it to the terror of Greek fire, incinerating dozens of its defenders with each burst. It is not clear whether his offensive had a clear strategic target. The Romans reduced Melitene, Samosata, and Theodosiopolis to the status of tributaries, along with the Qaysid towns north of lake Van (Mantzikert, Khliat, Berkri, and others). The Muslims often mounted a formidable resistance, but only locally, as they were politically and geographically fragmented. Tarsos led raids behind Kourkouas' back into Asia Minor to distract him, one reaching as far as Amorion and Ankyra (in 931). Azerbaijan was Islam's greatest regional power, but it was too distant, and Baghdad was unresponsive.[29] The towns agreed to pay tribute, but reneged as soon as the Romans left or another Muslim force came to the rescue. Kourkouas' campaigns were so extraordinary that someone wrote a panegyrical history of them in eight books, comparing him to Trajan and Belisarios and saying that he "doubled the size of Romanía."[30]

In 934 Kourkouas, Theophilos, and Melias invested Melitene, which surrendered on 19 May. This time, the conquest was meant to be permanent. The populace was required to choose between Christianity and Islam, and many Muslims converted to keep their properties and carry on with their lives, while the rest were escorted to Muslim-ruled territories (the same policy was implemented later by Nikephoros Phokas). Melitene and its territory became a *kouratoria*, an imperial estate run by, and for the benefit of, the crown.[31]

The crown gained a huge cash infusion from Melitene, but that crown was now worn by even more heads. Back in 924, Romanos had elevated two more of his sons, Stephanos and Konstantinos, to the imperial throne, bringing the total of crowned male heads to five (not counting Simeon of Bulgaria). Romanos intended for a younger son, Theophylaktos, to become patriarch, but he was only seven, so he was made *synkellos*. The regime was targeted by more plotters than the usual, or else Romanos was especially paranoid. However, he had given conspirators a range of junior emperors to back and use as vehicles for their ambitions. In 928, the *magistros* Niketas was accused of plotting on behalf of his son-in-law, the emperor's eldest son Christophoros. Niketas was tonsured and confined to a monastery. Christophoros died in 931, and Romanos did not promote his other sons ahead of Konstantinos VII. Theophylaktos was duly made patriarch in 933, at the age of twenty, and the regime increasingly relied on the eunuch Theophanes, a patrician. In 934, the latter managed to pay Magyar raiders to turn back from Constantinople and release their prisoners, a feat that no one in the rest of Europe was able to do, as the Magyars ravaged the continent from Spain and Italy to Germany.[32]

Expansion created both new friends and new enemies. Among the former were the Banu Habib, a force of 10,000–12,000 Arab cavalrymen from the region of Nisibis who went over to the Romans in the early 940s, converting to Christianity and enrolling in the imperial army. This was a major coup, because, like the Khurramites a century before, they were experienced fighters who had an intimate knowledge of the enemy and the terrain.[33] Foremost among the Romans' new enemies were the Hamdanids, a powerful Arab dynasty that sought to fill the void created by the collapse of Abbasid power along the frontier. At this time its chief representatives were the brothers Hasan and 'Ali, the first (and more senior) ensconced at Mosul with the title Nasir al-Dawla, whereas the second was more itinerant at first but eventually settled at Aleppo with the title Sayf al-Dawla ("the Sword of the Dynasty," i.e., the Abbasids). What they ruled were not exactly states but shifting coalitions of cities, tribes, and allies. The brothers had to keep these allies happy while jockeying for influence in Baghdad and fending off their many Muslim rivals. Nasir focused more on intrigue in Baghdad, while Sayf cultivated the image of a dashing warrior-prince who made war on the infidel. For this he received recruits and donations from across the Muslim world. He patronized poets, including the great al-Mutanabbi, who wrote his praises. For thirty years, Sayf was the Romans' greatest foe, even though he was constantly distracted by tribal disaffection and Muslim rivals. At best, he could harass the Romans, not do lasting damage.[34]

Sayf began his counteroffensive in the late 930s. In 938, he defeated Kourkouas in battle in Armenia, and by 939 he had wrested the Muslim cities of lake Van away from the empire and subordinated them to himself. He raided the theme of Koloneia and defeated the *domestikos* again on his return home.[35] Yet even when Sayf was distracted by rivals to the south, the Romans were unable to take full advantage of his absence because they were active on other fronts too. Imperial Italy in particular had become a quagmire, squeezed between the Muslims of

Sicily, who were demanding tribute, and Lombard aggression. It even appears that the imperial province was occupied in the early 930s by Landulf I, prince of Benevento and Capua. He withdrew when Constantinople sent a pair of fleets in 934–935 and made an alliance with Hugh of Provence, the king of Italy.[36] In the late 930s-early 940s, Romanos seems to have sent forces that occupied Taormina and the northeastern corner of Sicily.[37]

Constantinople was caught unprepared when a large Rus' fleet under king Igor attacked in June 941, eighty years after the Vikings' first appearance. The patrician eunuch Theophanes assembled an improvised fleet and equipped it with Greek fire. It ambushed and incinerated the attackers in the Bosporos. Theophanes had positioned the flamethrowers to fire in all directions from his ships. Igor fled, but many of his men escaped to the Asian coast, where they cruelly killed anyone whom they captured by crucifying them, staking them to the ground, or using them for target practice. The raiders were defeated in Bithynia by Bardas Phokas and Kourkouas, who had brought his army up from the east. The survivors of those battles sought to escape by sea, but were again defeated by Theophanes in a second naval engagement, which earned him the position of *parakoimomenos*. But when Romanos offered to marry Kourkouas' daughter to his grandson, "the other emperors," i.e., Stephanos and Konstantinos, intervened and forced the great general to retire. It was another sign, after the plot of Niketas, that Romanos did not fully control his family. He was now seventy.[38]

Still, Romanos began his third decade in power with a flurry of activity on the international stage. Hugh of Italy sought his aid against Fraxinetum, a Saracen base in the western Alps, asking specifically for ships with Greek fire. The ships were sent in 942 and did their part, but Hugh instead enlisted the Saracens as his own allies instead of destroying them, and the fleet was sent back. So the empire was still keeping a strong presence in the western Mediterranean. Corsica had gone silent, but the court recognized an *archon* of Sardinia, who is attested locally in a Greek inscription (Torkotorios, an imperial *spatharios*). It was likely from there that the assault on the Alpine coast was made. In exchange, Romanos asked for a daughter of Hugh to marry the newborn son of Konstantinos VII, another Romanos, named after him. The girl, Bertha, was sent to Constantinople in 944, renamed Eudokia after the wife of Basileios I, and married to Romanos, though both were children. A descendant of Charlemagne, she was a prestige match (see Figure 38).[39]

In 943, Theophanes the patrician persuaded yet another band of marauding Magyars to turn back, though some of them raided Greece. In 944, Romanos made a new trade treaty with the Rus'.[40] In the east, the imperial armies kicked back into motion in the early 940s, attacking Nisibis and Daras in Mesopotamia, places that had not seen a Roman army since the early seventh century. In 944, they besieged Edessa but offered to withdraw if the city surrendered to them

Figure 38 Ivory of Romanos II and Eudokia (Bertha). It measures 24.6 cm x 15.5 cm (Cabinet des Médailles, Paris
Photo by Clio20.

its most sacred relic, the *mandylion*, an imprint of Jesus' face that, according to legend, the Savior had personally sent to Agbar, the king of Edessa. The townspeople, who believed that it rendered their city impregnable, consulted Baghdad before taking such a grave step, which was authorized in exchange for the release of two hundred prisoners. Thus, the *mandylion* was sent to Constantinople, escorted by Theophanes himself. It was received by the court and populace on 15 August, in a religious procession shot through with triumphal pomp. After a reception in Hagia Sophia, the image was deposited in the palace Church of the Virgin at the Pharos, which was a museum of relics. The court of Konstantinos

VII later issued the *Tale of the Image of Edessa*, stressing the relic's miraculous powers and reception in Constantinople. This was a form of symbolic imperialism, a Christian version of the ancient Roman practice of taking the gods and images of subjugated people and absorbing them into a narrative of triumph.[41]

The scholarship of Konstantinos VII

The game of crowns ended swiftly for Romanos' interloper dynasty. In a palace conspiracy that involved more people than we can see, Stephanos and Konstantinos deposed their father Romanos in December, 944 and sent him to live as a monk on the island of Prote in the Sea of Marmara. They likely took this step because, in the current order of succession, Konstantinos VII was designated to follow Romanos. A tense standoff ensued between them and Konstantinos, while both sides jockeyed for support among the populace and court. The Macedonian heir won over the Phokades, Argyroi, the princes of Taron, and the people of the City, even the Amalfitan community. In January, 945, he sent his rivals to monastic exile on separate islands. Efforts in 947 to bring back Romanos and his sons were discovered and the plotters were exiled (including the eunuch Theophanes, who remained loyal to his old master) or faced worse punishments. It is likely that the Macedonian countercoup was planned not by Konstantinos himself but the Phokades, who were immediately placed in charge of the army, with Bardas as the *domestikos* of the *scholai* and his sons Nikephoros, Leon, and Konstantinos as *strategoi* of Anatolikon, Cappadocia, and Seleukeia respectively.[42] The Phokades would control the army on and off until 989.

Romanos died in 948 and was buried in his dynasty's tomb in the church of the Myrelaion monastery that he had built in Constantinople (see Figure 39). He had endowed it to provide 30,000 loaves of bread daily to the poor, a function that it continued to serve a century and a half later. Today it is the Bodrum mosque.[43]

Konstantinos VII was now sole emperor and henceforth appears bearded on his coins and seals; some of the latter even bore, for the first time, his moniker *Porphyrogennetos*. He insisted that people use it when referring to him.[44] His son Romanos II was crowned co-emperor at Easter, 945 or 946. Konstantinos had been excluded from power during the reign of Romanos I, whom he resented, calling him "an illiterate commoner, who was not bred in the palace, had no pedigree there . . . and usually acted in an arrogant and despotic way." This exclusion had left him embittered, with attitudes that verged on racism. He hated the Bulgarians (because they had intermarried with Romanos' dynasty), mocked the "Slavic face" of the *magistros* Niketas, and castigated as "Saracen-minded" some courtiers of his uncle Alexandros who had Arab origin. He believed that the races should keep apart and Romans should intermarry only with Franks, their sole peers (after all, his son had married one).[45] Yet his policies did not deviate from the direction that Romanos had charted and he never got out from under Romanos' shadow. Helene, his wife and ally against her brothers, was

Figure 39 Myrelaion church of Romanos I (Bodrum mosque, Istanbul)
Shutterstock/PavleMarjanovic

Romanos' daughter, and most of his top men were the products of Romanos' regime. Konstantinos also relied increasingly on the eunuch Basileios, an illegitimate son of Romanos and a "Scythian" woman. Basileios later became the most powerful man in the state.

Konstantinos VII was an inconsequential ruler, except for the area of scholarship, where he showed some initiative. He sponsored a corpus of textual compilations, which are attributed to his authorship or inspiration but carried out by ghostwriters and teams of anonymous scholars at the court.[46] The most successful was a series of biographies of the emperors from Leon V to Michael III ("Theophanes Continuatus"), discrediting them as heretics or bad rulers, followed by the *Life of Basileios I*. Their purpose was to legitimate the Macedonian dynasty and praise Konstantinos for adorning the imperial office with knowledge of history. This was as close to an "official history" as the palace of Constantinople ever produced, and even it did not monopolize views of the ninth century. Its heroic depiction of Basileios I was especially hard to believe. These texts did, however, revive the genre of imperial biography written in the classical style, which was followed by most subsequent Roman historians.

Konstantinos' team also produced a massive manual of protocols for the ceremonies of Constantinople, both political and religious, which drew on material as far back as the fifth century and aimed to restore a proper "order" (*taxis*) to the ceremonies of the capital (see Figure 40). There was also a survey

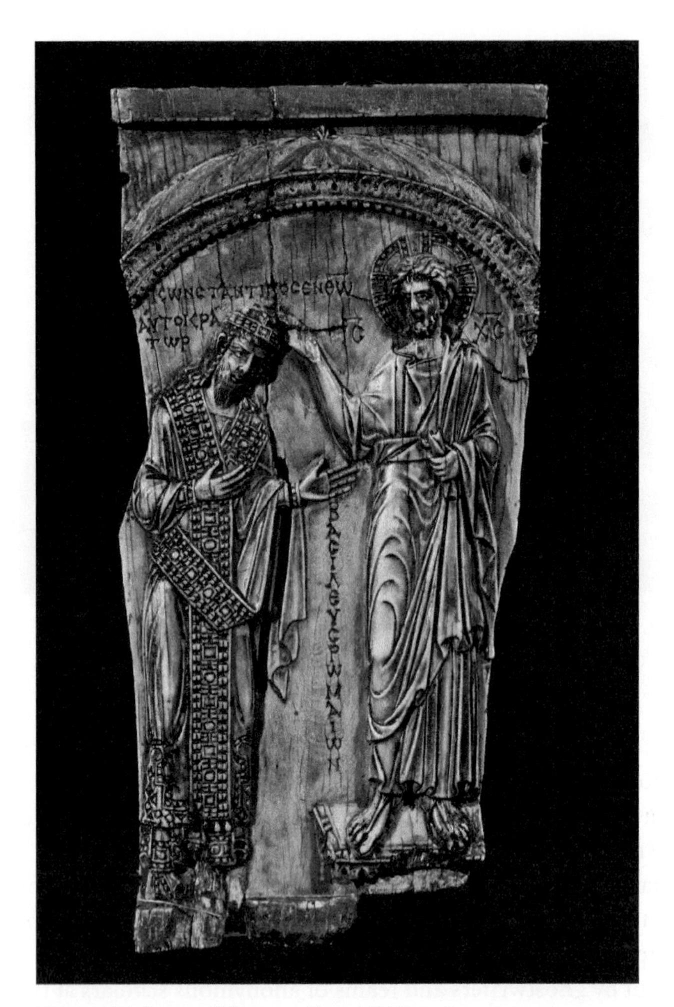

Figure 40 Ivory of Konstantinos VII Porphyrogennetos, representing the emperor of the Romans as crowned by Christ; 18.6 x 9.5 cm (Pushkin Museum, Moscow).
HIP / Art Resource, NY

of the empire's provinces, or themes, stressing antiquarian knowledge about their ancient history, going back to the origin of Roman rule in each place. These two works were complemented by a shoddy package of geographically arranged information about foreign peoples, from Spain to the Caucasus (excluding Bulgaria), to which early modern scholars gave the inaccurate title *De administrando imperio.* It was intended as a manual of advice for Konstantinos' heir Romanos II on how to deal with foreign peoples, written for clarity without literary pretension, but it is difficult to imagine that it was ever practically useful, even when its information was not hopelessly naïve or legendary. The oddest product of Konstantinian scholarship was the *Excerpta*, a massive edition in 53 volumes that contained excerpts from dozens of historians, mostly late ancient, arranged by topic: embassies, wars, customs, pithy sayings, and the like. The purpose of this monumental exercise of cut-and-paste remains elusive—this is no way to read the ancient historians—and the project failed: only one of the 53 volumes survives, along with parts of two more.[47] Konstantinos' patronage was also responsible for a manual on agriculture, the *Geoponika*, and another on equine veterinary science, the *Hippiatrika*, both containing repackaged ancient material. Konstantinos was essentially doing to these fields of knowledge what his father Leon VI had done to law and military science, in the *Basilika* and the *Taktika*. These works collected, anthologized, and consolidated knowledge from earlier periods and treated its preservation as a matter of urgent imperial attention.

The *Book of Ceremonies* and *De administrando imperio* are prized sources today because they preserve information that would otherwise have been lost. In fact, they played a formative role in fashioning modern views of "Byzantium" as a whole. But they had little contemporary impact and survive in one manuscript each (plus scattered bits). Twentieth-century scholarship lumped these products of Konstantinos' court under the rubric of "encyclopedism," which it took to be the defining intellectual trait of that era. But none are encyclopedias, strictly speaking. They are compilations of older texts and contemporary dossiers that were anthologized and rearranged.[48]

If these projects had an overarching agenda, it was to link the resurgent Roman polity of the tenth century to earlier Roman history, specifically to the glorious phase of Constantine the Great and Justinian, leapfrogging over the years of defeat and iconoclasm that followed them. Konstantinos VII was explicit that when he cited "prior emperors" as models he meant not the Isaurians, who were heretics, but "the great, famous, and saintly Constantine," and even Julian and Theodosius I.[49] He adorned the imperial box in the hippodrome with images of famous charioteers from the era of Anastasius and Justinian in order to foster an impression of continuity and return.[50] The *Book of Ceremonies* included model acclamations from the fifth and sixth centuries. The *Excerpta* drew heavily from authors of ancient Roman history and especially of late Roman history (over half the total comes from them). *On the Themes* classicized imperial geography. In sum, Konstantinos was appealing to a Roman past that was both classical and imperial-Christian, and jumping over the Biblical model of the Isaurians. The empire was expanding, both geographically and intellectually, and it needed more resources than Biblical fundamentalism to cope with the full range of its ancient patrimony as well as the growing complexity of its present circumstances.

Konstantinos' compilations were not always successful, useful, or elegant. But in the next generation this compilatory approach produced successful results. On the classics side was the *Souda*, which was an actual dictionary-encyclopedia with some 30,000 entries, in fact the most important one in the history of classical studies. Among many sources, its editors also used the historical *Excerpta*, which was kept in the palace library. On the Christian side, one Symeon (and his team) produced a massive collection of saints' lives that were rewritten to conform with more refined stylistic expectations (for which he was called Metaphrastes, or The Rewriter). Finally, the Church of Constantinople produced a definitive *Synaxarion*, a collection of entries on recognized saints, arranged according to their feast day in the liturgical calendar. As so much of our knowledge of the court, history, foreign relations, hagiography, and classical scholarship of the eastern empire come from these works, the mid-tenth century acquired a "paradigmatic" aspect in modern views of the culture.

These threads were interconnected. Consider the *magistros* Niketas, from Greece. He appears in the histories of the period as he was an important courtier, and the ceremonies by which he was elevated to the ranks of patrician and then *magistros* are described in the *Book of Ceremonies*. It was his granddaughter's marriage to the tsar of Bulgaria that infuriated Konstantinos VII in the *De administrando imperio* and his "Slav-face" that dominates the account of the Peloponnese in *On the Themes*. Niketas was also a classically educated writer and one of his compositions, a *Life of Theoktiste of Lesbos*, a fictional saint who was abducted by the Arabs of Crete, but whose biography was modeled on ancient texts, was included unchanged by Symeon Metaphrastes in his collection, for its prose style met with approval; a condensed version was included in the *Synaxarion* of Constantinople.[51] Finally, the classical references that Niketas drops throughout his letters are precisely the kind of learning that the *Souda* was designed to explain and facilitate.

Konstantinos VII inaugurated his reign with a flurry of diplomatic activity, whose purpose was as much to showcase his ascent to power as to negotiate with foreign powers. He sent embassies to Spain, Saxony, Tunisia, and the east, bearing expensive gifts, including books. They were received there with the same pomp as foreign ambassadors received in Constantinople. In the *Book of Ceremonies*, we have detailed instructions for the reception of foreign embassies in 946, soon after the coronation of Romanos II. These included emissaries from Tarsos to arrange a prisoner exchange from which the Romans made a good profit; emissaries from Amida, from Sayf al-Dawla, and from 'Abd al-Rahman III, the Umayyad caliph at Cordoba; and Olga in person, the ruler of Rus' and widow of king Igor (d. 945), who had so recently attacked Constantinople in 941. Olga was likely seeking Roman aid or neutrality in the Rus' war with the Pechenegs. During her stay, she agreed to be baptized, probably to flatter the court. Two Magyar chiefs (Bulscu and another with the title Gyula) were also baptized by the emperor and laden with gifts. In 949, the court was visited by Liudprand, the future bishop of Cremona in Italy and emissary of Berengar, the ruler of Italy.[52] These guests stayed for many months and were entertained with banquets featuring acrobatic performances and games in the hippodrome—no pork was served to the Muslims. The court turned out in full kit and formal dress to impress them. Organs blared while the diplomats bowed in the Magnaura hall before the "throne of Solomon," and the emperor was elevated by mechanical means so that he looked down on them from on high. While the negotiations took place, mechanical lions roared and the birds warbled: "I was prepared for this and not afraid," Liudprand wrote.[53]

Constantinople's diplomatic offensive was coupled with a resurgence of military aggression. Imperialism was back on the table. We know this because, starting around 900, court orators began to deny that warfare in the east was motivated by imperialism: it was only the Romans taking back their "ancestral inheritance" and restoring an older order. That, of course, is exactly the voice of imperialism.[54] The names of Trajan and Belisarios were brought up in connection with the conquests of Kourkouas. Romanos I had reminded Simeon that "the lands over which you now rule once belonged to our emperors," and that the Romans had not resigned themselves to their loss, they only blamed the past emperors who allowed it to happen. For his part, however, Simeon called them "the lands of my ancestors." These opposing perspectives contained the seeds of a titanic struggle. But for now, said a speaker celebrating the Roman-Bulgarian peace of 927, "the sons of Hagar [Muslims] quake at the news of our concord."[55]

In the late 940s, Bardas Phokas (*domestikos* since late 944) and his son Leon launched successful attacks on Adata (Hadath), Germanikeia (Marash), Theodosiopolis, and the region of Antioch, defeating Sayf al-Dawla when they encountered him.[56] In 949, the Romans occupied Theodosiopolis, the capital of their former province Armenia IV. This was a strategic point of access to the Caucasus. Constantinople was not planning action against the Georgian and Armenian principalities there, though some of them grew alarmed at this Roman expansion.[57]

With Sayf al-Dawla preoccupied with domestic rivals and Muslim enemies to the south, the moment was right for another landing on Crete. Sixty ships were assembled, mostly from the imperial fleet, with 10,000 marines and 5,700 full-time soldiers and foreign mercenaries, under the command of the eunuch Konstantinos Gongyles. The expedition was such a disaster that the Roman sources fail to say much about it; Gongyles was taken by surprise after landing on the island in August, 949, and fled.[58] Yet momentum was still on the Roman side. The caliphate was in terminal disarray, its lands ruled by whatever warlord could grab territory and establish a dynasty. Western Europe was also fragmenting into small, ineffectual principalities and cities. Only Umayyad Spain had its act together, and it was an ally of Constantinople. A poem addressed to Romanos II in 950 tells the young heir to help his tiring father write down the names of cities in the east, along with Crete and the Hamdanids, that were targets of the "loosed arrow" known as "Phokas."[59]

25

The Triumph of Roman Arms (950–1025)

The rhythm of raid and counterraid across the eastern frontier intensified in 950 and turned into a twenty-year war. Roman raids were increasingly conducted by large armies that sought to terrorize the enemy's civilian population, degrade defenses, often by demolishing the walls of temporarily occupied forts and cities, destroy places of worship, and capture prisoners for ransom. On the one side was the Roman professional army that targeted the entire arc from Antioch to Amida on the Tigris river. On the other was Sayf al-Dawla, whose forces were cobbled together from Arabs, Daylami, Turks, Kurds, Bedouin tribes, and jihadi volunteers from the caliphate, and allied to the militarized cities of the Cilician *thughur*, led by Tarsos.[1] On both sides, many forces were often operating at the same time in rapid coordinated movements along the border arc. Yet Sayf al-Dawla did not have the resources or the organization to inflict the same kind of damage on the Romans as they could on him. His raids into Romanía were fewer and restricted in scope. He could hope only to win brilliant set battles and attract more followers through the propaganda of his court poets, including his cousin Abu Firas (a half-Roman on his mother's side) and especially al-Mutanabbi, whose poems mocked the Romans and encouraged Sayf to reach the Bosporos. But Sayf was frequently ill and distracted by tribal enemies. His was an uphill struggle just to hold his forces together.

In 950, Leon Phokas, a master of the ambush tactics that the Romans had honed for centuries, trapped Sayf in a mountain pass on his return from a raid in Charsianon and annihilated his army; the emir barely escaped with his life. But Sayf tended to defeat the *domestikos* Bardas Phokas when the two met. The emir inflicted a crushing defeat on Bardas in 953 near Germanikeia, capturing his other son, Konstantinos, who died in captivity at Aleppo. After another Roman defeat before Adata in 954, the emperor retired Bardas, who was almost eighty and not a stellar commander, and replaced him with his son Nikephoros. A new phase of the war began.[2]

The conquest army

The imperial army, geared for centuries toward the defense of Asia Minor, had now taken on a more offensive stance. Its notional strength consisted of around 140,000 soldiers and another 12,000 in the fleet under the *droungarios*. The core of the conquest armies were the four *tagmata* with about 1,000 cavalry each. These were increasingly stationed closer to the frontier, now that offensive campaigns were launched on a nearly annual basis. There they were reinforced by the professional, full-time cores of the thematic armies and small units of elite foreign mercenaries. Al-Mutanabbi mocked the Roman soldiers for being so multilingual that they could not understand each other, but this was a gross distortion. In reality, the vast majority were Romans. The foreign units of Rus', Armenians, and Bulgarians, while colorful, were few and rarely numbered more than 700 men.[3] In a war of rapid-fire raids, most armies consisted of only a few thousand, but an expedition under a *domestikos* might number 12,000 infantry and 6,000 cavalry.[4] These were armies of conquest, larger than those sent out by Justinian in the sixth century, and expensive.

Imperial revenues were on the order of 2 to 3 million nomismata per year—that is a guess—most of it spent on the standing army, which amounted to about 1% of the population of the empire. The salaries of the top sixty officials and all holders of court titles has been estimated at between 200,000 and 300,000 nomismata. The Italian envoy Liudprand witnessed Konstantinos VII sit for three days before Easter behind a long table laden with silk garments and bags of gold, whose worth was labeled on the outside, personally handing them over in payment to his leading generals and court title-holders in descending order of rank. Some bags were so heavy that their recipients could not carry them but had to drag them away, assisted by their retinues. Under Leon VI, the top thematic generals received 40 lbs of gold each (2,880 nomismata), but the generals of the Balkan themes were not paid in the palace but directly from the local taxes. It was the eastern generals whom the court wanted to bind most closely to itself. Large-scale campaigns, such as those against Crete, cost between 100,000 and 200,000 nomismata.[5]

Starting in the tenth century, we hear of enlisted soldiers commuting their military service to cash payments to the state; in effect, they were waiving the tax exemptions that they enjoyed as soldiers in exchange for staying at home. This is called "fiscalization of *strateia*," a *strateia* being one's service duties. For example, instead of being sent to Italy in 934, some Peloponnesian soldiers opted to give over 1,000 horses and 100 lbs of gold. In 949, some soldiers of Thrakesion paid four nomismata instead of going to Crete (though this may have been a refund of an advance on campaign pay).[6] Fiscalization created the worry that, if soldiers were not called up, they would sell their arms and just become prosperous farmers.[7]

In the late 940s, Konstantinos VII reformed the property basis of military service. Claiming that "as the head is to the body, so is the army to the polity," and concerned to prevent the erosion of soldiers' lands, he locked those soldiers' properties down as "military lands" and forbade their alienation. The minimum was land worth four lbs of gold for a cavalryman and two for a sailor. They could sell personal property above and beyond that, and their "military lands" could be transferred over to, or inherited by, a relative (who thereby took on the military duties attached to that land) or by other soldiers in the same tax unit. Military service thus came to be attached to the land rather than the person, and could, as mentioned, be commuted to cash payments in some circumstances.[8]

The goal of this legal intervention was to protect soldiers' lands from being absorbed into larger estates owned by "the powerful." The latter included state officials, court titulars, churches, and powerful monasteries, who were getting richer as the economy continued to grow. The protection of soldiers' lands was an extension of a broader set of protections put into place initially by Romanos I in the 920s and 930s. Romanos decreed that relatives and neighbors in the same fiscal district had the right of first refusal when land was put up for sale; only if they declined to buy could it be put on the market. In 927–928, an unusually harsh winter followed by a famine forced many peasants to sell their land cheaply to "the powerful," or they were pressured by the latter to do so on extortionate terms. In 934, Romanos fulminated against such practices—"like gangrene in the body of the villages"—annulling many of those purchases (upon return of the purchase price) and giving the original owners of the land broad rights to reclaim it on favorable terms once their fortunes improved. "We do not introduce this legislation out of animosity or malice toward the powerful, but out of benevolence and protection for the poor and for public welfare."[9] The formalization of the military lands by Konstantinos VII was an extension of this effort to protect the lands of the "poor" or "weak." These terms referred not to the indigent but to small peasant farmers. Some soldiers belonged to the lower ranks of the powerful and could oppress others, whereas others were poor and could be oppressed. This stance enabled the emperors to act out a traditional role of benevolence and check the expansion of large estates into the village communes at the expense of the soldiery.[10]

Modern scholars have built two interrelated narratives on the back of these laws, one of which is conjectural and the other fictional. The conjectural one is that a massive socioeconomic transformation was taking place that consolidated most of the land in the empire into the hands of a landed aristocracy, turning the peasantry into its dependents. However, we have no data for the distribution of landed property and how it might have changed during this period. We have little evidence for the landed wealth of court officials. The laws in question remained in force and continued to be enforced in the eleventh century, possibly blocking the progress of this alleged transformation. It is also likely that the chief "aggressors" were churches and monasteries, not generals. A pious and ascetic military emperor, Nikephoros II Phokas (963–969), specifically targeted monastic properties on the grounds that "the acquisition of many possessions is an obstacle to salvation." In 996, Basil II intervened to slap the hands of grasping bishops. When he later issued a "solidarity" decree requiring large estates to make up the tax shortfalls of their neighboring villages, it was the patriarch who protested, not the "aristocracy," and to no avail at that.[11]

The second, fictional narrative attempts to fold the history of the eastern empire into a Marxist-lite model requiring a "feudal" phase. It claims that a "landed aristocracy" of "feudal Anatolian magnates"—the "powerful" mentioned in the land laws—challenged the centralized bureaucratic state of the Macedonian dynasty and eventually overturned it in pursuit of their own class interest. This narrative, however, is untenable, although it is entrenched in discussions of this period. The wealth of the "aristocrats" in question came primarily not from land but from the gold that they hauled away from the emperor's table in the week before Easter. They did of course buy land with it, but they were not a new socioeconomic force, only the same old class of army officers who were absolutely dependent on the state for their fortunes and status. Even when they rebelled against the throne, they accomplished nothing through their personal wealth and everything by suborning the state armies, in the typical Roman manner. When they periodically took power, as Nikephoros Phokas did in 963, they kept the same bureaucratic state in place, along with all the laws protecting small properties, and even added more such laws, further restricting the legal rights of the powerful. There was no class agenda here, no tension between magnates and the state, no solidarity of "landowners." Instead, Phokas, a military emperor, pandered to common soldiers, strengthening their fiscal and legal rights so that "they may undertake dangers on behalf of the emperors and all Christians in an exultant and eager spirit."[12] And far from cultivating their independence, the aristocracy of this period was so bound to the court that they tended to take on the emperors' first names. In the seventh and eighth centuries, they had preferred the names of saints.[13]

Moreover, unlike the Carolingian and Ottoman empires, Romanía did not engage in conquest in order to reward its aristocracy with new lands. It did so for strategic reasons of national defense, to increase the power of the state itself. There is no evidence that the military aristocracy massively expanded its landholdings in the conquered territories, though they probably did so to some degree. They continued to rely on state salaries as their primary source of wealth and on state titles for social prestige.

The armies of the conquest period were likely the best trained and most capably led, dangerous, and efficient fighting forces in the history of the eastern Roman empire. They were regularly called up, drilled, and put through their paces.[14] New military manuals were issued by leading generals to codify best practices, including manuals on siegecraft and naval warfare. The navy was regarded as "the glory of Romanía" and Nikephoros II Phokas could boast to a western envoy that he alone was the master of the Mediterranean. He mocked the discipline of the soldiers of Saxony.[15] Martial values gained widespread cultural appeal. An epic poem was written by the deacon Theodosios on the conquest of Crete (960–961) and a heroic martial history of the reigns of Phokas and Tzimiskes was written by the deacon Leon. Officers were raised since childhood in warlike pursuits and celebrated for their strength and dexterity, the number of men that they killed with their own hands, and their skill with javelin, bow, and horse. An officer could be praised for "loving war and his mother," or earn the nickname "Grim Reaper."[16] Ioannes Geometres brought forth the genre of military poetry, calling soldiers in his poem *On Roman Battle* "Seed of the Dragon, giant men killing each other in battle . . . in motion like fire, when challenged like lions."[17]

Victory in Roman culture called for triumphs, and the years 956–971 were packed with triumphal celebrations in Constantinople, awarded to generals and admirals. The City was drunk on victory, and its great monuments and churches were used as props for spectacles of conquest. Their choreographers copied the ancient Roman triumphs that they read about in history books. After he conquered Tarsos in 965, Nikephoros brought back Roman battle standards, liberating them from "captivity" and dedicating them in Hagia Sophia. From Manjib (Hierapolis) he extorted the Holy Tile relic on which Christ's features were impressed and brought that too to the City in a formal "relocation" ceremony.[18] The armies were methodically imbued with a fierce sense of religious purpose in the battle against the infidel. They attended mass, were blessed by priests detailed to military service and sprinkled with holy water, participated in mass prayers, fasted before battles, and witnessed the presentation of holy relics to sanctify their manly efforts on behalf of the Roman polity and all Christians.[19] We have a liturgy from this period commemorating fallen soldiers, who are called "the offspring of Rome" and "foundation of the fatherland." In the capital as well as in churches and monasteries across the empire, processional crosses and reliquaries featured inscriptions that prayed for Christ or the Virgin "to overthrow our enemies," "crush the impudence of the barbarians," and "put the tribes of the barbarians to flight."[20]

The conquest of Cilicia and Syria

Under Nikephoros Phokas, the Roman armies unleashed a savage barrage on northern Syria and Cilicia, following the tactics of Ioannes Kourkouas in Syria and Armenia a generation earlier. Rapid-fire raids from multiple directions devastated the agricultural hinterland, burned villages, massacred or enslaved peasants, and almost always defeated opposing armies.[21] We have good information about those wars from the eleventh-century chronicles of Yahya, an Egyptian Christian (Orthodox) writing in Antioch under Roman rule, and Miskawayh, a Persian official and philosopher at the Buyid court in Baghdad, also writing in Arabic. These sources are supplemented by Greek narratives, which tend to be rhetorical and less precise, but convey the devastation visited upon Syria and Cilicia. Even Roman military manuals instructed generals to burn crops, settlements, and pastures to create starvation; to blockade trade; and to make it known that Muslims, Armenians, and Syrians who did not surrender their fortresses would be beheaded when captured.[22] Muslims were expelled from conquered cities, becoming refugees in Muslim lands where they agitated for revenge, or else converted to Christianity, stayed at home, and became imperial subjects. This was methodical, state-sponsored violence.

The attacks of 955–959 were led by Nikephoros and Leon Phokas, Tzimiskes, and the *parakoimomenos* Basileios (the natural son of Romanos I). They targeted northern Syria and Mesopotamia (Adata, Samosata, and Mayyafariqin), degrading Sayf al-Dawla's economic base and ability to aid Cilicia. In 959, preparations began for another attack on Crete, which materialized in 960, after an imperial succession. Konstantinos VII had died on 9 November, 959, and was succeeded by his son Romanos II. The young emperor had an infant son by his second wife Theophano, Basil II, whom he crowned in 960. The only change in the leadership was that now Ioseph Bringas was *parakoimomenos* instead of Basileios. The latter had hoped to lead the Cretan campaign, and even had a manual of naval warfare prepared for him, but the command was given to Nikephoros Phokas.[23] We have two highly rhetorical Greek narratives of the Cretan campaign, a history and an epic poem. Nikephoros captured the Muslim capital, Chandax, on 6 or 7 March, 961, after a winter-long siege during which his forces were under attack from enemies in the mountains (whose severed heads he would catapult into the city).[24] Nikephoros settled Roman and Armenian colonists on the island, which became a theme. Its mosques were demolished, which sparked anti-Christian riots in Egypt. Muslims were expelled, enslaved, or converted, while the sons of its last emir joined the Roman army and became the powerful Anemas family. A wandering holy man from Cappadocia, Nikon, nicknamed "Repent!", came to the island to purge it of Islamic contamination. He had shown his quality earlier, when he expelled the Jews from Sparta. We have a letter from a Jew, Moshe Agura, who left Crete after it was "overthrown" and tried to rejoin his family in Egypt.[25]

The high military command was now split between a *domestikos* of the west (less prestigious, held by Leon Phokas) and the east (held by Nikephoros). While Nikephoros was on Crete with the cream of the Roman army, Leon held the line against invaders. With improvised forces, he ambushed and destroyed a Magyar invasion and, in 960, he again trapped Sayf al-Dawla in a mountain pass in the east and destroyed his army, replaying the ambush of 950. The emir barely escaped, again. But this time there would be no respite. Fresh from his victory on Crete and triumph in Constantinople, Nikephoros immediately went back on the offensive in Cilicia. The Romans captured Anazarbos and crushed the land army of Tarsos in battle (its fleet had been destroyed in 956). They then took Manjib (Hierapolis) in November 962, capturing its governor, the warrior-poet Abu Firas, Sayf's cousin. A half-Roman himself, Abu Firas spent four years in comfortable detention in Constantinople, writing his *Rummiyat* (i.e., *Roman Poems*). He was returned in the prisoner exchange of 966. The most stunning Roman success so far came in December, 962, when Nikephoros and Tzimiskes captured Aleppo, sacking it for a full week, except for its citadel. This broke Sayf's power and prestige. He was increasingly ill, faced more domestic rivals, and was unable to pay for 5,000 Khorasani volunteers who came in 964 to join his holy war. He had to send them back.[26]

Nikephoros II Phokas

Nikephoros was celebrated in Constantinople as a triumphant general, cheered by adoring crowds. He had earned his moniker The White Death of the Saracens. But when Romanos II died suddenly on 15 March, 963, he left behind two heirs, Basil and Konstantinos, in the care of their mother, the patriarch Polyeuktos, and the chamberlain Bringas. Many looked to Nikephoros, who was childless, as a possible interim emperor. The court reappointed him as *domestikos* and sent him off to Cappadocia, but he had to swear not to rebel against the two heirs, as "they had been proclaimed emperors by the entire people."[27] Yet at his command headquarters at Kaisareia, the armies, instigated by Tzimiskes, proclaimed Nikephoros emperor. He sent a letter to the court declaring his accession and pledging to respect the heirs' rights, but he also sent armies ahead to seize the Bosporos straits, and then arrived in person. Bringas secured the City and had Nikephoros proclaimed a public enemy. A standoff ensued during which each side tried to win over the populace. Bringas was an able administrator but "incapable of flattering public opinion in adverse circumstances." A crowd had assembled around Nikephoros' elderly father Bardas, who sought refuge in Hagia Sophia, and when Bringas failed to persuade them to disperse he threatened to cut off the City's bread supply. This led to fighting in the streets, and the mansions of Bringas' supporters were looted. Basileios, the former *parakoimomenos*, unleashed his own men to cause more chaos, and it was now Bringas' turn to seek sanctuary. At the invitation of the Senate, Nikephoros entered the City on 16 August and was crowned by the patriarch. He was fifty-one.[28]

Nikephoros appointed Tzimiskes as his *domestikos* of the east; his brother Leon Phokas as *logothete* of the *dromos* (with the imperial title *kouropalates*); and Basileios as *parakoimomenos* (with the title *proedros*, or president of the Senate). In September, Nikephoros married Theophano, mother of the two heirs, which led to a minor scandal within the Church because this was his second marriage and also because he was the two heirs' godfather. After spending almost a year in the capital to secure his position, Nikephoros returned to war. He dispatched a fleet in 964 to Sicily to aid the cities of Taormina and Rometta, which were under attack by the Muslim governor al-Hasan, but this expedition, like many Sicilian ventures in the past, was ignominiously defeated. Sicily fell again.[29] Yet victory in the east lay within reach. The Roman armies kicked into gear, raining a barrage of attacks on Cilicia. The fleet occupied Cyprus in 965, defeating some Egyptian ships that came to oppose the Roman annexation. The island was henceforth no longer shared with the Muslims. The appointment of a *kourator* (*curator*) there implies the confiscation of many lands, presumably from the island's Muslim minority.[30] Holding Crete and Cyprus, and following the destruction of the Tarsiot fleet in 956, the Romans now dominated the eastern Mediterranean.

The armies, "under the banner of the cross," intensified their attacks on the cities of the Cilician *thughur*—especially Tarsos and Mopsouestia—ravaging their agricultural hinterland and causing famine to such an extent that even the Roman armies sometimes had to leave. The cities finally capitulated in 965, along with Germanikeia. Muslims who survived the slaughters and did not want to convert were escorted to Antioch under guard. Nikephoros turned the main mosque of Tarsos into a stable and the cities were made into small military themes. These developments were greeted with outpourings of grief and anger in the Muslim world, but with celebration in Romanía. A church at Çavuşin in Cappadocia, the homeland of the Phokades, was adorned with colorful images of Nikephoros, Leon, Bardas, Tzimiskes, and Theophano.[31]

Nikephoros pushed into Syria, opening negotiations with a pro-Roman faction in Antioch, a city that was largely Christian, if mostly Arabic-speaking. He spent a week outside the city in October, 966, but the gates remained shut against him, so he left. Yet Sayf al-Dawla finally succumbed to his illness in February, 967, which opened more opportunities in Syria and Mesopotamia. Christians in the region also realized that the balance of power was dramatically shifting. A migration of Syrian Orthodox into the empire was facilitated by a deal struck between Nikephoros and their patriarch Yuhannan VII Sargita: the empire would tolerate their Church if he and his people relocated to Melitene. This was exactly the demographic and economic boost that the recently conquered areas needed. At this time the Syrian Orthodox were for all intents and purposes an ethnic group.[32]

In 967 or 968, the rulers of the Armenian principality of Taron, which was adjacent to Melitene, ceded their realm to the emperor in exchange for offices and titles. They went on to become the Roman Taronites, while their former realm was annexed into the regular thematic administration, subject to the basic land tax and featuring Chalcedonian sees and possibly military lands too. Some Armenian scribes overcompensated for their newfound affiliation with Rome by adopting a modified version of AUC dating—i.e., from the foundation of Rome in 753 BC—a system that eastern Romans themselves did not use.[33] Thus began the annexation of Armenia. It had been prepared in advance by soft-power strategies and the care taken by Constantinople not to treat Armenians and Georgians as enemies.[34] Even later, when more annexations were nudged along by force, the Romans did not celebrate triumphs over them.

For all that he was a brilliant general, Nikephoros turned out to be a bad politician, and his popularity hit an all-time low in 968, which he spent mostly in the capital. During a food shortage, his brother Leon the logothete was suspected of profiteering and the court staged lavish banquets to entertain foreign dignitaries. The emperor's father, the *kaisar* and former *domestikos*, also had a reputation for greed "to the point of mental illness."[35] Nikephoros alienated the Church and the formidable patriarch Polyeuktos by canceling subsidies and micromanaging the finances of the churches. Presumably, he was trying to raise money for his soldiers. He also limited future endowments of monasteries and charitable foundations in a law that criticized the worldly entanglements and greed of many monks, making the sarcastic observation that poverty suited them better. It is also alleged that he requested that fallen soldiers be regarded as martyrs, which the bishops rejected with outrage. But this is known from one hostile report, and anti-Phokas sentiment was producing a great deal of polemic at that time. Nikephoros was too indulgent of his soldiers and tolerated their abuses of civilians, "the very citizens who had made possible his rise to power." The presence of his soldiers in Constantinople led to tensions with the populace, and even brawls and riots. Nikephoros began to build a wall around part of the palace for security, which alienated the populace even more.[36]

The wars were generating plunder and revenue but apparently not enough to pay for themselves. Nikephoros had to become an oppressive tax collector, and he also issued a new gold coin, the *tetarteron*, that was one twelfth lighter than the standard nomisma (the *histamenon*) but was treated by the state as equivalent to it in value. This advantaged the state budget, but indicates that Nikephoros was looking for marginal efficiencies by mortgaging the credibility of the national currency, and it may have caused some inflation. In sum, the wars were popular but not the taxes that they entailed. As a contemporaneous Arab observer put it, "his subjects began to hate him . . . and killed him for it."[37] Thus we have two images of Nikephoros, a positive one that lionized his wars, disseminated by the Phokades and their clients, and a list of indictments by his critics.[38]

The most vicious image of Nikephoros came from another direction. It was written by Liudprand, now the bishop of Cremona in Italy, who came back to Constantinople in 968 as the representative of the German (Saxon) emperor Otto I, who was seeking a marriage alliance. Otto had defeated the Magyars in 955 and conquered the kingdom of Italy in 961. He was crowned in Rome in 962 and, like many of his predecessors, sought to enhance his standing through recognition by Constantinople. In the end, the marriage alliance fell through, probably because Otto was acting in bad faith: he had occupied Apulia and claimed it as a territory of his empire. When he returned home, Liudprand explained his diplomatic failure by attacking "the Greeks" as arrogant, delusional, ignorant, and tasteless, and cast Nikephoros as a hideously ugly dwarf. His *Embassy to*

Constantinople is a satire that deploys all the anti-Greek prejudices that were becoming standard in the west: "you are not Romans," "all heresies originate among you," "Greeks are faithless," and "Greeks eat disgusting food." The two empires skirmished against each other in Italy, but made no lasting gains.[39] It is instructive to compare Liudprand's satire with the poems that Abu Firas had written in Roman captivity only a few years earlier. Abu Firas indignantly defended the Arabs' martial valor when Nikephoros said that they were good only at wielding the pen. "You are the dogs," Abu Firas wrote, "we are like lions."[40] The Roman resurgence was putting everyone on the defensive.

In late 968, Nikephoros swept through northern Mesopotamia into Syria, from Mayyafariqin to Antioch, killing, plundering, and taking captives the whole way, after which he attacked Homs (Emesa) Tripolis, and ʿArqa. He obtained the surrender of Laodikeia by the coast, whose emir agreed to serve the empire in the capacity of a *strategos*. Laodikeia thereby became one of the empire's few Muslim protectorates. Nearby Antioch, a city torn between pro- and anti-Roman factions, was also effectively surrounded. Nikephoros left some forces there under Michael Bourtzes and one of his own retainers, the eunuch Petros, to blockade the city, and returned to Constantinople. No major opponent had emerged during the emperor's passage: the Romans no longer faced a credible enemy in the east. In October, 969, Bourtzes occupied a tower on Antioch's walls with help from inside. While he was under siege there, Petros pulled up with his forces and the city fell, although it was damaged by fires during the fighting. Bourtzes raced back to the capital with news of victory, but was deposed from his command by Nikephoros, who had wanted to take the city without damage (also, his father Bardas had just died). All of Syria lay open now to Roman attack.[41]

It was not Nikephoros who would lead those attacks. On the night of 10–11 December, 969, Tzimiskes, Bourtzes, and a few others approached the seaward side of the palace walls that Nikephoros had built and were hauled up in baskets by accomplices. They found Nikephoros asleep on the floor in his chambers and killed him. Tzimiskes proceeded to the throne room where he was acclaimed emperor, while Nikephoros' severed head prevented the imperial bodyguard from taking action. The coup had been planned carefully in advance, almost certainly by the *parakoimomenos* Basileios, who assisted Tzimiskes in winning over the palace, arresting the Phokades, and successfully keeping order in Constantinople during the transition. The Phokades had become too unpopular, and no one came to their defense. Tzimiskes himself had lost their favor in 965, and had dropped out of the historical record until that fateful night. Our sources claim that he was invited to seize the throne by Theophano, who either hated Nikephoros or loved Tzimiskes, though such stories were gossip from the start.[42] This murder is likely the most infamous in east Roman history—no small feat—in part because both the victim and the perpetrator were heroes, relatives, and comrades-in-arms who had fought together for decades.

Nikephoros proved easier to idolize in death. He was commemorated by the monks of Mt. Athos, because he had sponsored the foundation of a Lavra there by St. Athanasios (this was a relatively organized cluster of hermits). The monks wrote a liturgy honoring the murdered emperor as a martyr-saint who interceded with God on behalf of their prayers.[43] The soldier-poet Ioannes Geometres also wrote poems in the voice of Nikephoros: "For six years I held the godly reins of state . . . and yet, wretched me, I could not evade the hands of a feeble woman." "You can tear my portraits off the walls, but my victories abide."[44]

Ioannes I Tzimiskes

Tzimiskes (969–976) was one of the best military strategists in the empire's history, and also, despite his impetuous side, an astute politician. He had, by now, engineered two regime changes. "I always go into a situation with deliberation, but when it stands on the razor's edge you have to seize the moment. . . . Pluck up your courage and remember that you are a Roman," he once told his men.[45] He pledged to respect the two heirs to the throne and, to gratify the patriarch Polyeuktos, he rolled back Nikephoros' micromanagement of Church affairs. As someone had to atone for the murder of Nikephoros, Theophano was sent into monastic exile as its instigator and scapegoat. Tzimiskes then married a sister of Romanos II, linking himself to both the dynasty and the *parakoimomenos* Basileios (who was a son of Romanos I). The new emperor reversed Nikephoros' cuts to the senatorial salaries and promoted Bardas Skleros, a former in-law of his, to command the army as *stratelates*, an ad hoc position.[46] This created a rivalry between Skleros and the Phokades that cast a shadow over the next twenty years.

Tzimiskes was a capable peacemaker. He settled a dispute raging among the monks on Mt. Athos for and against the founder of the Lavra, Athanasios, who was Nikephoros' spiritual father. He issued the *Typikon of Tzimiskes* to regulate the affairs of the emerging monastic communities there, "finding that both parties were absolutely guiltless, strange as this may sound"—the trouble was all Satan's doing after all. The *Typikon* established a framework for coexistence on the Holy Mountain, which had some 3,000 monks at the time, along with a template for its future organization. By enabling the unfettered economic expansion of the more organized monasteries, it gave them a competitive advantage over the hermits.[47] Tzimiskes also cleared up the messes left behind by Nikephoros' dealings with non-Romans. Specifically, in violation of his agreement with the Syrian Orthodox, Nikephoros had arrested some of their Church leaders and forced them to answer for their non-Chalcedonian theology. They were now released and would not be troubled again for almost sixty years.[48] Tzimiskes also ended the war in Italy with Otto I by sending a bride for the latter's son, Otto II. Theophano, a distant relative of the emperor, married Otto II in Rome in

972. She is seen as a transmitter of eastern imperial culture to the medieval west, and imparted grand notions to her son, Otto III (996–1002). But she is never mentioned in Greek sources.[49]

In January, 970, Tzimiskes received another windfall. Nikephoros' former retainer, the eunuch-general Petros, had forced the surrender of Aleppo after a one-month siege. The Hamdanid regime was in disarray, and the city had come under the partial control of one Qarghuya. He now made a far-reaching agreement with Petros, called the treaty of Safar. Aleppo would henceforth be a quasi-autonomous but tributary client of the empire. It was required to help the Romans in their wars, especially by providing supplies and logistical support. While it would not have to fight other Muslims, it would block raids targeting Romanía. As a center of trade, goods passing through toward the empire would be taxed by imperial officials, and apostates from either religion would not be persecuted.[50] Thus Aleppo went from being the arch-enemy of Rome to a strategic and economic asset. Petros also settled the affairs of Antioch, which received a patriarch from Constantinople (an abbot handpicked by Tzimiskes himself) and a governor, namely Bourtzes, the city's conqueror and a co-conspirator in the murder of Nikephoros. Antioch was slated to become the forward operating base for Roman power in Syria.[51]

Having created peace at home, largely by making symbolic concessions that cost him little, Tzimiskes was in a position to tackle a crisis unfolding in Bulgaria. This was a more promising field for his real talents. King Sviatoslav of the Kievan Rus', the son of Olga who had visited Constantinople in 946, had expanded his realm eastward by destroying the Khazars in 965. He then turned to the Danube delta and began to conquer Bulgaria. With an army that included Magyars and Pechenegs, by early 970 he had overrun all of eastern Bulgaria to Philippopolis (Plovdiv). He took the Bulgarian tsar Boris II hostage, so that Bulgarians were fighting on his side too. Some sources claim that Sviatoslav had come at the invitation and payment of Nikephoros Phokas, who wanted to punish Bulgaria for not doing more to stop Magyar raids. But it seems more likely that he had his own plans, which emerged from the Viking tradition to which he belonged. "I prefer to live on the Danube," he is later said to have observed, "where all riches are concentrated: gold, silks, wine, and fruits from Greece, silver and horses from Hungary and Bohemia, and from Rus' furs, wax, honey, and slaves."[52]

The Rus' had twice before attacked Constantinople, and were now raiding Thrace, so Tzimiskes could not allow them to remain in Bulgaria, on the empire's doorstep. But before he could confront them, he first had to suppress a conspiracy backing the Phokades that broke out in 970. Leon (the former *kouropalates*) was quickly arrested but his son Bardas raised the standards of rebellion in Asia Minor. Skleros managed to put this down with few losses, and

Bardas was made a priest on Chios. The Phokades apparently believed they were entitled to the throne and had just enough support in the army to cause trouble, but not enough to prevail.[53]

We have two sources for the titanic war between the Romans and the Rus' that took place in 971, which ended in a spectacular victory for Tzimiskes. One is an epic narrative in Greek that was used independently by Leon the Deacon and Skylitzes, and cast its protagonists in the mold of classical heroes. The other is the so-called *Russian Primary Chronicle*, compiled in the twelfth century, the core of whose account is historical, though it embellishes it with much fiction and tries to pretend that Sviatoslav won. Tzimiskes activated the standard Roman strategy against Bulgaria: a fleet with Greek fire commanded the Danube while the emperor approached head-on from the south. Sviatoslav reacted too late and defensively. While he sat at Dorostolon (Silistra), he allowed Tzimiskes to defeat part of his army at Preslav and take the city by force, capturing the Bulgarian royal family. Tzimiskes then marched north, taking Pliska and defeating the Rus' again outside Dorostolon. He besieged them in the city both by land and with the imperial fleet in the river. During the siege, Leon Phokas again escaped from exile and attempted to take over the palace in Constantinople. But he, the twice-victor over Sayf al-Dawla, was arrested and blinded. By July, 970, the Rus' were hard-pressed from famine and Sviatoslav decided on a last stand. His army was again badly defeated by Tzimiskes and lost thousands, while the Romans' losses were in the hundreds. The latter included Anemas, the son of the last emir of Crete. The two rulers met to discuss terms for the Rus' surrender. Sviatoslav had shaved his beard and head, except for one lock that hung long on one side and a mustache. He pledged never to attack the Romans or their allies, and was given supplies for his departure. The Romans likely kept all the plunder that the Rus' had gathered from occupied Bulgaria. On the way back, Sviatoslav was ambushed by Pechenegs at the Dnieper rapids, and his skull was allegedly turned into a drinking cup.[54]

Tzimiskes staged an elaborate triumph in Constantinople, inspired by ancient precedents. He walked behind a chariot pulled by white horses, in which sat an icon of the Virgin taken at Preslav. Behind him walked the Bulgarian royal family. Tzimiskes then divested Boris II of his imperial regalia and dedicated them in Hagia Sophia. This symbolically terminated the Bulgarian state and annexed it to the Roman empire, though in practice only eastern Bulgaria had been occupied. After centuries of peaceful coexistence with Bulgaria, punctuated by bouts of war, the empire had retaken northern Thrace, which, its writers asserted, "had of old belonged to the Romans."[55] We have little evidence about how this territory was ruled during the first phase of Roman occupation (971–986), apart from a list of offices produced in ca. 971–975, the *Escorial Taktikon*. This list reflects a major innovation in military structure introduced by Tzimiskes, possibly building on a precedent from southern Italy. Clusters of adjacent themes along the empire's frontiers were placed under the command of top-level generals called *katepano* or *doukes* (singular: *doux*). In the Balkans, *doukes* were appointed at Adrianople, Thessalonike, and "Mesopotamia of the West," a short-lived *doukaton* probably in the lower Danube. The *doukes* were now entrusted with frontier defense in the conquered lands, and projected forward power.[56]

The same reform was carried out in the east, with *doukes* stationed at Antioch (facing Syria), Mesopotamia, and Chaldia (facing the Caucasus). A new geostrategic reality had by now emerged in the east. Iraq had been taken over by an Iranian (Daylami) dynasty, the Buyids, who ruled over a loose consortium of interrelated states. But they were unable to solve the problems that had brought down the Abbasids in the first place, making Baghdad ungovernable. No major threat would come from there against Rome. But in 969 Egypt had been taken over by the Fatimids, a Shia movement. This caliphate had begun in North Africa in the early tenth century, and its clients and governors in Sicily had been raiding Italy for decades. They even occupied Reggio in 952–956 and turned its cathedral into a mosque.[57] Holy war against the Romans was one of the Fatimids' professed goals. As soon as they secured Egypt, they sent an army into Palestine and Syria to take Damascus and then Antioch. But the defenses of Roman Antioch held against a five-month siege, and the Fatimid contingent was defeated near Alexandretta in mid-971.[58] The Fatimids would never again pose a direct threat to the empire. In fact, the balance of power between them and the Romans created a framework for stability in Syria. But for this to be achieved, it was necessary for Tzimiskes to reacquaint the region with Roman arms.

In late 972, Tzimiskes captured and plundered Nisibis and then besieged Mayyafariqin, but failed to take it. In 975, he returned to raid Syria, attacking Baalbek (Heliopolis), Damascus, Beirut, Byblos, and Tripolis in an ever-widening arc around the *doukaton* of Antioch. A later tale alleged that he reached Palestine and sought to liberate Jerusalem, but this post-crusade invention has no basis in fact. Tzimiskes' actual targets were either sacked (if captured) or forced to pay him to leave. He brought back a rich haul of plunder, but it is unlikely that the pledged tribute continued to flow after his departure. The empire had reached the limit of expansion here. The emperor's goal was not to conquer but to plunder and deter future aggression. Individual Roman generals could still be defeated—Melias, the *domestikos* of the east was defeated and captured in 973 by forces from Mosul—but a full imperial expedition faced no credible opponents, an advantage that the Romans would retain until the mid-eleventh century.[59] The contemporaneous Muslim geographer al-Muqaddasi said that in Syria "people [i.e., Muslims] live in dread of the Romaeans as if they were in a foreign land, for their frontiers have been ravaged and their border defenses shattered." His name for the Mediterranean was "the Romaean Sea."[60]

Tzimiskes fell ill during his return to Constantinople and died on 10–11 January at the age of fifty-one. Whereas he had buried Nikephoros in the imperial mausoleum, he arranged for his tomb to be placed in the chapel of the Savior at the Chalke Gatehouse. Rumor had it that he was poisoned by the *parakoimomenos* Basileios, who became alarmed when Tzimiskes discovered how much land the eunuch had accumulated in the conquered territories: "Are we fighting so that a eunuch can get rich?"[61] But accusations of poison can never be proven. Tzimiskes was remembered as a hero whose reputation was stained by the murder of his uncle—"My deeds were glorious, but my conscience trembles" was how the poet Geometres put it on his behalf. In visions of the afterlife he was seen begging for forgiveness from Nikephoros.[62] But that probably mattered little to the majority of his subjects. His reign was the first during which Asia Minor was not raided. His wars probably generated more money than they cost, so he did not have to raise taxes. Instead, he distributed grain efficiently during a scarcity, lowered taxes, and made generous gifts to churches and charities.[63]

The great civil wars

Basil II was now about eighteen, old enough to reign without a guardian, and one of his first acts was to bring his mother Theophano back from exile. Yet he still had a handler, the *parakoimomenos* Basileios, who was the most powerful politician from the 950s down to his dismissal in 985. He had military experience—Samosata in 958, for which he was awarded a triumph, and Bulgaria in 971—and was effectively in charge of foreign policy, as revealed by Liudprand of Cremona's meetings with him in 968 and the reports of other envoys. He was a major player in at least two coups (963 and 969) and was fantastically rich. We have some deluxe artworks that he commissioned, and he sponsored book production too, for example the final version of the *Book of Ceremonies*. It was he more than anyone who steered Roman policy during the years of conquest and then for fifteen more years after conquest gave way to detente. Basil II would later claim that "our opinions had no effect but his will and command prevailed in all matters."[64]

An aspiring successor to Phokas and Tzimiskes presented himself almost immediately: Bardas Skleros, the lead general under Tzimiskes and currently *doux* of Mesopotamia, who now rebelled in Melitene. This led to a three-year civil war (976–979), in which the court used Bardas Phokas (a former rebel himself and son of the *kouropalates* Leon) to suppress Skleros, who fled to Baghdad. After a seven-year period of tense peace, another civil war broke out in which both Phokas and Skleros sought the throne (987–989).

It was nothing new for generals to seek the throne. But the length, scope, and intensity of the conflicts of 976–989 are distinct and reminiscent of the civil wars at the end of the Republic. The two periods have much in common. The wars were fought by generals leading Roman armies of conquest that were stationed outside the national homeland. The conquests had increased the relative power of the military within the political system, and the generals sought to reap those dividends. An aristocracy of military service had emerged, wherein certain families had close ties with specific armies or regions, and they leaned on those clients for support. The armies, being personally attached to their generals after years of service, were willing to follow them even against the center, activating alliance networks among the emergent aristocracy. After Nikephoros II rose to the throne, the Phokades felt entitled to rule and even deployed propagandistic literature to bolster their claim. In these respects, the civil wars of 963, 970, 976–979, and 987–989 were not unlike those of Sulla, Caesar, and Pompey, although the Roman polity was now far more stable at its core. The Republican warlords had to find lands with which to reward their veterans, but in our period soldiers were already provided for. The major difference between the two periods was that there was now an established monarchy that commanded more resources and loyalty than did the rebel generals. Basil II would prevail.

Skleros had the more uphill battle as his name prestige and client network were not on the same scale as the Phokades; he had to win everything on the field of battle. In Lykandos, he defeated an imperial army under Bourtzes, the eunuch-general Petros, and Eustathios Maleïnos. Bourtzes then changed sides, bringing Antioch, his command, with him. Skleros appointed an Arab Christian, ʿUbayd Allah, possibly a recent convert, to govern the city for him. Skleros' followers also seized Attaleia, which brought him a fleet. In 977, he defeated another imperial army in Phrygia, and Petros, the conqueror of Antioch and Aleppo, was killed in the rout. Skleros then advanced to Nikaia, but his ships were prevented by the imperial fleet from reaching the capital. The court also suborned ʿUbayd Allah, who was promised a lifetime governorship of Antioch if he changed sides, which he did in early 978. And then Bardas Phokas was brought out of exile on Chios and made *domestikos* of the *scholai*. Leading western units, he snuck past Skleros to Kaisareia and joined Maleïnos; Bourtzes also defected back to the imperial side. The rebel now had to turn back into Asia Minor, and defeated Phokas at Amorion. Phokas fled to Upper Tao, whose ruler Davitʿ was known to him from the days when Phokas was *doux* of Chaldia. Davitʿ sheltered the Roman army and, in 979, gave to Phokas his own army, under the command of Tʿorʿnik. The two generals defeated Skleros in Charsianon, on 24 March, 979. A soldier in the Georgian army remembered this victory in a chapel that he later built in Georgia: "When Skleros rebelled, the *kouropalates* Davitʿ—may God exalt him—helped the holy emperor and sent us all on campaign. We forced Skleros to flee." Whereas the court could recover from multiple defeats, a rebellion was usually finished by just one. Skleros and his closest followers fled to Mayyafariqin and then Baghdad, seeking asylum with the Buyids.[65]

The Georgian general Tʿorʿnik had a fascinating story. He was a veteran officer of the Roman army who had retired with the rank of *patrikios* and became, around 970, a monk on Mt. Athos, in the Lavra of Athanasios, joining a small cluster of monks from Georgia. In 978, at the peak of Skleros' rebellion, the court invited T'or'nik from Athos to the capital and appealed to him to persuade Davit' to help. His superior, Athanasios, encouraged him to do as they said. This was the Phokas network in action. In Constantinople, T'or'nik found the *parakoimomenos* in charge of policy, but the empress Theophano also made an emotional appeal to him. T'or'nik "rebuked her for her misdeeds," alluding possibly to the murder of Nikephoros II, but agreed to help. When the war was over, T'or'nik returned to Mt. Athos and the court repaid his services with lavish gifts to the Holy Mountain and with assistance in founding a monastery there for Georgians (Iviron). Davit' of Tao was also richly compensated. He was given Theodosiopolis (Karin / Erzurum), a strategically located city, along with extensive lands to the south of Tao toward lake Van, though it is unclear whether he was to own them or only govern them on the empire's behalf.[66]

Phokas was made *domestikos* of the east and spent the next seven years patrolling the eastern frontier, consolidating his position in the army and enforcing the empire's position, such as the treaty of Safar with Aleppo, through occasional punitive raids. The court was also negotiating with the Buyids in Baghdad for the surrender of Skleros. Among the many embassies that were exchanged, we happen to have the report by one Ibn Shahram, who traveled to Constantinople in 981–982 after meeting first with Phokas. He reveals that Phokas was thinking of rebelling and that the *parakoimomenos* Basileios was the power behind the throne, though the blinded *kouropalates* Leon Phokas was also present, presumably to protect his family's interests. When the eunuch fell ill, Ibn Shahram and Basil II managed to make some progress toward a ten-year peace agreement, but the *parakoimomenos* was furious when he found out, and Basil had to appease him and tried to turn him against the Phokades. The emperor, now in his twenties, seems to have had little authority and knew that many are "indifferent to whether I or someone else is emperor." He did, however, have at least one supporter, the diplomat Nikephoros Ouranos.[67]

It is a sign of the empire's strength that, during the civil war, enemies did not invade. In 982, Otto II (973–973), the western "emperor of the Romans," tried to take over southern Italy, twenty years after his father had tried. With his Greek bride and infant son (Otto III) in tow, his army of German knights moved south ostensibly to protect Italy from Muslim raids, but really to reduce imperial cities, such as Taranto. But a Sicilian army, under the governor Abu Qasim, happened to invade Calabria just then. The Muslims decisively defeated the Germans at Stilo near Squilace, though Abu Qasim fell in the fighting and his army retreated to Sicily. Otto escaped by seeking refuge on an eastern tax vessel that chanced to be nearby, watching these two enemies of the empire so conveniently annihilate each other. Otto disguised his identity and secretly slipped away lest he be taken captive to Constantinople.[68] Constantinople struck back. The *katepano* of Italy, Kalokyros Delphinas, a Phokas ally, took Ascoli and Trani in 982–983. Constantinople's long reach now managed to install one of its clients, Boniface VII, as pope for eleventh months. It had been no idle boast, then, which the *parakoimomenos* Basileios had made to Liudprand back in 968, that the Roman Church would one day obey the emperor's nod.[69]

More trouble came also from the Bulgarians. Since the conquest of eastern Bulgaria in 971, the Bulgarian state had somehow reconstituted itself in the west, around Ohrid, and the figure who emerged as its leader was one Samuil. He was its leading general and the power behind the throne of tsar Roman, who was likely a eunuch. The events that led to this arrangement elude us, as does the ethnic makeup of the relocated state. Yet it is clear that tsar Roman (a son of tsar Petar) and Samuil (who became tsar after Roman) wanted their state to be understood as a continuation of the Bulgarian empire, and that is how it was understood by contemporaneous French, Armenian, and Arabic writers, both Christian and Muslim. We have an inscription of Ivan Vladislav (1015–1018), the last of the new tsars and a nephew of Samuil, which calls his state Bulgaria and his subjects Bulgarians. The Romans, however, refused to recognize Samuil as the tsar of the Bulgarians, for in their eyes the Bulgarian crown had been abolished by Tzimiskes in 971. Samuil for them was only a rebel troublemaker. Yet when the war was over, Basil II thanked God that "the Bulgarian state" was defeated by the Romans, and eleventh-century Romans consistently referred to Samuil as a Bulgarian.[70]

By the early 980s, Samuil was attacking the Romans' Balkan provinces, prompting Basil to take a number of fateful steps. Desiring military credentials to rival those of Phokas, in 985 he deposed and exiled the *parakoimomenos* Basileios, confiscating his wealth and annulling his acts.[71] He recalled Delphinas from Italy and demoted Phokas to *doux* of Antioch. Basil then prepared a campaign against Serdica (Sofia), which he personally led in 986. It was a disaster. After a twenty-day siege that accomplished nothing, Basil withdrew and was ambushed by Samuil in the pass of Trajan's Gate on 16 August. The army fled in panic and Basil barely escaped with his life. The historian Leon was serving as an imperial deacon and recounts how he "galloped off quickly before the enemy made it down the slope." The debacle was widely reported and mocked by the poet Geometres, a Phokas-partisan: among the trees, rocks, and mountains, he wrote, "the lion trembled before the doe." It was now plain that the emperor was an incompetent youth, and the *parakoimomenos* was no longer there to ease relations with the Phokades.[72]

The Buyids pounced immediately, releasing Skleros, his family, and followers to resume their rebellion. An eyewitness recorded the grand ceremony staged for Skleros in Baghdad after he agreed that, once he became emperor of the Romans,

Plate 1a Solidus of Constantine with image of Victoria. Solidi were struck at (ideally) 72 to the Roman pound (so about 4.5 grams of gold each).

Plate 1b Hagia Sophia, interior

Plate 2a Hagia Sophia, interior detail

Plate 2b Silk peplos given by Michael VIII Palaiologos to the city of Genoa (Comune di Genova—Museo di Sant' Agostino). For more, see p. 787.
Photo by David Hendrix

Plate 3a Justinian mosaic from Ravenna, San Vitale. Justinian brings the eucharistic bread to church, flanked by secular officials on the left and priests on the right (except for the head of the secular figure on his immediate right, who added himself in later). The positioning of the feet reveals who is front of whom in the procession.
Photo by David Hendrix

Plate 3b Theodora mosaic from Ravenna, San Vitale. The empress, who is bringing the wine, is escorted by eunuchs and handmaidens, and all are moving from right to left. The hem of her robe features the three Magi who brought offerings to the newborn Jesus.
Photo by David Hendrix

Plate 4a Konstantinos IV mosaic in the Sant' Apollinare church, Ravenna. Behind the emperor stand his brothers Herakleios and Tiberios and his son Justinian II. Konstantinos is handing over a document labeled "privileges" to the bishop.
Photo by David Hendrix

Plate 4b Mosaic of St. Demetrios (or another military saint) in his church in Thessalonike; from their clothes, the two children appear to be of aristocratic origin (probably seventh century).
Photo by David Hendrix

Plate 5a Narthex of Hagia Sophia, image of "Leo VI" performing proskynesis before Christ, beneath medallions of the Virgin (whose hands indicate that she is interceding for him) and the angel Gabriel. The text in Christ's hand says "Peace be upon you; I am the light of the world."
Shutterstock/imagebroker.com

Plate 5b Mosaic of Konstantinos IX Monomachos and Zoe from Hagia Sophia. The faces of the emperor and empress have been changed, in her case to update her profile, but in his because the original mosaic featured one of her previous husbands, whose names were shorter, and so "Konstantinos" had to be squeezed in at the top left. He brings the customary offering of gold to Hagia Sophia.
Photo by David Hendrix

Plate 6a Image of Alexios I Komnenos from the front pages (2r) of Zigabenos' Panoply (see p. 649). The manuscript is Vaticanus graecus 666. On the facing page (where Alexios is looking), a group of Church Fathers (clergy and monastic) are bringing him their collective learning.

Photo 12 / Alamy Stock Photo

Plate 6b Ioannes II Komnenos and Piroska (Eirene) mosaic from Hagia Sophia. The emperor is bring the customary gift of gold to the church.

Shutterstock/Ints Vikmanis

Plate 7a Theodoros Metochites, self-portrait from Chora, a monastery church that he renovated. He is bringing the church as an offering to Christ. See p. 820.
Photo by David Hendrix

Plate 7b Chora church, interior decoration of the side-chapel (parekklesion), which was a mortuary site. Above images of the Church Fathers is shown the Resurrection of Christ, who is pulling Adam and Eve out of their tombs. Above that is shown the Last Judgment, with Christ enthroned and flanked by rows of holy figures.
Photo by David Hendrix

Plate 8a Chora Mosaic, Enrollment of the Holy Family for taxation (see p. 834).
Photo by David Hendrix

Plate 8b Ms. image of Manuel II and Helene on the manuscript of pseudo-Dionysios that he sent to Saint-Denis, near Paris; for more, see p. 890.

he would be a peaceful ally of the Buyids, release all Muslim captives in the empire, and surrender seven border forts.[73] The Buyids did not, however, give him an army, as they had barely enough forces to control Iraq, so Skleros had to build up a coalition as he marched north, including tribal warriors, Armenians, a Kurdish emir, and the city of Melitene, which again declared for him. The court's response was to appoint Phokas *domestikos* again and charge him with defeating the rebel, but this time Phokas proclaimed himself emperor, at the estates of his relative Maleïnos in Charsianon, and entered into negotiations with Skleros for a partnership. But when the two partners met in Cappadocia, Phokas arrested and imprisoned Skleros. Phokas now controlled all the eastern armies and with them the whole of Asia Minor. He had been planning this for years and struck at the right moment. The western armies controlled by the court had just been defeated by the Bulgarians, who began to raid throughout Greece, Thessaly, and Macedonia. Probably already in 986, Samuil captured Larissa by starving it out, and transported its people and the relics of a local saint (Achilleios) to his base in the north, at Prespa.[74] By 987, Basil was squeezed between Samuil and Phokas, whose armies were now encamped by the Bosporos and Hellespont. The Phokades pumped out poems praising Nikephoros II Phokas, the rebel's uncle.[75]

In the first civil war, the court had sought the assistance of a foreign power, Davit' of Tao. But Davit' now sided with his old ally Phokas and helped him to defeat a small imperial force that was sent to disrupt Mesopotamia behind the rebel's lines. Basil turned instead to another power for help: Volodymyr (Vladimir), king of the Rus' and son of Sviatoslav. Basil offered him his born-in-the-purple sister Anna, the most desired match in Christendom at this time, whose hand had been sought in vain by the German emperors and Hugh Capet, the king of France. In exchange for this "unheard-of concession,"[76] Volodymyr would convert and give Basil an army to defeat Phokas. It seems like an uneven deal, but our sources for it are poor. The *Russian Primary Chronicle* recounts legends. It has Volodymyr enact a medieval trope, that of a heathen king sending out envoys to sample the religions of other nations and report back to him. They came back most awed by Hagia Sophia: "We knew not whether we were in heaven or on earth . . . . We know only that God dwells there among men, and their service is fairer than the ceremonies of other nations." In reality, Volodymyr was already planning to convert his realm to Christianity, probably as a way of centralizing his control, and wanted to offload a troublesome army of Varangians (i.e., Scandinavians) that he sent to Basil: "Don't let any of them come back here," he told the emperor. Thus Basil helped Volodymyr accomplish both goals and, by giving him Anna, raised his status to boot.[77]

Basil received the 6,000 Varangians in the summer of 988 and organized them into a new, supersized *tagma*. Probably in that year, he used them and his Roman forces to defeat Delphinas at Chrysopolis across the straits, hanging the former *katepano* on the spot. Early in 989, the two emperors, Basil and his brother Konstantinos VIII, crossed the Hellespont with their mixed Scandinavian-Roman army and confronted Phokas outside Abydos. On 13 April, right before battle was joined, Phokas fell dead from his horse. This ended his rebellion, as his relatives and supporters throughout the empire surrendered. They did, however, release Skleros from captivity, and he resumed his rebellion, with some former Phokas supporters. But he was almost seventy years old and infirm. By October, 989, he too negotiated a surrender. He agreed to retire to Thrace with the honorary rank of *kouropalates*, and died in 991. At his meeting with the emperor, Skleros was being carried by his attendants, and Basil exclaimed, "The man I have so long feared is being led by the hand!"[78]

This second round of civil war claimed few lives and did little damage to the empire. But it did leave some loose ends: allies to reward and enemies to punish. The Buyids could safely be ignored as they were too weak to harm the empire and they had already spent their bargaining chip. Basil made a treaty with the Fatimids instead. The incentive that emperors dangled before the eyes of Muslim powers was which caliph would be mentioned in the prayers of the mosques of Constantinople, a hugely prestigious feather in their caps.[79] Basil sent an army to punish Davit' of Tao, who had this time backed the wrong horse in a Roman civil war, but the Georgian ruler offered to bequeath his realm to the emperor upon his own death. Basil accepted, bestowing upon Davit' the rank of *kouropalates* and giving court titles to leading nobles of his principality in order to build up a cadre of local imperial officials. When Davit' died in 1000, Upper Tao was peacefully annexed.[80] Volodymyr, as agreed, was rewarded with Basil's sister Anna, who "departed with reluctance. 'It is as if I were setting out into captivity,' she lamented. 'Better to die at home.' But her brothers protested to her, 'Through you God is bringing the Rus' to repentance.'" Volodymyr, who was called by some *fornicator immensis*, married Anna at Cherson, and the priests who accompanied her set about organizing the Church among the Rus'. The Greek sources again say nothing about this process.[81]

Basil II's foreign wars

Basil would rule for another thirty-five years, becoming the longest-reigning Roman emperor in history (976–1025). Having lived through two interim emperors, a domineering eunuch-handler, and two major rebellions, Basil refused to delegate authority. He took personal command of the armies, sidelined his brother Konstantinos and the existing military families, and promoted his own officers, often from undistinguished origins, ensuring that they would be loyal to him.[82] It was from his officer class that the military aristocracy of the eleventh century emerged, including the families of Diogenes, Komnenos, Dalassenos, and others. He did not wage class war against the existing aristocracy, as is often thought. Basil merely kept them in check, in part by strengthening the land legislation of his predecessors. The Varangian Guard, a huge army personally loyal to him, was not encouraged to assimilate to Roman society precisely so that it would not meddle in politics. The guardsmen were regarded as savage foreigners, much like the German guards employed earlier by the Julio-Claudian emperors and the Khazar unit at the tenth-century court.[83] Basil also never married, which was unprecedented and not explained in the sources. He may have been apprehensive about allowing ambitious in-laws into the palace. In this, he followed the advice that the rebel Skleros is said to have given him: "depose all who accumulate too much power; don't let generals grow too rich; run them down with unfair taxes so that they are always busy with their private affairs; don't let a woman into the palace; don't be accessible; and don't let many know what you are thinking."[84]

There were long periods when Basil did not appoint a patriarch, especially in 991–996, and he is never shown interacting with the people. He seems to have consolidated all authority into his hands. But his reign is so poorly documented that it lacks a domestic history. On the night of 25 October, 989, as Skleros' rebellion was winding down, a powerful earthquake ruined many buildings in Constantinople and cracked the dome and apse of Hagia Sophia. Basil spent at least 1,000 lbs of gold on the repairs, which lasted between four and six years.[85] But it is unclear whether he personally spent much time in the City. He even chose to be buried outside Constantinople, at the church of St. John the Theologian at the military parade grounds of the Hebdomon. His epitaph boasts that "no one saw my spear lie idle. I stayed alert throughout my life . . . campaigning in both the west and east." The first-person voice in poetry was reserved for a confession of sins, but this epitaph is an exception, evincing "no humility . . . or trace of remorse."[86]

The major preoccupation of Basil's reign was the war with Bulgaria, which ended in 1018 with a definitive Roman victory. Arab and Roman sources explicitly state that this war lasted for thirty-five or forty years; even if we count it from 986, it would still be the single longest war in Roman history.[87] Unfortunately, they do not give a narrative of it, except for the years 1014–1018; before that we have only snippets. There are such huge gaps, including for the entire period 1003–1014, that we cannot even see the overall shape of the war. We do not know who controlled eastern Bulgaria in 986–1001. In the early 990s, Basil seems to have made some gains. He took Skopje, where he captured the eunuch-tsar Roman, the son of Petar, to whom he gave titles and the command of Abydos in Asia Minor. One of Basil's strategies throughout the war was to lure Bulgarians away from their allegiance to Samuil with offers of titles and offices. Meanwhile, Samuil raided Roman Macedonia and Greece as far as the Peloponnese, but he was badly defeated in 996 at the Spercheios river by Basil's trusted officer Nikephoros Ouranos, *doux* of Thessalonike. Ouranos ambushed the Bulgarians at night, and Samuil and his son hid among the bodies before escaping to Ohrid. The bones of the slain could still be seen decades later. Samuil was prepared to sue for terms, but just then the captive tsar Roman died, and Samuil proclaimed himself tsar of the Bulgarians. The war continued.[88]

We are better informed by Arabic sources about the eastern front, though no dramatic changes took place there. Basil's policy in the east was to maintain the status quo established in 970, treating Antioch as a Roman base and Aleppo as a client state. In this he was successful. Fatimid policy, by contrast, was to gain control over the quasi-independent cities of Syria (such as Damascus) and to wrest Aleppo and Antioch away from the Romans. In this they failed, but when the emperor was absent they made temporary advances. On 15 September, 994, their Turkish general Manju Takin destroyed an Aleppan-Roman army under Bourtzes and Leon Melissenos north of Apameia, and then invested Aleppo. Appeals from the city reached Basil "in the heart of Bulgaria," and he force-marched his army across the empire in under a month. Manju Takin fled at the news, and Basil took Apameia, Homs (Emesa), and many forts, burning and pillaging his way to Tripoli, which he besieged but failed to capture. There was apparently no one in the region willing to face him, and his campaign, like that of Tzimiskes twenty years before, was meant to demonstrate that. The emperor replaced Bourtzes with Damianos Dalassenos as *doux* and departed. But in his absence the Fatimids gradually clawed back their position. On 19 July, 998, their governor of Damascus, Jaysh, defeated and killed Dalassenos at Apameia, but was unable to make solid gains. Basil returned to the east in September, 999, and buried the bones of the Romans who had fallen at Apameia. He then rampaged in Syria, again failing to take Tripoli. Tripoli seems to have been the only additional place that the emperors wanted to acquire because of its strategic importance for naval operations. Basil appointed Ouranos as *doux* of Antioch, and retired to Cilicia.[89]

While Basil was wintering in Cilicia, Davit' of Tao died on 31 March, 1000. The emperor, taking the Varangians and followed at a distance by Ouranos and the army of Antioch, went on a tour of his Caucasian frontier. At this time he annexed Theodosiopolis (Erzurum) back into the empire, which had been loaned to Davit' after 979, and absorbed Tao itself as per the bequest agreement of 989. During the tour, Basil also bestowed titles on his local clients, including Bagrat III of Abkhazia (*kouropalates*), his father Gurgen of Kartli (*magistros*), and the emir Mumahhid al-Dawla of the Diyar Bakr, whom he made a *magistros* and *doux* of the region, with the authority to call on the armies of Taron and western Armenia. It was extremely rare, if not unprecedented, for a Muslim to obtain such a position in the Roman hierarchy. A Muslim writer even noted that Basil "was famed for his justice and affection toward Muslims."[90] The emperor also received the rulers of the Armenian principalities of Kars (Vanand) and Vaspurakan, giving them gifts but not titles (the ruler of Ani, Gagik, declined the invitation). Basil had already cultivated the goodwill of these princes in the past. In 983, he had sent a piece of the True Cross to the monastery of Aparankʿ in Vaspurakan, and its reception was celebrated by the poet-monk Grigor of Narek, who praised Basil explicitly. In these exchanges of goodwill, both sides ignored the theological differences between their Churches. When he reached Tao, Basil organized it as a province. It is not clear whether the *doukaton* of Iberia, with headquarters at Theodosiopolis, was formed now or later. But all the key positions were held by Romans, not locals.[91]

We have no direct information about the Bulgarian war during 1003–1014. It is possible that a Roman campaign had restored eastern Bulgaria (Preslav, Pliska, and the Danube delta) to imperial control in 1000/1,[92] but Samuil seems to have regained ground in Macedonia, as the fighting in and after 1014 was taking place in an arc around Thessalonike. When the curtain lifts, Samuil and Basil are facing each other across the Kleidion pass between the Strymon and Axios rivers, at which point Nikephoros Xiphias, the governor of Philippopolis, struck Samuil from behind. The tsar escaped again, and Basil blinded all the captured Bulgarian soldiers, between 14,000 and 15,000 of them, except for one out of every hundred, who was blinded in only one eye, to lead the others back home. Samuil, who was about seventy, allegedly fainted at this sight and died of a heart attack two days later, on 6 October. He was buried in the church of St. Achilleios on the island in lake Prespa, where his tomb was excavated in 1965 (see Figure 41).

Figure 41 Church of St. Achilleios at Prespa where Samuil was buried
Shutterstock/Panos Karas

Scholars have debated the historicity of Basil's atrocity, and the number of blinded soldiers seems certainly inflated; such a loss of manpower would have crippled the Bulgarian state, which nevertheless continued to fight on. In the modern imagination, the atrocity is associated with Basil's moniker "the Bulgar-Slayer," though that is not attested until the twelfth century. Still, Basil was not above inflicting spectacular punishments. In the east he amputated the hands of forty Bedouin raiders to discourage others, and he fed a treasonous secretary to a lion.[93] A famous manuscript, the Menologion of Basil II (Vaticanus graecus 1613), that was prepared for him, contains, on each page, a brief account of the life of a saint, usually a martyr, accompanied by a sadistic image of the distinctive method of his or her torture and execution.

The victory at Kleidion tipped the balance in favor of the Romans, but the Bulgarian state did not collapse overnight, even when the deceased tsar's relatives fought over the succession. Unfortunately, we know little about the organization, resources, and territorial extent of Samuil's state, but it must have been formidable to keep the Romans at bay for so long, at a time when no one could face them in the east. Basil had to move methodically and encountered stiff resistance, but made gradual progress. He took Melnik, Prilep, and Štip and burned the palace at Bitola in 1014. He captured Edessa and Moglena in 1015, and Beroia in 1017, returning to Constantinople at the end of each campaign. In February, 1018, the new tsar, Ivan Vladislav, was killed in a raid on Dyrrachion, leading to a collapse of the Bulgarian resistance. The leadership rushed to surrender, accepting titles and offices from Basil, who handed them out generously in exchange for cities and territories. The people at Ohrid greeted him with celebrations, and Basil gave the treasure of the last tsars, 720,000 nomismata, to his soldiers. He was gracious in his reception of Samuil's surviving family, and sent them along to Constantinople, as he planned to absorb them into the Roman aristocracy. In all, his tour of Bulgaria in 1018 and disposition of its new organization closely resembled his tour of Armenia and Tao in 1000. Basil then swung south to Athens, where he offered thanks to the Virgin in the Parthenon. In 1019, he returned to Constantinople and celebrated a triumph, his chariot proceeded by the Bulgarian royal family.[94]

Basil's conquest approximately tripled the extent of the empire's holdings in the Balkans, adding all the territory from Philippopolis to the Adriatic along the east-west axis, and from the mountainous core of western Greece in the south up to Vidin on the Danube in the north, with a long extension along the Danube that reached to Sirmium, on the borders of Hungary. Sirmium was acquired soon after the conquest of Bulgaria, by Konstantinos Diogenes, father of the future emperor. He ambushed and killed the city's ruler at a meeting, sent his wife to the capital to be married to a Roman senator, and annexed Sirmium, which had not been part of the empire for over four centuries. Effective control in the new lands reached from the Adriatic to the new theme of Naissos (Niš), encircling most of modern Serbia, but did not extend deeper into the former Yugoslavia.[95] Beyond that fortified line lay a number of Dalmatian, Serb, and Croat principalities that were now imperial clients. Their rulers were given titles and sometimes crowns by the emperor, and "invited" to Constantinople to confirm their loyalty, like the Lombard dukes and Armenian lords. Later in the century, a Roman essayist advised such toparchs to stay in their country and not be overly eager for court titles, because one day they might wake up to find themselves prisoners and their lands annexed. The Roman "Sun Kings" now had more satellites than ever.[96]

Conquered Bulgaria was carved up into military themes that were grouped into regional *doukata*. There was a *doux* of Bulgaria stationed at Ohrid (as an administrative term, this "Bulgaria" referred to the western Balkans conquered by Basil in 1018). Later in the century, another *doukaton* is attested along the Danube (Paristrion), with *strategoi* at Preslav, Pliska, and Varna; this too may have been created by Basil or an immediate successor to deal with the Pecheneg threat. The new *doukata* were buttressed to the south by the existing ones of Adrianople and Thessalonike, the latter being the main command headquarters during the war.[97] These commands were officered by Romans and constituted an occupation force. Forts were taken over by Roman soldiers or demolished, so that they could not become focal points for resistance. Basil arranged marriages between leading Bulgarians and Romans, "in order to put an end to their former mutual hatred,"[98] but apart from the royals and some top Bulgarian generals, who were absorbed into the Roman aristocracy, we do not hear of Bulgarian officers serving in the armies. The elimination of the Bulgarian court decapitated its nobility as well, though local society was probably unaffected and Basil allowed the Bulgarians to "carry on under their own leaders and customs." In particular, he allowed them to continue to pay taxes in kind, as they had under Samuil.[99]

In three charters (called *sigillia*), Basil confirmed the status of the Bulgarian Church as an autocephalous archbishopric based at Ohrid. However, this was not the Bulgarian Church of the empire of Simeon and Petar, but that of the western Balkan state of Samuil. Its jurisdiction included Ioannina, Kastoria, and other sees along the coast of southern Albania; Pelagonia, Beroia, Skopje, Strumica, Serdica, Vidin, and Niš in the central Balkans; Belgrade and Sirmium in the northwest; and Dorostolon (Silistra) in the northeast. The first appointee to this archbishopric was a Bulgarian, Ivan of Debar (1019–1036), but after him the position was held by Romans. Later in the eleventh century, the fiction would be invoked that Ohrid stood in for Justinian's creation Justiniana Prima, though there was no institutional continuity between the two nor precise overlap in their jurisdictions. That fiction, however, buttressed the restoration of Roman authority to the Balkans.[100]

In the east, the Romans retained a strong position throughout the rest of Basil's reign. The Hamdanids fell from power in Aleppo in 1004 and the emirate spiraled into political instability. When its rulers brought in the Fatimids in 1016, Basil took an extraordinary action which revealed the impressive infrastructural capabilities of the Roman state at this time: he placed an embargo on trade and travel with Syria and Egypt. This hurt Aleppo's economy enough that it submitted to the emperor, between 1017 and 1021. Another reason for Aleppo's reversal was the terrifying regime of the insane Fatimid caliph al-Hakim (996–1021), who issued bizarre decrees and tended to execute his officials at random. He demolished many churches, including, in ca. 1009, the Holy Sepulcher in Jerusalem, and he made life difficult for his Christian subjects. In 1013–1015, he allowed or coerced many of them to emigrate to Romanía, where they settled in Laodikeia, Antioch, and other cities; among them was the future historian Yahya.[101] Basil did not regard those actions as provocations and kept the peace for another five years. But by 1020, the situation was tense. Al-Hakim had received an offer of alliance from king Giorgi I of Abkhazia and Kartli, who was contesting the Roman annexation of Tao.[102] Basil was marching across Asia Minor—characteristically, he had told no one what his destination was—when he received news of the caliph's death. For years al-Hakim was in the habit of wandering alone at night outside Cairo. On 13 February, 1021, he did not return.

Whatever his original target had been, Basil now advanced against Giorgi of Abkhazia, moving east from Theodosiopolis into Vanand. This was the first war in centuries between an emperor and a Georgian or Armenian ruler, but it was not unprovoked; Giorgi had infringed on lands ceded to the empire by Davit' of Tao. Giorgi rebuffed Basil's diplomatic advances, but was defeated in battle in Vanand and fled north. While Basil wintered at Trebizond, Giorgi offered terms, including hostages. At this time, another Caucasian principality, Vaspurakan (east of lake Van), was voluntarily ceded to the emperor by its ruler Senek'erim (1003–1021), who was given titles and extensive lands around Sebasteia in Cappadocia. The king brought Armenian priests with him and was not required to convert to Orthodoxy. Conversely, when Basil turned Vaspurakan into a *katepanato* with Roman officers, Chalcedonian sees were established alongside those of the Armenian Church. The empire now bordered on Azerbaijan. Over the next decade, it would absorb the small Muslim emirates between lake Van and Roman Taron. During that same winter (1021–1022), Smbat III, king of Ani, also pledged his realm to the emperor, effective upon his death (which would be in 1041). It is possible that he had sided with Giorgi and feared direct military action by the emperor, thereby replaying the experience of Davit' of Tao back in 990. The emperor made Smbat a *magistros* and confirmed him in possession of his kingdom for his lifetime.[103] With little effort, the empire was absorbing Christian Transcaucasia.

At precisely that moment, when the war with Giorgi was heating up again, some officers mounted a military coup in Cappadocia, to the emperor's rear. They were Nikephoros Xiphias—who had ambushed the Bulgarians at Kleidion in 1014 and was now general of Anatolikon—and Nikephoros Phokas, a son of the rebel Bardas who held no office but was brought onboard for the military allure of his name. The Phokades tended to launch civil wars precisely when the empire was preoccupied with foreign wars, a tactic that would cost the empire dearly in the 1070s. But "the rebels' childish game was soon over, like a castle built on sand."[104] Phokas was executed and his head sent to his presumptive ally Giorgi of Abkhazia, while Xiphias was arrested and tonsured. Basil marched into the Basean valley and defeated the Abkhazians again, whereupon Giorgi sued for peace and gave up hostages. He was allowed to keep his kingdom. Basil then marched into Vaspurakan, his most recent acquisition, to organize its administration, after which he returned to Constantinople, in 1023.[105]

Basil had campaigned across the Balkans, as far east as Azerbaijan, and south to the Levantine coast. Everywhere he had "erected myriads of trophies" and expanded or fortified the empire of the Romans. "Witnesses of this," he boasted in his epitaph, "are the Persians and the Skythians, together with the Abkhazian, the Ismaelite, and the Iberian."[106] From a military standpoint, further conquest was feasible, but the empire was weary of incorporating Muslim populations, and mountainous regions, such as in the western Balkans were unprofitable. In fact, as we will see, it is likely that after the Bulgarian war the Roman state exercised little effective control over mountainous western Greece and Albania. But there was one area—southern Italy—where imperial authority could still be buttressed and one territory that could be profitably reconquered: Sicily.

Southern Italy was vulnerable from many directions. It was a regular target of Muslim raids from Sicily. Many of its governors in Bari were assassinated by Lombards, though it is not clear whether this violence stemmed from a generalized anti-Greek feeling. A bishop of Bari who died in 1035 is said to have hated the Greeks (despite, ironically, bearing the name "Bisantius"), and his successor, who was elected by the people, was arrested and taken to Constantinople.[107] Southern Italy was also periodically attacked by the nearby Lombard dukes and excited the interest of the German kings. Its distant link to Constantinople across the Adriatic could be severed by hostile fleets. Yet the imperial administration was entrenched in its Italian provinces. The thematic army organization penetrated down to the local level; officers sent from Constantinople were present throughout the land; and large investments were made in maintaining defensive fortifications. These created the conditions for prosperity and growth.[108]

Basil's administration ensured stability in Italy for a generation. In 992, he granted to the Venetians a favorable toll status for their trade at Constantinople and Abydos, in exchange for which they would help transport imperial armies to Italy and ensure stability in the Adriatic. In 1002, they indeed helped to lift an Arab siege of Bari. The doge of Venice received titles from the court just like the empire's other clients in Italy, Dalmatia, and the Caucasus.[109] Even Rome was again brought into the imperial orbit, when Byzantine diplomacy installed Ioannes Philagathos of Rossano, an imperial subject, on the papal throne as John XVI in 997–998. One of the diplomats involved admitted in a letter to a friend that Philagathos was a scoundrel: "I know that you're laughing at me but I suspect that you'll roar when you hear that I appointed Philagathos pope—when I ought to have strangled him and said 'serves him right!'" Philagathos was deposed by Otto III in 998 and mutilated.[110]

The imperial provinces remained vulnerable to Lombard adventurers. One Melo (Meles) of Bari made two attempts to take over Apulia, in 1009 and 1017–1018, both of which were defeated by the imperial *katepano*, but only after Melo had scored some initial successes and demonstrated that local support existed for such ventures. It is possible that local society was divided between pro- and anti-imperial factions.[111] Melo enjoyed the moral support of both pope Boniface VIII and the German emperor Heinrich II. His second defeat came at the hands of one of the most capable imperial officers of that age, Basileios Boioannes, who governed the south for ten years, until 1028. Boioannes fortified many cities along the border with the Lombard duchies, in the region that would come to be named, after his own office, as Capitanata; he also ensured the loyalty of Capua. When Heinrich II attacked the south in 1021–1022, he made no progress against the walls of Troia and departed. This was the high point of east Roman power in Italy. Boioannes promoted new settlements and the expansion of agriculture, and was widely popular. In anticipation of the emperor's arrival, in 1024, he crossed the Adriatic and arrested the family of the king of Croatia, sending it to Constantinople, whose palaces were filling up with hostage royal "guests." An advance imperial army for the conquest of Sicily arrived soon after, including Varangians and Bulgarians, but it was followed by news of the emperor's death in December 1025, and the campaign was called off.[112]

For an emperor who ruled for so long and changed the course of history, Basil remains an opaque figure. He consolidated power into his own hands to an extraordinary degree, stripping it down to himself and the army, keeping the army continually on the move and under his personal command. He did little to sponsor literary culture or non-military building, apart from the repair of Hagia Sophia in 989. He shunned the complications of family life and courtly culture, excluding his brother Konstantinos from the exercise of power. Yet he probably monitored everything taking place in his domain, "looking closely into every matter, whether great or small."[113] Most of his focus was on the practice of war, where he aimed at success rather than flair. Psellos later presented him as an austere and even ascetic general who micromanaged the battlefield according to "scientific" principles: he studied the military manuals, knew his armies, never took great risks, punished soldiers who broke formation even if they defeated the enemy, and kept his plans secret.[114]

Basil dramatically expanded the reach of his state, annexing the territories of its neighbors along with millions of non-Romans, all at a time of demographic and economic expansion. The Romans now ruled over previously foreign lands and peoples. This satisfied revanchist attitudes of Roman supremacy. In the first flush of victory, a patriarch could thank the Virgin "that the vile Scythians have been shattered" and "the Bulgarian race has lowered its head to the Roman yoke and learned to serve rather than rule."[115] But the dilemma of all empires was not long to appear. This was now a more complex society, with Bulgarians posted to defend Vaspurakan or conquer Sicily, with their royal family grafted to the Roman aristocracy; retired Armenian kings held vast estates in Cappadocia; and 6,000 Scandinavians, not all of them Christian, accompanied the emperor wherever he went. The Romans held an empire again, which paradoxically meant that the barbarians were inside the gates. Traveling to the frontier or settling in the new territories produced feelings of alienation and anguish. "I settled among alien nations with a strange religion and tongue," wrote one man who migrated to the Armenian badlands. "These stupid Cilicians have turned me into a barbarian," complained a governor of the province: "Tarsos is no friend of mine, nor do I love Antioch." The eastern borderlands were now full of anti-Chalcedonians, Muslims, and Nestorians. As Michael Psellos put it, "Roman and barbarian are not clearly distinguished now; we live all mixed up with one another."[116]

26

A Brief Hegemony (1025–1048)

Macedonian twilight

By refusing to marry, Basil knowingly consigned his dynasty to extinction. His brother Konstantinos VIII (1025–1028) had only daughters who were too old to have children. Yet a series of irregular marriages extended the dynasty's tail end through another generation. When Basil died, guardsmen brought his brother to Constantinople from Nikaia. Konstantinos also made no plans for the succession until he was about to die, when he summoned a former prefect of the City, Romanos III Argyros (1028–1034), and offered him a choice: Romanos could divorce his wife, marry one of Konstantinos' daughters (Zoe or Theodora), and become emperor, or else he would be blinded. In order to legally divorce, his wife had to "voluntarily" join a convent, which she was volunteered to do. There was another impediment, namely that Romanos and Zoe were kin of the seventh degree, and just then the Church was starting to ban such marriages. (To calculate degrees, you count inclusively up to the first common ancestor, and then down to the person you want to marry—an ancient Roman system.) During the eleventh century, marriage cases were shifting from the secular courts to the Church, but this particular ban was not made official until 1038, so the marriage of Zoe to Romanos was grudgingly accepted.[1]

Zoe then took up an affair with a strapping lad from Paphlagonia named Michael, who was subtly introduced to her by his brother, the influential court eunuch Ioannes, later known as the *orphanotrophos*. It was widely believed that Zoe and Michael conspired to murder Romanos. On the night that he died, the patriarch Alexios III Stoudites was summoned to the palace and asked to marry Zoe and Michael. This was irregular because the two were adulterers, possibly murderers, and Zoe had not mourned her first husband for the expected year. Alexios balked, but his qualms were assuaged by 50 lbs of gold for himself and another 50 for his clergy. Despite the manner of his rise to the throne, Michael IV the Paphlagonian (1034–1041) was a capable and dutiful emperor, who relied on his brothers, especially the Orphanotrophos, to govern. It is a testament to the impersonal and infrastuctural nature of state power in Romanía that holding office gave these former nobodies the authority to rule. Still, aristocratic grumblings were heard. Konstantinos Dalassenos, a career general and son of Basil II's *doux* of Antioch, "wondered aloud why, when there were so many excellent men of distinguished families, a vulgar and threepence-a-day man should be preferred."[2]

Michael gradually became estranged from Zoe, allegedly out of guilt for what they had done, and when he died (as a monk) he passed the throne to his nephew Michael V (1041–1042), whom Zoe formally adopted. When this Michael—known as Kalaphates, the "Caulker," after his father's profession—exiled Zoe from the palace, the populace of Constantinople rose up in a massive insurrection to defend their beloved empress. Michael hastily brought her back but it was too late. The palace was blockaded. Michael fled but he was arrested and blinded on the orders of Zoe and her sister Theodora. The crowd had extracted the latter from her convent and, against the wishes of both women, forced her to be co-empress. The two sisters now held a reverse bride show, interviewing candidates to marry Zoe and become the next emperor. They settled on Konstantinos IX Monomachos (1042–1055), a charming gentleman from a good family. However, this would be the third marriage for both. The patriarch Alexios refused to perform the service, but delegated it to a priest and then blessed the couple anyway. They did not undergo the required penance of five years. The mosaic of Zoe and Romanos III in Hagia Sophia had to be modified for Monomachos' image and name to take his predecessor's place (see Plate 5b).

Moreover, Monomachos already had a partner, Maria Skleraina, whom he introduced to the palace as a de facto wife, elevating her to the rank of Sebaste (the Greek translation of Augusta). The arrangement verged on bigamy. In 1044, Monomachos barely survived another popular insurrection, as the people believed that he too was also trying to set Zoe aside. Zoe died around 1050 and Monomachos in early 1055, whereupon the last Macedonian, Theodora, ruled in her own name for over a year (1055–1056), deciding, like Eirene, that she could do without a man. As she lay dying, Theodora (or the eunuchs around her) designated Michael VI Bringas as her successor (1056–1057), an old childless bureaucrat who ran the military budget. The people called him Michael the Old.

None of these emperors had a child who could become a dynastic heir and, by virtue of their marriage to Zoe, none could have one. Michael V was young but single, and his regime failed quickly. In a throwback to the fifth–sixth centuries, these emperors were acceptable to the polity at large and to the powerful interests that flanked the throne precisely because they were non-dynastic. Each of them was a temporary appointment with no future prospects that allowed the existing Macedonian dynasty to fade out while keeping powerful men content that at least their rivals were not entrenching themselves and their families on the throne. Even so, the emperors of this period faced many plots and conspiracies, real or alleged, from elements of the ruling class or the court, which we will not recount in detail. As no one had any "right" to the throne in the Roman system beyond what he or she could persuade others to recognize, power was always up for grabs. The two empresses were protected by the people of Constantinople, but when they died the game of thrones began in earnest.

None of these emperors had a military background. They were therefore vulnerable not only to plots and popular insurrections, but increasingly also to ambitious generals. To counter that threat, they relied on eunuchs to run the court and command the armies, alienating the "bearded" officer class. This approach peaked under Theodora and Michael VI, who were both old and childless and surrounded by eunuchs. As emperors grew weaker, generals increasingly tried to seize the throne in major military rebellions: Georgios Maniakes (1044), Leon Tornikios (1047), Bryennios (1055), and Isaakios Komnenos (1057). Thus, a rift opened within the leadership between the civilian or courtly interests (*politikon*) and the military (*stratiotikon*). This is how Psellos explained the putsch of 1057, when the dam finally burst:

> For a long time the soldiers had found the situation of the state to be intolerable . . . because the emperor was always chosen from the other side, I mean the civil servants. Even when a decision was to be made concerning the head of the army or the commander of a unit, leadership was entrusted to men inexperienced in war. Those who lived inside the cities received greater offices than those who endured the hardships of war . . . For these reasons they were ready to protest against this situation in a most violent manner, and they lacked only a spark to set off their explosion. And then it happened. No one asked them their advice concerning the appointment of the new emperor and they were held in contempt.[3]

These were not fixed "parties" within the political system but a broad divergence of interests within it. In practice, families and sometimes individuals played both sides of this fuzzy structural divide.[4]

Economic prosperity

Mounting budget deficits exacerbated the systemic tension. When Basil II died, he left a huge surplus, reported either as 43.2 million nomismata (implausible) or 14.4 million, excluding the plunder of war and the confiscated estates of rebels (more plausible). He built vast underground spiral vaults to hoard it. The bulk of these savings probably did not come from plunder—as we saw, he gave the Bulgarian treasury to his soldiers—but from stewardship and parsimony. Either Basil or his brother Konstantinos VIII remitted taxes in arrears in order "to go easy on the poor."[5] But by 1050, Monomachos was facing such deficits that he became a strict tax collector, "squeezing the rich dry" and sending out many assessors. He expanded the use of Phokas' smaller *tetarteron* coin and even began to devalue the gold coinage. The *roga*-salaries of court titulars were reduced by a seventh.[6] These were alarming signs of a fiscal crisis.

It is now understood that the economy was expanding during the eleventh and twelfth centuries, meaning that more lands were brought back into cultivation, reversing their abandonment in the seventh and eighth centuries. Sediment samples around lake Nar, which is not far from the former militarized border, suggest that agriculture picked up again in the tenth century.[7] Large landowners (including the major monasteries, churches, and the state) were better positioned to do this as they could afford to hire labor and invest in irrigation and reclamation projects. Psellos acquired the monastery of Medikion and its land even though it was in debt, because he was advised that if he bought animals, planted vineyards, and improved irrigation, it would repay the investment handsomely. Therefore, he wrote to the governor of Opsikion, a friend, for help in settling a legal case over the water rights and to ask him not to burden the place with his costly visits.[8]

Psellos' relationship to the monastery was that of a *charistikarios*. This was an institution devised by the emperors to aid struggling houses. A lay patron was appointed to oversee them, put their finances in order, and lobby on their behalf. Psellos appears to have been doing his duty, but other *charistikarioi* exploited their monasteries for personal profit, or to put their own people in them, leading to a major controversy over this practice at the end of the century that lasted well into the next.[9] Some monasteries became agribusinesses that traded their products, including wine, using their own fleets of ships. Conversely, other monasteries were endowed to act as trust funds for their founders' descendants, providing them with tax-exempt revenue—and prayers for their souls.[10]

Agricultural expansion implies population growth. Guesses as to its size in ca. 1025 reach as high as 19 million.[11] This growth was partially the result of increased security, which made it safer to invest in land reclamation. Asia Minor had been untroubled by raiding since the mid-tenth century, and the Balkan provinces were raided by the Bulgarians only during periods of war (917–924, 986–1018). A picture of life in Asia Minor in the eleventh century is provided by the *Life of Lazaros of Galesion*, a stylite saint who founded three monasteries near Ephesos. Previous saints helped provincials cope with raiders and captivity, but life's dangers now consisted of Armenian con men, mountain bears, and angry sheepdogs, though demonic possession remained a constant. One problem that we do not find in the *Life* is assaults on the property of the poor by the "powerful."[12] The latter were likely not the military aristocracy but the larger monasteries. "Ill with greed," a different source tell us, "they would force farmers to surrender their lands to them. And if they had to face them in court, they prevailed through the leverage of so much land and money and because they were exempt from giving an accounting on such matters."[13]

Asia Minor presented a vibrantly diverse, tessellated, and interconnected landscape. In addition to the village communes, which were taxed as units by the state, there were three kinds of large estates: those owned by private individuals; those belonging to the monasteries, around which settlements sometimes evolved; and imperial estates (*episkepseis*), run by state managers. This countryside was ancient, with continuity of land use and settlement going back to early Roman times. There were imperial estates in Thrace and Greece that went back to the reign of Augustus. The landscape was dotted with cities, which housed the civilian and ecclesiastical administration and celebrated festivals in honor of local saints, featuring both markets and pilgrimage sites, though some of the latter operated in rural areas too. Cities were denser in western Asia Minor, but the archaeological evidence for them in this period is not impressive.[14]

Pastoralism was more prevalent in the central plateau, where the military aristocracy had their estates, whereas in the western river valleys peasant holdings remained the norm. There were distinctive regional features, such as the horse farms of Cappadocia and rock-cut settlements in Phrygia and Cappadocia. The grid of the old Roman roads bound this landscape together, with station houses every 20 or 30 miles, equipped with 40 horses each, serviced by surrounding villages and overseen by the logothete of the *dromos*. Forts guarded mountain passes, and denser nodes of infrastructural control were provided by half a dozen *aplekta*, military depots and mustering grounds, such as at Malagina, Dorylaion, Koloneia, and Kaisareia.[15] Everywhere there were churches, along with ancient ruins. An earthquake in 1063 collapsed a temple at Kyzikos, "quite a sight to behold on account of its height and size."[16]

Trade was also booming. An Arab geographer refers to "the villas and estates lining both sides of the strait [the Bosporos] and innumerable vessels go back and forth, carrying all sorts of merchandise and provisions from these estates to the capital. The number of these ships cannot be estimated."[17] Rich families who lived in the City and wealthy monasteries and churches brought food and other goods into the capital from their country estates for their own use. But trade and markets were also flourishing. We have an evocative description of the annual fair of Thessalonike where buyers and sellers congregated from western Europe, the Balkans, and the east. Their stalls, offering everything from horses to furniture, were arranged in a long row like a centipede, with short extensions (its legs) poking out at intervals.[18] It appears that each guild of Constantinople had its own parade and festival. We have a poem on the carnivalesque procession of the notaries and a quasi-philosophical text on the festival of Agathe, celebrated by female textile workers who put their handiwork on display.[19] In general, this was a period of elevated consumption and ostentation. A poet praised an elaborate confection cooked by his (female) cousin, a pastry in the form of the zodiac, with different-sized eggs in the place of the stars. "Oh God, how many arts have you bestowed upon women, and what minds you have instilled in them."[20]

Women operated or owned workshops and shops and continued to manage property. Many cases before the courts involved women's properties, especially those originating in dowries. It has been estimated, albeit for a later period, that widows made up 20% of the overall population, so many of them would have managed the properties of their deceased husbands. In such situations, the women held the cards and were formidable economic agents. Some were adept at working the system, and even used stereotypes about "feminine weakness" to advantage, for example by invoking them to annul transactions that had been made under duress, or that had later turned out to be disadvantageous.[21] There was at least one school for girls in the capital, to which Psellos sent his daughter before she died at the age of nine. As a Platonist, Psellos believed that women were just as rational as men, but some parents did not want their daughters to learn how to read lest the immorality of classical texts corrupt them.[22]

Budget shortfalls

The emperors of the eleventh century were pulling in more revenue than at any time since the age of Justinian, in an economy, moreover, that was highly monetized.[23] Why, then, were Monomachos and his successors short of cash after 1050? Unfortunately we lack data for the size of the imperial budget and its single greatest expense, the army. The size of the army probably increased after all the conquests, but presumably in proportion to the resources of the conquered lands. We cannot tell to what extent military service was commuted to cash payments to the state, enabling emperors to hire smaller, more expensive, but more flexible, professional forces. Another explanation for the shortfall is that, starting in the late 1040s, the empire was engaged in simultaneous defensive wars on many fronts that cost money whether they were won or lost, but yielded few profits if won. The Romans did not know it yet, but those wars were part of a great turning point in medieval history that affected every place between England and Iran.

Emperors of this generation *had* to spend more than their predecessors. As they lacked dynastic and military credentials, they compensated by purchasing support from the senatorial classes, the Church, and the prominent monasteries, all at state expense, of course. Every new accession was marked by a round of "gifts," including cash payments, luxury objects, and court titles (it is unclear whether the emperors were giving away these titles along with their lifelong salaries, or "graciously" allowing more people to purchase them, which would have actually raised revenue). Each regime had its own favorites whom it had to placate, and even "the people" are occasionally mentioned as recipients of "gifts," though it is unclear what form they took. The year 1042 witnessed two rounds of gifts, once when the two sisters came to power after the fall of Michael V and then when they raised Monomachos to the throne. They obtained the money for the first round by squeezing Michael V's blinded uncle for the cash that he had squirreled away: 381,600 nomismata! When Theodora became sole empress in 1056, she declined to award new promotions and titles, saying that "she was not coming into power for the first time but had received it from her father."[24] Thus, political insecurity exacerbated deficits.

Figure 42 Daphni church, near Athens on the road to Eleusis
Shutterstock/Cortyn

In addition, the emperors began to build large churches again in the City. These were costly vanity projects intended to function as tombs; the last emperor buried in the old imperial mausoleum was Konstantinos VIII. Romanos III built a church of the Virgin Peribleptos; Michael IV built a church for the Anargyroi; and Monomachos built the church of St. George of the Mangana. All of these were lavishly decorated with luxury materials, given large endowments of land, and criticized by contemporaries for being expensive. Psellos blamed them for being immoral and unpatriotic: "all the imperial treasuries were opened up for these projects and streams of gold poured into them . . . disrupting the body politic." Worldly paradises were being constructed for the benefit of monks who had allegedly renounced the world but in reality ate their way through oceans of fish.[25] It was the biggest boom in construction since Justinian.

The eleventh century also witnessed impressive church construction in the Balkan provinces, such as on Mt. Athos, which became a monastic theme park from which women were legally excluded; in and around Athens (e.g., the church at Daphni), Boiotia (Hosios Loukas), and the Aegean islands, which were now free of Muslim raids (e.g., the large Nea Moni on Chios) (see Figures 42–43). Such large churches were being built in the Balkans but not in Asia Minor, whose archaeological profile in the eleventh century lags.[26] One explanation may be that emperors assisted financially in these new constructions, promoting them as nodes of imperial patronage in recently secured regions. They endowed some

Figure 43 Hosios Loukas church, Boiotia
Shutterstock/Anastasios71

of these foundations with annual grants of cash diverted from public taxes, ranging between 70 and 900 nomismata, and gave them exemptions and food deliveries. To be sure, these gifts were small compared to those routinely made to Hagia Sophia.[27] In addition, emperors continued to endow philanthropic institutions. These were churches endowed with tax-exempt provincial lands, annual cash grants, workshops such as bakeries and mills, and an administrative staff. Monomachos' church of St. George had such an endowment. An older one was the Orphanage; the eunuch Ioannes, brother of Michael IV, was its manager, whence his title *orphanotrophos*.[28] Thus, emperors, and especially Monomachos, acquired reputations for being *both* generous, even profligate, *and* parsimonious, strict tax collectors.

Minority groups in the east

Romanos III Argyros sought to gain military laurels in 1030 by leading an attack against Aleppo, which was ruled by the Mirdasid dynasty and not causing trouble. His generals tried to discourage him, proving that his motives were political and not geostrategic. The campaign was a disaster. Romanos foolishly allowed his army to be surrounded in a waterless location. When he tried to withdraw, a sudden Arab attack dispersed his column and the Romans fled, abandoning the imperial tent and its treasures to the enemy. But the emperor came out on top anyway. The generals he left behind, especially the *doux* of Antioch, Niketas of Mistheia, a eunuch, patched up the damage that Romanos had caused, and the Mirdasids were so divided, exposed to the Fatimids, and weak that Nasr, the ruler of Aleppo, came to Constantinople to renew the treaty of 970 and become an imperial vassal.[29] The emperor soon received another windfall. In 1031, one of his frontier generals, Georgios Maniakes, entered into negotiations with Sulayman, the Turkish governor of Edessa over the surrender of that city, in exchange for which Sulayman would receive money and lands inside the empire. Sulayman conveyed a sacred relic to Constantinople—the original correspondence in Syriac between Jesus and Abgar of Edessa—and Maniakes entered the citadel of Edessa. His occupation was contested. For months, Maniakes engaged in an urban standoff against rival factions that were all fighting each other, including forces sent by the Marwanid rulers of Mayyafariqin, but he prevailed. Taxes began to flow to Constantinople in 1033.[30] Maniakes is described as a giant of a man, with massive arms and a voice like thunder. He was marked for greatness.

The empire's southeast corner was its most culturally diverse. Antioch, Melitene, Edessa, and their territories were home to Roman settlers who followed the expansion, but they were a minority. The region was also home to Armenians (mostly non-Chalcedonians), the Syrian Orthodox (both preexisting and those who were invited to settle in and around Melitene by Nikephoros II Phokas), Melkites (i.e., Roman Orthodox but mostly Arabic-speaking), converted ex-Muslims, and Muslims. Many of these cities, therefore, hosted two or three parallel Churches. A later Coptic Christian text records that, in 1072, Edessa had 20,000 Syrians, 8,000 Armenians, 6,000 Romans, and 1,000 Latins (probably mercenaries).[31] The top secular positions were reserved for Romans, who retained local systems of social control and tax collection. Beyond the generals, imperial agents known as *basilikoi* ("the emperor's men") exercised supervision over the conquered cities, liaising with the *kouratores* of the imperial estates that were formed during the conquests.[32] But non-Roman groups were treated differently by the authorities based largely on how assimilable they were to Roman norms.

Muslims who did not convert were the furthest from that norm. They were mostly clustered in Laodikeia and its territory, which had surrendered to Phokas in 968 without violent expulsions or mass conversions. They had rebelled in 992, without success, and some had been resettled elsewhere in the empire by Bourtzes. In 1028–1032 there was another independence movement by the Muslims along the Phoenician coast, but it was suppressed by Niketas of Mistheia.[33] Ibn Butlan, a Nestorian Christian from Baghdad, wrote around 1050 that the main mosque of Laodikeia had been turned into a church but that the Muslims prayed at another mosque and had their own judge (*qadi*); other villages in Syria had mosques too. Presumably, the Roman authorities interfaced with the Muslims' leaders only and did not interfere more deeply in their affairs.[34] Muslims did not obtain offices in the Roman state, nor is it likely that Roman law applied to them.

As for the Syrian Orthodox, Phokas and Tzimiskes implemented a regime of toleration that lasted sixty years. Syriac sources are full of praise for Tzimiskes and Basil II. But in the late 1020s, there was a backlash, spearheaded by a faction of bishops in Constantinople around the patriarch Alexios the Stoudite. The Roman bishop of Melitene complained to Constantinople that Syrians were being treated effectively as Roman Chalcedonians by intermarrying with them, drafting legally valid wills, and testifying in court against them. While none that we know were appointed to political office, Roman officials were helping them in their ventures, such as establishing monasteries. Romanos III hauled some of their Church leaders to the capital for "debates," followed by exile to Thrace when they refused to see the light. The bishop of Melitene saw this as a matter of loyalty: "Wouldn't you accept the faith of the emperor?"[35] To this, the Syrian bishop Yuhannan VIII bar Abdun replied: "We are under the authority of the holy emperor in everything. But it is impossible to change our faith." In 1030, the Synod of Constantinople proclaimed that the rights enjoyed by the Syrians were illegal under Justinian's laws against Monophysites. It does not appear, however, that the Syrian laity suffered discrimination.[36] Romanos, who had a background in law, was likely doing the minimum necessary to appease a powerful faction of bishops.

The Melkites were mostly Arabic-speaking Christians in communion with Constantinople. During this period the Church of Jerusalem gradually adopted the liturgical texts and practices of Constantinople.[37] The emperors had lobbied with the Fatimids to be recognized as the official Christian patrons of Jerusalem, and Monomachos realized the dream of completing the rebuilding of the church of the Holy Sepulcher that had been demolished by al-Hakim; the project had begun under Michael IV. The emperors sent funds and architects, projecting their power to all Christian pilgrims who arrived at Jerusalem. The new church was admired by a Persian traveler in 1047, who commented on the "Roman" craftsmanship of the icons and mosaics.[38]

The Melkite community was, among all Near Eastern Christians, the most assimilable to Roman norms, and their numbers in the empire were boosted by refugees who fled from al-Hakim's Egypt. Their Church was dominant in Antioch and sometimes harassed the city's Armenian and Syrian Churches. Melkites who spoke Greek, as many did, were effectively indistinguishable from Romans, and could hold offices and titles. Antioch was a fascinating, multicultural city in this period. The Chalcedonian community was bicultural: some epitaphs were written in both Greek and Arabic, and texts and knowledge passed between the two languages, especially from Greek into Arabic. A Melkite, Petros Libellisios, was appointed governor of the city in 1068: "he was Assyrian by race, born in Antioch, and superbly educated in both Roman and Saracen wisdom and letters."[39]

The conquests also increased the empire's Jewish population, through both the physical incorporation of their communities and extensive immigration from lands that they deemed less hospitable, especially Fatimid Egypt and Palestine. They seem to have been drawn by economic opportunity, and settled in many places, such as Thessalonike but also a number of out-of-the-way towns, and some even intermarried with Romans. We know about these Jewish immigrants from the documents of the Cairo Genizah, for they stayed in communication with Jews elsewhere, corresponding with them in Hebrew, Arabic, and Greek written in Hebrew letters. The empire's Jews were split into two hostile groups, the majority Rabbanites and the minority Karaites, whose disputes were sometimes settled by the imperial government. By the twelfth century, if not earlier, the Jews of the City lived across the Golden Horn at Pera, but the two rival communities had built a wall between them.[40] References to real-life, contemporaneous Jews are extremely rare in Greek texts. An eleventh-century Nestorian bishop offers contradictory evidence about their standing: one the one hand, the Romans "tolerate a large population of Jews in their realm. They afford them protection, allow them openly to adhere to their religion, and to build their synagogues. . . . The Jew may adhere to his religion and recite his prayers." But at the same time "there is a large number of Jews who endure humiliation and the hatred of those men as well as of all others."[41]

The Paphlagonians

The regime of the Paphlagonians channeled its ambitions more to the west. Michael IV (1034–1041) "was neither from the royal clan, nor did he have the authority of a prominent officer," wrote an Armenian observer. "Rather, he was an insignificant functionary. The queen had lusted after him with a prostitute's diseased passion."[42] But Michael was talented and relied on his many brothers and nephews. One of them was always *doux* of Antioch and another was usually *doux* of Thessalonike. These two cities were now the control nodes of the empire, east and west. Michael himself spent time in Thessalonike, allegedly seeking a cure from St. Demetrios for his epilepsy (his retinue screened him when he had seizures). The bureaucracy was managed by his brother Ioannes the *orphanotrophos*, whom Psellos presents as a hard-working micromanager, a shrewd and dangerous manipulator, but not malicious. He and his sister Maria independently traveled to sites in Asia Minor to restore walls and sponsor pilgrimage sites. No imperial family had so dispersed itself across the empire before. A contemporary poet compared the brothers to the points of a compass and its center, which together formed the sign of the cross.[43]

The regime ably defended the empire against attacks, for example Muslim assaults on Edessa and Pecheneg raids across the Danube. The Aegean navy of the Kibyrraiotai appears to have been bolstered by Varangians brought by Harald, the future king of Norway (1046–1066), who was only about twenty at this time. Thus did the last Vikings, under Roman command, turn their longships against Sicilian Muslim raiders.[44] But just like Romanos III, the Paphlagonians sought military prestige, so they reactivated Basil II's final plan to conquer Sicily. Diplomacy established a bridgehead by supporting one side in a civil war among the Muslims in Sicily. When their candidate lost—he had been given the title *magistros* and his son was received in Constantinople—the regime sent an invasion force in 1038 under the fearsome Maniakes, with a fleet under Stephanos, Michael IV's brother-in-law. The army included units from the themes as well as Harald's Varangians and Norman knights from Italy. Later Norman and Scandinavian texts make it seem that their men were the real heroes, but in reality they were small players in a Roman operation. Maniakes defeated the Muslims in two major battles, and by 1040 he had conquered, or "liberated," the eastern part of the island. But he had a violent falling-out with Stephanos, after which he was arrested and taken back to Constantinople. His replacements lost his gains and withdrew to Italy; only Messina held out under Katakalon Kekaumenos, possibly until 1042. Thus Sicily was lost, for good this time, due to political infighting. But there was another reason why Maniakes' replacements withdrew to Italy: the army of conquest was recalled to deal with the greatest danger the empire had faced in a generation: a Bulgarian uprising.[45]

Occupied Bulgaria

According to one report, the proximate cause of the uprising was a demand by Ioannes the *orphanotrophos* that the Bulgarians pay their taxes in coin and not in kind, as Basil II had allowed after the conquest. Ioannes must have believed that their economy was sufficiently monetized, and perhaps he raised their taxes too. The underlying cause, as reported by all the Roman sources, was the Bulgarians' desire to "throw off the bonds of servitude" to the Romans and their "yearning for freedom." Unfortunately, we have no sources from the inside the rebellion, though later Bulgarian sources referred to this period as "the Greek slavery."[46]

A certain Deljan raised the standards of revolution in Belgrade, presenting himself as a descendant of Samuil and taking the regnal name Petar II in order to evoke the "milk-and-honey" reign of the saint-tsar Petar I.[47] As he marched south, he gathered followers who massacred all the Romans they found. Many Bulgarian soldiers and officers who were serving in the imperial armies joined his cause, and they soon reached Thessalonike, where Michael IV was residing; the emperor fled to Constantinople. Deljan now sent units south into Greece, and was even joined by the non-Bulgarian theme of Nikopolis, which was in the midst of its own tax protest against Constantinople. In September 1040, he was joined by Alusian, a son of the last tsar Ivan Vladislav, who had also served in the imperial army but had been cashiered by the *orphanotrophos*. Deljan gave him an army with which to attack Thessalonike, but the city was ably defended by the *doux* Konstantinos, the emperor's nephew, who then defeated Alusian in battle. When Alusian returned, he blinded Deljan and took his place as tsar. Michael IV was meanwhile suppressing more domestic plots against his throne—including one by Michael Keroularios, the later patriarch—and summoning his armies from both Sicily and the east. In mid-1041, Michael took the field in person, even though he was suffering from dropsy. But now Alusian negotiated secretly with the emperor, promising to betray the Bulgarian cause in exchange for money and titles, and he timed his defection to cause the maximum confusion and damage to the rebellion. Michael was able to sweep the opposition aside and march from Serdica to Prilep, extinguishing the uprising. He celebrated a triumph in Constantinople, with Deljan in tow, but was visibly ill: "he swooned on his horse as if attending a funeral." Michael died on 10 December after taking monastic vows, and refused to see Zoe when she came to visit him. He was buried in a humble ceremony by the church of the Holy Anargyroi that he had built outside the walls.[48]

The demography and geography of occupied Bulgaria, from Thrace to the Adriatic, was diverse, though we lack a proper ethnography. Its population was Orthodox (the "Bogomil" heresy had been taking root since the tenth century, but did not yet trouble the authorities). The project of translating Christian Greek literature into Slavonic continued during the period of the Roman occupation.[49] Given their common religion, difference was construed primarily in ethnic and linguistic terms. The Romans viewed the Bulgarians as a separate, subject, and inferior people. Some even believed that the Bulgarians had been civilized not when they had converted to Christianity—though that was definitely a step in the right direction—but when they had come under Roman rule. Psellos even claimed that it was *Basil II* who had "turned that nation toward God." They were associated with Scythian stereotypes such as living in wagons and wearing sheepskins. It was the conquest that had turned them from wild into tame animals.[50]

The Romans imposed their own fiscal and administrative apparatus on occupied Bulgaria, which, if we judge from the letters of the later eleventh-century archbishop of Ohrid, Theophylaktos, penetrated down to the most local level of peasant and tenant farmers. Those letters reveal a society of Roman lords and Bulgarian peasants, but not Bulgarian elites, whether local or higher. When the Bulgarians eventually formed a second empire in the 1180s, after another revolt, about three fourths of their legal and administrative vocabulary had a Roman origin, such was the impact of empire. On the other hand, it was presumably possible for Bulgarians to rise through the ranks of the Roman army, but, if they used Hellenized versions of their Christian names, they would remain invisible to us. The army of Bulgaria frequently performed loyal service to the empire.[51]

Two other named ethnic groups were absorbed into the empire with the conquest of Bulgaria: the Albanians and the Vlachs, pastoral groups that are first mentioned in Roman texts after the conquest. They lived in the mountains of the western Balkans and were not fully incorporated into the empire's bureaucratic apparatus. As "subjects," they probably interfaced with the empire via their own leaders to provide soldiers (who likely served in discrete ethnic units) and taxes. We know little about the Albanians at this time. The Vlachs (later Wallachians) spoke a Romance language and were likely the linguistic descendants, and possibly also the literal descendants, of the ancient Latin-speaking Romans of the western Balkans—Justinian's people. Now, four centuries after falling out of the empire, they were no longer regarded as Romans by Constantinople, but as "faithless and perverse" barbarians, whose wives and children the authorities were advised to keep as hostages during sensitive operations. Their cheese, however, was a delicacy. They had their own leaders and tribal groups, the *katuna*, which could include three hundred families. In the twelfth century, the governors of Greece had to use the army to suppress these "highway robbers and tax evaders" in Thessaly, which was also known as "Vlachia."[52]

Michael IV left the throne to his nephew Michael V, but he made nothing but poor decisions that resulted in his fall from power within five months. His primary base of support consisted of his uncles and Zoe, who had adopted him, and yet he quickly exiled his uncles, including Ioannes, and castrated all his male relatives who were not already eunuchs. He spared only one uncle, Konstantinos, who became his chief advisor and *nobelissimos*. Then, after Easter 1042, he exiled Zoe too. This resulted in a popular uprising and an assault on the palace by the people, who proclaimed Zoe and Theodora as empresses. The two sisters were enemies, but the crowd forced them to reconcile. Michael and Konstantinos fled to the Stoudios monastery, where they were blinded on the empresses' orders. Michael kicked and screamed through the ordeal, while Konstantinos endured it stoically. The Icelandic poets later claimed that the blinding was carried out by Harald himself. The populace had again defended the imperial rights of women, as they had in other times of children, against the ambitions of men who tried to force them out. For all the looting that accompanied such insurrections, the people were enforcing a sense of justice: Michael had violated his oaths to Zoe. A poet wrote about the wretched emperor who "lies now on the ground . . . craving the light he lost with his foolish aspirations."[53]

Konstantinos IX Monomachos

The sisters chose Konstantinos Monomachos to be the next emperor. He married Zoe on 11 June, 1042, and was crowned the next day. Monomachos had no military background and had not held high office. In fact, seven years earlier he had been exiled to Mytilene by Michael IV for participating in a conspiracy. He too, therefore, needed to buy support, and he proved to be an extraordinarily generous ruler to his three empresses, the Senate, and religious institutions, at least at first. He sent out a proclamation throughout the empire promising prosperity to all. As Psellos put it in an oration before the emperor in 1043, "the spigots of the treasury were opened and stayed there."[54]

Monomachos' reign was pivotal in the history of the empire. It was then that its geostrategic position began to change from hegemonic to defensive, and soon it would be fighting for survival. The change began during his reign, when the empire was attacked by the Normans in Italy, the Pechenegs on the Danube, and the Turks in the east. Assessments of his role have been negative, but they are unduly influenced by Psellos' caricature of his reign. Psellos had a splendid career under Monomachos. He revived the custom of delivering panegyrics at the court, had the emperor's ear, opened a school of philosophy, and was made supervisor of higher education with the newfangled title "Consul of Philosophers." His friends and fellow intellectuals also enjoyed court positions. Mauropous gave orations; Leichoudes became prime minister; and Xiphilinos was placed in charge of the emperor's new law school. Yet starting ca. 1050, this "regime of the philosophers" gradually lost influence and departed, hounded by unspecified enemies. In 1054, Xiphilinos and Psellos (who despised monasticism) had to become monks on Mt. Olympos in Bithynia. This lasted for only a few months until Monomachos died and Psellos could return, but he never forgave his former patron for hanging him out to dry. In his history, which is virtually a personal memoir, he satirizes him as a charming but irresponsible epicure, unconcerned about the empire's difficulties, and simply omits to discuss his foreign wars. This picture is false. Other accounts reveal that Monomachos took foreign threats seriously and responded to them vigorously, responsibly, and mostly successfully.[55]

The first five years of the reign reveal Monomachos' domestic vulnerability, but also his effective response to foreign challenges. Zoe had sent Maniakes back to Italy in 1042, but Monomachos recalled him. At this point Maniakes rebelled, killed his replacement, and marched on Constantinople. The hero of Edessa and Sicily, he was tired of being sent out and then arrested. He suspected that the court was biased against him because Skleros, brother of the emperor's girlfriend, was his personal enemy. And he was ambitious. Before reaching Thessalonike, he was met by an imperial army under the command of the eunuch Stephanos. Maniakes initially prevailed in the battle, but received a mortal wound and his army surrendered. Stephanos celebrated a triumph, parading the rebel's head on a stick. But the fallen giant continued to be regarded with awe. A "sweat-and-blood" epic poem was written about the fall of "the wild man Maniakes, the man of Mars," and another poet imagined him speaking from the grave.[56] Yet he had lacked political acumen.

Contrary to Psellos' happy-go-lucky image of Monomachos, the emperor was ruthless against suspected enemies. He suppressed a revolt by the general of Cyprus and had him paraded in the hippodrome in women's clothing. Another plot implicated the general of Melitene; Stephanos, the victor of Maniakes; and Ioannes the former *orphanotrophos*. The conspirators were tonsured and blinded.[57] In the same year, 1043, news arrived that the king of Rus', Jaroslav the Wise (son of Volodymyr), was preparing a naval assault on Constantinople, the last of the great Viking raids against the City (after 860 and 941). The pretext was a brawl in which a Rus' noble had been killed by some Romans. Monomachos pleaded with the king that this was no reason to disrupt good trading relations, but the massive armada sailed out anyway under the command of prince Volodymyr. It found Monomachos ready. All the Rus' in the City had been arrested and dispersed. The Roman fleet met the enemy in the Bosporos. Advance fireships incinerated the lead longships, after which the main Roman fleet engaged and defeated the rest. 15,000 corpses were later found on the beach. Survivors who reached the shore were cut down by the land army, which Monomachos had called up, and a force that tried to march back north along the Black Sea coast was defeated by Katakalon Kekaumenos, *doux* of Paristrion and hero of Messina. Later Rus' tradition tried to cover up the debacle by alleging that their fleet was destroyed by a storm before reaching "Tsargrad."[58]

As soon as this threat passed, Monomachos enforced the empire's claim to the Armenian realm of Ani, which had been pledged by its king Smbat III back in 1022. He died around 1041, and his nobles appointed his nephew Gagik II as his successor, intending to keep the kingdom independent, if loyal to Rome. But in 1044 Monomachos sent the *doux* of Iberia, Michael Iassites, to take the kingdom by force. He failed, so the emperor sent the eunuch *domestikos* Nikolaos, a former *parakoimomenos* of Konstantinos VIII, who had campaigned in the Caucasus twenty years previously. He brought enough pressure on Ani to force its surrender. Gagik traveled to Constantinople and was given land and titles in exchange for his crown. The kingdom of Ani became a new *doukaton*, closing the ring of annexed territories that now protectively encircled the empire. Ani was an important city in its own right, likely the most important center of trade in the region. Strategically, it was recognized as "a major bulwark, defending against any barbarians who intend to invade Iberia through that region."[59]

In 1045, Monomachos sent Iassites to pressure the Muslim emir of Dvin to surrender some of Ani's forts that he had taken. When Iassites failed again, he was replaced by Kekaumenos, and the eunuch-general Konstantinos was dispatched to keep up the pressure on Dvin. Eventually, the emir agreed to a peace. Monomachos, therefore, was not an idle emperor on the military front. He enforced the empire's claims and quickly replaced generals who failed. He also commanded authority abroad. When a Muslim preacher began to lead jihadist raids into imperial territory in 1047/8, Monomachos instructed the emir of Diyar Bakr to contain the problem or face one of his own. The emir told his men, "get him to stop, or he will bring the Romans down on us." The preacher was promptly arrested.[60]

Monomachos responded equally decisively to a Pecheneg attack. In those years, the Pecheneg khans and their armies were being driven westward by the Rus' and the Oghuz (another Turkic confederation moving in from Central Asia). In 1046, one Kegen and 20,000 of his people sought to enter the empire and take up service, which Monomachos granted gladly. Kegen was brought to the capital and honored, and his people were baptized and settled in the lower Danube. Following traditional stereotypes, Roman authors considered the Pechenegs to be uncivilized "Scythian" nomads, but imperial ideology allowed for their conversion and "taming."[61] They now raided north across the Danube against other Pechenegs, the followers of Tyrach, who invaded the empire in retaliation, in late 1046 or early 1047. Monomachos' armies kicked into action: the *doukes* of Paristrion, Adrianople, and Bulgaria converged on Tyrach's army, which was suffering from dysentery. The enemy surrendered and they were dispersed across Bulgaria, near Serdica and Niš, to work the land, pay taxes, and provide recruits. Tyrach was taken to Constantinople and publicly baptized.[62]

Yet somehow the Pecheneg situation became controversial, and Mauropous, who was scheduled to deliver a speech honoring the emperor on the feast of St. George (23 April, 1047), omitted that section at the last minute.[63] The army of Macedonia was agitated and Monomachos arrested and tonsured Leon Tornikios, a general believed to be plotting against him. Tornikios escaped to Adrianople, and began suborning the officers and soldiers of the Macedonian army. They were discontent with the emperor for "spurning" the army and proclaimed Tornikios as emperor. They marched on the City but were powerless against its walls. The emperor took his position on the battlements and hurled rocks at them with catapults. Tornikios' hope was that the people of Constantinople would abandon Monomachos, so a battle of slogans, insults, and sound bites ensued, shouted at and from the walls. "Open the gates! Your new emperor will be kind to you and increase the realm of the Romans with trophies against the barbarians!"—and the like. But the citizens remained loyal to Monomachos and the rebel's forces began to melt away, "forgetting their oaths that they would fight for him to the death." After some minor fighting in Thrace, Tornikios and his chief lieutenant Batatzes surrendered near Adrianople. Monomachos had them blinded.[64] Tornikios' rebellion revealed the ambitions of the military cadres that were entrenched in the Balkan provinces, the products of Basil II's long wars. There was now a "military aristocracy" there to rival that of Asia Minor. In fact, within a generation, the empire would flip its orientation and become a predominantly Balkan state. That transition was already underway.

In five years, Monomachos had suppressed two military coups and many conspiracies. He had defeated the Rus', the kingdom of Ani, and the initial wave of Pecheneg invaders, and he had intimidated Dvin and Diyar Bakr. His empire was, so far, on a sound footing.

The empire's Armenians

With the acquisition of Ani, it is likely that as many Armenians lived inside the Roman empire as outside it, or more. However, these annexations did not last long enough to leave much documentation, so we do not know how thoroughly the Roman administration penetrated these lands. We hear of tax officials, judges, and military administrators sent from Constantinople. Two imperial governors of Ani posted inscriptions, outside the doors of the city's cathedral, explaining the new system of requisitions, taxes, corvées on labor, and exemptions that was now in effect, a system with little precedent in Armenian tradition. So it appears that the center was at least planning on formatting this realm according to its own templates.[65] Somehow the imperial system also tamed the fractious and autonomist tendencies of the Armenian nobility, who caused little trouble during the period of Roman sovereignty. Rather, they reached for new opportunities. The nobleman Grigor of the Pahlavuni family surrendered his lands to the empire in exchange for others in Edessa, along with titles. He was made *doux* of Vaspurakan in the early 1050s, although he did not accept Chalcedon.[66] This was a notable accommodation on the part of Constantinople: while a parallel Chalcedonian Church was gradually being set up in Roman Armenia, state offices *were* given to Armenian noblemen who did not subscribe to Roman Orthodoxy, unlike the Syrians, who were not given offices. The discrepancy was due to the long history of Armenian service in the Roman armies, which had regularly turned a blind eye to religious differences, and the two Churches often preferred a policy of "don't ask, don't tell" regarding theology.[67] Moreover, unlike the Syrians, the Armenians had military and political experience governing their own realms, which was too useful to pass over.

Just as the emperors were establishing Chalcedonian sees in Armenia, the Armenian Church was expanding its sees in eastern Asia Minor. The *katholikos* Petros was, after the annexation of Ani, removed to Constantinople and then taken to various locations in Asia Minor. It does not seem, however, that his movements were forced, and he appears to have been honored in the capital.[68] There was an uptick in religious polemic against the Armenian Church in Constantinople during the eleventh century, much of it revolving around its use of unleavened bread (*azyma*) in the Eucharist, an "error" that linked the Armenians to the Latins in Roman eyes. But this did not result in actions against that Church's leadership or members (again, unlike the Syrians), though ethnic prejudice against Armenians endured. One Eustathios Boëlas found himself "exiled" in the Armenian borderlands around mid-century. He declared that "I settled among alien nations with a strange religion and tongue," i.e., Armenians, whom he mentions right after "snakes, scorpions, and wild beasts."[69]

In the eleventh century, Cappadocia became the new home of many former Armenian royals, especially from Vaspurakan and Ani, who had exchanged their principalities for lands and titles around Sebasteia and other eastern themes. They were sometimes appointed to be governors of those provinces. Gagik II "spent the rest of his charmed life in luxury and enjoyment of the properties and superlative titles that he was given."[70] Whether by choice or imperial order, these ex-royals stayed in Cappadocia and did not integrate into the Roman aristocracy. Along with most Armenians, they "remained alien and alienated—incorporated but not assimilated."[71] Later in the century, they acted as magnets for subsequent waves of Armenian immigrants who were pushed into the empire by the Turks.

Monomachos' social policies

The early part of Monomachos' reign offers a glimpse into the direction that Roman society might have taken were it not for the cataclysm of the Turkish conquest and the Norman attacks. That society would have been more civilian, less militarized. The more professional armies, including the *tagmata*, were now stationed in the recently annexed frontier *doukata*, and it is possible, though not certain, that many who owed service in the interior or Asia Minor commuted it to a cash payment instead, which the state used to hire more professional soldiers. The administration of the themes of the interior, in both Asia Minor and Greece, had also been demilitarized, with most functions passing from the general to the provincial "judge" (*krites*). The state invested substantially in this civilian infrastructure. A study of the lead seals of this period has found that officials on the judicial side of government were given increasingly higher titles and, presumably, salaries, compared to those of the other branches. Moreover, the disproportionately large number of seals surviving from the eleventh century reveal a significant expansion of the bureaucracy, far in excess of the expansion of the state's territories.[72] The pinnacle of a civilian career was the prestigious post of eparch of the City. We have a collection of decisions by Eustathios Romaios, a high judge in the City, who carefully applied Roman law to the cases before him. It reveals that access to his court was not limited to the powerful. The government reached intensively to the local level.[73]

Monomachos tried to centralize this trend further by requiring that all legal decisions in the provinces be forwarded to the capital for potential review. In ca. 1045, he created a new school of law under the *nomophylax*, or "Guardian of the Laws." The decree creating this new school was written by Mauropous and the first occupant was Xiphilinos, just as Psellos was made Consul of the Philosophers. Anyone was allowed to study at this school, regardless of background, and it also granted certificates of completion. This experiment, however, quickly failed as the *nomophylax* came in for criticism by the old guard. Mauropous, Xiphilinos, and Psellos were all forced out of the court during the early 1050s.[74]

Monomachos also expanded the social classes that were eligible to purchase or receive a court title so as to include "merchants," the "middle class," "working class," and "the people." Before his reign, social mobility could be described in this way: "among a thousand rich men just one unfortunate joins the lowly, while of all the countless wretched poor just three might prosper and join a higher rank." But now, Psellos claimed with typical hyperbole, Monomachos had broken the link between the status of fathers and sons. In reality, he was only slightly expanding the social elite to reflect (and benefit from) the growing wealth of merchants and the guilds as well as wealthy provincials who flocked to the capital in pursuit of the new opportunities opened up by empire.[75] Psellos himself, who did not come from an especially distinguished family but was a City native, was likely a beneficiary of this policy, and his school taught the sons of other beneficiaries. Monomachos was not handing titles away, but allowing "new money" to buy into the court system, so this was a mechanism for the state to capture cash being created through trade. By giving titles in exchange for money, the state satisfied its "thirst for gold" and ensured that it remained the arbiter of social status in emerging economic sectors.[76] This arrangement, however, would not survive the coming upheavals.

Monomachos' civilian priorities were reversed at the end of the eleventh century by a cabal of military aristocrats who fundamentally changed the business of politics at New Rome. The only part of Monomachos' cultural policy that survived was paradoxically that of Psellos, which blossomed in the twelfth century, after a time lag of two generations. Psellos was a polymath and versatile author. He was a master craftsman of words and images, enviably adept at working the forms of the rhetorical tradition. More than that, he fully grasped the plasticity of narrative composition, exhibiting in his history the self-conscious awareness of a cinematographer panning a camera across a moral tableau. He loved to refashion his authorial persona and imbued his accounts of others with his own experiences, making many of his texts covertly autobiographical. But beneath his witty turns of phrase and ambiguous presence lies an explicit understanding of the amorality of the art of persuasion and the hollowness of imperial rhetoric.

There was substance here too, not just form. Psellos advanced a program that greatly influenced his epigones in the twelfth century. He rejected the austere asceticism that his culture claimed to prize and insisted that he was composed of *both* body and soul, and the former had a moral claim on him too. In many works, he recuperated against the Orthodox ascetic tradition a positive view of the body and its pleasures. He delighted in subverting hallowed institutions, and despised monasticism in particular. He insisted that nature obeyed natural law and posited God as a distant and abstract principle. He even lectured an assembly of bishops or monks on the natural causes of the earthquake of 1063, and allegedly conducted scientific experiments in the classroom. There may also have been a dangerous side to his thought, as he instructed a generation of future churchmen and state officials to read and interpret Christian texts, both Scriptural and patristic, through the lens of Neoplatonism. The sincerity of his faith was called into question on a number of occasions, but the style of his writings guaranteed for him the devotion of posterity and a place of honor in the canon of great writers, a feat that few accomplished after the sixth century.[77] Had his works been lost, we would not have guessed how profoundly the experiments of the twelfth century were indebted to the thought of a single man of middling origin who had insinuated himself, through charm and learning alone, into the corridors of power.

PART EIGHT

A NEW PARADIGM

27

The End of Italy and the East (1048–1081)

Seljuks, Normans, and popes

History accelerated in the mid-eleventh century, not only for the Romans. The entire arc of the Christian and Muslim world, from Iran to England, witnessed momentous changes that ushered in new geopolitical challenges. Romanía was situated at the center of this arc and barely managed to survive the unleashing of forces that collided with its antique structures. It would be pulled back from the brink by Alexios I Komnenos (1081–1118), but only after huge losses, including its hegemony. In the twelfth century, a reformed Romanía was one great power among many, contending with peers in both east and west. Under Alexios' grandson Manuel I Komnenos (1143–1180), who made a dazzling effort to reassert Roman power, diplomacy and complex international relations came to the fore as never before in imperial history. That multipolar phase came to a crashing end in 1204, after which the Romans were relegated to second-rate status on the international stage, or worse.

The new challengers who most directly weakened the Roman empire was the Seljuk Turks, a dynasty of Turkmen nomads from Transoxiana who, under the leadership of their sultan Tughril Beg, conquered Iran in the 1040s and Iraq in the 1050s. The Seljuks overturned the Arab order that had been dominant since the seventh century. Their rise was accompanied by mass Turkmen migrations from Central Asia. The Seljuks were unable to control these movements and spent as much time suppressing internal rivals as conquering the Near East. Bands of raiders or settlers operated independently of their control and were sometimes redirected by them into the Caucasus and Asia Minor so as not to disrupt the establishment of the Seljuk state in the Near East. "They would invade our borders for their fill of captives and plunder," wrote one contemporary, but when they settled down they preferred pasturelands, or transformed agricultural lands into pasturelands "for their horses, mules, sheep, and camels." Already by 1080, a Roman witness claimed that "they have made the land of the Romans tributary or into grazing land for sheep."[1]

Major changes were also taking place in western Europe, which had entered a phase of agricultural and demographic growth and increased social complexity. Violent local lords were entrenching themselves by force in many regions, often by using cavalry, and dominated the countryside from their newly-built castles. The alliances that they formed through oaths, in order to contain the aggression, created a lattice of vassalage and lordship. But it was three developments in the west that impacted Romanía most severely. First, the papacy was captured by an ambitious reformist agenda that sought to centralize the Church of Rome and make it more autonomous from other states and secular institutions. This led to famous conflicts between popes and the German emperors, which are peripheral to our story. Part of the new agenda, however, was a reassertion of papal supremacy, the notion that Rome held sovereign authority over all Churches. This idea had troubled the relations between Rome and Constantinople from the start, especially during the so-called Acacian Schism, the Monothelite controversy, and the so-called Photian Schism, but it had ebbed and flowed over the centuries. Now it was entrenched at Rome. Papal supremacy became the north star of Rome's ideology, and it was alarmingly coupled with a sanctification of military violence by any party willing to enforce the pope's will on others, a legacy of the "Frankish turn" of the eighth century. Cynical interference by the popes in east Roman affairs and their blessing of Norman attacks were justified by appeals to St. Augustine's notion of Just War—"for the defense of the Church of Rome and our honor."[2] This was then coupled with the notion that "the Greeks" must be "returned to obedience" to the Roman Church, making conflict inevitable.

The second western development was the rise of the Normans. The Normans were Frenchified descendants of Vikings who had settled in northwestern France around 900, in a region that was named Normandy after them. Their culture was oriented around warfare, with leaders specializing in heavy-cavalry fighting. To support this expensive warrior lifestyle, they had to dominate and tax an agricultural base. But there was not enough land in Normandy to satisfy the ambitions of the military class, so the duchy exported mercenaries and exiles, who then destabilized other lands in their efforts to acquire lands and lordships. Surplus sons "left the country, seeking their fortune through the exercise of arms." They "abandoned little in order to acquire much . . . desiring to have all people under their rule."[3] At the highest levels, Normans specialized in state takeovers. Their armies targeted vulnerable states (England, Muslim Sicily, Constantinople) and tried to annihilate their armies in meat-grinding battles. Their own elites would then subjugate or displace the local ruling class and build keeps throughout their newly acquired territories "to the chagrin of the local inhabitants."[4] In the Roman order, fortifications were meant to protect the local population from foreign attack; by contrast, Norman forts enabled the new rulers to subjugate a population regardless of ethnicity, language, or religion, to extract tribute from it, and to attack the next target.

The Normans could occupy lands through infiltration too, as in southern Italy. Norman mercenaries sold their services to the Lombard duchies and cities, escalated their conflicts, and then turned on their employers or switched sides as soon as the opportunity presented itself. Their own propagandists were explicit about these cynical tactics,[5] through which they managed to entrench themselves and gain lordships. These then acted as a beacon for more Normans. New arrivals went out into the imperial provinces, terrorized the countryside with murders, kidnappings, and rapes, and forced the locals to pay protection money. "They tore up the vines and olive trees and seized the cattle and sheep."[6] One of their own called them "a shrewd people . . . avid for profit and domination, ready to feign or conceal anything." An east Roman called them "treacherous and greedy, and quick in minor setbacks to stir up blame and trouble and revolts."[7]

The Normans and the papacy were initially bitter adversaries, but, as the century wore on, they realized that their skills and ambitions were actually complementary and they joined forces, sometimes even to directly attack Romanía. The Normans saw Constantinople as a weak kingdom ripe for the plucking while the popes saw it as "disobedient" to themselves. This alignment would eventually feed into the third great development of the century, a series of assaults by Catholic armies on Muslim states. These would be dubbed "crusades," after they acquired a more or less formalized character. But the grounds for the so-called First Crusade of the 1090s were laid by attacks on the Muslims of Spain and Sicily in the 1060s, the latter by a Norman army blessed by a pope, as well as by a Norman attack on Romanía in the 1080s, blessed by another pope.

Thus Constantinople was squeezed between the rise of Turkish power on one side and the demands of papal supremacy and expansion of western lordships on the other. This set the framework for the remainder of east Roman history. It began during the reign of Monomachos.

To be sure, Monomachos had other pressing concerns that prevented him from identifying these developments as existential threats. But even in his time they acquired grave proportions. Tughril Beg's relatives began to raid Roman Armenia in the 1040s. Around 1045, his cousin Qutlumush passed through Vaspurakan, defeating and capturing its *doux*, Stephanos Leichoudes, nephew of the emperor's prime minister (*mesazon*). In 1048, Tughril Beg's nephew Hasan was defeated by the *doukes* of Vaspurakan and Ani (these were Aaron, son of the last Bulgarian tsar, and Katakalon Kekaumenos). This led to a major showdown between the two *doukes* and Tughril's half-brother Ibrahim Inal, leading a large force of Oghuz Turks from Transoxiana. At Kapetrou, near Theodosiopolis, on 18 September, 1048, the Turks seem to have defeated the Romans in battle, though Kekaumenos claimed it as a victory. The Turks departed with plunder and captives, including one Liparit, a Georgian who led a pro-Roman faction in his country. Negotiations between Monomachos and Tughril resulted in Liparit's release and the recognition of the sultan in the prayers recited in Constantinople's mosques, in place of the Fatimid caliph. In an awkward moment, this switch was witnessed by a Fatimid envoy, who informed his master in Cairo. The caliph responded with repressive measures against his Christian subjects and by stripping the emperor of his status as protector of the Church of Jerusalem. Placating one Muslim state would now offend the other. But Monomachos was acutely aware of the threat posed by the Turks: "from then on, he anticipated war with the sultan and, to the best of his ability, he sent agents to fortify the regions bordering on Persia." Monomachos reacted vigorously to military challenges. In 1048, he sent the eunuch-general Konstantinos, a former monk, to teach a lesson to the emir of Dvin, who was wavering as a client of the emperor. The emir had to leave his city and relocate to Ganja.[8]

The greatest challenge that Monomachos faced was an uprising of the Pechenegs whom he himself had settled along the lower Danube and in various Balkan provinces. Roman authors viewed these steppe peoples as irredeemably barbaric, or "Scythians," embodying the polar opposite of Roman civilization, even when they did go through the motions of converting.[9] The settlement had been controversial and, in 1049, its critics were proven right when the Pechenegs banded together, rebelled, and began to raid south across the Haimos mountains (Stara Planina). For the next four years, until 1053, they defeated or held their own against all the armies that Monomachos hurled against them. The emperor, who was reaching the end of his life and suffering from gout, "blamed the generals for cowardice and their inability to find a remedy." Our sources reveal a shocking level of failure, incompetence, and lack of coordination in the Roman command. Monomachos was nevertheless resourceful, and he ordered some of his units to improvise guerilla warfare against the enemy, which wore them down. Eventually, in 1053, the two sides made peace, which, like the Gothic war fought in the same provinces seven centuries earlier, recognized a quasi-autonomous barbarian enclave south of the Danube that nominally swore loyalty to the emperor.[10] The Pecheneg war was costly in men and money. It proved to be a historical fulcrum, marking a change in Constantinople's stance in the Balkans from dominant to defensive.

Monomachos found himself short on cash and had to devalue the gold coin and collect taxes more strictly. The expenses of the Pecheneg war, which dragged on for years while degrading the agricultural tax base of the eastern Balkans, likely contributed to this crunch. The emperor also faced periodic plots against himself at the court, though he managed to neutralize them. But trouble was brewing in Italy too, which was typically given a lower priority when the Romans were fighting on other fronts. This time it would doom the Italian provinces.

Specifically, some of the captains of the mercenary units of Lombards and Normans that Maniakes had led into Sicily in 1038 conspired, after their discharge in 1040, to take over Apulia with help from the Normans of Salerno. Among these captains were two sons of one Tancred of Hauteville, Guillaume Iron-Arm and Drogon, whose brothers Robert and Roger, once they were drawn into the action, would take the lead in creating a new Norman order in southern

Italy. In general, Norman mercenaries were fierce assets to have in battle, but they were treacherous and bent on carving out their own principalities at their employers' expense. Many modern historians defend their record, but they nearly always turned against the emperor during the eleventh century and did incalculable damage. In 1041, the Normans defeated two governors and set about reducing the cities of Apulia. In this project, they were assisted by local Lombards, including Argyrus, a son of the rebel Melo who had lived for years as a hostage in Constantinople. In 1042, Monomachos won Argyrus back to the imperial side with titles and power, and so Bari was recovered.[11]

There followed a long war of attrition and skirmishes whose outline is difficult to reconstruct. A hallmark of Norman aggression was the manufacture of legalistic pretexts that resulted from violence and then fueled its perpetuation. Even before they had actually conquered Apulia, the chief knights apportioned it into nominal fiefdoms; then, based on these fictional titles, they fought to claim lands that were "rightfully" theirs. Exactly this tactic would be used in the conquest of Muslim Sicily, which was "authorized" in advance by the pope, and then in 1204 by the crusaders before the walls of Constantinople, who notionally apportioned up among themselves a state that was not yet conquered. When Robert arrived in Italy in 1048, he was assigned to a region of Calabria, where he terrorized the locals (his own epitaph would later call him proudly "the terror of the world"). When his victims paid protection money to stave off attack and made "pacts" with him reinforced by oaths, this was treated as recognition of his right to rule them and as a justification for violence against those who resisted; resistance was equated with "treason." Needless to say, the "subjects" of these Norman lords hated their new masters. Robert earned the name Guiscard, the "Cunning," for these atrocities.[12]

The Normans' tactics made them many enemies, including Benevento, many of the Lombards of Apulia, and Leo IX (1049–1054), a reform-minded pope. Leo and Argyrus made an alliance in the early 1050s, but the Normans managed to defeat them separately before they could join forces, and took Leo captive after the battle of Civitate in 1053, though they treated him well. (When individual Norman bands caused trouble, their leaders speciously claimed that they could not control them, but when the Norman project as a whole was threatened, it was all hands on deck for them.) Leo now tried to persuade Monomachos to prioritize Italy and the Norman problem, especially as the Pecheneg wars were over. In 1054, he dispatched a cardinal (Humbert), papal chancellor (Friedrich), and bishop (Petrus of Amalfi), to Constantinople to forge an alliance.

Controversy marred the negotiations. The Church of Constantinople had already harassed the leadership of the Syrian Orthodox Church, and now some Greek bishops were reopening an old debate over the Armenian Church's use of unleavened bread (*azyma*) in communion. This quickly roped in the Latin

Church too. The patriarch Michael Keroularios (1043–1059) debated the *azyma* with Argyrus in Constantinople, had refused him communion over it, and it was alleged that he had closed down some Latin churches in the City. Meanwhile, Leon, the archbishop of Ohrid, sent a letter to a colleague in southern Italy arguing against the *azyma*. This was brought to the pope erroneously under Keroularios' name. Thus, even before the pope's emissaries departed for Constantinople, they believed that Keroularios not only rejected papal supremacy but was essentially a heretic. Whereas Keroularios was always conciliatory in his dealings with the pope, the papal side treated him consistently as an evil agitator and questioned his title "ecumenical patriarch."[13]

At this point, modern narratives tell the following story of the events of 1054. The legates arrived in Constantinople in late April and stayed until mid-July. While they were negotiating an alliance with the emperor, they also engaged in acrimonious confrontations with the arrogant and ambitious Keroularios. On 16 July, the legates entered Hagia Sophia and deposited an excommunication of the heretic Keroularios and all his "partisans," which targeted the issues raised in the letter of Leon of Ohrid and various other matters on which the legates believed that the Church of Constantinople deviated from that of Rome. They then left for Italy. But Keroularios, who was used to bullying Monomachos, instigated a riot against the emperor and forced him to authorize a counter-excommunication of the legates. Thus, the emperor's Italian policy was ruined.

This narrative, however, is a tissue of fictions and distortions. In reality, Keroularios met the legates only once, when they first arrived, and the acrimony at that meeting concerned only their seating arrangements and titles. The patriarch never met them again, or debated religious issues with them, or ever contradicted Monomachos. The emperor's chief concern was to work out the alliance, and to that end he gave the legates every indication that he and his people supported the agenda of papal reform. Emboldened by his support, the legates excommunicated Keroularios, probably in the (correct) belief that he opposed many articles of papal supremacy and Latin Church practice. Part of their brief, after all, was to answer the letter of Leon of Ohrid, which they (wrongly) believed came from Keroularios. The legates left two days afterward. When the patriarch had the excommunication translated, he took it to the emperor, who found it "shameless" and ordered the Synod to answer it. There was no "riot." Keroularios' Synod did exactly what the emperor ordered and pinned the blame on some interpreters, who were held responsible for the whole misunderstanding, and on Argyrus, who was out of favor with both the emperor and patriarch. The Synod did not condemn the pope. In fact, the legates returned to Italy believing that they had secured the alliance, won over the emperor, and condemned Keroularios.

The legates' excommunication of Keroularios was legally invalid, as pope Leo had died in the meantime, and the failure of the alliance was due to that and the death of Monomachos in January 1055. Technically, there was no new Schism. The emperor had worked hard to suppress open rupture between the two Churches, but there were prelates on both sides who wanted to drag the issues out into the daylight and provoke a showdown. Lists of the "Greek errors" had long circulated in Catholic circles. Soon Greek lists of the "errors of the Latins," such as clerical celibacy, the *azyma*, the *filioque*, and many more, also began to circulate and were attributed to Keroularios.[14] The grounds for conflict and Schism had existed for a long time, in fact since the fourth century. The issue was whether they could be overlooked to promote common goals, which at this point were military. For now it was still possible, but Schism would soon become the default setting.

The performance of the Roman armies under Monomachos was imperfect but they did get the job done. Despite suffering many defeats, they annihilated the Rus', captured Ani, subdued Dvin (twice), held their own against the Turks, and wore down the Pechenegs. They did not ultimately prevail in Italy, but the empire was never good at coping with many simultaneous threats, and Italy was always the lowest priority. Monomachos is often accused of "demilitarizing" the Iberian army in a way that later enabled the Seljuks to enter Asia Minor through that gap in the frontier. This accusation is based on sources which state that around 1050 Monomachos reformed the recruitment and payment of soldiers in the Iberian *doukaton*, but the nature of this reform remains opaque.[15] We can exclude the possibility that Monomachos was lulled into complacency by the "peace" of the eleventh century: his reign was not peaceful, and he had good reason to expect trouble in the east. Whatever this reform was, it did not immediately degrade the defenses of the east. When Tughril Beg invaded again in 1054, reaching as far as Theodosiopolis, he accomplished little because the population was secured behind forts and his scouts were cut down by Varangians. He turned back when he heard that a large Roman army was mustering at Kaisareia. He besieged Mantzikert on his way out, but failed to take it. The empire's defenses were solid, though Tughril was stripping away its Muslim clients along the periphery, such as the emirs of Diyar Bakr and Ganja (formerly of Dvin).[16] Contraction had begun in the east, but was yet perceptible only at the outer fringes.

At the same time, the slow end of the Macedonian dynasty was dragging Constantinople into a political crisis. The only emperor since 962 who had named a successor before dying was Michael IV. On his deathbed, Monomachos tried to pass the throne to the governor of Bulgaria, Nikephoros Proteuon, but Theodora staged a coup, exiled Proteuon, and took the throne for herself.[17] She did not intend to marry, and so became the second woman to rule the empire in her own name. This was indicated by a change in the image depicted on her seal, from the Virgin to Christ, the figure used more commonly by emperors. Theodora removed Monomachos' eunuchs and ruled through her own, especially Leon

Paraspondylos, a former priest. Historians of the period agree that her administration was just and her reign prosperous; only Keroularios openly said that the state needed a man, though others too were thinking it.[18]

Theodora died on 31 August, 1056. Just before that, prompted by her eunuchs, she nominated Michael VI Bringas as her successor, an old and childless man from the military bureaucracy. Thus, instead of an old and childless empress ruling through eunuchs, the eunuchs would now rule through an old and childless emperor. The Macedonian dynasty was finally extinct and so the game of thrones began in earnest. The element of the republic that was most disaffected were the army officers, who felt that they were insufficiently represented at the court or consulted in its decisions. The Norman mercenary captain Hervé Frankopoulos ("Son of the Frank") asked for a promotion to *magistros*, was denied, and so he, like most Normans to come, rebelled; he went over to the Turks. In his adventures beyond the frontiers, his men lost their lives and he ended up in prison.[19]

Isaakios I Komnenos

At Easter, 1057, when the Roman army officers came to the court for their salaries and honors, they felt disrespected and so they rebelled. The leaders included Isaakios Komnenos, who had been retired by Theodora (he was married to Aikaterine, daughter of the last Bulgarian tsar); his brother Ioannes Komnenos, married to Anna Dalassene and father of the later emperor Alexios; Katakalon Kekaumenos, who had been stripped of the command of Antioch; Michael Bourtzes, grandson of the conqueror of Antioch; Konstantinos Doukas, who was married to Eudokia, the niece of the patriarch Keroularios; his brother Ioannes, a friend of the philosopher Psellos (who had returned to court); as well as a Skleros, some Argyroi, and others. On 8 June, 1057, they proclaimed Isaakios Komnenos emperor at his estates in Paphlagonia. Many of the rebels did not hold official posts, so they had to intrigue and canvass for support among the soldiers and officers of the armies and the local notables, in some cases by forging fake letters of appointment, while trying to avoid exposing themselves to loyalists and risking arrest. Embedded in the history of Skylitzes we find a fascinating first-hand report on this canvassing by Kekaumenos, who later wanted to remind the emperor of the pivotal role he had played.[20] Kekaumenos belonged to the last generation of officers who governed the empire at its peak. He had fought Muslims in Sicily, the Rus' and then the Pechenegs in the Balkans, and the emir of Dvin in the Caucasus, and he had held Antioch against the Fatimids in the south. The opportunities for service on such a scale was soon to be lost as the empire contracted.

The rebels took Nikaia while the loyalists held Nikomedeia. On 20 August they fought a major battle at a place called Hades, which the rebels won with mass casualties of Roman soldiers on both sides. "Hands of sons were stained with the blood of fathers; brother struck down brother; and there was no pity or distinction made for close relations."[21] The emperor's position in the capital was weakened. He sent envoys to negotiate terms, including Monomachos' former *mesazon* Konstantinos Leichoudes, Leon Alopos, and Psellos. Eventually they agreed that Isaakios Komnenos would be proclaimed co-emperor and adopted by Michael VI as his son. But events in the capital raced ahead of this agreement. The people gathered at Hagia Sophia and chanted, "Give the throne to him who won the battle!"[22] The patriarch Keroularios had either instigated them to do this or was forced to go along with them. On 30 August, the clergy sided with the people, and Keroularios advised Michael to abdicate. Michael agreed, as he did not want more bloodshed. When he asked what he would get in return, he was told, "The kingdom of heaven." Komnenos, who was about fifty, was crowned on 1 September and thus "rebellion was transformed into lawful power."[23]

To announce the return of competent military leadership, Isaakios issued a coin that depicted him holding a drawn sword (see Figure 44). However, this was taken by many as a boast that his achievements did not come from God but his own prowess.[24] He staffed his regime with his fellow conspirators, who were mostly military men, and made his brother Ioannes, father of the future emperor Alexios I, *domestikos* of the west. Isaakios rewarded Keroularios by giving him authority over some fiscal and personnel matters of the Church.[25] During this reign, the employment of eunuchs in military positions, so prevalent during the late Macedonian dynasty, began to diminish. The dynasties of Komnenos, Doukas, and Diogenes reasserted the dominance of the "bearded" officer class.

Yet Isaakios, like Monomachos before him, faced a fiscal shortfall. This led him to became a strict tax collector, while at the same time he canceled many of his predecessors' gifts and awards of titles, eliminating or reducing the *rogai*

Figure 44 Coin of Isaakios I Komnenos brandishing sword

(salaries) attached to them. The policy of buying political support with "gifts" had been bankrupting the state. This made him unpopular with some, but he was still in a position of strength. He canceled grants of public land and curtailed gifts and tax exemptions that his predecessors had bestowed on wealthy monasteries. We know of one—the Vatopedi monastery on Athos—whose subsidy he cut in half. Secular-minded writers, such as Psellos and Attaleiates, applauded this, noting with ironic satisfaction that monks could now devote themselves to asceticism without worrying about material distractions. Psellos had jumped from Michael VI's ship to that of Isaakios during the negotiations after Hades, and was rewarded with the title of *proedros* (president) of the Senate. He compared the budget to a vast bloated monster with hundreds of limbs, like the ancient Titans, to which emperors had added an arm here, a leg there, while its body was fed with a steady diet of foul juices. Isaakios hacked away at the bloat, sickness, and putrefaction, cutting it down with surgery and cauterization.[26]

On 8 November, 1058, Isaakios sent the Varangians to arrest and depose Keroularios while he was conducting a service outside the walls and could not call on the populace for aid. We do not know the exact charges against him, if there were any. The sources say that the patriarch had been behaving imperiously toward the emperor, possibly in the belief that he was the prime mover in the coup of 1057: "I made you," he is supposed to have said about the emperor, "and I can unmake you." Keroularios was detained in Thrace but refused to tender his resignation. Formal proceedings were brought against him, but he died on 21 January, 1059, before they could be set into motion. He was replaced with Psellos' friend Leichoudes (1059–1063), though the emperor, whose eye was fixed on the budget, forced him to surrender the fund of St. George of Mangana before allowing him to take up sacred office. Psellos wrote a long speech of indictment against Keroularios, accusing him of wildly inflated sins, including satanic rituals. The philosopher had a grudge against the patriarch, who had hounded him in the early 1050s with accusations (probably true) of insincere belief. It was these that had driven Psellos out of Monomachos' court and into a brief monastic retreat in Bithynia, a painful and humiliating experience for this critic of monasticism. So this speech was payback. Yet later, for the benefit of the patriarch's nephews who were among Psellos' closest friends (and former pupils), he composed and delivered a laudatory funeral oration for Keroularios.[27]

Frontier defenses remained strong under Isaakios, even though the pressure was growing. Raiders attacked Chaldia, Keltzene, and Chorzane during the civil war of 1057, when the eastern armies were preoccupied in the west.[28] Worse came after Isaakios' coronation, when raiders reached Melitene. Following an agreement with the attackers, the population evacuated the city under cover of Roman forces, after which the raiders sacked the place for days. Yet Roman strategy ultimately prevailed. The raiders were forced to winter in Chorzane, in 1057–1058, and then ambushed three times and destroyed; prisoners and plunder were recovered. Over a century after its annexation, Melitene was now made into a *doukaton* and its walls repaired.[29] No raids had yet reached into the Roman heartland of Asia Minor, yet the army was reverting to its old ambush tactics from the eighth–ninth centuries. In 1059, Isaakios led a campaign in the Balkans against the Hungarians and some Pechenegs, but it is reported vaguely. The army suffered casualties during its return when a sudden storm swept away many soldiers and the tree under which Isaakios sought shelter was struck by lightning.[30] Psellos wrote letters to the emperor praising his campaigns, and added that the empress should also be credited as a joint victor, for her prayers ensured the goodwill of the Virgin Mary. Aikaterine had personal experience of Roman victories, for she had been paraded as a child in the triumph of Basil II over her people, the Bulgarians. Now she found herself on the winning side.[31]

Konstantinos X Doukas

In late 1059, after his return from the Balkan campaign, Isaakios fell ill and abdicated. He designated Konstantinos X Doukas (1059–1067) as his successor. Psellos, who was present, boasts that it was he who secretly orchestrated Doukas' proclamation, though he was likely only facilitating what others with real power had already decided. Isaakios had been raised as a child in the Stoudios monastery, and to it he now retired, as its doorman, before dying six months later.[32]

Konstantinos Doukas had been a lead conspirator in the putsch of 1057 and later told a Georgian monk that he had been "raised as a military person."[33] Yet there is no record of service on his part. Upon his accession, he spoke to the court and people promising justice, equality, and prosperity for all, and dispatched to the provinces a brief narrative of his accession, ghostwritten by Psellos, making the same promises: "we did not accept the power of the monarchy to make for ourselves a life of leisure, but in order to provide well for the public good."[34] Doukas was in his early fifties with three sons (Michael, Andronikos, and one who died), and had another son after his accession (Konstantios). The latter, a *porphyrogennetos*, was made co-emperor first, followed by Michael (VII), but all were children, and Michael proved to be a non-entity even as an adult. The pillar of the regime was the emperor's brother, Ioannes, who was appointed *kaisar*. He was a friend of Psellos and a formidable figure. He became the leading political fixer in the capital for the next generation. The empress Eudokia Makrembolitissa also had a mind of her own, but did not reveal it until after her husband's death.[35]

In April, 1060, soon after his accession, Doukas was targeted in an elaborate assassination attempt, which involved luring him onto a boat and dumping him out at sea. But he boarded the wrong vessel and survived. The conspiracy had been hatched by the City prefect and many officials, and was quashed by the *kaisar*. The conspirators were only exiled, in keeping with the regime's emphasis on mercy and piety. But the experience shook Doukas and led him to prioritize political survival over fiscal responsibility and defense. He emphasized justice, presiding over trials in person to ensure fairness, and piety, resuming the harassment of Syrian bishops and possibly Armenians too. Sources for his reign are poor, but they do say that he reversed Isaakios' austerity and restored the "honors" (and likely also the salaries) that Isaakios had cut. This may not have been universal, for we have a series of letters from Psellos to the retired general Katakalon Kekaumenos, now a monk, who complained that he was not receiving the salary due to him as a *kouropalates*. He was sending his agents to hound the emperor, patriarch, and Psellos about the matter, to no avail. Psellos had to console him with a vision of the heavenly riches that he was storing up by enduring "poverty" in the here and now.[36]

It is possible that Doukas paid for this political largesse by shortchanging the army. Psellos says that he downsized it and preferred diplomacy over war because it was cheaper. Attaleiates says that Doukas neglected the army and the frontiers; failed to ensure that soldiers were adequately equipped; and discharged the best and therefore more expensive soldiers, leaving only the dregs behind.[37] To be sure, Attaleiates was a partisan of Doukas' successor, Romanos IV Diogenes, and was trying to excuse his military failures by blaming Doukas, but Psellos was a partisan of the Doukes and an enemy of the memory of Romanos IV, so their agreement on this point regarding the army is significant.

Indeed, compared to Monomachos, who sent out army after army wherever there was a threat, Doukas was reluctant to respond at all to military aggression. Unfortunately, for events in the east we must rely on the twelfth-century Armenian historian Matthew of Edessa, who mixes history with romantic fantasy and writes from a strongly anti-Roman, Armenian nationalist position. Some of his reporting cannot be trusted without corroboration, such as an alleged sack of Sebasteia by the Seljuks in 1059/60. Raids targeted Chaldia, Koloneia, and Melitene, though they were sometimes beaten back successfully.[38] The major failure of the reign occurred in 1064, when the new sultan, Alp Arslan (1063–1072), moved up from Azerbaijan, subjugated Georgia, and then conquered the city of Ani after a brief siege. The Turks slaughtered the population and detached the city and its territory from the empire, a mere twenty years after its annexation. Attaleiates says that a certain Bargat (Pankratios) had persuaded Doukas to make him the *doux* of Ani, in exchange for which he would levy his salary and all military expenses locally and cost the court nothing. Naturally, he skimped on expenses in order to profit personally, and the city was unprepared for the attack. Such a "privatization" of government was bad enough, but Doukas did not respond to the Seljuk attack or try to retake the city. "And thus such a city was lost along with its villages and lands on account of greed and an untimely economizing."[39]

The Seljuks were now installing their own client rulers in territories taken from the empire. Ani was placed under the emir of Ganja, a former Roman client whom the Romans had chased out of Dvin under Monomachos. Strangely enough, it was the Seljuk expansion into the Transcaucasus that led to the Romans' last imperial acquisition, at the eleventh hour before the collapse of their empire in the east. Gagik-Abas, the Bagratid king of the Armenian kingdom of Vanand (Kars), opted to surrender his realm to the emperor in 1064/5 in exchange for estates in Cappadocia, rather than cope with Seljuk pressure. Seals attest a Roman *katepano* of Kars, though this was to prove a short-lived command.[40] By contrast, Balkan defenses were holding up. In the fall of 1064, an army of Oghuz Turks crossed the Danube, defeated the Danubian defense armies, and plundered the provinces. Our sources criticize Doukas for initially doing nothing, allegedly because "he was reluctant to pay the cost," and then for bowing to pressure and theatrically marching out with 150 guardsmen. But news quickly arrived that some of the Oghuz had recrossed the river while the rest were decimated by disease, famine, and the empire's Bulgarian and Pecheneg forces. Attaleiates claims that this was pure luck, but those forces were likely being coordinated by the capital.[41]

Southern Italy was meanwhile falling to the Normans. Robert Guiscard had led the Norman project since around 1057, and was joined by his younger brother Roger, though the two would frequently clash. By 1060, they had completed the conquest of Calabria and made an alliance with the reformist faction of the Church of Rome. In exchange for swearing loyalty to Rome, Robert was invested with a set of aspirational titles: "I, Robert, by the grace of God and St. Peter Duke of Apulia and Calabria, and in future, with the help of both, of Sicily."[42] None of these territories were the popes' to assign, and Sicily was still under Muslim rule. But open aggression, coupled with the cynical use of invented titles, was the circular process that propelled this new breed of military opportunists from the north and their papal backers. A striking demonstration of how it worked—at the level of an entire state and not just its outlying provinces—was given by William, the duke of Normandy, who conquered England in 1066.

William's countrymen in Italy intensified their attacks on Apulia in the 1060s, although the military history is hard to reconstruct. Moreover, Robert and Roger began the parallel conquest of Sicily in 1061, which slowed them down in Apulia. Normans had participated in Maniakes' short-lived conquest of Sicily in the 1040s, and so they knew how it could be done. Their strategy was to open as many fronts as possible to keep their followers busy, destabilize future targets, and create more legalistic pretexts for further conquest. In 1066, just as William was sailing against England, Geoffroi, the new Norman count of Taranto (taken in 1063), "wanted to attack Romanía, but was blocked" by the Roman admiral Michael Maurix.[43] Imperial agents financed a rebellion against Robert by some of his henchmen in 1067–1068, but they were defeated and fled to Constantinople.

Ultimately, the Norman advance could not be stopped without a major expedition from the east, and that was not forthcoming from Doukas. In 1068, Robert began the siege of Bari, which lasted until 16 April, 1071, when the city fell, ending the imperial presence in southern Italy.[44]

Anxiety ran high in Constantinople. Psellos' panegyrics began to refer to "the barbarians who are constantly pouring in against us," a theme absent from his previous orations. But Doukas was incapacitated with illness after October, 1066 and died on 22 or 23 March, 1067; he was buried at the monastery of St. Nikolaos outside the walls. His widow Eudokia Makrembolitissa took power, and she too changed her seal design from the Virgin to Christ.[45] But the collapse of the east was swift. In 1067, the *doux* of Edessa was captured by Seljuk raiders and had to be ransomed. Another group under Afshin finally broke into Asia Minor, sacked and burned Kaisareia, and plundered the church of the local saint, Basil the Great. They tried to profane his body, but his tomb was too solidly built, so they stripped it of valuables instead. Afshin then crossed to Cilicia, picked up reinforcements at Aleppo, and raided the territory of Antioch, taking away thousands of captives and animals. The Roman soldiers were allegedly too demoralized, ill-equipped, and underpaid to resist. In 1067–1068, Alp Arslan had returned to the Caucasus with a large army and the Romans feared that he would attack the empire "and destroy it." The empress Eudokia confided to Psellos that "our empire is withering and regressing."[46]

Romanos IV Diogenes

Eudokia and many at the court realized that the empire needed competent military leadership, and her eyes fell on the handsome general Romanos Diogenes, son of Basil II's general Konstantinos Diogenes and formerly the *doux* of Serdica. He had just been tried and exiled for intriguing with the Hungarians. Yet the wishes of Eudokia were blocked by her sworn oath never to remarry, an oath extracted by Doukas to protect his dynasty's future. She had signed it before the patriarch, Senate, *kaisar*, and her children, after which the senators and the patriarch (Psellos' other friend Ioannes Xiphilinos) had signed it too. We have the text of this oath, which calls on the sky, earth, elements, Trinity, Theotokos, Cherubim, Seraphim, and all orders of angels, prophets, apostles, martyrs, and saints, to witness the empress' pledge to be torn apart, burned, and thrown into the sea if she even thought about remarriage. But now, with disaster at hand, Eudokia, the patriarch, and the senators agreed that this oath, the jealous wish of a dying husband, "would harm the common good and contribute to the destruction of the Roman empire." They consented to her wish to marry Diogenes, except for the *kaisar* Ioannes and the Varangians, who opposed the move on the grounds that it would harm the interests of the sitting emperor, Michael VII. But Michael, who was about eighteen, consented, and so the opposition collapsed, for now. Diogenes swore to uphold the rights of the Doukas heirs, and he was married to Eudokia and proclaimed emperor on 1 January, 1068.[47] Finally, the Romans would march out to war, this time not to acquire but to salvage their empire.

It had been almost twenty years since the Roman army last conducted large-scale operations in the east. Most of the *tagmata*, the professional corps of the old themes, and mercenary units of Franks and Varangians were by now stationed in the frontier provinces.[48] The Roman heartland had not been raided in a century, and not intensively so in over two centuries. We do not know whether those who owned military lands were still liable to conscription and sent recruits, or whether the alternative option of "fiscalizing" their service and paying the state had been generalized. Fiscalization enabled the state to hire more expensive, professional soldiers, but it also tempted the court to use the money for other purposes, such as lavishing it on political support or decadence (as a moralizing Armenian historian complained).[49] Attaleiates, a legal scholar and historian who was among Diogenes' advisors, paints a sad picture of the armies in 1068: "It was something to see the famous units and their commanders now composed of just a few men, and these bent over by poverty and lacking proper weapons and war horses . . . little-by-little they were being defeated and routed by the enemy."[50] Attaleiates was excusing Diogenes' failure by blaming the Doukes. Yet his detailed account of Diogenes' campaigns reveals that the army was capable of performing strenuous, complex, and successful maneuvers.

Diogenes' campaigns, which he pursued with extraordinary vigor, had two strategic goals: to chase down and destroy raiding parties and to plug holes in the eastern defenses. In 1068, he received reports of raiders in Syria (Afshin and the forces of Aleppo were attacking Antioch) and Chaldia. He marched to Lykandos, but then heard that the northern raiders sacked Neokaisareia in Pontos. He swung north, pursued them, and destroyed them. Then he returned via Sebasteia to Syria, where he captured Manbij (Hierapolis) and defeated an Aleppan-Turkish army. Finally, he marched to the territory of Antioch and recaptured the fort of 'Artah. The campaign was a success, though Afshin had meanwhile slipped through the defenses of Melitene and sacked Amorion in central Asia Minor. Diogenes returned to Constantinople in January, 1069. One flaw in the imperial defenses had become apparent: local forces and commanders were reluctant to fight the Turks, leaving that to the emperor's army, but he was one and they were many and faster. But at least "the Romans were beginning to stand up to their enemies."[51]

Diogenes planned to chase raiders again in 1069, but first he had to deal with another rebellion by a Norman mercenary captain, Robert Crépin (Crispin). He was a veteran of the anti-Muslim wars in Spain, had then moved on to fight for the Normans in Italy, possibly against the empire, and had now taken up service under the emperor. Like Hérve, he too proved faithless and tried to seize some of the Armenian themes in the east, defeating an army that Diogenes sent against him. But when Diogenes arrived at Dorylaion, he submitted and was arrested.[52] While the emperor next chased down two raiding parties in the regions of Sebasteia and Melitene, Afshin managed to sack Ikonion. Diogenes tried to block the raiders' escape, but the *doux* of Antioch, Chatatourios (an Armenian name), failed to do so.[53] In 1070, Diogenes stayed in Constantinople to firm up his domestic position. Eudokia had given him a son (Leon) and another would follow (Nikephoros); she was the only empress to bear born-in-the-purple sons to two emperors. Diogenes had married an older son of his (from his first wife) to a Komnene, a niece of the former emperor Isaakios; she was the sister of Manuel, Isaakios, and Alexios (the future emperor, who was now in his teens). Diogenes was prying the Komnenoi away from the Doukes. The *kaisar* Ioannes Doukas, who hated Diogenes, retired to his estates.

Diogenes stayed in Constantinople in 1070 and entrusted that year's campaign to the young Manuel Komnenos. But Manuel was defeated at Sebasteia by the Turkish tactic of the feigned retreat. Meanwhile, another group of raiders sacked Chonai, in western Asia Minor, and plundered its famous church of the archangel Michael. The campaigns of 1068 and 1069 had failed to secure the passes into Asia Minor. Local defense forces could not, or would not, stop the invaders. But the leader who defeated Manuel, Arisghi (Chrysoskoulos), happened to be in rebellion against his brother-in-law, the sultan Alp Arslan, and he defected to the imperial side. In Constantinople, he divulged information about Seljuk tactics.[54] Diogenes was also funding the construction of forts inside Asia Minor, guarding the passes from the central mountainous plateau to the plains in the west. The interior was already being treated as a frontier zone, anticipating the strategic configuration of the twelfth and thirteenth centuries.[55]

Mantzikert

In 1071, Diogenes marched out to secure the Armenian frontier, especially at Mantzikert, which Alp Arslan himself had just taken and garrisoned. The sultan had subsequently marched to Edessa but failed to take it from the *doux* Basileios Alousianos, another descendant of the Bulgarian tsars. The sultan then failed to take Aleppo too, though its rulers accepted his suzerainty.[56] Diogenes marched by way of Kaisareia, Sebasteia, Koloneia, and Theodosiopolis. The latter had been abandoned, and its inhabitants had relocated to a more defensible location nearby. When he reached Mantzikert, he judged (correctly, as it turned out) that he could take it with only part of his army, so he sent the majority on to Khliat, his next target, under Ioseph Trachaneiotes, along with the Frank mercenaries under the Norman captain Roussel de Bailleul. Estimates of the total size of the army put it at 40,000, which, if correct, would be the largest expeditionary force assembled in recent Roman history.[57] Diogenes was not intending to fight the sultan and had no idea that he was nearby, or else he would not have sent the majority away. He reduced Mantzikert easily, but then learned that there was a Turkish force nearby. He did not know who they were, and it was too late to recall Trachaneiotes.

We have two conflicting accounts of what happened next, the most detailed by Attaleiates, who was in the camp. He says that Diogenes sent out Nikephoros Bryennios, *doux* of the western *tagmata*, to find the enemy and engage. Bryennios did so, but found the fighting harder than expected and requested reinforcements. Diogenes then sent Nikephoros Basilakes, *doux* of Theodosiopolis, and the Turks withdrew. Bryennios halted his pursuit but Basilakes foolishly plunged on and was captured. Toward evening, Turkish cavalry appeared outside the main Roman camp, its archers keeping the Romans pinned inside all night and all during the following day. "It was then that a tremendous fear took over; there was talk of disaster and incoherent cries." But the camp held, even though some "Scythians" in the imperial army defected to the Turkish side. The enemy then withdrew and peace envoys arrived. Diogenes eventually rejected their overtures and marched out on the third day, 26 August. He found the enemy ready for battle, but they fled before him. He pursued them but eventually stopped, so as not to fall into an ambush. But when he ordered his standard to be reversed, this was taken in the rear as a signal that the emperor had fallen, and the soldiers fled. It was alleged that the general Andronikos Doukas, son of the *kaisar*, deliberately withdrew and spread a rumor about the emperor's demise, causing a general panic. Some Turks pursued the fleeing soldiers back to the camp, where scenes of chaos reigned, while others surrounded the emperor. He fought valiantly but was captured. Attaleiates was at the camp: "What could be more pitiable than the entire imperial army in flight, chased by inhuman barbarians, the emperor defenseless and surrounded . . . and to see the whole Roman state overturned?"[58]

In Attaleiates' account there is no "battle" of Mantzikert, only a confused pursuit that ends in the emperor's capture. In the twelfth century, the historian and *kaisar* Nikephoros Bryennios, relying possibly on information passed down from his homonymous grandfather, the general, presents it more like a set battle on the final day, with left and right wings flanking Diogenes in the center, all fighting the Turks with variable results, until the emperor is captured.[59] "Mantzikert" quickly became a flashpoint for controversy, second-guessing, and recrimination among the high command, with Attaleiates and Bryennios both editorializing on what Diogenes should have done to avoid the fateful outcome. An emperor had not been captured since the third century AD, so the battle and its outcome became the stuff of legend in both eastern and western sources. It was also a morality tale for, as everyone including the Romans admitted, the sultan treated Diogenes with courtesy and compassion during his eight-day captivity. "What would you have done to me if our positions were reversed?" the sultan asked. Diogenes said, "I would have killed you cruelly," an answer whose honesty impressed Alp Arslan. Eventually, the two worked out a deal, though its terms are reported vaguely as they were never implemented. Some territory was ceded to the sultan (probably Vaspurakan), a marriage alliance was perhaps planned, and there were likely to be payments, though the emperor was candid: "I have used up the monies of the Romans . . . in the reorganization of the armies and in wars, and I have impoverished the nation." We know that this was true, because in setting out for war that year, Diogenes had no cash with which to pay senatorial salaries, only silk.[60]

The Roman leadership was in disarray. The army dispersed and each found his own way home. The initial reports reaching Constantinople were dire and contradictory. When he was released, and changed back from Turkish into Roman clothes, Diogenes sent a letter ahead to the capital to shore up his position, but his credibility as a leader was shot and the Doukes, meaning Ioannes and his sons Andronikos and Konstantinos, as well as Psellos, declared him deposed, and they confined Eudokia to a monastery; it was she, after all, who had brought him into the palace and bore his children.[61] But Diogenes, whose family was Cappadocian, enjoyed support in the eastern armies. A civil war ensued, at the worst possible moment. The Doukas army was initially led by Konstantinos and the Norman mercenary Crépin, who was released to perform this service. They defeated Diogenes' general Theodoros Alyates in the Armeniakon theme, and cruelly blinded him with tent pegs. Diogenes fell back to Cilicia, joined by his general Chatatourios. During the winter, the Doukes exiled the Komnenoi (Anna Dalassene and her sons) to the island of Prinkipos under suspicion of plotting with Diogenes, who was their in-law. In 1072 they sent another army under Andronikos Doukas and Crépin, which crossed the Tauros mountains to Cilicia and defeated Chatatourios.[62]

Diogenes was blockaded in Adana. Eventually, he agreed to surrender on condition that he not be harmed. The deal was accepted, and he was conveyed to the capital on a mule, a mark of humiliation. On 29 June, at Kotyaion (Kütahya), while the bishops who had stood as guarantors of the agreement watched helplessly, he was savagely blinded on orders from the court. Psellos, who later justified this deception and cruelty as necessary for the state, wrote a consolatory letter to the man whom he had once served and praised, explaining that everything happens for a reason and that the Sleepless Eye of Divine Justice sees all. Having lost his sight, Diogenes may now enjoy the divine light that God will ignite in his soul.[63] Diogenes was taken to the island of Prote, where he died on 4 August, 1072; Eudokia was allowed to bury him. Romanos IV Diogenes cut a tragic figure. He made a valiant effort to save his country, did no harm to his enemies even when they were in his power, and was repeatedly betrayed by them. In a satirical text of the following century, a Cappadocian visitor to the underworld sees his terrible ghost, broad-chested and with eyes gouged out.[64]

Mantzikert was a military disaster, the worst in Roman history since the Yarmuk (636 AD). It was not costly in terms of lives, nor was it lost to an enemy who was bent on the immediate conquest of Roman territory; Alp Arslan was looking elsewhere at the time.[65] It was a disaster because of its timing. It dispersed and demoralized the Roman armies precisely when quasi-independent Turkish groups were eager to expand into new lands. "Surging out of Persia, the Turks marched into the Roman themes, for there was no one to oppose them. They did not invade in scattered bands, as they had done before, but assumed control over everything in their path."[66] By the end of the decade, the Romans had lost control of Asia Minor, their heartland, the oldest part of the polity still in existence. But even this might not have happened but for another consequence of Mantzikert, namely its destabilization of imperial politics. It kicked off a vicious civil war, and the weak emperor who replaced Diogenes, Michael VII Doukas (1071–1078), was in no position to rally the suspicious Roman elite to defend Asia Minor. He was a non-entity, said to have the qualities appropriate to a bishop, and spent much of his time "trying to compose iambic verses under the tutelage of Psellos."[67] None of his poems survive.

Michael VII Doukas

The Doukes retained Diogenes' surviving generals. Nikephoros Botaneiates stayed in command of Anatolikon; Basilakes was posted to Paphlagonia and then Dyrrachion; Trachaneiotes to Antioch and his son Katakalon to Adrianople; Diabatenos to Edessa; and Bryennios to Bulgaria and Dyrrachion.[68] A marriage connection was made with the Komnenoi to bring them onside. The new emperor had married a beautiful Georgian princess, Martha, whom the Romans called Maria of Alania (though she was not from Alania). Her cousin now married Isaakios Komnenos, Alexios' older brother.[69] But the regime was strapped for cash. The coinage was debased even further until it reached a low of 10% gold content, fueling inflation.[70] Psellos, in a funeral oration for the patriarch, his friend Xiphilinos (d. 1075), focused on the problem of poverty in Constantinople, which imposed greater demands for charity on the Church. This was probably due to the loss of lands, revenue, and produce from the east, which was being overrun. The capital was also swelling with refugees from Asia Minor, as "large multitudes were fleeing those regions on a daily basis, and hunger afflicted everyone."[71] Such dire circumstances called for hard choices, and the regime brought in a eunuch called Nikephoritzes, a logothete with a background in administration and an expert at raising revenue. He was efficient, but quickly became detested.

Lacking cash to reward its favorites, the regime gave some of them imperial estates and their proceeds. In 1073, Andronikos Doukas, the victor and possible traitor of Diogenes, was given the large Alopekai estate in the Maeander valley and the Adam estate near Miletos, both in western Asia Minor, a region not yet overrun.[72] The Armenian-Georgian general Gregorios Pakourianos was given lands and villages in Bulgaria to compensate for the loss of his estates in the east to the Turks. His new lands were probably meant to enable him to carry out military duties for the emperor and build forts for the protection of the locals. In 1083, he used these lands to endow his monastery for Georgians at Bachkovo, from which Romans were excluded from key positions because, he claimed, they were too "violent and greedy."[73] This mechanism for rewarding followers would later be implemented by Alexios I on a vaster scale and it enabled some prominent families to relocate from eastern Asia Minor.

The loss of Asia Minor was not a foregone conclusion. Alp Arslan was killed in late 1072 and succeeded by his teenage son Malik Shah, who had to fight for the throne, so his attention was not on the west. Asia Minor was raided and occupied by independent bands, who could be defeated piecemeal. After all, the Roman armies had not been destroyed and their command structures along the periphery had not collapsed. Niketas, the *doux* at Belgrade, strenuously resisted a Hungarian attack in ca. 1071. He temporarily surrendered the city because of a fire, but it was later recovered. Sirmium, however, was possibly lost around this time.[74] Another Bulgarian uprising was suppressed in 1072 (or, less likely, 1073). Separatists at Skopje invited the ruler of Duklja, believed to be a descendant of tsar Samuil, to send his son Bodin "to liberate them from heavy-handed Roman oppression." At Prizren, Bodin was proclaimed as tsar Petar, and the rebels defeated the forces of the *doux* at Skopje, Damianos Dalassenos. The rebels then divided their forces, with Bodin going to Niš (Naissos) and his general Petrilos to Ohrid and Kastoria, where the pro-Roman element had regrouped. But Petrilos was defeated at Kastoria by the Roman generals, and the court dispatched Michael Saronites with an army of Romans, Franks, and Varangians, who crushed the remaining rebels. Bodin was exiled to Antioch.[75] This was the second large-scale attempt at Bulgarian independence, but the Roman command structure in the Balkans held.

In the east, the empire had irrevocably lost its Caucasian territories: Ani, Vaspurakan, and Taron. Trebizond was also taken by the Turks at some point in the 1070s, but they were driven off by a local officer, Theodoros Gabras, who set up a quasi-independent Roman marcher state. Theodosiopolis remained under the command of a *doux*, at least nominally; he was the Armenian-Georgian nobleman Gregorios Pakourianos. The *doukaton* of Mesopotamia was the corridor for many Turkish attacks, so control there had probably broken down. Nevertheless a *doux*, Nikephoros Palaiologos, is attested in 1077. Edessa was still under the command of Leon Diabatenos, though the city was increasingly difficult to govern. A wide swath of territory in the southeast, including Melitene, Germanikeia, Samosata, and later Edessa and Antioch, came under the rule of Diogenes' officer, Philaretos Brachamios, a Chalcedonian Armenian-Roman.

He did not recognize Michael VII, but would later recognize Nikephoros III Botaneiates (1078–1081). He too was a marcher Roman warlord. Antioch remained in Roman hands, and its *doux* even conducted successful operations against Aleppo in 1073.[76]

With Asia Minor in the balance, the final blow was delivered, once again, by Norman treachery. Robert Guiscard had taken Bari in 1071, and there was widespread apprehension that he would attack the Balkans, which kept Roman forces pinned down there that might otherwise have been deployed in the east. Yet far more damaging at this critical moment were the actions of Roussel de Bailleul, commander of the Franks in imperial service and a veteran of the Norman conquest of Sicily. He chose precisely this moment of Roman weakness to turn on his employers and carve out a Norman-style statelet for himself in Asia Minor. He timed his treason to undermine an expedition led by Isaakios Komnenos to reclaim Asia Minor in 1073. Without Frankish cavalry, Isaakios was defeated and captured by the Turks. Roussel then set up a protection racket, selling safety from the Turks to cities that would hire him (but, remember, paying a Norman means treating him as your lawful "lord"). In 1074, an army was sent out against him under the *kaisar* Ioannes Doukas and his son, the *domestikos* Andronikos, but its Franks also defected to Roussel. The Romans were defeated and their commanders captured, except for Botaneiates, who withdrew before the battle. There would now be no more expeditions to liberate central Asia Minor, which was overrun by Turks.[77]

Roussel marched to the Bosporos and burned Chrysopolis in view of the capital. He now led all the Franks formerly in imperial service, about 3,000 men. As he could not hope to win over the capital, he set up his captive, the *kaisar* Ioannes, as a puppet emperor to legitimate his fledging state in the interior of Asia Minor (this "fig-leaf legitimacy" would be practiced later by Robert Guiscard and the crusaders in 1203). The court now resorted to another strategy, which was to hire Turks to take down Roussel. The marauder Artuk, active in Bithynia, took up the contract and, with an army about twice the size of Roussel's, defeated him with a feigned retreat and took him and Ioannes captive. Yet Roussel's wife hastened to ransom him first, so he was set free to continue his predations in the Armeniakon. Yet another scheme failed in 1075, which was to borrow an army from the king of Georgia, Giorgi II. The commander of the mission, Nikephoros Palaiologos, did not have the cash to pay his Georgian soldiers and so they left.[78] Eventually, another contract was put out on Roussel, "that Frankish dog," which led to his capture in 1076 by Tutak (Artuk?). He was ransomed by the young Alexios Komnenos at Amaseia and taken to Constantinople, where he was tortured and imprisoned.[79]

The court had suppressed Roussel's emergent Normandy, but at the cost of sacrificing Asia Minor to the Turks. In a sense, the rest of Roman history was a struggle to steer a course between Frankish and Turkish predators, hiring the one to fight the other, a dynamic that expanded until it filled up the entire strategic horizon. Nikephoritzes, the power behind Michael VII's throne, had made his choice between the two, "preferring to see the land of the Romans under Turkish rule than to see Latins ensconced in any part of it, even if only to repel Turkish attacks." By contrast, the historian of those events, Attaleiates, was all for using Latins against Turks.[80] It is still unclear which of the two did more damage to Romanía.

Alexios' departure was essentially a farewell to Asia Minor. On the way back, dodging bands of Turkish marauders, he visited his grandfather's estate at Kastamone, but found it deserted. Many Romans were fleeing to the capital or the islands, and the fleet carried out evacuations. One farm between Pontos and Cappadocia was abandoned so quickly that the animals were left in their pens, where they died. "Not a nook escaped the attention of the godless."[81] The logothete Nikephoritzes recruited refugees into a new *tagma* called the Immortals, training them as cavalry lancers.[82] But many inland areas were depopulated, where agriculture collapsed or gave way to pastoralism. After 1100, both botanical and archaeological data indicate a sudden decline of agriculture on the central plateau. Coins became scarcer, though not in the still-militarized districts such as Antioch, which remained under tenuous control.[83]

During the 1070s, the court sent only men named Doukas, Komnenos, or Palaiologos into Asia Minor, families with roots there, and no one named Bryennios, Basilakes, or Trachaneiotes, who were based in the Balkans and who still had armies under their command, as we will see. The court, or the western generals, were unwilling to risk losing the Balkans in order to regain Asia Minor, what with a recent Bulgarian uprising and Robert threatening to invade from across the Adriatic. In 1074, the court bought Robert off with an extraordinary concession. He pledged to be an ally of Romanía and refrain from "violating our borders," in exchange for the marriage of his daughter to Michael's born-in-the-purple son Konstantinos and the right to distribute to his followers forty-four court titles whose salaries would be paid by Constantinople, to a maximum of 14,400 nomismata. The contract was drafted by Psellos and survives among his works.[84] This was extortion, with the added danger of making a contract with Normans, who viewed contracts as instruments of war, not peace.

Collapse into civil war

It is possible that the Doukes did not want the western Roman generals to pass through Constantinople with their armies, even to save Asia Minor, seeing them as a threat to themselves. Such fears would prove well founded as the regime became more unpopular. Nikephoritzes required all grain coming into the capital to be bought and sold at a single clearinghouse in Raidestos, which increased state fees but reduced competition, leading to lower prices for producers and higher cost to consumers. He also canceled subsidies to cities along the lower Danube, inciting them and the Pechenegs settled there to rebel and raid the provinces to the south. The Pechenegs were quasi-autonomous to begin with, but from this point on, until their destruction by Alexios Komnenos in 1091, they were entirely independent of imperial control.[85] Michael VII earned the nickname *Parapinakis*, "Cheapskate." By 1077, the regime had lost credibility and the dam burst.

One of the distinctive features of the Roman monarchy was that, lacking an order of succession to the throne, legitimacy was based on popularity and success. This was usually a strength of the system, but a regime perceived to be failing, especially in a foreign war, became vulnerable to would-be usurpers. Changes of leadership were often beneficial—"the situation needed management by a prudent, experienced, and magnanimous mind"[86]—but the concurrent civil wars that broke out in 1077–1081 exacerbated the empire's weakness in the face of foreign attack. With the sources focusing on domestic struggles, we learn little about how Romans in Asia Minor were coping under Turkish rule. We have only the most scattered glimpses, such as in a Latin narrative of the removal of the relics of St. Nicholas from Myra (in southern Asia Minor) to Bari in the late 1080s: the Baresi, and then the Venetians, found the town abandoned as the locals had sought refuge in their citadel from Turkish attacks.[87]

The rebellions came in pairs, one in the east and one in the west, and in waves. The first pair included Botaneiates (*doux* of Anatolikon) and Bryennios (*doux* of Dyrrachion). Botaneiates was almost eighty. A career officer born under Basil II, he had firsthand experience of the history that had brought the Romans to this pass. However, he had only 300 soldiers and had to hire Turks to bolster his numbers, while the court hired other Turks to suppress him.[88] Bryennios was more dangerous, because he commanded the stronger armies of the west. In addition to his brother Ioannes, he was joined by Katakalon Trachaneiotes (*doux* of Adrianople) and Nikephoros Basilakes (*doux* of Thessalonike), veterans of the Mantzikert campaign. But their rebellion played out like Tornikios' in 1047. Ioannes Bryennios marched to Constantinople but failed to persuade the people to open the gates and alienated them when his soldiers set fire to the suburbs. Meanwhile, the Pechenegs besieged the rebel himself in Adrianople and he had to pay them off.[89] The rebels went into winter quarters, while the court appointed Alexios Komnenos, who was around twenty, to suppress them. Over the objections of his mother Anna Dalassene, who hated the Doukes, Alexios married Eirene, the daughter of Andronikos Doukas, binding himself to the dynasty.[90]

Unexpectedly, it was Botaneiates who succeeded. He maneuvered his Turkish allies ably enough to be allowed into Nikaia, while his supporters were promoting his cause in the capital. Events played out as in 1057: a commotion in Hagia Sophia in late March, 1078, was followed by the liberation of prisoners, chanting in Botaneiates' favor, and the clergy of the Great Church joining his side. Michael VII abdicated and became a monk in the Stoudios monastery (and later the absentee bishop of Ephesos). Nikephoritzes was arrested and interrogated to divulge his riches, but he died under torture. Botaneiates entered the capital triumphantly in early April and was acclaimed emperor. He found the palace ransacked, but his reign was praised for generosity. His flatterers claimed that rivers of gold flowed from his hands, and he restored or confirmed grants to monasteries.[91]

No Roman emperor had ever taken hold of a more diminished territory than Botaneiates did now. Asia Minor was effectively lost, while most Balkan provinces were in the hands of rebels or periodically overrun by the Pechenegs of the lower Danube. Yet he followed the playbook of the emperors under whom he had come of age, by lavishly handing out more offices, titles, promotions, and tax exemptions, debasing the currency further in order to pay for it all. Although he had married twice already, he sought to legitimate himself through a dynastic connection. He considered first Eudokia Makrembolitissa, who was willing to return to power, but he was talked out of it by the *kaisar* Ioannes Doukas. He married Maria of Alania instead, but uncanonically, as her husband was still alive. In place of the logothete Nikephoritzes, Botaneiates ruled through two of his own servants, the "Scythians" Borilas and Germanos, who became just as hated as he.[92]

As planned by the previous regime, Alexios was sent out to fight Bryennios in the spring or summer of 1078, and defeated him at the battle of the Halmyros river, through a stratagem. The rebel was blinded on the orders of Borilas, then pardoned by the emperor. Bryennios had allegedly commanded an army of 10,000 men, while Alexios, as *domestikos* of the west, had an improvised force of Turkish allies from Asia Minor, Frankish mercenaries, the surviving Immortals, and scraps of Roman units. So instead of being used to destroy each other, Turks and Franks were now being deployed together to destroy the remaining Roman armies of the west.[93] The next contender, Basilakes, appeared immediately, still in 1078, his rebellion essentially an extension of Bryennios'. He brought up from Dyrrachion an army of 10,000 Romans, Bulgarians, and Albanians, along with some Franks from Italy, and based himself in Thessalonike. Alexios, the regime's improvisor-in-chief, "had barely shaken off the dust from the previous battle, or wiped down his sword," when he received orders to march against Basilakes. Near Thessalonike, Alexios defeated him through another ruse, then pursued him inside and captured him. Basilakes was sent to Botaneiates, who blinded him too. Alexios was elevated by the emperor and Senate to the dignity of *sebastos*, given to honored members of the imperial family.[94]

Now that the western armies had also been chewed up in civil conflict, the regime turned its attention to Asia Minor. Philaretos Brachamios had officially recognized the new emperor and had expanded his realm to include Antioch, but he was in practice independent. In 1079, an expeditionary force was assembled at Chrysopolis on the Asian side, but elements within it proclaimed Konstantinos Doukas (Michael VII's brother) as emperor. He was arrested and exiled, and the expedition was canceled.[95] Another would-be emperor, Nikephoros Melissenos, appeared at Nikaia, a willing puppet of the Turks. Alexios refused to campaign against him because they were brothers-in-law.[96] It was ironic that, in an age marked by so much defeat, so many leading Romans bore the name Nikephoros—"Bringer of Victory." They had been given that name a generation earlier, when the empire was at its peak.

Despite his youth, Alexios was the most prominent and successful member of Botaneiates' regime. The Komnenoi, who had powerful enemies at the court, made an alliance with the empress Maria of Alania, who was trying to safeguard the rights of her son Konstantinos, and she leaked palace news to them. When the aging emperor made a younger relative his heir, the Komnenoi rebelled, in the spring of 1081. Alexios' daughter Anna later claimed that they did this only to protect themselves from Borilas and Germanos, who wanted to arrest and blind them. Their chief accomplices were the Armenian-Georgian general Gregorios Pakourianos (promised the position of *domestikos*); the Norman Konstantinos Oumbertopoulos (i.e., "Son of Humbert"); Georgios Palaiologos (married to Alexios' wife's sister); and the *kaisar* Ioannes Doukas, now a monk but always ready for intrigue. The conspirators snuck out of the City, leaving their women behind to seek asylum in the churches, and joined the army in Thrace. But which brother would lead? Isaakios, who was married to a cousin of the empress Maria, was older, but the Doukes lobbied for their in-law, Alexios. He was, moreover, more capable and distinguished, and Isaakios had twice in the past been captured by barbarians and ransomed. Thus, the young *domestikos* was acclaimed by the assembled army.[97]

The rebels marched on the City. The walls were guarded by the Immortals, Varangians, and some Germans, but the *kaisar* knew that the Germans could be bribed, and they allowed the rebels to enter on 1 April, which was Thursday of Holy Week before Easter. But the rebels did not immediately occupy the palace, because their army, which was composed of both Romans and barbarians, engaged in a horrific spree of plunder and mayhem, stripping even the churches of their valuables. An offer from Botaneiates to adopt Alexios and make him co-emperor was refused, so the old emperor abdicated on 4 April and retired to a monastery. Alexios was duly crowned in Hagia Sophia, a usurper whose throne rested on a shaky coalition of intermarried aristocrats. The wars of the 1070s had swept away the Mantzikert-generation of generals and replaced them with a new cast arrayed around the new Komneno-Doukan dynastic configuration. But there were strong tensions within it, especially between the new emperor's mother, Anna Dalassene, and the Doukes, which delayed for a week the coronation of Alexios' fifteen-year-old wife Eirene Doukaina. There were even rumors that Alexios might repudiate her and instead marry Maria of Alania, who was living in the Mangana palace with her born-in-the-purple son, Konstantinos Doukas. The nucleus for the next century of Roman leadership was contained within that tense alliance, along with the seeds of its fateful demise.

Asia Minor was lost. The capital had been plundered. The Roman armies of the west had been decimated after years of civil war, and Robert was known to be preparing an invasion of the Balkans from Italy. "We were pressed on all sides by the bonds of death," a historian noted, and a bishop would later claim that when Alexios took power, his authority reached from the palace only as far as the Golden Gate.[98]

Causes of decline in the eleventh century

The eleventh-century decline had both exogenous and endogenous causes. Scholars have focused overwhelmingly on the latter, and there is a bias in favor of socioeconomic explanations. But the exogenous factors were critical here. In the years 1048–1081, the Romans were attacked by three formidable enemies—the Normans, Seljuks, and Pechenegs—of whom the first two represented novel geopolitical ambitions and new ways of fighting to which the Romans had little time to adjust.[99] The Seljuks brought greater manpower to the conflict than the Arabs ever had, and they were both more determined and ecologically better prepared to settle in Asia Minor than the Arabs. Arguments that local players in eastern Asia Minor cut deals with the Turks and destabilized the imperial order are misleading. A detailed study of those events reveals that it was the Turkish conquests that shook those players loose from the imperial framework, forcing them to fend for themselves, and not the reverse. This was not a case of spontaneous endogenous fragmentation. It was induced by outside attack.[100]

At the same time, Romanía was witnessing the slow and messy extinction of its longest-lived dynasty. The insecure interim emperors after Konstantinos VIII used revenues to buy political support, which, in combination with a massively expanded and expensive bureaucracy, eventually led to budget deficits when the wars multiplied and added to the cost. Salary payments were reduced and the coinage debased in response. The commutation of military service brought in cash, but there was no pledge that the emperors would use it to hire professional soldiers. They could use it instead to reward their followers or for luxury expenses, while some of the mercenaries they hired, especially the Normans, were extremely unreliable and prone to turn on the empire and kick it precisely when it was down. Fiscalization also meant that the interior of Asia Minor was hollowed out of its old defense forces, so that when the enemy broke through, there was virtually no one to defend the heartland.[101] Finally, the advancement of civilian government and the reliance on eunuchs even to lead the armies alienated the military aristocracy. As defeats on the border mounted, emperors lost credibility, which spurred military rebellions. Losses also made emperors seem weak, fueling even more rebellions in the 1070s, and these finally brought down the power structure.

These factors converged in the rise of Alexios Komnenos, who employed Frankish and Turkish mercenaries to destroy the remaining Roman armies of the west and then usurped the throne, backed by a cabal of military aristocrats. It was unclear whether he would be able to muster the resources to defend Romanía from the most sustained attack on its existence since the Arab assault of 717–718.

28
Komnenian Crisis Management (1081–1118)

For the reign of Alexios I Komnenos (1081–1118), we depend on the *Alexiad*, a heroic history written by his daughter Anna, whose title evokes the *Iliad*. It contains detailed and dramatic accounts of many of Alexios' wars but focuses on the first half of the reign, omits important events while presenting others out of chronological order, and commits many distortions. Anna was highly educated and supported a circle of scholars who wrote commentaries on the works of Aristotle. She was an accomplished writer in her own right and the first woman historian of western Eurasia. Scholars used to think that she wrote out of bitterness at being excluded from the throne, and they puzzled over her periodic lamentations in the text, but it has now been shown that these odd features of the work result from her ambitious attempt to be both a good matron and a historian, identities that Roman culture gendered in opposite ways.[1]

Alexios perched atop a fragile aristocratic coalition, resulting in a new system of court titles. As per Alexios' agreement with Maria of Alania, her son Konstantinos remained a nominal co-emperor and she lived in the palace built by Monomachos near St. George of the Mangana. Konstantinos had once been slated to marry Robert's daughter. When Anna, the future historian, was born in 1083, Alexios engaged him to her. Alexios also accommodated Nikephoros Melissenos, his sister's husband, who had rebelled against Botaneiates with Turkish assistance. Melissenos initially proposed that they divide the empire east-west between them, but in the end he settled for the title *kaisar* and the command of Thessalonike. This meant that Alexios had to concoct more elevated titles for his brothers and other relatives, and he did this with compounds of *sebastos*, such as *sebastokrator* for Isaakios and *protosebastos* for Adrianos and another in-law, Michael Taronites.[2] In time, all but these highest titles were gradually phased out, and the *roga* (salary) system was discontinued.[3] This had serious consequences for the relationship between the court and provincial elites, because titles and salaries had for centuries bonded the two. Now most provincials were excluded from the court system, while a coterie of intermarried military aristocrats ensconced themselves in the upper echelons that Alexios created for them.

The Norman war

The effects of these reforms would be felt later. In 1081, Alexios was facing a crisis, as "the empire was breathing its last." Guiscard was preparing to conquer what was left, citing as his pretext the dissolution of his daughter's betrothal to Konstantinos. He even found a man who claimed to be Michael VII and who was asking the Norman duke to reinstate him in exchange for money. A pretender was necessary because "the Roman people and army would never accept a barbarian such as Robert as their emperor."[4] Both pretexts were transparently false, but they were endorsed by pope Gregory VII, to whom Robert had just sworn another oath in 1080 after a decade of tense relations with the papacy. The pope presented the imminent Norman attack on Byzantium as an act of contrition and faith, an ideology that would before long fuel the crusades. The pope also excommunicated Alexios.[5] Rome, after all, stood to gain from the Norman conquests. It had regained some ecclesiastical jurisdiction over southern Italy and Sicily through them and hoped to extend it to the Balkans, its old diocese of Illyricum, a bone of contention with Constantinople since the eighth century. Pretexts aside, it was understood that Robert's goal was "to conquer the empire of Constantinople with the aid of God."[6]

We do not have reliable figures for the armies on either side, but Robert's invasion force may have numbered over 10,000 men, with 1,300 knights.[7] The Normans crossed the Adriatic in waves and occupied strategic locations on the coast, including Aulon and Kerkyra (Corfu). They besieged Dyrrachion on 17 June, 1081. Meanwhile, Alexios was scrambling to shore up his rule. He and his family made an elaborate show of pious contrition for the mayhem caused by his soldiers when they seized Constantinople in April. Taking a page out of the playbook of Theodosius I after the massacre of Thessalonike, he recast what was a failure of military control into a personal burden of guilt that could be expiated by fasting, sleeping on the floor, and wearing a sack under his purple robes for forty days. Through an imperial decree with a golden seal—or *chrysoboullon*—he gave plenipotentiary imperial authority to his formidable mother, Anna Dalassene, to act in his place while he was on campaign. "Whatever decisions she makes have the same validity as if they came from me." We have adjudications of property disputes which show that she used this power as late as her retirement in ca. 1099. Anna changed her seal to include the phrase "Mother of the Emperor."[8]

To fight the Normans, Alexios recalled the garrisons that were holding out against the Turks in a few towns in western Asia Minor. But his army consisted mostly of Roman Balkan units (Macedonians and Thessalians) as well as Frankish and Turkish mercenaries.[9] He was joined by the Venetians, who also stood to lose from a Norman empire spanning the Adriatic. Their fleet harried the Normans during the siege of Dyrrachion, which was defended by Palaiologos. When Alexios arrived, he decided to offer battle, which was risky, but he probably needed a spectacular victory to cow the gaggle of crowned heads and born-in-the-purple princes who accompanied him (Melissenos, Konstantinos Doukas, and two sons of Romanos IV Diogenes). He had a good battle plan, but Robert changed position at the last minute. Alexios was defeated when his Varangians broke ranks to pursue some Norman light soldiers, leaving the main Roman army to face the charge of the heavy cavalry. The Varangian unit at this time consisted of Englishmen who had emigrated after the conquest of their native land by William, and they hated Normans.[10] But they were now massacred and the Romans were routed with great losses. The defeat was also due to the heterogeneity of Alexios' army, whose elements had not trained to work together. Wounded, Alexios barely escaped with his life after furious fighting and wandered through the mountains to Ohrid, hoping to rally his army from Thessalonike. Dyrrachion, many of whose residents were from Amalfi and Venice, was either betrayed to the Normans or surrendered on 21 February, 1082.[11]

In March or April, Robert went on to capture Kastoria, whose garrison of 300 Varangians surrendered without a fight. But then he had to halt operations and personally return to Italy because rebellions had risen against him in southern Italy; moreover, the German emperor Heinrich IV was marching to Rome against his enemy, pope Gregory VII, who called on his Norman allies. Both the Italian rebellions and Heinrich's march had been spurred on by eastern diplomacy and funded by Constantinopolitan gold. It was with reason that westerners later compared Alexios to a scorpion: "he is not dangerous from the front, but watch the tail." Heinrich, who had his own motives to attack the pope, was promised 360,000 nomismata and salaries for dignities to be awarded by Constantinople to his men, like the deal made in 1074 with Robert.[12] When Robert returned to Italy, he entrusted the Balkan war to his son Bohemond, who prosecuted it for the next year and a half. Bohemond took Ioannina and made it his base. The Normans were slowly but steadily occupying Epeiros. But Alexios had no money left with which to raise a new army. He was so desperate that he took up a collection from family and supporters. Eventually he also expropriated Church treasures, the measure to which Herakleios had resorted during the darkest days of the Persian war. At a meeting of the Synod in late 1081 or early 1082, Isaakios Komnenos justified the expropriation by citing the canon that permitted it for the ransom of Christians from barbarian captivity. In August, 1082, Alexios issued an edict that justified his action with an appeal to the "misfortunes of Romanía, whose ship of state was about find itself under water." But he granted that his action had angered God and pledged to return the treasure as quickly as possible. He forbade any future expropriation.[13]

With the fate of the empire in the balance, Alexios also took the time to stage the condemnation of Ioannes Italos, a student of Psellos who had succeeded him as Consul of the Philosophers. Italos hailed from southern Italy and had been promoted by the Doukas regime. He was a more rigorous technical thinker than Psellos and prone to dialectics; he was also one of the first to admit that the Arabs had surpassed the Romans in philosophy.[14] Just as the sincerity of Psellos' faith had been questioned, Italos too had also been suspected of promoting philosophical heresies and he was now brought before a tribunal of the Church in March and April, 1081. Alexios, eager to buttress his reputation for piety and distract attention from his agents who were busy melting down Church plate, fully endorsed the prosecution, but it is not clear whether he instigated it to begin with. Italos was found guilty and forced to recant his views (which he did) and enter a monastery. Bishops who questioned the proceedings were intimidated.[15]

However, the heresies for which Italos was condemned (such as accepting the eternity of the world) do not match the positions that he expounds in his surviving works, though the latter might not reflect what he was teaching at the time. His greatest offense, in the end, may have been the pervasive use of pagan philosophy, especially Proklos, to explicate questions on which Christian dogma claimed a monopoly of truth.[16] Italos' prosecution inaugurated a series of trials of philosophers in the Komnenian period, which terminated Psellos' project of using Proklos to interpret the faith. The *Synodikon of Orthodoxy*, a document that was created to condemn heresies after the end of iconoclasm and was read out in church, was now expanded, like a reverse Bill of Rights, to anathematize such errors as "introducing the godless teachings of the Hellenes about souls, heaven, and earth into the Church . . . undergoing a course of Hellenic studies not merely for the sake of education but in order to believe them as truth . . . accepting the Platonic forms as true," and the like.[17]

Alexios marched out against Bohemond in May, 1082, soon after the Italos affair was settled. He foolishly risked battle against the Normans and was soundly defeated by Bohemond, once at Ioannina and then again in a subsequent battle. Alexios fled again and again. The Normans went on to occupy Ohrid (although the citadel held out) and Skopje. Bohemond now turned south and besieged Larissa, in Thessaly. Whatever reputation for military genius that Alexios had was now lost. He hired an army of 7,000 Turks from his "ally," the sultan,[18] and, in 1083, finally managed to inflict many defeats on the Normans at Larissa through ruses and ambushes. The Norman position collapsed. Invading armies are always at a disadvantage, and a single reverse can halt them. The Normans could not recruit locally and they faced a difficult terrain in a hostile land during a heavy winter. Alexios also sowed disaffection among the Norman elite successfully enough that Bohemond withdrew to the coast. In late 1083, the emperor recaptured Kastoria, but when he returned to Constantinople he faced discontent. Leon, the bishop of Chalkedon, had been protesting against the confiscation of sacred treasures, so Alexios convened another Synod in December, at

Blachernai, to defend his actions, though he admitted his guilt. Even so, there was a serious conspiracy against his throne, though Anna reports it vaguely.[19]

Bohemond returned to Italy, likely in early 1084, whereupon the Romans recovered Aulon and Kerkyra (though not the citadel), while the Venetians retook Dyrrachion. The Norman position appears to have collapsed, but Robert had in the meantime finished his work in Italy. In October, 1084 he launched a follow-up invasion, bringing his son and heir Roger Borsa with him. His forces captured Aulon and Butrint and came to the rescue of their men in Kerkyra's citadel. The Normans defeated a Roman-Venetian fleet that attacked them, though only after hard fighting. But Robert's forces were struck by an epidemic in winter quarters (1084–1085); it was said that 500 knights died along with thousands of common soldiers.[20] Bohemond fell ill and returned to Italy. In the spring, Robert moved southward, but he died upon reaching his next target, Kephalonia, on 17 July, 1085. He was seventy. The Venetians eventually returned Dyrrachion to Alexios. As so many times before, the Romans had lost the battles but won the war, in large part through diplomacy and subversion.

The Pecheneg wars

Alexios enjoyed only a brief respite before the next military crisis, a Pecheneg invasion, which did far more damage than the Norman one. In the capital, Leon of Chalkedon escalated his critique of the expropriation of Church plate, alleging that crimes were committed during it by the (now retired) patriarch Eustratios Garidas. Applying the familiar chain reaction of blame, Leon refused to commune with anyone who accepted that Garidas had even been a lawful patriarch. Leon was playing at being a new Theodoros of Stoudios and he appears to have had many followers, some of whom even saw him in visions. But he refused to provide evidence to back up his accusations. A commission appointed by Alexios investigated the matter, and Leon was deposed in January, 1086 and exiled to Thrace, where he remained defiantly critical of the regime, even when Alexios tried to improve his conditions. Leon argued that Alexios' actions were essentially a form of iconoclasm, as some of the implements melted down had images of Christ and the saints on them. A "schism" within the Church was reignited when Alexios violated his own pledge and expropriated more Church plate in order to face the Pecheneg invasions.[21]

Back in 1053, the Pechenegs had concluded a thirty-year peace treaty with Constantinople, which they honored for twenty years. In 1074, along with a number of cities along the lower Danube, they became effectively independent, and one of their leaders was Tatu, who ruled from Dorostolon (modern Silistra). This was effectively the kernel of a Pecheneg state, exactly where the Bulgars had established theirs four centuries earlier. They raided Thrace periodically in the 1070s and early 1080s, and Alexios' *domestikos* Pakourianos fought them at an unspecified time.[22] The problem escalated in the mid-1080s, possibly because more Pechenegs crossed the Danube and settled to the south. In 1085 or 1086, Pakourianos was killed in battle near Philippopolis by a large raiding party. Alexios immediately dispatched Tatikios, a personal confidant and childhood companion, with Oumbertopoulos, the commander of the Franks, and together they defeated them. Yet a new group of Pechenegs crossed the Danube in 1087, accompanied by Solomon, a deposed king of Hungary, and they managed to reach Charioupolis in southern Thrace, not far from the capital, before being defeated by two other Roman commanders; Solomon was killed in the pursuit.[23]

The Danube Pechenegs continued to plunder the surrounding districts, and Alexios found it intolerable that this group was "squatting on our land as if it were theirs." The younger members of his council advised war, though others, such as the blinded rebel Nikephoros Bryennios, urged the emperor to fortify the passes of the Haimos mountains and cede Paradounabon to the nomads. Alexios decided to destroy them once and for all, and set into motion the same strategy that emperors had traditionally used against the Bulgars. A fleet under Georgios Euphorbenos sailed into the Danube to strike from behind while an imperial army under Alexios, his brother the *domestikos* Adrianos, Tatikios, the *kaisar* Melissenos, the sons of Romanos IV, and many other commanders attacked frontally. This resulted in a catastrophic defeat at the battle of Dorostolon, in August, 1087. The emperor again had to flee and regroup. A critic later said that "he never returned from battle with the majority of his army."[24]

Our source for the battle, as well as for the four-year Pecheneg war that ensued, is Anna's *Alexiad*, but this text focuses on battle exploits and does not discuss strategy or offer coherent accounts of the movement of the armies across Thrace. It appears that the Roman defenses collapsed completely, from the Danube all the way to the capital, and Alexios had to resort again to guerilla warfare, conducted with patchwork forces against a more powerful mobile foe. A coherent narrative is beyond our reach, and it is unclear whether the Pechenegs were only raiding or also settling further south. When their host was finally defeated at Lebounion in 1091, it was accompanied by women and children. These movements must have caused considerable devastation in Thrace as they "plundered cities and regions." "Their countless multitudes spread throughout the land and ravaged everything." They even took Philippopolis in 1088.[25] A contemporary saint's life says that "everyone sought refuge in the forts because of the danger."[26]

To make matters worse, one Tzachas (Çaka), the Turkish ruler of Smyrna on the coast of Asia Minor, was creating a mini-empire for himself in the Aegean. He built a fleet and captured Mytilene (on Lesbos), Chios, Samos, and Rhodes, and terrorized the other islands so much that Christodoulos, the founder of the monastery of Patmos, had to flee to Euboia "because of the raids of the godless Turks." Tzachas even sought to ally himself with the Pechenegs for a joint assault on Constantinople. The fleets that the emperor sent against him now—first under Niketas Kastamonites and then under Alexios' relative Konstantinos Dalassenos—failed to dislodge him.[27] Moreover, the islands of Crete and Cyprus also rebelled, though the nature of those revolts is reported opaquely. They may have been tax revolts, as the state's remaining provinces were being squeezed to fund the wars.[28] Romanía was falling apart and the walls were closing in on Alexios again, worse than during the Norman war. His leadership was questioned and plots were formed against him.

The solution to the Pecheneg problem came from another nomadic group that had now established itself as dominant in the steppes north of the Black Sea: the Cumans (called Polovtsians in the Rus' sources). The Pecheneg leader Tatu was absent from the battle of Dorostolon (1087) because he had gone to seek Cuman help against the Romans. When the Cumans arrived, the battle was over, but they still demanded a share of the loot, leading to a fight between the two groups, which the Pechenegs lost. It is possible that the Pecheneg "migration" into the empire was caused by Cuman pressure, though Anna's narrative, with its gaps, does not let us see into that. Alexios managed to forge an alliance with the Cumans, who turned up in force in 1091 to help him against their common foe—another scorpion's tail. Anna makes it seem as if Alexios was surprised by the Cumans' arrival, but it was almost certainly arranged in advance (she makes the same error later regarding the crusaders). At Lebounion, in southern Thrace, on 29 April, 1091, the combined Roman and Cuman forces annihilated the Pechenegs. Thousands were killed—"a whole nation exterminated"—and many captives were executed later in the Roman camp. The Cumans departed to the north and Alexios restored Roman control back up to the Danube. His victory gave rise to a saying: "But for a day the Pechenegs didn't see the month of May."[29] "The Scythian tempest was calmed," the saint's life said.[30]

A new political paradigm

A decade into the reign, there are signs of grave discontent with Alexios. A prime exhibit is a speech by Ioannes Oxeites, patriarch of Antioch but resident in Constantinople, written or delivered two months before the battle of Lebounion. The speech thanks God for preserving Alexios for the good of the republic, but it also highlights the catastrophes now facing the state, which could only mean that God has withdrawn his favor. To explain this predicament, Oxeites delivers a scathing review of the regime's offenses. Alexios himself had usurped the throne; taxes were too many and too oppressive; Church treasures were melted down; and subjects were reduced to poverty, dying before their time or forced to emigrate. Oxeites advises Alexios, whose "hands are stained with blood," how to win back God's favor. He needs to seek forgiveness, "refrain from illegal revenues," and rein in "your family, which is a plague upon the monarchy and all of us. Each of them wants to live like a king, and they place personal profit over the common good." The emperor must instead consult with *all* his subjects.[31]

Oxeites' speech used to be read as purely hostile, but more recently it is seen as a programmatic call for reform that was endorsed if not orchestrated by Alexios himself, who was prone to public performances of contrition.[32] By 1091, Alexios had to answer for nothing less than a revolution in government that had harmed the interests of the old elite.

Facing a fiscal crisis, Alexios had further devalued the nomisma to the point where it had little gold content. Starting in the 1070s, emperors had increasingly rewarded their inner circle less with salaries than with gifts of land from imperial estates; with tax exemptions; or by assigning to them the proceeds of a tax district. The *kaisar* Melissenos, for instance, was given Thessalonike, while the *domestikos* Adrianos was assigned the taxes of the nearby Kassandreia peninsula.[33] Moreover, starting with a new census in 1088, the state began to confiscate vast tracts of land from individual landowners, churches, and monasteries, though we have detailed information only about the monasteries because their archives survive. The fiscal principle behind the confiscations was that one should not own more lands than one was paying taxes for. The Lavra on Athos lobbied successfully enough to mitigate some of the losses, and Maria of Alania intervened to protect some of the lands of Iviron, her countrymen, but they still lost about half. Overall, this was possibly the single greatest confiscation of lands in the history of the empire. It was what Oxeites meant when he said that "the wealthy are impoverished." We have a speech by an official early in the next century who, while praising Alexios, notes that his father had lost his property to the state. A later historian confirms that Alexios "confiscated senatorial estates" and "took away the houses of people who really owned nothing, on the basis of unjustly alleged debts [i.e., to the state]."[34] Alexios ruined a large part of the aristocracy in order to save the Roman polity from insolvency during the Pecheneg crisis.

But few of the confiscated lands became imperial estates managed directly by the central administration. Most were assigned to men in the emperor's inner circle as concessions, that is, as land that was understood to be public but was managed and exploited by members of the emergent Komnenian aristocracy. The taxes, fiscal burdens, and service owed by the populations living on those estates did not rise relative to those who lived on other lands, but their obligations were transferred from the imperial state to the beneficiary of the concession, such as the *sebastokrator* Isaakios Komnenos and the *protosebastos* Adrianos Komnenos. The crown was essentially outsourcing the management and revenue of public estates to men who exercised a quasi-imperial authority over them. These estates did not become their private property; it was only their revenues and benefits that were being awarded.[35] Alexios calmed the apprehensions of their residents, who are sometimes called *paroikoi*, by explaining that they would not be abused and that their legal rights remained intact; it was merely that "they would pay their state taxes" to, say, Adrianos.[36]

There were precedents for this arrangement. In the tenth century, salaries of the western generals were paid not by the emperor directly but from the taxes of their districts.[37] It is likely that the beneficiaries of Alexios' concessions used these revenues not just to live in style but to provide services that were essential to the state, such as bringing soldiers to Alexios' wars. In effect, by creating "public-private partnerships" at the expense of Balkan landowners, Alexios saved his extended family and followers from the financial ruin caused by the conquest of Asia Minor. But he also made sure that the state, i.e., the emperor, retained the final word on the assignment of these lands. *Paroikoi* remained free citizens, and their administrative subordination to a beneficiary held both pros and cons for them. They were not entirely segregated from the central administration. We know of one Bulgarian *paroikos* of the Church of Ohrid who conspired with imperial officials to create a great deal of trouble for the archbishop, Theophylaktos.[38]

At the same time, in 1092, Alexios reformed and stabilized the coinage. The new gold standard was the *hyperpyron*, with the same weight as the old nomisma but, despite its name, which meant "hyper-refined," it had only 20.5 karats instead of 24. Its shape, moreover, was curved like a cup rather than flat, a choice that is hard to explain beyond just impressing users with its technical virtuosity. The new coinage, issued in vast quantities from Constantinople and Thessalonike, came in many descending denominations that flexibly facilitated trade.[39] Yet many older coins of variable gold content were still circulating, and tax schedules were thrown into chaos as different locales and taxpayers had established different precedents and conversion rates for their own dues. In 1106–1109, by which point many older coins had likely dropped out of circulation, Alexios issued a uniform schedule for tax payments based on the "white *trachy*" (electrum) coin of the new currency, the second below the "hyper-refined" one. This standardization tended to hurt more prosperous taxpayers who had hoarded the older debased coins, so again Alexios embittered the old elites. The fiscal departments of the state were now placed under the *megas logariastes* ("Accountant-in-Chief")—one for the state offices and another for imperial properties—and the older bureaux receded in importance.[40]

Alexios' new tax schedules appear to have been onerous, though complaints tend to come from those who lost out *and* had the means to make their feelings known to us, including bishops such as Theophylaktos of Ohrid, who suspected that the *paroikoi* of his see were colluding with the taxman against him. Nikolaos Mouzalon resigned as bishop of Cyprus around 1100, complaining that the tax collectors were essentially torturers who "string up my flock and flail at them with rods." When one of them could not pay, they transferred the burden to another through the *allelengyon*, the collective responsibility on a district to pay all of its member's taxes.[41] Such abuses possibly became more common if, as seems likely, collection was falling increasingly into the hands of tax farmers, who secured the rights to a district by promising a higher haul or who were obligated to furnish what the schedule stipulated, while keeping a fee for themselves. Tax farmers may have squeezed out more revenue, but they were hated and so a political liability. Occasionally they needed to be punished. In 1104/5, one Demetrios Kamateros failed to extract twice the usual amount from Thrace and Macedonia as he had promised, and so Alexios confiscated his manor near the hippodrome.[42]

Alexios began to conduct foreign policy via concession too. It was likely in 1092 (rather than 1082, the traditional date) that he issued a chrysobull exempting Venetians from taxes on trade throughout the territory of the empire. This was not only to honor their services during the Norman war but to ensure their "goodwill toward Romanía and our imperial majesty" and stimulate trade and production by inviting foreign capital. The chrysobull conferred upon the doge and his successors the title of *protosebastos* (plus associated salary), upon the patriarch of Venice at Grado the title of *hypertimos* (plus salary), and it gave to the churches of Venice an annuity of 20 lbs of gold. The emperor also confiscated from certain monasteries a stretch of the City's coast along the Golden Horn and transferred it to the Venetians to use tax-free as their quarter, with all its associated workshops, wharves, and revenues. They were also given a church in Dyrrachion along with its properties. The rationale for these confiscations and concessions was the public interest, in which Venice was treated as something between a foreign state and a junior partner. In the long term, exemption from custom dues gave the Venetians a competitive advantage over Roman merchants and caused problems. It is unlikely, however, that the Venetians captured a significant share of trade at first, given their limited capacity; they probably stimulated the economy more than they depressed Roman merchants.[43] Romanía was now part of a new, multi-polar world, where survival required coalitions and trading partners. The empire was no longer an entire world—an *oikoumene*—unto itself.

Plots, heretics, and monks

In the early 1090s, Alexios dispatched a competent officer, Ioannes Doukas, grandson of the homonymous *kaisar* and brother of the empress Eirene, to expel Tzachas from the Aegean islands. He carried this task out successfully as *megas doux* of the fleet—the new admiralty position created by Alexios—assisted by Konstantinos Dalassenos. Tzachas was confined to his base at Smyrna and later murdered by a rival, the emir of Nikaia, whom Alexios had incited against him. "When two enemies of the Roman empire were fighting against each other, he would side with the weaker one, make gains at the expense of the stronger one, and then move on to take the next city." Doukas went on to reestablish imperial authority on Crete and Cyprus, which had revolted at some point before 1091. Anna provides a detailed account of the operations but no way to date them between 1092 and 1096.[44] Alexios also led a number of attacks against the Serbs to fortify the frontier against their raids, but these too cannot be precisely dated. It was during the last of them, probably in June, 1094, and while the army was still in Thrace, that Alexios uncovered a conspiracy against his life that aimed to replace him with Nikephoros Diogenes, a born-in-the-purple son of Romanos IV. Nikephoros was a charismatic figure and had built up strong support in the army, even among the emperor's inner circle. This was a moment of crisis for the regime.[45]

Unfortunately, Anna does not tell us why so many people—both elites and soldiers—were discontent with Alexios, nor does she reveal the identities of all the plotters. Nikephoros and some of the lead conspirators, including Taronites, the emperor's brother-in-law, were exiled (Nikephoros was blinded, allegedly not on Alexios' orders). Maria of Alania was implicated and permanently sidelined, and her son, the co-emperor Konstantinos Doukas (engaged to Anna), died later that year. Alexios effectively cleared the field of Doukas competitors, opening a path to the succession for his firstborn son Ioannes II, who had been crowned co-emperor in 1092 at the age of five.[46] Loyalties were generally tested in the early 1090s. Oumbertopoulos, a pillar of the regime from the beginning, was arrested and exiled for a separate conspiracy along with many other noblemen, and the son of the *sebastokrator* Isaakios was also accused, exposing a deep rift between Isaakios and his brother, the *domestikos* Adrianos. The latter appears to have retired from politics after 1095 and died as a monk in 1105.[47] In early 1095, Alexios healed the schism in the Church by reconciling with Leon of Chalkedon and restoring him to his see.[48]

Alexios continued to claim ultra-orthodox credentials throughout his reign by harassing or even prosecuting religious dissidents and errant theologians. The latter, including the monk Neilos and the priest Theodoros Blachernites, who were spreading their (vaguely reported) heresies in Constantinople, were brought before the Synod and excommunicated. These events cannot be dated as Anna's reporting here is thematic, not chronological.[49] Blachernites was linked to a wider problem that troubled the reign, namely a proclivity toward mystical "enthusiasm" labelled "Messalianism." Its nature remains unclear: it was likely not a doctrinal heresy but a desire for personal mystical experience of ecstatic visions. This was to date not a prominent aspect of Orthodox devotion, but it had been bolstered by the powerful mystical writings of Symeon the New Theologian, a eunuch-monk who lived under Basil II. Since it was not a formal doctrine, it eluded institutional control. In 1140, the Synod condemned and burned the writings of one Konstantinos Chrysomallos, whose notions of personal spiritual rebirth have been traced to Symeon. After that, mysticism went into abeyance again for two centuries.[50]

Alexios also targeted the Bogomils and Paulicians. These groups had their own leaders and theological views that deviated from the official Church, though those views are notoriously difficult to reconstruct from Orthodox polemics, which viewed and likely distorted them as dualists (or "Manichaeans"). A group of Paulicians had been settled by Ioannes I Tzimiskes in Philippopolis to defend the mountain passes. They were tolerated by the authorities, and even enlisted in the Roman armies, until Alexios began to pressure them to convert. In 1114, he forced their leaders to debate his philosopher, Eustratios, the bishop of Nikaia. Eustratios, a student of Ioannes Italos, was one of the sharpest philosophical minds ever produced by Constantinople. In 1117, he too was condemned by the Synod for Christological errors into which his study of Hellenic philosophy had led him. He was deposed but later sponsored by Anna Komnene to write commentaries on Aristotle for her.[51] In the intellectual life of the period, theology was dominant but also dangerous for its practitioners.

The nature and origins of the Bogomils are obscure and controversial, as the evidence is poor, hostile, and unreliable. By Alexios' time, it was believed that this "Manichean" and "Messalian" heresy originated in tenth-century Bulgaria. It was a threat to the Church as its adherents dissimulated their beliefs, pretending to be Orthodox. Alexios rounded up some of their suspected proponents and personally tried to convert them, which Anna plays up as proof of his "evangelical" nature. The sect's leader, one Basileios, he burned at the stake, a rare use of this severe (but legal) punishment. Anna places all this soon before Alexios' death, but it certainly happened before 1104, as his brother Isaakios took part in the inquisition; it may even have been in the 1090s.[52] Alexios, "realizing that the virus of heresy had infected every part of the Roman domain," commissioned a heresiological manual from Euthymios Zigabenos, who presented it to him in 1115 (see Plate 6a). This *Panoply of Doctrine* discussed and refuted all heresies from antiquity down to the Bogomils, of whose downfall it offers a full account. This manual treads lightly on the "Latin errors," treating the issue of unleavened bread in connection with the Armenians only.[53] Alexios was trying to be seen as a champion of Orthodoxy, a calculated strategy likely born of insecurity.

A political motivation may also be discerned behind Alexios' benefactions to monasteries. He gave money and gifts to many of them, including supplies of food (covering the transportation costs himself), but the sums were usually small and the recipients strategically dispersed for maximum public-relations impact. His female relatives were more involved in actually founding monasteries.[54] One of his major initiatives of the early 1090s was to expand St. Paul's Orphanage, which grew into a large campus on the acropolis of the City north of Hagia Sophia. In addition to the orphanage, it housed thousands of the elderly and disabled, schools (including one for choirs), churches, and adjacent monasteries. It was endowed with a portfolio of properties (a *sekreton*) to fund its activities.[55] This foundation, along with Alexios' harassment of the heretics, led some to praise him as "Equal to the Apostles," a new Constantine the Great.[56]

Alexios did not have especially close relations with Mt. Athos. The Holy Mountain was troubled by scandal during his reign, which we know through a strange collection of letters and documents assembled decades later. There was widespread apprehension about the (forbidden) presence there of women, children, and eunuchs, especially of a Vlach community of field workers on monastic lands, whose women sometimes dressed like men and provided "services" to the monks. This led to repeated embassies of monks to the capital and confusion about who had the authority to supervise the Athonite monasteries. Alexios indulged the monks but grew impatient with their repeated visits. To one of their complaints about the children he said, "And what do you want me to do about it? I am not king Herod!"[57]

Alexios was personally shaken by the Diogenes conspiracy of 1094, but he did not make major changes in response to it or lose confidence in the army. The campaign against Serbia went forward as planned in 1094 and, the following year, the Romans defeated a large Cuman invasion in Thrace and eastern Bulgaria. That operation involved many units acting separately but in efficient coordination with each other, especially during a month-long siege of Adrianople, which means that Alexios still trusted his commanders. The Cumans had brought with them a man claiming to be yet another son of Romanos IV Diogenes. Dressed in imperial garb, he tried to persuade the provincials to accept him as emperor, which some did, but he was captured and blinded when his barbarian backers were defeated. This was the second time in recent history that a foreign enemy used a pretender to justify an invasion, and this one, unlike Robert's marionette, may have been the real thing.[58] An even more serious challenge lay just over the horizon, namely that infighting members of the Komnenian extended aristocratic coalition would call in foreign aid to advance their political fortunes. Eventually, that would bring a crusade to Constantinople's doorstep.

The First Crusade

The First Crusade was invited by Alexios himself. It was the first time in the empire's history that armies marched across it to attack a foe on the other side, a sign of the increasing complexity of the international scene. Romanía found itself in the middle of a war that western Christendom chose to wage against Islam. Anna offers the only Roman view of the passage of the First Crusade, but she gets it wrong, depicting Alexios as startled by the news of its arrival.[59] In fact, he was well prepared, and the crusaders arrived expecting him to play a lead role.

The crusading movement emerged from a confluence of different trends. One was pilgrimage from Europe to Jerusalem. The overland route was, for the most part, a journey through Romanía. In 1064/5, the long trek was made by a group of thousands of German pilgrims. They were harassed by the Pechenegs in the Balkans, honored by the emperor, and cleared to exit the empire at Laodikeia. In the early eleventh century, the detente between Romanía and the Fatimids had smoothed the subsequent journey to Palestine, but in the tumult of the Seljuk wars the Germans encountered danger after they left the empire. In 1055, the Roman governor of Laodikeia "refused an exit-visa" to bishop Lietbert of Chambrai because conditions were too dangerous. The emperors sometimes provided an escort for pilgrims to make the rest of the journey.[60] But the Turkish conquest of Asia Minor after Mantzikert and the ongoing wars in Syria and Palestine had dramatically worsened conditions for travel. The monk Christodoulos, who later founded a famous monastery on the island of Patmos, explained why he could not stay in the east in the 1080s: "that was made impossible by the Saracen swarm, which fell upon the whole of Palestine like a lethal hailstorm, disrupting and obliterating Christian society there."[61] Horror stories about Muslim atrocities against Christians began to reach the west.

The leaders of the First Crusade had family traditions of pilgrimage to Jerusalem and knowledge of east Roman affairs. Robert I, duke of Normandy, the father of William the Conqueror and grandfather of the crusader Robert II of Normandy, had been buried at Nikaia in 1035 after his pilgrimage; he had been moved to Apulia on William's orders in ca. 1086. Robert I, count of Flanders and father of the crusader count Robert II, made the pilgrimage in the late 1080s and swore an oath to Alexios upon his return, promising to send him 500 knights. The brother and predecessor of Raymond, count of Toulouse, had made the journey in 1088.[62] Another crusader, Bohemond, the son of Robert Guiscard, was all too familiar with east Roman affairs. This group, then, was not a random selection of western lords, men whom the spirit moved when pope Urban II preached his sermon across Europe in 1095–1096. They were joined by Godefroy of Bouillon, duke of lower Lorraine; his brother Baldwin of Boulogne; Étienne, count of Blois; and Hugh, a Capetian count of Vermandois.

Recent scholarship has viewed "taking up the cross" as an expression of deep personal piety and has stressed its devotional aspects. Whatever the motives that set 50,000 men into motion, that mixture of guilt, fantasy, ecstasy, and calculation had no counterpart in east Roman culture and never would. And we must not lose sight of the wider geopolitical picture, which was understood better by Muslim observers. They saw that western Europe was, long before 1095, exporting its surplus aggression in a wave of wars against Muslims in Spain, Sicily, and Asia Minor (under Roussel, in the 1070s).[63] These wars were described at the time in proto-crusading terms, and were sanctioned in increasingly formal ways by the papacy, which benefited from them in terms of both jurisdiction and income.[64] The popes had not yet figured out the role of Constantinople within their growing ambitions. In 1073, pope Gregory VII received envoys from Michael VII Doukas promising Church Union in exchange for military aid, and the pope spent a year trying to mobilize armies that he would personally lead in an attack on the Saracens in the east, inviting, among others, Raymond of Toulouse.[65]

This was the first time that Constantinople asked Rome for military assistance in exchange for Church Union, a dynamic that would recur down to 1453. But those specific plans fizzled out and in 1081 Gregory reversed course and blessed Robert's attack on Romanía.

Urban II was Gregory's right-hand man and knew this history well. Before late 1095, he was contacted by Alexios, who was seeking to hire western soldiers. These contacts are reported vaguely in the sources, which has allowed historians to imagine *either* that Alexios was shocked at the turnout—50,000 men converging on his capital "like rivers flowing together from all directions"—*or* that he and Urban had jointly organized the First Crusade.[66] Pope and emperor had exchanged embassies back in 1088–1089, seeking to downplay the causes of division between the Churches. Urban terminated Gregory VII's excommunication of Alexios (from 1081).[67] The timing of the First Crusade—precisely when Alexios had pacified the Balkans and was ready to take on the challenge of Asia Minor—also suggests coordination. Alexios was prepared to receive the crusading armies, for when they arrived his officials, supply depots, and military escorts were ready to bring them safely to Constantinople and transport them to the Asian side, where the emperor had prepared installations and translators to receive them. In all, this was a massive logistical operation that likely only Romanía could pull off,[68] and it must have required a year's notice. The emperor had also prepared his strategy for bending the western lords to his will.

The so-called People's Crusade, associated with the charismatic preacher Peter the Hermit, arrived first. It was a violent rabble that had already attacked Jewish communities in Europe. When they reached Constantinople in the summer of 1096, they caused disturbances, so Alexios ferried them to Asia but warned them not to engage with the Turks. They ignored his advice and were massacred. Most of the princes' armies crossed the Adriatic and traveled to the City along the Via Egnatia, but Godefroy de Boullion and Étienne de Blois came from the north, via Belgrade, Serdica, and Adrianople, while Raymond of Toulouse marched along the Dalmatian coast to Dyrrachion. These armies were allowed to buy supplies without being gouged and so their passage went smoothly enough, barring some flare-ups. Bohemond deviated the most from his instructions, going south from the Egnatia to plunder Kastoria and its territory, which he had done during his father's invasion in the early 1080s. He then returned to the prescribed route, shadowed closely by Alexios' Pecheneg soldiers. Bohemond's motivations were suspect. His father had disinherited him in favor of his half-brother Roger, though Bohemond had managed through two revolts to win part of Apulia, including Taranto, Otranto, Bari, and Brindisi. He was looking for opportunities to seize more. The Romans suspected that he always had his eye on Constantinople.[69]

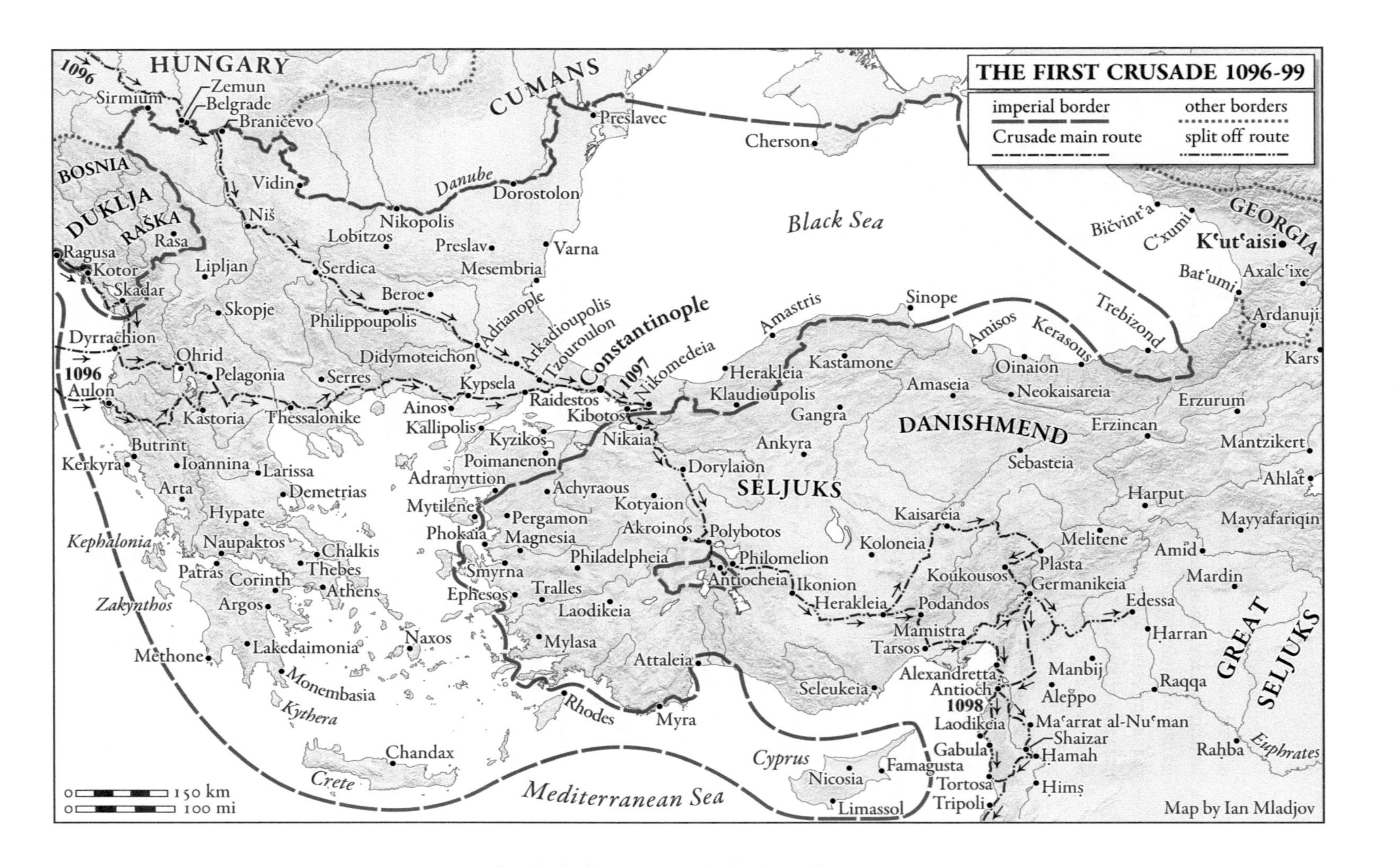
THE FIRST CRUSADE 1096-99
imperial border
other borders
Crusade main route
split off route
HUNGARY
CUMANS
BOSNIA
DUKLJA
RAŠKA
GEORGIA
DANISHMEND
SELJUKS
GREAT SELJUKS
Black Sea
Mediterranean Sea
Danube
Euphrates
1096
1097
1098
Sirmium
Zemun
Belgrade
Braničevo
Preslavec
Cherson
Vidin
Dorostolon
Nikopolis
Niš
Lobitzos
Preslav
Varna
Ragusa
Rasa
Kotor
Lipljan
Serdica
Mesembria
Skadar
Beroe
Skopje
Philippoupolis
Adrianople
Arkadioupolis
Tzouroulon
Constantinople
Dyrrachion
Ohrid
Didymoteichon
Pelagonia
Serres
Kypsela
Aulon
Raidestos
Nikomedeia
Kastoria
Thessalonike
Ainos
Kibotos
Kallipolis
Kyzikos
Nikaia
Butrint
Poimanenon
Dorylaion
Kerkyra
Ioannina
Larissa
Adramyttion
Achyraous
Arta
Demetrias
Kotyaion
Mytilene
Pergamon
Hypate
Akroinos
Polybotos
Phokaia
Magnesia
Kephalonia
Naupaktos
Chalkis
Philadelpheia
Philomelion
Thebes
Smyrna
Patras
Corinth
Antiocheia
Ikonion
Tralles
Athens
Ephesos
Zakynthos
Argos
Laodikeia
Heraklea
Podandos
Mylasa
Naxos
Mamistra
Methone
Lakedaimonia
Tarsos
Attaleia
Alexandretta
Monembasia
Seleukeia
Antioch
Kythera
Rhodes
Myra
Laodikeia
Gabula
Chandax
Cyprus
Famagusta
Crete
Nicosia
Tortosa
Limassol
Tripoli
Amastris
Sinope
Amisos
Kerasous
Trebizond
Herakleia
Kastamone
Oinaion
Klaudioupolis
Amaseia
Neokaisareia
Gangra
Ankyra
Sebasteia
Erzincan
Erzurum
Mantzikert
Ahlat
Harput
Kaisareia
Koloneia
Melitene
Mayyafariqin
Plasta
Amid
Koukousos
Germanikeia
Mardin
Edessa
Harran
Manbij
Raqqa
Aleppo
Ma'arrat al-Nu'man
Shaizar
Hamah
Hims
Rahba
Bičvint'a
C'xumi
K'ut'aisi
Bat'umi
Axalc'ixe
Ardanuji
Kars
150 km
100 mi
Map by Ian Mladjov

Alexios took advantage of the princes' staggered arrival in 1096–1097. As each arrived, his men were allowed into the City in small groups, while their lord was lavishly entertained in the palace, given impressive gifts, and pressured to swear an oath of loyalty to the emperor. Its gist was that all cities that formerly belonged to the emperors, probably as far as Antioch, would be restored to the empire, in exchange for which Alexios swore to provide all military aid and logistical assistance to the Franks. When the next lord arrived, the previous ones were there to add weight and precedent to Alexios' demand. Surprisingly, Bohemond acted energetically on Alexios' behalf and won the emperor's trust.[70] When Godefroy resisted, his supplies were withdrawn. When his men ravaged the City's suburbs, they were fired upon by men under the *kaisar* Nikephoros Bryennios (the rebel's son or grandson, Anna's husband). Godefroy submitted and took the oath in a formal ceremony.

> The emperor was seated, as was his custom, looking powerful on the throne of his sovereignty, and he did not get up to offer kisses to the duke nor to anyone, but the duke bowed down with bended knee, and his men also bowed down to kiss the exceedingly glorious and powerful emperor [who spoke], "I have heard about you that you are a very powerful knight and prince in your land, and a very wise man and completely honest. Because of this I am taking you as my adopted son, and I am putting everything I possess in your power, so that my empire and land can be freed and saved." The duke was pleased and beguiled by the emperor's peaceful and affectionate words, and he not only gave himself to him as a son, as is the custom of that land, but even as a vassal with hands joined, along with all the nobles who were there then.... And without any delay priceless gifts were taken from the emperor's treasury for the duke and all who had gathered there.[71]

Étienne de Blois wrote to his wife, the daughter of William the Conqueror, that Alexios "has no equal alive on earth today. He showers gifts on all our leaders. . . . Your father, my love, gave many great presents, but he was almost nothing in comparison with this man."[72] Yet Alexios did not distribute court titles or offices, even when Bohemond asked to be appointed *domestikos* of the east.[73]

The crusaders needed Alexios' support, and knew it in advance. "Without his aid and counsel we could not easily make the journey," as "we were about to enter a deserted and trackless land, one completely without goods of any kind," requiring "daily rations" that only he could provide.[74] Even more, the strategy that they pursued in Asia Minor was dictated by Alexios and advanced imperial interests above the goal of reaching Jerusalem. Urban II himself had intended for the crusade "to liberate the Churches of the East," including the east Romans ("Greeks"), and to secure the pilgrimage routes. No western pilgrims could be safe with Tzachas prowling the Aegean and eastern Mediterranean.[75] Alexios had promised the crusaders "that he would not permit anyone to trouble or vex our pilgrims on the way to the Holy Sepulcher," and for that he needed to reclaim Asia Minor.[76]

Alexios had once led Turks into battle against Franks; now he was leading a massive army of Franks against the Turks entrenched in Asia Minor. We know little about those Turks.[77] The most powerful group was ruled by a lateral branch of the Great Seljuks. Their chief Kilij Arslan I (1093–1107), who was based mostly at Nikaia, was the grandson of Qutlumush, the cousin and rival of Tughril Beg. His domain extended diagonally across Anatolia to Syria, but was flanked by other rulers. The Danishmend clan had established itself around 1080 in northeastern Anatolia, around Sebasteia and Koloneia, while other lords, such as Tzachas, operated along the coasts. Alexios had hired soldiers from the emirate of Nikaia to fight his Balkans wars and so had come to a provisional accommodation with it through treaties. He even granted the title of *sebastos* to one of their leaders who visited Constantinople and was entertained with races in the hippodrome. Alexios also commissioned a translation from Arabic of the popular eastern fable *Kalila wa-Dimna*; this was made by Symeon Seth, a bilingual intellectual, probably from Antioch. Seth had been injecting Arabic learning into Roman intellectual life since the 1070s, focusing on physics and medicine. The emperor wanted to access the cultural idiom of his eastern clients and attach it, as yet another appanage, to his imperial claims.[78]

Yet Alexios had also periodically tried to take Nikaia by force or buy it back from the Turks. Those efforts had failed. Elsewhere in Asia Minor he did make progress, taking back Sinope and other places along the Black Sea coast (in the late 1080s?); Kyzikos and Apollonias on the far side of the Sea of Marmara; and Nikomedeia (ca. 1090) with territory as far as the Sangarios river, whose defenses he bolstered with 500 Flemish knights.[79] Alexios' orators praised him for "restoring captured cities to the Roman state like daughters to their mother."[80]

The crusaders fully assembled only at Nikaia, which they placed under siege in May, 1097. The emperor was represented by Tatikios, while Alexios, based at Nikomedeia, ensured that they had abundant supplies. "We have spent more on them than anyone can count," he later wrote to the abbot of Monte Cassino, when he sent him some gifts.[81] Kilij Arslan rushed back from Melitene, but he was defeated by the Franks. The latter, however, could not make progress against the city, until Alexios portaged ships overland onto the lake, enabling the army to approach the city from the water. At that point the Turkish garrison surrendered, on 18 June, but only to the emperor, not the Franks. Alexios forbade the Franks from sacking the city, but appeased their leaders with gifts. The army then split into two parts. The Franks, accompanied by Tatikios, marched southeast into Asia Minor, while the Romans, under the formidable *doux* Ioannes Doukas, conquered western Asia Minor. Modern historians of the crusade usually focus exclusively on the Franks and overlook Doukas' campaign, but this was a joint operation, directed by the emperor, to restore the framework of imperial control. Doukas' brilliant campaign lasted until mid-1098, retaking Smyrna and Ephesos, then marching inland to Sardeis, Philadelpheia, Laodikeia, and Polyboton, routing the Turkish forces. The northwestern third of Asia Minor was restored to Roman rule, after a gap of almost twenty years. Alexios began to restore the thematic administration, with each theme under the command of a *doux*.[82]

Doukas was able to reach deep into Phrygia because the Franks had already passed through there in 1097, smashing the opposition. They had marched south, rather than along the more direct route east to Ankyra, probably in order to pave the way for Doukas' conquests. At Dorylaion on 1 July, 1097, Kilij Arslan had surrounded the Norman vanguard with his cavalry and came close to inflicting a defeat on them like that suffered by Romanos III Argyros at Aleppo or Romanos IV Diogenes at Mantzikert. But the French forces came to the rescue just in time and defeated the Turks. A series of losses broke Kilij Arslan's power and he withdrew into Anatolia, impeding the crusade no longer. The crusaders' journey after that need not be retold here, except to emphasize that as far as Antioch they followed established Roman strategies (probably pointed out to them by Tatikios) and were acting in the interest of the emperor, fulfilling their oath to him. This is grudgingly admitted in their accounts, which were written later in a context of increasing animosity toward the "Greeks." It is missing from Anna, because she did not understand the strategy of the campaign and some of its gains in the east proved to be short-lived, though they pointed toward a more ambitious conception. It is also absent from most modern accounts, who see the crusade exclusively through western eyes.

The crusaders were acting in the emperor's interests, as promised. Tatikios received the cities that they took on their circuitous march to Antioch, and made dispositions concerning their governance. The Franks, moreover, entered Syria from two directions, Cilicia and Kaisareia, which replicated Nikephoros Phokas' old strategy, and they made excursions to Germanikeia, Melitene, and Edessa, reconnecting those cities to the empire. They were currently ruled by Roman officers—Chalcedonians bearing imperial titles—who had survived the breakup of Philaretos Brachamios' marcher state. The framework for a reassertion of Roman authority already existed and was waiting to be activated.[83] The project began to falter when Baldwin took the city of Edessa, and then especially during the bitter siege of Antioch, from October, 1097 to June, 1098. The siege began with the intention of restoring the city to the emperor, but hardship led many Franks to believe that the emperor was not doing enough to help them (even though imperial and allied Italian ships were bringing them provisions).[84] Through intrigues that we need not scrutinize here, when Antioch fell in June,

1098 Bohemond seized the city for himself, alleging that the army had been betrayed by the emperor. Alexios, having just reconquered western Asia Minor, was at the critical moment of the siege marching east to help. But at Philomelion he was told, incorrectly, that all was lost at Antioch. He turned back, which was taken as betrayal. To justify (to themselves as much as anyone else) why they set their oaths aside, many in the army of God began to vilify Alexios and "the faithless Greeks" collectively. The emperor's role had been "pivotal," but the crusaders' debt to him later became embarrassing and so they reviled him viciously.[85]

Bohemond's perfidy was unsurprising. The career of his entire family had been premised on carving lordships out of the eastern Roman empire. He had no interest in Jerusalem, preferring instead to seize the *doukaton* of Antioch. It was perhaps too much to expect that the Franks would hand Antioch over after all that they endured before its walls, but to stake his claim Bohemond had to deceive his fellow crusaders too, which sowed dissension among them. Alexios was also uninterested in Jerusalem, prioritizing the safety of his own realm, as his Frankish critics complained.[86] Thus, the army of God fell to pieces as soon as it ceased to be under imperial direction. It was only a year later, in 1099, that some of its leaders scraped parts of it together and marched on Jerusalem, where they satiated their bloodlust and established a kingdom. Their success was due to their resolve but also to factors they could not have anticipated. The Seljuk world had fragmented into many local principalities that were not inclined to help each other, and all the major players—including the sultan Malik Shah, his vizier Nizam al-Mulk, as well as the Abbasid and Fatimid caliphs—had recently died. A later Muslim historian called it "the year of the death of caliphs and commanders,"[87] and it allowed the crusaders to slip through in all the chaos. Later crusades would not be so lucky.

The passage of the First Crusade was a tense experience for the Romans but had been tremendously advantageous, allowing the emperor to retake western Asia Minor. All things considered, it was ably handled by Alexios, who managed to assert himself as the crusaders' "father,"[88] at least for as long as they were in his realm. His gains altered the empire's strategic orientation. It now had a long and hazy land frontier with the Turks cutting diagonally across Asia Minor. It also had Franks to cope with in both west and east, and Romanía sat astride the routes that linked Europe to its acquisitions in Outremer. This was both a challenge and an asset. Would the emperor be regarded by the crusading Latins as a benevolent and generous ally or as an obstacle to their goals, a devious conniver and secret friend of the Muslims? Competing images emerged in the aftermath of the First Crusade, with Bohemond and many others spreading hostile views in the west, where many were already receptive to that message, while the emperor used the charm offensive of personal diplomacy and the wonders of Constantinople in order to recruit goodwill ambassadors in the west, whom he plied with gold, gifts, and titles. Alexios also ransomed many Franks from captivity to drive the message of his benevolence home.[89]

These competing images were put to the test when more western pilgrims and crusaders arrived, with mixed results. A second wave converged on the capital in 1101, for which Alexios used the same playbook: supplies at fair prices, oaths, gifts, and transport to Asia with a military escort. The Lombard contingent in the vanguard pillaged Bulgaria, and some broke into the palace at Blachernai, killing one of Alexios' relatives and his pet lion. The passage of armies was bound to cause such friction and leave bad feelings. But this wave also captured Ankyra and "restored it to the emperor's soldiers, because it was part of his kingdom and he had lost it by the Turks' unlawful invasion."[90] Yet the crusaders of 1101 made little effort to coordinate their movements, so they were cut down piecemeal by the Turks. Kilij Arslan had joined forces with the Danishmends and successfully applied tactics of encirclement, starvation, and ambush. Subsequent crusades would reveal that the success of the first had been a fluke, and despite the emperor's efforts many in the west blamed him for these failures and spread rumors that he was cynically feeding Christians to the Turks. This lie soon became a known fact, as it fit prevailing prejudices about "the Greeks," and it shaped accounts of the First Crusade into a "systematic defamation" of the empire.[91]

Alexios enjoyed public relations successes too. Some crusader lords, such as Raymond of Toulouse, became ardent champions of his cause, checking in with Constantinople before his every move, while others were equally captivated. The first pilgrim-king to pass through, in 1103, was Erik I of Denmark, whom Alexios honored in the palace; he died on Cyprus en route to Jerusalem. He was followed in 1111 by Sigurd I of Norway, whose longships had sailed through Gibraltar and across the Mediterranean. He returned to the north via Constantinople, where he was lavishly entertained. The king left many of his men to serve in the Varangian Guard as well as his dragon-headed ships, and Alexios put their prows on display before a church. In the Icelandic sagas, service in the Guard and gifts from the king of Miklagarðr—the "Great City"—were marks of great prestige.[92]

Between Franks and Turks

Alexios was unwilling to renounce his claim to the cities of the Roman east, especially Antioch. His fleet controlled the naval base of Attaleia on the southern coast of Asia Minor, though probably not much of its hinterland, as well as Cyprus. From there, in the chaotic years 1099–1104, he sent forces to take Cilicia from Seleukeia on the coast to Germanikeia inland, and Laodikeia on the Syrian coast, though Germanikeia and Laodikeia changed hands often in the years to come. Cilicia was now a militarized outpost facing Bohemond at Antioch. Yet by a stroke of luck Bohemond was captured by the Danishmends and held for three years (1100–1103), although his territorial claims were, during his absence, aggressively defended by his nephew, the irrepressible Tancred.

Another danger that emerged was the Italian fleets, especially of Pisa and Genoa, profiting from the crusader states' need for supplies and transport. As they were drawn into the complex politics of Outremer, they began to attack Roman islands (Kerkyra, Kephalonia) along the way. Venice, by contrast, remained loyal to its alliance with the empire. The imperial fleet under the *megas doux* Landulf (an Italian) and Tatikios had to patrol the seas and chase the other Italians away.[93]

Alexios, now in the third decade of his reign, was increasingly relying on the next generation of leaders, including Eumathios Philokales (*doux* of Cyprus), Kantakouzenos, Manuel Boutoumites, and Monastras (a half-barbarian). The first generation of Komnenoi brothers had mostly retired, and the next, their sons, were not yet ready for active duty. Anna Dalassene retired from the palace toward the end of the 1090s and died ca. 1101 in a convent, a year or two before the death of Alexios' brother, the *sebastokrator* Isaakios. The *kaisar* Melissenos died in 1104.[94] A generation that remembered the apogee of empire in the eleventh century was passing away. Around 1102, another conspiracy against Alexios was uncovered. A number of generals led by the Anemas brothers—descendants of the last emir of Arab Crete—plotted with some senators to murder the emperor and replace him with one of their own. The emperor's daughter, Anna, who was around twenty at the time, intervened to spare Michael Anemas from blinding. She provides an eyewitness account of the "parade of infamy" to which the plotters were subjected. Their heads and beards were shaved off and sheep guts were placed on them like crowns, and then they were paraded through the City seated sideways on cows, while people ridiculed them with bawdy poems.[95]

Alexios had lobbied hard to ransom Bohemond from the Danishmends, offering 260,000 nomismata, but they set him free in exchange for only 100,000 from his supporters, believing that he would cause trouble between Franks and Romans.[96] Bohemond was at a disadvantage in facing the Romans in Cilicia and Syria. He was nearer and could beat them in battle, but they had more money, their own fleet, and could send reinforcements and wait him out. He resolved on a characteristically bold plan. In 1105–1106, he traveled to Italy and France, spreading lies about "the Greeks" and drumming up forces for a war against them that followed in the footsteps of his father's campaign in the 1080s. Philippe I of France gave him his daughter in marriage. Many who signed up for this war believed that it was a crusade, for Bohemond presented it as such and pope Paschal II blessed it. At stake for Rome was also the extension of ecclesiastical control. Alexios was installing Greek-rite bishops in the areas that he reconquered, whereas the crusaders were installing Latin ones. At Antioch, they first retained the patriarch Ioannes Oxeites—he who had scolded Alexios in 1091—out of respect for the tortures he had endured at the hands of the Turks, but they soon replaced him with a Latin.[97] As for Bohemond, his goal was Constantinople itself, for, like his father before him, he brought with him a pretender to its throne, yet another alleged son of Romanos IV Diogenes.[98] He spent the year 1106–1107 preparing his forces in Apulia, though we lack reliable evidence for their size. In October he crossed the Adriatic and besieged Dyrrachion, which was commanded by the emperor's nephew, Alexios Komnenos, son of Isaakios *sebastokrator*.

But the emperor Alexios was now twenty years wiser. He had spent two years building up and training his army, mostly at Thessalonike, and was under no political pressure to secure a quick victory. Dyrrachion's defenses withstood the Norman siege engines and Greek fire repelled some of them. In early 1108, Alexios blockaded the invading army both by land and sea, killing foragers, guarding the passes, and starving the enemy. There were other ways to win, opined Anna, than by drawing the sword. Defectors were rewarded with gifts and titles. Dissension was sown in the Norman camp by leaking forged letters that implicated leading knights in collusion with the emperor, and units that Bohemond sent into the surrounding country were checked.[99] In September 1108, Bohemond surrendered and agreed to sign the Treaty of Devol (Diabolis), which Anna quotes verbatim to mark her father's crowning victory over the arrogant Frank. The treaty was cast partly in western feudal terms, and was ironclad. Bohemond pledged to be a "liege man" of Alexios and his son Ioannes II, and to fight against their enemies. He would keep Antioch, Germanikeia, and their territories during his own lifetime, but then they would revert to the emperor. Antioch's patriarch would be appointed by the emperor and "not be a man of our race." At Edessa Bohemond could leave a successor, but Cilicia and Laodikeia would immediately go to Alexios. He received the title of *sebastos* and an annuity of 200 lbs of gold to be paid in 1070s-era coins. Bohemond's signing was witnessed by Alexios' western allies and retainers to drive it home that the emperor's authority extended over Latins too. It was a humiliation for the Norman, to be sure, but sweetened with favorable terms.[100]

In the past, Bohemond had broken his agreement through his actions; this time, he did so through inaction. He returned to Apulia and stayed there until his death in 1111. His deputy in Antioch, Tancred, disregarded the treaty. No part of it was ever put into effect; Cilicia and Laodikeia were, for now, lost. Yet Alexios spent the next few years building up an alliance to enforce his legal claims in the region. In 1110, the Pisans swore vassal allegiance to the emperor and, in 1111, he granted to them concessions similar (but not as wide-ranging) as those of the Venetians, including a wharf and establishment to the east of the Venetians' in the City; a tax reduction on trade (4% instead of 10%); and reserved seats in Hagia Sophia and the hippodrome. In return, they vowed to be "loyal to Romanía" in its wars.[101] Alexios also began to dangle the carrot of Church Union before the eyes of pope Paschal II, which was now a standard tactic in the diplomatic repertoire of Constantinople. In 1112, Alexios presided over a debate on the *filioque* involving a former bishop of Milan on the Latin side and Eustratios of Nikaia and others on the Greek side. Theophylaktos, bishop of Ohrid and former court orator, wrote a treatise on the "errors of the Latins," arguing that most of them, such as their shaving and unleavened bread, were trivial differences of custom. The *filioque* was an inexcusable addition to the creed, but surely it would quickly be removed from the Latin text.[102]

Alexios deferred action in Cilicia and Syria in order to focus on Asia Minor. For a generation, its population had known only invasion and occupation by the Turks, with whom they had reached various forms of coerced accommodation. In addition to the west, Alexios managed to reclaim the coasts along the Black Sea in the north and Lykia in the south, but all places needed to invest now in defense. The landscape around Miletos "rapidly became dotted with agricultural towers and fortified farmhouses."[103] The frontier between the Romans and the Turks was an irregular series of passes and valleys between Phrygia and the central Anatolian plateau, and they too needed to be fortified and even reclaimed from local Romans who tried to be independent of both sides.[104] Some settlements in between, such as Amorion, were largely abandoned, their inhabitants probably moving west into the liberated Roman provinces. Back in 1098, Alexios had evacuated the population around Philomelion when he departed from there.[105] The legal system struggled for decades to match owners and displaced peoples with the properties that they had lost to "the barbarian sword."[106]

For a decade after the First Crusade, the Seljuks were preoccupied with the Franks, with rival Muslim powers in the east, and with their own internal disputes after the death of Kilij Arslan in 1107. Starting around 1109, they began to raid the Roman provinces again, often coming from Lykaonia and then fanning out in separate parties. These groups were chased down and usually defeated by the local governors, such as Eumathios Philokales (ca. 1109) and Konstantinos Gabras (ca. 1111). Eustathios Kamytzes was defeated and captured in ca. 1113, whereupon Alexios, who by this point in his life was suffering from gout, rushed to Bithynia and defeated the raiders. It was probably these wars, which are narrated by Anna, that scotched the Cilician project. In 1116, in response to a flurry of raids Alexios resolved to attack the capital of the sultanate, Ikonion (Konya). His forces reached as far as Amorion and Philomelion, but pushing forward was impractical, so they evacuated thousands of provincial Romans and marched back, enclosing the evacuees within a square formation while the Turks shot at them from a distance, howled at night, and lit fires. But all attacks were repulsed. Anna offers a striking image of this city on the move, which halted when women gave birth or to bury the dead. After this harrowing experience, Alexios and the sultan Shahinshah met and concluded a peace treaty.[107]

Alexios died on 15 August, 1118, in his early sixties. He had governed the empire for as long as Justinian and Basil II. Whereas Justinian found it strong and left it weak, and Basil had found it strong and made it stronger, Alexios found the empire on the verge of collapse and renewed it so that, under the reigns of his son and grandson, it could emerge again as a great power. Basil boasted in his epitaph that he patrolled the borders and conquered foreign nations, but Alexios, in a poem written for his son, is represented as desperately defending an empire assailed on all sides by "nations on the move."[108] He realized that the world was changing and the Romans had to build alliances and win over friends in order to survive. In this he was largely successful. Bountiful generosity helped, as did the fact that he did not keep grudges. He was secretive and better at winning through stratagems than pitched battles.[109]

International marriage ties were another instrument of Alexios' diplomacy. In 1104, he married his heir Ioannes II to Piroska, the daughter of the king (and later saint) Władysław I of Hungary (see Plate 6b). She was renamed Eirene after her mother-in-law and produced heirs (the twins Alexios and Maria) as early as 1106. Alexios had thus presided over the two first generations of Komnenoi in power, and by the time of his death the third was in adolescence. He personally arranged the marriages of his kin, including of his siblings' children, because the affairs of the Komnenoi were now effectively matters of state.[110] It is often said that during his reign the Roman republic became more like a family-run business. There is some truth in this. The impersonal character of the state, whose top positions had been staffed for almost a millennium by unrelated men of provincial origin, partly made way for a dynastic conception, in which social and political power belonged to an extended family network and its clients. The historian Ioannes Zonaras, a retired member of the bureaucratic class that was pushed down the political ladder by the rise of the Komnenoi, articulated a forceful critique of this transformation. Alexios himself, he says, was a good man, however

> an emperor must maintain the ancient orders of the polity. But Alexios . . . approached political affairs not as public matters of common interest, with himself as their trustee, but rather as their owner, treating matters of the monarchy as his own private household. . . . But when it came to his relatives and his retainers, he enriched them with cartloads of public money and bestowed on them hefty annual outlays. They became so rich that they surrounded themselves with retinues appropriate not to private citizens but to emperors, and they acquired manors as large as whole cities.[111]

It is often said that the Komnenian revolution represented the victory of the military aristocracy over the Roman state itself, but this is misleading. What happened instead was that one faction of the military aristocracy—the Komneno-Doukes—managed to survive the catastrophic losses that followed Mantzikert by grafting themselves onto the Roman state; their ascendancy came at the expense of the rest of the aristocracy, the Church, and the monasteries, many of whose lands Alexios had to confiscate. Alexios had reformed the currency, fiscal administration, system of court titles, judiciary, and army. He did this incrementally over a forty-year period, lurching in a stepwise fashion to meet the crisis of the moment. There was no revolutionary plan here. The family aspect of the regime grew under his son and grandson. It worked well as the basis of government for as long as they could tame their kin. After them, however, the flaws inherent in the Komnenian system brought down the entire polity.

Even so, Alexios' reign was a turning point. It was perhaps fitting that during it, in 1106, a gale finally toppled the colossal statue of Constantine-Apollo from the porphyry column in the forum, the City's symbolic focal point. That monument, which had survived fires and lightning, was a relic from a wildly different era. It was replaced with a cross by Manuel Komnenos.[112]

29

Good John and the Sun King (1118–1180)

The Komnenoi had more offspring than any other Roman dynasty. Their princes, princelings, princesses, and in-laws filled up the court, claiming the top positions and constituting an aristocracy that diminished the opportunities of provincial elites. Factions now formed around competing branches of the ruling clan, and politics was increasingly dominated by intra-family squabbles.

Ioannes II Komnenos

Toward the end of Alexios' reign, his empress Eirene favored the *kaisar* Nikephoros Bryennios (married to her daughter Anna) over her son Ioannes II, the designated heir, who was thirty-one (see Plate 6b). In his final years, Alexios started bringing Eirene with him on campaign. Anna claims that it was because of mutual affection, but lack of trust is possible. The transition was tense. Ioannes had to leave Alexios' side as he lay dying in the Mangana palace in order to secure the Great Palace, "to which he clung like an octopus on the rocks," even skipping the funeral. Alexios was buried at the monastery of Christ Philanthropos that he had founded. Meanwhile, Ioannes rallied his supporters, who included his brother Isaakios, now a *sebastokrator*, and Axouch, a Turk captured as a boy at the siege of Nikaia in 1097 and raised with Ioannes as a playmate; he was now made *megas domestikos*. Within a year the family tensions flared up again and Ioannes temporarily confiscated the properties of Bryennios and Anna. It was a later historian, Niketas Choniates, who made Anna the lead conspirator in order to highlight the unnatural character of Komnenian infighting; he even makes Anna reproach Nature for giving the penis to her husband rather than herself.[1] But the siblings were later reconciled. Anna, honored as a "tenth Muse" for her learning, was barred from meeting with powerful men but she did patronize an impressive group of scholars. Where she differed from Ioannes and, later, his son Manuel, was over policy: in contrast to them, she was anti-Latin and more pro-Turkish, a rift within the Roman leadership that had emerged in the 1070s and would continue to the end.[2]

Ioannes spent most of his long reign on campaign, "living in a tent away from the palace."[3] His wars were successful but resulted in few permanent gains. They were described in a perfunctory way by later historians, Kinnamos and Choniates, who name few of Ioannes' generals and omit campaigns that did not involve the emperor himself. They praised Ioannes but were more interested in his flamboyant successor. He thus remains an obscure figure.

Ioannes' focus was overwhelmingly on central Asia Minor, "to recuperate for the Romans lands and cities occupied by the Turks," to "restore populations long enslaved by the Persians [i.e., Turks]," and "to liberate cities of the Romans from bitter barbaric slavery."[4] Some lasting success was achieved in 1119–1120, when Ioannes opened the corridor between the Maeander valley and Attaleia in the south, taking Laodikeia and Sozopolis in Phrygia-Pisidia. In subsequent campaigns, he also pushed in the north against the Danishmends, who occasionally raided into Romanía. Kastamone in Paphlagonia changed hands often in the 1130s. Gangra was taken by the emperor in ca. 1134, then lost again. In 1139–1140, he advanced along the Black Sea coast all the way to Trebizond, a quasi-independent marcher state under Konstantinos Gabras, and he subjugated it and besieged Neokaisareia but departed before it fell. In sum, the Turks were firmly entrenched. Even when Ioannes defeated them, they regrouped when he left. The frontier that he defined around Attaleia and in Paphlagonia proved durable, though it required militarizing the interior. In ca. 1134, he made an alliance with the Turks of Ikonion (Konya) against the Danishmends, "knowing that he was no match for their combined forces," but it quickly fell apart.[5]

Not all Romans in Asia Minor wanted to be liberated. In 1141, Ioannes found that those of lake Beyşehir (near Konya) sided with the Turks against him. Sixty years after the conquests, they regarded the Turks as friends, neighbors, and trading partners. As Choniates famously put it, "time and custom had prevailed over race and religion."[6] The Seljuks were already laying down the foundations of a distinctive civilization of their own in the interior, one that mixed Turkish, Iranian, and Roman elements. By the mid-twelfth century, their leaders called themselves the sultans of the land of Rum, although this was only one part of their title and not the most common one, and the Danishmends also claimed to rule Rum, or a part of it.[7] As many ethnic Romans were ruled by Turkish leaders in Asia Minor and by Normans in Italy and Sicily as by the basileus himself.

In the west, Ioannes initially refused to confirm the privileges that his father had granted to the Venetians. When they sent a fleet in 1122 to aid in the crusader siege of Tyre, it wintered at Kerkyra against the locals' wishes and then attacked many Aegean islands along its return in 1124, taking captives in order to pressure the emperor to renew their privileges. Ioannes did so in August 1126. This was the second time that Romanía was attacked by a foreign power that hoped for trading concessions (the first was by Simeon of Bulgaria in the 890s). Venice was gradually regarded less as a junior partner of empire and more a predatory business associate who also slandered the "faithless" Greeks, despite having won the concessions. Its doge, Domenico Michiel, boasted on his epitaph that he was "the terror of the Greeks."[8]

The empire was increasingly vulnerable to seaborn attack, and Choniates accused Ioannes of skimping on naval expenditures on the advice of his finance minister, Ioannes of Poutzes, though evidence has turned up that he did build military ships and trained their crews in the late 1130s.[9] But on land the empire's defenses were ironclad. In ca. 1122, at a great battle near Beroe (Stara Zagora) Ioannes defeated the last great Pecheneg invasion from across the Danube. He settled some of the survivors in the western provinces, where "over time, they adapted to Roman ways and enlisted in the army." When Ioannes later defeated some Serb marauders, he resettled them by Nikomedeia to work the land and provide recruits.[10] He also faced a Hungarian invasion. The Hungarians were by now no longer marauders but a duly constituted Christian realm fully enmeshed in European diplomatic wrangling. Ioannes himself was married to a daughter of the Hungarian king Władysław I (1077–1095). King István II (1116–1131) was bellicose, but he accomplished little through his wars. He invaded Romanía in 1127 because a rival for the throne, his uncle Álmos (who had been blinded), had sought refuge there. The Hungarians advanced via Belgrade, Niš, and Serdica, and reached as far as Philippopolis, where they were repelled by Ioannes. The following year, Ioannes chased them back to the Danube and defeated them near the fort of Haram (Bačka Palanka in Serbia). The Romans fortified and occupied Braničevo. Skirmishing along the border continued until a treaty was signed in 1129.[11]

The Komnenian curse of infighting struck again in 1130 when the emperor's brother, the *sebastokrator* Isaakios, and his partisans seized the moment when Ioannes was absent on campaign to conspire against him. Ioannes rushed back to the capital to restore order and exile the plotters, but Isaakios and his son fled to the east. For eight years they roamed from court to court—Turkish, Latin, Armenian, and even the splinter Roman state of Trebizond before its reconquest—trying to stir up war against Ioannes. The latter had long since designated his son Alexios as his co-emperor (born in 1106, elevated by 1122), but Isaakios seems to have been motivated by a conceited sense of entitlement to the throne and did not balk at treason to attain it. In later times, after his return, he pointedly did not use his title of *sebastokrator* and used *porphyrogennetos* instead, associating himself, just like Anna, more with their father Alexios I than the current emperor. As the succession was moving inexorably away from them, the two siblings seem almost to have been pretending that 1118 had not happened.[12]

To bolster his popularity after another conspiracy in the capital in favor of Isaakios, in 1133 Ioannes revived the tradition of the triumph, celebrating one of his victories over the Turks. It deviated from tradition in starting not at the Golden Gate but on the seaward side of the City's acropolis, where Nikephoros II Phokas had placed the city gates of Tarsos. The celebration thus alluded back to the years of conquest, and Ioannes followed the example of Ioannes I Tzimiskes by placing an icon of the Virgin in the chariot, while he walked in front of it to Hagia Sophia. We have four poems for the occasion by Theodoros Prodromos, one of the most versatile writers of the era, who praised the emperor on behalf of

"Rome" and described the festivities: "The first to march in were the armed men of Ares . . . there followed a host of barbarian women, seated on horseback, each with her child."[13]

The Komnenoi were also endowing the City with prestigious monasteries. Adjacent to Alexios I's monastery of Christ Philanthropos, his wife Eirene built a convent for twenty-four nuns in honor of the Theotokos Kecharitomene ("Full of Grace"). Its leadership, she stipulated, should pass from her to Anna, and then to Anna's daughters, and so on. Aristocratic genealogies were making inroads into the monastic world, especially as one of the functions of these establishments was to offer prayers on behalf of the souls of designated family members. The convent's grounds included abutting apartments that Anna and other secular members of the family and visitors could use. Not far from the Holy Apostles and the old imperial mausoleum, Ioannes and Piroska-Eirene built the large Pantokrator monastery for eighty monks on a hill overlooking the Golden Horn (see Figure 45).

The Pantokrator featured a trio of interlinked churches in which the imperial couple intended to be buried, one of them being the largest of the cross-in-square type. It was completed in 1136, two years after Eirene's death, so its long *Typikon* was issued in Ioannes' name. The *Typikon* has drawn attention because of its detailed provisions for a hospital to operate on the grounds along with a home for the elderly and a leprosarium at a removed location. The hospital had fifty beds where patients

Figure 45 Pantokrator churches, Constantinople
Shutterstock/stocktr

of all social classes would be cared for by physicians with specialized tools, all paid for by the foundation's substantial endowments. Provisions were even made for full-time female doctors, who were paid 3/4 of their male counterparts' salary. No society had yet conceived an institution that resembled a modern hospital more than this, or endowed it so lavishly, though there were east Roman precedents. In the preamble, Ioannes referred to friends and relatives who "wickedly stood against me." Anna and Isaakios are excluded from the list of the commemorated, although another sister and even the *kaisar* Bryennios were included. Conversely, Anna herself excluded Ioannes from the list of emperors for whom she mourned, though that list included Bryennios, who was liked by everyone. Meanwhile, in the original arrangements that he made for his own burial, at the Chora monastery in Constantinople that he refurbished, Isaakios depicted his parents next to himself. These three siblings were, in different ways, competing over Alexios' mantle.[14]

Most of Ioannes' wars targeted the Danishmends in northern Asia Minor, but by the mid-1130s his failure to make gains was apparent. He thus turned his attention to Cilicia and Antioch, as the crusader forces there had been weakened and dealt a series of defeats, and Ioannes held the title to Antioch from the Treaty of Devol. In 1135, he tried but failed to arrange a marriage between his youngest son Manuel and Constance, the heiress of the principality of Antioch. To prepare for war, he first insured his western flank against attack by the newly self-proclaimed Norman king of Sicily, Roger II, who also claimed Antioch. Ioannes made an alliance with the German emperor Lothar III, who was also at odds with Roger. Lothar sent Anselm, bishop of Havelberg, to Constantinople, where, in 1136, he engaged in an (apparently cordial) discussion of the *filioque* and papal supremacy with Niketas of Nikomedeia. Anselm was hopeful that many differences could be put down to linguistic misunderstandings and cleared up.[15]

In 1137, Cilicia was divided between the Franks of Antioch and Edessa and Lewon, leader of the Armenian Rubenid dynasty that had established itself in the mountains and part of the plain of Cilicia. The Armenian presence went back to the migration that began during the eleventh century and had been facilitated, or at least allowed, by the emperors. In the chaos of the Seljuk conquests, the Armenians had established a number of principalities in the mountains but they were always eager to extend their power into the plain, as Lewon had done now. In the spring of that year, Ioannes marched from the Roman outpost of Seleukeia and quickly overran the Cilician plain, taking Tarsos, Adana, Mopsouestia, and Anazarbos away "from the Celtic and Armenian barbarians," as one panegyrist put it.[16] He installed garrisons and Greek bishops. Some of Ioannes' subjects expected him to take Antioch and possibly Aleppo and Damascus as well. This anticipation is revealed in a letter by a Jewish physician of Seleukeia, written in Arabic but with Hebrew letters. He was married to a Roman woman, was evidently prosperous, and referred to the army as "our commanders."[17]

Ioannes marched on to Antioch, which was governed by Raymond, a son of the duke of Aquitaine who had married the heiress Constance. The two men came to an agreement: Raymond would become a vassal of the emperor, Antioch would revert to the empire, but in exchange Ioannes would conquer and give to him Aleppo, Homs, and Shaizar (Larissa). The imperial standard was raised over the citadel of Antioch, though Ioannes did not yet enter the city and spent the winter in Cilicia. In 1138, the allied army marched on Aleppo and Shaizar, but failed to take them and returned to Antioch, although it had pulled in a rich haul of plunder. Ioannes, his sons, and the Roman army entered the city in a spectacular *adventus*, but when he demanded its surrender, the Franks balked at turning it over "to the effeminate Greeks." They instigated a popular uprising by spreading a rumor that the emperor was planning to deport the population. The city had been outside of effective Roman rule for over sixty years, and had been ruled by the Franks for almost forty. A realignment of local interests had evidently occurred during that time. Ioannes prudently withdrew to Cilicia and then Constantinople, not because he could not take the city by force—the Franks "were no match for the Roman army"—but because he did not want to instigate a broader war with the west.[18] He had taken the Cilician plain, which was enough.

War with the west was always a present danger. In March 1138, pope Innocent II had condemned Ioannes—calling him "the king of Constantinople"—for "disobedience" to Rome in his effort to reclaim Antioch, and he called on all Christians to dissociate from his service. The pope was probably most concerned about losing the patriarchate of Antioch, but these threats had teeth because the papacy had already learned to "brand its enemies as fit targets for holy war."[19] In his responses to Rome, Ioannes dangled "Church Union" as a carrot, implying that the two Churches were in a state of schism, though neither side explained when it had begun or why. The emperor's letters, which survive, were deluxe artifacts, with gold lettering on purple parchment, and were accompanied by Latin translations that showcased the eastern court's mastery of the western lingua franca.[20] The German alliance against Roger II was also renewed, even though Germany was no longer at war with Sicily. In 1140, the emperor's son Manuel was betrothed to Bertha of Sulzbach, sister-in-law of the German king Konrad III Hohenstaufen. Imperial princes, including Ioannes' heir Alexios, were married to foreign princesses from Georgia, Russia, and the west more frequently than ever before. This reflected an awareness of the multipolar world in which the empire now operated.[21] Moreover, Isaakios *sebastokrator*, the black sheep of the family, had returned to the fold in ca. 1137, after peregrinations in the east that had taken him as far as Jerusalem. Ioannes' successes made opposition to him futile, and the two were reconciled.

In 1142, after two years of campaigning in north and central Asia Minor, Ioannes marched back to Antioch and again demanded its surrender. Allegedly, he wanted to bundle Attaleia, Cyprus, Cilicia, and Antioch into "a semi-independent daughter state" for his son Manuel.[22] But everything changed during that winter while the emperor was in Cilicia and the negotiations dragged on. His son and heir Alexios died on 2 August, 1142, as did the next eldest son, Andronikos, who was sent to escort the body to Constantinople. Ioannes II was mortally wounded in a hunting accident on 1 April, 1143, and, before he died a week later, he designated Manuel, not his eldest surviving son Isaakios, as his heir. At twenty-five, Manuel was duly acclaimed emperor by the army.

For twenty-five years, Ioannes II ensured peace and a return to prosperity for many of his subjects. He was later remembered as Kaloiannes, or Good John, but also John the Moor because of his dark skin, a trait he passed on to Manuel.[23] He spent most of his reign on campaign, extending his dominion in Phrygia and the Pontos and fortifying the upland frontier against Danishmend and Seljuk raids. Those raids were a serious problem. Attaleia had to import food by sea because "the enemy" hindered the cultivation of its fertile hinterland. But our Jewish physician in nearby Seleukeia invited his Egyptian contact to emigrate to the land of the Romans: "you will not regret it. . . . I have built a house, and have 400 barrels of wine."[24]

Komnenian economy and administration

Ioannes and Manuel Komnenos seem never to have been short of cash, and Manuel in particular was famous for his extraordinary liberality. Allegedly he spent over 2 million gold coins on a failed invasion of Italy in the 1150s, a sum that, if true, exceeded the entire annual budget of the eighth-century empire. Yet its loss did not cause a fiscal crisis.[25] The Roman economy remained monetized, and its currency was regarded as a standard unit of value across the Mediterranean, the "dollar" of the Middle Ages, as it has been called. The treasury was clearly benefiting from demographic and economic growth, as well as the stability that Alexios had restored after so many wars. In Asia Minor the Romans had lost the more pastoral uplands but they recovered the agricultural and more urbanized western plains along the coasts. According to the state's tax offices, the land in western Anatolia was 30% more productive than that in the interior.[26]

Meanwhile, the Balkan provinces, which Constantinople called "the west," had emerged as the new economic powerhouse. Survey archaeology has revealed a great expansion of settlements in Greece, a region that had been untouched by war for a century. Athens now had at least forty recently-built churches, and Corinth and Thebes were booming centers of production and trade in wine, oil, and silk. With harbors on either side of the Isthmos, Corinth linked east-west trade routes. Ceramic containers from Greece, including some of high quality intended for a more refined market, are found throughout the empire as well as in the Near East and Italy. The trade concessions to the Italian cities stimulated production in the Balkan provinces because they enabled local producers to sell to larger markets than before. Italian merchant colonies and waystations included few people, but they were ubiquitous in coastal towns and outlets.[27] This perhaps explains why we see more prosperity in the regions closer to the sea. The picture was more complicated in the mountainous interior. In many places the Vlachs were basically autonomous and sometimes had to be suppressed by force. "Bulgaria" was considered pacified by conceited Roman writers, who compared it to a relatively prosperous farm of tamed animals. But the northern reaches of the Pindos mountains were described as largely uninhabited by many authors, and the emperors kept a depopulated zone along the frontier with Serbia and Hungary to discourage invasions.[28]

In many regions, the state outsourced the collection of taxes to officials who received land concessions. As a result, some tax revenue did not go back to the center but directly supported the regional branch office of the Komnenian administration; salaries were exchanged for tax concessions and exemptions. A legal writer at the end of the twelfth century, Theodoros Balsamon, wrote that the emperors had ceased to pay their high officials in person at a public ceremony during the reign of Konstantinos X Doukas, and that the practice was "lost to oblivion," unless one dug up old documents and learned about it. The advantages and drawbacks of the new system are still debated, though our understanding of it is murky, especially as every individual arrangement differs in its details.[29] Groaning about oppressive tax collection was common under the Komnenoi, and we hear it again from Greece in the late 1130s in an oration praising the governor for slapping down the taxman's greedy hands. At least they turned to imperial officials for recourse against the problems that the administration itself was causing.[30]

Choniates claims that Manuel used the concession system on a widespread scale to support individual soldiers. Specifically, he would assign the revenues due from those who farmed state lands (henceforth called *paroikoi*) to a soldier who would, on behalf of the state, receive their dues and services. This arrangement is called a *pronoia* ("forethought" or "solicitude," i.e., for the soldier), and its beneficiary is called a pronoiar. This was a financial instrument and not a social arrangement: the state merely allocated its dues from the land (taxes, rents, or services) to its beneficiary, but the lands continued to belong to their legal owners. The pronoiar did not necessarily even live anywhere near them. No comparison to western feudalism is warranted. These grants could be, and often were, reassigned by the authorities. We cannot assess how widely this instrument was implemented, and its pros and cons are debated. Choniates protested that, with their needs met, soldiers were not incentivized to perform well to earn their pay, and he objected to the fiscal subordination of "proud Roman peasants" to foreign soldiers who were "half-barbarian runts."[31] This system of pronoias and concessions was less consistent and uniform than what it replaced, for tax collecting was now carried out locally by a variety of non-professionals, which made the system feel unfair. It is unclear why the Komnenoi favored this decentralization of fiscal authority.

We are poorly informed about the Roman army of the Komnenoi. Native recruits from the Balkans probably accounted for the majority of its soldiers; they are called Macedonians, Thracians, and Thessalians in the sources. It is possible that some of the military lands still survived, along with their service obligations, while the rest had been fiscalized, paying cash to the state or to pronoiars. Foreign units—such as Varangians, Pechenegs, and Latins, "each with their own type of weapon"—were typically distinguished from native Romans and formed a large part of the army, possibly a greater proportion than before. The Komnenoi would often settle defeated foreign invaders on imperial lands and then recruit them.[32]

Komnenian literature

Meanwhile, under Alexios and Ioannes the foundations were being laid for a remarkable flowering of literature. In part, this was promoted by the Komnenian regime itself, and its appetite for panegyric. As praises had to be sung in an aristocratic and martial mode, panegyrists relied on classical language and imagery, as we see in Prodromos' verse praises of Ioannes. Likewise, in a work whose title evoked the *Iliad*, Anna depicted her father as a Homeric hero covered in the dust of battle and trading blows with Norman knights, not as an aloof bundle of abstract virtues, which is how good emperors used to be depicted. Yet somehow he also remained a paragon of Christian virtue, equal to the Apostles. This resulted in incongruous images. One orator praised Ioannes for wading through "oceans of barbarian blood" spilled by his sword, then called him "the heir of Christ."[33] The Komnenoi placed military saints on many of their coins and seals, overlooking the fact that these saints were martyred for disobeying orders and had not performed feats of martial valor. But they "looked" the part, what with their armor and weapons, and their posthumous miracles were often martial. Komnenian literature extolled noble lineage and feats of strength. Manuel, an ardent Latinophile, promoted jousting, and his court sponsored texts praising hunting and falconry.[34]

This was a fitting milieu for the composition of a heroic epic on the brawny frontiersman *Digenis Akrites*. It was written in quasi-vernacular Greek, a language that the poem calls "the Roman tongue." It is the sole east Roman text of its kind and is often regarded as the equivalent of the *Song of Roland*. We have only later versions, some of them fragmentary and incoherent, but they likely derive from an original that was produced in the twelfth century and was based on songs and tales about its hero. Digenis fights, hunts, feasts, rapes, and builds palaces, and yet is also conventionally pious, with God on his lips. The bard also invokes the military saints and spars with Homer.[35] In no way is Digenis' life a reflection of the actual frontier at any time in Roman history, as it is stripped of all institutions, such as the army, the tax collectors, and the Church. This allows the hero to roam without paperwork. The poem may well have originated in Constantinople, and it jibed with Komnenian values. Manuel was compared to Digenis by court poets.[36]

Psellos also exerted a large influence on Komnenian literature. He had experimented with genre, voice, and satire; skepticism of monastic ideals and an embrace of worldly experiences and even pleasures; a heightened openness to classical texts and ancient thought precisely because they explored values that Christianity did not, including heroism, romantic entanglements, and subversive wit; and, finally, a desire to study ancient philosophy in order to find new or more precise ways to express Orthodoxy, or alternatives to it. Psellos' epigones in the twelfth century picked up many of these threads and often acknowledged their debt to him. Psellos features prominently in a genre-bending satirical tale of a journey to Hades, the *Timarion*, a text with philosophical ambitions that was written under Alexios and contains sharp anti-Christian barbs.[37] The shift of the culture in this direction is indicated by the relative decline of hagiography and frequent complaints that monks and ascetics were hypocrites and obscurantist charlatans. Satire, finally let loose, had discovered its perfect target. To be sure, this was a marginal shift in one sector of elite opinion, not society as a whole, but it is striking. Later in the twelfth century, Eustathios, the bishop of Thessalonike and a former professor of Homer, wrote a treatise calling for a reform of monastic life to make it less hypocritical and more humanistic.[38]

The most versatile author of the mid-twelfth century was Prodromos, who exhibits many of these traits. In addition to philosophical essays, dialogues, and satires, he deployed a variety of ancient meters in his poems for the imperial family. He also wrote a parodic cento, *The Battle of Cat and Mice*, which mines Homer to mock Komnenian warfare. Prodromos was likely the first to don the persona of Ptochoprodromos ("Poor Prodromos") and write satirical poems in vernacular Greek. Even though some were presented to emperors—the first addresses Ioannes II as "Black John"—these poems tell the story of henpecked husbands, starving monks, and gluttonous abbots, mixing classical allusions (e.g., to Aristophanes) with bawdy sexual innuendos. It turns out that Ioannes and his court had a healthy sense of humor. The first poem includes a parody of a combat scene in *Digenis*, with the husband facing off against a broom-wielding wife.[39]

Spoken Greek, a language that was already being called "Romaic," had not previously been used for literature, so this was a significant development, similar to the emergence of vernacular Romance literature in the west. Another development was the return of the romance novel. It was Prodromos in the 1130s, sponsored by Anna's husband, the *kaisar* Bryennios, who wrote the first romance novel since antiquity, recounting the adventures of a young lovestruck couple (*Rodanthe and Dosikles*). The poem is in classical Greek, not Romaic. At least three more such romance narratives would appear during the next few decades from other authors. These romances imaginatively reconstructed antiquity in all its pagan glory, and were informed by high standards of classical scholarship. In these texts, authors and readers alike experimented with Hellenic personas.[40] Their interest in romantic love sat uneasily within Orthodox culture, which had shunned that topic for centuries, so when "it resurfaced in the twelfth century [it] had at first to pretend to be ancient and afterwards to be western, oriental, Homeric, allegorical or fairy-tale."[41]

The part of Psellos' project that fared the worst was its promotion of non-Christian philosophy, especially the Neoplatonism of Proklos. His student Italos and the latter's student Eustratios of Nikaia were progressively more analytical and better philosophers, but their trajectory was cut short by ecclesiastical censure. The project failed to launch and sought refuge in mere commentaries. Anna sponsored a circle of scholars to explicate the works of Aristotle, including Eustratios and one Michael of Ephesos. They occasionally express interesting ideas in these works (such as on the nature of money) and critiques of Komnenian monarchy inspired by Aristotle's *Politics*, but these were interesting thoughts, not original philosophy as such.[42] Nikolaos of Methone, a bishop with close ties to Manuel Komnenos, tried to bury that movement further by writing a massive *Refutation of Proklos*.[43] It was safer to study texts philologically than philosophically. In the long run, Eustratios had more influence on western European thought than at New Rome.

By contrast, classical scholarship and philology flourished, producing giants such as Eustathios of Thessalonike, who commented on Homer and other ancient authors. For no prior period can we name more teachers and schools active in Constantinople, ranging from private tutors and the schools of the Orphanage to the imperially-supported Master of Orators and the so-called Patriarchal Academy. The last is a modern term given by modern scholars to three teaching chairs—for the Psalms (or Old Testament), "the Apostle" (i.e., the Epistles), and the Gospels respectively. These seem to have been consolidated, and given an evangelical purpose, by Alexios I in 1107. It is likely that he did not want the likes of Psellos or Italos to be teaching those subjects to bureaucrats- and churchmen-in-training, as Psellos had done for decades. Alexios' attempt to give the clergy a prominent role in the world of education paid off, in that most writers of this period were affiliated with Hagia Sophia. Still, their interests ranged from the theological to the classical and took in the gamut of literary expression of the period, including the parodic, mythographical, and autobiographical. Alexios' professors also praised the emperor on formal set occasions. The three Scriptural professors, affiliated with Hagia Sophia, and nine other *maïstores*, associated with other churches, formed a faculty of twelve. They presided loosely over a sprawling network of private teachers, tutors, and grammarians. They formed a pool from which the exceptionally learned bishops of this period were drawn, redistributing the capital's intellectual assets to the provinces.[44]

These schools produced a surplus of specialized teachers, so for the first time we witness professional scholars such as Prodromos and Ioannes Tzetzes "begging" for work, looking for patronage, and complaining that their education had failed to improve their lot: better to have been a carpenter than a philologist! In the past, literature was something that well-off men did on the side, but these scholars were now trying to make a living from it. The new writerly class was self-conscious of its lower status compared to the Komnenoi lords from whom they sought employment, yet they had their own internal rivalries, hierarchies, and standards, which they brought to bear on the discerning critique of each other's works. The forum for this was the "theater," a term that referred to venues for the performance of rhetorical works. The court also hired these men to train foreign brides and catch them up on the classics. Tzetzes, for instance, produced some rudimentary allegories on Homer for Bertha, Manuel's wife, in addition to a host of didactic and pedagogic works in verse, which was easier to read and remember than prose. His corpus was as ample as his personality: "none of my peers has read as many books as I have, except when it comes to theology."[45] These were secular professional scholars.

Tzetzes also engaged in specialized scholarship, correcting manuscripts of Thucydides and annotating Aristophanes. The scholarly pinnacle of this era was the massive Homeric commentaries written by Eustathios, professor of rhetoric, court orator, and, from the 1170s, bishop of Thessalonike. These volumes were repositories of Homeric learning and analysis, and intended for expert use. But the court benefited from this activity. Cultural patronage ranked among the virtues of the Komnenian elite, which explains the proliferation of "occasional" pieces celebrating their births, weddings, and deaths, as well as their wars, hunts, and luxury accessories. Rhetoric moved into every space of the culture. Thus, while the writers did not themselves constitute the highest elite, they were its secretaries, spokesmen, and satirists.[46]

Eirene *sebastokratorissa*, the widow of Ioannes II's son Andronikos *sebastokrator* and likely a woman of foreign origin, commissioned many textbooks from Tzetzes, including a *Theogony* on the origin of the gods; a verse chronicle of Roman history from Konstantinos Manasses, which became immensely popular; and a grammar from Prodromos, in addition to the usual encomia and occasional poems. When he was not plotting treason, Isaakios, Ioannes' brother, wrote minor works on Homer and treatises on Proklos that Christianized his theology. But he too hired Prodromos to praise him as an "emperor" who, while seated upon a throne, is thanked by Philosophy for saving her from the tyranny of Ares. Isaakios must have projected a more refined and less militaristic alternative to Ioannes II, and was confined by him to the city of Herakleia.[47] The *Alexiad* of their sister Anna made a rival play for the appropriation of Alexios. Literary life was busier and more original under the Komnenoi than any previous time, possibly surpassing the era of Justinian.

This literary scene presented Manuel I Komnenos (1143–1180) with the means to fashion and project a glorious image of his reign as that of a Sun King. More panegyrics survive about him than any other emperor, and he micromanaged this whole production, from the manifold ceremonial settings in which his praises were performed to the gist of their contents. While his authors enjoyed some autonomy to fashion images, their messages followed the script of "press releases" that he dispatched from the front announcing his victories or the talking points released by the palace's "propaganda machine." Manuel was extoled in superlative terms.[48]

Manuel I Komnenos: assets and challenges

Manuel's praises did not stem from personal vanity. He needed an image to match the scale of his ambitions, which far outstripped those of his father and grandfather. But he also needed to shine more than the rest of his entitled clan, the gaggle of Komnenoi princes who always surrounded him and behaved as mini-emperors. Past emperors needed to rise only above their subjects and court functionaries. But Manuel had to outstrip the rest of his family, which included formidable individuals such as his uncle Isaakios *sebastokrator* and the latter's son, the future emperor Andronikos. The latter was, apparently, an awesome specimen of charismatic manhood, and as treasonous as his father.[49] The family constituted a social class in itself. By the 1160s it appears that just being a Komnenos, such as an imperial nephew or cousin, placed one above some actual title-holders. Young and inexperienced in-laws were sometimes given higher command positions than veteran generals, with less-than-ideal results. In the past, the court hierarchy shaped the elite, but now that family's notion of nobility determined the hierarchy.[50]

Like the name "Caesar" before it, Komnenos became a title and was used as such by the branch of the family that later ruled at Trebizond.[51] This development is reflected on the lead seals of officials. Before the tenth century, seals recorded one's Christian name and office. Surnames became common in the eleventh but in the twelfth, when even many peasants sported surnames, the elite sometimes did not record offices or titles, even when they had them, deeming their Komnenos (or Doukas) affiliation, or their specific relation to the emperor, to be a sufficient distinction. By ca. 1200, a certain Basileios Doukas Kamateros designated himself only as "the brother-in-law of the lord of the Ausonians" (an archaic label for the emperor of the Romans).[52] Kin relations thereby became as important as offices—they often entailed offices—and were recorded more punctiliously by historians. Not since the days of the Republic had the Romans fussed so much over lineage, bloodlines, and marriage politics.[53] Thus, Manuel had to manage the family, not just the state. This meant tightly regulating its marriages, especially with an eye toward foreign relations.[54] Thus, the elite, and by extension the rest of Roman society, were shaped by Manuel's foreign-policy goals. These differed significantly from his predecessors', as the international scene had changed dramatically.

For starters, the creation of Outremer meant that Romanía sat astride the lines of communication, trade, military alliances, and dynastic politics that joined the Levant to western Europe. The west now had a stake in what the Romans did in Syria, whereas previously their eastern and western fronts had been conveniently separate domains. Moreover, the set of players with a stake in this game included more peer monarchies than ever before, such as France and Germany. Even those that were not quite peers, such as the Norman kingdom of Sicily or Hungary, were protected by distance from the force of Roman arms and could still cause harm by raiding. This scene entailed more multilateral conflicts than the medieval world had yet seen. Constantinople had to enter into many bilateral agreements in order to advance its agenda and had to make deals with smaller players, such as the Italian city-states, because they might play a crucial role in the larger network that the emperor was building, for example in his effort to reconquer southern Italy in the first part of the reign, or to prevent Germany from dominating Italy in the second. Roman emperors had rarely in the past made deals with other monarchs as their equals, and Manuel struggled to preserve his superior status while in effect making bilateral deals. His treaties with the Genoese, for example, were pitched as concessions by a benevolent overlord to foreign hirelings, but the Genoese were in reality bargaining hard with him as equal and free partners.[55] The age of multilateral diplomacy had arrived.

Drawn into the decentralized world of western Europe, which included kingdoms, city-states, the papacy, and the German empire, Manuel adopted the language of feudal relations to make alliances. This was a bad fit with the Roman law that governed his own polity. In the eleventh century, emperors had begun to swear oaths and give guarantees in order to quell civil wars, but in the twelfth they had to swear oaths and make pledges in foreign policy, which detracted from their transcendent superiority. Manuel managed to remain the notionally superior party in all his agreements, but his successors increasingly had to enter into them as equals.[56] Moreover, Manuel had to navigate the mutual rivalries of his allies (e.g., Genoese and Venetians), which complicated dealing with any one of them. Not only did armies unrelated to his own projects, such as the Second Crusade, want to pass through his realm, his own allies would sometimes fight their own separate wars against each other within his own capital. Through extraordinary effort, Manuel managed to control the chaos. After him, however, the waves of these storms would overwhelm and sink the Roman state.

What were Manuel's assets and liabilities? On the personal side, he had a versatile mind, capable of grasping any issue, and a charismatic personality that made allies easily. He was a good at speaking, debating, and leading armies, and he cultivated a reputation for dashing valor. He drove a hard bargain yet was also patient and usually forgiving.[57] He also had vast amounts of cash, which he used as an instrument of foreign policy more extensively than his predecessors. The Roman economy was booming, but Manuel's subjects were likely squeezed too. As under Alexios and Ioannes, we hear complaints about "implacable and relentless" tax collection, not all of them from self-interested parties seeking exemptions.[58]

Manuel was able to defeat most foreign raids quickly. He faced no military rebellions, only attempted coups, mostly by relatives and in-laws. Constantinople provided Manuel with the most magnificent stage for the performance of imperial ceremonies, and he made good use of it. Its monuments and population—possibly as high as 400,000—overawed most visitors, especially the Latins, who had never seen anything like it. Even the most prejudiced called it "the glory of the Greeks, rich in renown and richer still in possessions . . . just as it surpasses other cities in wealth, so too does it surpass them in vice."[59]

Manuel pushed his resources and infrastructure into overdrive. He spent huge sums bribing men in key positions in foreign nations, so that "there was no city in Italy, or even farther away, where the emperor did not have agents sworn to promote his interests."[60] Fomenting internal discord beneath his enemies' thrones was a deliberate strategy during his reign.[61] Embassies bearing tempting gifts and promises were always on the move. In 1150, Manuel purchased the rights to the crusader county of Edessa after it was overrun by Nur al-Din, the ruler (*atabeg*) of Mosul. He later funded the resistance of the Lombard League to the German emperor Friedrich Hohenstaufen, while Ancona willingly served as a base from which his agents handed out "gifts," gained allies, and built networks.[62] He paid his enemies to attack each other, to keep them divided while he dealt with another theater, until such a time as could he could return in force to theirs. His armies sometimes ranged far outside his borders. In 1148, his fleet sailed up the Black Sea to attack the lands of some Cumans who were raiding the empire. In 1166, his armies crossed Transylvania to attack Hungary in a joint operation. In 1171, his agents pulled off one of the most impressive mass arrests in premodern history, targeting Venetians in a synchronized operation across the entire empire. In 1177, his fleet assisted the kingdom of Jerusalem to attack Egypt.[63] In 1180, shortly before Manuel's death, Eustathios of Thessalonike was urging him to get some rest from "council meetings every day; embassies as always, some going, others coming; drafting laws; rectifying verdicts; military planning;

conflicting reports, mostly from abroad, from the barbarians; budget formulas; scrutinizing decisions; and a horde of petitioners."[64]

What did Manuel hope to accomplish? His goals, which reveal his limitations and partly explain the collapse of his agenda after his death, emerged from his maximalist view of imperial authority and were also shaped by the early experiences of his reign.

The Second Crusade

From Cilicia, where he was acclaimed emperor, Manuel sent the *megas domestikos* Ioannes Axouch ahead to Constantinople to secure the capital and confine his brother, the *sebastokrator* Isaakios (the third of his name and title) in the Pantokrator monastery, to prevent him from seizing the throne. The brothers were reconciled when Manuel arrived and was crowned in Hagia Sophia, but the empire's neighbors quickly tested the new ruler for weakness. Antioch overran some Roman forts in Cilicia and the Turks of Konya raided western Asia Minor. In response, Manuel sent an army to Cilicia in 1144 that drove the Antiochenes out. At the same time, Zengi, the *atabeg* of Mosul, conquered Edessa and pressured Antioch from the north. Raymond of Antioch was left with no choice but to come to Constantinople as a suppliant, in 1145. Manuel ignored him until he performed his supplications at the tomb of Ioannes II in the Pantokrator. Raymond pledged to be Manuel's vassal (*lizios*), but this was only because the crusader states had run out of options. Yet Manuel's attention was always being pulled in many directions. In 1145–1146, he led campaigns against the sultanate of Konya, reaching as far as its capital, in order to punish the Turks for raiding, rebuild the Roman defenses, and remove part of the Roman population under Turkish rule, just as Alexios had done in 1116. In these battles, celebrated in the capital, the emperor always prevailed, and he extracted a peace treaty from the sultan Mas'ud.[65]

In January, 1146, Manuel finally wed his German bride Bertha-Eirene, who had been waiting in the capital for years. They had been betrothed when Manuel was unlikely to succeed to the throne, but, when he did, he kept his options open for a while. Bertha was unattractive, dour, and pious, while Manuel loved to party and even "fastened his buckle through a hole related to him by blood" (i.e., his niece). But in the end Manuel valued the German alliance too much, especially for promoting his designs in southern Italy, and Konrad III had even censured him about the delay in marrying Bertha.[66]

The German alliance was both supercharged and strained when Manuel learned that Konrad, along with the French king Louis VII, had decided to go on crusade in response to the fall of Edessa to Zengi. Like the First Crusade, the Second held both promise and peril for Constantinople, but mostly peril, as many Romans already believed that these expeditions were secretly aimed against them and because the success of this one could displace Manuel as the nominal overlord of Antioch. But as the new crusade could not be stopped at the source, Manuel made a virtue of necessity: he wrote letters to the kings and the pope pledging his "delighted" support of the project with supplies and guidance, though he required that "his honor be satisfied," i.e., that he receive the same oaths as were sworn to Alexios by the leaders of the First Crusade, namely that they would do no harm to Romanía and restore to him its lands and cities that were under occupation. Manuel received equivocal or no replies to this request, but he kept pressing the point as the expedition gathered steam, and secured partial and grudging assent. Behind his official delight, the emperor was "distrustful" of the Latins. He prepared for their arrival and repaired the walls of the City. The populace was frightened, and some wondered whether the walls were a sign of weakness rather than strength.[67]

Unfortunately, the crusade coincided, in 1147, with an attack by Sicily. Just as the armies of the kings set out on their march, Roger II seized the chance, while Manuel was distracted, to invade western Greece. The emperor and his writers called Roger the "western dragon" or "tyrant of Sicily" (because he was squatting on former imperial territory). Under the command of admiral Georgios, a Greek from Antioch, the Norman fleet occupied Kerkyra, allegedly with support from locals who resented paying Komnenian-level taxes. The Normans then raided the coasts and islands of Greece and sacked Thebes, taking its silk weavers away to Palermo (Thebes' silk industry had revived by 1160). Then they attacked Corinth, whose inhabitants had sought refuge on the Acrocorinth; the citadel fell and the invader returned to Kerkyra.[68]

Meanwhile, the Germans were marching across the Balkans on the road from Braničevo and Niš to Serdica and Adrianople, followed by the French. The emperor had prepared provisions for them, but his forces monitored them closely anyway because incidents of pillaging and violence did occur, especially involving Konrad's nephew Friedrich (the later emperor "Barbarossa"). The armies were accompanied by many civilians and priests, and Louis by his wife, the formidable Eleanor of Aquitaine. The German camp at Choirobakchoi in Thrace was washed away one night by a flooding river, with great loss of life. This delighted the Romans, who suspected that the true target of the crusade was Constantinople. Manuel wanted to steer the crusaders away from his capital but he failed to persuade the kings to cross at the Hellespont rather than the Bosporos. Konrad arrived in September, 1147 and sat before the City for about a month, his vast army ravaging the gardens and suburbs. He finally requested transport to Asia, and Manuel readily provided it. When the French arrived, some among them loudly urged Louis to ally with Roger of Sicily and attack Constantinople, "a city that was Christian in name only," arguing that the Greeks had attacked Latin Antioch. But Louis and Eleanor preferred to enjoy the emperor's hospitality inside Constantinople and then be ferried across to Asia.[69]

The two western hordes had ruined the gardens and suburbs outside the City, and the Romans were glad to see them go. Manuel's court poet immediately played this up as a great victory over those "wild beasts" who wanted to capture the City and impose a Latin patriarch on it who would use *azyma* (unleavened bread in communion). This hyperbole gratuitously relished in the crusaders' setbacks, such as the river flood. Public opinion among the populace must have regarded the Latins as nothing but hostile "barbarians," or else Manuel's court would not have pitched its messaging that way. There was little Christian brotherhood here, despite the rhetoric to that effect that Manuel deployed in his diplomacy with the Latins.[70]

Militarily, the Second Crusade was a fiasco. Both divisions of the German army were defeated by the Turks, the first near Dorylaion, proving that it was the First Crusade, not the Crusade of 1101, that was the fluke. The survivors joined up with the French at Nikaia and marched south along the coastal road, plundering Asia Minor as they went, but also complaining that the locals did not willingly sell them goods at discount prices. From Ephesos, Konrad sailed to Constantinople to spend the winter. Manuel tended to him personally when he was ill and provided him with ships that ferried him to Palestine. The French struck out from Laodikeia in early 1148 but, after some initial successes, were mauled by the Turks and diverted to the southern coast. From Attaleia, Louis sailed on to Syria but, as it was winter and there were few ships, the rest of his army had to march across the southern coast; few of them made it alive. The French army succumbed to its "bad timing, poor strategy, flawed diplomacy, and catastrophic logistics,"[71] in sum to its lack of all that the Romans could have provided, had the crusaders accepted Manuel's offers of leadership. This was more or less what Alexios had provided to the First Crusade. Arrogance had a cost.

The prime mover of the crusade in the west, St. Bernard, the abbot of Clairvaux, blamed the defeat on the collective sins of the Christians. But Odo of Deuil, Louis' chaplain who accompanied the expedition and wrote its history, blamed the humiliating failure on the "faithless" and "effeminate" Greeks, "a race of men hateful to me." They had allegedly undermined the Latins at every step and colluded with the Turks. Manuel, after all, had just made a truce with the Seljuks. It is likely that local Romans and Turks in Asia Minor did join forces to defend themselves against the invaders, regardless of what the emperor wanted. Influential voices in the west, including king Louis and Peter the Venerable (abbot of Cluny), echoed this view, which replayed the Norman propaganda emerging from the First Crusade. It was becoming a conventional trope in the west that crusades failed "because of the Greeks." A critical mass of resentment and racist and religious hatred was building up.[72]

The last Italian venture

Manuel's kind treatment of Konrad partially mitigated this public relations disaster. Besides, his army could not have escorted the crusaders, for it was fighting the Normans. Manuel confirmed his German alliance by giving his niece Theodora in marriage to Konrad's nephew Heinrich Jasomirgott, the duke of Bavaria, margrave of Austria, and member of the expedition. Manuel's court poet now struck a different tone: "Dance Alamania!" Heinrich, a (minor) star from the west, has come to bask in the "full daylight of the sun" that is Manuel.[73]

Manuel and Konrad met again at Thessalonike in the fall of 1148, after the former had repelled a Cuman invasion that required him to cross the Danube. His German counterpart (with Friedrich and other nobles in tow) was returning from Syria, having accomplished nothing. The two rulers reaffirmed their anti-Norman alliance and came to an agreement about Italy, though we do not know its precise terms. Manuel must have asserted his rights to the south and Sicily, a concession on Konrad's part that he likely cast as a dowry for Bertha. By now, Manuel had formulated two foreign-policy goals: first, to keep the western powers divided by bribing as many as he could to side with him or to harass his enemies, while he was paying the Muslims to stay quiet; and, second, to reconquer southern Italy and Sicily, with German consent. Manuel (correctly) perceived that western Christians were far more dangerous to his empire than Muslims, and he pursued a calculated strategy of divide-and-rule.[74]

Yet his enemies could also play that game. After a long siege, Norman-occupied Kerkyra surrendered in July, 1149, and Manuel placed a German garrison in its citadel. He had relied during the war on Venetian naval assistance, to obtain which he had issued a chrysobull confirming his father and grandfather's concessions, and then another expanding the Venetian quarter in Constantinople. (During the siege, the Venetians showed their quality when they got into an altercation with some Roman soldiers, seized the imperial barge, and dressed up a black African in the imperial regalia and acclaimed him emperor, just to mock Manuel, who was, like his father, dark-skinned.)[75] But when Manuel was ready to launch his attack on Italy, Konrad, who was ill and preoccupied with turmoil at home that had been stirred up by Roger of Sicily, wrote to excuse his absence from the campaign.[76] Moreover, Manuel had to spend the next few years (1149–1155) pacifying his northwestern frontier against raids by the Hungarians and the grand župan of Raška in Serbia, who were also allied to the "Sicilian Dragon" Roger. Manuel eventually prevailed on this front and imposed terms on the Serbs and Hungarians, but those wars had distracted him from Italy, as they were meant to do. Still, his orators spun them as major successes, comparing the wars in Raška to hunting jaunts: Manuel set his dogs on the župan, and the Serbs were like beasts to be chased over mountains and through forests. But an alarming revelation was made in 1154: Andronikos Komnenos, governor of Belgrade and Braničevo, was plotting with the Hungarian king Géza II to usurp the throne. He was imprisoned in the Great Palace.[77]

By 1155, Manuel was free to invade Italy, a venture that he believed would make him a New Justinian; indeed, his historian Kinnamos based his account of the expedition on Prokopios. Roger had died in 1154 and his successor, William I, was in a weak position and asked for peace, which Manuel refused. Konrad had died in 1152. His successor, Friedrich I Hohenstaufen, was playing a double game, pledging to the pope in 1153 that he would never let "the king of the Greeks" hold land "on this side of the sea," while simultaneously signaling support for Manuel's venture and urging it on. Friedrich had a maximalist view of his imperial status, styling himself as Emperor Augustus of the Romans (though he had not yet been crowned) and calling Manuel Emperor of Constantinople.[78] Manuel secured the support of Genoa through a deal similar to that with Pisa (from 1111), and sent agents loaded with money to buy allies in Italy. The invasion began in 1155 and was led by Michael Palaiologos and Ioannes Doukas, who were later reinforced by the *megas doux* Alexios Komnenos, a son of Anna. Their forces consisted mostly of small units of barbarians and relied on local support, exploiting the hostility that existed against the Normans in southern Italy and even, among Normans, against William. Manuel also offered money to the pope, Hadrian IV, to win him over. Hadrian desperately needed help against his domestic enemies, but it does not seem that he accepted the offer. At first the imperial army made impressive gains, taking Bari, Trani, and other towns. But it was decisively defeated at Brindisi in May 1156 by an army brought up from Sicily by William. Manuel's Italian dream was over. In 1158, he came to terms with the "Western Dragon" and recognized the kingdom of Sicily. His Italian strategy shifted to Ancona, which became a hub for the dissemination of his money and influence.[79]

A return to southern Italy was likely no longer feasible. Constantinople's hold on the region had been tenuous at times during the tenth and eleventh centuries, and was likely to be even more so now. The strategic wisdom of a play in Italy can also be doubted, just as under Justinian: Italian campaigns diverted forces away from homeland defense into a quagmire that sucked up money and men with little to show. Manuel's failed invasion was a waste of money "with no benefit for the Romans."[80] Success would likely have been worse than victory, entangling the empire in western feuds that would create many enemies and few friends. But such ventures were required by Manuel's exalted self-image and his determination that the Romans dominate in the emerging world order.

Collecting client kings

Manuel's goals changed after the failure in Italy. He now sought recognition of his status through dazzling public performances of hierarchy. He began with Antioch, where his authority had declined over the years. Specifically, the Armenian Rubenid prince Thoros had made inroads into Roman Cilicia in the late 1140s and defeated Andronikos, whom Manuel had sent in 1152 to restore control. The new prince of Antioch, the adventurer Raynald of Châtillon who arrived with the Second Crusade, had, unprovoked but aided by Thoros, plundered Cyprus in 1155, committing "abominable atrocities" on the population. This was regarded in western Europe as stupid and vile, for Cyprus was essential for provisioning Outremer.[81]

Manuel arrived in person in 1158, as soon as he had secured his western flank via the treaty with William of Sicily. He quickly overran the whole Cilician plain. Thoros initially fled, but Raynald of Châtillon, now isolated, came to the imperial camp at Mopsouestia. In the hair shirt of a penitent, with a rope tied around his neck, and surrounded by praying monks, Raynald flung himself on the ground before Manuel and begged forgiveness. This spectacle was staged to be witnessed by the envoys of all neighboring rulers who were in attendance. Baldwin III, king of Jerusalem, also attended upon Manuel. He had just married a niece of the emperor, Theodora, who was thirteen but came with a cash dowry of 100,000 hyperpyra and 10,000 for the wedding. The match allegedly corrected Baldwin's dissolute ways. Thoros also came to the camp, "a pitiable suppliant," and swore an oath of loyalty. Antioch was henceforth to be Manuel's client. It would provide military assistance when requested and accept a Greek patriarch (in 1165–1170). The new relationship was grandly staged in Manuel's *adventus* into Antioch in 1159, with Raynald on foot leading his horse and Baldwin riding without insignia. Manuel was satisfied with this symbolism; he had no intention of occupying the city, although he brought his Varangians with him into it. Equally symbolic, perhaps, was the joint campaign of the Latins and Romans against Nur al-Din. The *atabeg* released a few thousand prisoners and offered to assist Manuel with his wars in Asia Minor, which sufficed. Manuel was now, and for the rest of his reign, the chief protector of Outremer. He impressed the Antiochenes with his skill at jousting. Part of the objective, as the court orator Eustathios put it years later, was to gather up "living pearls and stones, from the whole earth . . . [to] encircle your crown."[82]

Manuel's goal was not to dominate the Latins, but to open his east Roman world to them and make them feel that it was also part of their own. This was an aspect of his notorious Latinophilia, which was criticized and resented by some of his subjects. Whether out of strategy or proclivity, Manuel adopted western cultural traits, such as chivalry, and it was even said that his personal gallantry was a means to impress his western wife, who expected that of a lordly husband.[83] More controversially, at a time when many Romans feared or hated the Latins, he opened his court to western advisors and his army to western soldiers and captains, possibly as a means of persuading the west that Romanía was not a foreign Other to be viewed with suspicion. For him, the Latins were both a mirror in which to see his own culture but also a source of anxiety, as he feared a western attack that "would deluge our lands like a swollen mountain stream that suddenly crests and sweeps away farmlands." But some of his subjects resented the flood of their own tax money that Manuel poured into his western projects and "friends." Allegedly he benefited those "money-grubbing barbarians" while "alienating native Romans who were honest and faithful."[84]

Manuel was playing a double game. To his subjects, his court propaganda often presented the Latins as dangerous barbarians, as during the passage of the Second Crusade. But the western brides imported to his court from France, Germany, and Hungary were cast in classicizing terms as "descendants of Julius Caesar" and Old Rome, no matter their actual origin.[85] When Bertha died in 1160, Manuel decided to marry a Latin from Outremer. His envoys "carefully scrutinized each detail and inquired into the life and conduct of the damsel, even to the most secret physical characteristics." Eventually Manuel chose Marie of Antioch, the fifteen-year-old daughter of the previous prince of Antioch, Raymond of Poitiers (she was also the granddaughter of Bohemond and great-granddaughter of Philippe I, king of France). Manuel married her on Christmas, 1161, in a grand ceremony in Hagia Sophia that was performed by the patriarchs of Constantinople, Alexandria, and Antioch, and followed by magnificent banquets and races to entertain the populace. When Baldwin III of Jerusalem died in 1163 and was succeeded by his brother Amalric (1163–1174), the latter also sought and, in 1167, obtained a Komnenian bride, a niece of the emperor named Maria. She came with officials from Constantinople who functioned as a standing "embassy" of sorts, and Amalric swore an oath to Manuel.[86]

Constantinople was now the chief patron of the crusaders states. When Amalric conceived a plan to invade and conquer Egypt, Manuel provided a fleet that did its part, under the command of his nephew, the *megas doux* Andronikos Komnenos Kontostephanos. The expedition failed, but through no fault of the Romans. As Nur al-Din continued to put pressure on Antioch and Jerusalem, and his lieutenant Saladin took Egypt, in 1171 Amalric sailed to Constantinople to renew his pledges of loyalty to Manuel in exchange for aid. However, he and his council had appealed first to all the major kings in the west, and turned to Manuel only when that got them nothing. The "Greeks" were thus not their first choice, but they were "nearer and richer" than the rest. Even so, Manuel ensured that Amalric and his retinue were received with all honors, "gifts," and tours of the City. Amalric's throne was lower than Manuel's at their joint appearance before the court.[87]

Manuel was not content to add only Latin jewels to his crown. After two campaigning seasons in Asia Minor (1159–1161), to which his Latin allies in the east dutifully sent contingents, Manuel forced the sultan of Konya, Kilij Arslan II, to accept terms that effectively subordinated him to the empire in military policy. The sultan also agreed to restrain his Turkmen raiders, though he only partially complied with that. Manuel's victory was capped by the sultan's visit to the City, a novelty "so awesome and amazing that I don't know if it has happened to any other emperor," Kinnamos wrote. The reception was orchestrated so that Kilij Arslan sat on a low chair next to Manuel's huge bejeweled throne, flanked by the Komnenoi who were arrayed by rank. The sultan was presented with races in the hippodrome, brilliant spectacles of Greek fire, and bounteous gifts. At the races, an Arab ventured to fly off a tower over the gates by flapping some mechanical wings, but he plummeted to his death. Emperor and sultan now corresponded as "father" and "son." And the Danishmend ruler of Sivas, Yaghibasan, who had assisted in the war against Konya, had long since proclaimed himself on his seal as "the slave of the *basileus*."[88] For good measure, Manuel strengthened the defenses of the cities of Asia Minor, which was later deemed to be "more beneficial to the common good" than his other, more symbolic ambitions. An orator hints that, according to a treaty, the Turks could pasture their animals on Roman territory, but had to pay rent.[89]

Through war and ceremony, Manuel was fashioning a ring of client rulers around himself. His goal was not to acquire their territory but to perform his superiority.[90] The empire had always sported client rulers along the periphery, but now they were vital for its security. Never before had so many of them been drawn up into such a complex network of alliances, and never had an emperor insisted so much on the ceremonial aspect of their subordination to him. Manuel had likewise made Louis VII of France sit on a lower seat beside him when he received him in 1147. One of his court orators stressed that it was "reigning kings who come and kneel before you" and not, as under Ioannes II, mere exiles and fugitive kings.[91] Manuel used both the Great Palace and the Komnenian palace at Blachernai for such events, equipping them with magnificent new throne rooms that featured murals of his victories (including those in Italy).[92] He staged half a dozen triumphs, following the route established by his father in 1133, from the eastern coast of the City, past the Orphanage, to Hagia Sophia. It was likely Manuel who introduced the ceremony of *prokypsis*: the emperor, standing or sitting on a raised platform, was suddenly revealed with a burst of music and light when the curtains were pulled away, an awesome performance of solar kingship.[93]

Having secured Asia Minor and Cilicia, Manuel spent seven years (1162–1168) enforcing similar arrangements in the Balkans. After many campaigns and a complex series of interventions in the Hungarian succession, Manuel succeeded here too. The unruly grand župan of Raška, Stefan Nemanja, was chastened by punitive invasions of his land. After the last of his "rebellions," in 1172, he was hauled to Constantinople where, like Raynald of Antioch, he prostrated himself before the emperor's feet and begged for mercy with a rope tied around his neck, "fearing the emperor more than wild beasts fear *their* king."[94] As for Hungary, official sources from the mid-1160s and afterward imply that Manuel already regarded it as a dependency, an impression that was ratified in July, 1167 by a decisive victory over a Hungarian army of 15,000 near Sirmium. The battle was won by the *megas doux* Andronikos Komnenos Kontostephanos, who rode behind his uncle in the ensuing triumph in Constantinople.[95] Just as Manuel had used forces from the Latin east against the Seljuks in 1159–1161, so too he used Seljuks in his Balkan wars, and later he used Serbs and Hungarians in his huge offensive against the Seljuks in the mid-1170s.

The victory over Hungary was not merely symbolic. The Romans regained Sirmium, which they had lost in the 1070s, in addition to territory to its northwest called Frangochorion (Fruška Gora) and a large swath of Dalmatia down to the coast, which was placed under a *doux*, possibly based at Split. These territories remained under Roman control only briefly (ca. 1166–1180), so we know little about their governance. Dalmatia remained under papal jurisdiction, and Manuel treated its bishops generously in order to persuade the papacy that a broader alliance with Constantinople could be mutually beneficial, at a time when both were suspicious of the German emperor. At the same time, Constantinople could project its power into Italy more effectively from the Dalmatian coast, as when its *doux* supported Ancona in 1173 during its great siege by Friedrich Barbarossa and the Venetians. Manuel's clients in Italy turned out and the siege failed.[96] Manuel controlled more of the Balkans than any emperor since the fourth century, though this dominion would be brief.

Manuel's involvement in the complexities of the Hungarian succession in the 1160s resulted in a strange development at his own court. Béla, the younger brother of king Istvàn III (1162–1172), had been allotted Sirmium and Dalmatia by his father. Manuel kept Béla, a teenager, at his court, pressing his rights to those territories as his proxy guardian (though in 1167 he annexed them outright). In 1163, he betrothed Béla to his daughter Maria (born to his first wife Bertha). Béla was renamed Alexios and, in 1165, Manuel shocked the court by designating him as his heir and giving him the quasi-imperial title of *despotes*, whose constitutional significance was opaque. Over twenty years into his reign now, Manuel still had not produced an heir and so a succession crisis was brewing. Manuel was half-Hungarian, but it was unprecedented to designate an actual foreigner to succeed to the throne, and some objected to it at the time, including Andronikos Komnenos, who had his eye on the throne. Scholars are unsure what Manuel was angling for here, or whether he was sincere. Some link this scheme to a prophecy according to which the dynasty would last another generation if the initials of its names formed AIMA ("blood"). Manuel was perhaps trying to co-opt the final "A" by renaming Béla. But his second wife gave birth to a boy in 1169, who was promptly named Alexios and crowned co-emperor in 1171. Manuel required the Church leadership to swear an oath that spelled out all contingencies regarding the succession. This was one of few efforts to create a "law of succession" in Constantinople. Béla's engagement to Maria was broken off and he was reduced to the rank of *kaisar*. When his brother died, he succeeded to the Hungarian throne (1173–1196) and was regarded by the "king of kings" Manuel as his client. Béla swore an oath that he would respect Roman interests.[97]

A loyal Hungary was seen as a buffer between Romanía and Friedrich's Germany, especially since Bertha, the link between the two empires, had died in 1160. The idea of a German attack on Romanía was aired vaguely in both eastern and western texts.[98] Constantinople had been allied with Germany against the Normans since at least the 1080s, and a possible alliance and new marriage link between the two continued to be discussed down to 1180. Manuel and Friedrich were never formally enemies, yet a cold war developed between them, because Friedrich tried to bring Italy under his control, backing an antipope, while Manuel blocked him by funding the Lombard League and backing a pope who later proved to be the "right" one, Alexander III. It was unprecedented for the pope and eastern emperor, with support from the Normans of Sicily and the French king, to oppose a German emperor. Scholars study this short-lived configuration as "the Problem of the Two Emperors," which revolves around their exclusive notions of *imperium* and the titles that they claimed for themselves and attributed to each other ("king of the Germans" and "king of the Greeks" when they were not being charitable). The plan was even floated that the pope would recognize Manuel rather than Friedrich as "emperor of the Romans," and Manuel tried hard to persuade the pope that he was sincere about Church Union. None of this came to pass, however.[99]

Eastern and western conceptions of empire were incommensurate and incompatible. In the east, the *basileus* was defined in relation to the surviving polity of the Roman people. In the west, by contrast, the Romanness of Friedrich's *imperium* had nothing to do with the existence of any Roman people, but was rather a superordinate title that had somehow passed from "the Greeks" to the Franks, Saxons, and Germans. This conception had no basis in Roman tradition. From the viewpoint of Constantinople, it was arrogant make-believe. East and west also assessed differently the relative standing of Old and New Rome in the Church, in imperial politics, and in history.[100] East Romans could not grasp the idea of an imperial title that could be bestowed only by the pope, while the pope, for his part, would have to overcome formidable barriers, both practical and ideological, before allowing Manuel onto the stage of Catholic powers, even if he could overcome entrenched western racism and religious bigotry against "the Greeks." The two systems simply did not mesh.[101]

Manuel I and the Church

They were also incompatible when it came to the Church. Like many emperors of the Romans, starting with Constantine the Great, Manuel had the authority, institutional means, and personal predilection to govern the affairs of his Church more directly than was the norm in the west. The autonomy of the imperial Church in religious matters was honored rhetorically, and it could be indignantly defended by dissidents who felt it was being violated, but for the most part the emperor had the power and tacit consent of the clergy to intervene where and how he wanted. This included routine administration as well as debates about policy and doctrine. It was emperors who had settled all the major theological controversies of the early centuries, whether by fiat or by putting their finger on the scales; and it was their laws that governed the organization and finances of the Church, even though in practice most emperors were content with a quiet status quo.

In the first part of his reign, Manuel was drawn into theological debates that were stirred up by various bishops, monks, and intellectuals who sought to clarify opaque areas of doctrine, or who used these in order to attack their rivals. The questions were typically inane, such as whether Christ offered himself up to himself as a sacrifice or only to the Father. They were confined to small groups of infighting bishops and teachers, and had no social impact. They were handled by the Synod in a manner similar to modern HR complaints, with Manuel leading the interrogations, as his grandfather Alexios had done on many occasions. He was invariably praised for his acuity and theological genius in the ensuing reports.[102] Manuel came to fancy himself an intellectual and theologian, and in the later part of his reign he was praised by flatterers as a philosopher-king devoted equally to Hermes as to Ares, despite his lack of formal training. He delivered catechetical orations, as "it was no use for a ruler to command the bodies of his subjects while not taking sufficient charge of their souls." He was "an excellent steward" and "wise teacher."[103] His intellectual vice was astrology, which he defended in a brief treatise against a monk of the Pantokrator who condemned it. Manuel argued that it was a science like any other. Celestial events marked momentous occurrences: "Had not experts predicted the comet that appeared when the Germans passed through the land of Romanía?" Most courtiers looked away from this, though one dissident, Michael Glykas, did refute the emperor's treatise. The historian Niketas Choniates excoriated the emperor for allegedly allowing astrology to influence his decisions, including his military strategy.[104]

In reports issued by the Synod in the early part of the reign, Manuel's role is described with the odd term *epistemonarches*, which literally means "master of knowledge." This was also the title of monastic officials who enforced the rules of the house, a kind of disciplinarian. Manuel was being hailed as an expert, even authoritative, voice in the resolution of disputes in the Church. He eventually adopted the term in his own pronouncements. In 1166, he thanked the Synod for bringing to him for approval or modification one of its decrees regarding marriage, thereby "preserving our *epistemonarchical* rights."[105]

In the same year, the Synod resolved a dispute that had been festering for six years over the verse "The Father is greater than I" (John 14:28), a throwback to the fourth-century Arian controversy. This dispute was more significant than the previous ones in that most of the Church was opposed to Manuel's view that the verse referred only to Christ's human nature. Moreover, the opposition identified Manuel's position as an error of Latin origin, and two members of his family (a Bryennios in-law and a Kontostephanos nephew) sided with the opposition—all this during the Béla affair, when the succession was in grave doubt. Manuel met with leading bishops individually, so they made a pact not to talk to him one-on-one lest he pry them away from the group. Yet after much agitation, the emperor had his way. The Synod met in the palace under his direction and reached the result that he wanted, in which he was possibly advised by his Pisan theological advisor, Ugo Eteriano, who believed that the Greek Church was generally in error. The patriarch Loukas Chrysoberges (1156–1169) was one of few bishops who had stuck with Manuel. When he died he was replaced with the Latinoskeptic Michael of Anchialos, perhaps a concession to the opposition.[106]

Manuel inscribed the synodal decision of 1166 in the form of an imperial edict "valid for all who live in the Roman jurisdiction" on a set of huge plaques that he mounted on the wall of the narthex of Hagia Sophia. His title in that edict is extraordinary, a throwback to the days of Justinian:

> Manuel, born-in-the-purple, *basileus* faithful in the God Christ, emperor of the Romans, most pious, Ever Revered, Augustus, *Isauricus, Cilicicus, Armenicus, Dalmaticus, Hungaricus, Bosnicus, Croaticus, Lazicus, Ibericus, Bulgaricus, Serbicus, Zechicus, Khazaricus, Gothicus*, who, led by God, is heir to the crown of Constantine the Great and holds all the rights that stem from it, at least in spirit, for some have illegitimately separated themselves from our power, [rights used for the benefit of] our entire Christ-loving populace, our Imperial City, which is guarded by God, and still more of all who live under our imperial authority in all territories, inland or coastal.[107]

Manuel begins the edict by praising St. Peter as the head of the Apostles, language that was meant to please the papacy at precisely the time when Manuel was seeking its support. But no pope would have associated himself closely with an emperor who governed the Church in this manner. Manuel's view of Church-state relations is reflected in the commentaries on canon law by Theodoros Balsamon, who later held the position of (absentee) bishop of Antioch. He is one of the most important canonists in the eastern Church tradition and a lively writer, if not always a reliable lawyer. Balsamon was a maximalist when it came to the power and jurisdiction of the Church of Constantinople and to the power of the emperor within or over the Church. His views are hard to pin down, but in some contexts he was willing to grant to emperors a quasi-sacerdotal status, and even appealed to the ancient emperors' title of *pontifex maximus*. As the "*epistemonarches* of the Church," the emperor could judge a patriarch "and his verdict answers to no one, given the supremacy of his throne."[108] By contrast, the historian Choniates, while not disputing that emperors had a legitimate role to play in ecclesiastical matters, accused Manuel of not fully understanding the issues before him.[109]

Manuel I and the Italians

The Latins that dominated Manuel's attention were the Italian merchant communities. A few thousand Italians now resided in imperial territory, mostly at Constantinople. The figure given in one source of 60,000 Latins in the City alone is impossible; a Genoese chronicle offers the more plausible figures of 1,000 Pisans and 300 Genoese in 1162.[110] The largest and most privileged group were the Venetians, who had their own *legatus* in Constantinople to resolve the community's internal disputes. Among the most successful Venetian merchants was Romano Mairano, who, starting in 1155, set up a network of business agreements with local partners in southern Greece and Constantinople, then in the eastern Aegean, and finally at Alexandria and Acre. He exported tons of oil from the Peloponnese to Alexandria and Venice. Komnenian tax demands, along with the incentives of Italian trade routes and the domestic safety guaranteed by Manuel, had stimulated local production in Greece, including a return of olive cultivation. A number of other Venetians, by contrast, settled in Romanía, taking Roman wives and living outside the Venetian quarter. Manuel created for them a distinct legal status—the *bourgesioi*, or permanent residents—who were required to swear oaths of loyalty to the Roman polity.[111]

The rival Italians sometimes attacked each other in Constantinople. In ca. 1160 the Pisans, with Venetian help, attacked and ruined the Genoese quarter. In 1168–1170, Manuel negotiated a new agreement with the Genoese, a tricky matter because the Genoese wanted to extract maximum concessions but did not want to pledge to support Romanía in case of a war with Friedrich. Both sides compromised.[112] But almost immediately afterward the Venetians destroyed the new Genoese quarter and refused to reimburse their victims, as Manuel demanded (the damages came to 5,674 hyperpyra). The Venetians went so far as to threaten Manuel with a piratical war like the one they had waged against his father in the 1120s. Venice's hostility was also due to Manuel's annexation of Dalmatia, which threatened their control of the Adriatic. In response to this provocation, Manuel launched one of the most impressive police actions in Roman history. On a preset day (12 March, 1171), his agents arrested all Venetians in the empire, some 20,000, and confiscated their properties. Romano Mairano managed to escape, but was financially ruined (he bounced back later). Venice responded by sending a fleet to ravage the Aegean in 1172, but it accomplished little and was stalked by the imperial fleet under the *megas doux* Andronikos Komnenos Kontostephanos. Kinnamos wrote what many Romans must have been thinking, that the Venetians were arrogant upstarts who had profited from their relationship with Romanía and were now foolishly turning against it. Eustathios called them "Adriatic scum and marsh-dwelling frogs."[113]

For years the Venetians lobbied unsuccessfully for reparations (1,500 lbs of gold), while the Genoese lobbied, equally unsuccessfully, to be given the generous concessions that their rivals had previously enjoyed. Venice joined in Barbarossa's attack on Ancona in 1173, Constantinople's forward operating base, but the siege failed. The leading Anconese were honored by a reception in Constantinople, sitting next to the emperor.[114] In sum, Romanía was not yet intimidated by, or dependent on, Italian financial interests and Italian naval power. In 1176, Eustathios crowed that the imperial fleet was manned with sailors who were "not from abroad, but indigenous, from ancient stock, most of them going back many generations, bred in the greatest of cities and never having left it."[115]

Myriokephalon

The empire's strategic situation shifted after the death of Nur al-Din in 1174. He had menaced the Seljuks from the east and required (or enabled) Manuel to act as protector of Antioch. But now Jerusalem began to look toward Friedrich Barbarossa as its patron, while the Seljuk Kilij Arslan annexed some Danishmend territories, whose lords came to Manuel for redress. Unchecked by Nur al-Din, Konya had become too powerful in Anatolia, and Manuel decided to cut it down to size in a campaign of Roman liberation. He commissioned a reliquary of the True Cross for the occasion; its inscribed poem said that Manuel "could not bear to see the free women's children enslaved to the slave-girl Hagar." The poem hopes for a victory like that which the Cross brought to Constantine the Great.[116] Manuel may also have wanted to reverse demographic changes that were taking place in southern Phrygia, as Turkish pastoralists were pushing out Roman agriculturalists.[117] In preparation, in 1175 he rebuilt the abandoned fortifications of Dorylaion and Soublaion on the central plateau to act as bases for expansion. In the fall of 1176, he assembled a huge army to lead against Konya, including units contributed by his foreign vassals. He also solicited crusader assistance from the west, via the pope. Manuel knew how to manipulate western rhetoric, but it is possible that it was the pope who cast the war as a crusade in his correspondence with western rulers. The campaign was not really a crusade, but a Roman war: "We fight for what is ours," proclaimed a court orator, "to restore the proper boundaries of the Roman empire."[118]

The campaign was a disaster, the worst Roman defeat since those suffered by Alexios in the 1080s and 1090s. Manuel failed to clear out a mountain pass through which his army had to pass to reach Konya, about a day's march from that city. Choniates, our main source, gets the location wrong, so we do not know where the attack took place, though the name that he gave to it, Myriokephalon, has stuck. On 17 September, the Turks fell on the center of the column as it was passing through, killing many and destroying the baggage and siege equipment. The Romans panicked and lost cohesion, but eventually they pushed through and regrouped. However, Manuel was now unable to continue the campaign and sued for terms to extricate his forces from what was, and would forever remain, enemy territory. Kilij Arslan quickly agreed, still terrified of a Roman force so near to his capital. Choniates wanted to tarnish Manuel's reputation and paints the defeat in emotive terms to suggest that the emperor's reckless ambitions resulted only in failure and humiliation. When Manuel returned home through the pass, he saw that "all the dead were scalped, many with their genitals removed"; in this way the Turks supposedly disguised the number of their own (circumcised) dead. Choniates and Manuel himself compared the defeat to that of Mantzikert, but it was not the same. The Roman defenses of Asia Minor held, as proved by the later defeat of Turkish raiders and Manuel's own successful, albeit defensive, campaigns in the region. Apart from "unbearable shame," Manuel had lost an opportunity to conquer Konya. But the battle changed little else, and Muslim sources paid it little attention.[119]

Manuel did not slow down after Myriokephalon. He sent a fleet to support another aborted attack by Jerusalem on Egypt in 1177; he campaigned in Asia Minor twice more; and he continued to expand his dynastic alliances. He scored his greatest success in that field when Louis VII of France agreed to send his eight-year-old daughter Agnes to marry Manuel's son and heir Alexios II. She arrived in 1179 to a magnificent reception celebrated by the entire City, and was betrothed to Alexios the following March. She was presented with an adorable booklet whose colorful images depict her journey and are accompanied by a poem in vernacular Greek. We also have Eustathios' speech of welcome, written in such a grand style that neither she nor anyone else present could have understood it.[120]

In 1180, Manuel scored his final victory over the Holy Synod, forcing it, after many contentious meetings, to change the formula that Muslim converts had to swear. The existing version required them to renounce Allah, who, in the Greek translation of the Quran, was described as "hammered together compactly." Manuel argued that Allah essentially meant "God" and should not be condemned along with the aspects of Islam that converts were required to abjure (Muhammad, the caliphs, the Quran, polygamy, and the like). It is unclear why Manuel wanted this change. It did not respond to, or cause, a wave of conversions. Eustathios, who was now the bishop of Thessalonike, vocally opposed the change, even though he was otherwise the emperor's cheerleader. In the end, Manuel again prevailed.[121]

Manuel took the monastic habit soon before his death on 24 September, 1180. He was buried in the central chapel, or imperial mausoleum, of the Pantokrator complex, and next to him was placed the Stone of Unction, a thin slab of dappled, red-and-white stone on which the body of Christ had been prepared for burial. Manuel had brought it from Ephesos in 1169 and had personally carried it on his back to the collection of relics in the Pharos chapel of the Great Palace.[122] He was the last emperor to be buried properly in the City for the next century and a half.

It is difficult to assess the phenomenon that was Manuel Komnenos. The man himself comes across as both ostentatiously glorious and all-too-human, the former in his court rhetoric, the latter in Choniates' snark. Manuel faced novel challenges: mastering a rapidly evolving and increasingly dangerous international scene, and commanding a fractious extended imperial clan. He invested in the exaltation of his person, in the symbolic subordination of neighboring rulers, and in marriage alliances. These were traditional tools of the monarchy, but never before used with such intensity and panache. He sought to graft onto the empire a complex network of western-style relations of vassalage, but these ties, as was their nature, adhered to himself personally and not to his crown, much less to the polity of the Roman people. The experiment collapsed when he died, because the two entities—the Roman polity and the western world of lordships and vassalage—had fundamentally different values, shapes, and origins. Previous emperors had never attempted anything like this, and later ones were in no position to emulate his approach, and so Manuel stands in glorious isolation, a passing experimental phase of Roman power.

Manuel understood better than his subjects that western Latin Europe was becoming more powerful and dynamic than ever before, and he tried to gain entry for Romanía into the western "club." He redirected the allegiance of many smaller players in Italy and Outremer to himself and bought the goodwill of others. Yet neither he nor his subjects truly belonged to that network. The Churches of Rome and Constantinople were not on good terms; Latinophobia was becoming rampant among the Romans; and, except for those whom he personally won over, the Latins increasingly disdained the "effeminate" and "faithless" Greeks. Manuel leveraged his significant assets in order to be accepted by the Latin club not only as a member but as one of their leaders. Yet for all that they would take his money, true acceptance was beyond his reach. Many Latins admired him personally: "a wise and discreet prince of great magnificence, worthy of praise in every respect"; "a right worthy man and the richest of all Christians who have ever been, and the most generous"; "the most blessed emperor of Constantinople, [at whose death] the Christian world incurred the greatest ruin and detriment."[123] But this love did not extend to his people or their polity, nor would it pass to Manuel's heirs. Thus, even his assets turned into liabilities, when the Latins whom he courted decided to *take* from the Greeks whom they despised rather than *receive*.

Domestically, Manuel governed a state that was significantly different from the Macedonian period. The upper echelons of the court and army were dominated by his own extended clan, some of whom behaved as entitled princelings. The old impersonal bureaucratic cadres, who, in the past, were drawn from the provinces and sometimes wielded real power, were now demoted to second-rate status. The court hierarchy, which previously reached into the provinces enticing their notables to invest in it, was now focused on the clan. This eroded, but did not displace, the national aspect of the Roman polity. One of Manuel's leading officials, Michael Hagiotheodorites, had been raised in an orphanage.[124] There were opportunities here, but overall fewer than before, for provincial elites to rise at the court. Without that binding layer, the government interfaced with the provinces mostly through the machinery of tax collection, recruitment, and administration. An exception were the bishops of this period, many of whom were provincials who were highly educated in Constantinople and then sent back out to the provinces to represent the center. Eustathios frequently quarreled with powerful interests at Thessalonike, both lay and monastic, and kept reminding his flock how much better things were in the capital. But others, such as Eustathios' former pupil Michael Choniates, the bishop of Athens, sided with his new city against Constantinople. Manuel held all this together through his personal majesty, effective governance, and promotion of peace and prosperity. The inscription under the cross that he placed on the column of Constantine sums up his ambitions for the polity as a whole: "Manuel, the pious emperor, renovated this holy monument, which was worn with time." But when his firm direction was removed, the system cracked, and Manuel's Latinophilia was exposed as widely unpopular. Romanía was torn apart by centrifugal forces just as it came under intense Latin attack.

30

Disintegration and Betrayal (1180–1204)

In accordance with the oath of 1171, Manuel's widow Marie of Antioch became a nun, taking the name Xene ("Foreigner"), and acted as regent for her eleven-year-old son Alexios II. The head of her government was the *protosebastos* Alexios Komnenos, the son of Manuel's brother Andronikos. Rumor had it that he and Marie were lovers. Opposed to them was a faction led by the *porphyregennete* Maria, Manuel's daughter by his German wife, whom Choniates called "reckless and masculine in resolve," and her husband, the young *kaisar* Ranieri, a son of the marquis of Montferrat (the title *kaisar* was bestowed by the Komnenoi on the most important in-law). The opposition included the City prefect, the two sons of Manuel's infamous cousin Andronikos, and others. When Marie-Xene and Alexios arrested many of their enemies in early 1181 and put them on trial for sedition, Maria and the *kaisar* sought asylum in Hagia Sophia and were supported by a large segment of the populace. Battle lines were drawn in the Augoustaion square between Hagia Sophia and the Great Palace, and the two sides clashed in May, shooting at each other from atop the City's monuments. The opposition lost and was driven inside the Great Church, but the *megas doux* Andronikos Komnenos Kontostephanos led a peace delegation from the palace, and order was restored. Manuel's death had been like the sudden removal of a support beam: everything started leaning in opposite directions.[1]

The empire's territorial contraction began immediately. Béla III of Hungary broke his oaths and, in 1180–1181, retook Dalmatia and Sirmium while his forces ravaged the territory of Belgrade and Braničevo. After all the effort that Manuel had put into the acquisition of Dalmatia and Sirmium—his only real conquests—they were lost swiftly and without notice in the Greek sources.[2] At the same time, the empire lost the Cilician plain to Antioch and the Armenians. It had changed hands often during the twelfth century, as it was too far from the rest of the empire and could be held securely only through direct imperial intervention, but this time the loss was permanent.[3] Also, Kilij Arslan took Sozopolis (which Ioannes II had acquired in 1120) and placed Attaleia under siege. It appears that Attaleia and the coast were cut off, probably permanently, from the rest of Roman Asia Minor.[4]

The empire was surrounded by predators who took advantage of Manuel's death to seize its lands. Many in the City began to look to Manuel's experienced cousin Andronikos to save the state. He was one of the most colorful and versatile personalities of the age. Tall and handsome, he was personally brave, but a poor strategist. In his treachery, Andronikos was an exaggerated version of his father, the *sebastokrator* Isaakios. For plotting against Manuel, Andronikos had been imprisoned in 1155 in the palace, from where he escaped twice, in cinematic ways. In the 1160s, he was reconciled with Manuel and sent in 1166 to govern Cilicia, but he deserted his post for Antioch, where he seduced Philippa, the sister of Manuel's second wife, Marie, jeopardizing the emperor's foreign policy. To avoid arrest, Andronikos fled to Jerusalem, where he seduced Theodora, the daughter of a cousin and widow of king Baldwin. The couple and their children wandered from court to court in the Near East for many years, until Theodora was captured by imperial agents. Andronikos returned to Constantinople in 1180, shortly before Manuel's death, and prostrated himself theatrically before him, begging forgiveness with a chain around his neck. Manuel sent him to govern Paphlagonia. Now in his early sixties, he was regarded by some as an elder statesman.[5]

East Roman Latinophobia

In early 1182, Andronikos advanced along the Black Sea, communicating with the opposition in the capital, spreading propaganda against the *protosebastos* Alexios, and posturing as the young emperor's champion. He defeated an imperial force that was sent against him under Andronikos Angelos. Angelos fled to the City but, fearing that he would be arrested for throwing the battle, fled again, this time to join Andronikos; he took with him his six sons, who included two future emperors, Isaakios and Alexios. Meanwhile, the *protosebastos* Alexios mobilized a fleet that included some Roman but mostly Italian ships, under the command of the *megas doux* Kontostephanos, a real elder statesman. But when Andronikos reached Chalkedon, Kontostephanos defected to him and the populace of the City were prepared to accept the rebel as "a god on earth." Many crossed the Bosporos to welcome him. The *protosebastos'* authority collapsed: he was arrested, hauled before Andronikos, and blinded. Andronikos then struck against the Latins of the City, in part because they had supported the regime of the empress and *protosebastos*, and in part because he sought to ride anti-Latin feeling to the throne. His fleet hemmed the Latins in the Golden Horn while their quarters were attacked by the populace. Men, women, and children were slaughtered, mostly Genoese and Pisans (as the Venetians had been expelled in 1171); properties were plundered and the quarters were set on fire. A papal legate was decapitated and his head tied to the tail of a dog, underscoring the religious dimension of the "hatred" that was unleashed. Still, forty-four ships escaped with refugees, and they recouped their losses, which the Genoese calculated at 228,000 hyperpyra, by ravaging the coasts on their way back home in April.[6]

Andronikos' propaganda cast the massacre as a defeat of "the tyranny of the Latins" and "a restoration of Roman affairs."[7] The event exacerbated anti-Greek feeling in Italy, and revealed the depth of anti-Latin sentiment in Romanía.

Likely a majority of Romans now regarded the Latins as religiously deviant or heretical in matters such as the *azyma* and *filioque*. The eastern Church rejected papal supremacy. Some, such as Kinnamos and Balsamon, even went so far as to claim for the Church of Constantinople the powers that Rome claimed for itself, on the grounds that it was now the seat of imperial power. After all, one of Rome's favorite proof texts, the (forged) *Donation of Constantine*, supported the notion that the pope's position was based on an act by Constantine, and Constantine had transferred his imperial power to the east. The Holy Synod even declared, around 1190, that "all churches of God must follow the custom of New Rome, that is Constantinople." When asked by the Melkite Church of Alexandria, now under the rule of Saladin, how to treat Latins, the Synod answered that the Church of Rome was no longer either Catholic or Orthodox, and so Latins could not be given communion.[8] Yet the Synod stopped short of declaring Rome heretical. That was a popular belief, not an official position.

The terms "Catholic" and "Orthodox" were not used in their modern senses at this time. The two Churches were differentiated primarily by language, Latin and Greek, a distinction that the east Romans accepted so long as the term Greek (*Graikos*) was used in a linguistic and not an ethnic sense. Their polemic against the Latins was to a considerable degree reactive, responding to centuries of westerners branding the "Greeks" as schismatic or heretical over their "disloyalty" to Rome as well as un-Roman and "effeminate." Religious hostility to the Greeks in Venice and Jerusalem had even created obstacles to Manuel's diplomacy. By the mid-twelfth century, westerners were complaining that the Greeks were washing down altars after Latins had used them and rebaptizing Latins before marrying them.[9]

Each side drew up lists of the "errors" of the other, but not everything in them was strictly about religion. Cultural differences were caught up in them too pertaining to food, social norms, and warfare. As was often the case in premodern ethnography, the two sides represented each other in gendered terms, with Greeks representing Latins as vicious and abusive men: they loved violence (even their priests fought in battle) and were arrogant and greedy (they would sell their wives for profit). Meanwhile, the Latins attributed to Greeks the vices of women: effeminacy, cowardice, subtlety, fickleness, and treachery. The Romans countered this by condemning the Latin custom of shaving because it "transformed men into women," or rather into "male women like the Hellenic hermaphrodites, who submit to men sexually no less than they mount women."[10] These stereotypes circulated broadly and explain the outburst of violence in April, 1182. The people of Constantinople knew that they were regarded as "faithless effeminate Greeks" by the Latins in their midst.

It is unlikely that the populace was angry at the trade concessions given to the Latins, for those did not yet have a major deleterious effect on the state budget or private fortunes, except among a small merchant class. It is more likely that resentment had built up at the favoritism that Manuel showed to the "barbarians." Latins had backed the regime of a foreign empress-regent (Marie of Antioch) and her corrupt Komnenian lover. The populace might well have feared, as Andronikos claimed, that the Latins were taking over the Roman state behind the scenes. It was a long-standing fear that the crusaders wanted to seize Constantinople. Manuel himself had encouraged such fears in 1147 in order to cast himself as the City's savior during the passage of the Second Crusade. We should not dismiss these fears as irrational, for many western authors of the twelfth century advocated precisely the capture of Constantinople and subjugation by force of the "faithless Greeks" to papal obedience.[11] A Greek envoy to the German court had denounced the papacy for betraying its religious calling by "gathering soldiers and inciting wars."[12]

By 1182, Latinophobia was pervasive in Roman society, especially in religious and popular circles, while Latinophilia was a niche attitude limited to a few secular elites who admired the Latins' martial qualities or benefited from their trade routes. After Manuel, suspicion was ascendant.

Andronikos I Komnenos

Andronikos methodically consolidated his own power under the cover of defending Alexios II. At Pentecost, 1182 (16 May), he had Alexios crowned again in Hagia Sophia, carrying him there on his own shoulders and swearing oaths to serve him. But the child was isolated. His half-sister Maria *porphyregennete* and her husband Ranieri died soon afterward, allegedly of poison administered by one of Andronikos' eunuchs. Alexios' mother Marie-Xene was also accused of sedition, tried, and convicted. She was confined to a monastery—she had, after all, taken vows after Manuel's death—then strangled, probably in early 1183. In 1182 or 1183, the *megas doux* Kontostephanos (the most senior Roman statesman), Andronikos Angelos, and their sixteen (!) sons, realizing what Andronikos was up to, formed a conspiracy against him. But they were betrayed. Kontostephanos and his sons were blinded. Angelos and his sons fled to Syria, possibly to Saladin.[13]

In September, 1183, Andronikos exploited a state of emergency to have himself proclaimed co-emperor. The Hungarians, aided by Serbs under Nemanja, had invaded the empire, overrunning Belgrade (which they kept), Niš, and Serdica. In addition, Nikaia and Prousa in Bithynia rebelled, the first under Theodoros Kantakouzenos and Isaakios Angelos (who had returned from Syria), the second under Isaakios' brother Theodoros Angelos. This crisis was an opportunity for Andronikos, whose yes-men "pressured" him to take the crown and save the republic. They were, perhaps, not entirely insincere: Andronikos had gotten this far because many believed that the state needed experienced leadership. He was acclaimed in the palace and, on the next day, when he was crowned in Hagia Sophia, his name was chanted before that of Alexios. The young heir was murdered soon afterward and his body dumped into the sea. Andronikos had "extirpated Manuel's family, pruning the imperial garden."[14]

The Hungarians were driven back by the general Alexios Branas, who then joined Andronikos in Bithynia in the spring of 1184. Nikaia was beseiged, and the emperor even strapped the mother of the Angeloi to a battering ram that he brought against the city. She was rescued by the defenders in a sally. The city surrendered and Isaakios was allowed to return to Constantinople under a pledge of security. Prousa, however, was taken by force. Many of its defenders were either executed or suffered horrendous punishments. Theodoros Angelos was blinded, placed on an ass, and forced to wander into the sultanate, where he was rescued and cared for by some Turks.[15]

For the reign of Andronikos, we rely on two hostile narratives: Eustathios' account of the capture of Thessalonike by the Normans in 1185, which was written in the immediate aftermath of that great disaster and of Andronikos' gruesome demise, and Choniates' history, which utilized Eustathios and depicts Andronikos as a classical tyrant, in fact as "surpassing all the tyrants who ever lived." His Andronikos is repressive, surrounded by vile yes-men, a dissimulator who suspects plots everywhere; he is driven by resentment against Manuel and has huge and creepy sexual appetites. He spent time and money on courtesans, and "was not ashamed, a man at the age of Kronos, to illegally marry his nephew's rosy-cheeked and tender bride [Agnes-Anna of France], who was barely eleven, an overripe dotard in the same bed with an unripe maiden, a wrinkly geezer next to a perky-breasted lass."[16] Andronikos' successors, the Angeloi, made it their official line that he had been a tyrant, and this was echoed in all texts addressed to them and their men. Weathervanes such as Theodoros Balsamon edited their texts, replacing *basileus* with *tyrannos* in references to him. But Andronikos was also an abiding source of fascination. Choniates used the formidable yet ambiguous image of Odysseus to capture his conflicting qualities, but he sometimes also became the fearsome Cyclops.[17]

Andronikos' was a reign of terror: spies everywhere, conspiracies real or alleged, night arrests, sham public trials, and spectacular punishments, including impalements, hangings, amputations, blindings, and burnings. He required the nobles to swear oaths of collective responsibility for each other's crimes. Eustathios alleges that the basis of his support was in the common people, that he wanted to wipe out the aristocracy and leave to his sons a polity of bakers and butchers.[18] This reign of terror was no literary invention, for it was reported in similar terms in western chronicles.[19] But the terror was balanced by positive initiatives that Choniates, to his credit, also reveals. Andronikos cracked down on abuses by tax collectors, curtailed supplementary taxes, and stopped selling offices, a practice that incentivized officials to fleece the provinces to recoup their "investments." Instead, he paid higher salaries to make his officials less corruptible and punished them for wrongdoing. He was receptive to accusations against them, and they "were petrified with fear of him, for they knew that he was not kidding around." Thus, the provinces grew prosperous and farmers "reclined in the shade of their trees with no fear of the tax man."[20]

That these measures bore fruit is confirmed by Michael Choniates, Niketas' older brother. Michael was among a class of provincials who were educated in Constantinople and then posted as bishops to provincial cities, in his case Athens. Michael's many letters and speeches are major sources for provincial society in the later twelfth century and reveal how bishops advocated for their cities, lamented the uncouthness of provincial culture, pined for the salons of Constantinople, but also excoriated official abuses. Michael in particular offers a fascinating glimpse into the attractions that the monuments of ancient Athens held for men of his cultural background. His residence was the Propylaia and his cathedral was the Parthenon church of the Virgin, whose statues still stood on the pediments while the interior was painted with Orthodox icons of the saints. Michael could not but compare the "ruined" city before him to the ideal polis of his imagination, and he commissioned a painting of ancient Athens in all its glory. The Parthenon was for him "the edge of heaven . . . a world-transcending chamber that projects spiritual energies" during the liturgy.[21]

During the reign of Andronikos, Michael praised the emperor for his justice, for cracking down on tax abuses, and allowing the cities to breathe again, and he praised the governors sent to Greece for their excellent qualities, comparing one of them to Tribonian. They prepared new tax registers that favored Athens, though these did not have time to go into effect. To be sure, this praise was formulaic, but Niketas was surely echoing information obtained from his brother when he praised the emperor's governance, and Michael asked his successor for more governors like his.[22] Andronikos, it appears, was responding to growing complaints about inequality, corruption, and a gap between Constantinople and the provinces. That he had to take such drastic measures—increasing salaries!—reveals uncomfortable truths about the public policy that Manuel had created. It is possible that serious domestic dysfunctions had long been disguised by Manuel's charisma.

However, Andronikos' reign of terror alienated the extended Komnenian aristocracy, especially by restricting their abuses. Many, including the Angeloi, fled to foreign courts, calling on their rulers to honor their pledges to Manuel and his son by attacking Andronikos.[23] Yet they found that those pledges had evaporated when Manuel died. Some rebelled. This was done by Isaakios Doukas Komnenos, a grandson of Isaakios *sebastokrator*, Manuel's brother. In 1184, using forged documents of appointment, he seized Cyprus and, from this point on, the island ceased to be part of the main Roman polity. Fragmentation had begun. Isaakios declared himself emperor and struck coins in his own name, but he lacked the means to export his rebellion, so he ruled Cyprus as an independent but peripheral Roman state until it was conquered by Richard the Lionheart of England in 1191, during the Third Crusade. Isaakios' reign is likewise described as tyrannical, marred by rapes, confiscations, and savagery. An aspiring saint on the island, the recluse Neophytos, described it as a period of evils: "he robbed the rich of their livelihood and imposed punishments on the lords so that they were in distress and sought to flee from his power."[24]

Inevitably, the entitled Komnenian princelings who fled from Andronikos found an opportunistic foreign leader willing to help them. This was William II (1166–1189), the king of Norman Sicily, whose ancestors had a tradition of attacking Romanía on behalf of alleged pretenders and who himself had been slighted by Manuel in a marriage proposal. His invasion forces, mustered in the summer of 1185, were accompanied by Alexios Komnenos (grandson of Manuel's brother Andronikos) *and* a child passed off as Alexios II, who had supposedly survived his murder. The Norman fleet of 220 ships quickly captured Dyrrachion on 24 June. Its army marched to Thessalonike, reaching it without opposition on 6 August, while the fleet sailed around Greece and arrived on 15 August. The walls were breached after a hard-fought siege and the city fell on 24 August. We have a detailed account by the archbishop Eustathios, who focuses on blaming the incompetence of the governor, David Komnenos. The conquerors raped, pillaged, and slaughtered for days. The dead were later counted at 7,000, a plausible figure, and Eustathios was asked to pay 4,000 hyperpyra for his ransom, though he could not. The ethnoreligious aspect of the violence inflicted by "the Roman-hating Latins" is also striking. They arranged the bodies of dead men and animals in sexual poses; killed priests in the churches, raped nuns, and urinated on sacred vessels; mixed lard with the bread so that their victims would have to break fasting rules; and violently cut off their beards, a sign of Latin gender insecurity. Eustathios considered the sack of his city as payback for the massacre of the Latins in 1182.[25]

Thessalonike was occupied until November. The Normans had also lost many men in the fighting and subsequently to disease and ambushes outside the walls. But, from the start, William had set his sights on Constantinople itself. The populace of the City was by now disenchanted with Andronikos' reign of terror and feared foreign conquest. The emperor had retired to a villa on the Asian side and considered executing all his political enemies at once. On 11 September, he also sent men to arrest Isaakios Angelos, who was twenty-nine and living quietly after surrendering Nikaia the previous year. Fearing for his life, Isaakios mounted a horse and charged at the man who came for him, splitting his skull with a sword. He then rode through the City to Hagia Sophia, waving the bloody weapon and calling on the populace to rally to his aid. The gambit paid off: the people of Constantinople massed at the Great Church and acclaimed Isaakios emperor, forcing the patriarch to crown him on the next day with the diadem of Constantine the Great that was suspended above the altar. Andronikos returned to the Great Palace and even shot arrows into the crowd from a tower, but realized that the situation was hopeless. Many of his guards had already melted away. He offered to abdicate in favor of his more popular son Manuel, but received insults in response. He therefore fled north, in a boat with Agnes and a concubine, but he was intercepted and hauled back. Andronikos thereupon suffered, over the course of many days, a gruesome dismemberment by the crowd, which included the widows of his victims. What was left of him was hung by the feet from a column in the hippodrome.[26]

Isaakios II Angelos

After a century of urban calm, owed to the competent if not always beloved rule by the first three Komnenoi, the people of Constantinople had emerged again as a force in politics. They had given the throne to Isaakios II (1185–1195), but had looted the Great Palace, including the treasury and armory, during the September commotions.[27] Meanwhile, the Norman war was in full swing, with the invaders advancing into Thrace. But just then an able leader emerged on the Roman side, the general Alexios Branas, who was entrusted with a war chest of 4,000 lbs of gold. He decisively defeated the Normans in November, 1185, first at Mosynopolis as they were heading toward the capital and then at the Strymon river. Branas captured their leaders, the counts Baldwin and Richard of Acerra, along with thousands of their soldiers, who would languish in captivity for years, many of them starving to death. While the Normans fled from Thessalonike, their fleet of 200 ships under Tancred of Lecce sailed into the Sea of Marmara but was repelled by the imperial fleet of 100 ships. Tancred attacked the coast around Nikomedeia but was again repulsed by land forces and by retrofitted merchant vessels manned by natives. Isaakios' orators, including the brothers Choniates, spun this as a great victory. Indeed it was, but that is how they would describe the emperor's every action for the next ten years, even the setbacks.[28]

Isaakios regained Dyrrachion in 1186, but the Ionian islands of Kephalonia, Ithaca, and Zakynthos were occupied by the Norman admiral Margaritone. They were permanently lost to the empire, and would pass to Venetian control after 1204. Margaritone's fleet also held some Aegean islands in 1186, subjecting them to tribute. Romanía was being chipped away at the edges.[29] In such circumstances, Isaakios could implement no grand agenda like that of Manuel, but he did try to rebuild Manuel's old network. Probably in early 1186, he married the ten-year-old daughter of Béla III, Margit (renamed Maria) to restore the Hungarian alliance. According to Isaakios himself, Béla swore to him the same oaths that he had given to Manuel, and pledged not to infringe on the "rights of Romanía" or to dominate the župan of Serbia.[30] But Isaakios was likely exaggerating the concessions that he extracted.

Isaakios aspired to rule more gently and compensated the victims of his predecessor's tyranny, but he was still ruthless against those who threatened his throne. He blinded Andronikos' sons as well as Alexios Komnenos, who incited the Normans.[31] On two occasions, he appointed men blinded by Andronikos to command armies, probably because they could not usurp the throne, but this hurt him in the more obvious way. An expedition against Cyprus in 1186, co-led by a blind general, failed miserably. The island's ruler, Isaakios Doukas Komnenos, defeated the imperial land army, while the Norman admiral Margaritone, who was sailing past Cyprus at that moment, took the seventy or eighty ships of the imperial fleet as they lay at harbor and sailed back to Sicily. This was effectively the end of the Roman imperial fleet as a formidable Mediterranean force.[32]

A greater blow against the empire was struck in the north: this was the independence movement that created the Second Bulgarian Empire. We know almost nothing about its socioeconomic background, and all discussion by scholars along these lines is pure guesswork. Our only narrative is by Niketas Choniates, who is hostile to the rebels and notes two of their grievances. In 1185 or 1186 (the date is unclear), the two brothers who founded the rebel state, Theodore (who later took the name Petar) and Ivan Asen, approached Isaakios at the mustering grounds of Kypsella in Thrace and asked, without success, to be enrolled in the army in exchange for receiving a pronoia in the Stara Planina. In their ensuing rebellion, they exploited disaffection among their people over the supplementary taxes that Isaakios levied to pay for his wedding with Margit. The sources suggest that the brothers were ethnic Vlachs, and they raised their rebellion in the territory between the Haimos mountains and the Danube, in the heartland of old Bulgaria, and so they pitched their movement as a revival of the Bulgarian empire. The name "Petar" harked back to the saintly tsar of the tenth century and the Bulgarian rebellions of the eleventh century (1040, 1072). Petar and Ivan Asen both claimed imperial status, the latter on one of his Greek seals as "*basileus* of the Bulgarians," while a Roman poet even called the former "Slavo-Peter." This was, then, a joint Vlacho-Bulgarian effort. The brothers rallied their followers around St. Demetrios, who, they argued, had abandoned Thessalonike. God now favored "the freedom of the Bulgarians and the Vlachs."[33]

The Vlachs spoke a language descended from Latin and, in the period 1000–1200, are attested in various mountainous regions of the former Bulgarian empire, including the Pindos and Stara Planina ranges as well as Thessaly (aka "Vlachia"). They were the linguistic descendants of the Latin speakers of the ancient Balkans, who passed out of imperial control after 600 and, by the eleventh century, were no longer regarded as Romans by the Greek speakers. Even though some believed that they originated in Italy—a connection prompted by their language—they were seen by Roman writers as nomadic barbarians. Their mountain dwellings were not seen as properly "pacified" from an imperial standpoint. The Vlachs had their own leadership. In 1066, some of them had staged a tax revolt in Thessaly. Now, a group in the Stara Planina led the dismemberment of the Roman empire.[34]

The rebels tried to take Preslav, but failed, and eventually Tarnovo became their capital. Their main activity in the years to come was to raid the Roman cities that ringed the Haimos range to the south and east. Whenever Isaakios was not preoccupied with another crisis, he campaigned against the rebels in their mountains, though never with lasting success. Choniates presents him as tiring quickly and fleeing back to the pleasures of the capital and his banquets. In 1186, for example, he overran their territory and forced Asen to flee across the Danube, but failed to adequately occupy the "gorges, mountains, and peaks," whereupon Asen returned with a host of Cuman allies.[35] Campaigns against the Vlachs, Bulgarians, and Cumans were now added to the docket of regular imperial business. Constantinople had lost more territory, and enemy raiding cut further into the revenues of Thrace.

Despite the panegyrics, which proclaimed Isaakios greater than Basil II, he was perceived as weak, which triggered many rebellions against him, even among his inner circle. In 1187, the general Alexios Branas was sent to deal with Bulgaria, but in April he was proclaimed emperor in his native city, Adrianople, after which he invested Constantinople. Branas appealed to the people to turn against Isaakios and open the gates, but they stood with the emperor whom they had created only two years before. But Branas did win over the commanders of both the Balkans and Asia Minor, isolating the capital. Isaakios did not have enough soldiers to prevail in battle. In an early skirmish, he even sent out Norman prisoners from the war of 1185, whom Branas defeated. Isaakios' salvation came from matrimonial diplomacy. Earlier that year he had married his sister Theodora to Conrad (Corrado), son of the marquis of Montferrat and brother of Ranieri (d. 1182) who had married Manuel I's daughter Maria. Choniates says that Conrad, elevated to the rank of *kaisar*, organized the defense. Yet we must be cautious here because Choniates often sets up virtuous Latins as foils for his degenerate Romans. With gold raised from monasteries, Conrad hired an additional force of 250 Latin knights, 500 infantry, plus assorted Turkish and Georgian mercenaries, who were joined by another 1,000 Romans provided by nobles loyal to Isaakios. With this improvised army, Isaakios and Conrad defeated and killed Branas outside the City walls. The rebel's head was kicked around at a celebratory banquet.[36]

Isaakios had no choice but to issue an amnesty for those who had joined Branas, but he allowed his Latin allies to ravage the homes of some peasants by the coast who had supported the rebel, and they were joined by people from the City while the navy sprayed the homes with Greek fire. Yet when the Latins returned to Constantinople they were set upon by other sectors of the populace.

An ethnic war was brewing, but passions were calmed by men of rank sent by the court. The City was becoming ungovernable. Conrad departed immediately for Outremer to fight against Saladin. He later became the king-in-exile of Jerusalem, severing his ties to Constantinople and even pretending that he had never been married to Theodora.

Two years into Isaakios' reign, the walls were closing in. Cyprus, the Ionian islands, and northern Bulgaria were lost, as was most of the imperial fleet. Asia Minor was periodically raided by Turkish emirs who had to be paid off to leave, and Thrace was raided by the Vlacho-Bulgarians. Thessalonike had been ruined by the Normans, and tax exemptions had to be granted to other victimized cities, which reduced revenue and forced the emperor's taxmen to squeeze other districts. Isaakios lacked the authority to master his nobles, many of whom had just supported the rebel Branas, and the populace of the City was increasingly restless. Over the next few years, a number of Komnenoi were arrested for plotting against the emperor and blinded. "Again and again this happened, it is impossible to say how often: like hollow bubbles they would emerge and then burst."[37]

To make matters worse, Romanía's coastlines and islands were increasingly harassed by what are called "pirates" in the sources and modern scholarship. They raided, murdered, plundered livestock, and sold their captives into slavery or held them for ransom. These were not random bandits but fleets from Norman Sicily and the Italian merchant republics, who were supplementing their earnings from trade, attacking rival Italians, or acting as para-statal agents on behalf of their cities in pressuring Constantinople. They became brazen in the 1180s and 1190s as the Romans no longer had an effective fleet. "The pirates now rule the seas and Roman lands near the coast suffer for it."[38] It was a return to the evils that had afflicted Romanía around 900, only with Italian instead of Muslim raiders. An eloquent witness to these ravages was Michael Choniates, for whom only tax collectors were worse. Athens, he laments, had once resisted Xerxes, but now Marathon and Eleusis were exposed to these killers, whom he identifies as Lombards. Aigina was virtually depopulated, although, alarmingly, some locals intermarried with the pirates and joined in their depredations, a sign of mounting provincial alienation from Constantinople.[39]

It is not surprising, then, that Isaakios renewed the trading and residential concessions of the Italian cities, first of Venice (1187, 1189), then Pisa and Genoa (1192). Romanía was simply too exposed to naval attack, and the theory behind the concessions was that they were granted by a benevolent emperor to loyal allies who would do their part in defending the polity that they so loved. The Venetians agreed to send fleets to aid the emperor in war, though he would pay most of their expenses and supply an equal number of ships (which in reality he could not do); the doge also was to swear an oath of loyalty to him. In return, Isaakios established a commission to track down and return the property confiscated from Venetians in the mass arrest of 1171. When this proved impractical, in 1189 he enlarged their quarter at the expense of smaller quarters given to the French and Germans, and undertook to pay the damages of 1171 himself (1,500 lbs of gold in installments). One chrysobull of 1192 stipulates that those whose properties were confiscated to endow the Genoese quarter (probably monasteries) could not sue the Genoese as they would be compensated by the fisc and that the confiscations were conditional on the beneficiaries' serving "the interests of Romanía."[40]

In reality, except for the restoration of the Latin quarters the terms of these treaties were never fully implemented. Venice never sent military aid, the emperor had no fleet, and probably no one was compensated. Isaakios was likely bullied into restoring the quarters and the chrysobulls stipulate ideal but unenforceable terms. This was a striking sign of Romanía's rapid decline to second-rate status. The chrysobull of June, 1189 to the Venetians, in which the emperor conceded far more than he received, was made under duress, for the massive army of Friedrich Barbarossa was approaching the City.

The Third Crusade

Few Romans reacted to the fall of Jerusalem to Saladin in 1187. One of them was Neophytos the Recluse on nearby Cyprus. He was outraged that the tomb of Christ fell into the hands of that "Muslim dog." Yet after the failure of the Third Crusade, he also opined that "Providence was not inclined to toss out the dogs and put wolves [Latins] in their place."[41] But in western Europe, the news of Saladin's success caused anguish and energized the pope and many kings to take action. Huge armies were raised through special levies and recruitment drives. Henry II of England and the German emperor Friedrich Barbarossa requested permission to pass through Romanía and receive supplies along the way; Henry even addressed Isaakios as "emperor of the Romans by the grace of God." Isaakios granted both requests in 1188 but his envoy to Friedrich, the logothete of the *dromos* Ioannes Doukas Kamateros, expressed the suspicion that Jerusalem was a pretext and the real target of the expedition was Constantinople; for Isaakios, this was "common opinion." Mutual assurances were therefore sworn.[42]

In the event, Henry died and his successor, Richard I, did not set out until 1190. Along with Philippe II of France, he chose to sail to Syria from Sicily. Barbarossa set out overland in 1189 with—according to sober scholarship—the largest army that the Balkans had ever seen: 20,000 knights and 80,000 infantry, too large and expensive to transport by sea.[43] Yet despite the agreement with Isaakios and the tight discipline of the German army, relations soured. The Germans were harassed by locals after Niš, and at Serdica, which they reached on 13 August, they discovered that there would be no markets and the way forward into Thrace was blocked. The Germans fought their way through and occupied Philippopolis in late August. The local governor was Niketas Choniates, who had first been instructed to repair the walls in anticipation of an attack and then, in a complete reversal, to demolish them so that the Germans could not hold the city securely. The Romans abandoned it, leaving only the Armenians, whose faith, from the Orthodox point of view, had common traits with the Latins (especially the use of *azyma*).[44] Harassed by imperial soldiers, the Germans held Philippopolis until November, when they moved to Adrianople and made plans to assault Constantinople. Friedrich had written to his son Heinrich in Germany to assemble a fleet from the Italian cities and meet him in March at Constantinople for a joint attack by land and sea. Heinrich was to get the pope to preach a crusade against the Greeks, the "enemies of the Cross." Their patriarch, he heard, had announced in Hagia Sophia that those who killed "pilgrims" (i.e., crusaders) would be forgiven by the Lord for their other sins.[45] Why had relations soured so badly?

Isaakios, his patriarch Dositheos, and probably most Romans did believe that Friedrich's real target was Constantinople. That was a long-standing fear. It did not help, moreover, that Friedrich met with the Serb Nemanja and was lobbied repeatedly by the Bulgarians, who now controlled the entire lower Danube as far as the Dobrudja, for an offensive alliance against Romanía. Isaakios feared that Friedrich planned to partition Romanía among his local allies and sons.[46] It was a self-fulfilling fear, as the Romans' hostility prompted Friedrich, who sincerely intended to march on to Jerusalem, to contemplate an attack. For their part, the Germans (and, soon, the entire Latin world) wrongly believed that Isaakios was in league with Saladin—the two had allegedly drunk each other's blood. The notion that Isaakios was undermining the crusade is still debated, though a convincing argument has been made that this was a Latin myth based on hatred and a more distant, albeit cordial, diplomatic relationship between Isaakios and Saladin. The former wanted the churches of Jerusalem to be given to Greeks, and the latter wanted his name, and that of the caliph whom he represented, to be mentioned in the prayers of the mosques in Constantinople.[47] Even though Isaakios later claimed, in seeking aid from Saladin, that he opposed the Germans as a service to him, Saladin knew that "the Roman king fears the Franks for the sake of his own realm, but if he succeeds against them, he will say that he did it for us."[48]

Isaakios' strategy was foolish. He could not realistically defeat or deflect Friedrich, who spent the winter occupying Thrace. He could only aggravate him and further inflame western opinion. Even if he were to win against the Germans, the consequences would be disastrous. For the Latins, "the Greeks" were already seen as uniformly "disobedient to Rome" and enemies of the crusades. However, Isaakios' actions may have been inspired by irrational beliefs. Choniates tells us that the emperor was susceptible to prophesies, conceits of divine invulnerability, and fantasies that he would personally conquer Palestine. Indeed, on 6 January,

1190, Choniates himself, speaking at the court, praised Isaakios as the emperor who would march Roman armies to Palestine. A court that could indulge in such delusions when the Vlacho-Bulgarians had seized the north and the Germans were occupying Thrace was probably not following a coherent strategy. In the process, Isaakios earned "the enmity of the Franks and their kin."[49]

The alliance between Constantinople and Venice, concluded months before the arrival of the German army and possibly intended as a safeguard against it, likely hindered Friedrich's agents in the west from raising the fleet that he wanted. And Constantinople finally came to its senses. Further negotiations resulted in an agreement over transport and supplies, in February, 1190. The Germans crossed the Hellespont, not the Bosporos, and marched into and across Asia Minor. They defeated the Turks and briefly took Konya, something that the Second Crusade and Manuel had failed to do. They moved on into Cilicia, where Friedrich fell into a stream and drowned in June 1190. His army subsequently melted away or died of disease, and those who stayed in Syria joined the grinding debacle of the Third Crusade. In retrospect, Choniates excoriated Isaakios for his stupidity and praised Friedrich as a noble emperor "whose passion for Christ burned brighter than in any Christian emperor of the time."[50] Choniates used Latins as a mirror to make his own people look bad.

Isaakios' obstructionism exacerbated Constantinople's evil reputation in the west. The Third Crusade also caused material damage to Romanía in May 1191, when Richard of England conquered Cyprus, removing it forever from Roman rule. His pretext was that its "tyrant" Isaakios Doukas Komnenos mistreated some of his men who landed on the island when they were blown off course. "We could not tolerate such an affront."[51] The reality was more political and premeditated. The crown of Jerusalem was being contested by two factions, that of Guy de Lusignan (backed by Richard, his liege) and the other by Conrad of Montferrat (the conqueror of Branas in 1187, backed by Philippe II of France). Isaakios Doukas Komnenos was allied with Conrad's faction, making him a target in Richard's eyes.[52] In 1192, when the crown went to Conrad, Richard gave Cyprus to Guy de Lusignan. Moreover, the strategic and material advantages that Cyprus offered to the crusaders were well known and not a merely incidental benefit of its conquest. Before moving to Syria, Richard removed from it "everything that was necessary for his expedition as if it had been collected for him."[53] Cyprus' occupation was a brutal colonial conquest and should not be romanticized in chivalric terms.

The Vlacho-Bulgarians and their Cuman allies continued to preoccupy Isaakios. He campaigned against them almost every year, without scoring decisive victories. Meanwhile, they raided widely in the early 1190s, attacking Anchialos, Varna, Serdica, Niš, Philippopolis, and Beroe. Isaakios scored a major success in a different quarter when, in 1190–1191, he defeated the Serbs and restored control over Braničevo and Niš. Nemanja's son (also named Stefan) was married to a daughter of the emperor's brother Alexios, and Isaakios met with his father-in-law Béla of Hungary. He secured Roman control over that northwestern corner of the frontier. And in 1192, he somehow drove a wedge between Asen (at Tarnovo) and Petar (at Preslav) by coming to some kind of arrangement with the latter.[54]

Despite this success, however, Romanía continued to fragment. In Asia Minor, one Theodoros Mangaphas rebelled in Philadelpheia in 1188, apparently taking the imperial title and minting silver coins. Isaakios marched against him in early 1189 and persuaded him to step down, but in the 1190s he defected to Konya, recruited Turkish soldiers with the sultan's permission, and raided the provinces.[55] His career pointed to two alarming developments. The first was local separatism. The likes of Mangaphas and Isaakios Doukas Komnenos on Cyprus may have claimed to be emperors, but in practice their movements remained local. The second was the greater frequency with which Romans crossed state and ethnic lines to form alliances with foreigners. In theory, it was supposed to be barbarians who assimilated to Roman manners and fought for Romanía against their former nation. Now defections began to cut in the other direction, a trend that had been pioneered by Isaakios *sebastokrator* and his sons.[56] Their treasonous interfaith alliances were now being replicated fractally on a local level, which was facilitated by the border's proximity and a century of contacts across it.

The Romans could now be pushed around, even slapped in the face, by midlevel powers. In 1192, some Genoese and Pisan "pirates" under the Genoese admiral Guglielmo Grasso conducted a murderous raid on Rhodes, after which they boarded a Venetian ship carrying Roman and Syrian ambassadors and gifts from Saladin. They killed many on board and seized the goods, whose worth Isaakios calculated at 96,566 hyperpyra. He lodged a formal protest with Genoa and Pisa and, under pressure by Roman merchants and "the anger of the populace of Constantinople," he tried to hold the recently reinstituted Genoese community in Constantinople financially liable for the crimes of their compatriots. The community handed over a security deposit of 20,000, but it is unlikely that full compensation was ever made. Genoese envoys pressured Isaakios to back off.[57]

Alexios III Komnenos

In late 1194, Isaakios' generals suffered a humiliating defeat by the Vlachs and Cumans near Arkadiopolis, not far from Constantinople itself. Calling on his father-in-law Béla of Hungary for assistance, Isaakios marched out in person in the spring of 1195. However, on 8 April, at the mustering grounds of Kypsella, he was arrested and blinded by a faction led by his older brother Alexios that included Branas, Palaiologos, Petraliphas, Raoul, and Kantakouzenos. The

City populace passively accepted this change and Alexios III (1195–1203) was crowned in Hagia Sophia, changing his name from Angelos to Komnenos, which is what he is called in official documents. Alexios called off the campaign and, in the manner of the eleventh-century emperors, used the funds saved up by his brother to buy political support. Our view of Alexios is dominated by the hostile account of Choniates, who managed his civilian administration as logothete of the *sekreta*. After 1204, Choniates revised his account, making it even more negative toward Alexios. He accuses the gouty emperor of wasting money on pleasures, being a "womanish man," and neglecting affairs of state, especially the wars.[58] This, as we will see, was untrue.

Choniates also accuses Alexios' wife Euphrosyne Doukaina Kamaterina of being too manly and meddling in politics; it was she who secured the capital during Alexios' coup and suppressed a countermovement to proclaim a Kontostephanos, son of the blinded *megas doux*, as emperor. Choniates accuses her of mutilating sculptures in the City in the magical belief that she could thereby avert certain evil outcomes. All this is stock gendered polemic and undermined by a careful reading of Choniates' own narrative. Alexios certainly did not neglect his duties. Instead, he responded with alacrity, if not always with success, to every rebellion and invasion. Choniates tends to elaborate disasters at great length, but spends only a line or two on Alexios' often successful responses to them. Romanía continued to lose territory and standing during Alexios' reign, but the rate of loss followed the same trajectory that set in after 1180. Moreover, despite the cruel way in which he came to power, Alexios was merciful, making rare use of blinding and mutilation and earning the nickname "Cotton-Rod."[59]

Euphrosyne was a powerful member of the regime, and sat next to Alexios on an equal throne for the reception of envoys. During the winter of 1196–1197, when some of her relatives accused her of adultery, she was banished to a monastery, but six months later she was back.[60] Her family, the Kamateroi, were among the most powerful in this period, holding top positions in the Church and administration, including two patriarchs. Writing to a Kamateros, Michael Choniates called them a "golden race." Some scholars see an uptick in the power of bureaucratic families at this time, including the Kamateroi, Kastamonites, and Hagiotheodorites.[61]

In Asia Minor, the Seljuks were mostly preoccupied with their own rivalries. Turkish raids did periodically occur, especially along the Maeander, though they did not change the strategic situation. The sultan Kilij Arslan II (1156–1192) had divided his realm among his many sons, who were now busy fighting each other. Alexios seems to have been paying those nearest him for peace, and they sent him soldiers. Most of the trouble came from a lower level, from Roman renegades who sought Turkish support, especially among borderland emirs, for their own attacks on Romanía. After Mangaphas (Philadelpheia), these included another pretender claiming to be Alexios II (ca. 1195–1197) and Isaakios Doukas Komnenos, the former emperor on Cyprus. After being freed from captivity at Antioch, he went to Konya where he vainly sought Turkish assistance to effect a return to power. These cross-border links were creating a fluid frontier. Even after supporting Mangaphas against the emperor, the sultan Kai Khusrow twice went to Constantinople seeking help against his brothers (in 1196 and 1200), and he was there when the Fourth Crusade arrived. Conversely, some Roman captives "preferred to resettle among barbarians rather than in the Greek-speaking cities, and happily quit their own fatherland."[62]

The main theater of war was now in the Balkans against the Vlachs, who continued to raid Thrace and Macedonia, as did the Cumans, whether with the Vlachs or on their own. Alexios III always responded, but his generals often were incompetent, fled, or rebelled against him. When Asen was murdered in 1196 at Tarnovo by one of his chiefs (Ivanko), the army sent by the emperor to take the city refused to cross the Haimos: "Turn back," they commanded their general, the *protostrator* Manuel Kamytzes, "and lead us to our own land." Thus Petar, based at Preslav, was able to secure Tarnovo.[63] When Petar too was assassinated, in ca. 1197, the Bulgarian empire was taken over by his younger brother Ivan (1197–1207), often called Ioannitsa (a diminutive), Kalojan ("Handsome John"), or, by the Romans, who came to hate him, "Bad Dog John."[64] In the 1180s, he had lived as a teenage hostage in Constantinople. He emerged as a vigorous monarch of the nascent Bulgarian state.

In the eyes of many westerners, Constantinople could now be bullied and intimidated. Barbarossa's son and heir, Heinrich VI, who had partly inherited and partly conquered the Norman kingdom of Sicily, wanted to pay for his planned crusade by extorting money from Alexios. He threatened to invade Romanía on the specious pretext that the Norman advance to Thessalonike in 1185 gave him rights to the western Balkans. He asked for 5,000 lbs of gold and Alexios agreed to pay part of it. The emperor announced a special "German tax" (*Alamanikon*), but when he convened an assembly of the populace to explain it, it was vehemently shouted down, and he repudiated the idea. He then did what no past emperor had dared: he plundered the tombs of his predecessors, except that of Constantine the Great, exhuming 7,000 lbs of silver and much gold from them. But Heinrich died on 28 September, 1197, removing the threat to Alexios. Choniates noted that all this prefigured the "oppressive slavery that would soon be imposed by the west on our entire race."[65]

The Venetians also extracted concessions. After intense negotiations, in 1198 Alexios issued a chrysobull expanding Venetian legal rights in the empire. Among other privileges relating to criminal trials and succession law, they gained the right to have some legal disputes between themselves and Romans tried by

Venetian judges. This was the first time in the empire's history that foreign judges displaced the jurisdiction of the imperial courts. As it happens, the Venetians were just then codifying the laws of their own city, and some of the privileges that they extracted from Alexios were based on the concessions that they had enjoyed in the crusading realms of the Levant. The chrysobull still treats the doge as a loyal subject of the emperor and exhorts Venetian judges to be impartial between their own people and the Romans. But this rhetoric barely disguised the humiliation of an emperor who had to agree in writing that he would prevent his own wife and in-laws from meddling in Venetian affairs.[66]

The imperial fleet had not been kept up to strength, allegedly because the admiral, the *megas doux* Michael Stryphnos, was corrupt. Moreover, the Romans had apparently lost the ability to manufacture Greek fire, which is last attested in the 1180s. To combat the Genoese pirate Cafforio, Alexios hired a Calabrian pirate, one Ioannes Steiriones, and gave him thirty ships. But Cafforio defeated Steiriones and took all his ships, whereupon Alexios offered the enemy 600 lbs of gold and a province (probably a pronoia) that could support 700 men. Meanwhile, the emperor built more ships, with which Steiriones and some Pisan allies defeated and killed Cafforio, likely in 1197.[67] Despite this success, the empire remained vulnerable to naval attack. And the right given to Steiriones, a former pirate, to collect taxes in order to maintain his force extended the problematic practice of outsourcing vital functions.[68]

In the late 1190s, the empire began to lose more territories to regional Vlach warlords, who were seeking to replicate the success of Asen and Petar. Dobromir-Chrysos was a Vlach who had fought for Alexios against the Bulgarian empire, but he rebelled and tried to create his own statelet in territory that Alexios had given him between the Vardar and Strymon rivers, specifically between the impregnable fort of Prosek and the town of Strumica (both now in modern North Macedonia, 130 km north of Thessalonike). A siege of Prosek by the emperor in ca. 1197 failed, after which Alexios tried to win over Dobromir-Chrysos by giving him the daughter of his cousin, the *protostrator* Manuel Kamytzes, in marriage (although both bride and groom were already married to others). Another siege of Prosek by Alexios failed again in 1199.

The next blow came from Philippopolis. Alexios had entrusted command of the city to Ivanko, the formidable Vlach who murdered Asen in 1196. He married the emperor's granddaughter and took the name Alexios, but in early 1200 he too rebelled, relying on Vlach support. The news reached the court during the double wedding of Alexios' daughters to Alexios Palaiologos and Theodoros Laskaris. The emperor had, for a change, chosen Romans to be sons-in-law. He lacked sons and needed to shore up his regime by appointing potential heirs, giving them, in succession, the title of *despotes*. Roman nativism was highlighted during Alexios' reign, including the fact that he was married to a Roman wife, not a foreigner like his predecessors. In fact, the double unions celebrated in early 1200 yielded the two last dynasties of the Roman state (the Laskarids and the Palaiologoi).[69]

Following Choniates, modern historians treat Alexios III as a disastrous emperor, incompetent and unconcerned. But this picture is false, as shown by the record of the next three years. The rebellions by Dobromir-Chrysos and Ivanko-Alexios almost led to a cascade of fragmentation, but Alexios III was up to the challenge. He immediately sent out Palaiologos, Laskaris, and Kamytzes to attack Ivanko, and they retook Philippopolis. Ivanko escaped to the mountains, where he ambushed and captured Kamytzes. He then began to raid Thrace, dismembering his Roman captives while treating non-Romans leniently. He also seems to have claimed imperial rank. In the spring of 1200, Alexios III marched out against him in person and captured him through trickery. The emperor next rushed over to Asia Minor to suppress a mutiny and defeat raiding Turks. He returned to Constantinople to find that Euphrosyne had suppressed yet another plot to elevate Alexios Kontostephanos. Alexios accomplished all this between the spring and mid-summer of 1200.[70]

Constantinople was becoming increasingly unruly. After some popular disturbances in mid-1200 that involved clashes with imperial soldiers, a coup was staged on 31 July, 1200, by Ioannes Komnenos Axouch, called "the Fat." His grandfather was Ioannes Axouch, a Turkish boy raised to become the right-hand man of Ioannes II, and his father was Alexios Axouch, Manuel I's high official who had married a granddaughter of Ioannes II but was arrested in 1167 for alleged pro-Turkish sympathies and conspiracy. Ioannes the Fat was backed by a powerful faction, but the accounts of his coup veil its exact composition. As the patriarch had gone into hiding, the plotters improvised a coronation in Hagia Sophia to considerable popular acclaim. The rebel encouraged chauvinistic slogans: "All will go well for us and for Romanía from now on! No barbarian will henceforth defeat us: they will lick the dirt from our shoes, and bow before us!" The revolutionaries seized the Great Palace, but not the Chalke, which was defended by the Varangian Guard. However, the emperor, who was at the Blachernai palace, sent Palaiologos with ships along the Golden Horn; he entered the Great Palace and killed Axouch. Axouch's grandfather's ethnic origins were held against him: "Once a Turk, always a Turk." This aspersion was necessary precisely because the rebel had presented himself as a Roman patriot.[71]

Alexios immediately departed for Asia Minor, where, after "bloodless" negotiations, he concluded a treaty with the sultan Rukn al-Din, returning a few days later to Constantinople. In the second half of 1200, Alexios returned to Asia Minor, where he defeated the rebel Michael Komnenos Doukas at Mylasa. The rebel (who later founded the Roman state in Epeiros) fled to Rukn al-Din, who now hated Alexios for allegedly sending assassins to kill him. Alexios spent the winter of 1200–1201 in the Great Palace. But meanwhile, Kamytzes had formed an alliance with his son-in-law Dobromir-Chrysos at Prosek, and they launched raids into Macedonia, reaching as far south as Greece. It seems that Kamytzes was trying to set up a statelet of his own in the south. But imperial diplomacy, and a new marriage between Dobromir-Chrysos and the emperor's own granddaughter, broke the rebels' alliance. Despite suffering from gout, Alexios spent the winter of 1201–1202 campaigning in the Balkans. He defeated Kamytzes in Thessaly and then arrested Dobromir-Chrysos when he accepted an invitation to a hunt with the emperor. All their territories were restored to imperial control. Another rebel, Ioannes Spyridonakis, governor of a theme in Macedonia, was simultaneously defeated by Palaiologos. Through his personal exertions, Alexios had restored order. The center had held, although, admittedly, many of the problems were caused by his reliance on treacherous associates.[72]

Moreover, the need to fight in the southern Balkans meant that losses had to be accepted in the north. Between 1198 and 1202, Kalojan conquered the region between Braničevo and Belgrade, while the Serbs took Niš and its territory. This northwestern corner of the empire, so recently restored by Isaakios, was now lost permanently and would henceforth be contested among Bulgarians, Serbs, and Hungarians. In late March, 1201, Kalojan conquered Varna on the Black Sea coast and buried his Roman captives alive in the siege pit. Eventually he would sport the name "Roman-Slayer," a response to Basil II's moniker. By 1203 Kalojan had also likely taken the territory of modern North Macedonia (including Skopje). The Romans had lost the entire northern Balkans, though they still held Dyrrachion in the far west.[73]

Romanía was losing international prestige. In the tenth and eleventh centuries, even foreign emperors found it hard to procure Roman brides. The Komnenoi reversed that policy and created a denser network of international marriage alliances, though still largely with kings. However, by the 1190s imperial brides were being given away to fourth-rate mountain bandits. Nor were they always respected. Isaakios II had given Alexios' daughter Eudokia in marriage to the heir of the grand župan of Raška, Stefan Nemanjić, who thereby became a *sebastokrator*. Stefan became župan in 1196. Probably in early 1199, and even though his father-in-law Alexios III was now emperor, Stefan repudiated his bride, stripping her to her undergarments and casting her out "like a whore."[74] Likewise Kalojan, who called himself domestically "tsar of the Bulgarians" and, in his letters to pope Innocent III, "emperor of the Bulgarians and Vlachs," preferred to accept a royal title (*rex*) from the pope rather than an imperial one from Alexios III (though he may have been lying to the pope about Alexios' offer, as a negotiating tactic). In exchange for recognizing Kalojan, Innocent received the formal submission of the Bulgarian Church to Rome, where, the pope believed, it

The Fourth Crusade

properly belonged before the Bulgarians were tricked by "the Greeks."[75] This realignment of Bulgaria with Rome was, however, short-lived.

Innocent III (1198–1216) was a dynamic young pope who wanted a new crusade and had little patience for limits on papal supremacy. In 1198–1202, he conducted intense negotiations with Alexios III, wanting to draw him into a new crusade, but only on condition that the Church of Constantinople recognize the Church of Rome as its sovereign. This was, of course, unacceptable in the east, as was, to the pope, Alexios' demand that Cyprus be returned to him. Alexios was in theory open to the idea of a general Council to discuss Union, possibly because he knew that Rome would reject that solution. The pope, who was planning his new crusade, issued barely veiled threats: "we may be forced to come against you and the Church of the Greeks." Meanwhile, in his own correspondence with the pope the patriarch Ioannes X Kamateros took umbrage at the threats and refuted the foundations of papal supremacy: no Gospel and no Council had ever established such a thing.[76] In the spring of 1202, as the crusade was assembling at Venice, a court orator praised the patriarch for standing up to the arrogant and murderous pope, like David to Goliath.[77] But a year later, on 24 June, 1203, the people of Constantinople awoke to the dread sight of a large fleet sailing past their City, 200 ships led by the vermillion-painted galley of the doge of Venice under the banner of the cross. A row of masts made "the sea seem to be covered in trees just like the land," yet these trees were "poisonous."[78] The Fourth Crusade had arrived.

The Fourth Crusade is the most controversial event in east Roman history. Niketas Choniates later argued that its outcome had been orchestrated in advance by the doge of Venice, Enrico Dandolo (1192–1205), who wanted to settle old scores with the Romans and enrich his city. In Choniates' mind, it was not a crusade at all but an invasion of Romanía from the start, like so many before it.[79] Modern scholarship has conclusively refuted that accusation and has carefully reconstructed the contingent events and decisions that diverted the crusade from its original targets to Constantinople. Yet alongside dispassionate analysis we still often find an apologetic, pro-crusading agenda, whose purpose is to insinuate that the crusaders were ultimately left with no choice but to conquer and burn down the greatest city in the Christian world. Cynical schemes, prejudice, and deceit are softened behind exculpating language ("miscalculations," "dilemmas," "anguished moral choices," "complexities," and "unintended consequences"). It is common to highlight the weakness of the "Greeks" (using the invaders' name for them), implying that the victim was somehow to blame. Some historians deploy orientalist tropes of "Byzantine" decadence and corruption to justify the conquest and add luster to the crusaders' manly chivalry, which is admired; or they claim that the invaders were welcomed by their victims, who were tired of their own degenerate leaders, an orientalist trope. It is common to downplay the role of the entrenched ethnic and religious prejudices that, at every step, predisposed the crusaders to attack Romanía.[80]

The crusade had been called by Innocent with traditional goals: to kill Muslims and retake Jerusalem. The call was answered by a number of mostly French counts, who signed a transport contract with Venice. However, their estimates were too high (33,500 men in 400 ships) and they failed to create a mechanism to steer all potential crusaders to Venice, so that many went off to Syria-Palestine on their own. This contributed to a significant shortfall in manpower and funds when the army assembled at Venice in the spring and summer of 1202. The counts and Venice had already agreed that the target of the crusade would be Egypt, the former for strategic and the latter for commercial reasons. The fall of the kingdom of Jerusalem to Saladin in the 1180s had created a consensus that Jerusalem could not be held without Egypt, where the Venetians desired to expand their presence. Yet this kind of thinking did not appeal to the common soldiers, who wanted an armed pilgrimage to Jerusalem for the expiation of their sins. Thus, the leadership kept the target secret from the rank and file so as not to jeopardize recruitment.[81]

For over a year, the Venetians invested large sums to create a huge fleet, designed with state-of-the-art technology specifically for an invasion of Egypt.[82] But the crusaders could not pay the agreed-upon sum. They could walk away from the debt, but that would end the crusade. Innocent himself did not step up to make good on the contract, even though it was he who had called the crusade, had approved the contract with Venice, and had a wide network for raising funds for crusading. Historians praise Innocent in grand terms for his "visionary" promotion of crusading, but he failed to take fiscal responsibility for the mess that he created. The only asset that the crusaders had was armed aggression, so the Venetians cynically turned this against the Christian city of Zara on the Adriatic coast, which they wanted for strategic reasons. Innocent prohibited this diversion on pain of excommunication for the Venetians, but the armada went through with it anyway, capturing Zara in late 1202. But this was only part one of the plan. Part two involved an attack on Constantinople.

Why did the crusade not just sail to Egypt as intended, under an emended agreement to give the Venetians a greater portion of the spoils, enough (and more) to pay off the contract? This is exactly what was agreed later about the conquest of Constantinople and Romanía, so it was a workable kind of agreement. It is likely that the large size of the original contract reflected the military resources that the leadership believed were necessary to conquer Egypt. But without more soldiers, or an injection of cash to hire mercenaries, that objective was beyond reach, especially as, precisely by early 1202, Saladin's formidable brother al-ʿAdil ("Saphadin") had secured control over Egypt and Syria. The Venetians, moreover, knew that Constantinople no longer had naval defenses. Manuel's once proud fleet of 200 ships had been reduced, in part thanks to the corruption of the *megas doux* Stryphnos, to "twenty rotting hulks."[83] The empire was far weaker than it was in 1185, when the Normans had last tried to conquer it. As recently as 1200, the Norman admiral Margaritone told the crusader king of France, Philippe II, that with a fleet he could make him emperor of Constantinople, an idea that the king briefly entertained. It was Margaritone who had captured the majority of the imperial fleet on Cyprus in 1186, so he knew of which he spoke.[84]

Yet it was not the Venetians who proposed the diversion to Constantinople; they merely agreed to it, in exchange for Zara. The diversion was the work of the circle around marquis Bonifacio of Montferrat, who had been elected as the leader of the crusade in 1201. Like many western invaders of Romanía in the recent past, Bonifacio had a puppet pretender to legitimate his intentions.

The pretext for the attack was provided by Alexios Angelos, son of the deposed and blinded Isaakios II. Alexios had fled to the west in the fall of 1201 and spent the winter looking for support to reclaim his father's throne. This was stunningly irresponsible on his part, but had ample precedent in the behavior of Komnenian princelings. After the pope turned him down, Alexios found more receptive ears at the court of Philipp of Swabia, his brother-in-law. Philipp was a son of Barbarossa and currently the German king (or *rex Romanorum*, as they were called). Now, Philipp of Swabia's cousin was none other than Bonifacio of Monferrat, who was staying at Philipp's court in the winter of 1201–1202 when Alexios arrived and the plan took shape. Bonifacio was the brother of Ranieri (who had married Manuel's daughter and was murdered by Andronikos in 1182) and of Conrad (who had married Isaakios II's sister and fought against Branas in 1187). Through their family connections, both Philipp and Bonifacio believed that they had "rights" in Romanía, and they began to lobby for the diversion to Constantinople *before* the shortfall of soldiers became apparent at Venice in the summer of 1202. In the fall of 1202, Innocent revealed to Alexios III that Philipp of Swabia had long been pushing for a war against Constantinople, though the pope claims that he opposed the plan ("but don't make me unleash him" is the subtext of his letter). In May, 1203, just as the crusade leadership was manipulating the rank and file to head to Constantinople, Philipp of Swabia, "King of the Romans," disclosed, in a treaty with the pope, his intention to subordinate "the kingdom of the Greeks" to his crown.[85] One of the architects of the diversion, Geoffroi de Villehardouin, the marshal of Champagne, reveals in his history of the crusade that when they set sail for Constantinople their objective was "to conquer lands for ourselves."[86]

When the contract shortfall did become apparent, the arguments of Philipp, Bonifacio, and the young Alexios sounded better to the rest of the leadership, for Alexios, prompted by his backers, was boasting that Constantinople had the cash to fund the crusade. We have to be careful on one point here. The sources written by the crusaders, which are followed here by much of the scholarship, depict the presence of Alexios as a weighty factor in the deliberations, as if he personally, or his alleged "rights," could not in good conscience be ignored by the counts, the marquis, and the Venetians. This impression was created by the need to maintain the fiction that they were diverting the crusade to the City in order to restore Alexios to his "rightful" throne ("What choice did we have?"). In reality, Alexios was a powerless twenty-year-old with no resources other than his name and no support or rights in Constantinople, as the leadership knew well. Alexios had not been crowned co-emperor by his father Isaakios and no one in the leadership had standing to intervene in Roman politics, for all their chivalric talk of "restoring" his throne. Innocent knew well that Alexios had no right to the throne. Moreover, as he correctly reminded the leadership in April, 1203, "it is not your business to judge the crimes" of Constantinople.[87] Alexios was a tool. The Fourth Crusade was not the story of Alexios recruiting a foreign army to rebel against his uncle. It was the story of yet another group of western warlords who, in the manner of Robert Guiscard, Bohemond, and William II, found a pliant Roman puppet to legitimate an attack on Romanía that they desired in advance.[88] This time it worked.

"Rights" were a pretext. In fact, to agree to the plan the Venetians had to violate their own recent treaty of 1198 with Romanía, in which they had explicitly waived all past grievances (including Manuel I's mass arrests of 1171) and sworn to be faithful allies of Alexios III Komnenos, whom they were now, only four years later, setting out to dethrone by war. Dandolo himself had sworn that oath.[89] It is unlikely that the Venetians would embark upon such grave treachery and overturn an advantageous agreement for a one-time cash grab from Constantinople. Along with Bonifacio and the others, they were planning to redefine the fundamentals of their relationship with Romanía through regime-change and the installation of a puppet emperor. These were calculated decisions, not "accidents" or "anguished moral choices."

The leadership knew that the diversion was unwelcome to the rank and file of their army, who were, in this sense, the first victims of these secret deals.[90] The diversion had, moreover, been strictly forbidden by Innocent. For this reason, the leadership engaged in another round of deception, hiding the pope's letters and prohibitions from the army and deluging the soldiers with propaganda. They methodically manufactured consent in the otherwise reluctant army by appealing to financial exigency; to the "honor" of the leadership and its need to save face before the Venetians; and the alleged "rights" of Alexios. The clinching argument was that the faithless "Greeks" had to be restored to "obedience" to the Church of Rome. This argument was put before the army at Zara, when the plan was finally disclosed, and it formed the main rallying cry before the final attack on the City in April, 1204. The priests who accompanied the army solemnly declared that the war was "just and lawful" because "the Greeks are schismatics," in fact "worse than Jews," and that "you are fighting to conquer this land and bring it under the authority of Rome."[91] Thus did the leadership inflame the religious prejudices of their soldiers to promote a plan that they had hatched for other reasons. But the leadership itself was not entirely immune to prejudice. They too were guided by anti-Greek stereotypes and were primed by their own chivalric literature, whose protagonists joyfully conquer and wreck Constantinople and sexually assault its women.[92]

The crusader fleet, ferrying more than 10,000 men-at-arms, sailed past the sea walls of Constantinople and on 24 June, 1203, reached Chalkedon, where the leadership occupied an imperial palace. The westerners gaped at the vastness of the City, the likes of which most had never seen, while the Romans, who had come out to the walls or stood on their roofs, also marveled at the size of the invasion fleet. Alexios III offered the crusaders money to leave, but they demanded his immediate resignation. They had come to seize power, not just money. They placed the young Alexios on a ship and paraded him along the sea walls calling out his name, but the populace rejected him.[93] The idea that the crusaders were disappointed at this and dismayed that they would have to fight is a modern apologetic fiction. They had come prepared for war.[94] After securing strategic locations on the Bosporos, on 5–6 July, the crusaders made the landing at Galata and forced the soldiers there to retreat to the head of the Golden Horn. A Latin camp was soon established there, opposite the Blachernai palace. It was subject to constant assault by Roman sorties. By taking Galata, however, the crusaders could disarm the chain that blocked entry into the Golden Horn, and so their fleet occupied that anchorage too. On 17 July, while the French land forces attacked the walls of Blachernai, the Venetian ships attacked the sea walls to the east of the palace. The French were repelled, but the Venetians managed to capture a number of towers around the Petrion gate. Even though he was blind, Dandolo led the charge by landing beneath the walls and his men erected scaling ladders. Venetian ships then dropped flying bridges onto the walls, allowing their marines to cross over to the battlements. When Alexios III sent an army to repel them, the Venetians started a fire that was quickly fanned by the wind and burned down about 125 acres of the city between the palace and the Euergetes monastery along the Golden Horn. Few Romans died, but thousands became homeless overnight.[95]

For the first time in its history, the City had been breached by a foreign foe, though it was not taken. Alexios III, probably fearing a coup, fled in the night, taking a heap of money and gems with him. This threw the high command and the court into confusion, and the decision was somehow made to restore Isaakios II Angelos to the throne. This disarmed the crusaders' pretext that they were there to restore legitimacy to the regime in Constantinople. After intense negotiation with the counts, Isaakios agreed to the terms that they had previously imposed on his son: Constantinople would pay the crusaders' expenses, fund their expedition, and its Church would submit to the authority of Rome. To seal the deal, Alexios, who was around twenty, was crowned co-emperor in Hagia Sophia on 1 August. He immediately began to hand over large sums of money to the leadership, almost all of which went to the Venetians, though he resorted to plundering the churches in order to obtain it, which instantly alienated his subjects.[96] Moreover, Alexios offered to renew the crusaders' "contract," paying them to stay on until March, 1204, at which point they could embark on their crusade, with his military and financial assistance. It would be naïve, however, to believe that this offer came from Alexios himself rather than the leadership. It was, they claimed, too late in the season for them to depart and they were not prepared for a long campaign.[97] It is not clear that they intended to leave at all: this extension was the first step in entrenching their position in Constantinople, which they now knew lacked significant armies. It was probably they who dictated to Alexios IV the letter of submission to the pope that he wrote on 25 August, pledging to "bend" the eastern Church to Rome's will, though no actions were (or could be) taken to enforce this.[98] Knowledge of this missive was likely hidden from the Roman populace, just as the pope's letters had been hidden from the crusader army.

Foreigners resident in the City reacted in remarkable ways to these events. Agnes of France, widow of Alexios II and Andronikos I and now married to a Branas, was angry with her former compatriots for what they did and refused to meet with them. She was in her early thirties and could no longer speak French. By contrast, the deposed sultan of Konya, Kai Khusrow, went to the crusaders and asked them to restore him too to his ancestral throne.[99] Although they declined his offer, he was not wrong to see them as mercenaries.

The French counts became honored guests and trusted advisors of the new regime. Isaakios, blind and lost in prophecies and superstition, faded from view, while Alexios IV had little support among his people, most of whom hated him for bringing this plague upon their heads. He quickly realized that he was out of his depth, holding not one but two wolves by the ear, both of which hated each other. The people of Constantinople were furious and, in a fit of misguided rage, attacked the City's Italian quarter, driving its long-time residents, many of whom were also unhappy at what the crusaders had done, across the harbor into the hands of the invaders encamped at Galata. This may have boosted the hostile force by as much as 15,000 people, turning potential allies into enemies, including Pisans (rivals of the Venetians) and Amalfitans, who had acculturated to Roman ways. In retaliation, some Latins crossed the Golden Horn on 19 August to attack a mosque by the harbor coast. When local Romans came out to defend the Muslims, the Latins set another fire, which was whipped by the strong winds into an inferno that spread southward across the City, raging for two days and nights. In that time, it crossed the forum of Constantine and reached the Sea of Marmara. As the wooden roof-beams of the porticos burned, the City resembled a "river of fire" with many tributaries, one of which came close to Hagia Sophia. Monuments, homes, shops, livelihoods, and libraries "vanished in a flash into thin air." Another 450 acres burned to ash, and between 50,000 and 100,000 people were left homeless. They began to leave the City, moved in with friends, became refugees in the churches and monasteries, or set up camp-towns in the remaining open areas. Choniates himself lost his mansion and his family moved into a small apartment that they owned near Hagia Sophia. The Romans and the Latins blamed each other for this disaster, which scotched any hope for peace.[100]

Alexios IV was regarded as an "abomination" by his subjects. He caroused in the Latins' camp, and spent part of the fall subduing Thrace to his rule through the force of his Latin backers. But eventually he ran out of funds with which to pay them, and relations cooled. By December, the leadership served Alexios with an ultimatum to fulfill his contractual obligations, while some crusaders plundered the estates around the capital. Meanwhile, a native resistance was forming. The people of the City formed militias that crossed over and attacked the enemy camp, calling themselves "true patriots." A certain Alexios Doukas, known as Mourtzouphlos because of his thick unibrow, distinguished himself in these attacks. On 1 January, the Romans tried to incinerate the Venetian fleet by launching fireships at it (not Greek fire, which no longer existed), but their plan was countered by the Italian pilots' skillful reaction. A Roman orator drafted a speech calling on Alexios IV to draw the sword against Old Rome, which was sucking the blood of New Rome. Finally, by late January, as Isaakios lay dying, the populace decided to terminate the Angelos dynasty. On the 25th, they assembled in Hagia Sophia. Yet after two days of intense debate and nominations, no one stepped forth to claim the throne. Recent decades had witnessed dozens of coups and plots, but now no one wanted to be emperor. On the 27th, a certain Nikolaos Kannabos was elected against his will. He was, for a few days, the emperor in Hagia Sophia. But Alexios Doukas Mourtzouphlos was meanwhile orchestrating a coup. He arrested Alexios IV and Kannabos and eventually had them executed. On 5 February, he was proclaimed emperor in Hagia Sophia and ordered the crusaders to depart. The army of God realized that, merely to survive in this hostile land, they would have to conquer the City all over again.[101]

In February and March, the two sides skirmished while Alexios V Doukas repaired and strengthened the sea walls and the crusaders prepared their ships for the assault. Dandolo, Bonifacio, count Baldwin of Flanders, count Louis of Blois, and count Hugh of Saint-Pol worked out the March Pact, a detailed agreement about the collection and division of the spoils, as well as rules for sacking the City (no killing of women and priests, and no raping, in theory at least). They also worked out the committees that would select an emperor of Constantinople from among them along with the next patriarch (a Latin, of course). The army was reassured that the attack was justified because it would bring the Greeks "back" into submission to Rome.[102]

The first attack was made on the sea walls along the northern stretch of the Golden Horn, where the first fire had broken out the previous year. It was repelled. But in a second attack on 12 April, led by the ships *Paradise* and *Pilgrimess*, the crusaders established a bridgehead on some towers. They began to slaughter the locals indiscriminately to create a dead zone, and set a third fire, which raged along the coast, toward the south this time where the former Latin quarters were situated. This fire consumed another 25 acres. During the night, the crusaders regrouped as they expected to be attacked in force, but Alexios V, like Alexios III before him, fled during the night. At dawn on 13 April, the crusaders found the City undefended and its populace in confusion. Bonifacio raced to secure the Great Palace, while Henri, the brother of Baldwin, secured the Blachernai palace. The sack then commenced in earnest and lasted for three days. No place in the Christian world had accumulated more treasures, antiquities, books, and holy relics than Constantinople in the nine centuries of its existence. These were now methodically plundered, burned, smashed, or desecrated as greed, whim, hatred, or fancy seized the looting conquerors. "Never since the Creation of the world was so much booty taken from a single city," declared one of the architects of the Fourth Crusade.[103]

What the conqueror could not appreciate, he destroyed. Whole chapters of ancient history, art, and literature were erased in mere hours. Choniates composed a separate section of his history to lament the destruction of ancient statues by the Latin barbarians. Choniates himself was briefly sheltered by a Venetian friend, a resident of the City, whom he, in turn, had protected during the anti-Latin riots of August. But despite these personal ties, the historian could not but conclude, upon reflection, that "between the Romans and the Latins there lies a huge gulf of difference: our mentalities are diametrically opposed, even when we join our bodies together and live in the same household."[104] The only union of bodies now was in the raping of Roman women. Choniates pointed out that when Saladin took Jerusalem in 1187, his men did not rape the Latin women in the same way. Men who defended their women were being slaughtered.[105]

Meanwhile, churches, including Hagia Sophia, were stripped of valuables and sacred treasures. The priceless altar of the Great Church was hacked to bits to be divided among the victors. A French prostitute dressed up in the patriarch's garb and put on a show. Much of the sacred loot was later shipped out to the west, where it remains today in museums, treasuries, and sacristies, especially in Venice. It included icons, relics, ancient statues (such as the porphyry

Tetrarchs and the so-called Horses of St. Mark), and even entire architectural elements (the co-called Pilastri Acritani, taken from the ruins of Anicia Juliana's church of St. Polyeuktos). The abbot of a Cistercian abbey in Alsatia made a beeline for the Pantokrator monastery, knowing that other Latins were not as aware of its significance. He threatened a monk there with death in order to seize the holy treasures that graced the tomb of Manuel Komnenos, ironically a Latinophile emperor. One of the pieces that he stole from there was a tablet that contained relics and depicted the Last Supper: he gave it to the German king Philipp of Swabia, one of the prime diverters of the crusade, explaining to him that the Greek emperors used to wear it around their neck on special occasions "as a token of their imperial power." This was as close as Philipp got to wielding eastern power.[106] A mosaic celebrating the capture of City was erected in a church in Ravenna, ironically a city that had once been Constantinople's forward operating base in Italy.[107]

For centuries, wealth and people had flowed into Constantinople; now they began to flow out. The Roman elite fled from the City rather than endure Latin rule, and many of the poor abandoned it as well. About a sixth of the City was a burned ruin, while the rest was stripped of valuables. Too late, the pope and others in the west realized that the project had been driven "more by price than by prayer."[108] As a result, "the beautiful City of Constantine, the common delight and boast of all nations, was consumed and blackened by fire, captured by force, and hollowed out of its wealth by these random western nations."[109] Constantinople would never fully recover. Nor would the Romans.

Causes of decline in the twelfth century

The lion's share of blame for the destruction of 1203–1204 lies squarely with the crusaders, and not just with the participants in the Fourth Crusade but with the crusading movement as a whole and the entire culture (that of medieval western Europe) that gave rise to it. Much recent scholarship on the crusades is apologetic, and studies of the Fourth Crusade in particular are master classes in the use of the passive voice ("mistakes were made," etc.). Yet those "mistakes" were shaped by underlying prejudices and ideologies, including the willingness of the leadership to put financial contracts over all other considerations; the readiness with which the Venetians broke their oaths to defend the eastern empire, in exchange for which they had received lucrative concessions; the decision to intervene in east Roman politics, where the crusaders had no legal standing; the Norman tradition of using puppet claimants to the throne of Constantinople as a pretext for aggression; the prejudice against "the Greeks" that, at every step, nudged the crusaders closer to violence against the Romans and cloaked naked aggression; the greed and envy with which many had regarded Constantinople; and the moral rottenness of crusading in general, which not only channeled hatred against perceived enemies of the faith but generated, armed, and funded it. Romanía was hated partly because it had showed insufficient enthusiasm for the crusading project.

Crusading may have been experienced by many as a pious pilgrimage for the expiation of sin, but it had quickly become a means by which to justify and drum up war against any opponent upon whom a crusade's leaders had set their sights, even for outright wars of conquest and against other Christians. Eventually, it generated doctrines, propagated at the highest levels of papal power, that any society that did not recognize the pope was a legitimate target of attack, even of preemptive war.[110] Innocent III initially opposed the diversion to Constantinople, but he quickly came around to accepting its results when he saw an opportunity to extend papal supremacy to the eastern Church. It was becoming hard to distinguish between religiously motivated attacks against Constantinople and cynical wars of aggression against it.

Romanía was already in trouble before the crusaders arrived, a fact that they knew and exploited. For starters, its own political culture was dysfunctional. Alexios IV's decision to recruit dangerous allies in order to destabilize a volatile political situation in Constantinople was reckless. Yet this was a broader structural flaw of the Komnenian aristocracy and no mere personal failing. Starting at least with Isaakios *sebastokrator* (Ioannes II's brother) and continuing with his son Andronikos I and many others, these entitled Komnenian princelings regularly fled their country and made deals with its neighbors, some of whom were its enemies. These foreign kings harbored claimants to the Roman throne or used them against the sitting emperor. Choniates laid the blame for the empire's fall on the Komnenoi for this reason: "by consorting with nations that were hostile to the Romans, they became a plague upon their country."[111]

But why were Komnenian princelings "consorting with foreign nations"? To be sure, seeking foreign help in a rebellion was not unprecedented in Roman history; witness Bardas Skleros in 979. But it was rare, and the differences were striking. Skleros was the leading general of his generation with a lifetime of service behind him, whereas some of the Komnenian princelings apparently believed that their family status alone entitled them to seek the throne by any available means. This sense of entitlement stemmed from the aristocratic mentality that the new system of government had inculcated. Aristocracies tend to form lateral ties with their counterparts in neighboring countries, regarding themselves as superior to the mass of their subjects at home.[112] Romanía had never before had an aristocracy of this kind. Its elite had been one of state service, drawn from the provinces, and families rotated in and out of power. That is why the Roman imperial elite had, for almost a millennium, not meshed well with its neighboring aristocracies. But in the twelfth century it had become an aristocracy conducive to lateral, international links, for its domestic power rested as much on personal ties as on institutional-statal positions. The Komnenian aristocracy was, moreover, densely intermarried with its neighbors, as Alexios, Ioannes, and Manuel had pursued matrimonial alliances to promote their foreign policies, something that emperors had resisted before the later eleventh century. Thus, Alexios IV found a sister at the German court, who harbored him and promoted his design with her husband Philipp of Swabia and his clients, including Bonifacio of Montferrat, the leader of the crusade (whose brother had married Alexios' aunt). Alexios was not only seeking foreign assistance through a coup: he was activating an extended family network. In reality, of course, it was using him.

These marriage alliances gave stakeholder status in the Roman polity to foreign predators, which blurred the line between domestic and foreign politics, as we see in the case of Montferrat. Moreover, this strategy of intermarriage failed to produce benefits to Romanía. It did not bring Antioch or Cilicia under control; the ties with Jerusalem were a vanity project on Manuel's part from the start; it yielded no benefits in Italy; and it generated no goodwill that helped the empire in moments of crisis, only more demands and legalistic pretexts for aggression. The strategy brought a crowd of ambitious foreign in-laws into an already tense political field. By the late twelfth century, they regarded themselves as peers of their Roman counterparts, entitled to a say in their politics. And so Manuel's desperate efforts to be accepted into the club of Latin states resulted in pathetic failure: the Latins took his money, but their contempt for "the Greeks" only grew, as did the Latinophobia of his own subjects. The crusades played a catalytic role here. Just when that movement was acting as a bonding agent on the otherwise fragmented polities of western Europe, the east Romans' lack of interest in it, in fact their fear and suspicion of its goals, isolated and marked them off as "other" in the eyes of western Christians. Choniates was right: the gulf between Romans and Latins was too wide. Aristocratic marriages brought meddling, not cultural understanding or fusion, and the crusades supercharged suspicion into hostility and war.

Romanía was also unlucky in its leadership after 1180. It is easy (though still correct) to point to the personal inadequacies of the Angeloi. They lacked the skills and charisma required by the unfolding crisis, which had been exacerbated by Andronikos' wild tyranny. The very legitimacy of the Angeloi was also shaky, given how they rose to power. Isaakios at least enjoyed popular support, but he was too weak to master his peers. The absence of compelling leadership is indexed also by the resurgence of popular power after 1180, which jostled with other elements (including the Church) to fill the vacuum left by a weak throne. The Komnenian aristocracy was by now too fierce a beast to be tamed by any one person. Manuel had done so, but he had come to power while the new regime was still maturing and, during his long reign, he carefully built up his own prestige to such extravagant levels that it outshone the entire extended clan. But when he died, no one inherited that prestige, and its power was dispersed to many other elements of the polity. Choniates rightly blamed Manuel for failing to make good provisions for the succession,[113] but a truer accusation would be that he created a system of dynastic governance that *no* successor could manage. This is why the years 1180–1204 were so thick with plots and rebellions in both the capital and the provinces: they reflected not just political instability, but incipient statal collapse.[114]

Why did Romanía begin to disintegrate? In the past, civil wars aimed only to replace the emperor; they did not jeopardize the polity's very integrity. To be sure, Isaakios on Cyprus and Mangaphas at Philadelpheia set themselves up as rival emperors, claiming the imperial title and minting coins. But their power was local, with no realistic prospect of making the leap to the capital, and others, such as Leon Sgouros in southern Greece, did not claim the imperial title to begin with. In the years before 1204, Greece and Asia Minor witnessed a proliferation of small-scale independence movements, whether they were supported by the locals or not (on Cyprus, at least, it appears not). For the most part they were led by local notables, not Komnenian types as on Cyprus. So why was this happening?[115]

Unfortunately, none of those men left accounts of their actions, but systemic analysis may explain them. In the past, provincial elites could rise up through state service and claim the highest offices. Many of the chief officials of all regimes between Constantine I and Alexios I were of provincial origin. But the options of provincials were curtailed by the Komnenoi and their in-laws, who monopolized the most powerful and lucrative positions. The court elite was not drawing provincials into itself at the same rates as before, and those who made it in were generally limited to supportive administrative posts. It is no accident that the most incisive critiques of the new system on this point came from historians who belonged to the bureaucratic class (Zonaras and Choniates).[116] Moreover, in the past provincials could purchase or be awarded high titles at the court, giving them a stake in the system, but this option too was abolished by Alexios I. This reform freed up capital for them to invest in the economy,[117] but it also weakened their ties to the center. Nor did the Komnenoi make an effort to co-opt the growing merchant class of this period. Finally, instead of marrying Roman brides from the provinces, which strengthened the cohesion of the polity, the Komnenoi chose brides from abroad or from within their own extended clan.

Provincials were less honored and cultivated by the Komnenoi. It is likely that they also felt more exploited, especially by governors who bought their offices. Michael Choniates' complaints from Athens are resounding. "What is it that you people lack?," he wrote to a sympathetic official in the capital. "You sit in peace in the City while the tax officials plunder the provinces. Doesn't all money eventually flow there to you, like rivers to the ocean?"[118] Michael drew up a memorandum for Alexios III in 1198/9, excoriating abusive tax collection and explaining how it worked. Athens had even secured an order preventing the governor of Greece (normally based at Thebes) from visiting the city, because such visits were used as opportunities to fleece the city with fees. But a recent governor had flouted that restriction on the pretext that he wanted to worship at the Parthenon, a famous shrine of the Virgin. Michael and his brother Niketas depict Constantinople as a parasite, exerting "fiscal violence" to feed the insatiable greed of a corrupt administration that was always taking but not giving back what Roman citizens expected from their government: justice and security.[119] The provinces, after all, had only limited means of self-defense against pirates and invaders; that is why they paid taxes to the center.

Taxes under the Komnenian empire were always high, but they came to be seen as unjust under Alexios III, exacerbating growing feelings of alienation from the center precisely when the empire was entering a crisis. The problem was not that the bureaucracy of taxation was breaking down, but that it was working all too well, at a peak of centralization, even by absentee governors who sent agents to the provinces to do the actual dirty work. As revenues were lost from regions that fell away (e.g., Bulgaria) and were ravaged by war (Thrace, Macedonia), or due to exemptions granted by the emperors to monasteries and their favorites, the state's remaining assets had to be squeezed more tightly, while the constant state of war drove up expenses.[120] Bulgarian independence was not only a blow to revenue but a source of instability, vulnerability, and expensive war. It is likely that, in a strictly military sense, the Romans could have prevailed over the new Bulgarian state, but their military efforts were undermined by political dysfunction, including frequent rebellions by imperial commanders and mutinies by the army.[121] Political control of both the army and the provinces was becoming tenuous. Alexios III created Vlach buffers against Kalojan by recruiting Ivanko and Dobromir-Chrysos, but both rebelled and had to be suppressed.

Many provincials were alienated from the Komnenian court in another sense too: their tax obligations were transferred to third parties, the pronoiars favored by the court. Thus, they dealt directly with the agents of that pronoiar and indirectly with their political leadership. This may have contributed to alienation from Constantinople and diluted the common purpose in which the institutions of the state had previously bound its provincials. In this context, the terms offered by a neighboring emir may have seemed more attractive, whereas in the past they would have been alien and unthinkable.

Finally, an explanation for the fall must account for the growing disparities between Romanía and the west. In the mid-eleventh century, the Roman empire was a superpower among Christian states. But the west experienced tremendous economic and demographic growth in the next century and a half. This enabled the Roman aristocracy, and especially Manuel, to treat their western counterparts as peers for the first time since the fourth century. Yet the moment of parity passed quickly, and was limited to the reign of Manuel. Moreover, Manuel's great-power panache masked systemic dysfunctions that led to a spiral of decline after his death. The Romans were losing ground and even mid-level foreign powers were closing the gap with them. Roman armies could still defeat a Hungarian or Norman invasion, but only narrowly and with a defender's advantage. They would not have stood a chance against Barbarossa in 1189. And a relatively small army of Frenchmen and Venetians was able to take the City twice in 1203–1204 because the Romans allowed their fleet to atrophy while the invader had spent a century honing skills in amphibian operations. The Romans had fallen behind militarily.

The Romans showed little interest in developing international trade networks like those of the Italians. Moreover, for all the undeniable advancements in scholarship, literature, and humanism that many of them made in the twelfth century, building in fascinating ways upon their late ancient heritage, they began to fall behind in philosophy and science. In part, this was because their intellectual life, like the rest of their society, was institutionally centralized, with their Church and state repressing any movement that challenged or even expanded upon official doctrines. By contrast, decentralization enabled the Latin world to experiment with new approaches not only in intellectual matters, but also in politics and economics. Centralization also made the Romans vulnerable if their leadership was weak at a critical moment. When the emperors fled at two critical moments (Alexios III in 1203 and Alexios V in 1204) the political system was paralyzed and resistance collapsed. When collapse came, it was swift. A Roman born in 1155 would have known peace, prosperity, and imperial greatness for a generation. By the time she was fifty, she was likely to be a refugee or living under colonial occupation. Paradoxically, the Romans became resilient again after 1204 precisely because they were fragmented and decentralized.

PART NINE
EXILE AND RETURN

31
"A New France": Colonial Occupation

"Divine Justice," wrote Baldwin of Flanders and Hainaut from the burned ruin of Constantinople, a city that was being abandoned by many of its citizens, "gave us a land overflowing with all good things. It is rich in produce, lovely in forests, waters, and pasture lands, spacious for settlement, and teperate in climate, with no equal in the world." Baldwin had been crowned "Augustus of Constantinople" in Hagia Sophia on 16 May, 1204, and he was recounting to pope Innocent III the "miracle" of the conquest. The Greeks had been punished by God for their perfidy, disobedience to the Church of Rome, and alliance with the Muslims. Baldwin asked the pope to sanction the defense of the new Latin empire as an ongoing crusade and "to inflame the inhabitants of the west" to emigrate and "serve our empire either for a while or for life." Exhilarated by this opportunity to extend papal supremacy to the Greek Church, Innocent forgot his prohibition of the crusade's diversion. God has restored the daughter to the mother and the limb to the head, he told his priests. The empire had been transferred from the Greeks to the Latins.[1]

The Latin empire

Baldwin had been elected by a committee of six Venetians and six non-Venetians, in accordance with the March Pact. It was widely assumed that marquis Bonifacio of Montferrat, the prime mover of the crusade's diversion and its military leader, would be elected, while the patriarchate and Hagia Sophia would go to the other party, i.e., the Venetians.[2] But Baldwin won the vote. A Venetian, Tommaso Morosini was duly appointed patriarch, though this decision, and the crusaders' entire handling of the Church of Constantinople, flouted canon law. Innocent was too ecstatic at the conquest and too far from events to substantively challenge these decisions. The pope instead went through the motions of deposing Morosini and then immediately reappointing him, to preserve the fiction of papal authority. Innocent did not care that a legally consecrated patriarch, Ioannes X Kamateros, was still alive, in flight in Thrace. Rome did not regard as legitimate any priest who did not accept the pope's authority as the pope himself defined it. The papacy had converted the pentarchy of five patriarchs into a monarchy focused on itself. It had now appointed its own Latin patriarchs to Constantinople, Antioch, and Jerusalem, though the last resided at Acre.[3]

The March Pact granted no rights or powers to any of the natives of Romanía. It stipulated that a committee of twenty-four (twelve Venetians and twelve non-Venetians) would divide Romanía up into fiefs, from which the enemies of the Venetians would be excluded. This was carried out during the summer and fall of 1204 and resulted in the *Partition of the Lands of the Empire of Romanía*, a document based on a Greek registry of Romanía's fiscal assets. The Venetians were to receive three eighths of Constantinople in addition to lands in Thrace, Epeiros, the Peloponnese, and the islands. Their doge henceforth sported the title "Lord of One Quarter and One Eighth of the Whole of Romania," and was not subject to the new Latin emperor. The latter was to receive Roman Anatolia and lands in Thrace, while other "pilgrims" would receive fiefs in Thrace, Macedonia, Thessaly, and Greece. All this, of course, required that the Latins actually conquered these territories, so it is no surprise that this partition, so neat on paper, did not become reality. Choniates noted that the Latins were counting up their revenues before they even set foot on these lands, and traded them among themselves like credit chips.[4]

The Latin empire ultimately fell because the Romans regrouped in Epeiros and Anatolia and fought back. The Latin emperors were fatally weakened in particular by their failure to secure Anatolia, for the *Partition* had assigned its provinces to them as their principle demesne. Without it, the emperors never had enough money to hire the soldiers they needed, as many of the original crusaders returned home after the fall of Constantinople.[5] Moreover, the Latin emperors could rarely ask their regional vassals to serve outside of their districts. Even in Thrace, the fugitive basileis Alexios III and Alexios V were organizing resistance, and Baldwin had to chase them out. The Latin leadership reached out to their Greek subjects with only symbolic gestures. In September, Baldwin hosted a feast for Greek nobles, where he dubbed 600 Latin knights and spoke on the glories of ancient Athens.[6] Bonifacio, nursing imperial ambitions of his own, married Margit, Isaakios II's Hungarian widow, who was now thirty. This linked him to both the previous imperial dynasty and the Hungarian crown.

But Bonifacio and Baldwin soon came to blows. After a tense standoff, Bonifacio strong-armed the fictitious "kingdom of Thessalonike" away from the emperor and proceeded to subjugate it, granting fiefs to his own followers. He then marched south to secure Greece against a rising Roman warlord from Nauplion in the Peloponnese, Leon Sgouros. Sgouros came from the local aristocracy and took advantage of the chaos of 1203 to establish his own statelet in the Argolid and Corinthia and then to advance into Attica, Boiotia, and Thessaly. At Larissa he joined with Alexios III, who gave him his daughter Eudokia (her third marriage, after Stefan Nemanjić and Alexios V), possibly along with the imperial title *despotes*. The only city that had successfully resisted Sgouros was Athens, under the leadership of Michael Choniates, who had fought him off from the Akropolis. However, in late 1204 Sgouros fled in the face of Bonifacio's advance, abandoning the Thermopylae pass. He holed up on the Acrocorinth, besieged by the Latins for three years. A later legend had him ride his horse off the citadel cliff.[7]

The cities along Bonifacio's path surrendered to him not because they saw him as a "liberator" or "welcomed" Latin rule but because they had no choice. Roman norms did not require civilians to fight to the death in the face of invasion, but to stay safe and await the return of Roman forces. Michael Choniates gave up Athens in 1205 and went into exile, leaving behind his beloved library and the Parthenon. He settled on the nearby island of Keos, where he acted as a shadow bishop of Athens, even ordaining priests for his see. Bonifacio made Othon de la Roche, a Burgundian knight, the "Grand Lord" of Athens, a fief that was later accounted a duchy. Othon soon acquired Boiotia, if it was not assigned to him already by Bonifacio. Then, two knights from Bonifacio's circle with an army of 500 initiated the conquest of the Peloponnese. They were Guillaume de Champlitte and Geoffroi de Villehardouin, a nephew of the marshal and historian of the Fourth Crusade. "Seeking glory and territory," they carved out for themselves the Principality of Achaea (or of the "Morea," probably named after the mulberry trees used locally in the production of silk). The lords of Athens and Achaea were in theory vassals of the king of Thessalonike, who was in turn a vassal of the Latin emperor. This arrangement made for a weaker emperor than was imagined in the *Partition*.[8]

The Latin empire did not issue its own gold coins but, as in all aspects of its existence, it scrapped together assets and resources made by others. Its titles and ceremonies were a novel pastiche of feudal and indigenous Roman elements.[9] Its very creation had fragmented the uniform administration of the Roman state and replaced it with a patchwork of feudal realms. It even had to share its capital with the Venetians, whose "state within a state" was headquartered at the Pantokrator monastery and led by their podestà and intricate system of councils.[10] Only a generation before, the Venetians of Constantinople had been arrested en masse by Manuel I Komnenos; now, they were ruling part of his City from his tomb.

The new political order came perilously close to collapse when its leaders died in the course of only a few years. In 1205, the Romans of Adrianople and Thrace rose up against the Latins "and began to kill the Franks, wherever they found them occupying the land." This threw the occupation armies into confusion, dispersed as they were throughout Greece and northwestern Anatolia securing their fiefs. They regrouped and converged on Adrianople, but in April, 1205, Baldwin was defeated outside that city by Kalojan, who was leading a raiding party of Vlachs and Cumans, probably in coordination with the Roman rebels. The Latin emperor was captured and taken into captivity, where he was killed: his arms and legs were cut off and he was tossed into a ravine as food for birds. This was a disaster for the Latin empire at the very moment of its inception. Adrianople had long been a Roman military base and Theodoros Branas, son of the rebel of 1187, was so powerful there that, in 1206, the Venetians ceded that city to him as a quasi-autonomous fief, along with the title *kaisar*. Branas was married to Agnes, daughter of the king of France Louis VII and sister of the current French king Philippe II, and so he interfaced directly with the Latins' feudal networks. Adrianople was nominally subordinate to the Latin emperors and initially helped them in their wars against Bulgaria. In the late 1220s, it fell into the orbit of the competing Roman states of Epeiros and Nikaia.[11]

The constant warfare among the Cumans, Romans, and Latins during those confusing years spread "horror" throughout Thrace, as civilian populations were targeted with atrocities, while refugees fled in all directions. The Latins had lost many men at Adrianople. In May, 1205, Dandolo died of natural causes and was buried in Hagia Sophia. The next to go was Bonifacio, the lord of Thessalonike, killed in an ambush by Vlachs and Cumans in September 1207. Thessalonike was left in the hands of his infant son Demetrios with Margit as regent. With the deaths of Baldwin, Dandolo, and Bonifacio, the Vlacho-Bulgarians were poised to make big gains in the wastelands of Thrace. Kalojan had forcibly transported thousands to his lands by the Danube. He had ruined cities and earned the moniker "Roman-Slayer." But then he too died, in his sleep in October 1207, while besieging Thessalonike. His death was duly attributed to St. Demetrios, the city's protector. Just as Bulgaria lost its most aggressive ruler, the Latin empire gained a competent one. Baldwin was succeeded by his brother Henri (1206–1216), who proved to be a good general and politician and put his state on a sounder footing. He proclaimed the infant Demetrios "king" of Thessalonike and, holding his noble French nose, even married a daughter of Kalojan to make peace with Bulgaria in 1213.[12]

The French conquest of the Morea trespassed on the Venetian "rights" to it granted by the *Partition*, yet Venice limited its claims to the fortified stations of Modon and Coron (Methone and Korone) in the southwest, which became crucial transit nodes in its growing overseas empire. The Republic and Villehardouin formalized this division of the Peloponnese in 1209.[13] The Roman trading city of Monembasia in the southeast resisted Latin occupation for at least two decades (see Figure 46). It was captured between 1223 and 1238, but liberated in 1261/2 in the initial phase of the Roman reconquest.[14] Venice instead invested most of its efforts into the colonization of Crete, in 1207–1211. Venice had no legal claim to the island—the background was complicated—but did not want to see it fall into the hands of the Genoese. The island was a large and wealthy overseas possession that Venice kept until 1669. It was called the realm of Candia (after its capital, modern Herakleion), was headed by a duke, and owed no allegiance to the Latin emperor of Constantinople.[15]

Figure 46 Monembasia
Shutterstock/Marianna Ianovska

Farther north, the Roman resurgence in western Greece excluded Venice from much of the territory in Epeiros to which it was "entitled." In 1207, Venice granted Kerkyra (Corfu) to ten of its nobles to exploit in its own name (not that of the Latin empire), but that island too was taken back by the Romans of Epeiros in ca. 1214 and kept until 1258.[16] By 1209, Venice had gained a foothold on Euboia (or Negroponte, as its main city Chalkis and the island as a whole were called). It began to expand its control there, transforming Euboia too into a major node for trade and transit.[17] The Aegean became a land of opportunity for adventurous Venetians. In 1214, Marco Sanudo, a nephew of Dandolo who had participated in the crusade, conquered many of the Cyclades islands, distributed them as fiefs among his followers, and called himself the duke of Naxos. Yet he placed this "duchy of the Archipelago" under the Latin emperor, not Venice.[18]

Thus Romanía was carved up among a gaggle of loosely affiliated French and Italian interests. They occupied fewer than half of the territories listed in the *Partition*, and fewer than half of those were occupied according to its terms. These new entities joined the French Lusignan kingdom of Cyprus in forming a network of colonial Latin states in the Greek-speaking lands (Cyprus was nominally subject to the German emperor until 1247). Some lasted for a generation (the kingdom of Thessalonike fell to the Romans of Epeiros in 1224) and some for two (the Latin empire of Constantinople fell to the Romans of Nikaia in 1261). One lasted for two centuries (the Principality of Achaea) and two for much more: French and then Venetian Cyprus lasted until the sixteenth century and Venetian Crete until the seventeenth. This was the *Frangokratia*, the period of Latin rule, as it is called today in Greece.

Colonial rule

There was much variation among the Latin states, but they were all essentially European colonial projects. Medieval historians—and historians of the crusades in particular—are squeamish when it comes to connecting the crusading conquests of the eleventh–thirteenth centuries to later European colonialism, even though there was no rupture in the history of expansion and exploitation between them or in their persistent religious justification. This reluctance stems in part from a school of thought, now in decline, that sought to define the crusades in narrowly pietistic terms in order to rehabilitate them, and also because medieval historians rarely study later phases of European colonialism.[19] In reality, there are strong lines of continuity between, say, Latin Greece after 1204 and the later phases of western colonialism. Small groups of military elites destroyed and dismantled native polities and displaced or subjugated their rulers, reducing the native population to a second-class status. The latter had few or no prospects of entering even the lowest tiers of the new ruling class, whereas new arrivals from the west were both welcomed and invited to settle in the new lands, partly in order to renew the links between the colonial elite and its former metropoles. The colonies became "lands of opportunity" for Europeans. The distinction between the Latin rulers and their "Greek" subjects was understood in fairly rigid ethnic and religious terms, codified in law, and reinforced by hefty doses of prejudice directed downward. Finally, and probably most importantly, both medieval and early modern colonialism were justified in religious terms; marked by extensive land confiscations to benefit the settlers; reduced most natives to the status of serfs; and adjusted trade networks to prioritize exchange with the colonial metropole.

It may be argued that in a strict sense only the Venetian acquisitions (such as Crete) fit a colonial model as only they were run as overseas territories for the direct benefit of the metropole. The rest of Latin Greece consisted of autonomous states that aimed to benefit themselves, or at least their rulers. But it is misleading to place them under the generic rubric of conquest, as opposed to colonialism. That would miss the manifold ways in which these new states remained tethered to western Europe and advanced the interests of its elites. For starters, the distinction between Latins and Greeks, and the biases associated with it, projected western ideologies. Latin Romanía was also understood to be "open for business" and "a land of opportunity" for western settlers, soldiers, and clerics, including for those who had debts to pay off or who had committed crimes. Baldwin explicitly called on them to immigrate, advertising its attractions. Pope Innocent

III echoed this plea and decreed that the defense of the Latin empire was an ongoing crusade.[20]

Moreover, the regimes that were now imposed on Greece were imported from the west and had little to do with native traditions.[21] Their new rulers desperately wanted to be seen in Europe as an overseas annex and so their systems were designed to be interchangeable with those of their metropoles, to such an extent that no purer form of feudal relations exists in medieval history than that codified for the Principality of Achaea. Local disputes in Latin Romanía were often referred for resolution to feudal overlords in the west, such as the king of France, belying any notion of local political independence.[22] The Latin lords also looked to the west for legitimacy even while they made pragmatic decisions on the ground. After all, the chief justification of the conquest was the subordination of the Greeks to the Church of Rome. The popes believed that they had the right to directly rule the eastern Church. Accordingly, Latin Romanía generated a series of ecclesiastical colonies whose metropole was Rome. A narrow definition of colonialism therefore misses many other lines of subordination and exploitation that bound Latin Romanía to western Europe.

What were the realities on the ground for subjugated Romans? The first act of the occupier everywhere was to confiscate land and distribute it to military colonists in the form of fiefs held by "feudatories" from the ruler or (in the case of Venice) the state.[23] These were likely the largest confiscations of land in Roman history. They swept up royal estates but also much Church, monastic, and private land, especially the estates of local magnates. The sweep was by no means total, though the Latin occupier always retained the option of making more confiscations and infeudations. On Cyprus, Richard of England proposed taking half the lands of the local elites in order to fund his crusade. His deputies suppressed the local uprising that ensued and Richard sold the island to the Templars, a militant monastic order. When they had to put down yet another uprising, with a great massacre, they returned it to Richard, who sold it to Guy de Lusignan. Guy arrived in 1192 and engaged in another round of confiscations to enfeoff his followers. A contemporaneous Latin historian complained that even lowly craftsmen, masons, and cobblers were given lands, as many refugees from the failed crusader states in Outremer had to be accommodated in the new crusader states in Romanía.[24] The remaining Roman elites (*archontes*) of Cyprus, having lost their properties, "sailed away secretly to foreign lands and to the Queen of Cities" (Constantinople was still free at that time). "As for those who stayed behind," wrote Neophytos the Recluse from his cell, "who could decry their sorrows, their trials, imprisonments, and the extortion of their money?"[25] In the rules that he later drew up for his hermitage, he noted that "our country has fallen to the Latins and all the people . . . have fallen into hard times."[26]

Elite flight left the Romans of Cyprus without leadership cadres to resist. Cyprus was thereafter free of rebellions and the Lusignan could exclude Romans from their ruling classes, employing them at most as secretaries, for only they knew how to operate the complex tax system and were also useful in crafting diplomatic correspondence, some of which took place in Greek. A western pilgrim, Wilbrand of Oldenburg, who visited Cyprus in 1211, noted that "the Greeks all obey the Franks, and pay tribute like slaves. Whence you can see that the Franks are the lords of this land, whom the Greeks and Armenians obey as serfs. They are rude in all their habits and shabby in their dress."[27] Neophytos in his cell was receiving reports that the island was becoming depopulated, and the Lusignan encouraged Syrian and Armenian immigration, which added to the ethnic diversity of their subjects.[28] By the fourteenth century, a few Romans had advanced in the urban society of Nicosia and made common cause with the Latin nobility. The Latin clergy also began to condemn mixed marriages that did not bring both spouses and their children under the jurisdiction of the Catholic Church, implying that such unions did take place.[29]

Constantinople and its hinterland were also abandoned by large segments of the Roman elite, most of whom fled to Anatolia, as well as by a large part of its native population. The industry of workshops that had previously been supported by the court collapsed, forcing many of its craftsmen to emigrate. Moreover, the City's population had also been maintained at artificially high levels, as finding the means to feed it was a core responsibility of the Roman emperors. But the Latin rulers had no interest in maintaining a large populace and lacked the means to do so, as they failed to secure the resources of Anatolia. In addition, sending food to a large royal center was no part of their practice of enfeoffment (which is why there was no megalopolis like Constantinople in western Europe). We may glimpse the fate of this dislocated population in the register of taxpayers carried out in 1219 in Lampsakos in the Troad, a city that remained under Venetian rule until 1224: one fifth of them were recently established peasants.[30] Eventually, the Latin emperors were also impoverished. Baldwin II (1228–1261) was known as "the Broke" and he spent much of his reign begging for funds in Europe; he even mortgaged his own son and heir to the Venetians. The latter expanded their trading operations in the City and yet, while they profited privately, the Venetian authorities had to borrow to provide for defense.[31]

Niketas Choniates lamented that he could not bear to stay in his beloved City because of the humiliation that he felt and the arrogance and violence of its new Latin lords. So many Romans fled from the City that the Latins had their choice of housing, even after the fires, and they could easily evict Romans from their homes. But many remained. The prospect of a chaotic emigration, after all, was daunting. The Latin emperors hired a skeleton crew of Roman officials and secretaries, who were necessary for the few functions of government that they retained, primarily tax extraction.[32] It was Henri who made the most successful overtures to the indigenous population. According to the historian Akropolites, writing after the Romans had retaken Constantinople, Henri, "even though he was a Frank by birth, behaved graciously to the Romans who were natives of the City and ranked many of them among his magnates, others among his soldiers, while the common populace he treated as his own people."[33] Yet Henri himself and other Latins admitted that the Latins were being called "dogs" both by the locals and by propaganda sent from the Romans at Nikaia.[34]

By contrast, we lack evidence for mass flight from Crete and Achaea. The Venetian government sent three waves of colonists to Crete (in 1211, 1222, and 1252), who were mostly expected to reside in the capital, Candia, and exploit their fiefs from a distance.[35] They formed the island's new ruling class, while the natives were excluded from their governing assemblies, even when later a few of them were allowed, in the third wave, to become feudatories of the lowest rank. Unlike the French in Achaea, Venice had a strong concept of the state and micromanaged the island's affairs. They imposed a policy of sociolegal apartheid on the locals, for example by banning intermarriage. The "Greeks" were not allowed to have any communal organizations. After all, even by the fourteenth century the Venetian colonists formed a small and vulnerable group of ca. 2,000 in a city with at most 8,000 and an island with at least 150,000.[36] But they failed to fully subdue the natives, whom they exploited ruthlessly; the Venetians' own sources document many abuses. Starting already in 1212 and throughout the thirteenth century, the Roman *archontes* and their followers rebelled often and violently against the Venetian presence, though they were not always united among themselves. Thus to establish their control over the island, the Venetians had to wage many bloody colonial wars of pacification. Even so, by rebelling the locals managed to extract concessions, including more property rights and guarantees of personal freedom, even for the *villani* (i.e., serf peasants) among them. Some social mingling and even intermarriage between Greeks and Latins occurred later in Candia, but in the first three centuries this did not significantly blur anyone's identity and was limited to small circles.[37] The Jewish community of Crete also interacted closely with its Christian neighbors without losing its identity.[38]

The princes of Achaea took a different approach. They conquered the peninsula in part through warfare but also by making treaties with local notables, allowing a small number of them to enter the lower echelons of the feudal elite of the Principality. "Give it to us in writing and with an oath," the Roman *archontes* are said to have demanded, "so that we and our children can have it securely that no Frank will ever force us to change our faith for that of the Franks, nor make us renounce our customs, the laws of the Romans."[39] But the extent to which this happened is likely exaggerated in our source, the *Chronicle of the Morea*, which was written in the fourteenth century when the Principality was facing a renewed

Roman push to reconquer the Peloponnese. Through such myths of partnership, the text was appealing desperately to the loyalty of Achaea's Roman feudatories. In reality, the Principality's top echelons at the time of its inception were formed by twelve French barons, who received the largest fiefs. Romans were never accepted as peers, nor could they aspire to high offices, and there was little intermarriage between them and the Latins. Even so, the Principality was relatively untroubled by native insurrections, in part because it allowed more Romans to keep their lands.[40]

Thus, the experience of Roman elites differed on Cyprus, Crete, the Morea, and Constantinople, though nowhere could they attain positions of true leadership or be accepted as peers, with the exception of Branas at Adrianople. Their insecurity is reflected in the huge number of coin hoards in Greece that date to the first decade of the century.[41]

The fate of common Romans, by contrast, was fairly uniform. While some remained free peasants in control of their own plots of land, most were reduced to the status of serfs (*villani* in Latin, *villeins* in French), working for the benefit of the feudatories to whom they had been assigned. They had lost not only their state and (in most places) their bishops, but also their personal legal freedom. They could be transferred from lord to lord, they could not marry without permission, and their testimony was weaker in court. They owed a more onerous burden of labor service to their Latin lords than previously to the Roman polity or the Komnenian aristocracy, though we do not know how or whether tax rates changed. Villeins were sometimes required to use their lord's presses, mills, and workshops (for a fee, of course), and some lords required all exports to go through them as intermediaries. These were all ways of fleecing the villeins. There was now almost no prospect for social mobility, which had still been possible in Komnenian society.[42]

In the Roman polity, the vast majority of the population was governed by a uniform set of laws, but in the Latin feudal order legal rights were defined by class, family, and ethnoreligious identity. These rights and responsibilities were specified in private legal collections known as *Assizes*, which were assembled for Cyprus and Achaea in the early fourteenth century.[43] The administration of justice varied from realm to realm. On Cyprus, the Latin feudatories, some 500 in number, headed by four barons, lived mostly in the capital, Nicosia, or in villas, and justice was dispensed by the king's courts. The majority of Romans on Cyprus brought their internal disputes to their own clergy, who adjudicated them based on whatever knowledge of imperial and canon law they had. In Achaea, by contrast, the feudal elite was dispersed, holding down the realm from their castles. The prince's own castle was the formidable Chlemoutsi, built near the Principality's capital, Andrabida, in the northwest triangle of the Morea (see Figure 47). Geoffroi de Villehardouin funded its construction by sequestering the proceeds of Church

Figure 47 Chlemoutsi castle
Shutterstock/Marianna Ianovska

lands.[44] Justice in the Principality was decentralized. The barons dispensed it in their own domains, while lower-ranked feudatories exercised more limited rights over their villeins. This was nothing like the former imperial system of justice. Without a Roman state, there could be no Roman justice, as one of the main functions of that state had been to curb elite abuses and provide standards of legal expertise. In Achaea, the state was essentially abolished.

Before the Latin conquest, much of the region's surplus wealth had flowed to Constantinople, but that flow now mostly dried up, meaning that more wealth remained local. This development did not necessarily benefit the Romans, as the surplus production was instead concentrated in the hands of the Latin feudatories. Latins generally displaced the local Roman *archontes* at the apex of consumption and trade. The region was, moreover, integrated as never before into western trading routes, which is where much of the surplus was now redirected. Western demand for Greek products grew.[45] This reshaped the economic geography, as bustling port-cities emerged that tapped into the Latins' routes. These included Candia and Negroponte in the Venetian network, and Famagusta (Ammochostos) on Cyprus. The whole Morea was reoriented away from Constantinople and to the west, following a new investment in the northwest "triangle": Glarentza (Clarence) was founded ca. 1255 as the Principality's main port near Andrabida (the capital) and Chlemoutsi (the prince's castle).[46] More trade was passing through coastal Greece than ever before, which dramatically increased monetization and banking. Western currencies began to circulate alongside the indigenous Roman coins and their regional imitations, especially Venetian torneselli, French tournois, and English pennies, each tending to predominate in its own economic zone. These developments in turn stimulated Italian, French, and Jewish immigration from the west.[47]

Church Schism

The Latin conquest profoundly changed the ecclesiastical profile of the occupied lands by eliminating or severely restricting the local Church hierarchy. It also changed the very nature of Orthodox identity by causing it to harden around a refusal to accept Catholicism. "Catholic" and "Orthodox" are modern terms of distinction (both Churches claim both labels in their official names). In our period, they were typically differentiated as "Latin" and "Greek," after their languages. In the eyes of the papacy and most Latins, the Greeks did not belong to a separate Church, as did, say, the Jacobites and Nestorians. They were, instead, disobedient and rebellious children of Mother Rome. Neither Church had formally excommunicated the other as heretical, nor would they do so, although many on both sides spoke as if that were the case. They each still believed that, in the end, they formed a single Chalcedonian Church. Ultimately, their schism was not so much over specific issues such as the *azyma* or the *filioque* but over the claim of papal supremacy, that is Rome's belief that the papacy had the right to govern the entire Church, including the Church of Constantinople and all its dependencies. After all, even the minor disputes quickly reduced to the question of who had the authority to resolve them, leading straight to the core issue. But the Greek Church had never accepted papal supremacy, nor the forgeries and fictions on which it rested, including the narrative that the eastern Church had once been subject to Rome but had later broken away from it and so had to be "returned to obedience," even through violence, a threat on which the crusade had delivered.

Constantinople always conceded to the pope a primacy of honor, but this did not entail administrative authority over other Churches. In eastern eyes, the differences between the Churches could be resolved only by general councils that produced consensus. By the twelfth century, the question of papal supremacy had become an intractable point of disagreement, and it remains so to this day. It was already a scoffing matter in the east. When the fleet of the Fourth Crusade stopped at Kerkyra in 1203, the local bishop, Basileios Pediadites, invited the Latin clergy to a meal and they got to disputing over the question. Pediadites remarked that he could think of no basis for the primacy of the See of Rome, except for the fact that it was Roman soldiers who had crucified Christ. Many years later, he turned down Innocent's invitation to attend the Fourth Lateran Council in Rome (1215) on the grounds that it was not representative of the entire Church, and because the lawful bishops of Athens, Ohrid, and Thessalonike had been driven into exile by the Latins.[48] Interestingly, on Cyprus the scene of Christ's Betrayal painted at the hermitage of Neophytos depicts the soldiers behind Judas as western crusaders, beneath the label "dogs," a term commonly used by many easterners, including the saint, for the Latins.[49]

For Innocent III, the ideal outcome was for the occupied lands to have a single unified Church structure that was under his own direction no less than the churches of Italy. Indeed, a truly optimal outcome would be for his authority to be extended to all Christians *tout court*, even beyond the borders of Latin Romanía. This would give Rome power over episcopal appointments, the final resolution of disputes in the Church, the clarification of ambiguities, the disposition of finances, and the definition of doctrine. Priests and even bishops could be Greeks, so long as they recognized Rome's supremacy. Innocent was otherwise (grudgingly) tolerant of local practices that deviated from those of Rome, such as clerical marriage and the use of leavened bread.[50] But local congregations had to genuinely accept papal supremacy. This was the model of Church governance that, through a stream of missives, Innocent tried to push the lords of Latin Romanía to enforce on their new subjects. He wanted obedience, not dialogue.

Only a small number of Greek bishops in Latin Romanía submitted to the Church of Rome and even they were suspected of insincerity. Others either went into exile (such as Michael Choniates) or were removed. Innocent allowed Greek bishops obedient to Rome to be appointed to mostly Greek-speaking areas, while Latin bishops ministered to Latin communities. This was the model that had prevailed in Norman Italy and Sicily, but Innocent himself had already cracked down on the Greek Church in those regions, pushing for a full Latin takeover. The old model was not followed in the newly conquered territories either, and Latins were appointed to most sees. These men arrived from the west often with profit in mind, and a number of bishoprics were amalgamated as each individually did not generate enough revenue to satisfy them. Thus, in most of the Latin empire, the Morea, and Crete there were almost no Greek bishops, only priests to minister to the population, in subjection to the Latin bishops.[51] The presence of the Latin Church was thin on the ground, with only a few bishops in the main towns, few priests overall, and almost none in the country. It is unlikely that Greek priests genuinely accepted papal supremacy or promoted it among their flocks. Dealings between them and their bishops likely took a "don't ask, don't tell" approach to this divisive issue.

By contrast, Greek bishops were allowed to operate in parallel to their Latin counterparts on Cyprus (though reduced from fourteen to four) and at Venetian Modon and Coron. These Greek bishops were stripped of all administrative power and, to disguise the uncanonical irregularity of having two bishops in the same city, they were required to live outside the towns where their Latin counterparts resided. A source of controversy on Crete and Cyprus concerned the ordination of Greek priests. This was supposed to be carried out by the Latin bishops but many went off to be ordained by Greek bishops in the free Roman states. In part, these secret ordinations were taking place because the Latin lords were capping the number of men who could become priests and monks in order not to lose villeins, but it also implied that the Romans did not accept the legitimacy of the Catholic hierarchy of the occupation.

The Catholic takeover also entailed a widespread confiscation of properties from the native churches and monasteries. Insofar as the Latin clergy mostly lived in the towns, this made the Catholic Church in Greece into another instrument of absentee landownership and exploitation. A number of monasteries were also appropriated by the western monastic orders that began to open branch offices in the new lands, in part to proselytize the local population. For example, the Daphni monastery near Athens was given to a branch of the Cistercians. Innocent and his successors tried to dictate from Rome the administrative and fiscal arrangements that governed the new Catholic presence, but their dictates were not always obeyed. Complicated wrangles over the division of the spoils emerged among the papacy, the feudal lords, the Catholic priests ("secular clergy"), and the western monastic orders ("regular clergy"). Overall, the feudal lords tended to get their way. Moreover, the Greek churches did not lose all their property and, over time, they began to accumulate more through donations, some of which were even made by Latins.[52]

Latins and Romans mingled in worship only to a limited degree, given how few of the former there were and how few Romans could interact with them in non-exploitative contexts. More importantly, the project of bringing the Greek Church to obey Rome failed utterly. Conquest and exploitation did not create an ideal context for winning over hearts and minds, and the quality of the Latin Church in the colonies was low. Its various factions feuded with each other over the division of the spoils and were visibly more interested in profit than in tending to the spiritual needs of the Greeks. On a macroscopic level, their failure can be measured by the insignificant levels of acceptance of the Church of Rome among the Orthodox, even in Latin states that lasted beyond the thirteenth century (by contrast, far more Romans were converting to Islam in Anatolia at the same time). It is measured also by the overwhelming popular resistance to Union that the Palaiologoi emperors had to cope with after the restoration of Roman rule to Constantinople. It can even be said that during this period the rejection of papal demands became, in the eyes of many, ingrained in Orthodox identity. In the early fourteenth century, the Venetian crusading theorist Marino Sanudo Torsello conceded that, even though the Latins had been able to conquer the lands of the Greek empire, they "were unable to bring the heart of the people to obey the Church of Rome."[53]

Greek resistance to papal demands was mostly passive and tacit. But when they were pushed to it, the spokesmen of the Greek Church could articulate their position clearly. In late 1204, a papal legate assembled the Greek clergy and monks of Constantinople in Hagia Sophia and demanded that "you Greeks submit to the Apostolic Throne." Ioannes Mesarites asked him to clarify what submission meant because, while their bodies were under the Latins' power, their souls recognized only the patriarch Ioannes X Kamateros. Another meeting was called in September, 1206, after Kamateros had died. The patriarch of the Latin Church was the Venetian Morosini, who demanded to be recognized by the Greeks now that their patriarch had died. He closed all Orthodox churches in the City until they did so. At the meeting, Mesarites rejected the Scriptural basis for papal supremacy and denied that St. Peter had been the bishop of Rome. At a follow-up meeting, the Greeks pointed out that Morosini had not been appointed patriarch through any process recognized by the Church of Constantinople. He could not even speak their language, so how could he be their patriarch? The exchange was written up in dialogue form by Ioannes' brother Nikolaos, who dramatized it and bolstered Ioannes' position with what were becoming Orthodox talking points and rallying cries. "We may have been deprived of all possessions, but we still have one source of wealth—our hallowed and orthodox faith, which you cannot take from us, however much pain you inflict on us."[54] Courting martyrdom was once a tactic used against heretical emperors; it was now used against Latin oppressors.

Pope Innocent's euphoria at the conquest of Constantinople began to fade along with the prospects for Union on his terms. He was also now receiving more accurate reports of the atrocities perpetrated during the City's capture, which had been hidden from him by the crusade's leadership. In an angry letter to his legate in Constantinople, he itemized the horrors inflicted by the Latins on the Greeks and wondered "how will the Greek Church, afflicted by persecution, return to unity and devotion to the Apostolic See . . . having seen in the Latins nothing but the works of Hell, so that it rightly detests them more than dogs?"[55] For Innocent, atrocities were problematic not in themselves but because they hindered the expansion of his power. The Greek clergy considered various compromises, but none of their suggestions, such as holding a council or being allowed to elect their own parallel patriarch, were acceptable to Rome. In the end, they petitioned Theodoros I Laskaris at Nikaia to appoint a patriarch-in-exile there, and in 1208 he appointed Michael IV Autoreianos.[56] The next papal legate to Constantinople, Pelagius, launched a vicious persecution of Greek priests and monks in 1213–1214, arresting them, closing their churches, and threatening them with death if they did not recognize the pope. This stopped only when they appealed to Henri. But the experience led to another wave of emigration from the City to Nikaia.[57]

Religious persecution in Latin Greece was rare, but when it did happen, it exacerbated the existing polarization. Soon after 1204, some Italian priests went to Mt. Athos and demanded that its monasteries commemorate the name of the pope, and they tortured those who refused. This created a schism between the monastery that complied (Iviron) and the rest, with the rest being unsure whether they should remain in communion with Iviron. The bishop whom they consulted in the Roman state of Epeiros, Demetrios Chomatenos of Ohrid, decreed that they should not, as Iviron had been contaminated. On top of that, the monasteries were periodically plundered by Latin lords and bishops.[58] A controversy that divided the Greek Church on Cyprus was over the demand that priests swear oaths of loyalty to their Latin bishops. Germanos II, the patriarch-in-exile at Nikaia, advised them not to do so, nor to have contact with those who did, which exacerbated the community's division. In 1231, thirteen Greek monks at Kantara on Cyprus were arrested, tortured, and executed because they would not desist from condemning the Latin *azyma* as a "heretical" practice. Their behavior was provocative, as no one was forcing them to change their own practice, but their martyrdom caused a scandal, eliciting protests from Germanos to the pope.[59] It appears, then, that authorities in the free Roman states, such as Chomatenos and Germanos, were urging their fellow Orthodox under Latin rule to take uncompromising stances toward the Catholics. Locals who favored more moderate stances saw this as divisive interference by men who did not have to endure the consequences.

The Catholic cause was hindered by the low quality of some of the bishops who came to Greece, sometimes for mercenary reasons. A particularly egregious example was Antelm "the Nasty," the first Latin archbishop of Patras (1205–ca. 1241) and one of the most powerful feudal barons in the Principality of Achaea. Among the many headaches that he caused to the popes, including embezzlement and uncanonical behavior, were scandals alleging his torture, blinding, and killing of Greek priests.[60] The western monastic orders, such as the Franciscans and the Dominicans, made almost no progress toward converting the Greeks.[61] The Latin empire was too weak and divided to promote a unified policy. Some of the popes tried to micromanage the situation through letters and legates, but they were too distant to respond in real time to developments and rampant abuse. Moreover, the popes had limited ability to enforce their will on the secular Latin lords, and spent much of their energy squabbling with them over the division of properties and the extraction of tithes for the Church. The Latin lords, in turn, mostly resisted calls to persecute the Greeks into compliance, because that would destabilize their fragile positions, and they did not really desire their Greek villeins to sincerely embrace Catholicism, because this would undermine the ethnic stratification and give their peasants more rights.[62] Finally, the Greeks were not inclined to abandon their religious identity in the dubious hope of gaining any advantage from their Latin rulers, whose nature they understood all too well. As the Venetian Marin Sanudo noted in the fourteenth century,

> despite the fact that these regions are ruled by the Franks and are subject to the Roman Church, still, almost their entire population is Greek: they cleave to this heresy and their hearts are devoted to Greek things and, when they will be able to express it freely, they will do so.[63]

In 1339, an envoy to the pope from Constantinople explained that the Greeks hate the Latins not so much because of doctrine but because of all the "evils" that they suffered at their hands. Religious Schism was only part of a story of conquest, colonization, and oppression.[64]

Roman loyalties

The other identity that the "Greeks" did not lose—in fact, they insisted on it—was national Romanness. This is hard for us to see today because Romans in the occupied territories produced almost no literature, and modern scholarship universally adopts the terminology of the western Europeans, calling them Greeks. But the Romans knew that the Greek label, when it was not being used in a purely linguistic sense, reflected ethnic prejudice. Other colorful terms used by the Latins included *personae indigenae* (in a document from Crete) and "Griffons" (mostly for the Romans of Cyprus, indicating their allegedly greedy and dangerous nature; a castle in Achaea was named Matagriffon, "Greek-killer", aka Akoba).[65] Whenever they could, these "indigenous persons" declared that they were really Romans. They did so for example in the Greek translation of the *Assizes* used on Cyprus (made ca. 1300), changing *grec* to *Romaios*. Again on Cyprus, a petition in Greek to a lord speaks on behalf of a community of "long-suffering Romans." Freed Greek slaves acquired "free Roman citizenship" and funds were established to ransom fellow Romans in Muslim captivity. As ethnic Romans were now divided among many states, the term "Romanites" emerged to designate a Roman from the free states, though it is rare.[66] In the treaty that Venice made with the Cretan rebel Alexios Kallergis in 1299, after years of fighting, the Latin term *Greco* is rendered *Romaios* in the Greek version. Kallergis was in a position of strength and could represent his people's identity as he chose.[67]

This dynamic played out differently in Achaea, whose feudal elite was partially open to Roman *archontes* in the lower echelons. The verse version of the *Chronicle of the Morea* may have been composed in vernacular Greek but it told the story and reflected the outlook of the French ruling class, large parts of which had learned Greek during the thirteenth century. The *Chronicle* consistently calls the natives "Romans," a major deviation from colonial practice elsewhere. The text tries not to disparage the local Romans, though it does disparage the Romans outside Achaea, especially those affiliated with the state of Nikaia who were trying to reconquer the Peloponnese. The text thus recognizes that Romanness, as an ethnic identity, cut across political boundaries, but it was working to retain the allegiance of Moreot Romans and prevent them from making common cause with outside Romans.

The *Chronicle* was addressing a serious problem facing the colonial states. The free state of Nikaia had reconstituted the offices of basileus and patriarch and in 1261 it regained Constantinople and parts of the Peloponnese. Nikaia also cultivated the allegiance of Romans under Latin rule. As we saw, clergy and monks in Constantinople urged Nikaia to reinstitute the patriarchate. The Greek Church on Cyprus also recognized the reconstituted patriarchate at Nikaia and often deferred to its spiritual authority. The monastic founder Neophytos assumed that the emperors at Nikaia were the legitimate rulers of his island.[68] Many priests from Cyprus and Crete traveled to the free Roman states to be ordained. In practice, however, it proved difficult to work out rules for the relations among the Greek and Latin Churches on Cyprus, the French rulers, and the emperors of Nikaia, each of whom had inherited a fragment of the authority that had previously been more unified.[69]

Romans under Latin rule could act as a fifth column. Guy de Lusignan is said to have feared that rebellions among his Roman subjects would be aided by the Roman emperors, while Henri, the emperor of Constantinople, feared that "all" his Greek subjects would help Theodoros I Laskaris in 1212 if he attacked Constantinople. When Laskaris' successor Ioannes III Doukas Batatzes of Nikaia did attack Constantinople in 1235, the City's Latin lords took steps to disarm its Roman population. Batatzes and other emperors also aided the rebellions on Crete.[70] In 1263, when Michael VIII Palaiologos was contemplating an attack on Cyprus, the pope warned the Latin regent of the Lusignan kingdom to beware because the "Greek Cypriots would gladly throw off the yoke of the nobles of Cyprus, if they could."[71]

Some Romans living under Latin rule proclaimed their loyalty to the Roman emperors. The decoration of a church on the island of Aigina (1289), when it was part of the duchy of Athens, mentions the emperor Andronikos II Palaiologos and the patriarch Athanasios I. The church reflects some western artistic influences, but Andronikos and Athanasios were anti-Union. Inscriptions in two fifteenth-century churches on Crete likewise invoke Ioannes VIII Palaiologos (1425–1448).[72] We do not know how widespread these loyalties were and they were rarely put to the test. Most Romans had little choice but to comply with Latin rule. Yet solidarity with the Roman polity was an option. Many Romans left Crete to serve the emperors in Constantinople "because they could not bear Italian rule."[73] Cretans formed an important contingent in the Roman army of Asia Minor.

By contrast, the Latin colonial elite always looked to western Europe and tried to replicate its environments in Greece, both to make itself feel at home and to maintain their cultural difference from the natives. At Candia, Negroponte, and elsewhere the Venetians redesigned their urban spaces around a church of San Marco facing the ducal palace or loggia, to evoke their home city.[74] The castles of the French Morea, such as Chlemoutsi, were a foreign import that revolutionized the landscape to facilitate western modes of feudal control over the Peloponnese. Bérard, the Burgundian bishop of Athens, sought to organize his see on a Parisian model, and the Burgundian dukes encased the Propylaia of the Akropolis inside a western-style ducal palace.[75] The French lords of Achaea took pride in the purity of their spoken French and their chivalric manners. Pope Honorius III referred to the conquered lands as "virtually a New France (*quasi nova Francia*),"[76] anticipating the naming practices of later European colonialism. Monumental art was also used to fashion narratives that legitimated the conquest. A lord of Thebes decorated his castle with scenes from the First Crusade, and the *Chronicle of the Morea* also begins with the tale of the First Crusade.[77] Another narrative of legitimation was the Trojan War. Many of the chroniclers of the Fourth Crusade cast the conquest of Constantinople as payback against the Greeks by the western descendants of the Trojans, which is what many western Europeans believed that they were, sparking the production of much Trojan-themed literature. The Latin archbishop of Patras painted a mural of the Trojan War in his palace, still visible in 1395.[78] It is not inconceivable that an image of an armed "Prophet Achilles," seen in the 1250s in a church in the Troad, was a Roman response to these Trojan claims.[79]

Ultimately, neither the Latins nor their subjects remained insulated from each other. Over time, artistic and architectural elements were borrowed in both directions, though this never resulted in a truly fused amalgam; it can always be classified as Latin or native with traces of the other. Scholars are still debating whether this borrowing was due to pragmatic factors, such as the employment of the same itinerant builders; to the naturalization of motifs in either culture (such that, after a while, they no longer appeared foreign to those who reproduced them); or whether hybridization encoded a thoughtful ideological stance toward "the other." But art and architecture perhaps give a skewed picture of how the Latins acculturated to their new environment. Their food, clothing, and other perishable objects of daily use must have quickly gone native, and it is hard to imagine that most of them did not become bilingual after the second or third generation. After all, their children were raised in a predominantly Greek linguistic environment, probably with Greek nurses and playmates. There is little evidence for such bilingualism on Lusignan Cyprus, but Geoffroi II de Villehardouin, prince of Achaea, is said in the *Chronicle of the Morea* to have spoken fluent "Romaic," i.e., Greek. The existence of the Greek version of the text—in fact, the likelihood that it was composed originally in that language around 1300—points to a Greek-speaking French aristocracy.[80]

In the fourteenth century, this aristocracy began to sponsor translations into vernacular Greek of some French chivalric romances. Along with the *Chronicle*, these works formed the largest corpus yet of "Romaic" literature. The Latins had no interest in or ability to produce classicizing Greek. In their realms, one could not be trained in it; only Latin was available, at most.[81] By contrast, the educational system in the Roman polities, both before and after 1204, was skewed entirely toward classicizing Greek. Thus, we have the paradox that the Latins did more to stimulate vernacular Greek literature than the Romans themselves ever had.

Romans in Anatolia

Millions of Romans also lived under Turkish Seljuk rule in central and eastern Anatolia. They formed the majority of the population; a western missionary reported that scarcely one in ten was a Turk, though this was too low an estimate.[82] The situation of the Romans there was not much different from that of the Romans under Latin rule, although by 1204 it was a century old. Their conquest by the Turks had caused tremendous damage and dislocation. Some Anatolian cities had been abandoned while others near the border were besieged and changed hands many times. Large populations emigrated or were subject to forced resettlement, and thousands were taken captive and sold as slaves. Raiding continued after the initial conquest, and the Romans of Anatolia also had to cope with the passage of crusades, the instability of the Seljuks and their endless civil wars, and then the Mongol invasions.[83] Religious life in Anatolia was disrupted, as many churches were destroyed or converted into mosques, while festivals and monastic centers lapsed. The religious and demographic landscape changed dramatically when Turkish, Arab, and Persian immigrants poured into Anatolia, with the Persian element acquiring a large role in the administration and literary production. Like many Muslim rulers before them, the sultans recruited slave armies, some from Christian children who were converted young, but they also hired Christian units of auxiliaries, including on occasion among their Roman subjects. Therefore, in its religious, cultural, and ethnic makeup, the Rum sultanate was more diverse than the Latin states of Greece.

As in the Latin states, ethnic Romans were largely excluded from the upper echelons of power in the sultanate. Exceptions have been found, but they are few for a state in which they formed the demographic majority and that lasted for a century and a half. Many of these appointments were "diplomatic" concessions to high-born deserters from Romanía, such as the disgruntled brothers of emperors or future emperors themselves, including Andronikos Komnenos in the mid-twelfth century and Michael Palaiologos in the mid-thirteenth. The Maurozomes family did well in the thirteenth century, but that is because it too began as a separatist regime along the frontier in the aftermath of 1204 that was eventually absorbed by the sultan; so too the Gabrades, who "treated the city of Trebizond as their own property" in the late eleventh century.[84] Trebizond's separatism would be taken to the next level after 1204, when it became a separate Roman state. But otherwise, the Romans of Romanía regarded their compatriots in the sultanate as "enslaved," that is stripped of political power, and subject to the will of their Muslim masters, even to religious persecution.[85]

Some ethnic Romans in Anatolia looked to the free Roman state of Nikaia. There are at least six Greek inscriptions from Seljuk Anatolia that recognize the basileus at Nikaia or (after 1261) at Constantinople, or the basileus and the sultan jointly.[86] But, unlike on Crete, there were no local Roman rebellions against the sultans or movements to rejoin the Roman polity. It is also unclear whether the emperors used the Church to penetrate Anatolia institutionally. Both before and after 1204 they took care to appoint bishops to the cities of the interior, but these bishops were mostly absentees who resided in Constantinople and Nikaia, where they attended the Synod. It was only in extraordinarily moments of alliance between the basileus and the sultan that some bishops were allowed to actually take up their posts.[87] Thus, most Romans of Rum were probably not in close contact with their compatriots in the free states.

Christians were second-class subjects in this Muslim empire. Even so, just as in some of the Latin states, Romans were employed in secretarial roles and in the bureaucracy, especially for tax collection. The sultans' diplomatic correspondence with Christian powers, even Latins ones, was often carried out in Greek, making Greek the lingua franca of the Aegean, also for the French.[88] Some of the sultans had Christian wives and mothers and absorbed their culture as children ("harem Christianity"). This gave them a Christian persona that they could activate when necessary, for example, when they fled to Roman courts seeking aid. Some of the sultans spoke Greek fluently, or could legitimately claim to have been baptized, a custom that some Muslims practiced, and to revere Jesus and the saints, whom they depicted on their coins. Some of their palaces included churches for Christian members of the court. Mixed marriages in the Seljuk realm were apparently more common than in Latin Greece. Among the offspring, boys were typically raised as Muslim and girls were allowed to choose.[89]

Other Muslims in Anatolia learned Greek too, not just the sultans. After all, it was the language of the majority population. Thus, a curious parallel emerged to the French Morea. In neither realm did the Romans produce Greek literature, but the foreign elites did. In Seljuk Anatolia, this was done by the politically influential Sufi poet and Persian émigré Rumi (d. 1273), along with his son Sultan Walad (d. 1313). They wrote poems in vernacular Greek, a language they called "Romaic," although they it wrote it phonetically in Arabic script. Some of Walad's courtship poems in Greek are impressively salacious: he had learned the most vulgar sexual words.[90] It was, then, conquerors and immigrants who shed the most light on the Greek spoken in the Morea and Anatolia in the thirteenth century, regions that had parted ways politically in the later eleventh century.

32
Romans West and Romans East (1204–1261)

Exile and lamentation

As Niketas Choniates fled from Constantinople, "some peasants mocked those of us who were from Byzantion, calling our poverty and nakedness a 'true political equality.'" The inequalities of the Komnenian system had alienated poor Romans from their formerly wealthy compatriots in the capital. But Niketas believed that their scoffing would choke in their throats when they too met "beef-eating Latins" who "had only arrogance and contempt for Romans." Once they were subjected to a racist feudal order, with the Latins moving into their homes and taking their lands, as well as to the horrors of war that were brought by the Bulgarians to Thrace, those scoffers would realize what the Roman polity had once done for them. For his part, when Niketas exited the City, he fell to the ground and asked the walls what they would be protecting now that all was lost. In his literary recollection, he performed a lament for the fallen capital. "Queen of Cities, song of songs and splendor of splendors, who has torn us away from you like children from their mother? Where shall we go now?"[1]

The fall of Constantinople shocked the Romans more than any other event in their history. A generation that had watched with growing unease as the polity unraveled experienced the unthinkable: their impregnable City was taken and the once mighty empire of Manuel I was destroyed by a ragtag army of western barbarians that had set sail from Venice, a city of sailors and merchants that used to be but a speck in the empire's backwater. Romanía was shattered. The Romans had become slaves and refugees in their own land. How had this happened? Most did not respond by analyzing the causes, beyond vaguely concluding that they must somehow have angered God. Surviving accounts lament the fall of the City and are shot through with seething anger at the Latins who had, unprovoked, perpetrated this atrocity. Lamentation runs through the writings of the generation that survived the fall, a trend that lasted for over a century. These lamentations were mixed into funeral speeches for relatives, which complained that the survivors now had to endure Latin oppression; into histories, which waxed indignant about the rape, murder, and plunder that accompanied the sack; and into treatises taking aim at the religious errors of the Latin aggressors.[2]

> Don't you tremble before the Latin race?
> How they oppress us, the Orthodox! . . .
> I was once rich, but today am poor.
> I had honors, but am now dishonored.
> I was envied, not envious, for income and rank.
> But they are all gone now, nothing is left
> of my golden icons, books, and home.[3]

The sack of Constantinople further poisoned the relations between the Churches. Writing in exile on *How the Latins Prevailed over Us*, the patriarch Ioannes X Kamateros explained why the Latins won despite their impiety. His answer was, "through the spear, not the cross." Kamateros branded the Latin religion with the sacrilegious offenses committed during the sack.[4] The bishop of Kyzikos Konstantinos Stilbes, a former rhetorician who in 1204 had to flee from his see and seek refuge at Nikaia, composed a list of 104 Latin errors, which, in addition to religious issues, called the hated Latins out for a wide range of cultural practices, including their food and shaving. He condemns the papacy as basically a criminal organization. Many items (76–98) are dedicated to the atrocities of 1204. Stilbes accused the Latins of being biased against Constantine the Great (because he founded New Rome, which they always envied) and St. Paul (who told the dirty truth about Old Rome in his Epistle to the Romans). After all, these Latins were not Romans at all, but barbarians, basically Vandals, who had conquered the west long ago and filled it with their heresies.[5] Stilbes' list was disseminated widely, for he deliberately wrote it in accessible Greek, unlike his more ornate rhetorical works.

The Roman response was not limited to texts of anger and pain. In fact, the Romans began to regroup even before the City fell, but in an uncoordinated way. "Like a large merchant ship, their empire had been smashed to pieces by the waves and wind, and everyone washed up on a different shore." Moreover, they did not initially collaborate. Choniates complained of disunion between the Romans of the east (Anatolia) and west (the Balkans).[6]

Trebizond

At a point that cannot be dated precisely (though possibly in 1203), Alexios and David Komnenos, the grandsons of the emperor Andronikos I Komnenos (via his popular son Manuel), traveled to the court of their aunt, the powerful queen of Georgia Tamar (1184–1213). With her aid, they took over Trebizond. The city and territory around it would be ruled by Alexios. His seal bears an image of the Resurrection

(*Anastasis*), a potent religious-political message. Alexios founded the dynasty that would rule from Trebizond until the mid-fifteenth century, outlasting the Palaiologan dynasty of Constantinople by almost a decade. Starting perhaps with the two brothers, or at any rate from the mid-thirteenth century, these rulers used the title Megas Komnenos—the Great or Grand Komnenos—indicating that, as the only male descendants of Andronikos, they were superior to other Romans who used that name to establish their royal credentials. While Alexios consolidated his rule over Trebizond, his brother David marched along the Black Sea coast to claim Roman Anatolia. It is possible that the brothers aimed at a full restoration of the Komnenian empire. By 1205, David had advanced beyond Sinope and had overrun Paphlagonia as far as Herakleia, a region that had been his grandfather's base back in 1182. He sent a general to take Nikomedeia, but he was defeated by Theodoros Komnenos Laskaris, who had just proclaimed himself basileus of the Romans in Bithynia.[7]

In 1214, the Seljuks seized Sinope, cutting Trebizond off from the western Roman states. The sultan also captured Alexios and required him to pay tribute to Konya. Thus, if the Grand Komnenoi had sought to reconstitute the Roman polity under their rule, that dream was dashed. Trebizond instead emerged as a regional Roman state that charted a separate course. Its territory consisted of a long and narrow strip of the southeastern coast of the Black Sea, about 400 km long, which was essentially a series of valleys in the Pontos. Tucked behind the mountains, it was protected against the Muslim and Caucasian neighbors who often raided its territories and even attacked its capital. But to the north it was advantageously open to the sea and maritime trade; at times it even held territories in the Crimea. In terms of ethnicity, Trebizond was a majority Roman state, and was understood that way by itself and others, being called *Rum* by the Muslims and *Greci* by the Latins. Its first rulers bore the title "basileus of the Romans," and its laws, liturgical calendar, offices, and titles were essentially those of Constantinople, with a few Turkish offices thrown in. Occupying the theme of Chaldia, its territory was divided into eight military *banda* that ran along the valleys into the sea, each under a *doux*. It probably had no more than 4,000 soldiers at any time and this force was never concentrated in one place. Battles, even under the basileus' command, were fought with far smaller units.[8]

Due to Trebizond's location, its population included large ethnic minorities, especially Georgians and Laz. The Mongol invasions intensified the migration of Armenian and Turkish groups to its relatively well protected territory, and brought Genoese and Venetian merchants who were taking advantage of the newly opened trade routes to the east. A tally of attested names suggests that in the fourteenth century about 35% of the overall population of some 250,000 were non-Roman. Many foreigners would have adapted to the local Roman culture, an assimilation that would not be visible in their names, yet at the same

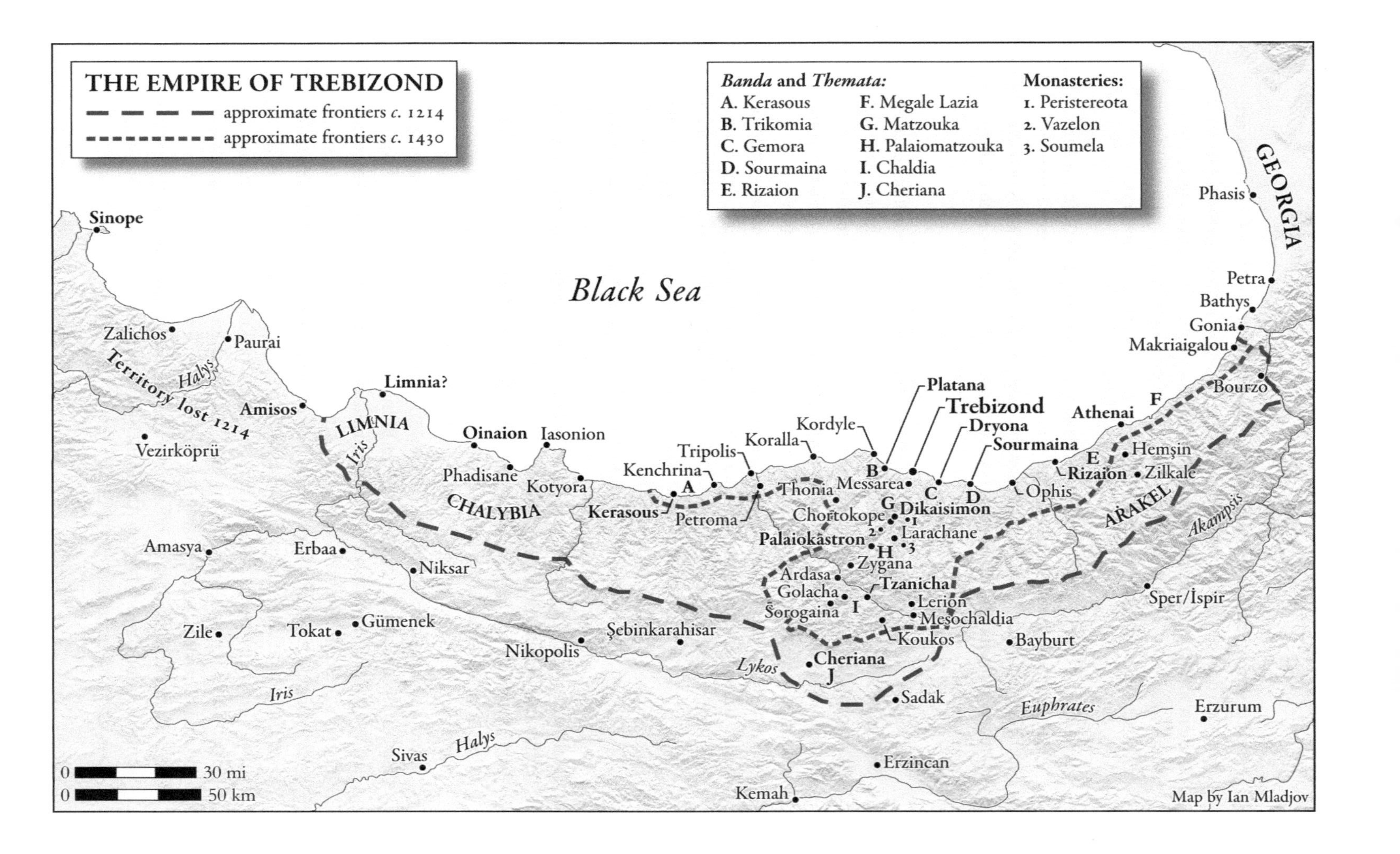
THE EMPIRE OF TREBIZOND
approximate frontiers c. 1214
approximate frontiers c. 1430
Banda and Themata:
A. Kerasous
B. Trikomia
C. Gemora
D. Sourmaina
E. Rizaion
F. Megale Lazia
G. Matzouka
H. Palaiomatzouka
I. Chaldia
J. Cheriana
Monasteries:
1. Peristereota
2. Vazelon
3. Soumela
Black Sea
GEORGIA
Phasis
Petra
Bathys
Gonia
Makriaigalou
Bourzo
Athenai
Hemşin
Rizaion
Zilkale
Ophis
ARAKEL
Akampsis
Sper/İspir
Erzurum
Euphrates
Bayburt
Sourmaina
Dryona
Trebizond
Platana
Kordyle
Koralla
Tripolis
Kenchrina
Kerasous
Petroma
Thonia
Messarea
Dikaisimon
Chortokope
Larachane
Palaiokastron
Zygana
Ardasa
Tzanicha
Golacha
Lerion
Sorogaina
Mesochaldia
Koukos
Cheriana
Sadak
Lykos
Erzincan
Kemah
Şebinkarahisar
Nikopolis
Iasonion
Oinaion
Kotyora
Phadisane
CHALYBIA
Limnia?
LIMNIA
Iris
Niksar
Erbaa
Amasya
Tokat
Gümenek
Zile
Sivas
Halys
Sinope
Zalichos
Paurai
Amisos
Territory lost 1214
Vezirköprü
0 30 mi
0 50 km
Map by Ian Mladjov

time the Roman culture of Trebizond was deeply influenced by ethnic styles, art, food, and dress.[9] The city itself might have had 5,000 residents, perhaps a quarter of them foreign.[10] Thus, a Roman from Nikaia might experience Trebizond as somewhat exotic, especially after it became a center of international trade. A native son of the city described it as follows in the early fifteenth century:

> As if our city were a common marketplace, you might see people from all over the world living here for most of the year, and it would not be hard to examine the more important races and languages. Just going to the market is enough to find out what is happening all over the world and what goods each country produces.[11]

In the early thirteenth century, Trebizond was periodically subordinated to the Seljuks and paid them tribute, and after 1243 it became nominally subject to the Mongols. Yet it was not ravaged by them and retained its de facto autonomy. Its basileis made many efforts to regain Sinope, but these never succeeded for long, with the last attempt made in 1277. This meant that Trebizond was effectively cut off from developments in the west, and could not compete effectively for leadership among the Romans of the west. The lead there was taken by Theodoros Komnenos Laskaris, who had pushed the Grand Komnenoi out of Paphlagonia.

Nikaia

Laskaris was about thirty when he set about creating a Roman state in Bithynia. He had married a daughter of Alexios III Komnenos and had received from him the title *despotes*, which marked him out as a potential heir. He used that title on his seals along with the designation "husband of the emperor's daughter Anna," as if that too were a title. Laskaris left the City in 1203, soon after Alexios III himself, and sought to enter Nikaia. After an initial refusal, the city eventually let him in. Laskaris had to lobby tirelessly for support, speaking at public events to rally support. He eventually became a magnet for most of the Roman high command, the clergy, and ordinary refugees who fled from areas under Latin rule. He established a mini-state-in-exile in Bithynia, acting in the name of Alexios III, but he faced significant obstacles, including the attack of David Komnenos of Trebizond. More serious were the Latin emperors, who were eager to subjugate Roman Anatolia because it was designated as their main demesne in the *Partition*. Latin forces scored victories over Laskaris in 1204–1205, enabling them to occupy parts of the Optimaton and Opsikion themes, including the Troad and Nikomedeia. However, the Latins were forced to halt their advance in order to respond to the crisis precipitated by the Bulgarian invasion, the death of Baldwin, and the Roman uprising at Adrianople in 1205. This gave Laskaris some breathing room. When Alexios III was arrested in Greece by Bonifacio, Laskaris proclaimed himself basileus.[12]

Another potential enemy of Nikaia was Konya, whose throne had just been reoccupied by the exiled sultan Kai Khusrow, who had left Constantinople at the same time. It took him a few years to consolidate his rule and so he was at peace with Laskaris. Moreover, the two men knew each other. While in Constantinople, Kai Khusrow had been spiritually adopted by Alexios III and this link passed now to his "brother" Laskaris.[13] A final challenge was presented by Roman *archontes* who exploited the chaos to assert themselves locally, such as Theodoros Mangaphas (again) at Philadelpheia and Manuel Maurozomes in the Maeander valley. With so many players on the field, alliances were arrangements of temporary convenience. The Latins allied with David Komnenos and then Kai Khusrow against Laskaris, and Laskaris allied with the Bulgarians against the Latins and with the Armenians of Cilicia against the Turks.[14] Meanwhile, individual Roman cities began to find their own political voice and made deals with the emperors as players in their own right. The Roman world became a looser coalition of regional statelets and cities that were trying to chart a safe, or advantageous, course through the storm, like the fragments of a shipwreck.

Through luck and skill, Laskaris survived and his vestigial Roman polity took hold. In 1207, Henri, who was hard-pressed by Kalojan, agreed to a two-year truce with Nikaia and gave up Kyzikos and Nikomedeia. Laskaris put the time to good use. At some point before 1214, he wrested Paphlagonia (including Amastris and Herakleia) from David Komnenos.[15] By this point, if not earlier, Laskaris was recognized by almost all of Roman Asia Minor. He had suppressed or absorbed the *archontes* and their lordships. His fleet had taken back some of the islands near the coast. In early 1208, he took a decisive step that upgraded his status and polity. In consultation with the clergy and priests of Constantinople, he appointed at Nikaia an exilic patriarch of Constantinople, Michael IV Autoreianos (1208–1213), who then formally crowned Laskaris emperor on Easter Sunday.[16]

Laskaris invited prominent Romans to join him at Nikaia, though not all did, such as the patriarch Ioannes X Kamateros (who died in 1206) and Michael Choniates (though he wished the new ruler well). Niketas Choniates, by contrast, did move to Nikaia, where, after a desperate search for patronage, he was allowed to write speeches for Laskaris and given a job. He saw himself as expelled from the paradise of Constantinople, "eking out a living from the churches at Nikaia, like a captive." He bitterly lamented the impoverishment, exile, and mass migration that he and his peers had endured.[17] An *archon* from Euboia named Chalkoutzes came to Laskaris' court armed with a letter of recommendation from Michael Choniates that praised him as a "Latin-hater who is most loyal to the Roman polity and has suffered at the hands of Latin tyranny."[18] Laskaris devoted himself to the salvation "of his own kind." "Those who had been enslaved by the Latins fled to him, and he received them all graciously and generously, giving them the means to live."[19] These newcomers appear in documentary texts as "foreigners, not registered in the local public records." Where we can compare their assets, they tend to have fewer than the locals.[20]

By contrast, grandees from the capital who were absorbed into the Laskarid system landed on their feet. The Latin conquest had sundered the large landowners of Constantinople, especially the churches and monasteries, from their estates in Anatolia. The Laskarids confiscated many lands from those absent landowners and thereby built up extensive crown lands. These could subsequently be reassigned to favorites of the new regime, including to local monasteries (such as the Lembiotissa near Smyrna) and in the form of pronoias to soldiers. Large estates were also assigned to support the new aristocracy of the court-in-exile.[21]

The leadership at Nikaia, both secular and ecclesiastical, was composed of middle-aged men who were previously part of the Constantinopolitan elite. Their outlook was dominated by feelings of loss, exile, humiliation, and fragmentation. They compared their experience to the Babylonian exile in the Old Testament and longed to return to their New Jerusalem. This was not just "imagery" for them: it formed the core of their political aspirations, which were laid out forcefully and programmatically in the texts that Choniates wrote for Laskaris. Like Alexios Komnenos at Trebizond, Laskaris also harped on the theme of the Resurrection of the Dead.[22] His reign heralded the liberation of "the common fatherland of the Romans," namely Constantinople, from the tyranny of that "foreign-speaking and mongrel race from the west."[23] The Romans at Nikaia were "bound to Constantinople in spirit, for all that we are separated from it in body." To make the body resemble the spirit, Nikaia was reconceptualized as a New Constantinople. Laskaris' successor Ioannes III Doukas Batatzes endowed the city with another set of walls and a moat to make it resemble New Rome.[24] Laskaris was cast as a new Noah and Nikaia as his Ark, "the acropolis of Roman affairs" that would preserve them during this deluge.[25]

The spokesmen for the Roman state at Epeiros projected the same ideology, creating tensions with Nikaia. Both states were conceived as irredentist national projects, postulating a single Roman people (identifiable by ethnic or national traits) whose union had been violently disrupted. Both states aspired to reunify the Romans, to "gather up the remnants of the Roman polity," and fight together against the hated Latin. Henri observed that Laskaris was inundating Greece with promises of liberation from the "Latin dogs." Michael Choniates was living in Greece when he wrote to Laskaris, exhorting him to drive the "Italian dogs" out of Constantinople. In a letter to pope Innocent of 1208, Laskaris branded the Latins as "apostates," for they had set out ostensibly to fight Muslims but really attacked other Christians.[26] Not all Romans adhered to this program, of course, not even their rulers at all times. But it meant that they could be called to account when they deviated from it. Niketas Choniates in particular kept hammering the national message home: Romans had a "duty" to unite against the Latins. He emphasized this especially when Laskaris was making pragmatic deals with them. Romans who strayed from this path showed that they were "foreigners in their thinking and traitors to their fatherland, even if they were of the same race." Likewise, the patriarchs-in-exile at Nikaia constantly exhorted their fellow Romans under Latin rule to hold fast to their Orthodox faith and not make concessions to the errors of Rome.[27] Even Michael Choniates, who heaped abuse on the Latins in his letters, took flak for his willingness to talk with them, and he counseled others to make pragmatic decisions when necessary.[28]

The hyper-nationalism of Nikaia is displayed in an official act addressed by the patriarch Michael IV Autoreianos to "the subjects of the basileus and all the soldiers," which was written in simple Greek to be understood. He forgave the sins of all who died "fighting for God and country on behalf of the common salvation and liberation of the nation." Never before had the Church of Constantinople countenanced the forgiveness of sins for fallen soldiers. Autoreianos begins with stirring nationalist rhetoric: "Roman Men! For this name suffices to recall your ancient valor, you who take pride in your ancestors." The literature of this period is full of exhortations to fight on behalf of the nation and the fatherland, while the rhetoric of the court downplayed Laskaris' lineage and played up his labors on behalf of the nation and the social values of fairness and equality. This was likely because Laskaris' family was not as distinguished as others among the aristocratic refugees at Nikaia; it had married into Komnenoi only recently.[29]

This nationalist rhetoric masked the ethnic diversity of Laskaris' army, which was revealed when hostilities erupted again between Nikaia and Konya in 1210. Kai Khusrow was now harboring the fugitive Alexios III Komnenos, who had been ransomed from Italian captivity and was demanding to be recognized as the legitimate basileus by his former clients at Nikaia. Laskaris refused. In the ensuing battle, in mid-1211 by Antioch on the Maeander, Laskaris fought with 800 Latin mercenaries and 1,200 Roman soldiers. The Latins fought well yet were annihilated in the first phase of the battle, but the tide turned in the Romans' favor when Laskaris personally defeated Kai Khusrow in a duel by cutting off the legs of his horse; the sultan was then decapitated. This win was duly celebrated in heroic terms and was the high point of Laskaris' career. Michael Choniates even called it a fitting revenge for Myriokephalon (1176). The sultan's was not the only colorful, peripatetic career ended by that battle. Alexios III was arrested there, blinded, and confined to the Hyakinthos monastery at Nikaia, where he later died and was buried.[30]

Laskaris made peace with the sultan's son and successor, Kai Kaus (1211–1220), but his army had been mauled at Antioch and the emperor Henri took note. Henri and pope Innocent were concerned about the presence of so many Latins on the Roman side, enticed there by Laskaris' pay. The pope had excommunicated any and all Latins who did this, for in his eyes maintaining the Latin empire was a crusading priority.[31] Henri quickly pounced. In 1211, he led a major incursion into Anatolia, defeating Laskaris' forces and reaching as far south as Nymphaion, near Smyrna. We have the affidavit of some farmers who worked the lands of the Lembiotissa monastery near Smyrna who were evacuated by the basileus' brother during this incursion by the "atheist Latins." They were taken into fortified cities or up to inaccessible mountains for their safety. But Henri lacked the forces to garrison this territory and he faced pressures elsewhere, and so he concluded a peace with Laskaris, possibly as early as 1212. Henri made gains north of Pergamon, which meant that the Nikaian state was now divided into two unequal parts linked by a narrow corridor: the region around Prousa and Nikaia in the north, and the Thrakesion theme in the south. Interestingly, Henri appointed a Roman, Georgios Theophilopoulos, to command his lands in Anatolia.[32] But the peace held for the remainder of Laskaris' reign. In 1219, Laskaris even took as his third wife Marie of Courtenay, the sister of the two Latin emperors who succeeded Henri, and in the same year he signed a deal with the Venetians of Constantinople, exempting them from trade taxes and promising not to send ships toward the old capital. It does not appear that the basileus received anything in return for these concessions.[33]

Epeiros

Laskaris' rapprochement with the Latins, his marriage to Marie, and his overtures to the papacy were criticized as a betrayal of Orthodox Romanía by Ioannes Apokaukos, the bishop of Naupaktos and spokesman for the Roman state of Epeiros. In his view, the Romans of the east and west should unite in their struggle against the Latins, their common persecutors, preferably under the leadership of his own ruler, Theodoros Komnenos Doukas.[34] Apokaukos had a point: while Nikaia had stalled, Epeiros was making huge revanchist strides.

The resistance in the "west" had also begun before the fall of the City, in 1203. While Laskaris was struggling to assert himself in Bithynia as *despotes*, his father-in-law Alexios III Komnenos was trying to rally the Romans in Thrace, and he may even have visited his old ally Roman Mstislavich, the Rus' prince of Galicia and Volhynia, in search of aid. When, in 1204, Alexios was joined at Mosynopolis by his other son-in-law, Alexios V Doukas ("Mourtzouphlos"), Alexios III blinded him. The crusaders eventually arrested Alexios V and executed him by throwing him from the spiral column of Theodosius I in Constantinople. The Latin armies then drove Alexios III out of Thrace. At Larissa, in Thessaly, he gave a daughter in marriage to the warlord Leon Sgouros, possibly along with the title of *despotes*, but Sgouros fled south before the Latin advance. Alexios went to Epeiros, where a cousin was organizing the Roman resistance. However, Alexios was arrested by Bonifacio, stripped of his royal insignia, and sent to Montferrat. He was the first emperor of Constantinople to visit Italy since Konstas II in the seventh century.[35] Links to Alexios III were used to legitimate the Roman states at both Nikaia and Epeiros.

Alexios' cousin in Epeiros was Michael Komnenos Doukas, who had a colorful career. He was a natural son of the *sebastokrator* Ioannes Doukas, a grandson of Alexios I. In 1189, he had been given as a young hostage by Isaakios II to Friedrich Barbarossa as the Third Crusade was passing through the Balkans. In 1200, while governor of Mylasa in Anatolia, Michael rebelled against Alexios III but was defeated by him, after which he fled to the court of the sultan Rukn al-Din. The sultan gave him forces with which to raid his former command. In 1204, Michael turned up in the entourage of Bonifacio of Montferrat, but abandoned him to create a separatist state in Epeiros. From his base at Arta, he quickly brought under his control a large territory reaching from Naupaktos in the south to the edges of Dyrrachion in the north. This had been allotted to Venice in the *Partition*, but Venice did not want the mountainous interior, only a few strategic points and islands along the long coast. From this base, Michael and his successor, his brother Theodoros, would reconquer most of central and northern Greece. Unfortunately, their brilliant campaigns and domestic politics were not recorded by contemporary historians and have to be reconstructed from stray notices in diplomatic texts, hostile Latin sources, and the history of Georgios Akropolites, who reflects the viewpoint of Nikaia and was dismissive of Epeiros. Yet the basic facts are clear. Michael and Theodoros were tremendously successful, bringing two assets to their task: tactical brilliance on the battlefield and the strategic violation of oaths. This cynical strategy was likely formulated in response to the Fourth Crusade, when the Venetians cynically broke their oath to defend the interests of Alexios III. After that, "the Romans never felt that they could trust a Latin oath again."[36]

In the sources Michael is surnamed Komnenos, Doukas, or Komnenos Doukas (and will here be called Michael Doukas). Strangely, he never took a title so there is no way to precisely define the nature of his state in Epeiros. In a treaty with Venice in 1210, he called himself merely "son of the *sebastokrator* Ioannes Doukas."[37] He defined himself by a purpose, to free as many Romans as he could from Latin tyranny. It is possible that, in the early years, he crossed the Corinthian Gulf and led the resistance against the French in the Peloponnese, but he was defeated near Modon.[38] Michael's state of Epeiros became a haven for Roman refugees from Constantinople and the Peloponnese. As at Nikaia, many of these refugees enrolled in the army and some were appointed to commands.[39] Ioannina was completely transformed after the influx of refugees, whom Michael resettled there. Families were broken up in the chaos. A woman came to Naupaktos from Corinth looking for her husband, not knowing whether he was there or had ended up among the Romans in Anatolia "during the great scattering of people caused by the Latin invasion." He turned up there but claimed not to know her—a different story.[40]

In late 1207, Michael Doukas defeated a contingent of crusaders that had crossed from Bari to Dyrrachion and were marching east to reinforce the empire of Constantinople.[41] He then made agreements with all neighboring Latin powers to fend off their attacks while he prepared a major assault against them. First, he placed his state under papal protection, which almost certainly entailed recognizing papal supremacy, at least nominally. In 1209, after Henri of Constantinople had suppressed a mutiny of the barons of Thessalonike and had marched down to the south, Michael came to an agreement with him too, accepting him as his lord. Henri correctly warned his envoys that Michael was a liar and traitor, but when Michael boasted to them that, "both by land and sea, there is no one as strong as I in the whole of Romanía," he was being truthful. Finally, in 1210, Michael signed a trade agreement with Venice: the latter recognized his hold on Epeiros while he pledged to be Venice's vassal and send a (symbolic) sum of 42 hyperpyra a year as tribute.[42] Thus Michael was "legalized" in the eyes of all three Latin powers. He also ransomed Alexios III from Italian captivity and kept him at Arta, presumably to validate his position in the eyes of the Romans, though he still took no title. In 1210, Michael sent Alexios with an escort to the court of the Seljuk sultan, which led to the battle of Antioch in 1211.[43] Michael possibly did this to destabilize the budding Laskarid regime. It was a nice reversal: in 1200 Michael had himself fled to Konya before Alexios III; now he was sending him there.

Epeiros had never come under Latin rule, and so its administrative system remained that of the Komnenian period.[44] Having secured his position, Michael launched his war of Roman liberation. Unfortunately, we have no narrative from the period, only the outraged responses of his targets. Between 1210 and ca. 1215, when he was assassinated in his sleep by one of his own men for unknown reasons, Michael launched a series of whirlwind campaigns, taking most of Thessaly and possibly Ohrid too. In the process, he broke, reaffirmed, and then again broke his agreements with Henri, who noted in a letter to the west that Michael had betrayed him four times. The pope was informed that Michael was cruel to Latin captives, crucifying a general and his companions and executing all Latin priests that he encountered. Michael had successfully driven a wedge between the Latin north (Thessalonike and Constantinople) and south (Athens, Thebes, and Salona). He broke his treaty with the Venetians too, annexing Dyrrachion and Kerkyra.[45] Refugees from the fall of Constantinople could be found on Kerkyra too. One of them, a Makrembolites, had fallen to the status of a *paroikos* farmer, while another, Pediadites, kept his rank of *pansebastos* in his "second fatherland," marrying the daughter of a local notable.[46]

Theodoros Komnenos Doukas

Michael's string of successes was continued without interruption by his brother Theodoros Komnenos Doukas (ca. 1215–1230). His big break came in 1217. After the death of Henri, the barons of Constantinople had elected as his replacement Pierre of Courtenay, who was crowned by the pope outside Rome in April, 1217. Pierre then crossed the Adriatic, failed to take Dyrrachion in a siege that he undertook jointly with the Venetians, and then set out for Constantinople. In mysterious circumstances, his army was defeated by Theodoros and he and his entire retinue were taken captive. Some western sources claim that Theodoros had sworn an oath of loyalty to Pierre and then betrayed him. Pope Honorius III (1216–1227) mounted a diplomatic offensive to secure the release of both Pierre and his own representative, the cardinal Giovanni Colonna. Honorius even threatened to divert to Epeiros forces from the crusade that he was organizing. Although Pierre would die in captivity, Theodoros Doukas did release Colonna and, like his brother before him, placed Epeiros under papal protection. Honorius called off the quasi-crusade and forbade the Venetians from attacking. But for Theodoros, like Michael before him, pledges were instruments of war, not peace. They gave him cover while he assaulted Latin positions in Greece with the aim of conquering Thessalonike.[47]

While Theodoros' brother Konstantinos annexed southern Thessaly—the territories around Lamia and Hypate (New Patras)—Theodoros began to encircle Thessalonike with his own conquests, starting with the fortress of Platamon in 1218 and then adding the formidable Prosek in 1219, a place that had given such trouble to Alexios III back in 1199. While we have no narrative of their conquest, Grebena, Kastoria, Prilep, Skopje, Beroia, Servia, Moglena, and Strumica also fell, followed by Serres, east of Thessalonike, possibly at the end of 1221. Thessalonike was cut off and invested in 1223.[48] Apokaukos crowed that the Thessalonians longed for Theodoros, "at least those among them who are of our religion, who speak the Hellenic tongue."[49]

The moment was opportune as the kingdom of Thessalonike was weak and divided. Bonifacio had been succeeded in 1207 by his infant son Demetrios, born to his Romanized Hungarian wife, Margit, the widow of Isaakios II. At times she had favored Roman interests but she was opposed by a faction of barons who wanted to give the kingdom to Bonifacio's much older son from Italy, Guglielmo VI, marquis of Montferrat. Soon before the siege began, Margit quit Thessalonike for her native Hungary, while her now teenage son Demetrios roamed Italy in search of aid. The new Latin emperor was Robert of Courtenay (1221–1228), the son of Pierre, and he sent an army to Serres. But this force retreated when news arrived of the heavy defeat of another army of the Latin empire by the basileus of Nikaia, Ioannes III Doukas Batatzes, at Poimanenon in Anatolia. Theodoros' forces annihilated the Latin soldiers withdrawing from Serres. Thus, in one year the Latin empire was defeated by both Nikaia and Epeiros, though the two Roman states were not coordinating their moves.[50]

Thessalonike had no choice but to surrender, probably in late 1224, on terms of safety for the Latins, who departed. But by 1220, pope Honorius realized that he had been duped by Theodoros. He broke off relations, excommunicated him, forbade any Latin from dealing with him, and tried to rally the powers of Latin Greece to aid Thessalonike. His efforts culminated in the first crusade to formally target the Romans of Greece, whom the pope now labeled "enemies of the faith" and "enemies of God." The link to Jerusalem in this iteration of crusading ideology was so tenuous as to be invisible. The expedition was led by none other than Guglielmo, the marquis of Montferrat. It landed at Halmyros in early 1225, but was stricken by an outbreak of dysentery. Guglielmo and many of his men died, and the rest dispersed. Apokaukos read this as a sign of divine support for the Romans for it prevented "the pollution of Latin bishops" from being reestablished in the cities.[51]

By 1225, Theodoros had been proclaimed as basileus but was postponing his formal coronation, perhaps in the hope of staging it in Constantinople.[52] His armies advanced victoriously into Thrace, taking back Christopolis (Kavala), Mosynopolis, and Didymoteichon. Theodoros also annexed Adrianople, a city that had only recently surrendered itself to Nikaia, which was gaining its first footholds in Europe, but the Nikaian officers left and were replaced by Epeirots. Theodoros then advanced to Bizye and almost to the walls of Constantinople itself.[53] But he was not ready for that challenge. He and his brother had liberated much of Greece, Macedonia, and Thrace, but had done so without holding an official title, unless they meant for their surnames (Komnenos and Doukas) to function as titles, for example on their coins. By 1225, Theodoros was being called basileus. He now made it official. The Synod of western bishops met in Arta in February, 1227, and resolved that Theodoros should be formally crowned in recognition of his many labors against the "atheist Latins" and for liberating so many sees from the "pollution" of Latin and Bulgarian bishops. "It is him alone that we recognize as basileus," they said, a snub aimed at Nikaia.[54]

The bishops of Nikaia, speaking for their basileus, Batatzes, sent a letter to Theodoros protesting his use of the title and urging him to renounce it. Batatzes allegedly offered to recognize him as a junior basileus. It was even brought up that in the 1200s, when Theodoros was at Nikaia, he had sworn an oath of loyalty to Laskaris before joining his brother Michael at Epeiros.[55] Moreover, the bishop of Thessalonike, Konstantinos Mesopotamites, also refused to recognize Theodoros as basileus. He had served as the empire's civilian administrator in the 1190s, and was restored to his see through Theodoros' liberation of Thessalonike. Yet despite Apokaukos' arguments that he should be grateful, he refused. Theodoros forged ahead with his plans anyway. Mesopotamites was removed from his office and the coronation was performed in 1227 by the archbishop of Ohrid (or "Bulgaria"), Demetrios Chomatenos. Like some of his predecessors, Chomatenos equated his archbishopric of Ohrid with that of Justiniana Prima, whose founder Justinian had decreed to be autocephalous. This, in his mind, boosted his quasi-patriarchal credentials for performing a coronation.[56] In reality, there had never been fixed rules for such ceremonies.

Epeiros and Nikaia found themselves in a tricky situation with no precedent in Roman history. Past conflicts had occurred between the basileus in the capital and a challenger in the provinces. The imperial tradition provided little guidance for two parallel Roman states that were vying over the same objective: to expel a foreign occupier and regain Constantinople. It was understood that "it was not in their interest, being people of the same race, to have two emperors and two patriarchs."[57] Epeiros and Nikaia did not want to fight each other but nor could they collaborate, for their rulers had no mechanism by which to coordinate their exclusive and sovereign titles and claims. The two basileis studiously ignored each other in a kind of cold war, as they had no interest in fighting an actual war. Besides, their spokesmen in the 1220s were aging bishops who had great respect for each other, in many cases through friendships forged before 1204. They wrestled with the underlying issues, specifically that of episcopal appointments.[58] Who had the right to appoint bishops?

Michael and Theodoros of Epeiros had, during the course of their wars, expelled the Latin and Bulgarian bishops from the towns that they conquered and, on the authority of the Synod of bishops at Arta, replaced them with Romans. In the previous imperial model, such appointments were made by the court and the patriarch at Constantinople, but that option was now unavailable. In 1213, the Epeirot bishops under the leadership of Apokaukos had drafted a request to the patriarch at Nikaia to confirm these appointments, but they received no reply for nine years. When a later patriarch finally did reply, he approved the existing appointments in a spirit of compassion but also demanded to control all future ones.[59] Yet Theodoros Doukas could not have his bishops sent from Nikaia, a rival state, and his subsequent proclamation as basileus complicated the matter. This set off a cold war within the Church and an exchange of fascinating texts, in which bishops struggled with this unprecedented situation and tried to preserve their unity in the face of political fragmentation. What kept them together was their common ethnic Roman identity, vision of national restoration, and shared Orthodoxy. This was effectively a new experience of Romanness, held together by ideas and identities and not, as before, also by unified institutions. Without those common elements, Nikaia and Epeiros would have spun off in separate directions, with no incentive to engage in anguished debate over unity.

Nikaia, and especially the patriarch Germanos (1222–1240), took a more hard-line approach. Germanos recognized neither the basileus nor the actions of the Church of Epeiros. He feared, however, that their separatism could lead to the creation of a rival patriarchate-equivalent in Epeiros.[60] The bishops of Epeiros were somewhat more flexible. They did not officially recognize the basileus of Nikaia, but they did occasionally speak of western and eastern

Romans in parallel terms, as "brothers" coping with the same crisis. Chomatenos, Apokaukos, and Georgios Bardanes (the bishop of Kerkyra, a former student of Michael Choniates) argued that Germanos was trying to enforce an order that no longer existed, as it presupposed a unified state. When Constantinople was retaken, which they hoped would be soon, that order would be reconstituted, but until then everyone had to make do with ad hoc arrangements.[61] Chomatenos could not resist getting some digs in. He noted that the "eastern" state was not expected to last for long anyway, surrounded as it was by enemies. Moreover, the Nikaians were not innocent of radical innovations too. "Whoever heard of one person serving as the metropolitan of Nikaia and simultaneously calling himself patriarch of Constantinople?"[62]

Epeiros managed to score only one hit against Nikaia, which was to take Adrianople from it (ca. 1226). But Nikaia had already scored a hit against Epeiros in ca. 1219, when it appointed an autocephalous archbishop for Serbia, a jurisdiction that had traditionally belonged to Ohrid (and thus to Chomatenos). The first to hold the new position was Sava, a younger son of the grand župan of Raška, Stefan Nemanja, who had often clashed with Manuel I Komnenos. Stefan abdicated in 1196 to become a monk. He and Sava founded the Serb monastery of Hilandar on Mt. Athos, obtaining recognition from Alexios III.[63] Meanwhile, Stefan's other son and successor Stefan Nemanjić was seeking to elevate his realm to the status of a kingdom, and he succeeded in ca. 1216, when pope Honorius awarded him a royal title (*kralj* in Serbian parlance). The domestic politics of Serbia in this period are opaque, but it is understandable why it turned not to Rome but to the Orthodox patriarchate in order to secure its ecclesiastical independence. Sava's religious career had unfolded entirely within the Orthodox orbit, and an autocephalous Orthodox archbishopric promised more genuine autonomy than anything that Rome was willing to offer. Chomatenos tried to persuade Sava to follow the canons and stay within the jurisdiction of Ohrid, but it was no use. The most that could be managed was a marriage of a daughter of Theodoros to Stefan's heir, Stefan Radoslav.[64] Serbia was poised to become a bigger player, but it remained within the Orthodox orbit.

Theodoros bestowed the rank of *despotes* on his two brothers Konstantinos and Manuel, an innovative use of that title. They held two regional commands, in Naupaktos in the southwest and probably Thessaly in the east. Compared with the state of Nikaia, we know much less about the political and military history of the state of Epeiros in this period, but more about its social history. This is due to the survival of the dossiers of Apokaukos and Chomatenos, which, in addition to internal administrative documents, include a number of legal verdicts issued by their episcopal courts at Naupaktos and Ohrid. Apokaukos complained bitterly about the administration of Konstantinos Doukas in his region, accusing him to Theodoros of harsh and even violent tax collection that had reduced people (and his priests) to poverty. Apokaukos and Konstantinos clashed to the point where the bishop was expelled from his episcopal residence. Konstantinos was also accused of confiscating lands from the Church in order to give them as pronoias to favorites. We hear of pronoias worked by Roman farmers that were assigned to Latin mercenaries. This was all like the Komnenian system: abuses were rampant but complaints were probably exaggerated, in traditional Roman style.[65] Epeiros was, then, getting by more or less in the same way as Nikaia.

The dossiers of the two episcopal courts also reveal the endemic violence of Epeirot society. Workers were tortured or beaten to death by landowners, officials, and even bishops. Conflicts over land spiraled into murder. Female fieldhands were sexually harassed or raped. A wife who could not endure her husband was locked up with him by the community so that the couple could "work it out." A thieving servant had his hands cut off and bled to death. A wife sought protection from the bishop against her husband who was demanding anal sex, and she threatened to kill herself if she were sent back to him. Officials used excessive violence. And couples sought divorce because they could just not get along, feared their spouse's black magic powers, or were married against their will, sometimes before the legal age of twelve.[66] These disorders may reflect a society under conditions of stress and dislocation. It is also possible that such social violence had always existed in the Roman provinces but only now, with the creation of a provincial state and the survival of the dossiers, do we see it in more granular resolution. Even in this case, however, we should beware the "nightly news" effect: court documents by nature preserve the most violent and salacious cases but leave it unclear whether they were aberrant or regular facts of life. At least we find that common people still had access to a responsive court system. Apokaukos and Chomatenos were compassionately inclined to grant divorces in many of these cases.

Epeiros was a Roman-majority state, but it included Albanians in the north, Vlachs in Thessaly, and Bulgarians in Macedonia and Thrace. These groups rarely appear in the sources and are not linked to troubles, whether military or social.[67] Religious minorities were smaller groups: Jews, Armenians, and Muslims. When Chomatenos was asked to explain why they were tolerated, he replied that by living among true Christians they might be persuaded to convert, though they were required to live within their own designated quarters. Moreover, they provided valuable services.[68]

Theodoros was positioning himself to retake Constantinople. Arta, like Nikaia, was reimagined as a surrogate capital, as seen in the new prominence given to the local monastery of Blacherna, which evoked Blachernai in the capital and was intended as a dynastic mausoleum. The iconography in the churches of other towns stressed the Biblical themes of exile, return, and liberation.[69] Theodoros often discussed the "liberation" of the Peloponnese and he praised one Moreot for "his loyalty to Romanía."[70] But even after taking Thessalonike, the basileus did not feel up to the challenge posed by Constantinople, so in September, 1228 he concluded a truce with the Latin empire, which established commercial relations and a right of return for refugees.[71] He instead attacked Bulgaria, with which he had also made a peace treaty sealed by a dynastic marriage. The rationale and goals of this strategic decision remain opaque. At this time, the rulers of Epeiros, Serbia, Bulgaria, the Latin empire, and Nikaia were densely intermarried, so that their strategic objectives cannot easily be inferred from their dynastic marriages. Their relations were also governed by a network of treaties, but treaties were, for the rulers of Epeiros, arrangements of convenience. In 1230, Theodoros marched up the Hebros river with an army of Romans and Latins. He met the Bulgarian-Cuman army of the tsar Ivan Asen II (1218–1241), who had hung the text of the broken treaty from his standards. At Klokotinitza the Romans were decisively defeated, and Theodoros and most of his captains were taken captive. This defeat ended Theodoros' grand ambitions. Ivan Asen freed the common Roman soldiers, but he advanced rapidly into Macedonia and Thrace, overrunning a huge swath of territory from Adrianople and Didymoteichon to Serres, Pelagonia, and Prilep, reaching to southern Albania.[72]

Ivan Asen proved to be a mild imperial overlord, unlike his uncle Kalojan, who had been psychotically sadistic to captives. In the church of the Forty Martyrs at Tarnovo, Ivan Asen set up a Cyrillic inscription celebrating his victory in battle, his conquest of the lands between Adrianople and Dyrrachion, and his belief that the Latin empire of Constantinople was now subordinate to him. In official texts, he claimed the imperial title "tsar of the Bulgarians and the Greeks."[73] Bulgaria had emerged as the major power in the Balkans, but its military capabilities were stretched too thin and the tsar could not place his own men in charge everywhere, so he allowed Romans to govern the most distant territories; it is not even certain whether they did so under his suzerainty or were fully autonomous. Thus Epeiros survived, albeit fragmented and reduced. Specifically, Thessalonike and its territory was taken over by Theodoros' brother, the *despotes* Manuel Doukas, who was Ivan Asen's son-in-law. Manuel's regime gave mixed signals as to whether he was a proper basileus or not, and he quickly recognized the Nikaian basileus (Batatzes) and patriarch (Germanos) in order "to heal the dissension among us Romans." In 1233, Germanos sent Christophoros, bishop of Ankyra, as his plenipotentiary representative (exarch) to the western churches. Chomatenos, whose see was autocephalous, remained aloof, but the other churches of the state of Epeiros fell in line with patriarchal control. Manuel also placed his state under papal protection, a tactic that both of his brothers had pursued in the past. Pope Gregory IX (1227–1241) warned him to learn from their fate and keep his word.[74]

The state of Epeiros eventually broke into three parts, which remained on good terms with each other. In the early 1230s, Michael II Doukas, the teenage son of the state's founder, returned to Epeiros from the Peloponnese, where his mother had fled (or been exiled) when Michael I was assassinated. Michael II now took over the western core of the Epeirot state, from Ioannina down to Naupaktos. Meanwhile, Theodoros Komnenos Doukas himself was issuing orders as basileus from Bulgarian captivity, but ca. 1234 he was blinded by Ivan Asen, likely as a concession to Bulgaria's new ally, Batatzes, the basileus at Nikaia. But in 1237, Ivan Asen temporarily lapsed from his Nikaian alliance and freed Theodoros. He returned to Thessalonike where he proclaimed his son Ioannes basileus so that he, Theodoros, could still rule behind the scenes despite his blindness. His brother Manuel, who was ejected from Thessalonike, ended up ruling in Thessaly after a series of adventures. When he died in ca. 1239, Michael II absorbed his lands.[75] Epeiros was thus no longer a unified state but a decentralized family operation of the Komneno-Doukes. And with the passing of the last generation educated in Constantinople before 1204, including Apokaukos and Chomatenos, Epeiros also lost its powerful spokesmen. Apokaukos had been desperate to find educated men to ordain as priests.[76] Epeiros became subordinate to Nikaia in both political and Church matters. Yet the regional lordships into which it collapsed—western Epeiros and Thessaly in particular—proved durable.

The former empire of the Romans was now fully fragmented into regional kingdoms and lordships. There were, at times, three or four men claiming the title basileus "of the Romans," including in Epeiros, Nikaia, and Trebizond, and even Ivan Asen boasted that he was tsar "of the Bulgarians and the Greeks" (i.e., the Romans). There was also a Latin "emperor of Constantinople" and the Seljuk sultan of Konya occasionally boasted that he was the ruler "of Rum" (i.e., the territory of Romanía), among other lands. The Serbs now had a kingdom and Armenian Cilicia had imperial pretensions of its own. Never before had there been so many kings and emperors packed into this territory, which had once been a single polity.[77]

Nikaian administration

Among these rivals, it was Nikaia that gained momentum under Ioannes III Doukas Batatzes (1221–1254), one of the most capable Roman rulers. He was the son-in-law of Theodoros I Laskaris, though he had not held the title of *despotes*. He did not officially use the name Batatzes, but he was (and still is) called that for disambiguation. His accession was opposed first by two of Laskaris' brothers and then, in 1224, by a major conspiracy against him during his first war with the Latins. However, we cannot reconstruct the deeper politics of his bumpy accession. The possibility that he seized power through a coup cannot be ruled out.[78] The sources for his reign are poor. Authors trained before 1204 continued to write down to ca. 1230 at most, but when they died there was only a handful to take their place, for most institutions of higher learning had lapsed. Few Romans managed to acquire a proper education in the years after 1204, so Batatzes' long reign is poorly documented.[79] The leading teacher of the reign was the irascible Nikephoros Blemmydes (1197–1272), whose memoirs, literally entitled *A Partial Account*, provided posterity with proofs of his brilliance and holiness. Batatzes commissioned Blemmydes to teach at the court, and his pupils included the royal heir Theodoros II. When he was not involved in some scandal, Blemmydes traveled to collect books and reconstitute the broken system of higher learning. Copyists of this time preferred rhetorical works from the twelfth century, the heyday of the Komnenian empire.

If Nikaia under Batatzes yielded a thin harvest of authors, it did at least enjoy a stable and perhaps growing agricultural production. We have reports of general prosperity, and the basileus ensured that all cities were well stocked with necessities, including weapons for defense. The disruptions and dislocations of 1204 had by now been smoothed over, and the Nikaian state had consolidated its management of the royal estates that it had created through the confiscation of (mostly monastic) lands. The government took regular and thorough censuses of both lands and taxpayers. Batatzes stimulated agricultural productivity through meticulous stewardship and stored up funds in his treasury at the city of Magnesia, for which he was remembered as a "Roman patriot."[80] In the economy he was a protectionist, discouraging imports and exhorting his subjects to be self-sufficient. Anecdotes circulated about how he practiced what he preached. He scolded his son and heir Theodoros II Laskaris for wearing gold and silver, for such items "could be purchased only by spending the blood of the Romans abroad. Don't you realize that the wealth of rulers is the wealth of their subjects?" To prosecute his Balkan wars, he cultivated good relations with the Seljuks, selling wheat to them during a famine. It was said that the empress' crown was paid for by the revenues of the royal poultry farms.[81]

Theodoros I Laskaris had established a second, winter court at Nymphaion, in the hills near Smyrna, and Batatzes spent more time there than at Nikaia, while his treasury (*vestiarion*) was at nearby Magnesia.[82] It was in the vicinity of those centers that Batatzes refounded a monastery dedicated to the Virgin, known as the Lembiotissa. We have a large archive of documents—a "chartulary"—from this monastery. It includes royal acts (chrysobulls), land surveys, and hundreds of documents regarding the monastery's village rights and bequests made to it. The collection, which still awaits a proper historical study, is our main source for the socioeconomic history of Nikaia and the complex mechanisms by which disputes were resolved by the court and the intervention of local officials. The chartulary mentions all the expected sociolegal categories, from landowners and pronoiars to tenant peasants whose status was defined by a variety of rights and duties. This dossier does not reflect significant change in the fundamentals of the Komnenian social order.[83] However, it does not illuminate demography or the overall patterns of landownership. The Lembiotissa looms large due to the survival of its dossier and not because the emperors endowed it with more lands and exemptions than they did other monasteries or, for that matter, the patriarchate.[84] We cannot put it properly into perspective.

The provinces of the Nikaian state included Paphlagonia; Optimaton and Opsikion (in Bithynia, fully recovered after 1225); Skammandros (or the Troad); Neokastra (including Pergamon and Sardeis); Thrakesion (including Smyrna and Ephesos); and Mylasa-Melanoudion in the south.[85] Each was commanded by a *doux* and had its own local defense forces, though these were increasingly called up to fight and garrison the state's expanding Balkan holdings. Relations with the Seljuks to the east were generally peaceful and, by mutual agreement, many Turks pastured their flocks in the lowlands during the winter. But Turkish war bands also raided the provinces to carry off children for the eastern slave markets, so the provinces were heavily fortified in this period, including the towns, monasteries, and private estates.[86] Roman settlers along the frontier were given tax breaks and pronoias to induce them to stay.[87] Unfortunately, we cannot estimate the size of Batatzes' field armies and we know little about their structure.

Like his predecessor, Batatzes hired Latin mercenaries and gave pronoias to those who joined his army on a permanent basis. But their commanders never rose higher than the lower echelons of his court hierarchy, mirroring the restrictions put on Roman *archontes* in the Principality of the Morea. Some Romans managed to climb from humble origins, through military service, to the top of the social ladder, and Batatzes educated pages (*paidopouloi*) at his court who were later given state responsibilities. We see some new names among the governors of the provinces, but the highest strata were still dominated by the old names, including Tornikes, Palaiologos, Kamytzes, Angelos, Kantakouzenos, Branas, Tarchaneiotes, Raoul, and Synadenos.[88] The basileus appointed these men to carry out the most important functions of state, both military and civilian, but this was done in an ad hoc way, often without regard to their exact titles or offices. For example, Andronikos Palaiologos was *megas domestikos* (commander of the armed forces) in the 1240s, but he was not replaced, and the basileus relied subsequently on officers with other ranks. Likewise, Demetrios Tornikios long held the post of *mesazon* (the basileus' chief-of-staff), but he too was not replaced, and Batatzes transferred his duties to "random people," including a bishop.[89] This strategy was reminiscent of the eleventh century, when emperors used flexible appointments to prevent the aristocracy from entrenching itself in administrative positions. However, a major difference from past practice was the vastly reduced use of eunuchs, only a handful of whom held important posts at Nikaia and Palaiologan Constantinople. This shift in court culture has not yet been adequately explained.

Honorific court titles had previously been distinct from offices linked to functions, but in the thirteenth century their amalgamation accelerated, resulting in a single court hierarchy in which titles and offices were jumbled together. Military functions were generally linked to offices, but high-placed men often carried out civilian or judicial functions on the authority of their title, e.g., *protosebastos*, which was not technically an office. Conversely, some offices lost any link to a function or department of state and became titles. For example, a *protovestiarites*, the title borne by Batatzes before his elevation to the throne, had no link to the *vestiarion*, the royal treasury. And certain men tended to carry out the same functions no matter what office or title they held, as was the case with Georgios Akropolites, who specialized in diplomacy and correspondence. We have little information about how titulars and office-holders were paid, beyond being awarded a pronoia. Finally, the Senate did not survive the fall of Constantinople as a discrete collective body. From now on, when the sources refer to the Senate they mean either the aristocracy generally, all court titulars and officers, or the basileus' advisory council, whose membership was at his discretion. The Komnenian aristocracy, therefore, had finally supplanted the Roman senatorial order.[90]

Batatzes' wars

Under Batatzes, Nikaia steadily expanded its territories, experiencing only minor temporary setbacks. Our main source is Akropolites, who recounts only the bare bones of the campaigns. Batatzes defeated the forces of the Latin empire in late 1223 or early 1224 at Poimanenon, pushing them out of most of Anatolia. "We were heating up, while they were cooling down."[91] It was this victory that enabled Theodoros of Epeiros, who was operating independently, to take Thessalonike. The Romans of Adrianople surrendered their city to Batatzes, but, as we saw, his garrison was withdrawn soon thereafter when Theodoros arrived. At a point that cannot be dated precisely, possibly ca. 1230, the Nikaian fleet took over the islands Lesbos, Chios, Samos, Ikaria, Kos, and possibly Rhodes. Rhodes was a special case, as it was ruled by a Roman dynasty, that of Gabalas, but eventually it too recognized Nikaian sovereignty.[92] The state of Nikaia had two naval bases, in the Hellespont for operations mostly against Constantinople and at Smyrna for the Aegean.[93]

In the early 1230s, Batatzes used diplomacy to prepare for the reconquest of Constantinople. He first explored the possibility of Union with Rome, which, if settled, would undercut a major justification for the Latin empire. Pope Gregory IX sent four friars—two Dominicans and two Franciscans—who participated in discussions at Nikaia and then Nymphaion in 1234, with Batatzes in attendance. Most of the debate concerned the procession of the Holy Spirit and the *azyma*, and Blemmydes provided the intellectual force behind the Orthodox side. Batatzes revealed his goals when he asked whether, in the eyes of the pope,

Union would entail the restoration of the patriarch to Constantinople. Batatzes also proposed to yield on the *azyma* if Rome would remove the *filioque* from its Creed. But the friars refused to budge on any point, and the meetings ended in acrimony: "You're the heretics!" "No, you are!" The Orthodox also denounced the sacrilegious atrocities committed by the Latins in 1204.[94]

Batatzes next turned his diplomatic efforts toward Bulgaria and found a ready ally in Ivan Asen, who had also been rebuffed by the Latins. Nikaia fully recognized him as a peer basileus and, in 1234, he gave his daughter Helene to marry Batatzes' son Theodoros II Laskaris. Nikaia also formally recognized the bishop of Tarnovo as an autocephalous patriarch, a concession that detached Bulgaria from the sphere of Rome and brought it back within an Orthodox orbit. Formal autocephaly had also been granted to the archbishop of Serbia in ca. 1219. With these moves, Nikaia dismantled the network of influence that the popes, by taking advantage of Constantinople's weakness, had painstakingly constructed in the Balkans in the late twelfth and early thirteenth centuries. Nikaia realized that the Roman polity was unlikely to reconquer Serbia and Bulgaria and so it converted their de facto independence into an anti-Latin asset by giving them what the pope would not: ecclesiastical autonomy. The elderly patriarch Germanos II (1222–1240), who had matured before 1204, was essentially creating an Orthodox federation of Churches. In his sermons, he preached total war against "the western people" who had brought "the darkness of tyranny" upon the Orthodox. He urged Batatzes "to send them packing, back to their own countries." Elsewhere, in a similar context, he refers strikingly to his people as the "humiliated generation" and encouraged Batatzes to rebaptize the Latins in their own blood. In a letter to the cardinals at Rome in 1232, Germanos refuted the foundations of papal supremacy and boasted that many great nations sided with the Greek Church and called it their "mother," including the Ethiopians, Syrians (Melkites), Georgians, "the vast nation of the Rus', and the victorious kingdom of the Bulgarians." The new Bulgarian patriarch Ioakim duly traveled to Nikaia to be ordained.[95]

Batatzes and Ivan Asen met at Kallipolis (Gallipoli) in the Thracian Chersonese, which Batatzes had just conquered. The tsar delivered his daughter to the basileus, and the two then conducted a joint war against the Latins in 1235. The Romans took most of southern Thrace, while the Bulgarians kept "the regions that faced to the north," whatever exactly that meant.[96] In 1235–1236, Batatzes and Ivan Asen jointly invested and attacked Constantinople by land and sea, with the Roman fleet led by Gabalas, the lord of Rhodes. The attacks, however, were foiled by the intervention of the Venetians and Geoffroi II de Villehardouin, lord of the Morea, who came to the rescue of the Latin emperor, his nominal overlord.[97]

Batatzes would presumably have continued his attack on Constantinople had the political landscape not suddenly changed. Ivan Asen switched sides and for two years was allied to the Latins. At the same time, all sides were watching with mounting apprehension as the Mongols, annihilating everyone in their path, advanced across the northern steppe and into Mesopotamia and the Caucasus in the south. This expansion made itself felt in the Balkans already in 1237, when an army of Cumans, fleeing before the Mongols, crossed the Danube and pushed through Bulgaria to Thrace. Some pillaged the countryside while others took up service with the Latins or the Bulgarians.[98] The core territories of Nikaia were safe for now, protected by Bulgaria, the Latin empire, and the Bosporos in the west and by the Seljuks of Rum in the east. But the Mongols were a growing worry.

Meanwhile, pope Gregory IX was planning a crusade against Batatzes, calling especially on Hungary and France to send soldiers. By this point, crusading was openly being used as a weapon against the enemies of the papacy, no matter their religion or location, for merely opposing or obstructing the pope's agenda was defined as "heresy." Batatzes was deemed "an enemy of God." In 1237, the pope threatened him with a crusade and exhorted him to become "a devoted son of the Roman Church." To this Batatzes responded with the most extraordinary letter written by any Roman emperor, so sarcastic that it was long considered an anti-papal forgery, though it is undoubtedly authentic. Batatzes mocked the pope's "arrogance and delusion" and affirmed his own commitment to fight for his people's freedom and to reconquer Constantinople, which was unjustly occupied by criminals who masked their greed under the sign of the cross and revealed their true nature in the atrocities of 1204. Send your armies, the basileus says, "we have the means to defend ourselves."[99]

Batatzes found an ally against the pope in Friedrich II Hohenstaufen, the German emperor. Friedrich was on good terms with the rulers of both Epeiros and Nikaia, seeing them as fellow victims of papal aggression. He saw their states as models of a political order oriented around secular rulers, not bishops. Still, in his official correspondence he referred only to himself as the basileus of the Romans, calling Batatzes the basileus of the *Graikoi*. Both Epeiros and Nikaia contributed men to Friedrich's Italian wars—the last east Roman soldiers to campaign in Italy, some seven centuries after Belisarios.[100] In exchange, Friedrich destabilized the papal alliance by recognizing Batatzes' claim to Constantinople and impeding the passage of Gregory's crusade through his lands. The crusade eventually reached the Balkans in 1239, led by the Latin emperor Baldwin II. Few had signed up for it, as many westerners believed that crusades should not target other Christians. In order to raise funds, Baldwin had mortgaged Constantinople's most sacred relic, the Crown of Thorns, to the Venetians for 13,134 hyperpyra; they then sold it to Louis IX of France. After marching across the Balkans, in 1240 Baldwin's army took back the fortress of Tzouroulon in southern Thrace, but that was all. Batatzes easily retook Tzouroulon in 1247.[101]

A second wave of Cumans fleeing the Mongols had crossed the Danube by 1241. Following a traditional imperial playbook, Batatzes resettled some 10,000 of them in Phrygia and the Maeander valley, so that they could provide light cavalry forces to his army; probably only a few hundred could be raised from a population group of that size. This force is attested down to the end of the thirteenth century, but within a generation they had been baptized and could speak Greek.[102] Batatzes was turning the disruptions of the Mongol advance to his advantage. But there was little that he could do if the Mongol juggernaut targeted him. In fact, everyone in eastern Europe and the Near East was exposed to the Mongols' sudden attacks. Yet as it happened, the Mongols invaded, defeated, and weakened the Romans' neighbors, but left the Romans themselves unscathed and therefore empowered relative to their local rivals. In part, this happened because the Romans were the most distant target along both of the Mongols' lines of advance, namely from the north into the Balkans or from the east into Anatolia. Specifically, in 1241–1242 a Mongol army commanded by Batu Khan, a grandson of Genghis Khan, rampaged through Poland, Hungary, Dalmatia, Serbia, and Bulgaria, leaving behind a swath of death and destruction. Baldwin II of Constantinople, who tried to resist, was dealt a defeat. Ivan Asen had died in early 1241 and his realm, ruled now by underage tsars who were tributaries of the Mongols, rapidly declined.[103] In the east, in 1243 a Mongol army crushed Kai Khusrow II, the Seljuk sultan of Rum, and his vassals and allies at the battle of Köse Dağ. These developments created opportunities for Batatzes.[104]

Batatzes' strategic objective in the early 1240s was not Constantinople but Macedonia and Epeiros. This reorientation made sense. Constantinople was a labor-intensive target that required joint sea-and-land operations, and the Latins could call on Venice, Achaea, and the pope for assistance. Another naval assault on the City had failed in 1241, when the resident Venetians counterattacked. Yet the western Roman lands were vulnerable, divided, under weak leadership, lacking allies, and a rich prize. Before launching his campaign, in 1241 Batatzes signed a treaty with Baldwin and Kaliman of Bulgaria.[105] He also renewed his ties with Friedrich II, who sent a Sicilian fleet to aid in the recovery of Thessalonike as well as his daughter, Anna (Constanza), for Batatzes to marry. Then, in 1241 or 1242, Batatzes' armies overran east Macedonia and invested Thessalonike. The city was ruled by the basileus Ioannes, son of the blind Theodoros Komnenos Doukas. After forty days, he agreed to give up his title and accept that of *despotes* from Batatzes, in exchange for which he was confirmed as lord of Thessalonike. This was an ad hoc arrangement made in haste, for news of the Mongol incursion into Anatolia forced Batatzes to return to Nymphaion to monitor developments. After the battle of Köse Dağ in 1243, he met with Kai Khusrow II and concluded an alliance with him too. The basileus explicitly regarded the Rum sultanate as a buffer between Nikaia and the Mongols. Subjects of the sultan immigrated to the state of Nikaia for protection. Batatzes ensured that Roman forts were stocked with provisions and carefully inventoried. The Mongols were an unknown and unpredictable quantity at this time: "No one knew why they had burst out of their homeland, or what their customs were. Some said they were the Dog-Headed people, others that they practiced cannibalism."[106]

After the battle of Köse Dağ, most of Anatolia recognized nominal Mongol overlordship. The basileus of Trebizond, Manuel I Grand Komnenos (1238–1263), exchanged his Seljuk master for a Mongol one, which brought him greater freedom of movement. But first, in 1246, he personally traveled to Karakorum in Mongolia to personally pay his respects to the new Great Khan Güyük, as did dozens of rulers from the Near East and Asia.[107] No Roman ruler had ever traveled that far. When he returned, Manuel consolidated his state. The silver mines controlled by Trebizond enabled him to issue a solid silver coinage that was used far and wide.[108] The Mongol conquests also shifted international trade away from Mesopotamia and toward the north, for example Tabriz, propelling Trebizond to become a major hub between Asia and the Italian networks, mainly Genoese and Venetian. The Italians set up their emporia in Trebizond and the city boomed.

Trebizond already sported a palace on the high ground between the two ravines, as well as the adjacent coronation church of the Panagia Chrysokephalos and the church of the city's patron saint Eugenios, above the marketplace and harbor. The Great Komnenoi placed their painted portraits, sporting full royal regalia, in all these buildings. Their palace featured a fascinating gallery of royal portraits going back, in genealogical succession, to the first Komnenos emperor in Constantinople, Isaakios (1057–1059). Manuel placed his portrait in the monastic church of Hagia Sophia that he built two miles west of Trebizond. Mounted on a platform, the church functioned also as a dynastic mausoleum (see Figure 48). Its name alluded to Constantinople, though its architecture drew also on Caucasian traditions. A relief and inscription in Greek above the south porch depicted "Adam sitting before Paradise, lamenting his nakedness," next to a scene of "God planting Paradise toward the east in Eden and placing there the man whom he created." This was likely a figured statement about the Grand Komnenoi themselves, their past, and their ambitions (see Figure 49). The iconography inside stressed themes of exile and Resurrection, as did the churches and rhetoric of the western Romans at that time. Yet the Grand Komnenoi no longer aspired to Constantinople and were reconciled to their eastern Eden, even under Mongol suzerainty.[109]

Batatzes had no intention of submitting to the Mongols. He sat tight for three years (1242–1245) waiting on developments. When the despot Ioannes of Thessalonike died in 1243/4, Batatzes appointed—or consented to the succession of—his brother Demetrios as despot. By 1245, the Mongols were "preoccupied with their own affairs" and the Latin empire was weak. When

Figure 48 Hagia Sophia in Trebizond, exterior
Photo by David Hendrix

Figure 49 Hagia Sophia in Trebizond, porch images and inscriptions
Photo by David Hendrix

Kaliman of Bulgaria died in late 1246, Batatzes marched quickly into Bulgarian-occupied Macedonia. He took Serres and Melnik and reached as far as Skopje and the Pelagonian plain. Most cities surrendered to him on condition that he confirm their existing "rights" and "customs," though we know little about the details; they likely concerned self-governance and tax exemptions. Thessalonike was also betrayed to Batatzes by a pro-Nikaian faction. Demetrios was deposed and the city became the base of the *megas domestikos* Andronikos Palaiologos. The latter's son Michael—the later Michael VIII—who was twenty-two, was put in command of Serres and Melnik. The state of Nikaia now reached as far as Epeiros, which was still ruled by Michael II Doukas. Between them lay a pocket of territory, including Ohrid, Prilep, and Vodena (Edessa), that was ruled by the blind Theodoros Komnenos Doukas.[110]

The title *despotes* was undergoing a significant shift. In the later twelfth century, it was given to the emperor's son-in-law and potential heir. In the early phases of Nikaia and Epeiros, it was given to the rulers' brothers. In the 1230s, Michael II of Epeiros and Manuel of Thessalonike were using it as a quasi-royal title, as its common meaning was "lord" or "master." Batatzes established a new usage when he awarded the title to Ioannes of Thessalonike and (with more certainty) around 1250 to Michael II of Epeiros. The latter regarded himself as autonomous, drawing legitimacy from his Komnenodoukan ancestry, but Nikaia regarded him as a subordinate. Batatzes thus inaugurated a system of regional Roman lordships governed by despots in the basileus' name. These lordships, misleadingly called "appanages" in the scholarship after the French feudal model, represented a new model of regional vassal states.[111] This system evolved out of the unusual circumstances of the thirteenth century. The relations between the states of Epeiros and Nikaia could no longer be normalized within the framework of the former Roman polity, which had a unitary conception of authority, so they repurposed older court titles in order to simulate notions of feudal vassalage that the Latins had introduced to Romanía. Oaths and other expressions of personal subordination were deployed to loosely glue together the fragments of a previously unitary system. It was not only interstate relations that were coordinated this way: Epeiros itself was fragmented internally in the same way, fractally divided among regional lords who jostled for status in quasi-feudal terms among themselves and with the basileus of Nikaia and later Constantinople.[112]

Epeiros and Nikaia came to blows again in 1251, when Michael II, aided by his uncle Theodoros Komnenos Doukas, attacked some of Nikaia's acquisitions in western Macedonia. Batatzes marched back to the west and, for the first time in his career, spent the winter in the Balkans, at Vodena, which his forces captured. His armies then forced Michael to sue for peace. Nikaia thereby acquired Ohrid, Diabolis, Kastoria, as well as the Albanian stronghold of Krujë not far from the Adriatic coast, probably as a loosely affiliated chiefdom. Some of these places went over to Batatzes through high-profile defections.[113] Nikaia's Balkan territory now consisted of a swath cutting directly across the peninsula, separating Bulgaria and Serbia in the north from Thessaly and Epeiros in the south. Thus, apart from Constantinople, southern Greece, and Crete, Batatzes had reassembled most of the pre-1204 empire, including most regions that were demographically Roman. This was Romanía sans imperial acquisitions. Overall command of the new provinces was entrusted to an official at Thessalonike, starting with Andronikos Palaiologos, the father of Michael VIII. The *megas logothetes* (and later historian) Georgios Akropolites held this post after 1256. Batatzes also bestowed titles and commands upon Epeirots who defected to him. Although he placed garrisons in the Macedonian towns, the latter were more loosely integrated into this reconstituted Roman polity than they had been before 1204, in part because they had joined it through bilateral agreements. The scope for "internal diplomacy" between the cities and the basileus had expanded, giving local notables more options.[114]

Batatzes presented himself as the legitimate ruler of all Romans, and he was recognized as such by many on Venetian Crete and in Seljuk Anatolia. When the Latins in Constantinople wanted to demolish some churches in order to sell their building materials, Batatzes bought them and ensured their survival. He paid for the repair of the Holy Apostles church after an earthquake, broadcasting his concern for the City that should have been his capital.[115] Batatzes initiated yet another round of negotiations over Church Union in 1249 with pope Innocent IV, who had prioritized the defense of the Latin empire. Batatzes' efforts at a diplomatic solution were, however, hindered by his ally Friedrich II, who was at war with the papacy (and aided by Nikaian soldiers). After lengthy negotiations, a proposal reached Rome in early 1254 from the patriarch Manuel II (1244–1254): Nikaia would accept a qualified version of papal supremacy in exchange for the return of Constantinople to the basileus. But Manuel, Batatzes, and Innocent all died in the second half of 1254, and the matter was shelved.[116]

Theodoros II Laskaris

Batatzes died at Nymphaion on 3 November, 1254, aged around sixty-two, and was buried at the monastery of Sosandra at Magnesia that he had founded. Before long, he was being revered as a saint, "John the Merciful," by a local constituency that was probably centered on Sosandra. His cult generated a saint's life and commemorative religious service. While it could not rival in scope that of St. Constantine the Great, it was more than any other Roman emperor had received.[117] This honor was due in part to Batatzes' qualities as a ruler and in part to a set of compounding rifts that emerged within Roman society after his death. These began with tension between Batatzes' son and heir, Theodoros II Laskaris, and the aristocracy of the Nikaian state, and it was then supercharged by the overthrow of the Laskarids by Michael VIII Palaiologos and the controversy over Union with Rome. "John the Merciful" was a useful hero for anti-Union partisans of the Laskarids.

Theodoros II Laskaris (1254–1258) was born around the time of Batatzes' accession in 1221. As a prince and then co-emperor, he governed Anatolia during his father's Balkan campaigns. He also received the finest education and wrote many original works, including essays on moral and political topics, treatises on philosophy and theology, a satire of his first tutor, orations, and hundreds of letters. As a record of literary and intellectual exploration that ranged far beyond the realm of his royal duties, Theodoros' corpus may be compared with that of only one other prior emperor, Julian (361–363). Both men died young and, interestingly, both were obsessed with ideas of Hellenism, though in vastly different contexts. Theodoros routinely refers to his subjects as Hellenes and to his realm as Hellas, though also as Romans and Romaïs (i.e., Romanía), without explaining how the two identities meshed. Theodoros' Hellenism was a national identity, combining culture, ethnic descent, and geography. Greece for him was located at the center of the world, and he even drew diagrams to illustrate the point. He developed this ideology in part to score points against the Latins, by showcasing the philosophical accomplishments of the Greeks, which far surpassed those of the Latins whom he debated: "every kind of philosophy and knowledge was either an invention of the Hellenes or was improved by them. . . . But you, O Italian, in whom do you boast? Nikaia is now comparable to Athens . . . the same air that was then, is now ours too; the Hellenic language is ours; and we are drawn from their blood. But what wisdom ever came from *you* to *us*?"[118]

Theodoros regarded war and philosophy as two sides of the struggle against the Latins: "the Hellenic sword was now avenging the murder of the Hellenes" in Constantinople in 1204.[119] Yet Theodoros was also worried over the recent silence of Hellenic wisdom and the prospect that philosophy might be abandoned by the Greeks and find a new home among the barbarians. This is the first sign of Roman intellectual insecurity vis-à-vis the Latin west.[120] Moreover, Theodoros remained alone in his proclamation of a Hellenic nationality. It did not catch on among his subjects, who clung to their Roman nationality. His Hellenism was, after all, an attempt to ameliorate the otherwise disparaging Greek identity that the west was projecting onto his subjects; he was trying to distinguish the culture of the eastern *Romaioi* from that of the western *Romani*. In the east-west debates of that time, more charitable thinkers than Theodoros recognized that both Greeks and Latins had common roots in the global Roman empire of antiquity and drew their shared name, culture, and religion from it.[121]

Nikaia's stated goal was still to recapture Constantinople and "to help our brothers, wherever they might be, against the foreign races." But most of Nikaia's leadership had by now been born and raised in Anatolia and their sense of "exile" was muted. Theodoros' "homeland" was Anatolia, and Nikaia was the new

Constantinople. Nikaia was the Queen of Cities, the new Athens of learning, while Constantinople was "now a slave." The basileus dedicated his victories to "the Holy Land, my mother Anatolia."[122]

Theodoros never got the chance to attack Constantinople during his brief reign. The Bulgarian tsar Mihail Asen I (1246–1256) took advantage of Batatzes' death to overrun a number of forts in Thrace. Akropolites claims that the tsar was aided by ethnic Bulgarians in those regions who "hated the Romans," as well as by a Bulgarian general in Roman service who attacked Melnik. The basileus led the Roman response personally and instantly, in spite of it being winter (early 1255). He chased the tsar away from Adrianople and regained the lost territories. The basileus then marched west to Thessalonike, Edessa, and on toward Ohrid, restoring his authority while both complaining and boasting in his letters about the long campaign, which lasted until the end of the year. He dismissed his senior generals Alexios Strategopoulos and Konstantinos Tornikes (son of the former *mesazon*) for incompetence verging on disloyalty, complaining about them to his confidant Georgios Mouzalon, the *megas domestikos* who was governing Anatolia. In early 1256, Mihail Asen called in an army of 4,000 Cumans to raid Thrace, but they were chased out, taking great losses. In June, 1255, the basileus and tsar agreed to a truce that restored the former boundaries (with Philippopolis, Sofia, and Skopje on the Bulgarian side). That summer, while in Thessalonike, Theodoros formalized a long-planned marriage alliance between his house and that of Michael II of Epeiros. In the process, he confirmed Michael II as despot but also twisted his arm to surrender Servia and Dyrrachion. Overall, Theodoros had good reason to boast of his successes.[123]

While Theodoros and his patriarch Arsenios were at Thessalonike, alarming news arrived regarding the canniest and most unscrupulous politician of that time: Michael Palaiologos had fled to the Turks. Like Theodoros II, he was a descendant of Alexios I and Alexios III Komnenos. In 1252, he had been tried by Batatzes on suspicion of treason and imprisoned for months. In addition to scheming with the empire's enemies, he was sporting in those days the royal name Komnenos and had commissioned a quasi-imperial encomium of his father, the *megas domestikos* Andronikos Palaiologos. Michael was eventually released on condition that he swear oaths of loyalty. He was married to Batatzes' great niece Theodora and made *megas konostaulos* (i.e., "constable"), the first known commander of the Latin mercenaries with that title.[124] Now, in 1256, he fled to Konya, ostensibly out of fear for his life. While in the sultan's service, Michael led the Christian forces of the sultanate in the battle of Aksaray (Koloneia) against the Mongols, which ended in a defeat for the sultan Kai Kaus II. In 1257, the sultan fled to Theodoros II, who had returned to Anatolia in haste to monitor the Mongol situation. The basileus harbored the sultan briefly before the latter returned to become a Mongol vassal. Michael also returned to the basileus after receiving oaths of safety, and was reappointed to his old position. He later said that "while I was with the Turks in body, I was with the Romans in spirit."[125]

Palaiologos was playing a dangerous game, but so was Theodoros. The basileus was at odds with the upper echelons of his aristocracy. He argued in theory against the notion of nobility of blood, advocating personal virtue as the basis of true nobility. His political philosophy rested on the notion of "friendship" between the ruler and his close associates, which in reality was a form of patron-client relationship based on trust. His practice matched this theory. Theodoros' closest associate, Georgios Mouzalon, did not have an aristocratic origin and was treated by the basileus as a close friend.[126] He appointed to high office many men "who came from the dregs," as Blemmydes and other critics put it.[127] This limited the elite's opportunities for advancement. Theodoros intervened in the aristocracy's marriage alliances, requiring their women (especially of the Palaiologos clan) to marry his favorites, but keeping his own daughters out of the marriage game. As a result, many of our sources are hostile to him, casting him as morose, suspicious, cruel, prone to anger, and terrified of magic. He deposed, blinded, and otherwise punished many of his aristocratic opponents and their kin, alienating families with names Strategopoulos, Palaiologos, Raoul, Tornikes, and Philes.[128]

One of the beneficiaries of the regime was Georgios Akropolites, who did not come from the highest elite but was married by Theodoros to a Palaiologos bride, made *praitor* of Thessalonike, and praised by the basileus for his learning. Yet in his *History*, written after the accession of Palaiologos, Akropolites goes out of his way to depict himself as a victim of the regime who was even beaten at the basileus' command for being friendly with Palaiologos. Blemmydes also turned against his former royal pupil, even though he too was honored by him. Blemmydes would have us believe that Theodoros offered him the patriarchate in 1254 but that he refused and scolded the basileus for treating the Church as a secular instrument of power. The office went to the monk Arsenios instead. Yet a cleric from Theodoros' entourage rewrote Akropolites' *History* to make it more favorable to the basileus and to Arsenios.[129] These battle lines—for and against Theodoros II—reflected the later partisan division between the Laskarids and Palaiologoi and exacerbated the debate over Union. The seeds of this later social division were being sown already in the mid-1250s.

Theodoros' reign ended unhappily. In early 1257, Michael II of Epeiros launched an all-out attack on the westernmost possessions of the state of Nikaia. Akropolites, as the governor of Thessalonike, was touring his domains and found that many of his subordinate officers, new men of humble origin appointed by the basileus, were either incompetent or disloyal, and some went over to Michael II. The latter overran Beroia and Ohrid. Eventually, Prilep was also betrayed to him and Akropolites was taken captive. Theodoros II sent Michael Palaiologos to fight back but did not give him enough forces to turn the tide. Michael II had Albanian and Serbian support and was building up a broader alliance with Guillaume II de Villehardouin, prince of Achaea, and Manfred of Sicily, the son of Friedrich II. Michael II married his daughters to those princes, with the former receiving a dowry of 60,000 hyperpyra. A document from February, 1258, reveals that Manfred was recognized as the overlord of Dyrrachion and Aulon, meaning that this portion of the Adriatic coast had been detached from Nikaian control, possibly with Michael's consent, and now alienated to western rule. Thus, Nikaia's position west of Thessalonike had collapsed, and Michael II hoped to capture that city as well. All that Theodoros II could do was form an alliance with new Bulgarian tsar, Konstantin Tih (1257–1277) by giving him his daughter in marriage; she was the granddaughter of Ivan Asen II, a desirable match for the tsar. But during 1258, Theodoros became increasingly more ill and, allegedly, paranoid. He died on 16 August after taking tonsure as a monk and was buried at the monastery of Sosandra beside his father.[130]

The rise of Michael Palaiologos

Theodoros had required all shareholders in the Roman polity—the Senate, army, clergy, and people—to swear that they would defend the succession of his son, Ioannes IV Laskaris, a child of six, and he appointed Mouzalon as regent until Ioannes came of age. But the revolution began immediately. Three days after Theodoros' funeral, at a memorial service for him at Sosandra a crowd of angry nobles with grievances against the regime, including Strategopoulos, Tornikes, Philes, Raoul, Zagarommates, and Alyates, caused a tumult. Mouzalon and his brothers were butchered by the Latin mercenaries, a corps that was under the command of the *megas konostaulos* Michael Palaiologos, who was the likely instigator of the coup. Soon afterward at Magnesia, Palaiologos, who was in his mid-thirties, was elected as the new regent for Ioannes and appointed *megas doux* and subsequently despot. "Let's not run the risk of putting an infant in charge of such weighty matters!" On 1 January, 1259, arguing that the crisis called for able and flexible leadership, his supporters proclaimed him, Michael Doukas Angelos Komnenos Palaiologos, as basileus at Nymphaion.

While Michael swore to uphold Ioannes' rights, at their joint coronation at Nikaia a few weeks later the patriarch Arsenios was pressured to crown Michael and his wife first, and the underage emperor received a lesser crown. Michael then purged many of Theodoros II's men from the government, appointed his own supporters, and spent money liberally from the public treasury to purchase wider support. The reversal of fortune was complete. Ioannes IV, whose succession was guaranteed by sacrosanct oaths, was sidelined, and Michael, a man who had once spent months in prison as a traitor, and who had later fled to the sultan and was robbed along the way by Turkmen, losing literally the clothes off his back, was now basileus of the Romans. The patriarch Arsenios felt tricked and ceased to perform his duties in protest. But others may have felt a whiff of destiny about Michael's remarkable career. This was due to more than his own unscrupulous genius: the Laskarids had created an aristocracy whose ambitions they could not contain, and Michael was their leader. A later historian called them "the golden chain," and Michael VIII was their strongest link.[131]

Before his proclamation, Palaiologos sent his brother Ioannes Komnenos (as *megas domestikos*) to confront Michael II of Epeiros. For Palaiologos, Epeiros was now led by "hostile fellow Romans."[132] Michael II hastily withdrew from Kastoria to western Epeiros to await his allies. In early 1259 Ioannes Komnenos retook Ohrid, Diabolis, and their territories, while Michael II gathered his coalition with units from Manfred (including 400 knights) and the entire army of Achaea led by its prince, Guillaume II himself. This allied force, which set out for Prilep, was too large for Ioannes Komnenos to face, so he kept his regular forces in the mountains and used Cuman and Turkish auxiliaries to wage guerilla operations in the plains; his rank had meanwhile been upgraded to *sebastokrator*. We have diverse reports about what happened next, probably near or in the plain of Pelagonia. Nikaian agitators or spies spread misinformation that induced Michael II to abandon his army at night, while his son Ioannes Doukas, the lord of Thessaly, went over the Nikaian side, allegedly because of a romantic quarrel with the French. The Epeirot Romans scattered while the Achaeans and Sicilians awoke to find the camp in confusion just as the Nikaians attacked. It was a rout, not quite "the battle of Pelagonia," as historians traditionally call it. Many were killed or taken captive as they fled. Guillaume II of Achaea was found hiding behind some hay near Kastoria, and recognized by his protruding teeth. He and most of his nobles were taken to Nikaia. Palaiologos had won a spectacular victory at the beginning of his reign.[133]

The armies of Nikaia pressed their advantage. Strategopoulos and Raoul marched into Epeiros and occupied the capital, Arta, liberating their compatriot Akropolites. The despot Michael II fled to the islands Leukas and Kephalonia. But the Nikaians had left the city of Ioannina unsubdued and under siege to their rear. The *sebastokrator* Ioannes then overran Thessaly and marched to Thebes, which he sacked, for the duchy of Athens was unable to resist after its losses at Pelagonia. However, he too had left Ioannes Doukas of Thessaly in his rear, and Doukas remained loyal to his father, the despot. The Nikaians mistreated and alienated the local population and were stretched too thin. When Michael II began to organize a resistance, the Nikaians withdrew their small garrisons from Greece. The borders reverted to their 1252 form, and the resilience of Epeiros was proven once again. Strategopoulos and the *sebastokrator* returned to the basileus to be rewarded for their victory; the former was made a *kaisar* and the latter a despot.

By his own account, Palaiologos was "reaching out to all the broken pieces of the empire of the Romans." He proffered a marriage alliance to Manuel I Grand Komnenos of Trebizond (1238–1263) in order "to unify the Romans." While that overture fell through, the negotiations yielded a symbolic but nevertheless potent diplomatic agreement, precisely the sort of thing at which Palaiologos would excel. His patriarch and Synod, made up of two dozen bishops from Bithynia, Thrace, and Epeiros, recognized the de facto autonomy of the Church of Trebizond, while the latter recognized the patriarchate's nominal suzerainty.[134] Palaiologos also had his eye on a prize greater than Greece or Trebizond: Constantinople. In early 1260, he besieged Galata, across the Golden Horn, hoping that the City proper would be betrayed to him by a contact inside. But it was not, and the siege of Galata failed. Yet during these operations, some of Michael's soldiers discovered the tomb of Basil II at the Hebdomon, which they identified by its inscribed verses. The corpse, found naked except for a flute in its mouth, was taken to Michael at Galata, and he had it reburied with honors at Selymbria, which he had just seized.[135]

Constantinople was a tough nut to crack, and Michael needed allies for a blockade and assault. He had neutralized the Achaeans and now he needed to counter the Venetians. In fact, an Italian chronicle at this time noted that, after Pelagonia, the Venetians were the City's last remaining Catholic defenders.[136] In March, 1261, at Nymphaion Michael made an alliance with their enemies, the Genoese. They would provide fifty ships to his campaigns, for which he would pay the cost, and they would be exempt from trade taxes throughout his realm, just as the Venetians had been in the twelfth century. The Genoese would also have access to Black Sea trade and their trade emporia in Romanía would be autonomous. Michael would give Smyrna to the Genoese and 500 hyperpyra per year to their city and 60 to their archbishop. In Genoa there survives a silk sheet depicting scenes from the life of St. Lawrence, who, together with an angel in the most prominent scene, escorts "the Most High Emperor of the Greeks Lord Michael Doukas Angelos Komnenos Palaiologos into the church of Genoa" (see Plate 2b). This item was likely a gift by the basileus, who, in agreeing to be called *Graecus*, was making yet another concession to his western allies.[137]

Before the alliance could be activated, Michael II of Epeiros resumed his aggression in Macedonia, and Michael VIII dispatched the *kaisar* Strategopoulos against him in 1261. When he arrived in Thrace, Strategopoulos made a detour to terrorize the Latins of Constantinople. He was there informed by local Romans "who had long hated the Latin yoke" that the Latin army and fleet of thirty ships were campaigning in the Black Sea against a small island owned by Nikaia; moreover, there was a gap in the defenses of the City that these locals would be thrilled to reveal to their fellow Romans. On 25 July, 1261, Strategopoulos' men passed through (or over) the walls, finding them poorly guarded. The Latins panicked and fled, including Baldwin II, who abandoned Blachernai for the Great Palace. Strategopoulos set fire to the Latins' homes along the sea, starting with those of the Venetians. The latter began to evacuate the City, taking Baldwin and their own stranded families with them. Ironically, Baldwin's horoscope, cast the year before, had predicted a prosperous and long reign for him. But the end of his empire was as ignominious as its origin was infamous. Baldwin had previously toured Europe seeking assistance for his impoverished realm; he would do so again now, with only an empty title to his name. But for the Romans, a dream had come true: "by divine providence, Constantinople again became subject to the basileus of the Romans."[138]

33
Union with Rome and Roman Disunity (1261–1282)

The return to Constantinople

Michael VIII Palaiologos staged his entry into Constantinople for maximum symbolic impact. Baldwin's imperial insignia had already been brought to him, marking the abolition of the Latin empire. Michael entered the City on 15 August, the Dormition of the Mother of God, the second most important celebration in the Orthodox calendar. He entered via the Golden Gate, reviving ancient triumphal practice. Before his entry, thirteen prayers written for the occasion by Akropolites were chanted from the top of the Gate by the bishop of Kyzikos, who clasped the icon of the Virgin Hodegetria. This was the City's most important palladium, which had been seized by the Venetians and kept in their headquarters in the Pantokrator monastery. Michael entered in a grand procession, walking with his family behind the icon, which he deposited in the Stoudios monastery. He then rode to a thanksgiving celebration in Hagia Sophia before retiring to the Great Palace. The Blachernai palace was not fit to receive him, for the Latins had left it full of soot and smoke from their feasts.[1]

Michael and those who accompanied him were conscious of fulfilling prophecies of their return that had circulated since 1204. When Michael was an infant, he had been put to sleep with lullabies about how he would enter the City as a conqueror.[2] "By God's gift," he now proclaimed, "it was returned to the Romans through us," for only God could make such an impossible feat so easy.[3] His followers explored the City and gawked at its sights, including the churches, monasteries, hippodrome, equestrian statue of Justinian in the Augoustaion, and royal columns. Most of them had never seen Constantinople before, except from afar.[4] The patriarch Arsenios, however, was notably absent, as was the dynastic heir Ioannes IV. The Latins who remained in the City were not molested and were allowed to live under their own laws, so long as they "kept quiet."[5] Nor were reprisals made against Romans who had worked for them. The mood was jubilant, not vengeful.

Michael had his work cut out for him. His priorities were to restore the City, transplant the Roman government to it, and elevate his dynasty at the expense of the Laskarids. While everyone was basking in his great success, he had Ioannes IV blinded on Christmas Day, 1261. In foreign policy, his priorities were to capitalize on his victory at Pelagonia and the captivity of Guillaume by gaining concessions in the Peloponnese and subordinating the Roman lordships of Epeiros to his rule; to prevent a Mongol attack through diplomacy; to interface peacefully with the Italian trading networks and temper their grasping nature and mutual rivalries; and to contain any blowback from the west over the recapture of Constantinople. He had no reason to think that the last point would become the defining challenge of his reign, nor that he would have to turn against his own people by imposing an unwanted Union with Rome on them in order to safeguard them from the most cynical and dangerous enemy to emerge from the west to date, Charles of Anjou. Michael, a cynic himself, would rather have play-acted the role of Most Orthodox Basileus.

Michael's propaganda stressed that he was personally destined by God for the throne, and he disseminated this idea through all media, including speeches, church paintings, the fine arts, and his monuments in the capital and monastic foundations. Reaching back into history, he linked himself to earlier periods of Roman greatness, for example by officially calling himself "New Constantine" in treaties, seals, and inscriptions, and expecting his supporters and officials to call him that in speeches, acclamations, and even in the churches that they founded in the provinces. He restored the porphyry column of the City's founder and depicted himself on coins with Constantine.[6] Michael also revived the performance of royal orations and the title *porphyrogennetos* for his children who were born after 1261, thereby treating his recoronation in Hagia Sophia later that year as a new start for his reign. Eventually, both palaces acquired a porphyry chamber for royal births.[7] Michael even revived, for the last time, the tradition of royal columns, erecting one beside the church of the Holy Apostles. It held up a remarkable statue group in bronze showing him kneeling before the Archangel Michael and offering to him a replica of the City. Bronze statues had not been set up in Constantinople since ca. 600. Michael needed to exalt himself, seeing as he was an unscrupulous usurper who had broken oaths to reach the throne. He also preempted criticism by repeatedly casting himself in a humble and penitential mode, while stressing his deep gratitude to God, which, of course, elevated him even further. Even on his gold coins, the basileus is shown kneeling, while a seated Christ touches his head. Michael perfected the art of triumphal humility.[8]

The obverse side of those hyperpyra depicted the walls of Constantinople enclosing a bust of the Virgin (see Figure 50). Michael made the City the centerpiece of his quest for legitimacy.[9] In a chrysobull of ca. 1270 assigning properties to the church of Hagia Sophia, Michael called Constantinople a New Zion and New Jerusalem and likened the "return of the Romans to their ancestral land" to the Hebrews' return from the Babylonian exile. Michael thus closed the rhetorical circle that Nikaia had opened, with references to the "despicable Italians, whose nation is worse than the Babylonian dragon. . . . God has decreed that my reign shall be the instrument of this renewal."[10] These themes were echoed by his

Figure 50 Gold coin of Michael VIII Palaiologos featuring a bust of the Virgin enclosed by the walls of the City on the obverse, and the emperor kneeling before Christ on the reverse

spokesmen.[11] But regaining the City was not the same as restoring it. Much of it had been destroyed in the fires and battles of 1203, 1204, and 1261. The invaders had destroyed and plundered its artwork. Countless books had been destroyed or lost, including much ancient literature, an irreparable loss. Precious relics had been stolen and sold in the west. To be fair, the Latins had built buttresses to prop up Hagia Sophia on the western side, but other churches had lost their valuables and even the lead and copper had been stripped from their roofs. The bronze sheathing of the column of Justinian had been pulled off, exposing and pockmarking the stonework beneath. Houses had been demolished to be used for firewood. In sum, Latin rapacity had turned "the Queen of Cities into a field of desolation, full of ruins and columns, its homes dug out or burned through. . . . Day and night the Latins had vandalized the City, as they had not really expected to live there for long."[12]

The losses were cultural and institutional, not just physical. Many of the monasteries of the capital had lost their land endowments under Latin rule and were in disrepair or ruin, or had been abandoned.[13] Palace ceremonial was stripped down to its essentials and the hippodrome races were no more.[14] The closing of the schools had dealt a grave blow to Hellenic learning. But the first order of business for Romans who returned was more mundane, to find homes. Even before his entry, Michael told his nobles to send men ahead to occupy the houses that they wanted, preferably their old family homes, and he authorized the *kaisar* Alexios Strategopoulos to assign lands and houses. A manuscript note tells the story of an official who occupied the house of an Anconitan, but in 1266/7 he was moved by royal command to the Blachernai district. "A huge crowd of common people" also joined the basileus in moving to the capital,[15] many from Greece too, not just Asia Minor. Michael himself later boasted that the City now echoed "not with the confused accents of a half-barbarian people, but the native inhabitants, all of them clearly articulating the polished Greek tongue and correctly pronouncing it."[16]

The rebuilding began with attention to food and water and the repairing of the walls, especially on the seaward side, which made sense given who was likely to attack them.[17] Michael also took the lead in founding, renovating, and endowing churches and monasteries in and around the City. He encouraged his family and the aristocracy to sponsor monasteries. Women eventually took a major role in this activity, leading to a major "reset" of monasticism in the capital.[18] But these efforts could not restore the City to its Komnenian state. Its population remained significantly smaller (though we have no reliable figures), many buildings remained empty, and much land inside the walls was used for farming, livestock, and orchards. According to a Dominican friar, "scarcely one third of it is inhabited, the rest is gardens and fields, or deserted." Constantinople used to be celebrated as an urban megalopolis, but now it had separate villages and suburbs within its walls, and authors, both Roman and foreign, praised its sylvan attractions too.[19]

A bitter work of social critique, the *Dialogue between the Rich and Poor*, written in the mid-fourteenth century, contrasted the brilliant chambers, baths, and tapestries that beautified the airy, three-story houses of the wealthy to the humble, dark, and dank homes of the poor. The early Palaiologan aristocracy flaunted its refined taste, wealth, and privilege, giving rise to moral censure by religious writers and even to class resentment by less fortunate Romans. Growing inequality was to be a major social problem of the Palaiologan period. Nobles always went around on horseback, and their behavior was often seen as arrogant.[20] But their position was precarious too. Michael Palaiologos was not their pawn and he did not run the government to benefit their interests. The model of a "feudal" Roman polity does not hold up.

The Palaiologan aristocracy

In searching for the basis of aristocratic wealth, scholars commonly assert that the Palaiologan elite, like its Macedonian and Komnenian predecessors, gobbled up the land of any remaining free peasants. But the open secret behind such theories is that they lack evidentiary support, not only in this phase but in all phases of east Roman history. (Moreover, historians who assert it for one phase do not explain the origin of the peasant landowners whom the next generation of feudal aristocrats allegedly absorbed.) Our evidence consists mostly of fiscal and legal documents relating to monastic properties (e.g., on Athos), or to specific concessions or exemptions granted by the basileus. These documents do not provide an overall picture of landowning patterns in any region, so we can draw only partial conclusions. Moreover, by definition they list only tenants and peasants whose lands had been assigned to pronoias, skewing the focus of historians toward these categories and making them seem normative. It is often forgotten that being given a pronoia did not make one a landowner; it meant only that one gained the taxes and other state dues on those lands. To be sure, the state could confiscate private lands and then gift them to its elites or to monasteries, but we cannot quantify that practice either. Yet what these documents *do* reveal is that relations between the basileus and his subjects were increasingly defined by grants of tax exemption or concessions of land.

Before the 1070s, the fortunes of the powerful came to a large degree from their court salaries, which they then invested in land. By contrast, it is unclear what the cash salaries of court officials were in the early Palaiologan period or whether they were sufficient to maintain them in style. Salaries seem mostly to have gone to the palace staff and certain categories of soldiers. Tax farming was a major source of income for many officials, and they may have banded together in consortia to raise the capital and insure against losses.[21] Complaints about the sale of offices, corruption, and extortion are as common in this period as any other. But all this likely accounted for a small part of elite incomes.

It is gradually becoming apparent that in the Nikaian and Palaiologan eras the court propped up its favorites—cities, individuals, and monasteries—through pronoias, land grants, and tax exemptions. Collectively these were often called an *oikonomia* and the beneficiary a *chrysoboullatos*, i.e., a recipient of a chrysobull guaranteeing the relevant privilege. Pronoias as such did not confer ownership and were not hereditary. They were a form of indirect salary drawn at the basileus' pleasure from lands assigned to a favorite. Michael talked of making some of them hereditary, but this was only for soldiers posted along the frontiers and likely not widely implemented (it became more common in the fourteenth century, though pronoia grants always retained their service obligations).[22] In 1264–1265, Michael sent an official, Chadenos, to Asia Minor to fix military pronoias at 40 hyperpyra of annual revenue. In a decree from 1272, Michael referred to additive grants to soldiers worth 24 and 36 hyperpyra (i.e., above whatever property threshold was supporting them until then). Thus, in the fourteenth century we hear of military pronoias generating around 80 hyperpyra. Tenant farmers (or *paroikoi*) seem to have been paying in rent (or tax) about 1/24 of the value of their land, or 20% of revenue per year (mathematics textbooks from the period use pronoia divisions among multiple shareholder as exercises). To put this income into perspective, records indicate that entire villages generated income for monasteries of between 77 and 240 hyperpyra. One of the wealthiest monasteries, the Lavra on Athos, may have received 12,000 from all its lands. Michael's born-in-the-purple son Konstantinos was said to have an *oikonomia* worth 60,000 hyperpyra.[23] That sounds ludicrously extravagant, but it isn't.

The difference between the lowest-paid soldier and a royal prince such as Konstantinos was equivalent to that today between an entry-level soldier in the US army and a CEO whose salary is $30 million. There are many people in 2023 who earn far, far more than $30 million. Thus, in terms of wealth gap the United States today is vastly more unequal than Romanía at peak aristocracy. To be sure, more Romans fell at the low end of the wealth scale, but on the other hand royal princes with vast pronoias were expected to use them to pay for soldiers, retinues, and public works, not just their own private enjoyment.[24] And it is unlikely that the top 1% owned or controlled 50% of total wealth, as with us.

The basileus could transfer a pronoia to a beneficiary's heirs, but this was at his discretion. Thus, insofar as elite wealth depended on concessions linked to service, which could be withdrawn when the basileus wanted to reward a different favorite, elite fortunes were precarious. Estates could also be confiscated if their owners were accused of treason, which happened often under the Palaiologoi, or for reasons of state, during an emergency.[25] In the *Dialogue between the Rich and Poor*, the rich state: "you overlook the anger and suspicion in which we are held by those in power."[26] As state territories began to shrink after Michael's reign, the competition over concessions become especially fierce. Moreover, the private land owned by the aristocracy diminished over time through partible inheritance, as all sons and daughters were legally entitled to a share. This would have made it hard for many families to stay at the top without state support.

This was a period of "governance by concession." The residents of entire cities on the European side were made tax-exempt, usually in order to induce them to surrender to Nikaia or Constantinople. The cities' strategic advantages and goodwill were just as valuable to the Palaiologoi as their cash, and the basileis could still appropriate and redistribute lands around the urban core. From these they could give land grants to their favorites, who were not limited to the aristocracy but also included many people of middling and even humble social status, provided they had a connection to the regime and could present themselves in their petitions as loyal assets. Thus, instead of giving them cash, the Palaiologoi purchased support by pledging to take less from them, by granting tax reductions. This required a vast amount of bookkeeping and census-keeping. It also produced data for historians to use. For example, the assessment of 1262 around Hierissos found that a quarter of households were led by widows, likely an effect of the wars. Paradoxically, this policy increased the power of the center over the distribution of land rights. This was not, therefore, a period of feudal devolution, as is often claimed, but a period of a growing state power that was consolidated through the politics of concession. As Andronikos II bluntly stated in a chrysobull, "no one, not even a monastery, has secure possession of any property, unless royal edicts confirm it." Proprietors were more than ever at the mercy of the royal will and were incentivized to support the basileus locally.[27]

Thus, the court and aristocracy were tightly bound together in mutual dependency: the basileus had to reward his men with concessions (lands, pronoias, exemptions, etc.) while the latter were sustained by his favor. This militates against the view that the state was, in a feudal manner, gradually alienating its holdings to "provincial magnates" over whom it lost control. According to that older view, decentralization fueled centripetal forces and led to state collapse. But it now appears that—foreign conquest aside—the Roman state never lost control of its lands or its aristocracy.[28] This was not why it eventually fell. Quasi-feudal relations emerged only on the diplomatic level with entities that were essentially separate states even if they were on Roman soil, such as Epeiros or the Genoese colony at Galata.

Michael VIII's foreign policy

Oddly, one of the first buildings erected by Michael in Constantinople was a mosque, which was ready to be shown in 1262 to an envoy of the powerful Mamluk sultan of Egypt, Baybars (1260–1277).[29] The decision to fast-track a mosque is explained by Michael's diplomacy. In the east, his primary concern was to prevent either of the two rival Mongol powers (the Ilkhanate in Iran and the Golden Horde in the north) from attacking him, a prospect that "terrified" him, just as in the west he was concerned to prevent anyone from restoring the Latin empire. In 1260, he made a peace treaty with Hülegü, grandson of Genghis Khan and founder of the Ilkanate. Both rulers needed a stable Anatolia. To reward the basileus, Hülegü forced the Latin prince of Antioch, Bohemond VI, to install an Orthodox patriarch in that city in place of the Latin one. But the next year, Hülegü drove out the sultan of Rum, Kai Kaus II ('Izz al-Din), replacing him with his brother. Michael wanted to remain on good terms with 'Izz al-Din too as he was a long-standing ally and friend and popular with the Romans of Anatolia, being half Roman himself. The sultan's sister was married to Berke, ruler of the Golden Horde, another grandson of Genghis Khan who could potentially attack Michael from the north. This was a narrow needle to thread for both sides. Michael received 'Izz al-Din with honor, treating him as a quasi-basileus in his own right, while the sultan and his entourage played the part of Christians by attending church; indeed, some were Christians or converted.[30]

Meanwhile, Berke of the Golden Horde, a Muslim, formed an alliance with Baybars of Egypt and 'Izz al-Din against Hülegü, and the only way they could coordinate was via Constantinople, which became a transit hub for their respective envoys. This angered Hülegü, who demanded that Michael block these communications, which he did. But Michael wanted to stay on the good side of Baybars too, a useful ally in the Mediterranean. Moreover, Mamluk power in Egypt depended on an annual supply of Kipchak (Cuman) slave-soldiers from the north, which could pass only through Constantinople; Baybars himself had been one of them. In return, Baybars allowed Michael to vet the Orthodox patriarch of Alexandria.[31] These alliances were giving Michael ecumenical sway in the eastern Churches, which the basileis had not wielded in centuries. But it proved impossible to please all sides. In 1264, 'Izz al-Din conspired with Berke and the Bulgarian tsar Konstantin Tih whose wife was a sister of Ioannes IV Laskaris and hostile to Michael. Tih had been leading raids into Roman Thrace, but that year's raid was reinforced by 2,000 Mongols from the north, who ambushed Michael as he was returning from a campaign in Greece. The Mongols devastated Thrace and freed the ex-sultan from what had become his Roman captivity at Ainos (he was later given a lordship in the Crimea). Michael barely escaped by embarking on Latin ships that happened to be anchored by the coast. He strengthened his ties to the Ilkhanate in 1265 by giving his daughter Maria in marriage to Hülegü, though he was dead by the time she arrived and so she married his successor Abaqa. Maria became a powerful patron of Christians in the Ilkhanate. The deaths of Hülegü and Berke calmed the tensions between the two rival Mongol superpowers. Michael was lucky to have suffered nothing worse by courting both of them while they were at war with each other.[32]

The 1264 campaign during which Michael was ambushed was part of a low-intensity war against Epeiros. In the early 1260s, Michael II of Epeiros seized almost every opportunity to strike against the interests of the basileus and scored notable successes, such as the capture of Alexios Strategopoulos, the liberator of Constantinople. In response, Michael VIII stationed his brother, the despot Ioannes, at Thessalonike to lead the defense and counterthrusts. Truces sealed by marriage alliances were planned and broken on an almost annual basis, until a truce finally took hold in 1265. When Michael II died two years later, his territory was divided into two lordships given to his sons, Epeiros (to Nikephoros) and Thessaly (to Ioannes).[33] The relationship between Epeiros and Constantinople was awkward. Michael VIII's writers, such as the historian Akropolites, pretended that the Epeirots were not true Romans and called them "those men in the west" (or the like) because they did not fully recognize the basileus at Constantinople. Of course, everyone knew that they were ethnically Roman, but Michael's regime was superimposing a loyalty criterion. In other texts, Michael admitted that he was opposed by some "apostates who are of the same Roman race as we are." By contrast, Michael VIII presented himself as "a Roman born of Romans" who had taken it upon himself to protect *all* the Romans, "the entire race," wherever they lived. He even made the curious (and false) argument that the rulers of Nikaia had not been proper basileis, though they "sometimes" called themselves that, because, unlike him, they had ruled only the Romans of the east.[34] He wanted to extend real and not only nominal control to Epeiros as well, and reminded Michael II that his lands "belonged of old to the basileia." Michael

II replied that his family had taken Epeiros by fighting against Latins, not against other Romans, as Michael VIII was now doing. The emotional rhetoric of Roman patriotism was claimed by both sides.[35]

The other irredentist war that Michael VIII launched in the early 1260s was in Achaea. He held its prince, Guillaume II, and many of his lords captive for two years after Pelagonia, trying to extract the most from them in exchange for release. Guillaume eventually ceded the forts of Monembasia, Mystras, Mani, and Geraki, which gave the Romans control of the southeastern Peloponnese. He also had to swear fealty to the basileus and received from him the title *megas domestikos*, the Greek version of the rank of "grand seneschal" that he held from the now extinct Latin empire. Guillaume was essentially exchanging one master in Constantinople for another, although the new one was more powerful. As the Latin empire had declined in the 1220s, Achaea had emerged as the leading Latin power in Greece. But Guillaume was now "domesticated" by Michael.[36] The power and prestige of the Principality were shattered as were Guillaume's ambitions.

Guillaume surrendered the forts as promised. But he then immediately broke his oaths and initiated an all-out war against the Romans. Michael sent another of his brothers, the *sebastokrator* Konstantinos, to Monembasia with an army of Romans and Turks, who were aided by many locals.[37] The aim of the *sebastokrator* was to conquer the entire Peloponnese,[38] and he came close to it when he made for Andrabida in 1263, but he was defeated. He was defeated again in 1264 while besieging Nikli when his Turks defected to the French because they had not been paid. By this point both sides were exhausted and arranged a truce. But the Romans had gained a foothold in the Morea and would slowly expand it, "building strong castles in the mountains and fortifying the passes." Local donors began to commemorate Michael in church inscriptions, in one case, on Kythera in 1275, calling him "the lord of Rome."[39]

Meanwhile, the fall of Constantinople had created a panic in the west, especially at Rome, where it was feared that Michael would scoop up all western colonial outposts. A "stupefied" Urban IV (1261–1264) admitted that the news about Constantinople was "like a spear piercing our heart." In the letters that he sent out in 1262 calling for a crusade against Palaiologos, "who calls himself emperor of the Greeks," he warned that Achaea was next. He also warned Lusignan Cyprus that Michael was coming for it too and that "Greek Cypriots would gladly throw off the yoke of the nobles of Cyprus." The doge of Venice, fearing the alliance between Michael and the Genoese, wrote to the pope in 1264 seeking a crusade to defend Crete, where Michael's agents had been fomenting rebellion against the Venetian colonists.[40] Indeed, Michael's orator Holobolos was publicly encouraging the basileus to recover all Roman lands that were under Latin occupation.[41]

Charles of Anjou

Michael had reason to believe that some western power, or a combination of them, might move against him, but did not know who, when, or where it would be. Neither did the pope. Urban called for a crusade against Michael, but there was little interest in such a project in the early 1260s, and the papacy was itself mired in a war against Manfred of Sicily, Friedrich II's heir in the south. The pope wanted to place Charles of Anjou, brother of king Louis IX of France, on the throne of Sicily. Meanwhile, Urban was unable to pry the Genoese away from their alliance with Michael, no matter how much he threatened them or invalidated their oaths to the basileus. As for the expelled emperor Baldwin, the kings of Europe had done little for him back when he had held Constantinople; they were even less inclined to help now that he had lost it. It did not help his case that Manfred emerged as his main sponsor. For his part, Michael set into motion an old strategy for deflecting Latin aggression, even while he was prosecuting the war in Achaea. Specifically, he tempted the pope with promises of Union. Urban, having cooled on Baldwin, took Michael up on this. The pope was operating along two parallel but contradictory tracks, urging "the most excellent emperor" Michael to swiftly implement Union while calling for a crusade "to expunge the schismatic race of the Greeks."[42] But Urban died before either plan gained traction.

The strategic environment was radically transformed in the mid-1260s by the ambitions of the ruthless Charles, count of Anjou, Provence, and Maine, whose wealth and forces rivaled those of his brother, the French king. In 1263, Charles accepted the pope's call to exterminate the Hohenstaufen in the Regno (southern Italy and Sicily). The war was cast by the papacy and Charles as a crusade. In 1266, Charles was crowned king of Sicily in Rome, defeated and killed Manfred, and consolidated his control over the south. This included Manfred's dominions in the Ionian Sea and along the coast, such as Kerkyra, despite the efforts made by Michael II of Epeiros and pope Clement IV to secure them for themselves or their favorites.[43]

One of Charles' strategies was to collect titles from those who had lost their kingdoms, and then use them as legalistic pretexts for expanding his own empire. No sooner had he taken over the Regno than he decided, following in the footsteps of its Norman rulers, to conquer Romanía too. Charles assembled his allies at the papal court of Viterbo in May, 1267, where the following agreements were ratified via dynastic marriages. Guillaume II de Villehardouin, who had fought alongside Charles and Louis IX in the Sixth Crusade against Egypt in 1249–1250, declared that he despaired of holding Achaea against Roman attack. He would lead the Principality for as long as he lived but his title would pass to Charles' heirs upon his death (which occurred in 1278), or to Charles himself. Thus, the Peloponnese would become an Angevin province. Then, Baldwin agreed to cede Achaea plus a third of the rest of his empire to Charles in exchange for military assistance in getting it back from the "schismatics"; if Baldwin's line was extinguished, his title would also pass to Charles or his heirs. The coalition also tempted Venice into joining by granting it its former rights in the Latin empire. The justification for all this was of course the good of Christendom, the Catholic faith, and ultimately the recovery of Jerusalem, in other words it was, at least in theory, a crusade.[44]

Charles spent two years (1268–1269) suppressing challengers, finding allies for his project from Spain to Hungary, and preparing his forces, some of which he began to send in stages to the Morea and the Albanian coast. He even concocted the fiction that the blinded Ioannes IV Laskaris had sought refuge at his court and was given a pension. This was the standard Norman play-book. Charles refused to recognize Michael as basileus, calling him instead a "usurper of the royal title."[45] Meanwhile, Michael VIII supercharged his diplomacy and made treaties with both Genoa and Venice. The Genoese had lost his favor by 1264, allegedly because they were plotting to betray Constantinople to Manfred, and he had expelled them from the City. But in 1267 Michael granted the whole of Galata (Pera) across the Golden Horn for them to settle as their own city, although only after he demolished its sea walls. At Galata they would be less dangerous to him and less irksome to the Romans. Their local governor (or podestà) was required to kneel before the basileus at formal receptions as if he were a royal official.[46]

The Venetians also sided with the basileus. Their profits from eastern trade had plummeted after the loss of Constantinople and because of the attacks against them by the Roman-backed Genoese. More importantly, they did not want the Angevins to straddle the Adriatic any more than they had wanted the Normans to do so. They accepted Michael's terms in 1268, even though his orator was calling them "an amphibian hydra." Specifically, they were exempted from trade taxes and their colonial possessions would not be attacked. In exchange, they would not assist the basileus' enemies or fight the Genoese. They were not given an emporion, and even addressed Michael as "emperor of the Romans."[47] For the next century and a half, while the Genoese were presumed to be allies and quasi-subjects of the basileus, the Venetians were presumed to be enemies who signed periodic five- or ten-year "truces" with Romanía. Their representatives were given inferior positions in palace receptions.

Michael also sent envoys throughout Europe and the Near East to counteract Charles' overtures. He relied on bilingual western secretaries and diplomats, and his chancery issued Latin documents. Two of his closest confidants and agents were the Genoese brothers Benedetto and Manuele Zaccaria, to whom, ca. 1267, he granted exclusive rights to mine alum in the hills above Phokaia, north of Smyrna, at "New Phokaia." Alum was a valuable commodity used mostly for dying textiles. The Zaccaria became hugely rich, and likely paid rent to the basileus. They secured Phokaia militarily and cleared the islands of pirates. There was something of Manuel I's Latinophile policies in the way that Michael recruited and patronized Latins. His investment in the Zaccaria would pay impressive dividends at the end of his reign.[48]

Michael knew that Charles had good chances of prevailing in a war and that the best way to stop him was by winning over the pope with promises of Union. He faced an uphill battle for the Latins believed that the Greeks were no better than "white Muslims."[49] He lobbied the new pope, Clement IV (1265–1268), promising to advance the cause of Union by hosting a Council or leading a crusade to the Holy Land, if the pope would but guarantee the security of his realm. But Clement rejected these proposals, replying that the basileus and Greek Church had to first unconditionally submit to Rome without any prior discussion of the issues, or else Rome would activate other options. When Clement died, Michael turned to Louis IX of France, begging him to mediate between him and Charles. Louis was sympathetic, but was warned by the cardinals at Rome that Michael was insincere and using delaying tactics.[50] But delaying, and talking instead of doing, paid off. Charles was held up by events that Michael could not have foreseen. Louis compelled Charles to join his ill-fated crusade to Tunis in 1270, where the king died. The crusading fleet was ruined in a storm as it returned under Charles' command. And then, the next pope, Gregory X (1271–1276), was receptive to Michael's overtures about Union. He believed that crusading should focus on the Holy Land and that the Greeks could contribute to that effort. Even though the pope was under great pressure from Charles, he forbade Charles from attacking Romanía, as that would not facilitate Union. Gregory's sincerity and zeal for genuine peace was praised in Constantinople.[51]

The debates over Union and Arsenios

Pretexts have disadvantages too, which cut against both Charles and Michael. Charles now had to put his holy war on hold, while the burden was on Michael to make good on his promises of Union. Gregory was planning a general Council of the Latin Church at Lyons, in 1274, to discuss organizational matters and the new crusade. He invited Michael to send representatives and recognize Rome's supremacy. Gregory offered the Greeks a choice of formulas by which to affirm their "agreement" with the Catholic Church. Against a background of low-intensity warfare with Charles' proxies in Achaea, the growth of Charles' forces in Albania—by 1272 he had secured Aulon and Dyrrachion—and the buildup of the Angevin fleet, Michael agreed to the pope's terms.[52]

Three of Michael's representatives reached Lyons in June, 1274. They were the *megas logothetes* Akropolites (the historian), the former patriarch Germanos III, and the bishop of Nikaia; two other secular envoys, along with all the gifts, were lost at sea on the way.[53] The envoys handed over the relevant documents, including Michael's letter acknowledging the pope as supreme, with the authority to adjudicate all appeals within the Church; professing his passion for Union; and promising to enforce Union on any of his subjects who proved recalcitrant. Prayers were chanted in both languages, including the *filioque* clause (three times). Union was formally proclaimed on 6 July, when the basileus' profession of faith (identical to that of Rome) was read to the Council, along with the concurring letter by the clergy of the eastern Church. There was no discussion or debate about the issues that divided the Churches. Akropolites, who had previously written against Latin theology, took an oath in Michael's name that he held to the faith of Rome, and more prayers were chanted (with the *filioque*, twice). The proceedings insisted on the pretense that Michael was accepting Roman supremacy voluntarily, indeed spontaneously.[54] Michael sent to Gregory a silk hanging with scenes from the life of Christ and the Apostles, captioned in both languages and featuring an image of the pope leading the basileus to St. Peter.[55]

The pope knew that the Greek clergy would resist Union, as Union meant capitulation to Rome, but he did not know the full extent of it and understandably took pride that he had accomplished a goal long desired by his predecessors. But for Michael, Lyons exacerbated a preexisting crisis of legitimacy by conjoining three sources of opposition to his policies that had separate origins but now joined forces: pro-Laskarid, Arsenite, and anti-Unionist.

The first was popular support for the Laskarids in Anatolia. Michael's rise to the throne was premised on oaths that he would honor Ioannes IV's rights, and oaths by the entire population that they would attack either of the two basileis if he moved against the other. After Michael had Ioannes blinded, some villages in Bithynia rose up in rebellion, in early 1262, following a youth who was presented to them as the young basileus. Their movement was brutally suppressed by the army, but loyalty to the old dynasty abided, and soon Ioannes III Doukas Batatzes was being revered as a saint.[56]

In the capital, the young secretary Manuel Holobolos (not yet the basileus' orator) expressed his sympathy for Ioannes IV so movingly that Michael mutilated Manuel's lips and nose. More dangerously, the patriarch Arsenios, who had been appointed by the Laskarids and administered the oaths, excommunicated Michael at the start of 1262 with the tacit consent of the Synod. Even so, this took a mild form, as the patriarch did not bar the clergy from commemorating Michael during the liturgy; Michael was allowed to attend services, but not to take communion. Arsenios apparently expected the basileus to abdicate and refused to assign him a specific penance. Michael begged him to lift the decree and performed acts of contrition—"a dove that will turn into a snake," the patriarch foresaw. Michael then threatened him with prosecution for treason, while the court concocted trumped-up charges. After three years of this tense stalemate, Arsenios barred the basileus from entering church, probably Hagia Sophia, causing a scene before bishops and high officials. By March, 1265, Michael had mustered enough support to bring charges against Arsenios before a synod of lay and ecclesiastical officials. The patriarch was deposed for failing to appear and answer them. He was exiled to an island and guarded by Varangians.[57]

Michael replaced Arsenios with Germanos III (1265–1266), an old associate, who put up banners in Hagia Sophia proclaiming Michael as a New Constantine (he was later a delegate to Lyons). Germanos pleaded on behalf of Holobolos, now a monk, securing his appointment as court orator, a position that was revived as part of the restoration of learning. In July 1265, Michael pressured Germanos and the Synod to excommunicate Arsenios for fomenting revolution. But the basileus gradually realized that the lifting of his own excommunication would not be convincing if done by Germanos. The patriarch's election was controversial, for he had been transferred from another see, which some viewed as uncanonical even though it happened often, and Germanos generally lacked authority. Critics even mocked his Laz origins. Germanos was persuaded to step down in September and was replaced by Michael's spiritual confessor, Ioseph I (1266–1275), an abbot. Ioseph lifted Michael's excommunication on 2 February, 1267, the feast of the Presentation of Jesus at the Temple. Michael had to remove his crown and fall to the ground before the patriarch in Hagia Sophia, tearfully confessing his guilt. Michael was practiced at humility and contrition, and was circulating comparisons of himself to the penitent David. He instituted an annual commemoration of his absolution.[58]

But discontent was growing, fueling opposition to the regime. Many were outraged not only by the blinding of Ioannes but by the illegal (as they saw it) deposition of Arsenios. These "Arsenites" were primarily lay and monastic, and decentralized. The movement's advocates believed that they had to break off all relations with those who recognized the new patriarch, leading to a chain reaction of schism. Their slogan—*"don't touch, don't discuss"*—was a call to self-segregate from those who were in communion with the official Church. It followed the old playbook of opposition that had been used, for example, by Theodoros of Stoudios against iconoclasm. They would preach in private homes against the basileus and his patriarch, dividing families and friends. The Arsenites were strongest in Anatolia but their movement spread to the capital and beyond. In 1268, the patriarch Ioseph tried to combat the movement head-on by going on a goodwill tour through Anatolia, but he received a chilly reception. Michael was determined to treat this dissent as treason against the throne, as he feared that it would spark armed opposition to him in Anatolia. He unleashed a savage repression, carried out by the *megas logothetes* Akropolites. Many were arrested, beaten, whipped, and paraded in humiliation.[59]

As the Arsenite problem grew, it was exacerbated by Michael's push for Union. Most of his subjects opposed the terms on which he was seeking it, which amounted to capitulation. Opposition to the Latins was, by now, part of Orthodox religious identity. Also, most Romans had negative views of the Latins generally, as did Michael himself, to judge from his numerous hostile statements against them. Even if these were insincere, they reveal what he thought his subjects wanted to hear. However, emperors had made overtures to Rome for Union many times in the past and had always failed, so few people were paying attention as Michael forged ahead into the deal that culminated at Lyons. By 1273, he was trying to sell the deal to his bishops, telling them that there was no real difference between the two faiths, and why not commemorate the pope? If Charles prevailed, the Romans would again be subject to the Latins and lose their freedom anyway. At a meeting of the Synod, the patriarch deferred the matter to his chief deputy (*chartophylax*) Ioannes Bekkos, who was widely respected. He confessed that he was torn between fear and respect for the basileus, but declared before the assembly that the Latins were heretics in all but name. He was quickly arrested on a trumped-up charge. In prison, however, he studied the Church Fathers and came around to the view that the Latins were not entirely heretical on the matter of the *filioque*. But meanwhile, the patriarch was pressured by his bishops to sign a document that he would never accept Union on the terms proposed by Michael. Rome had to remove the *filioque* from its creed, and Union could result only from a general Council that included the other patriarchs and fully discussed the underlying issues.[60]

But for Union to be ratified at Lyons, Michael needed his Church to agree to its terms in advance. The patriarch took himself out of the equation, retiring to a monastery and promising that, if Union actually went through on the basileus' terms, he would abdicate. Michael and Bekkos then leaned on the bishops. The basileus kept stressing that he was forced to accept Union because of the existential threat posed by Charles, thereby directly contradicting what his envoys would say at Lyons, that his actions were entirely voluntary. Michael also tried to convince the bishops by narrowing the points of Union to three: papal primacy (not primacy *and* supremacy as was proclaimed at Lyon); the right of appeal to Rome; and the commemoration of the pope in the liturgy. These articles, he argued, were merely symbolic, for the pope would never come to Constantinople to exercise his rights; hardly anyone would travel as far as Rome to appeal there (though, as he knew, many had in the past); and who could object to commemoration? Michael did not reveal, though he knew, that Rome would not agree to Union on such watered-down terms. But his bishops would not agree even to these. To show them what was at stake, Michael punished eleven lay and monastic objectors, one a woman and another the orator Holobolos, by having them whipped, roped together, covered in intestines, and paraded through the City. The bishops "begged him not to rage against them" and eventually they agreed to sign, on the condition that Michael produce a chrysobull pledging that Union would be limited to those three articles and that the faith would not be changed. He did so on Christmas, 1273.[61] The Church of Constantinople had, then, agreed to Union on those limited terms. It did not recognize Lyons as an Ecumenical Council nor accept of any of its provisions, only its own version of Union, and even that only as defined by the basileus.

In sum, when negotiating with the pope, Michael maximized the religious concessions he was willing to make and downplayed the role of Charles' threats, but in pressuring his Church to consent he minimized the religious concessions and played up the Angevin threat. The truth lay in what he was telling the bishops, as was understood by some in the west,[62] but even a limited Union did require some concessions, if only symbolic, and many Romans were loath to make even those.

When the delegates returned from Lyons in early 1275, the patriarch was deemed abdicated and a joint Greek and Latin liturgy was held in the Blachernai palace to commemorate the pope and recognize Peter as the chief of the apostles. Ioannes Bekkos, the convert to Union, was elected patriarch. Relations between Michael and pope Gregory remained constructive enough that the two discussed sending a crusade to the Holy Land through Anatolia, a venture from which the basileus probably hoped to reclaim Roman territory, as Alexios I had from the passage of the First Crusade. But Gregory's death in early 1276 ended that dream, and matters quickly soured.[63] Opposition to Union began to grow, not just to its terms but to the fact that Michael, a secular ruler, had rammed it down the throat of the Church. His appeals to *oikonomia* (the pragmatic bending of the rules) and his status as *epistemonarches* (disciplinarian of the Church) did not, argued the patriarch Ioseph, give him the right to elect or depose bishops, to excommunicate anyone, or generally to do a bishop's business.[64] Even so, in 1277 Michael's Synod decreed excommunication for dissenters, regardless of whether they were related to the basileus or were bishops, senators, monks, laymen, men, or women. The basileus required court officials to sign loyalty oaths. Meanwhile, the popes who succeeded Gregory began to demand more explicit confessions of obedience from all Greek priests, including acceptance of the *filioque*. They also required humiliating renunciations of the Schism, and requests for forgiveness from Rome made under the supervision of papal emissaries. According to Pachymeres, the list of signatories to these demands that were delivered by the basileus to Rome contained made-up names of bishops and imaginary sees.[65] Hard-line directives from Rome had backfired in the past, especially under Justin I, and they proved just as inflammatory and counterproductive this time too.

"Apart from the basileus, the patriarch, and a few associates, everyone hated the 'peace,'" i.e., the Union. Even Bekkos later admitted that everyone was against it, men and women; the old and the young; senators and priests; members of the royal family, as well as monks and laity.[66] On the legal grounds that this constituted treason against the throne, Michael launched a persecution to bring his subjects into line. This led to confiscations of property, arrests, imprisonments, whippings, exile, mutilation, and blindings. One of his goals was to convince Rome that he was doing everything to enforce Union. Papal emissaries were given tours of the prisons and monastic dissidents were sent to Rome (they were returned to Constantinople where one had his tongue cut out for calling Michael not a New Constantine but a New Julian). In 1278 Michael drew up, for papal edification, a list of punishments duly meted out to critics of Union. This was written by one of the basileus' Latin notaries, the Genoese Ogerio, who was also drafting the Latin professions of faith that Michael and Bekkos were required to send to the popes. Anti-Union literature was prohibited on pain of death. The Romans discovered that they had returned to Constantinople only to have *Latinismos* (Catholicism) forced down their throats more forcefully than it ever had been under Latin rule.[67]

Many churchmen conformed outwardly only, "with their lips, not in their hearts, or they yielded to force and commemorated the pope."[68] Scholars and bishops equivocated and hewed outwardly to royal policy, changing their tune later, when it was reversed. The Arsenites were as opposed to Union as the new group, the Josephites, the partisans of the deposed patriarch Ioseph, and the two groups sometimes joined together against Union and refused communion with the Unionists—*"don't touch, don't discuss."* But occasionally they clashed too because they championed rival patriarchs, "as opposed to each other today as they were to the Latins yesterday."[69] Even though Arsenios had died in 1273, his partisans did not recognize his successors. Fake news fueled hostilities, e.g., that Arsenios had excommunicated Ioseph or that Michael was taking communion with unleavened bread. One of the emperor's sisters was an Arsenite, the other a Josephite. "One person declared for this patriarch, another for the other."[70] As Bekkos later admitted, "Union" in reality meant fierce social division.[71]

Fugitives fled from Constantinople to Epeiros and Trebizond, chased out this time not by the Latins but by their own Roman basileus. The rulers of those lands presented themselves as more Orthodox than the basileus by condemning the Union. In 1276 and 1277, Nikephoros of Epeiros and Ioannes of Thessaly, who held their titles despot and *sebastokrator* from Michael, convened local counter-Synods that excommunicated Michael, Bekkos, and the pope. They were then counter-excommunicated by Bekkos, but the popes would not back Bekkos up in this even though Michael requested it, as Epeiros was an ally of Charles of Anjou, who was still waiting for the green light to pounce.[72] Despite Michael's persecution, Rome was receiving reports that he was insincere and the Union a farce.[73] Charles was meanwhile building up his alliance. In 1278, the Principality of Achaea came fully under his control and he began sending delegates (*baiuli*) to govern it in his name. However, indirect Angevin rule pushed the Principality even further into decline, and its nominal vassals, especially the duchy of Athens, did not always cooperate with Charles' men.

Michael VIII's final wars

Michael had begun counteroffensives. His forces occupied Butrint and Berat in the 1270s, hemming in Charles' men on the Adriatic coast at Dyrrachion. In 1272–1273, Michael sent an army under his brother, the despot Ioannes, to conquer Thessaly, but it was badly defeated when the duke of Athens, Jean de la Roche, provided cavalry assistance to Ioannes of Thessaly. However, in that year the royal fleet defeated the Latin pirate fleet of Euboia (Negroponte) and the adjacent islands at the battle of Demetrias in the Pagasetic Gulf. Those Latins made their living by raiding Roman territories. The Romans now took many of their ships and nobles captive, renewing Michael's hopes after the disaster in Thessaly.[74] The basileus had built up the royal fleet, "saying that the Romans could not hold on to the City unless they dominated the seas around it." He had between 60 and 80 ships, recruiting into it a group called the *gasmouloi*, born of mixed Roman-Latin marriages during the period of Latin rule. He also deputized Latin corsairs to harass enemy pirates and shipping, providing them with harbors, political cover, titles, and resources. Eventually he managed to bring most of the Aegean back under Roman control. A key lieutenant in this push was Licario, a Euboian Latin who, using mercenary forces in 1276, overran the entire island in the name of the basileus; the latter then gave it to him as a fief. Only the capital Negroponte held out. During that war, Licario defeated Jean de la Roche of Athens, and sent him to Constantinople. For the second time, a leading Latin lord of Greece had been captured and dispatched to Michael. Jean was released in 1279 in exchange for 10,000 hyperpyra and died the next year. As for Licario, Michael made him *megas doux* of the royal fleet. The basileus boasted that he had "purged the sea of pirates . . . and liberated the islands and Euboia."[75]

By 1277, Michael had persuaded the Venetians to renew their treaty with him for another two years, to be extended automatically thereafter unless one of the two parties gave six months notice. In addition to exempting Venetian trade from royal taxes, Michael conceded living quarters to them in the City, along the Golden Horn docks, though less than what they had had in the twelfth century. This agreement was cast in the form of a generous chrysobull concession by the basileus, not a bilateral treaty, and in order to secure it the Venetians even called him "emperor of the Romans."[76] Michael did, however, offer to pay damages for any acts of piracy committed against the Venetians by his subjects or for illegal fees imposed on them by his officials since 1268. In 1278, Venice duly presented him with a detailed list of over 300 itemized cases of piracy by "the emperor's men" (mostly Latins) or extortion, for which they were seeking 35,000 hyperpyra. This inventory provides fascinating glimpses into the perils of trade in the Aegean and Michael's use of corsairs to run a low-intensity war against his ostensible allies, the Venetians, who were themselves flirting with his enemy,

Charles of Anjou, in the matter of conquering Constantinople. It is unknown whether Michael paid this sum, but in 1285 his son Andronikos II reimbursed the Venetians 24,000 hyperpyra for a second batch of claims allegedly worth between 67,000 and 100,000.[77]

Venice was to prove an unreliable ally, and it never formally relinquished its claim to the lordship of Romanía. It was courted by Charles, whose coalition to attack Constantinople included Serbia, Bulgaria, Albania, Latin Greece, Epeiros, and Thessaly. When pope Nicholas III died in 1280, Charles ordered his regent in Albania, Hugues le Rousseau de Sully, to besiege Berat, the fortress that blocked his way into Macedonia. But in early 1281 an army sent by Michael destroyed this invasion force and captured Hugues himself. The giant warrior was paraded in the City, chained to his soldiers, and the Blachernai palace was adorned with paintings celebrating Michael's victory.[78] The road to Macedonia was, for now, closed to Charles, and Michael trolled his nemesis by sending ships to raid Apulia.[79] He was projecting his power into Italy. Michael also intervened in a dynastic dispute at Trebizond by backing Ioannes II Great Komnenos (1280–1297), who sought refuge in the City at one point. Ioannes II married Michael's daughter and conceded the title basileus of the Romans to the ruler of Constantinople. Henceforth, the ruler of Trebizond was deemed in Constantinople to be a despot, and thus notionally a subordinate, whereas back in the Pontos he styled himself either as basileus of Trebizond or as "emperor of the East, the Iberians [Laz], and the Lands Across [the Black Sea]." "East," of course, meant in relation to Constantinople, a striking admission of its centrality even to the Romans of Trebizond.[80] Constantinople was regaining its hegemony.

But meanwhile Venice had drifted into Charles' orbit, as its 1278 claims had not yet been satisfied by Michael, its shipping was still being harassed by corsairs, and most of the profits of eastern trade were likely going to Genoa. In July, 1281, Charles signed the treaty of Orvieto with Venice and Philippe of Courtenay (Baldwin II's heir) "for the recovery of the empire of Romanía." The allies recognized the doge as the lord of a quarter and an eighth of the empire. Moreover, a reversal of papal policy blessed the invasion of Romanía. In February 1281, Charles secured the election as pope of Martin IV, a Frenchman aligned with Angevin policy. To advance his patron's ambitions, on 18 October, 1281, Martin excommunicated Michael as a schismatic, without bothering to provide any proof that the policy of Union was failing or not being implemented in good faith. By the stroke of a pen, the basileus was declared to be a non-Catholic. He had tortured his own people to please the pope, and was now cast out by an Angevin puppet. War was again declared to be papal policy, and extensive preparations to attack Constantinople were set into motion.[81]

Yet upon the very threshold of Charles' assault, Michael was again saved by a combination of luck and cunning. Through his trusted agent, Benedetto Zaccaria (the Genoese lord of Phokaia), he had come to an agreement with Pedro III of

Aragon, who had a claim to Sicily. The two monarchs had jointly fomented and funded rebellion on the island against Charles. On 30 March, 1282, a chance altercation in Palermo sparked a bloody uprising against Angevin rule known as the Sicilian Vespers. It forced Charles to cancel the invasion and spend the rest of his life preoccupied with the collapse of his power in the south, as Pedro landed on Sicily with a fleet. The Venetians abandoned Charles and renewed their treaty with Constantinople, in 1285. As for Michael, he boasted that, with the help of God, he had "enabled the Sicilians to take up arms and liberate themselves."[82] It was a most cost-effective victory. As one of Michael's panegyrists had said, "he who fights with cleverness and wisdom is admired when he wins, but not mocked when he loses."[83]

Above all, Michael had safeguarded his own rule. Whether he had also kept his own people free depends on how they felt about the Union that he had forced on them. Most of them hated it. When Michael died, on 11 December, 1282, he was in Thrace, in the early stages of a war against Ioannes of Thessaly. His son and co-emperor, Andronikos II Palaiologos (1282–1328), who was about to repudiate his father's policies, buried him quietly in a minor monastery there. He was later moved to Selymbria and placed next to Basil II, whom Michael had reburied there in 1260.[84]

Michael VIII died excommunicated by both the Catholic Church and large swaths of the Orthodox Church. He was buried in obscurity and disowned by his people. His banners in Hagia Sophia and column-statue by the Holy Apostles were recast to honor Constantine the Great, not the New Constantine.[85] His victims were rehabilitated and heroized. Ioannes IV Laskaris was buried in the monastery of St. Demetrios that Michael had refounded, possibly where he had intended to be buried himself. The victims of his persecution were regarded as confessors of the faith. Andronikos II had Arsenios canonized; his remains were grandly received in Constantinople and treated as holy relics.[86] Thus, the Arsenites and Josephites were ultimately vindicated and claimed the moral high ground of east Roman society. Historians often cast them as intransigent religious zealots and Michael as a pragmatic ruler who put royal strategy first and religion second. In reality, both sides of the dispute manifested different but complementary aspects of the culture of New Rome: a rigorous adherence to rules on the one hand, without which there could be no lawful society, and pragmatic flexibility on the other, without which no state could survive in a dangerous world. These were present throughout the history of New Rome but rarely so starkly distinct in a single conflict. It was fitting that Michael prevailed in life, and accomplished what he had to, while his rigorist critics prevailed morally after death.

34

Territorial Retrenchment and Cultural Innovation (1282–1328)

At the age of three, in late 1261, Andronikos II Doukas Angelos Komnenos Palaiologos was acclaimed co-basileus with his father in Hagia Sophia, but he was not crowned until 1272. The separation between the proclamation of an heir and his coronation was an innovation of this period, and the full imperial title took the form "*basileus* and *autokrator* of the Romans." Just before his coronation, Andronikos was married to Anna, a daughter of the king of Hungary and, through her mother, a granddaughter of Theodoros I Laskaris.[1] His father Michael VIII then issued a unique document, a decree specifying Andronikos' rights and duties as heir, including when he could wear the purple eagle, when his movements were to be accompanied by trumpets, and how he was to resolve legal disputes.[2] This entrenchment of his dynasty belied Michael's earlier, cynical pledge to pass over his sons if they were unworthy.[3] When Anna died in 1281, Michael VIII proclaimed Andronikos' son, Michael IX, who was three, co-emperor. Following the new practice, Michael IX would not be crowned until 1294.[4]

The restoration of Orthodoxy

Andronikos had obediently followed his father's Unionist policy, signing all the relevant documents and sending his own professions of Catholic faith to Rome. But as soon as Michael died, Andronikos and his *megas logothetes*, Theodoros Mouzalon, immediately reversed course and annulled the Union, something that Martin IV had already done unilaterally on the papal side. Andronikos removed Bekkos as patriarch, restored Ioseph, and brought back all who had been exiled for their opposition to Union. He had every incentive to change course: Charles was neutralized, the Union was hugely unpopular, the persecution was tearing society apart, and the Arsenites were questioning the legitimacy of the dynasty. The triumphal return of the (dying) Ioseph satisfied his followers, and Andronikos allowed some prominent Arsenites, who "crawled out of their lairs," to participate in the restoration of Orthodoxy. Bekkos and his closest associates were charged with heresy and deposed after a Synodal hearing. When, in the spring of 1283, Ioseph died, he was replaced, apparently with the consent of both Arsenites and Josephites, by Gregorios II of Cyprus, a former classics teacher. He convened a Synod at Blachernai that, over the course of a week, tried and deposed all bishops who had accepted Union or were appointed by Bekkos. The opening address was given by Holobolos, who had suffered under Michael for expressing anti-Unionist views.[5] Unionist bishops in the provinces were duly expunged from local records and commemorations.[6]

Yet the architects of the restoration were themselves tainted by association with Unionist policy. Andronikos defensively claimed that he had dissimulated his anti-Unionist beliefs during his father's reign, and had signed off on Union under duress. He was now acclaimed as a restorer of Orthodoxy by his court writers.[7] His father had restored Constantinople to Roman rule, and Andronikos was now freeing his people from Catholic tyranny. Others faced more skepticism. The new patriarch Gregorios II was widely suspected of having supported Union before 1282. He admitted that under Michael "we carried on for ten years, against our convictions, a mockery to the nations around us."[8] Andronikos' own mother, Theodora, was subjected to a synodal inquiry and required to repudiate her husband's policies and accept that he would never be properly buried and commemorated. She went on to sponsor the convent of Lips in Constantinople, which she intended as a family mausoleum (only one basileus was buried there, her son Andronikos).[9] Konstantinos Akropolites, son of the signatory at Lyons, who also went on to hold the position of *megas logothetes*, honored his father for all that he had done for him but criticized him for breaking with the traditions of the Church. He did not include him among those whose names were commemorated at their family monastery.[10] Through these painful sacrifices, the regime regained Orthodox credentials.

This did not calm the storm raging inside the Church. Despite efforts by Andronikos and Gregorios to win them over, most Arsenites remained aloof from the imperial Church. It was feared that they were growing in number, going door-to-door to propagandize and subvert the regime.[11] In the spring of 1284, the basileus convened a council at Adramyttion in Anatolia, across from Lesbos, to resolve the dispute. Among the Arsenites in attendance were monks mutilated on Michael's orders. But no agreement could be reached, as the Arsenite view was that all patriarchs after Arsenios were illegitimate, along with the bishops whom they had appointed. This was principled but also cynical, as they hoped to take the posts held now by the Josephites. In the end, a number of Arsenites agreed to a trial by fire: both sides would place their written viewpoints in a fire and whichever one survived would prevail; if both burned, the Arsenites would rejoin the imperial Church. But when both burned, many Arsenites refused to uphold the agreement, and so Gregorios excommunicated them. The Arsenites now split into two, with a rigorist faction led by Ioannes Tarchaneiotes and a more moderate faction led by the monk Hyakinthos, which was willing to compromise. The latter were branded by the rigorists as "fire-lovers," after the embarrassment at Adramyttion. "You are attacking each other no less than the Church itself," a critic of both factions said.[12] Even so, Andronikos continued to court them in an effort to foster unity.[13] While the basileus was unwilling to condemn Ioseph, who symbolized resistance to Union and had, after all, crowned him, he was happy to honor Arsenios, whose body was returned triumphally to the capital to placate his followers.[14]

Another agitator was Bekkos himself, who continued to insist, apparently with justice, that his deposition in 1282–1283 had been flawed procedurally and that he had been removed on the grounds of heresy even though none of his positions regarding the procession of the Holy Spirit violated existing Orthodox doctrine (he did not have to defend papal supremacy, for not even during his own patriarchy had the eastern Church accepted it as Rome understood it). It also rankled with Bekkos that he had been replaced with someone from outside the establishment of the Constantinopolitan Church. Whereas he himself was, as he put it, "a Roman born and raised among Romans," Gregorios had been raised among the Italians on Cyprus and had changed his clothes and speech when he emigrated. Many Arsenites felt that way about this interloper.[15]

Bekkos got his hearing. Gregorios convened a synod at Blachernai in 1285 that repudiated Lyons, found Bekkos guilty of heresy, and excommunicated him and his associates. The synod ratified a formulation of the doctrine of procession of the Holy Spirit that was written by Gregorios himself. Bekkos had tried to argue that Catholic and Orthodox views were compatible, for the formula "through the Son" that had been used by some Church Fathers logically also entailed "from the Son." For his part, Gregorios countered this understanding of causation within the Trinity by distinguishing between procession and manifestation and engaging in much quibbling about the difference between "from" and "through" (echoing the quibbling that occurred in the fifth century over the difference between "in" and "from" when it came to Natures). The *Tomos* was duly signed by the bishops and thereby the Church of Constantinople acquired its first doctrinal formulation that formally set it at odds with Rome.[16] There was no communication with Rome during all this.

It was said that the healing waters of the Zoodochos Pege monastery, like a literal gauge of Orthodoxy, had ceased to flow during the period of Latin rule, began again when Michael VIII took the City, stopped when he pushed for Union, and restarted when Andronikos restored Orthodoxy.[17] But the Church was still unsettled even after 1285. "One declared for Kepha, another for Apollos, and a third for Paul," i.e., Arsenios, Bekkos, or Gregorios, "and you could see Christ broken into pieces."[18] To be sure, there were few Unionists, but from his exile on the Gulf of Nikomedeia Bekkos had the satisfaction of seeing Gregorios go down too, in 1289. In addition to Arsenite pressure verging on terrorism, many were skeptical that Gregorios' *Tomos* sufficiently distinguished Orthodox dogma from its Latin counterpart. Some extreme conservatives even wanted to ban the phrase "through the Son," despite its solid Patristic pedigree. Then, a treatise by a disciple of Gregorios to explain the *Tomos* was so muddled that the patriarch's personal enemies, of whom there were many, seized the opportunity to pounce and accused him of a number of minor infractions. In the end, Gregorios was persuaded to step down "for the sake of unity" on condition that his Orthodoxy not be impugned. The *Tomos* remained valid.[19] Andronikos replaced Gregorios with a cranky old Athonite monk, Athanasios I (1289–1293, 1303–1310). This stern disciplinarian and moralizer was what Roman society deserved just then.

The chaos in the Church was due not to its systemic flaws or predilection for infighting, but to Michael VIII. When past emperors wanted to impose their will on the Church, they carefully prepared the ground in advance and built up a sufficient consensus, often by bribing key players. Michael instead would make passionate but insincere pledges, then surprise everyone by breaking his word, and expect the relevant constituencies to ratify what he had done, whether it be the blinding of Ioannes IV or Union with Rome. Leon VI had behaved similarly with his fourth marriage in the tenth century, sparking a schism in the Church that also lasted for decades. Andronikos handled this mess with patience, prudence, and tolerance, and his reign was so long that he outlived the outrage. But in foreign policy, Andronikos was less successful.

The fall of Anatolia

Andronikos' most criticized decision was to disband the fleet of about eighty ships in ca. 1284, probably along with the network of Latin and mixed-race corsairs that his father had employed. His advisors wrongly argued that a navy was far more expensive than it was worth. Now that Charles was neutralized and the Romans were at peace with Genoa and Venice, the fleet was idle but still expensive. And with the Church at peace, God would provide all necessary assistance. So most of the ships were decommissioned and their crews discharged. They sought employment with the Latins, in agriculture or piracy.[20] This made travel and trade more dangerous, but it also made the Romans more dependent on the Italians and more vulnerable. In 1294, a few days after the coronation of Andronikos' heir Michael IX on 21 May, the scholar Maximos Planoudes delivered a speech praising the emperor but also Michael VIII for keeping up the fleet. This was a subtle critique of the regime that was soon proven right. For some years, the Italians upheld their agreements, but eventually the conflict between the Genoese and Venetians was exported to Roman shores. In 1296, a Venetian fleet of seventy-five ships attacked the Genoese colony at Pera, which was unfortified. The basileus managed to shelter the Genoese themselves in the City, but the Venetians burned their installations and some Roman houses. The City was exposed to attack, but, as a historian noted, the Romans had brought this upon themselves. The Italian war disrupted shipping in the Aegean, and at one point a royal barge with a valuable cargo was seized by Venetians off

Chios.[21] Andronikos was unable to respond except through diplomacy and by confiscating the property of Venetians in Constantinople. By the end of his reign, he had lost many of the Aegean islands that Michael VIII had acquired, including Euboia. Hegemony over the Aegean was Andronikos' first major loss.

The greatest loss suffered by the Romans under Andronikos was Anatolia. This was historically momentous and reduced the territory and revenues of the state by half. In the long term, it provided the crucible for the rise of the Ottomans. This loss unfolded in the twenty years before 1304, though our sources are poor and it is hard at times to understand the court's response (or non-response). The result was the termination of the 1,500-year history of Roman Asia Minor and the confinement of the Roman state to the Balkans.

A common understanding of this catastrophe, one first proposed by the contemporaneous historian Pachymeres, was that the loss of Anatolia was determined by the return to Constantinople in 1261. The state of Nikaia had been a success. The court had managed to integrate all sectors of the populace into a functional consensus oriented around local defense and economic prosperity. The system worked, the defenses held, and Nikaia brought much of the Roman Balkans under its power.[22] In regaining Constantinople, Michael VIII sought to revive the game of great power politics, but he based his international ambitions on a system that was designed for only local success. In fact, he *had* to think and act big in order to counter the western attack that the capture of Constantinople itself had sparked. Anatolia was deprioritized and national strength was exchanged for imperial weakness.[23] It was said that when news arrived of the capture of Constantinople in 1261, a court secretary "pulled out the hair of his beard and lamented the evils that will come now that the Romans have returned to the City." In search of money, Michael allegedly sent an official (Chadenos) to raise taxes on Anatolian soldiers. The Turks thereby overran the feeble and underpaid defenders in the east while Michael poured his money and forces into western conflicts. He is even said to have neglected and fleeced Anatolia in order to spite his political enemies, the Laskarid supporters.[24]

This interpretation can no longer stand.[25] There is no reliable evidence that Michael deliberately undermined the defenses of Anatolia. His official Chadenos performed an *exisosis*, or "equalization," a redistribution of royal pronoias to ensure that all soldiers had a minimum threshold of support (and, if possible, to also generate revenue for the state). Anatolian agriculture and production did not decline after 1261,[26] and it was not Michael who embroiled the armies of Nikaia in Balkan Wars. That was Batatzes, as early as the 1230s. Moreover, the Anatolian frontier had remained stable during the thirteenth century, first through the détente with the Seljuks and then the alliance with the Mongols. The eastern border was reasonably secure. The disruption came instead from the collapse of the Seljuk sultanate, which lost control of its nomadic Turkmen, many of them new arrivals. They cared nothing for states and borders, and their group formations were too fluid for a sultan or basileus to come to a binding agreement with them. They tended to spend the summer in the highlands with their flocks, and so were often beyond the reach of regular armies. Many of them began to overrun western Anatolia or fled there from the wars and political instability that were raging in the interior. Chiefs competed with each over followers and territory, and tried to build up coalitions of warriors that could stake a claim to Seljuk or Roman lands. These groups formed the nuclei of the later emirates (*beyliks*) of Karaman, Germiyan, Menteşe, Aydın, Osman, and others, that took over most of Anatolia.

In 1260 and again in 1261, so before he retook the City, Michael responded swiftly and decisively to the followers of one Mehmed-bey, who were raiding in the Maeander valley. When another attack came in 1263, Michael immediately sent his brother, the despot Ioannes, from the Balkans to the Maeander to counter it. Ioannes succeeded and stayed there until 1267 to put the defenses in order. Then there is a gap of thirteen years, while Michael was preoccupied with Charles of Anjou. Some units were transferred from Anatolia to the Balkans.[27] The Romans appear to have lost southern and eastern Karia, including Knidos, as well as Antioch-on-the-Maeander and Tralleis. Most of Paphlagonia was also overrun, except some coastal forts, such as Herakleia.[28] But Michael returned in force in 1280, countering a Turkish raid in Bithynia. This campaign, while otherwise successful, was marred by Michael's blinding of Ioannes Angelos Doukas, the son of Michael II of Epeiros who had been performing brave deeds against the Turks in Bithynia. The endemic suspicion of the Palaiologoi against their most competent and popular generals frequently undermined the war effort. At the same time, he dispatched Andronikos south to the Maeander, where the junior co-basileus rebuilt and resettled Tralleis as a defensive bulwark. Michael returned in 1281 and built a wooden wall along the right bank of the Sangarios river, to block incursions toward Nikomedeia. These efforts were successful at the time. Therefore, while Anatolia was not Michael's top priority and did suffer losses, he did not abandon it to its fate.[29]

It was Andronikos who lost Roman Anatolia. In 1284, Menteşe-bey took Tralleis, when a severe lack of water forced the city to surrender to him. There was apparently no Roman response to this loss, which was soon followed by the loss of many lands south of the Maeander, likely including Miletos. At that time, in 1283–1284, Andronikos was campaigning further north, from Nikaia to Nikomedeia and then down to Adramyttion, apparently winning some minor victories against other invaders. More importantly, he strengthened the fortifications of Anatolia, a project that would have been ongoing since the reign of his father and not carried out at one specific time.[30] After six years of absence, in 1290/1, Andronikos went south to Nymphaion, the former Laskarid capital. He stayed there for a full three years, returning to Constantinople in June, 1293. Such a long residence suggests that the basileus was taking the defense of Anatolia seriously, though we hear of no specific actions or reforms. It is possible that Andronikos resided at Nymphaion for a different reason, in order to stress the continuity between the Palaiologoi and the Laskarids and claim the loyalty that locals felt toward the state of Nikaia. This is suggested by his visit, before traveling to Nymphaion, to the blinded Ioannes IV in his prison in Bithynia. Andronikos softened the conditions in which Ioannes was held and sought forgiveness in exchange for recognition, a publicity stunt to win over the Arsenites. At the end of his stay at Nymphaion, Andronikos arrested his capable brother, the *porphyrogennetos* Konstantinos, on suspicion of treason, along with the general Konstantinos Strategopoulos. The historian Gregoras implies that these two were the bastion of Anatolian defenses, making this another example of Palaiologan insecurity undermining the interests of the state.[31]

Those generals were replaced with Alexios Philanthropenos, a nephew of both the basileus and Tarchaneiotes, the leader of the Arsenites. He was given an emergency command to save Anatolia, and that is exactly what he did, with an army that included a strong Cretan contingent. In 1294, he defeated some Turks who were threatening Achyraous in the north and then, in a series of brilliant campaigns, inflicted many defeats on the Turks of Menteşe. He retook many forts, cleared the way to Miletos, and in 1295 liberated that city too. "The Milesians now breathe the air of freedom and mix freely with people of their own kind," wrote Planoudes to Philanthropenos, his friend.[32] But the curse of the victorious general struck again. Philanthropenos rebelled against the basileus, whereupon another general, loyal to the regime, bribed some of his Cretan soldiers to arrest and blind him. Success had made Philanthropenos ambitious, and circumstances favored rebellion. Both the locals and the army preferred a present hero over a distant ruler with an indifferent reputation. Many soldiers had lost their pronoia-lands to the Turks, and Andronikos was slow in paying those who received cash salaries. Philanthropenos had reason to fear that his success would incur royal suspicion, so his rebellion was partly preemptive. The final straw was when Andronikos demanded that the general send to him all the plunder from the campaign, beyond the due that normally went to the basileus. Andronikos was possibly being more than greedy here: he was seeking to undermine his general's standing with his own soldiers.[33]

Philanthropenos had stabilized the situation, but after his arrest the army of Cretans and mercenaries melted away or were dispersed. In 1298, Andronikos made the odd choice to send Ioannes Tarchaneiotes, the leader of the hard-line Arsenites, to command in Anatolia. Tarchaneiotes had once been imprisoned on suspicion of disloyalty. While governing Anatolia, he was accused again of treason and impiety, this time by the patriarch Ioannes XII and Theoleptos, the bishop of Philadelpheia, an influential enemy of the Arsenites. Their accusations were backed, or instigated, by landholders who stood to lose from Tarchaneiotes' reforms of the land allotments. Andronikos had apparently allowed some of the soldiers' pronoias to become hereditary. But before he could implement an *exisosis* and endow all soldiers with lands, Tarchaneiotes was forced to abandon his post and clear his name with Andronikos in Thessalonike.[34] The war effort was again undermined by politics, not military failure.

When the Anatolian provinces were invaded again in force, in 1300–1301, Andronikos dispatched a force of between 5,000 and 8,000 Christian Alans who had recently emigrated to Romanía from the lands of the Golden Horde in the north. The basileus by now believed that "he could trust no Romans, and so he was dreaming of alliances with foreign nations." To arm and equip the Alans, tax collectors forcibly gathered up all the money, horses, and weapons that they could extract from the Romans. Thus, the expedition was accompanied by curses rather than prayers.[35] One joint Alan-Roman army was sent to Magnesia under the co-basileus Michael IX, "who may have been inexperienced in war, but was eager to help any Romans in trouble." However, he was persuaded by the Alans and his generals that their force was no match for the Turks, and so they withdrew to Pergamon in early 1303. He was followed by thousands of locals, who feared that they were being left behind. Refugees streamed north and even toward the islands and Greece, in the winter. The Turks overran the south in their wake, taking over the coast all the way to Adramyttion, except for Phokaia, which was in the hands of the Zaccaria. The city of Philadelpheia also remained free, albeit surrounded by Turkish bands. Other cities made what deals they could. The Sardians agreed to cede half their citadel to the Turks and divide it with a wall, so each group could live separately.[36]

Meanwhile, the governor of Bithynia, Leon Mouzalon, in command of another Roman-Alan army of about 2,000 men, was defeated by "Atman," i.e., Osman, the founder of the Ottoman dynasty, at the battle of Bapheus near Nikomedeia, on 27 July, 1302. So the north collapsed too, leaving the Romans in control of only a coastal strip along the Sea of Marmara as well as the walled cities Nikomedeia, Nikaia, and Prousa. Replaying the events of the late eleventh century, Turks appeared on the other side of the Bosporos by late 1302, ahead of another stream of refugees who fled to the City from Bithynia, many of them searching desperately for parents and children. The streets of the capital were filled with the hungry and homeless. Groups huddled in the porticos or by the walls, and the patriarchs, especially Athanasios I, tried to find food and relief for them. As the Church had lost most of its own lands in the east, Athanasios had to cajole, shame, and bully the capital's aristocracy to contribute to the charitable cause. To raise funds, he also reduced the economic perks of his own priests. Moreover, as the crisis became permanent, refugee issues were entrusted to a designated official, the *hetaireiarches*. Thrace, Macedonia, Greece, and the islands struggled to host fellow Romans, including children, monks, and soldiers, who needed new homes.[37] In the coming generations, peasants in Macedonia sported names that revealed their Anatolian origin, such as Prousenos, Nikaia, and Amasianos. A widow was named Anatolike.[38] Michael IX was given pronoias in the Balkans to compensate for the ones that he lost in Anatolia,[39] but such accommodations could not be made for everyone. Where once, a century ago, monks had fled from areas of Latin rule to Laskarid Anatolia, now they fled from Anatolia to the capital and the Balkans, and especially to Mt. Athos. This boosted Athos' profile in the landscape of Orthodox monasticism, with profound consequences for Church history.[40]

In just a century, the Romans had experienced a striking geographical whiplash. The grandparents or parents of the historian Georgios Pachymeres had fled from Constantinople to Nikaia after 1204. He was born there in 1242 and emigrated to Constantinople after 1261, for he regarded the City as his proper homeland. Yet by the time that he was writing in the early 1300s, the Anatolian state in which he was raised had collapsed and refugees were fleeing to the City from there.[41] The polity of Constantinople now consisted of a broad Balkan zone, about 150 km wide and 640 km long, stretching from Thrace to the Adriatic, which had been wrested by Batatzes from the Bulgarians, Latins, and Epeirots in the 1240s, when Pachymeres was born. It also controlled a few islands, a corner of the Peloponnese, and some beleaguered towns in Anatolia. It is indicative that Muslim rulers of this time regarded the basileus as simply the lord of Macedonia.[42] Roman literature began to exude despair and defeat. Before the 1290s, many feared that "Roman affairs are finished: there is no way for us to hold both west and east; one of the two will surely be lost."[43] By 1302, that prediction was confirmed.

The marcher emirates of Germiyan, Menteşe, Aydın, and Osman were establishing themselves in the territories of the former state of Nikaia. Germiyan (in Phrygia) was probably the most powerful, whereas Aydın came to dominate the Aegean coast. Using its ports and fleets, Aydın was poised to reap the profits from trade and piracy. Sometimes these emirates were rivals, but warriors from each often joined in the raids of the others, "received by them happily as allies."[44] It is difficult to see the early Ottomans in action because contemporary Greek accounts, while generally reliable, are scant and reflect the "distant" view of Constantinople, whereas the Turkish accounts, although they are fuller, are late, embellished with much legendary material, and ignore the international context, focusing on Osman. He was, at first, confined to the hills of southern Bithynia, squeezed between more powerful Muslim neighbors in the interior and the Roman forts closer to the coast. He was nominally subordinate to the Seljuk sultan of Rum, who was himself a Mongol puppet. His followers moved between winter and summer pastures, while raiding the Christians in order to capture livestock, slaves, and plunder. Gradually they expanded into the fertile lowlands of Bithynia, taking over the towns. Osman distributed the conquered lands among his followers, and converted some of the churches into mosques. This precipitated widespread conversions to Islam among the locals, who managed thereby to secure their socioeconomic conditions. In the battle of Bapheus, in 1302, Osman probably defeated a much smaller Roman force, and it seemed as though Bithynia would be opened up to him. But in 1307, he was defeated and pushed back to his upland base by a large Mongol army, a setback "forgotten" by the later Turkish tradition. Ottoman expansion was halted for the next twenty years because of it.[45] For now, the main cities of Bithynia—Nikaia, Nikomedeia, and Prousa—held out.

Palaiologan administration

The administration of the Palaiologan state remains opaque. The themes still existed as regional provincial units, and appear mostly in connection with taxation, sometimes subdivided into *katepanikia*. But the terminology in the sources is inconsistent and fuzzy, making it hard to know what is official and what literary language. Towns were placed under the military command of a *kephale*, i.e., a "head-man," with a number of them sometimes grouped together under a "catholic," i.e., "all-encompassing" *kephale*.[46] But the administration itself was by no means loose. The bureaucracy intensively surveyed, registered, and milked its subjects, keeping detailed records of its taxable assets and exemptions and concessions that had been granted. As noted previously, the citizens of some cities were given broad exemptions from taxation, but the state controlled the surrounding land. The population of a significant town at this time, such as Serres or Monembasia, was around 5,000–7000. Thessalonike and Constantinople had many more, though we are unable to say exactly how many.[47]

These cities had institutions of local self-governance, though these too are vaguely described. We hear of councils, leading citizens, and local lords, but it is unclear how formalized these were. The populace played a decisive role, sometimes by electing or choosing which of the notables would take the lead, and sometimes by negotiating with outside powers through its own representatives.[48] This was the final phase of the Roman city. In the early period, down to the seventh century, cities had formally constituted bodies of local government; in the middle period they were run by court officials; and now they enjoyed a loose autonomy and had their own leaders, though it is unclear whether these were formal "magistrates." Even in this final stage, Roman cities did not become independent enough of the center to develop their own separate states, economies, and cultures, as was happening in Italy. They always belonged to a regional power, whether by force or choice.

The administration of Constantinople itself is obscure too. It appears that Michael VIII brought back the office of the prefect to take charge of policing and provisioning, but the terminology for it is not precise and it had less status than before 1204. New to the political life in the capital were the *demarchs*, or leaders of the *demos*, who liaised between the populace and the court, and even participated in court functions. It is not clear how they were appointed, but likely they represented the capital's neighborhoods. The populace reasserted its political power under Andronikos, who was so desperate for confirmation of his legitimacy that he repeatedly convened public assemblies of the court and people, sometimes in the old hippodrome, and put questions of state to them. In 1296 it concerned a reform of the judiciary, because it was widely perceived as corrupt; the following year, the basileus delivered a point-by-point refutation of a pamphlet that came into his hands with accusations against him (not an advisable way to lay scandal to rest); and in 1303 it was to bring Athanasios I back to the patriarchal throne. The basileis regularly rode out into the City to receive petitions from their subjects.[49]

Andronikos was eager to be seen as extremely religious, and he was always in the company of monks and bishops and attending liturgies and litanies.[50] Given his shaky legitimacy, this was a matter of political survival, not just personal piety. His private life offstage is revealed by his many illegitimate children. He donated money and land to monasteries on Athos and elsewhere, even when funds were tight for national defense. In addition to their public-relations benefit, these acts authorized the basileus to call on the monasteries to pray on behalf of himself and all the Romans in times of crisis, buttressing the regime's legitimacy.[51]

Public assemblies often took place in the palace courtyards. Most of the old Great Palace was abandoned by this time, especially its wings down by the sea, but some of its ancient halls were still used for synods and ceremonies. The Blachernai palace was the main royal residence. It was taller and more compactly arranged around courtyards, where scaled-back versions of the *prokypsis* ceremony were staged. These took place twice a year on an outdoor platform built by Andronikos. The top floors of the palace afforded magnificent views of the City, Golden Horn, and Thracian fields. Ceremonies of this period are described in a manual known as pseudo-Kodinos, from the mid-fourteenth century. The palace banquets that it describes had shorter guest lists than in the tenth century, as in many respects this was a budget court operating on a smaller scale. For ease of access to the palace, many aristocrats situated their manors near Blachernai, which thereby became a posh neighborhood. Court dress—and Roman dress generally in this era—shunned western styles, though not necessarily western fabrics, which were imported and used to make Roman-style clothing. This choice has been linked to the rejection of Union, which under Andronikos became almost a core element of Roman identity. Foreign tastes looked instead to the east, leading to the adoption of turbans and caftans. Elite fashion sense fixated on hats, whose extravagant and exotic styles elicited commentary on the decline of Roman mores.[52] The most spectacular example is the parabolic turban sported by Theodoros Metochites, a leading intellectual and, after 1321, *megas logothetes*, in his donor portrait at the Chora monastery, which he renovated and transformed into a center of learning (see Plates 7a–b). His choice of headgear has been seen in light of his opposition to Union and affinity for eastern science.[53]

The court prayed that God would preserve Constantinople, a "salvific Ark for the state, in this flood of barbarians that we are enduring."[54] Soon after 1305, Metochites wrote the longest and most glorious of all orations in praise of the City, which is over a hundred pages long in the latest edition and full of beautiful and evocative imagery praising "the greatest city of all time." Constantinople is the center, beating heart, and highest point of the inhabited world, founded by the first and greatest Christian emperor in order to rule the world in an era when the world and the Roman state were coterminous. It is the mirror of cosmic Creation, a stage for the miracles of the Theotokos. And what Constantinople is to the world, Hagia Sophia is to Constantinople. Since the City is a universal norm, all people, not just the Romans, are at home in it: it is the "common polity of all people," no matter their ethnic origin.[55] This idealized picture reflected Metochites' privilege. The throngs of homeless refugees that filled Constantinople, along with provincial taxpayers, would have scoffed at his happy notion that the City collected taxes from the provinces and redistributed them to its inhabitants, enriching them.[56] Wealth inequality was at its peak, so much so that for the first time in Roman history a secular author wrote a treatise to decry it, the *Dialogue between the Rich and Poor*. The poor lived in hovels, while the rich had three-story manors full of opulent furniture. Metochites acknowledged this inequality, and after his fall from power he wrote a poem to lament the delights of his manor; he had even built a treasury inside it to store his valuables, sleeping with the key under his pillow.[57] It is striking that in his oration praising Constantinople he discusses the City's elite monuments but not its public places, which commoners used more. A random mention in an administrative document reveals that the area around Constantine's forum was given over to vineyards. It is likely that only the founder's column still stood in place, battered and burned after the centuries.[58]

The state was poor. Michael VIII had begun to slightly devalue the gold currency, a trend that Andronikos pushed further in an effort to squeeze more coins out of his shrinking revenues from almost fifteen carats to just below twelve. This, coupled with the mass of refugees in the City and the loss of provisions and income from Anatolia, caused price hikes and famine, especially in the first decade of the fourteenth century.[59] Starting already in 1283, in order to fund a successful campaign against Demetrias in Thessaly, all pronoiars were required to contribute a tenth of their proceeds to the treasury. This pronoia-surtax seems to have been retained thereafter, but many pronoiars paid it by squeezing their *paroikoi*.[60] By 1301, as Anatolia was overrun, Andronikos had ceased to pay the salaries of many officials, and in 1303 he confiscated, or rather recalled, all the properties given by the state to churches, monasteries, and members of the court in Bithynia. Even the patriarch Athanasios recognized the fiscal logic here, and sent an olive branch to the basileus as his reply. But the measure probably did not take effect, as the lands in question were overrun.[61] Reconquering Anatolia was now an imperative, but the Romans had no navy and could barely pay for more than a few thousand soldiers. Andronikos therefore resorted to a risky solution: he hired a western mercenary company to do the job for him.

The Catalan Company

Andronikos was diplomatically engaged with many western courts from the start of his reign, trying to build alliances through dynastic marriages. In 1284, after his first wife died, he married Yolanda of Montferrat (renamed Eirene) in order to neutralize one of the claims to the so-called kingdom of Thessalonike that was circulating in the west. In 1288–1294, he made a great effort to marry his son Michael IX to Catherine of Courtenay, the heiress of the title of the Latin empire of Constantinople, but this failed. Catherine eventually married Charles of Valois, the brother of the French king, who began to formulate plans for the conquest of Constantinople. The king of Cyprus also turned down a match to Michael IX by requiring prior papal consent—the popes had banned Catholic-Orthodox unions—so Michael eventually married an Armenian princess.[62] These negotiations required the dispatch of multiple embassies on long journeys, which was expensive. It is noteworthy that many of these envoys were scholars, such as Metochites. Lacking military superiority, or the funds that had once fueled Manuel I's extravagance, Constantinople was trying to impress the Latins with the one exclusive asset that it had left: classical learning and refinement, for which it was still the gold standard. This was a calculated effort to project soft power in an age of decline.

After Cyprus, Metochites went on another embassy in 1298–1299, this time to Serbia, which he regarded as a land of savage barbarian highlanders and cattle rustlers. Even so, Serbia was growing in power and encroaching on Roman lands, capturing Dyrrachion in 1296. It was with the kralj Stefan Uroš II Milutin (1282–1321) that Andronikos concluded the most humiliating agreement of his reign, in order to stop Serbian depredations. As the basileus' sister Eudokia absolutely refused to be sacrificed on that altar, Andronikos was forced to surrender to Milutin his precious five-year-old daughter Simonis, in 1299, over the objection of his churchmen who were concerned by the groom's dissolute lifestyle, multiple prior consorts, and advanced age. The wedding was performed in Thessalonike with the basileus, and his tearful mother Theodora, in attendance. The patriarch Ioannes XII Kosmas was so scandalized that he went on strike for a year.[63]

Yolanda (Eirene) of Montferrat was eleven when she married Andronikos, and even fifteen years later she found him to be "more ardent toward her than a husband ought to be." The couple did not get along and Yolanda did not take to Roman ways, as past princesses had done. She demanded that Andronikos divide the Roman polity "according to the Latin manner" into feudal lordships that she could distribute to her sons, but he utterly ruled this out: he would not turn the monarchy into a "polyarchy." Eventually, in 1303, Yolanda picked up and moved to Thessalonike, and she was based there until her death in 1317. Watched by her husband's officials, including Metochites, she presided over a quasi-autonomous court, promoting her sons' careers. Her second, Theodoros, became the marquis of Montferrat in 1306, the first east Roman prince to hold a western lordship. When he visited Constantinople, in 1317–1319 and 1325–1328, the Romans found him to be "a pure Latin in his outlook, religion, dress, haircut, and every other habit." He wrote a treatise, first in Greek and then translating it into Latin, advocating a more consultative form of monarchy, which Metochites slammed as an irresponsible advocacy of "democracy."[64]

Like Andronikos and Yolanda, Constantinople and the Latin west had never been so estranged as during this reign. And yet, just when Anatolia seemed lost for good, in 1303, Andronikos was contacted by one Roger de Flor, captain of a mercenary band of Catalans who had fought in the Sicilian war between Aragon and Anjou. Roger, a half-German and half-Italian adventurer who was on the run from justice in the west, promised that his newly formed Catalan Grand Company would clear western Anatolia of Turks in exchange for cash and titles for himself. It was clear to Andronikos that his Roman and Alan forces could not do the job. He obviously could not credibly ask the pope for a crusade to "save the Christian east." Yet Constantinople knew from hard experience that western mercenaries, whenever they became the dominant element of the armed forces, had only one goal, namely to conquer Roman territory for themselves and establish their own principalities by inventing new titles and cynically claiming that "the Greeks" had to be "restored" to papal obedience. In accepting Roger's offer, Andronikos made the biggest mistake of his reign, bringing ruin and misery upon himself and his subjects.[65]

Roger and Co. arrived in September, 1303 on leased Genoese ships. They were battle-hardened infantry soldiers, around 6,000 strong and accompanied by some women and children. The core was formed by the almogavars, light infantry fighters developed for the wars of Aragon, who coordinated tightly in battle with smaller contingents of heavy infantry and heavy cavalry; Andronikos had to supply the latter with horses. Roger was invested with the rank of *megas doux*—this was honorary, as there was no fleet for him to command—and married to a niece of the basileus. The pay that he had requested initially, for four months of service, is hard to calculate, but it certainly formed the largest item in Andronikos' expenses, as he had to stop paying salaries to palace officials and staff in order to raise it. As soon as they arrived at Constantinople, the Catalans clashed with the Genoese at Pera over the loan repayment, killing a number of them, including a Roman high official sent to mediate. Then additional contingents of Catalans arrived who were not part of the original arrangement. The basileus transported them all across the sea to Kyzikos, to spend the winter of 1303–1304. While there, they mistreated the local Romans, raping women and children. The basileus was angered, but could do nothing.[66]

The Company proved remarkably effective at fighting Turks. In 1304, it defeated groups around Kyzikos itself, then marched south to Philadelpheia, which was still being invested by the Karaman Turks. The Company defeated them and was welcomed inside as a liberator. It then marched west to Magnesia and Ephesos on the coast, where it was joined by more of their countrymen. The Catalans had proven again, as had Philanthropenos, that the Turks could be beaten. But they were the opposite of Philanthropenos in all other ways. The Catalans brutally extracted money and resources from the people they were ostensibly liberating and committed many atrocities, torturing monks and blinding and executing others to seize their wealth. They used ships to export their brutality to Chios, Lesbos, and Lemnos as well. Roger stored his ill-gotten gains in Magnesia, but the people there, led by one Attaleiotes and a band of Alans (who hated the Catalans), shut their gates behind the Company. While the Catalans were busy besieging Magnesia, the Turks made inroads in many places and the basileus received frantic and desperate calls from Anatolian Romans to recall his horrific army. The solution had proven far worse than the problem. After many efforts, Andronikos persuaded Roger to return in August, alleging that he needed the Company to help Michael IX fight the Bulgarians. The Company went into winter quarters at Gallipoli, in Thrace.[67]

Mutual recriminations built up during that winter. Michael IX, his Roman Anatolian refugee-soldiers, and the Alans were already suspicious of the Catalans. For their part, the latter complained about delays in payment. In October of 1304, Roger demanded 300,000 hyperpyra in back pay, to which Andronikos responded that he had already spent a million hyperpyra on the Catalans. The treasury had no more money. Andronikos had by now raised the tax on pronoias to a third of their proceeds, up from 10%, and Michael IX melted down personal valuables in order to pay his Balkan army. The Catalans balked at accepting the debased coin that Andronikos was paying, while heavy demands were being made on Thracian farmers to feed the guest army.[68] The arrival of Catalan reinforcements made the problem worse, as their leader, Berengar d'Estança, was a more intransigent and violent man, and he reinforced the links between the

Company and western kings who were planning attacks on Constantinople. He brought ties to Federico III of Sicily, though later the Company would drift into the ambit of Charles of Valois, who had acquired "rights" to the imperial title through his marriage to Catherine of Courtenay, the granddaughter of Baldwin II. Like Charles of Anjou, Valois was also building up a grand alliance to conquer Constantinople, except he lacked Anjou's resources. Both Federico and Valois, in sequence, regarded the Company as an advance army that was gaining a foothold in Romanía on their behalf. For their part, the Company was treating the title of *megas doux* as if it conferred feudal "ducal" rights over the coasts and islands of Romanía. Roger began to act as if his contract to liberate the east gave him claims to "the kingdom of Anatolia," a fictional realm that he hoped to create through force.[69] It was the Normans all over again.

Andronikos' Genoese allies warned him that the Company was scheming with western aggressors and was an enemy, not an ally. But Andronikos wanted to follow the old Roman playbook of cooption. He made Berengar *megas doux* in December, receiving from him an oath of loyalty, and made Roger a *kaisar* in the spring (which, of course, he interpreted as a rank of co-emperor). But on 30 April, 1305, Roger was assassinated by some Alans on a visit to the camp of Michael IX in Thrace. It is not clear who, if anyone, gave the order, but everyone in that camp would have hated him. The greatest poet of the age, Manuel Philes, wrote a short celebratory poem about "the slaughter of the Sicilian *kaisar*," comparing him to a stalk of wheat that had been cut and had to be ground into powder lest any part of it fall to the dirt and regrow. But it was too late. The Catalans had been raiding Thrace already from their fortified base in Gallipoli. After Roger's murder they killed all the Romans there, including the children, and initiated full-scale military operations against Romanía. They flew the banner of St. Peter from the tallest tower, flanked by those of Aragon, Sicily, and St. George.[70] The Company was posing now as a Catholic army fighting the treacherous "Greeks," and in May, 1305 it made a profit-sharing agreement with a Turkish group that defected from royal service. On 10 July, the Company and its allies defeated Michael IX and his army of Anatolian Romans, Alans, and Turks at Apros in Thrace.[71] Berengar now claimed the title "lord of Anatolia and the islands of the empire of Romanía," and the Company set their sights on "the kingdom of Thessalonike," devising official seals for it.[72]

For two years, 1305–1307, despite internal dissension and changes of leadership the Catalans devastated Thrace, raiding as far as Constantinople. They captured Raidestos, the grain hub of Thrace, after a year-long siege, but failed to take Adrianople. The Roman cities resisted them fiercely. But Thrace was so destabilized that travel between Thessalonike and Constantinople became risky, even for Yolanda.[73] The Bulgarians also took advantage of the chaos to seize Mesembria and Anchialos on the Black Sea.[74] This restricted Constantinople's ability to access grain from the north. The Genoese were the Romans' only ally in this war, but their help was limited to safeguarding their own commercial interests. They made excuses to Aragon for countering the Catalans, while rarely intervening decisively on the side of the Romans. In 1305, Chios was occupied by Benedetto Zaccaria, the Genoese lord of Phokaia, who alleged that, without the defense that only he could provide, the island would be overrun by Turks. Andronikos could not stop him, but extracted an agreement that Zaccaria would rule Chios as his representative, in renewable five-year terms. Thus, the wealth of the trade in mastic, an aromatic resin grown only on Chios and used as chewing gum and for oral hygiene, swelled the profits of the alum-lords of Phokaia.[75]

Meanwhile, the mainland was in chaos. Farmers in Thrace fled to the cities, including Constantinople, exacerbating the refugee problem from Anatolia and causing more grain shortages. In May, 1305, anti-Latin riots in the City targeted ethnic Catalans, including merchants, and even some Genoese. The populace was furious that Andronikos had scuttled the fleet back in the 1280s, which weakened their defenses. Andronikos was forced to give a speech in which he justified his policies by citing the precedent of Batatzes and Michael VIII, who had also hired Latin mercenaries. He then sent men throughout the City to require every citizen to swear an oath of loyalty to his regime. But his response was not merely defensive. The basileus built some ships and sent guards to protect farmers when they went out to cultivate their fields. He also solicited voluntary donations from his subjects in order to pay soldiers, a first in Roman history.[76] The poet Philes begged God to send the Romans a David who could fight against the "bloodthirsty Goliath."[77]

Absent a David, Andronikos implemented a harsh, but in the end effective, policy during the winter of 1306–1307. He discouraged farmers in Thrace from working their fields in order to starve out the Company, which brought famine to the entire region, including the City, where many sought refuge. The patriarch Athanasios protested this policy but the basileus would not budge. Athanasios railed against the corruption of the rich and of state officials who were seeking to make a profit from their stockpiles of grain, and the Genoese who were charged to bring cargoes of it would sell only to the richest. The patriarch demanded that profiteers be punished and he stopped paying his priests to raise money for soup kitchens and famine relief. Some aid came from outside. The Bulgarians made a treaty with Andronikos: he recognized their Black Sea conquests in exchange for grain to the City. Many died from hunger during that winter—"the bodies of the dead were piled up in the streets, and those who carried them away also fell dead into the graves"—but the strategy eventually worked.[78]

The Catalans had failed to dominate Thrace beyond the forts that they occupied by force, and they were now starved out by the damage that they themselves had caused to the region and by Andronikos' policy. So they moved on to Macedonia, ensconcing themselves in the Kassandreia peninsula. For two more years, 1307–1309, they ravaged that region too. They attacked the monasteries on Athos, burned the countryside, and besieged Thessalonike in 1308–1309, hoping to make it the capital of a new concocted principality, the "kingdom of Macedonia." In this they were aided by men sent by Charles of Valois. But they were fiercely opposed by the local population. The Romans had finally found their David, a certain Chandrenos, a refugee soldier from Anatolia, who organized the local resistance. The Catalans were enslaving the locals and selling them to western merchants, especially Venetians, though Andronikos tried to limit these sales, at least to the Genoese.[79] Finally, in spring, 1309, the Company was driven on by failure and lack of supplies to Thessaly, where it took up service under Gautier V de Brienne, the new duke of Athens, who was extending his realm in Thessaly. The Catalans proved as treacherous to him as to Andronikos. They fought and killed him at the battle of Halmyros, and took over his duchy. They recognized the Aragonese king of Sicily as their feudal overlord and ruled Athens from 1311 to 1388 in his name, introducing the laws of Aragon to Attica. Unsurprisingly, the Catalans proved to be the most oppressive of Athens' colonial rulers, and a piratical scourge to their neighbors.

Romanía survived the Catalan ordeal only by imposing desperate suffering on itself. The Catalans could ravage and destroy, but they created only victims, not subjects willing to be ruled by them. The Romans were also lucky in that the plans of Charles of Valois failed to materialize, and his crusading project was passed on to his heirs. The Romans had no allies during those years, apart from the Genoese and the Serbs (who were playing both sides). Had a western crusade attacked Constantinople during the crisis, there was no place where the Roman leadership could regroup. The damage caused by this ordeal was extensive. The treasury was empty, though it began to fill as soon as the Catalans moved on. Salaries had been slashed due to austerity measures: "and how we live now," wrote the priests to the patriarch, "is revealed by our hovels."[80] The army had been decimated and would have to be rebuilt. Thrace and Macedonia were ravaged, with thousands of people displaced, murdered, or starved. All hope of regaining Anatolia was lost. Mesembria and Anchialos were in Bulgarian hands; Chios was politely stolen by the Zaccaria; and, in 1306–1310, a predatory crusading order of martial monks, the Knights Hospitallers, who had been pushed out of Jerusalem to Tripoli and then to Cyprus, conquered Rhodes to use as their new headquarters, in the face of determined resistance by the Romans. The Knights asked Andronikos to hand it over to them so that they could fight the Turks, but he refused.[81] "We live," lamented Metochites, "in a few remnants of the body of our realm . . . like people who have had most, and the most essential, of their limbs amputated. . . . We are vulnerable and liable to perish easily from any small blow."[82]

Still, order began to return. In 1310, the Venetians renewed their treaty with Constantinople. They had been eager to join Charles of Valois' crusade, but their business interests suffered while they waited and so they reversed course. Andronikos agreed to pay them 40,000 hyperpyra in four annual installments, as compensation for damages. Such payments were now standard in treaties with the Italians, who expected the basileus to guarantee safety within his realm, even while they were destabilizing it through treaties with its enemies and piratical raids.[83] Diplomacy between Venice and Constantinople revolved around a small set of issues, including Romans and *gasmouloi* who were gaining Venetian citizenship in order to avoid paying taxes to the basileus (also an issue with Genoese citizenship); grievances against Roman officials who imposed illegal taxes on the Venetians or arbitrarily confiscated their cargoes; compensation for losses due to piracy in Roman waters; and restrictions by the basileus on the grain trade. Specifically, the first Palaiologoi prohibited the export of grain from their territories, lest there be a scarcity for their own subjects, but they also sought to restrict the import by the Italians of cheap Black Sea grain, lest it undercut local producers.[84] Overall, distrust prevailed. A Venetian put it well when he said that "the doge and the commune of Venice went from truce to truce with the emperor of the Greeks, but did not want to make peace."[85]

Also in 1310, the remaining Arsenites agreed to rejoin the official Church. It had been half a century since the outbreak of the controversy and tempers had cooled; moreover, the Arsenites' base in Anatolia been disrupted by the Turkish conquest. Andronikos was happy to grant the token concessions that they wanted, such as striking the name of the patriarch Ioseph from liturgical commemorations (though he was restored later in the century). The ceremony of reunion, held on 14 September, was remarkable: the corpse of Arsenios was seated in the patriarchal throne in Hagia Sophia, with a writ of forgiveness in its hand, which the current patriarch, Nephon, read aloud on his behalf.[86]

The Catalan mess was not fully mopped up until 1313. A group of 2,000 Turkish raiders under one Halil had allied with the Company but then broken off from it in 1309 to return to Anatolia. Instead, they ensconced themselves in a fort in Thrace and continued to raid the countryside, setting back the Roman recovery. They were defeated and massacred in 1313 by a joint Roman-Serb army supported by the Genoese.[87] The Catalans had been hired to defeat the Turks in Anatolia. Instead, they had introduced the first independent Turkish group to gain a military foothold in the Balkans.

Early Palaiologan literature

Writers of this period were overaware that Romanía was losing ground by the year. They were living through not a sudden collapse due to a single attack, such as the fall of 1203–1204, but a gradual decline, seemingly even a natural one akin to aging. In the twelfth century under Manuel I Komnenos, a blossoming

New Rome, free of wrinkles, could be contrasted to the superannuated Old Rome. But now, in the late thirteenth century, it could be admitted that New Rome had aged and had wrinkles too.[88] The end was in sight. The patriarch Athanasios warned Andronikos that without moral reform the realm would be enslaved to foreign nations, like Israel of old.[89] It was easy to attribute this decline to the sins of the Romans, and that is exactly what Athanasios did, aggravating everyone around him, but beyond such platitudes partisan polemics took over, with the Arsenites laying the blame on their opponents and vice versa, and likewise in the debate over Union. However, this period also produced less banal thinkers who reflected incisively on the causes and meaning of recent events. The Church bureaucrat and philosopher Georgios Pachymeres wrote a detailed and critical history of Michael VIII and Andronikos II that sought to identify specific decisions that led to loss of territory, money, and prestige. His work ranks among the best analyses of decline in Greek historiography.[90]

These subtle critiques rested on traditional foundations of classical study, which, despite the ongoing political retrenchment, enjoyed a golden age under the first Palaiologoi. Paradoxically, just as the Roman state was collapsing, its literary culture and art flourished and reached new heights. Michael VIII had prioritized the transfer of higher learning from Nikaia to Constantinople.[91] He even lifted his punishment of Holobolos for sedition so that he could teach in the refounded patriarchal school.[92] Most students there aspired to posts in the administration or Church, and the most ambitious sought to gain the attention and patronage of the aristocracy or the basileus, usually by delivering a riveting panegyric, a genre that flourished again under Andronikos. The rhetorical scene became so subtle and competitive that Nikephoros Gregoras, a student of Metochites, even composed a speech in the ancient Ionic dialect. Performances of encomia and other works of literature took place at ceremonial occasions and at literary gatherings, the *theatra*, a term that still referred to any occasion where orator and audience might interact. Some aspirants even mailed the text of their orations to colleagues or the basileus, hoping to be read and noticed.[93] But as Romanía shrank, so did the opportunities for advancement, resulting in heightened competition, which fueled rivalries and innovation.

The ideal outcome was experienced by Metochites. He was the son of an unrepentant Unionist who had been ejected from the court under Andronikos and relegated with his young son to Anatolia. But when the basileus moved to Anatolia in the early 1290s, Metochites, then about twenty years old, caught his attention with some nationalist speeches and was brought into the court system. Scholars who were noticed like this went on to enjoy careers in the administration or Church and were often sent on embassies. A few ended up wielding power. It is remarkable how many high officials of the state and Church not only had a classical education but continued to write and teach even while they carried out their official duties. Among secular officials, these included Georgios Akropolites (who studied under Blemmydes in the Nikaian state) and the *mesazontes* of Andronikos (in order, Theodoros Mouzalon, Nikephoros Choumnos, and Metochites), as well as the *megas logothetes* Konstantinos Akropolites (son of Georgios). The same was true of many clergymen. Gregorios II, who studied under Akropolites, was a teacher and classical scholar before he became patriarch and carried on with his scholarship while in office. His great enemy, Bekkos, the Unionist patriarch, had a mostly classical education before he turned to theology during Michael VIII's push for Union. The books that he left in his will included Thucydides, Lucian, Homer, and Aristotle.[94]

Remarkably, Andronikos allowed members of the royal family to marry the daughters of Choumnos, Metochites, and others ministers, thereby distinguishing their families. These men, and the learned class as a whole, were at best well-off but certainly not aristocratic: they were courtiers, secretaries, and scribblers with unimpressive names, so these marriages deviated from the dynastic practices of the Komnenian-Palaiologan superelite. Andronikos may have authorized them out of insecurity. It was precisely the upper echelons of the aristocracy—that is, his own extended family—that the basileus most suspected of plotting against him, and only one of them could realistically overthrow him. Yet that aristocracy trained for war more than anything, and avoided careers in the Church and civil service, which were open to men of humble origin. A Tarchaneiotes, praised by the poet Philes for painting his sword red in Bulgarian blood, even had scenes of his martial exploits depicted in the church of the Pammakaristos in the capital, which he renovated.[95] A small number of names recurs in the rolls of the realm's top military officers. Andronikos had to rely on his kin to command the armies and manage the largest pronoias. It is likely, therefore, that he promoted learned men, through elite marriages and by entrusting them with the civilian administration, as a counterweight to the aristocracy. Emperors of the eleventh century had used bishops and eunuchs in this way. In the process, these scholar-administrators became hugely rich, often through corrupt means. Choumnos confessed in a letter that his underlings were taking bribes, but noted in his own defense that he was taking less. Metochites was notoriously corrupt, "his money formed of the blood and tears of the poor." The two men famously feuded over their prose style.[96]

Scholarship and scientific learning also flourished. Most of it took place outside the political limelight and was carried out for intellectual reasons, not self-promotion. Classrooms and study halls were often literally cloistered, as many libraries were housed in monasteries, along with some leading scholars themselves. These collections were later broken up, yet by identifying their handwriting paleographers can reconstitute the history of individual codices and sometimes figure out who was working on which texts and where. The most important library was probably that of the monastery of Chora, especially after it was endowed by Metochites with funds, books, and the most spectacular mosaics and paintings, which exemplify the artistic efflorescence that was also taking place at this time (see Plates 7a–b, 8a).[97] In these scriptoria, scholars copied manuscripts of the ancient authors, to which we owe their survival.[98] Palaiologan manuscripts survive in greater numbers because, being late, they were less exposed to the vicissitudes of history. We are often lucky enough to have autograph copies of these scholars' work. But lateness was only one reason why their work looms so large in the history of classical scholarship. Palaiologan scholars gathered manuscripts to Constantinople and Thessalonike, where they prepared better editions, correcting errors in the transmission, in some cases by collating different manuscripts of the same text. They systematized the scholia that accompanied them in older editions and produced many collections, anthologies, lexica, textbooks, and commentaries. In two cases, liturgical texts were scraped off the page to make room for a Pindar and a lexicon.[99]

This activity is frequently called a "renaissance" but the Romans had never lost touch with the ancient sources of their culture or the ancient language. Early Palaiologan scholars were building on the work of their predecessors, and taking it to the next level. Modern classicists are indebted to their editorial work, especially to the labors of Maximos Planoudes, Pachymeres, Manuel Moschopoulos, Demetrios Triklinios, Thomas Magistros, Georgios Oinaiotes, and others. Triklinios in particular made major advances in the understanding of meter, which he used in his edition of Pindar. They were not all men. A niece of Michael VIII, Theodora Raoulaina, was a nun, patron of monasteries, and opponent of Union. She also copied ancient texts and corresponded with male colleagues.[100] Whether they know it or not, modern classicists stand in a tradition that goes directly back to these east Romans, a tradition that, a century later, was transported to the west and curated by the Italian humanists.

The intellectual life of this period also had distinctive traits. One was the beginning of a movement to learn Latin and translate works from it into Greek. The impetus here was to learn more about the western culture that was shaping not just the foreign policy but the social conflicts and even the faith of the east Romans. A small start was made by the anti-Unionist Holobolos, who translated philosophical works by Boethius, adding at the end of one of them that "you may wrap these syllogisms, friend, around the Latin's neck and strangle him."[101] Planoudes went much further, translating works by Ovid, Cicero, Macrobius, Augustine, and Boethius, and was a better philologist. He first supported Michael VIII's policy of Union, but changed his position under Andronikos. While he did bowdlerize the more risqué passages of Ovid, the goal of his project was probably less political and more literary, to give the Romans access to the "West's Greatest Hits."[102]

A second remarkable feature of the intellectual milieu was the emphasis that it placed on mathematics and astronomy. Even scholars who worked primarily on literature, and poetry at that, seriously studied technical fields. Planoudes wrote a treatise on Arabic numerals, which he called "Indian," not necessarily because that name was more accurate but because it was less tainted in Orthodox eyes. In this work he introduced his countrymen to the concept of "zero."[103] Triklinios wrote a brief treatise on lunar theory and, while he was running the empire, Metochites wrote a massive astronomical treatise upholding the Ptolemaic tradition against its more recent eastern rivals. It is likely that he was responding to the work of one Gregorios Chioniades, who around 1300 had traveled via Trebizond to Tabriz, the Ilkhanid Mongol capital, and returned with a store of "Persian" astronomical data, which he published in Greek translation.[104] The most impressive astronomical feats belonged to Nikephoros Gregoras, a student of Metochites and first-rate historian and philosopher. In 1324, Gregoras realized that the Julian calendar undercounted the length of the year by a small fraction each day. He put his findings before his scientific peers and explained them to Andronikos, who realized that he was right but decided not to go to the trouble of changing the calendar, which he said would create confusion; the basileus and clergy also feared a split in the Church over the matter. But Gregoras believed that in just two or three years everyone could be trained in the new system. In 1329, he wrote a letter to a colleague predicting three eclipses that would happen in the next year, one solar and two lunar, specifying the year, date, time of day or night, and duration of each eclipse.[105] Intellectually, the Romans were punching above their weight, but remained conservative. Gregoras' corrections to the calendar were not adopted and few used the Arabic numerals.

A third distinguishing mark of these writers was their willingness to take strident and sometimes unconventional positions, especially regarding politics. The impetus was the collapse of the Roman state, which called for both explanation and remedy, and they were enabled by the weakness of Andronikos, who did not want to jeopardize his shaky legitimacy by creating more enemies by persecution, as his father had done. While always suspicious, Andronikos preferred to talk it out, apologize for his own failings, and avoid imposing severe punishments. What many intellectuals did was double down on traditional Roman ideas whose strident expression melded into criticism of the regime and a diagnosis for what went wrong. For example, a strong emphasis was placed in rhetorical, didactic, and philosophical works on the public nature of the state and its assets, with reminders that the basileus was only a caretaker of the public good, not its owner or beneficiary. State revenue should be used solely to benefit the Romans as a whole, and not just a coterie of favorites. Taxes should not be farmed; offices should not be sold or given to inexperienced royal relatives; and national defense should be entrusted to native-born soldiers, not mercenaries. The Catalan debacle would have been on everyone's mind after 1304.[106]

The political thought of this period frequently innovated when it wrestled with the polity's rapidly declining circumstances. The gentleman-scholar Thomas Magistros wrote a work *On the Polity* addressed to his fellow Thessalonians. It treats the individual city, not the whole of Romanía, as the basic unit of self-governance and self-defense. Even women, he argues, should be trained to defend their city. Nikephoros Choumnos, apparently shocked at the corruption of the judicial system and the oppression of the poor by the rich, addressed a treatise to the people of Thessalonike advising them how justice should be administrated. As cities increasingly charted their own course, they acquired distinct identities. This reflected the looser, more contractual relationship that emerged between them and Constantinople after 1204.[107]

Striking analyses came from Metochites, Andronikos' prime minister, "a living library who spoke like a book." While he helmed "the shipwreck of the Roman empire" in the 1320s, he wrote a vast collection of essays in prose tangled "like a stormy sea."[108] Metochites developed original perspectives on topics of literature, history, and identity. Like Theodoros II Laskaris, he cast the ancient Hellenes as the ancestors of the modern Romans, seeking to appropriate their achievements to the credit of his own people, yet he too failed to explain how this Hellenic ancestry and identity meshed and interfaced with the Roman one. In contrast to Laskaris, Metochites was sharply critical of many Greek writers and thinkers, and he astutely recognized that Greek history was famous not because it was the most important but because it was recorded in brilliant texts. Other peoples throughout history had accomplished greater things than the Greeks, but they lacked a Thucydides. Moreover, Metochites was willing to extrapolate from current trajectories and conclude that the Roman monarchy—a world empire allegedly founded jointly by Augustus and Christ—would one day end. Not only that, he suspected that the Mongols, a nomadic culture that stood for the opposite of Roman civilization, was ascendant in world history and was possibly the wave of the future.[109]

The early Palaiologan revival of letters was not, as it is often presented, a paradox, occurring as it did during a time of political troubles. It was the result of the restoration of the state by Michael VIII, which invested in institutions of learning. All the leading intellectuals of this period and the following generation were produced during the optimistic years of the restoration. When the political project began to fail after 1300, the intellectual scene dried up too.

Ascendancy of the Church?

The Romans had no illusions: their polity could well fall and be replaced by a patchwork of Latin, Mongol, or Turkish states. This was already happening in many lands that Romanía had lost, from southern Italy to eastern Anatolia. Yet modern historians believe that a further shift in the balance of power was occurring within Roman society, namely the Church was gaining in importance relative to the state, even becoming ascendant over it. Treatises written by clergy argued that the basileus owed his legitimacy and office to the Church. The patriarch Athanasios believed that the Church was superior and in some respects autonomous, or "free," of the state, partly on the questionable grounds that it was older and more spiritual than it.[110] Common people turned more to the Church for material and spiritual succor. The patriarch and Synod became more assertive in matters of domestic and even foreign policy, and ecclesiastical networks sometimes survived the conquest of the Roman lands, giving the Church institutional reach beyond the shrinking borders of the state. Finally, the judicial functions of the patriarch and Synod expanded to include property disputes and even criminal cases and not just marriage and inheritance law. Andronikos empowered Athanasios to arbitrate disputes and decide which cases to refer to the basileus. As a result, long lines of people with envelopes full of paperwork formed every day at the patriarch's front door.[111]

There is some truth to the notion of a more prominent Church, but also much exaggeration, especially for the reign of Andronikos. The Church was in turmoil at this time, torn by division, instability, and poverty, and almost all the patriarchs were deposed on doctrinal, criminal, or procedural grounds because of internal enmities. The basileis could appoint and depose patriarchs almost at will, often in violation of canon law, and ultimately they had their way in almost any matter relating to the Church. They did so either through consensus building and the manufacture of consent or through intimidation and violence, but in the end they could steer the Church in the desired direction. They could also confiscate Church and monastic lands for reasons of state, and there was nothing that the Church could do to stop them, other than to note politely that this went against canon law. Athanasios could only send an olive branch when Andronikos tried to do this in Bithynia. In 1367, the Synod noted with resignation that, "if the holy basileus wants to take [these lands] on his own authority, which is what he wants to do, let him do so. It was he who gave them to the Church, so he can take them back if he wants to."[112]

The growing prominence of the Church is in part an illusion created by the survival of its sources, as we have no secular or state archives but ample monastic ones and two extraordinary collections of Synodal decisions from the period 1315–1402.[113] Once we correct for this bias, a different picture emerges: the Church was being deputized by the state to provide essential services. In particular, the expanded judicial role of the bishops served state interests in the same way that it had since the days of Constantine the Great: when the state was inundated with more casework than it could process—as it certainly was under Andronikos, given the massive disruptions affecting all aspects of life—it outsourced part of that load to the bishops, who were respected and often knew the law. This is also possibly why Andronikos transferred the administrative supervision of the monasteries of Mt. Athos from himself to the patriarch, casting it as the restoration of an original arrangement that had been distorted over time.[114] As for the treatises that argued for a dominant Church, some of them were written by radical Arsenites who did not speak for the mainstream of either the Church or society. Athanasios' views were also in the minority, as he was unable to control his clergy, who strongly resisted his efforts at their moral reform and forced him to resign twice. He also failed to persuade the basileus to back his causes, such as to monasticize the secular society of Constantinople, and his more idiosyncratic views were simply ignored. What the patriarch encountered and complained about was widespread "disregard of the commandments owed to the Church." He suspected that the basileus was tossing his petitions away, and when he could not even obtain a audience with him "my face filled with shame."[115] This was no champion of a Church ascendant. As he and Andronikos perceptively realized, there was a whiff of John Chrysostom in both his "spiritual wrath" and his failure.[116] The court was still calling the shots, but Church spokesmen dominated the airwaves.

Andronikos II and Andronikos III

After the Catalan storm, the 1310s were a period of relative calm. By 1321, Andronikos was allegedly pulling in revenues of one million (debased) hyperpyra per year. This sounds exaggerated, or represents an unusual haul. According to one estimate, the ordinary revenues were perhaps half a million per year and the total military expenses were not more than 150,000. Andronikos was prepared to give 50,000 to a general, the aristocrat and future basileus Ioannes Kantakouzenos, if he would fight the Catalans in Thessaly. He also gave 10,000 to his son Theodoros of Montferrat in 1318, either for his own use or to fund the Ghibelline faction in the Genoese civil war. These sums are a striking contrast to the court's poverty a decade previously. But Andronikos had to squeeze his subjects to collect these sums, giving him a reputation for oppressive taxation and fomenting discontent that advanced his grandson's rebellion in 1321.[117] Tax collecting was so important to his courtiers that Metochites placed an image of the Holy Family's Enrollment for Taxation, an otherwise rare theme, in a prominent position in the Chora church, adjacent to an image of the martyr St. Andronikos (see Plate 8a).[118]

The Romans both gained and lost territories in the 1310s. The greatest loss was the despotate of Epeiros. In order to maintain his independence from Michael VIII, the despot Nikephoros had made alliances that signaled his subordination to Charles of Anjou. In 1294, he gave his daughter Thamar in marriage to Philippe of Taranto, Charles' grandson, along with some cities along the Gulf of Corinth, such as Naupaktos, on condition that their inhabitants would be allowed to practice the Orthodox faith. Yet through the usual feudal legalism, Charles' heirs, Philippe and his father Charles II, twisted these alliances into an Angevin "claim" to the whole of the despotate, asserting "rights" to it just as they did to Albania, the principality of Achaea, Athens, Thessaly, and Constantinople. The basis of these alleged rights to Epeiros is reported only in western sources, so they cannot be entirely trusted. During those years, western Europe, especially France and Rome, was still abuzz with talk of a "crusade" to capture Constantinople, but until that materialized the Angevins launched military invasions to make good on their claims to Epeiros. However, Nikephoros' young son and heir Thomas Komnenos Doukas heroically defeated two invasions, in 1304 and 1306. But in 1318, Thomas was murdered by his nephew, Nicola Orsini, the count of Kephalonia and Zakynthos. The Orsini had ruled the islands since before the Fourth Crusade, and Nicola now exchanged that county for the despotate. His mother was Thomas' sister, so he was half-Roman himself, and he quickly married Thomas' widow (a daughter of Michael IX) and professed Orthodoxy in order to win over his Roman subjects. He refused to bow to Philippe of Taranto and obtained recognition from Andronikos, though he presently accepted Venice as his patron and was then murdered by his brother Giovanni in 1323. The despotate became a contested realm, switching rulers over the next century from the Orsini and Constantinople (1337–1348) to various Serb, Albanian, and ethnically mixed lords.[119]

Ioannina, however, chose a different path. Its people declared for the basileus and the city was immediately received into the Roman fold. In 1319–1321, Andronikos issued chrysobulls that, following the tradition established by Nikaia during its expansion in the Balkans, confirmed the local autonomy of the citizens of Ioannina and granted them extensive exemption from royal taxation, trading fees, and conscription into the royal army, except for the purpose of civic defense. The basileus rejoiced that the madness of division had finally been overcome and that such a magnificent city "was now wholeheartedly rejoining the common mother of their own race, namely the universal Church of those Christians who believe as we do and the joint association of all Romans in submission to our reign."[120] Meanwhile, Thessaly was fragmenting. The Catalans seized a number of towns in the south, including Neopatras (Hypate), Domokos, and Pharsala, while most of the rest stayed in the hands of local lords. The Synod of Constantinople wrote to the latter, pleading with them to "submit to the basileus so that the Roman state can again be unified, as it was before." But this did not accomplish anything.[121]

With the revenues that he now enjoyed, Andronikos planned to establish a fleet of twenty ships and station 1,000 cavalry in Bithynia and 2,000 more in Thrace and Macedonia.[122] But dynastic turmoil intervened. Specifically, his son and co-basileus Michael IX died at Thessalonike in October, 1320, at the age of forty-three. It was believed that the cause was grief at the death of his younger son Manuel, who was accidentally murdered in the capital by men whom Michael's older son, Andronikos III, had set to ambush a rival for the favors of a lover. This Andronikos was twenty-five and a co-basileus, but after this scandal Andronikos II began to withdraw his favor and signaled that he might divert the succession to Michael IX's brother, the despot Konstantinos. The senior basileus also began to suspect that Andronikos III and his circle of supporters were plotting rebellion. He sought to disperse them and hold them accountable. This precipitated what he most feared: Andronikos III slipped out of Constantinople in April, 1321, raced to Adrianople, and raised the standards of revolt with support from the armies of Thrace. The old basileus immediately ordered the Synod to proclaim his grandson an outlaw.[123] The Synod had taken over the functions of the Senate in proclaiming rebels as "enemies of the Roman people."

The ensuing conflict is recounted in extraordinary detail by two historians who were participants but often found themselves on opposite sides, Nikephoros Gregoras and Ioannes Kantakouzenos. Gregoras was with Metochites at the court of Andronikos II, whereas Kantakouzenos was Andronikos III's main supporter and was writing many years later to set the record straight in response to Gregoras, with whom he later clashed over theology too. Kantakouzenos justifies his later usurpation by insinuating, through fictitious speeches, that Andronikos II and III both regarded him, Kantakouzenos, as worthy of the throne. While both historians were biased, they were subtle narrators and did not hide the mistakes of their own side.

What led to this first civil war? Andronikos II was old and generally unpopular, especially in the provinces, which he had taxed heavily in order to restore his revenues. That is why Andronikos III immediately canceled taxes in Thrace and confiscated the money gathered by the collectors, distributing it to his followers and raising a large army.[124] Andronikos II was also perceived as a timid, tired, and unwarlike ruler who had failed to defend the Romans, especially in Anatolia. No triumphs had been celebrated in Constantinople during his reign. Andronikos III drove those points home and presented himself as a young warrior who would restore the Romans' arms and pride and even "expand their borders" by personally fighting in Bithynia.[125] Finally, there was a generational gap. Andronikos III was backed by younger men, such as Kantakouzenos, who saw little chance for rapid promotion in the gerontocratic court of Andronikos II and Metochites. Moreover, some of his supporters, including Kantakouzenos and Theodoros Synadenos, came from the retinue of his father, Michael IX, and they feared that the succession might be diverted to another branch of the royal family, leaving them in the cold. This is likely why the Thracian armies rallied to his cause. Andronikos III reassigned many pronoias in Thrace to his partisans and promoted his inner circle to high offices.[126]

When Andronikos III appeared before Constantinople with his army, Andronikos II came to terms. According to the power-sharing treaty of Region (June, 1321), Andronikos III would rule Thrace whereas Andronikos II would govern the rest and have authority over foreign policy. This division of the realm seems to be indicated on coins issued at this time bearing the basileus and the Prophet Ahijah, who foretold the division between the kingdoms of Israel and Judah.[127] But this experiment quickly broke down. Some of Andronikos III's supporters, notably one Syrgiannes Philanthropenos Palaiologos, defected to the senior basileus, who ordered his armies to attack his grandson from both the City and Thessalonike, where he had dispatched his son, the despot Konstantinos. But Andronikos III, whose rebellion was now being bankrolled by the hugely rich Kantakouzenos, his *megas domestikos*, survived this double attack. Moreover, the people of Thessalonike rose up against the despot Konstantinos and declared for the young basileus. Konstantinos was imprisoned at Didymoteichon, then tonsured and removed from the line of succession. Andronikos III's success led to a revised agreement with his grandfather at Epibates, in July, 1322. The realm was reunited; the appointments of Andronikos III's followers were confirmed; and the two basileis would rule jointly, with Andronikos III based at Didymoteichon. He would receive an allowance of 36,000 hyperpyra, excluding the cost of his army. That army, which both supported him and pressured him, seems to have included many displaced soldiers from Anatolia.[128]

The agreement of Epibates worked surprisingly well for five years, probably because the faction around Andronikos III won what it wanted. The grandson's militarism also paid off. The Bulgarians attacked Thrace in 1322, taking advantage of Roman dissension. They captured Philippopolis and raided as far as Adrianople. But Andronikos III and Kantakouzenos took Philippopolis back and, in 1323, also Mesembria. They could not bear "for the honor of the Roman state to be despised by barbarians." A Mongol invasion of Thrace was defeated in 1324. Around that time, the blind old general Alexios Philanthropenos, the one who had rebelled in Anatolia in 1295, was sent back there to relieve a Turkish siege of Philadelpheia, which he did successfully.[129] That city would remain a free Roman enclave until 1391, as it chanced to fall at the intersection of Germiyan, Aydin, and Saruhan, none of whom wanted the others to take it.[130] However, Prousa (Brusa) in Bithynia fell to the resurgent Ottomans in 1326 and became their capital city (Nikaia fell in 1331 and Nikomedeia in 1337). While Andronikos III was preoccupied with the military defense of Thrace, Andronikos II handled foreign diplomacy, but none too vigorously. He capitulated to the Venetians in the treaty of 1324, paying them the reparations that they demanded (even for Genoese hostilities against them) and allowing them to sell Black Sea grain anywhere in his realm.[131] Yet overall the two Andronikoi were in accord. On 2 February, 1325, the young basileus was crowned in Hagia Sophia, and a year later he married

Giovanna of Savoy, renamed Anna, a bride chosen by the elder basileus. At the ceremony, the groom crowned her Augusta and then engaged in jousting competitions with her Savoyard retinue.[132]

Both sides blamed each other for the outbreak of the second round of civil war in 1327. It began in a strange way. The governor of Thessalonike was the *panhypersebastos* Ioannes Palaiologos, a nephew of Andronikos II. In 1326, he declared that he would not be subject to a basileus and would independently rule the lands that he governed. He allied himself to the kralj of Serbia, Stefan Uroš III Dečanski, by giving him his daughter in marriage, and advanced with his forces to Serres. Andronikos II immediately recognized him as a *kaisar* and sent him the appropriate insignia, which he donned at Skopje. It has been proposed that all this was a plot by Metochites, as the bride was his granddaughter and the governors of Strumica and Melnik, who aided the rebel, were his sons. The court was aiming at another encirclement of the young basileus, even at the cost of dividing the realm. The unpopular faction around the *mesazon* had realized that it was only a matter of time until Andronikos III took over and completely froze them out of power. When the *panhypersebastos* Ioannes died suddenly of illness, Metochites wrote a long poetic lament in his honor. The period of harmony was over.[133]

This time the basileis sought outside allies. The court of Andronikos II sent envoys to the Serbian kralj, whose secret mission was to establish an alliance against Andronikos III. One of them was Gregoras, who wrote a colorful account of the journey and the Slavic-speaking brigands who infested the lands of western Macedonia. For his part, in May, 1327 Andronikos III personally met with the tsar of Bulgaria, Mihail Šišman, at Didymoteichon and made a treaty with him aimed against his grandfather. He then advanced toward the capital, trying to win the population over to his cause, even his grandfather's own emissaries. Andronikos II pressured the patriarch Esaias and the Synod to excommunicate him, but most of them refused. The patriarch was confined to the Mangana monastery. Andronikos III approached the walls of the City in November, but the guards would not open the gates, despite his growing popularity inside. The young basileus was promising a new age of military victory and tax relief. His uncle, Theodoros of Montferrat, who was visiting Constantinople, joined his cause too. Theodoros and Metochites appear to have been bitter rivals for the ear of Andronikos II. The marquis could not understand why his father listened to this evil philosopher who knew nothing about warfare, rather than to his own son.[134]

Meanwhile, the new governor of Thessalonike, the despot Demetrios (a son of Andronikos II), was confiscating the properties of the supporters of Andronikos III in Macedonia. But in December, 1327, the latter was informed that the people of Thessalonike had again declared for him. He rushed to the city, circumventing the guards posted by Demetrios, and entered in disguise. When he revealed his identity, he was given a hero's welcome and won over most Macedonian cities, including Edessa, Kastoria, Beroia, and Ohrid, though Prosek, Strumica, and Melnik stuck with his grandfather. Serbia had done little to help Andronikos II, though Bulgaria switched sides and joined his cause: Mihail Šišman sent a cavalry force to help defend the capital, perhaps in the hopes "of creating a single state for himself that stretched from Constantinople to the Danube," but neither basileus wanted him there and he was persuaded to withdraw. The writing was on the wall for the old regime. The populace of Constantinople was in a foul mood and hungry, as the Venetians and Genoese were at odds again and the former were not allowing the latter to unload Black Sea grain in the City. Metochites left his house and went to live with the old basileus. The two men huddled together in the palace as support drained away. It was inevitable that some guards would allow the young basileus to enter, which he did on the night of 23 May with some 800 men. Andronikos III entered the Blachernai palace to the accompaniment of chants of acclamation and found his grandfather clasping the icon of the Virgin Hodegetria in supplication, pleading to be spared: "Think how many years of my reign are now undone in one night." He had been basileus for 67 years, and senior emperor for 47. The victor put the old man under protective arrest and freed the patriarch Esaias. There was little looting, except for Metochites' townhouse, which was plundered by the populace. Knowing what was coming, the *megas logothetes* had distributed many of his valuables to friends and relatives in advance.[135]

Andronikos II was confined to the palace. In late 1329, the new basileus fell gravely ill and many who had a claim to the throne, including Andronikos II, were forced to become monks and take loyalty oaths; the old basileus now became the monk Antonios. When some priests were found commemorating the "basileus-monk Antonios," he was additionally required to renounce his claim to the throne. He was regularly visited by Gregoras and his own daughter Simonis, who had returned to Constantinople after the death of her Serb husband Milutin in 1321 to become a nun. Andronikos-Antonios died in 1332 and was buried in state at Lips, a monastery that his mother had refounded. As for Metochites, his properties were confiscated and he was exiled under harsh conditions to Didymoteichon, where he wrote philosophical poems on the vicissitudes of life. In 1330, he was allowed to return to Constantinople and become a monk at the Chora monastery, which he had refounded and where his precious (and mostly secular) library had survived. He was not allowed to speak with Andronikos, but he could from afar discern the ruins of his manor. Suffering from many ailments, Metochites died a month after his master and was buried at the Chora. Gregoras pronounced the eulogy at both funerals.[136]

The civil war between the Andronikoi was essentially a forced generational transfer of power from men in their sixties to men in their twenties. It was fought with remarkably little bloodshed, only skirmishes. We lack reliable data, but it appears that the armies mustered on either side were extremely small, and most operations were carried out with a few hundred men. When the rebels cut the City off from Macedonia and western Thrace, the old regime was apparently left with no armies; there was no Anatolian hinterland from which to draw up reserves. The contest was mostly to win over cities through persuasion and promises, so urban residents and local notables gained leverage in deciding the future of the kingdom as a whole. The Romans were fortunate that no foreign power took advantage of their discord to seize territory. It would not be so in future civil wars.

The Palaiologan dynasty would henceforth be extremely prone to division and internal conflict, and this first civil war revealed why. In the past, ambitious men fought for access to power at the court, but not necessarily for their personal fortunes, which were invested in land. However, with the loss of Roman territory and consolidation of state lands into pronoias, which the court could assign and then reassign to its favorites, the contest among elites was also over socioeconomic status and even survival. When one faction seized power, it could redistribute the pronoias among itself, without which its members would remain second-rate players or even lose their elite status. The victor was under extreme pressure to reward his followers with lands, and they might rebel against *him* in order to get them: Kantakouzenos' own son threatened that when his father won another civil war in 1347.[137] There was no lack of ambitious men, but resources could now maintain only a small elite and there was little resilience or redundancy left in the state economy, especially as the Balkans now had to accommodate Anatolian refugees. There was nothing to fall back on, which is why cities such as Adrianople and Didymoteichon, which were near fertile valleys, rose in relative importance.[138] Thus, Andronikos III's first measure upon becoming sole basileus was to restore confiscated lands to their prewar owners; he was being furiously lobbied on this point by partisans of both sides. Promises of land allotments was now the stuff of politics and rebellion.[139]

As more territory was lost to foreign conquest, the internal conflict over the remaining scraps became fiercer. Individuals and cities could be enticed to switch sides through concessions and tax exemptions.[140] Thus, the cause of Palaiologan infighting was the structure of the state economy, not some defect in the family's character. To their credit, the Palaiologoi gradually retired the practice of blinding or maiming defeated rivals, especially as the conflicts were increasingly localized within the family. The political cost of blinding Ioannes IV, for example, had been steep. At least now, in 1328, the Romans had a young basileus who promised to halt the decline and bring back the days of prosperity and victory.

PART TEN

DIGNITY IN DEFEAT

35
Military Failure and Mystical Refuge (1328–1354)

After the loss of Anatolia, most Romans understood that the very survival of their state and society was at stake. Their resources were limited and there was nowhere to fall back in case of another reversal. Their greatest fear in the recent past was of a western crusade, but that had now receded. Instead, they were surrounded by neighbors who were raiding their territories and nibbling away at their forts and lands. The Bulgarians were doing this on a small scale; Serb power was growing alarmingly in this period, and had detached many cities in the northwest from Romanía; and the Turks had settled into many regional emirates across Anatolia, from where they launched raids across the Hellespont into Thrace or across the Aegean to the islands on a regular basis. Romans traveling across their own lands, even high officials with escorts, often ran into marauders. Thousands were taken away into captivity and agricultural life was severely disrupted. Census documents from this period list some lands as "uninhabited because of the attacks of the Turks . . . the *paroikoi* have left and are living elsewhere."[1] A traveler in the 1320s saw "uninhabited places, burned by the barbarians; churches in ruins, icons trampled underfoot . . . people hunted down like prey." Many of the displaced had no choice but to turn to banditry.[2]

Even the popes were beginning to realize, as early as 1306, that the "Greek empire" was vulnerable to Turkish conquest, and if that happened it might be irrevocable.[3] The basileus could still be described in papal texts as "the enemy of the Roman Church and of all faithful Christians."[4] Yet a different view was emerging too. The Venetian Marin Sanudo Torsello advocated an anti-Turkish alliance among the western powers, including the Hospitallers of Rhodes and even the Greeks, if they would join. The Greeks were seen both as schismatics and potential allies. This presaged a major shift in crusading ideology from attacking them to helping them against the Turks, as the latter were now threatening western interests. An allied fleet—with no east Roman involvement—sailed to the Aegean in 1334, but accomplished little.[5]

Andronikos III Palaiologos

The reign of Andronikos III (1328–1341) was the last during which the Romans made a concerted effort not only to defend their territories with arms but to recover losses. Andronikos did not always succeed, but he was the last who tried. According to Gregoras, his armies were insufficient, but Kantakouzenos, the *megas domestikos*, presents a positive picture of the armed forces.[6] From the rare reliable numbers given in their narratives, it appears that a large campaign force of this period consisted of 2,000 men.[7] Andronikos himself disliked the pomp and ceremony of court life in the capital and preferred to live on campaign and spend his downtime at Didymoteichon, hunting if possible. He did not solicit panegyrics, poetry, or literature about himself. He was easygoing but aloof, and did not insist on formal distinctions of rank. He liked jousting, which Gregoras called the "Olympic games" of that time.[8] Kantakouzenos was also active in war and diplomacy (about half of his *History* is made up of speeches, often his own). The *protostrator* Theodoros Synadenos was placed in charge of Constantinople, while finances were entrusted to Alexios Apokaukos, an allegedly self-made tax official. All three had backed Andronikos' rebellion in 1321. After restoring their properties to those who had lost them during the civil war, Andronikos waived the taxes that weighed heaviest on the people of the capital and allowed them to have vineyards or homes on state lands rent-free.[9]

Andronikos and Kantakouzenos spent much of their time chasing down Turkish raiders in Thrace and Macedonia and defending Romanía against Serb and Bulgarian incursions. In the spring of 1329, they led an army to Anatolia to relieve Nikaia, which was besieged by the Ottomans, but they were badly defeated at Pelekanon and withdrew; the city fell in 1331.[10] In the fall of 1329, the basileus assembled a fleet and retook Chios from the Zaccaria of Phokaia. Martino Zaccaria had been successfully leading the fight against the Turks in the Aegean, some of whom he forced to pay him tribute, and he justified his hold on Chios by claiming that only he was able to defend it. He had obtained from Philippe of Taranto the nominal right to rule over Lesbos, Chios, Samos, and Kos, along with the title "king and despot of Asia Minor." The revenues from Chios were said to be 200,000 gold coins. But Andronikos put an end to his ambitions. He retook the island and Martino was arrested and sent to Constantinople, over the objections of the local Chiots who wanted to kill him there and then.

Andronikos then advanced on Phokaia, which let him in. He was recognized as its nominal ruler and left a few days later, entrusting it again to the Genoese. Thus, the web of fictional Latin "rights" to the eastern Aegean was shredded. Two things stand out about this campaign: first that the basileus was able to muster a fleet, allegedly of 105 ships, though many of them belonged to his allies such as the duke of Naxos or were merchant ships converted into transports for the campaign; and second, that Andronikos made alliances with two emirs, Saruhan and Mehmed of Aydın, meeting the former personally (the latter claimed to be too ill to pay his respects in person). In the Aegean war of all against all, the Romans were keeping their options open and making alliances with both Latins and Turks.[11] In 1333, the basileus went to Anatolia to relieve Nikomedeia, where he made a treaty with Orhan (1326–1360), the son and successor of Osman. The basileus would pay him 12,000 hyperpyra per year in exchange for peace for the remaining free Bithynian cities.[12] Orhan had emerged out from the shadow of his father's defeat by the Mongols in 1307. He was not a pastoral nomadic bandit but the ruler of a proper state Bithynia. His capital was at Bursa (Prousa), where he presided over a sophisticated bureaucracy and amassed considerable wealth. He struck his own coins and engaged in an extensive building program.

Andronikos was keen to restore the dignity of Roman arms, but not the exalted position of the basileus. He met with his peers and allies on the frontier, exchanged gifts with them, and made treaties, usually after they had raided and counterraided each other's territories. Basileus, tsar, and kralj were by now peer monarchs on the Balkan stage. And the balance of power among them was changing. In 1330, the Serbs defeated the Bulgarians at the battle of Velbažd, where the tsar himself was mortally wounded. The following year, the victorious kralj Dečanski was murdered by the supporters of his son, who took the throne as Stefan Uroš IV Dušan (1331–1355). Dušan aspired to conquer Roman Macedonia and so he made a lasting alliance with new Bulgarian tsar, Ivan Aleksandar (1331–1371). In 1332, when Andronikos III invaded Bulgaria, Ivan Aleksandar, reinforced by an army of Mongols, defeated him at Rosokastron. The Romans again lost Mesembria and Anchialos (these cities switched hands often).[13] Andronikos, always on the move, made up for these losses in 1333, when his armies annexed the chaotic marches of Thessaly, all the way down to the Catalan border. On his return to Thessalonike, Andronikos met with Dušan and came to an unspecified agreement with him.[14] Yet the next year, 1334, Dušan marched directly for Thessalonike and stopped only because the Roman traitor who was opening a path for him, Syrgiannes Philanthropenos Palaiologos, a former governor of Thessalonike, was assassinated by an agent of the basileus. Andronikos and Dušan met again outside the city and came to a new agreement. Serbia would keep Ohrid, Prilep, Strumica, and a few other fortified towns that Dušan had taken.[15]

The career and personality of Syrgiannes are bizarre. Between the 1310s and 1334, he changed sides so often in both civil and foreign conflicts that no sense can be made of his politics, nor can it be explained why the two Andronikoi failed to convict him even when he was repeatedly put on trial, and then reappointed him to sensitive posts, only to be betrayed again.[16]

In the second half of the 1330s, the regime hit its stride. In late 1335, the Genoese lord of Phokaia, Domenico Cattaneo, renounced his nominal allegiance to the basileus and, with naval assistance from Genoa, the duchy of Naxos, and the Hospitallers of Rhodes, seized Mytilene and overran most of Lesbos, minting coins as "Despot of Mytilene." Meanwhile, his countrymen at Galata fortified their city in preparation for reprisals. Andronikos' response was swift. He demolished some of the fortifications around Galata and assembled a fleet, variously reported as of 20 or 84 ships. Cattaneo was soon blockaded in Mytilene by the *pinkernes* Alexios Philanthropenos, the now elderly and blind rebel of 1295, while the basileus and Kantakouzenos blockaded Phokaia on the mainland. There they received assistance from the emir Saruhan and a visit by Umur, the emir of Aydın, the most fearsome raider in the Aegean, celebrated in a later Turkish epic. The basileus made an anti-Latin and anti-Ottoman treaty with him, while the emir and Kantakouzenos hit it off and became not only allies but friends. After a long blockade, in 1336 Mytilene was returned to Roman control and Phokaia surrendered, on condition that it still be governed by Cattaneo. The whole episode reinforced views of the Latins as faithless opportunists and reinvigorated Roman pride, so much so that a vernacular epic poem of this period, the *History of Belisarios*, fuses the achievements of Justinian's famous general with those of the widely admired Philanthropenos, who stayed on as Lesbos' governor.[17]

Even as Mongol and Turkish war bands raided Thrace, sometimes coming to blows among themselves "like dogs fighting over a corpse," Andronikos pursued his irridentist agenda. Only small units could be mustered to counter the raiders, but an opportunity that opened up in the west could not be missed. Giovanni Orsini, the ruler of the rump Epeirot state at Arta, died suddenly in 1335 and his heir, Nikephoros, was a child, while his widow, Anna, was a Palaiologina. In 1338, the basileus and Kantakouzenos were in the region of Berat, using an army of 2,000 Turks on loan from Umur to annihilate and enslave groups of Albanians, who at that time were migrating southward into Greece in large numbers. The Albanians were nomadic highlanders, who sought refuge in the mountains when trouble approached, but the Turks could follow them there. When Anna invited the basileus to confirm her son as despot, he and Kantakouzenos instead annexed Epeiros to the kingdom of the Romans. That, Kantakouzenos claimed, is where it belonged ever since it had been "unjustly" severed by the Latins in 1204. The Turks were sent home and the basileus toured his new domains, winning the locals over with grants and honors. Synadenos was appointed governor at Arta. Andronikos had, "without battles, restored to the Romans what had been lost to them since the days of Alexios III Angelos."[18]

Yet some Epeirot nobles had other plans. They whisked young Nikephoros off to Taranto so that he could be used in a counterplay by Catherine of Valois, the titular heiress of the old Latin empire and the Principality of Achaea. She even personally relocated to Achaea to monitor the revolution that was being fomented throughout Epeiros with Angevin support. Synadenos was imprisoned by the rebels. In response, Andronikos sent in an advance army in 1339 and came in person in 1340, with Kantakouzenos. After long sieges, eventually all the centers of resistance capitulated, more through diplomacy than force. In his speeches to the rebels, Kantakouzenos argued that Epeiros had belonged to the realm of the basileus "since the days of Caesar Augustus," and that Romans should not be bringing in "foreigners from Taranto." By contrast, the rebels regarded Epeiros as their "fatherland" and the Angeloi, not the basileis of Constantinople, as their proper lords. They needed to be convinced that service to the basileus would be preferable, but fear of his armies provided half the argument. Nikephoros was engaged to Kantakouzenos' daughter; Synadenos was posted to Thessalonike; and Arta was entrusted to Kantakouzenos' cousin, the *pinkernes* Ioannes Angelos. The "Despotate" of Epeiros had ended. That name for it had emerged among Latins (who regarded anything ruled by a despot as a "despotate") and was only formally recognized by Constantinople in 1342. Epeiros had survived for 130 years without specifying its nature as a state (except in the heady days of 1225–1230 when it had reached for the basileia), yet it had managed to sustain a separatist Roman identity of its own.[19]

Andronikos III's push to restore the pride of Roman arms ended when he died suddenly on 15 June, 1341, of an unspecified illness. Within a decade, his gains in the west would be wiped out, the Roman state would lose half of its remaining territories, and its population would be decimated by the Black Death. In the midst of these catastrophes, the cultural scene came to be dominated by Athonite monks who had different ideas about salvation.

Civil war, again

Andronikos' son Ioannes was nine when the basileus died. Ioannes had not been crowned and Andronikos had not appointed a formal regency, yet the four obvious choices came together to steer the ship of state: the basileus' widow, Anna of Savoy; the patriarch Ioannes XIV Kalekas (1334–1347); the *megas domestikos* Kantakouzenos; and Alexios Apokaukos, who was in charge of finances, the fleet (as *megas doux*), and the capital. Rivalries within this group, however, quickly tore it apart and led to another round of civil war that would last for six years (1341–1347). Unfortunately, our two narrative sources, Gregoras and Kantakouzenos, are both Kantakouzenist at this point and blame Apokaukos for everything, stigmatizing him as lowborn, greedy, and ambitious. Gregoras even fantasizes that, were it not for Apokaukos' machinations against Kantakouzenos, the Romans would have enjoyed a peace as deep as that of the ancient empire, when an unarmed man could walk safely from Cilicia to Bithynia and barbarians came in friendship to Greece to attend the Panathenaic festival. But Apokaukos probably came from a family with a long tradition of service in both the state and Church, and made his fortune in the same way as many aristocrats of that age. He even claimed the royal name "Doukas."[20] Unfortunately, we lack his view of the outbreak of the civil war. The latter, Katakouzenos admitted, "reduced the once mighty monarchy of the Romans into a pale shadow of its former self."[21]

It is just as possible that Kantakouzenos was trying to bully the regency as that they treacherously plotted against him. Be that as it may, Anna, Kalekas, and Apokaukos banded together against Kantakouzenos while he was with the army at Didymoteichon in late 1341. They proclaimed him a public enemy, stripped him of his offices and dignities, excommunicated him, and arrested his mother Theodora, whom they confined under such harsh conditions that she died during the winter. Letters were sent to every city denouncing him as a rebel and hurling anathemas on anyone who took his side. "Kantakouzenism" became a criminal offense. They also confiscated his properties. Kantakouzenos says that this cost him 5,000 head of cattle, 1,000 draft animals, 2,500 mares, 200 camels, 300 mules, 500 donkeys, 50,000 pigs, 70,000 sheep, and vast amounts of produce.[22] The state concessions and rents of his followers were reassigned to supporters of the regency.[23]

Kantakouzenos had support in the army, which he had been commanding and paying for two decades; he was literally its "wealth-giver."[24] In 1342, he had just performed an *exisosis* (or recalibration) of state grants to soldiers. While the politics of it are opaque, many soldiers came away grateful to the *megas domestikos*. An experienced tax collector loyal to him, Patrikiotes, carried this out and topped off the soldiers' grants with his own money, up to 140,000 hyperpyra, which he was willing to donate for the good of the Roman state out of remorse for the way in which he had collected it. The money, he now believed, should benefit the Romans since it was theirs to begin with.[25] On 26 October, at Didymoteichon, Kantakouzenos was proclaimed basileus and handed out dignities to his supporters, though he took care that Anna and Ioannes were proclaimed before his own name. His rebellion posed as "a tower to protect the heir's reign."[26]

Kantakouzenos also sent out letters seeking support in the cities of Thrace and Macedonia. At this point, his memoirs, our main source, take a fascinating turn. Kantakouzenos crafts a subtle picture of class conflict breaking out first in Adrianople and then in Thessalonike and other towns. The aristocracy allegedly took his side, whereas the vulgar masses opposed him. In this socioeconomic conflict, the populace almost always prevailed, expelling or arresting the "better element" and confiscating their property. The governor of Thessalonike, Synadenos, an associate of Kantakouzenos, was willing to turn the city over to him in 1342 but he too was expelled, whereupon a gang of populist thugs known as "the Zealots" took over, instituting a reign of terror against the aristocracy and ruling Thessalonike until 1350. Based on this biased reporting, and buttressed by a few factual errors added to the picture in the nineteenth century, many historians of the twentieth century posited a narrative of self-conscious class conflict. But it no longer holds up.

What really happened in Thrace and Macedonia in the 1340s was a war between the regency in Constantinople and a rebel general, Kantakouzenos, in which most Romans sided with the former and tried to keep the rebel out of their cities. He was supported by his soldiers—though in the darkest moments of his rebellion their number dwindled to only 500—and by a faction of the aristocracy (plus their clients and dependents) that was bound to him through ties of kinship and patronage. Kantakouzenos automatically presented his supporters as the better sort and his opponents as misguided vulgar nobodies. But in reality the aristocracy was split between himself and the regency. Common Romans seem to have mostly opposed him, so he despised them with all the class conceit that he could muster. Kantakouzenos was generally fussy about matters of protocol, decorum, prestige, and elite precedence, and hated popular interventions, but popular power was a formidable factor in civic politics at this time, and the populace was within its right to reject his bid for the throne.[27]

The traditional picture of the Zealots also dissolves upon inspection. Kantakouzenos himself says that the Zealots were a pro-regency faction, and took that name probably to indicate the intensity of their devotion to the dynasty.[28] They were not champions of the proletariat. They were headed initially by one Michael Palaiologos, who, based on his name, might have been affiliated with the regency. They came to power in conjunction with the arrival of the *megas doux* Alexios Apokaukos and his fleet of seventy ships, who beat Kantakouzenos to Thessalonike and empowered the local majority of anti-Kantakouzenists against the minority of about one thousand aristocrats and their clients who favored the rebel. The aristocrats' properties were confiscated because they were traitors, not because their enemies wanted to overturn the social order. The Zealots announced no socioeconomic agenda and do not seem to have circulated any manifestos or platforms. Apokaukos appointed his son Ioannes to govern the city as *megas primikerios* jointly with Michael Palaiologos, whose remit was to safeguard the city's traditional rights vis-à-vis Constantinople. Thus, in 1342–1347, and despite turnover in its leadership cadres, Thessalonike remained a city under the authority of Constantinople. Its institutions continued to function normally, including the council, courts, and assemblies. Ioannes Apokaukos settled disputes in the countryside as would any governor sent from the capital, and the city's bishop went on diplomatic missions representing the interests of the regency.[29]

The political ferment of the 1340s was not necessarily unusual. If we had detailed narratives of Thessalonike's political history between 1204 and 1342, we would likely find similar episodes. The city had a reputation for welcoming non-citizens and treating them as its own after they had acclimated.[30] It likely received many refugees after the fall of Anatolia and during the Catalan and civil wars. The prolonged war of the 1340s, during which the city was repeatedly approached by hostile Roman, Turkish, and Serbian armies, exacerbated social unrest and gave the populace more power, just as happened at Constantinople during the Catalan crisis. A later patriarch blamed the unrest in Thessalonike during the 1340s "not on our own people, but on barbarian aliens who gathered here from the outer limits of our state and the surrounding islands out of sheer necessity." He was possibly referring to the sailors of the fleet, which Apokaukos had used to keep Thessalonike tied to the capital.[31] But his description unfairly ethnicized what was essentially a Roman political problem. Unfortunately, the political interpretations of this disorder in our sources are shallow, from Kantakouzenos' moralizing tale of class conflict to Thomas Magistros' treatise *To the Thessalonians on Concord*, which urged his fellow citizens to just get along.

Kantakouzenos later wrote a detailed account of the war, presenting his desperate and failed effort to gain a hold in the cities as a titanic struggle on his part to promote justice and advance the common good of the Romans. As he was repeatedly turned away and his followers expelled or arrested, Kantakouzenos made a fateful decision that spelled the end of the Roman state and destroyed the policy of military assertiveness pursued by Andronikos III: he called on his foreign "friends" to provide him with military assistance. This, of course, gave them the opportunity to aggrandize themselves at Roman expense. In the summer of 1342, Kantakouzenos met with Dušan of Serbia at Skopje, "a city that used to belong to the Romans but was now long under Serb occupation," and made a deal with him. Dušan provided him with soldiers and specified that he expected to be given most of Macedonia in return. Kantakouzenos says that he rejected those terms, but he knew what he was getting into and yet still accepted the kralj's aid.[32] When his wife Eirene, whom he left in command of Didymoteichon, was hard pressed by the forces of the regency, she called tsar Ivan Aleksandar to her assistance, but the tsar, it turned out, had his own ideas, blockading Didymoteichon and hoping to take it for himself, while asking Dušan to arrest Kantakouzenos so that Bulgaria and Serbia could divide the Roman territories between them. But Dušan allowed the rebel to depart, and the latter then called on his old friend Umur of Aydın, who sailed up the Hebros with a large army and chased the Bulgarians away.[33] The Roman civil war thus drew in three foreign armies. Two of them were interested in conquest, while the Turks of Aydın were in it only for pillage and fun. Meanwhile, a number of colorful bandit warlords exploited the instability to sell their violence to either side, or to both.

Kantakouzenos relied heavily on his Turkish allies. In the winter of 1342–1343, Umur attacked the hinterland of Thessalonike and blockaded the city, but ultimately had to withdraw. The Thessalonians were packed inside their city with their sheep and cows, leading to disease and more death. Kantakouzenos' strategy was to force the cities into submission by attacking their hinterland and starving them out, "as if it were enemy land," he candidly admitted.[34] Umur repeatedly ravaged Thrace in an effort to force the cities to surrender simply to make the killing stop. He "set fire to the fields, killed livestock, and carried away men and women as slaves," leading to famine. Siege warfare rarely involved direct assaults on the walls anymore. Fortifications were by now too strong, and armies were too weak. Kantakouzenos' other strategy was to win over key aristocrats, even some who had previously deserted his cause, with promises of titles and wealth. The tax farmer Ioannes Batatzes had risen by buying the contracts for increasingly larger provinces, until he bought the governorship of Thessalonike from the regency in Constantinople. As he was prevented from taking it up, in 1344 Kantakouzenos won him over, along with his family and the Thracian towns that they controlled, by giving him a military title and "yearly revenues" for himself and his relatives.[35] It was precisely over these assets, after all, that the war was being fought. Many men, and with them cities in Thrace, changed sides during it; Batatzes himself changed sides three times in total, raking in "gifts" with each switch. The regency was also not above making territorial concessions. They gave some forts in Thrace, including the "great city of Philippopolis," to Ivan Aleksandar in exchange for help against Umur's Turks.[36]

Dušan and Serbia

The greatest beneficiary of the Roman civil war was Dušan, who did exactly what he informed Kantakouzenos he would do, namely occupy all of Macedonia. Dušan failed to take Thessalonike and, at first, Beroia, which was governed by Kantakouzenos' son Manuel, but he did take most of Epeiros and Thessaly. His forces reached as far east as Christopolis (Kavala). The Serbian kralj and his nobles had expertly played the regency and Kantakouzenos off each other, as both sides fed his "insatiable desire" for Roman land in order to win him over.[37] The gains of Andronikos III were thus instantly wiped out, and the Roman state was reduced on the mainland to part of Thrace, which was itself ravaged by the war. The sources of Roman resilience were therefore dried up, and there would be no more recoveries.

The Serbian monarchy was now more powerful than ever, but it was still beholden to its military nobility, so much so that Dušan probably embarked on a career of conquest in order to satisfy his nobles and prevent them from destroying him. Dušan was able to step into the role of the basileus in his newly conquered Roman provinces. Serbian churches and monasteries were already organized along east Roman lines, many Greek Orthodox writings circulated in Slavic translations, and much east Roman law had been adapted to royal use. Dušan had spent seven years of his childhood as a royal exile in Constantinople, and so he was personally immersed in Roman culture. Like other kings with a similar upbringing, including Simeon of Bulgaria, Dušan, at the peak of his conquests in 1345, began to style himself in both Greek and Slavonic as kralj of the Serbs and Greeks (or of the Serbs and Romanía). He then elevated the archbishop of Serbia, Joanikije, to the rank of patriarch in order, in turn, to be crowned basileus by him at Skopje, in April, 1346. Joanikije himself was sometimes called patriarch of the Serbs and Romans. After his coronation, Dušan called himself (in Greek) emperor of Serbia and Romanía or (in Serbian) emperor of Serbs and Greeks, and sometimes also of Bulgarians and Albanians. He was not claiming to rule the whole Roman state, only some of its territories and former subjects. Dušan commissioned a new law code for his empire, the *Zakonik*, in which he compared himself to Constantine and Justinian, and he issued Roman-style chrysobulls. Some were in Greek for use by his Roman subjects. His court imitated Constantinople also in its regalia, titles, and religious art.[38] According to Gregoras, "he changed his barbarian lifestyle and took on Roman customs."[39]

Dušan stressed that his subjects, both Serbs and Romans/Greeks, would be equal before the law, and he allowed Romans to live according to their customs. Many recognized his legitimacy, but likely only in order to have their properties, exemptions, and concessions confirmed. He seems to have avoided revolutionary changes, as his own position, after all, was tenuous in the face of his nobles. The Serb occupation was not especially violent, and there was no religious tension between conquerors and ruled. But Serbs did monopolize the top positions, Serb garrisons were installed in Roman towns, and lands were reassigned to Serb beneficiaries. The archives of Athos attest to lands that were lost by Roman proprietors to Serb occupiers. In 1347, Dušan visited Mt. Athos with his empress, in violation of the rules of the Holy Mountain, which exclude women entirely. He deposed the head (*protos*) of the monastic federation and appointed in his place a Serb from the Serbian Hilandar monastery.[40] In 1350, Dušan even sought support from Venice for an attack on Constantinople, a request that was declined. The plan likely stemmed from Dušan's opposition to Kantakouzenos, at a time when the latter controlled the City.[41] By then, Dušan had allied himself to the regency of Ioannes V. He recognized the Palaiologan dynasty and its basileia of the Romans as parallel to his own. (There was no sense here of a single "universal empire" over which these rulers were competing; that is a modern fiction.) In 1345, Dušan allowed the monks on Athos to mention the basileus of the Romans ahead of "my own krality" in their prayers.[42] For his Roman subjects, Dušan came closer to being a Roman basileus than any foreigner who had hitherto aspired to that position.

Dušan was not the only foreign ruler auditioning for the role. His brother-in-law Ivan Aleksandar of Bulgaria styled himself as a New Constantine in both texts and images, such as in the portrait of himself facing those of Constantine the Great and Helena, painted at the Bachkovo monastery, which was ceded to him by Anna during the war. He called himself the tsar and basileus of the Bulgarians and the Romans, an aspiration given force in the iconography and interventions made to the Bulgarian translation of the Roman history of Manasses: these argued that Tarnovo was the "New Tsargrad" and had inherited the mantle of Rome.[43]

Kantakouzenos' victory

Meanwhile, the Roman civil war was turning increasingly bitter. On 11 June, 1345, Alexios Apokaukos, the effective head of the regency, inspected the construction of a prison tower for Kantakouzenists in the Great Palace and was murdered by the inmates. His killers hoped that this would spark a regime change, but they were instead slaughtered by the armed sailors sent in by Apokaukos' widow and empress Anna. About two hundred were hacked to pieces. Apokaukos had, after all, relied on the fleet and so the sailors were his main clientele. He had funded the fleet by confiscating Kantakouzenist properties. His archenemy, Kantakouzenos, claims that Apokaukos intended to reform the economy away from land and toward finance and maritime trade, relying on the islands and treating Constantinople as an island. Yet Kantakouzenos cannot be trusted when he talks of other people's intentions, and the policies that Apokaukos actually implemented—heavier duties for shipping in the Bosporos, taxes on merchants, and the confiscation of aristocratic estates—did not favor trade and investment. It seems that, rather than unleash the forces of maritime trade to create surplus wealth, Apokaukos was simply extracting money by force to pay for his navy.[44]

A second massacre of Kantakouzenists occurred in Thessalonike a year later. The city's co-governors had fallen out with each other. In 1345, Apokaukos' son Ioannes, the *megas primikerios*, assassinated the Zealot Michael Palaiologos at a meeting, imprisoned the Zealot leadership, and barricaded himself in the citadel. Ioannes allegedly wanted to turn the city over to Kantakouzenos and lobbied in that direction. But in 1346, bloody battles broke out over that plan. One Andreas Palaiologos rallied the Zealots and brought his own political constituency into the fray too, the so-called people by the coast, referring either to the part of the city by the harbor or to its sailors. They arrested Apokaukos and his followers, but then, in a confusing melee that spread throughout the city, the populace rose up and massacred him along with hundreds of prominent men and suspected Kantakouzenists. They plundered their victims' properties and, in one case, allegedly used their body fat for cooking. The Zealots, it turned out, had limited influence over the populace. Andreas Palaiologos himself was, after all, no commoner, receiving titles and lands from the regency. In the end, Thessalonike stood by the regency, though in practice it remained quasi-independent.[45]

Both sides were now guilty of atrocities. Demetrios Kydones, a rising intellectual from Thessalonike and staunch Kantakouzenist, wrote a rhetorical *Lament for the Fallen in Thessalonike*, a text that may have been delivered and circulated as propaganda.[46] On 21 May, 1346, Kantakouzenos was formally crowned as basileus in Adrianople by Lazaros, the patriarch of Jerusalem. This was almost certainly a response to Dušan's coronation a month earlier. There were now four crowned basileis in the Balkans, all claiming to rule Romans in some capacity, and the prestige and power of the two actual Roman basileis was lower than ever. Kantakouzenos' main ally, Umur, was preoccupied with fighting crusading forces of Venetians and Hospitallers. Kantakouzenos and the regency were both courting the favor of Orhan, the Ottoman emir of Bithynia, who eventually allied himself with Kantakouzenos and was given his daughter as one of his wives. The ceremony was celebrated at Selymbria, although the groom himself did not attend. Instead, he sent thirty ships and some noblemen to represent him. The bride was unveiled on a *prokypsis*-stage and Kantakouzenos feasted the guests for many days. The affair was improvised and regarded as disgraceful and illegal by many Orthodox. Orhan, who was older than his father-in-law, would provide Kantakouzenos with armies for the struggles to come, but their purpose was as much to raid, plunder, and establish a Turkish presence in the Balkans as to help their nominal ally. The value of a royal Roman match had never before been so low, or its cost so high.[47] Kantakouzenos ought to have known better: Orhan was already presenting himself in inscriptions as a holy warrior for the expansion of Islam.[48] Yet Kantakouzenos always put his short-term interests ahead of the common good, even while he argued, at tedious length, the opposite.

On 19 May, 1346, an earthquake damaged Hagia Sophia, causing a third of the dome and a supporting arch to collapse. "This brought tears to the eyes of all, not just the Romans but foreigners too." The Muscovite king in Russia began to collect funds to help with its repair.[49] Makrembolites saw this as a sign of the End Times and the coming of the Antichrist.[50] It was a fitting image for the fracturing of the regency, which ultimately enabled Kantakouzenos to prevail. Anna and the patriarch Kalekas fell out and, in early 1347, she had him deposed by the Synod for selling Church offices and for heresy. The latter concerned the teachings of one Barlaam of Calabria; at any rate, the bishops' report seems designed to comply with Anna's request.[51] The court remained dominant over the Church to the extent that even a foreign queen with only a notional relationship to Orthodoxy could depose a patriarch and decide on the official theological position of the Church. But it availed her not, as Gregoras, an enemy of the theological position affirmed by the Synod, pointed out: on the very night after the Synod's meeting, 2 February, she fell from power. Ioannes VI Kantakouzenos, with about a thousand men and the help of supporters inside, broke through the walled-up arches of the Golden Gate and entered Constantinople.[52]

A standoff ensued, with Anna and Ioannes V blockaded in the Blachernai palace by Kantakouzenos. On 8 February, the two sides reached an agreement. There would be an amnesty, and Kantakouzenos would rule as senior basileus for ten years, after which he and Ioannes V would share power. Kantakouzenos would make no attempt to replace the Palaiologoi with his own dynasty, though Ioannes V would marry his daughter Helene. That marriage was performed a week after Kantakouzenos' second coronation, on 21 May, in the Blachernai church of the Virgin by the new patriarch Isidoros (Hagia Sophia could not be used because of the earthquake damage).[53] Those were the formalities of power. Its substance, by contrast, consisted of land grants to loyal followers who had suffered for the Kantakouzenist cause.[54] Kydones crowed that a new day had dawned and that the phoenix would be reborn from its ashes.[55] But the reality consisted only of ash. Kantakouzenos discovered that there was not enough money, whether public or private, to defend the state. Agriculture had been ruined by years of war, and even the crown jewels had been pawned to Venice by Anna as collateral for a loan of 30,000 gold ducats (about 60,000 hyperpyra) in 1343. There was no money left to redeem them. The jewels would in fact never be returned, a stinging humiliation for the Romans.[56] Royal banquets, Gregoras noted, now used vessels made of clay, not gold or silver. The treasury contained only air and dust, nothing but "the atoms of Epicurus."[57]

Hesychasm

Just as the Romans were losing their money, land, power, and status, some of them were accessing an ability to see something more precious: divine light. This claim was contested, fueling a theological conflict that raged alongside the civil war itself. It is usually named after Hesychasm, a monastic practice of spiritual quietude. *Hesychia* was long-established in the monastic lifestyle, but on Mt. Athos it was now associated with a striking theological claim, namely that the light seen by ascetics after they had fasted for days, turned their gaze inward, and recited the "Jesus prayer" a few hundred times, often while staring at their navels, was nothing other than a divine energy, a visible emanation of the Godhead itself that was not really part of the created world. It was identical to the Light of Tabor seen during the transfiguration of Jesus (also to the flames of Elijah's chariot and Moses' Burning Bush). It is unclear how developed these ideas were before they excited controversy. It was only when they were challenged by an immigrant philosopher, Barlaam of Calabria, that an Athonite monk from Constantinople, Gregorios Palamas, used them to craft a new articulation of Orthodox theology. Left undisturbed, these ideas might well have remained confined to small circles. But when they were challenged, a process was set into motion that catapulted them into the Church's definition of Orthodoxy. This, in turn, enabled the victorious side, the Palamites, to retroactively revise their understanding of the Orthodox tradition, making it seem as if it had always been leading up to Palamas. Moreover, Orthodoxy came to be strongly associated with mysticism and Athos, both of which had previously been marginal. In part, this happened because during the mid-fourteenth century all other institutions were collapsing, yielding to Athos a default position of cultural, political, and economic leadership. Neo-Palamism remains strong today, and its adherents uphold their hero as the "essence" of Orthodoxy.[58] To make this controversy even more toxic, western scholars (mostly Catholic) have traditionally attacked Palamas and sided with his critics, whom they see as more amenable to Union.[59]

Barlaam of Calabria was born in ca. 1290, in the same decade as Palamas, Gregoras, and Kantakouzenos. He was fluent in both Greek and Latin and was one of the most impressive philosophers and mathematicians of his age. Although he was a monk, his intellectual formation owed much to Greek Neoplatonism and formal logic, and little to Catholic thought or ascetic devotion, in which he was uninterested. He immigrated to Romanía in 1325, spending the next fifteen years between its two intellectual centers, Thessalonike and Constantinople. Eventually, he became the abbot of a monastery in the capital and acquired the patronage of Kantakouzenos and Andronikos III, who sent him on an embassy to the west in 1339. Barlaam was a pugnacious controversialist and his arrival on the intellectual scene led him to clash in the 1330s with Gregoras, the leading thinker of the age, especially over astronomy and the prediction of eclipses. Gregoras even wrote dialogues mocking this newcomer who originally spoke halting Greek but who had carefully changed his diction, facial hair, dress, and bearing in order to fit in and seem wise.[60] Gregoras was insecure, for Barlaam was challenging his intellectual hegemony.

A discussion over Church Union with some papal envoys in 1334 opened up a new controversy. Barlaam represented the Orthodox position, and both he and Gregoras subsequently wrote epistemologically radical treatises against the Latin *filioque*. Barlaam argued that apodeictic syllogisms were useless for solving these problems. The inner workings of the Trinity lie beyond the reach of our reasoning, and whatever truth is within our mental grasp was equally accessible to the pagan philosophers. Hence Barlaam found himself, philosophically speaking, in a position of Socratic ignorance. Belief beyond that was a matter of faith and obedience to the dogmatic tradition of the Church, making the *filioque* an unauthorized addition to the Creed. Gregoras took an even more extreme view, that theology is only a rough approximation of metaphysical truth that caters to the needs of simple people.[61] Both men had clearly gone too far into philosophy to represent the views of most churchmen, as applying their thinking consistently would wreak havoc on much of the theological tradition.

Somehow it was only Barlaam's position that elicited pushback from Palamas, who found out about it through a common friend, Gregorios Akindynos. Palamas responded that Barlaam's position undermined not only the Latin *filioque* but the Orthodox position as well, which, he believed, *was* provable by apodeictic syllogisms.[62] Paradoxically, this went against a great deal of Orthodox tradition which stressed the limits of syllogistic theology. For all that he relied on Platonic sources and put too fine an edge on his positions, Barlaam was more in line with the tradition here. The exchanges between the two men became more heated, until they snagged on the question of the knowledge of God that might be accessible to those who experience a mystical light in their prayers. Barlaam could not accept that real knowledge was contained in the hallucinations of ascetics who reported seeing "red and white lights." God cannot be grasped through physical means. He mocked these "monstrous" notions, which appalled him. Breathing techniques are of no use here, and truth does not enter the mind through nose and navel.[63]

In response, Palamas wrote the *Triads*, in which he argued that philosophy does not lead to salvation. Yet he defended the ascetics' ability to grasp divinity by drawing an Aristotelian distinction between the essence of the Godhead, which is unknowable, and the energies of God, which men who are on the path toward deification can see in the form of light. These energies belong neither to the essence of God nor to the created world, which is how they facilitate human salvation and why they exist (Palamas' opponents claimed that he was setting up a second type of God here). Hesychasts treated seeing these lights almost as a precondition for salvation. In an age of defeat and humiliation, Palamas was offering a way toward an "angelic dignity." Worldly things were like "dirt and dust," but illumination bestows upon man "the dignity of a prophet, Apostle, or angel of God."[64] It could be attained by anyone through prayer, and was not mediated by powerful men or institutions. In a period of inequality and social collapse, it was an appealing message.

Palamas referred to himself in the third person and claimed to be inspired by the Holy Spirit. For his part, Barlaam was good at making enemies and came across as arrogant. He lost Kantakouzenos' support and was warned to "stay in his lane of outer philosophy" and stop criticizing the monks, who had powerful friends. *Hesychia* was not his province.[65] But he plunged forward, accusing the Hesychasts of Messalianism, a form of excessive enthusiasm in monastic devotion, and lodged a formal accusation against Palamas before the Synod, demanding that the matter be investigated. The Synod was duly convened by Andronikos III in Hagia Sophia, in June, 1341, resulting in Barlaam's own condemnation. He had been naïve to hope that these issues would be adjudicated by philosophical merit, or that the Church would side with him, an outsider, against its monastic wing, which he had been "insulting." The Synod could (and did) censure him for bringing accusations against monks even though he was not a bishop. And when called upon to explain his positions, he digressed at length on prior matters of epistemology, confusing the assembly. Gregoras, who opposed both Barlaam and Palamas, absented himself from the Synod because of a migraine, but gloated over the outcome.[66] Barlaam departed for the west, where he converted to Catholicism, was ordained a bishop, and tried to teach Greek to the humanist Petrarch, with as much success as he had in teaching philosophy to the Holy Synod.

The Athonites' ascendancy was reversed during the civil war of the 1340s. Palamas himself and his supporters were correctly seen by the regency as too close to Kantakouzenos: they refused to condemn him and actively supported him in the civil war. Moreover, the background of the patriarch Kalekas was in the palace clergy, not the monastic world, and he disliked the idea of monks dictating "these foreign and newfangled doctrines" to the Church.[67] He took the position that the Synod of 1341 had only condemned Barlaam, not accepted the Orthodoxy of Palamas' teachings. Kalekas promoted Akindynos, a former student of Thomas Magistros and Palamas who emerged as the regency's leading anti-Hesychast. He argued that Palamas distorted the writings of the Fathers when he marshaled them to support his thought. Palamas was duly arrested by the regency and excommunicated in 1344. He spent the war imprisoned in the palace, defending his theology against Akindynos. The tables were turned when Kantakouzenos took the capital in 1347. A Synod was immediately convened, although only eleven bishops could be rounded up for its first session. It deposed Kalekas, excommunicated Akindynos, vindicated Palamas, and rammed through thirty-two Palamite episcopal appointments. Palamas was given the archbishopric of Thessalonike, although he could not take it up, for the city was held by anti-Kantakouzenists. The Synod declared that the machinations of Barlaam and Akindynos were stirred up by Satan to lead Christians away from their faith into atheism and polytheism. Akindynos and Kalekas, the Synod continued, were also complicit in the political plot against Kantakouzenos who "by the consensus of all Romans" had been entrusted with the guardianship of Ioannes V.[68] In reality, the young heir was now fifteen and chafing under his guardian.

Palamism remained extremely divisive among intellectuals and bishops. Opposition to it began to build up again immediately after the Synod of 1347, and this time the gauntlet was taken up by Gregoras, who had some bishops on his side. Gregoras became hysterically obsessive over the issue, filling up hundreds of pages of his history with screeds against Palamism and seeing it as the root cause of the decline of the Roman polity. He lost his friendship with Kantakouzenos over it. Kantakouzenos allowed Gregoras and the bishops who shared his views to present their case before the Synod in 1351, but the outcome was predetermined: Palamas was again vindicated and his critics excommunicated and deposed.[69] Palamas had been lucky that his three major opponents—Barlaam, Akindynos, and Gregoras—had come at him one at a time. Moreover, at the key moments in 1341, 1347, and 1351, Palamas enjoyed the backing of Kantakouzenos and the publicity machine of the Athonites. "Heavy beards stalked the palace," observed Kydones, another anti-Palamite.[70] By Synods comprising a couple dozen bishops at most, Orthodoxy was now redefined as Palamism. Gregoras was confined to the Chora monastery for years, from where he polemicized against Palamas and Kantakouzenos. According to one of his followers, when he died in ca. 1361 his body was mutilated by the Palamites.[71]

The Black Death

There is no evidence of popular interest in the Palamite controversy, which was confined to Church, monastic, and intellectual elites. Most people had other worries than the nature of hesychastic light. The 1340s was one of the worst decades in Roman history already, and it was about to get worse. In 1347, the Black Death arrived. It originated in China and reached Constantinople via the Genoese port of Caffa in the Crimea, after which it traveled along the trade routes to Egypt and western Europe. This was a more virulent form of the bubonic plague that had struck under Justinian and, in a series of outbreaks that recurred roughly every ten years or so, it killed between 30% and 60% of the population.[72] The Roman state was tiny—encompassing only southern Thrace, Thessalonike, a few islands, and a corner of the Peloponnese—and contained only a few hundred thousand people.

Kantakouzenos lost one of his sons to the disease and could not pass up the chance to endow his narrative with a moving Thucydidean set piece. But we have few other accounts of its initial outbreak because, like the Roman state itself, the literary scene had contracted too, as those educated under Andronikos II died off. The basileus' secretary Kydones wrote in a letter that "every day we bury some friend; the City is emptying of people and filling with graves."[73] Moreover, the impact of the plague is hard to pick out among the other disorders of that period, especially the civil war and the Turkish raids. Our data yields only macroscopic indexes. For example, depopulation and the abandonment of villages between 1321 and 1409 can be traced in the censuses of monastic land in Macedonia and Lemnos.[74] Survey archaeology suggests a decline of settlements in Laconia, while palynological evidence indicates a decline in cereal production.[75] Consistent with what we find in better-documented societies, it appears that urban wages rose, as labor became more valuable in relation to land.[76] Some *paroikoi* were able to demand better terms from their landlords, though labor was scarce also because people fled from Turks and pirates.[77] The plague constituted yet another source of trauma and helplessness, as neither science nor religion availed its victims.

Ioannes VI Kantakouzenos

As basileus, Ioannes VI Kantakouzenos (1347–1354) failed to remedy the ills of the Roman state. He was shrewd, "a mind with deep grooves,"[78] and he had more military and diplomatic experience than any Roman alive. Apparently, he could speak both Latin (Italian?) and Turkish. Yet the civil war that had ruined the Roman state was largely his own doing. Moreover, he had been played by his "friend" Dušan, who was consolidating his hold on Greece. In order to fight the regency, Kantakouzenos had brought Turkish war bands and fleets to Thrace, who were not only raiding but entrenching themselves there. Travel became extremely dangerous, not just for ordinary people. Kantakouzenos himself was ambushed in 1348 by a band of 2,000 Turks, who had crossed the Hellespont for some fun in Thrace. He bested them, but some among them had served under him in the past and knew the lay of the land.[79] When he sailed to take Thessalonike in 1350, he chanced upon 22 Turkish pirate ships at the mouth of the Strymon river and invited them to join his cause. He repeatedly apologized for bringing the Turks to Europe, for example in a letter to the pope and at an assembly of the populace of the City soon after his coronation in 1347.[80] It was humiliating when, in 1351, the Bulgarian tsar Ivan Aleksandar complained about raids on his territory by Kantakouzenos' Turkish mercenaries. The basileus apologized and invited the tsar to contribute money to the upkeep of the Roman fleet, which would prevent more Turks from crossing over. But Ivan Aleksandar could not trust the basileus. Indeed, some said that Kantakouzenos was using the funds collected by the Russian Church for the repair of Hagia Sophia to pay his Turks.[81] The work had been entrusted to the architect and politician Georgios Synadenos Astras and a Catalan colleague, Joan de Peralta.[82]

Kantakouzenos desperately needed money. Reconquering territory was out of the question. For one thing, he could not afford the mercenaries. At a public assembly in 1347, he laid out the state's fiscal crisis to the citizenry and called for voluntary contributions, with mixed success.[83] He could not borrow more money from the Venetians, as they were demanding repayment (with compound interest) of the loan that Anna had taken out to fight him, giving the crown jewels as collateral. They were also demanding compensation for cargoes lost to violence or extortion.[84] Moreover, the Genoese of Galata had a stranglehold on trade passing through the Bosporos. Their revenues amounted to 200,000 hyperpyra while the Romans were pulling in only 30,000. They also had a near monopoly on the City's grain supply, and could starve it out if they wanted. They were fortifying and expanding their commune at Galata against the basileus' wishes. In 1346, during the civil war, a Genoese adventurer named Simone Vignoso had attacked Chios and conquered it against heavy Roman resistance, after which he took both Old and New Phokaia. The Genoese were no less predatory than the Turks, despite their alliance with the Romans.[85]

To counter the Genoese ascendancy, Kantakouzenos invested in rebuilding the navy, both military and merchant. The Genoese immediately understood the threat that this posed and attacked the Roman shipyards to nip the project in the bud. This led to a series of battles, skirmishes, and incendiary assaults across the Golden Horn during 1348–1349. Most of the new Roman fleet was destroyed in a humiliating defeat when the Romans tried to attack Galata. The Genoese then used catapults against the City, damaging its famous churches, such as that of the Virgin at Blachernai, and dragged the imperial standards in the water in a show of contempt. But before hostilities could escalate further, envoys came from Genoa and made concessions to settle the dispute. Genoa would pay 100,000 hyperpyra in reparations; demilitarize Galata; and rent Chios for the price of 12,000 per year, while a Roman official governed the local population. Yet the damage was done: Romanía remained navally and fiscally boxed in. "Both sides suffered loss of life, but the Romans were, in addition, materially and politically harmed," noted Makrembolites, brimming with hatred for the Italians who had grown rich from Roman trade and were now behaving so insolently. In the face of widespread indignation at his failure, Kantakouzenos summoned a public assembly to explain that his revenues did not amount to millions upon millions, as some were saying, but only 50,000, and he had spent it on the fleet. All he could do now was raise taxes on some goods and lower the trade tariffs imposed on Roman merchants to 2% (down from 10%) so that they could compete with the Italians.[86]

Beyond the Genoese stranglehold, the Romans were squeezed in between Venice and Genoa, who went to war with each other in 1350. Kantakouzenos was pressured to take sides and eventually joined Venice. In the war, however, Venice repeatedly left him in the lurch to face the wrath of the Genoese of Galata, on his very doorstep. In early 1352, a naval battle was fought against the Genoese by a joint Venetian, Aragonese, and Roman fleet, but it was indecisive. The western allies abandoned the subsequent blockade of Galata and so, in May, 1352, the basileus had to make more concessions to the Genoese: their past privileges were confirmed, and they could fortify Galata as they wished. Roman sovereignty over Chios and Phokaia was not even mentioned. Chios was henceforth governed by a consortium of Genoese investors known as the Maona, which, during the next two centuries, profited from its mastic production.[87] Kantakouzenos had failed to obtain any advantage from his risky alliance with Venice.

On the positive side, Kantakouzenos had recovered Thessalonike. By 1349, the city was governed jointly by the Zealot leader Andreas Palaiologos and Alexios Metochites, the son of the philosopher. It had refused to recognize Kantakouzenos, even though he held Constantinople and settled his differences with the regency. Thessalonike's politics were volatile and exacerbated by an ongoing blockade by Dušan. Andreas Palaiologos and his associates were expelled in another popular uprising, indicating that the Zealots and the populace were not always on good terms. But when Alexios Metochites realized that a Zealot faction was negotiating to surrender the city to Dušan, he invited Kantakouzenos, his father's old enemy, to take possession of it. Unable to bear the thought that the Roman state would "lose one of its eyes," the basileus rushed to Thessalonike in the fall of 1349 and stayed there for over a year. He arrested the Zealot leaders and pushed the Serb garrisons out of their forts in the city's hinterland. Athos was brought back under Roman control, and a Roman was made its *protos* again. Also, Palamas was finally installed as the city's bishop. His inaugural sermon was a plea for reconciliation: it was Satan who instigated all the violence, but "heed me now that I am among you."[88]

Kantakouzenos left Ioannes V in charge of Thessalonike, under the eye of Kantakouzenos' father-in-law Andronikos Asanes. There was a risk that the Palaiologos heir would use the city as a base to resist Kantakouzenos and re-ignite the civil war, but the risk was greater that the city would be betrayed to the Serbs or go rogue again in the absence of a basileus.[89] Kantakouzenos also assigned the Morea to his son Manuel, to whom he gave the title of despot. Manuel held this position for life, until 1380 (though the Morea was not called "the Despotate," a term used only for Epeiros). Kantakouzenos also gave Didymoteichon to his eldest son Matthaios, "upon whom he bestowed no named title, but a rank greater than that of despot, directly below the basileus."[90] Kantakouzenos' dynastic plans remain unclear and were controversial even then. Did he intend to marginalize Ioannes V and promote Matthaios as the heir to the throne, as his critics charged? He always claimed that he was acting in the interests of the Palaiologos dynasty, but he had to say that to defuse any opposition. His plan may have been like that of Romanos I Lakapenos, namely to merge Ioannes V into his family and then marginalize him in favor of his own sons. But in the process, he essentially devised the late Palaiologan system of governance through regional commands assigned to members of the royal family. These are sometimes called "appanages" by modern scholars, a term taken from the French feudal model. It is a misleading term. These posts were not hereditary and did not entail ownership of the lands in question.[91]

The system in question evolved out of circumstances unique to the Roman state at the end of its life and owed nothing to western influence. Specifically, the three main territories of the state—Thrace, Thessalonike, and the Morea—were no longer contiguous and were separated by hostile agents. Each faced unique and sustained pressures, so it no longer made sense to dispatch short-term governors to them from the center on a rotating basis, nor was it practical or even safe to do so. Moreover, with the loss of most of its territories the court had also lost the ability to maintain its princes through large pronoias. Prominence in the hierarchy and the royal succession could now be demonstrated only by holding one of these regional commands, but there were only a few to go around, so they went to co-basileis and princes. These postings were also a way of removing an ambitious and potentially dangerous successor from the City and placing him in a provincial town where he would be moderately content but also preoccupied. Dynastic tension was a driver of this system, as Kantakouzenos needed to place his kin in positions of power to surround Ioannes V. For example, already in 1342, at the outset of the civil war, he gave the command of Thessaly along with the title of despot to his cousin Ioannes Angelos. The basileus issued a chrysobull stipulating that Angelos would rule Thessaly independently "for the rest of his life" but could not transmit it to his son (unless the basileus agreed) and was required to assist Kantakouzenos in operations west of Christopolis (Kavala).[92] The Roman state was henceforth a patchwork of interlinked domains whose histories began to diverge. Thessaly and Epeiros, for example, were conquered by Dušan before the decade was out.

This system of governance was flawed from the start as it gave regional power centers to royal princes who, incited by flunkies and yes-men, aspired to the throne in Constantinople. This forced Kantakouzenos to put out one political fire after another, and eventually it toppled his regime. Already in the summer of 1351, Ioannes V was pushed by the men around him to make an alliance with Dušan and restart the civil war "in order to reclaim his rightful patrimony." Kantakouzenos was preoccupied with the Genoese-Venetian war, so he sent Anna of Savoy to talk sense into her son, which she did, in an amazing feat of diplomacy, persuading even Dušan to withdraw from Thessalonike. Ioannes next asked to be transferred to Didymoteichon, which Kantakouzenos granted, while Anna took up the rule of Thessalonike, which she ruled capably until her death in 1365. She even reconciled with its bishop, Palamas, whom her regency had imprisoned during the civil war. However, giving Thrace to Ioannes meant that Matthaios Kantakouzenos had to be transferred to Adrianople.[93] Matthaios was long resentful about his ill-defined status. In 1347, "friends" had persuaded him that he was being sidelined in favor of Ioannes V, even though it was he and his father who had won the war. A mother again stepped in: Eirene Asanina talked him down.[94] Romanía had shrunk so much that its politics had become a game of musical chairs played by dynastic heirs, which often came down to mother-son relations.

Tensions escalated between Matthaios and Ioannes V, who were neighbors in Thrace, leading to war between them in 1352. Ioannes attacked Adrianople and was let in by the citizenry, who, like most Romans, preferred the Palaiologoi over the Kantakouzenoi. Both sides called in foreign allies, who were only too happy to interfere in the convulsions of the dying Roman state. Ioannes was given armies by Serbia and Bulgaria, and the Venetians loaned him 20,000 ducats in exchange for the island of Tenedos. Matthaios was backed by a Turkish army sent by Orhan to Kantakouzenos, under the command of the emir's son Süleyman. Foreshadowing what was about to happen in the Balkans over the next two decades, the Turkish army defeated the Serbs and Bulgarians by the Hebros river, near Didymoteichon. The survivors were chased down and killed. Few Romans were harmed, as they had become spectators in their own civil wars. Their role was merely to start them, after which they became the vehicles through which the Serbs and Turks contended over mastery of the Balkans. Kantakouzenos' destructive role in this process was perfectly understood and resented by his subjects. In fact, he was *paying* the Turks for this opportunity with treasures that he took from churches and monasteries.[95] The absurdity of it all was apparent. No one had done more to entrench the Turks in the Balkans than Kantakouzenos.

Kantakouzenos forced Ioannes V to relocate to Tenedos. Yet the faction around the young heir was determined to place him on the throne. In March, 1353, he sailed along the walls of Constantinople hoping to be let in, but Eirene Asanina secured the City's defenses and suppressed any popular demonstrations in his favor. Many in the Kantakouzenist camp now believed that the interdynastic project was unsalvageable and they urged the senior basileus to name Matthaios as his successor. Kantakouzenos, who was of the same mind, did this in a palace ceremony later that month. In his memoirs, Kantakouzenos presents himself as reluctant to take this fateful step, but in reality he rammed it through over the objections of the patriarch Kallistos, who threatened to resign, and actually did so, over this "usurpation" and the violation of oaths and agreements. Kantakouzenos appointed a new patriarch, Philotheos Kokkinos, who formally crowned Matthaios in the Blachernai church of the Virgin in February 1354. Ioannes V was no longer to be recognized in Constantinople. At long last, the dynastic coup had taken place. Had Kantakouzenos executed it earlier, he might have spared the Romans much fighting. Now he planned to give to Matthaios "some split-off portion of the Roman state for him to use during his lifetime, returning it to the basileus, whoever that was, at the time of his death."[96]

No sooner had this coup taken place than a dramatic development turned opinion decisively against the Kantakouzenoi. On 2 March, 1354, an earthquake demolished much of the strategic fortress of Gallipoli in the Thracian Chersonesos. Many died in the ruins, fled to surrounding towns, or were exposed to the elements in the freezing weather. Turkish raiders immediately descended on it and captured many to sell on the slave trade. Orhan's son Süleyman then led a force of Turkish soldiers, with their women and children, and occupied the site, with the intention of staying there permanently. In 1352, Süleyman had already occupied the nearby fort of Tzympe. To their horror, the Romans realized that the Turks now had strong bases in Europe. Kantakouzenos pleaded with his notional allies, Süleyman and Orhan, to return the cities and even offered them 40,000 hyperpyra, but the emir replied that he had but occupied an abandoned ruin.[97] The friendship between the two leaders was revealed as only an arrangement of convenience. The Turkish conquest of the Balkans had begun. Kantakouzenos holed himself up in the palace in fear of popular anger. He stood accused of "stripping the people of their freedom and turning them over to be the slaves of impious barbarians."[98]

Ioannes V made his move on the night of 29 November, 1354. He sailed to Constantinople from Tenedos and slipped into the City through the southern sea walls. The populace took up arms in his favor and pillaged the homes of top Kantakouzenists. In a reversal of the events of 1347, it was Kantakouzenos who was now besieged in the Blachernai palace. The two sides again came to a power-sharing settlement, but it did not last. On 10 December, Ioannes VI Kantakouzenos formally abdicated and became the monk Ioasaph.[99] Ioannes V Palaiologos (1341–1391) was now the senior basileus, and his mother already held Thessalonike. He deposed the patriarch Philotheos and restored his own loyalist Kallistos. Yet his brother-in-law Manuel Kantakouzenos continued to rule the Morea, capably, until his death in 1380, defeating attempts to have him replaced. As for Matthaios Kantakouzenos, he defiantly reigned as basileus in a small corner of Thrace. When he was captured by Serbs in 1357, he was ransomed by Ioannes V, who forced him to renounce his title; he was later allowed to join his brother Manuel at Mystras in the Morea.

The slave trade

As a handful of Kantakouzenoi and Palaiologoi jostled for the little power that was left in Romanía, their subjects were enduring deep trauma. A thriving slave trade had emerged in the Aegean that ensnared thousands of Romans who were captured by the Turkish conquerors of Anatolia as well as by the Turkish and Catalan raiders who preyed on the islands and coasts. Every military campaign was a new opportunity to round up dozens, hundreds, or thousands of helpless people from fields, villages, and sacked cities, and sell them at the nearest slave emporium run by Italians. Venetian Crete was a major clearinghouse. Therefore, it was not false to say that Kantakouzenos' civil wars literally enslaved his fellow Romans, for he knew what his Turkish allies were looking for as they ravaged the lands held by his political enemies. The slave trade was a huge part of the emerging economy of the Turkish emirates. If the victims were not lucky enough to be ransomed, they were conveyed as cargo by the Italians to Egypt and western Europe. The average price of a slave was about fifteen hyperpyra, around that of a mule.[100]

By contrast, the Roman army did not enslave people during its normal operations, in part because it rarely defeated the Turks or fought with the Latins much in this period, and there was a tacit agreement among the Orthodox rulers not to enslave each other's subjects (though Mongols were fair game).[101] The basileis protested repeatedly to Genoa and Venice about their role in the captivity of free Romans, and even argued to the pope that this impeded the cause of Union. But the slave trade only intensified after the Black Death, which had created an insatiable demand for labor and raised prices, incentivizing raids. The fragmentation of the Balkans, Aegean, and Anatolia meant that no power could guarantee the safety of its subjects. As Romans were the largest ethnic group in the region, they also made up a plurality of the victims. "You would not find an Italian on sale in Ephesos," observed Kydones, "but we are slaves everywhere."[102]

Even dead authors could be captured. A lively correspondence between Manuel II Palaiologos at Thessalonike and Kydones tells the story of a manuscript of Plato, which Manuel "liberated" in the 1380s from the monks at Mt. Athos, among whom the philosopher was dead, for the monks had long since renounced worldly wisdom. Yet this "Plato" was captured by Turkish pirates on his way to Kydones and had to be ransomed. After this "humiliation," Plato reached Kydones torn, soaked, and bedraggled.[103]

The most famous victim at this time was none other than Palamas himself, who was captured by Turkish raiders in the aftermath of the Gallipoli earthquake and taken to Bursa (Prousa), the Ottoman capital, until his ransom was paid a year later. He wrote an account of his captivity, containing fascinating information on Muslim-Christian relations in conquered Bithynia. The main purpose of the text is to showcase the deep respect that he inspired among his captors by his asceticism and ability to debate theology and religion. His narrative was embellished, if not largely fictional, but his deeper point was that Palamism could foster relations of mutual respect between conquered Romans and Turkish conquerors, such as could not exist between Romans and Latins. Yet his bitter enemy Gregoras wrote a strikingly different account of the experience. According to him, the Turks found much gold and silver secreted on Palamas' body and, after stripping him of it, they sodomized him. According to Gregoras, who was just as anti-Catholic as Palamas, Orthodox Romans were more likely to find safety and toleration under Latin rule, as one could see on Crete and Cyprus.[104] As the Romans faced the likely prospect of subjugation, they were increasingly divided over the question of east vs. west: Which foreign conqueror was the least bad?

36
The Noose Tightens (1354–1402)

Even after the loss of Anatolia, under Andronikos III the Romans remained a formidable Balkan power. But the civil war of the 1340s enabled the Serbs to annex Macedonia and central Greece, reducing the Roman state to second-rate status. It was no longer a serious contender for regional hegemony, so much so that none of its neighbors made it their chief target. The Serbs, Bulgarians, and Turks eyed each other over its head.

Trebizond

The Romans of Trebizond had also experienced a prolonged period of political instability and civil war, but had not lost ground in the same way. Protected by the formidable mountains of the Pontos, the Grand Komnenoi deftly navigated the changing political landscape of Anatolia. In order to preserve their functional independence, they periodically recognized the nominal suzerainty of Seljuk sultans and Mongol khans. They also recognized that their Church was notionally subordinate to New Rome and that their ruler, when he was visiting Constantinople, was only a despot compared to the basileus, but in practice Trebizond was an independent state. It skillfully adapted to the more fragmented world of the Turkish emirates that emerged in the fourteenth century. It has even been called, in that context, a "Greek emirate," but this is wrong.[1] It was a settled Roman state, not a coalition of nomadic warriors lording it over a conquered agricultural population in search of more land and plunder under the cover of holy war. Its identity was Roman, not Greek. A court poet at Trebizond proudly noted that the Latin enemies of Alexios III Grand Komnenos (1349–1390) were up against the descendants of ancient Romans, who had made Gelimer kneel before Justinian.[2]

The Grand Komnenoi dealt closely with the Italians because their city had emerged as a major hub of trade, starting especially in the mid-thirteenth century when the Mongol conquests opened up major trading routes. Also, the fall of Constantinople in 1204 opened the Black Sea to Italian merchants who supplied growing western markets with eastern goods (it was a six-month journey from Trebizond to Venice). We have vastly more information about the Venetian and Genoese merchant associations in Trebizond than we do about the city itself. It imported grain and salt (whose tax was a major source of revenue for the crown), and exported metals, wax, wine, and sulphates. Just as with Constantinople, the Italians always pushed for concessions, tax breaks, strategic points of control, and "restitutions" to the point of often engaging in hostilities against their hosts. These would be concluded with a new treaty, revised according to the outcome of battle. The city was home to many immigrants and was open to intellectual trends from the Muslim world too. Its harbor was "a marketplace for the world. . . . We intermingle with all foreign people, we interact with all races. We become wiser and better than them because we collect what is best from everywhere," wrote a native son, Bessarion, in the fifteenth century.[3]

Starting with Alexios III Grand Komnenos, the most famous of Trebizond's exports became its princess brides. In a calculated strategy of marital diplomacy, the Grand Komnenoi gave their daughters and sisters to foreign rulers regardless of ethnicity or religion, in order to create a network of advocates at foreign courts and prevent potential enemies "from ravaging their lands."[4] The brand value of the Komnenian brides was enhanced by a cultivated reputation for beauty. Yet the Komnenoi never took, or were never offered, Muslim brides in exchange.

The first half of the fourteenth century was a period of endemic political instability at Trebizond. Many Grand Komnenoi lost their throne to coups and sometimes mounted countercoups. A few sought refuge and marriage alliances in Constantinople, there to plot their return, but rarely received substantive aid from the basileis. Unfortunately, the political history of Trebizond in this period is known almost entirely from the chronicle of the Trapezuntine official Panaretos, who briefly records the dates of accessions, deaths, coups, and notable events, but never explains their background or significance. Modern historians have therefore supplied their interpretations, for example that the violence reflected a struggle of the great families of Constantinopolitan origin that dominated Trebizond against the local "feudal aristocracy"; or a structural tension between the monarchy and its aristocracy; or a struggle over land or foreign policy.[5] None of this can be proven. The instability was likely caused by factional disputes over power among the high officials of the realm, as only they appear in Panaretos' terse notices. It is not certain that some families were more ensconced in the capital and others in the provinces, as all of them produced office-holders *and* held lands. The prime mover in the last phase of troubles was the *megas doux* Niketas Scholarios, who backed the accession of Alexios III Grand Komnenos in 1349, then led the resistance against him in 1354–1355. He lost and was arrested, and Alexios III restored political stability for the rest of his long reign. Notably, the populace of Trebizond was a major political stakeholder that often intervened to settle the issue, just like its counterpart in Constantinople.

Thus, the histories of Trebizond and Constantinople converged in the 1340s and 1350s. They both experienced civil war, plague, and Genoese attacks. Alexios III married a daughter of Kantakouzenos' cousin in 1351.[6] By now, the two Roman states were roughly comparable in population and were coming under sustained Turkish attack, albeit from different directions. Alexios III and Ioannes V Palaiologos both had exceptionally long reigns, but the similarities ended there. For over forty years, Alexios vigorously defended his realm at the head of his armies.[7] By contrast, Ioannes V was reduced to humiliating beggary.

Challenges and points of pride

Soon after he became senior basileus, Ioannes V admitted in a chrysobull that the treasury was empty and he was forced to raise taxes on certain goods in order to pay for the army. In addition, he and his mother had borrowed 30,000 Venetian ducats (60,000 hyperpyra) to pay for the war against Kantakouzenos, on which they had to pay interest. Ioannes was the first Roman monarch who was heavily in debt to a foreign power.[8] Individual Romans had been borrowing from Venetians since at least the days of Andronikos II, a few thousand hyperpyra here and there, but Venetians had also borrowed from wealthy Romans.[9] The balance had now shifted as the Roman state became a permanent debtor and Italian bankers opened branch offices in its two main cities.[10] The hyperpyron was so devalued that foreigners were reluctant to accept it as payment, and sometimes they demanded to be paid in foreign currency or against the hyperpyron's bullion, not notional, value.[11] Thus, with revenues low and the economy saturated with foreign coin, Ioannes V ceased issuing hyperpyra. Until 1367, his highest-value coin was the silver *basilikon* (modeled on its Venetian counterpart), and after that the silver *stavraton*. These circulated mostly in the capital, and are found mixed with foreign coins. But the hyperpyron remained a notional unit of value that could be "paid in Venetian ducats," as Athonite documents put it.[12] A nationalist philosopher in the Morea, Georgios Gemistos Plethon, urged Ioannes' successor "to reform the currency. For it is absurd for us to be using these foreign counterfeit copper coins, which bring profit to others and ridicule upon us."[13]

The Romans also had few armies left. In 1354, Kantakouzenos poured cold water on the idea proposed at a war council that they go out and fight the Turks. The Turks were just as experienced, he said, and had far more men, preparedness, and eagerness, and they had vastly more territory and better morale.[14]

Shame, humiliation, and an awareness of decline are prominent themes in the literature of that time. "We have no provinces left, and we are slaves to people whom we used to command."[15] A recurring trope is the attempt to list, in anger or lamentation, the few cities and provinces that were left to the Roman state: a few lines usually sufficed.[16] But there was also a search for sources of pride and dignity. Kantakouzenos reminded his soldiers that they were descended from the Romans of old, who had conquered "almost the entire inhabited world." "Remember that we are Romans," Manuel II Palaiologos told the Thessalonians to boost their morale in 1383, adding that "the fatherland of Philip and Alexander is ours."[17] The glory of ancient Macedonia was another source of inspiration for the Romans of Thessalonike. Kydones reminded Kantakouzenos in 1345 "that the name of Macedonia inspires terror in the barbarians, as they remember

Alexander and how the few Macedonians with him conquered Asia. Show them, O basileus, that you too are Macedonians, that you differ from Alexander only in your age."[18] Even Alexios III of Trebizond, the ruler of a realm surrounded by "Persians," was compared by his court writers to Alexander. A deluxe illustrated copy of the Alexander Romance was prepared for him.[19]

Another source of pride was the very office of basileus of the Romans, who, regardless of his circumstances, "is greater and more prestigious than the kings or rulers of other people."[20] The Roman monarchy could be seen as superior in status and dignity to all others, just as Constantinople, "the eye of the *oikoumene*," was superior to all cites.[21] In the 1390s, the patriarch Antonios IV wrote to the Grand Prince of Moscow, Vasilij I, to remind him that the basileus of the Romans was the only monarch commemorated throughout the world seeing as it was his office that had established the universal Church and Christian empire. Vasilij, it seems, was arguing that the City had a Church but no longer a basileus, and had ended his commemoration in the Russian Church. The patriarch acknowledged that the Romans had lost their power, but their symbolic significance for all Christians, especially the Orthodox, remained intact.[22]

Ioannes V's reign began with a cascade of territorial losses and concessions. In 1355, he officially confirmed the Genoese possession of Chios, in exchange for a paltry (and symbolic) 500 hyperpyra per year.[23] In the same year, he married his sister Maria to the Genoese noble Francesco Gattilusio, who had helped him to reenter Constantinople in 1354. As his dowry, Gattilusio received Lesbos to rule autonomously and bequeath to his heirs, subject only to nominal recognition of the basileus' suzerainty. By maintaining a link to the dynasty, Gattilusio and his heirs were accepted by the local population, who numbered around 20,000 before the Black Death. This concession was not an act of supine indifference on Ioannes V's part. He likely did not have the forces to defend the island, and it might otherwise have fallen into the hands of Turks or hostile Genoese. (The Venetian governor in Constantinople even floated the idea that the Republic might take the City itself to prevent it from falling into Turkish hands.[24]) Lesbos would at least be held by an ally of the Palaiologoi. The Gattilusi employed ethnic Romans in their service to a greater degree than other Latin lords. The most famous was the historian Doukas, who recounted the fall of Constantinople while living on Lesbos. Doukas was in favor of Union with Rome, but the Gattilusi did not interfere much in the religion of their subjects. Overall, they charted an independent course, looking to their financial interests, and they did not help the Palaiologoi in their moment of crisis a century later.[25]

The Italians were unreliable allies. In competition with each other, they were always angling for more commercial advantages at the Romans' expense, while trying not to alienate their Turkish suppliers. Bulgaria was sometimes allied with Constantinople, but it was weak. The nearest power that might have resisted the Turks was Serbia; after all, it was Serb expansion that had fatally weakened Romanía. But when Dušan died in 1355, his state was revealed to be a ramshackle affair loosely held together by fractious nobles. "As they rebelled against each other, his state broke into ten thousand pieces, but," Kantakouzenos admitted, "the Romans were unable to seize the moment and reclaim what they had lost or repay the barbarians for their injustices."[26] The idea that Orthodox people would band together to resist their common enemy was rarely even entertained, much less put into practice.

Ioannes V Palaiologos and Union

Ioannes therefore turned to the west. His mother, after all, was a Catholic. In late 1355, he wrote to pope Innocent VI at Avignon asking for military help against the infidel and pledging, in return, to bring himself and his subjects into the fold of the Church of Rome. He laid out a detailed plan according to which his son and heir Andronikos IV, who was seven and already proclaimed basileus, would be tutored in Latin and Catholicism. A papal legate would be lodged in Constantinople to direct the transition. Should Ioannes fail to fulfill his pledge, he would abdicate and Andronikos would became basileus in his place.[27] This extraordinary offer was, at first, not taken at face value in Avignon, and it took years of correspondence for the popes to realize that Ioannes was sincere. Plans for a new crusade were always being hatched at this time, but the paradigms had changed. On the Latin side, the goal now was not to take Constantinople "back" from the Greeks but to make sure that it was not taken by the Turks. On the Roman side, promises of Union used to be made to *prevent* crusades, but from now on they would be made to *instigate* them.[28]

However, the crusading fleets of the 1350s and early 1360s either did not achieve much or attacked Egypt instead of the Aegean Turks. The Ottomans were meanwhile rapidly filling the power vacuum in the Balkans, and Ioannes V was unable to stem their advance in Thrace. Didymoteichon, Adrianople, Philippopolis, and Beroe fell during the 1360s and early 1370s. Thus, most of Thrace was lost and the hinterland of the City consisted henceforth of two coastal bands, one extending along the Sea of Marmara, including Selymbria, Herakleia, and Raidestos, and another along the Black Sea, sometimes reaching to Mesembria and Anchialos. These coastal cities were fortified and could be supplied by sea. In 1362, the City was visited by an outbreak of plague.[29] We know about these losses through brief chronicle entries. For commentary we have only the letters of Demetrios Kydones, who had become a major scholar of Latin and was engaged in a lifelong effort to translate the western theologians into Greek, including Augustine and Thomas Aquinas. He had learned Latin while serving Kantakouzenos as a secretary, and came to realize that the Latins were good not only at fighting, sailing, and trading, as many Romans dismissively believed, but had pulled ahead in understanding Aristotle too. Kydones eventually converted to Catholicism, impressed by the arguments in its favor and by western cultural dynamism, which contrasted to the stagnation of his own society. Yet he knew how deeply Latinophobic most of his countrymen were. "Don't consider us polluted for having eaten with [western] Romans," he said in a letter after his return from Italy, "we did not eat turtles and frogs."[30]

This made Kydones a figure of controversy and a target of attack, though he was protected by the basileis, especially Ioannes V, who was also moving toward Catholicism and declined to persecute anti-Palamites. The two issues were linked. Before the triumph of Palamas, major intellectuals (such as Gregoras) could be both anti-Latin and anti-Palamite. But after 1351, those who could not take the "red and white lights" seriously but wanted to be part of a thriving intellectual community had little choice but to go Catholic. Some scholars did so during the next century, following Kydones' lead, though they were a tiny fraction of the population. A larger group in the political leadership at Constantinople still hoped for help from the west and, while they would not renounce their religious identity, they were amenable to reconciliation with Rome. They needed men like Ioannes V and Kydones to keep channels open. But in mid-1364, Kydones had to admit that the Latins were better at promising aid than delivering it, and that it might take the fall of the City to motivate them. Many Romans doubted that they would come, and Turks jokingly asked, "Any news yet about the crusade?"[31]

Constantinople was now encircled both by land and sea. Turkish bands were reaching the walls and the people inside could see their fields and country homes burn. The Turks were preventing farmers from gathering crops, unless they first paid protection money. In effect, they were paying taxes to them, before even being conquered.[32] A steady trickle of emigration began, with some going to Italy or to the islands under Latin rule in search of safety, while others made deals with the Turks. The City's population gradually decreased, reduced as it was already by plague.[33] Among those who left in 1366 was the basileus Ioannes himself, though he did so in search of military aid in Hungary. Roman emperors had previously left the boundaries of the state only when they were on campaign. It was extraordinary that Ioannes paid a state visit to the "barbarians" on business that was deeply humiliating.[34] However, it was not unprecedented. Baldwin II, the last ruler of the Latin empire, known as the "Beggar Emperor," had done the same, and it was ironic that a Palaiologos, facing the same predicament, followed in his footsteps.

Hungary under Lajos I (Louis, 1342–1382) was a growing power and expanding against Serbia and Bulgaria. Ioannes sailed up the Black Sea coast and then the Danube to Buda, to avoid the overland route through Bulgaria. Lajos received him with great honor and was open to the idea of a crusade against the Turks, but he needed papal approval. Therefore, the two monarchs sent a joint embassy to Avignon. Pope Urban V welcomed the idea of a Hungarian crusade in the east, but solely for the benefit of Catholics, which the Greeks were not. The pope suspected that the Greeks were approaching the question of Union cynically and fraudulently, and he required, in order for them to qualify for aid, that the basileus, his clergy, and all the Greeks accept a long profession of faith, which he attached, by which they would capitulate unconditionally on all points that divided the two Churches. For their part, Orthodox Romans expected to receive aid before they would even begin to consider changing something as precious as their faith, so the two sides reached a stalemate: "You first!" Moreover, relations between Lajos and Ioannes soured during his six-month stay. The Hungarian required a hostage to allow Ioannes to leave—this was Manuel, Ioannes' son, who stayed behind for a few months—and even then Ioannes was held up at Vidin as the tsar blocked him from crossing his realm.[35] Bulgaria and Romanía were not on good terms at that time. The patriarch had even sent a letter to the tsar in 1364 simply to remind him of the virtues of harmony and concord.[36]

The stalemate was broken by an unexpected intervention. Amedeo VI, the chivalrous "Green Count" of Savoy and a cousin of the basileus, launched his own crusade against the Balkan Turks in 1366. As he had papal approval, this was an initial show of good faith by Rome, to match the personal pledge made by Ioannes to convert to Catholicism—neither moves were enough, but they were good starts. Amedeo's fleet sailed to the Hellespont and swiftly captured Gallipoli in August. It was a major success, for Gallipoli controlled the passageway between Asia and Europe. For Kydones, Amedeo's arrival became the prime exhibit of the Latins' willingness and ability to help against the Turks. Orthodox Serbs and Bulgarians were not helping, and they were poor and weak to boot, but "western Romans" such as Amedeo were the ideal allies for "our Romans." The links between Rome and New Rome, he argued, went back to antiquity; after all, Constantine the Great was a western Roman. Therefore, Kydones pleaded that Amedeo be admitted into the City, which he was, although against opposition.[37] The count then set about opening a path for Ioannes' return. He conquered a series of towns along the Black Sea coast held by the Bulgarians, including Sozopolis and Mesembria, and diplomatically pressured Ivan Aleksandar to allow the basileus to pass. The two cousins finally met at Sozopolis in January, 1367.[38]

Ioannes agreed to compensate Amedeo with 15,000 hyperpyra for his sea journey and Bulgarian war. The issue of Church Union proved trickier, and the two agreed to hold a debate between their representatives in Constantinople. As the patriarch Philotheos refused to debate Paulus, the Latin bishop of Smyrna and titular Latin patriarch of Constantinople, who was accompanying Amedeo, the task was taken up by Ioasaph, the retired basileus-monk Kantakouzenos, who later wrote an account of his impassioned performance before the assembled court in the summer of 1367. Paulus insisted on the need for absolute obedience to the pope, but Kantakouzenos, while favoring Union, rejected the pope's presumption of magisterial authority. That was no true Union. Even in armies, an area that he knew well, soldiers and generals consult each other. Papal absolutism would result in "terror and persecution," as under Michael VIII. True Union could be achieved only by convening a universal Council, including the patriarchs of the east. Paulus agreed to this proposal, although he had no authorization to do so, which created a serious misunderstanding between Constantinople and Rome.[39]

To advance the cause of Union, Ioannes had undertaken to travel to Rome and profess his spiritual submission to pope Urban. But Urban never agreed to a Council and expected to receive Ioannes' submission as a prelude to the universal conversion of the Greeks to Catholicism. Yet the populace of Constantinople, who were treated as shareholders in the negotiations, expected an Ecumenical Council. The patriarch Philotheos had already announced it to his bishops, with great enthusiasm.[40] But by 1368, it had become clear that no Council was in the offing. The Palamite Church of Constantinople quickly drew a line in the sand. The Synod condemned the anti-Palamite treatises of an Athonite monk and Latinist scholar, Prochoros Kydones, branding him as a follower of Barlaam, Akindynos, and, of course, Satan. This was a way of striking indirectly against his brother Demetrios, the basileus' *mesazon* who was the chief advocate and organizer of the upcoming trip to Rome, but was too powerful to touch directly. Demetrios was outraged and wrote a vicious response to Philotheos and the Palamite establishment. But the Synod had made its position clear: the basileus' conversion to Catholicism was of a private nature and not binding on his subjects. In the same act, the patriarch and bishops also pronounced Palamas a saint. This is one of the first extant cases of a formal canonization process in the Orthodox Church, which required documenting the saint's miracles. Palamas was pronounced a pillar of Orthodoxy, meaning that anyone who disagreed with him was excommunicate.[41] This indirectly erected yet another bulwark against Catholicism. Palamite authors of this period were as likely to polemicize against the Latins as against Barlaam and Akindynos.

Ioannes V set out for Italy in 1369, leaving his co-basileus Andronikos IV in charge of Constantinople and his second son Manuel in charge of Thessalonike, as despot. He took with him Kydones, Francesco Gattilusio, and some relatives and officials, but no clergy. They traveled by sea to Naples and then overland to Rome, arriving in September. Pope Urban was only briefly in Rome in 1367–1370, before returning to Avignon. On 18 October, the formal ceremony of Ioannes' conversion took place, using the same formula that Michael VIII had signed. Three days later, at a public ceremony Ioannes knelt before the pope and kissed his foot, knee, and cheek. The basileus had instructed his retinue "to muzzle themselves and not discuss any controversial issue" with their hosts. A century before, Michael VIII had professed Catholicism in order to avert an attack on Constantinople from the west; now, Ioannes V did the same in order to instigate an attack on the Turks from the west. The pope duly dispatched letters encouraging Catholic states to aid the basileus and his realm, though it was clear to all that no military operation was in the works, nor would the pope put much effort into organizing such a project. In fact, the climate of suspicion at the Curia was revealed in January, 1370, when the basileus was required to sign an additional document clarifying that by "Roman Church" he meant the one ruled by the pope; this was presumably to prevent him from secretly holding to the faith of his own fellow "Romans." Urban also issued a general letter to "the Greeks," encouraging them to follow their ruler's example and give up their "damnable schism." There would be no Ecumenical Council, for Rome already had all the answers and would be happy to provide instruction for anyone who was still confused.[42]

In the spring of 1370, Ioannes traveled to Venice to borrow more money.[43] The Venetians were demanding over 20,000 hyperpyra in reparations; over 30,000 ducats from the crown-jewels loan; and 5,000 ducats from another loan he took out in 1352. What they wanted was less for the basileus to repay his loans than for him to remain in their debt so they could extort concessions from him. Specifically, they wanted to buy the island of Tenedos from him in exchange for 25,000 ducats (a paltry sum, according to their own internal assessment of its worth), six ships, and the crown jewels. It is unclear whether this would also erase his other debts. The Venetians quibbled in order to prolong the negotiations into the summer, fall, and then the winter of 1371, because they knew that the basileus was running out of funds to cover his stay.[44] The papal and Venetian sources comment on the poverty of his retinue, and eventually he had to send for money from the Morea. It was his second son Manuel who brought it from Thessalonike, along with ships to escort his father back to Constantinople, which they reached in October, 1371. The stay in Venice had been a waste of time and money, and no deal was reached on the loans or regarding Tenedos.[45]

Turkish expansion

Ioannes reaped little benefit from his visit to Rome. He subsequently made no effort to remind his subjects that he had converted to Catholicism, and they, in turn, pretended that he had not. He returned home to an explosive situation. While most of the Serb lords of Dušan's fragmented empire were busy fighting each other, two important ones, kralj Vukašin and despot Uglješa, joined forces against the growing problem of Turkish raids. These were being carried out less by regular forces under sultan Murad I (1362–1389) and more by irregulars who raided, pillaged, and took slaves under the banner of holy war against the infidel (whence they are called *ghazis*, holy warriors). The most prominent among them was Evrenos, who supposedly lived for over a century. On 26 September, 1371, the combined forces of the raiders, including Evrenos and Lala Şahin Pasha, defeated Vukašin and Uglješa at the battle of Černomen on the Maritsa river. The Serbs were massacred and the Balkans were opened up to further Turkish penetration. The Romans also took advantage of the Serbian defeat, reestablishing their authority over parts of Macedonia in the early 1370s. In 1373, after Manuel had been crowned co-basileus, Ioannes issued a chrysobull ghostwritten by Kydones, which praised Manuel in superlative terms, thanking him for standing by his side in Hungary and Italy. It granted him power over any lands in Thessaly and Macedonia that he liberated. "For a basileus can give any part of his country to whomever he pleases."[46]

Conversely, the crown could also confiscate lands. In order to fund his army, Manuel confiscated half the lands owned by the monasteries of Athos and Thessalonike and turned them into military pronoias. "We are thinking of the common good, lest everything be lost."[47] Such confiscations were carried out at intervals into the fifteenth century and provoked at least one theologian, Nikolaos Kabasilas, a native of Thessalonike, to protest this injustice. In a treatise defending private property as the foundation of society—a revealing position for a mystical theologian to take—Kabasilas countered the arguments put forward by secular officials for the reallocation of Church land to secular purposes.[48] Yet Kabasilas offers no alternative for the defense of Romanía. He insists on the letter of the law at a time of sovereign collapse, and the views that he attributes to his opponents are fascinating: God's laws have expired and need to be replaced, he alleges that they said, and since soldiers are the ones who die in defense of the monks, the latter can at least feed them.[49]

The twenty years after Ioannes' return from Italy are poorly documented on all sides, except the Venetian. During this period, the Ottomans advanced across the Balkans, defeating and subordinating all the kingdoms and petty principalities that they encountered, even while they were also fighting against rival emirates in Anatolia. Instead of uniting to meet this existential threat, the Christians fought each other. The Serb empire had fragmented into warring pieces, and had been built at the Romans' expense to begin with. The Catalan duchy of Athens was attacked by a Navaresse mercenary company in 1379 and was then taken over by the Florentine banker-adventurer Nerio Acciaiuoli, who was buying up large tracts of the decrepit and leaderless Principality of Achaea. Venice and Genoa were perpetually at odds and fought one of their most vicious wars in this period, the Chioggia War (1376–1381), over who would get Tenedos from the basileus. The two Churches were in schism, as each waited for the other to make the first move toward reconciliation (submit to Rome or send military aid). The Romans were also prone to infighting. It was, after all, a civil war that had opened the Balkans to Turkish penetration in the first place, and now, in the 1370s and 1380s, another round of Palaiologan infighting, between Ioannes V and his son Andronikos IV, allowed the sultans to play the two sides against each other and thus consolidate their hold. The Palaiologoi, said Kydones, "forgot about those who are their enemies by nature [Turks] and turned on each other instead, squandering their energies against themselves and their subjects, not on those others." To fight each other, "they had to pay court to the barbarian, and so they ended up serving him more than their own subjects. . . . Each of them wanted to claim all power for himself, and threatened to go over to the barbarian and bring him in against his own fatherland and friend, if he did not get his way."[50]

Ironically, the only trend toward unity in this period was the recognition of Palamism by the Churches of Serbia, Bulgaria, and Russia. This was a conspicuous victory for Athos and Constantinople and a confirmation of their leadership in the broader Orthodox world.[51] Yet it too came at a cost. Palamism was divisive among Roman intellectuals, and even contributed to some of them converting to Catholicism. It also strengthened the barrier between the two Churches: on the one hand, Rome would never accept the new doctrines of the energies and lights, while on the other the patriarch risked losing his newly confirmed preeminence among the Orthodox Churches if he accepted Union. But the "international Palamism" of the Church brought almost no political, economic, or military advantages to any of its members.

At precisely this time of Christian strife, the Turks were moving toward unification and consolidation. At its core, the Ottoman project was no different than that of the other conquest-emirates of Anatolia. A dynastic warlord attracted nomadic fighters to his banners by delivering victories and the proceeds of raids, including revenues from land and slaves. The Ottomans happened to be the most successful emirate in the long term, in part for accidental reasons (battles, leadership, and the like) and in part because their Bithynian base enabled them to leap across the straits and expand in the Balkans at the expense of weak Christian powers. Ottoman expansion in the Balkans was promoted by freelance raiders, who would soften up future targets and create conditions of chaos in which the main Ottoman armies could intervene. The emirates and the raiders occasionally claimed to be waging a holy war to expand the domain of Islam, but this was not a hat that they wore on all occasions. For one thing, they were fighting each other too, and the rhetoric of holy war against the Christians was a method of enticing warriors away from rival leaders. The switch from mercenaries-for-hire to holy warriors could be accomplished quickly, as when Kantakouzenos' soldiers quickly became ghazis when they subsequently served under Süleyman, the son of Orhan.[52] Warrior bands do not require such beliefs to wage predatory raids. They tend to believe, Palamas observed when he was in their captivity, "that God approves everything that they do, such as murdering, pillaging, and taking slaves. This is why they have prevailed over the Romans."[53]

Roman society was by this point intimately familiar with Turks and Turkish culture. Thousands of Turks had immigrated to Romanía since ca. 1100, many as

OTTOMAN EXPANSION TO 1461

border in early 1402 — border in late 1453

Conquests of:
1 Osman I (1299–1326)
2 Orhan (1326–1362)
3 Murad I (1362–1389)
4 Bayezid I (1389–1402)
5 Mehmed I (1402–1421)
6 Murad II (1421–1451)
7 Mehmed II (1451–1481)
3, 7 repeated conquest
(4) temporary conquest

HUNGARY
Sirmium
Belgrade 7
Golubac 4, 6, 7
Târgoviște
Smederevo
6, 7
Severin
WALLACHIA
Hârșova
BOSNIA
SERBIA
Vidin
Danube
5
Dorostolon
5
Kruševac
Nikopolis
Pločnik
Niš
BULGARIA
Šumen
4, 5
Kaliakra
Varna
3, 6, 7
3
Priština
Serdica
4 Tărnovo
Kotor
Kosovo
6, 7
Zlatica
Mesembria
Anchialos
Skadar
4
3
Beroe
4, 7
Skopje
Philippoupolis 3
3
Krujë
(5)
4
Prilep
Strumica
Černomen
Edirne
Bizye
3, 7
Durazzo
6
Ohrid
Didymoteichon
Constantinople
Pelagonia
3
Tzouroulon
4
Berat
Serres
Xantheia
Raidestos
2, 5
Avlona
Nikomedeia
5
Kastoria
3
2
2, 6
7
Thessalonike
Ainos
3, 6
7
Gallipoli
Pegai
Argyrokastron
Butrint
Ioannina
Kerkyra
4
Larissa
6
Trikala
Lemnos
Arta
Zetounion 4, 6
(4)
Leukas
Mytilene
Salona
Bodonitsa 5
7 Phokaia
Kephalonia
4, 5
7
Negroponte
Chios
Glarentsa
Patras
Thebes
Corinth
Athens
Zakynthos
Argos
7
Mystras
Naxos
Modon
Koron
Monembasia
VENICE
Kythera
Crete
Candia
0 150 km
0 100 mi
Theodoro
Black Sea
Amastris 7
Sinope
CANDAR
Kastamone
4, 7
4, 5
Amisos
4, 6
CANIK
4, 6
Trebizond
7
Herakleia
4, 5
Gangra
Amaseia
4, 7
2
4
Tokat
SIVAS
Erzincan
2
Nikaia
Bursa
Söğüt
Ankyra
4
Sebasteia
(4)
1
Eskişehir
3
KARASI
2
Kütahya
3
3, 5
Harput
Pergamon
GERMIYAN
Kırşehir
SARUHAN
4, 5
Kaisareia
Magnesia
3, 5, 7
(4)
Melitene
Karahisar
Aksaray
Amid
4, 5
Philadelpheia 4
Philomelion
Smyrna
AYDIN
KARAMAN
DULKADIR
Ayasuluk
Laodikeia
(4)
Konya
Maraş
Edessa
4, 6
HAMIT
3, 5
RAMAZAN
Mylasa
4, 5
Laranda
Adana
MENTEŞE
TEKE
Tarsos
Ayas
Halikarnassos
Attaleia
Korykos
Aleppo
4, 6
4, 5
Antioch
Raqqa
Rhodes
Alanya
MAMLUKS
Euphrates
Laodikeia
CYPRUS
Mediterranean Sea
Hamah

Map by Ian Mladjov

soldiers who were resettled by the basileis, or as refugees from the Mongols. Back then, many had converted to Christianity and assimilated to Roman society, although sometimes they retained distinctive names such as Soultanos, Masgides ("Mosque-Man"), and Malik. Their food, words, and clothing styles entered the mainstream Roman mix.[54] There was such a thing as Turkish Romans.

During the fourteenth century, the balance tipped and the Muslim Turks became the dominant force. In the Balkans, the conquerors were a tiny minority and so Christian society and institutions survived. The Ottomans simply did not have the numbers to dominate local society, and so they preferred to divide its rulers and subordinate them to the sultan, who ideally would have to suppress no more than one or two Christian "rebels" at a time. Conquered Romans were not required or even invited to convert, only to pay tribute and accept subordination to the Muslim warrior class. After all, Christian *dhimmis* (protected minorities under Muslim rule) paid higher taxes. They were allowed to keep their religion and their ethnicity, in striking contrast to Latin imperialism, which recognized neither the Orthodoxy nor the Romanness of its "Greek schismatic" subjects. One victim of Michael VIII's pro-Union persecution noted that the "Muslim will dominate your body, but the heretic [i.e., the Latin] will take over your soul."[55] Many Romans were making that point: there were no good options here, but Muslim rule might be preferable.[56] The Ottomans incentivized this option by giving better terms to cities that surrendered, while slaughtering the people of those that resisted to the end (contrast the fate of Thessalonike in 1387 with 1430). Anti-Union Romans preferred the Ottomans to the Latins. Those who wanted western assistance, by contrast, or who were pro-Union, accused them of being too willing to deal with the Turks. Yet there was no "pro-Turkish" party as such.[57] Groups and individuals made whatever deals they had to in order to survive. Some churches and monasteries collaborated in order to keep part of their lands.[58] For their part, the Ottomans preferred to organize their subjects' lives around churches and monasteries rather than Roman political institutions that could muster armies and leadership cadres. The latter they dismantled, which is how in the long run the Church inherited the mantle of "Byzantium" by default.

In Anatolia, by contrast, more lands were confiscated by the Turkish rulers, towns abandoned, and churches and monasteries driven to extinction. The major difference was the influx of Turkmen migrants, who had changed the demographic and religious balance. In Anatolia, Romans converted to Islam in large numbers, as they were often stripped of their religious institutions, lost hope that the basileus would free them, and lived surrounded by Muslims, who enjoyed significant social and economic advantages. Manuel II admitted that converts wanted "wealth and glory and the pleasures of life, and so they chose to live according to the barbarian customs."[59] In one estimate, Muslims were a majority in Anatolia by the fourteenth century, as a result of both conversion and migration.[60] The number of Church sees gradually declined. Anatolian bishops who were not able to take up their posts often congregated in Constantinople, and the Synod sometimes took measures to ensure that they were supported, as the revenues from their sees had declined. One approach was to combine a see under occupation with one that was free (e.g., Smyrna and Chios) to provide the bishop with a salary.[61]

There was little that Constantinople could do for Anatolian Christians. In 1338, the patriarch was shocked to discover that the number of Christians in—of all places—Nikaia had dramatically declined. The Church, he reassured them, would always receive them back and "salvation is still possible even for those who practice their faith secretly" while outwardly conforming to Islam, seeing as the penalty for apostasy from Islam was death.[62] Kantakouzenos piously claims that his daughter, married to Orhan in 1346, helped many Romans return to the Christian faith.[63] Another strategy was to write martyrologies of those who were killed by the Muslims for apostasy, to bolster the resolve of the faithful. Through these narratives, Roman Christians also affirmed their identity in the face of an all-too-depressing reality.[64] They gradually became a minority among Turks and ex-Roman Muslims.

The founders of the Ottoman dynasty, Osman and Orhan, had originally little control over the raiders, mostly nomadic Turkmen, who flooded Anatolia. They were happy to lease them out to the basileis or funnel them into the Balkans, because otherwise they might disrupt the arrangements that the Ottomans were working out with the settled populations of Anatolia. But over time, and especially under Murad I, the Ottoman army became a more centralized force that deployed the raiders as auxiliaries and forerunners. The backbone of the army consisted of cavalry soldiers supported by pronoia-equivalents called *timars*. The sultan's personal corps consisted of the janissaries, who were reminiscent of the old Islamic slave armies. Janissaries had been captured in war as children, or removed from their families through the *devşirme* ("collection"), and raised to be Muslim soldiers loyal to the sultan. As the territories controlled by the dynasty expanded, the sultan could increasingly call upon the military assistance of vassal rulers, whom he had defeated but whose lands he had not annexed.[65] Thus, the emerging Ottoman state was oriented around the increasingly charismatic authority of the sultan, which was bolstered by the celebration of his virtues, a mythological aura, and his promotion of an Islamic-imperial social order. This was a dynastic state, lacking an equivalent concept to that of the impersonal "polity of the Roman people." It expanded not only through territorial conquest but by absorbing "defectors" and converts from the leading elements of Christian society, who brought their own retainers and resources to the project of empire.[66] Thus, the sultans were always surrounded by men who bore Islamic or Turkish names, but many of them were renegade ex-Romans, Serbs, Albanians, and the like, who were valuable assets in dealing with their former countrymen and with Christians generally. In time, ethnic cliques would form at the sultan's otherwise Muslim court.[67]

Vassals of the sultan

In the 1370s, the Roman basileus became a vassal of the Ottoman sultan. This did not happen in 1371, after the Maritsa battle, as is commonly believed, but in 1376. In May, 1373, Ioannes V and his eldest son Andronikos IV came to blows for unknown reasons (the sources for these events are late and contradictory), and Andronikos was arrested. He had Turkish allies, but these were likely not under Murad's orders.[68] Andronikos was a charismatic personality,[69] and only sixteen years younger than his father (they were born in 1348 and 1332 respectively). He had also tasted power when he governed Constantinople during his father's two prolonged absences, to Hungary and Italy. Now he and his son Ioannes (who was six) were imprisoned and blinded in order to preclude them from the succession, though they mysteriously regained their sight subsequently. A later historian, the Athenian Laonikos Chalkokondyles, says that the procedure was done with hot vinegar, after which their eyes eventually healed.[70] In September 1373, Manuel was proclaimed co-basileus. In either 1373 or 1374 Ioannes V traveled to the court of Murad in Anatolia to make a peace treaty. We know this primarily from two letters of Kydones, which do not suggest that the basileus was the sultan's vassal, yet the disparity in power between the two rulers was veering close to that reality. "I hope," Kydones wrote, "that the barbarian will be more gentle toward you." What Murad wanted from the basileus was the return of Gallipoli, but he did not get it.[71]

Meanwhile, the Venetians had been pressuring Ioannes over the matter of his debts and their reparations, and at some point the issue of Tenedos was raised again. By 1376, the two sides had reached an agreement as to its sale.[72] But the Genoese vehemently opposed this deal. Probably with their help, Andronikos escaped from prison and went straight to Galata. He made an alliance with them and Murad to overthrow his father. Murad happily fomented this civil war, in exchange for receiving Gallipoli from his puppet basileus. In the past, Romans would draw foreigners into their civil wars in exchange for concessions, but now foreigners were instigating Roman civil wars in order to win concessions. Our sources are poor, but it is clear that with help from the Genoese and the Turks Andronikos entered the City on 12 August, 1376, and took it over, possibly after street fighting that lasted for days. He imprisoned his father and brothers Manuel and Theodoros.[73] The new basileus immediately rewarded his Genoese allies with Tenedos. However, the island's inhabitants were loyal to Ioannes V, who had lived there for a while, and they resisted the Genoese, welcoming the Venetians instead. The Genoese "forced" Andronikos to attack the Venetians in Constantinople and to join them on a military expedition to Tenedos, bringing one ship. The campaign was a failure, and the new basileus was clearly following Genoese orders.[74] Genoa and Venice went on to fight a vicious all-out war, the Chioggia War, to which the Romans could contribute little but from which they suffered much, as trade was disrupted, causing famine, and the Venetians attacked the City's harbors.

Even more "dizzying" for Kydones was Andronikos' deal with Murad. He not only gave him Gallipoli, but the alliance amounted to subordination: "they are to receive countless money from us, order us around, and we have to obey him in all matters." Andronikos also pledged to provide Murad with soldiers, which he did in person in 1377, going to Anatolia, presumably to help Murad in his wars against the other emirates.[75] Andronikos thus became the first basileus to attend on a foreign ruler. His usurpation of power also split the Palaiologan dynasty into two, and then three, competing branches, which foreign powers, especially the sultans and the Genoese, played off against each other. This intra-dynastic conflict lasted for over two decades, but is poorly documented. The following are its main themes. First, it had become easy for rival Roman factions to break or sneak into Constantinople and take it over from the basileus ruling in Blachernai. This had happened already in 1328, 1347, 1354, and 1376, and it happened again in 1379, when Ioannes V and his sons escaped from confinement and returned to power in July. It happened again in 1390, when Ioannes VII, Andronikos' son, returned from Genoa to seize power, and again later that year, when Manuel II took the City back from Ioannes VII (his nephew). Constantinople's defenses were not weak or neglected, and foreign powers never considered that approach to taking the City. Instead, each dynastic faction had supporters inside who facilitated the takeover. Also, given their scant resources, the basileis could not properly reward their followers and so the latter frequently changed sides. At no time, however, did any of these factions or the populace consider letting the Turks into the City.[76]

Second, each dynastic faction was supported by foreign powers to the point of being their clients. Andronikos IV and his son Ioannes VII were backed by the Genoese and promised them Tenedos in return. When they lost the City in 1379, Andronikos and his son fled to Galata, taking as hostages Andronikos' mother Helene and her father, the monk-basileus Ioasaph-Ioannes VI Kantakouzenos, who was almost ninety. There, for over a year, they endured a blockade by Ioannes V and the Venetians. The latter had helped Ioannes V retake the throne and were fighting the Chioggia War against Genoa. A power-sharing agreement was finally reached in 1381/2, according to which Andronikos IV and Ioannes VII would be recognized as the heirs of Ioannes V but would reside in the highly fortified port town of Selymbria—all this for the "common good of the Romans and of all Christians everywhere."[77] The Venetians annexed Tenedos and relocated its population to other parts of their empire, but they did not pay Ioannes V for it.

Moreover, the two rival branches of the dynasty were still in a watchful state of near-war, even after Andronikos IV's illness and death in 1385. When Ioannes V wanted to complain that his grandson Ioannes VII was violating the agreement, he wrote to Genoa; and when Ioannes VII set out to overthrow his grandfather, which he briefly did in 1390, he went to Genoa to secure aid.[78] A correspondent of Kydones observed that "some demon has decided to turn the affairs of the Romans upside down, and to exterminate even the small trace of our race that still survives. The two basileis keep replacing each other and have caused a tremendous turmoil. They do not care at all about the common good but look only after their own pleasure, honor, and profit."[79]

The sultan was playing kingmaker. Murad backed Andronikos IV in 1376 and then Ioannes V in 1379 against Andronikos, even though the latter had performed loyal service as a vassal in 1377. Murad presumably raised the amount of tribute that Ioannes would pay him, up to 30,000 gold coins according to a later, garbled source.[80] He also demanded that Ioannes V's son Manuel II attend upon him at his court in Anatolia in 1381–1382, thus effectively excluding Manuel, Ioannes V's choice for the succession, from the negotiations over the power-sharing agreement.[81] Forcing Ioannes V to accept Andronikos IV as his heir in 1381 was likely intended to perpetuate the dynasty's division and provide both Turks and Genoese with future opportunities to intervene.

Third, conflicts over the throne in Constantinople were henceforth limited to members of the Palaiologan dynasty. The Roman political sphere had contracted to this one dynasty. But why, given its record of failure, did it last for so long? For starters, the old military aristocracy, which was still thriving under Andronikos III and which might have produced contenders for the throne, had disappeared along with the Romans' territories and armies. If the old military elite wanted to reside on what was left of its lands, it would have to bow to the Serbs or Turks who had conquered them. Otherwise, the top commands in the Roman polity were mostly given to Palaiologoi, and there were barely enough left for them. Thessalonike was given to Ioannes V's son Theodoros and then, when he was posted to the Morea, it was seized by Manuel II (in 1382–1387). Selymbria was allocated to Andronikos IV and then Ioannes VII. And in 1382, Ioannes V assigned Theodoros to the Morea, after the death of Kantakouzenos' sons, Manuel and Matthaios, who had governed it until then. Moreover, the Palaiologoi were in debt to the Italians and were vassals of the sultan, which gave those foreign powers an incentive to keep propping them up. Paradoxically, foreign dependence may have benefited the Palaiologoi and kept them on the throne.

The Roman aristocracy had lost most of its lands, and its political and military ambitions were severely curtailed. Kydones, for example, had lost many of his estates to the Serbs. Nor could state service compensate. Even Kydones wrote tersely to Ioannes V that if he wanted to be called a ruler he needed to give him the back pay that he owed him.[82] A small core of the old families survived, clustered tightly around the court. But alongside them we find a rising class of merchants, some from the Peloponnese. They became more prominent in this final phase of the polity, either because more Romans turned to trade or because the thinning of the military and political class made merchants more visible to the court. Many court officials became partners in trading ventures with Italians, though the volume of Roman trade was small by comparison. Georgios Notaras, the court interpreter of Andronikos IV, traded in fish. His grandson Loukas would be the last *mesazon*. Georgios Goudeles, the *mesazon* of Ioannes V, traded in grain, and when he was sent on an embassy to Genoa in 1390, it is not clear which of his two roles was primary: personal commerce or state diplomacy.[83] Missions to Italy were also a good opportunity to engage in banking. The problem of Romans obtaining, or at least claiming, Venetian and Genoese citizenship came to the fore, as that was a way to avoid paying taxes on trade. The basileus' own men were not paying their fair share.[84] Another problem was debt, as many loans were taken out, often from Italian bankers, to finance trading ventures. It is not surprising that a treatise was written at this time against those who charge interest, denouncing this evil banking practice as illegal and petty. "You don't work to earn interest, you just sit back and profit." Interestingly, it was written by the defender of the inalienable property rights of the Church, the mystic theologian and saint Nikolaos Kabasilas.[85]

Manuel II Palaiologos

The late Palaiologan civil war was won by Manuel II, though at times his prospects seemed dim. In 1382, aged thirty-two, he seized Thessalonike and ruled it as an independent basileus, breaking from his father and brother. He had ruled Thessalonike as a despot in 1369–1373, but the goal of his "new rule" was to defend the city from Turkish conquest.[86] He rejected his father's submission to the sultan, who sent his armies under Hayreddin Pasha to seize Macedonia in the 1380s. This wiped out the Roman gains of the 1370s. Yet in Thessalonike, Manuel met with passive resistance. The Thessalonians were divided not only over the issue of the Turks but along socioeconomic lines too. The rich were reluctant to contribute money to the war effort, or were seen that way and resented. They were, after all, cut off from the agricultural source of most of their wealth, and a settlement with the Turks would give them at least access to some of their lands. Many among the populace were also in favor of surrendering to the Turks, who began to blockade the city in 1383 after taking Serres. The defense was widely regarded as hopeless, as the blockade had cut the city off, leading to general "misery."[87] Thessalonike was given the choice of tribute or slaughter,[88] and many believed that Turkish rule was God's will. The archbishop, Isidoros Glabas, clashed with Manuel over the confiscation of Church property, and quit the city. Manuel lacked resources for a defense, and his few outside allies could not send help. He knew that people were hungry and demoralized, so he convened a public assembly where he delivered a rousing speech in favor of fighting on for liberty, appealing to the Thessalonians' pride in their Roman and Macedonian identity and the succor of St. Demetrios.[89] He failed, and not only because his speech was in convoluted classical Greek. In April, 1387, he fled from Thessalonike knowing that in a few days it would be surrendered to Hayreddin Pasha.

Turkish rule in Thessalonike was remote and apparently not cruel, though the tribute (*harac*) was heavy, many lands were confiscated, especially state land held in pronoia, and Turkish settlers were placed in strategic locations around the hinterland. Roman officials were replaced with Muslim ones and legal cases were settled by judges appointed by the sultan. But for the most part, Christians were given a degree a autonomy, a "tolerable slavery."[90] The social divisions persisted. In 1393, matters came to a head and the *archontes* threatened to resign in the face of popular hatred. The archbishop Isidoros Glabas urged the populace to respect their betters, who had the thankless task of mediating between Thessalonike and the Turkish authorities, incurring the risks of travel to the latter (located probably at Serres), and enduring the insults that they received there. In a sermon of 1395, Isidoros, who had objected to Manuel's use of Church property for the war effort, provides an early attestation of the child tax, the *devşirme*, which supported the sultan's slave army: "What suffering might one not experience, seeing his own child, whom he raised, over whom he shed tears praying for his happiness, being torn away from him violently by the hands of foreigners and forced to adopt a barbaric language, dress, and religion? A child who once attended churches is taught to murder his own kind!"[91]

Manuel had nowhere to go. He encamped on Lesbos, but was not allowed into Mytilene by its lord, Francesco II Gattilusio, and so moved on to Tenedos. He wrote a separate work, addressed to Nikolaos Kabasilas but intended as a circular apology, to complain about the Thessalonians, on whose attitude he blamed his failure.[92] Ioannes V still held him in disgrace, but Murad, who wanted to control all the rival factions of the dynasty, graciously invited him to Bursa. Ioannes V was thereby obliged to take Manuel back, but quickly dispatched him to Lemnos—all this in 1387. When Ioannes VII seized Constantinople in 1390 with help from the Genoese and the next sultan, Bayezid (1389–1402), Manuel was in the City, but he slipped out and recruited Latin allies. Bayezid had apparently given the City to Ioannes VII "as a gift," although it was not his to give, Manuel protested.[93] After two failed attempts, Manuel reentered the City with help from the Hospitallers of Rhodes and drove Ioannes VII out. A new agreement was brokered by the Genoese and Bayezid. Ioannes VII returned to Selymbria and Manuel II became Ioannes V's heir, which entailed military service to the sultan.[94] The new sultan, however, was the vehement Bayezid Yıldırım ("Thunderbolt"). He was cut from a different cloth than his father, Murad (who was struck down while decisively defeating the Serbs at the battle of Kosovo on 15 June, 1389). Manuel came to detest Bayezid. He had to pay a tribute so heavy that "even the poor had to be taxed, as the public revenue is barely enough to cover the cost."[95]

Bayezid wanted to centralize his power, annex the emirates in Anatolia, subordinate Balkan rulers to himself, and tie up loose ends, which included the conquest of Constantinople. In 1390–1391, Manuel and Ioannes VII were required to personally bring soldiers to Bayezid's campaigns in Anatolia. In 1391, Bayezid annexed the last Roman outpost in Anatolia, Philadelpheia; it is unclear whether Manuel personally witnessed this humiliation.[96] The sultan's efforts were then directed against the emirates in Anatolia. But he also demanded that Ioannes V demolish the fort that had been built around the Golden Gate of Constantinople, or else he would kill Manuel. The basileus had no choice but to comply, weakening the City's defenses.[97] Bayezid also demanded that a *qadi*, a Muslim religious judge, be placed in Constantinople to adjudicate disputes involving Muslim merchants.[98] When Ioannes V died on 16 February, 1391, Manuel rushed back to the capital to secure his accession, but quickly returned to the sultan, leaving his mother Helene Kantakouzene in charge. His honeymoon as chief basileus was to help the Ottomans consolidate their hold on Anatolia. In his letters, he describes it as a place of Roman ruins whose names had been forgotten, making him a stranger in the land of his ancestors.[99]

Manuel's campaign letters are remarkable. His experience was miserable, especially for having to attend Bayezid's drinking parties. To ameliorate this indignity, unprecedented for a basileus, Manuel fell back on his identity as a source of pride. He stressed his classical education, using Aristophanic allusions to mock Bayezid. During the winter in Ankyra, he worked on a text proving the superiority of his faith over Islam. This was the *Dialogue with a Persian*, the Persian being a Muslim scholar with whom Manuel was staying. Even here Manuel alluded to "the Comedian," drawing attention to the fact that his interlocutor could neither catch nor understand his classical allusions.[100] Yet on a pragmatic level, he still had to "fight alongside the Persians, because we would incur greater dangers by not doing so"; however, it was "unbearable to do so, for their increase, to which we are contributing, proportionately weakens us."[101]

On 10 February, 1392, Manuel married Helene Dragaš, the daughter of a Serbian ruler and fellow vassal of Bayezid. On the following day, the couple were crowned in a spectacular ceremony in Hagia Sophia that is described in detail by a Russian pilgrim to Constantinople. It took three hours for the procession to advance from the doors of the Great Church to the imperial thrones inside, or so it felt to him.[102] This display was meant to shore up Manuel's legitimacy, for many were skeptical of him and Ioannes VII enjoyed support. The Scriptural passages read on the occasion praised his "unshakable kingdom" and included the Parable of the Good Shepherd, a pointed injunction against usurpation.[103]

Bayezid's siege of Constantinople

Manuel's fear of his nephew Ioannes VII was an aspect of Turkish policy, as Bayezid fomented division among his vassals to neutralize resistance to his consolidation of power. In 1393, while his raiders reached as far as Greece, the sultan conquered and subjugated much of Bulgaria. In the winter of 1393–1394, he summoned his Serb and Roman vassals to attend him at Serres, but Manuel was spooked by the fact that his brother Theodoros was summoned from the Morea along with Ioannes VII. It felt like an ambush and prelude to a major shakeup. The basileus suspected that Bayezid and Ioannes VII were conspiring against him and he feared for his safety, as the sultan, whose "jaw gaped like Hades," was blinding and amputating the limbs of many in the princes' retinues. Manuel refused a return summons, fleeing to the City and barricading it, while Theodoros fled back to the Morea as Bayezid marched into Greece. This was effectively a declaration of war. Bayezid sent Evrenos to raid the Morea while he brought his forces to the walls of Constantinople. The sultan had decided to remove this thorn in the side of the Ottoman empire.[104] Kydones had been right: once they had subdued the Bulgarians and Serbs, the Turks would come for Constantinople.[105]

Bayezid's soldiers did occasionally assault the City's walls, as he watched from atop a tall hill, probably adjacent to Galata. From there he could see Hagia Sophia, which he dreamed of converting into a mosque.[106] But generally his strategy was to starve the City out through a blockade that lasted for eight years (1394–1402), while he continued to fight in the Balkans and Anatolia. Realizing that they could not defeat the Turks in battle, the Romans had invested in the fortification of their remaining cities along the coast and on Lemnos.[107] The basileus effectively controlled only the lands inside the walls: "Rule in there, then," Bayezid is reported to have said.[108] Ottoman ships patrolled the waters around the City to prevent the delivery of grain. Their domination of the sea was enhanced by Gallipoli and a fort, Anadolu Hisar, that the sultan built on the Asian side of the Bosporos.[109] Travel in and out of the City was not entirely blocked, but became difficult and dangerous. As much of the land inside was agricultural, some food was grown locally, but not enough. Venice sent one modest shipment per year, and other allies occasionally ran the blockade to deliver supplies. But over time privation, hoarding, and price gouging "ground people down with hunger and poverty."[110] The price of grain skyrocketed and those who could sneak it across from Galata made a killing. Small businesses such as bakeries and inns were shuttered or sold off at low prices. Debts went unpaid, properties were devalued, and dowries sold off illegally to procure the means to survive. Buildings fell into ruin and properties were abandoned as people left. Constantinople became a ghost town. The residents' fate is well documented in the records of the patriarchal court that adjudicated the inevitable disputes. People named Palaiologos,

Gabras, Raoul, and Philanthropenos also suffered the ill effects of the siege, and only those who were in a position to loan money profited.[111]

Manuel's diplomatic appeals to the west went into overdrive, as salvation could come only from the intervention of a foreign power. He soon discovered that king Sigismund of Hungary was organizing a campaign against Bayezid, for Turkish expansion was infringing on his borders, and so the two kings coordinated their plans. Manuel pinned all his hopes on the massive French and Hungarian army that was led by Sigismund south into the Balkans, but on 25 September, 1396, it was annihilated by Bayezid at the battle of Nikopolis on the Danube. Sigismund was evacuated down the Danube to Constantinople, where he delivered the news to a devastated Manuel. "This terrible disaster struck us with the utmost violence and tore up by the roots all the fairest hopes," the basileus wrote to Kydones, who had already emigrated from the City to Venice, to retire with honorary citizenship. Manuel acknowledged that some of his own subjects were thinking of converting to Islam, as this victory was a sign of God's favor for Bayezid.[112] Manuel offered to cede Constantinople or Imbros or Lemnos to the Venetians, if they would only undertake the City's defense in case he failed. The Republic politely declined, as it was not prepared to wage all-out war against the sultan. But they would not let go of Manuel's debts.[113] His subjects became desperate. Many were leaving the City. If, like Kydones, they had the connections and skills, such as classical learning, they tried for Venetian Crete or Italy. But others deserted to the Turks to escape hunger and poverty. Whole neighborhoods of the City were being abandoned.[114]

In 1399, Manuel resumed his appeals for aid from the west, "sending out a constant stream of envoys from the Aegean to the Pillars of Herakles."[115] The popes eventually began a collection to help beleaguered Constantinople, while the patriarch Matthaios requested money from the bishop of Kiev and All Russia. "Help us, we are hemmed in."[116] In 1399, the famous French marshal Jean II le Maingre, known as Boucicaut, a veteran of Nikopolis, arrived in Constantinople with about 1,000 men, 400 of them heavily armed. Joint Roman-French forces attacked Turkish positions around the City, even on the Asian side, but this provided only a temporary reprieve. Boucicaut's biography claims that it was he who persuaded Manuel to make his appeal to the western kings in person, and that he was instrumental in reconciling Manuel to Ioannes VII, who would rule the City in his absence.[117] Manuel had just called Ioannes a "despicable person rather than a nephew, a disaster for the Romans."[118] But there was support for Ioannes VII in Constantinople, and he was backed by men with commercial ties to Italy.[119] For unclear reasons, Ioannes had also broken from Bayezid and agreed to rule in Constantinople as a custodian-basileus while Manuel traveled in search of aid. Ioannes and his followers were received on 4 December, 1399, in a public display of reconciliation, and Manuel departed for the west six days later on a Venetian galley, accompanied by Boucicaut and his own family, which he entrusted to Theodoros in the Morea. Manuel knew that he might not have a home to which to return.

During his long absence and distant travels, Manuel failed to persuade any western ruler to take action. The only force on the horizon with the potential to challenge Bayezid was the terrifying Mongol warlord Timur (Tamerlane), who was busy creating a vast empire in Asia, reaching as far west as the Caucasus, but his movements seemed erratic. Timur and Ioannes VII were in diplomatic contact and making plans for an anti-Turkish alliance, and Bayezid was also watching Timur's movements closely. But the pressure on Constantinople did not relent and people inside began increasingly to agitate for the City to surrender and secure favorable terms. The patriarch Matthaios claims that he threatened to excommunicate any ambassadors to the sultan who dared to propose surrender. But the patriarch himself was accused of dealing secretly with the sultan to secure his own safety and office. He defended himself in a long apologia addressed to the clergy, magistrates, and populace of the City.[120]

When all seemed lost and the pressure to surrender grew, Timur invaded Anatolia and drew Bayezid's forces and attention away from Constantinople. A group of Roman officials set out to deliver the keys of the City to the sultan, fearing what he might do when he inevitably returned in triumph.[121] But before they could reach him, Timur destroyed the Turkish army at the battle of Ankyra on 28 July, 1402. Bayezid was captured and placed in a cage. This defeat threw the Ottoman empire into chaos and confusion, as it was not yet a settled state but still only an expansionist project linked to a dynasty of warlords. While Bayezid's heirs fought it out among themselves, the Roman polity was given an unexpected fifty-year extension. The Romans thanked the Virgin for protecting her City against "the great dragon." What a fitting "miracle" it was that his destruction came at the hands of another "monster from the north."[122]

The dignity of letters

Lacking arms, money, and ships, the Roman polity survived thanks to its thousand-year-old walls and the chance arrival of Timur. Its helplessness was evident during Manuel's four-year journey to Italy, France, and England. He was treated with honor but failed to receive substantive assistance. Western sources comment repeatedly that he was put up at his hosts' expense. One of them reflected on the decline of his empire: "your imperial greatness lies in ruins for all to see," yet in the past "you sat on the throne of majesty and ruled the entire world."[123] For his part, Manuel sought to salvage his dignity and show the world that, even in decline, the Romans were a cut above. He ably played the role of a wise, learned, august, and honorable king from the east who inspired "reverence tinged with pity" in all who met him. Both Latins and Muslims commented on his regal appearance.[124] His people imagined that foreign kings "regarded him as a demigod," as if he "appeared from the heavens."[125] It was a consolation of sorts.

The source of Manual's dignity could no longer be material. Even the holy relics that he brought as gifts to the monarchs of Europe were paltry, for all knew that the sacred treasures of Constantinople had been plundered after 1204 "and dispersed everywhere like water from a common font," as the basileus' friend and fellow diplomat Manuel Chrysoloras admitted.[126] The true asset that Manuel had was his identity and the literary education that enabled him to assert it eloquently. Just as he wrote a *Dialogue with a Persian* while on campaign with Bayezid, he wrote a treatise *On the Procession of the Holy Spirit* while staying at Paris and waiting for Charles VI to recover from bouts of madness. He politely but firmly asserted the Orthodox Palamite position, but this was intended for his subjects alone for it was in Greek. For their benefit, he cultivated a literary persona across many works that reaffirmed their Roman national identity, the value of Hellenic literature, and Orthodoxy. These were cultural assets that only the Romans held in their original, purest form. Manuel promoted scholarship, and disagreed with those who said that literature was a distraction.[127] If there was not much that he could do, he could still, through his writings, articulate the old ideals of his society, both political and religious. Chrysoloras, who served the basileus diplomatically in the west and became one of the first professors of Greek in Italy, urged Manuel "to save the nation" by establishing schools to advance "the study of the literature of the ancient Greeks and Romans, our ancestors." It would be absurd to neglect that patrimony now that the Italians were making such strides toward mastering it.[128]

Chrysoloras eventually converted to Catholicism. But on his own western journey, Manuel did not go to Rome. Instead, he reminded foreign nations how much they owed to the culture that had flowed out of Romanía. In 1407, via Chrysoloras, he sent a manuscript of pseudo-Dionysios the Areopagite to the royal abbey of St. Denis near Paris, which Manuel had visited on his journey. It bore an image of the theologian-saint dressed like an east Roman bishop and another of Manuel's family, with him and his wife prominently labeled "basileis and *autokratores* of the Romans" (see Plate 8b). This was a gentle reminder of the true origin of learning and imperial authority, including of French royal and religious identity itself. To Russia, by contrast, Manuel dispatched ecclesiastical vestments, astutely perceiving that his ties to Orthodox nations were forged through liturgy and ceremony. Through such symbolic gestures, which were calibrated to the interests of each recipient, the basileus used soft power to ameliorate the decrepit image of his polity and remind people what they owed to it. Constantinople projected itself as an "exemplary center" worthy of pilgrimage, especially to the people of the north but also to the Latins. It was a source of Christian culture and depository of sacred relics, which had miraculously reappeared after they had been plundered by the crusaders in 1204.[129] Although Romanía lay at the mercy of forces beyond its control, it still aspired to international eminence through its Hellenic intellectual culture, which it was exporting to Italy, and its foundational role in the creation of Orthodoxy.[130] If there is any redemption to be found in the sordid annals of the Palaiologoi, it is the cultured persona crafted by Manuel II and the ultimate sacrifice of his son, Konstantinos XI.

Yet Hellenic culture would not long remain a preserve of Constantinople. The misery of the siege drove many scholars to Crete and Italy, where the demand for Greek studies was growing, as evinced by Chrysoloras' success. Another cause of their departure was the Church's crackdown on anti-Palamites in the 1390s, which forced out a number of associates of Kydones such as Chrysoloras, Manuel Kalekas, Maximos Chrysoberges, and the latter's brothers. Manuel II was being disingenuous when he reproached them for fleeing from their native land even though no one was chasing them, for he allowed the Church to harass them at home.[131] They converted to Catholicism and, while few, they complicated the intellectual scene by forming a cadre of Greek Catholic thinkers. In the fifteenth century, it would include the likes of Isidoros of Kiev, Ioannes Argyropoulos, and Bessarion. They were ethnic Roman scholars who channeled Catholicism into their native Greek milieu.

Thus, Orthodoxy and Catholicism were no longer divided by language. The old debates could now be rehashed entirely in Greek. Greek Catholic thinkers, many of whom learned Latin, tended to downplay their countrymen's Roman ethnicity and emphasize the virtues of Hellenic ancestry.[132] The elder statesman of this group, Kydones, had argued that New Rome owed obedience to Old Rome as a colony did to its metropolis.[133] Chrysoberges argued that the sorry state of "the Greeks" was due to their disobedience to the pope, to which the anti-Latin and Palamite thinker Ioseph Bryennios responded that it was due instead to the geographical proximity of the Muslims. The disaster at Nikopolis proved that the Latins were no better.[134] The two men, Chrysoberges and Bryennios, debated the procession of the Holy Spirit on Crete in 1400, exchanging recycled talking points. "As time had caused the ship of the state to rot,"[135] Romanía was leaking out its culture and identity too.

37

The Cusp of a New World (1402–1461)

The Ottoman civil war

At Ankyra, Timur shattered the Ottoman empire. While the sons of Bayezid scattered for safety, positioning themselves for the internecine war to come, the Roman polity was unexpectedly extended for another fifty years. Timur restored the independence of the Anatolian emirates, such as Karaman and Aydın, to hinder the reemergence of Ottoman power. The fear that he might cross over to Europe was put to rest when he returned to Samarkand, though only after his forces sacked Bursa and he himself defeated the Hospitallers at Smyrna, leaving behind his trademark pyramid of skulls.

Constantinople had been on the cusp of surrender to Bayezid, but Ioannes VII suddenly found himself in a position of strength vis-à-vis the sultan's heirs. The one who seized Gallipoli was Süleyman, a veteran of both Nikopolis and Ankyra. He needed peace with the Romans to regroup, so in early 1403 he made a treaty with Ioannes and the other Christian powers, such as the Venetians, the Genoese of Chios, and the Hospitallers, which included favorable terms for the Romans. They would receive back Thessalonike, the hinterland of Constantinople, and the coasts of the Black Sea and Sea of Marmara; prisoners would be released; and the basileus would pay no more tribute. It seems that the Romans also received the coastal strip on the Asian side of the Sea of Marmara, running eastward from Skoutari almost to Nikomedeia, which they kept until 1419. Süleyman referred to Ioannes as his "father." When Manuel returned in the spring of 1403, he ratified the treaty and called Süleyman his "son."[1]

Manuel was still hostile to his nephew Ioannes, for all that he had handled the crisis well and remained true to their agreement. He confined him to Lemnos, but was persuaded to patch things up, partly because Ioannes had many followers, including the Gattilusi of Lesbos, and also because unity would serve the Romans better in this critical moment of Turkish infighting. Thus, Ioannes and his retinue took over the newly liberated Thessalonike, under the watch of Manuel's official Demetrios Laskaris Leontaris. The treaty with Süleyman stipulated that Turkish settlers would be removed, unless they had bought land legally, and that the city would continue to pay the same taxes to Ioannes as it had to Bayezid. As "basileus of All Thessaly," Ioannes governed it conscientiously and tried to improve stability and agricultural productivity in the city's hinterland, "on behalf," as he put it, "of our nation and the people of our blood." According to Ruy González de

Figure 51 The ivory pyxis of Ioannes VII (ca. 1404), showing the full imperial family and celebrating Ioannes' move to Thessalonike

Clavijo, a Spanish envoy passing through Constantinople on his way to the court of Timur, Manuel and Ioannes hatched a complex succession plan, whereby Ioannes would succeed his uncle after the latter's death and then their sons would alternate on the throne (see Figure 51).[2] The plan was inherently unworkable and rendered moot when Ioannes died in 1408. By then, Manuel had five sons (Ioannes, Theodoros, Andronikos, Konstantinos, and Demetrios), with another (Thomas) arriving in 1409. His branch of the dynasty had prevailed, though his sons Ioannes and Konstantinos would be the last basileis in Constantinople.

Even in the breathing space that they had been afforded, the Romans had few options. Manuel continued to send envoys to the west to plead for aid, but they sent back one disappointing missive after another, "nothing at all of what we had hoped for," he responded to a report by Chrysoloras in 1409.[3] The basileus had little money. He could issue only low-quality silver coins and his officials had to support themselves financially.[4] Affluent Romans were now vanishingly few, and typically made their fortunes by tapping into the massive flows of the Italian trade routes. Sources comment frequently on the extreme poverty of the majority of their countrymen, making wealth inequality a hot-button issue, especially in sermons and satires. But Manuel was unable to direct that wealth into his treasury. In 1418, when he was facing war with the Turks again, he imposed a tax on the wine consumed by the Venetians in their homes and taverns in the

City, explaining that his revenues had decreased because many of his subjects were falsely claiming Venetian exemptions and so not paying trade fees. This led to many taverns closing and vigorous protests by the Venetian government.[5]

Manuel could only hope that the Turkish civil war kept all sides distracted and weak, and he played the factions against each other in order to protract it. The sons of Bayezid were competing over the loyalty of local commanders, Turkish settlers, raiders (including the elderly Evrenos), and Christian allies. Initially, it was safer for Manuel to back Süleyman, who was opposed by his brother Mehmed in Anatolia. In 1403, Süleyman captured Bursa and forced Mehmed to withdraw to Ankyra and then farther east. After a long stalemate, in 1409 Mehmed sent their younger brother Musa to attack Süleyman's Balkan positions from Wallachia in the north. Manuel possibly helped Musa when he crossed over to Europe and sought Venetian assistance to block Süleyman from crossing, but when that request was declined the basileus went back to supporting Süleyman, and ferried him across in 1410. Because of his geographical position, Manuel was caught in the middle of a tangle of competing Christian and Turkish powers, but he had little leverage of his own. Süleyman stopped at Constantinople and renewed his alliance with Manuel.[6] Many battles between the rival sultans took place in the vicinity of Constantinople. Süleyman was initially victorious, but in 1411 he was killed, and Musa consolidated his hold on the Balkans. In reprisal against the Romans, he attacked Thessalonike, Constantinople, and Selymbria. Musa revived Bayezid's approach to conquest and firm centralization. He burned villages outside the City, forcing Manuel to evacuate them, and brought his navy into the straits.[7]

Manuel had no choice but to join forces with Musa's chief rival, his brother Mehmed in Anatolia. The two rulers met at Skoutari and Constantinople, and a few Roman soldiers participated in Mehmed's initial attack on Musa in 1412. This was unsuccessful and Mehmed fell back to Constantinople, where Manuel helped him regroup. In 1413, Mehmed defeated and killed Musa at a battle south of Sofia in Bulgaria. The outcome was a mixed blessing for the Romans. On the one hand, Mehmed I (1413–1421) was now the master of both the European and Anatolian halves of the Ottoman empire. Manuel had so far skillfully supported *all* the rival sultans in turn, but attempting to divide and conquer the Turks would henceforth be more difficult and much more dangerous. On the other hand, Mehmed was an ally who acknowledged his debt to the Romans: "Go tell my father, the basileus of the Romans," he said to Manuel's envoys, "that from now on I will obey him as a son does a father."[8] He spent most of his reign fighting the emirates in Anatolia.

The Roman Morea

During the Turkish civil war, Manuel visited his far-flung domains in order to inspect them, consolidate his authority, produce new censuses, resolve disputes, and install his sons

Figure 52 Aerial photo of Mystras, with the citadel at the top right and the palace of the despots at the bottom left; Sparta is in the distance.
Shutterstock/Leonid Andronov

in power. In 1406–1407, he traveled to Lemnos, Imbros, and the Peloponnese, turning the latter over to his eleven-year-old son Theodoros II after the death of the previous despot, the basileus' brother Theodoros I. Following the death of Ioannes VII, Manuel spent the winter of 1408–1409 in Thessalonike to install his even younger son, the despot Andronikos, who was handled by Demetrios Laskaris Leontaris. In 1414, Manuel set sail again from the capital. He took back by force the island of Thasos, which had been occupied by a Gattilusio, stopped at Thessalonike, and went on to the Peloponnese, where he spent an entire year, returning to the capital in March, 1416.[9] His priority in the Peloponnese was to fortify the Isthmos of Corinth. A number of local *archontes* objected to this imposition on their money and resources, and Manuel had to bring "these ungrateful people" to heel through force.[10] Yet despite this conflict, the Morea, and in particular its picturesque capital Mystras, was having a moment in the sun.

Mystras is its modern name (see Figure 52). The actual one was Myzithras, which is that of a delicious cheese, though writers often called it Sparta. It began as a Villehardouin fort atop a conical hill in the shadow of Mt. Taygetos that overlooked the valley of Lakedaimon. When it was ceded to the Romans after Pelagonia (1259), it acquired a thriving Roman settlement too, as people moved there from nearby Sparta. The territory that it controlled expanded into the central Morea by 1320 to include the fortresses of Akoba and Karytaina, and some Latin lords accepted Roman rule and assimilated to Roman ways.

The despot Manuel Kantakouzenos (1349–1380), son of the emperor Ioannes Kantakouzenos, governed this quasi-autonomous domain successfully.[11] He did face occasional revolts from the local lords, but the Roman Morea was a paragon of stability compared to the Latin sectors of the Peloponnese in the north and west. These cycled through a confusing series of competing rulers in the later fourteenth century, including the Angevins of Naples, the Hospitallers, Navarrese mercenaries, the Acciaiuoli of Florence, and the Tocco of the Ionian islands and Epeiros. The local Latin element had transitioned from French to mostly Italian through dynastic marriages and immigration, and Italian banking and trading interests had moved in too.

Manuel Kantakouzenos was succeeded in the Morea by Ioannes V's son Theodoros I Palaiologos (1382–1407), under whom the *archontes* appear to have become more defiant. The exact makeup of this oppositional group eludes us, but they were unwilling to obey the despot or pay taxes, and it is likely that control over towns and lands was also contested.[12] We know of Theodoros' struggles against them from a now-lost, long metrical inscription that he set up in 1389, on five pillars of a church, to commemorate their defeat. They were bringing in the Latins, likely the Navarrese, to fight against him, and so he brought in Evrenos' Turkish raiders, who defeated them. But then of course the Turks refused to leave, forcing Theodoros to travel to the "emir" (Murad I) to whom he likely had to pledge his loyalty before they were withdrawn.[13] This strategy of employing Turks to fight civil wars was the playbook of his grandfather Ioannes Kantakouzenos, and had led to the same outcome: subordination to the Ottomans.

Theodoros casts the Latins as his main foreign enemy in the inscription, and he did take Argos from the Venetians in 1388, putting him on bad terms with the Republic.[14] But the script was flipped in the 1390s, when some of his subjects denounced him to the sultan Bayezid and the latter sent raiders, including Evrenos, to attack the Morea in 1395–1402, during the siege of Constantinople.[15] This time the raiders allied themselves with the Navarrese, taking thousands of prisoners and causing mass dislocations. In desperate straits, the despot reconciled with Venice in 1394, returning Argos to them in exchange for help against the Turks. In 1395, he besieged Corinth, whose strategic location was "the key to his country." Possibly he hoped to block raiders at the Isthmos. His rival for possession of Corinth was Carlo Tocco, the Italian ruler of the Ionian islands, who had also allied himself to Bayezid and Evrenos against Theodoros. In the end, Tocco sold the rights to Corinth to the despot, but the latter was unable to maintain it and the Venetians refused to help him build the Hexamilion ("Six-Mile") wall across the Isthmos. So in 1397 he sold the city to the Hospitallers. Their recent Grand Master, one Juan Fernández de Heredia, had been eager to acquire the Morea for his order. He had even sponsored translations into

Aragonese of ancient and recent Greek histories of the Peloponnese, ranging from Thucydides to the *Chronicle of the Morea*.[16] Better the Hospitallers than the Turks, was the thinking. In 1400, Theodoros hatched a plan to sell the entire Roman Morea to the Hospitallers, and considered emigrating to Venice. This met with furious opposition by his subjects, especially at Mystras, and he backed down.[17] But the plan reflected the hopelessness of those years. Some had even considered surrendering Constantinople to Bayezid or to Venice, before Timur appeared.

Bayezid's defeat at Ankyra relieved the pressure on the Morea just as it did on Constantinople. Theodoros was able to consolidate his power. The agreement with the Hospitallers was officially canceled in 1404, and he bought Corinth back from them.[18] It is even possible that Theodoros expanded his sway into mainland Greece to the city of Zetounion (modern Lamia).[19] Manuel II's two visits to the Morea (in 1407 and 1415–1416) were intended to further consolidate the dynasty's control. Manuel pushed the Hexamilion project through, a wall seven km long, comparable in length to the land walls of Constantinople. The basileus knew that his nominal ally, the sultan Mehmed (whom he called the "enemy beast"), was unhappy with this project. Manuel shared with many a delusion that this wall would save the Peloponnese, though it turned out to be a dud. However, such projects allowed rulers to marshal the resources of their subjects and whip them into line, which is exactly what Manuel did. This is likely why they resisted the project, "threatening to kill the workmen."[20] In past centuries, Roman elites had drawn their wealth from the state and fought to defend it; now that their wealth came from private business in the context of a weak state, they resented its impositions. Their money was safer in the hands of Italian bankers. But many poor Romans also objected to the new taxes and labor corvées that the project required, and they emigrated to regions under Venetian control. Manuel had to ask for them back.[21]

Manuel wrote a long funeral oration for his brother Theodoros I, which was read out during both of his visits to the Morea. This argued that the plan to sell the Morea was really a misunderstood subtle strategy. The speech attacked the defiant notables, accusing them of betraying their Roman and Christian identity by selling out to the Turks, who would not be as tolerant as these ungrateful people hoped.[22] It was, all over again, the same problem that Manuel had encountered in Thessalonike in the 1380s: some of the rich were unwilling to give up their money for the common good (as defined by the basileus), and were open to a deal with the Turks.

"The Peloponnese is small and has few resources, barely enough for its own inhabitants," Kydones wrote in 1387. But it was agriculturally productive, exporting wine and oil.[23] "Go off to the Morea with your whole family," a character advised in a satirical text of ca. 1411, "and fill your belly with meat and olives, nectar and pork."[24] Yet in the wake of the Black Death labor remained at a premium, and both the Venetians and the Roman despots resettled thousands of Albanians ("Illyrians") as farmers and soldiers, though none of the figures given for the size of the despots' armies is believable.[25] During the fourteenth century, Albanians had migrated southward into Epeiros, where their regional dynasties intermarried with their Italian counterparts or fought against them. It was a small step from there to the Morea.[26]

Mystras itself cannot have had much more than a thousand inhabitants, but culturally it punched far above its weight. It featured a set of remarkable churches, some dating from the late thirteenth and early fourteenth centuries, which were adorned with a regionally distinctive style of painting and endowed with properties by the despots and basileis.[27] In the later fourteenth century, the town was also home to a small circle of philosophers with Hellenizing tendencies, who perhaps fled from the stifling Hesychast establishment of Constantinople. Around 1410, they were joined by a thinker of towering importance, Georgios Gemistos (ca. 1360–ca. 1452), who adopted the moniker Plethon, an Attic version of his surname that resonated with that of his intellectual master, Plato (Platon in Greek). Plethon had rejected Christianity on every level (metaphysical, ethical, political) and was a self-realized pagan Hellenist, though he had to conform outwardly. His main treatise of philosophical Platonism, the *Laws*, was later burned by Gennadios, the first patriarch of Constantinople after the fall, but it was only part of a broader project of Hellenic restoration that left traces in his other works and influenced western European thought. Plethon taught many of the luminaries of the fifteenth century, including staunch anti-Latin theologians (e.g., Markos Eugenikos); prominent ethnic-Roman Catholics such as Bessarion of Trebizond, who became a cardinal and almost pope; and other crypto-pagans such as the self-described "Hellene Lakedaimonian" Raoul Kabakes and the Athenian historian Nikolaos "Laonikos" Chalkokondyles. Plethon was the culmination of the growing engagement with ancient philosophy that had begun with Metochites, Gregoras, and Barlaam of Calabria, if not earlier, with Psellos himself. Unlike them, however, he "decided to cross the Rubicon" into pagan Hellenism.[28]

Plethon had served Manuel II as a judge and was later awarded pronoias in the Morea, where he was the nominal "head" of a fort and its district (the legal, social, and administrative framework of the Morea was the same as in other Roman territories).[29] In the late 1410s, Plethon composed two political memoranda for Manuel and his son, the despot Theodoros II, with proposals for radical overhaul in the governance of the Peloponnese, "the ancient fatherland of the Hellenes." This fatherland had to be "saved" from the Ottomans, whose way of life was geared to war. Plethon drew on ancient Spartan militarism and the division of classes in Plato's *Republic* to advocate a nationalist program of Hellenic autonomy, autarky, and nativism. This sounds utopian but it responded precisely to the dysfunctions of the Morea. According to Plethon, foreign trade was to be severely curtailed, the ruling class was not to participate in it, and land was to be redistributed to ensure the most efficient support for the army and reduce inequality, the scourge of Palaiologan society. There was no room for churches and monasteries in Plethon's vision.[30] His defensive nationalism made him a staunch partisan of the Hexamilion, and here he literally put his money where his mouth was: part of his pronoia revenues were earmarked for the wall's upkeep.[31] The Venetians, by contrast, whose territories were also behind the wall, declined to contribute.

Renewed Turkish attacks

The Romans would soon be manning all their defenses. Mehmed I died in May, 1421, and was succeeded by his seventeen-year-old son Murad II (1421–1451). The Roman leadership was of two minds regarding this succession. Manuel wanted to maintain good relations with the new sultan, but his son Ioannes VIII had a different plan. Ioannes was co-basileus and had just married Sophia of Montferrat. This marriage proved to be unhappy as Sophia had a beautiful body but a hideous face—the populace called her "Easter from the back but Lent from the front." Eventually she returned home after being neglected by her husband. Ioannes wanted to divide the Turks just as his father had done during the civil wars of 1402–1413. Specifically, he wanted to release Mustafa, yet another son of Bayezid who had challenged Mehmed in 1416 but lost. Mehmed had agreed to pay the Romans 20,000 hyperpyra to keep him in confinement. But in 1419, the sultan seized the Roman possessions in Asia along the Sea of Marmara, which they had regained in 1403.[32] Manuel, who was over seventy and ill, allowed Ioannes to have his way. Ioannes was not alone in believing that outside meddling could destabilize the Ottomans. The Turkish leadership itself had kept Mehmed's death a secret for over a month until Murad could take over, precisely because they feared Christian interference. Mustafa was therefore released in September, on condition that he surrender Gallipoli, and he was given Roman military assistance under Demetrios Laskaris Leontaris. Yet even though Mustafa took Gallipoli and Adrianople, he reneged on the agreement. However, he was quickly defeated and killed by Murad by early 1422, leaving the Romans exposed to the sultan's wrath. The Mustafa debacle cost them dearly.

In June, 1422, Murad besieged Constantinople while dispatching forces to Thessalonike and the Morea. We have an eyewitness account of the siege of the City, by Ioannes Kananos. Murad's general, Mihaloğlu Beg, built long earthworks to allow his soldiers to reach the land walls, and he brought massive siege engines to bear between the Romanos and Charisios gates, at the weak spot where the walls dipped into the old river bed. He even fired small cannons, though they were ineffective, failing to bring down a dilapidated tower that they targeted.

With prayers and prophecies the sultan signaled that this was a holy war for the victory of Islam, but the defenders, including women, peasants, and priests, successfully repelled the main assault in August. Meanwhile, Ioannes helped another Turkish rebel, Murad's brother, also named Mustafa, to rebel in Anatolia and attack Bursa, with the backing of the emirs. The basileus even provided Mustafa with military assistance. Murad lifted the siege on 6 September and crossed to Asia to suppress this new threat. The siege had given the City a foretaste of 1453. Then, at the end of October, Manuel suffered a debilitating stroke. The government was henceforth in the hands of his son Ioannes.[33]

Thessalonike proved less resilient. It had known a period of relative calm since its liberation in 1403, but this was likely not accompanied by prosperity. The tensions between the administration and the local *archontes* had not abated, as the latter were reluctant to pay for defense. There were tensions also between those who wanted an accommodation with the Turks and those who sought Latin aid, and between rich and poor. Little had changed since the 1380s. The city's bishop Symeon, a major theologian of this era, wanted neither the Latins nor the Muslims. He encouraged the populace to fight on and urged Constantinople to send help. But there were no resources to spare. After months of siege, in 1423 the despot Andronikos realized that Thessalonike could not be defended, at least not by him. With the court's consent, he offered the city to the Venetians on condition that they protect it and respect the religion and property of its inhabitants. Venice had previously declined to take on distressed cities but surprisingly, with 99 votes in the Senate in favor and 45 against, it accepted this offer, which promised more trouble than profit. Thus Thessalonike again left Roman rule, this time forever.[34]

The Venetian interlude was brief (1423–1430). The new masters imported food and a garrison, and they paid salaries to the notables and local soldiers, which was appreciated, but tensions quickly mounted. The garrison misbehaved, and the Venetian authorities curtailed the rights of the Orthodox Church. Salaries were then arbitrarily cut back, Venetian merchants broke into markets dominated by Romans, and the food supply was insufficient, leading to hunger and poverty. Thousands slipped away to find a future under the Ottomans, deeming life under the Venetian authorities to be "slavery." In reprisal, the authorities destroyed the houses of those who left. The population may have fallen as low as 10,000. The situation was untenable. Even the Venetian governors tried to resign, but no one was willing to replace them. After failing to persuade the city to surrender, Murad took it by force on 29 March, 1430. His men scaled the eastern walls and proceeded to slaughter, pillage, and enslave the population.[35] Ioannes Anagnostes, an eyewitness who wrote an *Account of the Last Sack of Thessalonike*, says that the Romans were coerced into fighting by the Venetians and implies that it would have been better to surrender from the start and not have to endure

Venetian oppression, the siege, and the sack. For their part, the Venetians lamented the funds that they poured into the project, some 740,000 ducats.[36]

The Hexamilion also failed to protect the Morea. In 1423, the forces of Turahan Beg, the Ottoman governor of Thessaly, tore down part of the wall, encountering no resistance, and launched a devastating raid inside the Morea, defeating the despot's Albanian mercenaries. The Romans were again out of options. Ioannes VIII followed in the footsteps of his father and grandfather and traveled to Venice, Milan, and Hungary in search of aid. The journey lasted from November, 1423, to November, 1424, and the basileus left his teenage brother Konstantinos in charge of Constantinople in his absence. But he obtained nothing beyond some funds from Venice to cover the cost of his travels and lectures from Sigismund on the need to repent and rejoin the Catholic Church. But during his absence, in February, 1424, his ailing father or brother sent emissaries to Murad, including Loukas Notaras and Georgios Sphrantzes, to sign a peace treaty. The Romans, who had already lost Thessalonike, now gave up most of their Black Sea possessions except for Mesembria and a few other forts. They would also pay the sultan an annual tribute of 300,000 silver Turkish coins (*aspra*), the equivalent of 21,000 hyperpyra. Thus, most of the gains achieved in 1403 were erased.[37] An anonymous Latin text from 1437 notes that the rulers of Constantinople governed "a territory that could be crossed in eight days by horse, and in barely two days in its width, but when they are at war they control only the coastal forts, while the infidels hold the rest." It also says that the population of the City was 40,000.[38]

Manuel died on 21 July, 1425. He was buried in the imperial Pantokrator monastery, a house that he had revived, in part by appointing the Athonite monk and theologian Makarios Makres as its abbot. Other members of the family were buried there too, including Ioannes VIII in 1448.[39] The dynasty was trying to forge associations with the glory days of the Komnenoi. But in a different sense, Manuel's death marked the end of an era. The men who replaced him had no memory of the fourteenth century, being born during the long siege and its aftermath. They included his sons and their high officials such as Loukas Notaras (*megas doux* and then *mesazon*) and Georgios Sphrantzes (a *protovestiarites* and diplomat), as well as many scholars and theologians such as Georgios Scholarios (the later patriarch Gennadios II), Bessarion (who became a cardinal), and Ioannes Argyropoulos. These men shaped the legacy that New Rome would leave behind after its death in 1453: the politicians by fighting the Ottomans to the end rather than surrendering; Scholarios by finding a path for the Church under Ottoman rule; and Bessarion by injecting Greek learning into western humanism.

The City itself was still admired by Latin and Russian travelers, pilgrims, and spies, who gazed upon its ancient monuments in wonder and adored its sacred relics. But they also commented on its wretched state: its populace was "sad and poor" and the City contained more open land than built. The Blachernai church of the Virgin was burned beyond repair by a lightning strike sent by God, according to the Spanish traveler Pero Tafur (1438), to punish the frequent sodomy that was committed in it. Tafur says that the royal ceremonies were kept up, but the basileus was "like a bishop without a see." Most of the Great Palace was in ruins, but in one chamber a splendid library of "ancient writings and histories" was still maintained. The history books told a depressing story. Ioannes Chortasmenos read the history of Choniates and asked in his marginal comments, "Where is this Greek Fire now?" "How great the palace once was, and look at it now!"[40] It is likely that, in all its scattered collections, Constantinople still housed more classical texts than survive today. A complete Diodoros of Sicily was seen in the palace library in 1453.[41] The Italian humanist Francesco Filelfo, who lived in the City in the 1420s, reported that the court idiom was Attic Greek.[42] In the midst of ruin, poverty, and decline, the last Romans were doubling down on ancient cultural assets: ceremony, religion, and classical culture. This was appealing even to some Turks. Yusuf, yet another son of Bayezid, lived quietly in Constantinople where he studied classical thought in Greek and was eventually buried as a Christian named Demetrios. In this way he also signaled to his brothers that he was not a danger to them and did not have to be strangled.[43]

Yet at the same time the Romans were now a small part of an expanding Turkish world, and this impacted their culture. Many were asking their religious leaders why the "impious" Turks were enjoying such success, and some converted to Islam. This elicited more treatises from Orthodox theologians.[44] Many transactions in Constantinople were carried out in Turkish coins. Turkish words had infiltrated spoken Greek, and many Romans, not just those from Anatolia, could speak Turkish. When Gennadios Scholarios sought to clear himself from the charge of being pro-Catholic because he knew Latin, he responded that "by this logic all of us are Muslims, for almost all of us use their language."[45] In 1432, a Burgundian spy observed the despot of the Morea and his retinue practicing a cavalry game in the hippodrome: flinging their hats into the air, they shot them with their bows, "one of the talents they have learned from the Turks."[46]

The despot in question was probably Konstantinos, not Theodoros II. There were by then three despots in the Morea, where the Romans were expanding and gobbling up the remaining fragments of the Latin Principality. They did this in part because Ioannes VIII had too many ambitious brothers and, after the loss of Thessalonike, not enough territories to give them. As neither he nor they yet had any sons, his brothers were also his prospective heirs, though Konstantinos was his closest ally and clear favorite. Ioannes needed lands to give them to prevent them from intriguing with the sultan against him, as Andronikos IV and

Ioannes VII had done against his father Manuel and grandfather Ioannes V. In fact, his brother Demetrios was precisely such an intriguer, and was periodically regarded as just as much a danger to the dynasty as the Ottomans.[47] But the only place where Roman lands were not surrounded by Turks was in the Morea, whose remaining Latin outposts were opportunely weak.

In 1427, Ioannes VIII and Konstantinos launched an offensive against Glarentza, eventually forcing its lord, Carlo Tocco of the islands and Epeiros, to surrender it along with the fortress Chlemoutzi through a marriage alliance (his niece Maddalena married Konstantinos, though she died soon after). Patras, a papal fiefdom held by its archbishop Pandolfo Malatesta, was invested by Konstantinos and eventually surrendered in 1429 (its citadel resisted for another year). The sultan objected to this expansion of Roman power, but, busy as he was with the siege of Thessalonike, he was handled diplomatically by Sphrantzes. Murad did, however, send Turahan Beg of Thessaly to ruin the Hexamilion again, where he faced no resistance. Meanwhile, the despot Thomas moved against the last Prince of Achaea, Centurione II Zaccaria, who was holed up in Chalandritsa in the north. Through another marriage alliance, followed by Centurione's death in 1432, Thomas inherited his lands too. The Principality of Achaea was no more, and the three despots played musical chairs with its former baronies in the now unified Roman Morea. They rewarded their men, including Latin lords who joined them, with pronoias and concessions. In 1434–1435, Konstantinos seems to have made a play for Athens too, following a crisis in the succession of its Florentine Acciaiuoli rulers, but this failed. As a result, a leading Roman family from Athens, the Chalkokondylai, emigrated to Mystras. Its scion, Nikolaos ("Laonikos"), studied under Plethon and later revived Athenian historiography in the manner of Thucydides.

The despots were not following a unified plan of Roman revival. They were carving out lands for themselves while jostling for the succession and eyeing each other warily. In 1436, Konstantinos and Thomas even skirmished against Theodoros, a conflict that ended only when Ioannes VIII intervened.[48] Palaiologan infighting continued to the very end.

The Council of Ferrara-Florence

The great project that preoccupied Ioannes VIII in the 1430s was a push for Union with Rome in the hope that it would result in a crusade against the Turks. Such crusades had achieved only minor successes in the past (e.g., Smyrna in the 1340s), and, given the growth of Ottoman power, would now require an army greater than that of Nikopolis (1396). But Ottoman expansion was threatening Hungary and the Adriatic too, and the Latin powers were increasingly anxious for their own safety, not just for their colonial possessions. The "reduction of the Greeks" (what Rome revealingly called Church Union) would give momentum to a crusade. Embassies and empty promises about

Union had been exchanged between Constantinople and the west fairly regularly, but the papacy had long been distracted by the split between popes and antipopes and, in the early fifteenth century, between popes and the conciliar movement. In the 1430s, pope Eugenius IV (1431–1447) and the Council (at Basel) were at odds with each other and competing over who would "reduce the Greeks." After complex negotiations with both sides, Ioannes VIII finally accepted the papal offer. For one thing, there could be no true Ecumenical Council in Orthodox eyes without the pope. This was a major concession by Eugenius to the eastern Church, namely that there be a Council with debates and not merely a ceremonial declaration of subordination to Rome, as at Lyons. In November, 1437, the basileus, the elderly patriarch Ioseph II, and hundreds more east Romans boarded the papal fleet and sailed for Italy. Konstantinos stayed behind as regent, advised by Notaras and Sphrantzes. Demetrios, who could not be trusted, was taken to Italy.[49]

The decision to pursue Union was controversial. Independently of how one felt about Union, there was a pragmatic argument against pursuing it sincerely that was attributed to Manuel II, who gave this advice to his heir: "Use Union in order to frighten the Turks with the prospect of a Latin attack, but don't pursue it too far, because our people will never accept it, and it may backfire, leaving us even more exposed to the infidel." Sphrantzes then has Manuel utter lines that have become famous: "My son [Ioannes], would make a good basileus, but our times instead call for a manager (*oikonomos*), not a basileus." "Basileus" here means a ruler with a grand strategy. Manuel was calling instead for a cautious caretaker, not the kind of debacle that Ioannes had created with Mustafa.[50] For his part, Plethon had correctly warned that a delegation of Orthodox bishops would be swamped out in Italy by their Catholic counterparts, who would function as their "jury."[51]

While most Orthodox were theoretically in favor of Union, they rejected the terms that Rome required and associated Catholicism with religious tyranny. The period is awash in anti-Latin treatises, including a debunking by Makarios of Ankyra of the *Donation of Constantine* as a forgery, decades before western philologists (most famously Lorenzo Valla) reached the same conclusion.[52] Yet it was unclear what would emerge from the Ecumenical Council in Italy and whether the basileus would or could impose its decrees on the Church. This again raised the thorny question of his powers over the Church, which was debated with renewed vigor. In 1380, Ioannes V had asked the Synod to define his legal powers in what we might call the "personnel matters" of the Church, which it did in a conservative document.[53] In practice, however, the basileus' powers were far more extensive and rarely contested. Every time one Palaiologos displaced another from the throne between 1376 and 1403, he also deposed his predecessor's patriarch and appointed his own, who dutifully carried out his royal patron's policies. None of this was even noted in the Synod's definition. When Makarios of Ankyra protested against Manuel's high-handed restoration of the patriarch Matthaios in 1403 and called the patriarch a lapdog, he, Makarios, was deposed and excommunicated by a compliant Synod. Many churchmen argued in this period that the basileus should not interfere in Church matters, but there is little basis in historical fact to say that the Church had become more independent. Manuel always had his way in Church affairs, even when there was initial opposition. He could expect the Synod to vote the way he wanted. Makarios himself, in his anti-Latin works, had touted the role of the basileus as the leader of the Church and teacher of the faith.[54] As Kydones had stated plainly, the patriarch "has one concern: to please the basileus. He governs the Church at the basileus' pleasure, and falls if he angers him."[55]

Ioannes VIII's intention was not to capitulate to Rome, as Michael VIII had done in 1274. He prepared for a genuine Council in which positions would be debated and opinions swayed, thereby yielding a Union born of persuasion. The Orthodox delegation consisted of some 700 people, including the basileus, the patriarch, two dozen bishops, and many clerics, along with their attendants. The bishops included representatives from Georgia, Wallachia, and Russia, the latter being the educated Isidoros of Kiev, an ethnic Roman. A number of learned men were made bishops in order to bolster the Orthodox cause at the Council, including Bessarion (of Nikaia), Markos Eugenikos (of Ephesos), and Dionysios (of Sardeis), the first two being students of Plethon.[56] For good measure, the basileus took lay thinkers with him too, such as Plethon, Scholarios, and Georgios Amiroutzes of Trebizond. Ioannes desired Union, but he would not humiliate or even humble himself in the process. During the long ordeal of the Council, which convened in 1438 at Ferrara and then in the first half of 1439 at Florence, the basileus regularly insisted on the honor due to his office, especially in relation to the pope, and rejected demands made by the Latins that would have disadvantaged his side. He certainly nudged the proceedings and deliberations in the direction of Union but, even as they were yielding to the Catholics, he was determined that the Orthodox retain their dignity. The patriarch refused to kiss the pope's foot at their first meeting. "What Council gave him this right?"[57] Latin Europe had deviated significantly from the modes and orders laid down by the first Christian emperors and their Councils a thousand years before, which still governed east Roman life.

Both sides were unquestionably sincere in their desire for Union, enduring months of deprivation, summer heat and winter cold, outbreaks of plague, petty tensions, frustration, and homesickness in order to get the job done. Their debates and planning sessions lasted for hours on end, and, to make their tedium worse, the proceedings were being translated. All hailed the expert services provided by the lead translator, Nikolaos Sekoundinos (Sagundino), an ethnic

Roman from Venetian Euboia who had witnessed the fall of Thessalonike in 1430 and had intellectual ties to Plethon.[58] The Council's expenses were covered by the pope, including stipends for the Orthodox, which was troubling, for the funds, and the hunger that ensued when they were withheld, could be used as leverage to force the Orthodox to capitulate.[59] At times this did happen, but the pope was also betting his legacy on the success of the Council, going deeply into debt and fearing that the Greeks might pack up and leave at any moment, leaving him with nothing to show for it. The Council was relocated to Florence in part because Cosimo de' Medici offered to pick up much of the tab.

After an inconclusive debate over Purgatory, a major item debated between the two sides at Ferrara was the addition of the *filioque* to the Nicaean Creed. The Orthodox were represented by the suave Bessarion and the more uncompromising Markos Eugenikos, who kept insisting that it was unlawful to make unauthorized additions to the Creed. But later the debate moved to the topic of the procession of the Holy Spirit, and here the Latins managed to persuade many of the Orthodox that some Greek Fathers had spoken of a double procession, from the Father *and* the Son, and it was useless to argue that all these texts had been tampered with. Moreover, the Orthodox realized that they were unprepared for the barrage of theological disputation that the Latins were hurling at them.[60] By the spring of 1439, a core group including Bessarion, Isidoros, and Scholarios was persuaded that the double procession of the Latin Creed was acceptable, and this formed the basis of Union. The basileus concurred and so, it seems, did the patriarch Ioseph, though he was ill for most of the Council and died on 10 June. He was the first patriarch of Constantinople to visit Italy, and he was buried there. Eventually most of the Orthodox signed off on Union, though Markos Eugenikos among the clergy and Plethon among the laity refused. The issue of the pope's rights over the eastern Church was addressed as an afterthought. But the affirmation of papal supremacy "without prejudice to the rights of the eastern patriarchs" was too vague a formula to be workable in the long term. By the end, everyone was impatient to declare the Council a success. After the signing ceremony, Union was celebrated with a liturgy in Latin on 6 July, in the recently inaugurated cathedral of Santa Maria del Fiore (also known as Il Duomo), in Florence, designed by Brunelleschi. Its dome was wider than Hagia Sophia's and reached to twice the height. The pope, however, refused to allow a parallel celebration of the Orthodox liturgy, which stung.

The experience of the Orthodox party at Ferrara-Florence marked the cusp between two worlds, the ancient Roman polity of the east that was ending and the emergence of western Europe and the Ottoman empire as the major players on the world scene. Ioannes VIII was like a basileus without a state, awarding titles and honors to his hosts that carried neither salaries nor functions.[61] Meanwhile, his party was overwhelmed by the wealth, resources, sophistication, and artistic and intellectual development of the Italians. They realized that they were hopelessly outclassed. Even their theology was lagging, not necessarily because the Latins had better arguments but because they had new paradigms of debate with which the east Romans could not engage. At Venice, they were poignantly reminded of the colonial background that exacerbated this inequality. As the patriarch Ioseph II and his priests toured the sacred treasures of San Marco, they came across items which the Venetians claimed came from Hagia Sophia, "according to the law of plunder. But we knew," wrote the priest Sylvestros Syropoulos, "based on inscriptions and images of the Komnenoi on them, that they came from the Pantokrator."[62]

There was still one asset that the east Romans had that their hosts craved: an expert knowledge of Greek and ancient books. They brought many such books to assist in the debates, not just the Church Fathers but Plato and Plutarch too.[63] The humanists in Florence drooled over this bounty of learning. At a time when few of them could access Plato's thought, Plethon dazzled them with his knowledge of the original texts of ancient philosophy. Ioannes VIII quoted poetry from memory, explaining first to his hosts that "there is a poet among the Greeks called Homer."[64] Yet even here the tide was turning. Leonardo Bruni, the chancellor of Florence, wrote a *Constitution of the Florentines* in passable classical Greek, which he gave to Plethon to correct. Even back home, some east Romans were beginning to realize that "wisdom has long since left Attica and is now living in Italy and its cities, or so we hear."[65]

For all the anguish of the Romans' compromises, and the toils and labors of the journey itself, the Council ultimately failed to unite the Churches or to succor Constantinople. Its immediate aftertaste was bitter in the mouths of the Orthodox delegation, smacking of coercion and duress. When they celebrated the liturgy in San Marco in Venice on the way back, they did not commemorate the pope and omitted the *filioque* (though the basileus was absent).[66] When they reached the City in early 1440, the popular reaction was mostly negative, and the court, rather than promulgate and double down on the attainment of Union, carried on as if nothing had happened.[67] Bessarion returned to Italy to become a cardinal, and when Isidoros tried to preach the Union in Russia, he was arrested. The Churches in Russia repudiated the Union and regarded Constantinople as lapsed from the faith.[68] Markos Eugenikos became a hero to many by denouncing the Council for selling out Orthodoxy. He called Latins "heretics" openly, whereas at Florence he had said that "they were heretics in all but name, though the Orthodox refrained from using that word."[69] Now he was using it. "No one has authority over our faith," he wrote to the Athonites, "neither a basileus, nor an archbishop, nor a false Synod," and he branded his lapsed countrymen as "Greek-speaking Latins."[70] Unionists were shunned and some who had signed off at Florence now changed tack. They included the priest

Sylvestros Syropoulos, who wrote a massive "secret history" of the Orthodox delegation, exposing its internal tensions and bitter infighting. In the angry climate emerging in Constantinople, his memoir was meant to explain "his grievous lapse in Italy," as it was called by one of his correspondents, Ioannes Eugenikos, the brother of Markos.[71]

Even the basileus' mother, Helene, criticized the Union.[72] His brother Demetrios seized the chance to become the anti-Unionists' political champion. In 1442, he blockaded the City with Turkish assistance, while Turkish ships besieged the despot Konstantinos in a town on Lemnos. Demetrios ended the hostilities after a few months, but not his troublemaking. The sultan was exploiting the divisions of the Palaiologoi, which were exacerbated by Union.[73]

For his part, pope Eugenius did proclaim a crusade against the Turks, though its primary purpose was to protect the Catholic kingdom of Hungary. The Hungarian army, under king Władysław III and his general János Hunyádi, invaded the Balkans in 1443 and scored some successes, after which they made peace with Murad. The sultan crossed over to Anatolia to fight the emirate of Karaman. But when an allied Venetian-Burgundian fleet arrived in 1444, sailing around Greece to the Bosporos, Władysław broke the truce and invaded again. Murad returned for the showdown. At Varna, on 10 November, 1444, the Hungarians were defeated and their king killed in the battle, though the sultan lost many men too in the carnage. Thus, for the Romans, the military aims of the Council had failed too. This outcome confirmed the predictions of many that Union would fail to deliver effective aid, but would cost the Church its soul by subjecting it to the pope.[74] Conversely, many westerners, knowing that the Greeks disliked Catholics, began to say that their agreement to the Union was insincere and self-interested.[75] This view was unfair to the Council participants. For their part, many Greeks believed that the Latins were unable to stop the Turkish advance.

Konstantinos XI Palaiologos

Murad did not blame the Hungarian war on Constantinople or the Council. The Hungarians, after all, had reason to attack him. But he made sure that the Romans did not benefit from the distraction. In the Morea, the despot Konstantinos had again fortified the Hexamilion and, in 1444, while the Varna crusade was in full swing, had taken over Boiotia and compelled Nerio Acciaiuoli of Athens to switch his allegiance to him. He even sent forces into Ottoman Thessaly. But in late 1446 Murad and Turahan marched south and forced Nerio to return to an Ottoman allegiance. In December, the Ottoman artillery bombarded the camp of the despots at the Hexamilion while the army stormed the wall and drove its terrified defenders away. Konstantinos and Thomas fled to Mystras, as they had bizarrely failed to prepare the Acrocorinth for a siege, though it was a formidable citadel. Murad slaughtered many prisoners and ritually sacrificed 600 of them in honor of his father's soul. He then raided the northern Peloponnese and departed with thousands of captives destined for the slave markets of Anatolia. Scholarios blamed the despots for this catastrophe along with the "wicked" inhabitants of the Morea, "the illegitimate heirs of the ancient Peloponnesians."[76] Bessarion had warned that Peloponnesian farmers were inadequately trained and too oppressed by their rich landlords to provide effective defense against the Turks.[77] The Morea became tributary to the sultan.

Ioannes VIII Palaiologos died on 31 October, 1448, at the age of fifty-six. He was buried in the Pantokrator, the last basileus of the Romans to receive burial. His brother Theodoros had died only months earlier, leaving Konstantinos as the next-eldest brother. Demetrios lobbied for the throne regardless, but their mother Helene and many high officials, including Notaras, backed Konstantinos. Murad also assented to his accession. Konstantinos reached the City in March, 1449, and sent Demetrios and Thomas to govern the Morea, where they mostly quarreled.[78] Konstantinos, however, was never crowned, only proclaimed basileus. Few were so legalistic as to make this a sticking point, as basileis were made by consensus, not specific rituals.[79] But it was odd. Konstantinos was also unmarried, and remained so to the end even though he sent Sphrantzes out on many missions to find a queen for him. Perhaps he was waiting to be crowned jointly with his wife. But no match emerged even though Konstantinos knocked on the doors of Aragon, Trebizond, and even proposed to the Serbian widow of sultan Murad himself. The king of Georgia agreed eventually to give his daughter, but by then it was too late.[80]

It is possible that the religious climate in the City was too divisive to stage a coronation. Konstantinos was being lobbied by Unionists, who demanded that he enforce Union on his subjects, and by anti-Unionists, who wanted him to reject Latin heresy and return to the Orthodox fold. Ioannes Eugenikos told the basileus that he had to condemn Union to be regarded as Orthodox by his group, and that a coronation by a Unionist patriarch would render him illegitimate.[81] Thus, forgoing a coronation paradoxically prevented Konstantinos from *losing* support. Another prominent anti-Unionist was Scholarios, who repudiated his own support for Union at Florence. He had broken with Bessarion and had been successfully recruited for the anti-Union cause by Eugenikos. Scholarios continued to admire Latin thought, Thomas Aquinas in particular, and was aware of the intellectual superiority of the Latin world. His theology was a kind of Thomistic Palamism, and he now headed up the Synaxis, a separatist Church that conducted its own ordinations.[82] Konstantinos arranged meetings between the rival groups, but compromise lay beyond reach. In the end, the basileus neither enforced Union on its increasingly vocal opponents, nor openly abandoned it. As a result he was criticized by both sides for failing in his duties, even though all seem to have liked him personally. In August, 1450, the patriarch Gregorios

III left the City, never to return. He had supported Union at Florence and served the basileis loyally, but by 1452 he was living in Rome on a papal pension.[83] The climate in Constantinople was too toxic for him. He preferred Rome even though its cultural environment was alien. At Ferrara he had observed that when he entered a Latin church he could not venerate the saints "because I can't recognize any of them."[84] Konstantinos could not replace him because any choice would elicit passionate opposition. Religious discord had resulted in political paralysis. The basileus lacked the means to take substantive action, and even symbolic actions would elicit furious resistance.

The siege and the fall of Constantinople

Into this volatile situation, just as the Romans were vulnerable and divided, there stepped a new sultan, Mehmed II (1451–1481). He was eighteen and, at first, underestimated by all. In a bizarre episode, his father Murad had abdicated in his favor in 1444, when Mehmed was only twelve, but then Murad had returned to power through a coup two years later, backed by elements of the Ottoman court who found Mehmed to be unfit. Now, in his second reign, the young sultan proved to be extraordinarily ambitious and dynamic, domineering, intellectually curious, resourceful, and tenacious. He was also secretive, paranoid, and, at times, horrifically cruel. By 1452, he had decided to terminate the Roman state at Constantinople, and he marshaled the resources of his empire to achieve that goal. His opening move was to build the fort of Rumeli Hisar on the European side of the Bosporos to complement Anadolu Hisar, which had been built by Bayezid on the Asian side. He equipped it with bombards (cannons), which, along with his newly expanded fleet, gave him control of the straits. It was therefore known as "The Throat-Cutter."[85] The Romans realized that this presaged a new siege, albeit one more methodically prepared. A prominent anti-Unionist wrote on 13 September, 1452, that the sultan "will return in spring to besiege the City with every imaginable piece of artillery and siege engine. But the City is bereft of any kind of assistance, whether from inside or outside, as it lacks money and men and has been ravaged by poverty, depopulation, enemy attacks, and by fear of what the future holds."[86]

Constantinople was "a city of ruins, from which all wealth has fled."[87] After so many blockades and outbreaks of the plague, its population had likely fallen to 25,000 or 30,000, significantly lower than is often assumed.[88] When Konstantinos asked Sphrantzes to make a census of adult men capable of fighting, even priests, he found 4,773 Romans and 200 foreigners (a figure that scholars have emended to 2,000, though it is likely correct, referring to foreign residents, not the reinforcements that arrived at the last minute).[89] Konstantinos had modest political skills and limited control over his officials, who quarreled and blocked the basileus in order to protect their own interests; Sphrantzes, for example, loathed Notaras.[90] Konstantinos also had little money. The Venetians had vigorously resisted even minor taxes imposed on their citizens for the purpose of defense. The wealthiest man in the City was the *megas doux* Loukas Notaras, and, while he did contribute to the effort, most of his assets were deposited in Italian banks, and he was greatly invested in Genoese public debt.[91] This was typical of his class, which derived wealth from trade and international contacts. Like their counterparts in Thessalonike, they too were now reviled for not contributing money to the common defense. But they were a rhetorically convenient target in the ensuing blame game.[92] Be that as it may, Konstantinos' poverty cost the Romans dearly. For example, he underpaid the Hungarian mechanic Urbanus, who transferred his services to the sultan and built for him a "monstrous" cannon that, during the siege, broke the City's ancient walls.[93]

Konstantinos sent out appeals for help in all directions. No military aid came from other Orthodox lands, the Gattilusi of Lesbos, or Venice.[94] In part, this was due to Mehmed's clever diplomacy, which isolated his targets as he came for them one by one. Meanwhile, the papal curia debated whether to help "the schismatic and heretical Greeks."[95] Pope Nicholas V informed Konstantinos that assistance depended on full implementation of Union, explaining to him that "the barbarian" was God's punishment for the Greeks' history of disobedience to Rome.[96] In late 1452, Nicholas sent cardinal Isidoros of Kiev to implement Union, and Isidoros rounded up some 200 mercenaries on the way to add to the City's defense. Thus, thirteen years after Florence, Konstantinos authorized the formal celebration of Union. This took place in Hagia Sophia on 12 December, 1452. As there was no patriarch, Isidoros himself presided, after which he and the basileus spoke to the crowd in attendance. The Synaxis and its followers boycotted this ceremony, which tainted Hagia Sophia in their eyes with Catholic contagion. Thus, even the City's jewel was dragged into the mire of discord. For many anti-Unionists, the Great Church had fallen to the enemy inside before the City itself had fallen to the enemy outside. This was its last known use as a Christian church.[97]

In the heated polemic and fake news of those days, the most hated figure was probably Notaras. An astute politician, he steered a middle course through the religious acrimony, with the result that each side thought that he belonged to the other. The pro-Union historian Doukas slanders Notaras by making him speak an infamous line: "Better the Turkish turban in the City than the Latin mitre." In reality Notaras followed the basileus on Union and was thick with the Latins. But many no doubt sympathized with that bitter sentiment, which had been circulating since the thirteenth century. Conversely, Kydones had argued that, if the Romans had to be slaves, it was better to be slaves of the Latins than the Turks. Ioannes Eugenikos said exactly the opposite to Notaras.[98] But in 1453, many Romans felt that they were being enslaved to *both* Catholicism and Ottoman imperialism. Their patriarch was at Rome, while most of Romanía was already in Turkish hands.

Konstantinos' strategy was as simple as his means were limited. With the grudging consent of the local Venetian authorities, he deputized Venetian ships to defend the Golden Horn behind the chain that was drawn across its entrance (see Figure 53). The defense of the land walls he entrusted to a Genoese nobleman, Giovanni Longo Giustiniani, who arrived in January, 1453 with 700 men. The Romans' greatest asset was the City's thousand-year old walls; in all other respects the sultan had what the basileus lacked. He did not need foreign powers to help, only to do nothing. Many did not believe that he was a serious threat, because of his youth, inexperience, and friendly diplomatic overtures. The Genoese of Galata assured him in advance of their neutrality, which in context was effectively taking his side. Moreover, the sultan's officers carried out his orders, usually with alacrity and fear, utterly unlike the situation that Konstantinos faced with his own grandees. Mehmed's forces were religiously diverse but they were not religiously divided, unlike the Romans, who were all Christians. While the sultan was not especially interested in religion, he successfully cast his attack as a war for the triumph of Islam over the Christian Roman enemy, a victory that

Figure 53 Fragment of the chain used to block the Golden Horn (Istanbul Archaelogical Museum)
Photo by David Hendrix

had long been foretold but eluded Muslim conquerors since the seventh century. His forces were reminded of this and infused with this religious message.

Rarely has a struggle for hegemony and survival, between a dying and an emerging empire, been fought so unequally. Mehmed's army was massive in comparison to the forces defending the City, possibly fifteen times larger. Unlike the defenders, they were well fed and well paid, and they stood to gain if they prevailed. He also built a significant fleet to cut the City off from provisions and aid during the blockade and bombardment. Constantinople had been attacked many times, but Mehmed's ace in the hole was his artillery. His engineers prepared the roads and bridges leading to the City to accommodate his dozens of cannons. The sultan's army arrived before the walls during the first week of April. Sultan and basileus faced off at the weakest point, at the center-north stretch where the walls dipped into the old river bed, around the Romanos gate, but other forces surrounded the City, by land and sea. Giustiniani was posted just to the north of the basileus. The bombardment began on 12 April, and by 21 April a tower had collapsed. As the walls cracked, Mehmed's soldiers would approach them with ladders while the defenders desperately tried to patch up the damage and devise countermeasures to blunt the force of the cannonballs, some of which weighed over 600 kg. The deafening and regular noise of the blasts was, at first, terrifying to the defenders, but it quickly became part of the background.

The basileus also had smaller cannons, but firing them from atop the walls shook them and was therefore counterproductive. On 20 April, one Roman and three Genoese ships broke through the Ottoman blockade, after outmaneuvering the sultan's, bringing joy to the defenders and embarrassment to the sultan, who had been shouting instructions to his crews from the shore. He confiscated his admiral's property and had him whipped publicly. In May, Mehmed opened a subterranean front in the siege. He sent sappers to dig tunnels beneath the towers and undermine them, but the Romans dug their own countertunnels and drove the Turks out with fire and sword. It was possible for the Romans to believe that their defenses would hold, as they had so many times in the past against the odds, and the sultan was being advised by many of his officials to call it off and cut his losses. But Mehmed had the resources and ingenuity to carry out impressive feats, which changed the both dynamic and the mood of the siege. To get his fleet into the Golden Horn, he portaged his ships overland around Pera, astounding the defenders. Their effort to burn his ships failed and Mehmed impaled his captives in full view of the City. He did not intend to take Constantinople from the Golden Horn, as the Venetians had done in 1204, only to force the defenders to divert scarce resources there away from the main point of attack, the land walls. Now that the City was entirely cut off and surrounded, he concentrated his assault on the dip in the walls at the Romanos gate. His final offer to accept Konstantinos' surrender was rejected by the basileus with these words, his final recorded words: "I do not have the right to give you the City, nor does anyone else of those who live in it. By a collective decision we will all willingly die and not try to save our lives."[99]

In the end, it was not cannons that sealed the City's fate but a frontal assault and the vicissitudes of battle. On the morning of 29 May, after a night of intense religious preparation on the part of his army, Mehmed ordered a full-on attack against the weakest point in the walls, where the moat had been filled in. For reasons that are unclear, Konstantinos and Giustiniani had chosen to defend the outer wall, in front of the moat, which was originally some 9 meters tall, and not the inner wall, which was between 15 and 20 meters tall. They did so possibly in order to carry out the many sorties that had disrupted Mehmed's operations during the past two months. On that day, the increasingly exhausted defenders repelled the first wave of irregulars, then the armies of Anatolia, but during the third-wave attack by the professional janissaries Giustiniani was wounded and retreated into the City, through a gate in the inner wall. Fearing that they were being abandoned by their commanders, the defenders panicked and fled. The basileus was killed in the fighting, though no one who later wrote of the siege witnessed this. His body was never recovered, which made him a figure of legend: somewhere he was waiting for the moment to return. History had come full circle, as a prophecy observed soon after the fall: the City would be lost by a basileus named Konstantinos, the son of Helene, just as it had been founded by one.[100] But the last basileus of the Romans had no crown, no wife, no heir, no patriarch, no money, no legions, no fleet, and no grave.

It is for others to tell of the slaughter that ensued when the City fell and the fate of those who survived it. The Roman polity of Constantinople came to an end that day, and Ottoman history advanced beyond its "prelude" phase. In the years to come, Mehmed mopped up the remaining pockets of Roman independence, taking the Morea in 1460 and Trebizond in 1461, along with Acciaiuoli Athens in 1456 and Gattilusi Lesbos in 1462. The narrative of the historian Doukas, writing on Lesbos, ominously ends during the bombardment of Mytilene. The despots of the Morea, Thomas and Demetrios, persisted in their sordid routine of infighting and incompetence to the end. They failed to collect taxes from their recalcitrant landowners and to deliver them to their Ottoman masters, and they had to call in the Turkish army of Thessaly in order to suppress local rebellions. Eventually, the sultan had enough and invaded in 1460, conquering the Peloponnese and taking thousands of captives.[101] Thomas fled to Italy, hawking relics and titles. Demetrios, who had long collaborated with the sultans and was anti-Union, surrendered Mystras and accepted retirement lands in Thrace.

The Ottoman sultans dismantled the secular and political institutions of the Roman state, leaving only the religious ones to continue, albeit in a much reduced and impoverished condition. This is how the Orthodox Church became the default heir of what was much later called "Byzantine" civilization. The anti-Union Scholarios was made patriarch, as it was in Mehmed's interest to perpetuate the separation between his Roman subjects and the Latin west. But the Church suffered major losses as well. The patriarch became essentially a tax collector for the Ottoman regime. Hagia Sophia and other churches were converted into mosques. The Holy Apostles was demolished, and Mehmed built his Fatih ("Conquest") mosque on its foundations. All of the imperial columns were gradually demolished, except that of Constantine, which survived minus its cross and encased in an Ottoman base. The old palace was abandoned to the elements. Mehmed began the repopulation of Constantinople by resettling conquered groups there from many regions of his extensive empire. The Roman people survived as one among many ethnic groups in the new Muslim empire. It was not until many centuries later that the *millet* system emerged, which ecclesiastically placed most Orthodox groups under the patriarch of Constantinople. Outside of this administrative arrangement, the *Rum* remained one ethnic group among others, distinct from the Bulgarians, Christian Albanians, Vlachs, and Serbs. Romans who emigrated to the west had to take on a "Greek" social profile, because that is how they were recognized there. It was only with the Greek Revolution of the nineteenth century that the Rum of Greece also changed their identity from Roman to Greek, with far-reaching consequences to this day. Only a few east Romans survive in modern Turkey.

The end

The Romans of the Palaiologan era present an unedifying picture. As so many complained at the time, their elites preferred their own financial advantage over the common good; the dynasty was prone to infighting, while failing dismally to defeat the Romans' common enemies; and their subjects were addicted to culture-war issues, especially over Union, "theologizing against the Latins at a time when their cities are being conquered," noted an expat in Rome.[102] But all this was to be expected. Intra-dynastic conflicts were merely a reduced version of the Roman civil wars of the past, not anything new in the political sphere. Moreover, the last Roman elites no longer derived their wealth and status from service to the state, so they were less bound to it than their counterparts in earlier times. They integrated successfully into Italian and Turkish networks and learned to navigate the complex world of early modernity. These skills would serve their descendants well for centuries to come under Ottoman and western colonial rule. Culture wars, meanwhile, were inevitable in a society trapped between competing imperialisms, from both east and west.

The Latins had broken the Roman polity in 1204 and thereafter kept its fragments weak in order to extract its resources cheaply and feed their insatiable markets back home. Western consumer society depended on these exports for a wide range of goods, and to this degree Latin colonialism in Romanía paid off handsomely. Huge volumes of trade passed through Roman lands, but the Roman state profited little from them. It had become "a rural hinterland whose relatively abundant natural resources were being creamed off at regular intervals by foreigners."[103] When the moment of crisis came, the Genoese and Venetians preferred to make deals with the sultan to salvage what they could of this profitable system. Meanwhile, the papacy clung to fantasies about "reducing the Greeks." Some Latins lamented the City's fall and called for a crusade, while others maintained that the schismatic Greeks had deserved their fate. But mostly they moved on, making deals with the Ottomans and worrying about where their expansion into the Christian world would end.

Konstantinos Palaiologos might have spared his subjects much suffering had he surrendered to Mehmed, and he was repeatedly given that opportunity. The last Grand Komnenos of Trebizond, David, surrendered his city rather than see it destroyed by the Ottoman armies, but his prudence availed him little. He and his family were hauled off to Constantinople, the sultan's new capital, and murdered in captivity. By contrast, the Romans of Constantinople in 1453 fought to the end. They had already weathered many sieges and the walls had been kept up. There is no sign of a will to surrender among them, so Konstantinos was echoing popular sentiment when he told Mehmed that "we will all willingly die and not try to save our lives."[104] In the eyes of posterity, Konstantinos' last stand and personal sacrifice redeemed his dynasty and brought a final glimmer of dignity to the end of Roman history. Constantinople did not bow its head and go quietly under the Turkish yoke. Konstantinos was a man of modest abilities, but he made sure the world knew that something epochal had just happened. An anonymous observer noted at the time that the basileus "died in the ruins that had been made in the Queen of Cities, alongside his leading men, and he earned the crown of martyrdom, for he refused to hand his kingdom over to the lawless ones, even though it was possible for him to escape the danger."[105]

The history of the New Roman empire had begun in antiquity, at a time when most of its subjects still worshipped Zeus. Even then the Roman empire was old. By 1453, Romanía was by far the oldest state in the world. It had survived to the very cusp of modernity, almost to the journeys of Columbus. At Florence, it is likely that Plethon met the mathematician Paolo Dal Pozzo Toscanelli, who is later said to have discussed geography with Columbus. Columbus' expeditions, in turn, were informed by Greek geographical texts that arrived in Italy along with east Roman émigré scholars.[106] The links were more than intellectual. It was the Ottoman conquest that pushed Italian trading routes westward, to Portugal and Spain and then into the Atlantic. Columbus' journeys were a response to Ottoman imperialism.[107]

How, then, did Romanía survive for so long, from Ptolemy to Columbus, through the most challenging millennium of human history, beset by enemies, and suffering repeated defeats at their hands that would have been fatal to other states?

The history of Romanía was one of resilience, marked by an extraordinary capacity to recover from setbacks and adapt to new circumstances. This durability was enabled by factors that are well known, most prominently the grid of overlapping, centralized institutions that bound Romanía together into a unified whole for most of its long history. A system of efficient taxation provided the resources for a national Roman army under central control that defended the borders of the state. A unified culture of law, religion, literature, and art buttressed a relatively homogenous Christian Roman society and endowed it with a heightened sense of its own place in the world. Imperial diplomacy and foreign policy were pragmatic and bolstered by a subtle deployment of soft power in the periphery. Constantinople positioned itself artfully as the arbiter of political prestige, elite culture, and religious authority. But there are also factors that have received less attention, which our story has tried to highlight. The government of Romanía extracted resources from its subjects enough to yield a bountiful surplus for state operations, while not exploiting them so much that they sought to free themselves from its grip. Separatist movements and agrarian revolts are few and far between in the millennial history of this polity. Moreover, the government was at all times careful to explain to its subjects that it was acting only for their common good, and for the most part it actually did so, by the standards of Roman political culture. It projected a persona of responsiveness and accountability. When subjects felt that their rulers were abusing their power, they let them know, sometimes in violent ways, usually resulting in a course correction and greater integration. The political culture valorized consensus. For the majority Roman population of this polity, it was no "empire."

The Ottoman conquest of Constantinople paradoxically restored the City's centrality as an imperial capital. A century later the territorial extent of the Ottoman empire eerily resembled that of the eastern empire around 500 AD. Yet the Ottoman and Roman empires were premised on radically different ideas about subject-ruler relations, which accounts for their divergent natures and trajectories. Recent claims to continuity between the two are vastly overstated. As it walked the fine line between taxation and exploitation, coercion and accountability, and power and persuasion, the Roman order successfully fostered cultures of loyalty toward itself and its official Church, resulting in deeply rooted identities among the overwhelming majority of its shareholders. This society was defined by traits that dated back to antiquity, including Orthodoxy, Roman ethnicity, the Greek language and its culture, and Roman political norms: they bound it together and provided the basis of its consensus. Over a century later, a historian writing in Greek with a flair for the dramatic put these words into Konstantinos XI's mouth before his death. "You know well, my brothers, the four things that we must all uphold in common, such that we would choose to die for them rather than live; first, our faith and religion; second, our fatherland; third, our basileus, the Lord's anointed; and, fourth, our relatives and friends."[108]

State Revenues and Payments to Foreign Groups, Fifth–Seventh Centuries

A list of indicative expenses and sources of revenue can help the reader calibrate the relative size of cash sums that appear in the narrative. The accuracy of these reports is not guaranteed, but overall they paint a consistent picture. To convert solidi sums into gold lbs, divide by 72.

STATE REVENUES AND EXPENSES	SOLIDI	SOURCE
Total state annual revenue	4–6 million (est.)	Hendy, *Studies*, 171; Haldon, *Empire*, 27–29
Marcian reserve, 457	7 million	Lydos, *On the magistracies* 3.43
North Africa campaign, 468	7–9 million	Kandidos, *History* fr. 2; Lydos, *On the Magistracies* 3.43
Anastasios reserve, 518	23 million	Prokopios, *Secret History* 19.7
Justinian's consular games, 521	288,000	Marcellinus, *Chronicle* s.a. 521
Relief to Antioch, 526	252,000	Malalas, *Chronicle* 17.16–17, 22
Hagia Sophia, 532–537	1 million (est.)	Lydos, *On the magistracies* 3.76 (extrapolated)
Church of Alexandria reserve, 610	576,000	Leontios, *Life of Ioannes the Almsgiver* 45
Payments by Mu'awiya, ca. 659 ff.	365,000 per year	Theophanes a.m. 6150, p. 347
Payments by 'Abd al-Malik, 685 ff.	365,000 per year	Eastern Source in Hoyland, *Theophilus*, 180–182

DATE	GROUP PAID	SOLIDI PER YEAR	SOURCE
420s ff.	Huns (Rua)	25,200	Priskos, *History* fr. 2
ca. 437 ff.	Huns (Attila)	50,400	Priskos, *History* fr. 2
447	Huns (Attila)	432,000 (one-time)	Priskos, *History* fr. 9.3
447 ff.	Huns (Attila)	151,200	Priskos, *History* fr. 9.3
ca. 460 ff.	Goths (Valamir)	21,600	Priskos, *History* fr. 37

473 ff.	Goths (Theoderic Strabo)	144,000	Malchos, *Byzantine History* fr. 2
478	Goths (Theoderic the Amal)	80,000 (one-time)	Malchos, *Byzantine History* fr. 18.3
478 ff.	Goths (Theoderic the Amal)	10,000	Malchos, *Byzantine History* fr. 18.3
480s ff.	Isaurians	108,000	Ioannes of Antioch, *History* fr. 239.4 (Mariev)
504	Persia (Kavad)	79,200 (one-time)	pseudo-Zacharias, *Chronicle* 7.5 (Prokopios, *Wars* 1.9.4 has 72,000)
532	Persia (Khusrow I)	792,000 (one-time)	Prokopios, *Wars* 1.22.3
545	Persia (Khusrow I)	144,000 (one-time)	Prokopios, *Wars* 2.28.10
551	Persia (Khusrow I)	187,200 (one-time)	Prokopios, *Wars* 8.15.3–7
556	client kings in the Caucasus	28,800 (one-time?)	Agathias, *Histories* 3.15.6, 4.20.9
561 ff.	Persia (Khusrow I)	30,000	Menandros, *History* fr. 6.1
574	Persia (Khusrow I)	45,000 (one-time)	Menandros, *History* fr. 18.2
574 ff.	Avars (Baian)	80,000	Menandros, *History* fr. 15.5, 25.1; Theophylaktos, *History* 1.37
575–577	Persia (Khusrow I)	30,000	Menandros, *History* fr. 18.3–4
576	Lombards / Franks	216,000	Menandros, *History* fr. 22
584 ff.	Avars (Baian)	100,000	Theophylaktos, *History* 1.3.13, 1.6.5–6
580s	Franks	50,000 (one-time)	Gregory of Tours, *History of the Franks* 6.42
598 ff.	Avars (son of Baian)	120,000	Theophylaktos, *History* 7.15.14
603 ff.	Avars (son of Baian)	>120,000	Theophanes a.m. 6096, p. 292
603	Lombards	12,000 (one-time?)	Paul the Deacon, *History of the Lombards* 4.32
623 ff.	Avars (son of Baian)	200,000	Nikephoros, *Short History* 13
ca. 637 ff.	Arab invaders	100,000 (Edessa)	Eastern Source in Hoyland, *Theophilus*, 118–119
636–639	Arab invaders	200,000 (Egypt)	Eastern Source in Hoyland, *Theophilus*, 109–114

Emperors of the Romans in the East

This is a list of senior emperors and the years during which they held that position, with junior co-emperors listed after them (though exceptions are made for unusual configurations). Rebels who held Constantinople for a few months or years before losing it to an existing senior emperor are indented.

311–324 Licinius (with son Licinius Caesar 317–324)
324–337 Constantine I (with sons Constantinus II, Constantius II, Constans, and nephew Dalmatius, Caesars)
337–361 Constantius II (with cousins Gallus Caesar 351–354 and Julian Caesar 355–361)
361–363 Julian
363–364 Jovian
364 Valentinian I (in west until 375, leaves east to brother Valens)
364–378 Valens
    365–366 Procopius
378–379 Gratian (in west 375–383, leaves east to Theodosius I)
379–395 Theodosius I (with sons Arcadius 383 and Honorius 393)
395–408 Arcadius (with son Theodosius II 402)
408–450 Theodosius II
450–457 Marcian
457–474 Leo I (with grandson Leo II 473)
474 Leo II (with father Zeno 474)
474–491 Zeno
    475–476 Basiliscus (with son Marcus Caesar)
491–518 Anastasius I
518–527 Justin I (with nephew Justinian I 527)
527–565 Justinian I
565–578 Justin II (with adopted son Tiberios II Konstantinos as Caesar 574, associated 578)
578–582 Tiberios II Konstantinos (with son-in-law Maurikios 582)
582–602 Maurikios (with son Theodosios 590)
602–610 Phokas
610–641 Herakleios (with sons Konstantinos III 613 and Heraklonas 638)
641 Konstantinos III (with brother Heraklonas)
641–642 Heraklonas (with brothers Tiberios and Martinos and nephew Konstas II 641)

642–669 Konstas II (with sons Konstantinos IV 654, Herakleios and Tiberios 659)
668–685 Konstantinos IV (with brothers Herakleios and Tiberios 668–681, with son Justinian II 681)
685–695 Justinian II (first reign)
695–698 Leontios
698–705 Tiberios III (Apsimar)
705–711 Justinian II (second reign; with son Tiberios 706)
711–713 Philippikos (Bardanes)
713–715 Anastasios II
715–717 Theodosios III
717–741 Leon III (with son Konstantinos V 720)
741–775 Konstantinos V (with son Leon IV 751)
742–743? Artabasdos (with son Nikephoros)
775–780 Leon IV (with son Konstantinos VI 776)
780–797 Konstantinos VI
780–802 Eirene
802–811 Nikephoros I (with son Staurakios 803)
811 Staurakios
811–813 Michael I Rangabe (with son Theophylaktos 812)
813–820 Leon V (with son Konstantinos 813)
820–829 Michael II (with son Theophilos 822)
829–842 Theophilos (with sons Konstantinos 829–831? and Michael III 840)
842–867 Michael III (with Basileios I 866)
867–886 Basileios I (with sons Konstantinos 869–879, Leon VI 870, and Alexandros 879)
886–912 Leon VI (with brother Alexandros, and with son Konstantinos VII 908)
912–913 Alexandros (with nephew Konstantinos VII)
913–959 Konstantinos VII (with in-laws 920–945; with son Romanos II 946)
920–944 Romanos I (senior co-ruler, with sons Christophoros 921–931, Stephanos and Konstantinos 923–945, and son-in-law Konstantinos VII)
959–963 Romanos II (with sons Basileios II 960 and Konstantinos VIII 962)
963–969 Nikephoros II Phokas (senior co-ruler)
969–976 Ioannes I Tzimiskes (senior co-ruler)
976–1025 Basileios II (with brother Konstantinos VIII)
1025–1028 Konstantinos VIII
1028–1034 Romanos III Argyros (marries Zoe, daughter of Konstantinos VIII)
1034–1041 Michael IV (marries Zoe)
1041–1042 Michael V (nephew, adopted by Zoe)
1042–1055 Konstantinos IX Monomachos (marries Zoe 1042–1050?, and with her sister Theodora)
1055–1056 Theodora

1056–1057 Michael VI Bringas
1057–1059 Isaakios I Komnenos
1059–1067 Konstantinos X Doukas (with sons Michael VII and Konstantios ca. 1060)
1067–1078 Michael VII Doukas (with brothers Konstantios and Andronikos; with son Konstantinos ca. 1075)
1068–1071 Romanos IV Diogenes (senior co-ruler, with the Doukes, see above)
1078–1081 Nikephoros III Botaneiates
1081–1118 Alexios I Komnenos (with Konstantinos Doukas 1081–1087?; with son Ioannes II 1092)
1118–1143 Ioannes II Komnenos (with son Alexios 1122–1142)
1143–1180 Manuel I Komnenos (with son Alexios II 1171)
1180–1183 Alexios II Komnenos
1183–1185 Andronikos I Komnenos (with younger son Ioannes)
1185–1195 Isaakios II Angelos (first reign)
1195–1203 Alexios III Komnenos (subsequently extramural emperor until 1205)
1203–1204 Alexios IV Angelos (with father Isaakios II, second reign)
1204 Alexios V Doukas Mourtzouphlos
1205–1221 Theodoros I Laskaris (with son Nikolaos ca. 1208- 1212?)
1221–1254 Ioannes III Doukas Batatzes (with son Theodore II ca. 1234)
1254–1258 Theodoros II Doukas Laskaris
1258–1261 Ioannes IV Doukas Laskaris
1259–1282 Michael VIII Palaiologos (senior co-ruler; with Ioannes IV until 1261; with son Andronikos II 1261 and grandson Michael IX 1281)
1282–1328 Andronikos II Palaiologos (with son Michael IX and grandson Andronikos III 1313)
1328–1341 Andronikos III Palaiologos
1341–1376 Ioannes V Palaiologos (first reign; with sons Andronikos IV 1352 and Manuel II 1373)
1347–1354 Ioannes VI Kantakouzenos (senior co-ruler; with son Matthaios 1353)
1376–1379 Andronikos IV Palaiologos (with son Ioannes VII)
1379–1390 Ioannes V Palaiologos (second reign; with sons Manuel II 1381 and Andronikos IV 1381–1385)
1390 Ioannes VII Palaiologos (regent 1399–1403; at Thessalonike 1403–1408, with son Andronikos V before 1407)
1390–1391 Ioannes V Palaiologos (third reign; with son Manuel II)
1391–1425 Manuel II Palaiologos (with nephew Ioannes VII and son Ioannes VIII by 1407)
1425–1448 Ioannes VIII Palaiologos
1448–1453 Konstantinos XI Palaiologos

Glossary

Fourth to seventh centuries

adaeratio: conversion of a tax paid in kind to a payment in cash.

annona: grain brought to Constantinople by the state or payments to its officials in the form of goods.

Augustus: a senior emperor (if there was a Caesar); a junior emperor after the mid-seventh century.

basileus: what Greek speakers called the emperor in (mostly) non-official contexts.

Caesar: a junior, subordinate emperor; later (as *kaisar*) a high court rank.

civitas: a city or municipality with its own laws, citizenship, and local government (Greek: *polis*).

collatio lustralis: a tax on urban trades instituted by Constantine and abolished by Anastasius (Greek: *chrysargyron*).

coloni: tenant farmers who were legally free but tied to the land they worked.

comes: high-ranking military officer or high government functionary (pl. *comites*), meaning "someone who accompanies" (i.e., the emperor).

comitatus: field army that accompanied the emperor; its soldiers were the *comitatenses*.

cubicularius: high-ranking court eunuch (from *cubiculum*, "bedchamber").

curiales: city councilors (sing. *curialis*), from *curia* ("senate," "council") (Greek: *bouleutai*).

decuriones: see *curiales*.

defensor civitatis: judicial official in the cities who protected the weak against the abuses of the strong.

diocese: regional administrative grouping of provinces.

domestici: corps of imperial bodyguards.

donative: large payment to the soldiers made on anniversary occasions, usually every five years.

dux: mid-level military officer (pl. *duces*).

exarch: title of the governors of North Africa and Italy after the later sixth century, who combined military and civilian authority.

excubitores: chief corps of imperial bodyguards after ca. 470, led by a *comes*.

foederati: Gothic auxiliary units of the army.

follis: the bronze (base) currency of the empire (pl. *folles*).

homoousian: someone who believes that the Father and Son are of the same substance (*ousia*), i.e., a Nicaean; *homoiousian*: that the Father and Son are of similar substance; *homoian*: that the Father and Son are similar, but not necessarily in substance; *heterousian*: that the Father and Son are not of the same substance; *anhomoian*: that the Father and Son are dissimilar.

hypostasis: Greek term for the essence of God or the personhood of the members of the Trinity.

illustris: highest rank of the senatorial order.

iugum: unit of taxable agricultural land (pl. *iuga*).

katholikos: head of the Armenian Church, and of the Church of the East.

limitanei (aka *ripenses*): soldiers posted along the frontier, contrasted to the *comitatenses*.

magister militum: highest-ranking general.

magister officiorum: high palatine official in charge of the palace, diplomacy, and many other matters.

Notitia dignitatum: list of military units and officers compiled, for the eastern empire, after 441.

nummi: the bronze (base) currency of the empire.

Oriens: the prefecture of the east, including Thrace, Asia Minor, Syria, Palestine, and Egypt; also the field army that defended the Mesopotamian border with Persia.

ousia: Greek for "substance," used in discussions of the essence of God.

patricius ("patrician"): high court title (not an office with functions).

phylarchos: imperially appointed leader of the empire's Saracen allies.

praesental army: two field armies "in the emperor's presence," stationed near Constantinople.

praetorian prefect: highest civilian official of the empire, in charge of the budget, tax collection, and the supervision of provincial governors; there was one per prefecture.

praitorion: the headquarters of a prefect or provincial governor.

prefecture: regional administrative cluster of dioceses, under the direction of a prefect. The eastern empire started with two, Illyricum and Oriens, and then added Italy and North Africa.

quaestor: the emperor's top legal official.

res privata: a financial department of the state, directed by a *comes*, that (among other minor functions) administered the crown lands.

res publica: the "public affairs" of the Roman people, what they called their state and society, aka a "republic" (Greek: *politeia*).

Romanía ("Romanland"): the proper name given to the empire by its inhabitants in this period, which became an official name in the tenth–eleventh centuries.

sacrae largitiones: a financial department of the state, directed by a *comes*, that (among other functions) operated the mints and handled the coin supply.

scholae palatinae: an imperial bodyguard instituted by Constantine that later became ceremonial.

silentiarius: a mid-level palace official in charge of palace order.

solidus: the empire's gold coin (pl. *solidi*); in Greek, a nomisma..

Theotokos: The Mother of God, what the eastern Church calls the Virgin Mary.

Seventh to fifteenth centuries

basileus: the main title of the monarch of Romanía (pl. *basileis*).

chrysobull: official document issued by the court, usually granting an exemption or concession and bearing the emperor's "golden seal."

domestikos: high military official; originally the commander of the *tagma* of the *scholai*, the *domestikos* often led the armies on campaign in the late tenth century.

doux: a high military office. After the late tenth century, *doukes* (or *katepano*) commanded clusters of *themata* and their *strategoi*; after the late eleventh, the military governors of most *themata* were *doukes*.

droungarios: admiral in the seventh–eleventh centuries.

eparchos: prefect of Constantinople, headquartered at the *praitorion*.

hyperpyron: the standard gold coin (and unit of value) after ca. 1100.

katepano: high military official equivalent to a *doux*.

kouropalates: high court title given to a relative of the emperor or foreign ruler favored by the court.

logothetes: head of the (mostly fiscal) bureaux of state (the *genikon*, *eidikon*, and *stratiotikon*), seventh–eleventh centuries. The logothete of the *dromos* was in charge of communications and foreign policy.

magistros: high court title of the middle period.

megas doux: admiral between the late eleventh and the fourteenth centuries.

mesazon: prime minister or chief of staff of the *basileus* in the late period.

nomisma: the gold coin of the empire (*solidus* in Latin). After ca. 1100, it was reissued as the *hyperpyron*.

oikonomia: a special dispensation granted in order to bend the rules for a good purpose.

paroikos: dependant farmer, usually one working land granted as a *pronoia*, whose taxes and labor dues went to the *pronoiar* rather than the state.

patrikios: a high court title of the early and middle periods.

pinkernes: a high military office of the later period.

porphyrogennetos: "born-in-the-purple" son or daughter of a sitting emperor, delivered in a special purple birthing room in the palace.

praitor: provincial governor (mostly civilian); performed military duties too in the thirteenth century.

prokypsis: phantasmagoric presentation of the emperor at a court ceremony, first devised probably in the twelfth century.

pronoia: an arrangement whereby the taxes and labor dues owed to the state by a piece of land and its tenants/owners were transferred to a beneficiary (the *pronoiar*), in lieu of direct payments by the state.

protasekretis: chief secretary of the imperial chancery.

protosebastos: see *sebastokrator*.

protospatharios: a court title of intermediate rank in the middle period.

protostrator: military office-*cum*-court title, prominent in the twelfth–fourteenth centuries.

roga: a state salary.

scholai: the most important *tagma*.

sebastokrator: one of many high court titles devised by Alexios I Komnenos from the word *sebastos*, "Augustus," to honor members of his immediate family.

sekreton: a fiscal bureau or endowment fund.

strategos: a general, Greek for *magister militum*. *Strategoi* (pl.) led the thematic armies and governed the themes in the ninth–eleventh centuries.

synkellos: no. 2 official in the Church after the patriarch, often serving as the emperor's representative to the patriarchate.

tagma: mobile field armies stationed in and around Constantinople between the eighth and the eleventh centuries, often serving as a counterweight to the thematic armies (pl. *tagmata*).

themes: the militarized provinces of the empire and the armies stationed in them, mainly eighth–twelfth centuries; afterward they were mostly administrative districts (pl. *themata*).

vestiarion: treasury of the later *basileis*.

Abbreviations

AA *Archives de l'Athos*
AASS *Acta Sanctorum*, 71 vols. (Paris 1886–1940)
ACO *Acta Conciliorum Oecumenicorum* (Berlin 1927–)
BGU Berlin, *Griechische Urkunden* (papyri from the Egyptian Museum)
BMFD J. Thomas and A. Hero, eds., *Byzantine Monastic Foundation Documents* (Washington, D.C. 2000)
BMGS *Byzantine and Modern Greek Studies*
BZ *Byzantinische Zeitschrift*
CIG *Corpus Inscriptionum Graecarum* (Berlin 1828–1877)
CIL *Corpus Inscriptionum Latinarum* (Berlin 1893–1986)
CJ *Justinianic Code (Codex Iustinianus)*
CTh *Theodosian Code (Codex Theodosianus)*
DAI *De administrando imperio*
DOP *Dumbarton Oaks Papers*
EEBΣ *Ἐπετηρὶς Ἑταιρείας Βυζαντινῶν Σπουδῶν*
EH *Ecclesiastical History*
EHB A. E. Laiou, ed., *The Economic History of Byzantium from the Seventh through the Fifteenth Century* (Washington, D.C. 2002)
FHG K. Müller, ed., *Fragmenta Historicorum Graecorum*, 5 vols. (Paris 1878–1885)
GRBS *Greek, Roman, and Byzantine Studies*
IG *Inscriptiones Graecae* (Berlin 1924–)
ILS *Inscriptiones Latinae Selectae* (Berlin 1892–1916)
JECS *Journal of Early Christian Studies*
JLA *Journal of Late Antiquity*
JöB *Jahrbuch der österreichischen Byzantinistik*
JRA *Journal of Roman Archaeology*
JRS *Journal of Roman Studies*
MGH *Monumenta Germaniae Historica*; all subseries: https://www.dmgh.de
MM F. Miklosich and J. Müller, *Acta et diplomata graeca medii aevi sacra et profana*, 6 vols. (Vienna 1860–1890)
PDTM W. Witakowski, *Pseudo-Dionysius of Tel-Mahre, Chronicle, Part III* (Liverpool 1996)
PG J.-P. Migne, ed. *Patrologia Graeca*, 161 vols. (Paris 1857–1866)
PL J-P. Migne, ed., *Patrologia Latina*, 217 vols. (Paris 1841–1855)

PLP	*Prosopographisches Lexikon der Palaiologenzeit*, eds. E. Trapp et al., 12 vols. (Vienna 1976–1996)
PLRE	*Prosopography of the Later Roman Empire*, eds. A. H. M. Jones et al., 3 vols. (Cambridge 1971–1992)
PmbZ	*Prosopographie der mittelbyzantinischen Zeit, 1. Abteilung (641–867); 2. Abteilung (867–1025)* (Berlin 1998–2013)
PO	*Patrologia Orientalis*
ΠΠ	*Παλαιολόγεια καὶ Πελοποννησιακά*, ed. S. Lambros, 4 vols. (Athens 1912–1930)
REB	*Revue des études byzantines*
RP	*Das Register des Patriarchats von Konstantinopel*, eds. H. Hunger et al., 3 vols. (Vienna 1981–2001)
SEG	*Supplementum Epigraphicum Graecum* (Leiden 1923–)
TM	*Travaux et mémoires*
ZPE	*Zeitschrift für Papyrologie und Epigraphik*

Notes

Introduction

1. *Life of Andreas the Fool* 36.
2. Malalas 13.7; Prokopios, *Wars* 5.15.8–14; Doukas 39.18.
3. A. Kaldellis, 'From "Empire of the Greeks" to "Byzantium": The Politics of a Modern Paradigm Shift,' in N. Aschenbrenner and J. Ransohoff, eds., *The Invention of Byzantium in Early Modern Europe* (Washington, D.C. 2021) 349–367.
4. E.g., in E. Jeffreys, ed., *The Oxford Handbook of Byzantine Studies* (Oxford 2008); D. Holton et al., *The Cambridge Grammar of Medieval and Early Modern Greek* (Cambridge 2019).
5. Edward Gibbon, *History of the Decline and Fall of the Roman Empire*, ch. 13 (v. 1, 359: Diocletian; 390: Constantine) (ed. Womersley). The term "eastern" is more appropriate for the brief period during which there was also a western empire (395–476 AD), after which it was the only one.
6. Manasses, *Historical Synopsis* 2320–2323.
7. J. Herrin, *Byzantium: The Surprising Life of a Medieval Empire* (Princeton 2007) xv.
8. See many theorists quoted in S. Weller, *The Idea of Europe: A Critical History* (Cambridge 2021).
9. A view classically codified in Montesquieu's *Considerations on the Causes of the Greatness of the Romans and Their Decline* (1734).
10. Theophanes Continuatus 4.17; Attaleiates, *History*, dedication.
11. A. MacIntyre, *After Virtue*, 3rd ed. (Notre Dame 2007) 31.

Chapter 1. New Rome and the New Romans

1. Kaldellis, 'Forum.' Apparition: Sozomenos 2.3; cf. *Greek Anthology* 14.115.
2. Hesychios of Miletos, *Patria* 41.
3. Konstantinos of Rhodes, *On Constantinople* 63, 84, 119–124.
4. *Anonymus Valesianus* 6.30.
5. Dagron, *Naissance*, ch. 1; N. Lenski, 'Constantine and the Tyche of Constantinople,' in J. Wienand, ed., *Contested Monarchy: Integrating the Roman Empire* (Oxford 2015) 330–352.
6. Philostorgios 2.17; cf. Theodoretos, *EH* 1.32.
7. Jerome, *Chronicle* s.a. 334.
8. Julian, *Letter* 48 (Loeb).

9. L. Grig and G. Kelly, eds., *Two Romes: Rome and Constantinople in Late Antiquity* (Oxford 2012) 11 ('Introduction'). Laws: e.g., *CTh* 14.17.5 (369 AD).
10. Theodosius I: *Parastaseis* 5 (unreliable); cf. Malalas 13.8; races: Konstantinos VII, *Book of Ceremonies* 1.79.
11. Marcian in the *Acts of the Council of Chalcedon* 2.1.2, p. 155.
12. Konstantinos VII, *Life of Basileios I* 1.
13. Sozomenos 7.9.2–3.
14. Tyche: Themistios, *Oration* 3.42a; metropolis and ancestors: 3.42b, 14.182a, 18.222b, 23.298a–b, 31.354c; Romulus-Constantine: 14.182a.
15. G. Bowersock, 'Old and New Rome in the Late Antique Near East,' in P. Rousseau and M. Papoutsakis, eds., *Transformations of Late Antiquity* (Farnham, UK 2009) 37–50, here 44–47. In later texts: e.g., Theodosios the Deacon, *On the Capture of Crete* 73–74; Theodoros Prodromos, *Poem* 19 (p. 311).
16. Herodian, *History after Marcus* 4.3.5–7.
17. R. Van Dam, '"Constantine's Beautiful City": The Symbolic Value of Constantinople,' *Antiquité tardive* 22 (2014) 83–94, here 90.
18. Cicero, *De re publica* 1.39.
19. Appianos, *Civil War* 2.37, 2.50; cf. Cicero, *Letters to Atticus* 7.11, 8.2–3.
20. Suetonius, *Gaius* 49; Cassius Dio, *Roman History* 63.27.2; A. Kaldellis, 'How Was a 'New Rome' Even Thinkable? Premonitions of Constantinople and the Portability of Rome,' in Y. Kim and A. McLaughlin, eds., *Leadership and Community in Late Antiquity* (Turnhout 2020) 221–247.
21. Herodian, *History after Marcus* 1.6.5.
22. Aurelius Victor, *De Caesaribus* 28 (tr. Bird).
23. Caracalla in *Papyrus Gissen* 40; "Divine Gift": *BGU* 2:655.
24. Ulpian in *Digest* 1.5.17; *Basilika* 46.1.14; see C. Ando, *Imperial Ideology and Provincial Loyalty in the Roman Empire* (Berkeley 2000) ch. 8.
25. Modestinus in *Digest* 50.1.33; *Basilika* 7.5.5, 38.1.6.
26. Carthage: Herodian, *History after Marcus* 7.5–6; Nikomedeia: Lactantius, *On the Deaths of the Persecutors* 7.8–10; Ammianus 22.9.3; Milan: *Panegyrici Latini* 11.12.2, 11.14.3; Serdica: Petros the Patrician, *History* fr. 211 (Banchich) = *Anonymous Continuer of Cassius Dio* fr. 15.1.
27. E. Marlow, 'The Multivalence of Memory: The Tetrarchs, the Senate, and the Vicennalia Monument,' in K. Galinsky and K. Lapatin, eds., *Cultural Memories in the Roman Empire* (Los Angeles 2016) 240–262, here 250.
28. Eusebios, *Life of Constantine* 2.53.
29. Athanasios, *History of the Arians* 35; *The Martyrdom of Saba* 4 (p. 218), 8 (p. 221); foreseen by Ailios Aristeides, *Oration* 26.61.
30. Orosius, *History against the Pagans* 7.43.5–6: *Romania . . . ut vulgariter loquar.*
31. Malalas 16.19; *Paschal Chronicle* [s.a. 531] (p. 622).
32. Themistios, *Oration* 7.94c–d.
33. R. Van Dam, *Rome and Constantinople* (Waco, TX 2010) 30.
34. Eutropius, *Breviarium* 9.

35. K. Hopkins, 'The Political Economy of the Roman Empire,' in I. Morris and W. Scheidel, eds., *The Dynamics of Ancient Empires* (Oxford 2009) 178–203, here 192; Tacoma, *Moving Romans*, 157–163.
36. Frier, 'Demography,' 814; Harper, *Fate*, 30–31, 319–320 n. 19; R. Van Dam, 'Bishops and Clerics during the Fourth Century: Numbers and Their Implications,' in J. Leemans et al., eds., *Episcopal Elections in Late Antiquity* (Berlin 2011) 217–242, here 228. I am moving half the estimate for the Danubian provinces from the west to the east.
37. R. MacMullen, *Corruption and the Decline of Rome* (New Haven 1988) 175–176; C. Whittaker, *Frontiers of the Roman Empire* (Baltimore 1994) 262–264. They may have owned land even without working it themselves: *CTh* 7.20.4.
38. C. Haas, *Alexandria in Late Antiquity* (Baltimore 1997) 77–80; C. Foss, *Byzantine and Turkish Sardis* (Cambridge, MA 1976) 18; control: R. Van Dam, 'Big Cities and the Dynamics of the Mediterranean during the Fifth Century,' in M. Maas, ed., *The Cambridge Companion to the Age of Attila* (Cambridge 2015) 80–97, here 91–93.
39. Banaji, *Agrarian Change*, 17–22, 180–181, 206, 215, esp. 263.
40. Prokopios, *Secret History* 6.2–3.
41. Sokrates 2.13; Themistios, *Oration* 23.292a; *CTh* 14.17.15.
42. John of Ephesos, *EH III* 2.41.
43. Gregory of Nazianzos, *Oration* 34.7.
44. Themistios, *Oration* 23.292a; transports and granaries: *Oration* 18.221a–c; *Civis Romanus*: *CTh* 14.17.5.
45. Eunapios, *Lives of the Philosophers* 463; Themistios, *Oration* 18.221c.
46. J. Koder, 'Fresh Vegetables for the Capital,' in Mango and Dagron, eds., *Constantinople*, 49–56.
47. T. Russell, *Byzantium and the Bosporus* (Oxford 2017) 157, 162; Frier, 'Demography,' 793.
48. Justinian, *Novels* 43.1, 59; *CJ* 1.2.4; É. Rebillard, 'Les formes de l'assistance funéraire dans l'empire romain,' *Antiquité tardive* 7 (1999) 269–282, here 274.
49. *CTh* 14.17.1.
50. Sozomenos 2.3.5; Zosimos 2.31; Hesychios of Miletos, *Patria* 40; cf. Eusebios, *Life of Constantine* 3.48.
51. A. Skinner, 'The Early Development of the Senate of Constantinople,' *BMGS* 32 (2008) 128–148, here 134–135.
52. Constantius II, *Letter to the Senate* 21b; cf. Themistios, *Oration* 26.326c–d. Magnentius: Moser, *Emperor*.
53. Themistios, *Oration* 34.13; Heather, 'New Men,' 11–33, here 18–20.
54. Basil the Great, *Homily to the Rich* 2; Gregory of Nyssa, *De beneficentia* (van Heck, 9:105).
55. Ca. 100 slaves in each *domus* in Rome: Tacoma, *Moving Romans*, 66; between 200 and 400: W. Eck, *Roma Caput Mundi* (Wellington, New Zealand 2001) 9–11.
56. E.g., *CTh* 6.2.16, 6.2.20.
57. *CTh* 13.1.21.
58. *Life of Olympias* 5, in *Analecta Bollandiana* 15 (1986) 413–414.

59. Libanios, *Oration* 1.279; cf. 18.146, 30.37, 48.3, 49.2.
60. Libanios, *Letter* 86; skeptical: *Letter* 62.
61. Burden: *Anonymous Valesianus* 6.30; Zosimos 2.32.1; Licinius' treasury: Julian, *Oration* 1.8.b–c; new taxes: Sozomenos 2.3.5; Zosimos 2.37–38; temple treasuries: Eusebios, *Life of Constantine* 3.54, and *Tricennial Oration in Praise of Constantine* 8; Firmicus Maternus, *The Error of the Pagan Religions* 28.6; Julian, *Oration* 7.228b–c; Anonymous, *De rebus bellicis* 2.1–2; Libanios, *Oration* 30.6, 30.37; Sozomenos 2.5. Some read Palladas in *Greek Anthology* 9.441, 9.528, 9.773, in this connection.
62. *Anonymous Valesianus* 6.30; Jordanes, *Getica* 28.143 (referring to 380 AD, possibly to sailors).
63. D. Feissel, 'Aspects de l'immigration a Constantinople,' in Mango and Dagron, eds., *Constantinople*, 367–377.
64. Sokrates 4.16.
65. Symeon Metaphrastes, *Life of Markianos the Presbyter* 4, in *PG* 114:433.
66. John Chrysostom, *Homily on the Martyr's Relics* 3, in *PG* 63:472.
67. Menandros Rhetor, *Treatise I* 60.10–16, 67.11–14, 68.10–14.
68. Diocletian in *Mosaicarum et Romanarum leges* 6.4; cf. *CTh* 13.12.1, 13.12.3.
69. Lavan, *Slaves*.
70. Julian, *Oration* 1.5c.
71. Augustine, *Expositions on the Psalms* 58.1.21, ed. E. Dekkers and J. Fraipont, *Augustinus: Enarrationes in Psalmos* (Tournhout 1956) = *Corpus Christianorum Series Latina* 38–40, here 39:744.
72. Eunapios, *Lives of the Philosophers* 487–488.
73. *Itinerarium Burdigalense* 566.7 (333–334 AD).
74. Aurelius Victor, *De Caesaribus* 39 (tr. Bird, mod.); cf. *Panegyrici Latini* 11.3.9.
75. Paulinus of Nola, *Poem* 17.214–216, 269–272; Claudian, *Panegyric for the Consulate of Flavius Manlius Theodorus* 38–41; Vegetius, *Epitoma rei militaris* 2.11, 4.12.
76. Theodoros, *Encomium for St. Theodosios* p. 45 (Usener); Anonymous Pilgrim of Piacenza, *Itinerarium* 37 (translators mistake it for "Persian"); Ioannes Moschos, *Spiritual Meadow* 157; cf. Jordanes, *Romana* 221, 283; *Getica* 12.73–75 (Jordanes was from this region). Arguments that these Bessians were really Georgians carry no weight.
77. *Oxyrhynchus Papyrus* 16.1903 (pp. 127–128).
78. C. Brixhe, 'Interactions between Greek and Phrygian under the Roman Empire,' in J. Adams et al., eds., *Bilingualism in Ancient Society* (Oxford 2002) 246–266, here 248, 252.
79. I take the "two languages" of Sokrates 5.23 to mean Gothic and Greek, not Phrygian.
80. Gregory of Nyssa, *Against Eunomios* 2.1.406; Basil of Kaisareia, *On the Holy Spirit* 29.74 (a dialect of Greek?). Iranians: Basil, *Letter* 258.4; Priskos fr. 41.1.
81. Theodoretos, *History of the Monks of Syria* 28.4.
82. Jerome, *Commentary on Galatians* 2 (pref.); J. Kelly, *Jerome: His Life, Writings, and Controversies* (London 1975) 26 (dependence on Lactantius).
83. Kyrillos of Skythopolis, *Life of Euthymios* 77.
84. Themistios, *Oration* 16.211c–d.

85. *Life of Symeon the Stylite the Younger* 189 (a dialect of Greek?).
86. *Laterculus Veronensis* 13.44, ed. O. Seeck, *Notitiae dignitatum* (Berlin 1876) 252.
87. Herodian, *History after Marcus* 3.1.4.
88. J.-L. Fournet, *The Rise of Coptic: Egyptian versus Greek in Late Antiquity* (Princeton 2020) 55, 61; cf. 47.
89. Heliodoros, *Aithiopika* 2.27; Julian, *Letter* 21.380d (Loeb).
90. Accent: *Miracles of Artemios* 17; Anastasios of Sinai, *Hodegos* 10.1.3; Caracalla: *Papyrus Gissen* 40. Anonymous, *Funeral Oration for John Chrysostom* 38; Ammianus 22.16.
91. Laniado, *Ethnos*, 7–8.
92. Listed by Theodoret, *Quaestiones in Octateuchum*, p. 303.
93. Rabbula: A. Butts, *Language Change in the Wake of Empire: Syriac in its Greco-Roman Context* (Winona Lake, IN 2016) 35. "Aramaic": see the codex cited by F. Millar, 'The Evolution of the Syrian Orthodox Church,' *JECS* 21 (2013) 43–92, here 60.
94. E.g., Herodian, *History after Marcus* 2.7.9; Julian, *Misopogon*; Eunapios, *Lives of the Philosophers* 496; and the *Historia Augusta* in B. Isaac, *The Invention of Racism in Classical Antiquity* (Princeton 2004) 349–350.
95. Iamblichos, *Babyloniaka*, note in the ms. of Photios, *Bibliotheca* 94.
96. F. Millar, *The Roman Near East, 31 BC – AD 337* (Cambridge, MA 1993) 17–24; M. Sartre, *The Middle East under Rome* (Cambridge, MA 2005) 365–368.
97. G. Bowersock, 'Roman Senators from the Near East,' in *Epigrafia e ordine senatorio (Tituli 5)* (Rome 1982) 651–668, here 655, 658.
98. W. Adler in M. Stone, *The Armenian Inscriptions from the Sinai* (Cambridge, MA 1982), Appendix II, pp. 183–185: *cessent Syri ante Latinos Romanos*.
99. Johnson, 'Introduction,' 26.
100. K. Holum, 'Identity and the Late Antique City: The Case of Caesarea,' in H. Lapin, ed., *Religious and Ethnic Communities in Later Roman Palestine* (Potomac, MD 1998) 157–177; population: C. Dauphin, *La Palestine byzantine* (Oxford: BAR Series 1998) 1:280–285.
101. I follow Schwartz, *Imperialism*, 101–176, having found no persuasive counterarguments.
102. A *piyyut* (liturgical poem) tr. in Sivan, *Palestine*, 148; cf. the poet Yannai at 226.
103. L. Levine, 'The Status of the Patriarch in the Third and Fourth Centuries,' *Journal of Jewish Studies* 47 (1996) 1–32; Schwartz, *Ancient Jews*, 118–123.

Chapter 2. Government and the Social Order

1. Potter, *Roman Empire*, 269–270.
2. Moser, *Emperor*, 215–228, 325.
3. Lactantius, *On the Deaths of the Persecutors* 23.2 (Galerius' 306 poll census included cities) (tr. Creed).
4. Themistios, *Oration* 8.113a–b (Valens); cf. Constantine in *Panegyrici Latini* 5.11–12; Julian in Ammianus 6.5.14; the prefect Anatolius in ibid. 19.11.3.

5. E.g., Tiberios II Konstantinos (575 AD) in Zepos, *Jus Graecoromanum*, 1:17–19.
6. Sokrates 2.16.2; Ioannes Lydos, *On the Magistracies* 2.20.
7. Slootjes, *Governor*.
8. Lactantius, *On the Deaths of the Persecutors* 7.3–4.
9. Jones, *Later Roman Empire*, 1411–1412 n. 44; Kelly, *Ruling*, 268 n. 10.
10. *CTh* 11.16.3 and 4.
11. Basil of Kaisareia, *Letter* 299.
12. Ulpian in *Digest* 1.16.6.3. Cf. Aurelius Victor, *De Caesaribus* 33.13, on military paymasters.
13. *CTh* 6.30.2; Cooper and Decker, *Cappadocia*, 50–53.
14. Theodoretos, *Letter* 42 (Sirm.).
15. R. Delamaire, *Largesses sacrées et res privata* (Rome 1989) 641–657. But contrast N. Lenski, *Constantine and the Cities* (Philadelphia 2016) 171–175, with S. Schmidt-Hofner, 'Die städtische Finanzautonomie im spätrömischen Reich,' in H.-U. Wiemer, ed., *Staatlichkeit und politisches Handeln im römischen Reich* (Berlin 2006) 209–248.
16. *CTh* 10.3.4; Jones, *Later Roman Empire*, 420, 732–733; complaints: Basil of Kaisareia, *Letter* 74.3; and Libanios, frequently, e.g., *Oration* 31.
17. Dorotheos of Gaza, *Teaching* 2.6, in *PG* 88:1648.
18. Augustine, *Sermon* 356.13, in *PL* 39:1580.
19. Bagnall, *Egypt*, 227; Banaji, *Agrarian Change*, 192–194; Ruffini, *Life*, 11.
20. John Chrysostom, *Homily 66 on Matthew* 3, in *PG* 58:630.
21. Bagnall, *Egypt*, 115, 119, 149; Brown, *Poverty*, 48; the evidence is consolidated in Dossey, *Peasant*, 8, and Caner, *Rich*, 166–167; Izdebski, *Rural Economy*, 13–21, 100–101.
22. I. Jacobs, '"Urbanized" Villages in Early Byzantium,' in B. Böhlendorf-Arslan and R. Schick, eds., *Transformations of City and Countryside in the Byzantine Period* (Heidelberg 2021) 13–23.
23. Bagnall, *Egypt*, 225–226, 310, 312.
24. *CTh* 11.1.14.
25. J.-M. Carrié, 'Colonato del Basso Impero,' in E. Lo Cascio, ed., *Terre, proprietari e contadini dell'impero romano* (Rome 1997) 75–150.
26. N. Lenski, 'The Late Roman Colonate – A New Status between Slave and Free,' in progress.
27. E.g., John Chrysostom, *Homily on Matthew* 61.3, in *PG* 58:591–593. Flight: S. Schmidt-Hofner, 'Barbarian Migrations and Socio-Economic Challenges to the Roman Landholding Elite,' *JLA* 10 (2017) 372–404, here 376–382.
28. Cf. K. Harper, *Slavery in the Late Roman World* (Cambridge 2011) with N. Lenski in many publications, e.g., 'Searching for Slave Teachers in Late Antiquity,' *Révue des études tardo-antiques* 12, suppl. 8 (2018–2019) 127–191.
29. Lenski, 'Slavery,' 467.
30. *CTh* 1.22.1; cf. Ulpian in *Digest* 16.1.2.2, 50.17.2; *Basilika* 2.3.2, 26.7.32; J. Beaucamp, *Femmes, patrimoines normes à Byzance* (Paris 2010) 1–56, 115–131.
31. John Chrysostom, *Which Women to Prefer*, in *PG* 51:231.
32. Prokopios, *Secret History* 10.2.

33. L. Brubaker, 'Dancing in the Streets of Byzantine Constantinople,' *Culture and History Digital Journal* 11.2 (2022).
34. A. Kelley, 'Searching for Professional Women in the Mid to Late Roman Textile Industry,' *Past and Present* 258 (2022) 3–43.
35. P. Thonemann, 'Estates and the Land in Late Roman Asia Minor,' *Chiron* 31 (2007) 435–478, here 453; Connolly, *Lives*, 71–72; cf. Bagnall, *Egypt*, 92–99, 130. Aphrodite: Ruffini, *Life*, 153.
36. John Chrysostom, *To the People of Antioch* 16.2, in *PG* 49:164; Augustine, *Treatise on the Gospel of John* 6.25 (*Corpus Christianorum, Series Latina* 36:66); Connolly, *Lives*, 134–136.
37. Ruffini, *Life*, passim, e.g., 26, 42.
38. F. Kenyon and H. Bell, *Greek Papyri in the British Museum* (Milan 1907) 3:229 (no. 983).
39. *Oxyrhynchus Papyrus* 46.3295 (284 AD, tr. J. Rea).
40. Justinian, *Novel* 74.4 (tr. Miller and Sarris).
41. Justinian in *CJ* 11.48.24; *Novel* 54 (537 AD).
42. Harper, *Fate*, 177; Dossey, *Peasant*, ch. 7; Connolly, *Lives*. The proof text of primitivist-isolationist readings is Synesios of Kyrene, *Letter* 148, a pastoral joke about a village deep in the Libyan hinterland. It repays closer study.
43. E.g., Justinian, *Novel* 80 (539 AD).
44. Anonymous, *De rebus bellicis* 2.1; Banaji, *Agrarian Change*, ch. 3; monetization: ibid. 60–65, 76–77, 87, 123, 158–159, 218–220, 265.
45. Anonymous, *De rebus bellicis* 2.2.
46. K. Harl, *Coinage in the Roman Economy* (Baltimore 1996) 158–175; G. Bransbourg, 'The Later Roman Empire,' in A. Monson and W. Scheidel, eds., *Fiscal Regimes and the Political Economy of Premodern States* (Cambridge 2015) 258–281, here 270–271.
47. Dossey, *Peasant*, 8, 87–88, 241 n. 11.
48. E.g., *CTh* 7.4.35 (423 AD).
49. Banaji, *Agrarian Change*, 70–75.
50. Ammianus 16.8.12–13.
51. *CTh* 7.4.1, 18, 20, 22, 31, 35–36; cf. Libanios, *Oration* 57.51.
52. *CTh* 6.36.1 = *CJ* 12.30.1.
53. *CTh* 6.2.15, 6.2.26; Marcian, *Novel* 2.4.
54. Hendy, *Studies*, 408.
55. Praetors: *CTh* 6.4; onerous: Libanios, *Letters* 252, 731, 952, 1277; Zosimos 2.38.3–4; consuls: *CJ* 12.3.2, 12.3.3; silver to gold: *CTh* 13.2.1.
56. *CJ* 12.1.15 (426–443 AD).
57. O. Kern, *Die Inschriften von Magnesia am Meander* (Berlin 1900) 108–113 (no. 122); Harper, 'Census,' 97.
58. Libanios, *Orations* 49.2, 62.64–66, 36.5.
59. Libanios, *Oration* 47.10, 29; cf. John Chrysostom, *Homily on Matthew* 61.2, in *PG* 58:590–591.
60. *CTh* 12.3.1.
61. Heather, 'New Men,' 21.
62. Libanios, *Oration* 48.7; restrictions: Jones, *Later Roman Empire*, 527–529, 741–745.

63. Libanios, *Oration* 25.43; cf. 39.10.
64. *CTh* 13.13.1–3; Libanios, *Oration* 18.193.
65. Basil of Kaisareia, *Homily 4 on Avarice (on Luke 12.18)* 4, in *PG* 31:269; cf. Asterios of Amaseia, *Homily* 3.7.
66. John Chrysostom, *Homily on Acts of the Apostles* 32.2, in *PG* 60:237.
67. Libanios, *Oration* 48.11–12; cf. Zosimos 4.29; Justinian, *Novel* 8; buying offices: Jones, *Later Roman Empire*, 393–396.
68. Libanios, *Oration* 46.22–23; Zosimos 2.38.2; Euagrios 3.39–41.
69. Pseudo-Joshua the Stylite, *Chronicle* 31; Anastasius: *CJ* 11.1.1.
70. Accessions: Ammianus 20.4.18; Leo I to Justin I in Konstantinos VII, *Book of Ceremonies* 1.100–103. Donative: pseudo-Zacharias, *Chronicle* 7.8f (denarius = solidus); Prokopios, *Secret History* 24.27–29.
71. Revenue: Hendy, *Studies*, 171; Haldon, *Empire*, 27–29; costs: W. Treadgold, 'Paying the Army in the Theodosian Period,' in I. Jacobs, ed., *Production and Prosperity in the Theodosian Period* (Leuven 2014) 303–318, here 316; Elton, *Warfare*, 124.
72. Libanios, *Oration* 2.39–40.
73. J. Rea and P. Sijpesteijn, *Corpus Papyrorum Raineri* (Vienna 1976) 5: no. 26 (early or mid-fifth century).
74. Themistios, *Oration* 8.113d.
75. R. McConnell, *Getting Rich in Late Antique Egypt* (Ann Arbor, MI 2017) 59–60.
76. Valentinian III, *Novel* 16.1; cf. Symmachus, *Relatio* 29.
77. John Chrysostom, *In principium auctorum* 4.2, in *PG* 51:98–99.
78. Sozomenos 2.5.1–3; see p. 934 n. 61 above.
79. J. Keenan, 'The Names Flavius and Aurelius as Status Designations in Later Roman Egypt,' *ZPE* 11 (1973) 33–63; 13 (1974) 283–304; S. Mitchell, 'Ethnicity, Acculturation and Empire in Roman and Late Roman Asia Minor,' in idem and G. Greatrex, eds., *Ethnicity and Culture in Late Antiquity* (London 2000) 117–150, here 137; Constantine as a Flavian: Van Dam, *Roman Revolution*, ch. 3.
80. A. Cameron, 'Flavius: A Nicety of Protocol,' *Latomus* 47 (1988) 26–33, here 33.
81. Diocletian: Aurelius Victor, *De Caesaribus* 39; Eutropius, *Breviarium* 9.26; savagery: R. MacMullen, *Changes in the Roman Empire* (Princeton 1990) 211.
82. S. James, 'The "Romanness" of the Soldiers: Barbarized Periphery or Imperial Core,' in L. Brody and G. Hoffman, eds., *Roman in the Provinces: Art on the Periphery of Empire* (Chicago 2014) 91–107.
83. *Panegyrici Latini* 10.3.3–4, to Maximian (tr. Nixon and Rodgers).
84. *CTh* 16.10.17–18, 15.7.3.
85. Kelly, *Ruling*, 212–216.
86. Parents: Diocletian, *Edict on Prices* pref.; "slaves" and "mother": Lavan, *Slaves*, 208–210; "born" and "liberator": Weisweiler, 'Populist Despotism,' 158.
87. Decius in Dexippos, *Skythika* fr. 26.5–7 (*FGrH*).
88. Constantine (or Constans) to Hispellum in *ILS* 1:158–159 (no. 705).
89. *CJ* 3.1.8.
90. *Pap.CairoIsid.* 1, ed. A. Boak, 'Early Byzantine Papyri from the Cairo Museum,' *Études de papyrologie* 2 (1934) 1–22 (mod.). Background: T. Barnes, *The New Empire of Diocletian and Constantine* (Cambridge, MA 1982) 230–231, and below.

91. Cf. Suetonius, *Gaius* 46.
92. Themistios, *Oration* 8.113a–114b; Ammianus 16.5.54.
93. Bransbourg, '*Reddite*,' 105; tax fairness: *CTh* 11.12.3; Valentinian III, *Novel* 10.4.
94. Justin II, *Novel* 149.2 (569 AD). Taxes and defense: Ammianus 20.11.5; Zosimos 3.33–34; Themistios, *Oration* 10.138b–139a; Gregory of Nazianzos, *Oration* 19.14, in *PG* 35:1061.
95. *Life of Hypatios of Gangra* 8, ed. S. Ferri, 'Il Bios e il Martyrion di Hypatios di Gangrai,' *Studi bizantini e neoellenici* 3 (1931) 69–103, here 80. Orosius, *Seven Books of History against the Pagans* 5.1.13 (tr. Fear).
96. Hebblewhite, *Emperor*, 135–136.
97. N. Kennell, 'An Early Byzantine Constitution from Ziporea,' *Epigraphica Anatolica* 26 (1996) 129–136.
98. J. Grubbs, *Law and Family in Late Antiquity* (Oxford 1995) 113.
99. *CTh* 11.16.3–4; *humanum*: *CJ* 4.44.2 (Diocletian).
100. A. Bryen, *Violence in Roman Egypt* (Philadelphia 2013) 96–100.
101. Lenski, *Failure*, 381–382. The *defensores* were later co-opted by city councils and weakened.
102. *CTh* 11.27.2; *CJ* 1.2.12; cf. Maurikios in *Life of Theodoros of Sykeon* 54.
103. Dossey, *Peasant*, 27, esp. 175–180, 194–195; petitions: Connolly, *Lives*.
104. Pseudo-Joshua the Stylite, *Chronicle* 29.
105. Priskos fr. 11.445–448. Anyone who is too cynical about Roman imperial justice should try suing a corporation today for polluting, or an employer for withholding overtime pay.
106. Weisweiler, 'Populist Despotism,' 152.
107. Neilos of Ankyra, *Letter* 102, in *PG* 79:102d; Brown, *Poverty*, 82–83.
108. *Digest* 1.4.1; *Basilika* 2.6.2.
109. Diocletian, *Edict on Prices* pref.; Galerius in Lactantius, *On the Deaths of the Persecutors* 34.1; Julian: Ammianus 15.8.14 (tr. Rolfe); Valentinian: 26.1.5 and 26.4.1; see Kaldellis, *Byzantine Republic*.
110. Ammianus 26.5.13; cf. Symmachus, *Oration* 1.19; Konstantinos VII, *Book of Ceremonies* 1.101.
111. A. Wardmann, 'Usurpers and Internal Conflicts in the 4th Century A.D.,' *Historia* 33 (1984) 220–237.
112. Ammianus 26.6.
113. Konstantinos VII, *Excerpta de insidiis* 35 (pp. 165–166).
114. *CTh* 7.20.2.1.
115. Symmachus, *Oration* 1.9.
116. Pacatus in *Panegyrici Latini* 2.31.2 (tr. Nixon and Rodgers).
117. Jerome, *Letter* 146.1.
118. Ammianus 30.10.1.
119. E.g., *CTh* 7.20.4 (325 AD).
120. Kaldellis and Kruse, *Field Armies*.
121. Julian at Strasburg (Ammianus 16.11.2, 16.12.2); Magnentius and Constantius at Mursa (Zonaras, *Chronicle* 13.8.17); Julian in Persia (Zosimos 3.12.5–3.13.1, 65,000 with possibly another 18,000 or 30,000 under Procopius and Sebastianus; see

Ammianus 23.3.5 for the latter figure, and F. Paschoud, *Zosime: Histoire nouvelle*, 2.1 [Paris 1979] 110–111).

122. Julian, *Letter to the Athenians* 286b.
123. 2.5% from retirement + 2.5% who did not make it to retirement: W. Scheidel, 'Marriage, Families, and Survival: Demographic Aspects,' in P. Erdkamp, ed., *A Companion to the Roman Army* (Malden, MA 2007) 417–434, here 426–427, 432. Adjust the numbers for a smaller army.
124. E.g., in *P.Michael.* 28 (313–314 AD), ed. D. Crawford, *Papyri Michaelidae* (Aberdeen 1955). A law of Valens (*CTh* 7.13.7) outlines the procedure (stressing commutation).
125. *The Greek Life of Pachomios* 4; Jones, *Later Roman Empire*, 618–619.
126. The Severan army: *Digest* 49.16.4.10; later: *BGU* 7:1680 ("everyone is doing it"); see Zuckerman, 'Two Reforms.' Laws dealing with reluctance to serve (*CTh* 7.13) stem from specific contexts: M. Whitby, 'Emperors and Armies, AD 235–395,' in S. Swain and M. Edwards, eds., *Approaching Late Antiquity* (Oxford 2013) 156–186, here 169–170.
127. *P.Lond.* 3:985, ed. F. Kenyon and H. Bell, *Greek Papyri in the British Museum* (London 1893) 3:228–229.
128. *CTh* 12.1.10, 12.1.13 (326 AD), 7.13.1 (353 AD), 12.1.38 (357 AD).
129. Bagnall, *Egypt*, 176 (recruitment); Sivan, *Palestine*, 88–89 (retirement, in the sixth century). Mostly Romans: Elton, *Warfare*, 136–152. Native soldiers defending eastern cities: Ammianus 18.9.3, 20.6.8, 20.7.1. The *Abbinaeaus Archive* (340s) shows that locals were recruited into the unit stationed between Dionysias and Arsinoe (in Egypt).
130. Lenski, *Failure*, 16–17.

Chapter 3. From Christian Nation to Roman Religion

1. Sozomenos 2.5.
2. Origen, *Against Kelsos* 8.75.
3. Eusebios, *On the Psalms* 50.21, 64.2–3, 86.2–4; citizenship: St. Paul, Phil. 3.20.
4. 1 Peter 2:9; A. von Harnack, *The Mission and Expansion of Christianity*, tr. J. Moffatt (London 1908) 1:240–253.
5. Army and school: Eusebios, *Evangelical Preparation* 1.5.10 and 14.3.4; nation: 1.2; *EH* 1.4.1–2, 10.4.19–20; Christ: *Evangelical Demonstration* 3.6.131c–d, 4.16.194a, and passim; Buell, *Why This New Race*; A. Johnson, *Ethnicity and Argument in Eusebius' Praeparatio Evangelica* (Oxford 2006).
6. Eusebios, *Evangelical Preparation* 1.2.2.
7. Eusebios, *EH* 5, pref. Augustus: 4.26 (a flattering appeal to the Romans, not necessarily a core belief); *Evangelical Demonstration* 3.7.30–35.
8. Eusebios, *Life of Constantine* 1.8.
9. Cicero, *Pro Flacco* 69; cf. *De officiis* 1.53; Marcus Aurelius in *CIL* 3:7106.11–15; see C. Ando, 'Religiöse und politische Zugehörigkeit von Caracalla bis Theodosius,' in L. Scheuermann and W. Spickermann, eds., *Religiöse Praktiken in der Antike* (Graz 2016) 61–73.

10. Ulpian in *Digest* 1.1.1.2 (tr. Watson).
11. Rives, *Religion*, 3–16, 59, 133, 235–240; E. Orlin, *Foreign Cults in Rome* (Oxford 2010) passim; moral: ibid. 24, 208; cf. Cicero, *Laws* 2.18 ff.
12. E.g., Justin Martyr, *1 Apology* 12, 17.
13. Lactantius, *On the Deaths of the Persecutors* 34.2; cf. Kelsos in Origen, *Against Kelsos* 8.17, 8.73, 8.75.
14. Rives, *Religion*, 253–261.
15. J. Rives, 'The Decree of Decius and the Religion of Empire,' *JRS* 89 (1999) 135–154.
16. *Acts of Cyprian* 1.1; cf. Tertullian, *Apology* 24.1 (*Romana religio*); *Acts of the Scillitan Martyrs* 2–3, 14; *Acts of Crispina* 1.3–4, 2.1, 2.4.
17. S. Berrens, *Sonnenkult und Kaisertum von den Severern bis zu Constantin I.* (Stuttgart 2004) 89–126.
18. *Mosaicarum et Romanarum leges* 15.3; cf. Constantine in *CTh* 16.2.5.
19. Lactantius, *On the Deaths of the Persecutors* 34.5, 34.1; E. Digeser, 'Why has the edict of AD 311 been ignored?' in *Serdica Edict (311 AD): Concepts and Realizations of the Idea of Religious Toleration* (Sofia 2014) 15–27.
20. Lactantius, *On the Deaths of the Persecutors* 48.2; Lenski, 'Significance.'
21. Eusebios, *Life of Constantine* 2.48–60, esp. 53.
22. *CTh* 16.10.2, 16.10.12, 16.5.63; cf. Tacitus, *Annals* 15.44.
23. E.g., Constantine in Eusebios, *EH* 10.7.2; *CTh* 16.2.16 (361 AD); *Christiana lex*: *CJ* 1.9.11. Judaism: R. Mathisen, 'The Citizenship and Legal Status of Jews in Roman Law During Late Antiquity,' in J. Tolan et al., eds., *Jews in Early Christian Law* (Turnhout 2013) 35–53, here 38.
24. Eusebios, *EH* 3.55.
25. *CTh* 16.1.2.
26. Augustine, *Letter* 87.7, citing Romans 13:2–4.
27. Themistios, *Oration* 5.70a.
28. Justin II, *Novel* 144.2.
29. *CTh* 16.5.7.
30. E.g., *Doctrina Jacobi nuper baptizati* 1.2 (Déroche pp. 71–72).
31. E.g., *ACO* 1.1.1, p. 112; Corippus, *Iohannis* 8.255–256; Prokopios, *Wars* 6.6.19; Theophylaktos Simokattes, *History* 2.3.5, 5.2.4, 5.3.4; Attaleiates, *History* 96.
32. Justinian, *Novel* 18, pref.; cf. *Novel* 86 pref.
33. *CIL* 6:32,323 (*ludi saeculares*, 17 BC); Horace, *Carmen Saeculare*; I. Pighi, *De ludis saecularibus populi romani Quiritium* (Milan 1941) 142 (*ludi saeculares*, 204 AD).
34. Constantius II and Julian in *CTh* 16.2.16; Justinian, *Deo Auctore* pref. (*Digest*).
35. Eusebios, *EH* 9.7.2.
36. Tertullian, *On Idolatry* 19.2; Vegetius, *Epitoma rei militaris* 2.5.
37. P. Photiadis, 'A Semi-Greek Semi-Coptic Parchment,' *Klio* 41 (1963) 234–235.
38. Eusebios, *Tricennial Oration in Praise of Constantine* 9.8.
39. E.g., Cyril of Jerusalem, *Letter to Constantius II* 8; pseudo-Joshua, *Chronicle* 27.
40. Text: F. Brightman, *Liturgies Eastern and Western* (Oxford 1896) 407–408; see McCormick, *Eternal Victory*, 237–252.
41. Holum, 'Inscriptions.'

42. Konstantinos VII, *Book of Ceremonies* 1.78 (2:221).
43. McGinn, 'Social Policy.'
44. Cf. W. Novak, 'The Myth of the "Weak" American State,' *American Historical Review* 113 (2008) 752–772.
45. Hippolytos of Rome, *Commentary on Daniel* 4.9; Origen, *Homily on Luke* 11.6; Lactantius, *Divine Institutes* 6.8.
46. B. Leadbetter, *Galerius and the Will of Diocletian* (London 2009) 9–10, 115, 118; E. Digeser, 'Citizenship and the Roman *res publica*: Cicero and a Christian Corollary,' *Critical Review of International Social and Political Philosophy* 6 (2003) 5–20; influence on Constantine: Lenski, 'Significance,' 48–49.
47. Eusebios, *Life of Constantine* 3.15, 3.10.3.
48. Eusebios, *Oration on the Holy Sepulchre* 16.4.
49. Sokrates 5 pref.
50. Origen, *Against Kelsos* 8.70; Lactantius, *Divine Institutes* 5.8.
51. Eusebios, *Life of Constantine* 2.68–70.
52. J. Rea, 'A New Version of P. Yale Inv. 299,' *ZPE* 27 (1977) 151–156.
53. Sokrates 1.24; Athanasios, *History of the Arians* 81. Allegedly the slaughter of (Donatist) Christians by the soldiers of a Christian ruler began in 317: *A Sermon on the Martyrs Donatus and Advocatus*, in M. Tilly, *Donatist Martyr Stories* (Liverpool 1996) 51–60.
54. John Chrysostom, *Homilies on John* 4.2, in *PG* 59:48; Gregory of Nyssa, *Oration on the Divinity of the Son and the Spirit*, in *PG* 46:557.
55. *CJ* 1.5.12.18–19. Shunning: Tannous, *Making*, 411.
56. Euagrios 4.10.
57. Julian in Ammianus 22.5.4. Cf. Kelsos in Origen, *Against Kelsos* 3.9–10; Eusebios, *Life of Constantine* 2.61.5 (mocked in the theaters); *EH* 8.1.7–9.
58. Alexandros of Lykopolis, *Against the Doctrines of the Manichaeans* 1.
59. Euagrios 2.5.
60. Sokrates 1.23.6; see Tannous, *Making*.
61. Ioannes Rufus, *Plerophoriae* 80.
62. Rives, *Religion*, 297; Buell, *Why This New Race*, 55; Brakke, *Demons*, 18, 24, 25, 27, 34, 35. Defend the name: Clement of Alexandria, *Stromateis* 4.10. Cf. 1 Corinthians 1:12, 3:4.
63. C. Ando, *Imperial Rome, AD 193 to 284* (Edinburgh 2012) 125.
64. Tertullian, *On the Flesh of Christ* 5.4; cf. J. Tooby, 'Coalitional Instincts,' *Edge* 2017: https://www.edge.org/response-detail/27168.
65. N. Klein, *No Logo* (New York 1999), esp. 16, 30.
66. K. Hopkins, 'Christian Number and Its Implications,' *JECS* 6 (1998) 185–226, here 198; S. Schwartz, 'Roman Historians and the Rise of Christianity,' in W. Harris, ed., *The Spread of Christianity in the First Four Centuries* (Leiden 2005) 145–160, here 160. Isis and others: M. Beard, J. North, and S. Price, *Religions of Rome*, v. 1: *A History* (Cambridge 1998) 307–310.
67. E.g., in Antioch: R. Wilken, *John Chrysostom and the Jews* (Berkeley 1983); J. Maxwell, *Christianization and Communication in Late Antiquity: John Chrysostom and His Congregation in Antioch* (Cambridge 2006).

68. Alexandros of Lykopolis, *Against the Doctrines of the Manichaeans* 1.
69. Augustine, *Enarrationes in Psalmos* 95.11; Gregory of Nazianzos, *Oration* 4.84.
70. Hilary of Poitiers, *Against Constantius* 11.
71. Athanassiadi, *Pensée unique*.

Chapter 4. The First Christian Emperors (324–361)

1. *CTh* 15.14.1–4. Licinius' legislation embedded in Constantine's: S. Corcoran, 'Hidden from History: The Legislation of Licinius,' in J. Harries and I. Wood, eds., *The Theodosian Code* (London 1993) 97–119.
2. Burgess, 'Summer,' 5.
3. Constantine, *Oration to the Saints* 18; but cf. Eusebios, *Life of Constantine* 2.50–51.
4. E. Fowden, 'Constantine and the Peoples of the Eastern Frontier,' in N. Lenski, ed., *The Cambridge Companion to the Age of Constantine* (Cambridge 2006) 377–398, here 390.
5. Themistios, *Oration* 4.58b.
6. Eusebios, *Life of Constantine* 2.24–42 (property: 2.35–41), 2.48–60 (esp. 2.56).
7. Arius in Athanasios, *On the Synods of Ariminum-Seleukeia* 15; Alexandros of Alexandria, *Letter to Alexandros of Byzantion* 26, 47, in Theodoretos, *EH* 1.4. "Second God": Eusebios, *Evangelical Preparation* 7.12–13.
8. E.g., Eusebios of Kaisareia, *Evangelical Demonstration* 4.3.13, 5.1.18–21.
9. L. Ayres, *Nicaea and its Legacy* (Oxford 2004) 48–49, 59, 62, 74. And some of them relied on faulty physics. The sun *is* diminished by its rays!
10. Eusebios, *Life of Constantine* 3.6.2.
11. Eusebios, *Life of Constantine* 3.10–13.
12. Eusebios in Athanasios, *Defense of the Nicaean Creed* 35; Theodoretos, *EH* 1.12.
13. Constantine in Athanasios, *Defense of the Nicaean Creed* 41.9–11; cf. Sozomenos 1.21.3–4.
14. Eusebios of Nikomedeia in Theodoretos, *EH* 1.6.
15. Philostorgios 2.4.
16. Zosimos 2.29.
17. Eusebios, *Life of Constantine* 3.29–44, 3.50–53 (quotation: 3.32).
18. Cyril of Jerusalem, *Catechetical Oration* 10.19; Ambrose, *On the Death of Valentinian II* 73.
19. Arius and Euzoïos in Socrates, *EH* 1.26; Sozomenos 2.27.
20. *ILS* 1:158–159 (no. 705), possibly issued weeks after Constantine's death by Constans: T. Barnes, *Constantine: Dynasty, Religion and Power* (London 2011) 22.
21. Gaddis, *There Is No Crime*, 57–59, 69; cf. Sokrates 1.10.
22. Constantine in Gelasios, *EH* 3.15.
23. Sokrates 1.14; Athanasios, *Apologia against the Arians* 59.
24. Athanasios, *History of the Arians* 4.
25. Epiphanios, *Panarion* 68.9.5; Barnes, *Athanasius*, is fundamental.

26. Athanasios, *Letter to Serapio on the Death of Arius*, followed by, e.g., Sokrates 1.38.
27. Eusebios, *Life of Constantine* 4.36; Theophanes a.m.5824, p. 29 (36,000 *modii*); Caner, *Rich*, 24–25.
28. Antioch: John Chrysostom, *Homilies on Matthew* 66.3, in *PG* 58:630; see Brown, *Poverty*.
29. Rapp, *Holy Bishops*, 212–214, 238, 282–283.
30. John Chrysostom, *On the Priesthood* 3.10.39–44.
31. Rapp, *Holy Bishops*, 242–252. I doubt the authenticity of the clause in *Sirmondian Constitution* 1 (333 AD) that allows only one party to remove a case to the bishop's court.
32. C. Humfress, 'Bishops and Law Courts in Late Antiquity: How (Not) to Make Sense of the Legal Evidence,' *JECS* 19 (2011) 375–400, here 386–387, 396.
33. Cooper and Decker, *Cappadocia*, 147.
34. McGinn, 'Social Policy'; Grubbs, *Law and Family*.
35. Justinian, *Novel* 117.10; Justin II, *Novel* 140.
36. *CJ* 3.12.3; Potter, *Roman Empire*, 379, 418–419, citing *Oxyrrhynchus Papyri* 3741 and 3759.
37. Burgess, 'Summer'; R. Van Dam, 'Eastern Aristocracies and Imperial Courts,' *DOP* 72 (2018) 1–24.
38. Julian in Libanios, *Oration* 14.29–30.
39. Eusebios, *Tricennial Oration in Praise of Constantine* 3.4.
40. *Origo Constantini* 35; many sources mention the bridge.
41. Constantine in Athanasios, *Apologia against the Arians* 89.
42. Themistios, *Oration* 10.135c; M. Kulikowski, 'Constantine and the Northern Barbarians,' in N. Lenski, ed., *The Cambridge Companion to the Age of Constantine* (Cambridge 2006) 347–376, here 360–361.
43. Libanios, *Oration* 50.89.
44. Philostorgios 2.5; Heather and Matthews, *Goths*, 124–143.
45. Armenia: Agathangelos, *History of the Armenians*; Georgia: Rufinus, *EH* 10.10.
46. Eusebios, *Life of Constantine* 4.9–13.
47. Libanios, *Oration* 59.66–70.
48. Eusebios, *Life of Constantine* 4.66–71, 4.58–60; sarcophagus: J. Bardill, *Constantine, Divine Emperor of the Christian Golden Age* (Cambridge 2012) 183–194.
49. John Chrysostom, *Against the Jews and Pagans* 9, in *PG* 48:825. C. Mango, 'Constantine's Mausoleum and the Translation of Relics,' *BZ* 83 (1990) 51–62, is fundamental. It is possible that the relics of Luke and Andrew were placed in the mausoleum in 336 and later translated to the church: R. Burgess, 'The *Passio S. Artemii*,' *Analecta Bollandiana* 121 (2003) 5–36, here 29–33.
50. Sokrates 2.39.42.
51. Van Dam, *Roman Revolution*, 11.
52. L. Koep, 'Die Konsekrationsmünzen Kaiser Konstantins und ihre religionspolitische Bedeutung,' *Jahrbuch für Antike und Christentum* 1 (1958) 94–104; J. Arce, 'Imperial Funerals in the Later Roman Empire,' in F. Theuws and J. Nelson, eds., *Rituals of Power from Late Antiquity to the Early Middle Ages* (Leiden 2000) 115–129.

53. Anna Komnene, *Alexiad* 12.4.5; Zonaras, *Chronicle* 13.3, 18.26; *Patria of Constantinople* 1.45a.
54. Mango, *Le développement urbain*, 28–29.
55. Burgess, 'Summer'; Libanios, *Oration* 18.10; Julian, *Letter to the Athenians*.
56. Libanios, *Oration* 59; *CTh* 11.12.1.
57. Fowden, *Empire*, 17–18.
58. Treaty: Petros the Patrician, *History* fr. 14 (ed. Müller); *regiones*: Ammianus 25.7.9; Festus, *Breviarium* 25; Prokopios, *Buildings* 3.1.17–28, 3.2.4–10; Lenski, *Failure*, 158–162; M. Marciak, *Sophene, Gordyene, and Adiabene* (Leiden 2017) 37–41; crown: *CTh* 12.13.6.
59. Ephrem the Syrian, *Hymns against Julian* 2.20, 4.15; fortifications: Lightfoot, *Eastern Frontier*, 46–49; miraculous powers: idem. 234, 251 n. 37.
60. Julian, *Oration* 1.26c–d.
61. Ammianus 14.10.16, 14.11.8, 21.16.15; Eutropius, *Breviarium* 10.15.2; *Epitome de Caesaribus* 42.18.
62. Eutropius, *Breviarium* 10.12 (tr. Bird); Zosimos 2.46.3. The casualty figures of 30,000 for Constantius and 24,000 for Magnentius are given by Zonaras, *Chronicle* 13.8.17 (3:42).
63. *CTh* 9.38.2.
64. Ammianus 14.5.6, 15.2–3.
65. Hebblewhite, *Emperor*, 127.
66. Vadomarius: Ammianus 21.3–4; Constantius' Goths: Libanios, *Oration* 59.92–93. Barbarian recruitment: M. Waas, *Germanen im römischen Dienst im 4. Jahrhundert nach Christus* (Bonn 1965); Elton, *Warfare*, 91–97, 129–153, 272–277. Settlements: G. De Ste. Croix, *The Class Struggle in the Ancient Greek World* (Ithaca, NY 1981) 509–518.
67. Ammianus 19.11; background: 17.12–13; Lenski, *Failure*, 350–351, for such incidents.
68. Mallobaudes: Ammianus 31.10.6; treason: 14.10.8, 16.12.2, 29.4.7, 31.10.3.
69. Ammianus 14.2; D. Goodblatt, 'The Political and Social History of the Jewish Community in the Land of Israel,' in S. Katz, ed., *The Cambridge History of Judaism*, v. 4 (Cambridge 2008) 404–430, here 411–413.
70. Ammianus 14.1, 14.7–9; Julian, *Letter to the Athenians* 271c–d.
71. Gregory of Nazianzos, *Oration* 4.75; Ambrose, *Consolation for the Death of Valentinian II* 21; Prudentius, *Apotheosis* 449 ff.
72. Julian, *Oration* 2.
73. Ammianus 17.5.3.
74. Ammianus 21.16.8.
75. For Julian on his predecessors, see the *Caesars* (a satire) and *Letter to the Athenians*.

Chapter 5. Competing Religions of Empire (337–363)

1. Athanasios, *On the Synods of Ariminum-Seleukeia* 23; Sokrates 2.10.
2. Athanasios, *On the Creed of the Council of Nicaea* 20.5.
3. Julius in Athanasios, *Apologia against the Arians* 22.3.

4. Sozomenos 3.8.4–6; Julius in Athanasios, *Apologia against the Arians* 21–35. The case of Paulos of Samosata had been referred by eastern bishops to the emperor Aurelian (270–275), who referred it to the bishops of Italy and Rome: Eusebios, *EH* 7.30.19.
5. Julius in Athanasios, *Apologia against the Arians* 35.
6. Athanasios, *On the Synods of Ariminum-Seleukeia* 22.2; Sokrates 2.10.4.
7. Athanasios, *Orations against the Arians* 1.3, written in 339–340.
8. W. Portmann, 'Die politische Krise zwischen den Kaisern Constantius II. und Constans,' *Historia* 48 (1999) 300–329.
9. Easterners in Hilarius, *Collectanea Antiariana Parisina*, ser. A, IV.12 (p. 57) (Feder). Right of appeal: Council of Serdica (343 AD), canons 3, 4, and 5 (sometimes numbered 3, 4, and 7); see H. Hess, *The Early Development of Canon Law and the Council of Serdica* (Oxford 2002) ch. 9.
10. Sokrates 2.22.
11. Sources: Hanson, *Search*, 307 n. 114; see esp. Constans in Sokrates 2.22.5; Constantius in Theodoretos, *EH* 2.16.21; Lucifer of Caralis, *On Athanasios* 1.29.28.
12. Constantius in Athanasios, *Apologia to Constantius* 30.
13. Athanasios, *History of the Arians* 31.
14. Eunomios in Gregory of Nyssa, *Against Eunomios* 3.9.27, 3.9.32; Hanson, *Search*, 598–636.
15. Philostorgios 4.12.
16. Basileios of Ankyra in Epiphanios, *Panarion* 73.4.3, 73.9.6.
17. Athanasios, *On the Synods of Ariminum-Seleukeia* 30; Theodoretos, *EH* 2.21. For this phase, see Brennecke, *Studien*; Barnes, *Athanasius*, 136–151.
18. Jerome, *Against the Luciferians* 19.
19. Iberia: Sokrates 1.20; Sozomenos 2.7; Frumentius: Constantius in Athanasios, *Apologia to Constantius* 31; Himyar: Philostorgios 3.4; in general: Fowden, *Empire*, 109–112.
20. Quoted in Athanasios, *History of the Arians* 44, 52; cf. 33.7, 34.1. The Donatists in North Africa had previously taken the same position—after their appeal for state intervention failed: Optatus, *Against the Donatists* 3.3.
21. John Chrysostom, *Homilies on Romans* 23.1, in *PG* 60:615.
22. *CTh* 16.10.2, 16.10.4, 16.10.6; Constantine: Potter, *Roman Empire*, 424–425.
23. Athens: Eunapios, *Lives of the Philosophers* 491; Alexandria: Sozomenos 4.30; Rome: Ammianus 19.10.4, 26.1.5; Ambrose, *Letter* 18.31; Libanios, *Oration* 30.34–35; in general: Trombley, *Hellenic Religion*.
24. Libanios, *Oration* 1.27; sacrifice as dangerous: *Orations* 1.119, 13.14, 14.41, 17.7, 18.23, 24.36, *Letter* 108.1; Julian, *Letter* 36; Claudius Mamertinus in *Panegyrici Latini* 3.23; John Chrysostom, *Discourse on Blessed Babylas* 74, in *PG* 50:533–572.
25. Eunapios, *Lives of the Philosophers* 503; Sozomenos 5.3, 5.5; Libanios, *Letters* 91 (Tarsos), 92.3–4 (Cilicia?), *Orations* 13.13, 14.63, 15.53, 17.7, 18.23, 24.36; Ammianus 15.8.22; John Chrysostom, *Discourse on Blessed Babylas* 41, in *PG* 50:533–572.
26. Gregory of Nazianzus, *Oration* 4.88 (Markos of Arethousa); also Sozomenos 5.10 (Markos); Theodoretos, *EH* 3.7 (Markos and Kyrillos of Heliopolis); Sozomenos 5.4 (Cappadocian Kaisareia), 5.9 (Gaza), 5.15 (Eleusios of Kyzikos); Libanios, *Letters*

103.7 (Arabia), 105.7 (the policy of the emperor), 1518.5 (the "Giants," i.e., Christians, in Greece).

27. Sozomenos 4.30, 5.7; Sokrates 3.2; Theodoretos, *EH* 3.18; Ammianus 22.11.4–8; Julian, *Letter* 21.
28. Firmicus Maternus, *The Error of the Pagan Religions* 16.4, 17.5.
29. Athanasios in Rufinus, *EH* 10.35; Sokrates 3.14.1; Sozomenos 5.15.3.
30. Julian, *Letter* 8.415c (Loeb); Ammianus 22.5.1; Libanius, *Oration* 18.114.
31. Julian, *Misopogon* 351d.
32. Equals: *Letter to Themistius* 261d; kisses and walk: Claudius Mamertinus in *Panegyrici Latini* 3.28.4, 3.29.4–30.3; Ammianus 22.7.1, 22.7.3, 22.9.13; Libanios, *Oration* 18.155–156; senators: *CTh* 9.2.1; Mamertinus 3.24.5, 3.29.4; Ammianus 16.7.6, 16.12.14–5, 22.7.3, 22.10.3, 25.4.16; Libanius, *Oration* 18.154; Eunapios, *History* fr. 28.2; Sokrates 3.1; fine: Ammianus 22.7.2. For Julian's political philosophy, see A. Kaldellis, 'Aristotle's *Politics* in Byzantium,' in V. Syros, ed., *Well Begun Is Only Half Done: Tracing Aristotle's Political Ideas in Medieval Arabic, Syriac, Byzantine, Jewish, and Indo-Persian Sources* (Tempe, AZ 2011) 121–143, here 129–132.
33. J. Matthews, *The Roman Empire of Ammianus* (London 1989) 235–237; cf. Ammianus 21.16.1; Gregory of Nazianzos, *Oration* 5.21–22; others in Libanios, *Oration* 1.129; Sokrates 3.1.
34. Temple lands: *CTh* 5.13.3, 10.1.8; civic: *CTh* 10.3.1; *CJ* 11.70.1; Libanios, *Oration* 13.45; Ammianus 25.4.15.
35. A contradiction noted by Athanassiadi, *Pensée unique*. Pontifical instructions: Julian, *Letter to a Priest*; *Letters* 20, 22.
36. Julian, *Letter* 58.401b.
37. R. Bradbury, 'Julian's Pagan Revival and the Decline of Blood Sacrifice,' *Phoenix* 49 (1995) 331–356.
38. Saloustios, *On the Gods and the World* 16. Daphne: Julian, *Misopogon* 362d. Restoration inscriptions: H. Teitler, *The Last Pagan Emperor: Julian the Apostate and the War against Christianity* (Oxford 2017) 49–51, with more at 150 n. 8.
39. *CTh* 12.1.50, 13.1.4; Julian, *Letter* 39; Libanios, *Oration* 18.148; Ammianus 25.4.21; Sozomenos 5.5.2, 6.3.4; Philostorgios 7.4; Theodoret, *EH* 3.6.5.
40. Gregory of Nazianzos, *Oration* 7.11–13.
41. Gregory of Nazianzos, *Orations* 4.64–65, 5.17. Christian soldiers: John Chrysostom, *Discourse on Blessed Babylas* 121, in *PG* 50:533–572.
42. "Ordered": Sozomenos 5.5. "Furious": Julian, *Letter* 41.436b; also *Letters* 37, 40, for more instructions. Careful not to create martyrs: Gregory of Nazianzos, *Oration* 4.27, 61, 68, 84, and 94 (order to not harm Christians).
43. Gregory of Nazianzos, *Oration* 4.27, 51, 57–62, 79.
44. Gaddis, *There Is No Crime*.
45. Ammianus 22.5.3–4; Sozomenos 5.5.7; Philostorgios 7.4; *Paschal Chronicle* s.a. 362. Many sources document the general pardon.
46. Council: *Tomus ad Antiochenos*, in *PG* 26:796–809; Julian, *Letters* 24, 46, 47.
47. Lightfoot, *Eastern Frontier*, 254 n. 51; sacrifice: D. Ullucci, *The Christian Rejection of Animal Sacrifice* (Oxford 2012) 145–146.

48. Julian, *Letter* 36; Kaldellis, *Hellenism*, 131–154.
49. Gregory of Nazianzos, *Oration* 4.92.
50. Kaldellis, *Hellenism*, 158–164.
51. P. Brown, *Power and Persuasion in Late Antiquity* (Madison, WI 1992) ch. 2.
52. Eunapios, *History* fr. 27.3–4; Libanios, *Oration* 1.133; army size: see p. 939 n. 121 above.
53. Sabinus in Ammianus 25.9.3, also 25.7.13; "necessary but shameful": Eutropius, *Breviarium* 10.17. Treaty: Ammianus 25.7.9–14; Zosimos 3.31.1–2. Denunciations: M. W. Graham, *News and Frontier Consciousness in the Late Roman Empire* (Ann Arbor, MI 2006) 169 nn. 4–5. Persian nobles: Payne, *State of Mixture*, 137.
54. Ephrem, *Hymns against Julian* 3.3–4, tr. S. Griffith, 'Ephraem the Syrian's Hymns against Julian,' *Vigiliae Christianae* 41 (1987) 238–266, here 248.
55. Cf. Libanios, *Oration* 18.279.
56. Cassius Dio, *Roman History* 75.3.3.
57. Themistios, *Oration* 5.69b–c. Temple lands: *CTh* 10.1.8.
58. M. Marcos, 'Emperor Jovian's Law of Religious Tolerance,' in M. Escribano Paño and R. Testa, eds., *Política, Religión y legislación en el imperio Romano* (Bari 2014) 153–177.
59. Eunapios, *History* fr. 29.
60. Konstantinos VII, *Book of Ceremonies* 2.42 (3:241).

Chapter 6. Toward an Independent East (364–395)

1. Eunapios, *History* fr. 31.
2. Ammianus 31.14.5; Zosimos 4.4.1.
3. Themistios, *Oration* 8.113d–114b; Ammianus 31.14.2; *Epitome de Caesaribus* 46.3; Sokrates 4.1.11.
4. Zosimos 4.3.1.
5. *CTh* 11.1.13 (365 AD); 12.6.10 = *CJ* 10.72.3 (365 AD); Basil of Kaisareia, *Letter* 21; *Oxyrrhynchus Papyrus* 48.3393; see Petronius below.
6. Ammianus 26.6–9; Zosimos 4.5–8; Themistios, *Oration* 7.
7. Lenski, *Failure*, 106–108.
8. Procopius in Ammianus 26.7.16.
9. Ioannes Lydos, *On the Magistracies* 3.19.
10. Themistios, *Oration* 8.113d–114a; during the Gothic war: Zosimos 4.10.3–4; *CTh* 7.4.15; in general: Ammianus 30.9.1, 31.14.2.
11. Lenski, *Failure*, 264–307 (little guy: 281). Inscriptions: Harper, 'Census.'
12. Themistios, *Orations* 8.119c, 10.136c–137a; Ammianus 26.4.5, 26.6.11; Zosimos 4.10.1; contingent: Ammianus 26.10.3 (3,000 men), 27.5.1; Zosimos 4.7.1–2 (10,000 men); resettlement: Eunapios, *History* fr. 37. For the war of 367–369, see Ammianus 27.5; Zosimos 4.10–11; Themistios, *Oration* 10.
13. Themistios, *Oration* 8.113–114 (tr. Heather and Matthews).

14. Treaty: Themistios, *Oration* 10.135c–d; Lenski, *Failure*, 136; trade prohibited in *CJ* 4.41.1. Borders: G. Greatrex, 'Roman Frontiers and Foreign Policy in the East,' in R. Alston and S. Lieu, eds., *Aspects of the Roman East* (Turnhout 2007) 103–173.
15. Themistios, *Oration* 10.
16. Ammianus 18.2.14.
17. E.g., after the battle of Strasbourg: Ammianus 17.1.12–13, 17.10.3–4.
18. McCormick, *Eternal Victory*; P. Heather, 'The Late Roman Art of Client-Management,' in W. Pohl et al., eds., *The Transformation of Frontiers: From Late Antiquity to the Carolingians* (Leiden 2001) 15–68.
19. See the *Life of Sabas*, addressed to the Church of Cappadocia (led by Basil of Kaisareia); Basil of Kaisareia, *Letters* 155, 164–165 (missionaries and contacts). Relevant texts: Heather and Matthews, *Goths*, 96–123.
20. Sokrates 4.33.1–4; chronology: N. Lenski, 'The Gothic Civil War and the Date of the Gothic Conversion,' *GRBS* 36 (1995) 51–87.
21. Lenski, *Failure*, 174–176.
22. *Epic Histories* 5.33 (tr. Garsoïan).
23. E.g., *CTh* 9.16.8 = *CJ* 9.18.8 (370 AD).
24. Ammianus 29.1–2 (libraries: 29.2.4); Zosimos 4.14–15; Libanios, *Oration* 1.171–173; Eunapios, *Lives of the Philosophers* 480–481. John Chrysostom, *Homilies on Acts of the Apostles* 38.5, in *PG* 60:274–275. Christians and magic: D. Rohmann, *Christianity, Book Burning, and Censorship in Late Antiquity* (Berlin 2017).
25. Sacrifice: Libanios, *Oration* 30.7; *Letter* 1147.
26. *CTh* 9.16.9 (371 AD; tr. Pharr), referring to an earlier law; praised: Ammianus 30.9.5; criticized: Theodoretos, *EH* 4.24.2–3, 5.21.3–4. For the ban on nocturnal rites and its revocation, see *CTh* 9.16.7; Zosimos 4.3.2–3.
27. Sozomenos 6.7.2; Theodoretos, *EH* 4.6.6–7.
28. [Athanasios], *Historia acephala* 5.1–7 (Martin); Sokrates 4.12–13; Sozomenos 6.10; doubt: Errington, *Policy*, 180–185. Baptism: Jerome, *Chronicle* s.a. 366; Epiphanios, *Panarion* 69.13.1–3; Theodoretos, *EH* 4.12.2–4.
29. Hilarius, *Against Constantius* 12; Athanasios, *On the Synods of Ariminum-Seleukeia* esp. 12, 41; Basil of Kaisareia, *Letter* 263; Epiphanios, *Panarion* 73.36. Sokrates and Sozomenos also document aspects of this rapprochement.
30. Basil of Kaisareia, *Letter* 239.2.
31. Gregory of Nazianzos, *Oration* 43.51–53; N. McLynn, 'The Transformation of Imperial Churchgoing in the Fourth Century,' in S. Swain and M. Edwards, eds., *Approaching Late Antiquity* (Oxford 2013) 235–270, here 253–255. Armenia: Rousseau, *Basil*, 281–287.
32. Brennecke, *Studien*, 181–242.
33. Theodoretos, *EH* 4.21–22; Epiphanios, *Panarion* 68.11.4–6.
34. Cyril of Jerusalem, *Catechetical Oration* 18.26.
35. Ephrem the Syrian, *Hymn against Heresies* 22.5.
36. Philostorgios 8.2–5, 9.4; Sokrates 4.13; Prokopios, *Secret History* 1.15; see P. Van Nuffelen, 'Episcopal Succession in Constantinople (381–450 C.E.),' *JECS* 18 (2010) 425–451, here 435–441.

37. E.g., John Chrysostom, *Homily on 1 Timothy* 1.3, in *PG* 62:507.
38. John Chrysostom, *Homilies on Acts of the Apostles* 33.4, in *PG* 60:243.
39. Themistios in Sokrates 4.32; Sozomenos 6.36.
40. Isaurians: Zosimos 4.20.1–2; Eunapios, *History* fr. 43.4; Saracens: Lenski, *Failure*, 204–207.
41. R. Errington, 'Church and State in the First Years of Theodosius I,' *Chiron* 27 (1997) 21–72, here 27–30.
42. *CTh* 7.13.7 (375 AD).
43. Ammianus 31.4.4; cf. 19.11.7 (Limigantes); Sokrates 4.34; cf. the consistory debate in Eunapios, *History* fr. 42.
44. Kaldellis, 'Classicism.'
45. Ammianus 31.4.9–11, 31.5.1; Eunapios, *History* fr. 42 (figure); Jerome, *Chronicle* s.a. 377; Jordanes, *Getica* 26.134–137; defenders: Lenski, *Failure*, 354–355.
46. Basil of Kaisareia, *Letter* 268.
47. Sokrates 4.38; Sozomenos 6.39.
48. Ammianus 31.13.18.
49. John Chrysostom, *To a Young Widow* 5, in *PG* 48:606.
50. Themistios, *Oration* 16.206d; see N. Lenski, 'Initium malum Romano imperio: Contemporary Reactions to the Battle of Adrianople,' *Transactions of the American Philological Association* 127 (1997) 129–168.
51. John Chrysostom, *To a Young Widow* 4, in *PG* 48:605.
52. Ammianus 31.16.7.
53. Libanios, *Oration* 24.15–16.
54. Pacatus in *Panegyrici Latini* 2.12.1; cf. Themistios, *Oration* 14.182b; R. Errington, 'The Accession of Theodosius I,' *Klio* 78 (1996) 438–453.
55. Illyricum: Errington, 'Theodosius and the Goths'; Trajan: Kaldellis, 'Genealogies.'
56. Zosimos 4.25.1, 4.27.1; Pacatus in *Panegyrici Latini* 2.21.2–5, 2.47.3; *Epitome de Caesaribus* 48.9.
57. Ammianus 31.16.8; Zosimos 4.26; C. Zuckerman, 'Cappadocial Fathers and the Goths,' *TM* 11 (1991) 473–486, here 480–486.
58. *CTh* 7.13.8–11, 7.22.9–19; Zuckerman, 'Two Reforms,' 115–116 for papyri.
59. Zosimos 4.30.
60. Zosimos 4.31–32 (garbled).
61. Libanios, *Oration* 30.52.
62. *CTh* 16.1.2; *CJ* 1.1.1; cf. *CTh* 16.5.6. Sozomenos 7.4.6, explains *infamia*.
63. *CTh* 16.5.5.
64. Themistios, *Oration* 15.
65. Invitation: Gregory, *De vita sua* 595–608, in *PG* 37:1070–1071; small group: ibid. 587–589; *Oration* 42.2; "anger" etc.: *De vita sua* 1325–1341. The *Theological Orations* are nos. 27–31 (380 AD). Gregory in Constantinople: McGuckin, *St Gregory*, 236–369.
66. Sokrates 5.8.1; Sozomenos 7.7.1.
67. Gregory on bishops: McGuckin, *St Gregory*, 188, 192, 195, 257, 352–366, 371–377, 381–384; populace: e.g., 241, 244, 281.
68. Sokrates 5.8.12; Theodoretos, *EH* 5.9.15.

69. Our first source for the Creed of Constantinople is the Acts of the Council of Chalcedon (451 AD).
70. Bishops: *CTh* 16.1.3; heretics: 16.5.11–24; civic rights: Sozomenos 7.12.11–12; persuasion: Gregory, *De vita sua* 1293–1294; Sozomenos 7.12.11–12.
71. *CTh* 16.4.2.
72. Errington, *Policy*, 6–7.
73. Gregory of Nazianzos, *Oration* 33.2 (379 AD).
74. Errington, 'Theodosius and the Goths,' 17–19.
75. Treaty: Heather, *Goths and Romans*, 157–181. Undefeated: Themistios, *Oration* 16.209b, 211a. Separate laws: Synesios, *On Kingship* 19.
76. Eunapios, *History* fr. 59. Intermarriage had been prohibited by Valentinian: *CTh* 3.14 (I am unpersuaded that this law does not mean what it says).
77. Pacatus in *Panegyrici Latini* 2.32.3.
78. Themistios, *Oration* 16; previous *Orations* 14 (mid-379 AD), 15 (19 January, 381 AD); "hounds": 15.199a.
79. Libanios, *Orations* 19.22, 20.14.
80. Tomi: Zosimos 4.40; Greuthungi: 4.35.1, 4.38–39; Claudian, *Panegyric on the Fourth Consulship of Honorius* 623–637; triumph and date: *Consularia Constantinopolitana* s.a. 386. Phrygia: P. Heather, 'The Anti-Scythian Tirade of Synesius' *De Regno*,' *Phoenix* 42 (1988) 152–172, here 156–157.
81. Zosimos 4.37.3; Libanios, *Orations* 49.3, 30.44–51; *Consularia Constantinopolitana* s.a. 388; G. Fowden, 'Bishops and Temples in the Eastern Roman Empire,' *Journal of Theological Studies* 29 (1978) 53–78, here 62–67.
82. Theodoretos, *EH* 5.21; Sozomenos 7.15; law: *CTh* 16.10.16; Trombley, *Hellenic Religion*, 1:123–129.
83. Libanios, *Oration* 30, between 385 and 387.
84. Poem: Libanios, *Letter* 990.
85. Zosimos 4.43.2–3.
86. Blockley, *Policy*, 42–44. "Garment": Ghazar, *History* 1, tr. R. Thomson, *The History of Łazar P'arpets'I* (Atlanta, GA 1991).
87. Goths: Zosimos 4.45.3; Eunapios, *History* fr. 55; "suspicious": Pacatus in *Panegyrici Latini* 2.32.3. Laws: *CTh* 15.14.6–8.
88. In particular speeches by Libanios and John Chrysostom; see F. van de Paverd, *St. John Chrysostom, The Homilies on the Statues* (Rome 1991). Donative: Libanios, *Oration* 22.4; a demon: *Oration* 19.29–34; foreigners and the Devil: John Chrysostom, *Homilies on the Statues* 12.3, 15.4, 17.5; name: 21.7–9.
89. Sokrates 5.13.
90. Ambrose, *Letter* 74; McLynn, *Ambrose*, 298–309.
91. Payne, *State of Mixture*, 47–48.
92. Sozomenos 7.25; analysis: McLynn, *Ambrose*, 315–330.
93. Heather, *Goths and Romans*, 184–188.
94. Rufinus, *EH* 11.22–23, 11.28 ("every city"); Eunapios, *Lives of the Philosophers* 472; Sokrates, 5.16–17; Sozomenos 7.15. Library: Ammianus 22.16.12; cf. Aphthonios, *Progymnasmata* 60; Epiphanios, *On Weights and Measures*.

95. Konstantinos of Rhodes, *On Constantinople* 178–201; Choniates, *History* 648.
96. Kaldellis, 'Genealogies'; J. Bardill, 'The Golden Gate in Constantinople,' *American Journal of Archaeology* 103 (1999) 671–696.
97. Errington, *Policy*, 165–167.
98. B. Croke, 'Reinventing Constantinople: Theodosius I's Imprint on the Imperial City,' in S. McGill et al., eds., *From the Tetrarchs to the Theodosians* (Cambridge 2010) 241–264, here 249–254.
99. L. Brubaker and C. Wickham, 'Processions, Power, and Community,' in W. Pohl and R. Kramer, eds., *Empires and Communities in the Post-Roman and Islamic World* (Oxford 2021) 121–187.
100. Sozomenos 7.21.5; *Paschal Chronicle* s.a. 391. "Reverse": Kelly, 'Stooping,' 239.
101. Theodoretos, *EH* 5.19.2–3.
102. Eunapios, *History* fr. 57; Zosimos 4.52; Asterios of Amaseia, *Homily* 4.9; Claudian, *Against Rufinus* 1.245–250; *Paschal Chronicle* s.a. 393; ban lifted in 393 AD via *CTh* 9.38.9; inscriptions: Kelly, *Ruling*, 257 n. 65; acts: *CTh* 9.42.12 (plus 11.1.23), 9.42.13, 12.1.131, 14.17.12; S. Rebenich, 'Beobachtungen zum Sturz des Tatianus und des Proculus,' *ZPE* 76 (1989) 153–165.
103. Eunapios, *History* fr. 58.2; Zosimos 4.53–54.
104. Philostorgios 11.2.
105. Zosimos 4.57.2–3; Eunapios, *History* fr. 60; Gaïnas' background: Anonymous, *Funeral Oration for John Chrysostom* 47, 50–51; Sokrates 6.6; Sozomenos 8.4. Alaric: Zosimos 5.5.4; Sokrates 7.10.1.
106. Sources: Liebeschuetz, *Barbarians*, 26 n. 9, 30 n. 42.
107. Zosimos 4.58.2; Orosius, *History against the Pagans* 7.35.19 (10,000 of them); cf. Jordanes, *Getica* 28.145 (he had taken 20,000 Goths with him).
108. Ambrose, *Commentary on the Gospel of Luke* 10.10 (380s); Jerome, *Letter* 60.16.

Chapter 7. City and Desert: Cultures Old and New

1. *SEG* 45:412; Remijsen, *Athletics*, 56 for Delphi.
2. Kallinikos, *Life of Hypatios* 33; Gaddis, *There Is No Crime*, 203–204.
3. John Chrysostom, *Homily on Matthew* 85.4, in *PG* 58:762–763; R. MacMullen, *Christianizing the Roman Empire* (New Haven 1984) 83.
4. P. Athanassiadi, 'The Fate of Oracles in Late Antiquity: Didyma and Delphi,' *Δελτίον της Χριστιανικής Αρχαιολογικής Εταιρείας* 15 (1989–1990) 271–278; in general: Trombley, *Hellenic Religion*.
5. 1 Corinthians 1:26–28; cf. 4:13; 2 Corinthians 10:3–4; 2 Timothy 2:4; and Maria in Luke 1:52–53.
6. S. Schwartz, *Were the Jews a Mediterranean Society?* (Cambridge 2010) 5, 20, 30–32.
7. 2 Corinthians 12:10.
8. Aristotle, *Nicomachean Ethics* 4.3.
9. Kelsos in Origen, *Against Kelsos* 3.62; *Sayings of the Desert Fathers: Alphabetical Collection*, Sarmatas 1.

10. Ephesians 6.11–17; Eusebios, *EH* 5 pref.
11. *Anonymous Funeral Speech for John Chrysostom* 31.
12. G. Woolf, 'Inventing Empire in Ancient Rome,' in Alcock et al., eds., *Empires*, 311–322, here 319. Cf. R. MacMullen, 'What Difference Did Christianity Make?' *Historia* 35 (1986) 322–343.
13. Cf. *CTh* 7.20.2 with *CJ* 12.46.1.
14. Sokrates, book 5 pref., responding to Eusebios.
15. *Bohairic Life of Pachomios* 84 (tr. Veilleux, mod.).
16. Kelly, *Ruling*, 232–245, here 234 (233 for Chrysostom).
17. Eusebios, *Life of Constantine* 4.54; e.g., *CJ* 1.5.18.5; *Paschal Chronicle* s.a. 530.
18. John Chrysostom, *Against the Games and Theatres*, in *PG* 56:263–270; John of Ephesus, *EH* 3.26; for choice expressions, see Brown, *Body*, 313–315; R. Webb, *Demons and Dancers: Performance in Late Antiquity* (Cambridge, MA 2008).
19. *Anonymous Funeral Speech for John Chrysostom* 13.
20. Philosophy: John Chrysostom, *Homily on John* 51.3, in *PG* 59:286; J. Whittaker, 'Christianity and Morality in the Roman Empire,' *Vigiliae Christianae* 33 (1979) 209–225. Blasphemer: John Chrysostom, *Homily on the Statues* 1.32.
21. Kelsos in Origen, *Against Kelsos* 1.4.
22. Antony: Athanasios, *Life of Antony* 2. Castration: D. Caner, 'The Practice and Prohibition of Self-Castration in Early Christianity,' *Vigiliae Christianae* 51 (1997) 396–415. Itinerant: Caner, *Wandering*; community: Eusebios, *EH* 2.17; Basil of Kaisareia, *The Long Rules* 35, in *PG* 31:1004–1008; Ioannes Cassianus, *Conferences* 12.2, 18.5.
23. Elm, *Virgins*.
24. Athanasios, *Life of Antony* 3; Rousseau, *Pachomius*, ch. 3.
25. Basileios of Ankyra, *On The True Incorruptibility of Virginity* 1, in *PG* 30:669, 721c.
26. Sokrates 2.43; and Canons 1, 9, 13–15, 17 of the Synod of Gangra.
27. Romans 12:2.
28. Gregory of Nazianzos, *Orations* 2.29, 21.19, 43.62–66; Jerome, *Letter* 22.33–34.
29. Palladios, *Lausiac History* 17.10.
30. M. Gleason, 'Visiting and News: Gossip and Reputation Management in the Desert,' *JECS* 6 (1998) 501–521.
31. Brakke, *Demons*, 48.
32. Bagnall, *Egypt*, 295–297; Brakke, *Demons*, 60. Dwellings: D. Brooks Hedstrom, 'Divine Architects: Designing the Monastic Dwelling Place,' in R. Bagnall, ed., *Egypt in the Byzantine World* (Cambridge 2007) 368–389; archaeology: eadem, *The Monastic Landscape of Late Antique Egypt* (Cambridge 2017); geography, dwellings, and economy: E. Wipszycka, *Moines et communautés monastiques en Égypte* (Warsaw 2009) 107–225, 471–565.
33. Elm, *Virgins*, 345.
34. *The First Sahidic Life of Pachomios* 17 (tr. Veilleux).
35. Rousseau, *Pachomius*, 74–75, but see E. Wipszycka, *The Second Gift of The Nile: Monks and Monasteries in Late Antique Egypt* (Warsaw 2018). Nitria: Chitty, *Desert*, 30–31, esp. Palladios, *Lausiac History* 7.2 (5,000), 13.2; Scetis: ibid. 20.1 (500), 29.2, 58.1.

Shenute's federation: the figure is in the Arabic *vita*, corrected by L. Blanke, *The Archaeology of Egyptian Monasticism* (PhD dissertation, University of Copenhagen 2014) 216. Zacharias, *Life of Severos* 141 (early sixth century), gives 30,000 as only a part of the monks of Egypt.

36. Caner, *Rich*, 17.
37. Curials: *CTh* 12.1.63; monks: Jerome, *Chronicle* s.a. 375; N. Lenski, 'Valens and the Monks,' *DOP* 58 (2004) 93–117.
38. K. Cooper, *The Virgin and the Bride: Idealized Womanhood in Late Antiquity* (Cambridge, MA 1996) 85–87.
39. Athanasios, *Life of Antony* 14; Palladas in *Greek Anthology* 11.384.
40. Euagrios, *On Harmful Thoughts* 21.
41. Rousseau, *Pachomius*, 156–158.
42. *Sayings of the Desert Fathers: Alphabetical Collection*, Arsenios 36.
43. Augustine, *On the Work of Monks* 25.33.
44. Ioannes Cassianus, *Institutes* 4.9; Rousseau, *Pachomius*, 139–140; Brakke, *Demons*, 77, 150–151.
45. *Sayings of the Desert Fathers: Alphabetical Collection*, Ammonas 3; Palladios, *Lausiac History* 23.3.
46. J. Barns, 'Shenute as a Historical Source,' in J. Wolski, ed., *Actes du Xe Congrès international de papyrologues* (Warsaw 1961) 151–159.
47. D. Raynor, 'Non-Christian Attitudes to Monasticism,' *Studia Patristica* 18 (1989) 267–273.
48. Ioannes of the Klimax, *The Ladder of Divine Ascent* 15, in *PG* 88:880. For the first view, see Brown, *Body*, 225–226; the second is more amply documented, for example in Basileios of Ankyra, in Elm, *Virgins*, 114.
49. Kelsos in Origen, *Against Kelsos* 4.23.
50. Ioannes of the Klimax, *Ladder to Heaven* 25, in *PG* 88:997. Euagrios: Brakke, *Demons*, 67; in general: P. Canivet, 'Erreurs de spiritualité et troubles psychiques,' *Recherches de science religieuse* 50 (1962) 161–205.
51. *CJ* 1.3.30.5 (469 AD).
52. *Sayings of the Desert Fathers: Anonymous Greek Collection* 244.
53. *The Tenth Sahidic Life of Pachomios* 3 (= *Pachomian Koinonia* 1:452); *The Bohairic Life of Pachomios* 35.
54. E.g., Chitty, *Desert*, 33.
55. Elm, *Virgins*, 257; Brown, *Body*, 217, 242–249. Automatic rape: *Draguet Fragment II* 7 (= *Pachomian Koinonia* 2:117). Cf. John Chrysostom, *Homily on Matthew* 7.7, in *PG* 57:81, among many passages.
56. G. Radle, 'The Veiling of Women in Byzantium,' *Speculum* 94 (2019) 1070–1115.
57. Brown, *Body*, 260.
58. John Chrysostom, *Homily on Matthew* 7.7, in *PG* 57:81, and 8.5, in *PG* 57:88–89.
59. "Worldly": John Chrysostom, *Against the Judaizers* 8.4.1, in *PG* 49:932; treatise: *PG* 47:319–386.
60. Pachomios in Rousseau, *Pachomius*, 170; Rapp, *Holy Bishops*, 138. Ioannes Cassianus, *Institutes* 11.18; cf. 11.14–16.
61. Athanasios, *Life of Antony* 47.1.

62. John Chrysostom, *Discourse on Blessed Babylas* 42, in *PG* 50:533–572; cf. Jerome, *Life of Malchus* 1; *Letters* 52.5, 125.16.
63. Athanasios, *Letter* 49.9.
64. *CTh* 16.3.1 (390 AD), 16.3.2 (392 AD).
65. Gaddis, *There Is No Crime*, 262–264.
66. Basil of Kaisareia, *Letters* 14, 2; cf. Gregory of Nazianzos, *Letters* 4, 5 (for the slaves that he kept until the end of his life, see his will in *PG* 37:389–396); Annisa retreat: Elm, *Virgins*, 60–105.
67. Elm, *Virgins*, 76–77; Rousseau, *Basil*, 190–232.
68. S. Holman, *The Hungry Are Dying: Beggars and Bishops in Roman Cappadocia* (Oxford 2001).
69. Gregory of Nazianzos, *Oration* 43.61–63; Basil, *Letter* 94 (*nosokomoi* and *iatroi*); in general: Caner, *Rich*, 55–57; Valens: Lenski, *Failure*, 254; name: Sozomenos 6.36. Hospitals: Miller, *Birth*, to be preferred over its critics.
70. Image: G. Bowersock et al., *Late Antiquity: A Guide to the Postclassical World* (Cambridge, MA 1989), Plate 8. We can disregard the bizarre idea that this proves an ignorance of Roman tradition in the east.
71. Caner, *Rich*, 65.

Chapter 8. The Political Class Ascendant (395–441)

1. G. and M. Greatrex, 'The Hunnic Invasion of the East of 395,' *Byzantion* 69 (1999) 65–75. Destroyed: John of Ephesos quoted at 70; *foederati*: the Syriac tale of *Euphemia and the Goth*, quoted at 71; *foederati* = Goths: Laniado, *Ethnos;* Addaeus: *PLRE* 1:13.
2. Zosimos 5.12.1; Philostorgios 11.3; Synesios, *On Kingship* 14.
3. Eunapios, *History* fr. 62.1.
4. Zosimos 5.4.2.
5. Claudian, *The Gothic War* 166–204, 610–614; Synesios, *On Kingship* 21; P. Heather, *Empires and Barbarians: Migration, Development and the Birth of Europe* (London 2009) 191–194.
6. Heather, *Goths and Romans*, 199–201.
7. Claudian, *Against Rufinus* 2.108–110; cf. *On Stilicho's Consulship* 1.152–160.
8. Cameron, *Claudian*, 168; 159–168 for analysis.
9. Illyricum: Cameron, *Claudian*, 60–62; guardianship: Zosimos 5.4.3; Claudian, *Against Rufinus* 2.4–6; *On Stilicho's Consulship* 2.53–55; *Panegyric on the Third Consulship of Honorius* 151–153 (private meeting); *Panegyric on the Fourth Consulship of Honorius* 430–433.
10. Philostorgios 11.3; Claudian, *Against Rufinus* 2.436–439; Jerome, *Letter* 60.16; date: Sokrates 6.1.4.
11. *CTh* 9.42.14; *PLRE* 1:780.
12. Ammianus 18.4.3.
13. S. Tougher, *The Eunuch in Byzantine History and Society* (London 2008) 42–53; C. Messis, *Les eunuches a Byzance* (Paris 2014).

14. Palladios, *Dialogue on the Life of John Chrysostom* 5 (p. 29); Sozomenos 8.2.
15. Claudian, *Against Eutropius* 1.234–282, 2(pr).55–56.
16. A. Brown, 'Banditry or Catastrophe? History, Archaeology, and Barbarian Raids,' in R. Mathisen and D. Shanzer, eds., *Romans, Barbarians, and the Transformation of the Roman World* (Farnham, UK 2011) 79–96; I. Jacobs, 'Prosperity after Disaster? The Effects of the Gothic Invasion in Athens and Corinth,' in eadem, ed., *Production and Prosperity in the Theodosian Period* (Louven 2014) 69–89.
17. Villas: P. Heather, 'Goths in the Roman Balkans,' *Proceedings of the British Academy* 141 (2007) 163–190, here 169–171. Walls: T. Gregory, *The Hexamilion and the Fortress* (Princeton 1993).
18. War: Cameron, *Claudian*, 168–176, 474–477; command: Heather, *Goths and Romans*, 204–206.
19. Synesios, *On Kingship* 20.
20. M. Kulikowski, 'The Failure of Roman Arms,' in J. Lipps et al., eds., *The Sack of Rome in 410 AD: The Event, Its Context and Its Impact* (Wiesbaden 2013) 77–83.
21. Herakles: Synesios, *Letters* 41, 113; *Katastasis* 2.303a; cavalry: *Letter* 108; artillery: *Letter* 133; comedies (examples): *Letters* 5, 148; terms: *Letter* 105 (cf. Sokrates 5.22 for episcopal marriages). See J. Bregman, *Synesius of Cyrene: Philosopher-Bishop* (Berkeley 1982).
22. Synesios, *On Kingship*, 14–21. Synesios in Constantinople: Cameron and Long, *Barbarians*.
23. Themistios, *Oration* 16.212b.
24. *CTh* 4.6.4; Libanios, *Oration* 1.145.
25. C. Davenport, 'Imperial Ideology and Commemorative Culture in the Eastern Roman Empire,' in D. Dzino and K. Parry, eds., *Byzantium, its Neighbours and its Cultures* (Leiden 2017) 45–70, here 60–62; A. Burnett, *Coinage in the Roman World* (London 1987) 148.
26. Cameron, *Claudian*, 60–62; Liebeschuetz, *Barbarians*, 58–60, 98 n. 28.
27. Zosimos 5.11.1.
28. Eunapios, *History* fr. 71.3; Cameron and Long, *Barbarians*, 247–249.
29. Claudian, *Against Eutropius* 2.174–229; Tribigild: *PLRE* 2:1125–1126; main narrative: Zosimos 5.13–18; the armies: Kaldellis and Kruse, *Field Armies*, 28–30.
30. *CTh* 9.40.17; empress: Philostrogios, *EH* 11.6; sermon: John Chrysostom, *Homily on the Patrician Eunuch Eutropius*, in *PG* 52:391–396; Sokrates 6.5.
31. Zosimos 5.18.6–10; Sokrates 6.6.1; Sozomenos 8.4.5.
32. *Anonymous Funeral Oration for John Chrysostom* 50.
33. John Chrysostom, *When Saturninus and Aurelianus Were Exiled* 1, in *PG* 52:415; date: Cameron and Long, *Barbarians*, 173–175.
34. Zosimos 5.18.10–22.3; Sokrates 6.6; Sozomenos 8.4; Philostorgios 11.8; and, for what it's worth, Synesios, *The Egyptians or On Providence* 2.1–3. Cameron and Long, *Barbarians*, 205–211, fail to persuade that Gaïnas did not introduce Gothic soldiers into the City. The evidence of *all* the sources is against them, including the *Anonymous Funeral Oration for John Chrysostom* 47, which they do not cite. Church: Chrysostom established it for orthodox Goths, and preached to them there: *Homily in the Church of the Goths*, in *PG* 63:500–510.
35. Zosimos 5.21.5–6; Eunapios, *History* fr. 69.2, 69.4, 71.2–4; execution: Cameron and Long, *Barbarians*, 236–252.

36. J. Matthews, 'Viewing the Column of Arcadius at Constantinople,' in D. Brakke, ed., *Shifting Cultural Frontiers in Late Antiquity* (Farnham, UK 2012) 211–224.
37. Claudian, *Against Eutropius* 1.242, with a grain of salt.
38. Eunapios, *History* fr. 59, 69.2, 71.3; Zosimos 4.56; Sokrates 6.6.39; Philostorgios 11.8.
39. Sokrates 6.6.4.
40. Subsidies: Jordanes, *Getica* 29.146 (compressed chronology); Alaric's movements: Heather, *Goths and Romans*, 206–213.
41. Elton, *Warfare*, 148, 173.
42. A summary of the acts in Photios, *Bibliotheca* 59.
43. *Lithomania*: Sokrates 6.7.15; Sozomenos 8.12.6; Palladios, *Dialogue on the Life of John Chrysostom* 6; Isidoros of Pelousion, *Letter* 1.152, in *PG* 78:285 (hostile sources).
44. E. Clark, *The Origenist Controversy* (Princeton 1992) proposed that the real target was the Origenist monastic theorist Euagrios. Theophilos against Origenism: N. Russell, *Theophilus of Alexandria* (London 2007) 18–27, especially the *Second Synodal Letter* of 400 at 93–99 (= Jerome, *Letter* 92).
45. Palladios, *Dialogue on the Life of John Chrysostom* 7; Sozomenos 8.13; see Kelly, *Golden Mouth*, 191–210.
46. Sokrates 6.3.14, 6.4–5; Sozomenos 8.8.6.
47. Sozomenos 8.9.
48. Sokrates 6.15; Sozomenos 8.16; Palladios, *Dialogue on the Life of John Chrysostom* 6.
49. Zosimos 5.23.4–5; T. Gregory, 'Zosimos 5,23 and the People of Constantinople,' *Byzantion* 43 (1973) 63–81; cf. *Anonymous Funerary Speech for John Chrysostom* 79.
50. Palladios, *Dialogue on the Life of John Chrysostom* 9; John Chrysostom, *Letter* 1 (to pope Innocent I, p. 80), is a key source.
51. John Chrysostom, *When He Returned from Exile*, in *PG* 52:443–448; Sozomenos 8.18.8.
52. Sokrates 6.18; Sozomenos 8.20. The sources give conflicting testimony about when John said this. It is echoed in the *Anonymous Funerary Speech for John Chrysostom* 3, 36, 138 (I am not persuaded by the translators, Barnes and Bevan, that he never used such language: 26–28).
53. John Chrysostom, *Letter* 14.1, in *PG* 52:612.
54. Palladios, *Dialogue on the Life of John Chrysostom* 11.
55. J. Liebeschuetz, 'Friends and Enemies of John Chrysostom,' in A. Moffatt, ed., *Maistor: Classical, Byzantine and Renaissance Studies* (Canberra 1984) 85–111.
56. Kelly, *Golden Mouth*, 287–290.
57. Council: Palladios, *Dialogue on the Life of John Chrysostom* 3 (p. 64): letter: *Collectio Avellana* no. 38; synod of 405: Kelly, *Golden Mouth*, 278. Innocent I's letters and embassy: Sozomenos 8.26, 8.28; Palladios, ibid. 4.
58. Philostorgios 11.6.
59. Sokrates 7.1; Synesios, *Letters* 26, 73, 91, 111, 112, 118, and especially 123.
60. Stilicho's embargo: *CTh* 7.16.1; 4,000: Sozomenos 9.8.6; Zosimos 6.8.2 (emended); Prokopios, *Wars* 3.2.36; embargo of 410: *CTh* 7.16.2.
61. Themistios, *Oration* 18.222b–233a.
62. *CTh* 15.1.51 (413 AD), 7.8.13 (422 AD); nine years: W. Lebek, 'Die Landmauer von Konstantinopel und ein neues Bauepigram,' *Epigraphica Anatolica* 25 (1995) 110–119, 138.

63. Illyricum: *CTh* 11.17.4, 15.1.49, 12.1.177; *CJ* 10.49.1; fleet: *CTh* 7.17.1 (412 AD). Cities required to build walls in 396: *CTh* 15.1.34. Archaeology: Jacobs, 'Creation.'
64. Sozomenos 9.5; *CTh* 5.6.3.
65. Marcellinus Comes s.a. 409; *Paschal Chronicle* s.a. 412 (wrong date); fund: *CTh* 14.16.1; law: 13.5.32.
66. See the inventory at the back of R. Janin, *Constantinople byzantine* (Paris 1964); P. Magdalino, 'Aristocratic *oikoi* in the Tenth and Eleventh Regions of Constantinople,' in Necipoğlu, ed., *Byzantine Constantinople*, 53–69; for example, Theodosius II's sisters in *Paschal Chronicle* s.a. 396.
67. *Paschal Chronicle* s.aa. 406, 411; Jerome, *Against Vigilantius* 5; see also *Paschal Chronicle* s.a. 415 for the inauguration of the second Hagia Sophia.
68. Liebeschuetz, *Barbarians*, 142–144.
69. Pulcheria: Sozomenos 9.1; monastery: Sokrates 7.22.3–4; shirt: Ioannes Rufus, *Plerophoriae* 99; Gospels: Nikephoros Xanthopoulos, *EH* 14.3, in *PG* 146:1064; Ignatius of Smolesk in G. Majeska, *Russian Travelers to Constantinople* (Washington, D.C. 1984) 96–97, 294–295.
70. J. Harries, 'Men without Women: Theodosius' Consistory and the Business of Government,' in Kelly, ed., *Theodosius*, 67–89, esp. the incident at 73. Appeals: *CJ* 7.62.32; Senate: *CJ* 1.14.8.
71. D. Lee, 'Theodosius and his Generals,' in Kelly, ed., *Theodosius*, 90–108, here 90–91; Ares: 98 (= *SEG* 41.1408).
72. Cameron, 'Empress' (too dismissive of paganism). "Romance": Malalas 14.3–8; *Paschal Chronicle* s.aa. 420, 421, 444; Ioannes of Nikiou, *Chronicle* 87; T. Braccini, 'An Apple between Folktales, Rumors, and Novellas: Malalas 14.8 and its Oriental Parallels,' *GRBS* 58 (2018) 299–323. A historical account in Sokrates 7.21.8–9; skepticism in Euagrios 1.21.
73. Signature: Millar, *Greek Roman Empire*, 63; signing: Theophanes a.m.5941, p. 101; ring: J. Biers, 'A Gold Finger Ring and the Empress Eudocia,' *Muse* 23–24 (1989–1990) 82–99.
74. Greatrex and Lieu, *Frontier*, 36–43; soldiers transferred from the Balkans: Theophanes a.m.5943, p. 104. Huns: B. Croke, 'Evidence for the Hun Invasion of Thrace in A.D. 422,' *GRBS* 18 (1977) 347–367; subsidy: Priskos fr. 2.
75. Olympiodoros, *History* fr. 43; Sokrates 7.23 (angel); J. Matthews, *Western Aristocracies and Imperial Court, AD 364–425* (Oxford 1975) 378–381.
76. E.g., in Hydatius, *Chronicle* s.a. 424.
77. Theodosius II, *Novel* 1.1 (438 AD, the ratification of the *Code*).
78. *CTh* 1.1.5–6; Theodosius II, *Novel* 1.3; J. Matthews, *Laying Down the Law: A Study of the Theodosian Code* (New Haven 2000).
79. Hierokles, *Synekdemos* pref. (pp. 7, 12); cf. Sozomenos 2.3, projecting a similar definition onto Constantine.
80. Priskos fr. 2.
81. Prokopios, *Wars* 3.3.35; Euagrios 2.1; Theophanes a.m.5931, p. 95, and a.m.5943, p. 104.
82. Sokrates 7.7.

83. Sokrates 7.13–14 (quotation: 7.13.9); Ioannes of Nikiou, *Chronicle* 84.89–99.
84. Sokrates 7.15.2; beauty: Damaskios, *Life of Isidoros / Philosophical History* 43A; gender: well put by E. Watts, *Hypatia: The Life and Legend of an Ancient Philosopher* (Oxford 2017) 105.
85. Sokrates 7.15; Damaskios, *Life of Isidoros / Philosophical History* 43E; Ioannes of Nikiou, *Chronicle* 84.101–103 (victory).
86. Condemnation: e.g., Sokrates 7.15; Damaskios, *Life of Isidoros / Philosophical History* 43E (bribery); Malalas 13.39. Laws: *CTh* 16.2.42–43; G. Bowersock, '*Parabalani*: A Terrorist Charity in Late Antiquity,' *Anabases* 12 (2010) 45–54.
87. Schwartz, *Imperialism*, 179–180, 207; the new synagogues: ch. 7–10.
88. D. Nirenberg, *Anti-Judaism: The Western Tradition* (New York 2013) 1–12.
89. Constantine: *CTh* 16.8.1 ("nefarious"); tax exemptions: 16.8.2, 4; dissidents: 16.8.8; A. Linder, *The Jews in Roman Imperial Legislation* (Detroit 1987); C. Nemo-Pekelman, *Rome et des citoyens juifs (IVe-Ve siècles)* (Paris 2010).
90. Conversions: *CTh* 16.8.7, 19, 22; slaves: 16.9; protections: 16.8.9 (quotation), 12, 20, 21, 25, 26, and 7.8.2.
91. *CTh* 2.1.10.
92. *CTh* 16.8.20, 16.8.24; Theodosius II, *Novel* 3 (438 AD).
93. Theodosius II, *Novel* 3.2 (438 AD).
94. *CJ* 1.9.7; Schwartz, *Ancient Jews*, 133–134.
95. G. Stemberger, *Jews and Christians in the Holy Land* (Edinburgh 2000) 269–297. Rabbis: H. Lapin, *Rabbis as Romans: The Rabbinic Movement in Palestine, 100–400 CE* (Oxford 2012); N. Dohrmann, 'Law and Imperial Idioms: Rabbinic Legalism in a Roman World,' in eadem and A. Reed, eds., *Jews, Christians, and the Roman Empire* (Philadelphia 2013) 63–77.
96. The bishops of Palestine to Theophilos of Alexandria in Jerome, *Letter* 93.
97. *CTh* 16.8.22, 25, 27.
98. *CTh* 16.2.45 (412 AD) = *CJ* 1.2.6; cf. *CJ* 11.21.1; Thessalonike as vicariate: e.g., pope Siricius, *Letter* 4, in *PL* 13:1148–1149; pope Innocent I, *Letter* 1, in *PL* 20:463–465; letters between the courts: Boniface I, *Letters* 10–11, 13, in *PL* 20:769–777; see V. Limberis, 'Ecclesiastical Ambiguities: Corinth in the Fourth and Fifth Centuries,' in D. Schowalter and S. Friesen, eds., *Urban Religion in Roman Corinth* (Cambridge, MA 2005) 443–457, here 444–449.
99. Sokrates 7.29, 7.31; Barhadbeshabba, *History* 20, in *PO* 9:521 (a Nestorian history in Syriac, ca. 600); Bevan, *New Judas*, 84.
100. Barhadbeshabba, *History* 21, in *PO* 9:529.
101. R. Price, 'Marian Piety and the Nestorian Controversy,' *Studies in Church History* 39 (2004) 31–38; Bevan, *New Judas*, 85–90 (and passim).
102. See, e.g., Nestorios' sermons translated by Marius Mercator in *ACO* 1.5, pp. 40–46; origin of the controversy: Sokrates 7.32; Nestorios to Ioannes of Antioch in Loofs, *Nestoriana*, 185.
103. Cyril of Alexandria, *Paschal Homily* 17; *Letters* 19, 4; *Five Books against Nestorios*, in *ACO* 1.6 (from early 430).
104. Bevan, *New Judas*, 100–101, 111–112.

105. Cyril of Alexandria, *Twelve Anathemas* esp. 4 and 12; *Letter* 17 (approved as canonical by the Council of Ephesos).
106. Kelly, *Doctrines,* 290–297; R. Norris, *Manhood and Christ: A Study of the Christology of Theodore of Mospuestia* (Oxford 1963) 81–122. Athanasios: Hanson, *Search,* 646–647.
107. Nestorios in *ACO* 1.1.2, p. 49. Theodoros: Kelly, *Doctrines,* 303–309; Bevan, *New Judas,* 42–57.
108. P. Galtier, 'Saint Cyrille et Apollinaire,' *Gregorianum* 37 (1956) 585–609.
109. E.g., Nestorios in Loofs, *Nestoriana,* 224, 280, on which J. McGuckin, *St. Cyril of Alexandria: The Christological Controversy, Its History, Theology and Texts* (Leiden 1994) 160–163. Cyril of Alexandria, *Letters* 4.3 (quotation), 39.9, and 46.3; also Cyril to Aristolaos in *ACO* 1.4, p. 206 (Christ is passible as a man but impassible as God).
110. *Sacra* of Theodosius II in *ACO* 1.1.1, p. 115, esp. line 23.
111. "New Judas": Deposition in *ACO* 1.1.2, p. 64.
112. The Easterners to Theodosius II: *ACO* 1.1.5, p. 134 (esp. line 29).
113. Bevan, *New Judas,* 160–163.
114. Demonstrations: memo of the Cyrillians in Constantinople: *ACO* 1.1.2, pp. 65–66; Nestorios, *Book of Herakleides* pp. 240–241 (tr. Nau) = pp. 271–273 (tr. Hodgson and Driver); and W. Kraatz, *Koptische Akten zum Ephesinischen Konzil vom Jahre 431* (Leipzig 1904) 47–49. Hagia Sophia: Kraatz, *Koptische Akten,* 49–55; the clergy of Constantinople to the Cyrillians at Ephesos: *ACO* 1.1.3, p. 14. Danger: Eirenaios in *ACO* 1.1.5, p. 136.
115. Gregory, *Vox populi.*
116. *ACO* 1.1.3, pp. 47–48.
117. *ACO* 1.1.7, p. 142.
118. *ACO* 1.4, p. 59.
119. Cyril of Alexandria in *ACO* 1.1.5, pp. 15–20 = *Letter* 39.
120. Epiphanios (Cyril's *synkellos*) to Maximianos (the new bishop of Constantinople) in *ACO* 1.4, pp. 224–225. Accusations of bribery: Bevan, *New Judas,* 183, 199, 200, 207, and 221–222. Bribes as "prayers": Theodoretos, *Letter* 110.
121. Alexandros of Hierapolis to the mines: *ACO* 1.4, p. 203; burning: *CTh* 16.5.66.
122. Cyril of Alexandria, *Letters* 44–46 = *ACO* 1.1.4, pp. 35–37; 1.1.6, pp. 151–162.
123. Theodoretos, *Letter* 180.
124. *CTh* 16.10 passim, esp. 16.10.21 on service; Theodosius II, *Novel* 3.8 (438 AD); *CJ* 1.11.7.
125. Isidoros of Pelousion, *Letter* 1.270; Theodoretos, *Therapy for the Hellenic Maladies* 6.87; Theodosius II in *CTh* 16.10.22; W. Kaegi, 'The Fifth-Century Twlight of Byzantine Paganism,' *Classica et Mediaevalia* 27 (1966) 243–275.
126. Cyril of Alexandria, *Against Julian: Address to Theodosios II* 4–5; Theodoretos: see *Therapy for the Hellenic Maladies* 6.87.
127. Malchos fr. 23.
128. Theodoretos, *Letter* 68; Zacharias, *Life of Severos* 60 (tr. Brock and Fitzgerald).
129. I am unpersuaded by the recent rush to proclaim Nonnos a Christian.
130. Marinos, *Life of Proklos* 9.

131. *Life of Rabbula* pp. 74–75 (tr. Doran); Gaddis, *There Is No Crime*, 168. Hierokles: Damaskios, *Life of Isidoros / Philosophical History* 45B; code: P. Athanassiadi, 'Persecution and Response in Late Paganism,' *Journal of Hellenic Studies* 113 (1993) 1–29, here 18. Isokasios: *PLRE* 2:633–634. Alexandria: E. Watts, *City and School in Late Antique Athens and Alexandria* (Berkeley 2006) ch. 8.
132. Jacobs, 'Creation,' 129.
133. C. Foss, 'Late Antique and Byzantine Ankara,' *DOP* 31 (1977) 29–87, here 65–66.
134. *CTh* 14.9.3, 15.1.53.
135. Synesios, *Dion, or on My Way of Life* 4.42b; cf. *Letter* 154 to Hypatia.
136. Brakke and Crislip, *Selected Discourses*, 39.
137. Entrechius: Zacharias, *Life of Severos* 28–32; B. Caseau, 'Le crypto paganisme et les frontières du licite: Un jeu de masques?' in P. Brown and R. Lizzi, eds., *Pagans and Christians in the Roman Empire* (Vienna 2011) 541–571.
138. Egypt: D. Frankfurter, *Religion in Roman Egypt: Assimilation and Resistance* (Princeton 1998) 31, 45, 47, 187–189, 193–197, 257–262; in general: R. MacMullen, *Christianity and Paganism in the Fourth to Eighth Centuries* (New Haven 1998) ch. 4. Sacrifices: *Life of Nikolaos of Sion* 55; A. Kaldellis, 'Lesbos in Late Antiquity,' in W. Caraher et al., eds., *Archaeology and History in Medieval and Post-Medieval Greece* (Aldershot, UK 2008) 155–167.
139. E.g., Augustine, *City of God* 22.9; Gregory of Nazianzos in *Greek Anthology* 8.175.
140. A. Kaldellis, 'The Kalends in Byzantium,' *Archiv für Religionsgeschichte* 13 (2012) 187–203; Isis: Ioannes Lydos, *On the Months* 4.45.
141. D. Frankfurter, *Christianizing Egypt: Syncretism and Local Worlds in Late Antiquity* (Princeton 2018) 248–252.
142. Kaldellis, *Parthenon*, ch. 1; Marinos, *Life of Proklos* 30.
143. Lucian, *On the Syrian Goddess* 28–29; J. Lightfoot, *Lucian: On the Syrian Goddess* (Oxford 2003) 417–417.
144. Euagrios 1.13, with 1.14 for the site and women.
145. Theodoretos, *Historia Religiosa* 24.11.
146. "Frozen": *Life of Daniel the Stylite* 52–53; epigram: ibid. 36 (tr. Dawes and Baynes, mod.) = *Greek Anthology* 1.99.
147. Euagrios 1.21. Hell: *Sayings of the Desert Fathers*: Zeno 6. Theodoretos, *Historia Religiosa*.
148. C. Markschies, 'Körper und Körperlichkeit im antiken Mönchtum,' in B. Feichtinger and H. Seng, eds., *Die Christen und der Körper* (Munich 2004) 189–212, here 202–204.
149. John Chrysostom, *Homily on 1 Thessalonians 4* 6.1, in *PG* 62:420, an old term of abuse.
150. Jerome, *Letter* 22.34; later: Ioannes Tzetzes, *Letters* 57, 104.
151. Caner, *Wandering*, ch. 4.
152. G. Dagron, 'La monachisme à Constantinople jusqu'au Concile de Chalcédoine,' *TM* 4 (1970) 229–276, here 253 n. 125.
153. Council of Chalcedon, canons 4, 8, 23; Marcian's instructions at *ACO* 2.1.1, pp. 156–157 (= *Chalcedon* 6.16–17). Tightly run: Gaddis, *There Is No Crime*, 315–317. *Status* or *fortuna*: *CJ* 1.3.26 (Leo I).

154. *Syriac Life of Simeon the Stylite* 56, 60; Theodoretos, *Historia Religiosa* 26.26. Thesis: Brown, 'Rise and Function,' but see R. MacMullen, 'The Place of the Holy Man in the Later Roman Empire,' *Harvard Theological Review* 112 (2019) 1–32, for miracles.
155. Brown, 'Rise and Function,' 100–101.
156. P. Brown, 'The Rise and Function of the Holy Man in Late Antiquity, 1971–1997,' *JECS* 6 (1998) 353–376, here 355–356.
157. Leontios, *Life of Ioannes the Almsgiver* 2; John Chrysostom, *Homily on Matthew* 66.3, in *PG* 58:630; cf. Markos the Deacon, *Life of Porphyrios of Gaza* 94 (how much, but not to how many).
158. Ambrose of Milan, *Letter* 18.16.
159. Theodoretos, *EH* 5.36 (Eunomios); cf. Ammianus 20.7.7–8; R. Marcus, 'The Armenian Life of Marutha of Maipherkat,' *Harvard Theological Review* 25 (1932) 47–73.
160. *Life of Rabbula*, p. 90 (tr. Doran).
161. Council of Chalcedon, canon 26; Rapp, *Holy Bishops*, 218–219; audits: Brown, *Poverty*, 30. Scandals: Athanasios, *Apologia against the Arians* 18; Sozomenos 4.25.3–4; possibly *Life of Rabbula*, pp. 172–173, 190 (ed. Overbeck).
162. Theodoretos, *Letter* 42; Iakobos: *Historia Religiosa* 21.
163. Sozomenos 4.24.15 (359 AD); Rapp, *Holy Bishops*, 206.
164. *ACO* 1.1.4, p. 64.
165. Caner, *Wandering*, 218–220.
166. Sozomenos 7.12.
167. The praetorian prefect Taurus in *ACO* 1.4, p. 155. Markos the Deacon, *Life of Porphyrios of Gaza* 40–41, while fictional, is revealing.
168. *CTh* 15.8.2; Theodosius II, *Novel* 18.
169. K. Harper, *From Shame to Sin: The Christian Transformation of Sexual Morality in Late Antiquity* (Cambridge, MA 2013) brilliantly sketches the ideal types.
170. K. Gaca, *The Making of Fornication: Eros, Ethics, and Political Reform in Greek Philosophy and Early Christianity* (Berkeley 2003).
171. Grubbs, *Law and Family*, 62, 87, 250–253; D. French, 'Maintaining Boundaries: The Status of Actresses in Early Christian Society,' *Vigiliae Christianae* 52 (1998) 293–318.
172. Webb, *Demons*.
173. *Actuarius*: *CTh* 8.7.21–22; numbers: Theophylaktos 8.7.11; see Cameron, *Circus Factions*; C. Roueché, *Performers and Partisans at Aphrodisias in the Roman and Late Roman Periods* (London 1993); Liebeschuetz, *Decline*, ch. 6.
174. Isidoros of Pelousion, *Letter* 5.185, in *PG* 78:1436–1437; cf. Michael the Syrian 11.1.
175. John Chrysostom, *On the verse, 'Give greetings to Priskilla'* 1, in *PG* 51:188.
176. Amphilochios of Ikonion, *Poems to Seleukos* 150–170.
177. Sunday: *CJ* 3.12.6 (389 AD), *CTh* 15.5.5 (416 AD), and *CJ* 3.12.9 (469 AD); no crosses: *CJ* 1.3.26. Cosmology: G. Dagron, *L'hippodrome de Constantinople* (Paris 2011) ch. 2–4.
178. É. Patlagean, 'Une image de Salomon en basileus byzantin,' *Revue des études juives* 121 (1962) 9–33. The image also influenced the Byzantine Alexander Romance.

179. Prokopios, *Wars* 1.24.1–6; *Secret History* 7.1–42.
180. Prokopios, *Secret History* 29.28–28; Malalas 14.19 = Konstantinos VII, *Excerpta de virtutis* 13 (pp. 162–163), 14.32, 14.34. Swapping out: Malalas 15.12, 16.6.
181. Cf. Prokopios, *Wars* 1.24.2 with Euagrios 2.5; Bell, *Social Conflict*, 140. Cf. Sozomenos 3.13.4–6.
182. Cameron, *Circus Factions*, ch. 9.
183. J. Toner, *Popular Culture in Ancient Rome* (Cambridge 2009) ch. 5; sixth century: Liebeschuetz, *Decline*, 217; in general: Kaldellis, *Byzantine Republic*.
184. J. C. Moreno García, *The State in Ancient Egypt* (London 2020) 35, 149.

Chapter 9. Barbarian Terrors and Military Mobilization (441–491)

1. Millar, *Greek Roman Empire*.
2. Theophanes a.m.5940–5942, pp. 98–102 (dispersed); Ioannes of Nikiou, *Chronicle* 87.29–33. The key study is Cameron, 'Empress.'
3. Marcellinus Comes s.a. 444; Priskos fr. 14.35–37.
4. Priskos fr. 8 (the last clause is ambiguous); Cyrus: *PLRE* 2:338. Switch to Greek: Ioannes Lydos, *On the Magistracies* 2.12; judges: *CJ* 7.45.12; wills: Theodosius II, *Novel* 16.8. Sea walls: *Paschal Chronicle* s.a. 439, but cf. C. Mango, 'The Shoreline of Constantinople in the Fourth Century,' in Necipoğlu, ed., *Byzantine Constantinople*, 17–28, here 24–25 (the passage in Germanos can mean "were unmanned").
5. Malalas 14.17 (with variants); Cameron, 'Empress,' 243–244. Chrysaphius' role: *Life of Daniel the Stylite* 31. Succession anxieties were likely responsible for the execution of Paulinos, ex-*magister officiorum*: Marcellinus Comes s.a. 440.
6. Victor of Vita, *History of the Vandal Persecution* 1.2; Prokopios, *Wars* 3.5.18–19 (the same number, but all warriors, which is unlikely).
7. Valentinian III, *Novel* 9 (440 AD).
8. Prosper Tiro, *Chronicle* s.aa. 441 and 442 (= *Chronica Minora* 1:478–479); Theophanes a.m.5942, pp. 101–102 (misdated); Nikephoros Xanthopoulos, *EH* 14.57 (1,170 ships).
9. Theodoretos, *EH* 5.37.5; Marcellinus Comes s.a. 441; Prokopios, *Wars* 1.2.11–15 (garbled).
10. T. Barfield, 'The Shadow Empires: Imperial State Formation along the Chinese-Nomad Frontier,' in Alcock et al., eds., *Empires*, 10–41.
11. Priskos fr. 2 (subsidy), 4 (Viminacium, Naissus), 11.2.50–55 (bones); Marcellinus Comes s.aa. 441, 442; increased subsidy: inferred from Priskos fr. 9.3; chronology: Maenchen-Helfen, *World*, 108–125.
12. Marcellinus Comes s.a. 441; Priskos fr. 13.2–3.
13. Theodosius II, *Novel* 24.
14. Kaldellis and Kruse, *Field Armies*.
15. Nestorios, *Book of Herakleides*, p. 366 (tr. Driver and Hodgson).

16. *CIL* 3.734 = *ILS* 823; *Greek Anthology* 9.691 (sixty days). Events: Priskos fr. 9; Marcellinus Comes s.a. 447; Malalas 14.22; Jordanes, *Romana* 331; *Paschal Chronicle* s.aa. 447, 450. "In reverse": Kelly, 'Stooping,' 239 (sources at 221–222).
17. Kallinikos, *Life of Hypatios* 52.
18. I. Topalilov, 'The Barbarians and the City,' in D. Dzino and K. Parry, eds., *Byzantium, its Neighbours and its Cultures* (Leiden 2017) 223–244; A. Poulter, 'The Transition to Late Antiquity,' *Proceedings of the British Academy* 141 (2007) 1–50, here 39–40.
19. Priskos fr. 9.3 (fear and terms); fr. 11.1.8–14 (territory); disease: Maenchen-Helfen, *World*, 121–123 (based on the Syriac writer Isaakios of Antioch's *Homily on the Royal City*).
20. Priskos fr. 9.3.22–34.
21. See pp. 49, 919 above.
22. Olympiodoros, *History* fr. 41.2; cf. Gerontius, *Life of Melania the Younger* 2.15 (ca. 1,666 lbs). But the Roman aristocracy exaggerated its wealth: Ammianus 14.6.10; Justinian, *Edict* 7.2; for the figures, see A. Cameron, 'The Antiquity of the Symmachi,' *Historia* 48 (1999) 477–505, here 492–499.
23. N. Lenski, 'Captivity among the Barbarians,' in M. Maas, ed., *The Cambridge Companion to the Age of Attila* (Cambridge 2015) 230–246, here 231–237.
24. Paintings: Priskos fr. 22.3; *magister*: 11.2.627–636; cf. Shapur I in Lactantius, *On the Deaths of the Persecutors* 5.3.
25. Priskos fr. 11–15; strip: 15.4.
26. Bevan, *New Judas*, 288–306.
27. Edict: *ACO* 1.1.4, p. 66 (= *CJ* 1.1.3). Confinement: Theodoretos, *Letters* 71, 79, 80 (quoting the order); Theodosius II in *ACO* 2.1.1, p. 69 (= *Chalcedon* 1.24).
28. G. Bevan and P. Gray, 'The Trial of Eutyches: A New Interpretation,' *BZ* 101 (2008) 617–657. I differ regarding the position of the court. Eutyches' age: letter to pope Leo I in *ACO* 2.4, p. 144.37.
29. Soldiers: Eutyches in *ACO* 2.1.1, pp. 94–95 (= *Chalcedon* 1.85) and p. 177 (= 1.834), and the minutes at pp. 137–138 (= 1.463). Florentius' interventions: cf. pp. 144–145 (= 1.541, 1.549) with p. 172 (= 1.776, 1.778).
30. Leo I, *Letters* 20–24, 26–28, the last being the "Tome"; Greek version: *ACO* 2.1.1, pp. 10–20 (= *Chalcedon* 1.11).
31. Theodosius II in *ACO* 2.1.1, p. 73 (= *Chalcedon* 1.51; tr. Price and Gaddis), confirmed by Nestorios, *Book of Herakleides*, pp. 341–343 (tr. Driver and Hogdson).
32. Taxes and communion: Nestorios, *Book of Herakleides*, pp. 341–343 (tr. Driver and Hogdson). Dioskoros and Theodoretos: Theodosius II in *ACO* 2.1.1, pp. 68–69 (= *Chalcedon* 1.24). No vote: *ACO* 2.1.1, p. 72.21–24 (= 1.49).
33. *ACO* 2.1.1, p. 143 (= *Chalcedon* 1.527–529).
34. *ACO* 2.1.1, p. 118 (= *Chalcedon* 1.304).
35. *ACO* 2.1.1, p. 88 (= *Chalcedon* 1.134), also pp. 75–76 (= 1.60), and elsewhere.
36. Nestorios, *Book of Herakleides*, p. 345 (p. 302 Nau); Chadwick, 'Exile.'
37. *ACO* 2.1.1, p. 191 (= *Chalcedon* 1.964); flee: Prosper Tiro, *Chronicle* s.a. 448; Leo I, *Letter* 50; Theophanes a.m.5941, p. 100. Their remit: Leo I, *Letters* 28–32, 34–35.

38. Theodoros of Klaudiopolis: *ACO* 2.1.1, p. 76 (= *Chalcedon* 1.62); for more, see Gregory, *Vox populi*, 149.
39. Leo I, *Letter* 95 (to Pulcheria in 451 AD).
40. Western letters: Leo I, *Letters* 43–46, 50–51, 54–58; Theodosius' replies: Leo I, *Letters* 62–64; the ideological context: Demacopoulos, *Invention*, 59–72.
41. R. Burgess, 'The Accession of Marcian,' *BZ* 86–87 (1993–1994) 47–68; C. Zuckerman, 'L'empire d'orient et les Huns: Notes sur Priscus,' *TM* 12 (1994) 159–182, here 171–176; and M. Whitby, *The Ecclesiastical History of Evagrius Scholasticus* (Liverpool 2000) 60 n. 12.
42. Tribute: Priskos fr. 20.1, 23, 24.2; taxes: Marcian, *Novel* 2 (quotation: 2.6); *CJ* 12.2.2.
43. Theodoros Anagnostes 355.
44. "Clergy and people": Theodoros Anagnostes 357; Pulcheria to Leo I in *ACO* 2.3, pp. 18–19 = Leo I, *Letter* 77 (Flavianos and exiled bishops). Synod: Chadwick, 'Exile,' 31–32. Theodoretos, *Letter* 139.
45. Meliphthongos of Iouliopolis in *ACO* 2.1.1, p. 158 (= *Chalcedon* 1.634).
46. Leo I, *Letters* 73, 76, 79, 83, 89, 90, 95.
47. R. MacMullen, *Voting about God in Early Church Councils* (New Haven 2006) 79–81.
48. *ACO* 2.1.1, p. 70 (= *Chalcedon* 1.44).
49. *ACO* 2.1.1, p. 94 (= *Chalcedon* 1.181–184).
50. *ACO* 2.1.1, pp. 118–119 (= 1.308–327).
51. *ACO* 2.1.2, pp. 129–130 (= *Chalcedon* 5.34; tr. Price and Gaddis).
52. Euagrios 2.5.
53. E.g., Theodoros Anagnostes 483–484; Kyrillos of Skythopolis, *Life of Sabas* 30; Monophysite: Leontios of Jerusalem, *Questions to Those Who Posit a Compound One-Nature Christ*, in *PG* 86B:1849A; Diphysite: Severos, *Select Letters* 1.60 (tr. Brooks, 2.1:182).
54. S. Brock, 'Miaphysite, not Monophysite!,' *Cristianesimo nella Storia* 34 (2013) 299–310. "Miaphysite" is a neologism designed for ecumenical rapprochement, which is not our aim.
55. Bevan, *New Judas*, 318.
56. *ACO* 2.1.3, pp. 7–11 (= *Chalcedon* 9 Greek = 8 Latin).
57. See p. 961 n. 153 above.
58. Debate over Canon 28: *ACO* 2.1.3, pp. 86–99 (= *Chalcedon* 17 Greek). Letter to Leo: Leo, *Letter* 98; farce; Demacopoulos, *Invention*, 69–70. Marcian was more candid: Leo, *Letter* 100.
59. Initial concern: Leo, *Letters* 104 (Marcian), 105 (Pulcheria), 106 (Anatolios); Marcian to Leo in early 453: *Letter* 110 (Leo admitted the truth of this in *Letters* 117, 124, and 130); relents: *Letters* 114–115 (more complaints in 116, 119, 127).
60. "Discuss": *ACO* 2.1.2, pp. 120–121 = *CJ* 1.1.4; "write" etc.: *CJ* 1.5.8–11 (tr. Blume et al., mod.).
61. Priskos fr. 28.1; Zacharias, *EH* 3.2; Ioannes Rufus, *Plerophoriae* 77.
62. Zacharias, *EH* 3.3–5; Ioannes Rufus, *Life of Petros the Iberian* 76–81; *On the Death of Theodosios*; and *Plerophoriae* 10, 25, 29, 39, 54, 56, 87, 91; Kyrillos of Skythopolis, *Life of Euthymios* 27 ("Scripture"); Euagrios 2.5.

63. Ioannes Rufus, *Plerophoriae* 38, 40.
64. *Life of Rabbula* p. 92 (tr. Doran), for Marcionites.
65. Ioannes Rufus, *Plerophoriae* 9.
66. Marcian in *ACO* 2.1.3, pp. 124–127.
67. Zacharias, *EH* 3.8–9; Ioannes Rufus, *On the Death of Theodosios*; and *Plerophoriae* 54.
68. Hydatius, *Chronicle* s.a. 452; threat: Priskos fr. 24.2.
69. Kyrillos of Skythopolis, *Life of Euthymios* 30; cf. Leo I, *Letter* 123, for prior contacts.
70. *Foederati*: Theophanes a.m.5931, p. 94, and Ariobindus, *comes foederatorum* in 422: *PLRE* 2:145. Support: Jordanes, *Getica* 52.270. Barbarians: Prokopios, *Wars* 3.11.3–4, 8.5.13–14, with Laniado, *Ethnos;* Aspar as their patron: A. Laniado, 'Aspar and His phoideratoi,' in U. Roberto and L. Mecella, eds., *Governare e riformare l'impero al momento della sua divisione* (Rome 2015) 1–18; Heather, *Goths and Romans*, 253–263.
71. M. McEvoy, 'Becoming Roman? The Not-So-Curious Case of Aspar and the Ardaburii,' *JLA* 9 (2016) 483–511, here 485, 494–498. I disagree that ethnicity was inconsequential.
72. Malalas 14.40.
73. Prokopios, *Wars* 3.6.3; Theophanes a.m.5961, p. 116, based on an earlier source.
74. Konstantinos VII, *Book of Ceremonies* 1.100; Aspar's *curator*: Theophanes a.m.5961, p. 116; cf. Kandidos fr. 1.4, 1.26.
75. *ACO* 2.5, pp. 11–17 (Proterios' followers to Leo); Ioannes Rufus, *Life of Petros the Iberian* 83–95, and *Plerophoriae* 66; Zacharias, *EH* 3.11–4.2; Theodoros Anagnostes 368–370; Euagrios 2.8; Theophanes a.m.5950, pp. 110–111.
76. Seleukos of Amaseia in *ACO* 2.5, p. 85.29–35.
77. *Codex*: *ACO* 2.5, pp. 9–98 (an incomplete Latin translation); narratives: Zacharias, *EH* 4.5–10 (with claims of violence but the text is corrupt); Euagrios 2.9–10; Theodoros Anagnostes 371–373; Theophanes a.m.5952, pp. 111–112.
78. Euagrios 2.12–13; Zonaras, *Chronicle* 14.1 (3:124–125: Aspar); Kedrenos, *Historical Compendium*, 1:609–611; Kaldellis, 'Forum,' 718–719.
79. Ardabur: Jordanes, *Romana* 336; Anthemius: Sidonius, *Carmina* 2.224–298; Dengizich: Marcellinus Comes s.a. 469; *Paschal Chronicle* s.a. 468.
80. Priskos fr. 37; Jordanes, *Getica* 52.271.
81. Priskos fr. 45; meeting: *Life of Daniel the Stylite* 55. Reconstruction: B. Croke, 'Dynasty and Ethnicity: Emperor Leo I and the Eclipse of Aspar,' *Chiron* 35 (2005) 147–203, wrongly dismissing ethnicity.
82. Reform: Ioannes Lydos, *On the Magistracies* 1.16; oak and boots: Corippus, *In Praise of Justin II* 3.165–179; "tall" and Justin: Prokopios, *Secret History* 6.2–3; A. Kaldellis, 'Leo I, Ethnic Politics, and the Beginning of Justin I's Career,' *Zbornik radova Vizantološkog instituta* 55 (2018) 9–17.
83. Sidonius, *Carmina* 2.30–34 (tr. Anderson, mod.).
84. Kandidos fr. 2: 7 million plus change; Ioannes Lydos, *On the Magistracies* 3.43: ca. 9 million (Marcian left 7 million solidi in reserve); Prokopios, *Wars* 3.6.1–2. Anastasius left 23 million in 518: Prokopios, *Secret History* 19.17.
85. Prokopios, *Wars* 3.6.3–4; Hydatius, *Chronicle* s.a. 468 (contemporary).

86. Priskos fr. 53; Prokopios, *Wars* 3.6.10–26. "Phantoms": Ioannes Lydos, *On the Magistracies* 3.44.
87. Malalas 14.40, from Konstantinos VII, *Excerpta de insidiis* 31 (p. 160).
88. *Life of Markellos* 34, ed. G. Dagron, 'La vie ancienne de saint Marcel l'Acémète,' *Analecta Bollandiana* 86 (1968) 271–321, here 316–318; Malalas 14.40, from Konstantinos VII, *Excerpta de insidiis* 31 (p. 160); Theophanes a.m.5961, p. 116; Zonaras, *Chronicle* 14.5–7 (3:122–123).
89. Priskos fr. 64; letter: Malalas 14.45.
90. Malchos fr. 2, usually dated to 473, on the assumption that Malchos did not cover earlier events; numbers: Heather, *Goths and Romans*, 254.
91. Jordanes, *Getica* 51.283–288; population: Heather, *Goths and Romans*, 248; wagons: Malchos fr. 20.245.
92. Kandidos fr. 1.46–47. Zonaras, *Chronicle* 14.1.28 (3:126): Leo had concerns about Zeno's fitness.
93. Marcellinus Comes s.a. 440.1.
94. Ioannes of Antioch fr. 229 (Mariev); *CJ* 9.12.10.
95. Marcellinus Comes s.a. 473.
96. Konstantinos VII, *Book of Ceremonies* 1.103.
97. *Life of Daniel the Stylite* 67; Kandidos fr. 1.48–49.
98. Unwarlike: Malchos fr. 5.1; ugly: Zonaras, *Chronicle* 14.1.28 (3:126), 14.2.2 (3:128); hated: pseudo-Joshua the Stylite, *Chronicle* 12.
99. *Life of Daniel the Stylite* 69; *Anonymous Valesianus (post.)* 9.41.
100. Ioannes of Antioch fr. 233 (Mariev); death of Herakleios: Malchos fr. 6.
101. Massacre: Kandidos fr. 1.57; deal: Malchos fr. 15.21–22 (reliance on Gothic soldiers?), 18.4.17; Theophanes a.m.5970, p. 126; guard: *Life of Daniel the Stylite* 75.
102. Encyclical: Zacharias, *EH* 4.12–5.4; Euagrios 3.4–6; and E. Schwartz, 'Codex Vaticanus gr. 1431,' *Abhandlungen der bayerischen Akademie der Wissenschaften, philosophisch-philologische und historische Klasse* 22.6 (Munich 1927) 49–51. The original version is debated: see G. Greatrex, ed., *The Chronicle of Pseudo-Zachariah Rhetor* (Liverpool 2011) 177 n. 22.
103. *Life of Daniel the Stylite* 70–85; Malchos fr. 9.3; Zacharias, *EH* 5.4–5; Euagrios 3.7.
104. Kandidos fr. 1.52–72; *Life of Daniel the Stylite* 69; *Souda* s.v. Harmatus.
105. Malalas 15.5; Kandidos fr. 1.68–70; *Anonymous Valesianus (post.)* 9.42–44; Euagrios 3.24.
106. Zonaras, *Chronicle* 14.2.22–24 (3:130–131); Kedrenos, *Historical Compendium*, 1:564, 616.
107. *CJ* 8.10.12.
108. Malchos fr. 14; Marcellinus Comes s.a. 476. Insignia: *Anonymous Valesianus (post.)* 12.64. Dalmatia: I. Basić and M. Zeman, 'What can epigraphy tell us about *partitio imperii* in fifth-century Dalmatia?' *JLA* 12 (2019) 88–135.
109. Ioannes Rufus, *Plerophoriae* 89 (probably Timotheos the Cat).
110. Malchos fr. 15.
111. Malchos fr. 15, 18.2.13, 20.171–172; *Anonymous Valesianus (post.)* 9.42.
112. Strabo in Malchos fr. 18.2.33–38.

113. Malchos fr. 20.6–19.
114. Deal: Malchos fr. 18.4; Dyrrachion: fr. 20 (quotation: 20.76); Heather, *Goths and Romans*, 272–293.
115. Ioannes of Antioch fr. 234.1–2 (Mariev); Kandidos fr. 1.89–94.
116. Ioannes of Antioch fr. 234.3–4 (Mariev); Euagrios 3.26; Theophanes a.m.5971, pp. 126–127.
117. Malchos fr. 22.
118. Ioannes of Antioch fr. 234.5 (Mariev); Euagrios 3.25.
119. Marcellinus Comes s.aa. 482–483; Ioannes of Antioch fr. 236, 237.3 (Mariev).
120. Euagrios 3.8–9; Zacharias, *EH* 5.5; depositions: V. Grumel, *Les regestes des actes du patriarchat de Constantinople*, v. 1.1 (Paris 1932) 113 (no. 150); Kosiński, *Zeno*, 108–118.
121. Theodoros Anagnostes 427. Parrot: R. Kosiński, 'Peter the Fuller,' *Byzantinoslavica* 68 (2010) 49–73, here 70–71.
122. Zacharias, *EH* 5.5.
123. Simplicius to Zeno and Akakios in *Collectio Avellana* nos. 66–67 (479 AD).
124. Nikephoros Xanthopoulos, *EH* 16.12, in *PG* 147:136; *Henotikon*: Euagrios 3.12–16; Zacharias, *EH* 5.7–8 (including Mongos' sermon).
125. Euagrios 3.18–21; Kosiński, *Zeno*, 179–184. Monk: Liberatus, *Breviarium* 17.125, in *ACO* 2.5, p. 131; "no notice": Theodoros Anagnostes 434; Theophanes a.m.5980, p. 132. The texts are Felix, *Letters* 6–8 (Thiel).
126. J.-M. Kötter, *Zwischen Kaisern und Aposteln: Das Akakianische Schisma (484–519)* (Stuttgart 2013).
127. Pseudo-Joshua the Stylite, *Chronicle* 14 (tr. Trombley and Watt).
128. Ioannes of Antioch fr. 237 (Mariev); pseudo-Joshua the Stylite, *Chronicle* 13–17; Malalas 15.13–14. Verina's letter: Konstantinos VII, *Excerpta de insidiis* 35 (pp. 165–166); disjointed but important notices in Theophanes a.m.5972–5980, pp. 127–132.
129. Horoscope: *Catalogus codicum astrologorum Graecorum*, 8.4:221–224; Damaskios, *Life of Isidoros / Philosophical History* fr. 113C, also 77B; sacrifices: Zacharias, *Life of Severos* 54; cf. his *Life of Isaiah* 10 (Gaza); Pamprepios: Malchos fr. 23; Kosiński, *Zeno*, 154–167; E. Livrea, 'The Last Pagan at the Court of Zeno: Poetry and Politics of Pamprepios of Panopolis,' in A. de Francisco Heredero et al., eds., *New Perspectives on Late Antiquity in the Eastern Roman Empire* (Newcastle-upon-Tyne 2014) 1–29.
130. E. Watts, *Riot in Alexandria: Tradition and Group Dynamics in Late Antique Pagan and Christian Communities* (Berkeley 2010).
131. Prokopios, *Buildings* 5.7.1–9; Malalas 15.8. Samaritan sources are late (fourteenth century) and fictional. The events are traditionally dated to 484 because that is where the *Paschal Chronicle* (probably arbitrarily) places one of them (Kaisareia). L. Di Segni, 'The Samaritans in Roman-Byzantine Palestine,' in H. Lapin, ed., *Religious and Ethnic Communities in Later Roman Palestine* (Bethesda, MD 1998) 51–66, tries to fuse the two, fails, and concludes that one might have been fictional.
132. Ioannes of Antioch fr. 237.7–8 (Mariev).
133. Prokopios, *Wars* 1.8.3, 5.16.2.

134. Ioannes of Antioch fr. 239.4 (Mariev); Jordanes, *Romana* 354; Euagrios 3.35 (5,000 lbs—impossible).
135. Prokopios, *Wars* 5.1.10.

Chapter 10. Political Consolidation and Religious Polarization (491–518)

1. Aristakes of Lastivert, *History* 9; others: Kaldellis, *Byzantine Republic*, 114.
2. Ulpian in *Digest* 30.39.9.
3. Konstantinos VII, *Book of Ceremonies* 1.101.
4. Theodoros Anagnostes 446, whence Euagrios 3.32; Theophanes a.m.5983, p. 136.
5. Prokopios of Gaza, *Panegyric for Anastasius* 5.
6. Ioannes Lydos, *On the Magistracies* 3.50 is revealing.
7. Ioannes of Antioch fr. 239 (Mariev); Marcellinus Comes s.a. 491; Theophanes a.m.5984–5985, p. 137; *PLRE* 2:688 (Longinus 3), 689–690 (Longinus 6); Haarer, *Anastasius*, 21–28.
8. Euagrios 3.35.
9. B. Croke, 'Poetry and Propaganda: Anastasius as Pompey,' *GRBS* 48 (2009) 447–466.
10. *Greek Anthology* 9.656 (possibly by Christodoros of Koptos).
11. *CJ* 11.1.1–2; pseudo-Joshua the Stylite, *Chronicle* 31; and many sources. Bonfire: Zosimos 2.38; Prokopios of Gaza, *Panegyric for Anastasius* 13; Priscianus, *Panegyric for Anastasius* 152–153, 164–166; Euagrios 3.39.
12. Malalas 16.7; the reform is poorly understood: Haarer, *Anastasius*, 197–199.
13. Prokopios, *Secret History* 19.17.
14. See the list in D. Stathakopoulos, *Famine and Pestilence in the Late Roman and Early Byzantine Empire* (London 2004).
15. Malalas 18.54.
16. *CJ* 10.27.2.10; cf. Malalas 16.3; Euagrios 3.42; A. Sarantis, 'Military Provisioning in the Sixth-Century Balkans,' *JLA* 12 (2019) 329–379, here 353–355.
17. See pp. 226–231 below, on cities.
18. W. Treadgold, *Byzantium and Its Army, 284–1081* (Stanford, CA 1995) 153. Justinian: P. Rance, 'The Army in Peace Time: The Social Status and Function of Soldiers,' in Y. Stouraitis, ed., *A Companion to the Byzantine Culture of War* (Leiden 2018) 394–439, here 399–400.
19. Marcellinus Comes s.a. 498; "ordered": Malalas 16.12; Hendy, *Studies*, 475–478.
20. Constructions: Malalas 16.21; Ioannes Lydos, *On the Magistracies* 3.47; Haarer, *Anastasius*, ch. 7. Relief: Malalas 16.17–18; Lydos, *On the Magistracies* 3.47–48; pseudo-Joshua the Stylite, *Chronicle* 42, 66, 78, 84, 87, 92–93, 99; pseudo-Zacharias, *Chronicle* 7.5; 1,000 lbs for ransom: Marcellinus Comes s.a. 517.
21. Especially Theodoros Anagnostes. Other verdicts: Justin I in *CJ* 2.7.25 (stingy); Ioannes Lydos, *On the Magistracies* 3.49; Euagrios 3.42; Ioannes of Antioch fr. 243 (Mariev); *Oracle of Baalbek* 168–170; *Greek Anthology* 11.270–271.

22. Significant syntheses in H. Saradi, *The Byzantine City in the Sixth Century* (Athens 2006); and I. Jacobs, *Aesthetic Maintenance of Civic Space: The 'Classical' City from the 4th to the 7th c. AD* (Leuven 2013).
23. A. Poulter, *Nicopolis ad Istrum: A Late Roman and Early Byzantine City* (Oxford 2007) 25–26.
24. Kaldellis, *Parthenon*; C. Foss, *Ephesus after Antiquity: A Late Antique, Byzantine and Turkish City* (Cambridge 1979).
25. A. Brown, *Corinth in Late Antiquity* (London 2018) ch. 5.
26. Slootjes, *Governor*, 77–89.
27. I. Uytterhoeven, 'A Change of Appearance: Urban Housing in Asia Minor during the Sixth Century,' in I. Jacobs and H. Elton, eds., *Asia Minor in the Long Sixth Century* (Oxford 2019) 9–27.
28. L. Lavan, 'From *polis* to *emporion*? Retail and Regulation in the Late Antique City,' in Morrisson, ed., *Trade and Markets*, 333–377.
29. Remijsen, *Athletics*, 103–104.
30. Constantine in Eusebios, *Life of Constantine* 3.18.
31. *Miracles of Thekla* 33, also 26; Tarsos: 4; others: Ammianus 18.8.14 (Amida); pseudo-Joshua, *Chronicle* 35 (Arsamosata); Theodosius, *De situ terrae sanctae* 85 (forty days at Aegeae in Cilicia); Prokopios, *Wars* 8.25.23 (central Greece).
32. G. Dagron, 'Le Christianisme dans la ville byzantine,' *DOP* 31 (1977) 3–25.
33. Theodoretos, *Letter* 79, also 81; Rapp, *Holy Bishops*, 220–223.
34. Sokrates 6.7.15; Sozomenos 8.12.6; Palladios, *Dialogue on the Life of John Chrysostom* 6; Isidoros of Pelousion, *Letter* 1.152, in *PG* 78:285 (hostile sources); Gaddis, *There Is No Crime*, 263.
35. Jones, *Later Roman Empire*, 726–727, 731; *principales*: A. Norman, *Libanius: Selected Works* (Cambridge, MA 1977) 2:411–416.
36. Text and translation in C. Foss, *Byzantine and Turkish Sardis* (Cambridge, MA 1976) 110–113. M. di Branco, 'Lavoro e conflittualità sociale in una città tardoantica: Una rilettura dell'epigrafe di Sardi CIG 3467,' *Antiquité tardive* 8 (2001) 181–208, reads it as repressive.
37. Majorian, *Novel* 7.1 (458 AD), a western law, but true for the east. Selling land: Leo I in *CJ* 11.32.3; *defensor*: Anastasius in *CJ* 1.4.19; bishops: *CJ* 1.4.17–18, 10.27.3.
38. Rapacity: Priscianus, *Panegyric of Anastasius* 193–198; *vindex*: Ioannes Lydos, *On the Magistracies* 3.49 ("undoing"); Malalas 16.12 ("Romanía"); Euagrios 3.42.
39. Liebeschuetz, *Decline*, esp. ch. 3; better is Laniado, *Recherches*, and 'From Municipal Councillors to 'Municipal Landowners',' in M. Meier and S. Patzold, eds., *Chlodwigs Welt* (Stuttgart 2014) 545–565.
40. K. Holum, 'The Survival of the Bouleutic Class at Caesarea in Late Antiquity,' in idem and A. Raban, eds., *Caesarea Maritima: A Retrospective after Two Millennia* (Leiden 1996) 615–627.
41. *CJ* 12.1.15; Dagron, *Naissance*, 164–170.
42. Theodosius II, *Novel* 15.1.2 and 15.2.3 (439 and 441 AD; tr. Pharr, mod.).
43. Ioannes Rufus, *Life of Petros the Iberian* 103.

44. Justinian, *Edict* 8.3.1; Malalas 18.29; see A. Laniado, 'Social Status and Civic Participation in Early Byzantine Cities,' in C. Brélaz and E. Rose, eds., *Civic Identity and Civic Participation in Late Antiquity and the Early Middle Ages* (Turnhout 2021) 111–144.
45. Brown, *Poverty*, 52.
46. Ruffini, *Life*, 93; L. Koenen, 'The Carbonized Archive from Petra,' *JRA* 9 (1996) 177–188.
47. Marcellinus Comes s.a. 510; Theodoros Anagnostes 482; Ioannes Lydos, *On the Magistracies* 3.17. Estates: Bransbourg, 'Capital.'
48. Pseudo-Joshua the Stylite, *Chronicle* 8–10, 18–23; Priskos fr. 41.1.3–20 and 47; Ioannes Lydos, *On the Magistracies* 3.52–53; Theophanes a.m.5996, p. 144; Prokopios, *Wars* 1.7.1–2; Blockley, *Policy*, 50–51, 61.
49. Pseudo-Joshua the Stylite, *Chronicle* 48–89; pseudo-Zacharias, *Chronicle* 7.3–6; Prokopios, *Wars* 1.7–9; Theophanes a.m.5996–5998, pp. 144–149; Greatrex and Lieu, *Frontier*, ch. 5.
50. Prokopios, *Buildings* 3.2.4–8.
51. Prokopios, *Wars* 1.7.4; "no worthwhile army": Theophanes a.m.5996, p. 144; monks: Pseudo-Zacharias, *Chronicle* 12.7.l.
52. Prokopios, *Wars* 1.8.4.
53. Pseudo-Joshua the Stylite, *Chronicle* 90; Marcellinus Comes s.a. 518; pseudo-Zacharias, *Chronicle* 7.6.
54. C. Roueché, *Aphrodisias in Late Antiquity: The Late Roman and Byzantine Inscriptions* (London 1989) 227–228.
55. *Excubitores*: Malalas 16.4; *Paschal Chronicle* s.a. 498; ban: Ioannes of Antioch fr. 101 in Konstantinos VII, *Excerpta de insidiis* 101 (pp. 142–143); pseudo-Joshua the Stylite, *Chronicle* 46; Marcellinus Comes s.a. 501; Prokopios of Gaza, *Panegyric for Anastasius* 15–16; cf. Priscianus, *Panegyric for Anastasius* 223–227; Antioch: Malalas 16.6.
56. A. Cameron, *Porphyrios the Charioteer* (Oxford 1973) 232–244.
57. *Greek Anthology* 15.41–50; *Planudean Anthology* 335–387.
58. Herakleia: Gelasius, *Letter* 26 (495 or 496 AD) = *Collectio Avellana* nos. 95.21–27 (pp. 376–378); "Greeks": *Letter* 7.2 = *Collectio Avellana* no. 79 (p. 220), and *Letters* 26.12, 27.11–12; "arrogant": *Letters* 10.9, 12.12.
59. Euagrios 3.30; R. Kosiński, 'Euphemios, Patriarch of Constantinople,' *JöB* 62 (2012) 57–79.
60. Philoxenos: Euagrios 3.31–32; Severos: Zacharias, *Life of Severos*; *Anonymous Life of Severos*.
61. Theodoros Anagnostes 477, 479; Theophanes a.m.6002, pp. 152–153 (with caution).
62. Severos of Antioch, *Letter* 108, in *PO* 14:266–267; debates: Zacharias, *Life of Severos* 152; *Anonymous Life of Severos* 45.
63. Theodoros Anagnostes 483–486; Theophanes a.m.6003, p. 154. Severos' letter: J. Dijkstra and G. Greatrex, 'Patriarchs and Politics in Constantinople in the Reign of Anastasius,' *Millennium* 6 (2009) 223–264, here 242.
64. Theodoros Anagnostes 487–492; pseudo-Zacharias, *Chronicle* 7.8 (the letter of presbyter Simeon); Theophanes a.m.6004, pp. 154–156. For "corruption of Scripture," see also Severos of Antioch, *Letter* 108, in *PO* 14:266–267.
65. Gelasius, *Letter* 12.10, p. 357 (Thiel).

66. Euagrios 3.32–33; "resistance": Philoxenos, *Letter to Maro of Anazarbos* 27–32, ed. and tr. J. Lebon, 'Textes inédits de Philoxène de Mabboug,' *Le Muséon* 43 (1930) 17–84, 149–220, here 76–80.
67. Severos, *Inaugural Address*, in *PO* 2:324.
68. Malalas 16.19; Marcellinus Comes s.a. 512; Euagrios 3.44.
69. Cf. R. Price, 'The Development of a Chalcedonian Identity in Byzantium (451–553),' *Church History and Religious Culture* 89 (2009) 307–325.
70. Severos, *Select Letters* 1.19 (tr. Brooks, 2.1:68).
71. *Collectio Avellana* no. 139.
72. Dorotheos of Thessalonike in *Collectio Avellana* no. 105. See Haarer, *Anastasius*, 157–164; Hatziantoniou, *Η θρησκευτική πολιτική*, 115–133, 158–163 (I am less certain of Anastasius' convictions).
73. Under Anastasius: G. Greatrex, 'Flavius Hypatius, *quem vidit validum parthus sensitque timendum*,' *Byzantion* 66 (1996) 120–142.
74. Vacillator: Severos, *Select Letters* 5.5 (tr. Brooks, 2.2:292–292); "no difference": ibid. 7.4 (2.2:374–375).
75. Leontios of Jerusalem, *Testimony of the Saints*, p. 152.
76. K. Appiah, *The Lies that Bind: Rethinking Identity* (New York 2018) 30.
77. S. McGill and E. Watts, eds., *A Companion to Late Antique Literature* (Malden, MA 2018), part I; Coptic: M. Choat, 'Language and Culture in Late Antique Egypt,' in P. Rousseau, ed., *A Companion to Late Antiquity* (Malden, MA 2012) 342–356.
78. Edessa: J. Flemming, *Akten der Ephesinischen Synode vom Jahre 449 syrisch* (Berlin 1917) 15–17. Jacob: R. Schröter, 'Trostschreiben Jacob's von Sarug an die himyaritischen Christen,' *Zeitschrift der deutschen morgenländischen Gesellschaft* 31 (1877) 360–405, here 388. Pseudo-Joshua the Stylite, *Chronicle* 67–68.
79. F. Millar, 'The Evolution of the Syrian Orthodox Church in the Pre-Islamic Period: From Greek to Syriac,' *JECS* 21 (2013) 43–92, is excellent.
80. Cf. A. Louth, 'Why Did the Syrians Reject the Council of Chalcedon?' in R. Price, ed. *Chalcedon in Context: Church Councils 400–700* (Liverpool 2009) 107–116.
81. Riot: Malalas 16.19. Severos, *Select Letters* 1.24 (tr. Brooks, 2.1:84), 5.12 (2.2:341). Devotion to Theodoretos: see the story told at the Council of Constantinople II (553): Session 7.12, in *ACO* 4.1, p. 199.
82. Ioannes of Antioch fr. 242 (Mariev); Theodoros Anagnostes 509; Marcellinus Comes s.a. 514–515 ("Gothic dagger"); Malalas 16.16; Jordanes, *Romana* 357–359; Euagrios 3.43. I reject the reported numbers (50,000 or 60,000 soldiers for Vitalianus, 80,000 for Hypatius). In Persian war: pseudo-Joshua the Stylite, *Chronicle* 60; Prokopios, *Wars* 1.8.3; no office, and ancestry: A. Laniado, 'Jean d'Antioch et les débuts de la révolt de Vitalien,' in P. Blaudeau and P. Van Nuffelen, eds., *L'historiographie tardo-antique et la transmission des savoirs* (Berlin 2015) 349–379. The chronology of the revolt is debated: based on Marcellinus, I prefer a condensed chronology.
83. Anastasius in *Collectio Avellana* nos. 109 and 107; Vitalianus: ibid. 116.7; Hormisdas: ibid. 108 and 110 (letters), 116a–b (*indiculus* and *libellus*), and Appendix 4, pp. 800–801 (*professio*).
84. Anastasius in *Collectio Avellana* no. 125.

85. Malalas 16.16 features a tale about a sulphur weapon used by Marinus.
86. Severos, *Hymn on Vitalianus*, in *PO* 7:710–711, and *Homily* 34.
87. *Greek Anthology* 16.350, 15.50, also 16.347–348; A. Cameron, *Porphyrius the Charioteer* (Oxford, 1973) 126–130.
88. Anastasius in *Collectio Avellana* no. 138.
89. Ioannes Lydos, *On the Magistracies* 3.43; Prokopios, *Secret History* 19.7.
90. Prokopios, *Wars* 5.1.4.
91. I deliberately draw attention to the lucid treatment by a Byzantinist: M. Whittow, 'The Second Fall: The Place of the Eleventh Century in Roman History,' in M. Lauxtermann and M. Whittow, eds., *Byzantium in the Eleventh Century* (London 2017) 109–126. Economies: Wickham, *Framing*.
92. Ioannes of Antioch fr. 235.5 (Mariev).
93. Malchos fr. 18.3.41; M. Whitby, 'The Long Walls of Constantinople,' *Byzantion* 55 (1985) 560–582. J. Crow and A. Ricci do not refute this dating with arguments in their 'Investigating the Hinterland of Constantinople: An Interim Report on the Anastasian Long Wall,' *JRA* 10 (1997) 235–262, here 239.
94. One can produce a coherent and sophisticated account of the American Civil War in which slavery is not the major factor, but it would also be a false account.
95. Prokopios, *Wars* 5.1.25–31, a jab at Justinian; Jordanes, *Getica* 57–58.
96. Marcellinus Comes s.a. 505 and 508; Jordanes, *Getica* 58.300–301; *Romana* 356; Cassiodorus, *Variae* 1.16, 1.25, 2.38.
97. Cassiodorus, *Variae* 1.1 (tr. Hodgkin, mod.).
98. *Anonymous Valesianus (post.)* 12.64.
99. Avitus of Vienne, *Letters* 78, 93 (tr. Shanzer and Wood).
100. Gregory of Tours, *History of the Franks* 2.38.
101. Y. Pyatnitsky, 'New Evidence for Byzantine Activity in the Caucasus during the Reign of the Emperor Anastasius I,' *American Numismatic Society* 18 (2006) 113–122; R. Gildina et al., 'The Nevolino Culture in the Context of the 7th-Century East-West Trade,' *TM* 17 (2013) 865–930, here 868.
102. Priskos fr. 33, 44; *Life of Daniel the Stylite* 51.
103. Amorkesos: Malchos fr. 1, hostile to Leo; Anastasius: Theophanes a.m.5990, p. 141. Iotabe was briefly lost and recaptured soon before 535: Chorikios of Gaza, *Praise of Aratios and Stephanos* 67–78. Was it a port?: P. Mayerson, 'A Note on Iotabe and Several Other Islands in the Red Sea,' *Bulletin of the American Schools of Oriental Research* 298 (1995) 33–35.
104. Menandros fr. 9.11.31.
105. Ammianus 14.4.1; an excellent survey in Fisher, ed., *Arabs and Empires*.
106. Priskos fr. 26 (ca. 453 AD); Barsauma of Nisibis, *Letter* 2 (484/5 AD), tr. in Fisher, ed., *Arabs and Empires*, 217; in the 490s: Euagrios 3.36; Theophanes a.m.5990, p. 141, and a.m.5994, p. 143; during the Persian War: Kyrillos of Skythopolis, *Life of Ioannes the Hesychast* 13.
107. Pseudo-Joshua the Stylite, *Chronicle* 79, 88.
108. Theophanes a.m.5995, p. 144 (tr. Mango and Scott); *phylarchos*: Nonnosos in Photios, *Bibliotheca* 3; affiliation: P. Edwell et al. in Fisher, ed., *Arabs and Empires*, 221.

Chapter 11. Chalcedonian Repression and the Eastern Axis (518–531)

1. Konstantinos VII, *Book of Ceremonies* 1.102.
2. Malalas 17.2; pseudo-Zacharias, *Chronicle* 8.1; Euagrios 4.2.
3. Theodoros Anagnostes 524; cf. Justinian to Hormisdas in *Collectio Avellana* no. 147 (518 AD).
4. Theophanes a.m.6010, p. 164; ambiguous: Severos of Antioch, *Letter* 6.1 (tr. Brooks, 2.2:360–361).
5. *ACO* 3, pp. 71–76 (no. 27); monks: pp. 67–71 (no. 26).
6. A. Papadakis, 'Byzantine Monasticism Reconsidered,' *Byzantinoslavica* 47 (1986) 34–46, here 40.
7. *ACO* 3, pp. 62–66 (no. 25); executions: Prokopios, *Secret History* 6.26; martyrs: A. Vasiliev, *Justin the First* (Cambridge, MA 1950) 104–106.
8. John of Nikiou, *Chronicle* 90.1; John of Ephesos, *Lives* 13, in *PO* 17:187.
9. Euagrios 4.4; pseudo-Zacharias, *Chronicle* 8.2.
10. Ioannes in *ACO* 3, p. 77; his letters to them and their acts at pp. 77–106.
11. Menze, *Justinian*, 75. *Libellus*: *Collectio Avellana* no. 116b.
12. Reception: Dioscurus to Hormisdas in *Collectio Avellana* no. 167.
13. Menze, *Justinian*, 76–86.
14. The legates were governed by a papal *indiculus*: *Collectio Avellana* no. 158 (p. 608 for the "concession").
15. *Collectio Avellana* no. 167.9.
16. Justin in *Collectio Avellana* no. 160.4.
17. Justin in *Collectio Avellana* no. 241–242; Menze, *Justinian*, 48–55.
18. Marcellinus Comes s.a. 526; *PDTM*, 50–51.
19. List of deposed bishops: John of Ephesos in *PDTM*, 17–18; *Chronicle to the Year 846* pp. 171–173 (ed. Brooks and Chabot); Michael the Syrian 9.13. 2,500: Rusticus (a nephew of pope Vigilius), *Against the Acephali*, in *PL* 67:1251D–1252A.
20. John of Ephesos in *PDTM*, 21–44, 46–47; idem, *Lives* 35, in *PO* 18:607–623; pseudo-Zacharias, *Chronicle* 8.5; Michael the Syrian 9.14–16. Some of these stories concern the persecution of 536, not of the 520s. Monasteries: Menze, *Justinian*, ch. 3.
21. Brock, 'Conversations,' 113–117.
22. Justin and Justinian in *Collectio Avellana* nos. 192.3, 232.3, 196, 200, and 235.
23. Hormisdas in *Collectio Avellana* no. 238.
24. E.g., Justin in *Collectio Avellana* no. 193.
25. Prokopios, *Secret History* 6.27–28; Victor of Tunnuna, *Chronicle* s.a. 523 (mistaken year); Jordanes, *Romana* 361.
26. *ACO* 3, pp. 85, 86, 103 (late 518 AD).
27. Prokopios, *Secret History* 24.17; Agathias 5.16.1–6.
28. Prokopios, *Secret History* 6.18–19, 8.2, 18.33, 18.45, 23.1, 24.29, 24.33.
29. Adoption: *Greek Anthology* 1.97. Justinian calls Justin his father in many laws.
30. General: Victor of Tunnuna, *Chronicle* s.a. 520; games: Marcellinus Comes s.a. 521.
31. Prokopios, *Secret History* 9.35–46; Malalas 17.12; Ioannes of Nikiou, *Chronicle* 90.17–19.

32. John of Ephesos, *Lives* 13, in *PO* 17, p. 189; cf. Prokopios, *Secret History* 9.
33. *CJ* 5.4.23; Prokopios, *Secret History* 9.47–54.
34. Obvious: the *quaestor* Proculus in Prokopios, *Wars* 1.11.16; Caesar: Victor of Tunnuna, *Chronicle* s.a. 525; possibly Konstantinos VII, *On the Themes* 1.12, p. 76.
35. *Greek Anthology* 1.10.
36. *Collectio Avellana* nos. 187.5, 218.1–3, 190.4.
37. Prokopios, *Buildings* 1.4.1–2; *Greek Anthology* 1.8; Sergios and Bakchos: Croke, 'Justinian' (epigram: 47–48).
38. Marcellinus Comes s.a. 525; *Book of Pontiffs* 55 (I doubt the coronation).
39. *CJ* 1.5.12.17 (527 AD).
40. Malalas 14.15; John of Ephesos in *PDTM*, 44–46; Prokopios, *Buildings* 2.7.5.
41. Malalas 17.16–17, 22; Prokopios, *Wars* 2.14.7 gives 300,000; reconstruction: Ioannes Lydos, *On the Magistracies* 3.54.
42. Theophanes a.m.6021, pp. 177–178; Malalas 18.29; *PDTM*, 72–73.
43. Palace: *Paschal Chronicle* s.a. 527; Delphax: Konstantinos VII, *Book of Ceremonies* 1.104; hippodrome: Zonaras, *Chronicle* 14.39–41 (3:151); chronicle: Marcellinus Comes s.a. 527. Date: Justinian, *Novel* 47. Justinian combines all elements of this accession (God, Justin, and the people) in *Novel* 28.4.
44. Malalas 17.9; *Paschal Chronicle* s.a. 522; Prokopios, *Wars* 1.11.28–31; regalia: Agathias 3.15.2; in general: D. Braund, *Georgia in Antiquity* (Oxford 1994) ch. 9. For the Persian garb of king Gobazes, see p. 248 above.
45. Agathias 3.5.4.
46. Menandros fr. 6.1.545–603.
47. Iberia: Prokopios, *Wars* 1.12.1–19, 2.15.6; Persarmenian raids: ibid. 1.12.20–22; 528 war in Lazica: Malalas 18.4 (the Greek version omits Belisarios, but the Slavic has him); *Paschal Chronicle* s.a. 528; Ioannes of Nikiou, *Chronicle* 90.52–53; Theophanes a.m.6020, p. 174. Notary: Petrus 27 in *PLRE* 2:870.
48. *CJ* 1.29.5; Prokopios, *Buildings* 3.1.27–29; Malalas 18.10.
49. Justinian, *Edict* 3 (535 AD); *Novels* 21, 31 (536 AD; tr. Miller and Sarris); T. Greenwood, 'A Contested Jurisdiction: Armenia in Late Antiquity,' in Sauer, ed., *Sasanian Persia*, 199–220.
50. Proklos' "Tome": *ACO* 4.2, pp. 187–195.
51. R. Thomson, 'Armenia (400–600),' in J. Shepard, ed., *The Cambridge History of the Byzantine Empire* (Cambridge 2008) 156–171; Stopka, *Armenia*, 54–76; and W. Baum and D. Winkler, *The Church of the East* (London 2003).
52. Z. Rubin, 'The Reforms of Khusro Anushirwan,' in A. Cameron, ed., *The Byzantine and Early Islamic Near East* (Princeton 1995) 3:227–297; Payne, *State of Mixture*, 145.
53. Pourshariati, *Decline*, is unmatched in prosopographical attention.
54. Prokopios, *Wars* 1.17.46–48; Flavios: R. Hoyland, 'Late Roman Provincia Arabia, Monophysite Monks and Arab Tribes,' *Semitica et Classica* 2 (2009) 117–139, here 119–120.
55. Against tribal labels: Fisher, *Between Empires*; against both tribal and dynastic labels: R. Hoyland, 'Insider and Outsider Sources: Historiographical Reflections on Late Antique Arabia,' in Dijkstra and Fisher, eds., *Inside and Out*, 267–280, here

267–273. Lakhmid is attested epigraphically for a client king of the shah in ca. 300: H. Humbach and P. Skjaervø, *The Sassanian Inscription of Paikuli* (Wiesbaden 1983) 92.

56. Kyrillos of Skythopolis, *Life of Euthymios* 10, 47.
57. Prokopios, *Secret History* 11.25.
58. Malalas 18.35; *Paschal Chronicle* s.a. 530 ("fear"); pseudo-Zacharias, *Chronicle* 9.8; tax relief: Kyrillos of Skythopolis, *Life of Sabas* 70–72; Prokopios, *Secret History* 11.24–30 ("destitute"). Repressive laws: *CJ* 1.5.12–13, 17–19, 21.
59. Pseudo-Joshua the Stylite, *Chronicle* 57.
60. For these terms, see John of Ephesos, *EH III* 6.3–4.
61. Pseudo-Zacharias, *Chronicle* 8.3; *Martyrdom of Arethas* 25; captives: Prokopios, *Wars* 1.17.44; Nonnosos in Photios, *Bibliotheca* 3.
62. C. Robin, 'The Peoples beyond the Arabian Frontier in Late Antiquity,' in Dijkstra and Fisher, eds., *Inside and Out*, 33–79; and idem, 'Himyar, Aksum, and Arabia Deserta in Late Antiquity,' in Fisher, ed., *Arabs and Empires*, 127–171.
63. G. Bowersock, *The Throne of Adulis: Red Sea Wars on the Eve of Islam* (Oxford 2013); martyrs: Beaucamp et al., eds., *Juifs et chrétiens*. Christian lobbying against Yusuf: e.g., pseudo-Zacharias, *Chronicle* 8.3g; Justin's intervention: *Martyrdom of Arethas* 27–29 (Greek text), doubted by C. Robin, 'Arabia and Ethiopia,' in S. Johnson, ed., *The Oxford Handbook of Late Antiquity* (Oxford 2012) 247–332, here 283; and J. Beaucamp, 'Le rôle de Byzance en Mer Rouge sous le règne de Justin: Mythe ou réalité?' in eadem et al., eds., *Juifs et chrétiens*, 197–218. Himyar tributary: Prokopios, *Wars* 1.20.8.
64. Greatrex and Lieu, *Frontier*, 82–87; al-Mundhir's raids: pseudo-Zacharias, *Chronicle* 8.5 (human sacrifice); Theophanes a.m.6021, p. 178; Prokopios, *Wars* 2.28.13.
65. Malalas 18.44.
66. Prokopios, *Wars* 1.13–14; Malalas 18.50.
67. Malalas 18.54; Theophanes a.m.6021, pp. 178–179; also pseudo-Zacharias, *Chronicle* 9.8.
68. Prokopios, *Wars* 1.15–18; Malalas 18.60–61.
69. Pseudo-Zacharias, *Chronicle* 9.6, 9.17; Prokopios, *Wars* 3.9.25; Malalas 18.61.
70. Prokopios, *Wars* 1.20.9–13, probably the same embassy in Malalas 18.56; for Prokopios' Qays, see Nonnosos in Photios, *Bibliotheca* 3.
71. *Greek Anthology* 4.4.28–30.

Chapter 12. The Sleepless Emperor (527–540)

1. *CJ* 7.37.3.4.
2. Justinian, *Novel* 31 (tr. Miller and Sarris).
3. *Const. Deo auctore* pref. 10.
4. *Const. Cordi* 4 (confirming the second *Codex*): *varia rerum natura*; Sarris, 'Introduction,' 13.
5. *Const. Summa* 2 (confirming the first *Codex*); *Const. Haec* 3 (authorizing its making).
6. *Const. Summa* 1; *Const. Cordi* pref. Prior calls for clarity: *CJ* 5.27.9, 7.47.1.

7. But cf. *Const. Summa* pref. (*Codex*); *Const. Imperatoriam maiestatem* (*Institutes*).
8. *Const. Deo auctore* pref. (tr. Watson ed., mod.).
9. *Const. Imperatoriam maiestatem* (*Institutes*).
10. *Const. Omnem* 2–9 (*Digest*).
11. B. Stolte, 'Legal Thought,' in Kaldellis and Siniossoglou, eds., *Intellectual History*. 141–167.
12. E.g., conflicts of interest: *CJ* 1.51.14; procedures: 2.55.4–5, 4.20; abuses: 1.53.1, 12.63.2.
13. E.g., *CJ* 1.5.18.12, 2.2.4, 12.63.2.2.
14. *CJ* 3.1.13, 9.44.3.
15. *CJ* 1.2.25.
16. *CJ* 1.4.25, 1.4.34, 3.43.1.3; camels: Malalas 18.47.
17. Malalas 18.18; Theophanes a.m.6021, p. 177; Prokopios, *Secret History* 11.34–36, 16.18–28, 20.9; earthquakes: *Novels* 77, 141; cf. *Institutes* 4.18.4. Science: Agathias 2.15.9–13; 5.6–5.8.
18. Justinian, *Novels* 14, 51, following up on *CJ* 1.4.33, 5.4.29, 6.4.4.2 (freeing prostituted slaves). Theodora's role: Malalas 18.24.
19. Cf. Prokopios, *Buildings* 1.9.2–3 with *Secret History* 17.5–6; Ioannes of Nikiou, *Chronicle* 93.3.
20. Manicheans: *CJ* 1.5, 1.11.10. Persia: Zacharias, *Seven Anathemas against the Manichaeans*, ed. M. Richard, *Iohannis Caesariensis opera quae supersunt* (Turnhout 1977) xxxiii–xxxix; pamphlet: Zacharias, *Against the Manichaeans*, in A. Demetrakopoulos, *Ἐκκλησιαστικὴ Βιβλιοθήκη* (Leipzig 1866) 1:1–18.
21. *CJ* 1.11.10; cf. 1.5.16. "Tolerant": *CJ* 1.5.12 pref.
22. John of Ephesos in *PDTM*, 77–78; *Lives* 47, in *PO* 18:681; *EH III* 2.44–45, 3.3.36–37; Michael the Syrian 9.24 (they preached Chalcedon, which was still better than paganism); Menze, *Justinian*, 256–265. For logistics, see F. Trombley, 'Paganism in the Greek World at the End of Antiquity,' *Harvard Theological Review* 78 (1985) 327–352, here 329–334; surviving paganism: Bell, *Social Conflict*, 238–246, 315.
23. Purge of 529: Malalas 18.42; Theophanes a.m.6022, p. 180 (better because probably based on the unabridged Malalas); purge of 545/6: John of Ephesos in *PDTM*, 76–77; Phokas: Kaldellis, 'Hagia Sophia.'
24. *Souda* s.v.; Delphic: Justinian, *Novel* 3 pref.; hidden Plato: *Novel* 74.4 pref.; for more, see G. Lanata, *Legislazione e natura nelle Novelle giustinianee* (Naples 1984); faked orthodoxy: *CJ* 1.5.16.4, 1.5.18.5; cf. 1.11.6.
25. Barsanouphios, *Letters* 774–775.
26. General law: *CJ* 1.11.10.2 (tr. Miller and Sarris); Athens: Malalas 18.47; S. Corcoran, 'Anastasius, Justinian, and the Pagans,' *JLA* 2 (2009) 183–208.
27. Agathias 2.30–31, here 2.30.3–4.
28. A. Frantz, *The Athenian Agora XXIV: Late Antiquity A.D. 267–700* (Princeton 1988) 44–47, 88–89; T. Shear, 'The Athenian Agora: Excavations of 1971,' *Hesperia* 42 (1973) 121–179, here 156–164.
29. C. Moss, 'Jacob of Sarugh's Homilies on the Spectacles of the Theater,' *Le Muséon* 48 (1935) 87–112, here 109; I quote the paraphrase by D. Potter, *Theodora: Actress, Empress, Saint* (Oxford 2015) 45. Dice playing: *Miracles of Artemios* 18.

30. *Akta dia Kalopodion*: Theophanes a.m.6024, pp. 181–186 (tr. Mango and Scott). Nika: *Paschal Chronicle* s.a. 531; Malalas 18.71; Prokopios, *Wars* 1.24.
31. Ioannes Lydos, *On the Magistracies* 3.70; pseudo-Zacharias, *Chronicle* 9.14; corruption: Prokopios, *Wars* 1.24.11–16.
32. Prokopios, *Secret History* 14.8.
33. Strategios, *Capture of Jerusalem* 3.8 (ed. Garitte); *Patria of Constantinople* 3.201; Michael Glykas, *Annals*, p. 496.
34. Ioannes Lydos, *On the Magistracies* 3.70 (tr. Bandy).
35. *Greek Anthology* 16.44; Smith, *Greek Epigram*, 115–117.
36. Dates: Kedrenos, *Historical Compendium*, 1:651; Continuation of Marcellinus Comes s.a. 537; Romanos Melodos, *Canticum* 54, str. 22.5–6 (p. 470 Trypanis) says that work began "the next day." Cost: Ioannes Lydos, *On the Magistracies* 3.76; estimate: E. Stein, *Histoire du Bas-Empire* (Paris 1949) 2:459–460. A legendary text, the *Narrative about the Construction of Hagia Sophia* 25, claims that the church cost 320,000 lbs of gold, which is impossible. Architects: combine Kaldellis, 'Hagia Sophia,' with N. Schibille, *Hagia Sophia and the Byzantine Aesthetic Experience* (Farnham, UK 2014); also the extraordinary study by B. Pentcheva, *Hagia Sophia: Sound, Space, and Spirit in Byzantium* (University Park, PA 2017); capacity: ibid. 3. Staff: Justinian, *Novel* 3.1.
37. Prokopios, *Buildings* 1.1.29, 1.1.46, 1.1.54; cf. Homer, *Iliad* 8.19, a key verse for Platonists.
38. Romanos Melodos, *Kontakion* 54, str. 17–19, 21; cf. 31, str. 16; 33, str. 16.
39. Prokopios, *Wars* 1.22; Agathias, *History* 2.31.4; Christians: E. Nechaeva, 'Seven Hellenes and One Christian in the Endless Peace Treaty of 532,' *Studies in Late Antiquity* 1 (2017) 359–380.
40. J. Howard-Johnston, 'The India Trade in Late Antiquity,' in Sauer, ed., *Sasanian Persia*, 284–304, here 293.
41. Justinian, *Novel* 30.11.2; Ioannes Lydos, *On the Magistracies* 3.55.
42. Prokopios, *Wars* 3.8.3–4; cf. Justinian in *CJ* 1.27.1.4; persecutions: Victor of Vita, *History of the Vandal Persecution*.
43. Prokopios, *Wars* 3.10.18–21; Victor of Tunnuna, *Chronicle* s.a. 534.
44. Prokopios, *Wars* 3.9.1–5; Moors: Y. Modèran, *Les Maures et l'Afrique romaine* (Rome 2003); E. Fentress and A. Wilson, 'The Saharan Berber Diaspora and the Southern Frontiers of Byzantine North Africa,' in S. Stevens and J. Conant, eds., *North Africa under Byzantium and Early Islam* (Washington, D.C. 2016) 41–63.
45. Pseudo-Zacharias, *Chronicle* 9.17; Prokopios, *Wars* 4.5.8; merchants: ibid. 3.20.5–6.
46. Brubaker and Haldon, *History*, 493–495; in general: A. Harris, *Byzantium*; E. Campbell, *Continental and Mediterranean Imports to Atlantic Britain and Ireland, AD 400–800* (York 2007).
47. Justinian to Gelimer: Prokopios, *Wars* 3.9.10–13; cynicism: C. Pazdernik, 'Procopius and Thucydides on the Labors of War,' *Transactions of the American Philological Association* 130 (2000) 149–187; "generals": Prokopios, *Wars* 3.10.4; Antonina: *Secret History*, passim.
48. John of Ephesos in pseudo-Dionysios of Tel-Mahre, *Chronicle*, p. 29; pseudo-Zacharias, *Chronicle* 8.5.

49. John of Ephesos, *Lives* 24, in *PO* 18:515–519; Elias, *Life of Yuhannan of Tella* 59, tr. J. Ghanem, *The Biography of John of Tella (d. A.D. 537) by Elias* (PhD dissertation, University of Wisconsin 1970) 83. Cf. Severos, *Select Letters* 1.59 (tr. Brooks, 2.1:178–179); see Menze, *Justinian*, 175–193.
50. Chalcedonian: *ACO* 4.2, pp. 169–184; anti-Chalcedonian: Brock, 'Conversations'; also pseudo-Zacharias, *Chronicle* 9.15.
51. *ACO* 4.2, p. 173; unless the reference by Severos of Antioch is earlier: *Letter to Ioannes the Hegoumenos*, in F. Diekamp, *Doctrina patrum de Incarnatione Verbi* (Münster 1907) 309.
52. Prokopios, *Wars* 5.3.6–8. Cf. *Secret History* 18.29.
53. Prokopios, *Wars* 3.11.1–21.
54. Prokopios, *Wars* 3.21.6.
55. Prokopios, *Wars* 4.7.20–21.
56. Prokopios, *Wars* 4.9.1–16.
57. Justinian in *CJ* 1.27.1.8 (civilian), 1.27.2 (military). Iustiniana: *Novel* 37; Prokopios, *Buildings* 6.5.8–11. Cost: Hendy, *Studies*, 165–166.
58. *Institutes* pref.; *Const. Tanta* pref. (*Digest*); cf. *CJ* 1.4.34; *Novel* 36 pref.
59. Prokopios, *Wars* 4.10–13; D. Pringle, *The Defence of Byzantine Africa from Justinian to the Arab Conquest* (Oxford 1981).
60. Prokopios, *Wars* 5.3–5; murder: *Secret History* 16.1–5, and Cassiodorus, *Variae* 10.20–21.
61. Prokopios, *Wars* 4.4.10–12, 4.5.1, 4.7.17, 4.9.1, and esp. 4.14.17–18; cf. 2.22.4.
62. Assessment: Prokopios, *Wars* 4.8.25; *Secret History* 18.10; Vandal lands: *Wars* 3.5.14, 4.14.8–10; *Secret History* 18.11; law: Justinian, *Novel* 36 (1 January 535).
63. *Collectio Avellana* no. 85; pope Agapetus to the African bishops: ibid. no. 87; Agapetus to Justinian: ibid. no. 88 (thanking him).
64. Prokopios, *Wars* 4.14.11–21; Justinian, *Novel* 37 (1 August 535). I am not convinced of an initially flexible and tolerant approach on Justinian's part. Prior law: *CJ* 1.5.12.17 (527 AD).
65. Prokopios, *Wars* 4.15.2–4, 4.16.3.
66. Justinian, *Novel* 11 (14 April 535); Prokopios, *Buildings* 4.1.19–27. Agapetus: *Collectio Avellana* no. 88.12–13. In 545, Justinian confirmed papal authority over the new archbishop: *Novel* 131.3.
67. Sarantis, *Justinian's Balkan Wars*, 153.
68. Justinian, *Novel* 30.11.2 (March 536).
69. Severos' declination in 532: pseudo-Zacharias, *Chronicle* 9.16; hiding: Severos, *Select Letters* 5.12 (tr. Brooks, 2.2:339, 341), 5.15 ("loneliness": 2.2:358–359).
70. Theodora: pseudo-Zacharias, *Chronicle* 9.19–20; Euagrios 4.10; condemned: e.g., Kyrillos of Skythopolis, *Life of Sabas* 71; Novatai: John of Ephesos, *EH III* 4.6–9; both sides: Prokopios, *Secret History* 10.15, 13.19, 14.8, 27.13; cf. Euagrios 4.10; "no peace": Severos in *PO* 2:302–303 = John of Ephesos, *Lives* 48, in *PO* 18:687.
71. Pseudo-Zacharias, *Chronicle* 9.19; *Book of Pontiffs* 59.
72. Menas: *ACO* 3, p. 181; Justinian, *Novel* 42. Hormisdas: John of Ephesos, *Lives* 48, in *PO* 18:686.

73. Pseudo-Zacharias, *Chronicle* 10.1.
74. Menze, *Justinian*, 160–163, has great stories.
75. Croke, 'Justinian,' 32, 39–40.
76. John of Ephesos, *Lives* 25, in *PO* 18:534.
77. Justinian, *Novel* 109 (541 AD).
78. Severos, *Select Letters* 1.63 (tr. Brooks, 2.1:197–199, mod.).
79. *Anonymous Life of Severos* 78.
80. Omen: Prokopios, *Wars* 4.14.5–6; wine: John of Ephesos in *PDTM*, 70–71; also Cassiodorus, *Variae* 12.25; Ioannes Lydos, *On Omens* 9c.
81. Prokopios, *Wars* 5.14.14.
82. Prokopios, *Wars* 6.29.17–41.
83. Prokopios, *Wars* 7.1.4–22.
84. Prokopios, *Secret History* 4.13; *bucellarii*: Hickey, *Wine*, 111–112; Liebeschuetz, *Barbarians*, 43–47; abuses: P. Sarris, *Economy and Society in the Age of Justinian* (Cambridge 2006) 162–175.
85. Prokopios, *Wars* 7.1.28–33.
86. Prokopios, *Wars* 2.3.
87. Nocturnal: Prokopios, *Secret History* 12.20–27, 13.28, 15.11; *Buildings* 1.7.8–9; throngs: *Secret History* 30.27–30; Theodora: 15.6–9; Scripture: 12.20, 18.29, *Wars* 7.32.9.
88. Respectively: Justinian, *Novels* 8 pref. (cf. 37 pref.); 30.11.2; *Edict* 13 pref. (cf. *Novel* 64.2); and 15 ep., among many similar statements.
89. Didyma inscription: Feissel, *Documents*, 266.
90. Prokopios, *Secret History* 12.20–22.
91. T. Honoré, *Tribonian* (Ithaca, NY 1978) 16; Ioustinianopoleis: Feissel, *Documents*, 318–321; name: Prokopios, *Secret History* 11.2.
92. Justinian, *Novel* 47.
93. Justinian, *Novel* 105; Ioannes Lydos, *On the Magistracies* 2.8; see M. Kruse, *The Politics of Roman Memory from the Fall of the Western Empire to the Age of Justinian* (Philadelphia 2019) ch. 4.
94. Justinian, *Novel* 7.1 (535 AD).
95. S. Corcoran, 'Roman Law and the Two Languages in Justinian's Empire,' *Bulletin of the Institute of Classical Studies* 60 (2017) 96–116, here 114–115. Prefecture: Kelly, *Ruling*, 32–36.
96. Brown, *Gentlemen*, 50–51.
97. Sarris, 'Introduction,' 26; Lenski, 'Slavery,' 463–465.
98. Justinian, *Novel* 8 pref. (tr. Miller and Sarris).
99. Justinian, *Novel* 8 pref. (tr. Miller and Sarris); the reform *Novels* are: 24 (Pisidia), 25 (Lykaonia), 26 (Thrace), 27 (Isauria), 28 (Helenopontos), 29 (Paphlagonia), 30 (Cappadocia), 31 and 21 (Armenia, discussed above), 102 (Arabia), 103 (Palestine), 104 = 75 (Sicily), *Edict* 4 (Phoenice Libanensis), and *Edict* 13 (Egypt), preceded by *CJ* 1.27 (North Africa). Military and civilian commands were not amalgamated everywhere. Appeals: *CJ* 7.63.5; *Novels* 23, 20, and 50 (five provinces).
100. Justinian, *Novels* 8.10.2, 30.11.2.

101. Ioannes Lydos, *On the Magistracies* 3.66; Kelly, *Ruling*, 71–81.
102. Justinian, *Novel* 24.1.
103. Justinian, *Novel* 17; oath: *Novel* 8 app.; Prokopios, *Secret History* 21.5–25.
104. Justinian, *Novel* 30; *Edict* 13.
105. Justinian, *Novel* 64.
106. Feissel, *Documents*, 223–250 (the later names can be interpreted differently).
107. R. McConnell, *Getting Rich in Late Antique Egypt* (Ann Arbor, MI 2017); also Hickey, *Wine*; Apion estate: Bransbourg, 'Capital.'
108. Bransbourg, 'Capital,' 405.
109. Marcian, *Novel* 1 pref. (tr. Pharr, mod.).
110. Justinian, *Novel* 80; Prokopios, *Secret History* 20.9–14; Ioannes Lydos, *On the Magistracies* 3.70 (misdated); profiling: Laniado, *Ethnos*, 173–254; hostel: Prokopios, *Buildings* 1.11.27. Consumption figures: P. Magdalino and N. Necipoğlu, eds., *Trade in Byzantium* (Istanbul 2016) 102 (J. Koder on salt), 108 (C. Morrisson on wood).
111. Justinian, *Novel* 13; Prokopios, *Secret History* 20.9–14, 11.37, 16.19–20, 18.33; deacon: *Anonymous Sayings of the Desert Fathers* N.640 (Wortley).
112. Justinian, *Novel* 80.5.
113. Prokopios, *Buildings*, book 1; Holy Apostles dedication: Malalas 18.109.
114. Prokopios, *Buildings* 1.10.11–20; Malalas 18.85.
115. Prokopios, *Buildings* 1.11.12–15; Malalas 18.17, 18.91.
116. S. Cuomo, *Technology and Culture in Greek and Roman Antiquity* (Cambridge 2007) 139–141, 163; Theodoros: Prokopios, *Wars* 2.13.26.
117. Prokopios, *Buildings* 5.6; Kyrillos of Skythopolis, *Life of Sabas* 72–73; Y. Tsafrir, 'Procopius and the New Church in Jerusalem,' *Antiquité tardive* 8 (2000) 149–164. Dome of the Rock: L. Nees, *Perspectives on Early Islamic Art in Jerusalem* (Leiden 2016) 108.
118. Prokopios, *Buildings* 1.8.5.
119. Prokopios, *Buildings* 5.1.4–6; *Greek Anthology* 1.91, 1.95. For a new proposal, see N. Karydis, 'The Evolution of the Church of St. John at Ephesos during the Early Byzantine Period,' *Jahreshefte des österreichischen archäologischen Institutes in Wien* 84 (2015) 97–128.
120. I. Ševčenko, 'The Early Period of the Sinai Monastery in the Light of its Inscriptions,' *DOP* 20 (1966) 255–264; Prokopios, *Buildings* 5.8, with P. Mayerson, 'Procopius or Eutychius on the Construction of the Monastery at Mount Sinai,' *Bulletin of the American Schools of Oriental Research* 230 (1978) 33–38.
121. Feissel, 'Les édifices,' 93.
122. Prokopios, *Buildings* 6.1.4.

Chapter 13. "Death Has Entered Our Gates" (540–565)

1. Prokopios, *Secret History* 18.30. I use "decimate" in its original sense.
2. Prokopios, *Secret History* 11.12, 18.28–29; *Wars* 2.1.12, 2.3.47, 2.10.16.

3. Prokopios, *Wars* 2.5–14; *Secret History* 2.25; artwork: Ioannes Lydos, *On the Magistracies* 3.54; John of Ephesos in *PDTM*, 69, 91; 570s: John of Ephesos, *EH III* 6.19. The mosaic was described by the poet al-Buhturi. Better Antioch: De Giorgi and Asa Eger, *Antioch*, 208.
4. Prokopios, *Secret History* 24.12–14; installations: Gândilă, 'Heavy Money,' 367 n. 24. Coin finds suggest that the reform was limited to Palestine, Prokopios' home province: P. Casey, 'Justinian, the *limitanei*, and Arab-Byzantine Relations in the 6th C.,' *JRA* 6 (1996) 214–222; Sivan, *Palestine*, 88–89.
5. Prokopios, *Wars* 2.15–19; access: 2.15.27, 2.28.23, 8.7.12, and Agathias 2.18.7; renamed: Justinian, *Novel* 28.
6. Prokopios, *Wars* 1.25; *Secret History* 2.1–16, 17.38–45; Malalas 18.89.
7. Prokopios, *Secret History* 3.4, 3.12
8. Prokopios, *Wars* 2.22, esp. 2.22.9 (movement), 2.22.23 (doctors). I thank Merle Eisenberg for advice on this section.
9. M. Keller et al., 'Ancient *Yersinia pestis* genomes,' *Proceedings of the National Academy of Sciences of the Unites States of America* 116 (June 18, 2019) 12363–12372.
10. Prokopios, *Wars* 2.23.
11. Malalas 18.92.
12. Euagrios 4.29, 6.23; *Life of Symeon the Stylite the Younger* 233.
13. John of Ephesos in *PDTM*, 79–109 (tr. Witakowski); "Death": cf. Jeremiah 9.21.
14. Barsanouphios, *Letter* 569.
15. Cf. J. Durliat, 'La peste du VIe siècle,' in J. Lefort and C. Morrisson, eds., *Hommes et richesses dans l'empire byzantin* (Paris 1989) 1:107–119, with Harper, *Fate*, esp. 226, 232–234, 244, 343 n. 75; against the maximalist position: J. Haldon et al., 'Plagues, Climate Change, and the End of an Empire,' *History Compass* 16 (2018), part 3; L. Mordechai and M. Eisenberg, 'Rejecting Catastrophe: The Case of the Justinianic Plague,' *Past and Present* 244 (2019) 3–50.
16. Justinian, *Edict* 7 (tr. Miller and Sarris); cf. *Edict* 9.
17. Justinian, *Novel* 122; cf. Prokopios, *Secret History* 20.1–5, 25.13, 26.19, 26.36. Egyptian wage data: Hickey, *Wine*, 88.
18. Church: Justinian, *Novel* 120; taxation: *Novel* 128 (esp. 7–8); 535 law: *Novel* 17.14.
19. Prokopios, *Secret History* 23.20–21.
20. Bransbourg, 'Capital,' 320–321, 325, 364, esp. 399–400; at 333–334 he rejects a one-time "plague discount" in 544, but it remains a possibility. John of Ephesos in Michael the Syrian 9.28 (tr. Moosa, p. 351).
21. Justinian, *Novels* 117, 157, 125, 119, 124.
22. Prokopios, *Secret History* 22.17–19. Farmers: *Life of Nikolaos of Sion* 52.
23. M. McCormick, 'Tracking Mass Death during the Fall of Rome's Empire,' *JRA* 29 (2016) 1004–1046; but see L. Mordechai et al., 'The Justinianic Plague: An Inconsequential Pandemic?' *Proceedings of the National Academy of Sciences of the Unites States of America* 116 (December 17, 2019) 25546–25554. Inscriptions: M. Meier, 'The "Justinianic Plague": An "Inconsequential Pandemic"? A Reply,' *Medizinhistorisches Journal* 55 (2020) 172–199, here 182.

24. Prokopios, *Secret History* 22.38; cf. P. Sarris, 'Bubonic Plague in Byzantium: The Evidence of Non-Literary Sources,' in L. Little, ed., *Plague and the End of Antiquity* (Cambridge 2007) 119–132, here 127–128, with Hendy, *Studies*, 492–493.
25. Prokopios, *Wars* 2.24.8–12.
26. Prokopios, *Buildings* 1.2.1–12; cf. Homer, *Iliad* 22.26–31; date: Malalas 18.94.
27. Prokopios, *Secret History* 4.1–37; Continuation of Marcellinus Comes s.a. 545.3.
28. Prokopios, *Wars* 2.24–28, 8.14.35–37; Jesus' letter: 2.12; Continuation of Marcellinus Comes s.a. 546.4; limited: Agathias 2.18.3.
29. Prokopios, *Wars* 8.15.1–7, 14–18; cf. Menandros fr. 20.2.17–21. *Aerikon*: Prokopios, *Secret History* 21.1–2.
30. Prokopios, *Wars* 2.28.12–14; Michael the Syrian 9.33; *Life of Simeon the Stylite the Younger* 186–187. Armistice: Agathias 4.30.7–10.
31. Konstantinos VII, *Book of Ceremonies* 1.98–99; Prokopios, *Wars* 8.15.20.
32. Prokopios, *Secret History* 25.13–16; *Wars* 8.17.1–8; reconstruction: C. Zuckerman, 'Silk "Made in Byzantium": A Study of Economic Policies of Emperor Justinian,' *TM* 17 (2013) 323–350, refuting, at 343, the suggestion that silk was produced in fifth-century Syria. Canes: Theophanes of Byzantium in Photios, *Bibliotheca* 64.26a–b.
33. Paulos Silentiarios, *Ekphrasis of Hagia Sophia* 755–805.
34. Prokopios, *Wars* 4.28.52; Theodora: *Secret History* 5.28–33; plague: Corippus, *Iohannis* 3.343–393.
35. Thrace: Prokopios, *Wars* 7.10.1–4; nothing: *Secret History* 5.1–2.
36. Continuation of Marcellinus Comes s.a. 543.2.
37. Greece: Prokopios, *Wars* 8.22.17–32; Sardinia and Corsica: 8.24.31–36; overtures: 7.21.18–20, 7.37.6–7, 8.24.4.
38. Prokopios, *Secret History* 5.7–15.
39. Prokopios, *Wars* 7.39.
40. Prokopios, *Wars* 8.26.5–17; Agathias 2.4.10.
41. Malalas 18.140.
42. Agathias 1.12.4, 1.16.2; Prokopios, *Wars* 6.13.16.
43. Sacrifices: Prokopios, *Wars* 6.25.9–10; famines in 538/9: 6.20.15–33; abuses: 7.9.1–4; general ruin: *Secret History* 18.13–14. Archaeologically the damage of this period is hard to distinguish from that of the subsequent Lombard invasion. For a survey, see Christie, *From Constantine*, esp. 458–460. Poorer: Wickham, *Framing*, 649, 654.
44. Justinian, *Novels: Appendix* 7 (tr. Miller and Sarris).
45. 528 (Huns): Malalas 18.21; Theophanes a.m.6031, pp. 217–218 (misdated). 529 (Huns and Goths?): Malalas 18.46; Theophanes a.m.6032 (misdated). 530 (Bulgars): Marcellinus Comes s.a. 530. 531–534 (Sklavenoi and Antai): Prokopios, *Wars* 7.14.1–6. 534/5 (Bulgars): Marcellinus Comes s.a. 534. *Questura*: Justinian, *Novels* 41, 50. The standard study is now Sarantis, *Justinian's Balkan Wars*; 161–198 for fortifications, along with Prokopios, *Buildings*, book 4; amphorae: Brubaker and Haldon, *History*, 496.
46. Prokopios, *Wars* 2.4.4–11, 7.13.15–16; *Buildings* 4.10.9; eyewitness: John of Ephesos in pseudo-Dionysios of Tel-Mahre, *Chronicle*, p. 89.

47. Prokopios, *Wars* 6.14, 7.33.13; Marcellinus Comes s.a. 512.11. Sarantis, *Justinian's Balkan Wars*, is fundamental.
48. Prokopios, *Wars* 7.14.22–30.
49. Antai and Sklavenoi: Prokopios, *Wars* 7.14.31–34 (545 AD); Jordanes, *Getica* 5.34–35; for the rest, see the next paragraph. Slavic origins: P. Heather, *Empires and Barbarians: Migration, Development and the Birth of Europe* (London 2009) ch. 8.
50. Prokopios, *Wars* 7.38.20. Raid of 545: 7.13.24–25; of 548: 7.29.1–3; of 549/50: 7.38; of 550: 7.40.1–7; of 551: 7.40.31–45; of 552: 8.25.1–6, 8.25.10–14.
51. Heruls' defection: Prokopios, *Wars* 6.15, 7.34.43; Gepids ferry raiders: 8.18.13–18; Kutrigur settlers: 8.19.6–7; raiders of 551: 8.21.18–22; Sklavenoi raiders of 552: 8.25.1–6 (ferried by Gepids).
52. Prokopios, *Wars* 8.27; Jordanes, *Romana* 52; Paul the Deacon, *History of the Lombards* 1.23.
53. Prokopios, *Secret History* 8.5–6, 11.5–11, 19.13–17, 21.26; *Wars* 8.5.16–17, 8.18.19.
54. Jordanes, *Getica* 58.303 (it is unlikely that Liberius led the expedition); Isidore of Seville, *History of the Kings of the Goths* 47; Gregory of Tours, *History of the Franks* 4.8; J. Fossella, '"Waiting only for a pretext": A New Chronology for the Sixth-Century Byzantine Invasion of Spain,' *Éstudios bizantinos* 1 (2013) 30–38. *Magister militum*: *CIL* 2:3,420.
55. O. Olesti Vila, R. Andreu Expósito, and J. Wood, 'New Perspectives on Byzantine Spain: the *Discriptio Hispaniae*,' *Journal of Ancient History* 6 (2018) 278–308; and Wood, 'Spain,' pushing back against minimalist readings.
56. Justinian, *Novel* 30.11.2.
57. Agathias 5.13.7; calculations: Haldon, *Warfare*, 100; W. Treadgold, *Byzantium and Its Army* (Stanford, CA 1995) 46–49, 59–64; but see now Kaldellis and Kruse, *Field Armies*.
58. Kaldellis, 'Classicism.'
59. Prokopios, *Wars* 7.11.11–16; critique: Agathias 5.13.8.
60. Brock, 'Conversations,' 108.
61. Justinian to Hormisdas in *Collectio Avellana* nos. 187, 191 (Vitalianus' role: p. 648), and 188; the formula: Menze, *Justinian*, 171–173; J. McGuckin, 'The "Theopaschite Confession",' *Journal of Ecclesiastical History* 35 (1984) 239–255.
62. Conference: *ACO* 4.2, p. 183,8; edict: *CJ* 1.1.6.5–6 (but 1.1.7.4, 1.1.7.7 is qualified: "incapable of suffering as a deity"); John II: *CJ* 1.1.8 (note 31–33 against the Sleepless Monks) and *Collectio Avellana* no. 84; Agapetus: *Collectio Avellana* no. 91.3 (esp. p. 343).
63. Menze, *Justinian*, 174.
64. Albertella et al., *Drei dogmatische Schriften*, 6–78, distorting the Crucified addition.
65. Edict: Schwartz, 'Vigiliusbriefe.' For various accounts of its intention, see Justinian, *Letter* to the First Session of the Council of Constantinople II, in *ACO* 4.1, p. 10, pleading the problem of Nestorianism; Liberatus, *Breviarium* 24 (a distorted view of the influence of Theodoros Askidas, bishop of Kaisareia in Cappadocia); a "concession" to Monophysites: Leontios of Byzantion, *De sectis* 6.6, in *PG* 86.1:1238D.
66. John of Ephesos, *Lives* 49, in *PO* 18:691–695, and 50, in *PO* 19:156–158.
67. John of Ephesos, *Lives* 25, in *PO* 18:538.

68. Facundus of Hermiane, *In Defense of the Three Chapters* 4.4.2–9.
69. Fulgentius Ferrandus of Carthage, *Letter* 6.3, in *PL* 67:921–928.
70. Justinian, *Letter on the Three Chapters*, possibly of 549/50, ed. in Albertella et al., *Drei dogmatische Schriften*, 82–126.
71. Wall: Vigilius, *Dum in Sanctae Euphemiae*, in Schwartz, 'Vigiliusbriefe,' 5 (tr. Price); heavy: Theophanes a.m.6039, p. 225.
72. *ACO* 4.1, pp. 8–14.
73. Vigilius' *Constitutum* in *Collectio Avellana* no. 83.305–306 (p. 318).
74. Victor of Tunnuna, *Chronicle* s.a. 555 ff.; opposition collapses: R. Price, *The Acts of the Council of Constantinople of 553* (Liverpool 2009) 1:31–32; J. Conant, *Staying Roman: Conquest and Identity in Africa and the Mediterranean, 439–700* (Cambridge 2012) 316–330; Italy: C. Sotinel, 'The Three Chapters and the Transformations of Italy,' in C. Chazelle and C. Cubitt, eds., *The Crisis of the* Oikoumene: *The Three Chapters and the Failed Quest for Unity* (Turnhout 2007) 84–120. Narses: Pelagius, *Letter* 60.
75. Prokopios, *Wars* 8.3.12–21, 8.9.10–30; castration: Justinian, *Novel* 142 (558 AD).
76. Prokopios, *Wars* 1.15.19–25; "human beings": *Buildings* 3.6.12; Justinian, *Novels* 1 pref., 28 pref.; 558: Agathias 5.1–2 (the general Theodoros).
77. Agathias 2.15–16; Malalas 18.112; John of Ephesos in *PDTM*, 132–136.
78. Malalas 18.128, 18.143; John of Ephesos in *PDTM*, 131–132; *Paschal Chronicle* s.a. 563; dome: Agathias 5.9.
79. Agathias 5.10; Malalas 18.127.
80. Malalas 18.119, 135, 138, 150, 151; Theophanes a.m.6053, pp. 235–236; a.m.6055, p. 237; a.m.6055, p. 239; John of Ephesos in *PDTM*, 127–128; wills: Justinian, *Novel* 129.
81. Agathias 5.14.1–2; Menandros fr. 5.1.16–26.
82. Agathias 5.11–25; Theophanes a.m.6051, pp. 233–234; Menandros fr. 2; Sykai: Victor of Tunnuna, *Chronicle* s.a. 560. Return: Konstantinos VII, *Three Treatises on Imperial Military Expeditions*, Treatise C (Haldon). Hun raid in 562: Theophanes a.m.6054, p. 236.
83. Theophanes a.m.6053, pp. 234–235; and a.m.6055, pp. 237–239; Malalas 18.141; Paulos Silentiarios, *Ekphrasis of Hagia Sophia* 24–39. Justin II, *Novel* 148 pref.; Corippus, *In Praise of Justin II* 2.401.
84. Menandros fr. 6, here 6.1.30–32.
85. Theophanes a.m.6056, p. 240.
86. Theophanes a.m.6057, p. 240.
87. Euagrios 4.39; John of Ephesos in *PDTM*, 144–145; Theophanes a.m.6033, p. 241; Eustratios the Presbyter, *Life of Patriarch Eutychios*, pp. 31 ff. (Laga).
88. Corippus, *In Praise of Justin II* 1.274–296, 3.1–61.
89. Euagrios 5.1; Prokopios, *Secret History*.
90. Prokopios, *Secret History* 13.7.
91. Stephanos, bishop of Herakleiopolis Magna, *A Panegyric on Apollo, Archimandrite of the Monastery of Isaac* 8 (ca. 600 AD, tr. Alcock).
92. *Book of Pontiffs* 59 (Agapetus); Facundus of Hermiane, *In Defense of the Three Chapters* 12.4, in *PL* 67:844C.

93. Prokopios, *Secret History* 13.2; Justinian, *Novel* 74.4.
94. H. Kennedy and J. Liebeschuetz, 'Antioch and the Villages of Northern Syria in the Fifth and Sixth Centuries,' *Nottingham Medieval Studies* 32 (1988) 65–90; Foss, 'Syria.'
95. E.g., pseudo-Joshua the Stylite, *Chronicle* 49; Prokopios, *Wars* 7.29.17–19; *Secret History* 1.5–9; Agathias 5.5.1–3.
96. Prokopios, *Secret History*; Ioannes Lydos, *On the Magistracies* 3.57, 3.62; Agathias 5.14; Euagrios 4.30.
97. Euagrios 5.1 (tr. Whitby).

Chapter 14. The Cost of Overextension (565–602)

1. John of Ephesos, *EH III* 2.10; A. Cameron, 'The Empress Sophia,' *Byzantion* 45 (1975) 5–21.
2. Euagrios 5.1–3; John of Biclaro, *Chronicle* 4 (s.a. 568); Eustratios the Presbyter, *Life of Patriarch Eutychios*, pp. 69 ff. (Laga).
3. Justin II, *Novel* 149; Italy: *Novels: Appendix* 7.12; Laniado, *Recherches*, 225–252.
4. Justin II in Corippus, *In Praise of Justin II* 2.259–264 (tr. Cameron); repayment: 2.361–403; also Justin II, *Novel* 148 pref. (loans and arrears); Theophanes a.m.6060, p. 242. Divorce: *Novel* 140, against 117.10 and 134.11.
5. A. Cameron and A. Cameron, 'Anth. Plan. 71: A Propaganda Poem from the Reign of Justin II,' *Bulletin of the Institute of Classical Studies* 13 (1966) 101–104.
6. Corippus, *In Praise of Justin II* 1.259–262, 3.354–355 (tr. Cameron); rebuff in 565: 3.231–401; Menandros fr. 8; John of Ephesos, *EH III* 6.24.
7. Menandros fr. 5.1–2; Malalas 18.125; John of Ephesos, *EH III* 6.24; also Agathias 5.14.1 for criticism; hair: Theophanes a.m.6050, p. 232; Corippus, *In Praise of Justin II* pref. 4; Agathias 1.3.4.
8. 20,000: a Turkish envoy in Menandros 10.1.83; in general: Pohl, *Avars*, 37. Danube petition: Menandros fr. 5.4; Euagrios 5.1; Agathias 4.22.7.
9. 566: Theophylaktos 6.10.7–13; 567 and negotiations: Menandros fr. 12 (quotation: 12.5.57–63); Paul the Deacon, *History of the Lombards* 1.27; treasury: John of Biclaro, *Chronicle* 19 (s.a. 572). Gepids: Pohl, *Avars*, 274–276; Sirmium: I. Popović et al., eds., *Sirmium à l'époque des grandes migrations* (Leuven et al. 2017), briefly held by Justinian in 535–536.
10. Menandros fr. 10; John of Ephesos, *EH III* 6.23; Michael the Syrian 10.10; Turkish delegation: Menandros fr. 19.1; anti-Persian alliance: ibid. fr. 13.5.
11. Sindual in *PLRE* 3:1154–1155.
12. The likeliest scenario is reported by the earliest writer, Marius Aventicensis (d. 596), *Chronicle* s.a. 568. John of Ephesos, *EH III* 1.39 says that Narses died in Italy and his body was returned to the City.
13. Lombard advance: the earliest narrative is the *Origin of the Lombard People* (ca. 643), ed. G. Waitz, *Scriptores rerum Langobardicarum et Italicarum saec. VI-IX* (Hannover 1878) 2–6, embellished by Paul the Deacon, *History of the Lombards* 2.7–30; plague

and famine: ibid. 2.26–27; *Book of Pontiffs* 64; skull: N. McLynn, 'Death in Verona,' *Kyoyo-Ronso* 123 (2005) 135–171; cf. Gregory of Tours, *History of the Franks* 4.41; a reconstruction in Wickham, *Italy*, 30–32. Populations: P. Tedesco, 'Exploring the Economy of Byzantine Italy,' *Journal of European Economic History* 2 (2016) 179–193, here 182.

14. Theophanes a.m.6058–6064, pp. 241–244.
15. John of Ephesos, *EH III*, book 1 (persecution), 2.5 (mice), 2.50 (writing); prior discussions: Michael the Syrian 9.30 (end), 10.2, and 10.3–9 for persecution; the edict is quoted in Greek by Euagrios 5.4.
16. Winlock and Crum, *Monastery*, 1:29–31, 331–341.
17. Ioannes of Epiphaneia, *History* 1.2, in *FHG* 4:274; Theophanes of Byzantion in Photios, *Bibliotheca* 64; Tabari, *History*, 1:945–958; cf. Prokopios, *Wars* 1.20.3–8 on Abraha. Abraha's Himyar: C. Robin, 'Himyar, Aksum, and *Arabia Deserta* in Late Antiquity,' in Fisher, ed., *Arabs and Empires*, 127–171; Persian-controlled Himyar: I. Gajda, *Le royaume de Himyar à l'époque monothéiste* (Paris 2009) 149–167.
18. Greatrex and Lieu, *Frontier*, 136.
19. Greatrex and Lieu, *Frontier*, 137–142, 149, esp. Menandros fr. 16.
20. Pseudo-Sebeos, *History* 8 (67–68); John of Biclaro, *Chronicle* 15 (s.a. 571); Theophanes of Byzantion in Photios, *Bibliotheca* 64.
21. Ioannes of Epiphaneia, *History* 1.3–5, in *FHG* 4:274–275; Euagrios 5.8–10; John of Ephesos, *EH III* 6.2–7 (virgins: 6.7; their mass suicide en route is doubtful). Apameia: Foss, 'Syria,' 205–226 ("shadow": 224).
22. John of Ephesos, *EH III* 3.2.
23. Menandros fr. 15.3; Euagrios 5.11; Theophanes a.m.6066, p. 247.
24. Menandros fr. 15.5, 25.1, and 18.1–4 (funeral: 19.1); Euagrios 5.12; John of Ephesos, *EH III* 6.8; "ugly": ibid. 6.45. Inscription: E. Ross and V. Thomsen, 'The Orkhon Inscriptions,' *Bulletin of the School of Oriental Studies* 5 (1930) 861–876, here 864.
25. Baduarius: John of Biclaro, *Chronicle* 38 (s.a. 576). Bribes: Menandros fr. 22, 24.
26. John of Ephesos, *EH III* 3.7, 3.11, 3.14; patriarch: ibid. 1.37; latter attacks: 2.37–41, 3.15–16; law: Tiberios, *Novel* 163.
27. Garmul: John of Biclaro, *Chronicle* 8, 11, 16, 48; refugees: S. Adamiak, *Carthage, Constantinople and Rome: Imperial and Papal Interventions* (Rome 2016) 30.
28. Caspian: Theophylaktos 3.15.1–2; cf. John of Ephesos, *EH III* 6.10.
29. John of Ephesos, *EH III* 3.14, 3.23; Gregory of Tours, *History of the Franks* 5.19.
30. John of Ephesos, *EH III* 3.25 (tr. Smith, mod.).
31. Euagrios 5.14; Theophanes a.m.6074, pp. 251–252; recruitment: Theophylaktos 3.12.4.
32. John of Biclaro, *Chronicle* 41 (s.a. 576), 60 (s.a. 581); settlements: John of Ephesos, *EH III* 6.25; Michael the Syrian 10.18; numbers: Menandros fr. 20.2.150–155; joint operation: ibid. fr. 21.
33. Menandros fr. 25, 27; inscription: R. Noll, 'Ein Ziegel als sprechendes Zeugnis einer historischen Katastrophe,' *Anzeiger der philosophisch historischen Klasse der österreichischen Akademie der Wissenschaften* 126 (1989) 139–154; fire: John of Ephesos, *EH III* 6.33.

34. *Paschal Chronicle* s.a. 582; Theophanes a.m.6074, pp. 251–252; Theophylaktos 1.1–2.
35. Whitby, *Maurice*.
36. John of Ephesos, *EH III* 5.18–19 (family), 5.14 (Theodosius); *Paschal Chronicle* s.a. 602.
37. C. Toumanoff, *Studies in Christian Caucasian History* (Washington, D.C. 1963) 380–382 (based on vague sources); Greatrex and Lieu, eds., *Frontier*, 167–172.
38. John of Ephesos, *EH III* 3.40–43, 6.16–17; Euagrios 5.20, 6.2; Theophylaktos 3.17.5–10.
39. Theophylaktos 2.2.5, 2.10.6–7; Fisher, *Between Empires*, 174–184.
40. Theophylaktos 1.3.7, 1.6.5–6, 7.15.14. Totals and box: Pohl, *Avars*, 232–233; A. Gandila, *Cultural Encounters on Byzantium's Northern Frontier, c. AD 500–700* (Cambridge 2018) 233–234, 263.
41. Pohl, *Avars*, 224–228.
42. E.g., Theophylaktos 3.7.10, 3.10.7 (Persian), 5.11.4, 7.7.1–2 (numbers depleted by war), 8.3.11; Whitby, 'Recruitment,' 100–101.
43. *Miracles of Demetrios* 1.13.128; Whitby, *Maurice*, 98, 117.
44. "Broom": John of Ephesos, *EH III* 5.20; Arabissos and army: 5.22.
45. Agathias 5.13.7–14.4.
46. Tiberios, *Novel* 163; Harper, *Fate*, 237–238.
47. A. Poulter, 'The End of Scythia Minor: The Archaeological Evidence,' in M. Mullett and R. Scott, eds., *Byzantium and the Classical Tradition* (Birmingham 1979) 198–204; Madgearu, 'Town Life'; Sarantis, 'Raiding.'
48. Bransbourg, '*Reddite*,' 102; 'Capital,' 343, 388–389, 393; Banaji, *Agrarian Change*, 27, 59, 96.
49. Gândilă, 'Heavy Money,' 370, 379.
50. 588: Theophylaktos 3.1–4 ("accountant": 3.2.8); Euagrios 6.4–13 (Gregorios); 594: Theophylaktos 7.1.2–9.
51. W. Goffart, 'Byzantine Policy in the West under Tiberius II and Maurice,' *Traditio* 13 (1957) 73–118; Wood, 'Spain,' 310–314. Comenciolus: *CIL* 2:3,420, and A.-K. Wassiliou-Seibt, 'From *magister militum* to *strategos*: The Evolution of the Highest Military Commands in Early Byzantium,' *TM* 21 (2017) 789–802, here 791 n. 16.
52. Gennadius 1: *PLRE* 3:510–511; F. Shlosser, 'The Exarchates of Africa and Italy,' *JöB* 53 (2003) 27–45.
53. John of Biclaro, *Chronicle*, 70 (s.a. 584); Gregory of Tours, *History of the Franks* 6.42 (money back), 8.18, 9.25, 10.1–4; Paul the Deacon, *History of the Lombards* 3.16–17, 3.22, 3.29, 3.31, 4.3; E. Fabbro, 'The Frankish Job: A Reassessment of the Frankish Italian Campaigns (584–590),' *JLA* 12 (2019) 519–549 (less convincing on imperial strategy, spelled out by Romanos at 541–542). Correspondence: *Letters* 3.40–41, in *MGH Epist.* 3:145–148.
54. Gregory I, *Register* 2.38 (tr. Martyn); cf. 5.36.
55. "Swords" and "*res publica*": Gregory I, *Register* 5.36; Leontios: 11.4; Brown, *Gentlemen*, 152–153. Pelagius I: *Letters* 4, 85. Gregory's diplomacy: W. Pohl, 'The Empire and the Lombards: Treaties and Negotiations in the Sixth Century,' in idem, ed., *Kingdoms of the Empire: The Integration of Barbarians in Late Antiquity* (Leiden 1997) 75–133, here 98–112.

56. Paul the Deacon, *History of the Lombards* 4.23–28, 4.32, 4.35.
57. Paul the Deacon, *History of the Lombards* 3.18–19 (tr. Foulke, mod.); Africa: Gregory I, *Register* 9.9; see *PLRE* 3:425–427.
58. M. Starr in *Science Alert* 13 April 2018; M. Brown in *Archaeology* July/August 2018.
59. Pourshariati, *Decline,* esp. 122–130, 397–414 for Bahram. Right of resistance: Z. Rubin, 'Nobility, Monarchy and Legitimation under the Later Sasanians,' in J. Haldon and L. Conrad, eds., *The Byzantine and Early Islamic Near East*, v. 6 (Princeton, NJ 2004) 235–273.
60. Theophylaktos 4.11.2; terms: 4.13.24; pseudo-Sebeos, *History* 11 (76–80); concessions and objections: ibid. 11 (76), 12 (84); John of Nikiou, *Chronicle* 96.10–13.
61. Theophylaktos 5.9.4; *Chronicle to 1234* 7–8, tr. Palmer, *Seventh Century*, 116–117. Pseudo-Sebeos, *History* 11 (77) mentions 15,000 for the Armenian field army (mistaking it for a national Armenian army) and 11 (70) mentions 8,000 allied Persians.
62. Ananias of Shirak in T. Greenwood, 'Armenia,' in Johnson, ed., *Handbook*, 115–141, here 133.
63. Pseudo-Sebeos, *History* 15–20 (86–93), 30 (104–105), romanticized; "bread": *Narratio de rebus Armeniae* 102 (p. 40, Garitte); Stopka, *Armenia*, 78–81.
64. 580s: John of Ephesos, *EH III* 5.14, 5.21. 590s: cf. Michael the Syrian 10.23 with Euagrios 6.22.
65. Euagrios 6.21; Theophylaktos 5.13–14.
66. Gregory I, *Register* 3.67; legends: Payne, *State of Mixture,* 164–166.
67. Euagrios 6.22; *Khuzistan Chronicle*, pp. 19–20, tr. Greatrex and Lieu, eds., *Frontier*, 231–232; Fisher, ed., *Arabs and Empires*, 357–362.
68. Maurikios, *Strategikon* 11.2; stirrups: F. Curta, 'The Earliest Avar-Age Stirrups, or the 'Stirrup Controversy' Revisited,' in idem, ed., *Other Europe*, 297–326. Transfer: Theophylaktos 5.16.1; pseudo-Sebeos, *History* 18 (90–91), 20 (91–93).
69. Avar destruction: Madgearu, 'Town Life.' Slavs: Maurikios, *Strategikon* 11.4; Thessalonike: *Miracles of Demetrios* 1.13–15; Athens: D. Metcalf, 'The Slavonic Threat to Greece *circa* 580,' *Hesperia* 31 (1962) 134–157; cave: *Andritsa Cave – Fateful Refuge* (Byzantine and Christian Museum, Athens, 2005 exhibition); in general: F. Curta, *The Making of the Slavs* (Cambridge 2001) 90–99.
70. Theodoros Synkellos, *On the Attack by the Atheist Barbarians and Persians on this God-Protected City* 9 (p. 301, Sternbach, re-ed. Makk).
71. Sarantis, *Justinian's Balkan Wars*, 385.
72. Theophylaktos 6.6–10; reconstructions: Whitby, *Maurice*, 156–165; Pohl, *Avars*, 171–197, with reservations by J. Liebeschuetz, 'The Lower Danube Region under Pressure: From Valens to Heraclius,' *Proceedings of the British Academy* 141 (2007) 101–134.
73. 598: Theophylaktos 7.15.2 (plague), 7.15.14 (treaty); 599: 8.5.8–6.1.
74. Theophylaktos 8.6.10 (foraging), 8.6.9–7.7 (Phokas); Ioannes of Antioch fr. 318 (Roberto).
75. Theophylaktos 8.1–9–10; Ioannes of Antioch fr. 316 (Roberto); Theophanes a.m.6092, pp. 278–280.

76. Theophanes a.m.6093, p. 283; Ioannes of Antioch fr. 317 (Roberto); context: Theophylaktos 8.4.11–5.1; poem: tr. (mod.) and commentary in G. Horrocks, *Greek: A History of the Language and its Speakers*, 2nd ed. (Malden, MA 2010) 327–330.
77. Theophylaktos 8.6–15; *Paschal Chronicle* s.a. 602; Theophanes a.m.6094, pp. 283–286 (legends); Priskos: ibid. a.m.6093, p. 294.
78. Euagrios 3.41.
79. *Life of Theodoros of Sykeon* 119.
80. A. Kaldellis, *Ethnography after Antiquity: Foreign Lands and People in Byzantine Literature* (Philadelphia 2013) ch. 1; China: É. de la Vaissière, 'Theophylact's Turkish *Exkurs* Revisited,' in V. Schiltz, ed., *De Samarcande à Istanbul: Étapes orientales* (Paris 2015) 2:91–102.
81. *Res publica*: John of Biclaro, *Chronicle* 69; Romulus: Venantius Fortunatus, *Poems: Appendix* 2.93; statue: Zemarchos in John of Ephesos, *EH III* 6.23; coins: Kosmas Indikopleustes, *Christian Topography* 2.77, 11.17; cf. Pliny, *Natural History* 6.24.85.
82. Ioannes Philoponos, *Commentary on Aristotle's Physics* 17:683 (Vitelli).
83. Prokopios, *Secret History* 26.1–11.
84. Alexandria: G. Fowden, 'Alexandria between Antiquity and Islam,' *Millennium Jahrbuch* 16 (2019) 233–270; law schools: Sarris, 'Introduction,' 24–25.
85. H. Maehler, 'Byzantine Egypt: Urban Élites and Book Production,' *Dialogos* 4 (1997) 118–136, here 128; Lauxtermann, *Byzantine Poetry*, 1:47.
86. D. Gutas, *Greek Thought, Arabic Culture: The Graeco-Arabic Translation Movement* (London 1998) 20–27, 34–45; J. Walker, 'The Limits of Late Antiquity: Philosophy between Rome and Iran,' *Ancient World* 33 (2002) 45–69, esp. 60–63, 66. Romans who knew this: Priskianos of Lydia, *Solutions to Questions Posed by King Chosroes*, ed. I. Bywater, *Supplementum Aristotelicum*, (Berlin 1886) 1.2:39–104; Agathias 2.28; John of Ephesos, *EH III* 6.20.
87. John of Ephesos, *EH III* 3.27–35; Gregorios of Antioch: ibid. 5.17; Euagrios 5.18.
88. Cities: A. Busine, 'The Conquest of the Past: Pagan and Christian Attitudes toward Civic History,' in D. Engels and P. Van Nuffelen, eds., *Religion and Competition in Antiquity* (Brussels 2014) 220–236; Alexandria: Ioannes Moschos, *Spiritual Meadow* 77; Constantinople: e.g., H. Klein, 'Constantine, Helena, and the Cult of the True Cross in Constantinople,' in B. Flusin and J. Durand, eds., *Byzance et les reliques du Christ* (Paris 2004) 31–59; exempla: C. Rapp, 'Old Testament Models for Emperors in Early Byzantium,' in P. Magdalino and R. Nelson, eds., *The Old Testament in Byzantium* (Washington, D.C. 2010) 175–197.
89. Euagrios 3.26; Theophylaktos, *History*: Dialogue; Georgios of Pisidia, e.g., *Heracliad* 1.78, 2.21.
90. O. Dalton, *Catalogue of Early Christian Antiquities and Objects from the Christian East* (London 1901) 81–86.
91. Corippus, *In Praise of Justin II* 2.1–83, 2.427; seals: B. Pentcheva, *Icons and Power: The Mother of God in Byzantium* (University Park, PA 2006) 19–21.
92. Mikhail, *Egypt*, 154–155; but see J. Beaucamp, 'Byzantine Egypt and Imperial Law,' in R. Bagnall, ed., *Egypt in the Byzantine World* (Cambridge 2007) 271–287.
93. Tannous, *Making*, 21–22, and passim for ignorance.

94. Eratosthenes *scholastikos* in *Greek Anthology* 5.242; see Smith, *Greek Epigram*.
95. L. MacCoull, *Dioscorus of Aphrodito* (Berkeley 1988); and the chapters by J.-L. Fournet and A. Papaconstantinou in S. Johnson, ed., *Languages and Cultures of Eastern Christianity: Greek* (Farnham, UK 2015) 221–248 and 249–260, respectively.

Chapter 15. The Great War with Persia (602–630)

1. Reception: Gregory I, *Register*, App. 8 (tr. Martyn); letter: 13.32 (tr. Kaldellis).
2. Olster, *Politics*.
3. Theophanes a.m.6101, pp. 296–297 (misdated); *Paschal Chronicle* s.a. 603; Kedrenos, *Historical Compendium*, 1:709.
4. Theophylaktos 8.11.2–4, 8.13.3–6, 8.15.8–9; Narses 10 in *PLRE* 3:935; transfer and payment: Theophanes a.m.6096, p. 292.
5. Greatrex and Lieu, *Frontier*, 184; slaughter: pseudo-Sebeos, *History* 31 (107).
6. Theophanes a.m.6097, pp. 292–293; cf. pseudo-Sebeos, *History* 31 (106–107).
7. Theophanes a.m.6098, p. 293; a.m.6099, pp. 295; and a.m.6101, p. 297; *Paschal Chronicle* s.a. 605; Kedrenos, *Historical Compendium*, 1:711.
8. Pseudo-Sebeos, *History* 31–33 (107–111); *Narratio de rebus Armeniae* 109–113 (pp. 41–42, Garitte); chronology: Greatrex and Lieu, *Frontier*, 186–187.
9. Greatrex and Lieu, *Frontier*, 185–186; Chalcedonian bishops expelled: *Chronicle to 1234* 21, in Palmer, *Seventh Century*, 125–126; fighting: Howard-Johnston, *Last Great War*, ch. 1.
10. Howard-Johnston, *Last Great War*, 42.
11. Egypt: John of Nikiou, *Chronicle* 107.1–29; factions and Bonosos: Strategios, *Capture of Jerusalem* 3.8–12, ed. and tr. G. Garitte, *La prise de Jérusalem par les Perses en 614* (Leuven 1960); pseudo-Sebeos, *History* 31 (106–107) (quotation tr. Thomson); *Miracles of Demetrios* 1.10.82–85; analysis in Olster, *Politics*, ch. 6; Kourtzian, 'L'incident'; inscriptions: P. Booth, 'Shades of Blues and Greens in the *Chronicle* of John of Nikiou,' *BZ* 104 (2011) 555–601, here 594–595.
12. Strategios, *Capture of Jerusalem* 4.1–5; other sources: Olster, *Politics*, 101–102.
13. John of Nikiou, *Chronicle* 107.30–109.17; papyri: R. Bagnall and K. Worp, *Regnal Formulas in Byzantine Egypt* (Missoula, MO 1979) 66–67.
14. Zacharias: *Paschal Chronicle* s.a. 609; Ioannes: C. Rapp, 'All in the Family: John the Almsgiver, Nicetas and Heraclius,' *Νέα Ῥώμη* 1 (2004) 121–134; 8,000 lbs: Leontios, *Life of Ioannes the Almsgiver* 45. 30%: Hendy, *Studies*, 172, 620–621.
15. *Paschal Chronicle* s.a. 610; Ioannes of Antioch fr. 321 (Roberto); John of Nikiou, *Chronicle* 109.25–110.13; "proclaimed": Nikephoros, *Short History* 2. Zar: C. Zuckerman, 'Epitaphe d'un soldat africain d'Héraclius,' *Antiquité tardive* 6 (1998) 377–382.
16. Theophylaktos, *History*: Dialogue 4–6; Georgios of Pisidia, *Heracliad* 2.11; *Avar War* 53.
17. Pseudo-Sebeos, *History* 33 (111–112); *Paschal Chronicle* s.a. 609; *Chronicle to 1234* 14, in Palmer, *Seventh Century*, 122; quotation: *Chronicle to 724* AG 921, in ibid. 17.

18. Families: Pourshariati, *Decline,* 118–140; *spahbeds*: R. Gyselen, 'Spahbed,' *Encyclopedia Iranica,* s.v. (2004); Vistahm's rebellion: pseudo-Sebeos, *History* 22–29 (94–104).
19. "Son": Euagrios 6.17; Theophylaktos 5.3.11, 8.15.7 (pretext); *Chronicle to 1234* 7, 14 (mourning), in Palmer, *Seventh Century,* 116, 121; Michael the Syrian 10.25.
20. *Life of Theodoros of Sykeon* 152.
21. Pseudo-Sebeos, *History* 33 (112), 34 (113); Nikephoros, *Short History* 2; *Life of Theodoros of Sykeon* 153–154 (terror).
22. Pseudo-Sebeos, *History* 34 (114–115); *Life of Theodoros of Sykeon* 153–154; "heels": *Chronicle to 1234* 20 and 23, in Palmer, *Seventh Century,* 125 (127 for the battle); refugees at Emesa: *Chronicle to 724* AG 922, in ibid. 17.
23. Strategios, *Capture of Jerusalem* 3.2.
24. Strategios, *Capture of Jerusalem* 4.8, partial tr. F. Conybeare, 'Antiochus Strategus' Account of the Sack of Jerusalem in A.D. 614,' *English Historical Review* 25 (1910) 502–517. Strategios' account is a compilation of separate sources, though it is unclear whether the accounts of the siege and the exile had different authors: J. Howard-Johnston, *Witnesses to a World-Crisis: Historians and Histories of the Middle East in the Seventh Century* (Oxford 2010) 165. Other accounts: pseudo-Sebeos, *History* 34 (115–116); *Paschal Chronicle* s.a. 614; Theophanes a.m.6106, pp. 300–301.
25. Zacharias, *Letter,* in *PG* 86b:3229b, 3232c.
26. Sophronios, *Anacreontica* 14 (*On the Fall of Jerusalem*); cf. *Anonymous Life of Ioannes the Almsgiver* 9 (a lamentation); graves: G. Avni, 'The Persian Conquest of Jerusalem (614 C.E.) – An Archaeological Assessment,' *Bulletin of the American Schools of Oriental Research* 357 (2010) 35–48; building: D. Ben-Ami et al., 'New Archaeological and Numismatic Evidence for the Persian Destruction of Jerusalem in 614 CE,' *Israel Exploration Journal* 60 (2010) 204–221. Population: L. di Segni and Y. Tsafrir, 'The Ethnic Composition of Jerusalem's Population in the Byzantine Period,' *Liber Annuus* 62 (2012) 405–454, here 411–412. It has been proposed that Roman Jews sided with Persia because the latter sided with the Jews of Himyar. The connection is tenuous and invisible.
27. Pseudo-Sebeos, *History* 3–36 (116–121); Alexandria: Leontios, *Life of Ioannes the Almsgiver* 20; *Khuzistan Chronicle* p. 27, tr. Greatrex and Lieu, *Frontier,* 235. See Payne, *State of Mixture,* 184.
28. *Anonymous Life of Ioannes the Almsgiver* 9; Leontios, *Life of Ioannes the Almsgiver* 7; monks and Saracens: Antonios, *Life of Georgios of Khoziba* 7.31; cf. 8.34–35.
29. *Paschal Chronicle* s.a. 615; see the following note.
30. The earliest sources do not say that Shahin took the city: *Paschal Chronicle* s.a. 615; *Life of Anastasios the Persian* 8; Nikephoros, *Short History* 6–7; pseudo-Sebeos, *History* 38 (122–123). Cf. Theophanes, Michael the Syrian, and others who used the common eastern source: Hoyland, *Theophilus,* 66. Unlike Flusin, *Saint Anastase,* 2:83–93, I cannot make sense of the confusing reports in pseudo-Sebeos and the *Life* about Philippikos' maneuvers in the east.
31. Foss, 'Persians'; *contra*: F. Trombley, 'The Decline of the Seventh-Century Town: The Exception of Euchaita,' in S. Vryonis, ed., *Byzantine Studies in Honor of Milton V. Anastos* (Malibu 1985) 65–90, here 75–81; Russell, 'Persian Invasions,'

especially 63–71, whose own view of a late sixth-century decline, based on a couple of buildings, is also contestable. See A. Wilson, 'Aphrodisias in the Long Sixth Century,' in I. Jacobs and H. Elton, eds., *Asia Minor in the Long Sixth Century* (Oxford 2019) 197–221, for a possible attack on Aphrodisias.

32. C. Foss, 'Late Antique and Byzantine Ankara,' *DOP* 31 (1977) 27–87, here 70–71.
33. *Chronicle to 724* AG 934, in Palmer, *Seventh Century*, 18. The attack on Cyprus in 617 is a phantom: Metcalf, *Byzantine Cyprus*, 377–378, 383–385. Slavic naval raids: *Miracles of Demetrios* 2.1.179.
34. Foss, 'Persians,' 730–733; I. Touratsoglou and E. Halkia, *Ο θησαυρός της Κρατήγου Μυτιλήνης* (Athens 2008); Eupalinos: G. Greatrex, 'The Impact on Asia Minor of the Persian Invasions,' in C. Şimşek and T. Kaçar, eds., *The Lykos Valley and Neighborhood in Late Antiquity* (Istanbul 2018) 13–26, here 17. Edessa: *Chronicle to 1234* 19, in Palmer, *Seventh Century*, 124.
35. Leontios, *Life of Ioannes the Almsgiver* 44b.
36. "Bloodshed": *Chronicle to 1234* 24, in Palmer, *Seventh Century*, 128; Cypriot monk: Ioannes in Theodoros of Paphos, *Life of Spyridon* 20, ed. P. Van den Ven, *La légende de s. Spyridon évêque de Trimithonte* (Louvain 1953). Coptic sources and archaeology: Gariboldi, 'Social Conditions,' 325–327, and 330–331 for the general; Foss, 'Roman Near East,' 165. The most detailed narrative of the fall of Alexandria is the *Khuzistan Chronicle* pp. 25–26, tr. Greatrex and Lieu, *Frontier*, 235, but it appears fanciful.
37. Women: Winlock and Crum, *Monastery*, nos. 433 (p. 264) and 300 (pp. 233–244); Pesenthios: Gariboldi, 'Social Conditions,' 337.
38. Foss, 'Roman Near East'; Howard-Johnston, *Last Great War*, 153–173; a mere "jolt": G. Bowersock, *Empires in Collision in Late Antiquity* (Waltham, MA 2012) 47.
39. *Praitorion*: *Life of Anastasios the Persian* 17–18; "countless": Theophanes a.m.6098, p. 293 (misdated but valid).
40. Khusrow's Better Antioch: Theophylaktos 5.6.9–7.3. Herakleios: Theophanes a.m.6118, p. 322. Deportations: B. Dignas and E. Winter, *Rome and Persia in Late Antiquity* (Cambridge 2007) 254–263.
41. *Martyrdom of Pushai*, tr. Payne, *State of Mixture*, 65.
42. MacCoull, 'Coptic Egypt,' 311; Maria: Winlock and Crum, *Monastery*, no. 170, p. 199; widow: J. Drescher, 'A Widow's Petition,' *Bulletin de la société d'archéologie copte* 10 (1944) 91–96; permit: Gariboldi, 'Social Conditions,' 348; Foss, 'Roman Near East,' 167–168. For coping with violence previously, see Ruffini, *Life*, ch. 2.
43. Antonios, *Life of Georgios of Khoziba* 9.38, 9.42; Saracens: 8.31, 8.34; Theophanes a.m.6104, p. 300; Antiochos of Mar Saba, *Letter to Eustathios, Abbot of Attalina in Galatia*, in *PG* 89:1424c, 1425b.
44. Russell, 'Persian Invasions,' 55–57; Arabia: M. Piccirillo, 'The Province of Arabia during the Persian Invasion,' in K. Holum and H. Lapin, eds., *Shaping the Middle East: Jews, Christians, and Muslims in an Age of Transition* (Bethesda, MD 2011) 99–114.
45. Russell, 'Persian Invasions,' 52–55; H. Pottier, *Le monnayage de la Syrie sous l'occupation perse* (Paris 2004), with introduction by C. Foss. Insult: cf. the ungrammatical Spanish signs posted by the US government at the Mexican border.

46. *Chronicle to 1234* 31, in Palmer, *Seventh Century*, 133–134; conversion rates: Hendy, *Studies*, 480–481; Justinian: Prokopios, *Buildings* 1.1.65; Alexandria: Leontios, *Life of Ioannes the Almsgiver* 45.
47. Cf. Gariboldi, 'Social Conditions,' 341–342, with Banaji, *Agrarian Change*, 27, keeping in mind that the former figures are one-thirds and the latter for the whole year. The occupation force: P. Sänger, 'The Administration of Sasanian Egypt,' *GRBS* 51 (2011) 653–665.
48. Kitchen: *BGU* 2:377; prices: Gariboldi, 'Social Conditions,' 348, for wheat; MacCoull, 'Coptic Egypt,' 311: 1,375 lbs of linen per solidus.
49. 43%: ibn Khordadbeh, *Kitab al-Masalik Wa'l-Mamalik*, ed. M. de Goeje, *Bibliotheca Geographorum Arabicorum* (Leiden 1889) 6:12; luxury: Tabari, *History* 1:1041–1042, cf. the tradition of Theophilos of Edessa in Hoyland, *Theophilus*, 66–67; Herakleios: Theophanes a.m.6118, p. 322. Arabs: Kennedy, *Conquests*, 111–124, 129.
50. The title appears in pseudo-Sebeos, *History*, e.g., 37 (121) and probably dates to the reign itself.
51. Payne, *State of Mixture*.
52. Union of 616: Michael the Syrian 10.26–27; Johnson, 'Introduction,' 45; court debates: pseudo-Sebeos, *History* 46 (149); Payne, *State of Mixture*, 186–188; Monophysite bishops: Flusin, *Saint Anastase*, 2:112–114.
53. *Khuzistan Chronicle* p. 25, tr. Greatrex and Lieu, *Frontier*, 234; also Strategios, *Capture of Jerusalem* 19.4, 20.4–5 (tr. Conybeare, pp. 512–513); *Life of Anastasios the Persian* 7.
54. Anastasios: Michael the Syrian 10.27 (tr. Moosa, p. 443), 11.3 for "tribulations." "Grace": Gariboldi, 'Social Conditions,' 329, 334; in general: Mikhail, *Egypt*, 179, 181, 191; in prior wars: Hatziantoniou, *Η θρησκευτική πολιτική*, 196–200.
55. P. Photiades, 'A Semi-Greek Semi-Coptic Parchment,' *Klio* 41 (1963) 234–236.
56. John of Nikiou, *Chronicle* 109.18–24.
57. *Miracles of Demetrios* 2.1.179–181.
58. *Miracles of Demetrios* 2.2.198–215; Isidore of Seville, *Chronicle* s.a. 614.
59. Georgios of Pisidia, *Heracliad* 2.95; cf. 2.75.
60. *Paschal Chronicle* s.a. 615; Hendy, *Studies*, 494–495, 498; mints: Russell, 'Persian Invasions,' 59–62. Battle cry: Maurikios, *Strategikon* 12B.16.
61. Leontios, *Life of Ioannes the Almsgiver* 12; cf. 15 for an unspecified money-making scheme; bread: *Paschal Chronicle* s.a. 618; Nikephoros, *Short History* 8 (Carthage).
62. Prigent, 'Provinces d'Occident'; Brubaker and Haldon, *History*, 490–491, 686–687.
63. Theophanes a.m.6113, pp. 302–303; Nikephoros, *Short History* 11.
64. Georgios of Pisidia, *Persian War*, paraphrased by Theophanes a.m.6113, pp. 302–306, who says the general was Shahrbaraz.
65. *Paschal Chronicle* s.a. 623; Theodoros Synkellos, *On the Attack by the Atheist Barbarians and Persians on this God-Protected City* 9 (Sternbach, re-ed. Makk, p. 301) (vague reference to the treaty); Nikephoros, *Short History* 10, 13; Theophanes a.m.6110 and 6111, pp. 301–302 (misdated). 70,000: Georgios the Monk, *Chronicle*, 2:669, probably the correct version of the 270,000 in Nikephoros.
66. *Paschal Chronicle* s.a. 624; pseudo-Sebeos, *History* 38 (124–125), with additions from Thomas Artsruni, *History of the House of the Artsrunik'* 2.3 (tr. Thomson, p. 159),

on pollution; Theophanes a.m.6113, pp. 302–303; Georgios of Pisidia, *Heracliad* 2.160–230; Movses Dasxuranci, *History of the Caucasian Albanians* 2.10 (tr. Dowsett, pp. 78–81). I follow the excellent reconstruction by J. Howard-Johnston, 'Heraclius' Persian Campaigns and the Revival of the East Roman Empire, 622–630,' *War in History* 6 (1999) 1–44, except as modified below. Fiction: A. Kaldellis, *Romanland: Ethnicity and Empire in Byzantium* (Cambridge, MA 2019) 182–185.

67. Theophanes a.m.6114–6116, pp. 307–314; see also previous note. I follow C. Zuckerman, 'Heraclius in 625,' *Revue des études byzantines* 60 (2002) 189–197.
68. Letter: pseudo-Sebeos, *History* 38 (123–124); speeches and dispatches: Theophanes a.m.6114–6116, pp. 307–314. Pseudo-Sebeos, *History* 38 (124–125) impossibly gives Herakleios an army of 120,000, of which 20,000 were elite. The latter figure is plausible. At 38 (125) he gives Shahin 30,000.
69. Theophanes a.m.6117, p. 315; 12,000: *Paschal Chronicle* s.a. 626 (p. 718); but see Howard-Johnston, *Last Great War*, 260–271.
70. *Paschal Chronicle* s.a. 626; Theodoros Synkellos, *On the Attack by the Atheist Barbarians and Persians on this God-Protected City*; Georgios of Pisidia, *Avar War*; Nikephoros, *Short History* 12–13.
71. Kaldellis, 'Union.'
72. Movses Dasxuranci, *History of the Caucasian Albanians* 2.11 (tr. Dowsett, pp. 81–83); C. Zuckerman, 'The Khazars and Byzantium - The First Encounter,' in P. Golden et al., eds., *The World of the Khazars* (Leiden 2007) 399–432, esp. 413–417, whose chronology I follow below.
73. Campaign of 627–628: Herakleios' dispatches in Theophanes a.m.6117–6118, pp. 316–327; *Paschal Chronicle* s.a. 628; also Nikephoros, *Short History* 12–15; Movses Dasxuranci, *History of the Caucasian Albanians* 2.11 (from one source), 2.12–14 (from a more reliable source) (tr. Dowsett, pp. 85–95); pseudo-Sebeos, *History* 38–39 (126–127). The *Chronicle to 1234* 37, in Palmer, *Seventh Century*, 137, and related eastern texts (along with Nikephoros) reveal that the Turks accompanied Herakleios (they are wrongly called "Khazars" in some sources); also Michael the Syrian 11.3. Ziebel: É. de la Vaissière, 'Ziebel Qaghan Identified,' *TM* 17 (2013) 761–768. I reject the tale of Shahrbaraz and the intercepted letters.
74. Theophanes a.m.6109, p. 301.
75. Nikephoros, *Short History* 15; pseudo-Sebeos, *History* 39 (128).
76. *Chronicle of 1234* 38–40, 43, in Palmer, *Seventh Century*, 138–142; the eunuch Narses in Palestine: Strategios, *Capture of Jerusalem* 24.2–6.
77. Pseudo-Sebeos, *History* 40 (129–130); his prior refusal to evacuate: 39 (128); Nikephoros, *Short History* 17; Arabissos and border: *Chronicle to 724* AG 940, in Palmer, *Seventh Century*, 18.
78. Maranci, *Art of Armenia*, 37–42.
79. Theophanes a.m.6119, pp. 327–328; Nikephoros, *Short History* 18–19. Chronology of the Cross: C. Zuckerman, 'Heraclius and the Return of the Holy Cross,' *TM* 17 (2013) 197–218.
80. Maximos, *Letter* 8, in *PG* 91:445A; also *Letters* 28–31; Sophronios, *Poem* 18 (*On the Holy Cross*) 77–84.

81. Kaegi, *Heraclius*, 89; Wood, 'Spain,' 301.
82. *Return of the Relic of the Martyr Anastasios the Persian* 1 (Flusin).
83. Pseudo-Sebeos, *History* 41 (131); also *Khuzistan Chronicle*, p. 30, tr. Greatrex and Lieu, *Frontier*, 237; *Return of the Relic of the Martyr Anastasios the Persian* 3 (Flusin).
84. *Basileus* in a law: J. Konidaris, 'Die Novellen des Kaisers Herakleios,' *Fontes Minores* 5 (1982) 33–106, here 57–60.
85. *Return of the Relic of the Martyr Anastasios the Persian* 1 (Flusin) ("republic"); Georgios of Pisidia, *On the Restoration of the Cross* (the defeat of the barbarians and refutation of false religion); the *Return of the Cross to Jerusalem*, appended as ch. 24 to Strategios' *Capture of Jerusalem*; Nikephoros, *Short History* 18 (based on a slightly later account by a contemporary); pseudo-Sebeos, *History* 41 (131) (a later seventh-century perspective). Hum of eschatology: *Life of Theodoros of Sykeon* 134; Antonios, *Life of Georgios of Khoziba* 4.18. There is one bona fide prophecy, albeit attributed to Khusrow and without Christian coordinates (Theophylaktos 5.15.5–7); and *possibly* also the Syriac *Alexander Legend* (I am not fully convinced that the prophecy refers to Herakleios, and, even if it does, the text cannot be linked to the court).
86. H. Sivan, 'From Byzantine to Persian Jerusalem: Jewish Perspectives and Jewish/Christian Polemics,' *GRBS* 41 (2000) 277–306; W. van Bekkum, 'Jewish Messianic Expectations in the Age of Hercalius,' in G. Reinink and B. Stolte, eds., *The Reign of Heraclius (610–641)* (Leuven 2002) 95–112. The Christian polemical text *Doctrina Jacobi nuper baptizati* responds to Jewish expectations (e.g., at 4.5–5.9).
87. Correspondence: Theodosius II in *ACO* 2.2.1, p. 8; monograms: Feissel, 'Les édifices,' 90–91; cf. in literature, *Greek Anthology* 1.11 (Sophia to Justin II); *basileia*: e.g., Justinian, *Novel* 47 (also on papyri); Christ: Justinian, *Const. Imperatoriam maiestatem* (*Institutes*).
88. Jerusalem: Theophanes a.m.6120, p. 328; Khusrow in pseudo-Sebeos, *History* 34 (116). Edessa: ibid. 42 (134); cf. *Chronicle of 1234* 39, in Palmer, *Seventh Century*, 139–140; reprisals are attested in the *Annals* of the tenth-century Melkite patriarch of Alexandria Eutychios, which often mix fact with legend: in *PG* 111:1089–1091.
89. R. Devreesse, 'La fin inédite d'une lettre de saint Maxime,' *Revue des sciences religieuses* 17 (1937) 25–35, giving the previously unpublished end of his *Letter* 8. Constantinople: *Doctrina Jacobi nuper baptizati* 5.20.20–40 (Déroche, p. 217). Later sources: the Slavic preface of the *Doctrina* (ibid. p. 70); Fredegar, *Chronicle* 4.65 (tangled in dreams and eschatology); Michael the Syrian 11.4 (bare mention). See G. Dagron and V. Déroche, 'Juifs et Chrétiens dans l'Orient di VIIe siècle,' *TM* 11 (1991) 17–46, here 28–32.
90. Antioch: cf. Anastasios of Sinai, *Homily* 3: *Against the Monotheletes* 1, and Theophanes a.m.6121, pp. 329–330, with Michael the Syrian 11.3. Ishoyahb: *Chronicle of Seert* 93, in *PO* 13.4:557–561. Armenia: pseudo-Sebeos, *History* 41 (131–132); *Narratio de rebus Armeniae* 121–143 (Garitte, pp. 43–46). Booth, *Crisis*, 200–208.
91. Kyros of Alexandria, *Letter to Sergios of Constantinople*, in *ACO* ser. 2, 2.2 (p. 592); the nine articles of union are laid out on pp. 596–600. Persecution: Coptic sources in Booth, *Crisis*, 206–208.

92. Sophronios in Alexandria and Constantinople: Sergios of Constatinople, *Letter to pope Honorius* in *ACO* ser. 2, 2.2 (pp. 538–543); Maximos, *Opusculum* 12, in *PG* 91:143. Honorius' response: *ACO* ser. 2, 2.2 (pp. 548–558). "Communion": Anastasios of Sinai, *Homily* 3: *Against the Monotheletes* 1.
93. Sophronios, *Letter to Sergios of Constantinople*, in *ACO* ser. 2, 2.1 (pp. 410–494); Stephanos of Dora: *PmbZ* 6906.

Chapter 16. Commanders of the Faithful (632–644)

1. Names: Lindstedt, '*Muhajirun*'; Bible and Seven Sleepers: R. Hoyland, 'The Jewish and/or Christian Audience of the Qur'an and the Arabic Bible,' in F. del Río Sánchez, ed., *Jewish Christianity and the Origins of Islam* (Turnhout 2018) 31–40; Alexander: K. van Bladel, 'The *Alexander Legend* in the Qur'an 18:83–102,' in G. Reynolds, ed., *The Qur'an in its Historical Context* (London 2008) 175–203; local religious context: A. Al-Azmeh, *The Emergence of Islam in Late Antiquity: Allah and His People* (Cambridge 2014), not easy to follow; R. Hoyland, 'Writing the Biography of the Prophet Muhammad,' *History Compass* 5 (2007) 1–22, here 13; ship: P. Crone, *Meccan Trade and the Rise of Islam* (Princeton 1987) 5 n. 9.
2. Y. Ragheb, 'Les premiers documents arabes de l'ère musulmane,' *TM* 17 (2013) 679–729.
3. P. Crone and G. Hinds, *God's Caliph: Religious Authority in the First Centuries of Islam* (Cambridge 1986).
4. Shoshan, *Tradition*.
5. F. Donner, 'Centralized Authority and Military Autonomy in the Early Islamic Conquests,' in A. Cameron, ed., *The Byzantine and Early Islamic Near East*, v. 3 (Princeton, NJ 1995) 337–360. But cf. Shoshan, *Tradition*, 29.
6. Donner, *Conquests*, 116–119, 177; see p. 384 below for Muslim attitudes toward non-Muslim Arabic speakers.
7. Baladhuri, *Origins* 108, 135 (tr. Hitti, 1:167, 207); Donner, *Conquests*, 119.
8. Theophanes a.m.6123–6124, pp. 335–336 (*Arabes*); Nikephoros, *Short History* 20 (an alternative, but still economic motivation); *Doctrina Jacobi nuper baptizati* 5.16; see Hoyland, *Theophilus*, 93–94; Donner, *Conquests*, 116, 126 (date). In ca. 700, this was remembered as one of two major engagements (with Yarmuk): Anastasios of Sinai, *Homily* 3: *Against the Monotheletes* 1. I am skeptical that we can make any sense of the battle of Mu'ta (allegedly 629 AD in the Muslim tradition).
9. Sophronios (probably), *Preface to the Spiritual Meadow*, ed. H. Usener, *Sonderbare Heilige I. Der heilige Tychon* (Leipzig 1907) 91–93; Sophronios, *Homily on the Nativity and the Saracen Disorder*, ed. H. Usener, 'Weihnachtspredigt des Sophronios,' *Rheinisches Museum für Philologie* 41 (1886) 501–516, esp. 514. He refers to Saracen invasions in his *Letter to Sergios of Constantinople*, in *ACO* ser. 2, 2.1 (p. 492). Muslim sources for 634: Donner, *Conquests*, 119–131.

10. Theodoros: Hoyland, *Theophilus*, 96–98; Sophronios, *Homily on the Theophany*, ed., Papadopoulos-Kerameus, Ἀνάλεκτα, 5:151–168, here 166.
11. Translated by Michael the Syrian 11.7 as "rest in peace, Syria"; Baladhuri, *Origins* 137 (tr. Hitti, 1:210).
12. Hoyland, *Theophilus*, 109–114, 118–119; W. Kaegi, *Byzantium and the Early Islamic Conquests* (Cambridge 1992) 159–167; Booth, 'Last Years,' 513. Early attack on Egypt: Hoyland, *Seeing Islam*, 574–581.
13. M. Levy-Rubin, *Non-Muslims in the Early Islamic Empire* (Cambridge 2011); 'Umar's letters to provincials: Tabari, *History* 1:2405–2407; Yuhannan: tr. in Hoyland, *Seeing Islam*, 195–197.
14. E.g., from Damascus: Baladhuri, *Origins* 123 (tr. Hitti, 1:189), who mentions more cases; in general: Ditten, *Ethnische Verschiebungen*, 54–65.
15. Tabari, *History* 1:2498–2505; cf. 2594; *Chronicle of 1234* 79–80, in Palmer, *Seventh Century*, 164–165.
16. New reading of John of Nikiou, *Chronicle* 111–112 in P. Booth, 'The Muslim Conquest of Egypt Reconsidered,' *TM* 17 (2013) 639–670; Kyros: Nikephoros, *Short History* 23, 26; Booth, 'Last Years'; and the Eastern Source in Hoyland, *Theophilus*, 109–114.
17. John of Nikiou, *Chronicle* 113.4 (tr. Charles, mod.).
18. Foss, 'Egypt,' 271. Fall of Babylon: John of Nikiou, *Chronicle* 117.3.
19. John of Nikiou, *Chronicle* 120.17–27 (Kyros and 'Amr), 120.36–38 (Kyros' death); defeat of the Roman generals seen from Constantinople: Nikephoros, *Short History* 23. Treaty of Egypt: Tabari, *History* 1:2588–2589.
20. Ibn 'Abd al-Hakam and others in Banaji, *Agrarian Change*, 267–268; households: 152–159, 170.
21. Kaisareia: John of Nikiou, *Chronicle* 118.10–12 (horrors) (tr. Charles); damages: Holum, 'Archaeological Evidence,' 74, 80, 83, who unnecessarily argues against his evidence; Hijaz: Baladhuri, *Origins* 142 (tr. Hitti, 1:218); Tripolis: ibid. 127 (tr. Hitti, 1:194–195).
22. *Doctrina Jacobi nuper baptizati* 3.10, 3.12; al-Tabarani quoted by D. Cook, 'Syria and the Arabs,' in P. Rousseau, ed., *A Companion to Late Antiquity* (Malden, MA 2012) 467–478, here 468.
23. Tabari, *History* 1:2632, 2722.
24. Anastasios of Sinai, *Homily* 3: *Against the Monotheletes* 1.
25. *Anti-Jewish Dialogue*, ed. D. Afinogenov et al., 'La recension γ des *Dialogica polymorphia antiiudaica* et sa version slavonne,' *TM* 17 (2013) 27–103, here 62–65; cf. C. Schiano, 'Les *Dialogica polymorphia antiiudaica* dans le Paris. Coisl. 193,' *TM* 17 (2013) 139–170, here 161.
26. Mikhail, *Egypt*, 179–181, 191; Kennedy, *Conquests*, 148–149, 153, 155, 167–168, 350–356; B. Palme, 'Political Identity versus Religious Distinction? The Case of Egypt in the Later Roman Empire,' in W. Pohl et al., eds., *Visions of Community in the Post-Roman World* (Farnham, UK 2012) 81–98; Sarantis, 'Raiding,' 255 n. 292.
27. John of Nikiou, *Chronicle* 115.9–10; J. Moorhead, 'The Monophysite Response to the Arab Invasions,' *Byzantion* 51 (1981) 579–591; likewise the Jews: S. Leder, 'The

Attitude of the Population, Especially the Jews, toward the Arab-Islamic Conquest of Bilad al-Sham,' *Die Welt des Orients* 18 (1987) 64–71.

28. *Chronicle of 1234* 84, in Palmer, *Seventh Century*, 166.
29. *Doctrina Jacobi nuper baptizati* 5.16; see S. Anthony, 'Muhammad, the Keys to Paradise, and the *Doctrina Jacobi*: A Late Antique Puzzle,' *Der Islam* 91 (2014) 243–265 (and 244 for Thomas the Presbyter).
30. S. Anthony, *Muhammad and the Empires of Faith: The Making of the Prophet of Islam* (Berkeley 2020) 40, 192–193.
31. John of Nikiou, *Chronicle* 121.10, 120.36. For the earliest texts, see Hoyland, *Seeing Islam*; Kourtzian, 'L'incident,' 180–184.
32. Genealogies: H. Kennedy, 'From Oral Tradition to Written Record in Arabic Genealogy,' *Arabica* 44 (1997) 531–544; A. Elad, 'Community of Believers of 'Holy Men' and 'Saints' or Community of Muslims?,' *Journal of Semitic Studies* 47 (2002) 241–308, here 277–278; formularies: G. Khan, 'The Pre-Islamic Background of Muslim Legal Formularies,' *Aram* 6 (1994) 193–224; ethnic perception of the conquerors: Tannous, *Making*, 307, 525–531.
33. Apostle: Quran 4:79, 34:28; cf. 49:13; Arabic Quran: 12:2, 39:28, 41:3, 41:44, 42:7, 43:2.
34. *Maronite Chronicle* in Palmer, *Seventh Century*, 32. Cf. Quran 9.29.
35. Hawting, *First Dynasty* 4–5, 9, 37.
36. R. Humphreys, 'Consolidating the Conquest: Arab-Muslim Rule in Syria and the Jazirah, 630–775 CE,' in Dijkstra and Fisher, eds., *Inside and Out*, 391–405, here 400; P. Webb, *Imagining the Arabs: Arab Identity and the Rise of Islam* (Edinburgh 2017) 134–135. The *Doctrina Jacobi nuper baptizati* 5.17 implies that "the Jews" or "the Saracens" might use force to get a Christian to renounce Christ. But this is a polemical text whose notions of persecution were shaped by early Christian history. Egyptian converts: John of Nikiou, *Chronicle* 114.1.
37. Kennedy, *Conquests*, 104; R. Hoyland, 'Early Islam as a Late Antique Religion,' in Johnson, ed., *Handbook*, 1053–1077, here 1060. See the episodes in Tabari, *History* 1:2508–2509; Baladhuri, *Origins* 136 (tr. Hitti, 1:208–209).
38. A. Grohmann, *From the World of Arabic Papyri* (Cairo 1952) 113–116 (the Arabic portion of the papyrus gives no proper name for 'Abdallah's companions); Magaritai: P. Crone, 'The First-Century Concept of *hiǧra*,' *Arabica* 41 (1994) 352–387, esp. 359; Gadara and Nessana: Webb, *Imagining the Arabs*, 150.

Chapter 17. Holding the Line (641–685)

1. Factions: Booth, 'Last Years'; titles: Nikephoros, *Short History* 27–32 (based on a contemporary source), with C. Zuckerman, 'Titles.' Fall of Martina: Theophanes a.m.6133, p. 341; John of Nikiou, *Chronicle* 120.39–55 (tr. Charles, mod.); pseudo-Sebeos, *History* 44 (141).

2. 75%: Haldon, *Empire*, 27–29; also Hendy, *Studies*, 171–172, 619–626; donative: Kedrenos, *Historical Compendium*, 1:753 (based on a contemporary source). Hijaz: Foss, 'Egypt,' 260, 268.
3. Hoyland, *Theophilus*, 124–125; Michael the Syrian 11.8; raid patterns: Baladhuri, *Origins* 163–164 (tr. Hitti, 1:253); list: Lilie, *Reaktion*, 63–83, to be updated at many points.
4. Pseudo-Sebeos, *History* 44 (142–143); Theophanes a.m.6136, p. 343; possibly John of Nikou, *Chronicle* 120.61–63 (in which case misdated); attack on the Arabs: Booth, 'Last Years,' 538–539.
5. Feissel, 'Jean de Soloi,' 219.
6. Pseudo-Sebeos, *History* 42–49 (139–168); cf. Ghewond, *History* 2; the tradition in Hoyland, *Theophilus*, 139 has Konstas turn back at Kaisareia. According to Fredegar, *Chronicle* 4.81, Konstas bought the truce for 1,000 solidi per day.
7. Baladhuri, *Origins* pp. 197–204 (tr. Hitti, 1:309–321); Hoyland, *Theophilus*, 140; pseudo-Sebeos, *History* 52 (174).
8. Pseudo-Sebeos, *History* 45 (147), 49 (169); Hoyland, *Theophilus*, 138.
9. Hoyland, *Theophilus*, 131–134; Baladhuri, *Origins* 152–153 (tr. Hitti, 1:235–236). Cf. Metcalf, *Byzantine Cyprus*, 395–414, with Zavagno, *Cyprus*, 72–79; Ioannes: Feissel, 'Jean de Soloi'; Dead Sea: Anastasios of Sinai, *Questions and Answers* 28.16.
10. Konstantinos VII, *On the Themes* 1.15, p. 81.
11. L. Conrad, 'The Arabs and the Colossus,' *Journal of the Royal Asiatic Society* ser. 3, 6 (1996) 165–187.
12. Hoyland, *Theophilus*, 141–144; pseudo-Sebeos, *History* 50 (170–171); Cosentino, 'Constans,' with the evidence of the *Apocalypse of Daniel* and Tabari, *History* 1:2888–2889.
13. Theophanes a.m.6150, p. 347; 'Abd al-Rahman: *Chronicle to 819* AG 971, in Palmer, *Seventh Century*, 77.
14. Herakleios, *Ekthesis*, in *ACO* ser. 2, 1, p. 160 (Lateran Synod of 649); Honorius, *Letter to Sergios* in *ACO* ser. 2, 2.2 (Constantinople III), pp. 548–558, esp. 550; echoed by Pyrros of Constantinople in his *Letter to Pope John IV* in *ACO* ser. 2, 1, p. 338 (cf. *ACO* ser. 2, 2.2, p. 626).
15. *Maximos' Disputation with Pyrros*, in *PG* 91:287–354; see J. Noret, 'La redaction de la *Disputatio cum Pyrrho* (*CPG* 7698) de sainte Maxime le Confesseur?' *Analecta Bollandiana* 117 (1999) 291–296; *Book of Pontiffs* 75 (Theodore); eastern monks: J.-M. Sansterre, *Les moines grecques et orientaux à Rome aux époques byzantine et carolingienne* (Brussels 1983). Greek learning: Ekonomou, *Byzantine Rome*, 6–24, 134.
16. Context: Booth, *Crisis*, 259–269; "Two Wills": 268; papal preeminence: 269–276; *imperium*: Maximos, *Opusculum* 12, in *PG* 91:144B-C (preserved in Latin translation). Assaults: Paulos of Constantinople, *Letter to Pope Theodore*, in *ACO* ser. 2, 1, 196–204.
17. Kaegi, *Muslim Expansion*. ch. 6. Maximos' support is alleged in *Record of the Trial* 2, in Allen and Neil, *Maximus*, 50–53.

18. *Typos*: *ACO* ser. 2, 1, pp. 208–210. Sixth Ecumenical: Maximos, *From a Letter Written in Rome*, in *PG* 91:137D (possibly spurious). The priority of the Greek Acts was established by R. Riedinger in papers later gathered in *Kleine Schriften zu den Konzilsakten des 7. Jahrhunderts* (Turnhout 1998).
19. Pope Martin, *Letters* 12–13, in *PL* 87:182–198.
20. No theological difference?: R. Price, 'Monotheletism: A Heresy or a Form of Words?' *Studia Patristica* 48 (2010) 221–232; Three Wills: Maximos, *Opusculum* 9, in *PG* 91:125–128; no compromise: e.g., *Maximos' Disputation with Pyrros*, in *PG* 91:300, 305–308; and *Dispute at Bizye* 12, in Allen and Neil, *Maximus,* 110–111; see Booth, *Crisis,* 218–219, 314–316.
21. Olympios: I distrust the narrative in the *Book of Pontiffs* 76, but Martin's involvement was later held against him: Theodoros Spoudaios, *Account of the Exile of Pope Martin* 6, 16–17, ed. B. Neil, *Seventh-Century Popes and Martyrs: The Political Hagiography of Anastasius Bibliothecarius* (Turnhout 2006). Punitive measures against Rome?: *Book of Pontiffs* 78. Martin unpopular: Ekonomou, *Byzantine Rome,* 158–159.
22. Trial: *Record of the Trial*; no compomise and "villain": *Dispute at Bizye* 4 and 12, in Allen and Neil, *Maximus,* 88–89, 110–111.
23. Justinian II, *Letter to Pope John V*, in *ACO* ser. 2, 2.2, p. 886. Opsikion: J. Haldon, 'More Questions about the Origins of the Imperial Opsikion,' in A. Beihammer et al., eds., *Prosopon Rhomaikon: Ergänzende Studien zur Prosopographie der mittelbyzantinischen Zeit* (Berlin 2017) 31–42; navies: Cosentino, 'Constans,' 602–603.
24. Theophanes a.m.6149, p. 347; Perberis: *Record of the Trial* 13, in Allen and Neil, *Maximus,* 72; Belegezites: cf. *Miracles of Demetrios* 2.1.179–180 with 2.4.254. For Theophanes' use of the term "Sklavinia," possibly an anachronism, see E. Chrysos, 'Settlements of Slavs and Byzantine Sovereignty in the Balkans,' in Belke et al., eds., *Byzantina Mediterranea,* 123–135.
25. Maurikios, *Strategikon* 11.4 (tr. Dennis); Pohl, *Avars,* 135, 159–161; see 444 n. 70 and 445 n. 85 for bibliography on the Slavic settlements.
26. D. Pettegrew, 'The Busy Countryside of Late Roman Corinth,' *Hesperia* 76 (2007) 743–784, here 778–779.
27. J.-M. Martin, *Byzance et l'Italie mérdionale* (Paris 2014) 39–47, 123–138; E. Kislinger, *Regionalgeschichte als Quellenproblem: Die Chronik von Monembasia und das sizilianische Demenna* (Vienna 2002). Sicily: Ekonomou, *Byzantine Rome,* 177–179.
28. Zuckerman, 'Titles,' 881.
29. *PmbZ* 7797; Booth, *Crisis,* 318–319.
30. Movses Dasxuranci, *History of the Caucasian Albanians* 2.22, 3.15; cf. pseudo-Sebeos, *History* 52 (175); C. Zuckerman, 'Jerusalem as the Center of the Earth in Anania *Širakac'i's Ašharhac'oyc*',' in M. Stone et al., eds., *The Armenians in Jerusalem and the Holy Land* (Leuven 2002) 255–274, here 259–261. Eagles and monograms: Maranci, *Art of Armenia,* 43–44.
31. Ecclesiastical condemnation: Makarios of Antioch in the Acts of the Sixth Ecumenical Council: *ACO* ser. 2, 2.1, p. 230; "short": Theodoros Spoudaios, *Commemoration* 4, in Allen and Neil, *Maximus,* 153–154.

32. Gregory I, *Dialogues* 3.38, tr. Christie, *From Constantine*, 41, also 1, 5, 61, 200–202, 460; Wickham, *Italy*, 65, 80–81, 87, 94, 148; people: Harper, *Fate*, 263; material decline of Ravenna: D. Deliyannis, *Ravenna in Late Antiquity* (Cambridge 2010) 288–289.
33. Wickham, *Italy*, 19, 27, 75–76; Deloglu, 'The Post-Imperial Romanness,' 157–171.
34. Isaakios: *PLRE* 3:719–721; *PmbZ* 3466; confiscation: *Book of Pontiffs* 73; epitaph: *CIG* 4.9869, tr. from Lauxtermann, *Byzantine Poetry*, 1:221–223 (mod.). Exarchs: Brown, *Gentlemen*.
35. Fredegar, *Chronicle* 4.71; Paul the Deacon, *History of the Lombards* 4.45; archaeology: N. Christie, *The Lombards: The Ancient Longobards* (Oxford 1995) 95.
36. Paul the Deacon, *History of the Lombards* 5.6; *Book of Pontiffs* 78; coins: Curta, 'Beginning,' 152; Opsikion: Haldon, 'Questions,' 38. The traditions in the Eastern Source (Hoyland, *Theophilus*, 150–151) are doubtful.
37. Agnellus, *Book of Pontiffs of Ravenna* 110; privilege: *Rerum Italicarum Scriptores* 2.1 (p. 146); Herrin, *Ravenna*, 259–266.
38. *Book of Pontiffs* 78; campaigns: Paul the Deacon, *History of the Lombards* 5.7–11.
39. Haldon, *Tale*, 107–109. Raids: Hoyland, *Theophilus*, 152–153; the table in Jankowiak, 'Siege,' 264–269.
40. Theophanes a.m.6159, pp. 348–351; Hoyland, *Theophilus*, 153–161.
41. Jankowiak, 'Siege'; see 290–291 for the Companions. Demons: Anastasios of Sinai, *Beneficial Tales* 1, ed. S. Heid, 'Die C-Reihe erbaulicher Erzählungen des Anastasios vom Sinai,' *Orientalia Christiana Periodica* 74 (2008) 78–114.
42. Theodoros and Andreas: Theophanes a.m.6160, p. 351 (they are *PmbZ* 7312 and 353); assault: ibid. a.m.6165, pp. 353–354 (confused); the *Maronite Chronicle* in Palmer, *Seventh Century*, 32–33; other sources in Jankowiak, 'Siege,' 292–300. Thomas: *ACO* ser. 2, 2.2, p. 614.
43. Hoyland, *Theophilus*, 162–164.
44. Mango, *Le développement urbain*, 54.
45. Cf. Hoyland, *Theophilus*, 162–164 with *Book of Pontiffs* 79 (Adeodatus); Jankowiak, 'Siege,' 309–314 (313–314 for the Arab raid).
46. Theophanes a.m.6159, p. 351.
47. Hoyland, *Theophilus*, 166–168; garbled in Nikephoros, *Short History* 34; Egypt: Jankowiak, 'Siege,' 279–280.
48. Jankowiak, 'Siege,' 260, 274–275.
49. Hoyland, *Theophilus*, 169–170; see A. Asa Eger, *The Islamic-Byzantine Frontier: Interaction and Exchange among Muslim and Christian Communities* (London 2012) 295–299.
50. Belegezites: *Miracles of Demetrios* 2.4.254; Perboundos: ibid. 2.4.235; "other war": 2.4.257; raiding: 2.4.277.
51. "Schism": *ACO* ser. 2, 2.1, p. 2; Sergios etc.: p. 20; Agatho against the One Will: pp. 122–148; Makarios on Honorius: p. 22; condemnation of One Will: Session 13. See also *Book of Pontiffs* 81 (Agatho). For the schism of the 670s, see Jankowiak, 'Siege,' 283–285.
52. *ACO* ser. 2, 2.2, pp. 674–680.

53. *Book of Pontiffs* 82–84; Herrin, *Ravenna*, 266.
54. J. Tannous, 'In Search of Monotheletism,' *DOP* 68 (2014) 29–67.
55. Jankowiak, 'Notitia 1' (lowest number: 449).
56. Theophanes a.m.6161, p. 352, and a.m.6173, p. 360 (misdated); S. Brock, 'A Syriac Fragment on the Sixth Council,' *Oriens Christianus* 57 (1973) 63–71; Michael the Syrian 11.13.
57. Nikephoros, *Short History* 35–36; Theophanes a.m.6171, pp. 356–359; date: *ACO* ser. 2, 2.2, p. 694,27. Settlement: U. Fiedler, 'Bulgars in the Lower Danube Region,' in Curta, ed., *Other Europe*, 151–236.
58. Hoyland, *Theophilus*, 180–182; Baladhuri, *Origins* 160 (tr. Hitti, 1:247); Jankowiak, 'Siege,' 255–256.
59. Kosmas Indikopleustes, *Christian Topography* 2.75; Andreas of Kaisareia, *Commentary on Revelation* 55 (on 18:21–24), 64 (on 20:9–10); pseudo-Methodios, *Apocalypse* 10.6.

Chapter 18. Life and Taxes among the Ruins

1. Adamnán of Iona, *De locis sanctis* 3.1 (ed. and tr. Meehan, p. 107); Bede, *Ecclesiastical History* 5.16.
2. Isidore of Seville, *Etymologies* 18.2.2–3, 15.1.42 (tr. Barney et al., p. 303); Agatho in *ACO* ser. 2, 2.1, pp. 58, 122; also pope Leo II in ibid. p. 882.
3. Mango, *Le développement urbain*, 54.
4. Agatho in *ACO* ser. 2, 2.1, p. 132; M. Lapidge, 'The Career of Archbishop Theodore,' in idem, ed., *Archbishop Theodore: Commemorative Studies on His Life and Influence* (Cambridge 1995) 1–29, here 9, 13.
5. Haldon, *Empire*, 27–29.
6. *Life of Theodoros of Sykeon* 134.
7. Curta, 'Beginning,' 145, 172, 196. Anglo-Saxons: the poem *The Ruin* 2 (*enta*); and their verb *timbran*.
8. Ivison, 'Amorium,' 43. Surveys: W. Brandes, *Die Städte Kleinasiens im 7. und 8. Jahrhundert* (Berlin 1989); Decker, *Dark Ages*, ch. 3; Brubaker and Haldon, *History*, ch. 7.
9. Theophanes a.m.6208, p. 388; Tabari, *History* 3:1240–1243 (838 AD).
10. E.g., Leon VI, *Taktika* 17.59.
11. Canon 18 of the Council in Troullo, in *ACO* ser. 2., 2.4, p. 33; Galatian emigrants: Canon 95, in ibid. p. 58; Council of 680: Jankowiak, 'Notitia 1.'
12. Pseudo-Methodios, *Apocalypse* 11.5.
13. Leon VI, *Novel* 46.
14. J. Haldon, '"Cappadocia Will be Given over to Ruin and Become a Desert": Environmental Evidence for Historically-Attested Events,' in Belke et al., eds., *Byzantina Mediterranea*, 215–230; Nar: Haldon, *Empire*, 234–237. In general: J. Haldon et al., 'The Climate and Environment of Byzantine Anatolia: Integrating

Science, History, and Archaeology,' *Journal of Interdisciplinary History* 45 (2014) 113–161, esp. 139; Izdebski, *Rural Economy*.

15. Olson, *Environment*, ch. 3–4.
16. African Red Slip: McCormick, *Origins*, 55, 102, 511; eastern merchants: A. Harris, *Byzantium;* M. Decker, 'Export Wine Trade to West and East,' in M. Mango, ed., *Byzantine Trade, 4th-12th Centuries* (Farnham, UK 2009) 239–252; tin: E. Campbell and C. Bowles, 'Byzantine Trade to the Edge of the World,' in ibid. 297–313; Alexandria: Leontios, *Life of Ioannes the Almsgiver* 10; Constantinople: P. Magdalino, 'The Merchant of Constantinople,' in idem et al., eds., *Trade*, 181–191, here 181–182; *Miracles of Artemios* 27. In general: Decker, *Dark Ages*, 61–72; Brubaker and Haldon, *History*, ch. 6.
17. Haldon, 'Commerce,' 103–107, 111.
18. Prigent, 'Provinces d'Occident'; Brubaker and Haldon, *Byzantium*, 490–491, 686–687.
19. Kaldellis, 'Borders.'
20. Monetary break: C. Morrisson, 'Byzantine Money,' in *EHB*, 955–958 and the tables 6.1–11; Haldon, 'Commerce,' 108–112; exceptions: Morrisson and Prigent, 'Monetazione'; Curta, 'Beginning,' 151–156; C. Lightfoot, 'Business as Usual? Archaeological Evidence for Byzantine Commercial Enterprise at Amorium,' in Morrisson, ed., *Trade and Markets*, 177–191; bathhouse: Ivison, 'Amorium,' 46.
21. Hendy, *Studies*, 499; Jankowiak, 'Siege,' 315.
22. Thessalonike: *Miracles of Demetrios*; Euchaïta: Haldon, *Tale;* the Virgin: Kaldellis, 'Union'; Artemios: *Miracles of Artemios*.
23. Ephesos: Theophanes a.m.6287, pp. 469–470; festivals: S. Vryonis, 'The *Panêgyris* of the Byzantine Saint,' in idem, *Byzantine Institutions, Society and Culture* (New Rochelle, NY 1997) 1:251–292; Athens: Kaldellis, *Parthenon;* names: Jankowiak, 'Notitia 1,' 440.
24. Malakope: Theophanes a.m.6298, p. 482; Troglodytes: Leon the Deacon 3.1; Cooper and Decker, *Cappadocia*, 19–20, 32–42.
25. Morrisson and Prigent, 'Monetazione.'
26. Brubaker and Haldon, *History*, 490.
27. McCormick, *Origins*, 719–726; catalogue: A. Muthesius, *Byzantine Silk Weaving* (Vienna 1997) 163–203; Brubaker and Haldon, *Sources*, 80–108.
28. Anastasios of Sinai, *Questions and Answers* 65.4, 101; *Homily* 3: *Against the Monothelites* 1. Blame game: Haldon, *Empire*, 84–87.
29. Buddha: *Miracles of Artemios* 32; Islam: D. Olster, *Roman Defeat, Christian Response, and the Literary Construction of the Jew* (Philadelphia 1994); *contra*: V. Déroche, 'Polémique anti-judaïque et emergence de l'Islam,' *REB* 57 (1999) 141–161.
30. *ACO* ser. 2, 2.4; G. Nedungatt and M. Featherstone, eds., *The Council in Trullo Revisited* (Rome 1995); pseudo-pagan customs: A. Kaldellis, 'The Kalends in Byzantium,' *Archiv für Religionsgeschichte* 13 (2012) 187–203.
31. *ACO* ser. 2, 2.4, pp. 17–20; signature: p. 62.
32. Troullo Canon 19.
33. Humphreys, *Law*, 77–79.

34. Dome: R. Hoyland, 'New Documentary Texts and the Early Islamic State,' *Bulletin of the School of Oriental and African Studies* 69 (2006) 395–416, here 409; "Muslims": Lindstedt, '*Muhajirun*.'
35. Hoyland, *Theophilus*, 180–182; Sebastopolis: ibid. 185–187; cf. Baladhuri, *Origins* 160 (tr. Hitti, 1:247).
36. Lamb: Troullo Canon 82; coins: R. Hoyland, 'Writing the Biography of the Prophet Muhammad,' *History Compass* 5 (2007) 1–22, here 14–16; M. Humphreys, 'The 'War of Images' Revisited: Justinian II's Coinage Reform and the Caliphate,' *The Numismatic Chronicle* 173 (2013) 229–244.
37. *On Strategy* 43, ed. Dennis, *Military Treatises*, 124–125.
38. Wickham, *Framing*, 131–144, 251–255; Sahner, *Christian Martyrs*, 195.
39. Quran 3.102–107, 49.9–10. Factions: Hawting, *First Dynasty*. For the nexus of taxation, identity, and military service, see P. Crone, *From Arabian Tribes to Islamic Empire: Army, State and Society in the Near East* (Burlington, VT 2008) esp. IX.
40. *Book of Pontiffs* 83 (Benedict II).
41. Nikephoros, *Short History* 39–40; Theophanes a.m.6187, pp. 368–369.
42. *Ekloge* 12.6.
43. *On Strategy* 3.38–44, ed. and tr. Dennis, *Military Treatises*, 15–17.
44. *Farmer's Law* 18–19, ed. W. Ashburner, 'The Farmer's Law,' *Journal of Hellenic Studies* 30 (1910) 85–108 and 32 (1912) 68–95. This likely dates to the second half of the eighth century: Humphreys, *Law*, ch. 5. The present section follows Brubaker and Haldon, *History*, ch. 10–11. Villages and taxation: Haldon, *Seventh Century*, 138–141.
45. *Farmer's Law* 40.
46. Brubaker and Haldon, *History*, 717. Konstantinos V: Nikephoros, *Short History* 85; *Antirretikos* 3.75, in *PG* 100:513d–516a; Theophanes a.m.6259, p. 443.
47. Choniates, *History* 442.
48. Konstantinos VII, *Book of Ceremonies* 2.45 (clothes: 3:339).
49. Zuckerman, 'Learning,' 125–134.
50. *On Strategy* 2.18–21, ed. and tr. Dennis, *Military Treatises*, 12–13.
51. Brubaker and Haldon, *History*, 682–695.
52. Haldon, *Empire*, 258–266; Cooper and Decker, *Cappadocia*, 245–247; J.-C. Cheynet, 'Quelques nouveaux sceaux de commerciaires,' in Magdalino et al., eds., *Trade*, 25–54 (tentatively endorses this interpretation). F. Montinaro, 'Les premiers commerciaires byzantins,' *TM* 17 (2013) 351–538, dissents.
53. Konstantinos VII in N. Svoronos, *Les Novelles des empereurs macédoniens* (Athens 1994) 118.
54. Estates: Hendy, *Studies*, 637–640; Treadgold, *Army*, 24–25, 171–178; Cooper and Decker, *Cappadocia*, 240–243; barbarians: Whitby, 'Recruitment,' 112–114; "various means": W. Kaegi, 'Review of R.-J. Lilie,' *Speculum* 53 (1978) 399–404, here 403; Italy: S. Cosentino, 'Politics and Society,' in idem, ed., *A Companion to Byzantine Italy* (Leiden 2021) 29–67, here 41–44. The billeting-and-acquisition theory has been promoted especially by J. Haldon in many publications, e.g., *Seventh Century*, 130, 153, 221, 227–228, 249.
55. Leon VI, *Taktika* 11.9.

56. *Ekloge* 16; Theodoros of Stoudios, *Letter* 7.61–63; *Life of Euthymios the Younger* 3; see Brubaker and Haldon, *History*, 744–746 (n. 77 for soldiers' tax exemptions). Four-year rotation: Hendy, *Studies*, 648–651.
57. Leon VI, *Taktika* 12.57 (and passim); fatherland: *On Strategy* 4.11, ed. Dennis, *Military Treatises*, 20–21; *Sylloge Tacticorum* 13.2, ed. A. Dain, *Sylloge Tacticorum quae olim "Inedita Leonis Tactica" dicebatur* (Paris 1938); in general: Kaldellis, *Romanland;* S. Eshel, *The Concept of the Elect Nation in Byzantium* (Leiden 2018).
58. See p. 69 above.
59. A. Pertusi, 'Una Acoluthia militare inedita del X secolo,' *Aevum* 22 (1948) 145–168, here 157.
60. Pseudo-Zacharias, *Chronicle* 8.1 (tr. Greatrex et al.); citing Psalm 112.7.
61. Zepos, *Jus Graecoromanum*, 1:33.
62. Skylitzes 483 (Kekaumenos).
63. Leon III, *Ekloge*, pref.; cf. Justinian, *Novel* 25.2.
64. "Anti-nobiliary": C. Toumanoff, *Studies in Christian Caucasian History* (Washington, D.C. 1963) 39; Basil II, *Novel of 996* prol. 3, in McGeer, *Land Legislation*, 114–116. See E. Ragia, 'Social Group Profiles in Byzantium,' *Byzantina Symmeikta* 26 (2016) 309–372.
65. Brubaker and Haldon, *History*, 525–526, 599–600.
66. The first surviving ranking of dignities is the *Taktikon Uspenskij* (mid-850s), ed. Oikonomidès, *Listes*, 46–63; payments: Liudprand, *Antapodosis* 6.10; *roga*: Konstantinos VII, *Book of Ceremonies* 2.49; Oikonomides, 'Role,' 1008–1010.
67. Leon III, *Ekloge* preface and 18; *Appendix to the Ekloge* 11.3–5 (from the *Digest*); *Farmer's Law* 81. See Kaldellis, *Byzantine Republic*, 194–196 (imperial pronouncements), 40–41 (oaths).
68. *Souda* s.v. *basileia*.
69. Theophanes a.m.6258, p. 440; Michael Glykas, *Annales*, pp. 527–528; Kaldellis, *Romanland*, ch. 4.
70. Leon VI, *Taktika* 18.95.
71. Kaldellis, *Romanland*, 127–132.
72. Kaldellis, *Romanland*, ch. 5; Armeniakon: ibid. 174–177 (see, e.g., Theophanes a.m.6285, p. 469).
73. Theophanes a.m.6207, pp. 385–386; *Lives of David, Symeon, and Georgios of Mytilene* 34.
74. Yazid: *PmbZ* 2656.
75. Kaldellis, *Romanland*, 185–186.

Chapter 19. An Empire of Outposts (685–717)

1. Frier, 'Demography,' 814; A. Laiou, 'The Human Resources,' in *EHB*, 47–51.
2. Skylitzes 41.
3. R. Hoyland, *Khalifa ibn Khayyat's History on the Umayyad Dynasty* (Liverpool 2015) 85–86.

4. *Book of Pontiffs* 84 (tr. Davis, p. 80); Kaegi, *Muslim Expansion*, esp. 108–110, 153, 226–249, 254.
5. Nikephoros, *Short History* 41; Theophanes a.m.6190, pp. 370–371.
6. Septem: Justinian in *CJ* 1.27.2.2; Prokopios, *Wars* 4.5.6; *Buildings* 6.7.14–16; exile: Nikephoros, *Short History* 30; *Septensiansis*: Justinian II, *Letter to Pope John V*, in *ACO* ser. 2, 2.2, p. 886; Julian: Montenegro and del Castillo, 'Theodemir's Victory,' 408–410. Balerics: Prokopios, *Wars* 4.5.7; Georgios of Cyprus, *Descriptio Orbis Romani*, ed. H. Gelzer (Leipzig 1890) 34; Kaegi, *Muslim Expansion*, 257–259. *Archons*: L. Zavagno, *Cyprus between Late Antiquity and the Early Middle Ages* (London 2017) 87–91.
7. Tax: *Book of Pontiffs* 78 (Vitalian); army: ibid. 79 (Adeodatus); Justinian II, *Letter to Pope John V*, in *ACO* ser. 2, 2.2, p. 886; Barbaricini: Prokopios, *Wars* 4.13.44; *Buildings* 6.7.13; pope Gregory I, *Register* 4.25, 4.27; monks: Allen and Neil, *Maximus the Confessor*, 124–131; inscription: Cosentino, 'Sardinia,' 344. Augustine: Bede, *Martyrology*, in H. Quentin, *Les martyrologes historiques du Moyen âge* (Paris 1908) 109.
8. Corsica: pope Gregory I, *Register* 7.3; attack: *Chronicle of 754* 87.1, in K. Wolf, *Conquerors and Chroniclers of Early Medieval Spain* (Liverpool 1999) 151; Montenegro and del Castillo, 'Theodemir's Victory.'
9. Konstantinos VII, *On the Themes*, p. 94.
10. M. Nichanian and V. Prigent, 'Les stratèges de Sicile,' *REB* 61 (2003) 97–141. Malta: Georgios of Cyprus, *Descriptio Orbis Romani*, ed. H. Gelzer (Leipzig 1890) 30; exile and *doux*: Nikephoros, *Short History* 24; B. Bruno, *Roman and Byzantine Malta: Trade and Economy* (Malta 2009) 7–11, 52–53, 84–85, 208–211.
11. T. Brown, 'A Byzantine Cuckoo in the Frankish Nest? The Exarchate of Ravenna and the Kingdom of Italy,' in C. Gantner and W. Pohl, eds., *After Charlemagne: Carolingian Italy and its Rulers* (Cambridge 2021) 185–197.
12. Noble, *Republic*, ch. 1; Deloglu, 'The Post-Imperial Romanness,' 157–171. Losses in Apulia: Paul the Deacon, *History of the Lombards* 6.1.
13. Justinian in *ACO* 4.1, p. 25.12–13; Union: patriarch Ioannes in *Collectio Avellana* no. 159.2.
14. *Book of Pontiffs* 86 (Sergius I).
15. Agnellus, *Book of the Pontiffs of Ravenna* 137–145 (quotation: 140, tr. Deliyannis, mod.). Agnellus attributes the attack to Justinian's desire for revenge for his first deposition; also *Book of Pontiffs* 90 (Constantine); Theophylaktos: ibid. 87 (John VI). Herrin, *Ravenna*, 294.
16. *Book of Pontiffs* 88 (John VII), 90 (Constantine), and 91 (Gregory II, revealing that Troullo was discussed at Nikomedeia) (tr. Davis).
17. H. Ohme, 'The Causes of the Conflict about the Quinisext Council,' *The Greek Orthodox Theological Review* 40 (1995) 17–43.
18. Brandes, 'Schweigen,' 187–201.
19. C. Lambot, *Oeuvres théologiques et grammaticales de Godescalc d'Orbais* (Louvain 1954) 208.

20. A. Petranović and A. Margetić, 'Il Placito del Risano,' *Centro di ricerche storiche di Rovigno: Atti* 14 (1983–1984) 55–75.
21. McCormick, 'Imperial Edge,' 51.
22. Konstantinos VII, *DAI* 29.61–66, 86–88, 30.58–59, 123–126; survey: Curta, *Southeastern Europe*, 100–107; treaty: Dölger, *Regesten*, 1.1:47.
23. Hellas: Nikephoros, *Short History* 40; Theophanes a.m.6187, p. 368. Karabisianoi: *Miracles of Demetrios* 2.5.295; Justinian II, *Letter to Pope John V*, in *ACO* ser. 2, 2.2, p. 886; their end: Brubaker and Haldon, *History*, 729–730, 739. Thessalonike: A. Gkoutzioukostas, 'The Prefect of Illyricum and the Prefect of Thessalonike,' *Byzantiaka* 30 (2012–2013) 45–80.
24. Thessalonike: *Miracles of Demetrios* 2.4; Huneberc of Heidenheim, *Hodoeporicon of Saint Willibald* in *MGH SS* 15.1:93; assimilation: *Miracles of Demetrios* 2.4.235 and 254; Kaldellis, *Romanland*, 136–147, 218–221.
25. Theophanes a.m.6180, p. 364. Strymon: Konstantinos VII, *On the Themes*, p. 89; Curta, *Edinburgh History*, 109, 131 n. 34. See also Nikephoros, *Short History* 38; Michael the Syrian 11.15; Ditten, *Ethnische Verschiebungen*, 86–88, 216–234 (224–225 on numbers).
26. N. Khrapunov, 'Continuity in the Administration of Byzantine Cherson According to Seals and Other Sources,' in H. Ivakin et al., eds., *Byzantine and Rus' Seals* (Kiev 2015) 179–192; *archon*: Theophanes a.m.6203, pp. 377–378; Khazars: ibid. a.m.6196, pp. 372–373; Nikephoros, *Short History* 42; archaeology: A. Aibabin, 'Early Khazar Archaeological Monuments in Crimea,' in C. Zuckerman, ed., *La Crimée entre Byzance et le khaganat Khazar* (Paris 2006) 31–65.
27. Nikephoros, *Short History* 42; Theophanes a.m.6196–6198, pp. 372–375, and a.m.6203, pp. 377–381; relying possibly on Traïanos the patrician: Forrest, 'Theophanes' Byzantine Source'; golden nose: Agnellus, *Book of the Pontiffs of Ravenna* 137. Seals: Jonathan Shea, pers. comm.
28. Nikephoros, *Short History* 42.61–64; seal: Petkov, *Voices*, 2; inscription: ibid. 5, but see Pohl, *Avars*, 518 n. 300; M. Ivanova, 'The Madara Horseman and Triumphal Inscriptions,' in M. Kinloch and M. MacFarlane, eds., *Trends and Turning Points: Constructing the Late Antique and Byzantine World* (Leiden 2019) 166–184; ceremony: *Souda* s.v. *Boulgaroi*; treaty: Theophanes a.m.6305, p. 497 (looking back); Curta, *Southeastern Europe*, 83.
29. Hoyland, *Theophilus*, 191–192.
30. Theophanes a.m.6209, p. 391; Ghewond, *History* 10; see B. Martin-Hisard, 'La domination byzantine sur le littoral oriental du Pont Euxin,' *Byzantino-bulgarica* 7 (1981) 141–156.
31. Haldon, *Empire*, 65–70.
32. E.g., Vasiliev, *Byzance*, 2.1:375; Romanos I in Theodoros Daphnopates, *Letter* 6.19–34.
33. Haldon and Kennedy, 'Arab-Byzantine Frontier'; Lynch, 'Cyprus,' 542; Kaldellis, 'Borders'; Mardaïtes: see pp. 400, 403 above; removed: Theophanes a.m.6176–6179, pp. 361–364.
34. Theophanes a.m.6178, p. 363; Baladhuri, *Origins* 152–154 (tr. Hitti, 1:235–237); Tabari, *History* 1:2826 (both antedated); Nea Ioustinianoupolis: Troullo Canon 39;

Hoyland, *Theophilus*, 185–187; a legendary account of their return in Konstantinos VII, *DAI* 47; Muslim jurists: Lynch, 'Cyprus.' Crown: Ioannes of Antioch fr. 321 (Roberto).

35. Officials: Zavagno, *Cyprus*, 43, 82, 87; trade: 47–48 and ch. 6; Muslim minority: 85. Al-Walid: Baladhuri, *Origins* 154 (tr. Hitti, 1:238); Tabari, *History* 2:1769. Eyeball: *ACO* ser. 2, 3.2, p. 410.
36. See pp. 382–383 above. Taxation and navy: Foss, 'Egypt,' esp. 275.
37. M. Vaiou, *Diplomacy in the Early Islamic World: A Tenth-Century Treatise on Arab-Byzantine Relations* (London 2015) 89 (mod.).
38. Suspicion: Sahner, *Christian Martyrs*, 231–232; raids: Baladhuri, *Origins* 127 (tr. Hitti, 1:195), 133 (tr. p. 204); Foss, 'Egypt,' 22, 269.
39. Niketas, *Life of Andreas of Crete*, in Papadopoulos-Kerameus, *Ἀνάλεκτα*, 5:171–179 ("enemies": 173).
40. Agnellus, *Book of the Pontiffs of Ravenna* 142 (tr. Deliyannis); Nikephoros, *Short History* 45; Theophanes a.m.6203, p. 381.
41. Nikephoros, *Short History* 40–53; Theophanes a.m.6187–6207, pp. 368–386; see Forrest, 'Theophanes' Byzantine Source.'
42. Theophanes a.m.6203–6204, pp. 381–382; Agathon the Deacon, *Epilogos* in *ACO* ser. 2, 2.2, pp. 898–900, whose claims of persecution are generic. Only the bishop of Sinope dissented: pseudo-Germanos, *Account of the Heresies and Synods* 38. Rome: *Book of Pontiffs* 90 (Constantine). See G. Tsorbatzoglou, 'Η εκκλησιαστική πολιτική του αυτοκράτορα Βαρδάνη-Φιλιππικού,' *Kosmos* 1 (2012) 229–304.
43. Agathon the Deacon, *Epilogos* in *ACO* ser. 2, 2.2, p. 900; Theophanes a.m.6204, p. 382; a.m.6205, p. 383.
44. Hoyland, *Theophilus*, 194–196, 201–202, 205.
45. Nikephoros, *Short History* 49–51; Theophanes a.m.6206–6207, pp. 383–386. Feared populace: Agapios in Hoyland, *Theophilus*, 208.
46. Nikephoros, *Short History* 52; Theophanes a.m.6208, pp. 386–390; date: a.m.6232, p. 412. "Slaughtering": Hoyland, *Theophilus*, 211; graffiti: F. Imbert, 'Graffiti Arabes de Cnide et de Kos,' *TM* 17 (2013) 731–758, here 734, 746, 749–750.
47. Nikephoros, *Short History* 52, 54, 56; Theophanes a.m.6209–6210, pp. 395–399; Hoyland, *Theophilus*, 209–215. Muslim sources are late and embroidered. Grammarian: Lauxtermann, *Byzantine Poetry*, 1:48, 2:37–41; Germanos: V. Grumel, 'Homélie de Saint Germain sur la deliverance de Constantinople,' *REB* 16 (1958) 183–205; and the letter of pope Gregory II to Germanos: Brubaker and Haldon, *History*, 90–94.
48. Nikephoros, *Short History* 55, 57, 60; Theophanes a.m.6210, p. 398; a.m.6211, p. 400; a.m.6218, p. 405.
49. Blankinship, *Jihâd State*, 32–34; Roman raids: 287 n. 133; laws: Sahner, *Christian Martyrs*, 244.
50. S. Bashear, 'Apocalyptic and Other Materials on Early Muslim-Byzantine Wars,' *Journal of the Royal Asiatic Society* ser. 3, 1 (1991) 173–207, here 191 (mod.).

Chapter 20. The Lion and the Dragon (717–775)

1. E. Brooks, 'The Campaign of 717–718, from Arabic Sources,' *Journal of Hellenic Studies* 19 (1899) 19–31, here 22.
2. Theophanes a.m.6209, p. 391.
3. Sicily: widely different reconstructions in Chiarelli, *History*, 15–17; V. Prigent, 'Notes sur l'évolution de l'administration byzantine en Adriatique,' *Mélanges de l'école française de Rome* 120.2 (2008) 393–417, here 397; and Blankinship, *Jihâd State*, 139–140, 165. Crete: Niketas, *Life of Andreas of Crete* 8, in Papadopoulos-Kerameus, *Ἀνάλεκτα*, 5:177; date: F. Trombley, 'Mediterranean Sea Culture between Byzantium and Islam,' in E. Kountoura-Galake, ed., *Οι σκοτεινοί αιώνες του Βυζαντίου* (Athens 2001) 133–169, here 162–163.
4. Theophanes a.m.6218, pp. 405–406; Huneberc of Heidenheim, *Hodoeporicon of Saint Willibald* in *MGH SS* 15.1:101; raids: Blankinship, *Jihâd State*, 119–121, 162–163, 168–170; inscription: A. Schneider, *Die Stadtmauer von Iznik (Nicaea)* (Berlin 1938) 49 no. 29.
5. *Ekloge* 17.20, 17.38.
6. Humphreys, *Law*, 124.
7. *Ekloge*, pref., lines 32–34, 95–96; Humphreys, *Law*, 103–104, 128; *Mosaic Law*: 171–179.
8. Stephanos the Deacon, *Life of Stephanos the Younger* 9.
9. Mathews, *Dawn*.
10. Mathews, *Dawn*, 171–184, but cf. Niewöhner, 'Significance,' 215 n. 127; Paulos Silentiarios, *Ekphrasis of Hagia Sophia* 682–719, 755–805.
11. Church Fathers: John of Ephesos, *EH III* 2.27, 3.16 (dissidents); Milion and Chalke: Agathon the Deacon, *Epilogos* in *ACO* ser. 2, 2.2, pp. 898–900.
12. Respectively: Gregorios of Nyssa, *On the Divinity of the Son and Holy Spirit*, in *PG* 46:572; *Life of Maria of Egypt* 23; Brakke and Crislip, *Selected Discourses*, 37; Sophronios, *Miracles of Kyros and Ioannes*, pref. 7; Asterios of Amaseia, *Ekphrasis of the Martyr Euphemia*.
13. John of Ephesos, *EH III* 3.29; Agathias in *Greek Anthology* 1.34; Smith, *Greek Epigram*, 19, 77.
14. E.g., *Life of Theodoros of Sykeon* 8; *Miracles of Artemios* 18, 34. Arculf: e.g., Adamnán of Iona, *De locis sanctis* 3.4–5 (ed. and tr. Meehan, pp. 110–119).
15. A. Kaldellis, 'The Military Use of the Icon of the Theotokos,' *Estudios bizantinos* 1 (2013) 56–75, here 59–60.
16. Niewöhner, 'Significance.'
17. Troullo Canon 82; evolution: E. Kitzinger, 'The Cult of Images in the Age before Iconoclasm,' *DOP* 8 (1954) 83–150; sources: J. Elsner, 'Iconoclasm as Discourse: From Antiquity to Byzantium,' *Art Bulletin* 94 (2012) 368–394, here 372. Dialogue: Alexakis, 'Dialogue.' Brubaker and Haldon, *History*, 143 n. 269 are skeptical of its date.
18. Skepticism: L. Brubaker, 'Icons before Iconoclasm?' *Settimane di Studio del Centro Italiano di Studi sull'Alto Medioevo* 45 (1998) 1215–1254, relying on the oeuvre of Paul Speck. But see R. Price, 'Acta, Treatises, and Hagiography,' in M. Humphreys, ed., *A Companion to Byzantine Iconoclasm* (Leiden 2021) 230–260.

19. E.g., Latin: Brubaker and Haldon, *History*, 53–54; Syriac: pseudo-Zacharias, *Chronicle* 7.4e, 12.4b.
20. Meeting: Theophanes a.m.6221, pp. 408–409; Nikephoros, *Short History* 62; Gregory II: *Book of Pontiffs* 91.17 and cf. 23–24 for what Leon allegedly did in Constantinople (tr. Davis).
21. Chalke: Auzépy, *L'histoire*, 145–178; Brubaker and Haldon, *History*, 128–135; Germanos: ibid. 79–80, 123–126.
22. Gregory I, *Register* 9.209, 11.10; Maranci, *Art of Armenia*, 52; Mathews, *Dawn*, 209–211; Brubaker and Haldon, *History*, 67–68.
23. C. Sahner, 'The First Iconoclasm in Islam: A New History of the Edict of Yazid II,' *Der Islam* 94 (2017) 5–56.
24. Alexakis, 'Dialogue'; anti-Jewish dialogues: see the papers in *TM* 17 (2013) 5–169, e.g., at 46, 164; and Dagron and Déroche, *Juifs*; for a defense of the authenticity of Leontios, see A. Louth, *St. John Damascene: Tradition and Originality in Byzantine Theology* (Oxford 2002) 211–212. Germanos: *Letter to Ioannes of Synada* and *Letter to Thomas of Klaudiopolis* in *ACO* ser. 2, 3.2, pp. 442–479.
25. Theophanes a.m.6218, p. 406.
26. Niewöhner, 'Significance,' 240–241.
27. *Book of Pontiffs* 91.15–18; Theophanes a.m.6217, p. 404, and 6224, p. 410; Agnellus, *Book of Pontiffs of Ravenna* 153. Poll tax: Zuckerman, 'Learning,' 94–101 (with a different sequence). Brandes, 'Schweigen,' argues that the *patrimonium* was confiscated after the loss of Ravenna in 751, and because of it.
28. J. Osborne, *Rome in the Eighth Century* (Cambridge 2020) ch. 5; army of Rome (*exercitus Romanus*): Lambakis et al., *Βυζαντινά στρατεύματα*, 206–213.
29. Paul the Deacon, *History of the Lombards* 6.54; Gregorius in John the Deacon, *History of Venice*, p. 67, ed. G. Monticolo, *Cronache Veneziana antichissime*, v. 1 (Rome 1890); I follow Zuckerman, 'Learning,' 87–94.
30. Theophanes a.m.6231, p. 411; Blankinship, *Jihâd State*, 169–170.
31. Nikephoros, *Short History* 64–66; Theophanes a.m.6233–6235, pp. 414–421. "Slanders": Nikephoros, *Antirretikos* 2.3, in *PG* 100:340B-C; embassy: *Book of Pontiffs* 93.20.
32. Defecation: *Adversus Constantinum Cabalinum* 20, in *PG* 95:337A-B; Theophanes a.m.6211, p. 400; "pernicious" etc.: a.m.6232, p. 414 (tr. Mango and Scott); music and men: a.m.6259, pp. 442–443; scenes: Stephanos the Deacon, *Life of Stephanos the Younger* 26, 28 ("dragon"); dragonslayer: *Gesta episcoporum Neapolitanorum*, p. 423, ed. G. Waitz, *MGH*: *Scriptores rerum langobardicarum et italicarum saec. VI-IX* (Hannover 1878), with Auzépy, *L'histoire*, 317–328. "New Constantine": *ACO* ser. 2., 3.3, p. 778.
33. Nikephoros, *Short History* 63; Theophanes a.m.6232, p. 412; walls: B. Meyer-Plath and A. Schneider, *Die Landmauer von Konstantinopel* (Berlin 1943) 126–134. Eirene: Niewöhner, 'Significance,' 219–223.
34. Nikephoros, *Short History* 67–68 (quotation); *Antirretikos* 3.65, in *PG* 100:496B; Theophanes a.m.6238, pp. 422–424; a.m.6247, p. 429; a.m.6258, p. 440; Theodoros the Stoudite, *Praise of Abbot Platon* 1.3, in *PG* 99:805D.

35. Nikephoros, *Short History* 67, 70, 73; *Antirretikos* 3.72–73, in *PG* 100:508D-509A, 512B (forts in Thrace); Theophanes a.m.6237, p. 422; a.m.6243, p. 427; a.m.6247, p. 429; Hoyland, *Theophilus*, 289–290; raids: Lilie, *Reaktion*, 162–171; populations: Ditten, *Ethnische Verschiebungen*, 178–193.
36. Initial raid: Nikephoros, *Short History* 73; Theophanes a.m.6247, p. 429 (dishonest); campaigns: Brubaker and Haldon, *History*, 165; Curta, *Southeastern Europe*, 84–88; "images": *ACO* ser. 2, 3.3, p. 780; Nikephoros, *Antirretikos* 1.27, in *PG* 100:276B.
37. Haldon, *Praetorians*, 205–234.
38. Nikephoros, *Short History* 86; Theophanes a.m.6259, p. 443; R. Cormack and E. Hawkins, 'The Mosaics of St. Sophia at Istanbul: The Rooms above the Southwest Vestibule and Ramp,' *DOP* 31 (1977) 175–251.
39. Theophanes a.m.6244, p. 427; Theosteriktos, *Life of Niketas of Medikion* 29. *Peuseis*: S. Gero, *Byzantine Iconoclasm during the Reign of Constantine V* (Louvain 1977) 37–52.
40. *Horos*: Price, *Acts*, 668–684; forum: Theophanes a.m.6245, p. 428; Mansour: Anthony, 'Fixing.'
41. Magdalino, *Studies*, IV:8.
42. Brubaker and Haldon, *History*, 199–212; Polyeuktos: Mathews, *Dawn*, 173–182; Niewöhner, 'Significance,' 215 n. 127; Blachernai: Stephanos the Deacon, *Life of Stephanos the Younger* 29; Nikephoros, *Refutation of the Synod of 815* 71. Provincial churches: Signes Codoñer, 'Melkites,' 142.
43. Oath: Alexander, *Nicephorus*, 13 n. 2.
44. "Scorn": Theophanes a.m.6257, p. 437; a.m.6260, p. 443; Nikephoros, *Short History* 81. Stephanos the Deacon, *Life of Stephanos the Younger* 39–40; for this text see M.-F. Auzépy, *La vie d'Étienne le Jeune par Étienne le Diacre* (Aldershot, UK 1997) 5–42.
45. Nikephoros, *Short History* 80, 83; Theophanes a.m.6257, pp. 436–438. Cf. Maurikios in Gregory I, *Register* 3.61.
46. Magdalino, *Studies*, IV:6–10.
47. Theophanes a.m.6259, p. 443; a.m.6262–6263, pp. 445–446; Stephanos the Deacon, *Life of Stephanos the Younger* 59 (chronologically problematic).
48. "Iconoclast" monks: S. Gero, 'Byzantine Iconoclasm and Monachomachy,' *Journal of Ecclesiastical History* 28 (1977) 241–248; K. Ringrose, 'Monks and Society in Iconoclastic Byzantium,' *Byzantine Studies* 6 (1979) 130–151; Brubaker and Haldon, *History*, 240–241, 244.
49. Cf. M. Humphreys, 'Images of Authority? Imperial Patronage of Icons from Justinian II to Leo III,' in P. Sarris et al., eds., *An Age of Saints? Power Conflict and Dissent in Early Medieval Christianity* (Leiden 2011) 150–168, with D. Krausmüller, 'Contextualizing Constantine V's Radical Religious Policies,' *BMGS* 39 (2015) 25–49.
50. *Book of Pontiffs* 93.12–17 (early 740s), 94.8–9 (early 750s). Athenian: Konstantinos VII, *DAI* 27.16.
51. *Book of Pontiffs* 94.25–29 (Stephen), 94.43–45 (envoys); Noble, *Republic*, 49–94.
52. Konstantinos VII, *On the Themes*, p. 94.
53. Stephen in *MGH Epist.* 3:506; C. Gantner, 'The Label "Greeks" in the Papal Diplomatic Repertoire in the Eighth Century,' in W. Pohl and G. Heydemann, eds., *Post-Roman*

Transitions: Christian and Barbarian Identities in the Early Medieval West (Turnhout 2013) 303–349.

54. Noble, *Republic*, 77, 96–97.
55. Naples: T. Brown, 'Byzantine Italy, c. 680-c. 876,' in R. McKitterick, ed., *The New Cambridge Medieval History*, v. 2 (Cambridge 1995) 320–348, here 341–342. Arechis: pope Hadrian to Charlemagne in *MGH Epist.* 3:617.
56. Wilson, *Holy Roman Empire*, 23; also A. Ekonomou, *Byzantine Rome and the Greek Popes: Eastern Influences on Rome and the Papacy from Gregory the Great to Zacharias* (Plymouth, UK 2007).
57. Brandes, 'Schweigen,' 200. 785: pope Hadrian to Charlemagne in *MGH Epist.* 5:57.

Chapter 21. Reform and Consolidation (775–814)

1. *Royal Frankish Annals* s.a. 757.
2. T. Lounghis, *Les ambassades byzantines en Occident* (Athens 1980) 151–152.
3. Dagron, *Idées*, 454.
4. *Book of Pontiffs* 96.23; Brubaker and Haldon, *History*, 172–173.
5. Kaldellis, *Parthenon*; J. Darrouzès, 'Les listes épiscopales du Concile de Nicée (787),' *REB* 33 (1975) 5–76.
6. Theophanes a.m.6261, p. 444; Konstantinos VII, *Book of Ceremonies* 1.50.
7. Theophanes a.m.6262, p. 445; a.m.6289, p. 472; Konstantinos VII, *Book of Ceremonies* 2.21–22, 1.51.
8. Konstantinos VII, *Book of Ceremonies* 1.69.
9. Theophanes a.m.6260, pp. 443–444; Konstantinos VII, *Book of Ceremonies* 1.52.
10. Theophanes a.m.6268, pp. 449–451.
11. Theophanes a.m.6272, p. 453. For the legend of Eirene as a secret icon-worshipper, see J. Herrin, *Women in Purple: Rulers of Medieval Byzantium* (Princeton 2001) 71–73.
12. Theophanes a.m.6270–6271, pp. 451–452; Baladhuri, *Origins* 189–190 (tr. Hitti, 1:295–296); Tabari, *History* 2:485–486, 493.
13. Theophanes a.m.6273, p. 454.
14. Theophanes a.m.6273–6274, pp. 454–456.
15. Theophanes a.m.6274, p. 455; *Royal Frankish Annals* s.a. 781.
16. Theophanes a.m.6274, p. 456; Tabari, *History* 2:503–505 (the text is corrupt; I thank Kevin van Bladel for his help).
17. Theophanes a.m.6275–6276, pp. 456–457; N. Sharankov and D. Yankov, 'A 784 AD Inscription of Constantine VI and Irene from Beroe-Irenopolis,' *Archaeologia Bulgarica* 12 (2008) 77–86.
18. *Sacra* of Konstantinos and Eirene to the Council, in *ACO* ser. 2, 3.1, pp. 44–46; Tarasios in ibid. p. 10, and Theophanes a.m.6277, p. 459.
19. Ignatios the Deacon, *Life of Tarasios* 4–6; Hadrian: *ACO* ser. 2, 3.1, pp. 165–167; delegates: Price, *Acts*, 198–202.

20. *ACO* ser. 2, 3.1, pp. 12–16; cf. Theophanes a.m.6278, pp. 462; Ignatios the Deacon, *Life of Tarasios* 26–27. Ten bishops: Price, *Acts*, 84. 6,000: *Life of Ioannes of Gotthia* 4, in *AASS* 7 June (1867), pp. 167–171. *Vigla*: Haldon, *Praetorians*, 236–245.
21. *ACO* ser. 2, 3.3, p. 826 (tr. Price, mod.); cf. Basil of Kaisareia, *On the Holy Spirit* 18.45; tabernacle: Exodus 25:18–20; L. Brubaker, 'The Elephant and the Ark: Cultural and Material Interchange across the Mediterranean in the Eighth and Ninth Centuries,' *DOP* 58 (2004) 175–195, here 178–180.
22. Brubaker and Haldon, *History*, 352–354.
23. Brubaker and Haldon, *History*, 133–135, 294–297, 309–315; Ignatios the Deacon, *Life of Tarasios* 49–52, 56.
24. Theophanes a.m.6281, pp. 463–464; see Treadgold, *Byzantine Revival*, 92 for Italy.
25. Theophanes a.m.6282–6289, pp. 464–473; forum: Nikephoros, *Chronographikon*, p. 100, ed. C. de Boor, *Nicephori archiepiscopi Constantinopolitani opuscula historica* (Leipzig 1880).
26. Petros, *Life of Ioannikios* 5–7.
27. Treadgold, 'Unpublished Saint's Life.'
28. Theophanes a.m.6290–6294, pp. 473–475; Konstantinos VII, *Book of Ceremonies* 1.5, 1.19; Theodoros Stoudites, *Letter* 7.
29. Humphreys, *Law*, 235–242; laws: Humphreys, *Laws*, 164–168.
30. Haldon and Kennedy, 'Arab-Byzantine Frontier,' 106–115; C. Bosworth, *The Arabs, Byzantium and Iran* (London 1996) XIV; 790s: Brubaker and Haldon, *History*, 289; deal: Treadgold, *Byzantine Revival*, 113.
31. *Book of Pontiffs* 98.23; *Royal Frankish Annals* s.a. 801.
32. Hadrian in *MGH Epist.* 3:587; Aachen: Wilson, *Holy Roman Empire*, 36; Deliyannis, 'Silver Tables'; D. Rollason, *The Power of Place: Rulers and Their Palaces, Landscapes, Cities and Holy Places* (Princeton 2016) 273–289.
33. Price, *Acts*, 68–73; Brubaker and Haldon, *History*, 281, 282 n. 140.
34. J. Davis, *Charlemagne's Practice of Empire* (Cambridge 2015) 1, 3, 178, 343–379, 412.
35. *Annales Laureshamenses* s.a. 801, p. 33: *cessabat a parte Graecorum nomen imperatoris, et femineum imperium apud se abebant.*
36. Theophanes a.m.6293, p. 475.
37. Theophanes a.m.6295, pp. 476–479; *Royal Frankish Annals* s.a. 803.
38. Theophanes a.m.6295–6296, pp. 479–480; Theophanes Continuatus 1.1–3; I do not believe that he was *monostrategos* of Asia Minor; sources: *PmbZ* 766.
39. Anthony, 'Fixing,' 627.
40. *ACO* ser. 2, 3.3, pp. 782–784.
41. Auzépy, *L'histoire*, 69–74, 209–220; Signes Codoñer, 'Melkites,' 159–160; florilegia: A. Alexakis, *Codex Parisinus Graecus 1115 and Its Archetype* (Washington, D.C. 1996); *Adversus Constantinum Caballinum*: *PG* 95:309–344; wizard: *ACO* ser. 2, 3.2, pp. 590–594.
42. Auzépy, *L'histoire*, 119–144.
43. A. Binggeli and S. Efthymiadis, *Les nouveaux martyrs à Byzance* (Paris 2021) I.
44. Hatlie, *Monks*, 244–250; new foundations: 284–287.
45. *ACO* ser. 2, 3.1, p. 230; see Price, *Acts*, 33–35, 55–56. Relative: Hatlie, *Monks*, 289–290.

46. Theophanes a.m.6287–6288, pp. 469–471; Alexander, *Nicephorus*, 82–101.
47. Numbers: Hatlie, *Monks*, 322–325; reforms: 274–276, 338–352; minuscule: 416–417; A.-M. Talbot, *Varieties of Monastic Experience in Byzantium* (Notre Dame 2019) 16–25.
48. R. Taft, *The Byzantine Rite* (Collegeville, MN 1992) 52–84.
49. Brubaker and Haldon, *History*, 360.
50. Theodoros of Stoudios, *Praise of Platon* 35.
51. Theodoros of Stoudios, *Letter* 22.
52. Petros, *Life of Ioannikios* 36.
53. Dagron, *Idées*, 545–562.
54. Synod: Theodoros of Stoudios, *Letter* 48; P. Henry, 'The Moechian Controversy and the Constantinopolitan Synod of January 809,' *Journal of Theological Studies* 20 (1969) 495–522; Hatlie, *Monks*, 327 n. 54; C. Zuckerman, 'Theophanes the Confessor and Theophanes the Chronicler, Or, A Story of Square Brackets,' *TM* 19 (2015) 31–52.
55. Theodoros of Stoudios, *Letters* 33–34; Gouillard, 'Origines'; Brubaker and Haldon, *History*, 83 n. 52; in general: Dagron, *Emperor and Priest*, ch. 5.
56. Hagiography: Prieto Domínguez, *Literary Circles*, ch. 1; Bulgars: Sophoulis, *Byzantium*, 38–39.
57. Brubaker and Haldon, *History*, ch. 10, esp. 682, 697, 709–711, 716, 752. *Taktikon Uspenskij*: Oikonomidès, *Listes*, 46–63; date: E. Kislinger, 'Dyrrachion und die Küsten von Epirus und Dalmatien im frühen Mittelalter,' *Millennium* 8 (2011) 313–352, here 338, 342–344.
58. A.-K. Wassiliou-Seibt, 'Reconstructing the Byzantine Frontier on the Balkans,' *REB* 73 (2015) 229–239; T. Živković, 'The Date of the Creation of the Theme of Peloponnese,' *Βυζαντινά Σύμμεικτα* 13 (1999) 141–155.
59. *Chronicle of Monembasia*, pp. 18–22, ed. I. Dujčev, *Cronaca di Monemvasia* (Palermo 1976), on which see I. Anagnostakis and A. Kaldellis, 'The Textual Sources for the Peloponnese, A.D. 582–959,' *GRBS* 54 (2014) 105–135, here 106–115. Dispute: Konstantinos VII, *DAI* 49; K. Belke, 'Einige Überlegungen zum Sigillion Kaiser Nikephoros I. für Patrai,' *JöB* 46 (1996) 81–96.
60. Theophanes a.m.6302, p. 486; settlements in Thrace in 806/7: a.m.6299, pp. 482–483; Brubaker and Haldon, *History*, 744–755, assume immediate universal application.
61. Ivison, 'Amorium,' 31; *Hikanatoi*: Niketas David, *Life of Ignatios* 3; Theophanes Continuatus 1.10; Haldon, *Praetorians*, 245–246; but see Petros in *PmbZ* 6046.
62. Theophanes a.m.6302–6303, pp. 486–489; "orthodox": *Life of Niketas of Medikion* 31.
63. Theophanes a.m.6298, p. 482; 6300, p. 483; Tabari, *History* 2:708–711.
64. Sophoulis, *Byzantium*, 185.
65. Theophanes a.m.6302, pp. 485–486.
66. *Chronicle of 811*, in P. Stephenson, '"About the emperor Nikephoros and how he leaves his bones in Bulgaria": A Context for the Controversial Chronicle of 811,' *DOP* 60 (2006) 87–109; Theophanes a.m.6303, pp. 490–491; archaeology: Fiedler, 'Bulgars,' 176–177, 184; Sophoulis, *Byzantium*, 63–64, 205; inscription: ibid. 207 n. 204.
67. Michael the Monk, *Life of Theodoros of Stoudios B* 28, in *PG* 99:272A-B.

68. Theophanes Continuatus 1.1; *Chronicle of 811*, p. 216; J. Wortley, 'Legends of the Byzantine Disaster of 811,' *Byzantion* 50 (1980) 533–562.
69. Theophanes a.m.6304, pp. 494–495; Nikephoros, *Letter to Pope Leo*, in *PG* 100:169–200; Michael the Monk, *Life of Theodoros of Stoudios B* 28, in *PG* 99:272–273; "prudently": *Scriptor Incertus de Leone Armenio*, p. 335.
70. Petkov, *Voices*, 6.
71. Theophanes a.m.6305, pp. 497–503; *Scriptor Incertus de Leone Armenio*, pp. 336–340; Theophanes Continuatus 1.5; Skylitzes 12. The story that Leon (Anatolikon) threw the battle is compromised by iconophile polemic.
72. Hatlie, *Monks*, 329.
73. Theophanes a.m.6305, pp. 502–503; *Scriptor Incertus de Leone Armenio*, pp. 342–346; Symeon Logothetes 131.9; 40,000 captives: *Synaxarion of Constantinople*, p. 415.
74. E.g., *MGH Legum* 3, *Concilia* 2.2:475.
75. *Royal Frankish Annals* s.a. 810–814; Konstantinos VII, *DAI* 28; treaty: Dölger, *Regesten*, 1.1:47; Nicol, *Byzantium*, 16–19; M. Ančić et al., eds., *Imperial Spheres and the Adriatic: Byzantium, the Carolingians and the Treaty of Aachen (812)* (New York 2018); patrician: C. Baltrame, 'On the Origin of Ship Construction in Venice,' in S. Gaspari and S. Gelichi, eds., *The Age of Affirmation: Venice, the Adriatic and the Hinterland between the 9th and 10th Centuries* (Turnhout 2017) 129–146; Kephalonia theme: Brubaker and Haldon, *History*, 757.
76. A critical survey in E. D'Amico, 'Approaches and Perspectives on the Origins of Venice,' *Memoirs of the American Academy in Rome* 52 (2017) 209–230.
77. *Scriptor Incertus de Leone Armenio*, pp. 347–348.

Chapter 22. Growing Confidence (815–867)

1. Theophanes Continuatus 1.19.
2. Theophanes a.m.6303, pp. 488–489; a.m.6304–6305, pp. 496–497, 501; Nikephoros, *Antirretikos* 3.62–94, 3.70–72, in *PG* 100:492–493, 504–508; *Apologetikos* in ibid. 556B-D; *Scriptor Incertus de Leone Armenio*, p. 349; Treadgold, *Byzantine Revival*, 413 n. 249. Shaving: Stephanos the Deacon, *Life of Stephanos the Younger* 38.
3. *Scriptor Incertus de Leone Armenio*, pp. 349–355; Theosteriktos, *Life of Niketas of Medikion* 31.
4. *Scriptor Incertus de Leone Armenio*, pp. 355–362; Theosteriktos, *Life of Niketas of Medikion* 32–35 ("child of the Church"); Theophylaktos, *Life of Theophylaktos of Nikomedeia* 11 ("wolf"), 12–13 (meetings), ed. A. Vogt, 'S. Théophylakte de Nicomédie,' *Analecta Bollandiana* 50 (1932) 71–82. "Bones": Nikephoros, *Refutation of Pseudo-Epiphanios* 6, ed. J. Pitra, *Sancti Nicephori Antirrheticus liber quartus* (Rome 1858) 292–380.
5. P. Alexander, 'The Iconoclastic Council of S. Sophia (815),' *DOP* 7 (1953) 35–66; naïveté: fr. 7; "idols": fr. 16. Pledge: Nikephoros, *Refutation and Overthrow of the Council of 815* 4.

6. Treadgold, *Byzantine Revival*, 213–214, 418 n. 290; Hatlie, *Monks*, 384; Theodoros of Stoudios: cf. *Letter* 38 with 407.
7. Theophanes Continuatus 1.13, 1.20; Genesios 1.12; inscriptions: Petkov, *Voices*, 7–8; date: W. Treadgold, 'The Bulgars' Treaty with the Byzantines in 816,' *Rivista di studi bizantini e slavi* 4 (1984) 213–220; terms: Curta, *Southeastern Europe*, 154–156; Erkesija: idem, 'Linear Frontiers in the 9th Century: Bulgaria and Wessex,' *Quaestiones Medii Aevi Novae* 16 (2011) 15–31; Fiedler, 'Bulgars,' 167.
8. Theodoros of Stoudios, *Letters* 128, 245; iconophile hagiography: Prieto Domínguez, *Literary Circles*.
9. Alexander, *Nicephorus*, 140–147; Brubaker and Haldon, *History*, 375–382; Hatlie, *Monks*, 376; Thaddaios: ibid. 265; retroactive distortion: ibid. 360–362.
10. Hatlie, *Monks*, 423 n. 52; expunged: Prieto Domínguez, *Literary Circles*, 45.
11. Theophanes Continuatus 1.19. No chains: Theosteriktos, *Life of Niketas of Medikion* 47.
12. Michael II, *Letter to Louis the Pious*, in *MGH Legum* 3, *Concilia* 2.2:475–480; Theophanes Continuatus 2.9–20; Genesios 2.2–9; P. Lemerle, 'Thomas le Slav,' *TM* 1 (1965) 255–297.
13. Theophanes Continuatus 2.8. Athinganoi: I. Panagiotopoulos, *Περὶ Ἀθιγγάνων: Πολιτικὴ καὶ θρησκεία στὴ βυζαντινὴ αὐτοκρατορία* (Athens 2008).
14. Theodoros of Stoudios, *Letters* 417, 469; cf. 429, 532 (to the emperors).
15. Theodoros of Stoudios, *Letter* 28.92.
16. Michael II, *Letter to Louis the Pious*, in *MGH Legum* 3, *Concilia* 2.2:478–479. Cf. Theodoros of Stoudios, *Letter* 17.
17. B. Anderson, 'Images Down Low,' in S. Feist, ed., *Transforming Sacred Spaces: New Approaches to Byzantine Ecclesiastical Architecture from the Transitional Period* (Wiesbaden 2020) 161–187.
18. Hilsdale, *Byzantine Art*, 238–239: manuscript: Paris BN Ms. gr. 437.
19. Theophanes Continuatus 2.21–26; Genesios 2.10–13; C. Makrypoulias, 'Byzantine Expeditions against the Emirate of Crete, c. 825–949,' *Graeco-Arabica* 7–8 (2000) 347–362.
20. Chiarelli, *History*, 20–32 (Arabic sources); V. Prigent, 'La carrière du tourmarque Euphèmios, Basileus des Romains,' in A. Jacob et al., eds., *Histoire et culture dans l'Italie byzantine* (Rome 2006) 279–310.
21. *PmbZ* 8167 (p. 629).
22. Symeon Logothetes 130.2–5; cf. *Life of the Empress Theodora* 3; W. Treadgold, 'The Historicity of the Imperial Bride-Shows,' *JöB* 54 (2004) 39–52.
23. Oikonomides, 'Role,' 981. C. Morrisson, 'Byzantine Money,' in *EHB*, 947–950; Brubaker and Haldon, *History*, 487, 517, 703–704.
24. Cf. Haldon, *Empire*, 29, with idem, 'Late Rome,' 363. Reserves: cf. Theophanes Continuatus 4.20 with Konstantinos VII, *Life of Basileios I* 27.
25. Theophanes Continuatus 3.8, 3.42–44, 4.21; Konstantinos VII, *Life of Basileios I* 29; Symeon Logothetes 130.9.
26. Theophanes Continuatus 3.9, 4.27.

27. Symeon Logothetes 130.6, 10; Theophanes Continuatus 3.1, 3.3; *Timarion* 32–33; 100,000: Hatlie, *Monks*, 259.
28. Theophanes a.m.6302, p. 487; P. Magdalino, 'The Merchant of Constantinople,' in idem and Necipoğlu, eds., *Trade*, 183–191; in general, McCormick, *Origins*, 115–119, 433–441. Ship: Theophanes Continuatus 3.4; Genesios 3.20.
29. M.-F. Auzépy, 'Miracle et économie à Byzance (VIe–IXe siècle),' in D. Aigle, ed., *Miracle et karâma: Hagiographies médiévales comparées* (Turnhout 2000) 2:331–351.
30. C. Pulak et al., 'Eight Byzantine Shipwrecks from the Theodosian Harbour Excavations,' *The International Journal of Nautical Archaeology* 44 (2015) 39–73.
31. E. Batuman, 'The Big Dig,' *The New Yorker*, August 31, 2015.
32. 770s: Theophanes a.m.6265, p. 447; Baladhuri, *Origins* 189 (tr. Hitti, 1:294); al-Jarmi: Treadgold, *Army*, 64–69; Haldon, *Warfare*, 101–103.
33. 5,000: Nikephoros II, *On Skirmishing* 17 (p. 204); Leon VI, *Taktika* 18.148–149.
34. Equids: Cooper and Decker, *Cappadocia*, 84–88; cost: Treadgold, *Army*, 128.
35. Protocol: Haldon, *Constantine*, 146–151; in general: Signes Codoñer, *Theophilos*, ch. 14.
36. Theophanes Continuatus 1.5; Khurramites: Kaldellis, *Romanland*, 127–132.
37. Michael the Syrian 12.19; Tabari, *History* 3:1234–1236; Theophanes Continuatus 3.29; Genesios 3.11–13; "flowers": Haldon, *Constantine*, 150–151.
38. Tabari, *History* 3:1236–1256; Michael the Syrian 12.20; Theophanes Continuatus 3.30–35.
39. Ivison, 'Amorium.'
40. Greek translation in H. M. Hassan, 'Το ποίημα του Αμπού Ταμμάμ για την άλωση του Αμορίου το 838 μ.Χ.,' *Journal of Oriental and African Studies* 13 (2004) 33–72.
41. Theophanes Continuatus 3.29, 3.38; "extinct": Genesios 3.7; other sources: Kaldellis, *Romanland*, 127–132; rebellion: Signes Codoñer, *Theophilos*, ch. 12.
42. Methodios, *Life of Euthymios of Sardeis* 12–14; *Lives of David, Symeon, and Georgios of Mytilene* 22.
43. *Life of Methodios* 4–6, in *PG* 100:1248–1249; *Lives of David, Symeon, and Georgios of Mytilene* 22; Theophanes Continuatus 2.8. *Daniel*: P. Alexander, *The Byzantine Apocalyptic Tradition* (Berkeley 1985) 61–72; W. Treadgold, 'The Prophecies of Methodios,' *REB* 62 (2004) 229–237; Hatlie, *Monks*, 389.
44. Lazaros: Theophanes Continuatus 3.13; *Book of Pontiffs* 106.33, with Brubaker and Haldon, *Sources*, 72–73; in general: Brubaker and Haldon, *History*, 392–403.
45. Theophanes a.m.6305, p. 499; Ditten, *Ethnische Verschiebungen*, 66–68; Michael et al.: Auzépy, *L'histoire*, 216–220, 248–251; Hatlie, *Monks*, 267–269, 322, 389–391. Verses: Theophanes Continuatus 3.14; Symeon Logothetes 130.38; *Lives of David, Symeon, and Georgios of Mytilene* 23.
46. Theophanes Continuatus 3.9.
47. L. Westerink, 'Leo the Philosopher: *Job* and Other Poems,' *Illinois Classical Studies* 11 (1986) 193–222; V. Laurent, 'Une homélie inédite de l'archevêque de Thessalonique Léon le philosophe,' in *Mélanges Eugène Tisserant* (Vatican City 1964) 2:281–302; accusations: P. Matranga, *Anecdota graeca* (Rome 1850) 2:555–559.
48. Theophanes Continuatus 3.18; Symeon Logothetes 130.11–14; *PmbZ* 195. Slavs: Ignatios the Deacon, *Life of Gregorios Dekapolites* 52.

49. Theodoros of Stoudios, *Letter* 162.
50. *Passion of the Martyrs of the Chalke*, in *AASS* 2 Aug, pp. 434–447 (Maria); *Synaxarion of Constantinople*, pp. 828–830 (Theodosia); ibid. pp. 613–614 and C. Mango, 'St. Anthusa of Mantineon and the Family of Constantine V,' *Analecta Bollandiana* 100 (1982) 401–409; Theophanes a.m.6258, pp. 439–440 (relics of Euphemia); Treadgold, 'Unpublished Saint's Life,' and Kedrenos, *Historical Compendium*, 2:19–20 (Eirene); Symeon Logothetes 131.2 and Theophanes Continuatus 3.5–6 (Theodora); Brubaker and Haldon, *History*, 398; see S. Efthymiadis, 'Γυναίκες, μοναχισμός και αγιολογία στη μεσοβυζαντινή και την υστεροβυζαντινή περίοδο,' in E. Kountoura-Galake and E. Mitsiou, eds., *Women and Monasticism in the Medieval Eastern Mediterranean* (Athens 2019) 31–48.
51. Theophanes Continuatus 3.2; *Life of the Empress Theodora* 7.
52. *Synodicon Vetus* 156; *Life of the Empress Theodora* 10; *Lives of David, Symeon, and Georgios of Mytilene* 26–30; Theophanes the Abbot, *Exile and Translation of the Relics of Nikephoros* 7–8, ed. Th. Ioannou, *Μνημεῖα ἁγιολογικά* (Leipzig 1884) 115–128, here 122–123; procession: Konstantinos VII, *Book of Ceremonies* 1.37.
53. Theophanes the Abbot, *Exile and Translation of the Relics of Nikephoros* 11–13; Ioannes: Theophanes Continuatus 4.9; images: K. Corrigan, *Visual Polemics in Ninth-Century Byzantine Psalters* (Cambridge 1992).
54. B. Zielke, 'Methodios I. (843–847),' in R.-J. Lilie, ed., *Die Patriarchen der ikonoklastischen Zeit* (Frankfurt 1999) 183–260, here 231–247; Hatlie, *Monks*, 391–393. Repentance: e.g., *Lives of David, Symeon, and Georgios of Mytilene* 28.
55. O. Prieto Domínquez, 'The Iconoclast Saint: Emperor Theophilos in Byzantine Hagiography,' in Tougher, ed., *Emperor*, 216–234.
56. Niewöhner, 'Significance,' 187.
57. Sicily: Chiarelli, *History*, 32–39; Italy: Kreutz, *Normans*, ch. 2; migration: McCormick, 'Imperial Edge,' 33; Deliyannis, 'Silver Tables.'
58. Aigina: *Life of Hosios Loukas of Steiris* 2–3; *Life of Theodora of Thessalonike* 3; patrols: *Life of Petros of Argos* 9; *Life of Theodoros of Kythera* 5; M. Leontsini, 'The Byzantine and Arab Navies in the South Aegean and Crete,' *Graeco-Arabica* 12 (2017) 170–231, here 206–211.
59. Ignatios the Deacon, *Letter* 37; campaign: Symeon Logothetes 131.3–4; Arabic source: V. Christides, 'The Cycle of the Arab-Byzantine Struggle in Crete in Skylitzes,' *Graeco-Arabica* 11 (2011) 17–50, here 35–37.
60. Symeon Logothetes 131.4–5.
61. Theophanes a.m.6304, p. 495; Theodoros of Stoudios, *Letters* 94, 455; Ignatios the Deacon, *Life of Nikephoros*, pp. 158–159; Sabas, *Life of Makarios of Pelekete* 14; Petros of Sicily, *History of the Paulicians* 175–176.
62. Theophanes Continuatus 4.16; Petros of Sicily, *History of the Paulicians* 37; exodus: ibid. 177–185.
63. Tabari, *History* 3:1417–1418; Vasiliev, *Byzance*, 1:212–217; G. Levi Della Vida, 'A Papyrus Reference to the Damietta Raid of 853 A.D.,' *Byzantion* 17 (1944–1945) 212–221.
64. Symeon Logothetes 131.45.

65. Cf. Symeon Logothetes 131.22–23 with Theophanes Continuatus 4.20.
66. Niketas David, *Life of Ignatios* 17.
67. Psellos, *Chronographia* 6.1.
68. T. Papamastorakis, 'Tampering with History: From Michael III to Michael VIII,' *BZ* 96 (2003) 193–209, here 194–199: Pharos: Photios, *Homily* 10.
69. Vasiliev, *Byzance*, 1:223, 233–236.
70. Symeon Logothetes 131.26; Genesios 4.15; Theophanes Continuatus 4.25; Tabari, *History* 3:1509; campaign: H. Huxley, 'The Emperor Michael III and the Battle of Bishop's Meadow,' *GRBS* 16 (1975) 443–450; triumph: McCormick, *Eternal Victory*, 150–152.
71. Vasiliev, *Byzance*, 1:219–222.
72. Photios, *Homily* 3.1, 4.2–4 (tr. Mango, pp. 82, 98–102); date: F. Cumont, *Anecdota Bruxellensia* (Ghent 1894) 1:33; Niketas David, *Life of Ignatios* 28.
73. Photios, *Letter* 2 (p. 50); cf. Theophanes Continuatus 4.33.
74. Pope Nicholas I, *Letter* 88 to Michael III (865 AD), in *MGH Epist.* 6:479.23–29.
75. *PmbZ* 2666 (esp. pp. 174–175); resignation: Dvornik, *Photian Schism*, ch. 2.
76. Ignatios and learning: Anastasius the Librarian, *Preface to the Eighth Ecumenical Council*, in Mansi, *Sacrorum Conciliorum*, 16:6 = Leonardi and Placanica, eds., *Gesta*, 13. Photios: W. Treadgold, 'Photius before his Patriarchate,' *Journal of Ecclesiastical History* 53 (2002) 1–17.
77. Photios, *Homilies* 10, 17.
78. Nicholas, *Letter* 82 to Michael III (860 AD), in *MGH Epist.* 6:433–439. Serdica: H. Ohme in W. Hartmann and K. Pennington, eds., *The History of Byzantine and Eastern Canon Law to 1500* (Washington, D.C. 2012) 66–74; cf. Photios, *Letter* 290.339–341. Scribe: J. Morton, *Byzantine Religious Law in Medieval Italy* (Oxford 2021) 90.
79. E. Chrysos, 'New Perceptions of *Imperium* and *Sacerdotium* in the Letters of Pope Nicholas I to Emperor Michael III,' *TM* 22 (2018) 313–339.
80. Paulos of Kaisareia in V. von Glanvell, *Die Kanonessammlung des Kardinals Deusdedit* (Paderborn 1905) 603.
81. Photios, *Letter* 290 (861 AD); Nicholas, *Letter* 85 to Michael III (862 AD), in *MGH Epist.* 6:442–446, and *Letter* 86 to Photios (6:447–451); synod of 863: *Letter* 91 (6:512–533). John VII, *Letter* 37 to Boris, in *MGH Epist.* 7:294.
82. Nicholas, *Letter* 27, in *MGH Epist.* 6:293 (864 AD); Theophanes Continuatus 4.13–15; Symeon Logothetes 131.25.
83. S. Ivanov, *"Pearls before Swine": Missionary Work in Byzantium* (Paris 2015).
84. F. Curta, *Eastern Europe in the Middle Ages (500–1300)* (Leiden 2019) ch. 11; Venice: *Life of Constantine-Cyril* 16; M. Ivanova, 'Re-Thinking the *Life of Constantine-Cyril the Philosopher*,' *Slavonic and East European Review* 98 (2020) 434–463.
85. Nicholas, *Letter* 88 to Michael III, in *MGH Epist.* 6:454–487 (*princeps omnem terram*); Chrysos, 'War of Languages.'
86. Nicholas, *Letter* 99 (*Response to the Bulgarians*), in *MGH Epist.* 6:568–600; *Letter* 92 (6:533–540); heresy: Chrysos, 'War of Languages,' 271–272. Cremations: Fiedler, 'Bulgars,' 157–158. Cf. Aeneas of Paris, *Liber adversus Graecos*, in *PL* 121:685–762, here 686–689; Ratramnus of Corbie, *Contra Graecorum*, in *PL* 121:225–346.

87. Photios, *Letter* 2.55–107; T. Kolbaba, *Inventing Latin Heretics: Byzantines and the Filioque in the Ninth Century* (Kalamazoo, MI 2008) ch. 4.
88. Dvornik, *Photian Schism*, 121 n. 1, 128–129; and *Synodicon Vetus* 161. Destruction of Acts: C. Mango, *Homilies of Photius* (Cambridge, MA 1958) 299. Ecumenical: Niketas David, *Life of Ignatios* 52.
89. Photios, *Letter* 18.
90. *Royal Frankish Annals* s.a. 802, 810; Notker, *Life of Charlemagne* 2.9.
91. *On Strategy* 1.17–22, 3.16–17, 3.63–64, ed. Dennis, *Military Treatises*, 10–11, 14–17.
92. Einhard, *Life of Charlemagne* 16.
93. P. de Gayangos, *A History of the Mohammedan Dynasties in Spain* (London 1843) 2:115 (6.4); E. Manzano Moreno, 'Byzantium and al-Andalus in the Ninth Century,' in L. Brubaker, ed., *Byzantium in the Ninth Century: Dead or Alive?* (Aldershot, UK 1998) 215–227.
94. *On Strategy* 43.7–13, ed. and tr. Dennis, *Military Treatises*, 124–125.
95. P. Frankopan, 'Some Notes on Byzantine Foreign Policy in the 9th-11th Centuries,' *Journal of Medieval and Islamic History* 3 (2003) 1–11; J. Olsson, 'Coup d'état, Coronation and Conversion: Some Reflections on the Adoption of Judaism by the Khazar Khaganate,' *Journal of the Royal Asiatic Society* 23 (2013) 495–526, here 513–515.
96. Kaldellis, *Ethnography*, ch. 2.
97. A. Kaldellis, 'Did the Byzantine Empire have "Ecumenical" or "Universal" Aspirations?,' in C. Ando and S. Richardson, eds., *Ancient States and Infrastructural Power* (Philadelphia 2017) 272–300.
98. G. Prinzing, 'Byzantium, Medieval Russia and the So-Called Family of Kings,' in A. Alshanskaya et al., eds., *Imagining Byzantium: Perceptions, Patterns, Problems* (Mainz 2018) 15–30.
99. Kaldellis, *Romanland*, ch. 6.
100. S. Griffith, 'Byzantium and the Christians in the World of Islam,' *Medieval Encounters* 3 (1997) 231–265.
101. Gutas, *Greek Thought*, 84–87; language: Kaldellis, *Romanland*, 104–105.
102. R. Forrai, 'The Sacred Nectar of the Deceitful Greeks: Perceptions of Greekness in Ninth Century Rome,' in A. Speer and P. Steinkrüger, eds., *Knotenpunkt Byzanz: Wissensformen und kulturelle Wechselbeziehungen* (Berlin 2012) 71–84.
103. A. Kaldellis, 'The Byzantine Role in the Making of the Corpus of Classical Greek Historiography,' *Journal of Hellenic Studies* 132 (2012) 71–85.
104. A. Kaldellis, 'Translations into Greek in the Byzantine Period,' in D. Gutas, ed., *Why Translate Science? Documents from Antiquity to the 16th Century* (Leiden 2022) 397–444.
105. Lemerle, *Humanism*, 82.
106. Theophanes Continuatus 4.26–29; Genesios 4.17.
107. Lemerle, *Humanism*, 178–180; P. Pattenden, 'The Byzantine Early Warning System,' *Byzantion* 53 (1983) 258–299; use: Theophanes Continuatus 4.35; local: Nikephoros II, *Skirmishing Warfare* 2; Italy: Noyé, 'New Light,' 184.

108. C. Brockmann, 'Scribal Annotation as Evidence of Learning in Manuscripts from the First Byzantine Humanism: The "Philosophical Collection",' in J. Quenzer et al., eds., *Manuscript Cultures: Mapping the Field* (Berlin 2014) 11–34.
109. Gutas, *Greek Thought*, 184–185.
110. *Life of Constantine-Cyril* 7; Theophanes Continuatus 4.27.

Chapter 23. A New David and Solomon (867–912)

1. Konstantinos VII, *Life of Basileios I* 7; cf. Liudprand, *Antapodosis* 3.32.
2. A. Markopoulos, 'An Anonymous Laudatory Poem in Honor of Basil I,' *DOP* 46 (1992) 225–232, here 230; cf. Psalm 77.70.
3. Arabs: El Cheikh, *Byzantium*, 88–89; Chinese: Dagron, *Emperor and Priest*, 13; Khazar: *Life of Constantine-Cyril* 9.
4. Haldon, *Seventh Century*, 155–160, 382; Neville, *Authority*, 18–20.
5. V. Vlysidou, *Αριστοκρατικές οικογένειες και εξουσία (9ος-10ος αι.)* (Thessalonike 2001); Cheynet, *Byzantine Aristocracy*, esp. I.
6. Photios: cf. Anastasius the Librarian, *Preface to the Eighth Ecumenical Council*, in Mansi, *Sacrorum Conciliorum*, 16:6, with Symeon Logothetes 132.5. Skepe and envoys: Niketas David, *Life of Ignatios* 53.
7. *Book of Pontiffs* 108.25–33; Hadrian, *Letters* 39–40 to Ignatios and Basileios, in *MGH Epist.* 6:750–758; Mansi, *Sacrorum Conciliorum*, 16:122–131, 372–380 = Leonardi and Placanica, eds., *Gesta*, 230–248.
8. *Book of Pontiffs* 108.40.
9. E. Chrysos, 'The Council of Constantinople in 869–870: A Minority Council,' *Annuarium Historiae Conciliorum* 49 (2018–2019) 138–161; Dvornik, *Photian Schism*, ch. 5. First session: Niketas David, *Life of Ignatios* 61; Anastasius: Mansi, *Sacrorum Conciliorum*, 16:45, 190.
10. *Book of Pontiffs* 108.44 (tr. Davis); Anastasius in Mansi, *Sacrorum Conciliorum*, 16:29.
11. Dvornik, *Photian Schism*, 150–151; cf. canon 21 of the Council.
12. *Book of Pontiffs* 108.46–63; Anastasius in Mansi, *Sacrorum Conciliorum*, 16:11–13. Hadrian, *Letter* 41 to Basileios, in *MGH Epist.* 6:759–761; condition: Dvornik, *Photian Schism*, 155–157.
13. *PmbZ* 23548.
14. Konstantinos VII, *Life of Basileios I* 53, 55; Sicily: Vasiliev, *Byzance*, 2.1:21–26.
15. Konstantinos VII, *Life of Basileios I* 53; *DAI* 29.88–104.
16. Bari: *Annales Bertiniani* s.a. 869; Louis II, *Letter to Basileios I*, in *MGH Epist.* 7:391–392.
17. Louis II, *Letter to Basileios I*, in *MGH Epist.* 7:385–394; Kaldellis, *Romanland*, 20–21.
18. Lambakis et al., *Βυζαντινά στρατεύματα*, 305–306; Kreutz, *Normans*, 55–60; John VIII, *Letters* 47 and 245, in *MGH Epist.* 7:45–46, 214.

19. Theodosios: Vasiliev, *Byzance*, 2.1:71–72 n. 6; Konstantinos VII, *Life of Basileios I* 69–70; Genesios 4.33; Nikolaos Mystikos, *Letter* 75.58–60; Nea: Symeon Logothetes 132.12, with P. Magdalino, 'Observations on the Nea Ekklesia of Basil I,' *JöB* 37 (1987) 51–64.
20. Konstantinos VII, *Life of Basileios I* 62; Genesios 4.34; in general: V. Prigent, 'Cutting Losses: The Unraveling of Byzantine Sicily,' K. Wolf and K. Herbers, eds., *Southern Italy as Contact Area* (Cologne 2018) 79–100.
21. Ephesos: Genesios 4.35; Petros: Lemerle, 'L'histoire.'
22. Konstantinos VII, *Life of Basileios I* 41–43; Genesios 4.36–37; Lemerle, 'L'histoire,' 103–108.
23. Lemerle, 'L'histoire,' 108; Ditten, *Ethnische Verschiebungen*, 203–207.
24. Vasiliev, *Byzance*, 2.1:43–52, 79–94; cf. Konstantinos VII, *Life of Basileios I* 39–40, 46–49 (quotation: 49). Protocol: Haldon, *Constantine*, 140–147.
25. Konstantinos VII, *Life of Basileios I* 59–64; Vasiliev, *Byzance*, 2.1:52–65.
26. Many episodes in A. Kaldellis and I. Polemis, *Saints of Ninth- and Tenth-Century Greece* (Cambridge, MA 2019).
27. Leon VI, *Taktika* pref. 5, 12.57, 18.17–19.
28. Mosaic: Konstantinos VII, *Life of Basileios I* 89.77–78; Photios: ibid. 44; Dvornik, *Photian Schism*, 161–164; hymns: A. Markopoulos, 'Οι μεταμορφώσεις της «μυθολογίας» του Βασιλείου Α′,' in V. Leontaritou et al., eds., *Antecessor: Festschrift für Spyros N. Troianos* (Athens 2013) 945–970, here 951–953.
29. Forgery: Niketas David, *Life of Ignatios* 89–90; Leon VI, *Homily* 14.126–142; "son": Yovhannes Drasxanakertcʻi, *History of Armenia* 29.13 (tr. Maksoudian); Konstantinos VII, *Book of Ceremonies* 2.48 (3:61); Kaldellis, *Romanland*, 193.
30. Mansi, *Sacrorum Conciliorum*, 17:513C.
31. Reconciled: Mansi, *Sacrorum Conciliorum*, 17:424; Dvornik, *Photian Schism*, ch. 6; deposed bishops: 161–163, 167; J. Meijer, *A Successful Council of Union: A Theological Analysis of the Photian Synod of 879–880* (Thessalonike 1975).
32. John VIII, *Letter* 259 to Basileios I, in *MGH Epist.* 7:229.
33. Mansi, *Sacrorum Conciliorum*, 17:420, 488; John VIII: see previous note.
34. J. Fine, *The Early Medieval Balkans* (Ann Arbor, MI 1983) 126–130.
35. Konstantinos VII, *Life of Basileios I* 100–102; Symeon Logothetes 132.23–24; Kourkouas: *PmbZ* 22824; Michael III: Symeon Logothetes 133.2; Tougher, *Reign*, 67.
36. Purge: *Life of the Patriarch Euthymios* 2; sermon: Leon VI, *Homily* 22; trial: Tougher, *Reign*, ch. 3.
37. Symeon Logothetes 133.25–28.
38. Lambakis et al., *Βυζαντινά στρατεύματα*, 313–342. Date: Zuckerman, 'Squabbling Protospatharioi,' 207; Baladhuri, *Origins* 234 (tr. Hitti, 1:371).
39. Photios, *Letter* 297.
40. Erchempert, *History of the Lombards of Benevento* 48, 54–56, 67, 79, in *MGH, SS rer. Lang.* 255, 257, 260, 263; and *Catalogus regum langobardorum* in idem., 496; Kreutz, *Normans*, 63–64, 72–74.

41. *Notitia* 7, ed. J. Darrouzès, *Notitiae episcopatuum Ecclesiae Constantinopolitanae* (Paris 1981) 273, 283; Stephen V, *Letter* 18 in *MGH, Epist.* 7:343–344; see J.-M. Martin, *Byzance et l'Italie mériodionale* (Paris 2014) ch. 12 for theme organization.
42. Leon VI, *Taktika* 15.32, 18.84; Konstantinos VII, *Life of Basileios I* 71; Kaldellis, *Romanland*, 222–223.
43. Holo, *Jewry*, 107–110.
44. Holo, *Jewry*, 45–46; sources in Starr, *Jews*, 123–141; cf. Leon VI, *Novel* 55; critique: Dagron and Déroche, *Juifs*, 313–357.
45. *Life of Nikon* 33–35; cf. Michael Choniates, *Encomium for Niketas of Chonai* 88 (1:53).
46. Basileios I, *Hortatory Chapters for Leon* 1.66; Tougher, *Reign*, 122–132.
47. "Emperor and priest": forged papal letters in Gouillard, 'Origines,' 298–305; propaganda: *Record of the Trial* 4 in Allen and Neil, *Maximus the Confessor*, 54–59; polemic: John of Damascus, *Against the Enemies of the Icons* 2.16. For hints of a quasi-sacerdotal authority in imperial texts, see the *Address* of the Council of Troullo to Justinian II: *ACO* ser. 2, 2.4, pp. 17–20; Leon III, *Ekloge*, preface.
48. "Cleansing": *Eisagoge*, pref. Dates: T. van Bochove, *To Date and Not to Date: On the Date and Status of Byzantine Law Books* (Groningen 1996).
49. Leon VI, *Novels* pref.; Kaldellis, *Byzantine Republic*, 9–14; marriage: *Novel* 89.
50. Kaldellis, *Byzantine Readings*, ch. 1.
51. *Life of Blasios of Amorion* 666E, in *AASS* Nov. 4, 656–669; "the Wise": Tougher, *Reign*, ch. 5.
52. T. Antonopoulou, '"What agreement has the temple of God with idols?" Christian Homilies, Ancient Myths, and the "Macedonian Renaissance",' *BZ* 106 (2013) 595–622.
53. Wilson, *Scholars*, ch. 6; trial: R. Jenkins and B. Laourdas, 'Eight Letters of Arethas on the Fourth Marriage of Leo the Wise,' *Ἑλληνικά* 14 (1956) 293–372, here 347–351 (political subtexts are unnecessary); "lesbian": Parisinus Graecus 451, 124v., on Clement, *Paidagogos* 3.3.21.3.
54. Magdalino, *L'Orthodoxie*, 70–79; Julian: Arethas, *Opus* 21, in *Scripta Minora*, 1:200–212.
55. O. Prieto Domínguez, 'On the Founder of the Skripou Church,' *GRBS* 53 (2013) 166–191; Photios, *Letter* 209.
56. Yovhannes Drasxanakertc'i, *History of Armenia* 31.1–8.
57. *Russian Primary Chronicle* 31–37 (pp. 64–68), 46–54 (pp. 73–78); Leon VI, *Novel* 63 (on *CJ* 4.41.2 = *Basilika* 19.1.86).
58. Prefect: *Eisagoge* 4.1–11; staff: Philotheos, *Kletorologion*, p. 113; dress: Christophoros Mytilenaios, *Poem* 30; foreigners: *Book of the Eparch* 20; Syria: ibid. 5.
59. A. Laiou, 'Exchange and Trade,' in *EHB*, 711, 723–730.
60. Kaldellis, 'Borders.'
61. Symeon Logothetes 133.15.
62. Liudprand, *Antapodosis* 3.29; *Oration on the Treaty with the Bulgarians* 16, ed. and tr. Dujčev, 'Treaty,' 278–279.
63. Curta, *Southeastern Europe*, 213–224.
64. Arethas, *Opus* 67, in *Scripta Minora*, 2:27.
65. Symeon Logothetes 133.16–21; Leon VI, *Taktika* 18.42; Konstantinos VII, *DAI* 40 ("emigrated"); "ferocious": Regino of Prüm, *Chronicle* s.a. 899, in *MGH Scriptores SS* 1:599–600; Tougher, *Reign*, 172–181.

66. Vasiliev, *Byzance*, 2.1:142–152; Lambakis et al., *Βυζαντινά στρατεύματα*, 343–349; prisoners: *Life of Elias the Younger* 43; Taormina: ibid. 49–55 ("flood": 50); recriminations: Symeon Logothetes 133.34; Nikolaos Mystikos, *Letter* 75 (from 920).
67. Leon: Kaminiates, *Capture of Thessalonike* 24 (refugees: 12.6; Naxos: 70.1); Theophanes Continuatus p. 366; cf. Nikolaos Mystikos, *Letter* 9.31–33; Samos etc.: Symeon Logothetes 133.12, 133.30, 133.35; Tabari, *History* 3:2185 (898 AD); Vasiliev, *Byzance*, 2.1:157–181; Tougher, *Reign*, 183–193.
68. Nikolaos Mystikos, *Sermon on the Fall of Thessalonike* 111–115 (= *Miscellaneous Writings*, p. 14); *Letter* 326.64–66; Kaminiates, *Capture of Thessalonike*, passim (I am unpersuaded that the text is a fifteenth-century forgery).
69. Symeon Logothetes 133.41; *Life of the Patriarch Euthymios* 15.
70. Leon VI, *Taktika* 18.132: Doukas: *PmbZ* 20405.
71. Symeon Logothetes 133.52–57; *Life of the Patriarch Euthymios* 13–14.
72. Nikolaos Mystikos, *Letter* 1.16–21; *Life of Demetrianos of Chytroi* 13, in *AASS* 3 Nov., here 306–307; cf. Leon VI, *Taktika* 20.212; Vasiliev, *Byzance*, 2.1:196–216.
73. Konstantinos VII, *Book of Ceremonies* 2.44; J. Haldon, 'Theory and Practice in Tenth-Century Military Administration,' *TM* 13 (2000) 201–352.
74. See the parents of the saint in the *Life of Euthymios the Younger* 3.4–5.
75. Kaminiates, *Capture of Thessalonike* 63, 73.
76. Symeon Logothetes 133.23; cf. *Life of the Patriarch Euthymios* 8; concubine: R. Guilland, 'Les noces plurales à Byzance,' *Byzantinoslavica* 9 (1947–1948) 9–20.
77. Symeon Logothetes 133.32; law: Leon VI, *Novel* 90; cf. Nikolaos Mystikos, *Letter* 32.77–86.
78. Leon VI, *Novel* 91.
79. Symeon Logothetes 133.47–49; Nikolaos Mystikos, *Letter* 32.45–54; *Life of the Patriarch Euthymios* 11.
80. Arethas, *Opera* 67–69, in *Scripta Minora*, 2:56–93, esp. 61 for the smallness of the group; Nikolaos: *Letter* 32.108–128; *Life of the Patriarch Euthymios* 11; "rapist": Arethas, *Opus* 87, in *Scripta Minora*, 2:169.
81. *Life of the Patriarch Euthymios* 12.
82. Symeon Logothetes 133.50; *Life of the Patriarch Euthymios* 13–15; new law: Oikonomides, 'Leo VI,' on *Procheiros Nomos* 4.25–27.
83. Arethas, *Opera* 1–2, 45–47 in *Scripta Minora*, 1:1–18, 306–319; *Life of the Patriarch Euthymios* 15.
84. *Life of the Patriarch Euthymios* 16–17; Symeon Logothetes 133.49, 133.60.

Chapter 24. A Game of Crowns (912–950)

1. Lauxtermann, *Byzantine Poetry*, 2:94.
2. Arethas, *Opus* 8, in *Scripta Minora*, 1:89–91; *Life of the Patriarch Euthymios* 20–21; Symeon Logothetes 134.
3. Symeon Logothetes 135.12; *Life of the Patriarch Euthymios* 17a.

4. *Life of the Patriarch Euthymios* 17a–19; Leon's will and mosaics: Oikonomides, 'Leo VI,' 166–168.
5. Symeon Logothetes 135.3–9; *Life of the Patriarch Euthymios* 21; *Life of Basileios the Younger* 1.14–19; cf. Theophanes Continuatus p. 373 (another prophecy).
6. Shepard, *Emerging Elites*, III:6–8; seals: III:11.
7. *Oration on the Treaty with the Bulgarians* 13, ed. and tr. Dujčev, 'Treaty,' 274–275; Symeon Logothetes 134.8, 135.10–11; Nikolaos Mystikos, *Letters* 5–6, esp. 6.31–37; I. Mladjov, 'The Crown and the Veil: Titles, Spiritual Kinship, and Diplomacy in Tenth-Century Bulgaro-Byzantine Relations,' *History Compass* 13 (2015) 171–183.
8. *Life of the Patriarch Euthymios* 21; Symeon Logothetes 135.12–13.
9. Symeon Logothetes 135.14–16; Nikolaos Mystikos, *Letter* 16.71–75.
10. Yovhannes Drasxanakertc'i, *History of Armenia* 54–56; Symeon Logothetes 135.15; Step'anos of Taron, *History* 3.6; Takirtakoglou, *Αρμενία*, 275–285; Vasiliev, *Byzance*, 2.1:229–234.
11. Liudprand, *Antapodosis* 2.52–54; Lambakis et al., *Βυζαντινά στρατεύματα*, 356–360.
12. Skylitzes 263; Vasiliev, *Byzance*, 2.1:307–311; Chiarelli, *History*, 81–84; Donnolo: Starr, *Jews*, 149.
13. Symeon Logothetes 135.18–30 ("obliterate"); Skylitzes 205–209; allegations: Nikolaos Mystikos, *Letter* 9.89–95, 181; quotation: 10.33; unprovoked: 18.54–56, 21.39–60.
14. Symeon Logothetes 136.1–13; R. Jenkins, *Byzantium: The Imperial Centuries* (London 1966) 239. Writ: L. Westerink, *Nicholas I, Patriarch of Constantinople: Miscellaneous Writings* (Washington, D.C. 1981) no. 200 (56–71), with Oikonomides, 'Leo VI,' 169–170.
15. Symeon Logothetes 136.13–18; coins: Marić, 'Lost.'
16. Raids: *Life of Hosios Loukas of Steiris* 24, 32–34; Peloponnese: Konstantinos VII, *DAI* 50; *Life of Petros of Argos* 12; Curta, *Edinburgh History*, 170–173.
17. Symeon Logothetes 136.17–20, 136.23–24, 136.27.
18. *Life of Maria the Younger* 23–25 (pp. 700–702).
19. Seals: Petkov, *Voices*, 33–34 (no. 35); atrocities: Nikolaos Mystikos, *Letters* 23.49–50, 23.79 ff., 24.58 ff., 26.25–26, 26.44–47, 28.10–11, 29.32–40; imperial pretensions: 10.27, 18.30–32, 18.105–106, 19, 21.59–60, 21.127, 25.84–100, 28.72–73; "West": 27.72. I am skeptical of the story in Skylitzes 264 about Simeon's Fatimid alliance.
20. Symeon Logothetes 136.29–37; terms: Theodoros Daphnopates, *Letter* 5.135–141, 6.142–149.
21. Romanos in Theodoros Daphnopates, *Letter* 5.20–50.
22. Symeon Logothetes 136.46–51; *Oration on the Treaty with the Bulgarians*, passim; *Life of Maria the Younger* 26 (p. 702); title: Petkov, *Voices*, 34 (no. 36); Liudprand, *Embassy to Constantinople* 19; war party: Shepard, *Emerging Elites*, III:14.
23. Leon VI, *Taktika* 18.59.
24. Qudama in H. Kennedy, 'Frontiers of Islam,' in K. Wolf and K. Herbers, eds., *Southern Italy as Contact Area* (Cologne 2018) 51–64.
25. Miskawayh, *Experiences of the Nations*, 2:56–60.
26. "Empty": Konstantinos VII, *On the Themes*, p. 75; Melias: *PmbZ* 25041; new themes and Tekes (= Manuel in *PmbZ* 24875): Konstantinos VII, *DAI* 50.92–166;

E. Kountoura-Galake et al., eds., *Η Μικρά Ασία των θεμάτων* (Athens 1998) 307–335.

27. N. Oikonomidès, 'L'organisation de la frontière orientale de Byzance aux Xe-XIe siècles,' in M. Berza and E. Stănescu, eds., *Actes du XIVe Congrès international des études byzantines* (Bucharest 1974) 285–302, here 286–288, 297–298; J.-C. Cheynet, 'Les Arméniens dans l'armée byzantine au Xe siècle,' *TM* 18 (2014) 175–192.
28. Symeon Logothetes 136.22; Konstantinos VII, *DAI* 45–46, esp. 46.163–165; house: 43.
29. Vasiliev, *Byzance*, 2.1:261–270; Qaysids: Konstantinos VII, *DAI* 44; Theodosiopolis: Theophanes Continuatus p. 428.
30. Theophanes Continuatus pp. 426–428.
31. Symeon Logothetes 136.53.
32. Symeon Logothetes 136.38, 136.54, 136.62, 136.66, 136.69; J. Shepard, 'Byzantine Writers on the Hungarians in the Ninth and Tenth Centuries,' *Annual, Department of Medieval Studies, Central European University* 10 (2004) 97–123.
33. Ibn Hawqal in Vasiliev, *Byzance*, 2.2:419–421, with 2.1:270–273.
34. Bikhazi, *Hamdanid Dynasty*.
35. Vasiliev, *Byzance*, 2.1:282–290.
36. Landulf: *PmbZ* 24272; Hugh: *PmbZ* 22637; Zuckerman, 'Squabbling Protospatharioi,' 210–215, 224.
37. V. Prigent, 'La politique sicilienne de Romain Ier Lépanène,' in D. Barthélemy and J.-C. Cheynet, eds., *Guerre et société, Byzance - Occident* (Paris 2010) 63–84.
38. Symeon Logothetes 136.71–76; Liudprand, *Antapodosis* 5.15; *Life of Basileios the Younger* 3.23–28; *Russian Primary Chronicle* 44–45 (pp. 71–73).
39. Symeon Logothetes 136.78; Liudprand, *Antapodosis* 5.9–17; Charlemagne: Konstantinos VII, *DAI* 26. Sardinia: *Book of Ceremonies* 2.48; Cosentino, 'Sardinia,' 347–351.
40. Symeon Logothetes 136.77; *Life of Hosios Loukas of Steiris* 61; *Russian Primary Chronicle* 45–54 (pp. 72–78).
41. Symeon Logothetes 136.80–81; Yahya, *PO* 18.5:730–733; Konstantinos VII, *Tale of the Image of Edessa*, ed. and tr. M. Guscin, *The Image of Edessa* (Leiden 2009) 8–69.
42. Skylitzes 238; coups: J.-C. Cheynet, 'Une querelle de famille: La prise du poivoir par Constantin VII,' *TM* 23.1 (2019) 121–139.
43. Liudprand, *Antapodosis* 5.21–23; Symeon Logothetes 136.83–137.8; Skylitzes 233–237; loaves: Theophanes Continuatus p. 430.
44. Marić, 'Lost,' 120–122.
45. Konstantinos VII, *DAI* 13.105–186, 50.202–208; *On the Themes*, pp. 84, 85, 91; *Life of Basileios* I 12.
46. I. Ševčenko, 'Re-reading Constantine Porphyrogenitus,' in J. Shepard and S. Franklin, eds., *Byzantine Diplomacy* (Aldershot, UK 1992) 167–196.
47. A. Németh, *The Excerpta Constantiniana and the Byzantine Appropriation of the Past* (Cambridge 2018).
48. Cf. Lemerle, *Humanism*, ch. 10, with P. Van Deun and C. Macé, eds., *Encyclopedic Trends in Byzantium?* (Leuven 2011).
49. Konstantinos VII in Haldon, *Constantine*, 97.
50. Lauxtermann, *Byzantine Poetry*, 1:178.

51. K. Jazdzewska, 'Hagiographic Invention and Imitation: Niketas' *Life of Theoktiste* and Its Literary Models,' *GRBS* 49 (2009) 257–279; *Synaxarion of Constantinople*: 9 November.
52. Konstantinos VII, *Book of Ceremonies* 2.15; *DAI* 40.51–67; Skylitzes 239–240; see C. Zuckerman, 'Le voyage d'Olga et la première ambassade espagnole à Constantinople en 946,' *TM* 13 (2000) 647–672; profit: al-Mas'udi in Vasiliev, *Byzance*, 2.2:407–408.
53. Liudprand, *Antapodosis* 6.5.
54. Arethas, *Opus* 62, in *Scripta Minora*, 2:33–34.
55. Romanos in Theodoros Daphnopates, *Letter* 5.116–124; Simeon in Tabari, *History* 3:2152 (896 AD); speaker: *Oration on the Treaty with the Bulgarians* 18, ed. and tr. Dujčev, 'Treaty,' 280–281.
56. Vasiliev, *Byzance*, 2.2:317–319.
57. Step'anos of Taron, *History* 3.7; Yahya, *PO* 18.5:768; Konstantinos VII, *DAI* 45.
58. Konstantinos VII, *Book of Ceremonies* 2.44–45; Leon the Deacon 1.2; Skylitzes 245–246; with C. Zuckerman, 'Campaign Blueprints of an Emperor Who Never Campaigned in Person,' *TM* 22 (2018) 341–382.
59. P. Odorico, 'Il calamo d'argento: Un carme inedito in onore di Romano II,' *JöB* 37 (1987) 65–93.

Chapter 25. The Triumph of Roman Arms (950–1025)

1. McGeer, *Sowing*, 229–246.
2. Vasiliev, *Byzance*, 341–355; Bikhazi, *Hamdanid Dynasty*, 705–779; failure: Skylitzes 241.
3. Mutanabbi in Vasiliev, *Byzance*, 2.2:333; cf. McGeer, *Sowing*, 209; G. Theotokis, 'Rus, Varangian and Frankish Mercenaries in the Service of the Byzantine Emperors,' *Byzantina Symmeikta* 22 (2012) 125–156.
4. Nikephoros Phokas, *On Skirmishing*, ed. Dennis, *Military Treatises*, and *Praecepta Militaria*, ed. McGeer, *Sowing*; Haldon, *Warfare*, 101–104.
5. Haldon, 'Late Rome,' 363–365; Liudprand, *Antapodosis* 6.10; salaries: Konstantinos VII, *Book of Ceremonies* 2.50.
6. Konstantinos VII, *DAI* 51.199–204; *Book of Ceremonies* 2.45 (3:321).
7. *Campaign Organization* 28, ed. Dennis, *Military Treatises*, 318–319.
8. Konstantinos VII in McGeer, *Land Legislation*, 68–76.
9. Romanos I in McGeer, *Land Legislation*, 37–60, here 54; winter famine: Symeon Logothetes 136.57–58.
10. R. Morris, 'The Powerful and the Poor in Tenth-Century Byzantium,' *Past and Present* 73 (1976) 3–27; H. Saradi, 'On the "*archontike*" and "*ekklesiastike dynasteia* and "*prostasia*" in Byzantium,' *Byzantion* 64 (1994) 67–117; Chitwood, *Legal Culture*, 83–86.
11. Nikephoros II in McGeer, *Land Legislation*, 86–103, here 92; Basil II in ibid. 122–126; "solidarity": Skylitzes 347, 365; ecclesiastical encroachments: Symeon Logothetes, *Letter* 5, in Darrouzès, *Epistoliers*, 101–102; see Kaldellis, *Streams*, 13–18; M. Whittow in J. Howard-Johnston, 'Introduction,' in idem, ed., *Social Change in Town and*

Country in Eleventh-Century Byzantium (Oxford 2020) 1–15, here 6, and idem, 'General Reflections,' in ibid. 220–247, here 231–233; monasteries: Morris, *Monks*, ch. 7; encroachments: Attaleiates 61–62.

12. Nikephoros II, *On Skirmishing* 19.
13. Cotsonis, 'Onomastics,' 20.
14. Leon the Deacon 3.1, 3.9.
15. Kekaumenos, *Strategikon* 87; Liudprand, *Embassy to Constantinople* 11. The *Naumachika*, issued under Leon VI, were recopied for the *parakoimomenos* Basileios.
16. Leon the Deacon 4.3 on Tzimiskes; Bryennios, *Materials* 1.1 on the Komnenoi; mother: ibid. 1.12; reaper: 1.2.
17. Geometres, *Poem* 7, in *PG* 106:910; M. Lauxtermann, 'John Geometres - Poet and Soldier,' *Byzantion* 68 (1998) 356–380.
18. McCormick, *Eternal Victory*, 159–178; standards: Leon the Deacon 4.4; Skylitzes 270; relics: D. Sullivan, 'Siege Warfare, Nikephoros II Phokas, Relics, and Personal Piety,' in idem et al., eds., *Byzantine Religious Culture* (Leiden 2012) 395–409; ancient models: Kaldellis, 'Original Source.'
19. Menze, 'Sacralization of War,' esp. 159–160.
20. T. Détokaris and J. Mossay, 'Un office inédit pour ceux qui sont morts à la guerre,' *Le Muséon: Revue des études orientales* 101 (1988), 183–211, esp. vv. 43–44, 101; R. Nelson, 'The Byzantine Art of War in the Tenth Century,' *DOP* 65–66 (2011–2012) 169–192.
21. Yahya, *PO* 18.5:825–826.
22. Nikephoros Ouranos, *Taktika* 63, 65.
23. C. Mazzucchi, 'Dagli anni di Basilio Parakimomenos,' *Aevum* 52 (1978) 267–316, here 302.
24. Theodosios the Deacon, *On the Capture of Crete*; Leon the Deacon 1.2–2.8.
25. Yahya, *PO* 18.5:782–783; *Life of Nikon Metanoeite* 20–21; J. Holo, 'A Genizah Letter from Rhodes,' *Journal of Near Eastern Studies* 59 (2000) 1–12.
26. Kaldellis, *Streams*, 39–40; A. Miquel, *Abû Firâs al-Hamdânî: Les Byzantines* (France 2010).
27. Leon the Deacon 2.12.
28. Leon the Deacon 3.7; Konstantinos VII, *Book of Ceremonies* 1.105; quotation: Skylitzes 257.
29. Kaldellis, *Streams*, 45–46.
30. Skylitzes 270; Yahya, *PO* 18.5:794–795; *kourator*: V. Prigent, 'Chypre entre Islam et Byzance,' in J. Durand et al., eds., *Chypre entre Byzance et l'Occident* (Paris 2012) 79–93, here 87; minority: ibid. 82; Zavagno, *Cyprus*, 38, 85.
31. Kaldellis, *Streams*, 43–49; cross: Leon the Deacon 4.1; mosque: Miskawayh, *Experiences of the Nations*, 2:225; Çavuşin: L. Jones, 'Visual Evidence for the Mutability of Identity,' in K. Durak and I. Jevtić, eds., *Identity and the Other in Byzantium* (Istanbul 2019) 129–142; Muslim reactions: El Cheikh, *Byzantium*, 168–178.
32. Michael the Syrian 13.4; Vest, *Geschichte*, 1077–1107; B. Romeney, 'Ethnicity, Ethnogenesis and the Identity of the Syriac Orthodox Christians,' in W. Pohl et al., eds., *Visions of Community in the Post-Roman World* (Ashgate 2012) 183–204.

33. Skylitzes 279; Step'anos of Taron, *History* 3.8; Greenwood, 'Social Change,' 202–203, 209–212.
34. Takirtakoglou, *Αρμενία*, 397, 411, 417–420.
35. Skylitzes 241, 277–278; Leon the Deacon 4.6; Liudprand, *Embassy to Constantinople* 34, 44.
36. Skylitzes 273–274; monasteries: McGeer, *Land Legislation*, 90–96.
37. J. Kramer and G. Wiet, *Ibn Hauqal: Le configuration de la terre*, 2 vols. (Paris 1964) 193–194; Kaldellis, *Streams*, 51–54.
38. R. Morris, 'The Two Faces of Nikephoros Phokas,' *BMGS* 12 (1988) 83–115.
39. Kaldellis, *Streams*, 59–60.
40. N. Hermes, 'The Byzantines in Medieval Arabic Poetry,' *Byzantina Symmeikta* 19 (2009) 35–61, here 49–50.
41. Yahya, *PO* 18.5:807, 813–816, 822–826; Leon the Deacon 4.10–5.5; Skylitzes 271–273.
42. Yahya, *PO* 18.5:827–829; Leon the Deacon 5.5–9; Skylitzes 279–280.
43. L. Petit, 'Office inédit en l'honneur de Nicephore Phocas,' *BZ* 13 (1904) 398–420.
44. Geometres, *Poems* 61, 80 (van Opstall) = *PG* 106:927, 932.
45. Tzimiskes in Leon the Deacon 8.3 (tr. Talbot and Sullivan, mod.).
46. Leon the Deacon 6.3–5, 7.9; Skylitzes 285–286, 294.
47. *Typikon of Tzimiskes*, tr. G. Dennis in *BMFD*, 232–244. 3,000: Morris, *Monks*, 221.
48. Michael the Syrian 13.4.
49. A. Davids, ed., *The Empress Theophano: Byzantium and the West at the Turn of the First Millennium* (Cambridge 1995).
50. Yahya, *PO* 18.5:824–825; Farag, *Byzantium*, 167–183.
51. Yahya, *PO* 18.5:824, 832; Leon the Deacon 6.6; Skylitzes 286. Antioch in this period: Todt, *Dukat*.
52. *Russian Primary Chronicle* 67 (p. 86); Nikephoros: Kaldellis, *Streams*, 54–57.
53. Leon the Deacon 7.1–9; Skylitzes 291–294; Yahya, *PO* 18.5:831–832.
54. Leon the Deacon 7.9–9.12; Skylitzes 287–310; *Russian Primary Chronicle* 69–74 (pp. 87–91); Kaldellis, 'Original Source.'
55. Leon the Deacon 6.8–9.
56. Oikonomidès, *Listes*, 262–263, 344–346; occupation: Stephenson, *Balkan Frontier*, 55–58.
57. F. Russo, *Storia della Chiesa in Calabria* (Soveria Mannelli, CZ 1982) 1:176–180.
58. Skylitzes 287; P. Walker, 'A Byzantine Victory over the Fatimids at Alexandretta (971),' *Byzantion* 42 (1972) 431–440.
59. P. Walker, 'The "Crusade" of John Tzimiskes,' *Byzantion* 47 (1977) 301–327; Kaldellis, *Streams*, 76–79.
60. Al-Muqaddasi, *The Best Divisions for Knowledge of the Regions*, tr. B. Collins, rev. M. Hamid al-Tai (Reading, UK 1994) 139.
61. Leon the Deacon 10.11; Skylitzes 311–312; Rudhrawari, *Continuation of Miskawayh*, 6:6.
62. Geometres, *Poem* 2, in *PG* 106:903–905; J. Baun, *Tales from Another Byzantium: Celestial Journey and Local Community in the Medieval Greek Apocrypha* (Cambridge 2007) 15, 72, 222–225.
63. Leon the Deacon 6.8; Skylitzes 311; Morris, *Monks*, 141, 189, 231.

64. Basil II, *Novel of 996* 6.1, tr. in McGeer, *Land Legislation*, 128–130; Psellos, *Chronographia* 1.20; see S. Wander, *The Joshua Roll* (Wiesbaden 2012) 93–132. Theophano: Skylitzes 314; Yahya, *PO* 18.5:831. For Basil II, C. Holmes, *Basil II and the Governance of Empire* (Oxford 2005) is fundamental.
65. Leon the Deacon 10.7; Skylitzes 314–328; Yahya, *PO* 23.3:372–378, 399; Step'anos of Taron, *History* 3.15; inscription: Forsyth, *Chronicle*, 386–387.
66. *Life of John and Euthymios* 4–8, tr. Grdzelidze, *Georgian Monks*, 57–63; J. Lefort et al. in *AA* 14 (= *Iviron* 1) 3–32; concessions: Step'anos of Taron, *History* 3.15.
67. Rudhrawari, *Continuation of Miskawayh*, 6:23–34 (tr. Amedroz and Margoliouth); Kaldellis, *Streams*, 90–94.
68. Thietmar of Merseburg, *Chronicon* 3.20–23.
69. Delphinas: *PmbZ* 23632; Liudprand, *Embassy to Constantinople* 18.
70. Inscription: Petkov, *Voices*, 39 (n. 53). Writers: Adémar of Chabannes, Step'anos of Taron, Yahya of Antioch, and al-Rudhrawari, in addition to Psellos, Attaleiates, Kekaumenos, and others. Basil: H. Gelzer, 'Ungedruckte und wenig bekannte Bistumsverzeichnisse der orientalischen Kirchen,' *BZ* 2 (1893) 22–72, here 42, 46. Leon the Deacon, writing in the 990s, calls both the subjects of Petar and armies of Samuil "Mysians" (e.g., 1.5, 10.8–10); his classicizing terminology is usually consistent.
71. Yahya, *PO* 23.3:417; Skylitzes 335; Psellos, *Chronographia* 1.19–21.
72. Leon the Deacon 10.8; Skylitzes 330–331; Yahya, *PO* 23.3:419. Geometres, *Poem* 90 (von Opstall).
73. Rudhrawari, *Continuation of Miskawayh*, 6:115–117; Qalqashandi in Farag, *Byzantium*, 127–135.
74. Skylitzes 330; Kekaumenos, *Strategikon* 73.
75. Kaldellis, *Streams*, 96–99.
76. Liudprand, *Embassy to Constantinople* 15.
77. *Russian Primary Chronicle* 108 (p. 111), 79 (p. 93) (tr. Cross and Sherbowitz-Wetzor); Yahya, *PO* 23.3:423–424; Ste'panos of Taron, *History* 3.43; Rudhrawari, *Continuation of Miskawayh*, 6:118–119; Skylitzes 336; C. Raffensperger, *Reimagining Europe: Kievan Rus' in the Medieval World* (Cambridge, MA 2012) 159–163.
78. Skylitzes 339; Kaldellis, *Streams*, 98–99.
79. Forsyth, *Chronicle*, 434; Farag, *Byzantium*, 236.
80. Yahya, *PO* 23.3:429–430; Ste'panos of Taron, *History* 3.43; Skylitzes 339; Forsyth, *Chronicle*, 465–470, 517–518.
81. Thietmar of Merseburg, *Chronicon* 7.72; *Russian Primary Chronicle* 110–113 (pp. 112–114).
82. Psellos, *Chronographia* 1.30.
83. Blöndal, *Varangians*; Khazars: Symeon Logothetes 133.16; Konstantinos VII, *Book of Ceremonies* 2.15 (3:113); A. Vasiliev, 'Harun-ibn-Yahya and his Description of Constantinople,' *Seminarium Kondakovianum* 5 (1932) 149–163, here 156.
84. Psellos, *Chronographia* 1.28; Kaldellis, *Streams*, 115–119.
85. Skylitzes 331–332; Leon the Deacon 10.10; Yahya, *PO* 23.3:428–429.

86. Lauxtermann, *Byzantine Poetry*, 1:218, 236–238.
87. Rudhrawari, *Continuation of Miskawayh*, 6:119, 229, 232; Yahya, *PO* 23.3:444; Attaleiates 229; Skylitzes 348.
88. Skylitzes 341–342, 364; Yahya, *PO* 23.3:446–447; Kaldellis, *Streams*, 112–115.
89. Kaldellis, *Streams*, 105–110.
90. Rudhrawari, *Continuation of Miskawayh*, 6:119.
91. Steʿpanos of Taron, *History* 3.43; Yahya, *PO* 23.3:460 (positions); Aristakes of Lastivert 1.3–4; Skylitzes 339; Kaldellis, *Streams*, 110–111.
92. Skylitzes 343–344.
93. Skylitzes 348–349; Kekaumenos, *Strategikon* 19; Attaleiates 230; cf. Stephenson, *Legend*, 92.
94. Skylitzes 349–365.
95. Skylitzes 365–366; Stephenson, *Legend*, 44.
96. Kekaumenos, *Strategikon* 89–90; Sun-king: e.g., Psellos, *Orationes panegyricae* 1.3.
97. B. Krsmanović, *The Byzantine Province in Change (On the Threshold between the 10th and the 11th Century)* (Belgrade and Athens 2008) 196–197; A. Madgearu, *Byzantine Military Organization on the Danube, 10th-12th Centuries* (Leiden 2013) 63–64.
98. Yahya, *PO* 47:407.
99. Skylitzes Continuatus 162; Skylitzes 412.
100. Ivan: *PmbZ* 23365. Justiniana Prima: M. Panov, *The Blinded State: Historiographic Debates about Samuel* (Leiden 2019) 111–114.
101. Yahya, *PO* 47:401–405, 417–419; Kaldellis, *Streams*, 127–130.
102. Yahya, *PO* 47:461.
103. Aristakes of Lastivert 2.11–13, 2.16, 3.19; Yahya, *PO* 47:461–463; Skylitzes 354–355, 435; Smbat, *The Tale of the Bagratids* 58–59, tr. Rapp, *Studies*, 350–367; *Georgian Chronicles* 282–283; priests: Greenwood, 'Social Change,' 202–203; emirates: A. Ter-Ghewondyan, *The Arab Emirates in Bagratid Armenia*, tr. N. Garsoïan (Lisbon 1976) 106, 115–116.
104. Aristakes of Lastivert 3.18–19.
105. Aristakes of Lastivert 3.18–4.23; Skylitzes 366–367; Yahya, *PO* 47:465–469; Smbat, *The Tale of the Bagratids* 61–63, tr. in Rapp, *Studies*.
106. Lauxtermann, *Byzantine Poetry*, 1:236–238.
107. *Annales Barenses* s.a. 1035, in *MGH SS* 5:54.
108. Noyé, 'New Light,' 166–184.
109. V. von Falkenhausen, 'Between Two Empires: Southern Italy in the Reign of Basil II,' in P. Magdalino, ed., *Byzantium in the Year 1000* (Leiden 2033) 135–159; Kaldellis, *Streams*, 134–136. Venetian pact: Pozza and Ravegnani, *Trattati*, 21–25; Nicol, *Byzantium*, 40–42.
110. Leon of Synada, esp. *Letters* 1, 6 (quotation), 8–11; *PbmZ* 23486.
111. Noyé, 'New Light,' 184–189.
112. Kaldellis, *Streams*, 136–138.
113. Yahya, *PO* 47:483.
114. Psellos, *Chronographia* 1.32–34; *Orationes panegyricae* 2.123–132.

115. Antonios III Stoudites, *Logos* (970s), ed. L. Sternbach, *Analecta Avarica* (Krakow 1900) 45.
116. Respectively: Vryonis, 'Will,' 264; Philetos Synadenos, *Letters* 7, 11, ed. Darrouzès, *Epistoliers*, 254, 257; Psellos, *Letter* 88 (p. 187).

Chapter 26. A Brief Hegemony (1025–1048)

1. A. Laiou, 'Imperial Marriages and Their Critics in the Eleventh Century,' *DOP* 46 (1992) 165–176; shift: Leidholm, *Kinship*, 65; debate over degrees: ch. 3.
2. Skylitzes 393–394 (tr. Wortley).
3. Psellos, *Orationes funebres* 1.49; Kaldellis, *Streams*, 225–226.
4. Cheynet, *Pouvoir*.
5. Yahya, *PO* 47:482–483; Psellos, *Chronographia* 1.31; Skylitzes 373 (quotation).
6. Attaleiates 50–51; Skylitzes 476. Coins: Hendy, *Studies*, 3–6, 233–236; C. Kaplanis, 'The Debasement of the "Dollar of the Middle Ages",' *Journal of Economic History* 63 (2003) 768–801. *Roga*: N. Oikonomides, 'Title and Income at the Byzantine Court,' in H. Maguire, ed., *Byzantine Court Culture from 829 to 1204* (Washington, D.C. 1997) 199–215, here 208.
7. Haldon, *Empire*, 234–237.
8. Psellos, *Letters* 91, 350; Harvey, *Expansion*, 47–58, 134–135, 159–162; Laiou and Morrisson, *Economy*, 46–47 and ch. 4.
9. Morris, *Monks*, 263–270.
10. Harvey, *Expansion*, 42–43, 238–241; Morris, *Monks*, ch. 7; M. Kaplan, 'Monks and Trade in Byzantium,' in Magdalino and Necipoğlu, eds., *Trade*, 55–64; trust funds: Lemerle, *Cinq études*, 65–113.
11. Laiou and Morrisson, *Economy*, 93; D. Stathakopoulos, 'Population, Demography, and Disease,' in E. Jeffreys, ed., *The Oxford Handbook of Byzantine Studies* (Oxford 2008) 309–316, here 312.
12. *Life of Lazaros of Galesion* 9, 25, 26, 64.
13. Attaleiates 61–62.
14. See the papers in Niewöhner, ed., *Archaeology*, 55–57, 216, 279; J.-C. Cheynet, 'La société urbaine,' in *TM* 21.2 (2017) 449–482; estate continuity: Sarris, 'Beyond the Great Plains,' 84–85.
15. Cooper and Decker, *Cappadocia*, 83–94; K. Belke, 'Transport and Communication,' in Niewöhner, ed., *Archaeology*, 28–38, here 32–33; J. Crow, 'Fortifications,' in ibid. 90–108.
16. Attaleiates 90.
17. Mas'udi, *Meadows of Gold*, tr. P. Lunde and C. Stone (London 1989) 322.
18. *Timarion* 5–6; D. Jacoby, 'Byzantine Maritime Trade, 1025–1118,' *TM* 21.2 (2017) 627–648.
19. Christophoros Mytilenaios, *Poem* 136; Psellos in Kaldellis, *Mothers and Sons*, 179–186.
20. Christophoros Mytilenaios, *Poem* 42; A. Kazhdan and A. Epstein, *Change in Byzantine Culture in the Eleventh and Twelfth Centuries* (Berkeley 1990) 74–83.

21. A. Laiou, 'The Role of Women in Byzantine Society,' *JöB* 31.1 (1981) 233–260; L. Neville, 'Taxing Sophronia's Son-in-Law: Representations of Women in Provincial Documents,' in L. Garland, ed., *Byzantine Women* (Aldershot, UK 2006) 77–89.
22. Kaldellis, *Mothers and Sons*, 21–22.
23. Morrisson, 'Byzantine Money,' in *EHB*, 958–961, with tables 6.1–11.
24. Psellos, *Chronographia* 3.6, 4.10–11, 6.5, 6.7, 6A.3 (Theodora), 7.53; Skylitzes 375–376, 393, 417, 422–423 (uncle).
25. Psellos, *Chronographia* 3.14–16 (quotation), 4.31, 4.36, 6.185–188, 7.59; Skylitzes 392, 476; endowments: Lemerle, *Cinq études*, 272–285.
26. P. Niewöhner, 'What Went Wrong? Decline and Ruralization in Eleventh-Century Anatolia,' in Howard-Johnston, ed., *Social Change*, 98–132.
27. E.g., Harvey, *Expansion*, 82–83, 188; S. Hondridou, *Ο Κωνσταντίνος Θ′ Μονομάχος και η εποχή του* (Thessalonike 2002) 329–332.
28. Oikonomides, 'St. George'; Miller, *Orphans*, ch. 7.
29. Yahya, *PO* 47:493–509; Skylitzes 377–385; Psellos, *Chronographia* 3.7–11; Matthew of Edessa 1.57.
30. Matthew of Edessa 1.57; Skylitzes 387; Yahya, *PO* 47:515–519; Aristakes of Lastivert 7.34–36.
31. A. Atiya and Y. Abd al-Masih, eds., *History of the Patriarchs of the Egyptian Church, Known as the History of the Holy Church of Sawirus* (Cairo 1959) 2.3:305.
32. C. Holmes, "How the East Was Won" in the Reign of Basil II, in A. Eastmond, ed., *Eastern Approaches to Byzantium* (Farnham, UK 2001) 41–56; judges: J. Howard-Johnston, 'Military and Provincial Reform in the East in the Tenth Century,' *TM* 21.1 (2017) 285–309, here 306–307.
33. Yahya, *PO* 23.3:439, and *PO* 47:501–515; Skylitzes 382–383.
34. J. Schlacht and M. Meyerhof, *The Medico-Philosophical Controversy between Ibn Butlan of Baghdad and Ibn Ridwan of Cairo* (Cairo 1937) 54–57.
35. Michael the Syrian 13.6 (tr. Moosa, p. 596).
36. G. Ficker, *Erlasse des Patriarchen von Konstantinopel Alexios Studites* (Kiel 1911) 17, 28–42; Vest, *Geschichte*, 1196–1223; Chitwood, *Legal Culture*, 133–149.
37. D. Galadza, *Liturgy and Byzantinization in Jerusalem* (Oxford 2018).
38. R. Ousterhout, 'Rebuilding the Temple: Constantine Monomachus and the Holy Sepulchre,' *Journal of the Society of Architectural Historians* 48 (1989) 66–78. Naser-e Khosraw, *Book of Travels*, tr. W. Thackston (New York 1986) 37–38.
39. Attaleiates 110; epitaph: G. Dagron and D. Feissel, 'Inscriptions inédités du Musée d'Antioche,' *TM* 9 (1985) 421–461, here 457–459; translations: A. Roberts, *Reason and Revelation in Byzantine Antioch* (Berkeley 2020); in general: Todt, *Dukat;* De Giorgi and Asa Eger, *Antioch*, 299–317.
40. Holo, *Jewry*, 50–77, 146; Italy: S. Bowman, 'The Jewish Experience in Byzantium,' in J. Aitken and J. Paget, eds., *The Jewish-Greek Tradition in Antiquity and the Byzantine Empire* (Cambridge 2014) 37–52. Wall: Benjamin of Tudela, *Itinerary*, pp. 13–14, ed. and tr. M. Adler (London 1907).
41. Starr, *Jews*, 190.
42. Aristakes of Lastivert 9.37 (tr. Bedrosian); Kekaumenos, *Strategikon* 83.

43. Christophoros Mitylenaios, *Poem* 18; Psellos, *Chronographia* 4.12–14; Skylitzes 393–408.
44. Kaldellis, *Streams*, 166–169; Blöndal, *Varangians*, 59–60.
45. Skylitzes 398–407; Attaleiates 8–9; Kekaumenos, *Strategikon* 81; J. Shepard, 'Byzantium's Last Sicilian Expedition,' *Rivista di studi bizantini e neoellenici* 14–16 (1977–1978) 145–159; Lambakis et al., *Βυζαντινά στρατεύματα*, 428–431.
46. Skylitzes 409, 412; Attaleiates 9–11, 34, 54; Psellos, *Chronographia* 4.39–40; *Orationes panegyricae* 2.340–344 (p. 32); cf. Petkov, *Voices*, 254.
47. Petkov, *Voices*, 196.
48. Skylitzes 409–413; Attaleiates 9–10; Psellos, *Chronographia* 4.39–50, 4.53–54; Kekaumenos, *Strategikon* 31, 42.
49. E. Bakalova et al., eds., *Medieval Bulgarian Art and Letters in a Byzantine Context* (Sofia 2017).
50. Psellos, *Orationes panegyricae* 17.69–73 (p. 146); Kaldellis, *Ethnography*, 126–139.
51. Kaldellis, *Romanland*, 234–239.
52. Kekaumenos, *Strategikon* 75; Anna 5.5.3, 8.3.4, 8.4.5; Euthymios Malakes in A. Papadopoulos-Kerameus, *Noctes Petropolitanae* (St. Petersburg 1913) 145; Kaldellis, *Romanland*, 239–242. Cheese: Ptochoprodromos, *Poems* 3.118, 4.211.
53. Psellos, *Chronographia* 5; Attaleiates 10–17; Skylitzes 416–421; poem: Christophoros Mytilenaios, *Poem* 52 (tr. Bernard and Livanos); Blöndal, *Varangians*, 93–94.
54. Psellos, *Orationes panegyricae* 2.663–669; *Chronographia* 6.29–30; Skylitzes 423; Christophoros Mytilenaios, *Poem* 55.
55. "Philosophers": Lemerle, *Cinq études*, ch. 4; A. Kaldellis and I. Polemis, *Psellos and the Patriarchs* (Notre Dame, IN 2015); rehabilitation: Kaldellis, *Streams*, ch. 8–9.
56. M. Bruggini, 'Il carme Εἰς τὸν Μανιάκην περὶ τοῦ Μούλτου attribuito a Cristoforo Mitileneo,' *Porphyra* 15 (2011) 14–34; Christophoros Mytilenaios, *Poem* 65; Skylitzes 427–428; Psellos, *Chronographia* 6.79–82; Attaleiates 18–20.
57. Skylitzes 429–430; Attaleiates 20.
58. Skylitzes 430–433; Psellos, *Chronographia* 6.90–95; Attaleiates 20–21; *Russian Primary Chronicle* 154 (p. 138); J. Shepard, 'Why Did the Russians Attack Byzantium in 1043?' *Byzantinisch-neugriechische Jahrbucher* 22 (1985) 147–212.
59. Attaleiates 79–80; Skylitzes 435–438; Aristakes of Lastivert 10.53–61; Matthew of Edessa 1.74–85; chronology: Leveniotis, *Πολιτική κατάρρευση*, 74–81.
60. W. Felix, *Byzanz und die islamische Welt im früheren 11. Jahrhundert* (Vienna 1981) 165; Dvin: Skylitzes 437–439; Aristakes of Lastivert 10.62; Matthew of Edessa 1.87.
61. Kaldellis, *Ethnography*, 106–126.
62. Skylitzes 455–459; Attaleiates 30–31; Mauropous, *Oration* 182.
63. J. Lefort, 'Rhétorique et politique: Trois discours de Jean Mauropous en 1047,' *TM* 6 (1976) 265–303.
64. Skylitzes 438–442; Psellos, *Chronographia* 6.99–123 (quotations); Attaleiates 22–30; Mauropous, *Oration* 186.
65. J.-P. Mahé, 'Ani sous Constantin X, d'après une inscription de 1060,' *TM* 14 (2002) 403–414; Kaldellis, *Romanland*, 244–245.
66. Aristakes of Lastivert 10.60; Garsoïan, 'Armenian Integration,' 53–124, here 65, 87, 91, 99–100.

67. Stopka, *Armenia*, 87–97; Takirtakoglou, *Αρμενία*, 367–368, 383.
68. Garsoïan, 'Armenian Integration,' 71, 76, 80–81.
69. Vryonis, 'Will,' 264–265; prejudice: Kaldellis, *Romanland*, 187–189; polemic: Kolbaba, *Byzantine Lists*, 37–38, 68–69.
70. Attaleiates 80; Skylitzes 437.
71. Garsoïan, 'Armenian Integration,' 124.
72. J. Shea, *Politics and Government in Byzantium: The Rise and Fall of the Bureaucrats* (London 2020); also H. Ahrweiler, 'Recherches sur l'administration de l'empire byzantin aux IX-XIème siècles,' *Bulletin de correspondance hellénique* 84 (1960) 1–111, here 50–52, 67–78; expansion: Cotsonis, 'Onomastics,' 3.
73. J. Howard-Johnston, 'The *Peira* and Legal Practices in Eleventh-Century Byzantium,' in Lauxtermann and Whittow, eds., *Byzantium*, 63–76, here 74.
74. Attaleiates 21–22; Kaldellis, *Streams*, 188.
75. Christophoros Mitylenaios, *Poem* 13 (tr. Bernard and Livanos, mod.); cf. *Poem* 55; Psellos, *Orationes panegyricae* 1.77–99; Attaleiates 18; Hondridou, *Κωνσταντίνος Θ΄*, 56–77, 98–103.
76. Oikonomides, 'Role,' 1021.
77. Kaldellis, *Hellenism*, ch. 4; S. Papaioannou, *Michael Psellos: Rhetoric and Authorship in Byzantium* (Cambridge 2013).

Chapter 27. The End of Italy and the East (1048–1081)

1. *Georgian Chronicles* 323; Attaleiates 116; background: Peacock, *Early Seljuk History*; Beihammer, *Byzantium*.
2. Gregory VII, *Register* 8.5–7, 91.7; background: C. Morris, *The Papal Monarchy: The Western Church from 1050 to 1250* (Oxford 1989).
3. Respectively: Geoffrey Malaterra, *Deeds of Count Roger* 1.5 (tr. Wolf); Amatus of Montecassino, *History of the Normans* 1.2 (tr. Dunbar and Loud).
4. Geoffrey Malaterra, *Deeds of Count Roger* 3.1 (Rossano).
5. William of Apulia, *Deeds of Robert Guiscard* 1.140–161.
6. Geoffrey Malaterra, *Deeds of Count Roger* 1.10 (tr. Wolf).
7. Geoffrey Malaterra, *Deeds of Count Roger* 1.3; Skylitzes Continuatus 135 (tr. McGeer and Nesbitt); also Anna 14.4.6; background: Loud, *Robert Guiscard*.
8. Skylitzes 448–454 (quotation: 454), 464; Attaleiates 148; Aristakes of Lastivert 11.68–13.89; Matthew of Edessa 1.92–94; *Georgian Chronicles* 295; Leveniotis, *Πολιτική κατάρρευση*, 147–152; Beihammer, *Byzantium*, 74–80, and 95 for Fatimid relations. Liparit: B. Martin-Hisard, 'Regards croisés du XIe siècle, byzantine et géorgien, sur Lip'arit' et sa famille,' *TM* 21.1 (2017) 399–450.
9. Kaldellis, *Ethnography*, 117–126.
10. Skylitzes 460–476; Attaleiates 31–43 (quotation: 35).
11. Loud, *Robert Guiscard*, 92–110; Lambakis et al., *Βυζαντινά στρατεύματα*, 432–440.

12. Pro-Norman sources: Amatus of Montecassino, *History of the Normans*, esp. 3.7–11 for Robert in Calabria; Geoffrey Malaterra, *The Deeds of Count Roger of Calabria and Sicily and of His Brother Duke Robert Guiscard*, esp. 1.16–19, 1.28 ("treason"); and William of Apulia, *Deeds of Robert Guiscard*, esp. 1.235–237 on concocting fictional titles of lordship in advance and then enforcing them through violence; 2.297–363 on Calabria; also Anna 1.11; reconstruction: Loud, *Robert Guiscard*, ch. 3, with 111–116, 126, 154, and 170 for local hatred. Epitaph: William of Malmesbury, *Gesta Rerum Anglorum*, pp. 484–485 (ed. Mynors).
13. Sources: C. Will, *Acta et scripta quae de controversiis ecclesiae graecae et latinae* (Leipzig 1861); reconstruction: A. Kaldellis, 'Keroularios in 1054,' in Chrissis et al., *Byzantium*, 9–24.
14. Kolbaba, *Byzantine Lists*.
15. Attaleiates 44–45; Skylitzes 476; Kekaumenos, *Strategikon* 20; Kaldellis, *Streams*, 210–213.
16. Skylitzes 462–464; Aristakes of Lastivert 16.92–107; Attaleiates 46–47; Matthew of Edessa 2.3; Beihammer, *Byzantium*, 58, 61, 80–84.
17. Skylitzes 477–478; Attaleiates 51.
18. Attaleiates 52; Psellos, *Chronographia* 6A.4, 6, 17; *Orationes funebres* 1.46; seals: Cotsonis, 'Onomastics,' 15.
19. Skylitzes 484–488; A. Simpson, 'Three Sources of Military Unrest in Eleventh Century Asia Minor,' *Mésogeios* 9–10 (2000) 181–207.
20. Skylitzes 490–491.
21. Attaleiates 55; also Skylitzes 487–495; Psellos, *Chronographia* 7.5–14.
22. Psellos, *Orationes funebres* 1.50.
23. Psellos, *Orationes funebres* 1.51; J. Shepard, 'Isaac Comnenus' Coronation Day,' *Byzantinoslavica* 38 (1977) 22–31.
24. Attaleiates 60; Skylitzes Continuatus 103; Matthew of Edessa 2.5. It was imitated by William the Conqueror in England.
25. Psellos, *Chronographia* 7.45; Attaleiates 60.
26. Psellos, *Chronographia* 7.51–60; Attaleiates 60–61; Skylitzes Continuatus 103–104. Vatopedi: Harvey, *Expansion*, 83.
27. Psellos, *Orationes forenses* 1; *Orationes funebres* 1.55–60; *Chronographia* 7.65–67; Attaleiates 62–66; Skylitzes Continuatus 104–105; Mangana: Zonaras, *Chronicle* 18.5; Oikonomides, 'St. George.'
28. Aristakes of Lastivert 18.122–19.130.
29. Aristakes of Lastivert 21.134–140; Matthew of Edessa 2.8–9; Michael the Syrian 15.1; Vest, *Geschichte*, 1298–1315.
30. Attaleiates 66–68; Psellos, *Chronographia* 7.76–70; Skylitzes Continuatus 107; Matthew of Edessa 2.5; Anna 3.8.6–10.
31. Psellos, *Letter* 139 (p. 375).
32. Attaleiates 69; Psellos, *Chronographia* 7.72–9, 7A.8–14; Skylitzes Continuatus 108–109; Bryennios 1.4–5.
33. *Life of Giorgi* 25, tr. Grdzelidze, *Georgian Monks*, 144.

34. Psellos, *Chronographia* 7A.14; *Oratoria minora* 5.5–61 (quotation); Attaleiates 70–71.
35. D. Polemis, *The Doukai: A Contribution to Byzantine Prosopography* (London 1968).
36. Psellos, *Letters* 101–103; Kaldellis, *Streams*, 233, 235.
37. Attaleiates 71–79; Psellos, *Chronographia* 7A.2–3, 16–24.
38. Matthew of Edessa 2.12–13, 2.15–19; Attaleiates 78–79.
39. Attaleiates 79–82 (quotation: 82); al-Athir, *Annals*, in Richards, *Annals*, 152–155; Matthew of Edessa 2.20–22; Aristakes of Lastivert 24.163–165; *Georgian Chronicles* 299–300.
40. Matthew of Edessa 2.23; Leveniotis, *Πολιτική κατάρρευση*, 116–118.
41. Attaleiates 83–87; Skylitzes Continuatus 113–116; Psellos, *Chronographia* 7A.23; *Orationes panegyricae* 14; Matthew of Edessa 2.24.
42. Loud, *Robert Guiscard*, 188.
43. Lupus Protospatharius, *Chronicle* s.a. 1066; fears of an attack by Robert: Geoffrey Malaterra, *Deeds of Count Roger* 2.43 (end); Kekaumenos, *Strategikon* 74; Bryennios 3.3.
44. Amatus of Montecassino, *History of the Normans* 5.4, 5.27; Geoffrey Malaterra, *Deeds of Count Roger* 2.40, 2.43; William of Apulia, *Deeds of Robert Guiscard* 2.478–3.166; Loud, *Robert Guiscard*, 131–134.
45. Psellos, *Orationes panegyricae* 9–10; Attaleiates 92; Cotsonis, 'Onomastics,' 15.
46. Matthew of Edessa 2.27–29, 48–49; Attaleiates 93–96, 100 (quotation); Psellos, *Chronographia* 7B.6 (quotation). Afshin: Beihammer, *Byzantium*, 120–121.
47. Attaleiates 97–102, 106; Psellos, *Chronographia* 7B.10.
48. E.g., Skylitzes 490.
49. Aristakes of Lastivert 17.108; fiscalization: Harvey, *Expansion*, 110–112.
50. Attaleiates 103–104; Skylitzes Continuatus 125.
51. Attaleiates 103–122 (quotation: 119); Kaldellis, *Streams*, 241–248; Beihammer, *Byzantium*, ch. 3.
52. Attaleiates 122–125; Amatus of Montecassino, *History of the Normans* 1.5–8.
53. Attaleiates 125–138.
54. Attaleiates 138–142; Bryennios 1.11, 1.18; Matthew of Edessa 2.54; Arisghi: Peacock, *Early Seljuq History*, 143–144.
55. Foss, 'Defenses,' 153.
56. Attaleiates 159; Matthew of Edessa 2.56; al-Athir, *Annals*, in Richards, *Annals*, 169–170; for Aleppo, see Zakkar, *Emirate*, 175–180.
57. J. Haldon 'La logistique de Mantzikert,' in D. Barthélemy and J.-C. Cheynet, eds., *Guerre et société: Byzance - Occident (VIIIe-XIIIe siècle)* (Paris 2010) 11–25, here 14.
58. Attaleiates 142–167 (quotation: 165).
59. Bryennios 1.16–17.
60. S. Vryonis, 'The Greek and Arabic Sources on the Eight Day Captivity of the Emperor Romanos IV,' in C. Sodé and S. Takácks, eds., *Novum Millennium: Studies on Byzantine History and Culture Dedicated to Paul Speck* (Farnham, UK 2001) 439–450; silk: Skylitzes Continuatus 142.
61. Attaleiates 168–169; Psellos, *Chronographia* 7B.23–31; Bryennios 1.18–20.
62. Attaleiates 169–179; Bryennios 1.21–25; Psellos, *Chronographia* 7B.32–42.

63. Psellos, *Letter* 39.
64. *Timarion* 20–22.
65. Cheynet, *Byzantine Aristocracy*, XIII.
66. Skylitzes Continuatus 156–157 (tr. McGeer and Nesbitt, mod.).
67. Attaleiates 303; Skylitzes Continuatus 171; Psellos, *Chronographia* 7C.4.
68. Cheynet, *Pouvoir*, 349–350.
69. L. Garland and S. Rapp, 'Mary "of Alania": Woman and Empress between Two Worlds,' in L. Garland, ed., *Byzantine Women: Varieties of Experience, 800–1200* (Aldershot, UK 2006) 91–124.
70. C. Kaplanis, 'The Debasement of the "Dollar of the Middle Ages",' *Journal of Economic History* 63 (2003) 768–801, here 770–771.
71. Psellos, *Orationes funebres* 3.21; Attaleiates 211 (quotation).
72. Vranousi and Nystazopoulou-Pelekidou, *Βυζαντινὰ ἔγγραφα*, 1: no. 1; 2: no. 50; Thonemann, *Maeander*, 259–270, 302–306.
73. P. Gautier, 'Le typikon du sébaste Grégoire Pakourianos,' *REB* 42 (1984) 5–145; Bartusis, *Land*, 125–128.
74. Kaldellis, *Streams*, 254.
75. Skylitzes Continuatus 163–166; *Chronicle of the Priest of Dioclea (Duklja)* 40.
76. Gabras: Anna 8.9; Leveniotis, *Πολιτική κατάρρευση*, 120–125, 246–251; 285–286; Palaiologos: Bryennios 3.15; Diabatenos: Matthew of Edessa 2.71; Philaretos: C. Yarnley, 'Philaretos: Armenian Bandit or Byzantine General?' *Revue des études arméniennes* 9 (1972) 331–353; Cheynet, *Société*, 390–410; Aleppo: Zakkar, *Emirate*, 172, 180–187.
77. Attaleiates 183–207; Bryennios 2.3–27; Anna 1.1–3 (esp. 1.1.2 for his timing); Sicily: Geoffrey Malaterra, *Deeds of Count Roger* 2.33; in detail: G. Leveniotis, *Το στασιαστικό κίνημα του Νορμανδού Ουρσελίου (Ursel de Bailleul) στην Μικρά Ασία (1073–1076)* (Thessalonike 2004).
78. *Georgian Chronicles* 303–310.
79. "Dog": Ioannes Oxeites in Gautier, 'Diatribes,' 23.
80. Attaleiates 199; P. Magdalino, *The Byzantine Background to the First Crusade* (Toronto 1996) 29–34.
81. Kastamone: Bryennios 2.26; refugees: Attaleiates 200, 211, 267; Christodoulos of Patmos, *Rule* 5, in *MM* 6:61–62 ("nook"); fleet: Michael the Syrian 15.4; farm: Izdebski, *Rural Economy*, 37; Sarris, 'Beyond the Great Plains,' 78.
82. Bryennios 4.4; Attaleiates 243.
83. J. Haldon et al., 'The Climate and Environment of Byzantine Anatolia,' *Journal of Interdisciplinary History* 45 (2014) 113–161, here 151; depopulation and coins: Harvey, *Expansion*, 67, 88–89.
84. Psellos, *Orationes forenses: Actum* 5; Skylitzes Continuatus 170; Amatus of Montecassino, *History of the Normans* 7.26.
85. Attaleiates 201–209; Skylitzes Continuatus 166; Laiou and Morrisson, *Byzantine Economy*, 135–136, 162; Kaldellis, *Streams*, 263; Meško, 'Pecheneg Groups.'
86. Skylitzes Continuatus 171.
87. A. Grant, 'Byzantium's Ashes and the Bones of St Nicholas,' in Kinloch and MacFarlane, eds., *Trends*, 247–265, here 250, 255.

88. Attaleiates 215, 240; O. Karagiorgou, 'On the Way to the Throne: The Career of Nikephoros III Botaneiates before 1078,' in C. Stavrakos et al., eds., *Hypermachos: Studien zu Byzantinistik, Armenologie und Georgistik* (Wiesbaden 2008) 105–132.
89. Attaleiates 242–262; Skylitzes Continuatus 172–176; Bryennios 3.3–14.
90. Attaleiates 252–255; Bryennios 3.26.
91. Attaleiates 255–277, 283–284; Bryennios 3.15–24; grants: F. Dölger, *Regesten der Kaiserurkunden des oströmischen Reiches* (Munich 1995) 2:76–85.
92. Attaleiates 273–275, 283, 304; Skylitzes Continuatus 181–182; Bryennios 3.25–4.2, Anna 3.2.3–6.
93. Attaleiates 284–296; Skylitzes Continuatus 179–181; Bryennios 4.2–18; Anna 1.4–6.
94. Attaleiates 297–300; Skylitzes Continuatus 182–183; Bryennios 4.16–28; Anna 1.7–9 (quotation: 1.7.3).
95. Attaleiates 306–309.
96. Bryennios 4.31–40; G. Leveniotes, 'Το θέμα/δουκάτο των Ανατολικών κατά το δεύτερο ήμισυ του 11ου αι.,' *Byzantiaka* 25 (2005–2006) 33–101, here 64–71, 86–87.
97. Anna 2.1–3.1, 3.5; Zonaras, *Chronicle* 18.20; ransomed: Bryennios 2.5, 2.29.
98. Attaleiates 198; Oxeites in Gautier, 'Diatribes,' 35.
99. Haldon, 'L'armée,' 585.
100. Beihammer, *Byzantium*. Beihammer's data are often misread, starting in the book's promotional material.
101. Haldon, 'L'armée,' 587–588, though I disagree regarding mercenaries (582, 589, 590): Kaldellis, *Streams*, 271–279.

Chapter 28. Komnenian Crisis Management (1081–1118)

1. Neville, *Anna*.
2. Anna 2.8, 3.4, 6.8.3–5; Cheynet, *Byzantine Aristocracy*, VI.
3. Bryennios 4.1; Zonaras, *Chronicle* 18.21 (3:733).
4. Anna 1.15.6, also 1.10.2, 1.12.2–10; 3.9.1 ("breathing").
5. Gregory VII, *Register* 8.6, 9.17; H. Cowdrey, *Pope Gregory VII* (Oxford 1998) 482–486.
6. Contemporary note added to Amatus of Montecassino, *History of the Normans* 5.3 (tr. Dunbar).
7. Geoffrey Malaterra, *Deeds of Count Roger* 3.24; Orderic Vitalis, *EH* 4.16–17; cf. Anna 1.16.1; Theotokis, *Norman Campaigns*, 21–22, 143. Anna offers the most detailed narrative; for her reliance on William of Apulia, see J. Howard-Johnston, 'Bilingual Reading, the *Alexiad*, and the *Gesta Roberti Wiscardi*,' in Shawcross and Toth, eds., *Reading*, 467–498; in general: Loud, *Robert Guiscard*, 209–223.
8. Anna 3.5–6; Vranousi and Nystazopoulou-Pelekidou, *Βυζαντινὰ ἔγγραφα*, 1:331–335, 342–351; *AA* 13 (*Docheiariou*) no. 2, 58–59; seal: N. Oikonomides, 'The Usual Lead Seal,' *DOP* 37 (1983) 147–157, here 156.

9. Anna 3.9.3, 4.4.
10. Geoffrey Malaterra, *Deeds of Count Roger* 3.27; Theotokis, *Norman Campaigns*, 85–86; battle-plan: M. Meško, 'Some Thoughts on the Military Capabilities of Alexios I Komnenos,' *Graeco-Latina Brunensia* 24 (2019) 143–161.
11. Anna 5.1.1.
12. Scorpion: William of Tyre 10.13; Heinrich: Ekkehard of Aura, *Universal Chronicle* s.a. 1083, in *MGH SS* 6:205; Anna 3.10, 5.3.1–6; Shepard, 'Scorpion.'
13. Anna 5.2; Alexios I, *On the Holy Vessels*, in *PG* 127:921–926; Glavinas, *Ἡ ἐπὶ Ἀλεξίου Κομνηνοῦ*, ch. 2–3.
14. Psellos, *Oratoria minora* 19.
15. L. Clucas, *The Trial of John Italos* (Munich 1981); J. Gouillard, 'Le procés officiel de Jean l'Italien,' *TM* 9 (1985) 133–174.
16. M. Trizio, 'Ancient Physics in the Mid-Byzantine Period: The *Epitome* of Theodore of Smyrna,' *Bulletin de philosophie médiévale* 54 (2012) 77–99, esp. 95–96.
17. *Synodikon of Orthodoxy* 184–249, ed. J. Gouillard, 'Le Synodikon de l'Orthodoxie,' *TM* 2 (1967) 1–316, here 56–61; trials: M. Trizio, 'Trials of Philosophers and Theologians under the Komnenoi,' in Kaldellis and Siniossoglou, eds., *Intellectual History*, ch. 27.
18. Anna 5.5.2.
19. Anna 6.3–4; Glavinas, *Ἡ ἐπὶ Ἀλεξίου Κομνηνοῦ*, 80–92.
20. William of Apulia, *Deeds of Robert Guiscard* 5.143–228; Anna 4.3 misplaces this.
21. Alexios I, *Memorandum on the Deposition of Leon of Chalkedon*, ed. I. Sakkelion, 'Documents inédits,' *Bulletin de correspondance hellénique* 2 (1878) 113–128; Leon of Chalkedon, *Letter to Nikolaos of Adrianople*, ed. E. Lauriotes, 'Ἱστορικὸν ζήτημα ἐκκλησιαστικόν,' *Ἐκκλησιαστικὴ ἀλήθεια* 20 (1900) 403–407, 411–416, 445–447, 455–456; Glavinas, *Ἡ ἐπὶ Ἀλεξίου Κομνηνοῦ*, 99–177; visions: e.g., Anna 7.4.1; second expropriation: ibid. 5.2; Oxeites in Gautier, 'Diatribes,' 31–33, 49; Zonaras, *Chronicle* 18.22.
22. P. Frankopan, 'A Victory of Gregory Pakourianos against the Pechenegs,' *Byzantinoslavica* 57 (1996) 278–281; in general: Meško, 'Pecheneg Groups'; dating: idem, 'Notes sur la chronologie de la guerre des Byzantins contre les Petchénègues,' *Byzantinoslavica* 69 (2011) 134–148.
23. Anna 6.14–7.1.
24. Oxeites in Gautier, 'Diatribes,' 35.
25. Anna 7.2–8.3; quotations: 7.6.3, 8.3.1; women: 8.5.9; Choniates, *History* 14.
26. Nikolaos Kataskepenos, *Life of Kyrillos Phileotes* 29.1.
27. Anna 7.8, 8.3, 9.1.9, 9.5.1; Zonaras, *Chronicle* 18.22; Christodoulos of Patmos, *Private Testament* 3, in *MM* 6:81.
28. Oxeites in Gautier, 'Diatribes,' 35, 41; Anna 9.2.
29. Anna 7.5, 8.3–8.6; alliance: Theophylaktos of Ohrid, *Oration to Alexios*, pp. 219–221 (early 1088).
30. Nikolaos Kataskepenos, *Life of Kyrillos Phileotes* 29.11.
31. Oxeites in Gautier, 'Diatribes,' 29–43.
32. Ryder, 'Role.'
33. Bartusis, *Land*, ch. 4.

34. Smyrlis, 'Fiscal Revolution'; Oxeites in Gautier, 'Diatribes,' 31–33, 43; P. Gautier, 'Le dossier d'un haut fonctionnaire d'Alexis Ier Comnène, Manuel Straboromanos,' *REB* 23 (1965) 168–204, here 183; Zonaras, *Chronicle* 18.21, 18.25 (3:733, 737).
35. Zonaras, *Chronicle* 18.29 (3:767).
36. *AA* 5 (*Lavra* 1) nos. 46.12–17, 48.23–27, 51.
37. Konstantinos VII, *Book of Ceremonies* 2.50 (3:389); Ani: Attaleiates 80.
38. K. Smyrlis, 'Social Change in the Countryside of Eleventh-Century Byzantium,' in Howard-Johnston, ed., *Social Change*, 62–75, here 70–74.
39. M. Hendy, *Coinage and Money in the Byzantine Empire, 1081–1261* (Washington, D.C. 1969); J. Jarrett, 'Why Did the Byzantine Coinage Turn Concave?' in M. Caltabiano, ed., *XV International Numismatic Congress, Taormina 2015: Proceedings* (Rome 2017), Addendum: 1–4.
40. Alexios I in Zepos, *Jus Graecoromanum*, 1:334–340; Harvey, *Expansion*, 90–102; 'Financial Crisis and the Rural Economy,' in Mullett and Smythe, eds., *Alexios*, 167–184.
41. A. Harvey, 'The Land and Taxation in the Reign of Alexios I Komnenos: The Evidence of Theophylakt of Ochrid,' *REB* 51 (1993) 139–154; S. Doanidou, 'Ἡ παραίτησις Νικολάου τοῦ Μουζάλωνος,' *Ἑλληνικά* 7 (1934) 109–150.
42. Alexios I in Zepos, *Jus Graecoromanum*, 1:334; Oikonomides, 'Role,' 1027.
43. Pozza and Ravegnani, *Trattati*, no. 2:38–45; Anna 6.5.10; P. Frankopan, 'Byzantine Trade Privileges to Venice in the Eleventh Century,' *Journal of Medieval History* 30 (2004) 135–160; Smyrlis, 'Private Property'; limited impact: D. Jacoby, 'Byzantine Maritime Trade, 1025–1118,' *TM* 21.2 (2017) 627–648, here 643–646.
44. Anna 9.1–3; "weaker": 6.11.2.
45. Anna 8.7.2, 9.1.1, 9.4–9; Zonaras, *Chronicle* 18.23 (3:741–742); date: P. Frankopan, 'Challenges to Imperial Authority in the Reign of Alexios I Komnenos,' *Byzantinoslavica* 64 (2006) 257–274.
46. Doukas: Kouroupou and Vannier, 'Commémoraisons,' 67; Ioannes: Anna 6.8.5; V. Stanković, 'John II Komnenos before 1118,' in Bucossi and Rodriguez Suarez, eds., *John II*, 16–17.
47. Anna 8.7–8; 1095: Glavinas, *Ἡ ἐπὶ Ἀλεξίου Κομνηνοῦ*, 182; 1105: Kouroupou and Vannier, 'Commémoraisons,' 62.
48. Glavinas, *Ἡ ἐπὶ Ἀλεξίου Κομνηνοῦ*, 179–193.
49. Anna 10.1.1–6; J. Nilsson, 'The Emperor Is for Turning: Alexios Komnenos, John the Oxite and the Persecution of Heretics,' in Kinloch and MacFarlane, eds., *Trends*, 185–202.
50. C. Messis, 'Public hautement affiché et public réellement visé: Le cas de l'*Apologie de l'eunuchism* de Théophylacte d'Achrida,' in P. Odorico, ed., *La face caché de la littérature byzantine* (Paris 2012) 41–85, here 69–78; Chrysomallos: Magdalino, *Empire*, 276, 368.
51. Anna 6.2, 14.8–9; Zonaras, *Chronicle* 18.26; M. Trizio, *Il neoplatonismo di Eustrazio di Nicea* (Bari 2016).
52. Anna 15.8–10; Tia Kolbaba, pers. comm.
53. Zigabenos, *Panoply* pref., in *PG* 130:21B; Bogomils: Title 27; Anna 15.9.1.

54. P. Armstrong, 'Alexios I Komnenos, Holy Men and Monasteries,' in Mullett and Smythe, eds., *Alexios*, 219–231; Morris, *Monks*, 280–282; food: Nikolaos Kataskepenos, *Life of Kyrillos Phileotes* 47.12.
55. Anna 15.7.3–9; P. Magdalino, 'Innovations in Government,' in Mullett and Smythe, eds., *Alexios*, 146–166, here 157.
56. Nikolaos Kataskepenos, *Life of Kyrillos Phileotes* 47.6; Anna 14.8.8.
57. P. Meyer, *Die Haupturkunden für die Geschichte der Athosklöster* (Leipzig 1894) 163–184; Morris, *Monks*, 275–280.
58. Anna 10.2–4; *Russian Primary Chronicle* 226–227 (p. 180); P. Frankopan, 'Unravelling the *Alexiad*,' *BMGS* 29 (2005) 147–166.
59. Anna 10.5.4.
60. E. Joranson, 'The Great German Pilgrimage of 1064–1065,' in L. Paetow, ed., *The Crusades and Other Historical Essays* (New York 1928) 3–43; S. Runciman, 'The Pilgrimages to Palestine before 1095,' in K. Setton, ed., *A History of the Crusades* (Madison, WI 1969) 1:68–78, here 76; escorts: Kaldellis, *Streams*, 345 n. 11.
61. Christodoulos of Patmos, *Rule* 3, in *MM* 6:60.
62. Kaldellis, *Streams*, 283–284; Flanders: Anna 7.6.1.
63. P. Cobb, *The Race for Paradise: An Islamic History of the Crusades* (Oxford 2014).
64. Chevedden, 'Crusade.' See the proto-crusading language and practices in Amatus of Montecassino, *History of the Normans* 1.5; Geoffrey Malaterra, *Deeds of Count Roger* 2.33.
65. H. Cowdrey, 'Pope Gregory VII's "Crusading" Plans of 1074,' in B. Kedar et al., eds., *Outremer: Studies in the History of the Crusading Kingdom of Jerusalem* (Jerusalem 1982) 27–40.
66. Harris, 'Byzantium and First Crusade,' esp. 129–130 for Alexios' appeal. Anna 10.5.6.
67. W. Holtzman, 'Die Unionsverhandlungen zwischen Kaiser Alexios I und Papst Urban II im Jahre 1089,' *BZ* 28 (1928) 38–67; excommunication: Bernold of Constance, *Chronicle* s.a. 1089, ed. I. Robinson, *Die Chroniken Bertholds von Reichenau und Bernolds von Konstanz* (Hanover 2003).
68. Cf. K. Leyser, *Communications and Power in Medieval Europe: The Gregorian Revolution and Beyond* (London 1994) 77–95; translators: Anna 10.5.9; logistics: 11.1.1.
69. Anna 10.5.10, 10.9.1, 10.11.7; Alexios in Robert the Monk, *History of the First Crusade* 2.14; other sources: Kaldellis, *Streams*, 289–292.
70. J. Shepard, 'When Greek Meets Greek: Alexius Comnenus and Bohemond in 1097–98,' *BMGS* 12 (1988) 185–277; oath: Harris, 'Byzantium,' 137, 139.
71. Albert of Aachen, *History of the Journey to Jerusalem* 2.16, tr. S. Edgington (Farnham 2013).
72. Stephen, *Letter to Adela* 1, tr. M. Barber and K. Bate, *Letters from the East: Crusaders, Pilgrims and Settlers in the 12th-13th Centuries* (Farnham 2013) 15–17, 22–25.
73. Anna 10.11.7. I am not convinced that Alexios made the offer and Bohemond turned it down.

74. Fulcher of Chartres, *A History of the Expedition to Jerusalem* 1.9.3, tr. F. Ryan (Knoxville 1969); and Robert the Monk, *History of the First Crusade* 2.19, tr. C. Sweetenham (Farnham 2005).
75. "Liberate": Chevedden, 'Crusade,' 217; also H. Cowdrey, 'Pope Urban II's Preaching of the First Crusade,' in Madden, ed., *Fourth Crusade*, 15–29.
76. *Gesta Francorum* 2.6, ed. and tr. R. Hill, *The Deeds of the Franks and the Other Pilgrims to Jerusalem* (London 1962).
77. Beihammer, *Byzantium*, ch. 5, 7; K. Belke, 'Byzanz und die Anfänge des rumseldschukischen Staates,' *JöB* 61 (2011) 65–79.
78. Anna 6.10.9–10; D. Gutas, A. Kaldellis, and B. Long, 'Intellectual Exchanges with the Arab World,' in Kaldellis and Siniossoglou, eds., *Intellectual History*, 79–98, here 92–98.
79. Anna 6.9–13 (garbled), 7.7.4, 10.5.1–3; treaties with Nikaia: 3.11.5, 6.9.1.
80. Theophylaktos, *Oration to Alexios*, p. 227.
81. Alexios I, *Letter to Oderisius*, ed. H. Hagenmeyer, *Epistulae et chartae ad historiam primi belli sacri spectantes: Die Kreuzzugsbriefe aus den Jahren 1088–1100* (Innsbruck 1901) 152–153; supplies: Kaldellis, *Streams*, 296 n. 62.
82. Anna 11.5; Shepard, 'Scorpion,' 125–126; E. Ragia, 'Η αναδιοργάνωση των θεμάτων στη Μικρά Ασία τον δωδέκατο αιώνα,' *Byzantina Symmeikta* 17 (2005) 223–238.
83. Kaldellis, *Streams*, 297–299; Beihammer, *Byzantium*, 288–289, 293–293; Tyerman, *God's War*, 132.
84. Tyerman, *God's War*, 136–137; J. France, *Victory in the East: A Military History of the First Crusade* (Cambridge 1994) 208–220.
85. Tyerman, *God's War*, 162; but cf. Bartolf of Nangis in Phillips, 'Crusader Perceptions,' 107.
86. Raymond d'Aguilers, *Historia Francorum qui ceperunt Iherusalem* 41, tr. J. and L. Hill (Philadelphia 1968); Anna 11.6.4.
87. Ibn Taghribirdi in C. Hillenbrand, 'The First Crusade: The Muslim Perspective,' in J. Philips, ed., *The First Crusade: Origins and Impact* (Manchester 1997) 130–141, here 132–133.
88. Shepard, 'Scorpion,' 81.
89. Shepard, 'Scorpion,' 76–80; idem, 'Significant Others,' 146–147.
90. Albert of Aachen, *History of the Journey to Jerusalem* 8.9; Anna 11.8.
91. Albert of Aachen, *History of the Journey to Jerusalem* 8.45–48; Ekkehard of Aura, *Universal Chronicle* s.a. 1101, in *MGH SS* 6:219–223; William of Tyre 10.12–13; Lilie, *Byzantium*, 53–60 ("defamation": 60); Beihammer, *Byzantium*, 318–323.
92. Blöndal, *Varangians*, 131–141; K. Ciggaar, *Western Travellers to Constantinople* (Leiden 1996) ch. 4; F. Androshchuk et al., eds., *Byzantium and the Viking World* (Uppsala 2016).
93. Attaleia: Anna 11.9.3; naval operations: 11.10–11; Lilie, *Byzantium*, 62–72.
94. Zonaras, *Chronicle* 18.24 (3:747); Kouroupou and Vannier, 'Commémoraisons,' 51, 56.
95. Anna 12.5–6 (Isaakios was alive, so before 1104).
96. Lilie, *Byzantium*, 71.

97. Ryder, 'Role,' 93.
98. Orderic Vitalis, *EH* 11.12; crusade: Tyerman, *God's War*, 259–263.
99. Anna, books 12–13 ("sword": 13.4.3).
100. Anna 13.12–14.1; territories: E. Honigmann, *Die Ostgrenze des byzantinischen Reiches von 363 bis 1071* (Brussels 1935) 125–129.
101. Pisans: G. Müller, ed., *Documenti sulle relazioni della città toscane coll'Oriente cristiano e coi Turchi* (Florence 1879) 52; Alexios: *MM* 3:9–13; Lilie, *Byzantium*, 88–91.
102. Theophylaktos, *On the Accusations against the Latins*, pp. 246–285; Shepard, 'Significant Others,' 144–145; I. Augé, *Byzantins, Arméniens et Francs au temps de la Croisade* (Paris 2007) 151–156.
103. Thonemann, *Maeander*, 262.
104. Anna 14.3.5.
105. C. Lightfoot, 'Amorium,' in P. Niewöhner, ed., *Archaeology*, 333–341, here 341; evacuation: Anna 11.6.4–5.
106. *MM* 4:324–325; K. Smyrlis, *La fortune des grands monastères byzantins* (Paris 2006) 169–170.
107. Anna books 14–15; Zonaras, *Chronicle* 18.27; Beihammer, *Byzantium*, 363–373.
108. "Alexios I Komnenos," *Muses* 1.324–325.
109. Anna 1.2.2.
110. Zonaras, *Chronicle* 18.22 (3:739–740), 18.24 (3:746–747); Magdalino, *Empire*, 202–209.
111. Zonaras, *Chronicle* 18.29 (3:766–767).
112. Anna 12.4.5; Zonaras, *Chronicle* 13.3, 18.26.

Chapter 29. Good John and the Sun King (1118–1180)

1. Zonaras, *Chronicle* 18.26–29; Anna 12.3, 15.11; Choniates, *History* 8–10.
2. Anna 14.3.9, 14.7.6; Neville, *Anna*. Muse: Prodromos, *Epithalamium for the Kaisar's Son*, p. 347, ed. P. Gautier, *Nicéphore Bryennios histoire* (Brussels 1975).
3. Choniates, *History* 43.
4. Kinnamos 1.2, 1.9; Prodromos, *Historical Poems* 4.111–120.
5. Choniates, *History* 19–20; Kinnamos 1.6.
6. Choniates, *History* 37; Kinnamos 1.10; geography: Hendy, *Studies*, 109–131.
7. D. Korobeinikov, '"The King of the East and the West": The Seljuk Dynastic Concept,' in A. Peacock and S. Yıldız, eds., *The Seljuks of Anatolia* (London 2013) 68–90; Shukurov, 'Turkoman.'
8. Devaney, 'Byzantine-Venetian Conflict'; Kinnamos 6.10.
9. Choniates, *History* 55; Nikolaos, ho tou Kataphloron, *Oration for the Governor of Greece* 32–34; commentary and dating: I. Polemis, *Κείμενα για την Ελλάδα στην περίοδο των Κομνηνών* (Athens 2020) 16–23.
10. Kinnamos 1.3; Choniates, *History* 16.

11. Kinnamos 1.4; Choniates, *History* 17–18; Makk, *Árpáds*, 21–27.
12. Barzos, *Γενεαλογία*, 1:238–243; K. Linardou, 'Imperial Impersonations: Disguised Portraits of a Komnenian Prince and his Father,' in Bucossi and Rodriguez Suarez, eds., *John II*, 155–181.
13. Prodromos, *Historical Poems* 6.116–124; Choniates, *History* 18–19; reconstruction and translation: P. Magdalino, 'The Triumph of 1133,' in Bucossi and Rodriguez Suarez, eds., *John II*, 53–70.
14. *Typika*: tr. R. Jordan in *BMFD* 649–781, esp. 738 ("wickedly"), 742 (commemorations); Isaakios' burial: *Typikon of the Kosmosoteira* in ibid. 838; hospital: Miller, *Birth*, 14–21, 141–166; S. Kotzabassi, ed., *The Pantokrator Monastery in Constantinople* (Berlin 2013); Anna 14.7.6.
15. Embassy: *Annales Magdeburgenses* s.a. 1135, in *MGH SS* 16:185 (and other chronicles); Anselm of Havelberg, *Anticimenon: On the Unity of Faith and the Controversies with the Greeks*, tr. A. Criste and C. Neel (Collegeville, MN 2010); see Phillips, 'Crusader Perceptions,' 110. Constance: Kinnamos 1.7.
16. Michael Italikos, *Oration 43 to Ioannes Komnenos*, p. 253.
17. Goitein, 'Letter.'
18. Kinnamos 1.7–8 ("match"); Choniates, *History* 21–32; William of Tyre 14.24, 14–30–15.5 ("effeminate"); Orderic Vitalis, *EH* 13.34; Michael Italikos, *Oration 43 to Ioannes Komnenos*, pp. 261–266; Gregory the Priest, *Continuation of Matthew of Edessa's History* 1; Lilie, *Byzantium*, 103–131.
19. Tyerman, *God's War*, 248.
20. D. Stathakopoulos, 'John II Komnenos,' in Bucossi and Rodriguez Suarez, eds., *John II*, 1–10, here 5.
21. Otto of Freising, *Deeds of Frederick Barbarossa* 1.25; others: A. Panagopoulou, *Οι διπλωματικοί γάμοι στο Βυζάντιο* (Athens 2006) part 4.
22. Kinnamos 1.10; "daughter": Lilie, *Byzantium*, 139.
23. Otto of Freisig, *The Two Cities* 7.28; William of Tyre 15.23; Anna 6.8.5.
24. William of Tyre 16.26; raids: Kinnamos 2.9; Seleukeia: Goitein, 'Letter,' 300.
25. Choniates, *History* 97.
26. J. Lefort, 'The Rural Economy,' in *EHB*, 299–300.
27. P. Armstrong, 'Greece in the Eleventh Century,' in Howard-Johnston, ed., *Social Change*, 133–156; harbors: Choniates, *History* 74; ceramics: Laiou and Morrisson, *Economy*, 117–118; currency: 153–155; in general: Curta, *Southeastern Europe*, 319–327.
28. Kaldellis, *Romanland*, 240–242; *Ethnography*, 132–134; frontier: Hendy, *Studies*, 35–39.
29. Balsamon in Rallis and Potlis, *Σύνταγμα*, 5:523–524; see Laiou and Morrisson, *Economy*, 159; Bartusis, *Land*, 132–152; Smyrlis, 'Fiscal Revolution,' 608–609.
30. Nikolaos, ho tou Kataphloron, *Oration for the Governor of Greece* 28–29, 35.
31. Choniates, *History* 208–209, tr. and analysis in Bartusis, *Land*, 65, 46–49, 88–95; relationship and residence: ibid. 406, 408–409.
32. "Weapon": Choniates, *History* 30; a list of ethnic units in Alexios' chrysobul to Patmos: Vranousi and Nystazopoulou-Pelekidou, *Βυζαντινὰ ἔγγραφα*, 1:61; support: Bartusis, *Land*, 105–111, 123.

33. Nikephoros Basilakes, *Oration for Ioannes Komnenos* 1 (*Or. et ep.* pp. 49–50); Kaldellis, *Hellenism*, 243–244 for more.
34. A. Kazhdan and A. Epstein, *Change in Byzantine Culture in the Eleventh and Twelfth Centuries* (Berkeley 1985) 104–116; seals: Cheynet, *Société*, 113–123; C. Messis and I. Nilsson, 'The *Description of a Crane Hunt* by Constantine Manasses,' *Scandinavian Journal of Byzantine and Modern Greek Studies* 5 (2019) 9–89; L. Jones and H. Maguire, 'A Description of the Jousts of Manuel I Komnenos,' *BMGS* 26 (2002) 104–148.
35. Jeffreys, 'Afterlife.' "Tongue": *Digenes G* 1.115; Homer: 4.27; saints: 1.20–29, 6.700–701.
36. Ptochoprodromos 4.189, 4.544; "Manganeios Prodromos" in Magdalino, *Empire*, 449.
37. A. Kaldellis, 'The *Timarion:* Toward a *Literary* Interpretation,' in P. Odorico, ed., *Le face cachée de la littérature byzantine* (Paris 2012) 275–288; idem, *Hellenism*, 276–283; Psellos' influence: ibid. 225–228, 241–247, 297–299. Psellos not alone: P. Magdalino, 'Cultural Change? The Context of Byzantine Poetry from Geometres to Prodromos,' in F. Bernard and K. Demoen, eds., *Poetry and its Contexts in Eleventh-Century Byzantium* (Farnham, UK 2012) 19–36, here 27–29.
38. P. Magdalino, 'The Byzantine Holy Man in the Twelfth Century,' in S. Hackel, ed., *The Byzantine Saint* (London 1981) 51–66; Kaldellis, *Hellenism*, 253–255, and ch. 5 passim; S. Paschalides, 'The Hagiography of the Eleventh and Twelfth Centuries,' in S. Efthymiadis, ed., *The Ashgate Research Companion to Byzantine Hagiography* (Farnham, UK 2011) 1:143–171; K. Metzler, *Eustathius: De emendanda via monachica* (Berlin 2006).
39. A. Kazhdan, *Studies on Byzantine Literature of the Eleventh and Twelfth Centuries* (Cambridge 1984) ch. 3 (outdated); Ptochoprodromos: Jeffreys, 'Afterlife,' 147–148; M. Janssen and M. Lauxtermann, 'Authorship Revisited: Language and Meter in the *Ptochoprodromika*,' in Shawcross and Toth, eds., *Reading*, 558–584, here 562–564.
40. E. Jeffreys, *Four Byzantine Novels* (Liverpool 2012); "reconstruction": Kaldellis, *Hellenism*, 256–276; "Romaic": Kaldellis, *Romanland*, 97–108.
41. Lauxtermann, *Byzantine Poetry*, 2:101.
42. C. Barber and D. Jenkins, eds., *Medieval Greek Commentaries on the* Nicomachean Ethics (Leiden 2009); money: Laiou and Morrisson, *Economy*, 162–163; monarchy: A. Kaldellis, 'Aristotle's *Politics* in Byzantium,' in V. Syros, ed., *Well Begun Is Only Half Done: Tracing Aristotle's Political Ideas* (Tempe, AZ 2011) 121–143.
43. M. Trizio, 'Eleventh- to Twelfth-Century Byzantium,' in S. Gersh, ed., *Interpreting Proclus* (Cambridge 2014) 182–226.
44. Nesseris, *Παιδεία*, esp. Part I; Magdalino, *Empire*, 325–330; C. Messis, 'Ο Θεόδωρος Βαλσαμών και η παρουσία του στο λογοτεχνικό περιβάλλον,' in V. Vlysidou, ed, *Byzantine Authors and Their Times* (Athens 2021) 306–323, here 306–308.
45. P. Leone, ed., *Ioannis Tzetzae Carmina Iliaca* (Catania 1995) 129.
46. Magdalino, *Empire*, 335–356; Kaldellis, *Hellenism*, ch. 5; Pontani, 'Scholarship,' 430–471.
47. E. Jeffreys, 'The *sebastokratorissa* Irene as Patron,' in M. Mullett and M. Grünbart, eds., *Female Founders in Byzantium and Beyond* (Vienna 2014) 177–194; Isaakios: Nesseris, *Παιδεία*, 2:304–306; Herakleia: Kinnamos 2.2. Prodromos: E. Kurtz, 'Unedierte Texte aus der Zeit des Kaisers Johannes Komnenos,' *BZ* 16 (1907) 69–119, here 112–117.

48. M. Jeffreys, 'Versified Press-Releases on the Role of the Komnenian Emperor,' in G. Nathan and L. Garland, eds., *Basileia: Essays on Imperium and Culture* (Virginia, Queensland 2011) 27–38; Magdalino, *Empire*, 314, 414, 445.
49. Choniates, *History* 280; Kinnamos 2.7.
50. Well put by Magdalino, *Empire*, 183–185; positions: Stephenson, *Balkan Frontier*, 259–260.
51. Macrides, 'What's in the Name.'
52. Dumbarton Oaks seal BZS.1958.106.1544. Neville, *Authority*, 33 for legal documents. Peasant names: Bartusis, *Land*, 50.
53. Leidholm, *Kinship*; entailing office: Choniates, *History* 400.
54. Magdalino, *Empire*, 209–217, 257.
55. Day, *Genoa's Response*, ch. 2.
56. A. Laiou, 'The Emperor's Word,' *TM* 14 (2002) 347–362.
57. Michael Italikos, *Imperial Oration for Manuel Komnenos* (no. 44); Kinnamos 1.10; Choniates, *History* 42–46.
58. E.g., Choniates, *History* 54–55, 73, 186, 204, 230; Georgios Tornikes, *Letter* 27; M. Choniates, *Address to Demetrios Drimys* 40 (1:174–175); Neophytos in Galatariotou, *Neophytos*, 190–193.
59. Odo of Deuil, *Louis VII's March to the East* 4 (tr. Berry, pp. 63–65, mod.); population: Magdalino, *Studies*, I:61–63.
60. Choniates, *History* 201; Kinnamos 5.9.
61. Eustathios, *Funeral Oration for Manuel Komnenos* 17.
62. William of Tyre 17.16; Abulafia, 'Ancona.'
63. Kinnamos 3.3, 6.3, with Curta, *Southeastern Europe*, 316–317; fleet: Lilie, *Byzantium*, 215–220.
64. Eustathios, *Oration* K, p. 185 (ed. Wirth).
65. Kinnamos 2.3–2.11; Choniates, *History* 52–53.
66. Choniates, *History* 54, tr. Magdalino, *Empire*, 4; Basileios of Ohrid, *Epitaph for the Empress Eirene*; Otto of Freising, *Deeds of Frederick Barbarossa* 1.25.
67. Choniates, *History* 61–62; V. Grumel, 'Au seuil de la deuxième croisade: Deux lettres de Manuel Comnène au pape,' *REB* 3 (1945) 143–167; Lilie, *Byzantium*, 150–153; weakness: Tzetzes, *Letter* 59.
68. Kinnamos 3.2; Choniates, *History* 62, 72–73; Otto of Freising, *Deeds of Frederick Barbarossa* 1.34; "dragon": Manuel I in Zepos, *Jus Graecorormanum*, 1:376. Revived: Benjamin of Tudela, *Itinerary*, p. 10 (tr. Adler); Choniates, *History* 461.
69. Odo of Deuil, *Louis VII's March to the East*; Kinnamos 2.12–19; Choniates, *History* 60–72; Otto of Freising, *Deeds of Frederick Barbarossa* 1.47; William of Tyre 16.18–27.
70. "Manganeios" in Jeffreys, 'Wild Beast.'
71. Tyerman, *God's War*, 328.
72. Odo of Deuil, *Louis VII's March to the East* 3, p. 57 (tr. Berry); William of Tyre 16.20–21; others: Magdalino, *Empire*, 52; but see J. Phillips, *The Second Crusade* (New Haven 2007) 274–276; T. Reuter, 'The "non-crusade" of 1149–50,' in J. Phillips and M. Hoch, eds., *The Second Crusade* (Manchester 2001) 150–163.

73. Jeffreys, 'Wild Beast,' 114; Magdalino, *Empire*, 52 n. 93.
74. Choniates, *History* 199–200; Kinnamos 3.4–5. Thessalonike: ibid. 2.19; Stephenson, *Balkan Frontier*, 223–224.
75. Choniates, *History* 86; concessions: Tafel and Thomas, *Urkunden*, 1:109–124, 189–194; Nicol, *Byzantium*, 85–86.
76. Konrad: *MGH Diplomata* 9:404–406 (*DD Ko III*).
77. Kinnamos 3.6–19; Choniates, *History* 89–94, 100–102; "Dragon": Prodromos, *Historical Poems* 30.194–204; Michael the Rhetor in Regel and Novosadskii, *Fontes*, 158–163; Serbs: Kaldellis, *Ethnography*, 135–136; wars: Magdalino, *Empire*, 54–56, 443; Stephenson, *Balkan Frontier*, 224–238.
78. Cf. Kinnamos 4.10 with Prokopios, *Wars* 5.24 and 8.1.11. William: Kinnamos 3.12; Friedrich in Wibald of Stablo and Corvey, *Letters* 386–387, in *MGH Epistolae: Briefe d. dt. Kaiserzeit*, 9.3:814–818, with Duggan, '*Totius*,' 111–115, 121.
79. Kinnamos 4.1–15; Choniates, *History* 91, 95–99; Magdalino, *Empire*, 57–61; Lambakis et al., *Βυζαντινά στρατεύματα*, 453–467; Abulafia, 'Ancona.' Genoa: Day, *Genoa's Response*, 23–26; pope: Duggan, '*Totius*,' 122.
80. Choniates, *History* 100.
81. William of Tyre 18.10, 18.23; Kinnamos 3.14–15, 4.17; Lilie, *Byzantium*, 166–169.
82. William of Tyre 18.22–25; Gregory the Priest, *Continuation of Matthew of Edessa's History* 38–40; Kinnamos 4.17–21; Choniates, *History* 102–110; panegyric: "Manganeios" in E. and M. Jeffreys, 'A Constantinopolitan Poet Views Frankish Antioch,' *Crusades* 14 (2015) 49–151; Eustathios, *Oration* O, p. 263 (ed. Wirth), tr. Stone, *Eustathios*, 19–20; Lilie, *Byzantium*, 176–183; Theodora: Barzos, *Γενεαλογία*, 327–346.
83. Kinnamos 2.7.
84. Choniates, *History* 203–205 (tr. Magoulias, mod.); Georgios Tornikes, *Letter* 10; Magdalino, *Empire*, 222–223.
85. Kaldellis, *Hellenism*, 299.
86. William of Tyre 18.32, 20.1; Kinnamos 5.4, 5.13.
87. William of Tyre 20.22–24; Kinnamos 6.10; Eustathios, *Oration* M, p. 214 (ed. Wirth); Lilie, *Byzantium*, 198–209.
88. Kinnamos 4.22–24, 5.3; Choniates, *History* 116–125; Euthymios Malakes, *Encomium for Manuel Komnenos*, ed. Papadopoulos-Kerameus, *Noctes*, 162–187; seal: Shukurov, 'Turkoman,' 275.
89. Choniates, *History* 150; Eustathios, *Oration* M, p. 205 (ed. Wirth); see Foss, 'Defenses.'
90. Magdalino, *Empire*, 69.
91. Kinnamos 2.17; Euthymios Malakes, *Encomium for Manuel Komnenos* 7, ed. Papadopoulos-Kerameus, *Noctes*, 168.
92. Choniates, *History* 206; P. Magdalino, 'Manuel Komnenos and the Great Palace,' *BMGS* 4 (1978) 101–114.
93. M. Jeffreys, 'Byzantine Court Culture,' in D. Sakel, ed., *Byzantine Culture* (Ankara 2014) 331–341, here 336–338.
94. Kinnamos 6.11; Choniates, *History* 159 (dated earlier); Eustathios, *Oration* M, p. 217 (ed. Wirth); see Stone, *Eustathios*, 108–109.

95. Subordination: Michael the Rhetor in R. Browning, 'A New Source on Byzantine-Hungarian Relations in the Twelfth Century,' *Balkan Studies* 2 (1961) 173–214, esp. 202–203; Kinnamos 5.1, 5.5 (μεταποιεῖσθαι); and Mango, 'Edict,' 324 (οὐγγρικός). Victory: Kinnamos 6.7; Choniates, *History* 151–158; see Makk, *Árpáds*, 79–106; Stephenson, *Balkan Frontier*, ch. 8.
96. Kinnamos 5.17; Abulafia, 'Ancona'; Stephenson, *Balkan Frontier*, 261–266; see also p. 692 below.
97. Kinnamos 5.5, 6.11; Choniates, *History* 112, 128, 137, 169–170; "king": Eustathios, *Oration* M, p. 215 (ed. Wirth); subordination: Konstantinos Manasses, *Oration to the Emperor Manuel Komnenos*, ed. E. Kurtz, 'Eshche dva neizdannykh proizvedeniya Konstantina Manssi,' *Vizantijskij Vremennik* 12 (1905) 88–98, esp. 92; see Makk, *Árpáds*, 106–107; Magdalino, *Empire*, 200, 215. Oath: Papadopoulos-Kerameus, *Ἀνάλεκτα*, 4:109–113.
98. Kinnamos 5.1, 5.5, 5.9, 6.4; Godfrey of Viterbo, *Gesta Friderici* 21, in *MGH SS rer. Germ.* 30:19; cf. *Chronica regia Coloniensis* s.a. 1161, in *MGH SS rer. Germ.* 18:108.
99. Magdalino, *Empire*, 83–95; J. Harris and D. Tolstoy, 'Alexander III and Byzantium,' in P. Clarke and A. Duggan, eds., *Pope Alexander III (1159–81)* (Farnham, UK 2012) 301–313; E. Tounta, *Το δυτικό sacrum imperium και η βυζαντινή αυτοκρατορία* (Athens 2008); E.-D. Hehl, 'Zwei Kaiser – (k)ein Problem? Byzanz, das westliche Kaisertum und ein missverständlicher Forschungsbegriff,' in L. Körntgen et al., eds., *Byzanz und seine europäischen Nachbarn* (Mainz 2020) 41–76.
100. A. Kolia-Dermitzaki, 'Byzantium and the West – the West and Byzantium,' in Kolias et al., eds., *Aureus*, 357–380, e.g., 365.
101. E.g., Kinnamos 5.7, 5.9, 6.4.
102. Magdalino, *Empire*, 277–285.
103. Eustathios, *Funeral Oration for Manuel Komnenos* 35 (tr. Bourbouhakis); Hermes: Kinnamos 6.2; more: Magdalino, *Empire*, 465–467.
104. Manuel and Glykas in F. Cumont and F. Boll, *Catalogus codicum atsrologorum Graecorum* (Brussels 1904) 5.1:108–140 (quotation: 115); Magdalino, *L'Orthodoxie*, ch. 5; Choniates, *History* 95–96, 154, 169, 220–221.
105. *Memorandum on the Deposition of the Patriarch Kosmas Attikos*, in Rallis and Potlis, *Σύνταγμα*, 5:309; *Memorandum on the Heresy of Soterichos Panteugenos*, in *PG* 140:188; Manuel in Zepos, *Jus Graecoromanum*, 1:409.
106. Kinnamos 6.2; E. Stavropoulos, *Le dialogue institutionnel entre imperium et sacerdotium sous l'empereur Manuel Ier Comnène* (PhD dissertation, Université Paris-Saclay, 2017) 241–245; Eteriano: Magdalino, *Empire*, 90–91.
107. Mango, 'Edict,' 324.
108. Rallis and Potlis, *Σύνταγμα*, 2:467, 3:149; Dagron, *Emperor and Priest*, 248–267.
109. Choniates, *History* 209–212.
110. Eustathios, *Capture of Thessalonike* 28; Caffaro, *Genoese Annals* s.a. 1162, in *MGH SS* 18:33.
111. *Legati*: Penna, 'Venetian Judges,' 137; Mairano: Nicol, *Byzantium*, 104–106; *bourgesioi*: Kinnamos 6.10; Thessalonike: Eustathios, *Capture of Thessalonike* 72. Olive: Olson, *Environment*, 178.

112. G. Day, 'Byzantino-Genoese Diplomacy,' *Byzantion* 48 (1978) 393–405.
113. Kinnamos 6.10; Eustathios, *Oration* M, p. 211 (ed. Wirth), tr. Stone, *Eustathios*, 94; Choniates, *History* 171–173; Nicol, *Byzantium*, 96–100; Genoese damages: Day, *Genoa's Response*, 27.
114. Boncompagno da Signa, *The History of the Siege of Ancona*, ed. and tr. A. Stone (Venice 2002); Abulafia, 'Ancona,' 213.
115. Eustathios, *Oration* M, p. 213 (ed. Wirth), tr. Stone, *Eustathios*, 98.
116. S. Lambros, 'Ὁ Μαρκιανὸς κῶδιξ 524,' *Νέος Ἑλληνομνήμων* 8 (1911) 3–59, here 51.
117. Thonemann, *Maeander*, 162.
118. K. Bonis, 'Εὐθυμίου τοῦ Μαλάκη, Μητροπολίτου Νέων Πατρῶν (Ὑπάτης), Δύο Ἐγκωμιαστικοὶ Λόγοι,' *Θεολογία* 19 (1941–1948) 524–558, here 535, 539; E. Chrysos, '1176 – A Byzantine Crusade?' in J. Koder and J. Stouraitis, eds., *Byzantine War Ideology* (Vienna 2012) 81–86.
119. Choniates, *History* 175–212 (scalping: 190); Kinnamos 7.1–3; Neophytos the Recluse in Galatariotou, *Neophytos*, 213–216; Michael the Syrian 20.1–6 (Kilij Arslan terrified: 20.5); "shame": Michael Choniates, *Letter* 179.3; topography: Thonemann, *Maeander*, 163–169; A. Vasiliev, 'Manuel Comnenus and Henry Plantagenet,' *BZ* 29 (1929–1930) 233–244; Muslim sources: Mecit, *Rum Seljuqs*, 63–67, 79.
120. Magdalino, *Empire*, 99–100; C. Hilsdale, 'Constructing a Byzantine "Augusta": A Greek Book for a French Bride,' *Art Bulletin* 87 (2005) 458–483; Eustathios, *Oration* Ξ (ed. Wirth).
121. Choniates, *History* 213–220; C. Hanson, 'Manuel I Comnenus and the "God of Muhammad",' in J. Tolan, ed., *Medieval Christian Perceptions of Islam* (New York 1996) 55–82; C. Simelidis, 'The Byzantine Understanding of the Qur'anic Term al-Samad,' *Speculum* 86 (2011) 887–913.
122. I. Drpić, 'Manuel I Komnenos and the Stone of Unction,' *BMGS* 43 (2018) 60–82.
123. Respectively: William of Tyre 20.22 (tr. Babcock and Krey); Robert de Clari, *The Conquest of Constantinople* 18 (tr. McNeal, p. 46); L. Belgrano and C. Imperiale di Sant' Angelo, *Annali genovesi de Caffaro e de'suoi continuatori* (Rome, 1890–1901) 2:14–15.
124. Miller, *Orphans*, x–xii.

Chapter 30. Disintegration and Betrayal (1180–1204)

1. Eustathios, *Capture of Thessalonike* 14–20; Choniates, *History* 223–243 ("reckless": 230; "beam": 224); William of Tyre 22.5; key players: Barzos, *Γενεαλογία*, 2:189–218, 439–452.
2. Makk, *Árpáds*, 115–116; Belgrade: Choniates, *History* 267.
3. F. Hild and H. Hellenkemper, *Kilikien und Isaurien* (Vienna 1990) 74.
4. Choniates, *History* 262; Lilie, *Byzantium*, 224 n. 10.
5. Choniates, *History* 103–108, 129–132, 138–142, 226–227; Kinnamos 3.15–18, 5.11, 6.1.

6. William of Tyre 22.10–13; Eustathios, *Capture of Thessalonike* 21–31 ("god": 24); Choniates, *History* 228–252; Roberto de Monte, *Chronicle* s.a. 1182, in *MGH SS* 6:533. Damages: Day, *Genoa's Response*, 28.
7. M. Choniates, *Address to Demetrios Drimys* 14–16 (1:163–164).
8. Rallis and Potlis, *Σύνταγμα*, 4:449, 460; against papal supremacy: A. Siecienski, *The Papacy and the Orthodox* (Oxford 2017) 267–277; cf. Anna 1.13.4; Kinnamos 5.7.
9. Odo of Deuil, *Louis VII's March to the East* 3 (tr. Berry, pp. 55–57); Ugo Eteriano in A. Dondain, 'Hughes Ethérien et Léon Toscan,' *Archives d'histoire doctrinale et littéraire du Moyen Âge* 19 (1952) 67–134, here 126–127. Diplomacy: Devaney, 'Byzantine-Venetian Conflict,' 144; Tyerman, *God's War*, 231, 273; Lilie, *Byzantium*, 204.
10. M. Choniates, *Encomium for Niketas of Chonai* 63 (1:43); C. Messis, 'Lectures sexuées d'altérité: Les Latins et identité romaine menacée les derniers siècles de Byzance,' *JöB* 61 (2011) 151–170; cultural differences: Kolbaba, *Byzantine Lists*; Anna 6.6.4, 10.8.8, 11.2.2.
11. S. Kindlimann, *Die Eroberung von Konstantinopel als politische Forderung des Westens im Hochmittelalter* (Zurich 1969).
12. Peter the Deacon, *Chronicle* 3.116, in *MGH SS* 7:833.
13. William of Tyre 22.13; Eustathios, *Capture of Thessalonike* 31, 35–36; Choniates, *History* 259–260, 265–267; Saladin: Magnus of Reichersberg, *Chronicle* s.a. 1189, in *MGH SS* 17:511 (untrustworthy).
14. Eustathios, *Capture of Thessalonike* 38–43; Choniates, *History* 269–272, 277 (quotation: 269); Makk, *Árpáds*, 117–118.
15. Choniates, *History* 280–289.
16. Choniates, *History* 275 ("surpassed": 321); Eustathios, *Capture of Thessalonike* 44.
17. V. Tiftixoglu, 'Zur Genese der Komentare des Theodoros Balsamon,' in N. Oikonomides, ed., *Το Βυζάντιο κατά τον 12ο αιώνα* (Athens 1991) 483–532, here 487; Simpson, *Niketas*, 158–164, 236–237.
18. Choniates, *History* 343; Eustathios, *Capture of Thessalonike* 37–38, 45; cf. M. Choniates, *Letter* 39.
19. S. Neocleous, 'Andronikos I Komnenos: Tyrant of Twelfth-Century Europe,' *The Medieval History Journal* 22 (2019) 92–130.
20. Choniates, *History* 325–328, 330–331.
21. M. Choniates, *Letter* 63.2; Kaldellis, *Parthenon*, ch. 6.
22. E.g., M. Choniates, *Address to Demetrios Drimys* 39–48 (1:174–178); *Letters* 30, 32, 40 (request).
23. Eustathios, *Capture of Thessalonike* 46–47; Choniates, *History* 264.
24. Neophytos the Recluse, *Letter* 1.70–76, in A. Karpozilos, ed., *Ἁγίου Νεοφύτου τοῦ Ἐγκλείστου Συγγράμματα* (Paphos 2005) v. 5, on whom see Galatariotou, *Neophytos*, 199–200, 211–213; also Choniates, *History* 290–296, 340; Michael the Syrian 21.5; Metcalf, *Byzantine Cyprus*, 185–186, 534, 558–565.
25. Eustathios, *Capture of Thessalonike*, esp. 51–54, 98–119; quotation: 116; *Annales Ceccanenses* s.a. 1185, in *MGH SS* 19:287; Choniates, *History* 296–308 (derivative); Broadhurst, *Ibn Jubayr*, 354–356, contains independent information, esp. about the intent to attack Constantinople.

26. Choniates, *History* 335–354; Michael the Syrian 21.3.
27. Choniates, *History* 347.
28. Choniates, *History* 320, 357–367; orators: Brand, *Byzantium*, 357 n. 57.
29. Choniates, *History* 361; Gregorios Antiochos, *Speech of Welcome to Isaakios Angelos*, in Regel and Novosadskii, *Fontes*, 300–301; islands: Theodosios of Byzantion, *Encomium of Saint Christodoulos of Patmos* 12, ed. Boïnes, *Ἀκολουθία*, 177; Brand, *Byzantium*, 356 n. 46; P. Soustal, *Nikopolis und Kephallenia* (Vienna 1981) 168, 176.
30. Isaakios II in Demetrios Tornikes, *Letter* 33 (p. 343).
31. Choniates, *History* 355–356, 368; *Oration* E.
32. Theodosios of Byzantion, *Encomium of Saint Christodoulos of Patmos* 12–13, ed. Boïnes, *Ἀκολουθία;* Choniates, *History* 369–370; Magnus of Reichersberg, *Chronicle* s.a. 1189, in *MGH SS* 17:511–512.
33. Choniates, *History* 368–371, 468 (Vlach language); Akropolites 11; Magdalino, *Empire*, 195 n. 99; Madgearu, *Asanids*, esp. 53–54 (date), 58–60 (ethnicity), 46–49 (titles), and 76 (seal); "Sthlavopetros": A. Rhoby, 'The Poetry of Theodore Balsamon,' in idem and N. Zagklas, eds., *Middle and Late Byzantine Poetry* (Turnhout 2018) 111–145, here 130.
34. Kinnamos 6.3; Kekaumenos, *Strategikon* 74–75; Anna 5.5.3, 8.3.4, 10.2.6–3.1.
35. Choniates, *History* 372–373 (cf. 437, 441); *Oration* B (pp. 7–9).
36. Choniates, *History* 377–390; M. Choniates, *Encomium of Isaakios Angelos* 66–73 (1:246–250); Simpson, *Niketas*, 211, 264–265.
37. Choniates, *History* 367–368, 421–422 (Turks), 445 (taxes), 423–426, 435–436 (plots); quotation: 423.
38. Choniates, *History* 55.
39. M. Choniates, *Letters* 20, 46; also 14, 27, 44; *Address to Nikephoros Prosouchos* 16 (1:147); *Address to Basileios Kamateros* 10 (1:315: Lombards); Magdalino, *Empire*, 138–140; M.-L. Favreau, 'Die italienische Levante-Piraterie und die Sicherheit der Seewege nach Syrien,' *Vierteljahresschrift für Sozial- und Wirtschaftsgeschichte* 65 (1978) 461–510.
40. Penna, *Byzantine Imperial Acts*; Nicol, *Byzantium*, 110–117; compensations: Smyrlis, 'Private Property,' 125.
41. Neophytos the Recluse, *Letter* 1.17–18 (Karpozilos); Galatariotou, *Neophytos*, 206–207.
42. Henry: Ralph de Diceto, *Ymagines historiarum* s.a. 1188, ed. W. Stubbs, *Radulfi de Diceto . . . opera historica* (London 1876) 2:52–53; Friedrich: *Historia de expeditione Friderici imperatoris,* in *MGH SS rer. Germ. N.S.* 5:15; Choniates, *History* 401–402.
43. Tyerman, *God's War*, 389, 418.
44. Choniates, *History* 402–403.
45. *Historia de expeditione Friderici imperatoris,* in *MGH SS rer. Germ. N.S.* 5:42–43.
46. Choniates, *History* 404; *Historia de expeditione Friderici imperatoris,* in *MGH SS rer. Germ. N.S.* 5:46; Magnus of Reichersberg, *Chronicle* s.a. 1189, in *MGH SS* 17:510; Bulgarians: Madgearu, *Asanids*, 88–104.
47. S. Neocleous, 'The Byzantines and Saladin: Some Further Arguments,' *Al-Masaq* 25 (2013) 204–221.

48. Al-Fadil in Abu Shama, *Le livre des deux jardins*, in *Recueil des historiens des croisades: Historiens orientaux* (Paris 1898) 4:509.
49. Choniates, *History* 404, 432–433; *Oration* Θ, p. 94; "enmity:" Baha al-Din, *The Rare and Excellent History of Saladin*, tr. D Richards (Aldershot, UK 2001) 122.
50. Choniates, *History* 416.
51. Richard I in W. Stubbs, ed., *Chronicles and Memorials of the Reign of Richard I* (London 1865) 2:347.
52. Nicolaou-Konnari, 'Conquest,' 36–38.
53. H. Nicholson, *Chronicle of the Third Crusade: A Translation of the 'Itinerarium peregrinorum et gesta regis Ricardi'* (Aldershot, UK 1997) 195; see J. Harris, 'Collusion with the Infidel as a Pretext for Western Military Action against Byzantium,' in Lambert and Nicholson, eds., *Languages*, 99–117, here 113–114.
54. Sergios Kolybas, *Address to the Emperor Isaakios Angelos*, in Regel and Novosadskii, *Fontes*, 293; Madgearu, *Asanids*, 77–81, 98–108; Serbs: 102; Choniates, *History* 434, 437; A. Simpson, 'Byzantium and Hungary in the Late 12th Century,' in Chrissis et al., *Byzantium*, 192–205.
55. Choniates, *History* 399–401.
56. A. Beihammer, 'Defection across the Border of Islam and Christianity,' *Speculum* 86 (2011) 597–561; Korobeinikov, *Byzantium*, 126.
57. Isaakios in *MM* 3:41; D. Penna, 'Piracy and Reprisal in Byzantine Waters,' *Comparative Legal History* 5 (2017) 36–52.
58. Choniates, *History* 549, and passim.
59. Choniates, *History* 453 app. (and elsewhere).
60. Choniates, *History* 446–461, 484–489.
61. M. Choniates, *Letter* 129; M. Angold, 'The Road to 1204,' *Journal of Medieval History* 25 (1999) 257–278, here 268–269. For Euphrosyne, cf. Mesarites, *The Coup of Ioannes Komnenos "the Fat"* 24.
62. Choniates, *History* 495–496, also 461–464, 474–475, 493–496; Korobeinikov, *Byzantium*, 96–97, 118–120, 124–125; payments: also Broadhurst, *Ibn Jubayr*, 240, 355.
63. Choniates, *History* 471.
64. See the mss. scholia in Van Dieten, *Niketas*, 132.
65. Choniates, *History* 476–479; Tyerman, *God's War*, 489–490.
66. Penna, 'Venetian Judges'; eadem, *Byzantine Imperial Acts*, 62–100; Tyerman, *God's War*, 179–180.
67. Choniates, *History* 481–483, 491; J. Haldon, '"Greek Fire" Revisited: Recent and Current Research,' in E. Jeffreys, ed., *Byzantine Style, Religion and Civilization* (Cambridge 2006) 290–325, here 309.
68. M. Choniates, *Memorandum to Alexios III Komnenos*, ed. Stadtmüller, *Michael Choniates*, 282–286.
69. Choniates, *History* 487, 497–498, 502–509; non-foreign wife: N. Choniates, *Oration* Z, pp. 67–68; *despotes*: Barzos, *Γενεαλογία*, 2:746–747.
70. A. Kaldellis, 'The Chronology of the Reign of Alexios III Komnenos,' *Byzantina Symmeikta* 32 (2022) 59–82.

71. Mesarites, *The Coup of Ioannes Komnenos "the Fat"* 3; Euthymios Tornikes, *Oration* 1.12 (to Alexios III); Choniates, *History* 523–528; M. Angold, 'The Anatomy of a Failed Coup: The Abortive Uprising of John the Fat,' in Simpson, ed., *Byzantium,* 113–134.
72. Choniates, *History* 533–535; *Oration* IA; Nikephoros Chrysoberges, *Oration* 2, ed. M. Treu, *Nicephori Chrysobergae ad Angelos orationes tres* (Breslau 1892) 20–21; M. Choniates, *Letter* 78; Van Dieten, *Niketas*, 127.
73. Kalojan: Madgearu, *Asanids*, 116–123; Dyrrachion: 129. Roman-Slayer: Akropolites 13. I attach little significance to the peace with Kalojan in ca. 1202. It was one among many annual truces, and should not be exaggerated as "formal recognition."
74. Choniates, *History* 531; marriage: Georgios Tornikes, *Address to the Emperor Isaakios Angelos*, in Regel and Novosadskii, *Fontes*, 277; date: Barzos, *Γενεαλογία*, 2:746 n. 83.
75. Madgearu, *Asanids*, 125–135.
76. Innocent III, *Register* 2:202; A. Papadakis and A.-M. Talbot, 'John X Camaterus Confronts Innocent III,' *Byzantinoslavica* 33 (1972) 33–41; J. Powell, 'Innocent III and Alexios III,' in Bull and Housley, eds., *Experience*, 196–212.
77. Browning, 'Unpublished Address.'
78. Vermillion: Robert de Clari, *Conquest of Constantinople* 13; masts: Mesarites, *Funeral Oration for his Brother Ioannes* 28; 200 ships: Queller and Madden, *Fourth Crusade*, 68–69.
79. Choniates, *History* 538–539.
80. Queller and Madden, *Fourth Crusade*, is a solid reconstruction vitiated by apologetics, including tendentious parsing of crusader motives and legalistic moralisms (always finding for the crusaders). Van Tricht, *Latin Renovatio*, 1–39, is an extreme example.
81. Geoffroi de Villehardouin, *Conquest of Constantinople* 30 (Faral). Geoffroi was part of the planning throughout.
82. J. Pryor, 'The Venetian Fleet for the Fourth Crusade,' in Bull and Housley, eds., *Experience*, 1:103–123.
83. Choniates, *History* 541; see 82 note.
84. Roger of Hoveden, *Chronicle* s.a. 1199 (Stubbs, 4:121–122); A. Kiesewetter, 'Preludio alla Quarta Crociata? Megareites di Brindisi,' in Ortalli et al., eds., *Quarta Crociata,* 317–358.
85. Innocent, *Register* 5:121; Philipp of Swabia, *Treaty with Innocent III*, in *MGH Dipl.* 2:9 (clause 7); Choniates, *History* 536 (even before 1201). Queller and Madden, *Fourth Crusade*, 35–39, 64 are unconvincing on this point; see M. Angold, 'The Anglo-Saxon Historiography of the Fourth Crusade,' in Ortalli et al., eds., *Quarta Crociata,* 301–316; cf. Tyerman, *God's War*, 518–519.
86. Geoffroi de Villehardouin, *Conquest of Constantinople* 120 and 122 (Faral).
87. Innocent III, *Register* 6:101, tr. Andrea, *Contemporary Sources*, 62–63; also *Register* 5:121, tr. ibid. 35.
88. See esp. Robert de Clari, *Conquest of Constantinople* 17, 29–30, 33.
89. Tafel and Thomas, *Urkunden*, 1:255.

90. D. Queller et el., 'The Fourth Crusade: The Neglected Majority,' *Speculum* 49 (1974) 441–465.
91. Sources: Tyerman, *God's War*, 551–552.
92. E. Boeck, 'Fantasy, Supremacy, Domes, and Dames: Charlemagne Goes to Constantinople,' in Slootjes and Verhoeven, eds., *Byzantium*, 142–161.
93. Robert de Clari, *Conquest of Constantinople* 40; Geoffroi de Villehardouin, *Conquest of Constantinople* 138–147 (Faral).
94. M. Meschini, 'The "Four Crusades" of 1204,' in T. Madden, ed., *The Fourth Crusade: Event, Aftermath, and Perceptions* (Aldershot, UK 2008) 27–42, here 35.
95. Chain: J. and Y. Takeno, 'The Mystery of the Defense Chain Mechanism of Constantinople,' in T. Koetsier and M. Ceccarelli, eds., *Explorations in the History of Machines and Mechanisms* (New York 2012) 199–211; fires: Madden, 'Fires.'
96. Choniates, *History* 551–552, 555–556, 559–560.
97. Geoffroi de Villehardouin, *Conquest of Constantinople* 184–191 (Faral).
98. Innocent III, *Register* 6:209, tr. Andrea, *Contemporary Sources*, 77–79; Hugh of Saint Pol, *Letter to R. of Balues*, tr. ibid. 199–200.
99. Robert de Clari, *Conquest of Constantinople* 52–53.
100. Geoffroi de Villehardouin, *Conquest of Constantinople* 205 (15,000 Latins) (Faral); Choniates, *History* 552–556 (Amalfitans: 552); Mesarites, *Funeral Oration for his Brother Ioannes* 27–34 ("vanished": tr. Angold); cf. Simpson, *Niketas*, 113; Ibn al-Athir, *Annals*, sets the Latins of Constantinople at 30,000: D. Richards, *The Chronicle of Ibn al-Athir for the Crusading Period* (London 2008) 3:76; estimates: Madden, 'Fires,' 88; J. Russell, *Late Ancient and Medieval Population* (Philadelphia 1958) 99.
101. Baldwin I in Innocent, *Register* 7:152; Choniates, *History* 557–564; Robert de Clari, *Conquest of Constantinople* 54–63; Geoffroi de Villehardouin, *Conquest of Constantinople* 206–231 (Faral); Gunther of Pairis, *Hystoria Constantinopolitana* 13; speech: C. Brand, 'A Byzantine Plan for the Fourth Crusade,' *Speculum* 43 (1968) 462–475.
102. Pact: Innocent III, *Register* 7:205, tr. Andrea, *Contemporary Sources*, 140–144, as well as the western narrative sources.
103. Geoffroi de Villehardouin, *Conquest of Constantinople* 250 (Faral); for specifics, see Robert de Clari, *Conquest of Constantinople* 80–84; the Anonymous of Soissons in Andrea, *Contemporary Sources*, 223–238; and below.
104. Choniates, *History* 301, 586–593; statues: 647–655; P. Chatterjee, 'Sculpted Eloquence and Nicetas Choniates's *De Signis*,' *Word & Image* 27 (2011) 396–406; the same sentiment by Chrysoberges in Browning, 'An Unpublished Address,' 58.
105. Choniates, *History* 576; Mesarites, *Funeral Oration for Ioannes Mesarites* 34.
106. Gunther of Pairis, *Hystoria Constantinopolitana* 19, 25.
107. C. Fiori and E. Tozzola, *San Giovanni Evangelista a Ravenna* (Ravenna 2014) 67–78.
108. Konrad, bishop of Halberstadt, in *The Deeds of the Bishops of Halberstadt*, in *MGH SS* 23:118.15, tr. Andrea, *Contemporary Sources*, 253; Innocent at ibid. 166: "temporal wages." Exodus: Robert de Clari, *Conquest of Constantinople* 80.
109. Choniates, *History* 585.

110. Cf. Tyerman, *God's War*, 308, 488–489; J. Riley-Smith, *What Were the Crusades?* 4th ed. (New York 2009) 9–12; Chrissis, *Crusading*, 15–20.
111. Choniates, *History* 529.
112. E. Gellner, *Nations and Nationalism* (Ithaca, NY 1983) ch. 2.
113. Choniates, *History* 220; cf. 203–204.
114. Cheynet, *Pouvoir*, 427–458.
115. Past discussions: J. Hoffmann, *Rudimente von Territorialstaaten im byzantinischen Reich (1071–1210)* (Munich 1974); R.-J. Lilie, 'Des Kaisers Macht und Ohnmacht: Zum Zerfall der Zentralgewalt in Byzanz vor dem vierten Kreuzzug,' *Poikila Byzantina* 4 (1984) 9–120; Savvides, *Κινήματα*.
116. P. Magdalino, 'Aspects of Twelfth-Century Byzantine *Kaiserkritik*,' *Speculum* 58 (1983) 326–346.
117. Laiou and Morrisson, *Economy*, 139.
118. M. Choniates, *Letter* 50.9–10; *Encomium of Isaakios Angelos* 51 (1:237); N. Choniates, *History* 483, 537.
119. M. Choniates, *Memorandum to Alexios III Komnenos*, ed. Stadtmüller, *Michael Choniates*, 282–286. "Violence": Magdalino, *Empire*, 172–173, 249; J. Herrin, 'Realities of Byzantine Provincial Government: Hellas and Peloponnesos, 1180–1205,' *DOP* 29 (1975) 253–288.
120. K. Smyrlis, 'Sybaris on the Bosporos: Luxury, Corruption and the Byzantine State under the Angeloi,' in Simpson, ed., *Byzantium*, 159–178.
121. M. Ritter, 'Die vlacho-bulgarische Rebellion und die Versuche ihrer Niedershlagung durch Kaiser Isaakios,' *Byzantinoslavica* 71 (2013) 162–210.

Chapter 31. "A New France": Colonial Occupation

1. Innocent III, *Register* 7:152–154, tr. Andrea, *Contemporary Sources*, 98–126 (quotation, mod.: 109).
2. Pact: Innocent III, *Register* 7:205. The presumption for Bonifacio is in the Pact and Gunther of Pairis, *Capture of Constantinople* 18.
3. D. Mureşan, 'Le patriarcat latin de Constantinople comme paradoxe ecclésiologique,' in H.-M. Blanchet and F. Gabriel, eds., *Réduire le schisme? Ecclésiologies et politiques de l'Union entre Orient et Occident* (Paris 2013) 277–302. Innocent on Morosini: *Register* 7:203, tr. Andrea, *Contemporary Sources*, 138–139.
4. Choniates, *History* 595; A. Carile, 'Partitio terrarum imperii Romaniae,' *Studi veneziani* 7 (1965) 125–305; background: Saint-Guillain, 'Comment les Vénitiens.'
5. Lock, *Franks*, 36 n. 2, 56–57.
6. *Corpus Chronicorum Flandriae*, in Tafel and Thomas, *Urkunden*, 1:302.
7. Choniates, *History* 604–611; *despotes*: pseudo-Skoutariotes, *Chronicle*, p. 453 (Sathas); Cheynet, *Pouvoir*, 138–139. There is no evidence that Sgouros' aggression began before the crusaders' arrival, nor that the *megas doux* Stryphnos' visit to Athens (ca. 1200–1202) was related to him.

8. For the complexity of the conquests, see Lock, *Franks*, 68–75 ("welcomed": 68). "Glory": *Chronicle of the Morea* 1818–1819 (Greek). Choniates: Angold, *Church*, 207–212.
9. A. Stahl, 'Coinage and Money in the Latin Empire of Constantinople,' *DOP* 55 (2001) 197–206; Van Tricht, *Latin Renovatio*, with a different interpretation; appropriation of indigenous elements: Shawcross, 'Conquest Legitimized.'
10. D. Jacoby, 'The Venetian Government and Administration in Latin Constantinople,' in Ortalli et al., eds., *Quarta Crociata*, 19–79.
11. Geoffroi de Villehardouin, *Conquest of Constantinople* 336–375; "killing": 336 (Faral); Choniates, *History* 613–617, 642; treaty: Tafel and Thomas, *Urkunden*, 2:17–19; F. Van Tricht, 'The Byzantino-Latin Principality of Adrianople,' *DOP* 68 (2014) 325–342.
12. Robert de Clari, *Conquest of Constantinople* 116–118; "horrors" in Thrace: Choniates, *History* 612–637; Akropolites 13.
13. Tafel and Thomas, *Urkunden*, 2:96–100; A. Nanetti, ed., *Il patto con Geoffroy de Villehardouin per il Peloponneso, 1209* (Rome, 2009 = *Pacta Veneta* 13).
14. Saint-Guillain, 'Conquest of Monemvasia.'
15. Saint-Guillain, 'Comment les Vénitiens.'
16. Tafel and Thomas, *Urkunden*, 2:54–56; Gasparis, 'Land,' 75–76.
17. Tafel and Thomas, *Urkunden*, 2:89–96; D. Jacoby, *Latins, Greeks, and Muslims* (Farnham, UK 2009) IX.
18. S. Saint-Guillain, 'Les conquérants de l'archipel,' in Ortalli et al., eds., *Quarta crociata*, 125–238.
19. See now Demacopoulos, *Colonizing Christianity*.
20. Chrissis, *Crusading*, 12; Innocent III, *Register* 7:152–154, tr. Andrea, *Contemporary Sources*, 98–126, and esp. *Register* 8:70 (May 1205). Debts and crimes: Marin Sanudo Torsello, *History of Romania* 1, p. 104.
21. Jacoby, 'Encounter'; and *Byzantium*, VIII.
22. E.g., Marin Sanudo Torsello, *History of Romania* 1, p. 112.
23. Gasparis, 'Land.'
24. Nicolaou-Konnari, 'Conquest,' 62–71, and the papers in A. Nicolaou-Konnari and C. Schabel, eds., *Cyprus: Society and Culture, 1191–1374* (Leiden 2005). Contemporary: Continuer of William of Tyre in M. L. de Mas Latrie, *Histoire de l'isle de Chypre sous le règne des princes de Maison de Lusignan* (Paris 1861) 1:43–44.
25. Neophytos the Recluse, *Letter* 1.33–44 (Karpozilos); Galatariotou, *Neophytos*, 175, 201; Nicolaou-Konnari, 'Greeks,' 42.
26. Neophytos the Recluse, *Typikon* 10, tr. C. Galatariotou in *BMFD* 1353 (mod.).
27. C. Cobham, *Excerpta Cypria* (Cambridge 1908) 13; secretaries: A. Beihammer, 'Multilingual Literacy at the Lusignan Court,' *BMGS* 35 (2011) 149–169.
28. Galatariotou, *Neophytos*, 60–67, 202–203; Schabel, 'Religion,' 160–170.
29. Schabel, 'Religion,' 182–183; B. Arbel, *Cyprus, the Franks and Venice* (Aldershot, UK 2000) VI.
30. Jacoby, *Byzantium*, VI:173–181.
31. Jacoby, 'Economy'; idem, *Byzantium*, VII; cf. L. Robbert, 'Rialto Businessmen and Constantinople,' *DOP* 49 (1995) 43–58.

32. Choniates, *History* 634–635; housing: Geoffroi de Villehardouin, *Conquest of Constantinople* 251 (Faral); 266 for flight; Gunther of Pairis, *Capture of Constantinople* 20; Robert de Clari, *Conquest of Constantinople* 79–80; Jacoby, 'Greeks.' Fiscal system: Jacoby, *Byzantium*, VI.
33. Akropolites 16 (tr. Macrides).
34. Prinzing, 'Brief,' 415; Robert de Clari, *Conquest of Constantinople* 72.
35. Venice's initial plans are spelled out in the *Concessio* of 1211: Tafel and Thomas, *Urkunden*, 2:129–142. Colonists: D. Jacoby, *Latins, Greeks, and Muslims* (Farnham, UK 2009) IV; in general: C. Maltezou, *Η Κρήτη στη διάρκεια της περιόδου της Βενετοκρατίας* (Herakleion 1990); McKee, *Uncommon Dominion*, ch. 1.
36. McKee, *Uncommon Dominion*, ix, 91.
37. McKee, *Uncommon Dominion*, with the corrections by D. Tsougarakis, 'Venetian Crete and the Myth of Novel Ideas,' *Θησαυρίσματα* 31 (2001) 43–64. The revolts remain understudied: S. Xanthoudides, *Ἡ Ἐνετοκρατία ἐν Κρήτῃ καὶ οἱ κατὰ τῶν Ἐνετῶν ἀγῶνες τῶν Κρητῶν* (Athens 1939).
38. R. Lauer, *Colonial Justice and the Jews of Venetian Crete* (Philadelphia 2019).
39. *Chronicle of the Morea* 2091–2095 (Greek); D. Jacoby, 'Les *archontes* grecs et la féodalité en Morée franque,' *TM* 2 (1967) 421–482.
40. *Chronicle of the Morea* 1644–1648, 2820–2823 (Greek); Jacoby, 'Encounter,' 902–903; common identity: T. Shawcross, 'Greeks and Franks after the Fourth Crusade,' in Lambert and Nicholson, eds., *Languages*, 141–157.
41. J. Baker, 'Money and Currency in Medieval Greece,' in Tsougarakis and Lock, eds., *Companion*, 217–254, here 230.
42. Nicolaou-Konnari, 'Greeks,' 31–37; D. Jacoby, 'The Economy of Latin Greece,' in Tsougarakis and Lock, eds., *Companion*, 185–216, here 201–203.
43. P. Topping, *Feudal Institutions as Revealed in the Assizes of Romania, the Law Code of Frankish Greece* (Philadelphia 1949); D. Jacoby, *La féodalité en Grèce médiévale: Les "Assises de Romanie"* (Paris 1971).
44. *Chronicle of the Morea* 2648–2658.
45. D. Jacoby, 'The Economy of Latin Greece,' in Tsougarakis and Lock, eds., *Companion*, 185–216, here 190, 205–206; also C. Morrisson, 'L'ouverture des marchés après 1204: Un aspect positif de la IVe croisade?' in Laiou, ed., *Urbs Capta*, 215–232.
46. A. Tzavara, *Clarentza, une ville de la Morée latine* (Venice 2008); D. Athanasoulis, 'The Triangle of Power: Building Projects in the Metropolitan Area of the Crusader Principality of the Morea,' in Gerstel, ed., *Viewing the Morea*, 111–152.
47. D. Jacoby, *Commercial Exchange across the Mediterranean* (Aldershot, UK, 2005); J. Baker, *Coinage and Money in Medieval Greece* (Leiden 2020); migration: Jacoby, *Byzantium*, IX.
48. *The Deeds of the Bishops of Halberstadt*, in *MGH SS* 23:118.23–27, tr. Andrea, *Contemporary Sources*, 254; H. Sieben, 'Basileios Pediadites und Innozenz III,' *Annuarium Historiae Conciliorum* 27–28 (1995–1996) 249–274.

49. A. and J. Stylianou, 'The Militarization of the Betrayal and its Examples in the Painted Churches of Cyprus,' in E. Kypraiou, ed., *Εὐφρόσυνον: Αφιέρωμα στον Μανόλη Χατζηδάκη* (Athens 1991–1992) 2:573–581.
50. A. Andrea, 'Innocent III and the Byzantine Rite,' in Laiou, ed., *Urbs Capta*, 111–122; Chrissis, *Crusading*, 45–51.
51. Coureas, 'Churches'; Schabel, 'Religion'; bishops: J. Richard, 'The Establishment of the Latin Church in the Empire of Constantinople,' *Mediterranean Historical Review* 4 (1989) 45–62; Angold, *Fourth Crusade*, 171–172. Exceptional cases of Greek bishops on Crete: ibid. 156–157; in the Morea (Mani): Demetrios Chomatenos, *Opus* 22.193. The data in Van Tricht, *Latin Renovatio*, 312–334 is more persuasive than his interpretation. Norman lands: P. Herde, 'Das Papsttum und die griechische Kirche in Süditalien,' *Deutsches Archiv* 26 (1970) 1–46.
52. Schabel, 'Religion,' 184–190; Nicolaou-Konnari, 'Greeks,' 45–49; Latin donations: Kalopissi-Verti, 'Monumental Art,' 374–376; conversions of churches and monasteries: ibid. 371–372.
53. Quoted in W. Norden, *Das Papsttum und Byzanz* (Berlin 1903) 687 n. 1.
54. Nikolaos Mesarites, *Funeral Oration for Ioannes Mesarites* 37–38, 41–49 (tr. Angold, mod.); and *Disputation with Morosini*; see Hoeck and Loenertz, *Nikolaos-Nektarios*, 30–54.
55. Innocent III, *Register* 8:127, tr. Andrea, *Contemporary Sources*, 166 (mod.); Demacopoulos, *Colonizing Christianity*, ch. 3.
56. Petitions to Innocent: Mesarites, *Funeral Oration for Ioannes Mesarites* 50; and *PG* 140:293–298; to Laskaris: Mesarites, *Petition to Theodoros Laskaris*.
57. Akropolites 17; Mesarites, *Fourth Lenten Sermon* 16–32; context: Jacoby, 'Greeks,' 64–65; Hoeck and Loenertz, *Nikolaos-Nektarios*, 54–62.
58. Chomatenos, *Opus* 54; Demacopoulos, *Colonizing Christianity*, 77–81; plundered: Angold, *Fourth Crusade*, 177.
59. *The Thirteen Martyrs of Crete*, ed. K. Sathas, *Μεσαιωνικὴ Βιβλιοθήκη* (Venice 1873) 2:20–39; Schabel, 'Religion,' 194–197.
60. C. Schabel, 'Antelm the Nasty, First Latin Archbishop of Patras,' in A. Beihammer et al., eds., *Diplomatics in the Eastern Mediterranean 1000–1500* (Leiden 2008) 93–138.
61. N. Tsougarakis, *The Latin Religious Orders in Medieval Greece* (Turnhout 2012).
62. Cf. Jacoby, *Byzantium*, VIII:24.
63. Marin Sanudo Torsello, *History of Romania* 3, pp. 166–169.
64. Barlaam of Calabria: Gill, *Byzantium*, 197–198.
65. Nicolaou-Konnari, 'Conquest,' 88–89; McKee, *Uncommon Dominion*, 103.
66. *Assizes*: K. Sathas, *Μεσαιωνικὴ Βιβλιοθήκη* (Venice 1877) 6; petition, etc.: S. Lambros, 'Κυπριακὰ καὶ ἄλλα ἔγγραφα,' *Νέος Ἑλληνομνήμων* 14 (1917) 50; 15 (1921) 152–153, 337 (also for *Romanites*); for all terms, see A. Nicolaou-Konnari, 'Ὅλος ὁ τόπος ἦτον γεμάτος Ῥωμαῖοι: αυτό-/ετεροπροσδιορισμοί και ταυτότητα/-ες στην Κύπρο,' in O. Katsiardi-Hering et al., eds., *Ἕλλην Ρωμιός Γραικός: Συλλογικοί προσδιορισμοί και ταυτότητες* (Athens 2018) 145–163. For the politics of ethnic labels in this period, see Kaldellis, *Hellenism*, 338–360.

67. S. Xanthoudides, 'Συνθήκη μεταξὺ τῆς Ἐνετικῆς Δημοκρατίας καὶ Ἀλεξίου Καλλιέργου,' *Ἀθηνᾶ* 14 (1902) 283–331, here 313, 325.
68. Galatariotou, *Neophytos*, 216–219, 224–225; Schabel, 'Religion,' 211; Van Tricht, *Latin Renovatio*, 359–360.
69. A. Beihammer, 'A Transcultural Formula of Rule: The Byzantine-Frankish Discourse on the Formation of the Kingdom of Cyprus,' in G. Christ et al., eds., *Union in Separation: Diasporic Groups and Identitites in the Eastern Mediterranean* (Rome 2015) 435–452, here 444–447.
70. Henri: Prinzing, 'Brief,' 414–415. Batatzes: Philippe Mouskes, *Chronique rimée* 29044–29058, ed. F. De Reiffenberg (Brussels 1838) 2:614; Guy: Machairas, *Chronicle* 22 (a projection of later fears?).
71. Pope Urban IV, *Letter* g-8, in C. Schabel, *Bullarium Cyprium*, v. 2: *Papal Letters Concerning Cyprus, 1261–1314* (Nicosia 2010) 18–21.
72. Kalopissi-Verti, 'Monumental Art,' 396; Jacoby, *Byzantium*, 25; Kaldellis, *Hellenism*, 350.
73. Pachymeres 9.8 (3:235).
74. M. Georgopoulou, 'The Landscape of Medieval Greece,' in Tsougarakis and Lock, eds., *Companion*, 328–368, here 329, 344–346.
75. Athens: Innocent, *Register* 11:113; J. Longnon, 'L'organisation de l'église d'Athènes par Innocent III,' *Archives de l'Orient chrétien* 1 (1948) 336–346; T. Tanoulas, *Τα Προπύλαια της αθηναϊκής Ακρόπολης κατά τον Μεσαίωνα* (Athens 1997).
76. Cited in G. Page, 'Literature in Frankish Greece,' in Tsougarakis and Lock, eds., *Companion*, 288–325, esp. 290–292.
77. *Chronicle of the Morea* 8080–8085.
78. T. Shawcross, 'Re-inventing the Homeland in the Historiography of Frankish Greece,' *BMGS* 27 (2003) 120–152 (Patras: 136).
79. Nikephoros Blemmydes, *Letter 19 to Theodoros II Laskaris* (p. 310).
80. *Chronicle of the Morea* 4130; T. Shawcross, *The Chronicle of Morea: Historiography in Crusader Greece* (Oxford 2009); Venetians on Crete: McKee, *Uncommon Dominion*, 115; Cyprus: G. Grivaud, 'Literature,' in Nicolaou-Konnari and Schabel, eds., *Cyprus*, 219–284, here 223; Baldwin II: Shawcross, 'Conquest Legitimized,' 201; in general: Lock, *Franks*, 298–299.
81. Gregorios of Cyprus, *Concerning his own Life*, ed. W. Lameere, *La tradition manuscrite de la correspondance de Grégoire de Chypre* (Brussels 1937) 176–191.
82. *The Mission of Friar William of Rubruck*, p. 276 (Jackson and Morgan).
83. Vryonis, *Hellenism*, ch. 3.
84. Anna 8.9.1 ("property"); Kinnamos 2.8 (an ethnic Roman).
85. E.g., Eustathios of Thessalonike, *Oration* N, p. 236 (Wirth); persecution: Theodoros Mouzalon, *Oration for the New Martyr Niketas*, ed. D. Samara, *Θεόδωρος Μουζάλων* (Thessalonike 2018) 127–173.
86. S. Métivier, 'Byzantium in Question 13th-Century Seljuk Anatolia,' in Saint-Guillain and Stathakopoulos, eds., *Liquid*, 235–257.
87. Vryonis, *Hellenism*, 194–210.

88. Vryonis, *Hellenism*, 229–234; M. Delibaşi, 'Greek as a Diplomatic Language in the Turkish Chancery,' in N. Moschonas, ed., *Η ἐπικοινωνία στο Βυζάντιο* (Athens 1993) 145–153.
89. Shukurov, 'Harem Christianity'; idem, 'Christian Elements in the Identity of the Anatolian Turkmens,' *Settimane di Studio della Fondazione Centro italiano di studi sull'alto medioevo* 51 (2004) 707–764; V. Takinalp, 'Palace Churches of the Anatolian Seljuks,' *BMGS* 33 (2009) 148–167.
90. Poems: http://www.opoudjis.net/Play/rumiwalad.html; Shukurov, 'Harem Christianity,' 130–132.

Chapter 32. Romans West and Romans East (1204–1261)

1. Choniates, *History* 591–593.
2. A selection is discussed by M. Angold, 'Laments by Nicetas Choniates and Others for the Fall of Constantinople,' in M. Alexiou and D. Cairns, eds., *Greek Laughter and Tears* (Cambridge 2017) 338–352; also Neophytos the Recluse in Galatariotou, *Neophytos*, 207–210; Choniates' orations, e.g., *Oration* ΙΓ, p. 126; Sergios the Deacon, *First Didaskalia*, ed. M. Loukaki, 'Première didascalie de Serge le Diacre,' *REB* 52 (1994) 151–173; Akropolites 4; Ioannes Staurakios and Konstantinos Akropolites in F. Dall'Aglio, 'The Bulgarian Siege of Thessalonike in 1207,' *Eurasian Studies* 1 (2002) 263–282, here 267–268, 272; and many more (see throughout this chapter).
3. Euthymios Tornikes, *To a Foolish Bishop of Seleukeia*, ed. W. Hörandner, *Facettes de la littérature byzantine* (Paris 2017) 91–140 (condensed).
4. Ed. in Arkhimandrit Arsenii, *Tri stat'i neizviestnago grecheskago pisatelia nachala XIII vieka* (Moscow 1892) 84–112.
5. J. Darrouzès, 'Le mémoire de Constantin Stilbès contre les Latins,' *REB* 21 (1963) 50–100.
6. Choniates, *History* 625; "ship": Gregoras 1.3 (p. 13).
7. Choniates, *History* 626; Panaretos, *The Grand Komenoi of Trebizond*, p. 61 (Lampsidis); Macrides, 'What's in the Name'; Barzos, *Γενεαλογία*, 2:743; seal: P. Gounaridis, 'Ενα μολυβδόβουλο του Αλεξίου Α΄ Μεγαλοκομνηνού,' *Byzantina Symmeikta* 13 (1999) 247–261.
8. Basileus: inscription of Manuel I Grand Komnenos: Eastmond, *Art and Identity*, 139–141 (liturgy: 66), with Karpov, *Ιστορία*, 183. Law and organization: ibid. 186–192; Roman identity: ibid. 134, 184, 405; Panaretos, *The Grand Komenoi of Trebizond* passim, in addition to stray references in other authors.
9. R. Shukurov in Karpov, *Ιστορία*, 388–400; population: A. Bryer, *The Empire of Trebizond* (London 1980) V:121.
10. Savvides, *Ιστορία*, 49.
11. Bessarion, *Encomium on Trebizond*, 45–46 (tr. Kennedy, mod.).

12. Choniates, *History* 602, 626; Geoffroi de Villehardouin, *Conquest of Constantinople* 313, 319–323 (Faral); Akropolites 6–7; dates: Schreiner, *Byzantinischen Kleinchroniken*, 1:74; Macrides, *George Akropolites*, 82–83; seal: G. Zacos and A. Veglery, *Byzantine Lead Seals* (Basel 1972) 1.3:1570–1571.
13. Korobeinikov, *Byzantium*, 120–136.
14. Akropolites 6–7; *archontes*: Savvides, *Κινήματα*.
15. Choniates, *History* 640–641; Geoffroi de Villehardouin, *Conquest of Constantinople* 482–489 (Faral); Paphlagonia: Akropolites 11 (undated, but David died in December 1212 as a monk).
16. Choniates, *History* 638; Akropolites 7; dates: Karpozilos, *Ecclesiastical Controversy*, 22–23.
17. Niketas Choniates, *Oration* ΙΓ, p. 126.23; *History* 635, 645 (quotation); Simpson, *Niketas*, 22–31; cf. Michael Choniates, *Letter* 137.
18. M. Choniates, *Letter* 136.
19. Pseudo-Skoutariotes, *Additions to Akropolites* 20 (Heisenberg, p. 282).
20. *MM* 2:249, 6:179; F. Kondyli, 'Meeting the Locals: Peasant Families in 13th-Century Lemnos,' in Saint-Guillain and Stathakopoulos, eds., *Liquid*, 75–90, here 88.
21. Bartusis, *Land*, 172–228; Angold, *Byzantine Government*, 124.
22. Niketas Choniates, *Orations* ΙΓ, p. 128; ΙΔ, pp. 133, 138; Iς, p. 172.
23. E.g., Niketas Choniates, *Orations* ΙΕ, p. 147; Iς, p. 175; ΙΓ, p. 128; Michael Choniates, *Letter* 94.6; Angelov, 'Ideological Reactions,' 297–299.
24. Choniates, *History* 579; Pitamber, *Replacing Byzantium*.
25. Sources: Chrissis, 'Contestations,' 250; S. Eshel, *The Concept of the Elect Nation in Byzantium* (Leiden 2018) 175–180. "Acropolis": Theodoros Metochites, *Nicene Oration* 16 (Foss).
26. Prinzing, 'Brief,' 415; Michael Choniates, *Letter* 94.6 (also "remnants"); Laskaris: Innocent III, *Register* 11.44.
27. Choniates, *History* 637–639; "traitors": *Oration* ΙΔ, pp. 136.35–136.1 (Maurozomes); reminding Laskaris: Chrissis, 'Contestations.' patriarchs: M. Angold, 'Greeks and Latins after 1204,' *Mediterranean Historical Review* 4 (1989) 63–86, here 69–70.
28. T. Shawcross, 'The Lost Generation (c. 1204–1222): Political Allegiance and Local Interests under the Impact of the Fourth Crusade,' in J. Herrin and G. Saint-Guillain, eds., *Identities and Allegiances in the Eastern Mediterranean after 1204* (Farnham, UK 2011) 9–45, here 20–24.
29. N. Oikonomidès, 'Cinq actes inédits du patriarch Michel Autôreianos,' *REB* 25 (1967) 113–145, here 117–119; Kaldellis, *Hellenism*, 366–367; fairness etc.: Angelov, 'Ideological Reactions,' 303–304; undistinguished: Korobeinikov, *Byzantium*, 67.
30. Akropolites 8–10; pseudo-Skoutariotes, *Chronicle*, pp. 454–457 (Sathas); Niketas Choniates, *Oration* Iς; Michael Choniates, *Letter* 179. Georgios of Pelagonia, *Life of the Saint Emperor Ioannes III the Merciful* 24, gives 3,000 for the size of the Roman army.
31. Prinzing, 'Brief,' 414; Innocent, *Register* 13.184 (= *PL* 216:353–354); crusading: Chrissis, *Crusading*, ch. 1.

32. Akropolites 15–16; Prinzing, 'Brief'; Macrides, *George Akropolites*, 149–153; farmers: *MM* 4:35; alternative dating: Van Tricht, *Latin Renovatio*, 354–356.
33. Pieralli, *Corrispondenza*, 115–118; Jacoby, 'Economy,' 206.
34. Apokaukos, *Letter* 15, in Vasilievsky, 'Epirotica,' 266–267.
35. Choniates, *History* 556, 608–609, 612, 620; Akropolites 5, 8; Geoffroi de Villehardouin, *Conquest of Constantinople* 306–308 (Faral); Robert de Clari, *Conquest of Constantinople* 108–109; A. Maiorov, 'Angelos in Halych: Did Alexios III Visit Roman Mstislavich,' *GRBS* 56 (2016) 343–376.
36. Choniates, *History* 622; Michael: Barzos, *Γενεαλογία*, 2:669–674; Macrides, *George Akropolites*, 117 n. 12; territory: Choniates, *History* 631 (app.), 638; Akropolites 8.
37. Tafel and Thomas, *Urkunden*, 2:119.
38. Geoffroi de Villehardouin, *Conquest of Constantinople* 328 (Faral); Lappas, *Πολιτική ιστορία*, 69–72.
39. Konstantinos Maliasenos from Demetrias in Thessaly: *MM* 4:345–347; army: Henri de Valanciennes, *History of the Emperor Henri of Constantinople* 693.
40. Apokaukos, *Letter* 13 in N. Bees, 'Unedierte Schriftstücke aus der Kanzlei des Johannes Apokaukos,' *Byzantinisch-neugriechische Jahrbücher* 21 (1971–1974) 57–160; Ioannina: A. Papadopoulos-Kerameus, 'Περὶ τοῦ συνοικισμοῦ τῶν Ἰωαννίνων μετὰ τὴν Φραγκικὴν κατάκτησιν τῆς Κωνσταντινουπόλεως,' *Δελτίον τῆς ἱστορικῆς καὶ ἐθνολογικῆς ἑταιρείας τῆς Ἑλλάδος* 3 (1891) 451–455; Theodoros Doukas in Chomatenos, *Opus* 22.141–152 (Peloponnesians); for more see Nicol, *Studies*, IV:13–14, 20–21.
41. Choniates, *History* 631 app.; Chrissis, *Crusading*, 28–29.
42. Innocent III, *Register* 12.96 (= *PL* 216:106–107); Henri de Valanciennes, *History of the Emperor Henri of Constantinople* 689–694; Tafel and Thomas, *Urkunden*, 2:119–123.
43. Iob the Monk, *Life of the Empress Theodora*, in *PG* 127:904C; Akropolites 8; escort: Macrides, *George Akropolites*, 130 n. 1.
44. G. Prinzing, 'Studien zur Provinz- und Zentralverwaltung im Machtbereich der epirotischen Herrscher,' *Ἠπειρωτικὰ Χρονικά* 24 (1982) 73–120 and 25 (1983) 37–112; 'Das Verwaltungssystem im Epirotischen Staat der Jahre 1210–ca. 1246,' *Byzantinische Forschungen* 19 (1993) 113–126.
45. Henri: Prinzing, 'Brief,' 411–412; Innocent III, *Register* 13.184 (= *PL* 216:353–354); Lappas, *Πολιτική ιστορία*, 89–96.
46. Chomatenos, *Opus* 41, 50, 65.
47. Van Tricht, *Latin Renovatio*, 242–244; Chrissis, *Crusading*, 61–67.
48. Lappas, *Πολιτική ιστορία*, 104 n. 350, 106–113.
49. Apokaukos, *Letter* 4 in Vasilievsky, 'Epirotica,' 248.
50. Thessalonike: Van Tricht, *Latin Renovatio*, 247–248, 382–383; Margit: Coureas, 'Churches,' 154; Chrissis, *Crusading*, 68–69; Poimanenon and Serres: Akropolites 22; Philippe Mouskes, *Chronique rimée* 23180–23194, ed. F. De Reiffenberg (Brussels 1838) 2:408–409.
51. Apokaukos, *Letter* 26 in Vasilievsky, 'Epirotica,' 296; see Chrissis, *Crusading*, 68–78 ("enemies": 75).

52. A. Stavridou-Zafraka, *Νίκαια και Ήπειρος τον 13ο αιώνα* (Thessalonike 1991) 67–69.
53. Akropolites 24; anticipation for Constantinople: Apokaukos, *Letter* 25 in Vasilievsky, 'Epirotica,' 288.
54. Synod: Apokaukos, *Letter* 24 in Vasilievsky, 'Epirotica,' 285–286; context: A. Stavridou-Zafraka, 'The Political Ideology of the State of Epiros,' in Laiou, ed., *Urbs Capta*, 311–323, here 318–320.
55. Letter: Blemmydes, *Autobiography* 1.23; oath: Akropolites 14; conceeded by Bardanes in R. Loenertz, 'Lettre de Georges Bardanes,' 115.
56. Akropolites 21; Apokaukos, *Letter* 20 in Vasilievsky, 'Epirotica,' 280–282; date: Stavridou-Zafraka, *Βυζάντιο*, 145–146; Mesopotamites: Simpson, *Niketas*, 33–34, 75; Justiniana Prima: Chomatenos, *Opus* 114.11; G. Prinzing, 'A Quasi-Patriarch in the State of Epiros,' *Zbornik radova Vizantološkog instituta* 41 (2004) 165–182.
57. Blemmydes, *Autobiography* 1.23 (ca. 1226).
58. Karpozilos, *Ecclesiastical Controversy*; and see n. 52 above.
59. Apokaukos and Manuel in *Letters* 16–17 in Vasilievsky, 'Epirotica,' 268–278. Bulgarian bishops; Chomatenos, *Opus* 8, 146.
60. G. Prinzing, 'Die "Antigraphe" des Patriarchen Germanos II an Erzbischof Demetrios Chomatenos von Ochrid,' *Rivista di studi bizantini e slavi* 3 (1984) 21–64: Chomatenos' response: *Opus* 114.
61. Chomatenos, *Opus* 112.49; Apokaukos, *Letters* 17 and 27 in Vasilievsky, 'Epirotica,' 276–277 and 294; Loenertz, 'Lettre de Georges Bardanes,' 113, 116–117.
62. Chomatenos, *Opus* 114.3–4.
63. *AA* 20 (= *Chilandar* 1) nos. 4–5, pp. 107–110, 114–116; V. Jankovic, 'The Serbian Tradition on Mount Athos,' in G. Speake and K. Ware, eds., *Mount Athos: Microcosm of the Christian East* (Bern 2012) 79–96.
64. Chomatenos, *Opus* 86 (Sava), 10 (marriage).
65. Stavridou-Zafraka, *Βυζάντιο*, V:86 (*despotes*); IV:318, 322 (pronoias), 325–327 (Konstantinos); Bartusis, *Land*, 228–235 (pronoias).
66. Stavridou-Zafraka, *Βυζάντιο*, IV:324–333; T. Kiousopoulou, *Ο θεσμός της οικογένειας στην Ήπειρο κατά τον 13ο αιώνα* (Athens 1990); Angold, *Church*, ch. 10–12.
67. Nicol, *Studies*, IV:22–26; B. Dimou, 'Εθνολογικά στοιχεία στα έργα του Δημητρίου Χωματιανού,' in Chrysos, ed., *Πρακτικά*, 279–302.
68. Chomatenos, *Responses to Konstantinos Kabasilas of Dyrrachion* in *PG* 119:977.
69. L. Fundić, 'Art and Political Ideology in the State of Epiros,' *Byzantina Symmeikta* 23 (2013) 217–250.
70. Chomatenos, *Opus* 22.105–128.
71. R. Cessi, *Deliberazioni del Maggior Consiglio di Venezia* (Bologna 1950) 1:209–210.
72. Akropolites 25; J. Ransohoff, 'An Empire "Between Three Seas"? Mapping Late Medieval Bulgaria,' *Balkanistica* 30.2 (2017) 233–255.
73. Inscriptions: Petkov, *Voices*, 425–426; titles: Madgearu, *Asanids*, 202–205.
74. *MM* 3:59–65; plenipotentiary: E. Kurtz, 'Christophoros von Angyra als Exarch des Patriarchen Germanos II,' *BZ* 16 (1907) 120–142, here 141; papacy: A. Tautu, *Acta*

Honorii III (1216–1227) et Gregorii IX (1227–1241) (Vatican City 1950) 232; Lappas, *Πολιτική ιστορία*, 137–150; Macrides, *George Akropolites*, 183–184.

75. Akropolites 26, 38–39; Macrides, *George Akropolites*, 182–183, 214; Madgearu, *Asanids*, 202.
76. Stavridou-Zafraka, *Βυζάντιο*, IV:330.
77. G. Prinzing, 'Das byzantinische Kaisertum im Umbruch,' in R. Gundlach and H. Weber, eds., *Legitimation und Funktion des Herrschers* (Stuttgart 1992) 129–183; Eastmond, *Art and Identity*, 2–4, 160.
78. Akropolites 22–23; Gregoras 2.1.
79. C. Constantinides, *Higher Education in Byzantium in the Thirteenth and Early Fourteenth Centuries* (Nicosia 1982). P. Agapitos, 'The Insignificance of 1204 and 1453 for the History of Byzantine Literature,' *Medioevo greco* 20 (2020) 1–58, fails to account for the generational lag between conquest and its impact on literary production.
80. Pachymeres 1.23–24; also pseudo-Skoutariotes, *Additions to Akropolites* 33 (Heisenberg, pp. 285–287); Angold, *Byzantine Government*, 102–104, 124, 210–214 (censuses); Jacoby, 'Rural Exploitation.'
81. Pachymeres 1.14, 1.23; Gregoras 2.6.
82. Blemmydes, *Partial Account* 1.12; pseudo-Skoutariotes, *Additions to Akropolites* 33 (Heisenberg, p. 286); Pachymeres 1.23; Pitamber, *Replacing Byzantium*, 215–233. *Vestiarion*: Kontogiannopoulou, *Εσωτερική πολιτική*, 210–213.
83. *MM* 4:1–289; H. Ahrweiler, 'L'histoire et la géographie de la région de Smyrne,' *TM* 1 (1965) 1–204.
84. Angold, *Byzantine Government*, 47–48, 127–129.
85. Angold, *Byzantine Government*, 99–100, 244–249.
86. Thonemann, *Maeander*, 4, 7, 14, 276; C. Foss, *Cities, Fortresses, and Villages of Byzantine Asia Minor* (Aldershot, UK 1996) V–VI.
87. Pachymeres 1.4.
88. Latins: Bartusis, *Army*, 28–29; mobility: Akropolites 60; elites: Korobeinikov, *Byzantium*, 75, 59–66; pages: Angold, *Byzantine Government*, 176–177.
89. Angold, *Byzantine Government*, 155–159, 182–184, 201; Korobeinikov, *Byzantium*, 70–73; "random": Akropolites 49, with Macrides, *George Akropolites*, 254–255.
90. Kyritses, *Byzantine Aristocracy*, 22, 38, 52–55; Macrides et al., *Pseudo-Kodinos*, 291–301; Kontogiannopoulou, *Εσωτερική πολιτική*, 72–81; *protovestiarites*: Angelov, *Byzantine Hellene*, 18–19, 33.
91. Akropolites, *Funeral Oration for Ioannes III Batatzes* 8 (p. 17); *History* 22–24.
92. Gregoras 2.3; Macrides, *George Akropolites*, 187–188; Savvides, *Κινήματα*, 301–341.
93. H. Ahrweiler, *Byzance et la mer* (Paris 1966) 301–327.
94. J. Brubaker, '"You Are the Heretics!" Dialogue and Disputation between the Greek East and Latin West,' *Medieval Encounters* 24 (2018) 613–630.
95. "Packing": Germanos, *Catechetical Oration* in S. Lagopates, *Γερμανὸς ὁ Β′ πατριάρχης Κωνσταντινουπόλεως-Νικαίας* (1913) 347; "humiliated": *Sermon on the Holy Cross* in *PG* 140:641B; letter: C. Arampatzis, 'Ἀνέκδοτη ἐπιστολὴ τοῦ πατριάρχη Κωνσταντινουπόλεως Γερμανοῦ Β′ πρὸς τοὺς Καρδιναλίους τῆς Ῥώμης,' *ΕΕΒΣ* 52

(2004–2006) 363–378, here 377. Tarnovo patriarchate: Macrides, *George Akropolites*, 196; Ioakim: Petkov, *Voices*, 256–257, 438–440.

96. Akropolites 31–33.
97. J. Langdon, 'The Forgotten Byzantino-Bulgarian Assault and Siege of Constantinople,' in S. Vryonis, ed., *Byzantine Studies in Honor of Milton V. Anastos* (Malibu 1985) 105–135.
98. Akropolites 35.
99. Batatzes in Pieralli, *Corrispondenza*, 119–126; V. Grumel, 'L'authenticité de la lettre de Jean Vatatzès,' *Échos d'Orient* 29 (1930) 450–458; Chrissis, *Crusading*, 104–111.
100. J.-M. Martin, '*O Felix Asia!* Frédéric II, l'empire de Nicée et le "Césaropapisme",' *TM* 14 (2002) 473–483; soldiers: Chrissis, *Crusading*, 89, 118; Macrides, *George Akropolites*, 180.
101. Akropolites 37, 47; crusade: Chrissis, *Crusading*, 120–126; Crown: Nicol, *Byzantium*, 168–171.
102. Akropolites 40, 76 (Greek); Gregoras 2.5β; Theodoros II, *Encomium for Ioannes III Batatzes* 3; Angold, *Byzantine Government*, 105, 188; Macrides, *George Akropolites*, 217.
103. Madgearu, *Asanids*, 228–235.
104. Korobeinikov, *Byzantium*, 175–179.
105. Attack: Angelov, *Byzantine Hellene*, 91–92; treaty: Albricus the Monk, *Chronicle* s.a. 1241, in *MGH SS* 23:950.
106. Akropolites 40–41; Gregoras 2.6α; quotation: Pachymeres 2.25; Friedrich: J. Langdon, *John III Vatatzes' Byzantine Imperium in Anatolian Exile* (PhD dissertation, UCLA 1978) 251; date: Macrides, *George Akropolites*, 216; immigration: Theodoros II Laskaris, *Encomium for Ioannes III Batatzes* 3.
107. A. Bryer, 'The Grand Komnenos and the Grand Khan at Karakorum in 1246,' in R. Curiel and R. Gyselen, eds., *Itinéraires d'Orient* (Bures-sur-Yvette 1994) 257–261.
108. A. Bryer and D. Winfield, *The Byzantine Monuments and Topography of the Pontos* (Washington, D.C. 1985) 303–304.
109. Eastmond, *Art and Identity*, 66–73, 100–114; portraits: Karpov, *Ιστορία*, 501–502; palace: Oikonomides, 'Chancery,' 322–323.
110. Akropolites 41–46.
111. Stavridou-Zafraka, *Βυζάντιο*, V.
112. P. Gounaridis, 'Η φεουδαρχία στο δεσποτάτο της Ηπείρου,' in E. Chrysos, ed., *Πρακτικά*, 37–45, here 41; Angelov, *Imperial Ideology*, 334–344.
113. Akropolites 49; date: K. Murata, 'The Mongols' Approach to Anatolia and the Last Campaign of Emperor John III Vatatzes,' *GRBS* 55 (2015) 470–488.
114. Angold, *Byzantine Government*, 23–25, 175–176, 288–294.
115. Pseudo-Skoutariotes, *Additions to Akropolites* 33 (Heisenberg, p. 287).
116. Chrissis, *Crusading*, 159–172. A. Franchi, *La svolta politico-ecclesiastica tra Roma e Bisanzio (1249–1254)* (Rome 1981) is crucial.
117. L. Ciolfi, 'John III Batatzes: History, Myth and Propaganda,' in M. Lau et al., *Landscapes of Power* (Frankfurt 2014) 273–288.

118. Theodoros II, *On Christian Theology* 7, pp. 137–143; Kaldellis, *Hellenism*, 372–379; Angelov, *Byzantine Hellene*, ch. 10 (diagrams: figs. 29–30).
119. Theodoros II, *On Christian Theology* 7, p. 142.
120. Theodoros II, *Letter* 5 (p. 8).
121. E.g., Akropolites, *Against the Latins* 2.27.
122. Goal: Akropolites, *Funeral Oration for Ioannes III Batatzes* 21 (p. 28); "brothers": Theodoros II, *Treatise to Georgios Mouzalon* 4 (pp. 125–126); "slave": *Encomium for Georgios Akropolites* 4 (p. 101); Nikaia: *Encomium of Nikaia*, passim; "mother": *Letters*, App. 1, p. 281; Angelov, *Byzantine Hellene*, 39–42, 208.
123. Akropolites 54–63, to be read with pseudo-Skoutariotes' additions; Theodoros II, *Letter* 204 (generals), 44 (boast), *Letters* App. 1 (pp. 280–282: treaty).
124. Pachymeres 1.7, is better than Akropolites 50; Macrides, *George Akropolites*, 72–74. Encomium: Iakobos of Ohrid, *Funeral Oration for Andronikos Palaiologos*, ed. A. Mercati, *Collectanea byzantina* (Rome 1970) 1:66–73.
125. Michael VIII, *Typikon of the Monastery of St. Demetrios* 5, tr. (mod.) G. Dennis in *BMFD* 1243; Akropolites 64–65, 69; Pachymeres 1.9–10; Niketas Karantenos, *Letter to the Abbot of St. John's on Patmos*, ed. M. Nystazopoulou, 'Γρᾶμμα τοῦ ἱερέως καὶ νομικοῦ τῶν παλατίων Νικήτα Καραντηνοῦ,' in *Χαριστήριον εἰς Ἀναστάσιον Κ. Ὀρλάνδον* (Athens 1966) 2:286–308.
126. Angelov, *Imperial Ideology*, ch. 7; *Byzantine Hellene*, 111–112, 123–127; see esp. Theodoros II, *Treatise to Georgios Mouzalon*.
127. Blemmydes, *Partial Account* 1.88; Akropolites 60, 76; Pachymeres 1.8.
128. Akropolites 75; Pachymeres 1.8; Angelov, *Byzantine Hellene*, 161.
129. Blemmydes, *Partial Account* 1.74–80; cf. pseudo-Skoutariotes, *Additions to Akropolites* 35 (Heisenberg, pp. 288–291). Akropolites a victim: *History* 63–64.
130. Akropolites 66–73, 76; Pachymeres 1.10–13; dowry: *Chronicle of the Morea* 3127–3128; Dyrrachion: *MM* 3:239–242; Lappas, *Πολιτική ιστορία*, 198–214; Angelov, *Byzantine Hellene*, 175–179.
131. Arsenios, *Testament* 4, in *PG* 140:949C-D; Akropolites 75–78; Pachymeres 1.14–29, 2.1–10 ("chain": 1.21' "infant": 1.27), 2.15 (Arsenios); Gregoras 3.3–4; full name: *AA* 18 (= *Iviron* 3) no. 58, p. 92; A. Failler, 'Chronologie et composition dans l'Histoire de Georges Pachymère,' *REB* 38 (1980) 5–103, here 24–44.
132. Michael VIII, *Typikon for the Monastery of St. Michael at Mt. Auxentios* 15, tr. G. Dennis in *BMFD* 1231 (mod.).
133. Akropolites 80–81; Pachymeres 1.30–31; Gregoras 3.5; *Chronicle of the Morea* 3549–4200 (Greek).
134. Ch. Siderides, 'Ἔλεγχος τῆς ἐκδόσεως . . . Πατριάρχου Νικηφόρου,' *Νέα Σιών* 6 (1907) 707–747, here 746–747; Karpov, *Ιστορία*, 217–219.
135. Akropolites 82–83; Michael VIII, *Typikon of the Monastery of St. Demetrios* 7, tr. G. Dennis in *BMFD* 1244; Pachymeres 1.32, 2.11, 2.14, 2.20–21 (Basil II); Gregoras 4.1δ.
136. *Chronicon Marchiae Tarvisinae et Lombardiae*, ed. L. Botteghi in *Rerum Italicarum Scriptores*, n.s., 8.3:47 (Città di Castello 1916).

137. Text: Pieralli, *Corrispondenza*, 129–151; study: Geanakoplos, *Emperor Michael*, 81–91; silk: Hilsdale, *Byzantine Art*, ch. 1.
138. Akropolites 85 (tr. Macrides, mod.); Pachymeres 2.26–27; Gregoras 4.2 ("hated"). Van Tricht, *Horoscope*.

Chapter 33. Union with Rome and Roman Disunity (1261–1282)

1. Akropolites 87–88; Pachymeres 2.29–31; Holobolos, *Oration* 2, pp. 73–74; Hodegetria: Macrides, *George Akropolites*, 385 n. 5.
2. Pachymeres 2.23, 2.27; A. Pertusi, 'Le profezie sulla presa di Costantinopoli,' *Studi veneziani* 3 (1979) 13–46.
3. Michael VIII, *Typikon of the Monastery of St. Demetrios* 8, tr. G. Dennis in *BMFD* 1245.
4. Holobolos, *Oration* 2, pp. 76–77.
5. Pachymeres 2.32.
6. Agoritsas, *Κωνσταντινούπολη*, 51–55, 60; Hilsdale, *Byzantine Art*, 99–108; Eastmond, *Art and Identity*, 108, 116, 142, 142–143.
7. Macrides et al., *Pseudo-Kodinos*, 27 n. 2; Agoritsas, *Κωνσταντινούπολη*, 247–248. Orations: Angelov, 'Ideological Reactions,' 305.
8. Hilsdale, *Byzantine Art*, 109–151 (statue), 155–169 (coins).
9. Hilsdale, *Byzantine Art*, 155–157, 169–185.
10. Zepos, *Jus Graecoromanum*, 1:659–666; D. Geanakoplos, *Constantinople and the West* (Madison, WI 1989) 173–188.
11. Agoritsas, *Κωνσταντινούπολη*, 48–49, 136.
12. Gregoras 4.2στ; houses: 4.1δ; column: 7.12δ; also Holobolos in *Oration* 2, p. 61, and Previale, 'Panegyrico,' 18; roofs: Angold, *Fourth Crusade*, 148, for two testimonia; Agoritsas, *Κωνσταντινούπολη*, 66–67. A more positive (and apologetic) picture in Van Tricht, *Horoscope*, ch. 7. Buttresses: E. Swift, 'The Latins at Hagia Sophia,' *American Journal of Archaeology* 39 (1935) 458–474.
13. K. Smyrlis, *La fortune des grands monastères byzantins* (Paris 2006) 176–177.
14. R. Macrides, 'The Citadel of Byzantine Constantinople,' in S. Redford and C. Chabon Aslan, eds., *Cities and Citadels in Turkey* (Leuven 2013) 277–304.
15. Pachymeres 2.30, 2.33; Gregoras 4.2; official: P. Schreiner, 'Die topographische Notiz über Konstantinopel,' in I. Ševčenko and I. Hutter, eds., *AETOS: Studies in Honour of Cyril Mango* (Stuttgart 1998) 273–283, here 276; "crowd": Holobolos, *Oration* 2, p. 72.
16. Michael VIII, *Typikon for the Monastery of St. Michael at Mt. Auxentios* 1, tr. G. Dennis in *BMFD* 1216 (mod.).
17. Pachymeres 3.9, 5.10; Holobolos, *Oration* 2, p. 58 (water); Talbot, 'Restoration.'
18. Talbot, 'Restoration,' 253–257; Agoritsas, *Κωνσταντινούπολη*, 111–120, 325–328.
19. C. Beazley, 'Directorium ad Faciendum Passagium Transmarinum, II,' *American Historical Review* 13 (1907) 66–115, here 84; Agoritsas, *Κωνσταντινούπολη*, 189–191.

20. Alexios Makrembolites, *Dialogue between the Rich and Poor*, p. 209; Agoritsas, *Κωνσταντινούπολη*, 304–308.
21. Kyritses, *Byzantine Aristocracy*, 199–202; Kontogiannopoulou, *Εσωτερική πολιτική*, 149; tax system: A. Kontogiannopoulou, 'La fiscalité à Byzance sous les Paléologues,' *REB* 67 (2009) 5–57; salaries: Macrides et al., *Pseudo-Kodinos*, 313–313.
22. Pachymeres 1.28, 2.1, 2.5; Bartusis, *Land*, 274–280, 442–469; *oikonomia*: ibid. 251–258.
23. Pachymeres 1.5, 8.19; Heisenberg, *Geschichte*, 40; Laiou-Thomadakis, *Peasant Society*, 5; Bartusis, *Army*, 170–175; Lavra and textbooks: Bartusis, *Land*, 532–533, 350–351; Preiser-Kapeller and Mitsiou, 'Hierarchies,' 250.
24. Pachymeres 3.21 for the despot Ioannes Palaiologos, Michael's brother; 4.29 for his pronoias (Lesbos and Rhodes).
25. Kyritses, *Byzantine Aristocracy*, 172–174, 210–212; Michael no pawn: 304–305.
26. Alexios Makrembolites, *Dialogue between the Rich and Poor*, p. 212.
27. Smyrlis, 'Wooing'; and many of his other publications on this period, are fundamental; also D. Kyritses, 'The "Common Chrysobulls" of Cities,' *Byzantina Symmeikta* 13 (1999) 229–245; Macrides et al., *Pseudo-Kodinos*, 313–314. Andronikos: *MM* 5:254. Hierissos: S. Gerstel, *Rural Lives and Landscapes in Late Byzantium* (Cambridge 2015) 100.
28. Estangüi Gómez, *Byzance*, passim, e.g., 3, 63, 71, 85, 119, 395.
29. Talbot, 'Restoration,' 252–253.
30. Pachymeres 2.24; Gregoras 4.5γ; D. Korobeinikov, 'Byzantine Emperors and Sultans of Rum: Sharing Power?,' in Tougher, ed., *Emperor*, 83–111.
31. Pachymeres 3.3; Gregoras 4.7α.
32. Pachymeres 3.25; Gregoras 4.6α; B. Lippard, *The Mongols and Byzantium* (PhD dissertation, Indiana University 1983) 188–198; Korobeinikov, *Byzantium*, 203–206.
33. Lappas, *Πολιτική ιστορία*, 250–268.
34. Akropolites 50 ("born"), 81 (Epeirots were Romans); Michael VIII, *Typikon for the Monastery of St. Michael at Mt. Auxentios* 15 ("on behalf of the Romans") and 16 ("apostates" and "basileis"), tr. G. Dennis in *BMFD* 1232–1233 (mod.); *homoethneis*: Gregorios of Cyprus in C. Rapp, 'Ein bisher unbekannter Brief des Patriarchen Gregor von Zypern,' *BZ* 81 (1988) 12–28, here 18.
35. Pachymeres 3.16.
36. Pachymeres 1.31; *Chronicle of the Morea* 4210–4512 (Greek); Marin Sanudo Torsello, *History of Romania* 1, pp. 114–117; Saint-Guillain, 'Conquest of Monemvasia,' 263 n. 70, 265 n. 73 ("domesticated").
37. *Chronicle of the Morea* 5603–5610 (Greek).
38. Pachymeres 3.16; cf. *Chronicle of the Morea* par. 382 (French).
39. Foskolou, 'In the Reign.' "Castles": Marin Sanudo Torsello, *History of Romania* 2, p. 125.
40. Achaea: J. Guiraud, *Les registres d'Urbain IV* (Paris 1946) 2: nos. 131 and 187; M. Barber, 'Western Attitudes to Frankish Greece in the Thirteenth Century,' *Mediterranean Historical Review* 4 (1989) 111–128, here 116–117; Crete: ibid., 119–120, with Geanakoplos, *Emperor Michael*, 184. Cyprus: Urban IV, *Letter* g-8,

in C. Schabel, *Bullarium Cyprium*, v. 2: *Papal Letters Concerning Cyprus, 1261–1314* (Nicosia 2010) 18–21.

41. Holobolos, *Oration* 3, p. 89.
42. Chrissis, *Crusading*, 182–200 (quotations: 197 n. 66, 199 n. 73).
43. Pachymeres 6.32; Chrissis, *Crusading*, 202–204.
44. Treaties: C. Perrat and L. Longnon, *Actes relatifs à la principauté de Morée* (Paris 1967) 207–211; J. Buchon, *Recherches et matériaux* (Paris 1840) 1:30–37; *Chronicle of the Morea* 6265–6492 (Greek). Venice: Chrissis, *Crusading*, 215.
45. Geanakoplos, *Emperor Michael*, 217–222; "usurper": I. Filangieri et al., *I registri della cancelleria angioina* (Naples 1950) 1:91 no. 3.
46. Pachymeres 2.35, 5.10; *Annali Genovesi* (Rome 1926) 4:107–108 (s.a. 1267); kneeling: Macrides et al., *Pseudo-Kodinos*, 153, 183, 387.
47. Tafel and Thomas, *Urkunden*, 3:93–100; "hydra": Holobolos, *Oration* 2, p. 70.
48. Pachymeres 5.30, 12.34; Marin Sanudo Torsello, *History of Romania* 3, p. 173; S. Mergiali-Sahas, 'In the Face of a Historical Puzzle: Western Adventurers, Friars and Nobility in the Service of Michael VIII,' in Chrissis et al., eds., *Byzantium*, 275–285; concession: S. Efthymiades and A. Mazarakis, 'Φωκαϊκά Σπαράγματα,' *Δελτίο Κέντρου Μικρασιατικών Σπουδών* 15 (2008) 39–163, here 105–108; alum: Doukas 25.4–5.
49. Pachymeres 5.10.
50. Chrissis, *Crusading*, 201–217; Geanakoplos, *Emperor Michael*, 216–228.
51. Pachymeres 5.11, 6.15.
52. Chrissis, *Crusading*, 217–225; J. Wilksman, 'The Conflict between the Angevins and the Byzantines in Morea in 1267–1289,' *Byzantina Symmeikta* 22 (2012) 31–70.
53. Pachymeres 5.17, 5.21.
54. Gill, *Byzantium*, 133–141; B. Roberg, *Das zweite Konzil von Lyon* (1274) (Paderborn 1990); the main narrative source is Franchi, *Concilio*.
55. Hilsdale, *Byzantine Art*, 46.
56. Pachymeres 2.2–4 (oaths), 3.12–13.
57. Pachymeres 3.11, 3.14, 3.19, 4.1–8; Gregoras 4.4; Varangians: Arsenios, *Testament* 9, in *PG* 140:956A–B; L. Rickelt, 'Die Exkommunikation Michaels VIII. Palaiologos,' in M. Grünbart, ed., *Zwei Sonnen am Goldenen Horn? Kaiserliche und patriarchale Macht im byzantinischen Mittelalter* (Berlin 2011) 97–125.
58. Pachymeres 4.13, 4.17–25; I. Sykoutris, 'Συνοδικὸς Τόμος τῆς ἐκλογῆς τοῦ πατριάρχου Γερμανοῦ τοῦ Γ',' *ΕΕΒΣ* 9 (1932) 178–212; D. Angelov, 'The Confession of Michael VIII Palaiologos and King David,' *JöB* 56 (2006) 193–204.
59. Pachymeres 4.10–11, 4.19, 4.28, 5.2, 5.23; A. Kontogiannopoulou, 'Το σχίσμα των Αρσενιατών,' *Byzantiaka* 18 (1998) 177–235; Gounarides, *Κίνημα*. For the catch-phrase, see Colossians 2:21.
60. Pachymeres 5.12–16; Gregoras 5.2; oath: Laurent and Darrouzès, *Dossier*, 302–305; response to the basileus (embellished later): ibid 134–301.
61. Pachymeres 5.17–20; Laurent and Darrouzès, *Dossier*, 306–319.
62. Franchi, *Concilio*, 86.246–249; Geanakoplos, *Emperor Michael*, 264 n. 24.
63. Pachymeres 5.22–26; crusade: Gill, *Byzantium*, 162.

64. Pachymeres 5.18, 6.15; Gregoras 5.2γ; *MM* 5:247; Zepos, *Jus Graecoromanum*, 1:503, 660; Ioseph: Laurent and Darrouzès, *Dossier*, 236–239.
65. Pachymeres 6.14, 6.17; Geanakoplos, *Emperor Michael*, 305–325; Gill, *Byzantium*, 166–169; A. Riebe, *Rom in Gemeinschaft mit Konstantinopel: Patriarch Johannes XI. Bekkos as Verteidiger der Kirchenunion von Lyon (1274)* (Wiesbaden 2005).
66. Pachymeres 6.30; Bekkos, *On the Injustice of his Deposition* 2, in *PG* 141:952D–953A; and in Laurent and Darrouzès, *Dossier*, 465; V. Puech, 'The Byzantine Aristocracy and the Union of the Churches (1274–1283): A Prosopographical Approach,' in Saint-Guillan and Stathakopoulos, eds., *Liquid*, 45–54.
67. Pachymeres 6.16–18, 6.23–24, 7.3; D. Nicol, *Byzantium: Its Ecclesiastical History and Relations with the Western World* (London 1972) VI:130–135; *Latinismos*: idem, 'Popular Religious Roots of the Byzantine Reaction to the Second Council of Lyons,' in C. Ryan, ed., *The Religious Roles of the Papacy* (Toronto 1989) 321–339, here 337–338; anti-Latin texts: Agoritsas, *Κωνσταντινούπολη*, 466–467. Ogerio: R.-J. Loenertz, 'Mémoire d'Ogier,' *Orientalia Christiana Periodica* 31 (1965) 374–408; Pieralli, *Corrispondenza*, 88–95.
68. Meletios in Laurent and Darrouzès, *Dossier*, 111.
69. Pachymeres 5.23; Bekkos in Laurent and Darrouzès, *Dossier*, 481.21–26.
70. Theoleptos in Sinkewicz, *Critical Edition*, 76; Gounarides, *Κίνημα*, 89–119.
71. Bekkos in Laurent and Darrouzès, *Dossier*, 465.
72. Gill, *Byzantium*, 164–165, 169–170; flight: Gregoras 5.2δ.
73. Pachymeres 6.15.
74. Pachymeres 3.9, 4.31–5.1; Gregoras 4.9–10; Marin Sanudo Torsello, *History of Romania* 2, pp. 130–143; Nicol, *Despotate*, 12–20; Lappas, *Πολιτική ιστορία*, 274–280.
75. Michael VIII, *Typikon of the Monastery of St. Demetrios* 8, tr. G. Dennis in *BMFD* 1245; see Pachymeres 2.33, 3.9, 4.26 ("dominated"), 5.30; Gregoras 4.6ε; M. Angold, 'Michael VIII Palaiologos and the Aegean,' in Saint-Guillain and Stathakopoulos, eds., *Liquid*, 1–18.
76. Pieralli, *Corrispondeza*, 267–302.
77. Tafel and Thomas, *Urkunden*, 3:159–281; G. Morgan, 'The Venetian Claims Commission of 1278,' *BZ* 69 (1976) 411–438; Nicol, *Byzantium*, 197–206; Laiou, *Constantinople*, 58–59, 66.
78. Pachymeres 6.32–33; Gregoras 5.6; Marin Sanudo Torsello, *History of Romania* 2, pp. 144–147; Lappas, *Πολιτική ιστορία*, 293–301.
79. Geanakoplos, *Emperor Michael*, 336–337.
80. Pachymeres 6.34; Oikonomides, 'Chancery,' 324–330; Ioannes II: Karpov, *Ιστορία*, 222–225.
81. Chrissis, *Crusading*, 238–249; Orvieto: Tafel and Thomas, *Urkunden*, 3:287–308.
82. Michael VIII, *Typikon of the Monastery of St. Demetrios* 9, tr. G. Dennis (mod.) in *BMFD* 1246; S. Runciman, *The Sicilian Vespers* (Cambridge 1958); Geanakoplos, *Emperor Michael*, 344–367.
83. Previale, 'Panegirico,' 35.
84. Pachymeres 6.36, 7.37; Gregoras 5.7.

85. Hilsdale, *Byzantine Art*, 110, 147–148.
86. T. Shawcrosss, '"In the Name of the True Emperor": Politics of Resistance after the Palaiologan Usurpation,' *Byzantinoslavica* 66 (2008) 203–227, here 218–224.

Chapter 34. Territorial Retrenchment and Cultural Innovation (1282–1328)

1. Akropolites 89; Pachymeres 4.29; Gregoras 4.9γ; Macrides, 'New Constantine,' 37–38; Macrides et al., *Pseudo-Kodinos*, 421–422.
2. Heisenberg, *Geschichte*, 37–41.
3. Pachymeres 2.1.
4. Pachymeres 7.33, 9.1.
5. Pachymeres 7.2–19 ("lairs": 7.12); Bekkos, *On the Injustice of his Deposition* 2, in *PG* 141:949–1009; Georgios Metochites, *Dogmatic History* VIII.2, pp. 90–104 (Cozza-Luzi); Gregoras 6.1β; Gounarides, *Κίνημα*, 121–137.
6. E.g., Foskolou, 'In the Reign,' 460.
7. Gregoras 6.1β; Agoritsas, *Κωνσταντινούπολη*, 54–55.
8. Gregorios II, *Encomium of Andronikos II Palaiologos*, in J. Boissonade, *Anecdota Graeca* (Paris 1829) 1:381; Gounarides, *Κίνημα*, 140–141 n. 84.
9. Pachymeres 7.19; A.-M. Talbot, 'Empress Theodora Palaiologina,' *DOP* 46 (1992) 295–303.
10. Macrides, *George Akropolites*, 19.
11. Pachymeres 7.12–13; Methodios the Monk, *Against the Schism* 5, in *PG* 140:785C; Gregorios II, *Letter* 124 (pp. 291–292), 132 (pp. 12–13); Theoleptos of Philadelphia in Sinkewicz, *Critical Edition*, 78.
12. Pachymeres 7.21–22, 8.12; Gregoras 6.1ε; critic: Ioannes Chilas in J. Darrouzès, *Documents inédits d'ecclésiologie byzantine* (Paris 1966) 358.
13. Andronikos II, *Novel* 36, in Zepos, *Jus Graecoromanum*, 1:553.
14. Pachymeres 7.31; Gregoras 6.2θ.
15. Pachymeres 7.34; Bekkos, *Against the Tomos* 1, in *PG* 141:865B-C; Georgios Metochites, *Dogmatic History* VIII.2, pp. 36–37 (Cozza-Luzi); Gregoras 6.1ζ; Ragia, 'Confessions.'
16. Pachymeres 7.34–35, 8.1–3; *Tomos*: *PG* 142:233–246; Bekkos, *Against the Tomos*, in *PG* 141:863–926; A. Papadakis, *Crisis in Byzantium: The filioque Controversy in the Patriarchate of Gregory II of Cyprus* (New York 1983), a partisan account.
17. Nikephoros Xanthopoulos, *On the Miracles of Zoodochos Pege*, ed. A. Pamperis, *Λόγος διαλαμβάνων*... (Leipzig 1802) 64–65.
18. Ioseph Kalothetos, *Life of the Patriarch Athanasios* 23, ed. D. Tsames, *Ἰωσὴφ Καλοθέτου συγγράμματα* (Thessalonike 1980) 453–502.
19. Pachymeres 8.3–13; Gregoras 6.4.
20. Pachymeres 7.26; Gregoras 6.3.
21. Pachymeres 9.18; Gregoras 6.11; Nicol, *Byzantium*, 218–220. Planoudes: Angelov, *Imperial Ideology*, 174–176.

22. Angold, *Byzantine Government*, 277.
23. Angold, *Byzantine Government*, 294-296; Thonemann, *Maeander*, 1; Agoritsas, *Κωνσταντινούπολη*, 46–47.
24. Pachymeres 2.28, 1.5–6, 3.22, 4.27, 6.29.
25. Korobeinikov, *Byzantium*, ch. 7–8.
26. Jacoby, 'Rural Exploitation,' 248.
27. Nikephoros Choumnos, *Encomium for Andronikos II Palaiologos*, in J. Boissonade, *Anecdota Graeca* (Paris 1830) 2:30.
28. E. Ragia, *Η κοιλάδα του κάτω Μαιάνδρου στη βυζαντινή εποχή* (Thessalonike 2009) 279–285. Paphlagonia: Pachymeres 4.27; Marin Sanudo Torsello, *History of Romania* 3, pp. 168–171.
29. Korobeinikov, *Byzantium*, 226–227, 245–251; Doukas: Pachymeres 6.24.
30. Metochites, *Oration* 7.20, 27–28, referring to the early 1280s; C. Foss, 'Byzantine Malagina and the Lower Sangarius,' *Anatolian Studies* 40 (1990) 161–183.
31. Korobeinikov, *Byzantium*, 250–251, 256–261; Pachymeres 7.36; Gregoras 6.8γ.
32. Planoudes, *Letter* 119.
33. Korobeinikov, *Byzantium*, 264–269; A. Laiou, 'Some Observations on Alexios Philanthropenos,' *BMGS* 4 (1978) 89–99.
34. Pachymeres 9.25, 10.2; hereditary: Nikolaos Lampenos, *Encomium for Andronikos II Palaiologos* 65 (pp. 67–68).
35. Gregoras 6.10β; Pachymeres 10.16.
36. Pachymeres 10.16–22 (quotation: 10.17), 11.16 (Sardeis), 11.21, 12.34 (Phokaia); Gregoras 6.10β-γ.
37. Pachymeres 10.25–26; Gregoras 6.11, 7.1α. Bosporos: Athanasios, *Letter* 37. Refugees: A. Kontogiannopoulou, 'Εσωτερικές μεταναστεύσεις στο ύστερο Βυζάντιο,' *Byzantina Symmeikta* 27 (2017) 211–238; Agoritas, *Κωνσταντινούπολη*, 488–493. *Hetaireiarches*: Macrides et al., *Pseudo-Kodinos*, 94–95 (and passim); Athanasios, *Letter* 60; cajoling: *Letters* 22, 78; Boojamra, *Church*, ch. 5.
38. Laiou-Thomadakis, *Peasant Society*, 108–129; Shukurov, *Byzantine Turks*, 366.
39. Pachymeres 11.18.
40. Agoritsas, *Κωνσταντινούπολη*, 329–332. Refugee-saint: Philotheos of Selymbria, *Life of Maximos Kausokalybites*.
41. Pachymeres 1.1, 2.27.
42. Kantakouzenos 4.14 (p. 94); K. Jahn, *Histoire universelle de Rašid al-Din*, v. 1: *Histoire des Frances* (Leiden 1951) 21–22.
43. Metochites, *Oration* 7.14 (*Second Imperial Oration*); more: Agoritsas, *Κωνσταντινούπολη*, 498–514.
44. Kantakouzenos 3.96; for what follows, see Foss, *Ottoman Empire*.
45. Pachymeres 13.38.
46. Kontogianopoulou, *Εσωτερική πολιτική*, 134–155.
47. Kiousopoulou, *Οι «αόρατες» βυζαντινές πόλεις*, 37–38.
48. Kiousopoulou, *Οι «αόρατες» βυζαντινές πόλεις*, 91–92, 118–120; A. Kontogiannopoulou, *Τοπικά συμβούλια στις βυζαντινές πόλεις: Παράδοση και εξέλιξη (13ος-15ος αι.)* (Athens 2015).

49. Kontogianopoulou, *Εσωτερική πολιτική*, 81–86, 125–131; eadem, 'The Notion of ΔΗΜΟΣ and its Role in Byzantium during the Last Centuries,' *Byzantina Symmeikta* 22 (2012) 101–124; Agoritsas, *Κωνσταντινούπολη*, 223–225, 312–314.
50. E.g., Pachymeres 7.36; Metochites, *Oration* 5.20–30 (*First Imperial Oration*).
51. E.g., *AA* 21 (= *Vatopédi* 1) nos. 55–57 (unknown date); Smyrlis, 'Financial Crisis,' 80–81; idem, 'Τα μοναστήρια στο ύστερο Βυζάντιο,' in I. Kolovos, ed., *Μοναστήρια, οικονομία και πολιτική* (Herakleion 2011) 53–68.
52. Macrides et al., *Pseudo-Kodinos*, passim, esp. 315–316 (banquets), 324–325 (hats), 357 (turbans); Agoritsas, *Κωνσταντινούπολη*, 75, 196; M. Parani, 'Encounters in the Realm of Dress: Attitudes toward Western Styles in the Greek East,' in M. Brownlee and D. Gondikas, eds., *Renaissance Encounters: Greek East and Latin West* (Leiden 2013) 263–301.
53. Zachariadou, 'Mosque.'
54. J. Verpeau, *Pseudo-Kodinos: Traité des offices* (Paris 1966) 339.
55. Metochites, *Oration* 11.96–97 (*Byzantios*).
56. Metochites, *Oration* 11.78.
57. Metochites, *Poem* 19; Gregoras 9.5β; Kantakouzenos 3.27 (pp. 164–165); Alexios Makrembolites, *Dialogue between the Rich and Poor*, p. 209.
58. *RP* 3:68 (no. 184).
59. Pachymeres 12.8; P. Grierson, *Catalogue of the Byzantine Coins* (Washington, D.C. 1999) 5.1:44, 128–134; Kontogiannopoulou, *Εσωτερική πολιτική*, 272–273. Famine: Athanasios, *Letters* 72–73.
60. Pachymeres 7.25 (10.2: Demetrias); Smyrlis, 'Financial Crisis.'
61. Pachymeres 10.9, 11.9, 11.13.
62. Laiou, *Constantinople*, 44–54. Cyprus: Pachymeres 9.5.
63. Pachymeres 9.30–10.5; Gregoras 6.9; Metochites, *Oration* 8; Laiou, *Constantinople*, 93–101.
64. Gregoras 7.5, 9.2η; Pachymeres 11.5; Kontogiannopoulou, *Εσωτερική πολιτική*, 167–168; clash: Kaldellis, *Ethnography*, 180–182.
65. Main sources: Pachymeres, books 11–13; Gregoras 7.3–4, 7.6–7; Ramon Muntaner, *Chronicle* 199 ff.; study: Laiou, *Constantinople*, 127–229.
66. Muntaner 200–202; Pachymeres 11.12–14, 11.17, 11.21; numbers: Jacoby, 'Catalan Company.'
67. Pachymeres 11.21–27, 11.31, 12.3; Gregoras 7.3; Muntaner 203–210.
68. Pachymeres 11.28, 12.7–8; Muntaner 210.
69. Muntaner 199, 209, 212.
70. Pachymeres 12.7–25; Gregoras 7.4; Muntaner 210–216, 219. Manuel Philes, *Carmina* II, p. 288 (Miller) with G. Papazoglou, "Ο κώδικας Μετοχίου 351,' *Θεολογία* 40 (1989) 176–186, here 182.
71. Pachymeres 12.32, 13.4, 13.14–15, 13.22; Muntaner 215, 220–221, 228.
72. A. Rubió y Lluch, *Diplomatari de l'Orient català (1301–1409)* (Barcelona 1947) 15 (no. 14); seal: Muntaner 225.
73. Pachymeres 13.12; Manuel Moschopoulos, *Letter* 3 (Levi); Muntaner 222–230.
74. Pachymeres 13.18.
75. Kantakouzenos 2.10 (p. 370); Argenti, *Occupation*, 1:55–56.

76. Pachymeres 12.26, 12.31–32, 13.4; ships: Laiou, *Constantinople*, 165.
77. Manuel Philes, *Carmina* II, p. 50 (Miller); Catalan merchants: Agoritsas, *Κωνσταντινούπολη*, 174.
78. Pachymeres 13.27; Athanasios, *Letters* 67, 73, 93, 106; "bodies": Ioseph Kalothetos, *Life of Patriarch Athanasios* 105, ed. A. Pantokratorinos, 'Βίος καὶ πολιτεία Ἀθανασίου Α',' *Θρακικά* 13 (1940) 56–107, here 101; A. Laiou, 'The Provisioning of Constantinople during the Winter 1306–1307,' *Byzantion* 37 (1967) 91–113.
79. Pachymeres 13.34, 13.38; Thomas Magistros, *Oration for Chandrenos*, in *PG* 145:353–373; Gregoras 7.6; Muntaner 231–233; slaves: Jacoby, 'Catalan Company,' 165; destruction: Laiou-Thomadakis, *Peasant Society*, 241, 261.
80. Pachymeres 13.37 (extracts, p. 723).
81. A. Failler, 'L'occupation de Rhodes par les Hospitaliers,' *REB* 50 (1992) 113–135; cf. Pachymeres 13.33.
82. Metochites, *Semeioseis gnomikai* 39.3 (tr. Hult, mod.).
83. Nicol, *Byzantium*, 226–227.
84. Laiou, *Constantinople*, 261–262, 271–277, 308–311; Nicol, *Byzantium*, 228–245.
85. Marin Sanudo quoted in Laiou, *Constantinople*, 67.
86. V. Laurent, 'La fin du schisme arsénite,' *Bulletin de la section historique de l'Académie Roumaine* 26.2 (1945) 225–313; Gregoras 7.9γ-δ.
87. Gregoras 7.7–8, 7.10.
88. Sources: Ševčenko, 'Decline,' 182.
89. Athanasios, *Letters* 82, 6.
90. S. Lampakis, *Γεώργιος Παχυμέρης* (Athens 2004).
91. C. Constantinides, *Higher Education in Byzantium in the Thirteenth and Early Fourteenth Centuries* (Nicosia 1982); Agoritsas, *Κωνσταντινούπολη*, 82–89.
92. Macrides, 'New Constantine.'
93. Angelov, *Imperial Ideology*, ch. 1 (75: Gregoras; 57: Gabras); N. Gaul, 'Performative Reading in the Late Byzantine Theatron,' in Shawcross and Toth, eds., *Reading*, 215–233.
94. Ragia, 'Confessions,' 42; I. Pérez Martín, *El patriarca Gregorio de Chipre* (Madrid 1996).
95. H. Belting, C. Mango, and D. Mouriki, *The Mosaics and Frescoes of St. Mary Pammakaristos (Fethiye Camii) at Istanbul* (Washington, D.C. 1978) 12; Manuel Philes, *Carmina* II, p. 248 (Miller); war: Bartusis, *Army*, 242; no Church careers: Kyritses, *Byzantine Aristocracy*, 275–277.
96. Choumnos, *Letter* 156, ed. J. Boissonade, *Anecdota Nova* (Paris 1844) 178–179; "money": Gregoras 9.6η; I. Ševčenko, *Études*.
97. Books: D. Bianconi, *Tessalonica nell'età dei Paleologi* (Paris 2005); 'La biblioteca di Cora tra Massimo Planude e Niceforo Gregora,' *Segno e Testo* 3 (2005) 391–438; art: O. Demus, 'The Style of the Kariye Djami,' in Underwood, ed., *Kariye Djami*, 4:107–160.
98. Pontani, 'Scholarship,' 472–508; E. Fryde, *The Early Palaeologan Renaissance* (Leiden 2000).

99. H. Hunger, *Schreiben und Lesen in Byzanz* (Munich 1989) 20.
100. A. Riehle, 'Καὶ σὲ προστάτιν . . . Theodora Raulaina als Stifterin und Patronin,' in L. Theis et al., eds., *Female Founders in Byzantium and Beyond* (Vienna 2014) 299–316.
101. B. Bydén, '"Strangle Them with These Meshes of Syllogisms!": Latin Philosophy in Greek Translations of the Thirteenth Century,' in J. O. Rosenqvist, ed., *Interaction and Isolation in Late Byzantine Culture* (Stockholm 2004) 133–157; A. Kaldellis, 'Translations into Greek in the Byzantine Period,' in D. Gutas, ed., *Why Translate Science? Documents from Antiquity to the 16th Century in the Historical West* (Leiden 2022) 397–444.
102. E. Fisher, 'Planoudes, Holobolos, and the Motivation for Translation,' *GRBS* 43 (2002) 77–104.
103. A. Allard, *Maxime Planude: Le grand calcul selon les Indiens* (Louvain-la-Neuve 1981).
104. B. Bydén, *Theodore Metochites' Stoicheiosis Astronomike* (Güteborg 2003). Chioniades: see the account by Georgios Chrysokokkes in S. Lambros, 'Τὰ ὑπ᾽ ἀριθμὸν 91 καὶ 92 κατάλοιπα,' *Νέος Ἑλληνομνήμων* 15 (1921) 332–339.
105. Gregoras 8.13; *Letter* 40.
106. Angelov, *Imperial Ideology*, passim (e.g., 113, 139 for Andronikos' "philanthropy"); Thomas Magistros and others on mercenaries: ibid., 303; Kyriakides, *Warfare*, 118–135.
107. Laiou, *Constantinople*, 193; Angelov, *Imperial Ideology*, 303–305. Choumnos: J. Boissonade, *Anecdota Graeca* (Paris 1830) 2:137–187.
108. Quotations: Gregoras 7.11; Metochites, *Miscellanea* 28 (p. 193).
109. Kaldellis, *Ethnography*, 160–166, 180–185; idem, *Byzantine Readings*, ch. 6; Hellenes: A. Garzya, 'Byzantium,' in K. Dover, ed., *Perceptions of the Ancient Greeks* (Cambridge, MA 1992) 29–53; in general: Ševčenko, 'Theodore Metochites.'
110. Angelov, *Imperial Ideology*, ch. 11; Boorjama, *Church*.
111. Pachymeres 11.1.
112. *MM* 1:507–508; Smyrlis, 'The State, the Land.'
113. C. Gastgeber, 'Diplomatics of the Patriarchate of Constantinople,' in idem et al., eds., *A Companion to the Patriarchate of Constantinople* (Leiden 2021) 246–285.
114. *AA* 7 (= *Protaton*) nos. 11–12, 243–254.
115. Athanasios, *Letters* 104, 14 (tr. Talbot); also 23, 49, 58, 60, 80; cf. Pachymeres 8.16, 13.23, 13.37; Gregoras 6.5.
116. Athanasios, *Letter* 2.15; Gregoras 7.1δ, 6.7α.
117. Gregoras 8.6ε-ζ; Kantakouzenos 1.18–19 (pp. 88, 93–94); Laiou, *Constantinople*, 265–266; estimates: Bartusis, *Army*, 147–148.
118. R. Nelson, 'Heavenly Allies at the Chora,' *Gesta* 53 (2004) 31–40.
119. Lappas, *Πολιτική ιστορία*, 324–350; Nicol, *Despotate*, 44–82.
120. Andronikos II in *MM* 5:77–87, here 79; events: *RP* 2:94–104 (no. 110).
121. Gregoras 7.13γ; P. Magdalino, 'Between Romaniae: Thessaly and Epirus in the Later Middle Ages,' *Mediterranean Historical Review* 4 (1989) 87–110, here 98.
122. Gregoras 6.8ε.

123. Gregoras 8.6ζ; Kantakouzenos 1.19 (p. 93).
124. Gregoras 8.6ζ.
125. Gregoras 8.1β, 9.2β; Kantakouzenos 1.45 (pp. 220–221).
126. Gregoras 8.4ς, 8.11β; Kantakouzenos 1.4 (p. 23), 1.8 (p. 38), 1.20 (p. 101); Kyritses, *Byzantine Aristocracy*, 338–339.
127. Gregoras 8.7θ; Kantakouzenos 1.24; coins: Hilsdale, *Byzantine Art*, 195, a reading by P. Grierson.
128. Gregoras 8.11–12; Kantakouzenos 1.30–34; funds: 1.28 (pp. 136–137); Anatolia: Estangüi Gómez, *Byzance*, 40–41.
129. Kantakouzenos 1.35–39 (quotation: p. 184); Gregoras 8.12γ.
130. Foss, *Ottoman Empire*, 178, 224.
131. Nicol, *Byzantium*, 247–249.
132. Gregoras 8.14α, 8.15α; Kantakouzenos 1.41–42.
133. Gregoras 8.14β; Kantakouzenos 1.43; Metochites, *Poem* 9; Kyritses, *Byzantine Aristocracy*, 343–345.
134. Ševčenko, *Études*, 165.
135. Gregoras 9.1–6; Kantakouzenos 1.44–59.
136. Gregoras 9.10δ-θ, 9.14–10.2; Metochites, *Poems* 17–20; Ševčenko, 'Theodore Metochites,' 33–37; Kantakouzenos 2.14–18.
137. Gregoras 16.5γ (p. 818).
138. R. Estangüi Gómez, 'Andrinople et Didymotique aux 13e-14e siècles,' in A. Kontogianopoulou, ed., *Πόλεις και εξουσία στο Βυζάντιο κατά την εποχή των Παλαιολόγων* (Athens 2018) 161–203.
139. Kantakouzenos 2.1 (p. 312); Gregoras 10.7α.; lobbying: Michael Gabras, *Letters* 330, 378, 391, 421, etc.
140. E.g., Kantakouzenos 1.48 (p. 238); Smyrlis, 'Wooing,' 660; the preambles written by Gregoras: Angelov, *Imperial Ideology*, 151–160.

Chapter 35. Military Failure and Mystical Refuge (1328–1354)

1. *AA* 19 (= *Iviron* 4) 108 (no. 87), from 1341.
2. Text transcribed in Agoritsas, *Κωνσταντινούπολη*, 506.
3. *Regestum Clementis Papae V* (Rome 1885–1888) 1:40–41 (no. 243).
4. In 1318: G. Thomas and R. Predelli, *Diplomatarium veneto-levantinum* (Venice 1880–1899) 1:111.
5. Laiou, *Constantinople*, 313–314; Chrissis, 'Crusades,' 36–42.
6. Cf. Gregoras 9.8α with Kantakouzenos 2.3 (pp. 326–327).
7. Bartusis, *Army*, 258–266.
8. Gregoras 10.3α, 11.11.
9. Kantakouzenos 2.2 (pp. 322–323).
10. Gregoras 9.9α-δ; Kantakouzenos 2.6–8 (pp. 341–363).
11. Gregoras 9.9ς; Kantakouzenos 2.10–13; Argenti, *Occupation*, 1:59–68.

12. Schreiner, *Byzantinischen Kleinchroniken*, 8.7 (1:80; 2:243–244). Kantakouzenos 2.24 omits the terms.
13. Gregoras 10.4; Kantakouzenos 2.26–27.
14. Kantakouzenos 2.28.
15. Gregoras 10.7; Kantakouzenos 2.25 (misdated); forts: Soulis, *Serbs*, 8.
16. *PLP* 27167.
17. Gregoras 11.1–2; Kantakouzenos 2.29–31; poems, coins, and other sources: Kaldellis and Efthymiades, *Prosopography*, 126–128, 131–133, 164–166; chronology and events: P. Lemerle, *L'émirat d'Aydin* (Paris 1957).
18. Gregoras 11.3α, 11.4a-γ, 11.6; Kantakouzenos 2.32–33 (quotation: p. 504).
19. Gregoras 11.9; Kantakouzenos 2.34–38 (esp. pp. 520–524); Constantinople's ideology also in *RP* 2:96–98 (no. 110); name: Kantakouzenos 3.53 (p. 321); B. Osswald, 'The State of Epirus as Political Laboratory,' in C. Stavrakos, ed., *Epirus Revisited* (Turnhout 2020) 13–36, here 22–23.
20. Gregoras 12.7ε; Apokaukos: C. Malatras, 'The Social Aspects of the Second Civil War,' in Congourdeau, ed., *Thessalonique*, 99–116, here 106–107.
21. Kantakouzenos 3.1 (p. 12).
22. Kantakouzenos 3.30 (p. 185; "Kantakouzenism": pp. 177, 212, 235, 385, 572); letters: Gregoras 12.12ϛ.
23. Estangüi Gómez, *Byzance*, 88–90.
24. Gregoras 12.5α.
25. Kantakouzenos 3.8; Gregoras 12.6ϛ.
26. Kantakouzenos 3.27; Gregoras 12.12β.
27. See the papers in Congourdeau, ed., *Thessalonique*; Kyritses, *Byzantine Aristocracy*, 363–387.
28. Kantakouzenos 3.38 (p. 233); Gregoras 13.10ε.
29. Congourdeau, 'Vivre.'
30. Planoudes, *Letter* 86 (p. 110); Nikephoros Choumos, *Advice to the Thessalonians on Justice*, in J. Boissonade, *Anecdota Graeca* (Paris 1830) 2:147–148; D. Jacoby, 'Foreigners and the Urban Economy in Thessalonike,' *DOP* 57 (2003) 85–132.
31. Philotheos Kokkinos, *Life of Saint Sabas the Younger* 3 (Tsames); P. Katsoni, 'Η κοινωνική διαστρωμάτωση της Θεσσαλονίκης στα χρόνια του κινήματος των Ζηλωτών,' *Μακεδονικά* 43 (2018–2019) 65–90, here 78–81.
32. Kantakouzenos 3.42–43 (quotation: p. 259); Gregoras 13.2–3.
33. Kantakouzenos 3.56; Gregoras 13.4.
34. Gregoras 13.12α; 13.10γ; Kantakouzenos 3.49 (p. 292).
35. Kantakouzenos 3.76 (pp. 475–476); Macrides et al., *Pseudo-Kodinos*, 314.
36. Kantakouzenos 3.66 (pp. 406–407).
37. Gregoras 15.1α; Soulis, *Serbs*, 26.
38. J. Shepard, 'Manners Maketh Romans? Young Barbarians at the Emperor's Court,' in E. Jeffreys, ed., *Byzantine Style, Religion and Civilization* (Cambridge 2006) 145–148; Soulis, *Serbs*, 19, 29–31, and ch. 3 (with reservations); B. Krsmanović and L. Maksimović, 'Byzantium in Serbia: Serbian Authenticity and Byzantine Influence,' in D. Vojvodić and D. Popović, eds., *Sacral Art of the Serbian Lands in the Middle Ages*

(Belgrade 2016) 41–56. Titles: N. Oikonomides, 'Emperor of the Romans,' in *Βυζάντιο και Σερβία κατά τον ΙΔ΄ αιώνα* (Athens 1996) 121–128; but cf. Kantakouzenos 3.89 (p. 552); Gregoras 15.1α ("of the Romans").

39. Gregoras 15.1β.
40. Kantakouzenos 4.18–19 (pp. 120, 127, 131); M. Bartusis, 'The Settlement of Serbs in Macedonia,' in Ahrweiler and Laiou, eds., *Internal Diaspora*, 151–159; properties: Estangüi Gómez, *Byzance*, 91–103; *protos*: idem, 'Séjour,' 64.
41. Nicol, *Byzantium*, 270–271.
42. *AA* 22 (= *Vatopédi* 2) 197–198 (no. 92).
43. E. Boeck, *Imagining the Byzantine Past: The Perception of History in the Illustrated Manuscripts of Skylitzes and Manasses* (Cambridge 2015) 77–85, 245–247; Soulis, *Serbs*, 27–29.
44. Gregoras 14.10; Kantakouzenos 3.87–88; property: ibid 3.36 (p. 225); policies: ibid. 3.85; *pace* K.-P. Matschke, *Fortschritt und Reaktion in Byzanz im 14. Jahrhundert* (Berlin 1971).
45. Kantakouzenos 3.93–94; Kydones, *Letter* 7 (Council massacred); Andreas: Congourdeau, 'Vivre,' 50–53; date: D. Mureşan, 'Pour une nouvelle datation du massacre,' in Congourdeau, ed., *Thessalonique*, 117–132.
46. *PG* 109:639–652.
47. Doukas 8.1–2 is preferable to Kantakouzenos 3.95 and Gregoras 15.5β; A. Bryer, 'Greek Historians on the Turks,' in R. Davis and J. Wallace-Hadrill, eds., *The Writing of History in the Middle Ages* (Oxford 1981) 471–493.
48. C. Heywood, 'The 1337 Bursa Inscription,' *Turcica* 36 (2004) 215–232.
49. Gregoras 28.34–35, 36.30–31; I. Ševčenko, 'Notes on Stephen, The Novgorodian Pilgrim,' *Süd-ost Forschungen* 12 (1953) 165–175.
50. Alexios Makrembolites in S. Kourouses, 'Αἱ ἀντιλήψεις περὶ τῶν ἐσχάτων τοῦ κόσμου,' *ΕΕΒΣ* 37 (1969–1970) 211–250, here 235–240.
51. Text: A. Rigo, 'Il *Rapporto dei metropoliti ad Anna Paleologa*,' *Byzantion 85* (2015) 285–339.
52. Gregoras 15.7–9, 18.4 (p. 887); Kantakouzenos 3.98–99; Philotheos Kokkinos, *Life of Gregorios Palamas* 78; sources for the Synod: Melichar, *Empresses*, 195.
53. Kantakouzenos 3.100–4.1, 4.4; Gregoras 15.8, 15.11.
54. Gregoras 15.12ζ; e.g., Congourdeau, 'Vivre,' 44–47 for Nikolaos Kabasilas.
55. G. Cammelli, 'Demetrii Cydonii ad Ioannem Cantacuzenum imperatorem oratio altera,' *Byzantinisch-neugriechische Jahrbücher* 2 (1923) 77–83.
56. Kantakouzenos 4.5 (p. 33); Barker, *Manuel*, 443–445; Nicol, *Byzantium*, 259–260.
57. Gregoras 15.12γ-ς.
58. M. Trizio, 'Byzantine Philosophy as a Contemporary Historiographical Project,' *Recherches de théologie et philosophie médiévales* 74.1 (2007) 247–294.
59. N. Russell, *Gregory Palamas and the Making of Palamism in the Modern Age* (Oxford 2019).
60. Gregoras, *Florentios*, pp. 65, 71–72 (Leone); Moschos, *Πλατωνισμὸς*, 35–36.
61. M. Trizio, '"Una è la verità che pervade ogni cosa": La sapienza profana nelle opere perdute di Barlaam Calabro,' in A. Rigo, ed., *Byzantine Theology and its Philosophical*

Background (Turnhout 2011) 108–140; Gregoras 10.8, with Moschos, *Πλατωνισμὸς*, 38–40.

62. Palamas, *Two Apodeictic Treatises on the Procession of the Holy Spirit*, and his *Letters* to Akindynos and Barlaam.
63. Barlaam, *Letters* 3, 5. Practical guides to meditative prayer: Nikephoros of Mt. Athos, *On Vigilance and Guarding the Heart*, in *PG* 147:945–966; Anonymous, *Method of Sacred Prayer*, ed. I. Hausherr, 'La méthode d'oraison hésychaste,' *Orientalia christiana* 36 (1927) 101–209; and the works of Gregorios of Sinai.
64. Palamas, *Triads* 3.1.36; see 1.3.39, 2.3.28, 2.3.32 (St. Basil).
65. Philotheos Kokkinos, *Life of Gregorios Palamas* 45; Akindynos, *Letters* 8, 10.
66. *RP* 2:205–256 (no. 132.3–6); Gregoras 11.10.
67. Kalekas, *Patriarchal Logos*, in *PG* 150:892–894; Palamites: G. Weiss, *Johannes Kantakuzenos* (Wisebaden 1969) 113–122.
68. *RP* 2:346–382 (no. 147).
69. 1351: *Tomos* in *PG* 151:717–764; Kantakouzenos 4.23–24; Gregoras books 18–21; Moschos, *Πλατωνισμός*.
70. Kydones, *Letters* 50, 88.
71. Ioannes Kyparissiotes, *On the Crimes of the Palamites* 10, in *PG* 152:733–736.
72. Estimates: A. Bresson, 'Review of Kyle Harper,' *JRS* 110 (2020) 233–246, here 239. Spread: N. Varlik, *Plague and Empire in the Early Modern Mediterranean World* (Cambridge 2015) 97–107; waves: ibid. 118–126.
73. Kantakouzenos 4.8; Kydones, *Letter* 88; Gregoras 16.1ε.
74. A. Laiou, 'The Agrarian Economy, Thirteenth-Fifteenth Cenuries,' in *EHB*, 315–317, 365–366; J. Lefort, 'Population et peuplement en Macédoine orientale,' in V. Kravari et al., eds., *Hommes et richesses dans l'Empire byzantin* (Paris 1991) 2:63–82, here 79–81.
75. P. Armstrong, 'The Survey Area in the Byzantine and Ottoman Periods,' in W. Cavanagh et al., eds., *The Laconia Survey: Continuity and Change in a Greek Rural Landscape* (London 2002) 339–402; A. Izdebski et al., 'Exploring Byzantine and Ottoman Economic History with the Use of Palynological Data,' *JöB* 65 (2015) 67–110, here 89.
76. S. Pamuk, 'The Black Death and the Origins of the "Great Divergence" across Europe,' *European Review of Economic History* 11 (2007) 289–317, here 300–301.
77. K. Smyrlis, '"Our Lord and Father": Peasants and Monks in Mid-Fourteenth-Century Macedonia,' *TM* 16 (2010) 779–791.
78. Gregoras 9.8δ.
79. Kantakouzenos 4.41 (p. 303: Latin), 4.10 (pp. 65–66).
80. Kantakouzenos 4.5 (p. 37), 4.9 (pp. 53–54), 4.17 (pp. 116–117).
81. Kantakouzenos 4.22; Gregoras 28.36; R. Radić and D. Korać, 'Enemy at the Gates: An Alliance Ridiculed,' in P. Armstrong, ed., *Ritual and Art: Byzantine Essays for Christopher Walter* (London 2006) 236–245.
82. Estangüi Gómez, *Byzance*, 151.
83. Kantakouzenos 4.5–6.
84. Nicol, *Byzantium*, 268–271.

85. Gregoras 15.6α-γ, 17.1β (revenues); Kantakouzenos 3.95 (pp. 583–584); Argenti, *Occupation*, ch. 3.
86. Alexios Makrembolites, *Historical Account*, ed. Papadopoulos-Kerameus, *Ἀνάλεκτα*, 1:144–159, here 153; Kantakouzenos 4.11–12; Gregoras 17.1–7.
87. Nicol, *Byzantium*, 271–277; Argenti, *Occupation*, ch. 4.
88. Kantakouzenos 4.15–17 (quotation: p. 108); chronology: Estangüi Gómez, 'Séjour'; Palamas, *Homily* 1.
89. Estangüi Gómez, 'Séjour,' 87–88.
90. Kantakouzenos 4.5 (p. 33).
91. J. Barker, 'The Problem of Appanages in Byzantium,' *Βυζαντινά* 3 (1971) 103–122.
92. Kantakouzenos 3.53.
93. Kantakouzenos 4.28; Gregoras 27.27–29; Anna in Thessalonike: Melichar, *Empresses*, 198–206.
94. Kantakouzenos 4.7–8 (pp. 47–49); Gregoras 16.2–3.
95. Kantakouzenos 4.33–34; Gregoras 28.2–7.
96. Kantakouzenos 4.35–38 (quotation: pp. 280–281); Gregoras 28.18–19.
97. Kantakouzenos 4.38; Gregoras 28.67–29.4.
98. Gregoras 29.27.
99. Kantakouzenos 4.39–42; Gregoras 29.27–30.
100. S. Mergiali-Sahas, 'Οι Βυζαντινοί ως εμπορεύσιμο αγαθό στο δουλεμπόριο της Μεσογείου,' in V. Leontaritou et al., eds., *Αντικήνσωρ: Τιμητικός τόμος Σπύρου Ν. Τρωιάνου* (Athens 2013) 2:971–996, with bibliography, esp. E. Zachariadiou, *Trade and Crusade: Venetian Crete and the Emirates* (Venice 1983).
101. Kantakouzenos 1.35 (p. 171); 1.39 (p. 190).
102. Kydones, *Advice to the Romans*, in *PG* 154:981C.
103. Manuel II, *Letter* 3; Kydones, *Letters* 258, 276, 259.
104. Kaldellis, *Ethnography*, 148–156.

Chapter 36. The Noose Tightens (1354–1402)

1. M. Angold, 'Byzantium in Exile,' in D. Abulafia, ed., *The New Cambridge Medieval History*, v. 5 (Cambridge 1999) 543–568, here 547.
2. Stephanos Sgouropoulos, *Poem Praising Alexios III*, ed. Papadopoulos-Kerameus, *Ἀνάλεκτα*, 1:435–436.
3. Bessarion, *Encomium of Trebizond* 41, 45 (tr. Kennedy); Karpov, *Ιστορία*, 150–178.
4. Chalkokondyles 9.27; list in Savvides, *Ιστορία*, 213–219.
5. E.g., Karpov, *Ιστορία*, 145, 188, 210, and 196 for A. Bryer; Savvides, *Ιστορία*, 91.
6. Panaretos, *On the Emperors of Trebizond* 43–56.
7. R. Shukurov, 'Between Peace and Hostility: Trebizond and the Pontic Turkish Periphery,' *Mediterranean Historical Review* 9 (1994) 20–72.
8. L. Perria, 'Due documenti greci del XIV secolo,' *JöB* 30 (1981) 259–297; debts: P. Katsoni, *Μια επταετία κρίσιμων γεγονότων: Το Βυζάντιο στα έτη 1366–1373* (Thessalonike 2002) 73.

9. Agoritsas, *Κωνσταντινούπολη*, 300, 309; Kyritses, *Byzantine Aristocracy*, 206–208.
10. K.-P. Matschke, 'The Late Byzantine Urban Economy,' in *EHB*, 481–486.
11. Agoritsas, *Κωνσταντινούπολη*, 488 n. 377.
12. C. Morrisson, 'Byzantine Money,' in *EHB*, 933–934, 961–962.
13. Plethon, *Memorandum to Manuel Palaiologos*, in *ΠΠ* 3:262.
14. Kantakouzenos 4.40 (pp. 295–296).
15. Makrembolites, *Dialogue between the Rich and Poor*, p. 213; Ševčenko, 'Decline.'
16. A. Kaldellis, *A New Herodotos: Laonikos Chalkokondyles* (Washington, D.C. 2014) 214–215 n. 16; Ševčenko, 'Decline,' 173.
17. Kantakouzenos 2.6 (pp. 344–345), 3.40 (p. 244), 3.41 (p. 251); Manuel II, *Speech of Advice to the Thessalonians*, p. 297.
18. Kydones, *Letter* 8.
19. N. Trahoulias, 'The Venice Alexander Romance,' in R. Macrides, ed., *History As Literature in Byzantium* (Aldershot, UK 2010) 145–165.
20. Kantakouzenos 3.7 (p. 53), 1.40 (p. 196).
21. Angelov, *Imperial Ideology*, 104–105.
22. *MM* 2:190–192.
23. Argenti, *Occupation*, 2:173–177.
24. Nicol, *Byzantium*, 296.
25. Kaldellis and Efthymiades, *Prosopography*, 138–140; C. Wright, *The Gattilusio Lordships and the Aegean World* (Leiden 2014) esp. ch. 5; population: Preiser-Kapeller and Mitsiou, 'Hierarchies,' 266.
26. Kantakouzenos 4.43 (p. 315).
27. Greek and Latin texts in A. Theiner and F. Miklosich, *Monumenta spectantia ad unionem ecclesiarum* (Vienna 1872) 29–37.
28. Well put by Chrissis, 'Crusades,' 54.
29. Nerantzi-Varmazi, *Βυζάντιο*, 26–27, 57.
30. Kydones, *Letter* 107; in general, see his *Apologia* I; J. Ryder, *The Career and Writings of Demetrius Kydones* (Leiden 2010).
31. Kydones, *Letter* 93; east Roman Catholics: Gill, *Byzantium*, 221.
32. Kydones, *Speech of Advice to the Romans*, in *PG* 154:968A, 997B-C; in the 1370s: *Speech of Advice regarding Gallipoli*, in *PG* 154:1012D.
33. V. Nerantzi-Varmazi, 'Η μετανάστευση από την Κωνσταντινούπολη το β′ μισό του 14ου αιώνα,' *Βυζαντιακά* 1 (1981) 89–97.
34. Kydones, *Speech of Advice to the Romans*, in *PG* 154:1002A.
35. Nerantzi-Varmazi, *Βυζάντιο*, 61–107. Ioannes' account in Z. von Lingenthal, 'Prooemien zu Chrysobullen,' *Sitzungsberichte der königlich preussischen Akademie der Wissenschaften* (1888) 1409–1422, here 1419.
36. Philotheos Kokkinos in *MM* 1:453–454.
37. Kydones, *Speech of Advice to the Romans*, in *PG* 154:977–980.
38. Nerantzi-Varmazi, *Βυζάντιο*, 109–126.
39. J. Meyendorff, 'Projets de concile oecuménique en 1367,' *DOP* 14 (1960) 149–177; Paulus, *Letter to the Pope*, in *PG* 154:836–837.

40. *MM* 1:491–493: populace: Schreiner, *Byzantinischen Kleinchroniken*, 9.22 (1:94); Tautu, *Acta Urbani*, 201–215 (nos. 124–132a).
41. *Synodal Tomos against Prochoros Kydones*, in *PG* 151:693–716, and A. Rigo, 'Il Monte Athos e la controversia palamitica,' in idem, ed., *Gregorio Palamas e oltre* (Florence 2004) 1–117. Kydones: Mercati, *Notizie*, 293–338.
42. Gill, *Byzantium*, 219–220; profession: Tautu, *Acta Urbani*, no. 167; "Roman": ibid. no. 181; "Greeks": ibid. no. 184; "muzzle": Manuel II, *Discourse to Iagoup*, quoted from an unpublished edition by Çelik, *Manuel*, 55 n. 3.
43. Kydones, *Letter* 71.
44. Ioannes in Tinnefeld, 'Prooimien,' 181.
45. Katsoni, *Επταετία*, 68–81, 101–102.
46. Ioannes V in Tinnefeld, 'Prooimien,' 178–183; chronology: Estangüi Gómez, *Byzance*, 202–230.
47. *AA* 23 (= *Vatopédi* 3) no. 199; Smyrlis, 'The State, the Land,' 69–71.
48. I. Ševčenko, 'Nicolas Cabasilas' "Anti-Zealot" Discourse,' *DOP* 1957 11 (1957) 79–171.
49. Siniossoglou, *Radical Platonism*, 359–369.
50. Kydones, *Letters* 222, 442.
51. D. Obolensky, *The Byzantine Inheritance of Eastern Europe* (London 1982) XVII.
52. Oikonomides, *Society*, XX; E. Zachariadou, 'Holy War in the Aegean,' *Mediterranean Historical Review* 4 (1989) 212–225.
53. Palamas, *Letter to His Church from Captivity* 8.
54. Shukurov, *Byzantine Turks*.
55. Meletios, *Against the Italians* 228–231, in Laurent and Darrouzes, *Dossier*, 562.
56. E.g., the apocryphal, late thirteenth-century *Dialogue between the Patriarch Michael III and Emperor Manuel I*, in Laurent and Darrouzes, *Dossier*, 367; Metochites and others in Zachariadou, 'Mosque'; Ioseph Bryennios in Ševčenko, 'Decline,' 180.
57. M. Balivet, *Byzantins et Ottomans* (Istanbul 1999) 31–47.
58. Smyrlis, 'Occupation'; Necipoğlu, *Byzantium*, 92; collaboration: Siniossoglou, *Radical Platonism*, 115, 342–343.
59. Manuel II, *Funeral Oration for Theodoros Palaiologos*, p. 129.
60. S. Vryonis, 'Nomidization and Islamisation in Asia Minor,' *DOP* 29 (1975) 41–71, here 59.
61. Laiou, *Constantinople*, 247–248; Preiser-Kapeller and Mitsiou, 'Hierarchies,' 251, 265; Vryonis, *Hellenism*, ch. 4; and J. Pahlitzsch, 'The Greek Orthodox Communities of Nicaea and Ephesus under Turkish Rule,' in A. Peacock et al., eds., *Islam and Christianity in Medieval Anatolia* (Farnham, UK 2015) 147–164.
62. *RP* 2:132–137 (no. 116).
63. Kantakouzenos 3.95 (p. 589).
64. B. Kitapçı Bayrı, *Warriors, Martyrs, and Dervishes* (Leiden 2020) 96–157.
65. P. Fodor, 'Ottoman Warfare, 1300–1453,' in K. Fleet, ed., *The Cambridge History of Turkey*, v. 1 (Cambridge 2009) 192–226.
66. C. Kafadar, *Between Two Worlds: The Construction of the Ottoman State* (Berkeley 1995); H. Lowry, *The Nature of the Early Ottoman State* (New York 2003).

67. N. Malcolm, *Agents of Empire: Knights, Corsairs, Jesuits and Spies in the Sixteenth-Century Mediterranean World* (London 2015) 224–229, 267–270, 356–357.
68. Katsoni, *Επταετία*, 91–166; date: Schreiner, *Byzantinischen Kleinchroniken*, 9.24 (1:95).
69. Katsoni, *Ανδρόνικος*, 64 n. 3.
70. Chalkokondyles 2.4; cf. Doukas 12.2–4. The story that Andronikos colluded with a son of Murad is not credible.
71. Kydones, *Letters* 193–194; Katsoni, *Επταετία*, 156–158. Chalkokondyles' account conflates this visit and later events. Gallipoli: Kydones, *Speech of Advice regarding Gallipoli*, in *PG* 154:1009–1036.
72. Nicol, *Byzantium*, 308–313.
73. Katsoni, *Ανδρόνικος*, 92–106.
74. Kydones, *Letter* 167; Chrysostomides, *Byzantium*, II:148–159.
75. Kydones, *Letter* 167; Schreiner, *Byzantinischen Kleinchroniken*, 9.34 (1:96); Chalkokondyles 2.5.
76. C. Wright, 'Constantinople and the Coup d'État in Palaiologan Byzantium,' *DOP* 70 (2016) 271–292.
77. *MM* 2:25–27; Doukas 12.4, 14.2. Genoese ratification: L. Belgrano, 'Prima serie di documenti riguardanti la colonia di Pera,' *Atti della Società Ligure di Storia Patria* 13 (1877) 133–140.
78. Katsoni, *Ανδρόνικος*, part II.
79. Theodoros Potamios, *Letter* 12 to Kydones.
80. Chalkokondyles 2.6; cf. Kydones, *Letter* 224.
81. Kydones, *Letters* 218–220.
82. Kydones, *Letter* 70. Lands: Estangüi Gómez, *Byzance*, 111.
83. Katsoni, *Ανδρόνικος*, 144–147, 195–196; in general: Laiou, *Gender*, VII-VIII; K.-P. Matschke, 'Commerce, Trade, Markets, and Money,' in *EHB*, 771–806; Estangüi Gómez, *Byzance*, 196–201.
84. J. Harris, 'Constantinople as City-State,' in idem et al., eds., *Byzantines, Latins, and Turks in the Eastern Mediterranean World* (Oxford 2012) 119–140, here 129.
85. Nikolaos Kabasilas, *On Interest*, in *PG* 151:728–750; M.-H. Congourdaeau, 'Nicolas Cabasilas et son discours sur les intérêts,' in C. Gastgeber et al., eds., *Pour l'amour de Byzance: Hommage à Paolo Odorico* (Frankfurt 2013) 73–88.
86. Kydones, *Letter* 264.80; G. Dennis, *The Reign of Manuel II Palaeologus in Thessalonica* (Rome 1960); Çelik, *Manuel*, ch. 3.
87. Kydones, *Letter* 299; divisions: Necipoğlu, *Byzantium*, part II.
88. Isidoros Glabas, *Homily 1 for Saint Demetrios*, p. 31; Kydones, *Letter* 324.
89. Manuel II, *Letter* 4; *Speech of Advice to the Thessalonians*.
90. Makarios Makres, *Encomium of Archbishop Gabriel of Thessalonike* 25; Necipoğlu, *Byzantium*, 77–78, 84–102; Smyrlis, 'Occupation'; Estangüi Gómez, *Byzance*, 290–313.
91. Isidoros Glabas, *Homily* 4.1 (*On the Abduction of Children*); Doukas 23.2, 23.9.
92. Çelik, *Manuel*, 111–118.
93. Schreiner, *Byzantinischen Kleinchroniken*, 7.21 (1:68); Manuel II, *Dialogue on Marriage* 709–719 (pp. 98–100).

94. Barker, *Manuel*, 57–79; agreement: Katsoni, *Ανδρόνικος*, 222–223.
95. Kydones, *Letter* 442 (p. 407).
96. Necipoğlu, *Byzantium*, 129 n. 39.
97. Doukas 13.4; Ignatius of Smolensk, *Journey to Constantinople*, pp. 102–105 (Majeska); Barker, *Manuel*, 467–468.
98. Necipoğlu, *Byzantium*, 138–139.
99. Manuel II, *Letters* 16, 19; Kydones, *Letter* 432.
100. Çelik, *Manuel*, 130–157; Hilsdale, *Byzantine Art*, 214–218.
101. Manuel II, *Letters* 14, 19.
102. Majeska, *Russian Travelers*, 104–113 (Ignatius of Smolensk), 416–436 (commentary).
103. S. Reinert, 'Political Dimensions of Manuel II Palaiologos' 1392 Marriage and Coronation,' in C. Sode and C. Takàks, eds., *Novum Millennium* (Aldershot, UK 2001) 291–304; divided loyalties: *MM* 2:151; Kydones, *Letter* 432; Doukas 14.3.
104. Manuel II, *Funeral Oration for Theodoros Palaiologos*, pp. 132–157; Chalkokondyles 2.13, 2.25–27; Doukas 13.6.
105. Kydones, *Speech of Advice regarding Gallipoli*, in *PG* 154:1024A-B, 1028A-D.
106. Gautier, 'Récit inédit,' 108; *Anonymous Bulgarian Chronicle* 20, in I. Bogdan, 'Ein Beitrag zur bulgarischen und serbischen Geschichtsscheibung,' *Archiv für slavische Philologie* 13 (1891) 481–543, here 526–543.
107. Estangüi Gómez, *Byzance*, 149–166.
108. Doukas 13.5, 15.1; Kydones, *Letter* 442.
109. Gautier, 'Récit inédit,' 106; K.-P. Matschke, *Die Schlacht bei Ankara und das Schicksal von Byzanz* (Weimar 1981) 77–78. Siege: Hatzopoulos, *Πρώτη πολιορκία*.
110. Manuel Kalekas, *Letter* 48, to Manuel Chrysoloras in Florence.
111. Necipoğlu, *Byzantium*, ch. 7; Hatzopoulos, *Πρώτη πολιορκία*, 225–240; A.-M. Talbot, 'Agricultural Properties in Palaiologan Constantinople,' in A. Berger et al., eds., *Koinotaton Doron: Das späte Byzanz* (Berlin 2016) 185–195.
112. Manuel II, *Letter* 31 (tr. Dennis).
113. Barker, *Manuel*, 146–147.
114. E.g., in Manuel II, *Letters* 30, 62; Gautier, 'Récit inédit,' 106; Chalkokondyles 2.27.
115. Isidoros of Kiev, *Panegyric for Manuel II and Ioannes VIII*, in *ΠΠ* 3:161.
116. *MM* 2:359-361; Chrissis, 'Crusades,' 60; Hatzopoulos, *Πρώτη πολιορκία*, 138–141.
117. D. Lalande, *Livre des fais du bon messire Jehan Le Maingre, dit Bouciquaut* (Geneva 1985) 1.30–34 (pp. 132–152); Clavijo, *Embassy to Tamerlane* 2 (tr. Le Strange, pp. 51–52).
118. Manuel II, *Dialogue on Marriage* 698–699 (p. 98).
119. Doukas 14.3–4; Necipoğlu, *Byzantium*, 133–135.
120. Doukas 14.1, 14.4; Matthaios in *MM* 2:463–467.
121. Schreiner, *Byzantinischen Kleinchroniken*, 22.28 (1:184); Gautier, 'Récit inédit,' 110; Clavijo, *Embassy to Tamerlane* 2 (tr. Le Strange, p. 52).
122. P. Gautier, 'Action de grâces de Démétrius Chrysoloras,' *REB* 19 (1961) 340–357.
123. C. Given-Wilson, *The Chronicle of Adam of Usk* (Oxford 1997) 121 (mod.). Manuel's travels: Barker, *Manuel*, 165–199.
124. Hilsdale, *Byzantine Art*, 223; Çelik, *Manuel*, ch. 7; e.g., Sphrantzes 11.2.

125. Doukas 14.5; Isidoros of Kiev, *Panegyric for Manuel II and Ioannes VIII*, in *ΠΠ* 3:162.
126. Manuel Chrysoloras, *Comparison of Old and New Rome* 58; Hilsdale, *Byzantine Art*, 228–230.
127. Manuel II, *Letter* 19; Leonte, *Imperial Visions*.
128. Manuel Chrysoloras, *Discourse to Manuel II* 18–19.
129. J. Shepard, 'Imperial Constantinople: Relics, Palaiologan Emperors, and the Resilience of the Exemplary Center,' in Harris et al., eds., *Byzantines*, 61–92.
130. Hilsdale, *Byzantine Art*, ch. 4–5.
131. Çelik, *Manuel*, 180–186, 240.
132. Kaldellis, *New Herodotos*, 225–226.
133. Kydones, *Apology I*, in Mercati, *Notizie*, 372.
134. Ioseph Bryennios, *Letter* 10, in E. Boulgaris, ed., *Ἰωσὴφ μοναχοῦ τοῦ Βρυεννίου τὰ εὑρεθέντα* (Leipzig 1784) 3:148–155.
135. Manuel II, *Dialogue on Marriage* 662 (p. 96).

Chapter 37. The Cusp of a New World (1402–1461)

1. G. Dennis, *Byzantium and the Franks* (London 1982) VI; Doukas 18.2; Asian side: Shukurov, *Byzantine Turks*, 147–156; succession wars: Kastritsis, *Sons of Bayezid*.
2. Doukas 18.2; *AA* 23 (= *Vatopédi* 3) no. 191; Clavijo, *Embassy to Tamerlane* 4 (tr. Le Strange, p. 87); cf. the *pyxis* in Hilsdale, *Byzantine Art*, 210–213. Ioannes in Thessalonike: Estangüi Gómez, *Byzance*, 323–332, 347–352; "blood": *AA* 23 (= *Vatopédi* 3) no. 197.
3. Manuel II, *Letter* 55.
4. S. Bendall and P. Donald, *The Later Palaeologan Coinage* (London 1979).
5. Chrysostomides, *Byzantium*, III:308–310; Laiou, *Gender*, VII:216.
6. Kastritsis, *Sons of Bayezid*, 135–149.
7. Kastritsis, *Sons of Bayezid*, 168–171.
8. Doukas 19.10–12, 20.1; Chalkokondyles 4.12–18.
9. Estangüi Gómez, *Byzance*, 373–384.
10. Manuel II, *Letter* 68; Mazaris, *Journey to Hell*, pp. 82–84; Necipoğlu, *Byzantium*, 259–262.
11. D. Zakythinos, *Le despotat grec de Morée*, 2 vols. (Athens 1932–1953) is outdated but still standard; 1:94–118 for Manuel.
12. Manuel II, *Funeral Oration for Theodoros Palaiologos*, p. 123; Necipoğlu, *Byzantium*, ch. 9.
13. R.-J. Loenertz, 'Res gestae Theodori Ioann. F. Paleologi,' *EEBΣ* 25 (1955) 206–210; Evrenos: Schreiner, *Byzantinischen Kleinchroniken*, 33.14 (1:244); civil war: Kydones, *Letters* 293, 313; and the letter in Chrysostomides, *Monumenta*, 58 (no. 27).

14. Chrysostomides, *Monumenta*, 99–105 (nos. 46–47).
15. Manuel II, *Funeral Oration for Theodoros Palaiologos*, pp. 127–135; Chalkokondyles 2.25; Necipoğlu, *Byzantium*, 240–242.
16. Necipoğlu, *Byzantium*, 257; Chrysostomides, *Byzantium*, IV ("key": 95); A. Luttrell, 'Juan Fernandez de Heredia's History of Greece,' *BMGS* 34 (2010) 30–37.
17. Chrysostomides, *Monumenta*, 415–416 (no. 213); Manuel II, *Funeral Oration for Theodoros Palaiologos*, pp. 175–211, esp. 185 for opposition; Chalkokondyles 2.45.
18. Chrysostomides, *Byzantium*, IV:100; Manuel II, *Funeral Oration for Theodoros Palaiologos*, pp. 208–211 (n. 130–131); documents: Chrysostomides, *Monumenta*, 515–532 (nos. 269–279).
19. Estangüi Gómez, *Byzance*, 320–322.
20. Mazaris, *Journey to Hell*, p. 82; Chalkokondyles 4.19; Necipoğlu, *Byzantium*, 259–262; T. Gregory, *Isthmia V: The Hexamilion and the Fortress* (Princeton 1993); "beast": Manuel II, *Letter* 68 (p. 217).
21. Necipoğlu, *Byzantium*, 262–267.
22. Manuel II, *Funeral Oration for Theodoros Palaiologos*, pp. 131, 161.
23. Kydones, *Letter* 342; D. Jacoby, 'Rural Exploitation and Market Economy,' in Gerstel, ed. *Viewing the Morea*, 212–275, esp. 274.
24. Mazaris, *Journey to Hell*, p. 8.
25. Kyriakidis, *Warfare*, 106; Bartusis, *Army*, 265–266.
26. B. Osswald, 'The Ethnic Composition of Medieval Epirus,' in S. Ellis and L. Klusáková, eds., *Imaging Frontiers, Contesting Identities* (Pisa 2007) 125–154, here 133–139.
27. T. Papamastorakis, 'Myzithras of the Byzantines / Mistra to Byzantinists,' in Kiousopoulou, ed., *Βυζαντινές πόλεις*, 277–296; and many of the papers in Gerstel, ed., *Viewing the Morea*, esp. by Papamastorakis.
28. Siniossoglou, *Radical Platonism*, 277.
29. *AA* 23 (= *Vatopédi* 3) no. 204; Bartusis, *Land*, 575–578.
30. Shawcross, 'New Lykourgos.' Siniossoglou, *Radical Platonism*, ch. 7.
31. Chrysobull of Ioannes VIII in *ΠΠ* 3:331.
32. Doukas 22.3–27.7; Chalkokondyles 4.44–45, 4.61–5.9; Sphrantzes 7.1–9.4; Barker, *Manuel*, 340–344. Asia: Shukurov, *Byzantine Turks*, 147–156.
33. Ioannes Kananos, *On the Siege of Constantinople*; Chalkokondyles 5.10–20; Doukas 28; Sphrantzes 10–11.
34. Necipoğlu, *Byzantium*, 44, 53, 59–83.
35. Necipoğlu, *Byzantium*, 102–112; merchants: D. Jacoby, 'Foreigners and the Urban Economy in Thessalonike,' *DOP* 57 (2003) 85–132, here 110–112.
36. Antonio Morosini in J. Melville-Jones, *Venice and Thessalonica, 1423–1430: The Venetian Documents* (Padua 2002) 220.
37. Barker, *Manuel*, 371–381; treaty: Sphrantzes 12.4; Doukas 29.1; conversion rates: T. Bertelé and C. Morrisson, *Numismatique byzantine* (Wetteren, Belgium 1978) 89–90. Bertrandon de la Broquière, *The Voyage d'Outremer*, p. 104 (tr. Kline), puts the tribute at 10,000 ducats, which is about right.

38. V. Rose, *Die Handschriften-Verzeichnisse der königlichen Bibliothek zu Berlin* (Berlin 1905) 13.2.3:1344.
39. N. Melvani, 'The Tombs of the Palaiologan Emperors,' *BMGS* 42 (2018) 237–260, here 248–250.
40. Ševčenko, 'Decline,' 173 n. 23.
41. Clavijo (in 1403), *Embassy to Tamerlane* (tr. Le Strange); Johann Schiltberger (in the 1420s), *The Bondage and Travels of Johann Schiltberger* (tr. Telfer); Bertrandon de la Broquière (in 1432), *The Voyage d'Outremer*, pp. 96–106 (tr. Kline); Pero Tafur (in 1438), *Travels and Adventures*, pp. 117, 138–148 (tr. Letts); also Majeska, *Russian Travelers*. Diodoros: Konstantinos Laskaris, *De scriptoribus Graecis Patria Siculis*, in *PG* 161:917–918.
42. H. Lamers, 'Hellenism and Cultural Unease in Italian Humanism: The Case of Francesco Filelfo,' in J. De Keyser, ed., *Francesco Filelfo, Man of Letters* (Leiden 2019) 22–42, here 40.
43. Doukas 20.4; Sphrantzes 3.
44. Makarios Makres, *Orations Addressed to Those Scandalized by the Success of the Impious*.
45. Shukurov, *Byzantine Turks*, 359–380.
46. Bertrandon de la Broquière, *The Voyage d'Outremer*, p. 101 (tr. Kline).
47. Sphrantzes 25.6; Necipoğlu, *Byzantium*, 141.
48. Philippides, *Constantine XI*, 106–139; grants: Necipoğlu, *Byzantium*, 269–270.
49. Gill, *Council*, ch. 2–3.
50. Sphrantzes 23.5–7.
51. Syropoulos 6.19.
52. D. Angelov, 'The Donation of Constantine,' in idem, ed., *Church and Society in Late Byzantium* (Kalamazoo, MI 2009) 91–157.
53. V. Laurent, 'Les droits de l'empereur en matière ecclésiastique: L'accord de 1380/82,' *REB* 13 (1955) 5–20.
54. Çelik, *Manuel*, 300–306; Leonte, *Imperial Visions*, 27–31, 48–54.
55. Kydones, *Apology I*, in Mercati, *Notizie*, 373.
56. Syropoulos 3.23.
57. Syropoulos 4.33.
58. C. Caselli, 'Interpreter, Diplomat, Humanist: Nicholas Sagundinus as a Cultural Broker,' in Slootjes and Verhoeven, eds., *Byzantium*, 226–244.
59. A refrain in Syropoulos, e.g., *Memoirs* 2.19.
60. Gill, *Council*, 227–229.
61. *ΠΠ* 3:345–352.
62. Syropoulos 4.25.
63. Gill, *Council*, 163–164; R. Nelson, 'The Italian Appreciation and Appropriation of Illuminated Byzantine Manuscripts,' *DOP* 39 (1995) 209–237.
64. J. Gill, *Quae supersunt actorum Graecorum concilii Florentini Pars I* (Rome 1953) 106.
65. Ioannes Chortasmenos, *Letter* 44; Bruni: Kaldellis, *New Herodotos*, 92–93.
66. Syropoulos 11.9.

67. G. Demacopoulos, 'The Popular Reception of the Council of Florence in Constantinople,' *St. Vladimir's Theological Quarterly* 43 (1999) 37–53.
68. E. Boeck, *The Bronze Horseman of Justinian in Constantinople* (Cambridge 2021) 402–405.
69. Syropoulos 9.10.
70. Markos Eugenikos, *Letter* 4, in *ΠΠ* 1:25; *Encyclical Letter against the Graikolatinoi*; cf. patriarch Gregorios III, *Response to the Letter of Markos Eugenikos*, in *PG* 160:116.
71. Ioannes Eugenikos, *Letter* 21 to Syropoulos, in *ΠΠ* 1:191.
72. Ioannes Eugenikos, *Oration to the Basileus Konstantinos Palaiologos*, in *ΠΠ* 1:125.
73. Philippides, *Constantine XI*, 171–177.
74. E.g., Ioseph Bryennios in Leonte, *Imperial Visions*, 42.
75. E.g., Bertrandon de la Broquière, *The Voyage d'Outremer*, p. 95 (tr. Kline).
76. Georgios Scholarios, *Funeral Oration for Theodoros II Palaiologos*, in *ΠΠ* 2:6–8; Chalkokondyles 7.17–28; Philippides, *Constantine XI*, 177–190.
77. Bessarion, *Letter to Konstantinos Palaiologos*, in *ΠΠ* 4:34–35.
78. Sphrantzes 28.7–29.7.
79. Philippides, *Constantine XI*, 221–222.
80. Philippides, *Constantine XI*, 240–249.
81. Ioannes Eugenikos, *Consolatory Address to Konstantinos Palaiologos*, in *ΠΠ* 1:125–129.
82. M.-H. Blanchet, *Georges-Gennadios Scholarios* (Paris 2008). Arguments that Scholarios never supported the Union of Florence have to argue that a number of texts are forgeries. While not impossible, this is apologetic.
83. J. Harris, 'The Patriarch of Constantinople and the Last Days of Byzantium,' in C. Gastgeber et al., eds., *The Patriarchate of Constantinople in Context and Comparison* (Vienna 2017) 9–16.
84. Syropoulos 4.46.
85. Doukas 34.5–8; Chalkokondyles 8.1–3; Kritoboulos 1.6–11.
86. Theodoros Agallianos in Schreiner, *Byzantinischen Kleinchroniken*, App. 6 (2:636).
87. Scholarios, *Letter* 2 (4:405).
88. K. Moustakas, 'Μεθοδολογικά ζητήματα στην προσέγγιση των πληθυσμιακών μεγεθών της υστεροβυζαντινής πόλης,' in Kiousopoulou, ed., *Βυζαντινές πόλεις*, 225–251.
89. Sphrantzes 35.6.
90. Sphrantzes 32.7, 34.2–6.
91. Nicol, *Byzantium*, 388–392; T. Ganchou, 'Le rachat de Notaras,' in M. Balard and M. Ducellier, eds., *Migrations et diasporas méditerranéennes* (Paris 2002) 149–229.
92. Philippides, *Constantine XI*, 241–244; J. Harris, 'Constantinople as City-State,' in Harris et al., eds., *Byzantines*, 119–140; Necipoğlu, *Byzantium*, 225–227.
93. Doukas 35.1; Chalkokondyles 8.6.
94. Sphrantzes 36.
95. J. Hankins, 'Renaissance Crusaders,' *DOP* 49 (1995) 111–207, here 148–168.
96. Pope Nicholas V, *Letter to Konstantinos Palaiologos*, in *ΠΠ* 4:49–63.
97. Doukas 36.2–6, 39.19; M. Philippides and W. Hanak, *Cardinal Isidore, c.1390–1462* (London 2018) 150–159.

98. Doukas 37.10; Kydones, *Advice to the Romans*, in *PG* 154:997D; Ioannes Eugenikos, *Letter to Notaras*, in *ΠΠ* 1:142; Necipoğlu, *Byzantium*, 215–218.
99. Doukas 39.1.
100. Philippides and Hanak, *Siege*, 219–220.
101. Chalkokondyles 8.33–43, 9.1–13, 9.37–62; Kritoboulos 3.1–9.
102. Theodoros Gazes, *Letter to his Brothers in Constantinople*, in *ΠΠ* 4:46.
103. Shawcross, 'New Lykourgos,' 434.
104. Doukas 39.1.
105. Anonymous in Schreiner, *Byzantinischen Kleinchroniken*, 14.107 (1:155).
106. N. Wilson, *From Byzantium to Italy* (London 2017) 64–65.
107. F. Cervantes, *Conquistadores: A New History* (London 2020) 5.
108. Pseudo-Sphrantzes, *Chronicon Maius*, p. 416.

Bibliography

Most scholarship is cited only once, and fully, in the notes. This bibliography contains items that are cited in more than one note (and are abbreviated there). For reasons of accessibility, and the convenience of the vast majority of present and future readers of this book, these items are mostly in English. For reasons of space, there is no bibliography of the primary sources, nor are full citations to their editions and translations given in the notes, unless they are obscure. Readers can easily find that information online. I have used the most recent editions of sources available at the time of writing.

Abulafia, D., 'Ancona, Byzantium and the Adriatic, 1155–1173,' *Papers of the British School at Rome* 52 (1984) 195–216.

Agoritsas, D., *Κωνσταντινούπολη: Η πόλη και η κοινωνία της στα χρόνια των πρώτων Παλαιολόγων (1261–1328)* (Thessalonike 2016).

Ahrweiler, H., and A. Laiou, eds., *Studies on the Internal Diaspora of the Byzantine Empire* (Washington, D.C. 1998).

Albertella, R., et al., *Drei dogmatische Schriften Iustinians*, 2nd ed. (Milan 1973).

Alcock, S., et al., eds., *Empires: Perspectives from Archaeology and History* (Cambridge 2001).

Alexakis, A., 'The "Dialogue of the Monk and Recluse Moschos concerning the Holy Icons": An Early Iconophile Text,' *DOP* 58 (1998) 187–224.

Alexander, P., *The Patriarch Nicephorus of Constantinople* (Oxford 1958).

Allen, P., and B. Neil, *Maximus the Confessor and his Companions* (Oxford 2002).

Andrea, A., *Contemporary Sources for the Fourth Crusade* (Leiden 2000).

Angelov, D., 'Byzantine Ideological Reactions to the Latin Conquest of Constantinople,' in A. Laiou, ed., *Urbs Capta.*

_____, *Imperial Ideology and Political Thought in Byzantium* (Cambridge 2007).

_____, *The Byzantine Hellene: The Life of Emperor Theodore Laskaris* (Cambridge 2019).

Angold, M., *A Byzantine Government in Exile: Government and Society under the Laskards of Nicaea* (Oxford 1975).

_____, *Church and Society in Byzantium under the Comneni 1081–1261* (Cambridge 1995).

_____, *The Fourth Crusade: Event and Context* (Harlow, UK 2003).

Anthony, S., 'Fixing John Damascene's Biography,' *JECS* 23 (2015) 607–627.

Argenti, P., *The Occupation of Chios by the Genoese* (Cambridge 1958).

Athanassiadi, P., *Vers la pensée unique: La montée de l'intolérance dans l'Antiquité tardive* (Paris 2010).

Auzépy, M.-F., *L'histoire des iconoclastes* (Paris 2007).

Bagnall, R., *Egypt in Late Antiquity* (Princeton 1993).

Banaji, J., *Agrarian Change in Late Antiquity* (Oxford 2012).

Barker, J., *Manuel II Palaeologus (1391–1425): A Study in Late Byzantine Statesmanship* (New Brunswick, NJ 1969).

Barnes, T., *Athanasius and Constantius: Theology and Politics in the Constantinian Empire* (Cambridge, MA 1993).

Bartusis, M., *The Late Byzantine Army* (Philadelphia 1992).
_____, *Land and Privilege in Byzantium: The Institution of the Pronoia* (Cambridge 2012).
Barzos, K., *Ἡ γενεαλογία τῶν Κομνηνῶν* 2 vols. (Thessalonike 1984).
Beaucamp, J., et al., eds., *Juifs et chrétiens en Arabie aux Ve et VIe siècles* (Paris 2010).
Beihammer, A., *Byzantium and the Emergence of Muslim-Turkish Anatolia* (London 2017).
Belke, K., et al., eds., *Byzantina Mediterranea: Festschrift für Johannes Koder* (Vienna 2007).
Bell, P., *Social Conflict in the Age of Justinian* (Oxford 2013).
Bevan, G., *A New Judas: The Case of Nestorius in Ecclesiastical Politics* (Leuven 2016).
Bikhazi, J., *The Hamdanid Dynasty of Mesopotamia and North Syria* (PhD dissertation, University of Michigan 1981).
Blankinship, K., *The End of the Jihâd State: The Reign of Hisham Ibn 'Abd al-Malik and the Collapse of the Umayyads* (Albany, NY 1994).
Blockley, R., *East Roman Foreign Policy* (Leeds 1992).
Blöndal, S., *The Varangians of Byzantium* (Cambridge 1978).
Boïnes, K., *Ἀκολουθία ἱερὰ τοῦ ὁσίου . . . Χριστοδούλου* (Athens 1884).
Boojamra, J., *The Church and Social Reform: The Policies of Patriarch Athanasios of Constantinople* (New York 1993).
Booth, P., *Crisis of Empire: Doctrine and Dissent at the End of Late Antiquity* (Berkeley 2014).
_____, 'The Last Years of Cyrus, Patriarch of Alexandria (d. 642),' *TM* 20 (2016) 509–558.
Brakke, D., *Demons and the Making of the Monk: Spiritual Combat in Early Christianity* (Cambridge, MA 2006).
Brakke, D., and A. Crislip, *Selected Discourses of Shenoute the Great* (Cambridge 2015).
Brand, C., *Byzantium Confronts the West, 1180–1204* (Cambridge, MA 1968).
Brandes, W., 'Das Schweigen des Liber pontificalis: Die "Enteignung" der päpstlichen Patrimonien Siziliens und Unteritaliens in den 50er Jahren des 8. Jahrhunderts,' *Fontes Minores* 4 (2014) 97–203.
Bransbourg, G., 'Capital in the Sixth Century: The Dynamics of Tax and Estate in Roman Egypt,' *JLA* 9 (2016) 305–413.
_____, '*Reddite quae sunt Caesaris, Caesari*: The Late Roman Empire and the Dream of Fair Taxation,' in R. Lizzi Testa, ed., *Late Antiquity in Contemporary Debate* (Newcastle-upon-Tyne 2017) 80–112.
Brennecke, H., *Studien zur Geschichte der Homöer der Osten* (Tübingen 1988).
Broadhurst, R., *The Travels of ibn Jubayr* (London 1952).
Brock, S., 'The Conversations with the Syrian Orthodox under Justinian (532),' *Orientalia Christiana Periodica* 47 (1981) 87–121.
Brown, P., 'The Rise and Function of the Holy Man in Late Antiquity,' *JRS* 61 (1971) 80–101.
_____, *The Body and Society: Men, Women, and Sexual Renunciation in Early Christianity* (New York 1988).
_____, *Poverty and Leadership in the Later Roman Empire* (Hanover, NH 2002).
Brown, T., *Gentlemen and Officers: Imperial Administration and Aristocratic Power in Byzantine Italy* (Rome 1984).
Browning, R., 'An Unpublished Address of Nicephorus Chrysoberges,' *Byzantine Studies* 5 (1978) 37–68.
Brubaker, L., and J. Haldon, *Byzantium in the Iconoclast Era (ca 680–850): The Sources: An Annotated Survey* (Burlington, VT 2001).
_____, *Byzantium in the Iconoclast Era, c. 680–850: A History* (Cambridge 2011).

Bucossi, A., and A. Rodriguez Suarez, eds., *John II Komnenos, Emperor of Byzantium* (London 2016).
Buell, D., *Why This New Race: Ethnic Reasoning in Early Christianity* (New York 2005).
Bull, M., and N. Housley, eds., *The Experience of Crusading* (Cambridge 2003).
Burgess, R., 'The Summer of Blood: The "Great Massacre" of 337,' *DOP* 62 (2008) 5–51.
Cameron, A., *Claudian: Poetry and Propaganda at the Court of Honorius* (Oxford 1970).
_____, *Circus Factions: Blues and Greens at Rome and Byzantium* (Oxford 1976).
_____, 'The Empress and the Poet: Paganism and Politics at the Court of Theodosius II,' *Yale Classical Studies* 27 (1982) 217–289.
Cameron, A., and J. Long, *Barbarians and Politics at the Court of Arcadius* (Berkeley 1993).
Caner, D., *Wandering, Begging Monks: Spiritual Authority and the Promotion of Monasticism in Late Antiquity* (Berkeley 2002).
_____, *The Rich and the Pure: Philanthropy and the Making of Christian Society in Early Byzantium* (Berkeley 2021).
Çelik, S., *Manuel II Palaiologos (1350–1425): A Byzantine Emperor in a Time of Tumult* (Cambridge 2021).
Chadwick, H., 'The Exile and Death of Flavian of Constantinople,' *Journal of Theological Studies* 6 (1955) 17–34.
Chevedden, P., '"A Crusade from the First": The Norman Conquest of Islamic Sicily, 1060–1091,' *Al-Masaq* 22 (2010) 191–225.
Cheynet, J.-C., *Pouvoir et contestations à Byzance (963–1210)* (Paris 1996).
_____, *The Byzantine Aristocracy and its Military Function* (Aldershot, UK 2006).
_____, *La société byzantine: L'apport des sceaux* (Paris 2008).
Chiarelli, L., *A History of Muslim Sicily* (Malta 2011).
Chitty, D., *The Desert a City* (Oxford 1966).
Chitwood, Z., *Byzantine Legal Culture and the Roman Legal Tradition, 867–1056* (Cambridge 2017).
Chrissis, N., *Crusading in Frankish Greece: A Study of Byzantine-Western Relations and Attitudes, 1204–1282* (Turnhout 2012).
_____, 'Ideological and Political Contestations in post-1204 Byzantium,' in Tougher, ed., *Emperor*, 248–263.
_____, 'Crusades and Crusaders,' in Tsougarakis and Lock, eds., *Companion*, 23–72.
_____, et al., eds., *Byzantium and the West: Perception and Reality (11th–15th c.)* (London 2019).
Christie, N., *From Constantine to Charlemagne: An Archaeology of Italy* (Farnham, UK 2006).
Chrysos, E., ed., *Πρακτικά διεθνούς συμποσίου για το Δεσποτάτο της Ηπείρου* (Arta 1992).
_____, 'A War of Languages? Greek and Latin in the Confrontation between Pope Nicholas and Patriarch Photius,' in M. Caroli et al., eds., *Per respirare a due polmoni: Chiese e culture cristiane tra Oriente e Occidente* (Bononia 2019) 261–278.
Chrysostomides, J., *Monumenta Peloponnesiaca: Documents for the History of the Peloponnese in the 14th and 15th centuries* (Camberley 1995).
_____, *Byzantium and Venice, 1204–1453*, ed. M. Heslop and C. Dendrinos (London 2011).
Congourdeau, M.-H., ed., *Thessalonique au temps des Zélots* (Paris 2014).
_____, 'Vivre à Thessalonique sous les Zélots,' in eadem, ed., *Thessalonique au temps des Zélotes (1342–1350)* (Paris 2014) 23–54.
Connolly, S., *Lives behind the Laws: The World of the Codex Hermogenianus* (Bloomington, IN 2010).

Cooper, J., and M. Decker, *Life and Society in Byzantine Cappadocia* (New York 2012).
Cosentino, S., 'Byzantine Sardinia between West and East,' *Millennium* 1 (2004) 329–367.
_____, 'Constans II and the Byzantine Navy,' *BZ* 100 (2007) 577–603.
Cotsonis, J., 'Onomastics, Gender, Offices, and Images on Byzantine Lead Seals,' *BMGS* 32 (2008) 1–37.
Coureas, N., 'The Latin and Greek Churches in Former Byzantine Lands under Latin Rule,' in N. Tsougarakis and P. Lock, eds., *A Companion to Latin Greece* (Leiden 2015) 145–184.
Croke, B., 'Justinian, Theodora, and the Church of Saints Sergius and Bacchus,' *DOP* 60 (2006) 25–63.
Curta, F., *Southeastern Europe in the Middle Ages* (Cambridge 2006).
_____, ed., *The Other Europe in the Middle Ages: Avars, Bulgars, Khazars, and Cumans* (Leiden 2008).
_____, 'The Beginning of the Middle Ages in the Balkans,' *Millennium* 10 (2013) 145–214.
_____, *The Edinburgh History of the Greeks, c. 500 to 1050: The Early Middle Ages* (Edinburgh 2011).
Dagron, G., *Naissance d'une capital: Constantinople et ses institutions* (Paris 1984).
_____, *Emperor and Priest: The Imperial Office in Byzantium*, tr. J. Birrell (Cambridge 2003).
_____, *Idées byzantines* (Paris 2012).
Dagron, G., and V. Déroche, *Juifs et chrétiens en Orient byzantin* (Paris 2010).
Darrouzès, J., *Epistoliers byzantines du Xe siècle* (Paris 1960).
Day, G., *Genoa's Response to Byzantium, 1155–1204* (Urbana and Chicago 1988).
De Giorgi, A., and A. Asa Eger, *Antioch: A History* (London 2021).
Decker, M., *The Byzantine Dark Ages* (London 2016).
Deliyannis, D., 'Charlemagne's Silver Tables: The Ideology of an Imperial Capital,' *Early Medieval Europe* 12 (2003) 159–178.
Deloglu, P. 'The Post-Imperial Romanness of the Romans,' in Pohl et al. eds., *Transformations*, 157–171.
Demacopoulos, G., *The Invention of Peter: Apostolic Discourse and Papal Authority in Late Antiquity* (Philadelphia 2013).
_____, *Colonizing Christianity: Greek and Latin Religious Identity in the Era of the Fourth Crusade* (New York 2019).
Dennis, G., *Three Byzantine Military Treatises* (Washington, D.C. 1985).
Devaney, T., 'The Byzantine-Venetian Conflict of 1119–1126,' in T. Madden et al., eds., *Crusades – Medieval Worlds in Conflict* (London 2010).
Dijkstra, J., and G. Fisher, eds., *Inside and Out: Interactions between Rome and the Peoples on the Arabian and Egyptian Frontiers* (Leuven 2014).
Ditten, H., *Ethnische Verschiebungen zwischen der Balkanhalbinsel und Kleinasien vom Ende des 6. bis zur zweiten Hälfte des 9. Jahrhunderts* (Berlin 1993).
Dölger, F., *Regesten der Kaiserurkunden des oströmischen Reiches* (Hildesheim 1976).
Donner, F., *The Early Islamic Conquests* (Princeton 1981).
Dossey, L., *Peasant and Empire in Christian North Africa* (Berkeley 2010).
Duggan, A., '*Totius christianitatis caput*: The Pope and the Princes,' in B. Bolton and A. Duggan, eds., *Adrian IV the English Pope (1154–1159)* (Aldershot, UK 2003) 105–155.
Dujčev, I., 'On the Treaty of 927 with the Bulgarians,' *DOP* 32 (1978) 219–295.
Dvornik, F., *The Photian Schism: History and Legend* (Cambridge 1948).
Eastmond, A., *Art and Identity in Thirteenth-Century Byzantium: Hagia Sophia and the Empire of Trebizond* (Aldershot, UK 2004).

Ekonomou, A., *Byzantine Rome and the Greek Popes* (Plymouth, UK 2007).
El Cheikh, N., *Byzantium Viewed by the Arabs* (Cambridge, MA 2004).
Elm, S., *'Virgins of God': The Making of Asceticism in Late Antiquity* (Oxford 1996).
Elton, H., *Warfare in Roman Europe, AD 350–425* (Oxford 1996).
Errington, R., 'Theodosius and the Goths,' *Chiron* 26 (1996) 1–27.
_____, *Roman Imperial Policy from Julian to Theodosius* (Chapel Hill 2006).
Estangüi Gómez, R., *Byzance face aux Ottomans: Exercise du pouvoir et contrôle du territoire sous les derniers Paléologues* (Paris 2014).
_____, 'Le séjour de Jean VI Kantakouzènos à Thessalonique,' in M.-H. Congourdeau, ed., *Thessalonique au temps des Zélotes (1342–1350)* (Paris 2014) 55–88.
Farag, W., *Byzantium and Its Muslim Neighbours during the Reign of Basil II (976–1025)* (PhD dissertation, University of Birmingham 1977).
Feissel, D., 'Les édifices de Justinien au témoignage de Procope et de l'épigraphie,' *Antiquité tardive* 8 (2000) 81–104.
_____, *Documents, droit, diplomatique de l'Empire romain tardif* (Paris 2010).
_____, 'Jean de Soloi, un évêque chypriote au milieu du VIIe siècle,' *TM* 17 (2013) 219–236.
Fiedler, U., 'Bulgars in the Lower Danube Region,' in F. Curta, ed., *The Other Europe in the Middle Ages: Avars, Bulgars, Khazars, and Cumans* (Leideon 2008) 151–236.
Fisher, G., *Between Empires: Arabs, Romans, and Sasanians in Late Antiquity* (Oxford 2011).
_____, ed., *Arabs and Empires before Islam* (Oxford 2015).
Flusin, B., *Saint Anastase le Perse et l'histoire de la Palestine au début du VIIe siècle. 2 vols.* (Paris 1992).
Forrest, S., 'Theophanes' Byzantine Source for the Late Seventh and Early Eighth Centuries,' *TM* 19 (2015) 417–444.
Forsyth, J., *The Byzantine-Arab Chronicle (938–1034) of Yahya b. Sa'id al-Antaki*, 2 vols (PhD dissertation, University of Michigan 1977).
Foskolou, V., '"In the Reign of the Emperor of Rome . . . ": Donor Inscriptions and Political Ideology in the Time of Michael VIII Paleologos,' *Δελτίον τῆς Χριστιανικῆς Ἀρχαιολογικῆς Ἑταιρείας* 27 (2006) 455–462.
Foss, C., 'The Persians in Asia Minor and the End of Antiquity,' *English Historical Review* 90 (1975) 721–747.
_____, 'The Defenses of Asia Minor against the Turks,' *Greek Orthodox Theological Review* 27 (1982) 149–204.
_____, 'Syria in Transition, A.D. 550–750: An Archaeological Approach,' *DOP* 51 (1997) 189–269.
_____, 'The Persians in the Roman Near East,' *Journal of the Royal Asiatic Society* ser. 3, 13 (2003) 149–170.
_____, 'Egypt under Mu'awiya,' *Bulletin of the School of Oriental and African Studies* 72 (2009) 1–24 (Part I) and 259–278 (Part II).
_____, *The Beginnings of the Ottoman Empire* (Oxford 2022).
Fowden, G., *Empire to Commonwealth: Consequences of Monotheism in Late Antiquity* (Princeton 1993).
Franchi, A., *Il Concilio II di Lione (1274)* (Rome 1965).
Frier, B., 'The Demography of the Early Roman Empire,' in *The Cambridge Ancient History, v. 11: A.D. 70–192* (2000) 787–816.

Gaddis, M., *There Is No Crime for Those Who Have Christ: Religious Violence in the Christian Roman Empire* (Berkeley 2005).
Galatariotou, C., *The Making of a Saint: The Life, Times and Sanctification of Neophytos the Recluse* (Cambridge 1991).
Gândilă, A., 'Heavy Money, Weightier Problems: The Justinianic Reform of 538 and its Economic Consequences,' *Revue numismatique* 168 (2012) 363–402.
Gariboldi, A., 'Social Conditions in Egypt under the Sasanian Occupation,' *Parola del Passato* 64 (2009) 321–353.
Garsoïan, N., 'The Problem of Armenian Integration into the Byzantine Empire,' in H. Ahrweiler and A. Laiou, eds., *Studies on the Internal Diaspora of the Byzantine Empire* (Washington, D.C. 1998) 53–124.
Gasparis, C., 'Land and Landowners in the Greek Territories under Latin Dominion,' in N. Tsougarakis and P. Lock, eds., *A Companion to Latin Greece* (Leiden 2015) 73–113.
Gautier, P., 'Un récit inédit du siège de Constantinople par les Turcs (1394–1402),' *REB* 23 (1965) 100–117.
_____, 'Diatribes de Jean l'Oxite contre Alexis Ier Comnène,' *REB* 28 (1970) 5–55.
Geanakoplos, D., *Emperor Michael Palaeologus and the West* (Cambridge, MA 1959).
Gerstel, S., ed., *Viewing the Morea: Land and People in the Late Medieval Peloponnese* (Washington, D.C. 2013).
Gill, J., *The Council of Florence* (Cambridge 1959).
_____, *Byzantium and the Papacy, 1198–1400* (New Brunswick, NJ 1979).
Glavinas, A., *Ἡ ἐπὶ Ἀλεξίου Κομνηνοῦ (1081–1118) περὶ ἱερῶν σκευῶν, κειμηλείων, καὶ ἁγίων εἰκόνων ἔρις (1081–1095)* (Thessalonike 1972).
Goitein, S., 'A Letter from Seleucia (Cilicia),' *Speculum* 39 (1964) 298–303.
Gouillard, J., 'Aux origines de l'iconoclasme: Le témoignage de Grégoire II,' *TM* 3 (1968) 243–307.
Gounarides, P., *Τὸ κίνημα τῶν Ἀρσενιατῶν* (Athens 1999).
Grdzelidze, T., *Georgian Monks on Mount Athos* (London 2009).
Greatrex, G., and S. Lieu, *The Roman Eastern Frontier and the Persian Wars, Part II: AD 363–630* (London 2002).
Greenwood, T., 'Social Change in Eleventh-Century Armenia,' in J. Howard-Johnston, ed., *Social Change in Town and Country in Eleventh-Century Byzantium* (Oxford 2020) 196–291.
Gregory, T., *Vox populi: Popular Opinion and Violence in the Religious Controversies of the Fifth Century A.D.* (Columbus, OH 1979).
Grubbs, J., *Law and Family in Late Antiquity* (Oxford 1995).
Gutas, D., *Greek Thought, Arabic Culture: The Graeco-Arabic Translation Movement in Baghdad and Early 'Abbasid Society* (London 1998).
Haarer, F., *Anastasius I: Politics and Empire in the Late Roman World* (Liverpool 2006).
Haldon, J., *Byzantine Praetorians: An Administrative, Institutional, and Social Survey of the Opsikion and tagmata, c.580–900* (Bonn 1984).
_____, *Byzantium in the Seventh Century: The Transformation of a Culture* (Cambridge 1990).
_____, *Constantine Prophyrogenitus: Three Treatises on Imperial Military Expeditions* (Vienna 1990).
_____, *Warfare, State and Society in the Byzantine World* (London 1999).

_____, 'Commerce and Exchange in the Seventh and Eighth Centuries,' in C. Morrisson, ed., *Trade and Markets in Byzantium* (Washington, D.C. 2012) 99–122.
_____, 'Late Rome, Byzantium, and Early Medieval Western Europe,' in A. Monson and W. Scheidel, eds., *Fiscal Regimes and the Political Economy of Premodern States* (Cambridge 2015) 345–389.
_____, *A Tale of Two Cities: The Martyrdoms and Miracles of Saints Theodore 'the Recruit' and 'the General'* (Liverpool 2016).
_____, *The Empire that Would not Die: The Paradox of Eastern Roman Survival, 640–740* (Cambridge, MA 2016).
_____, 'L'armée au XIe siècle,' *TM* 21.2 (2017) 581–592.
_____, 'More Questions about the Origins of the Imperial Opsikion,' in A. Beihammer et al., eds., *Prosopon Rhomaikon* (Berlin 2017) 31–41.
Haldon, J., and H. Kennedy, 'The Arab-Byzantine Frontier in the Eighth and Ninth Centuries,' *Zbornik Radova Vizantinoloskog Instituta* 19 (1980) 79–116.
Hanson, R., *The Search for the Christian Doctrine of God: The Arian Controversy 318–381* (Edinburgh 1993).
Harper, K., 'The Greek Census Inscriptions of Late Antiquity,' *JRS* 98 (2008) 83–119.
_____, *The Fate of Rome: Climate, Disease, and the End of an Empire* (Princeton 2017).
Harris, A., *Byzantium, Britain and the West: The Archaeology of Cultural Identity AD 400–650* (Stroud, UK 2003).
Harris, J., 'Byzantium and the First Crusade: Three Avenues of Approach,' *Estudios bizantinos* 2 (2014) 125–141.
Harris, J., et al., *Byzantines, Latins, and Turks in the Eastern Mediterranean World* (Oxford 2012).
Harvey, A., *Economic Expansion in the Byzantine Empire, 900–1200* (Cambridge 1989).
Hawting, G. *The First Dynasty of Islam: The Umayyad Caliphate*. 2nd ed. (London 2000.)
Hatlie, P., *The Monks and Monasteries of Constantinople ca. 350–850* (Cambridge 2007).
Hatziantoniou, E., *Η θρησκευτική πολιτική του Αναστασίου Α΄ (491–518)* (Thessalonike 2009).
Hatzopoulos, D., *Ἡ πρώτη πολιορκία τῆς Κωνσταντινουπόλεως ἀπό τούς Ὀθωμανούς* (Athens 2004).
Heather, P., *Goths and Romans, 332–489* (Oxford 1991).
_____, 'New Men for New Constantines?,' in P. Magdalino, ed., *New Constantines* (Aldershot, UK 1994) 11–33.
Heather, P., and J. Matthews, *The Goths in the Fourth Century* (Liverpool 1991).
Hebblewhite, M., *The Emperor and the Army in the Later Roman Empire* (London 2017).
Heisenberg, A., *Aus der Geschichte und Literatur der Palaiologenzeit* (Munich 1920).
Hendy, M., *Studies in the Byzantine Monetary Economy* (Cambridge 1985).
Herrin, J., *Ravenna: Capital of Empire, Crucible of Europe* (Princeton 2020).
Hickey, T., *Wine, Wealth, and the State in Late Antique Egypt* (Ann Arbor, MI 2012).
Hilsdale, C., *Byzantine Art and Diplomacy in an Age of Decline* (Cambridge 2014).
Hoeck, J., and R. Loenertz, *Nikolaos-Nektarios von Otranto, Abt von Casole* (Ettal 1965).
Holo, J., *Byzantine Jewry in the Mediterranean Economy* (Cambridge 2009).
Holum, K., 'Archaeological Evidence for the Fall of Byzantine Caesarea,' *Bulletin of the American Schools of Oriental Research* 286 (1992) 73–85.
_____, 'Inscriptions from the Imperial Revenue Office of Byzantine Caesarea Palaestinae,' *JRA Supplementary Series* 14 (1995) 333–345.

Hondridou, S. *Ο Κωνσταντίνος Θ' Μονομάχος και η εποχή του* (Thessalonike 2002) 329–332.
Howard-Johnston, J., ed., *Social Change in Town and Country in Eleventh-Century Byzantium* (Oxford 2020).
_____, *The Last Great War of Antiquity* (Oxford 2021).
Hoyland, R., *Seeing Islam as Others Saw It* (Princeton, NJ 1997).
_____, *Theophilus of Edessa's Chronicle* (Liverpool 2011).
Humphreys, M., *Law, Power, and Imperial Ideology in the Iconoclast Era* (Oxford 2015).
_____, *The Laws of the Isaurian Era: The Ecloga and its Appendices* (Liverpool 2017).
Ivison, E., 'Amorium in the Byzantine Dark Ages,' in J. Henning, ed., *Post-Roman Towns, Trade and Settlement in Europe and Byzantium* (Berlin 2007) 25–55.
Izdebski, A., *A Rural Economy in Transition: Asia Minor from Late Antiquity into the Early Middle Ages* (Warsaw 2013).
Jacobs, I., 'The Creation of the Late Antique City: Constantinople and Asia Minor during the 'Theodosian Renaissance',' *Byzantion* 82 (2012) 113–164.
Jacoby, D., 'The Encounter of Two Societies: Western Conquerors and Byzantines in the Peloponnesus,' *The American Historical Review* 78 (1973) 873–906.
_____, *Byzantium, Latin Romania and the Mediterranean* (Aldershot, UK 2001).
_____, 'The Catalan Company in the East,' in G. Halfond, ed., *The Medieval Way of War* (London 2015) 153–182.
_____, 'The Economy of Latin Constantinople,' in Laiou, ed., *Urbs Capta*, 197–214.
_____, 'The Greeks of Constantinople under Latin Rule,' in Madden, ed., *The Fourth Crusade*, 53–73.
_____,'Rural Exploitation in Western Asia Minor . . . in the Thirteenth Century,' in Kolias et al., eds., *Aureus*, 243–256.
Jankowiak, M., 'Notitia 1 and the Impact of the Arab Invasions on Asia Minor,' *Millennium* 10 (2013) 435–462.
_____, 'The First Arab Siege of Constantinople,' *TM* 17 (2013) 237–320.
Jeffreys, E., 'The Afterlife of *Digenes Akrites*,' in P. Roilos, ed., *Medieval Greek Storytelling* (Wiesbaden 2014) 141–161.
Jeffreys, E., and M. Jeffreys, 'The "Wild Beast from the West",' in A. Laiou and R. Mottahedeh, eds., *The Crusades from the Perspective of Byzantium and the Muslim World* (Washington, D.C. 2001).
Johnson, S., ed., *The Oxford Handbook of Late Antiquity* (Oxford 2012).
_____, 'Introduction,' in idem, ed., *Languages and Cultures of Eastern Christianity: Greek* (Farnham, UK 2015).
Jones, A. H. M., *The Later Roman Empire* (Baltimore 1964).
Kaegi, W., *Heraclius, Emperor of Byzantium* (Cambridge 2003).
_____, *Muslim Expansion and Byzantine Collapse in North Africa* (Cambridge 2010).
Kaldellis, A., 'Classicism, Barbarism, and Warfare: Prokopios and the Conservative Reaction to Later Roman Military Policy,' *American Journal of Ancient History* n.s. 3–4 (2004–2005 [2007]) 189–218.
_____, *Mothers and Sons, Fathers and Daughters: The Byzantine Family of Michael Psellos* (Notre Dame, IN 2006).
_____, *Hellenism in Byzantium: The Transformations of Greek Identity and the Reception of the Classical Tradition* (Cambridge 2007).
_____, *The Christian Parthenon: Classicism and Pilgrimage in Byzantine Athens* (Cambridge 2009).

_____, '"A Union of Opposites": The Moral Logic and Corporeal Presence of the Theotokos on the Field of Battle,' in C. Gastgeber et al., eds., *Pour l'amour de Byzance: Hommage à Paolo Odorico* (Frankfurt am Main 2013) 131–144.

_____, *Ethnography after Antiquity: Foreign Lands and People in Byzantine Literature* (Philadelphia 2013).

_____, 'The Original Source for Tzimiskes' Balkan Campaign (971),' *BMGS* 37 (2013) 1–18.

_____, *A New Herodotos: Laonikos Chalkokondyles on the Ottoman Empire, the Fall of Byzantium, and the Emergence of the West* (Cambridge, MA 2014).

_____, 'The Making of Hagia Sophia and the Last Pagans of New Rome,' *JLA* 6 (2014) 347–366.

_____, *Byzantine Readings of Ancient Historians* (London 2015).

_____, *The Byzantine Republic: People and Power in New Rome* (Cambridge, MA 2015).

_____, 'The Forum of Constantine,' *GRBS* 56 (2016) 714–739.

_____, *Streams of Gold, Rivers of Blood: The Rise and Fall of Byzantium, 955 A.D. to the First Crusade* (Oxford 2017).

_____, *Romanland: Ethnicity and Empire in Byzantium* (Cambridge, MA 2019).

_____, 'The Politics of Classical Genealogies in the Late Antique Roman East,' in I. Tanaseanu-Döbler and L. von Alvensleben, eds., *Athens II: Athens in Late Antiquity* (Tübingen 2020) 259–277.

_____, 'Byzantine Borders Were State Artifacts, Not "Fluid Zones of Interaction",' in D. Tor and A. Beihammer, eds., *The Islamic-Byzantine Border in History: From the Rise of Islam to the End of the Crusades* (Edinburgh 2023) 100–124.

Kaldellis, A., and S. Efthymiades, *The Prosopography of Byzantine Lesbos* (Vienna 2010).

Kaldellis, A., and M. Kruse, *The Field Armies of the East Roman Empire, 361–630 AD* (Cambridge 2023).

Kaldellis, A., and N. Siniossoglou, eds., *The Cambridge Intellectual History of Byzantium* (Cambridge 2017).

Kalopissi-Verti, S. 'Monumental Art in the Lordship of Athens and Thebes,' in Tsougarakis and Lock, eds., *Companion*, 369–417.

Karpov, S., *Ιστορία της αυτοκρατορίας της Τραπεζούντας*, tr. E. Kritsefskaja and A. Eustathiou (Athens 2017).

Karpozilos, A., *The Ecclesiastical Controversy between the Kingdom of Nicaea and the Principality of Epiros* (Thessalonike 1973).

Kastritsis, D., *The Sons of Bayezid: Empire Building and Representation in the Ottoman Civil War of 1402–1413* (Leiden 2007).

Katsoni, P., *Μιά επταετία κρίσιμων γεγονότων: Το Βυζάντιο στα έτη 1366–1373* (Thessalonike 2002).

_____, *Ανδρόνικος Δ΄ Παλαιολόγος* (Thessalonike 2008).

Kelly, C., *Ruling the Later Roman Empire* (Cambridge, MA 2004).

_____, 'Stooping to Conquer: The Power of Imperial Humility,' in idem., ed., *Theodosius II: Rethinking the Roman Empire in Late Antiquity* (Cambridge 2013) 221–243.

_____, ed., *Theodosius II: Rethinking the Roman Empire in Late Antiquity* (Cambridge 2013).

Kelly, J., *Early Christian Doctrines* (New York 1960).

_____, *Golden Mouth: The Story of John Chrysostom* (London 1995).

Kennedy, H., *The Great Arab Conquests* (Philadelphia 2007).

Kinloch, M., and A. MacFarlane, eds., *Trends and Turning Points: Constructing the Late Antique and Byzantine World* (Leiden 2019).

Kiousopoulou, T., ed., *Οι βυζαντινές πόλεις (8ος-15ος αιώνας)* (Rethymno 2012).

_____, *Οι «αόρατες» βυζαντινές πόλεις στον ελλαδικό χώρο (13ος–15ος αιώνας)* (Athens 2013).

Kolbaba, T., *The Byzantine Lists: Errors of the Latins* (Urbana 2000).

Kolias, T., et al., eds., *Aureus: Volume Dedicated to Professor Evangelos K. Chryssos* (Athens 2014).

Kontogiannopoulou, A., *Η εσωτερική πολιτική του Ανδρόνικου Β΄ Παλαιολόγου* (Thessalonike 2004).

Korobeinikov, D., *Byzantium and the Turks in the Thirteenth Century* (Oxford 2014).

Kosiński, R., *The Emperor Zeno: Religion and Politics* (Cracow 2010).

Kouroupou, M., and J.-F. Vannier, 'Commémoraisons des Comnènes dans le typikon liturgique du monastère du Christ Philanthrope,' *REB* 63 (2005) 41–69.

Kourtzian, G., 'L'incident de Cnossos (fin Septembre/début Octobre 610),' *TM* 17 (2013) 173–196.

Kreutz, B., *Before the Normans: Southern Italy in the Ninth and Tenth Centuries* (Philadelphia 1991).

Kyriakides, S., *Warfare in Late Byzantium* (Leiden 2011).

Kyritses, D., *The Byzantine Aristocracy in the Thirteenth and Early Fourteenth Centuries* (PhD dissertation, Harvard University 1997).

Laiou, A., *Constantinople and the Latins: The Foreign Policy of Andronicus II* (Cambridge, MA 1972).

Laiou-Thomadakis, A., *Peasant Society in the Late Byzantine Empire: A Social and Demographic Study* (Princeton 1977).

_____, *Gender, Society, and Economic Life in Byzantium* (London 1992).

_____, ed., *Urbs Capta: The Fourth Crusade and its Consequences* (Paris 2005).

Laiou, A., and C. Morrisson, *The Byzantine Economy* (Cambridge 2007).

Lambakis, S., et al., *Βυζαντινά στρατεύματα στη Δύση* (Athens 2008).

Lambert, S., and H. Nicholson, eds., *Languages of Love and Hate: Conflict, Communication, and Identity in the Medieval Mediterranean* (Turnhout 2012).

Laniado, A., *Recherches sur les notables municipaux dans l'empire protobyzantin* (Paris 2002).

_____, *Ethnos et droit dans le monde protobyzantin* (Geneva 2015).

Lappas, N., *Πολιτική ιστορία του κράτους της Ηπείρου κατά τον 13ο αι.* (PhD dissertation, University of Thessalonike 2007).

Laurent, V., and J. Darrouzès, *Dossier grec de l'Union de Lyon* (Paris 1976).

Lauxtermann, M., *Byzantine Poetry from Pisides to Geometres* 2 vols. (Vienna 2003–2019).

Lauxtermann, M., and M. Whittow, eds., *Byzantium in the Eleventh Century* (London 2017).

Lavan, M., *Slaves to Rome: Paradigms of Empire in Roman Culture* (Cambridge 2013).

Leidholm, N., *Elite Byzantine Kinship, ca. 950–1204* (Leeds 2019).

Lemerle, P., 'L'histoire des Pauliciens d'Asie Mineure d'après les sources grecques,' *TM* 5 (1973) 1–144.

Lemerle, P., *Cinq études sur le XIe siècle byzantin* (Paris 1977).

_____, *Byzantine Humanism: The First Phase*, tr. H. Lindsay and A. Moffatt (Canberra 1986).

Lenski, N., *Failure of Empire: Valens and the Roman State in the Fourth Century A.D.* (Berkeley 2002).

_____, 'The Significance of the Edict of Milan,' in E. Siecienski, ed., *Constantine: Religious Faith and Imperial Policy* (London 2017) 27–56.

_____, 'Slavery in the Byzantine Empire,' in C. Perry et al., eds., *The Cambridge World History of Slavery*, v. 2 (Cambridge 2021) 453–481.

Leonardi, C., and A. Placanica, eds., *Gesta Sanctae ac Universalis Octavae Synodi quae Constantinopoli congregata est* (Florence 2012).

Leonte, F., *Imperial Visions of Late Byzantium: Manuel II Palaiologos and Rhetoric in Purple* (Edinburgh 2020).

Leveniotis, G., *Η πολιτική κατάρρευση του Βυζαντίου στην ανατολή* (Thessalonike 2007).

Liebeschuetz, J., *Barbarians and Bishops: Army, Church, and State in the Age of Arcadius and Chrysostom* (Oxford 1990).

_____, *Decline and Fall of the Roman City* (Oxford 2001).

Lightfoot, C., *The Eastern Frontier of the Roman Empire with Special Reference to the Reign of Constantius II* (PhD dissertation, Oxford University, 1982).

Lilie, R.-J., *Die byzantinische Reaktion auf die Ausbreitung der Araber* (Munich 1976).

_____, *Byzantium and the Crusader States*, tr. J. Morris and J. Ridings (Oxford 1993).

Lindstedt, I., '*Muhajirun* as a Name for the First/Seventh Century Muslims,' *Journal of Near Eastern Studies* 74 (2015) 67–73.

Lock, P., *The Franks in the Aegean, 1204–1500* (London 1995).

Loenertz, R., 'Lettre de Georges Bardanes, Metropolite de Corcyre, au patriarch oecumenique Germain II,' *EEBΣ* 33 (1964) 87–118.

Loofs, F., *Nestoriana: Die Fragmente des Nestorius* (Halle 1905).

Loud, G., *The Age of Robert Guiscard: Southern Italy and the Norman Conquest* (New York 2000).

Lynch, R., 'Cyprus and Its Legal and Historiographical Significance in Early Islamic History,' *Journal of the American Oriental Society* 136.3 (2016) 535–550.

MacCoull, L., 'Coptic Egypt during the Persian Occupation,' *Studi classici e orientali* 36 (1986) 307–313.

Macrides, R., 'What's in the Name "Megas Komnenos"?' *Ἀρχεῖον Πόντου* 35 (1979) 238–245.

_____, 'The New Constantine and the New Constantinople – 1261?,' *BMGS* 6 (1980) 13–41.

_____, *George Akropolites: The History* (Oxford 2007).

Macrides, R., et al., *Pseudo-Kodinos and the Constantinopolitan Court* (London 2013).

Madden, T., 'The Fires of the Fourth Crusade in Constantinople, 1203–1204,' *BZ* 84–85 (1991–1992) 72–93.

_____, ed., *The Fourth Crusade: Essential Readings* (Malden, MA 2002).

Madgearu, A., 'The End of Town Life in Scythia Minor,' *Oxford Journal of Archaeology* 20 (2001) 207–217.

_____, *The Asanids: The Political and Military History of the Second Bulgarian Empire* (Leiden 2017).

Maenchen-Helfen, J., *The World of the Huns* (Berkeley 1973).

Magdalino, P., *The Empire of Manuel I Komnenos* (Cambridge 1993).

_____, *L'Orthodoxie des astrologues: La science entre le dogme et la divination à Byzance* (Paris 2006).

_____, *Studies on the History and Topography of Byzantine Constantinople* (Aldershot, UK 2007).

Magdalino, P., and N. Necipoğlu, eds., *Trade in Byzantium* (Istanbul 2016).

Majeska, G., *Russian Travelers to Constantinople in the Fourteenth and Fifteenth Centuries* (Washington, D.C. 1984).
Makk, F., *The Árpáds and the Comneni* (Budapest 1989).
Mango, C., 'The Conciliar Edict of 1166,' *DOP* 17 (1963) 315–330.
_____, *Le développement urbain de Constantinople* (Paris 2004).
Mango, C., and G. Dagron, eds., *Constantinople and its Hinterland* (Aldershot, UK 1995).
Mansi, J. D., *Sacrorum Conciliorum Nova et Amplissima Collectio* v. 16–17 (Venice 1771).
Maranci, C., *The Art of Armenia* (Oxford 2018).
Marić, I., 'Lost on Reverse? Constantine VII Porphyrogennetos's Vying with Romanos I Lekapenos,' in N. Gaul et al., *Center, Province and Periphery in the Age of Constantine VII Porphyrogennetos* (Wiesbaden 2018) 103–123.
Mathews, T., with N. Muller, *The Dawn of Christian Art in Panel Paintings and Icons* (Los Angeles 2016).
McCormick, M., *Eternal Victory: Triumphal Rulership in Late Antiquity, Byzantium and the Early Medieval West* (Cambridge 1990).
_____, 'The Imperial Edge: Italo-Byzantine Identity, Movement and Integration,' in H. Ahrweiler and A. Laiou, eds., *Studies on the Internal Diaspora of the Byzantine Empire* (Washington, D.C. 1998) 17–52.
_____, *Origins of the European Economy: Communications and Commerce, A.D. 300–900* (Cambridge 2001).
McGeer, E., *Sowing the Dragon's Teeth: Byzantine Warfare in the Tenth Century* (Washington, D.C. 1995).
_____, *The Land Legislation of the Macedonian Emperors* (Toronto 2000).
McGinn, T., 'The Social Policy of Emperor Constantine in *Codex Theodosianus* 4,6.3,' *Tijdschrift voor Rechtsgeschiedenis* 67 (1999) 57–73.
McGuckin, J., *St Gregory of Nazianzus: An Intellectual Biography* (Crestwood, NY 2001).
McKee, S., *Uncommon Dominion: Venetian Crete and the Myth of Ethnic Purity* (Philadelphia 2000).
McLynn, N., *Ambrose of Milan* (Berkeley 1994).
Mecit, S., *Rum Seljuqs: Evolution of a Dynasty* (London 2014).
Melichar, P., *Empresses of Late Byzantium* (Berlin 2019).
Menze, V., *Justinian and the Making of the Syrian Orthodox Church* (Oxford 2008).
_____, 'Byzantine Sacralization of War,' in N. Gaul et al., *Center, Province and Periphery in the Age of Constantine VII Porphyrogennetos* (Wiesbaden 2018) 153–167.
Mercati, G., *Notizie di Procoro e Demetrio Cidoni* (Vatican City 1931).
Meško, M., 'Pecheneg Groups in the Balkans (c. 1053–1091),' in F. Curta and B.-P. Maleon, eds., *The Steppe Lands and the World Beyond Them* (Iași 2013) 179–205.
Metcalf, D., *Byzantine Cyprus* (Nicosia 2009).
Mikhail, M., *From Byzantine to Islamic Egypt: Religion, Identity and Politics after the Arab Conquest* (London 2016).
Millar, F., *A Greek Roman Empire: Power and Belief under Theodosius II* (Berkeley 2006).
Miller, T., *The Birth of the Hospital in the Byzantine Empire*, 2nd ed. (Baltimore 1997).
_____, *The Orphans of Byzantium*, 2nd ed. (Washington, D.C. 2022).
Montenegro, J., and A. del Castillo, 'Theodemir's Victory over the Byzantines,' *Byzantion* 74 (2004) 403–415.
Morris, R., *Monks and Laymen in Byzantium, 843–1118* (Cambridge 1995).
Morrisson, C., ed., *Trade and Markets in Byzantium* (Washington, D.C. 2012).

Morrisson, C., and V. Prigent, 'Le monetazione in Sicilia nell'età byzantina,' in L. Travaini, ed., *Le zecche italiane fino all'Unità* (Rome 2011) 427–434.
Moschos, D., *Πλατωνισμὸς ἢ Χριστιανισμός; Οἱ φιλοσοφικὲς προϋποθέσεις τοῦ Ἀντιησυχασμοῦ τοῦ Νικηφόρου Γρηγορᾶ* (Athens 1998).
Moser, M., *Emperor and Senators in the Reign of Constantius II* (Cambridge 2018).
Mullet, M., and D. Smythe, eds., *Alexios I Komnenos* (Belfast 1996).
Necipoğlu, N., ed., *Byzantine Constantinople: Monuments, Topography and Everyday Life* (Leiden 2001).
_____, *Byzantium between the Ottomans and the Latins: Politics and Society in the Late Empire* (Cambridge 2009).
Nerantzi-Varmazi, V., *Το Βυζάντιο και η Δύση (1354–1369)* (Thessalonike 1993).
Nesseris, I., *Η παιδεία στην Κωνσταντινούπολη κατά τον 12ο αιώνα* (PhD dissertation, University of Ioannina 2014).
Neville, L., *Authority in Byzantine Provincial Society* (Cambridge 2004).
_____, *Anna Komnene: The Life and Work of a Medieval Historian* (Oxford 2016).
Nicol, D., *The Despotate of Epiros, 1267–1479* (Cambridge 1984).
_____, *Studies in Late Byzantine History and Prosopography* (London 1986).
_____, *Byzantium and Venice: A Study in Diplomatic and Cultural Relations* (Cambridge 1988).
Nicolaou-Konnari, A., 'The Conquest of Cyprus by Richard the Lionheart,' *Επετηρίδα του Κέντρου Επιστημονικών Ερευνών* 26 (2000) 25–123.
_____, 'Greeks,' in eadem and Schabel, eds., *Cyprus*, 16–62.
Nicolaou-Konnari, A., and C. Schabel, ed., *Cyprus: Society and Culture* 1191–1374 (Leiden 2005).
Niewöhner, P., ed., *The Archaeology of Byzantine Anatolia* (Oxford 2017).
_____, 'The Significance of the Cross Before, During, and After Iconoclasm,' *DOP* 74 (2020) 186–242.
Noble, T., *The Republic of St. Peter: The Birth of the Papal State, 680–825* (Philadelphia 1984).
Noyé, G., 'New Light on the Society of Byzantine Italy,' in J. Howard-Johnston, ed., *Social Change in Town and Country in Eleventh-Century Byzantium* (Oxford 2020) 157–195.
Oikonomidès, N., *Les listes de préséance byzantines des IXe et Xe siècles* (Paris 1972).
_____, 'Leo VI's Legislation of 907 Forbidding Fourth Marriages,' *DOP* 30 (1976) 173–193.
_____, 'The Chancery of the Grand Komnenoi,' *Ἀρχεῖον Πόντου* 35 (1979) 299–332.
_____, 'St. George and Mangana,' *DOP* 34–35 (1980–1981) 239–246.
_____, *Society, Culture and Politics in Byzantium* (Aldershot, UK 2005).
_____, 'The Role of the Byzantine State in the Economy,' in *EHB*, 1008–1010.
Olson, A., *Environment and Society in Byzantium, 650–1150* (Cham, Switzerland 2020).
Olster, D., *The Politics of Usurpation in the Seventh Century* (Amsterdam 1993).
Ortalli, G. et al., eds., *Quarta Crociata* (Venice 2006) 317–358.
Palmer, A., *The Seventh Century in the West-Syrian Chronicles* (Liverpool 1993).
Papadopoulos-Kerameus, *Ἀνάλεκτα Ἱεροσολυμίτικης σταχυολογίας*, 5 vols. (St. Petersburg 1891–1898).
_____, *Noctes Petropolitanae* (St. Petersburg 1913).
Payne, R., *A State of Mixture: Christians, Zoroastrians, and Iranian Political Culture in Late Antiquity* (Berkeley 2015).
Peacock, A., *Early Seljuk History: A New Interpretation* (London 2010).
Penna, D., 'Venetian Judges and their Jurisdiction in Constantinople,' *Subseciva Groningana* 8 (2009) 135–146.

_____, *The Byzantine Imperial Acts to Venice, Pisa and Genoa, 10th-12th Centuries* (PhD dissertation, University of Groningen 2012).

Petkov, K., *The Voices of Medieval Bulgaria* (Leiden 2008).

Philippides, M., *Constantine XI Dragaš Palaeologus (1404–1453)* (London 2019).

Philippides, M., and W. Hanak, *The Siege and the Fall of Constantinople in 1453* (Farnham, UK 2011).

Phillips, J. 'Crusader Perceptions of Byzantium,' in Chrissis et al., eds., *Byzantium*, 102–117.

Pieralli, L., *La corrispondenza diplomatica dell'imperatore bizantino con le potenze estere nel tredicesimo secolo* (Vatican City 2006).

Pitamber, N., *Replacing Byzantium: Laskarid Urban Environments and the Landscape of Loss* (PhD dissertation, UCLA 2015).

Pohl, W., *The Avars: A Steppe Empire in Central Europe* (Ithaca, NY 2018).

Pohl, W., et al., eds., *Transformations of Romanness* (Berlin 2018).

Pontani, F., 'Scholarship in the Byzantine Empire (529–1453),' in F. Montanari, ed., *History of Ancient Greek Scholarship* (Leiden 2020) 373–529.

Potter, D., *The Roman Empire at Bay, AD 180–195*, 2nd ed. (New York 2014).

Pozza, M., and G. Ravegnani, *I trattati con Bisanzio, 992–1198* (Venice 1993).

Pourshariati, P., *Decline and Fall of the Sasanian Empire* (London 2008).

Preiser-Kapeller, J., and E. Mitsiou, 'Hierarchies and Fractals: Ecclesiastical Revenues . . . in the Early 14th Century,' *Byzantina Symmeikta* 20 (2010) 245–308.

Previale, L., 'Un panegyrico inedito per Michele VIII Paleologo,' *BZ* 42 (1943–1949) 1–49.

Price, R., *The Acts of the Second Council of Nicaea (787)* (Liverpool 2020).

Prieto Domínguez, Ó., *Literary Circles in Byzantine Iconoclasm* (Cambridge 2020).

Prigent, V., 'Le rôle des provinces d'Occident dans l'approvisionnement de Constantinople,' *Mélanges de l'École française de Rome, Moyen Âge* 118 (2006) 269–299.

Prinzing, G., 'Der Brief Kaiser Heinrichs von Konstantinopel vom 13. Januar 1212,' *Byzantion* 43 (1973) 395–431.

Queller, D., and T. Madden, *The Fourth Crusade*, 2nd ed. (Philadelphia 1997).

Ragia, E., 'Confessions of an Ingenious Man: The Confessions of Faith of John XI Bekkos,' in M-H. Blanchet and F. Gabriel, eds., *L'Union à l'épreuve du formulaire* (Paris 2016) 39–75.

Rallis, G., and M. Potlis, *Σύνταγμα τῶν θείων καὶ ἱερῶν κανόνων*, 6 vols (Athens 1852–1859).

Rapp, C., *Holy Bishops in Late Antiquity* (Berkeley 2005).

Rapp, S., *Studies in Medieval Georgian Historiography* (Leuven 2003).

Regel, V., and N. Novosadskii, *Fontes rerum byzantinarum* (St. Petersburg 1892–1917).

Remijsen, S., *The End of Greek Athletics in Late Antiquity* (Cambridge 2015).

Richards, D., *The Annals of the Saljuq Turks: Selections from al-Kamil fi'l-Ta'rikh of 'Izz al-Din Ibn Al-Athir* (London 2002).

Rives, J., *Religion and Authority in Roman Carthage* (Oxford 1995).

Rousseau, P., *Pachomius: The Making of a Community in Fourth Century Egypt* (Berkeley 1985).

_____, *Basil of Caesarea* (Berkeley 1994).

Ruffini, G., *Life in an Egyptian Village in Late Antiquity: Aphrodito before and after the Islamic Conquest* (Cambridge 2018).

Russell, J., 'The Persian Invasions of Syria/Palestine and Asia Minor,' in E. Kountoura-Galake, ed., *Οι σκοτεινοί αιώνες του Βυζαντίου* (Athens 2001) 41–71.

Ryder, J., 'The Role of the Speeches of John the Oxite in Komnenian Court Politics,' in T. Shawcross and I. Toth, eds., *Reading in the Byzantine Empire and Beyond* (Cambridge 2018) 93–115.

Sahner, C., *Christian Martyrs under Islam: Religious Violence and the Making of the Muslim World* (Princeton 2018).

Saint-Guillain, G., 'Comment les Vénitiens n'ont pas acquis la Crète,' *TM* 16 (2010) 713–758.

_____, 'The Conquest of Monemvasia by the Franks,' *Rivista di studi bizantini e neoellenici* 52 (2015) 242–294.

Saint-Guillain, G., and D. Stathakopoulos, eds., *Liquid & Multiple: Individuals & Identities in the Thirteenth-Century Aegean* (Paris 2012).

Sarantis, A., *Justinian's Balkan Wars: Campaigns, Diplomacy and Development in Illyricum, Thrace and the Northern World A.D. 527–65* (Prenton, UK 2016).

_____, 'The Socio-Economic Impact of Raiding on the Eastern and Balkan Borderlands of the Eastern Roman Empire,' *Millennium* 17 (2020) 203–264.

Sarris, P., 'Beyond the Great Plains and the Barren Hills: Rural Landscapes and Social Structures in Eleventh-Century Byzantium,' in M. Lauxtermann and M. Whittow, eds., *Byzantium in the Eleventh Century* (London 2017) 77–87.

_____, 'Introduction,' in D. Miller and P. Sarris, eds., *The Novels of Justinian* (Cambridge 2018) 1–51.

Sauer, E., ed., *Sasanian Persia: Between Rome and the Steppes of Eurasia* (Edinburgh 2017).

Savvides, A., *Βυζαντινὰ στασιαστικὰ καὶ αὐτονομιστικὰ κινήματα στὰ Δωδεκάνησα καὶ στὴ Μικρὰ Ἀσία, 1189-c.1240 μ.Χ.* (Athens 1987).

_____, *Ιστορία της αυτοκρατορίας των Μεγάλων Κομνηνών της Τραπεζούντας*, 2nd ed. (Thessalonike 2009).

Schabel, C., 'Religion,' in Nicolaou-Konnari and C. Schabel, eds., *Cyprus: Society and Culture 1191–1374* (Leiden 2005) 156–218.

Schreiner, P., *Die byzantinischen Kleinchroniken*. 3 vols. (Vienna 1975).

Schwartz, E., 'Vigiliusbriefe, 2: Zur Kirchenpolitik Justinians,' *Sitzungsberichte der bayerischen Akademie der Wissenschaften: Phil.-hist. Abt. 1940*, no. 2, 73–81.

Schwartz, S., *Imperialism and Jewish Society, 200 B.C.E. to 640 C.E.* (Princeton 2001).

_____, *Ancient Jews from Alexander to Muhammad* (Cambridge 2014).

Ševčenko, I., 'The Decline of Byzantium Seen through the Eyes of its Intellectuals,' *DOP* 15 (1961) 167–186.

_____, *Études sur la polémique entre Théodore Métochite et Nicéphore Choumnos* (Brussels 1962).

_____, 'Theodore Metochites, the Chora, and the Intellectual Trends of his Time,' in P. Underwood, ed., *The Kariye Djami* (New York 1975) 4:17–91.

Shawcross, T., 'Conquest Legitimized: The Making of a Byzantine Emperor in Crusader Constantinople,' in J. Harris et al., *Byzantines, Latins, and Turks in the Eastern Mediterranean World* (Oxford 2012) 181–220.

_____, 'A New Lykourgos for a New Sparta,' in Gerstel, ed., *Viewing the Morea*, 419–452.

Shawcross, T., and I. Toth, eds., *Reading in the Byzantine Empire and Beyond* (Cambridge 2018).

Shepard, J., '"Father" or "Scorpion": Style and Substance in Alexios' Diplomacy,' in M. Mullet and D. Smythe, eds., *Alexios I Komnenos* (Belfast 1996) 68–132.

_____, *Emerging Elites and Byzantium in the Balkans and East-Central Europe* (London 2011).

_____, 'The Emperor's "Significant Others": Alexios I Komnenos and his "Pivot to the West",' in S. Tougher, ed., *The Emperor in the Byzantine World* (London 2019) 135–155.

Shoshan, B., *The Arabic Historical Tradition and the Early Islamic Conquests* (London 2016).

Shukurov, R., 'Turkoman and Byzantine Self-Identity,' in A. Eastmond, ed., *Eastern Approaches to Byzantium* (Aldershot, UK 2001) 259–276.

_____, 'Harem Christianity: The Byzantine Identity of Seljuk Princes,' in A. Peacock and S. Nur Yıldız, eds., *The Seljuks of Anatolia* (London 2013) 115–150.

_____, *The Byzantine Turks, 1204–1461* (Leiden 2016).

Signes Codoñer, J., 'Melkites and Icon Worship during the Iconoclastic Period,' *DOP* 67 (2013) 135–187.

_____, *The Emperor Theophilos and the East* (Farnham, UK 2014).

Simpson, A., *Niketas Choniates: A Historiographical Study* (Oxford 2013).

_____, ed., *Byzantium, 1180–1204: 'The Sad Quarter of a Century'* (Athens 2015).

Siniossoglou, N., *Radical Platonism in Byzantium* (Cambridge 2011).

Sinkewicz, R., *A Critical Edition of the Anti-Arsenite Discourses of Theoleptos of Philadelphia* (Toronto 1988).

Sivan, H., *Palestine in Late Antiquity* (Oxford 2008).

Slootjes, D., *The Governor and his Subjects in the Later Roman Empire* (Leiden 2006).

Slootjes, D., and M. Verhoeven, eds. *Byzantium in Dialogue with the Mediterranean* (Leiden 2019).

Smith, S., *Greek Epigram and Byzantine Culture* (Cambridge 2019).

Smyrlis, K., 'The First Ottoman Occupation of Macedonia,' in A. Beihammer et al., eds., *Diplomatics in the Eastern Mediterranean, 1000–1500* (Leiden 2008) 327–339.

_____, 'Private Property and State Finances: The Emperor's Right to Donate his Subjects' Land in the Comnenian Period,' *BMGS* 33 (2009) 115–132.

_____, 'The State, the Land, and Private Property,' in D. Angelov, ed., *Church and Society in Late Byzantium* (Kalamazoo, MI 2009) 58–87.

_____, 'Financial Crisis and the Limits of Taxation under Andronikos II,' in D. Angelov, ed., *Power and Subversion in Byzantium* (Farnham, UK 2013) 71–82.

_____, 'Wooing the Petty Elite: Privilege and Imperial Authority in Byzantium,' in O. Deluis et al., eds., *Le saint, le moine et le paysan* (Paris 2016) 657–682.

_____, 'The Fiscal Revolution of Alexios I Komnenos,' *TM* 21.2 (2017) 593–610.

Sophoulis, P., *Byzantium and Bulgaria, 775–831* (Leiden 2012).

Soulis, G., *The Serbs and Byzantium during the Reign of Tsar Stephen Dušan* (Washington, D.C. 1984).

Stadtmüller, G., *Michael Choniates, Metropolit von Athen* (Rome 1934).

Starr, J., *The Jews in the Byzantine Empire* (New York 1939).

Stavridou-Zafraka, A., *Βυζάντιο 13ος αιώνας: Από την κατάρρευση στην ανασυγκρότηση* (Thessalonike 2016).

Stephenson, P., *Byzantium's Balkan Frontier: A Political Study of the Northern Balkans, 900–1204* (Cambridge 2000).

_____, *The Legend of Basil the Bulgar-Slayer* (Cambridge 2003).

Stone, A., *Eustathios of Thessaloniki: Secular Orations* (Leiden 2013).

Stopka, K., *Armenia Christiana: Armenian Religious Identity and the Churches of Constantinople and Rome* (Cracow 2017).

Tacoma, L., *Moving Romans: Migration to Rome in the Principate* (Oxford 2016).

Tafel, T., and G. Thomas, *Urkunden zur älteren Handels- und Staatsgeschichte der Republik Venedig*, 3 vols. (Vienna 1856–1857).
Takirtakoglou, K., *Η Αρμενία μεταξύ Βυζαντίου και Χαλιφάτου (885–929)* (Athens 2019).
Talbot, A.-M., 'The Restoration of Constantinople under Michael VIII,' *DOP* 47 (1993) 243–261.
Tannous, J., *The Making of the Medieval Middle East: Religion, Society, and Simple Believers* (Princeton 2018).
Tautu, A., *Acta Urbani P.P. V* (Vatican City 1964).
Theotokis, G., *The Norman Campaigns in the Balkans, 1081–1108* (Woodbridge, UK 2014).
Thonemann, P., *The Maeander Valley: A Historical Geography from Antiquity to Byzantium* (Cambridge 2011).
Tinnefeld, F., 'Vier Prooimien zu Kaiserurkunden,' *Byzantinoslavica* 44 (1983) 13–30, 178–204.
Todt, K.-P., *Dukat und griechisch-orthodoxes Patriarchat von Antiocheia in mittelbyzantinischer Zeit (969–1084)* (Wiesbaden 2020).
Tougher, S., *The Reign of Leo VI* (Leiden 1997).
_____, ed., *The Emperor in the Byzantine World* (London 2019).
Treadgold, W., 'An Unpublished Saint's Life of the Empress Irene,' *Byzantinische Forschungen* 8 (1982) 236–251.
_____, *The Byzantine Revival, 780–842* (Stanford, CA 1988).
_____, *Byzantium and Its Army, 284–1081* (Stanford, CA 1995).
Trombley, F., *Hellenic Religion and Christianization*, 2nd ed. (Leiden 2001).
Tsougarakis, N., and P. Lock, eds., *A Companion to Latin Greece* (Leiden 2015).
Tyerman, C., *God's War: A New History of the Crusades* (London 2006).
Underwood, P., ed., *The Kariye Djami*, v. 4 (New York 1975).
Van Dam, R., *The Roman Revolution of Constantine* (Cambridge 2008).
Van Dieten, J.-L., *Niketas Choniates: Erläuterung zu den Raden und Briefen nebst einer Biographie* (Berlin 1971).
Van Tricht, F., *The Latin Renovatio of Byzantium* (Leiden 2011).
_____, *The Horoscope of Emperor Baldwin II* (Leiden 2019).
Vasiliev, A., et al., *Byzance et les Arabes* (Brussels 1950–1968).
Vasilievsky, V., 'Epirotica saeculi xiii,' *Vizantijski Vremmenik* 3 (1896) 233–299.
Vest, B., *Geschichte der Stadt Melitene und der umliegenden Gebiete: Vom Vorabend der arabischen bis zum Abschluss der türkischen Eroberung (um 600–1124)* (Hamburg 2007).
Vranousi, E., and M. Nystazopoulou-Pelekidou, *Βυζαντινὰ ἔγγραφα τῆς Μονῆς Πάτμου* (Athens 1980).
Vryonis, S., 'The Will of a Provincial Magnate, Eustathius Boilas (1059),' *DOP* 11 (1956) 263–277.
_____, *The Decline of Medieval Hellenism in Asia Minor and the Process of Islamization from the Eleventh through the Fifteenth Century* (Berkeley 1971).
Webb, P., *Imagining the Arabs: Arab Identity and the Rise of Islam* (Edinburgh 2017).
_____. *Demons and Dancers: Performance in Late Antiquity* (Cambridge, MA 2008).
Weisweiler, J., 'Populist Despotism and Infrastructural Power in the Later Roman Empire,' in C. Ando and S. Richardson, eds., *Ancient States and Infrastuctural Power* (Philadelphia 2017).
Whitby, M., *The Emperor Maurice and his Historian: Theophylact Simocatta on Persian and Balkan Warfare* (Oxford 1988).

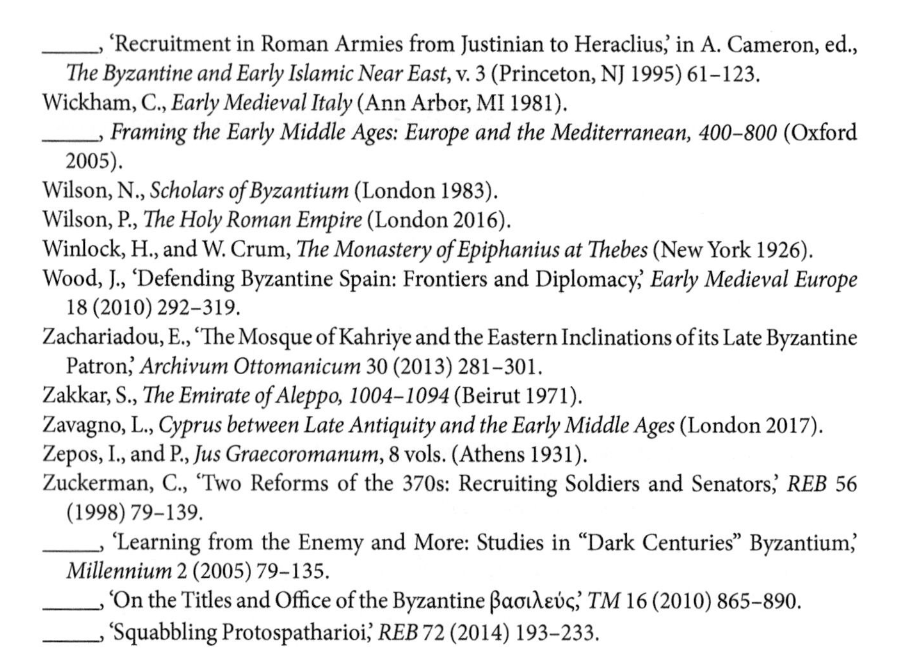

_____, 'Recruitment in Roman Armies from Justinian to Heraclius,' in A. Cameron, ed., *The Byzantine and Early Islamic Near East*, v. 3 (Princeton, NJ 1995) 61–123.

Wickham, C., *Early Medieval Italy* (Ann Arbor, MI 1981).

_____, *Framing the Early Middle Ages: Europe and the Mediterranean, 400–800* (Oxford 2005).

Wilson, N., *Scholars of Byzantium* (London 1983).

Wilson, P., *The Holy Roman Empire* (London 2016).

Winlock, H., and W. Crum, *The Monastery of Epiphanius at Thebes* (New York 1926).

Wood, J., 'Defending Byzantine Spain: Frontiers and Diplomacy,' *Early Medieval Europe* 18 (2010) 292–319.

Zachariadou, E., 'The Mosque of Kahriye and the Eastern Inclinations of its Late Byzantine Patron,' *Archivum Ottomanicum* 30 (2013) 281–301.

Zakkar, S., *The Emirate of Aleppo, 1004–1094* (Beirut 1971).

Zavagno, L., *Cyprus between Late Antiquity and the Early Middle Ages* (London 2017).

Zepos, I., and P., *Jus Graecoromanum*, 8 vols. (Athens 1931).

Zuckerman, C., 'Two Reforms of the 370s: Recruiting Soldiers and Senators,' *REB* 56 (1998) 79–139.

_____, 'Learning from the Enemy and More: Studies in "Dark Centuries" Byzantium,' *Millennium* 2 (2005) 79–135.

_____, 'On the Titles and Office of the Byzantine βασιλεύς,' *TM* 16 (2010) 865–890.

_____, 'Squabbling Protospatharioi,' *REB* 72 (2014) 193–233.

Index

For the benefit of digital users, indexed terms that span two pages (e.g., 52–53) may, on occasion, appear on only one of those pages.

The Index focuses on people and places, while including some broad topics too, though it was impossible to be comprehensive about either. Places, groups, and institutions that appear with great regularity are not indexed (e.g., Constantinople, Rome, Romans, Romanía, Persia, Egypt, Thrace, Armenia, Venice, Turks, most offices, and broad regions such as the Balkans and Asia Minor). Emperors, empresses, and relatives with imperial rank also do not appear; readers can find them in the relevant sections of the narrative. Only significant mentions of them *outside* those sections are referenced here. Most topics of broad interest are signaled in the sub-headings of the text, not here. Coverage has necessarily been selective. Some items are clustered together under a common heading, specifically named Battles, Churches, and Councils.